THE UNITED STATES IN ITS WORLD RELATIONS

McGRAW-HILL SERIES IN AMERICAN HISTORY

Blake	A Short History of American Life
Blake & Barck	The United States in Its World Relations
Dupuy & Dupuy	Military Heritage of America
Gewehr, Gordon, Sparks, & Stromberg	The United States: A History of a Democracy
Rae & Mahoney	The United States in World History
Riegel & Long	The American Story
	VOLUME I: Youth
	VOLUME II: Maturity

THE UNITED STATES
IN ITS WORLD RELATIONS

Nelson Manfred Blake

Professor of History
Maxwell School
Syracuse University

Oscar Theodore Barck, Jr.

Professor of History
Maxwell School
Syracuse University

New York   Toronto   London

1960   McGRAW-HILL BOOK COMPANY, INC.

THE UNITED STATES
IN ITS WORLD RELATIONS

PREFACE

The United States no longer has a choice between isolation and deep involvement in world affairs. After we dropped our first atomic bomb and the Russians launched their earliest sputnik, the foreign relations of the United States became matters of life and death in the most literal sense. Today Washington and New York City stand in greater danger of destruction from enemy attack than London and Paris did in 1939. To say this, is not to aim at sensationalism, but to face up to the sober facts of the nuclear age.

Obviously we need to understand as thoroughly as possible the relations of our nation with the rest of the world. Nor can these relations be studied only in their present-day aspect. Nations, like individuals, are deeply conditioned by earlier experience, and American diplomatic history therefore offers many insights for the better comprehension of our contemporary predicament.

The present work traces the history of United States foreign relations from their simple beginnings to their present complexity. Our first objective has been to present the essential facts as directly and clearly as possible. Our second has been to suggest lines of interpretation and reflection. In this we have tried to avoid pontificating. Diplomatic history is particularly inviting territory to second-guessers who know just what Madison should have done differently to avoid the War of 1812, or what Polk, McKinley, Wilson, F. D. Roosevelt, or Truman should have done to keep out of later conflicts. We are not so sure that we possess this superior wisdom. On such issues we think our duty lies not in the passing of thundering judgments, but in a sober discussion of all sides of the situation. The task of interpretation is never an easy one, nor should students be led to think it is. Merely to justify all that has been done is to encourage a kind of fatalism and to deny that rational human beings ought to be able to learn from their past mistakes. On the other hand, to censure

v

harshly on the basis of hindsight is often to show a lack of understanding of the actual situation confronting the men who had hard decisions to make. We have tried, therefore, to keep a healthy middle ground, attempting first to explain why men did what they did and then suggesting what alternatives of policy there may have been. Final judgments we have usually left to the reader.

Since no work of this scope can be based on more than partial firsthand examination of the sources, our greatest indebtedness is to scores of fellow scholars who have contributed useful studies on various phases of American diplomatic history. Some of the evaluation of this literature will be found in the Suggestions for Further Reading at the end of the present volume.

Nelson Manfred Blake
Oscar Theodore Barck, Jr.

CONTENTS

Preface   v

Part One. The Diplomacy of Nascent Nationalism (1776–1815)   1

  1. The Struggle for Independence   4
  2. Peace and Its Problems   23
  3. Politics and Diplomacy of the New Federal Union   43
  4. Wrestling with France and Spain   63
  5. Jefferson Flies the Flag   78
  6. Dilemma of a Neutral   94
  7. Peace Again   117

Part Two. Continental Expansion (1815–1890)   131

  8. The Florida Question   133
  9. The Monroe Doctrine   147
 10. Repairing Relations with France and England   166
 11. Frontier Pressures   183
 12. Manifest Destiny   199
 13. Looking for New Worlds to Conquer   220
 14. Diplomacy and the Slavery Issue   240
 15. Civil War Diplomacy   263
 16. Post–Civil War Expansionists   286
 17. War Scares and Peaceful Settlements   306
 18. Diplomacy in Low Gear   331

Part Three. The Age of Imperialism (1890–1917)   351

 19. The New Imperialism   353
 20. The United States Emerges as a World Power   376
 21. John Hay and the Open Door   401
 22. Roosevelt Gets His Canal   415

23. Roosevelt and World Politics   437
24. Dollar Diplomacy   458
25. The Diplomacy of Morality   470

Part Four. The Search for World Order (1917–1945)   489

26. The Ideal of Peace   492
27. World War I: The Trials of a Neutral   509
28. The Light That Failed   541
29. Republican Peace Efforts   565
30. Shifts of Policy   588
31. Good Neighbors—and Bad   615
32. Between Peace and War   645
33. The Great Coalition   677

Part Five. Diplomacy of the Atomic Age (since 1945)   701

34. From One World to Two   705
35. The Struggle for Asia   729
36. Nuclear Stalemate   755

Suggestions for Further Reading   789

Index   813

PART ONE

The Diplomacy of Nascent Nationalism

Diplomatic history deals with the relations of independent nations with each other. Within their own boundaries, national governments exercise such clear powers as making and enforcing laws, levying taxes, and requiring military service of their citizens or subjects. But in their relations with other governments, they have to operate on a different basis. Despite periodic aspirations for world government, the nations have never in modern times surrendered any significant part of their cherished sovereignty. They obey no clearly formulated body of law and acknowledge no superior authority.

Yet no nation can live entirely isolated from the rest of the world. Often two or more countries depend on the same river for access to the sea. How is the use of this common waterway to be regulated? Outlaws on one side of a national boundary may assault and rob on the other. How are they to be disciplined? One country produces a surplus of one commodity, which might profitably be exchanged for the surplus of a second country. How are merchants to be protected in carrying on this desirable trade?

Out of these necessary transactions of one country with another the usages of diplomacy have evolved over the course of many centuries. The most important diplomatic documents are treaties by which two or more governments exchange their solemn promises. They may agree to respect each other's independence, to accept certain boundaries between their contiguous territories, to allow the citizens of each to travel and trade in the territory of the other, or to help each other in case of war. Ranking below treaties are various other protocols, conventions, and executive agreements.

1

To negotiate these documents and to communicate on other matters, a variety of diplomatic agents are employed. At first the United States was represented at foreign capitals only by ministers; the bestowal of the rank of ambassador on its most important diplomats after 1893 was a mark of the nation's assumption of great-power status.

Through scrupulous observance of treaties and friendly diplomacy, nations often maintain harmonious relations over many decades. Yet diplomatic history deals repeatedly with the use of force among governments. The reason is obvious. When one nation attempts to dominate or dictate to another, or when the two are unable to settle serious disputes through diplomacy or arbitration, then the absence of a superior authority leaves the parties with no recourse except to attempt to injure each other through economic reprisals or acts of war.

To understand diplomatic history requires an analysis of many factors. A first consideration must be that of national interest. What does a country consider essential to its security and welfare? Occasionally its goals will have sufficient continuity over the years to become cornerstones of foreign policy. Isolation, or freedom from overseas commitments, was until relatively recently a jealously guarded principle of American foreign policy; more recently, this has had to give way to the ideal of mutual security. The Monroe Doctrine and the Open Door have been other traditions of great force in American diplomatic history. Besides these larger interests, each period reveals its own immediate goals.

Diplomatic history also involves emotional factors. Hate and fear between the people of one country and those of another may gain such force that it will be difficult for the two governments to maintain friendly relations. Stories of insults and atrocities will fan the war spirit. On the other hand, a disposition to friendship and a will to peace will usually smooth the way to the settlement of even the most difficult disputes.

Since force has always been the final resort in international affairs, diplomatic history necessarily involves a consideration of one country's potential ability to injure another. From one point of view, the oceans have always been America's best defenses, usually saving her from serious fear of invasion. Yet the oceans have also provided the means of communication between America and the rest of the world, and the United States has always jealously opposed any domination of the sea lanes by a hostile power. Different weapons and changing methods of warfare have profoundly influenced international relations. A new navy and new conceptions of sea power made Hawaii and the Panama Canal vital to American security around 1900; a half century later the development of strategic air power and ballistic missiles appeared to require American bases in Western Europe and North Africa.

If a realistic study of American diplomacy requires attention to ideas of national interest, popular emotions, and military factors, this does not mean that moral principles have had no influence. On the contrary, ideals like republicanism, democracy, self-determination, and freedom have again and again played a powerful role in determining American foreign policy. Often, of course, motives have been mixed. To promote democracy and freedom abroad has seemed essential to defending it at home.

Between 1776 and 1815, the United States won its independence, organized its government, and laid the basis of its political life. During this period of nascent nationalism the goals of its foreign policy were clear. First, it sought recognition of its independence and such foreign aid as might be necessary to win this. Second, it demanded living space —generous boundaries that would give it room for growth and keep dangerous neighbors at a distance. Third, it needed rights to trade—for its frontiersmen to use the Mississippi and for its merchants to trade in the West Indies and in Europe. Finally, as a new nation, it felt the need for respect—for freedom from foreign intrigue both among the Indians and in domestic politics.

During these years the infant nation was all too deeply involved in the affairs of Europe. To win independence, she had to fight England and accept the aid of France, Spain, and Holland. Then in the postwar years she faced the possibility of war with Spain, fought an undeclared naval conflict with France, and finally collided in a second war with England. It is little wonder that Americans yearned to cut loose from the clashing ambitions of the Old World.

1

THE STRUGGLE FOR INDEPENDENCE

On July 2, 1776—two days before the famous Declaration of Independence was adopted—the Continental Congress brought a new nation to birth by approving the resolution introduced by Richard Henry Lee of Virginia:

> That these United Colonies are, and of right ought to be, free and independent States, that they are absolved from all allegiance to the British Crown, and that all political connection between them and the State of Great Britain is, and ought to be, totally dissolved.

With these few words, George III's rebellious American Colonies took an audacious and historic step. Renouncing all dependence on Great Britain, they claimed for the United States the proud rights of a sovereign nation: to make war and peace, to conclude treaties and exchange diplomatic representatives with foreign states, to make and enforce its own laws, to tax, and to coin money.

Like every newcomer in the family of nations, the United States desired prompt recognition of its new status by other countries. An even more urgent need was to obtain powerful European friends to assist the Americans in their desperate military struggle with England. The necessity of such aid was one of the principal arguments by which the radicals induced Congress to accept the idea of independence—an idea which American conservatives had been very reluctant to entertain. Lee's resolution for independence had in fact contained a second clause: "That it is expedient forthwith to take the most effectual measures for forming foreign Alliances." Congress acted on this even before approving the resolution for independence when, on June 11, 1776, it appointed a committee "to prepare a plan of treaties to be proposed to foreign powers." The following day, John Dickinson, Benjamin Franklin, John Adams, Benjamin Harrison, and Roger Morris were named as committee members.

4

The expediency of seeking alliances became more and more obvious during the summer and fall of 1776. As Washington's armies suffered discouraging defeats around New York City and retreated wearily across New Jersey, the prospects for American independence appeared far from bright. Unless foreign military and naval help could be obtained, the history of the United States seemed likely to be short.

Appointment of Diplomatic Agents

Long before the resolution for independence was adopted, the Continental Congress had sent out cautious feelers to foreign governments. Although the Congress [1] was in origin an extralegal body, created to coordinate the efforts of the thirteen Colonies in demanding recognition of their rights within the British Empire, it had gradually assumed the powers of a *de facto* [2] government by raising an army, maintaining a postal service, and issuing paper money. Exercising a loose conglomeration of legislative, judicial, and executive powers, Congress carried out most of its functions through committees. One such body, appointed November 29, 1775, was the so-called Committee of Secret Correspondence, charged with the duty of "corresponding with our friends in Great Britain, Ireland, and other parts of the world." This was the forerunner of the State Department of later days.

The natural leader among the five men appointed to this Committee of Secret Correspondence was Benjamin Franklin. Now sixty-nine years old, Franklin was probably the most famous American then alive, at least as far as Europe was concerned. "Rags-to-riches" success stories were as popular in the eighteenth century as today, and no such theme could be better illustrated than that of how Franklin had arrived in Philadelphia as a hungry runaway youth and worked his way up to the position of wealthy printer and leading citizen. Franklin's fame had spread throughout Europe after he began experimenting with electricity. An able letter writer, the Philadelphia savant had built up a remarkable correspondence with kindred spirits throughout the Colonies, in England, and in many other countries. He had enlarged this circle of acquaintances and had learned much of European politics during several years of residence in London as a colonial agent.

Among Franklin's colleagues on the Committee of Secret Correspond-

[1] This was the Second Continental Congress, which met at Philadelphia in May, 1775, after hostilities had broken out at Lexington and Concord. The First Continental Congress had met in 1774 to deal with the situation created by the Boston Tea Party and the English Coercive Acts.

[2] A *de facto* government is one that is actually functioning, even though it did not come into power through regularly established means. Such a government is to be distinguished from a *de jure* one, which has a clear legal basis for its existence.

ence, two men of undoubted ability also deserve mention. One was John Dickinson, a wealthy Philadelphia lawyer who had gained fame as the author of the *Letters of a Farmer in Pennsylvania* during the controversy over the Townshend Acts. The other was John Jay, a brilliant young lawyer from New York.

As one of its first steps, the Committee communicated with Arthur Lee, who was still residing in London despite the outbreak of hostilities. Lee, a member of the famous Lee family of Virginia, had been educated in England and served as a colonial agent. He was thoroughly loyal to the colonial cause and possessed useful abilities: he had traveled widely and spoke fluent French, Italian, and Spanish. Unfortunately he was jealous and suspicious by nature and proved a difficult colleague for other American diplomats. On December 12, 1775, the Committee informed Lee that Congress would like "to know the disposition of foreign powers towards us." The Virginian was asked to explore the situation with "great circumspection and impenetrable secrecy."

Franklin also believed that an alert agent in The Hague, a cosmopolitan city where ambassadors from all European nations were stationed, might pick up information of great value. Therefore he enlisted the help of Charles William Frederick Dumas, a naturalized Dutchman who made a precarious living by tutoring, translating, and writing. Dumas was typical of the many foreign scholars who had come to idolize Franklin and had exchanged ideas with him by letter.

As long as the moderates in Congress clung to the hope of reconciliation with the mother country, the work of the Committee of Secret Correspondence was confined to a cautious gathering of information regarding the disposition of foreign governments. As the quarrel between America and England grew in bitterness, however, the Committee turned to stronger measures. In March, 1776, Silas Deane of Connecticut was sent to France to seek an audience with the Count de Vergennes, Louis XVI's Minister of Foreign Affairs. He was to impress that official with the value to France of American friendship and ask for men and supplies, which would be paid for as soon as the Americans could safely export produce to France.

The latest entry into the infant American diplomatic service was a graduate of Yale, who had studied law but had soon abandoned this profession for the occupation of merchant. Deane had been active in pre-Revolutionary politics in Connecticut and had represented that colony in the Continental Congress. Although he worked energetically in the American cause during his mission abroad, he became involved in unfortunate quarrels with the suspicious Arthur Lee. Deane's carelessness in confusing the business that he did as an agent of Congress with business done in his private capacity as merchant contributed to his difficulties.

Background of American Foreign Relations

To understand the situation that confronted such agents as Lee, Dumas, and Deane requires some acquaintance with earlier history. From the moment that news of Columbus's discovery of the New World reached Europe, the control of these overseas territories had been an object of Old World diplomacy. Spain and Portugal had made an audacious attempt to divide all these new lands between them. In 1493, Pope Alexander VI proclaimed the first so-called Demarcation Line, but the following year Spain and Portugal modified this in the Treaty of Tordesillas with a second Demarcation Line farther to the west.

Other European states did not admit the legality of this partition of the colonial world, but they lacked the incentive and effective power to challenge it at the time. Throughout most of the sixteenth century, therefore, Portugal dominated the East Indies, the coasts of Africa, the islands of the eastern Atlantic, and Brazil, while Spain controlled the rest of the Americas, the West Indies, and the Philippines. By 1600, however, England, France, and the Netherlands had grown strong enough to contest this monopoly. The defeat of the Spanish Armada by the English in 1588 and other disasters to the Spanish and Portuguese arms opened the way for merchants of other countries to organize trading companies and colonial projects that carried the English, French, and Dutch flags into India, the East and West Indies, Africa, and North America.

The new imperial powers were soon involved in conflicts among themselves. During the seventeenth century the English and Dutch engaged in three wars that resulted in a serious weakening of Dutch sea power and the annexation of New Netherland by the English. This was only a prelude to a much broader and more bitterly contested struggle between the French and the English. Between 1689 and 1763, these two powers engaged in four major wars.[3] Each was fought on a world-wide scope: on the continent of Europe, where Prussia, Austria, Spain, and the Netherlands became involved as the allies of one or another of the contestants; in India, Africa, and the West Indies; and on the North American continent.

The last of these great intercolonial struggles—the Great War for the

---

[3] These were: (1) the War of the League of Augsburg—known in America as King William's War (1689–1697); (2) the War of the Spanish Succession or Queen Anne's War (1702–1713), ended by the Treaty of Utrecht, under which England gained some territory from France in North America and Gibraltar from Spain; (3) the War of the Austrian Succession or King George's War (1744–1748), which like the first ended in stalemate; and (4) the Great War for the Empire or the Seven Years' War or the French and Indian War (1754–1763).

Empire, known in Europe as the Seven Years' War and in America as the French and Indian War—ended in bitter humiliation for France. By the Treaty of Paris of 1763, she was stripped of valuable territories in many parts of the world. On the continent of North America she lost everything; Canada had to be ceded to England, along with all French claims east of the Mississippi River, while Louisiana—New Orleans and all of North America between the Mississippi and the Rocky Mountains—was transferred to Spain to compensate this ally of France for its loss of Florida to England.

The Treaty of Paris represented a striking triumph for England. Rarely, if ever, had Britain's position in world politics seemed as secure as it did between 1763 and 1775. Yet there were ominous clouds on the horizon that more prudent statesmen than those who directed English destinies during these years might well have heeded. France and Spain found their second-rank status intolerable and were impatiently awaiting an opportunity to revenge themselves on Britain. Other European powers were also jealous of the English and disliked the highhandedness of the British navy during wartime.

Most dangerous of all to English supremacy was the growing discontent in her own Colonies. The quarrel that eventually resulted in the American Revolution had, of course, many causes: disputes over taxation and the right of representation, resentment against mercantilist restrictions, mob action in the Colonies, and unwise measures of coercion on the part of the mother country. Among these sources of friction might be listed colonial impatience with a situation wherein foreign policy and Indian policy were determined by British officials—often without regard to American opinion. In the earlier intercolonial wars, for example, American lives and money were expended in expeditions to conquer French posts that were sometimes handed back to the enemy in exchange for some bit of territory in another part of the world where the Americans had no interest.[4] Similarly resented were such decisions of British bureaucracy as the Proclamation of 1763, which closed—at least temporarily —the territory beyond the Appalachians to white settlement as a measure to pacify the Indians. Such measures might be wise and necessary, but they encountered sharp criticism from land-hungry colonists.

One important force driving the colonists toward independence was the feeling that by cutting the tie with the mother country, the Americans could free themselves from involvement in England's many wars. This impulse toward isolationism, avoiding entanglement in Europe's

---

[4] For example, Louisburg, important French fortress on Cape Breton Island, had been conquered by an expedition from Massachusetts in 1745, only to be returned to the French in exchange for Madras in India by the Treaty of Aix-la-Chapelle in 1748 —without asking the Americans.

quarrels, was one of the earliest factors influencing America's foreign relations. In *Common Sense*, Thomas Paine's famous pamphlet in favor of American independence, heavy stress was placed on this argument. " 'Tis the true interest of America," asserted Paine, "to steer clear of European contentions, which she never can do while by her dependence on Britain she is made the makeweight in the scale of British politics." Yet the ironic predicament of the Americans in 1776 was that in order to win this isolation from Old World politics, they had first to involve themselves in them. Foreign aid and alliance appeared essential to winning independence.

In many ways it might seem that provincial Americans were poorly equipped to play the game of international diplomacy. The world of colonial printing shops, rural law offices, and tobacco plantations appeared to have little in common with the world of European court society. Yet the rusticity of the colonials is likely to be exaggerated. Literate Americans of the Revolutionary generation were far from ignorant of European politics. Colonial newspapers published extensive dispatches from foreign ports—often almost to the exclusion of purely domestic news. Many books and journals were imported from England and other European countries. Some of the wealthier Americans had studied or traveled abroad; others had engaged in trade with the Old World. A few, like Franklin and Arthur Lee, had learned lessons easily transferable to the field of diplomacy from their experience as colonial agents in London.

Just as generations of participation in colonial politics had prepared Americans for the governmental responsibilities of independence, so these miscellaneous contacts between the New World and the Old had provided them with the knowledge necessary to conduct the foreign relations of the new state.

European Intrigue

American prospects for obtaining foreign aid were in fact excellent. Even before the colonial agents were ready to ask, certain foreign governments were preparing to give. The policy of France and Spain toward the American Revolution is not to be explained on the grounds of sympathy with the colonial cause. On the contrary, Old World diplomats prided themselves on their ability to formulate policy on completely hardheaded considerations, uninfluenced by weak sentimentality.

The French government had in fact been watching the American situation very closely for over a decade. French foreign policy from 1758 to 1770 had most of the time been directed by the energetic Duc de Choiseul, who had gained power as the favorite of Madame Pompadour, the mistress of Louis XV. After the great humiliation of the Treaty of Paris in 1763, Choiseul started preparing for an eventual war of revenge against hated England. The French army and navy were re-organized at his insistence, and efforts—unfortunately unsuccessful—were made to reform the national finances. In the diplomatic field Choiseul not only strengthened the Family Compact, the defensive alliance that linked the Bourbon thrones of France and Spain, but also worked to im-prove French relations with Austria and Prussia. In the event of another war between France and England, the French Minister hoped that Britain would find no allies at all on the European continent.

For obvious reasons Choiseul was delighted when the American colonists became involved in heated controversies with the mother coun-try over such issues as the Stamp Act and the Townshend Acts. He sent secret agents to America to investigate the situation and learn whether these quarrels might develop into armed revolt. At first the news from the Colonies was highly encouraging to French designs, but modifications of British policy around 1770 resulted in a partial reconciliation between the colonists and the home government—much to Choiseul's disappoint-ment.

After the death of Madame Pompadour, Choiseul became the target for the intrigues of Madame Du Barry, another of the King's mistresses. This, combined with other misfortunes, led to Choiseul's dismissal in 1770. He hoped to return to power after the indolent and dissolute Louis XV died in 1774, but the new King, the well-intentioned but slow-witted Louis XVI, chose instead as his Foreign Minister the Count de Vergennes. Vergennes was a man with many years of experience in the French diplo-matic service, extraordinarily industrious and eager to rebuild his nation's prestige. He practiced diplomacy according to European standards of the day, not hesitating to resort to intrigue or deceit when he thought that his monarch's interest could thus be served. But American diplomats were to learn that despite these methods the French Minister was more depend-able than the men who held similar posts in other European countries. Vergennes was patient and intelligent, a man with whom the American representatives could profitably do business.

The possibilities of exploiting the quarrel between England and her Colonies were forcefully pointed out to Vergennes by Caron de Beau-marchais, one of the most fascinating personalities of the eighteenth cen-tury. Originally trained to follow his father's craft of watchmaker, Beaumarchais had won favor with Madame Pompadour and Louis XV through his wit and intelligence, and he became an influential courtier. He had turned to music and literature with equal success, writing *The Barber of Seville* and other highly popular plays. Discovering still other talents in the clever Beaumarchais, the French government had used him for various confidential missions to foreign countries. It was while this watchmaker–courtier–playwright–secret agent was in England in 1775 that he met Arthur Lee, from whom he received firsthand information about the American situation. Beaumarchais was a man of enthusiasms, and the story of the colonists' taking up arms to obtain a recognition of their rights was one to fire his imagination. He crossed the Channel several times to urge the French government to make secret help available to the rebels.

Vergennes needed little persuasion. As early as September, 1775, he sent a secret agent, Archard de Bonvouloir, to America. Bonvouloir was instructed to assure the Continental Congress of French sympathy, to allay American fears that France wanted to recover Canada, and to suggest that French ports might be opened to American ships, but he was to avoid specific commitments. This mission had important results. On the one hand, the Committee of Secret Correspondence was encouraged to send Silas Deane to Europe; on the other, Bonvouloir was able to report that the Americans were moving steadily toward independence.

During the early months of 1776, Vergennes became personally convinced that his government must secretly supply the Americans with arms and money. In a memorandum to the King and Council, he argued that since England was her natural enemy, France should seize every opportunity to weaken this great rival. If the American Colonies won their independence with her assistance, France would reap great benefits. England's power would be lessened and France's proportionately increased. England's trade would be irreparably damaged, while France's would expand. In addition, France might recover the valuable Newfoundland fisheries and other possessions she had lost in earlier wars.

Beaumarchais may have suggested some of the arguments used in Vergennes's memorandum. In any event, on February 29, 1776, the playwright submitted a similar document of his own to the King. Beaumarchais warned that if French help were denied, the colonists might become sufficiently discouraged to patch up their quarrel with the mother country and then collaborate with her in an attack upon the French West Indies. A few millions spent now to aid the Americans might save France from war and serious trouble. "If it is replied that we cannot aid the Americans without drawing upon us a storm, I reply that this danger can be averted if the plan be adopted which I have so often proposed, to aid the Americans secretly."

Vergennes and Beaumarchais encountered serious opposition to their proposals. Many nobles saw a dangerous precedent in encouraging revolution, while Baron Turgot, the controller general of finance, feared such a policy would involve France in war and financial disaster. But Louis XVI overruled these objections—which actually made much sense from the standpoint of the welfare of France—and decided upon the secret aid policy. On May 2, 1776, the King authorized a grant of 1 million livres [5] to the Americans. Vergennes immediately informed Grimaldi, the Spanish Foreign Minister, of this new policy and suggested that Charles III, the Spanish King, grant a similar amount to this promising cause. Grimaldi readily obtained his royal master's consent to the grant.

Period of Secret Aid

Because neither France nor Spain was ready to risk war with England, elaborate precautions were taken to deceive the British with professions of friendship while aid to the Americans was transmitted through secret channels. With characteristic ingenuity Beaumarchais organized a fictitious commercial firm, Roderigue Hortalez & Company, to serve as a front for these transactions. Hortalez & Company in Paris was soon engaged in mysterious communications with "Mary Johnston" in London —and Mary Johnston was none other than Arthur Lee.

This was the situation when Silas Deane, whom the Committee of Secret Correspondence had sent abroad to seek aid, arrived in Paris on July 7, 1776. Although Deane professed to be only a private merchant engaged in purchasing goods for the Indian trade, the English were not deceived and promptly set spies to watch the American's every move. Despite this surveillance, Deane accomplished a great deal, since he was only asking for what the French government had already determined to give. The American representative, in secret interviews with Vergennes, was assured of French sympathy but not of open assistance. Deane soon learned that Beaumarchais was the intermediary through whom he was expected to do business.

Within a few months a steady stream of gunpowder, guns, cannon, and other supplies was crossing the Atlantic. These munitions were the main reliance of the Continental armies during the critical campaigns of 1777.

From the beginning, however, the financial relations of the American agents with Beaumarchais were hopelessly confused. During his early negotiations with the French playwright, Arthur Lee had gained the impression that the supplies from France were to be given as *subsidies*, with no expectation of repayment. When Beaumarchais learned, however, that Deane was authorized by Congress to *purchase* supplies, he negotiated a contract whereby Deane committed Congress to pay Hortalez & Company in goods or money at some later date. Congress ratified this agreement and exported tobacco and other supplies to France until the British blockade made this difficult. Before the end of the war, however,

[5] Equivalent to about $200,000 in eighteenth-century dollars.

the Americans regretted this arrangement, suspecting, on the basis of Lee's reports and other evidence, that Beaumarchais was demanding payment for supplies which the kings of France and Spain had intended to provide as gifts. Consequently, Congress refused to settle the Hortalez & Company claims. This was hardly just, however, because Beaumarchais had purchased extensively for the Americans on his own account over and above the 2 million livres advanced by the French and Spanish governments.[6]

Once committed to a policy of secret aid, Vergennes saw to it that more and more assistance was forthcoming. Subsidies totaling 2 million livres were transmitted to American agents in 1777, and larger amounts in subsequent years, so that the total amount granted by Louis XVI without expectation of repayment was 10.5 million livres, or about 2 million dollars in eighteenth-century money. Moreover, Congress obtained loans through French governmental channels of an additional 35 million livres (6.3 million dollars). The Spanish monarchy was also feeding money through secret channels to keep the American rebellion going. Exactly how much was thus transmitted is impossible to determine, but the total amount—including the grant to Beaumarchais in 1776—has been established at about $400,000. In addition to these subsidies, the Americans were able to borrow about $248,000 from Spanish sources.

France also aided in other ways. Vergennes insisted that French ships had a right to ply between the ports of the mother country and those of the French West Indies without British interference. This made it possible to accumulate munitions and supplies in Haiti and Martinique, where they could be easily transferred to the Americans. With cheerful deception Vergennes publicly closed French harbors to American privateers, while clandestinely allowing these vessels to equip themselves and dispose of their prizes on French soil. The British secret service was well aware of France's unneutral conduct, but the British government, anxious to avoid an enlargement of the war, pretended to accept Vergennes's bland assurances at face value.

The French Foreign Minister was highly pleased with the American assertion of independence in July, 1776, since this seemed to assure a final and complete breach between America and England. In August of that year Vergennes seriously considered whether the moment had not come for France and Spain to declare war on England. He obtained Louis's consent to propose such a policy to the Spanish government, which eagerly supported the idea—not out of any enthusiasm for American independence—

[6] The troublesome problem was not finally resolved until 1835, long after Beaumarchais's death, when the United States finally paid 800,000 livres to his heirs to settle claims that had totaled over 3.6 million livres—an act of substantial though delayed justice in a case where exact justice was impossible.

but because of the opportunity to conquer Portugal, Britain's long-time ally. Just when events were developing in this direction, however, news of a most discouraging nature reached Europe. The defeat of Washington on Long Island and the dreary succession of subsequent defeats and retreats during the fall of 1776 chilled all of Vergennes's enthusiasm for open intervention. Therefore he resumed his policy of watchful waiting.

The Plan of 1776

The work of the Committee of Secret Correspondence in formulating American foreign policy was greatly clarified by the Declaration of Independence. The new government of the United States clearly needed recognition of its status by foreign states, treaties to define American rights to trade in foreign ports, and additional help in maintaining its independence.

In September, 1776, Congress approved a model commercial treaty, which its agents were to propose first to France and then to other governments. This document, known as the Plan of 1776, was of historic importance in fixing the American position on certain points of international law that had been in dispute for many generations before 1776 and were destined to remain so long afterwards. These issues had particular reference to rights of neutral trade during wartime. The Plan of 1776 accepted the principle of "free ships, free goods"—that is, except for contraband of war, cargoes of neutral ships, whatever their ownership or destination, should be exempt from seizure by belligerent naval vessels or commerce raiders. Contraband consigned to a belligerent port was subject to seizure, but it was to be narrowly defined to include only actual implements of war, while excluding food, clothing, naval stores, and similar goods. Neutrals should have the right to carry goods from one belligerent port to another—this was a repudiation of the British "Rule of 1756," which asserted that a power that had prohibited its colonial trade to foreign vessels in time of peace could not reverse its policy in time of war. All in all, the Americans were taking their stand for a broad interpretation of neutral rights. This was an effective bid for the support of all European governments that resented British highhandedness on the seas and was also in shrewd anticipation of their own interest during future European wars.

The Mission of Benjamin Franklin

To obtain such a treaty of friendship and commerce with France, Congress, on September 26, 1776, appointed a commission composed of Benjamin Franklin, Silas Deane, and Thomas Jefferson. The serious illness of his wife and other personal problems prevented Jefferson's accepting this mission, and the choleric Arthur Lee was substituted.

One of the most interesting chapters in Franklin's long life of adventure opened when the seventy-year-old American arrived in France in December, 1776. The name of the famous citizen of Philadelphia who had drawn lightning from the clouds was already familiar to Frenchmen of all classes, and the news that he had come to represent his country at the French court was greeted with extraordinary enthusiasm. Although Franklin had long outgrown his artisan origins and become a polished gentleman, he shrewdly adopted the dress and mien that his French admirers looked for in the simple sage of an unspoiled New World society. French opinion assumed Franklin to be a Quaker, so he gladly accepted that role, despite his long-held deistic and rationalist views. To protect himself from the wintry blasts of the Atlantic voyage Franklin wore a fur cap. When he found that the French were enchanted with this simple headgear, he wore it instead of the fashionable powdered wig. Similarly he delighted Paris by wearing his spectacles all the time, instead of reserving them for his study according to the custom of the day. Altogether, Franklin was just the quaint and homely figure the French wanted him to be. Delineated in prints, busts, and ornamented snuffboxes, the American's picture was to be seen everywhere. Writing in amusement to his daughter, Franklin asserted that his face was now as well known as that of the moon and that "he durst not do anything that would oblige him to run away, as his phiz would discover him wherever he should venture to show it."

Although Franklin's popularity in France was largely a deserved recognition of his own character and achievements, it was his good fortune to arrive when the ideas of the philosopher Jean Jacques Rousseau were permeating upper- and middle-class society. Rousseau had condemned the artificialities and corruptions of civilized society and exalted the virtues of natural man living in a simple and unspoiled society. Through the eyes of romanticism, Franklin seemed the embodiment of these pristine virtues and America itself was regarded as a land of ideal promise.

By skillfully playing his assumed role and by writing anonymous pamphlets and other bits of propaganda, Franklin prepared French public opinion for whatever joint action with America the French government might take. A generous sympathy for the American cause impelled the young Marquis de Lafayette to cross the Atlantic, where he served under Washington with great distinction. Franklin was able to recommend another useful officer in Baron von Steuben, a German professional soldier who helped drill the raw Continental militiamen into real soldiers. There were many other European volunteers for commissions in the American army, but Franklin had to discourage most of them as irresponsible adventurers in search of money and glory.

Meanwhile Vergennes refused to be hurried. Throughout most of 1777 the news from America was bad. General Howe captured Philadelphia and forced the Continental Congress into undignified retreat. General

Burgoyne, invading New York State from Canada, captured Fort Ticonderoga with little opposition. Under these circumstances, the French government was little inclined to go further in helping the Americans than the policy of secret aid dictated.

Early in December, 1777, the exciting news reached France that Burgoyne's entire army had surrendered at Saratoga. Prospects that the United States would make good its claim of independence were now excellent. If France intended to avenge herself upon Britain, the time for action had arrived. Vergennes began immediately to press for the negotiation of treaties of friendship and alliance.

This turn of events also impelled the British government to new measures. To terminate the struggle in America and avert the threat of French intervention, Lord North's ministry formulated a proposal for reconciliation based upon repeal of the offending parliamentary legislation that had brought on the Revolution and the grant of a large degree of autonomy to the American Colonies. By now Congress was resolved to accept nothing less than independence, and the North plan had little chance of success. But awareness of what was under discussion revived the old French fear that the English and the Americans might patch up their quarrel and together swoop down on the French West Indies. Franklin and Deane shrewdly pressed their advantage, and Vergennes suddenly decided to abandon his cautious delay and adopt a program of action.

The Treaty of Alliance

On February 6, 1778, the diplomatic representatives of the United States and France affixed their signatures to a treaty of amity and commerce, drawn up in close conformity with the principles of the Plan of 1776, and a treaty of alliance, stipulating that, if war should break out between France and Great Britain during the present conflict between the United States and England, France and the United States would act as allies. The objective of the alliance was to be the maintenance of the absolute sovereignty and independence of the United States. If the United States should conquer Bermuda or Canada, the extension of her rule over these areas would be recognized by France, which renounced any claim to them. On the other hand, France was to have the right to retain any conquests in the British West Indies. The United States and France mutually promised not to make any truce or peace treaty with England without first obtaining the formal consent of the other party, and they agreed not to lay down their arms until the independence of the United States was assured. Finally, the two parties agreed to mutual guarantees "from the present time and forever." The United States guaranteed to the King of France all the possessions that he then held in the American area as well as any that he might acquire in the future treaty of peace, while the King of France guaranteed to the United States "their liberty, Sovereignty, and Independence absolute, and unlimited, as well in Matters of Government as commerce and also their Possessions, and the additions or conquests that their Confederation may obtain during the war. . . ."

This historic treaty of alliance was at first intended to be secret, but a full report on it was transmitted to London through the ubiquitous English spy system almost before the ink on the document was dry. The British government, still reluctant to have France as an active belligerent, took no immediate action, but war between the two ancient rivals could not long be delayed. On March 13, 1778, the French Ambassador at London notified the British government that his King had concluded a treaty of amity and commerce with the United States, and a week later formal recognition of the new nation was symbolized when Louis XVI received Franklin—still wigless and bespectacled—together with his fellow commissioners, at Versailles. On the evening of June 17, 1778, units of the French and British navies exchanged shots off the French coast, and the War of the American Revolution thereupon entered upon its international phase.

So closely had England guarded the lines of communication across the Atlantic that Congress had had no word of Franklin's activities in France for more than a year. Great was the excitement, therefore, when the first rumors of the French alliance reached America late in April, 1778, to be followed within a few days by the actual texts of the two treaties. Although the commissioners had somewhat exceeded their instructions, Congress enthusiastically ratified the agreements and passed resolutions of grateful acknowledgment of the French King's "truly magnanimous conduct."

The consummation of the alliance occurred just as the British government's attempt at reconciliation with the Colonies reached its final phase. A British commission, headed by Lord Carlisle, arrived in America in June, but the new arrangement with France made its prospects, never bright, completely hopeless. The irony of the situation was revealed when the Americans used some wine and turtles given them by the British peacemakers to entertain Conrad-Alexandre Gérard, King Louis's Minister to the United States, who reached Philadelphia in July with the fleet of the Count d'Estaing. From this time on the French navy and French expeditionary forces became increasingly important factors in the war.

Relations with Spain

From the moment he first adopted the policy of secret aid to the Americans, Vergennes had hoped that France and Spain could act in close collaboration. Spain had cooperated to the extent of supplying money to keep the American insurrection alive, but she had little enthusiasm for the idea of a strong and independent United States. An open sore in the British Empire was one thing; the emergence of an aggressive new republic in America was something else again. The example of the United States might incite rebellion in the Spanish New World colonies; rapid growth of population and assertive nationalism might lead the new nation into a policy of expansionism that would threaten the Spanish Empire. Determined to act only in line with its own interests, the Spanish government rejected Vergennes's proposal that Charles III should unite with Louis XVI in allying with the United States.

The primary objective of Spanish foreign policy was to recover the fortress of Gibraltar that Spain had been compelled to cede to England in 1713 after the War of the Spanish Succession. The new situation created by France's entry into the War of the American Revolution seemed to offer Spain an opportunity for achieving this end. Throughout 1778 Spain remained neutral and expressed a desire to mediate among the belligerents to bring the war to a close. Floridablanca, the new Spanish Foreign Minister, hoped the British would return Gibraltar to keep Spain permanently out of the war. England, however, was not prepared to pay so high a price, and in April, 1779, events moved to a showdown. The British government rejected the peace terms contained in a Spanish ultimatum, and the Spanish government promptly signed a treaty of alliance (the so-called Convention of Aranjuez) with France. Spain was to enter the war against England, and the two allies were not to make peace until Gibraltar was restored to Spain. The latter power was also promised territory in Florida and other parts of the British Empire that she might conquer. The following June Spain declared war on England.

Spanish entry into the war was not an unmixed blessing for the Americans. Spain's alliance was with France, not with the United States. Indeed, the Spanish government continued to refuse to recognize the independence of the New World republic. Even after hostilities opened between Spain and England, Floridablanca secretly negotiated with the enemy, looking toward a possible bargain under which Spain would get Gibraltar while England would retain those sections of the American Colonies then within her military lines. George III's stubbornness, so injurious to the Americans before the war, now benefited them. The English King would not relinquish the "rock." Spanish military and naval effort in the war was largely concentrated on a clumsy and unsuccessful attempt to conquer the famous fortress by siege and blockade. Spain's only military activity in North America was to occupy West Florida.

Hoping for a direct alliance with Spain and more extensive aid, Congress sent John Jay to Madrid, but his mission was almost completely unsuccessful. Floridablanca refused to receive him officially or to do anything else that would imply recognition of American independence. Jay was able to negotiate a few small loans for the purchase of supplies, but the principal result of his long stay in Spain was to give him a disillusioning education in the wiles of European diplomacy.

The Spanish problem also complicated the relations of the United States with France. Vergennes, eager to get and keep Spain in the war, instructed Minister Gérard to protect Spanish interests as well as those of France. Gérard tried to induce Congress to give Spain a free hand in Florida and to recognize Spain's right to control not only the Mississippi River, but even areas to the east of that river. The French Minister's attempts to influence American policy in this direction served only to arouse American suspicions that France, like Spain, would bear watching.

Holland Enters the War

Despite the delicacy of the situation in which France found herself in trying to maintain alliances with both the United States and Spain, the Spanish declaration of war on England had been a major victory for the French in their principal diplomatic objective—to keep England isolated in her hour of troubles. Developments elsewhere in Europe contributed to the same end.

Most Dutchmen were indifferent to the issues of the American Revolution and wished to keep their country free from involvement in the New World contest. Neutrality, in truth, promised to be very profitable to the Dutch. The Dutch West Indian island of St. Eustatius became a busy mart where American blockade runners picked up vast quantities of munitions and supplies. Many of the shipments from Beaumarchais's Hortalez & Company utilized this route. After France entered the war, new opportunities for profit opened for the Dutch, who became heavily involved in transporting naval stores from Baltic ports to France. The obvious policy for Vergennes to follow was not to encourage the Netherlands to enter the war against England, but to keep her neutral so that France could benefit both from the Dutch carrying trade and the opportunities to borrow from rich Amsterdam bankers.

Dutch neutrality, however, was difficult to maintain. The Netherlands government insisted upon its right to carry naval stores to the French ports; the British government protested that these were contraband of war. The situation was complicated by the existence of two century-old treaties between the two countries. An Anglo-Dutch treaty of 1674 supported the Dutch contention that naval stores were not to be considered contraband, but a treaty of 1678 required each to come to the support of the other in case of war. The British government tried to use the alliance treaty to induce the Netherlands to restrict its trade with France. The Dutch government, artfully influenced by French diplomacy, rejected this proposal and voted to protect its cargoes of naval stores with convoys.

English policy toward the Netherlands now stiffened. The London government called upon the Dutch to enter the war on the British side in conformity with the old alliance. If the Netherlands were to comply, the profitable trade with France and America would be immediately cut off. The Dutch, however, were by no means ready to alter their policy. Instead they turned to a desperate attempt to win support among the nations linked in the Armed Neutrality, presently to be discussed.

At just this juncture the British government found a convenient pretext for declaring war on the Netherlands. Henry Laurens of South Carolina, whom the Continental Congress had sent to seek aid from the Dutch government, was captured by the English at sea before he ever reached his destination. Among his papers was found the draft of a proposed commercial treaty between the Netherlands and the United States. The draft had resulted from discussions through strictly unofficial channels and was not intended to be acted upon until the British government had recognized the independence of her former colonies. Nevertheless, the English used the document to charge that the Dutch had entered into a secret agreement with the Americans. Citing this and other reasons, the British government declared war on the Netherlands in December, 1780.

The Dutch were ill-prepared to defend themselves and suffered severely. English warships and privateers searched the seas for Dutch vessels and took scores of easy prizes. The British navy wiped out the annoyance of St. Eustatius by swooping down on that island, capturing it, and seizing a rich store of plunder. Although the elimination of this source of supplies was a blow to the Americans, the episode had more than compensating advantages. While the British Admiral Rodney was thus occupied, the French Admiral Count de Grasse slipped out of the West Indies for the American mainland, where he eventually played a decisive part in the Yorktown campaign.

Congress, delighted to see another nation drawn into the war, ordered John Adams—already in Europe on another mission—to proceed to The Hague to obtain recognition of American independence, a commercial treaty from the Netherlands government, and a loan from the great Dutch banking houses. At first the New Englander received a discouragingly cool reception, but his dogged persistence eventually won out. On October 8, 1782, the Netherlands government agreed to a treaty of commerce and friendship with the United States—the second such treaty in American history. Adams was also able to complete arrangements with Dutch bankers for a loan of 5 million guilders (about 1 million dollars) to the United States in 1782.

The Armed Neutrality

Meanwhile other European governments had become deeply involved in the problem of neutral rights. At the Russian court of the masterful Catherine the Great, the French and English ambassadors were engaged in a contest of intrigue, each trying to influence Russian policy to benefit his own particular cause. Catherine became equally indignant with all the belligerents, especially after a succession of incidents in which American privateers seized British prizes off the Russian coast, Spanish ships claimed the right to stop all Mediterranean-bound neutral cargoes ultimately destined for Gibraltar, and British naval vessels attempted to break up neutral trade in naval stores. The Empress mobilized her naval strength to protect Russian shipping against all belligerents and announced the principles of international law which she intended to maintain. This Russian Declaration of February 28, 1780, addressed to the British, French, and Spanish governments, closely resembled the American Plan of 1776 and the Franco-American commercial treaty of 1778 in asserting that neutral vessels should have the right to navigate freely from one belligerent port to another, that the cargoes of neutral vessels should be exempt from seizure except as contraband of war, and that contraband should be narrowly defined and should not include naval stores and provisions. A new and important principle incorporated in Catherine's Declaration provided that a port could only be legally blockaded by stationing naval vessels sufficiently near to render access to the port clearly dangerous.

The Russian government invited other neutral states to join it in defending these rights. Denmark acceded to this so-called Armed Neutrality in July, 1780; Sweden and the Netherlands joined later in the same year. In 1781 Prussia and Austria added their signatures, to be followed finally by Portugal in 1782 and the Kingdom of the Two Sicilies in 1783. Vergennes, eager to turn this development to French advantage, announced that his country's navy would observe these principles, and the Spanish government, at French insistence, took a similar stand. Britain, reluctant to give up the advantages that superior naval power afforded her, did not accept this charter of neutral rights. However, the English were not eager to bring still other powers into the war against them, so in practice they modified their policy toward neutral shipping.

Congress, ever hopeful of turning these European developments to the advantage of the United States, sent Francis Dana, who had been serving as John Adams's secretary, to St. Petersburg. But Dana's efforts to obtain recognition for his government and an invitation to join the League of the Armed Neutrality were unavailing. Catherine was by no means disposed to encourage upstart republicanism by entering into diplomatic relations with the American government, nor did she wish to jeopardize the possibility of seizing the center of the diplomatic stage by acting as mediator between the two belligerent camps.

In the end, therefore, American Revolutionary diplomacy only achieved one military alliance for the United States and two commercial treaties. And even in the case of France and the Netherlands, self-interest, rather than enthusiasm for American independence, was the motivating force. Yet if the United States received a rather cool reception into the family of nations, the general European situation worked greatly to American advantage. If the English had not been involved in war with the French after 1778; if they had not been obliged to defend Gibraltar against a determined Spanish siege; if they had not been harassed by controversies over neutral rights; if their hands had been free, in short, to devote all their energies to breaking the American rebellion, the independence of the United States would have been much more difficult to achieve. England's difficulty was indeed America's opportunity.

2

PEACE AND ITS PROBLEMS

Like a stone thrown into a pool, the American Revolution had sent out concentric circles of influence touching more and more countries. That the Americans would make good on their claim of independence appeared increasingly certain after 1778, but just how and when peace would be finally achieved depended on complex diplomatic factors. The situation was not without serious dangers for the infant United States, since there was an ever-present danger that in the diplomatic bargaining American interests might be sacrificed to obtain advantages for European powers. It is a remarkable tribute to the ability and shrewdness of Benjamin Franklin, John Jay, and John Adams that these pioneer American diplomats more than held their own in contending for the rights of the United States at the conference table. But even after a satisfactory treaty of peace was signed, the new republic was confronted with alarming perils to its welfare, particularly along the sparsely settled borders between the United States and the neighboring possessions of Britain and Spain.

Congress Appoints Peace Commissioners

As early as 1779 Congress was confronted with the problem of appointing a peace commissioner and drawing up instructions to guide his conduct. At this time—just before Spain entered the war as the ally of France —the Spanish government was attempting to play the role of mediator. Vergennes, eager to cooperate, sent word to Philadelphia through the French Minister, Conrad Gérard, that it would be wise for Congress to grant Benjamin Franklin full powers to represent the United States at any peace conference that might result from the Spanish maneuver. The French diplomat worked hard for several months not only to get this post for Franklin, but to have the latter's instructions framed in such a way that Spain's claims to both banks of the Mississippi would not be challenged. Fearing that Franklin was too much under the influence of Vergennes, Congress appointed John Adams peace commissioner instead. In his instructions Adams was ordered to make it "a preliminary article to any negotiation that Great Britain shall agree to treat with the United States as sovereign, free, and independent." The boundaries to be claimed included the Mississippi River on the west and the 31st parallel on the south. To the north, Congress emphasized the importance of obtaining Canada and Nova Scotia and equal rights in the fisheries, but did not make these terms unconditional. Adams was to be guided by the advice of America's allies and by his own discretion.

If it were intended to give this mission to a man of sturdy independence, Congress could not have found a better agent than John Adams. The Massachusetts lawyer and patriot leader possessed many sterling virtues—persistence, honesty, erudition, and devotion to duty. Yet he had his conspicuous failings also; he was pompous, vain, irritable, and incurably suspicious of other men's motives. He was in most respects the opposite of the urbane and tolerant Franklin, and he made no secret of his disapproval of the old philosopher. It especially offended the strait-laced New Englander that Franklin "at the age of seventy-odd had neither lost his love of beauty nor his taste for it"—in other words, that Franklin still liked the company of lovely ladies.[1] If Adams could not get along with his famous American compatriot, it was scarcely to be expected that he would do so with the polished and devious Vergennes. The peace commissioner and the French Foreign Minister promptly took a strong dislike to each other. Adams went to the Netherlands in disgust, and Vergennes pulled wires either to have Adams's commission transferred to some other agent or to have new instructions sent out requiring the American to accept French advice.

By this time the prospects for immediate peace talks were not bright. The Spanish mediation proposals had failed, and Spain was attempting to obtain Gibraltar and other objectives by force. But a series of events, beginning in December, 1780, renewed hope that the belligerents could be brought together at the conference table. Catherine the Great, eager to play the role of peacemaker and to advance the recently formulated principles of the Armed Neutrality, offered her services as mediator. The British government, hopeful of appeasing Russia, accepted this offer in principle and suggested Austria as a co-mediator.

---

[1] Prior to Adams's appointment as peace commissioner, Franklin, Arthur Lee, and Adams had been fellow commissioners to the court of France. Adams had taken the place of Silas Deane, who was recalled in December, 1777. This arrangement had been terminated in February, 1779, when Franklin received an appointment as sole Minister Plenipotentiary to France.

The Vergennes Truce Proposal

The French government replied to the proposal cautiously, but by no means unfavorably. Vergennes was in fact anxious to bring the war to a close. The enormous expenses were threatening to bankrupt French finances, and the news from the battlefronts was far from encouraging. A secret memorandum prepared by the French Foreign Minister in February, 1781, gives evidence of the extremes to which France would have gone to obtain peace. She would have assented to a long-term truce between Britain and the United States, leaving in British possession all the American territories then occupied by English troops, except New York. Peace on this basis would have deprived the new republic of large sections of North Carolina, South Carolina, and Georgia, as well as most of Maine and the fortified posts in the Great Lakes area.

Vergennes's hope to buy peace at America's expense—if such a course of action became necessary—made it important for France to get not only more pliant American peace commissioners than the stubborn Adams, but also new instructions from Congress that would bind the American negotiators more closely to their French allies. The Chevalier de la Luzerne, who succeeded Gérard as French Minister to the United States in 1779, used his wealth and engaging manners to win an extraordinary influence over Congress. At his prompting the American lawmakers on June 15, 1781, enlarged the peace commission to include Benjamin Franklin, John Jay, Henry Laurens, and Thomas Jefferson. In its new instructions Congress laid down only two essential conditions: the commissioners were not to sign any treaty unless it recognized the independence and sovereignty of the United States and left the American treaties with France in full force. As to other terms, the commissioners were given wide discretion, but were instructed

> ...to make the most candid and confidential communications upon all subjects to the ministers of our generous ally, the King of France; to undertake nothing in the negotiations for peace or truce without their knowledge and concurrence; and ultimately to govern yourselves by their advice and opinion.

Adams and Jay protested vainly against what seemed to them Congress's unwarranted trust in the disinterested benevolence of the French government.

The Rockingham Ministry

Peacemaking on the basis of Austro-Russian mediation made no further progress during 1781, largely because George III still refused to accept the loss of his American Colonies. But the fateful news that Cornwallis had surrendered his entire army at Yorktown in October, 1781, spurred the parliamentary opposition to a spirited attack upon the whole system by which the King had so long dominated policy. Under this storm of criticism, Lord North, the Prime Minister, finally resigned on March 20, 1782. The distraught monarch threatened to abdicate rather than accept the opposition leaders as ministers, but in the end he had to swallow this bitter pill. Lord Rockingham, always an advocate of generous measures toward America, became Prime Minister, and Lord Shelburne and Charles James Fox, representatives of rival Whig factions, took over the principal cabinet posts. As Secretary for Home Affairs, Shelburne was in charge of colonial matters; as Secretary for Foreign Affairs, Fox had responsibility for diplomatic problems. Until American independence was formally recognized, negotiations with the former colonists would, therefore, be in the hands of Shelburne.

Immediately after taking office, Shelburne initiated policies that he hoped might drive a wedge between the United States and France. Sir Guy Carleton, the new commanding general who replaced Henry Clinton at New York, was instructed to avoid battle and to seek a local armistice that would permit the peaceful withdrawal of British troops for use against France and Spain on other fronts. Washington and Congress, however, refused to consider any deal that would violate the spirit of the French alliance. Shelburne's other moves were more effective. To sound out John Adams, then in the Netherlands, the British Minister paroled Henry Laurens, who had been a prisoner of war since his capture in 1780. To make contact with Benjamin Franklin in France, Shelburne employed Richard Oswald, a wealthy Scotch merchant whose slave-trading activities and land purchases had given him an interest in American affairs. As a young man Oswald had lived in Virginia; in later years he had developed a taste for philosophy and philanthropy. All in all, he was the kind of person whom Shelburne hoped Franklin would find congenial.

Anglo-American Negotiations

Franklin and Oswald did in fact take to each other at once. During their preliminary conversations in April, 1782, the American let it be known he would be glad to treat for peace, but only after first consulting with his fellow peace commissioners. Furthermore, Franklin insisted, the Americans would negotiate only in concert with their allies. The shrewd old philosopher suggested that one of the best ways for Britain to cement good relations with the United States would be to cede Canada to the new republic.

Despite these promising overtures, several months of diplomatic sparring were required before really serious peace negotiations could begin. On the British side, the rivalry of Fox and Shelburne made a consistent policy impossible. This conflict of counsels at London was reflected at Paris, where Oswald continued to serve as Shelburne's agent in negotiating with the Americans, while Thomas Grenville represented Fox in dealings with the French government. The lines of authority were finally cleared in July, when Rockingham died, Shelburne became Prime Minister, and Fox resigned.

On the American side, there was delay and difficulty in assembling the five commissioners. Jay had to wind up his affairs in Madrid and did not arrive in Paris until late in June. Adams, reluctant to leave the Netherlands until he had completed negotiations for the commercial treaty and loan, did not reach the French capital until October. Laurens, ill and discouraged by personal misfortunes, tried to avoid serving at all and only appeared late in November when negotiations were nearly completed. Delayed by the illness and death of his wife and other troubles, Jefferson never left America. Consequently, the responsibility for peacemaking rested essentially with Franklin, Jay, and Adams.

Jay brought with him a lively suspicion of Spanish diplomacy. Soon after his arrival in France, conversations with the Count of Aranda, the Spanish Ambassador, antagonized the American still further. Far from conceding Jay's claim that the western and southern boundaries of the United States should follow the Mississippi and the 31st parallel, Aranda demanded that the line run some three or four hundred miles to the east of the Mississippi. Jay's suspicion of Spain was extended to France when Gérard de Rayneval, Vergennes's private secretary, proposed a compromise that would have left the territory north of the Ohio River in the possession of England and established an Indian buffer state to the south of that river. It looked, in Franklin's phrase, like a plan "to coop us up within the Allegheny Mountains."

Jay was still further upset by the news that Rayneval had departed on a mysterious mission to London. Convinced that the French were attempting to undermine the American position, Jay, without even consulting Franklin, sent his own personal emissary to Shelburne to suggest that if the British cabinet gave new instructions to Oswald, the American and English negotiators might reach an agreement. Shelburne, still hoping to drive a wedge between the United States and France, acted promptly on this hint. On September 19 the British cabinet voted to empower Oswald "to treat with the Commissioners appointed by the Colonys, under the title of Thirteen United States, inasmuch as the Commissioners have offered under that condition to accept the Independence of America as the First Article of the Treaty." Although this language was far from clear, Jay and Franklin chose to interpret it as constituting the prior

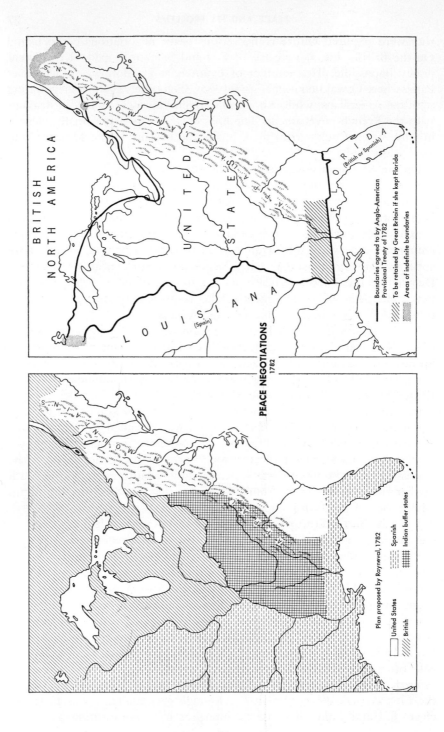

PEACE NEGOTIATIONS
1782

Top map labels:

BRITISH NORTH AMERICA

UNITED STATES

LOUISIANA
(Spain)

FLORIDA
(British or Spanish)

Boundaries agreed to by Anglo-American Provisional Treaty of 1782

To be retained by Great Britain if she kept Florida

Areas of indefinite boundaries

Bottom map legend:

Plan proposed by Rayneval, 1782

United States

British

Spanish

Indian buffer states

recognition of independence upon which they had been insisting. Formal negotiations were instituted early in October when Jay handed Oswald the first draft of a proposed treaty.

The British government was by no means prepared to accept the American terms on all points. Indeed, news of the failure of the latest Spanish effort to capture Gibraltar reached London at just this time, thereby stiffening the English attitude. Shelburne sent a second representative, Henry Strachey, to Paris to assist Oswald with orders to oppose some of the American claims for fishing rights and to demand that the Americans recognize the right of the Tories to recover their confiscated estates and that of British merchants to collect their old colonial accounts. During November there was hard bargaining on all of these points. Adams, now present on the American side of the table, agreed with Jay that the negotiations be carried on without consulting the French. With some reluctance Franklin acquiesced in this procedure—one which clearly violated the commissioners' instructions from Congress.

The Provisional Treaty

On November 30, 1782, the American and English commissioners affixed their signatures to a provisional treaty of peace, not to become effective until Great Britain and France had agreed on terms. By the first article the King of England acknowledged the United States to be "free Sovereign and independent States," to which he relinquished all governmental and proprietary claims. The second article defined the boundaries of the United States. On the north, the line was irregularly drawn to follow the St. Croix River from its mouth to its source, thence due north to the watershed between the St. Lawrence River and the Atlantic Ocean and then to follow various landmarks, parallels of latitude, and bodies of water through the Great Lakes and northwestward to the Lake of the Woods, from which the line was to run due west to the Mississippi River. The western boundary followed the middle of the Mississippi River to the 31st degree of north latitude. The southern boundary followed the 31st parallel to the Chattahoochee River, and thence in irregular fashion to the Atlantic Ocean. In a separate and secret article the Americans agreed that in case Britain should recover West Florida in the final peace treaty, the southern boundary should run from the mouth of the Yazoo River due east to the Chattahoochee. (This would mean a line drawn at approximately 32°30'.)

The provisional treaty gave valuable fishing rights to the Americans— rights of particular importance to John Adams's fellow New Englanders. United States citizens were to continue to enjoy the right to fish on the Grand Banks of Newfoundland and also in other customary places in the

Gulf of St. Lawrence and along the coasts of the British North American possessions. The right to cure and dry fish on the beaches was restricted to the unsettled parts of Nova Scotia, the Magdalen Islands, and Labrador.

On the issues upon which the British negotiators had put up their most stubborn fight, the Americans agreed to provisions which permitted the English government to save face, but gave little actual protection to the affected interests. Article Four stated that creditors on both sides should "meet with no lawful impediment to the Recovery of the full value in Sterling Money of all bona fide Debts heretofore contracted." Article Five stipulated that Congress should "earnestly recommend" to the legislatures of the respective states that they provide for the restitution of the confiscated estates and properties of all Loyalists except those who had borne arms against the United States. Article Six provided that no future confiscations should be made, nor any prosecutions commenced, against any person by reason of any part he might have taken during the war.

The remaining articles provided for the mutual release of prisoners, for the evacuation of British forces from previously defined United States "with all convenient speed," and for free navigation of the Mississippi from source to mouth by both British subjects and American citizens.

Vergennes's first comment about this provisional treaty was mildly critical. The hasty signing, he said, "had not been particularly civil to the king." But the French Minister conceded the Americans had obtained good terms and that English recognition of American independence might facilitate a general peace treaty. A few days later Vergennes had an opportunity to express himself in more positive terms. Franklin had asked the French government to make still another loan to the impoverished government of the United States; Vergennes replied in a letter that politely but pointedly referred to the American commissioners' disregard of their instructions from Congress and their failure to consult with the French government before reaching an understanding with England. How did the Americans propose to carry out their obligations as allies in the future? "When you shall be pleased to relieve my uncertainty I will entreat the king to enable me to answer your demands." Franklin responded to this courteous rebuke with an adroit letter, admitting that he and his colleagues had been guilty of neglecting a point of propriety, but denying that this reflected any want of respect for Louis XVI, "whom we all love and honour. . . . *The English, I just now learn, flatter themselves they have already divided us.* I hope this little misunderstanding will therefore be kept a secret and that they will find themselves totally mistaken." Franklin's soft answer mollified the Minister, and the French government, although desperately short of funds, paid the first installment on a new loan of 6 million livres to the United States.

The Definitive Treaties

Actually the Anglo-American provisional treaty helped, rather than injured, France. The government of Louis XVI needed peace and could not afford to have the war prolonged while Spain launched more offensives against stubborn Gibraltar. News of the provisional treaty precipitated a new round of diplomatic bargaining among the other belligerents, and on January 20, 1783, a general armistice was achieved when English negotiators signed preliminary peace treaties with both France and Spain. The definitive treaties formally terminating the war were not signed until nine months later, largely because of a political overturn in England. Although Shelburne's policy appears today to have been statesmanlike, it was then unpopular in his own country. The terms of the settlements were severely criticized in Parliament, and in February Shelburne was forced out of office. The new ministry was based upon an unnatural coalition between Charles James Fox and Lord North, formerly bitter political enemies. New English agents failed to achieve better terms, and on September 3, 1783, definitive treaties of peace between England on the one hand and the United States, France, and Spain on the other were signed.[2]

In its settlement with Spain, England retained Gibraltar, but gave up East and West Florida and the Mediterranean island of Minorca and also accepted a limitation upon its claims to the Honduran coast in Central America. To France the British made a number of similar minor territorial concessions. They ceded the island of Tobago in the West Indies and slave-trading posts in the Senegal region of West Africa. They also turned over to the French the small islands of St. Pierre and Miquelon in the Gulf of St. Lawrence as fishing stations, but not as naval bases. For a nation compelled to defend an empire spread all the way from America to India against a formidable array of enemies, the English had not done badly. Nevertheless, when George III was compelled to recognize the independence of the United States, he signed away his most populous and valuable colonies. This constituted the real revenge of France and Spain against the power that had humiliated them in 1763.

When news of the provisional treaty first reached America, it received a mixed reception. Its terms were highly satisfactory, but the possibility that the American peace commissioners had antagonized France caused some anxiety. Congress debated whether its agents should not be recalled or reprimanded for their failure to follow instructions. Before any such step could be taken, however, further news indicating that Vergennes's

[2] The final Anglo-Dutch peace treaty was not signed until May 20, 1784.

annoyance with the peace commissions had been short-lived and that France and Spain were ready to make their own settlements with England threw an entirely new light on the situation. Franklin, Jay, and Adams received the credit they deserved for an assignment brilliantly performed. Some students have reserved their warmest praise for Jay and Adams on the grounds that their realism and boldness saved the United States from the mistakes which Franklin might have made because of his advanced age and excessive trust in France. But an examination of the earlier phase of the negotiations, when Franklin was dealing alone with Oswald, will demonstrate that the grand old man was still well able to take care of himself. All the essential American demands were formulated at that time. Even without the assistance of Jay and Adams, Franklin would undoubtedly have gained a good treaty. While he would probably have treated Vergennes with more deference during the negotiations, there is no reason to believe that he would have sacrificed any American interest to Spanish and French intrigue. The leading authority on the diplomacy of the Revolution gives equal credit to each of the three men for what he calls "the greatest victory in the annals of American diplomacy." [3]

Growth of the Diplomatic Service

American diplomatic success had resulted from favoring international factors and a shrewd capitalizing on opportunity, rather than from careful planning and administrative efficiency. Actually the agencies of the new United States government for dealing with foreign affairs were being fashioned during these years through a process of trial and error—and often error seemed to prevail.

A strong faction in the Continental Congress, led by such famous patriots as Samuel Adams and Richard Henry Lee, opposed all proposals for concentrating executive responsibility in permanent departments or individual officers. As long as this group was dominant, Congress itself attempted to conduct the foreign affairs of the nation, drafting instructions to agents abroad in sessions at which the French Minister was often present. To assist it in these duties Congress depended on a system of committees. The Committee of Secret Correspondence, created in 1775, was renamed the Committee for Foreign Affairs on April 17, 1777.

These administrative arrangements became increasingly unsatisfactory as time went on. The most conscientious member of the Committee for Foreign Affairs was James Lovell, a Boston schoolmaster, but often he was discouraged. In 1779 he wrote: "There is really no such thing as a committee of foreign affairs existing—no secretary or clerk further than

[3] Samuel Flagg Bemis, *The Diplomacy of the American Revolution* (New York: Appleton-Century-Crofts, Inc., 1935), p. 256.

I persevere to be one and the other." Communications from American agents abroad sometimes went unopened and unanswered for months, and anything like consistent policy was impossible because of the changing personnel of the committee and Congress's unwillingness to delegate any real authority.

Franklin advised the new government to follow the traditional practices of diplomacy and send ministers only to those governments which had extended recognition to the United States. He believed, in his own characteristic phrase, that "a virgin State should preserve its virgin character and not go about suitering for alliances, but wait with decent dignity for the application of others." But Congress had little patience with such Old World conventions. "Militia" diplomats, like militia troops, thought John Adams, "sometimes gain victories over regular troops, even by departing from the rules." In keeping with this philosophy, Congress sent diplomatic militiamen to most European courts to demand not only recognition, but subsidies. Arthur Lee was commissioned to go to Madrid, with Berlin as an alternative; William Lee was directed to go to Vienna, Francis Dana to St. Petersburg, John Adams to The Hague, and Ralph Izard to Florence. This policy was completely unrealistic. Since only France was even contemplating recognition of the brash new republic, these agents were rebuffed when they tried to carry out their missions. For the most part, however, they made no such attempt, but settled in Paris instead. Their maintenance burdened Congress with unnecessary expense, and Franklin was hampered with their bickering and conflicting advice.

In 1781 the lines of authority for dealing with foreign affairs were somewhat clarified. The Articles of Confederation, finally ratified in March, prohibited the individual states from levying war or maintaining diplomatic relations with foreign governments, and vested these powers in the central government. Even before the articles went into effect, the nationalist faction in Congress had obtained the passage of a law authorizing the appointment of a single Secretary of Foreign Affairs. After several months of wrangling, Robert R. Livingston of New York was elected to the new post, largely through the influence of La Luzerne, the French Minister.

The new Secretary was an able man, who tried to bring some order into the handling of foreign affairs, but he found serious obstacles in his path. His relationships with Congress were imperfectly defined, and that body continued to interfere with the day-by-day conduct of diplomacy. Believing himself underpaid, Livingston resigned to become Chancellor of the State of New York in 1783. Congress, after considerable discussion, finally elected John Jay, who took office late in the year 1784. To assist the new Secretary in his duties, Congress provided for an undersecretary and a small staff of clerks and interpreters. Determined to make the most of his authority, Jay insisted that all correspondence with foreign governments go through his office. Since he regularly attended Congress and served on its committees, the Secretary of Foreign Affairs now became one of the most powerful men in the Confederation government.

The United States continued to be well represented in foreign capitals. In 1784 Congress sent Thomas Jefferson to Europe to serve as a fellow commissioner with Franklin and Adams in negotiating commercial treaties with the various European powers. A year later this assignment was significantly modified. The old and ailing Franklin was permitted to return to America; Adams was appointed Minister to England, and Jefferson Minister to France.

Negotiating Commercial Treaties

Rosy dreams of the great commercial advantages to be won by independence did not all come true. The world of the 1780s was one in which the ideal of free trade among nations had only weak support. Responsible statesmen still cherished the illusions of mercantilism, hoping to reserve as many economic privileges as possible for their own country's merchants and to make as few concessions to foreigners as possible. The United States, an infant republic, would not have been in a strong bargaining position in any case, but its position was made all the weaker by the Articles of Confederation under which each state could regulate its own commerce.

Nevertheless, some progress was made in the opening of foreign ports to American shipping. The United States already had commercial treaties with France and the Netherlands. With the former state, however, trade was still heavily encumbered by mercantilist restrictions and royal monopolies. Jefferson persistently pressed the French government to modify its laws to provide a better market for American goods. By the time he returned to America in 1789, he had won substantial concessions. The practical result, however, was small, since the French Revolution and the wars that followed soon disrupted all normal trade relations.

Sweden agreed to a commercial treaty with the United States in 1783, and Prussia followed in 1785. The Prussian treaty was a particularly enlightened one, providing not only for the liberal definition of neutral rights laid down in the American Plan of 1776, but incorporating additional clauses in which the two parties agreed, in case of war between them, not to commission privateers and not to seize contraband without compensation.

Before the Revolution, American ships sailing the Mediterranean had been protected from the molestation of the piratical Barbary States of North Africa by English treaties and the British navy, but now the Americans were on their own. With the Sultan of Morocco the United States made a satisfactory agreement in 1787, but the potentates of Algiers, Tunis, and Tripoli proved impossible to deal with. Two American ships with their crews were seized by the Algerians in 1785, and an outrageous sum was demanded for their ransom. Adams advised the United States to follow the general European practice of making regular payments to the Barbary rulers; Jefferson advocated a stronger navy and forceful protection of American rights. Neither policy was feasible, because the United States had neither the money to pay tribute nor the naval power to compel recognition of its rights. Consequently Congress did nothing. The problem of the Barbary pirates, like so many other problems of the 1780s, was insoluble until the United States had established a stronger government and acquired greater resources.

Difficulties with England

The treaty of peace clearly defined the new political relationship between England and her former American Colonies. The question of their commercial relationship, however, was not easily resolved. Despite American annoyance with some features of the old Navigation Acts, a generally prosperous trade had characterized the pre-Revolutionary British Empire. English merchants and manufacturers had done a thriving business in providing the colonists with fabricated goods, while the Americans had found in England their principal market for naval stores, tobacco, rice, and indigo. Even more profitable had been the trade between the mainland Colonies and the British West Indies, with the Americans supplying the islanders with provisions, lumber, and slaves, and receiving payment in sugar and molasses. Was American independence to result in the disruption of all these familiar patterns of commerce?

A number of influential Englishmen urged that Britain's true interest lay in the adoption of a liberal trade policy toward the former Colonies. Adam Smith, the great Scottish economist, advocated this, as did Lord Shelburne, Edmund Burke, Charles James Fox, and William Pitt. On practical rather than theoretical grounds English merchants and West Indies planters also urged generous concessions. With the rank and file of members of Parliament, however, such proposals were highly unpopular. Since the Americans had taken themselves out of the British Empire, let them suffer the consequences. The Navigation Acts had made England the world's greatest shipping and trading nation; therefore these laws should not be relaxed on the basis of dubious economic theories and sentimental hopes for reconciliation with the United States.

The conservatives who opposed concessions to the Americans were ably led by the Earl of Sheffield, a wealthy landowner who felt that he had a mission to preserve English supremacy in shipping and shipbuilding. In 1783 he published *Observations on the Commerce of the United States,* in which the case for a tough policy was persuasively stated. From Sheffield's point of view:

> It is now to be decided whether we are to be ruined by the independence of America or not. The peace, in comparison was a trifling object; and, if the neglect of any one interest more than another deserves impeachment, surely it will be the neglect of this, which involves in it, not merely the greatness, but even the very existence of our country.

The Earl argued that no special concessions to the United States were necessary. English manufacturers would inevitably capture the American market, since foreign competitors could not afford to extend the necessary credit. There was no need to fear American retaliation because of the weakness of the Confederation government.

During the crucial year 1783, when British policy toward the former Colonies was being formulated, Lord Sheffield and his conservative allies completely routed the liberals. A bill introduced by William Pitt to treat American ships carrying American goods as if they were British ships was defeated. The possibility of incorporating the principle of Anglo-American commercial reciprocity in the final peace treaty was discussed by the American commissioners and David Hartley, who represented the Fox-North ministry, but these discussions came to nought because of increasing English opposition to all such concessions. Instead Parliament merely repealed the Prohibitory Act, which since 1775 had banned trade between the American Colonies and the loyal parts of the British Empire. The actual rules for future trade were to be formulated by the Privy Council. By an order in council of July, 1783, American ships were excluded from the British West Indies carrying trade. Certain commodities like tobacco, provisions, and naval stores might be imported into the islands from the United States, but only in British ships. Trade with Canada was even more narrowly restricted: no American goods could be imported except in times of emergency. Commerce between the United States and England itself, however, was placed on a much more favorable basis: American ships were allowed to bring unmanufactured goods except whale oil into English ports on the same terms as in pre-Revolutionary days.

The British decision to exclude American ships from the West Indies was based on the assumptions that the profits of this carrying trade could be captured by English shippers and that Nova Scotia and the other British maritime provinces could supply a major portion of the provisions needed in the islands. These premises proved faulty. West Indies planters knew from experience that they could be more cheaply and conveniently supplied from the familiar American sources than from any other. When their pleas for a modification of British policy went unheeded, the planters connived with American sea captains in wholesale defiance of the regulations. Complaisant colonial governors declared frequent states of emergency in order to admit American ships, or allowed the forbidden vessels to enter the ports under the convenient fiction that they were in need of repairs. Another gaping loophole in the British system was the proximity of French, Dutch, and Spanish islands to which American goods could be taken and thence smuggled to the British islands.

The English refusal to negotiate a liberal commercial treaty was thus more an annoyance to the Americans than a serious handicap to their commerce. Within two or three years after the war, powerful economic forces were pushing trade back into the old familiar channels despite all restrictions. The United States was receiving some 90 per cent of its imports from England, and finding in England and other parts of the British Empire the best markets for its own products. Yet it was galling to American pride that this trade had to be conducted either through subterfuge or under unilateral British orders, rather than on terms mutually agreed upon by the two nations. Although individual American states expressed their irritation by placing restrictions on British ships entering their ports, any uniform policy of retaliation was impossible, because the Articles of Confederation had not delegated the power to regulate foreign commerce to the central government.

The Northwest Posts

Even more exasperating from the American point of view was British policy toward the Northwest posts, which had been built originally during the earlier wars with the French at strategic points to control access to the Great Lakes and other waterways. The Treaty of Paris provided that these posts, of which the most important were Detroit, Niagara, and Oswego, were to be within United States territory and thus should be evacuated by the British "with all convenient speed." The fur traders of Montreal, headquarters for a business grossing perhaps a million dollars a year, were particularly upset by this provision. A major portion of the furs came from Indians living south of the Great Lakes, and surrender of the posts threatened this trade on two scores. Much of it might now pass into American hands to be diverted through Albany and New York, while American military control would ultimately open the Northwest to white settlement, dislodge the Indians, and destroy the fur trade for both English and Americans. Since the business was enormously profitable to British importers and to the Exchequer, the British government had reason to take a serious view of the situation.

Also disquieting were the reports sent to London from British military commanders in Canada. Many of the Indian tribes of the Northwest had fought in the Revolutionary War as allies of the English and had been taught to hate and fear the Americans. These Indians, the British officers warned, would regard the Treaty of Paris as a betrayal of their interests. Although an attempt was made to keep the savages in ignorance of the boundary provisions, the news soon spread. The resulting Indian anger and resentment threatened to erupt in a general frontier war in which the tribes would attack English and Americans alike. This situation provided the British with further reasons for keeping their garrisons in the Northwest posts.

In July, 1784, when Lieutenant Colonel William Hull was sent to Canada to fix the details for the evacuation, he was informed by Governor General Frederick Haldimand that no orders had been received from England for the delivery of the posts. Haldimand added that in his "private opinion" one reason for the delay was the harsh treatment that returning Loyalists were receiving in the United States. As time went on, American failure to carry out the provisions of the treaty in regard to Tories and the pre-Revolutionary debts provided the English with a more plausible pretext for refusing to surrender the posts.

In the beginning, probably, the English had intended to delay the evacuation for only a few months to ease the blow to the fur traders and the Indians. But soon they began to act as though they intended to hold on to the disputed posts indefinitely. The British Department of Indian Affairs, under Sir John Johnson, encouraged the savages to resist American attempts to win them over by a policy of conciliation. The tribes were told to stand firm on their rights under the Treaty of Fort Stanwix of 1768, which had recognized as Indian territory the districts north of the Ohio River, much of northwestern Pennsylvania, and western New York. Although avoiding direct incitement, English agents gave their savage allies provisions, guns, and ammunition from British stores.

The Canadian officials also took advantage of dissensions and weak government across the border to try to foster separatist movements in the American frontier settlements. Special concessions to trade with Canada by way of Lake Champlain and the Richelieu River were granted to the restless Vermonters led by Ethan Allen. British agents dangled similarly tempting bait before the eyes of American frontiersmen in the Ohio River area.

The United States government soon concluded that effective occupation and settlement of the Northwest Territory would be almost impossible unless the British gave up the disputed posts. Yet every American remonstrance that England was violating the peace treaty was countered by a British retort that the Americans themselves were guilty of denying justice to Loyalists and British creditors.

Under the Articles of Confederation Congress could do no more than recommend that the individual states accommodate their laws to the provisions of the treaty. At first such requests had little effect, since popular indignation against the Tories was great and times were so hard that debtors could scarcely pay their American creditors, to say nothing of the ones overseas. Within a few years, however, there was in each state a conservative party, eager to strengthen its ranks by facilitating the return of the former Loyalists and committed to the principle of the strict collection of debts. By the end of the Confederation period the grossest violations of the treaty had been corrected. The laws forbidding the return of Tory exiles had been repealed, and in many cases the Loyalists had either recovered their confiscated estates or received some form of compensation for their losses. Mutual concessions had eased the way for British merchants to collect the pre-Revolutionary debts. In an agreement negotiated by Thomas Jefferson and John Adams, the British merchants had consented to forego the interest accumulated during seven years of war and to accept payment in five annual installments. Congress responded in 1786 with a successful appeal to the states to repeal their laws which were in conflict with the Treaty of Paris. The Virginia law, however, was not to go into effect until the British should evacuate the Northwest posts or pay for the slaves they had taken from the state during the war.

Despite the very real progress made toward carrying out these treaty provisions, the British government still refused both to negotiate a commercial treaty and to give up the disputed posts. No British minister to the United States was appointed, and John Adams left England in disgust in 1788, thereby breaking off the first attempt to establish normal diplomatic relations between the two governments.

Clashing Interests with Spain

Even while giving limited aid to the Americans during the Revolution, Spain had not concealed its desire to restrict the boundaries of the new republic. For this reason, the terms of the Treaty of Paris granting the United States the free navigation of the Mississippi and a southern boundary along the 31st parallel were by no means acceptable. Indeed, from the Spanish point of view, the English had granted what was not theirs to give. The treaty of peace between Spain and England contained no provision for the navigation of the Mississippi, and East and West Florida were ceded to Spain without defining their boundaries. The Spanish asserted that the boundary of West Florida lay at least as far north as the mouth of the Yazoo River. Facts tending to support the Spanish claim —although unknown to the Spanish authorities in 1783—were that the British themselves had defined the boundary of West Florida along the Yazoo line in a proclamation of 1764, and that the secret clause in the Anglo-American provisional peace treaty of 1782 had stipulated that this northern line should be the boundary in case Britain retained the Floridas in the final treaty.

Although the Spanish government did not formally protest the terms of the Anglo-American treaty, it ignored them. Spanish troops continued to occupy the important post of Natchez in the disputed territory, and local officials negotiated treaties of alliance with the Indian tribes of the area. Indeed, the principal objective of Spanish policy was to create a strong Indian buffer state between the American frontier settlements and the Spanish colonies. As in the Northwest, control of the fur trade was a major prize in the contest. The Spanish were handicapped in their inability to supply the traditional European goods demanded by the Indians. But the Florida authorities met this situation by giving extensive privileges to Alexander McGillivray and William Panton, two Georgia Loyalists banished by the Americans during the Revolution. These two merchants, who marketed their furs in England, used their extraordinary influence over the Indians of the Southwest to make trouble for the hated Georgians.

The Spanish government feared the American frontier movement as a threat both to Louisiana and the Floridas. During the Revolution more and more pioneers had crossed the Appalachians into the regions now known as Kentucky and Tennessee, but at that time under the jurisdiction of Virginia and North Carolina. This first wave of migration across the mountains was obviously the precursor of much larger ones to follow. Soon after the war, the Spanish authorities were disturbed by news of grandiose projects of land speculation that would open up to American settlement the Natchez district and other areas claimed either by the Spaniards themselves or by their Indian allies. The Spaniards succeeded in thwarting these schemes, but in so doing they aroused dangerous resentment among the American land speculators, fur traders, and frontiersmen.

In 1784 Spain tried to strangle the American West by ordering the navigation of the Mississippi closed to all but Spanish ships. This was a crippling blow to the settlers of Kentucky and Tennessee, whose economic health depended upon floating their produce on flat boats down the great interior river system to New Orleans, where it could be transferred to oceangoing vessels to be carried to markets in the eastern United States and in Europe. In another document Spain laid claim to a huge area on the east bank of the Mississippi as far north as the Ohio and the

Tennessee Rivers. To obtain the consent of the United States to these claims—or as much as possible of them—the Spanish government sent over a mission headed by Don Diego de Gardoqui, a Spanish merchant who had arranged secret aid to the Americans during the Revolution.

Gardoqui's assignment was not quite as hopeless as might be assumed. A strong faction in Congress, reflecting the conservative interests of the Northeast, regarded the frontier movement with dislike, since it drained population from the older districts, reduced land values, and threatened to create new states that would dilute the political influence of the older ones. These Easterners were not unwilling to see the growth of the West retarded for reasons of their own. Moreover, an agreement to accept the closure of the Mississippi would be doubly acceptable, if it could be coupled by commercial concessions that would open the ports of the Spanish Empire to American ships. This trade appealed to Eastern conservatives, not only because it would be profitable, but because it would attract a flow of Spanish gold dollars into the United States to bolster the sagging monetary system.

John Jay, the Secretary of Foreign Affairs, viewed the problem largely from this Eastern point of view. Accordingly he went before a secret session of Congress in August, 1786, to urge that his instructions be modified to permit a compromise with Spain. Since the latter power could not be dislodged from control of the Mississippi except by a war which the United States was unprepared to wage, and since free navigation of the Mississippi would not really be necessary to the Americans for the next twenty-five or thirty years, Jay argued that the nation should consent to the closure of the river for a period of years in return for commercial concessions and a reasonable settlement of the boundary question. After a long and bitter debate Congress finally empowered Jay to negotiate a treaty along these lines.

But the projected Jay-Gardoqui treaty was never concluded. Although the deliberations in Congress were supposedly secret, news of the affair soon leaked out and resulted in severe condemnation. Both the West and the South regarded the proposed settlement as a betrayal of vital national interests. Although Gardoqui advised his government that popular disapproval would make it impossible to negotiate any treaty under which the United States would give up its rights to navigate the Mississippi, the Spanish diplomat stayed on in America. In 1788 he received new instructions from Madrid that offered important concessions to the American position. Had these proposals come two years earlier, a treaty would probably have been concluded, but by this time the Confederation government was in its last and weakest phase. The Spanish question was left to be dealt with by the new government soon to be established under the Constitution.

Meanwhile, the Spanish government had abruptly altered its policy toward American frontiersmen. Well aware that the settlers in Kentucky and Tennessee were boiling with indignation against Congress, the Spanish officials sought to capitalize on the resulting separatist sentiment. When James Wilkinson, a rascally Kentucky merchant, visited New Orleans in 1787 with a plan for extending Spanish influence in the Southwest by permitting privileged individuals to use the Mississippi, he received a sympathetic hearing and his project was referred to Madrid. Several other prominent frontier leaders, speculating on the possibility of seceding from the United States and founding an independent trans-Appalachian nation, also flirted with the Spaniards.

In the end the Spanish government did not accept any of these proposals, but adopted two significant new policies in 1788. To promote better relations with the Kentucky and Tennessee settlers, Spain partially opened the Mississippi. Americans could now use the river as far south as New Orleans subject to the payment of a 15 per cent duty on their goods. This duty might be reduced to 6 per cent in individual cases at the discretion of the local officials.[4] Furthermore, Americans were now to be encouraged, by offers of liberal commercial privileges and religious toleration, to settle in Louisiana in order to increase the population of that Spanish colony.

The weaknesses of the Confederation government obviously exposed the new nation to perils of a most serious character. Unless the central government could be sufficiently strengthened to enable it to assert American claims successfully against England and Spain, the territorial integrity of the republic was far from secure. The generous boundaries achieved in the Treaty of Paris were in danger of becoming a mockery.

[4] Upon payment of an export tax of 6 per cent the American goods might be shipped from New Orleans to certain specified markets—the French and Spanish West Indies, Spain, and France—but not to the ports of eastern United States.

3

POLITICS AND DIPLOMACY
OF THE NEW FEDERAL UNION

The adoption of the Constitution was as important for the history of American foreign relations as it was for that of domestic politics. The new document set up carefully balanced machinery to control such vital government functions as making war, negotiating treaties, and appointing ambassadors. No less significant than the Constitution itself were the precedents established during the Washington administration that determined how the President, the Senate, and the House of Representatives would carry out their respective functions. During these years, moreover, it became obvious that American foreign policy would be powerfully influenced by public opinion, which in turn would reflect the ambitions of party politics.

Constitutional Provisions

When the Constitutional Convention met in Philadelphia in May, 1787, the inadequacies of the Articles of Confederation causing chief concern were those related to domestic matters. In the field of foreign affairs the articles had appeared to be more satisfactory, because of the broad powers they had granted to Congress. In the actual exercise of these powers, however, Congress had been continually embarrassed by the general weaknesses of the central government. Without authority to levy import duties or retaliatory embargoes and without adequate revenues to maintain an efficient army and navy, the United States could not command respect for the rights it claimed.

The new Constitution bestowed extensive executive powers upon the President. He was to be Commander in Chief of the Armed Forces and to receive the ambassadors and ministers of foreign states—both significant duties in the determination of foreign policy. In the allocation of other key powers, there was difference of opinion. Some delegates favored giving the President the sole power to appoint all officers of the government, while others advocated entrusting the appointment of ambassadors and judges to the Senate. The eventual compromise was that the President should appoint ambassadors and other public ministers and consuls "by and with the Advice and Consent of the Senate."

In the draft originally presented to the Convention on August 6, 1787, the power to make treaties was vested in the Senate alone. The resulting debate reflected both fear that the Senate might become too powerful and suspicion that one section of the country might use the treaty-making power to its own advantage. Several delegates argued, as have many critics since, that it would be better to require the approval of a simple majority of both Houses of Congress rather than to give to a minority of senators what was essentially a veto power over treaties. But this proposal to include the House of Representatives in the treaty-making power was rejected by the Convention, largely because the House was too large to maintain the secrecy then believed essential to the consideration of foreign affairs. At least one delegate preferred to grant the treaty-making power to the President alone, but such a complete delegation had little support. In the end the Convention adopted the compromise proposal that the President should make treaties "by and with the Advice and Consent of the Senate . . . provided two thirds of the Senators present concur." This article gave reasonable assurance to the South and West that no such unpopular treaty as the proposed Jay-Gardoqui agreement would ever be approved. At the same time, by requiring the approval of two-thirds of the senators present instead of two-thirds of the entire membership, the Constitution would prevent any such paralysis of business through nonattendance as had afflicted government under the Articles of Confederation.[1]

Perhaps the most critical power the Convention had to allocate was that of declaring war. In European countries this had always been considered a prerogative of the executive, and at least one delegate was willing to follow precedent by vesting the entire responsibility in the President, confident that he "will not make war but when the Nation will support it." Another delegate urged that this duty be entrusted to the superior wisdom and discretion of the Senate. But the great majority of delegates agreed that the power to declare war should be included among those delegated to the whole Congress. The significance of this step was stressed by Thomas Jefferson:

[1] Under the Articles of Confederation the assent of nine out of the thirteen state delegations was required for the approval of a treaty.

We have already given, in example, one effectual check to the dog of war, by transferring the power of letting him loose from the Executive to the Legislative body, from those who are to spend to those who are to pay.

Also vested in Congress were such other powers pertinent to the conduct of foreign relations as those of granting letters of marque and reprisal,[2] of raising and supporting armies, providing and maintaining a navy, and calling out the militia to repel invasions.

The machinery of checks and balances, so highly esteemed in eighteenth-century political thought, was implicit in most of these constitutional provisions. Control over the day-by-day conduct of diplomacy had been entrusted to the President, but his freedom of action was limited by the necessity of obtaining senatorial approval for his appointments, and appropriations from Congress to support the diplomatic establishment. Congress's power to declare war was similarly checked by the President's veto power and the more practical limitation that the President's direction of diplomacy and conduct as Commander in Chief might result in the nation's becoming involved in hostilities without a formal declaration. However, the possibility that the executive could for very long wage war without the consent of Congress was obviated by the legislature's control of the purse. Even the treaty-making power was modified by the constitutional provision that all money bills must originate in the House of Representatives. Time was to prove that treaties for which the President had obtained the assent of the Senate might run into stormy weather in the lower house, if appropriations of money were necessary to carry out their provisions.

The Constitution provided that all treaties made under the authority of the United States should be part of the supreme law of the land, binding upon states, anything in their constitutions or laws notwithstanding. This clause, enforced as it soon was by the Federal courts, gave assurance that the central government would not suffer such embarrassments as it had under the Articles of Confederation, when it was unable to compel the states to make their laws consistent with the nation's treaty obligations. The supreme law of the land clause, however, could not guarantee that American foreign relations might not be complicated by factors arising out of the federal form of government. Since the power to define and punish ordinary crimes and to regulate property holding and education had been reserved to the states, difficult problems involving the rights of foreign nationals in the United States were likely to arise. In such cases the Federal government could take no direct action.

[2] Letters of marque and reprisal were commissions given to the owners of merchant vessels, authorizing them to use their ships as privateers to capture enemy-owned merchant vessels in time of war.

The Machinery of Diplomacy

The Constitution did not specify how the executive branch of the government was to be organized, but incidental references to the "principal officers in each of the executive departments" and to the "heads of departments" clearly indicated that the framers expected a division of responsibilities along departmental lines. Indeed, the precedents for such an organization had been clearly laid out during the Confederation period when departments of foreign affairs, finance, war, marine, and post office had been established.

Therefore, shortly after George Washington had been inaugurated, Congress began organizing the requisite departments. On July 27, 1789, it established a Department of Foreign Affairs, headed by "the secretary for the department of foreign affairs." By a subsequent act, signed on September 15, 1789, the names of the department and its principal officer were changed to Department of State and Secretary of State respectively. This was the result of the decision to enlarge the Secretary's duties by making him the custodian of the great seal of the United States and the official with whom statutes and commissions were deposited for safekeeping and official publication.

Actually the transition from the Department of Foreign Affairs under the Confederation to the Department of State under the Constitution was far from abrupt. Among the men best equipped by experience to deal with foreign affairs, Benjamin Franklin was too old, John Adams was ineligible because of his election to the vice presidency, and John Jay preferred to be appointed Chief Justice. Only Thomas Jefferson was available for the new secretaryship, and he was still in France. When he returned to America for a visit in November, 1789, President Washington offered him the office. At first, eager to return to France and foreseeing that the secretaryship might involve him in political strife, Jefferson was reluctant to accept. At length, however, he acceded to Washington's urging and assumed the duties of the new office in March, 1790. In the interval since the inauguration of the new government John Jay had continued to act as unofficial head of the department.

Foreign Relations and Party Politics

In his extensive knowledge of history and law and in the experience gained during his mission to France, Jefferson was splendidly equipped to become the nation's first Secretary of State. He had, moreover, the patience and flexibility of mind necessary to direct American foreign policy during a crucial transitional period. Yet Jefferson's position in the

Washington administration soon became a most difficult one. When he joined the Cabinet, the brilliant Secretary of the Treasury, Alexander Hamilton, had already become the dominant figure in the new government. His financial program, designed to increase the prestige of the national government and to win the support of the business classes, almost immediately aroused the suspicion of Jefferson, who opposed both centralization and special favors to privileged groups. The two men were also at odds in their attitude toward foreign affairs. Hamilton admired British institutions and desired close Anglo-American ties as a spur to commerce. Jefferson disliked England and was sympathetically inclined toward France, an agrarian nation.

Hamilton and Jefferson were not unique in their respective pro-English and pro-French learnings. As early as 1790, Congress was clearly divided along similar lines, and the schism soon pervaded public opinion generally. The Federalist party, soon to take form, generally was pro-English, while the Democratic-Republican party was strongly pro-French.

The Nootka Sound Incident

In 1790, the situation was complicated by the strong possibility that England and Spain would become involved in war. Spain, claiming the whole Pacific Coast, captured three English ships in that region, imprisoned their crews, and expelled an English fur-trading settlement along Nootka Sound on Vancouver Island. The British government countered with stiff demands, not only for restitution and indemnity, but for recognition of the right to settle throughout the Pacific Northwest, north of the area actually occupied by Spain.

American opinion was both divided and confused over what policy the United States should take in case the expected Anglo-Spanish war broke out. Since the Bourbon Family Compact was still in existence, France would presumably go to Spain's assistance. Should the United States in this case strengthen its ties with France and use the occasion to attempt to capture the disputed Northwest posts from the British? Or should the United States ally itself with England and engage in a joint campaign to expel the Spaniards from the Mississippi?

Washington's advisers were fairly well agreed that the country should try to keep out of war, but there was a strong possibility that American neutrality would not be respected. Were England to request permission to cross United States territory to attack Spanish posts in Louisiana, what, asked the President, should the American reply be? Although Hamilton and Jefferson agreed that the American army was unprepared to stop the English in such an event, the two men were not in accord on the best policy to pursue. Hamilton advised giving the British formal permission to cross American territory; Jefferson preferred to make no reply, thereby avoiding the appearance of acquiescence.

Fortunately, the Spanish government acceded to the English demands and the Nootka Sound controversy was peacefully settled. The Washington administration therefore did not have to decide the questions it had found so perplexing in the summer of 1790, but the older grounds of dispute between the United States and the European powers still remained.

Jefferson's difficulties were increased because the United States and England had not yet established formal diplomatic relations. Instead of appointing a regular minister, the British government preferred to deal with the Americans through unofficial agents. On this basis, the Washington administration sent Gouverneur Morris to London in 1790 to discuss outstanding difficulties. Although the English gave Morris some encouragement, his mission had no real success. The favorite English intermediary was George Beckwith, a lieutenant colonel in the British army, who made several visits to the United States between 1787 and 1791. He and Hamilton had become fast friends before Jefferson took over the State Department, and they continued to exchange confidential communications thereafter—much to Jefferson's annoyance.

The Secretary of State favored using the new powers granted by the Constitution to bring pressure upon the British government. Bills, introduced in the House of Representatives by Jefferson's friend, James Madison, would have imposed retaliatory tariffs or exclusion from American ports against any nation refusing to negotiate a satisfactory commercial treaty with the United States. The Hamilton faction blocked these measures temporarily, but Colonel Beckwith warned his government that anti-British legislation would ultimately be enacted unless American opinion were appeased. The British cabinet had already decided to send a properly accredited minister to America, and Beckwith's advice confirmed the wisdom of this policy. As a result, regular diplomatic relations between the two nations were established in 1791. George Hammond, a young diplomatist with only limited experience, became the first British Minister to the United States, while Thomas Pinckney, a South Carolinian who had been educated in England and France and had had a distinguished political career in his native state, was appointed the first regular United States Minister to Britain.[3]

Unfortunately, Hammond was not empowered to negotiate seriously on either of the major sources of controversy: the British retention of the Northwest posts and unsatisfactory commercial relations. Instead, he and Jefferson became involved in a fruitless exchange over which

[3] John Adams had served as Minister under the Articles of Confederation, but Britain scarcely considered him as an official representative.

country was the more guilty of violating the peace treaty. In such a duel of wits the British Minister was no match for the more experienced Secretary of State. Upset by Jefferson's vigorous assertion of the American case, Hammond complained to Hamilton, who consoled him by deploring the "intemperate violence of his colleague." Hamilton assured the British Minister that Jefferson's policy did not have the support of the President or the other Cabinet members. In this instance, and in many others as well, Jefferson discovered that his diplomatic efforts were being frustrated through his rival's interference.

Hammond, taking full advantage of this situation, conferred regularly with the Secretary of the Treasury and negotiated with Jefferson only when necessary. Although Hamilton was extraordinarily sympathetic to the British point of view, he was not entirely insensitive to his own country's interests. When Hammond tried to persuade the United States to accept English mediation in its difficulties with the Indians of the Northwest Territory, Hamilton left no doubt that such matters were entirely American domestic problems in which no foreign interference would be tolerated.

America and the French Revolution

Meantime, Americans were following the unfolding drama of the French Revolution with lively interest. The aid of Louis XVI, the Marquis de Lafayette, and the French nation generally in the winning of American independence was remembered with profound gratitude, and most Americans wished for France's happiness and prosperity. Therefore, public opinion was almost unanimously favorable to the events of 1789, when the French Estates General transformed itself into a National Assembly and undertook a program of far-reaching reform. Even American conservatives could at first see little but good in a process whereby the Old Regime in France seemed to be giving way to a constitutional monarchy.

Secretary of State Jefferson was particularly optimistic regarding this trend of events. During the last months of his mission to France, his house had been a meeting place for Lafayette and other liberal leaders devoted to the cause of reform. Even after the Revolution entered its violent phase with the deposition and execution of the King and the imprisonment of moderates like Lafayette, Jefferson did not lose his faith that the great upheaval would benefit mankind. Most Federalists, on the contrary, regarded the Terror as proof that the French Revolution was a threat to law and order everywhere.

As far as the general public was concerned, enthusiasm for the French Revolution was at a peak during the last months of 1792 and the first half of 1793. When France became involved in war with Prussia and Austria, American sympathies were definitely in favor of the French, who appeared to be championing the cause of liberty against the forces of reaction. Consequently, news of the French victory at Valmy was greeted with as much jubilation as though the Americans themselves had won the battle. Even more welcome was the knowledge that the French assembly had deposed the King and proclaimed a republic. The sober town of Boston was enthusiastic about these events. On January 24, 1793, many of its citizens turned out for a "Civic Feast." A roasted ox, bedecked with ribbons, was carried through the streets. From one gilded horn streamed the Stars and Stripes; from the other, the tricolor. When the ox and the accompanying wagonloads of bread and punch reached State Street, they were eagerly devoured by the happy throng. Each child was given a little cake bearing the words "liberty and equality," and the gilded ox horns were hoisted to the top of a 60-foot liberty pole erected in Liberty Square, newly named to commemorate the occasion. In all the large towns and many of the smaller ones there were similar demonstrations. Gallic fever seemed to infect everybody except a few dour conservatives.

The Problem of Neutrality

In the midst of this enthusiasm it was not easy to view calmly the serious problems created by England's declaration of war on France on February 1, 1793, news of which reached America in April. Washington's Cabinet immediately considered its implications. In the Treaty of Alliance of 1778 the United States had agreed to guarantee forever "the present possessions of the Crown of France in America, as well as those which it may acquire by the future peace treaty." This clause would seem to obligate the United States to assist France in defending her West Indies in case of British attack. Additional entanglements were contained in the commercial treaty of 1778 whereby French privateers and their prizes were to be admitted to American ports, while France's enemies were to be prohibited from fitting out privateers in those ports.

In responding to President Washington's request for advice, Jefferson and Hamilton agreed that the United States should remain at peace, but differed as to how it should do so. Hamilton favored an immediate proclamation of neutrality; Jefferson wanted to delay any such announcement until an attempt had been made to obtain concessions from the British. The Secretary of State also raised a constitutional objection. Since a proclamation of neutrality was a decision *not* to go to war, did not Congress, rather than the President, have the authority to make such a declaration? To meet these difficulties, Washington decided upon a carefully worded proclamation in which the word neutrality did not appear. The document noted that war existed between France and her several enemies, stated that the duty and interest of the United States required it to pursue a conduct "friendly and impartial toward the belligerent Powers," and warned American citizens to avoid all acts that might jeopardize this position.

Despite the somewhat circuitous language employed, the document was really a proclamation of neutrality and was so recognized at the time. Although Jefferson acquiesced in its issuance, many of his political followers criticized the President's action. Hamilton and Madison debated the issue in the newspapers. The former argued by analogy with the British Constitution that the power to proclaim neutrality clearly belonged to the executive branch; Madison warned against the danger of making the prerogatives of the King of England the standard for judging such issues in republican America. Despite these misgivings, the power of the President to define a policy of neutrality was eventually conceded, and the example of the first President was followed by later Chief Executives, regardless of party.

The Genêt Affair

The real issue, however, was not whether the United States would enter the war, but what kind of neutrality would be maintained. Would a cold impartiality between the belligerents be observed, or would the American government slant its policy to give maximum benefits to France? This kind of ultrabenevolent neutrality was obviously what the authorities of the French Republic had in mind when they drafted secret instructions for the new French Minister to the United States, Citizen Edmond Genêt. He was to insist on the letter of the existing treaties, particularly in those articles that would forbid the equipping of all except French privateers in American ports. He was to encourage Kentucky frontiersmen to attack Spanish garrisons in Louisiana. He was to propose new treaties that would tighten the bonds between the United States and France both politically and commercially.

Even before Genêt arrived, the Washington administration was divided on how he should be received. Some thought he should be accepted without reservation as the representative of a nation to which the United States was closely bound by treaty. Others thought he should be received with cautious qualifications, calculated to impress him with the fact that the American government doubted whether the old treaties were still in effect. Hamilton argued that the United States had made these agreements with Louis XVI, a monarch who had since been deposed, tried, and guillotined. Therefore, as long as a revolutionary regime of dubious legality controlled the government of France, the treaties should be regarded as either terminated or suspended. Jefferson vigorously denied this theory when he wrote:

> I consider the people who constitute a society or nation as the source of all authority in that nation, as free to transmit their common concerns by any agent they think proper, to change these agents individually, or the organization of them in form or function whenever they please: that all acts done by those agents under the authority of the nation, are the acts of the nation, are obligatory on them, & enure to their use, & can in no wise be annulled or affected by any change in the form of the government, or of the persons administering it.

Since the treaties of 1778 had been made with Louis Capet not as an individual, but as the representative of the French people, the contracts were still in effect despite the change in government. If they contained provisions that were impossible to fulfill or were self-destructive, the parties might seek release from these obligations, but must base their conduct on the same moral laws governing the relations of individuals.

On this issue, Washington agreed with Jefferson. Genêt was received without reservations, and the treaties were regarded as still in force. The precedent was an important one for future American foreign relations. The United States based its subsequent policy upon the Jeffersonian principle—which was also that of the best authorities on international law—that treaties and agreements were to be interpreted as the acts, not of the individuals who negotiated them, but of the nations that these individuals represented. Such agreements continued to be binding despite political upheavals and changes in the form of government. The reception of Genêt also established another precedent. The general practice of the United States would be to recognize *de facto* governments without attempting to pass judgment upon how they had come into power. Not until the twentieth century did the United States make major departures from this policy.

Citizen Genêt, a handsome young man still in his twenties, was a member of a prominent French family who had held responsible diplomatic posts under the Old Regime. After the deposition of Louis XVI, however, he had become an ardent advocate of republicanism. By education and experience he seemed a good choice to represent the French Republic in America, but fatal defects of character caused his mission to be one of the most spectacular failures in the history of diplomacy. Vain, excitable, and stubborn, he committed a series of mistakes that soon alienated even as sympathetic a friend of France as Thomas Jefferson.

Instead of sailing directly to the capital at Philadelphia, Genêt landed in Charleston, South Carolina, in April, 1793. There the citizens, already aflame with the Gallic fever, gave him such a tumultuous welcome that his head was completely turned. He promptly authorized French consuls in the United States to act as courts of admiralty in condemning prizes brought into American ports by French warships and privateers. Then he endeavored to provide these tribunals with business. He purchased American vessels, commissioned and equipped them as privateers, manned them with French and American crews, and sent them out to prey upon British commerce—all with the tacit assent of the obliging Governor William Moultrie of South Carolina. Genêt also enlisted the help of George Rogers Clark, a Revolutionary hero, who accepted a French commission to organize an army of American frontiersmen for an attack upon New Orleans.

After performing these miscellaneous deeds so compromising to American neutrality, Genêt at last set out for Philadelphia. The journey northward through predominantly Democratic-Republican territory was a triumphant procession. The most extraordinary scenes of all took place in Philadelphia, where Genêt's welcome was climaxed by a banquet at which French and American republicans donned red liberty caps, drank numerous toasts, and sang "*La Marseillaise.*"

After receiving so many effusive tributes, the French Minister was deeply disappointed by the cool manner in which the President received him. Washington regarded Genêt's delay in presenting his credentials as an act of discourtesy, and his conduct in Charleston—of which the British Minister had already complained—as a serious breach of American neutrality. Moreover, Genêt had flouted the diplomatic code by becoming involved in American party politics; the numerous banquets he had attended had been used as rallies for the Democratic-Republicans, who denounced the English, the aristocratic Federalists, and the Proclamation of Neutrality. Nor had Washington himself escaped the attacks; he was even depicted as a king with his head under the guillotine. It was easy, therefore, for Hamilton and Secretary of War Henry Knox to convince the President that the democratic societies springing up throughout the country were incubators of sedition, threatening to overthrow the government.

On the other hand, Secretary of State Jefferson at first made light of Genêt's indiscretions and was inclined to collaborate closely with him. Indeed, for a few days after the French Minister's arrival in Philadelphia, it seemed that Jefferson would establish as close an intimacy with Genêt as Hamilton had with the British Minister, Hammond. The Secretary of State defended Genêt's actions in Cabinet sessions and expressed bitter disappointment when the President sided with Hamilton and Knox.

Even though Jefferson's heart might be with Genêt and the French Republic, his head told him American neutrality must be preserved.

Reluctantly, therefore, he insisted that the French obey the principles of international law. In a series of reports and diplomatic notes, Jefferson now defined a neutral nation's rights and duties in a manner that provided excellent precedents for the future. Moreover, he quickly put these theories into practice: he ruled the French capture of an English ship in American waters illegal and ordered the vessel returned to the English; he denied the right of the French to man and equip privateers in neutral ports; and he refused to accept Genêt's interpretation of the commercial treaty of 1778 that the article binding the United States not to permit the enemies of France to fit out privateers in its ports implied that France should be permitted to exercise such a privilege. To Jefferson, impartial neutrality required the United States to enforce the same prohibition against France as well.

For some three months Jefferson tried to preserve American neutrality without forcing a break with the ebullient French Minister, but Genêt's own folly made a showdown necessary. Genêt apparently broke his word by defiantly allowing a prize ship, the *Little Sarah* (which had been renamed *La Petite Démocrate*), to slip out of Philadelphia as a French privateer. To make matters worse, the French Minister was threatening to appeal his action to the people over the head of the President. The embarrassed Jefferson and his allies, knowing that Washington was still deeply revered by the general public, feared that open villification of the national hero would seriously weaken the cause of the French Republic and the Democratic-Republicans. As Jefferson himself explained the matter in a letter to Madison: "Finding at length that the man was absolutely incorrigible, I saw the necessity of quitting a wreck which could not but sink all who should cling to it."

With the unanimous approval of Washington and the other members of the Cabinet, Jefferson firmly but courteously requested Genêt's recall on August 16, 1793. This had to be done not only to ensure the "constant and unabating" friendship of the United States for France, but to prevent injury to the interests of France herself.

Even before Jefferson's request reached France, a new turn of the revolutionary wheel had deposed the Girondist faction that had commissioned Genêt. Although the new Jacobin regime was in general more radical than its predecessor, it did not approve the indiscretions of the French Minister. In a stern rebuke Genêt was ordered "to treat with the Government and not with a portion of the people, to be the mouthpiece of the French Republic before Congress, and not the leader of an American party.... We must not, we cannot recognize in America any legitimate authority other than that of the President and of the Congress."

Repudiated both by the American and French governments, Genêt's days as a diplomat were obviously numbered. Yet communications were then so slow that Joseph Fauchet, his successor, did not arrive until February, 1794. During the interval, Citizen Genêt retained his post and behaved no better than before. He continued to take a lordly tone in his dealings with Jefferson, to engage in more or less open attacks upon Washington, to meddle in American politics, and to plan expeditions against New Orleans. More than once the Cabinet considered ordering him to leave the country immediately. The new Minister brought an order for Genêt's arrest and return to France, but Washington refused to send him back to almost certain death on the guillotine. Instead, the ex-Minister was permitted to remain in New York, where he married a daughter of Governor George Clinton and settled down to the unexciting but safe life of an American country gentleman.

After the hectic months during which he had had to struggle with the problems created by Genêt, Thomas Jefferson gladly retired to Monticello in January, 1794. He had wanted to resign two years earlier, when his differences with Hamilton had started, but President Washington, reluctant to admit the existence of party divisions, had persuaded him to continue in office. Hamilton's growing influence over Washington and his constant interference in the field of diplomacy, however, made the Secretary of State's position increasingly difficult, and the President finally accepted Jefferson's resignation on December 31, 1793.

To fill the vacancy Washington promoted Edmund Randolph, who had been Attorney General. Randolph, a Virginian and a cousin of Jefferson, had wavered between the Federalists and the Democratic-Republicans during the early party disputes. In his new post he inclined toward an anti-English and pro-French position, but his influence over diplomacy was negligible. Much more than while Jefferson was in the Cabinet, Hamilton now controlled the foreign policy of the nation.

War Scare of 1794

Even with the Anglophile Hamilton at the peak of his influence, American relations with England deteriorated almost to the point of war during the early months of 1794. All points of friction between the two nations were rubbed raw by a series of exasperating incidents.

After the American expedition headed by General St. Clair had been badly defeated by the Northwest Indians in 1791, President Washington sent General Anthony Wayne to the Ohio country to subdue the natives and open the region to settlement. Determined that this campaign should be successful, Wayne spent many months drilling his troops and gathering provisions. These preparations alarmed the British authorities in Canada, who feared that the ultimate American objective might be to capture the disputed Northwest posts and perhaps to invade Canada itself. These officials considered an Anglo-American war very likely, and some of them actually hoped for such a conflict, since it would terminate the peace treaty of 1783 and make possible English reconquest of the Northwest Territory.

The British continued to intrigue with the Indians. The tribes were encouraged to reject American proposals for a peaceful settlement and were supplied with British arms and provisions. News of these actions inflamed American opinion against England, as did reports that the British had warned American settlers to stay out of areas indubitably within the United States and had built new fortifications of their own on American soil. Particularly resented was a speech of Lord Dorchester, the Governor General of Canada, to a delegation of Northwest Indians in February, 1794, assuring them that the English King and the Americans would soon be at war, and that then the Indians together with the King's warriors could draw a new boundary line.

Even more inflammatory were reports of British highhandedness on the seas. Determined to make full use of their vast sea power to win the war in Europe, the English government issued orders in council that showed little respect for neutral rights. By the so-called Provision Order of June 8, 1793, British naval commanders were directed to bring in all neutral ships bound for French ports with cargoes of grain or flour. These provisions were to be confiscated, but with compensation to the owners.[4] This policy by which foodstuffs were treated as contraband conflicted sharply with the American interpretation of international law contained in treaties with France and other countries, but Jefferson's protests were fruitless.

Even more drastic was the order in council of November 6, 1793, directing the seizure of all neutral ships engaged in trade with the French West Indies. The British based the new order on the so-called Rule of 1756, under which British admiralty courts had held that a belligerent which had prohibited its colonial trade to foreign nations in time of peace could not reverse the practice in time of war. Actually, however, the order of 1794 was much more stringent than this, since it applied to many types of trade that France had permitted Americans to engage in before the war began. Perceiving that it had gone too far, the British government modified its policy by a third order in council of January 8,

---

[4] Although the British claimed that legally they had the right to confiscate such commodities, they softened their actions by paying the owners. Thus they would be obtaining needed supplies and at the same time would be preventing the owners from complaining so bitterly to their neutral countries that war might ensue.

1794, which followed the Rule of 1756 more closely. But the Americans were far from conceding that this rule, which provided for the detention of American ships carrying the produce of the French colonies to European ports, was valid.

The way in which British naval officers enforced these orders was even more exasperating than the orders themselves. By March 1, 1794, about 250 American ships had been stopped and subjected to rigorous search and time-consuming legal proceedings in British West Indian ports. One hundred fifty of these ships were condemned, and their unfortunate crews were left stranded far from home. Some of the sailors suffered personal mistreatment and were stripped of their clothing by their greedy captors; others, asserted to be British subjects, were impressed into the King's navy.

Lurid, and no doubt exaggerated, accounts of these outrages filled the American newspapers during the early months of 1794. The democratic societies, which had been lying low since Genêt's disgrace, now found an issue on which they could carry on an impassioned propaganda. Even the Federalists lost patience with England. Hamilton condemned the British conduct as "atrocious" and advocated recruitment of a Federal army of 30,000 men and fortification of American ports.

The President sent Congress papers showing both the American grievances and the discouraging reports sent back by Thomas Pinckney, the United States Minister to England. Federalists and Democratic-Republicans alike took a serious view of the situation and prepared for possible hostilities. Requisitions for militia were sent to the states, and a thirty-day embargo was imposed upon all shipping from American ports. The latter measure, eventually extended to sixty days, was intended to bring pressure to bear upon England by cutting off her supplies from the British West Indies.

The Democratic-Republicans in Congress were eager for more drastic steps. Madison's proposals of 1791 for imposing retaliatory duties and regulations against any nation with which the United States did not have a commercial treaty were revived and hotly debated. Other legislators introduced bills to prohibit all commercial intercourse with England until she rescinded her objectionable orders and to sequester all debts due to British creditors in order to compensate victims of British seizures.

Alarmed lest the United States be swept into a disastrous war, Federalist party leaders now convinced President Washington that one last effort should be made to settle Anglo-American difficulties through diplomacy. Hamilton was first suggested for special envoy, but Democratic-Republican bitterness against him made such a nomination impossible. Instead, the post was given to Chief Justice John Jay. Neither the idea of the mission itself nor the nomination of Jay, whose Federalist sympathies were well known, was popular with the Democratic-Republicans. Nevertheless, the Senate confirmed the appointment by a vote of 18 to 8, and on May 12, 1794, the special envoy embarked for England.

Jay's Treaty

John Jay's able service as peace commissioner during the Revolutionary War and his experience as Secretary of Foreign Affairs under the Confederation appeared to provide excellent qualifications for this new responsibility. The Chief Justice was a man of fine intelligence, honest, high-minded, and patriotic. But, as one of its agents informed the British Foreign Office, "almost every man has a weak spot and Mr. Jay's weak spot is Mr. Jay." The American envoy liked to hear himself praised, and his British hosts saw to it that he was flattered with every attention from the time he arrived in England. Much pleased with his reception, Jay failed to negotiate with the stubborn persistence that a man like John Adams might have displayed.

But even if the American envoy had behaved differently, it is doubtful whether he would have been much more successful. In so far as the issues under discussion involved British policy toward neutral shipping, no major concessions to the American point of view were likely. Since the English government considered it was fighting on behalf of law and order against a dangerous threat to civilized society, it was determined to make the most effective possible use of its supremacy on the seas.

Jay's position was also weak because the Federalists were eager to sign a treaty on almost any terms, and the English knew this. However great were Hamilton's abilities in the realm of finance, his ventures into diplomacy were usually harmful. The Secretary of the Treasury's indiscreet conversations with George Hammond were as damaging to the efforts of his political ally, Jay, as they had been to those of his political enemy, Jefferson. While the important negotiations in London were still in progress, Hammond informed his government that Hamilton sympathized with the British application of the disputed Rule of 1756 and that there was no danger of the United States joining with Sweden and Denmark in a revival of the League of Armed Neutrality.

Holding poor cards in the first place and robbed of the few possible winners that he did have by Hamilton's indiscretions, Jay finally signed on November 14, 1794, one of the most controversial treaties in the history of American diplomacy. While the United States gained a few valuable concessions, and the agreement was by no means as bad as its rabid Democratic-Republican critics asserted, several of its provisions were, nevertheless, extremely humiliating to the pride of a young nation.

The first advantage implicit in the treaty was the fact that it did in a

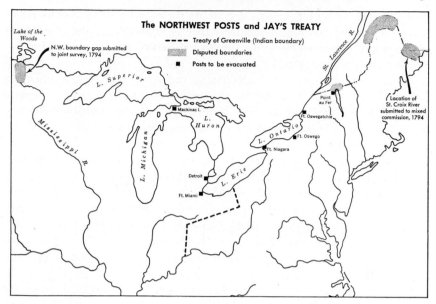

The NORTHWEST POSTS and JAY'S TREATY

- - - - Treaty of Greenville (Indian boundary)
▨▨▨ Disputed boundaries
■ Posts to be evacuated

Lake of the Woods

N.W. boundary gap submitted to joint survey, 1794

Location of St. Croix River submitted to mixed commission, 1794

L. Superior

Mississippi R.

Mackinac I.

L. Michigan

L. Huron

Point au Fer

Ft. Oswegatchie

L. Ontario

Ft. Oswego

Ft. Niagara

St. Lawrence R.

Detroit

L. Erie

Ft. Miami

sense complete the recognition of the United States. Hitherto, the British government had acknowledged American independence and exchanged diplomatic representatives, but had stubbornly refused to negotiate the treaty of amity and commerce customary among sovereign nations. The second clear gain was the British pledge—at long last—to evacuate the Northwest posts on or before June 1, 1796.

The treaty articles relating to commerce for the most part simply codified the regulations under which trade between the two nations was already being conducted. One new concession was the admission of American ships to the British East Indies; another was the permission granted reciprocally to whites and Indians on both sides of the Canadian boundary to pass freely into each other's territory and to carry on trade, except in the areas reserved to the Hudson's Bay Company. On the critical issue of the West Indies trade, article 12 of the treaty was far from satisfactory. For the duration of the Anglo-French war and for two years thereafter, American ships of less than 70 tons were to be allowed to exchange products with the British West Indies. In return for this concession the United States had to promise to prohibit the export to foreign nations of any molasses, sugar, coffee, cocoa, or cotton produced either in the British islands or in the United States itself.

The treaty made an important contribution to the practice of international arbitration by referring certain disputed issues to mixed commissions. One such body, to be composed of two commissioners nominated by the United States and two by Great Britain with a fifth chosen either by agreement or by lot, was to determine the compensation due to either party on account of illegal seizures, that is, through irregular captures of American merchant ships by the British navy or captures of English vessels by French privateers illegally equipped in American ports. A similar mixed commission was to determine the amount of indemnification due to British creditors from the American government to compensate them for losses sustained through state legislation incompatible with the peace treaty of 1783. A third commission was to decide which was the St. Croix River mentioned in the peace treaty in order to define the northeastern boundary of the United States. To clarify still another boundary problem, the treaty provided for a joint survey of the line between the Lake of the Woods and the Mississippi.

The least satisfactory articles of the treaty were those dealing with neutral rights. Although the British promised to consider after the war such crucial issues as the definition of contraband and whether free ships made free goods, they would consent only to modifications of their own interpretation of international law while the war was still in progress. In this particular, therefore, the Jay Treaty represented a retreat from the principles that the United States had laid down in its commercial treaty with France in 1778 and in later treaties with the Netherlands, Prussia, and Sweden. On the issue of impressment of American sailors—destined to be so important a cause of controversy during the next decade—the treaty was entirely silent.

The Democratic-Republicans had not ceased to denounce the Jay mission throughout the negotiations and were prepared to condemn the treaty whatever its terms. The actual text of the treaty remained secret until after the Senate had been specially convened to approve it. Article 12 was so unsatisfactory that most of its provisions were suspended. The rest of the treaty was approved 20 to 10, strictly along party lines and without a vote to spare.

But there still remained danger that it would prove impossible to carry the agreement into effect. One Democratic-Republican senator secretly gave a copy of the treaty to a printer, who published it in pamphlet form. When the actual text thus became public, condemnation of the treaty took violent form. In towns and villages all over the country mass meetings were held, where the iniquitous document was denounced and copies publicly burned. The feature event of the evening was oftentimes the hanging of John Jay in effigy. At Philadelphia the dummy representing Jay was first exposed on the public pillory, then guillotined, set on fire, and finally blown up with gunpowder. Washington himself was bitterly criticized for betraying the national interest.

The Federalists attempted to defend the treaty by publishing pamphlets and circulating petitions. But the agreement was so unpopular that it was dangerous to speak publicly in its favor. When Hamilton tried to do so at a meeting in New York, he was pelted with stones and compelled to retire with blood streaming down his face. A protreaty man in Charleston was ducked at the public pump until he was almost drowned.

When Congress convened in regular session in December, 1795, there was a Democratic-Republican majority in the House of Representatives, where, under the Constitution, the bills necessary to appropriate the money called for by the treaty had to originate. The majority party contended that the House had power to review the whole negotiation before passing the requested sums; the Federalists held that the treaty, having been properly ratified, was now the supreme law of the land and that Congress was morally bound to pass the necessary implementing legislation. When the House called upon the President to submit all papers relating to the negotiation, Washington, upon the advice of his Cabinet, refused to comply because the papers were unrelated to any functions of the House unless it were considering his impeachment. The House responded with a resolution asserting its right to call for the papers and defending its power to deliberate upon the expediency of carrying the treaty into effect.

In the end, thanks in part to an extraordinarily effective speech by the Massachusetts Federalist, Fisher Ames, the House voted the necessary appropriations, 51 to 48. But this did not settle the constitutional issue. Spokesmen for the House of Representatives continued to contend that in cases where a treaty required the appropriation of money or some other act of Congress to carry it into effect, the agreement must in practice receive the consent of both Houses. Since the House could not be coerced in such instances, this precedent at length became established.

Carried into effect, therefore, despite bitter opposition, Jay's Treaty provided a final disposition for some issues that had troubled Anglo-American relations for many years. The Northwest posts were evacuated on schedule. This event, following as it did Wayne's decisive victory over the Indians at the battle of Fallen Timbers (August 20, 1794) and the Treaty of Greenville (August 3, 1795), by which the Indians ceded most of the lands in the present state of Ohio, laid the basis for rapid American settlement in the Old Northwest.

It proved impossible to settle the question of the pre-Revolutionary debts through the mixed commission established by Jay's Treaty, but a special convention of 1802 finally disposed of the issue, with the United States government paying $2,664,000 to injured British creditors. The Spoliations Commission eventually awarded $5,849,082 to American claimants for irregular British seizures and $2,807,428 to English claimants for damages caused through the illegal fitting out of French privateers in American ports. The commission to identify the St. Croix River did so, but other uncertainties arising out of the interpretation of the Treaty of 1783 left the northeast boundary still a matter of dispute. Nor did the survey provide a final solution for all the problems involved in defining the boundary west of the Lake of the Woods.

Jay's Treaty, therefore, settled a few issues and left many others to be dealt with in the future. Most important, it removed the very real threat of an Anglo-American war—a war that would have been very dangerous to the young and still weak republic. Whether the United States could also avoid serious trouble with Spain and France still remained to be seen.

4

WRESTLING WITH FRANCE AND SPAIN

Prior to 1795 the Washington administration had avoided full commitment to the Federalist or the Democratic-Republican party. Although Hamilton continued to be the strongest influence on the government even after his return to private life in January, 1795, Edmund Randolph's presence in the Cabinet emphasized the fact that the President had not entirely surrendered to Federalist influence. But Randolph's position as Secretary of State, never very secure, became untenable when he opposed the Jay Treaty. In July, 1795, he was forced to resign as a consequence of the Fauchet affair, in which the Secretary was accused of having solicited bribes from Joseph Fauchet, the French Minister—a charge that Randolph vigorously denied.

When President Washington appointed Timothy Pickering of Massachusetts as the new Secretary of State, the Federalist victory was complete. For the remaining months of the Washington administration and for the four years of the ensuing Adams administration, the conservative party was in undisputed command. In foreign policy this meant, in the first place, a firm reliance on the reconciliation with England that had been achieved in Jay's Treaty. With Spain also the Federalists were able to effect a diplomatic settlement. The Pinckney Treaty, which solved the troublesome problems of the southern border and the navigation of the Mississippi, was in fact a much more satisfactory document than the Jay Treaty.

With republican France, however, Federalist diplomacy had difficulties of the gravest character. The Paris government of these years was so arbitrary and corrupt that even a sympathetic State Department would have had trouble in maintaining friendly relations. For the Federalists, with their natural affinity for England and dislike for France, the difficulty of course was much greater. Indeed, Federalist partisans seemed to welcome the prospect of war between the United States and France. Not only would such a conflict permit America to join England in repressing the French threat to law and order, but it would provide an opportunity to consolidate Federalist control of the government and to crush Jeffersonian opposition. Fortunately President Adams preferred honorable peace to party advantage and so opposed the extremists of his own party.

Intrigue in the Old Southwest

American relations with Spain were strongly influenced by the westward movement of American frontiersmen. Kentucky had a sufficient population to obtain statehood in 1792, and Tennessee was admitted to the Union four years later. The rapid expansion of settlement whetted the appetites of land speculators, who were restlessly concocting new schemes. In 1789, for example, three companies of such adventurers obtained large land grants from the state of Georgia in the Yazoo country of the present state of Mississippi. These tracts lay in territory whose ownership was disputed between Spain and the United States, and the Yazoo land speculators sought to protect themselves by proposing to Spain that the new settlements should either acknowledge Spanish sovereignty or maintain the status of an independent buffer state between the two contesting nations.

The readiness of the Yazoo speculators to court favor with Spanish colonial officials was matched by the flirtations that prominent Kentucky politicians continued to carry on with the Spaniards. Although President Washington entrusted him with a brigadier generalship in the United States Army in 1792, James Wilkinson still drew a secret pension from Spain. Also deeply involved in intrigue were two other Kentucky leaders: Congressman John Brown and Federal District Judge Harry Inness. Throughout the early 1790s the danger persisted that the Western settlements might declare their independence in order to obtain from Spain the right to navigate the Mississippi and transship their merchandise at New Orleans. The doubtful loyalty of the West to the new Federal government arose out of both the old suspicion that Eastern politicians were indifferent to frontier needs and of newer grievances against the financial policies and aristocratic tone of the Washington administration.

On the other hand, few Westerners really liked the Spaniards, and it was always easy to recruit conspirators for proposed attacks upon New Orleans. During the Nootka Sound crisis, for instance, some frontier leaders planned combined operations in which the Americans would fall upon the Spanish garrison by land while the British navy would strike from the Gulf. These projects came to nought when the expected war between England and Spain failed to materialize. A few months later, however, new plots for invading Spanish territory were hatched, with the backing of the troublemaking French Minister, Citizen Genêt.

Under the circumstances, it is little wonder that Spanish colonial authorities were unable to formulate a consistent policy. Part of the time they attempted to combat the American frontier movement by extending their military posts into the disputed territory and stirring up their Indian allies to attack American settlements. At other times they courted the Americans by extending the privilege of navigating the Mississippi and of trading at New Orleans or by offering generous terms to Americans who wanted to settle on Spanish lands.

What was obviously needed was a treaty between Spain and the United States, definitely fixing the boundary line and clarifying the respective rights. But at first the Washington administration seemed no more able to conclude such a settlement than had its weak predecessor, the Confederation government. At the invitation of Spain, two American envoys, William Short, who had been American chargé d'affaires at Paris, and William Carmichael, chargé at Madrid, were sent to Madrid in 1792. Since Spanish pride was somewhat wounded that more illustrious personages had not been named, the negotiations began poorly. A more important handicap, however, was the international situation. The French Revolution had terminated the traditional Bourbon Compact between Spain and France and had brought about an alliance between Spain and England instead. Because relations between England and the United States were bad in 1793, the Spaniards had no reason to fear any joint Anglo-American threats to Spanish America. The Madrid government could therefore see no reason to concede the American demands.

In 1794, however, the situation changed. Spain's brief participation in the war against the French Republic brought only defeats and heavy expenditures. Manuel de Godoy, Duke of Alcudia, the youthful Chief Minister of Charles IV, became convinced that Spain must seek peace even at the expense of alienating England. News of the Jay mission to London alarmed the Spanish Minister, since it posed the threat of an Anglo-American alliance dangerous to Spanish control of Louisiana and the Floridas. The Madrid government therefore adopted a more conciliatory policy, promising to restrain the Indians from attacking the American frontier and inviting the United States to send some illustrious person on a new mission to Spain.

The Treaty of San Lorenzo

Although the Washington administration was still pessimistic about the prospects for a diplomatic settlement, it seemed wise to accept the invita-

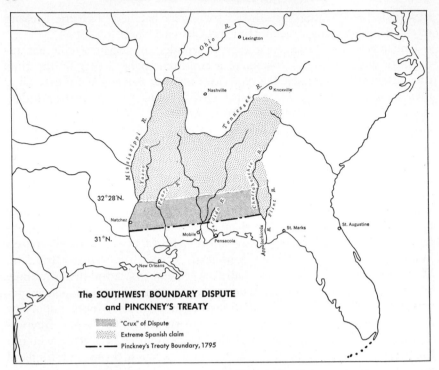

The SOUTHWEST BOUNDARY DISPUTE
and PINCKNEY'S TREATY

"Crux" of Dispute
Extreme Spanish claim
Pinckney's Treaty Boundary, 1795

tion if only to placate the restless Kentuckians. Accordingly, Thomas
Pinckney, who had played a leading role in the Revolutionary politics of
South Carolina and was now United States Minister to England, was sent
to Madrid. When he arrived there at the end of June, 1795, the situation
was unusually advantageous to American diplomacy. Spain was in the
final stages of the ultrasecret negotiations for a peace treaty with France.
Since this news might result in drastic retaliation from England, Godoy
was eager to settle with the United States on almost any terms. The
Spanish Minister was in all the greater hurry because his rivals at court
were intriguing against him and he needed to clear his desk of foreign
complications.

The Treaty of San Lorenzo, signed October 27, 1795, granted to the
United States all it had been seeking since 1783. The boundary line between the Floridas and the United States was fixed at the 31st parallel, and
the line between Louisiana and the United States was defined as the middle channel of the Mississippi River. Spanish subjects and American citizens were to be allowed free navigation of that river. For three years
Americans were to be permitted to deposit their merchandise at the port
of New Orleans and to export their cargoes without paying any other
fees than a fair price for warehousing. At the conclusion of this period,

the King of Spain promised either to continue this right of deposit at New Orleans or to substitute similar privileges somewhere else on the lower Mississippi. In its other provisions the Pinckney Treaty regularized commercial relations between the two nations and defined neutral rights in accordance with the liberal French treaty of 1778, rather than following the retrograde Jay Treaty of 1794. Finally both parties mutually promised to restrain Indians living within their boundaries from attacking settlements across the borders.

The treaty, unanimously ratified by the United States Senate, did not prevent future disputes between the neighbors. On the contrary, Spanish delays in evacuating the disputed territory created new friction, and the land north of the 31st parallel was not finally cleared of Spanish garrisons until 1798. Nevertheless, the Treaty of San Lorenzo was a major achievement of Federalist diplomacy, for, in addition to the specific terms, it facilitated the settlement of the West and quieted separatist agitation in Kentucky.

Friction with France

In 1794, President Washington appointed James Monroe as Minister to the French Republic to succeed Gouverneur Morris, whose ill-concealed hostility to the Paris government had led to a request for his recall. The appointment of Monroe, an ardent follower of Jefferson, was designed both to quiet Democratic-Republican criticism at home and to reassure the French at a time when Jay's mission to England had aroused serious misgivings.

When Monroe arrived in Paris, he received a warm welcome, to which he reciprocated with fervent protestations of admiration for the French Republic. After an extraordinary round of festivities, the new Minister began the serious business of trying to remove grievances that had accumulated between the two nations. The French were complaining about the Washington administration's refusal to allow French privateers to equip themselves and sell their prizes in American ports. The Americans were protesting over French seizure of neutral ships and over the many annoying restrictions on American trade in French ports. During the early months of his mission, Monroe appeared to be making good progress toward convincing the French government that it should demonstrate its good will by reverting to the liberal principles of the Franco-American commercial treaty of 1778.

All the ground that Monroe had gained, however, was lost as a result of two developments in the latter half of 1795. In August, the text of Jay's Treaty reached Paris, together with the assurance that the document did not conflict with the Franco-American alliance. Monroe's attempts to defend the new treaty were lame and unconvincing—the more so because he himself was strongly opposed to it. To add to the Minister's problems, another turn of the revolutionary wheel brought to an end the government of the National Convention and substituted that of the Directory. The new regime was less radical than its predecessor, but it was more cynical in its foreign policy. Any effort to appeal to the Directors on grounds of sentiment and common ideals was not likely to succeed.

Prevented by his own prejudices from fully understanding the situation in America, Monroe made serious mistakes. First, he predicted the Senate would reject Jay's Treaty. When this prophecy proved wrong, Monroe intimated that the Federalists would be voted out of office in the elections of 1796.

Monroe's indiscretions and the advice sent home by French envoys in the United States confirmed the Directory in the delusion that American foreign policy could be controlled by meddling in American domestic politics. Joseph Fauchet and Pierre Adet, successive ministers to the United States, were involved in a network of intrigue. They sought to influence Congress and supplied anti-Federalist editors and writers with propaganda and sometimes even with money. Their great objective was to prevent the reelection of Washington for a third term or the choice of any other Federalist to succeed him. They worked instead to have Jefferson established in the Presidency.

As part of this campaign to influence the American election, the French government increased its restrictive measures against American shipping. This was intended to demonstrate French displeasure with the Jay Treaty and to convince American voters that it would be impossible to achieve better relations with France as long as the Federalists remained in office.

President Washington deeply resented both the tactics of the French government and the increasingly personal criticism to which he was being subjected by the Democratic-Republicans at home. In August, 1796, he recalled Monroe and appointed Charles Cotesworth Pinckney, a South Carolina Federalist, to replace him. This action only added fuel to the flames. Monroe wrote a pamphlet defending his conduct and condemning the Washington administration's policy, while the Directory determined not to receive Pinckney.

Washington's Farewell Address

Meantime, Washington had decided that he should issue a message declining a third term and offering fatherly advice to his fellow citizens on their future conduct. He had been thinking of doing this ever since 1792, when he sought Madison's advice on how he might convey to the public his wish to retire. On the earlier occasion, Washington had been persuaded to accept a second term, but now he was determined to quit the noisy political arena for the serenity of Mount Vernon. Significantly he turned this time to Alexander Hamilton, rather than to Madison, for assistance in composing his farewell message. The resulting document, one of the most notable in American history, represented skillful collaboration. The ideas were Washington's; the felicitous language in which they were expressed was largely Hamilton's.

Much of the Farewell Address was devoted to domestic affairs. After explaining the reasons for his determination to retire, Washington went on to stress the importance of national unity and to warn of the perils of sectionalism. Somewhat unrealistically, he deplored "the baneful effects of the spirit of party generally." In an obvious reference to French intrigues of the day, Washington asserted that the rise of political parties "opens the door to foreign influence and corruption, which find a facilitated access to the government itself through the channels of party passion."

In the most famous part of the address, the first President turned to the field of foreign affairs. "Observe good faith and justice toward all nations," he enjoined. Then, speaking in general terms, but in language clearly applicable to the relations of the United States toward England and France, Washington warned against "permanent, inveterate antipathies against particular nations and passionate attachments for others." Excessive attachment to a foreign power would involve America in foreign quarrels without adequate justification. "Against the insidious wiles of foreign influence," asserted Washington, "the jealousy of a free people ought to be *constantly* awake, since history and experience prove that foreign influence is one of the most baneful foes of republican government."

Washington pointed out that Europe had a set of primary interests with which America had a very remote relation. "Hence, therefore, it must be unwise in us to implicate ourselves by artificial ties in the ordinary vicissitudes of her politics or the ordinary combinations and collisions of her friendships or enmities." The United States should take advantage of its "detached and distant situation" to strengthen its government and command foreign respect for its rights.

> Why forego the advantages of so peculiar a situation? Why quit our own to stand upon foreign ground? Why, by interweaving our destiny with that of any part of Europe, entangle our peace and prosperity in the toils of European ambition, rivalship, interest, humor, or caprice?

The nation's true policy, declared the president, was to "steer clear of permanent alliances with any portion of the foreign world." He hastened to add that he was not advocating repudiation of existing obligations.

These should be scrupulously observed, but it would be unnecessary and unwise to extend them. If the nation made adequate provision for defense, it might "safely trust to temporary alliances for extraordinary emergencies."

The Farewell Address was destined to be quoted on many future occasions, usually by isolationists eager to cite Washington's warning against foreign entanglements. Oftentimes the first President's words were taken out of context and given a somewhat twisted meaning. It should be noted that Washington did not advocate American isolation under all circumstances. On the contrary, he stressed the sanctity of existing treaties and suggested that alliances of a temporary character might be necessary to meet future emergencies. His advice was against the kind of permanent alliance that might involve the United States in quarrels of a strictly European character. Moreover, his advice was predicated on America's "detached and distant situation," a situation drastically modified in later years by the steamship and the airplane. Although Washington was giving advice which he hoped would be useful in the future, his particular concern was with the very specific situation existing in 1796, when the nation's relations with France were dangerously involved in the imminent presidential election.

The XYZ Affair

As soon as Washington definitely removed himself from consideration, the election of 1796 developed into a contest between Federalist John Adams and Democratic-Republican Thomas Jefferson. The rivalry between the parties became ever more bitter, and the balloting was extremely close. In the end, Adams was elected President by a narrow margin, while Jefferson, through the operation of the peculiar electoral machinery provided in the original Constitution, became Vice President.

To emphasize the continuity between his own administration and the preceding one, Adams retained Washington's entire Cabinet in office. This proved a serious mistake, because Secretary of State Pickering and most of his colleagues looked to Alexander Hamilton for leadership. Eventually Adams asserted himself and gained control over his own administration, but this victory for a moderate policy did not take place until after the Hamiltonian faction had brought the country close to all-out hostilities against France.

The most important problem confronting Adams when he took office was the disruption of diplomatic relations between the United States and France. When C. C. Pinckney had arrived in Paris in December, 1796, the Paris government lost no time in demonstrating its displeasure. The Directors refused to receive the new Minister, threatened him with arrest, and ordered him out of the country. Pinckney thereupon retired to Holland to await further instructions from home. To underline further their rebuke to the American Federalists, the Directors bade a most affectionate farewell to Monroe. Paul Barras, the most powerful man in the government, took this occasion to make a speech bitterly denouncing the American administration and appealing to the American people to repudiate Federalist leadership.

President Adams was not a man to allow such provocations to go unanswered. He summoned Congress in special session in May, 1797, to hear an indignant message, which the Democratic-Republican opposition bitterly denounced as a "war whoop." The President condemned the French refusal to receive Pinckney and the insulting speech of Barras, and asked Congress for appropriations to strengthen the Navy. Yet the President's real wish was for peace. He announced that a special commission would be sent to France to seek an honorable settlement of the differences between the two nations.

Adams's first impulse was to send Jefferson, Madison, and Hamilton, but political rivalries were too bitter to make such a bipartisan approach possible. Handicapped by the suspicions of both Democratic-Republicans and Federalists, the President finally named Pinckney, the rejected Minister, John Marshall, a brilliant young Virginia lawyer, and Elbridge Gerry of Massachusetts. Pinckney and Marshall were staunch Federalists; Gerry was a man of somewhat uncertain politics who had opposed the Hamiltonian program in the early Congresses, but had supported his friend, John Adams, for the Presidency in 1796. The inclusion of this almost-Democratic-Republican on the commission was strongly attacked by Secretary of State Pickering and the rest of the Hamiltonian faction.

This American commission arrived in Paris early in October, 1797—a highly inauspicious time for requesting modification of French policy. The military genius of General Napoleon Bonaparte had recently been demonstrated in his first Italian campaign, and a bold show of power by the same general had suppressed all domestic opposition to the regime. Bonaparte's vaulting popularity was ominous for the future of the Directory, but its immediate result was to place the government in a position where it felt able to dictate terms to all its neighbors. Even the British government was discouraged with the progress of the war and was considering peace proposals.

As Foreign Minister, the Directors had appointed Charles Maurice de Talleyrand. This brilliant and unscrupulous man, born of aristocratic parentage, had been educated for the clergy and had risen to the rank of bishop before the French Revolution. Because of his rationalism and support of the anticlerical policy of the National Assembly, he had been expelled from the Church by the Pope. His ability and training had made him useful to the early revolutionary government as a diplomat, but fear for his life during the Terror drove him into exile. For more than two years he had lived in the United States, but the experience had not imbued him with any love for the new nation or respect for the American character. Talleyrand had returned to Paris during the period of conservative reaction, and he had soon risen to a position of influence he was to retain under three successive regimes: the Directory, the Empire of Napoleon, and the restored monarchy of Louis XVIII.

Although Talleyrand received the American commission soon after its arrival in Paris, he put off all attempts at negotiation. While Adams's envoys waited disconsolately in their rooms, the French government demonstrated its power with an intensified campaign of seizures of American vessels. After the first two weeks of delay, the commissioners received mysterious visits from certain private individuals [1] who claimed to know what was in the mind of Talleyrand and the Directors. They warned the Americans that the French government was so seriously displeased with the United States that war was likely, but they confided the interesting suggestion that American dollars might assuage these French wounds. What was proposed was a concealed loan of an unspecified amount from the United States to France and a secret bribe of $250,000 to go to Talleyrand and the Directors. Once these financial arrangements were made, the Paris government would renew diplomatic relations and negotiate on outstanding grievances.

Immoral and insulting though this proposal was, it was not unusual for the day. The French Republic had on earlier occasions extorted tribute from its neighbors. Portugal had recently bribed the Directors to obtain a treaty with France, and Britain was seriously considering a similar course.

The American commissioners were sorely troubled by the proposition, not so much because it was dishonorable as because a loan to France would compromise American neutrality. They reported the matter to their home government and remained in Paris, hoping the Directory would adopt a more reasonable attitude. For some five months this strange situation continued, with Talleyrand persisting in his refusal to negotiate directly and insisting through secret channels that money must be paid. Pinckney and Marshall, the thoroughgoing Federalists, favored a stiff attitude. "No, no; not a sixpence!" was Pinckney's indignant response when a French emissary became too demanding. Marshall transmitted to the French government a formal statement of the American position, defending the Jay Treaty and protesting that the retaliatory decrees of

---

[1] The principal go-betweens were two bankers named Hottinguer and Bellamy, and a merchant named Hauteval. A lovely lady, Madame de Villette, likewise became involved, as did also the famous Beaumarchais.

the Directory had not been justified. But Gerry, with his Democratic-Republican sympathies, favored a more flexible policy; he thought the threat of war was very real and that it might be worth while to pay money to avoid it.

The French government, still confident of its ability to overturn the Federalists by collaborating with the Jeffersonian party, worked hard to capitalize on the disagreements among the American commissioners. Talleyrand let it be known that the American case might have a better chance were Marshall and Pinckney to go home and leave the negotiations to Gerry.

Finally, in April, 1798, Marshall and Pinckney abandoned their futile mission. Marshall sailed directly home; Pinckney, unwilling to hazard the life of his seriously ill daughter with a long ocean voyage, retired to the south of France. Despite the remonstrances of his fellow commissioners, Gerry remained in Paris until August. He received much flattering attention from the wily Talleyrand, but no solid concessions. The New Englander's conduct was bitterly condemned in the Federalist press as a violation of his instructions.

Although communications across the Atlantic had been unusually slow during the months that all three commissioners had been in Paris, President Adams was in possession of their earlier dispatches by March 19, 1798, when he sent a somber message to Congress, announcing that the mission had been a failure, that it was impossible to agree with France "on terms compatible with the safety, the honor, or the essential interests of the nation, and that the United States should prepare for war." Refusing to believe Adams's statement of the case, the Democratic-Republicans loudly demanded publication of the diplomatic correspondence. The Federalists, well informed on the dynamite contained in the papers, also urged publication. Early in April, therefore, the documents were sent to Congress and soon were printed in the newspapers. For the actual names of the intermediaries who had solicited bribes, the cryptic letters W, X, Y, and Z were substituted; hence the origin of the term "XYZ Affair."

War Clouds

The story of what had happened in Paris stirred most Americans to indignation. The Democratic-Republican leaders weakly remonstrated that the nation should remain calm, that the infamous X, Y, and Z might have been imposters, and that the French government would presently set the records straight. But such counsels of caution were unpopular. "*Ça ira*," the recently popular song of the French Revolution, was now greeted with hisses and groans; "The President's March" was played by vociferous demand at every theatrical performance. On April 25, 1798, when a Philadelphia theater audience heard the first singing of "Hail, Columbia," with words by Joseph Hopkinson set to the tune of "The President's March," the scene was one of wild excitement. Other new patriotic songs soon appeared; "American clubs" were organized; spirited youths wearing black cockades engaged in street brawls with those who still stubbornly displayed the tricolored cockades of the pro-French faction.

At the height of the excitement, John Marshall returned to the United States. Both at New York, where he landed, and at Philadelphia, where he hastened to report to the President and Secretary of State, the envoy who had resisted the insulting French demands received a hero's welcome with parades and banquets. It was at one of the latter that some inspired participant proposed the toast: "Millions for defense but not a cent for tribute." This defiant phrase seemed so appropriate a response for Pinckney to have made in Paris that popular legend soon attributed the words to him.

This patriotic tidal wave swept President Adams and his party to an unwonted peak of popularity. Eagerly responding to the popular mood, the Federalist majority in Congress passed a series of sweeping measures. All treaties with France were abrogated, and commercial intercourse between the United States and areas under French rule was prohibited. American merchant vessels were authorized to arm themselves for defense. Armed French ships were declared subject to capture by American naval vessels and even by American merchant ships in case the latter were attacked. Frigates long in process of construction were rushed to completion and new ships authorized. As news came in of the success of the infant American Navy in capturing or driving away French war vessels and privateers that had been hovering off the Atlantic Coast, patriotic fervor was still further inflated.

Although French and American frigates were now exchanging fire in what has been called the undeclared war, the situation had not yet developed to the stage of full-scale war. In anticipation of widened hostilities, the Federalist majority in Congress authorized the raising of an army. Command was placed nominally in the hands of the venerable George Washington; actually the reins of authority were entrusted to the eager Alexander Hamilton, whom Adams appointed reluctantly—and at Washington's insistence—to the influential post of Inspector General. Hamilton, eager to win military glory, devoted all his energies to recruiting soldiers, organizing and training regiments, and making ready for the day when he would take the field against the French.

The Federalists, intoxicated by their sudden popularity, attempted to take advantage of the war scare to crush their political opponents. They hurried into law the controversial Alien and Sedition Acts and began petty persecution of Democratic-Republican editors and politicians who had been overly critical. When Dr. George Logan, a well-meaning but blundering Philadelphia Quaker and Democratic-Republican, undertook to patch up the quarrel with France by going on his own unofficial peace mission, he was subjected to savage Federalist criticism. Congress enacted a law providing fine and imprisonment for any person entering into such unauthorized negotiation with a foreign power (the so-called Logan Act, which is still on the books). Such evidences of vindictiveness reacted against the Federalists, however, and public opinion in 1799 began once again to turn toward the Democratic-Republicans.

The Convention of 1800

Meanwhile, President Adams had received intimations that France was ready to negotiate on a more reasonable basis. From the ridiculed Dr. Logan, from the Francophile Connecticut poet, Joel Barlow, and from other sources came rumors that the Directory desired a reconciliation. One reason for this undoubtedly was the recognition by Talleyrand that French recalcitrance had had an opposite effect from that intended. Instead of overturning the Federalists and bringing the Democratic-Republicans to power, it was rallying the American public to the Federalists.

Adams was most impressed by news from William Vans Murray, American Minister to Holland, who had been assured by a French diplomat that if a new minister were sent to Paris, he would be treated with respect. Although indirectly transmitted, this amounted to a promise by Talleyrand. The President thereupon sent to the Senate the nomination of Murray as Minister to France. The Hamiltonian faction bitterly opposed the idea, and Adams had to accept a compromise under which a commission of three would be sent to Paris to renew negotiations on the old grievances. Murray, Chief Justice Oliver Ellsworth of the Supreme Court, and Governor William R. Davie of North Carolina were chosen for the mission.

In accepting the French overtures and opening new negotiations, John Adams acted with characteristically sturdy independence. The Democratic-Republicans still distrusted the President and criticized his every action. The Hamiltonian faction in his own party was equally troublesome. Indeed, Secretary of State Pickering was so much opposed to Adams's policy that he delayed the actual departure of the commission for several months. In the end, the President had to act decisively, overriding the obstructionists and ordering the envoys to sail. Extraordinarily bad weather, however, delayed their arrival in Paris until March, 1800.

By this time the political situation in France had again changed drastically. By a *coup d'état* Napoleon Bonaparte had overthrown the Directory and seized dictatorial authority as First Consul. The wily Talleyrand had ridden safely through this political storm and emerged as Napoleon's Foreign Minister. Since the First Consul approved Talleyrand's policy of reconciliation with the United States, the American commissioners were hospitably received. Despite this auspicious beginning, it still proved difficult to settle the old grievances. The American envoys' hands were tied by Pickering's stiff instructions; they were obliged to insist that France pay indemnity for its spoliations against American neutral shipping. Napoleon steadfastly refused to make any such concession, and the negotiations bogged down for several months more. Contributing to the delay was the fact that the First Consul was far more interested in concluding the secret agreement of San Ildefonso with Spain.

In the end, the American commissioners disregarded their instructions and accepted the best terms they could get. By the so-called Convention of 1800, signed on September 30, the United States and France terminated their quasi-war by mutual restoration of all captured public ships and such private ships as had not been judicially condemned. Normal commercial relations between the two nations were to be resumed, and neutral rights were defined in the old liberal terms that had been set forth in earlier Franco-American treaties. Contraband was limited to actual munitions of war, and the principle of free ships–free goods was recognized. The spoliation claims were postponed for future negotiations, and, pending their settlement, the famous old treaties of 1778, the treaty of alliance and the treaty of commerce, were suspended.

The Hamiltonian faction, reluctant to allow the war spirit to die, condemned the convention as unsatisfactory. This opposition resulted in significant reservations being attached to the Senate's approval of the agreement. Article 2, dealing with spoliations and suspension of the old treaties, was rejected, and the duration of the treaty was limited to eight years. Napoleon accepted these changes on condition that the spoliations claims be finally abandoned. The end result, therefore, was that the United States had to give up its claims for indemnity; in return, however, it obtained honorable release from the old alliance, a commitment that had become increasingly troublesome.

Gift horses bearing Napoleon's greeting card would always bear examination, and this was true of the settlement of 1800. French policy was motivated primarily by selfish interests. Napoleon's solicitude for neutral rights was shrewdly related to his country's relative weakness on the seas and its need to rely on neutral shipping for its own supply. Moreover, the general consideration underlying Talleyrand's reconciliation policy was to avoid driving the United States into an alliance with England that might result in American capture of New Orleans. Already France was intriguing to get Louisiana for itself.

However cynical and calculating Napoleon's policy may have been, the Convention of 1800 was, nevertheless, advantageous to the United States. Successfully, although somewhat clumsily, John Adams had walked the tightrope and avoided the dangers threatening on either side —that of compromising American independence by spiritless submission to French highhandedness on the one hand, and of committing the nation to full-scale war against France on the other.

5

JEFFERSON FLIES THE FLAG

Since Federalists and Democratic-Republicans had always differed sharply on issues of foreign policy, it might have been expected that the inauguration of Thomas Jefferson in 1801 would be followed by drastic changes in the relations of the United States with foreign powers. Such changes eventually did occur, but the shift in American policy was by no means rapid. If the quasi-war with France during the administration of John Adams is to be regarded as the logical result of anti-French prejudices of the Federalists, then the War of 1812 during Madison's term may be considered the natural outcome of long-existing anti-British bias of the Democratic-Republicans. Actually, however, circumstances influenced American foreign policy much more than did party prejudices, and events during the early years of Jefferson's Presidency were so compelling that the Democratic-Republicans seriously considered the possibility of allying with England in war against France.

Jeffersonian Principles

President Jefferson did not want war, to be sure, with either England or France. "Peace, commerce, and honest friendship with all nations, entangling alliances with none" was the formula for American foreign policy that he laid down in his first inaugural address. Since this attitude had also been the essential content of Washington's Farewell Address, it is obvious that the early statesmen of the Republic were in fundamental agreement on the ideals that should underlie the relations of the United States with the rest of the world.

Yet Washington and Jefferson differed on how these ideals should be attained. The first President had believed that a strong central government and constant military preparedness were the essential conditions. Jefferson, on the other hand, thought the central government should have a minimum of power, leaving as much responsibility as possible to the states. He also was of the opinion that a large army and navy were dangerous to the liberties of the people and unnecessarily expensive to the taxpayers. In time of peace the nation could depend largely upon a citizen militia; in case of war a liberty-loving people would quickly spring to arms to repel any foe. The navy, consisting primarily of small craft, should be used principally for coastal defense. Jefferson did not for a moment concede that reduction of the armed forces would expose the nation to indignities at the hands of foreign powers. "Our commerce," he wrote, "is so valuable to them that they will be glad to purchase it when the only price we ask is to do us justice." In other words, the President was confident that the most effective way to enforce respect for American rights was to refuse to trade with any recalcitrant power.

Albert Gallatin, Jefferson's able Secretary of the Treasury, was even more firmly committed to the idea that military appropriations should be reduced. While most victorious political parties come into office committed to a program of lowering government expenses and cutting taxes, the Jeffersonians took this pledge with unusual seriousness. For political reasons the new administration felt it imperative to reduce the debt and to repeal the hated Hamiltonian excise taxes; therefore it was vital to find ways of saving money. The Adams administration had already begun to retrench by cutting naval appropriations after the termination of the quasi-war with France; the new administration not only gladly continued this policy, but extended it to the army as well.

Unfortunately, the protection of American interests abroad without the use of force was a much more difficult task than cutting the budget at home. Therefore a certain inconsistency between Jeffersonian principles and Jeffersonian practice was almost inevitable.

Disciplining the Barbary Pirates

The original difficulties encountered by the Confederation government in protecting American shipping in the Mediterranean from the depredations of the Barbary pirates have already been related. This problem continued to cause trouble throughout the Washington and Adams administrations.

The Dey of Algiers, the Pasha of Tripoli, and the Bey of Tunis supposedly served under the suzerainty of the Sultan of Turkey; the Emperor of Morocco was regarded as an independent sovereign. Actually all four of these Moslem dignitaries maintained a *de facto* independence and used their power to wage sporadic war against the commerce of the hated Christians. Barbary corsairs ranged throughout the Mediterranean and even ventured occasionally through the Straits of Gibraltar into the

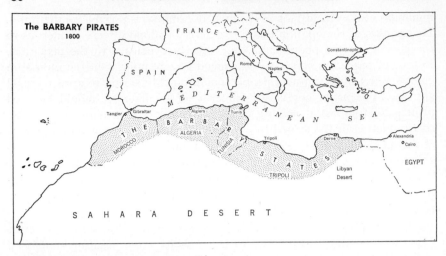

Atlantic. They enriched themselves by seizing ships and cargoes and by heartlessly selling captured crews into slavery. Only by paying heavy ransom could the various Christian governments obtain the release of these unhappy prisoners.

Strange though it seems, European governments had tolerated this situation for generations. Instead of taking individual or collective action to terminate this piracy, the Christian powers had bought temporary immunity for their shipping by making treaties with the Barbary rulers that provided for payment of annual tribute. The principal reason for this policy appears to have been commercial greed; each treaty power hoped to enrich itself by enjoying special privileges while the trade of its rivals was being disrupted. One reason for anti-British feeling in the United States during the 1790s was the series of rumors that English agents were encouraging Barbary attacks on American shipping.

During the Washington administration at least eleven American ships were captured by raiders from Algiers, and the total number of American captives in Algerian hands rose to 119. It was this situation that led Congress in 1794 to authorize the construction of six naval vessels. The following year tension was reduced by resort to customary means. The American government promised to pay $642,500 in cash and $21,600 annual tribute in naval stores; the Dey of Algiers agreed in turn to release the American captives and to refrain from future seizures. This treaty was followed by agreements between the United States and the other Barbary states; each of these involved liberal gifts to the Barbary rulers, but no annual tribute.

Until such time as the United States had at least a minimum of naval strength, the only alternatives open to the American government were either to satisfy the demands of the North African rulers or to abandon American trade in the Mediterranean. After the settlement with Algiers in 1795, the naval building program was cut in half, and it was not until two years later that the first three frigates of the American Navy were ready for service. During the trouble with France, a number of other ships were authorized, and President Adams planned to dispatch a fleet of these new ships to the Mediterranean as soon as good relations with France were restored.

The idea of making a show of force against the Barbary states appealed strongly to President Jefferson despite his well-known love for peace. Since the days of his mission to France during the Confederation period, he had been an advocate of strong measures to end this particular nuisance. "I am an enemy to all these douceurs, tributes & humiliations," he wrote to James Madison, his Secretary of State. "I know nothing will stop the eternal increase of demands from these pirates but the presence of an armed force, and it will be more economical & more honorable to use the same means at once for suppressing their insolencies." Contributing to this feeling was recent information that the Dey of Algiers had compelled Captain William Bainbridge of the *George Washington* to transport the Algerian Ambassador to Turkey in 1800.

The Tripolitan War

In May, 1801, Jefferson sent Commodore Richard Dale with four naval vessels to the Mediterranean under orders either to make new agreements with the Barbary states or, failing that, to wage war on them. The administration did not regard this expedition as inconsistent with its economy program, for, as Madison pointed out, it would cost almost as much to maintain these ships at home as abroad.

By coincidence, just a few days before this decision was made in Washington, the Pasha of Tripoli had ordered the flagstaff on the American consulate cut down. This was the Barbary symbol for a declaration of war and reflected the Pasha's discontent with American unwillingness to pay him more money. The American squadron on its arrival in the Mediterranean was able to cripple one of the Tripolitan ships and to hamper enemy commerce, but its strength was not adequate to win a decisive victory.

In 1803, a larger American fleet under Commodore Edward Preble was able to command more respect. When the Emperor of Morocco suddenly attacked American shipping, Preble's countermoves were so swift and decisive that the Emperor promptly came to terms. But the Pasha of Tripoli continued hostile and, in October, 1803, he gained an important advantage when the frigate *Philadelphia* ran aground and was captured by the Pasha's forces. In a famous act of heroism, Stephen Decatur took a small boat into the enemy harbor and set fire to the *Philadelphia*, thereby preventing the frigate's guns from ever being turned against her sister ships. This feat, however, did not alter the fact that the Pasha now held 307 American sailors, whom he put to hard labor and threatened with worse punishment if the United States did not meet his demands.

Gallatin, worried by mounting expenses for these Mediterranean operations, believed that it might be better to resume tribute payments, but Jefferson continued to support strong measures, even reversing earlier policy to the extent of asking for larger naval appropriations. Recognizing the need for a flexible policy, however, he sent Tobias Lear, who had once been President Washington's secretary, to the scene of hostilities with wide discretionary powers to make peace on the best possible terms.

During the summer of 1804, Commodore Preble carried on hostilities against Tripoli more energetically than ever, running close to shore and bombarding the capital city on more than one occasion. Further operations were also carried on by Commodore Samuel Barron and Commodore John Rodgers, who succeeded Preble in the Mediterranean command. Despite these punishing attacks, the Pasha remained obdurate, demanding first a million dollars, then lesser sums, as his price for releasing the American prisoners and for agreeing to a satisfactory treaty.

It was General William Eaton, an adventuresome native of Connecticut and former American consul at Tunis, who did much to bring Tripoli to terms by a bold, dramatic stroke. The Pasha of Tripoli, Yusuf Karamanli, had usurped the throne at the expense of his weak elder brother, Hamet Karamanli. Early in 1805, Eaton sought out Hamet in Egypt, where the Tripolitan prince was living in exile. Eaton promised to restore Hamet to power with American arms if the Tripolitan would make a permanent treaty of friendship with the United States. Thereupon Eaton recruited a motley army of some 10 Americans and 400 other volunteers of miscellaneous Christian and Moslem background. With this force he crossed 500 miles of barren and waterless Libyan desert to attack the Tripolitan outpost at Derne. With the help of three American ships, which bombarded the town from the sea, Eaton captured the place and then planned an attack upon the city of Tripoli itself.

The Treaty of Peace

Further adventuring on Eaton's part was prevented by a treaty of peace, signed by Tobias Lear and Pasha Yusuf on June 10, 1805, under which the United States promised to evacuate Derne, to give up its support of Hamet, and to pay $60,000 ransom for the *Philadelphia* captives. On his part, the Pasha pledged to respect American trading rights without any annual tribute. In the event of future conflict, the Tripolitan government promised to treat captured Americans as prisoners of war, not as slaves.

This treaty did not escape criticism in the United States, especially from the Federalists. Lear was condemned for having sacrificed the interests of Hamet and Eaton. The naval leaders were denounced for not having made better use of their ships. And the agreement to pay ransom for American prisoners was challenged as an abandonment of the principle for which the United States had been fighting. The administration, however, strongly defended Lear's diplomacy. If the Americans had insisted upon unconditional surrender and launched a full-scale attack upon the city of Tripoli, the Pasha might well have carried out his threat to massacre the prisoners.

The country as a whole was highly pleased with the outcome of the fighting in North Africa. The United States had freed itself from the ignominy of buying protection for its Mediterranean trade.[1] This resolute policy raised the prestige of the new republic in the eyes of many Europeans and gave the Americans themselves a greater sense of national pride.

The Mississippi Question Arises Again

As the trans-Appalachian states grew with unexpected rapidity, the unencumbered use of the Mississippi River and the port of New Orleans became ever more important. When the Spaniards, in customary fashion, delayed compliance with the Treaty of San Lorenzo, American indignation rose dangerously. Nor did Spanish evacuation of the disputed posts in 1798 immediately end the threat of serious trouble. Spain was closely tied to France during these years, and Americans suspected some kind of deal between the two powers by which France would regain Louisiana.

During the quasi-war with France in 1798 and 1799, Inspector General Alexander Hamilton had dreamed of settling the Mississippi question once and for all by an American conquest of Louisiana and Florida. Indeed, Hamilton's projects even included the possibility of a joint Anglo-American naval expedition against South America in collaboration with the Venezuelan adventurer and patriot, Francisco de Miranda.

The hopes of the Federalist war hawks had been dashed by President Adams, who accepted Talleyrand's peace overtures. With diplomatic relations restored with France and the Spanish colonial officials now faith-

---

[1] Algiers, however, continued to expect annual deliveries of naval stores and became increasingly insolent after the withdrawal of the American fleet in 1807. Not until Commodore Decatur took a squadron to the Mediterranean in 1815 did Algiers sign a satisfactory treaty.

fully complying with the Treaty of San Lorenzo, the prospects for peace appeared excellent at the time of Jefferson's inauguration.

Spain's Loss of Interest in Louisiana

This calm, however, was merely on the surface. In secret European negotiations decisions of fateful importance were being made. As early as 1795, the Spanish government had concluded that Louisiana was a hopelessly unprofitable colony. The costs of its administration far exceeded the local revenues, thereby making necessary an annual subsidy from the rich province of Mexico. In addition, perennial rumors of impending invasion by American frontiersmen made the defense problem a constant cause of anxiety. Attempts to increase the strength and prosperity of Louisiana by offering inducements to American immigrants had succeeded only in undermining Spanish religious and mercantilist policy. The grant of the right of deposit at New Orleans had opened the door to wholesale smuggling.

The Madrid government therefore regarded Louisiana as a mere pawn in the diplomatic game, which it would gladly give up in exchange for some more valuable piece. In 1796, Spanish and French negotiators had actually arranged a treaty whereby Louisiana would have been returned to France, but the Directory disapproved the terms and refused to ratify the agreement. Four years later, when the question was reopened on the initiative of Spain, a mutually satisfactory bargain was effected.

The Treaty of San Ildefonso

In return for Louisiana, Napoleon promised to try to obtain for the Prince of Parma, the Spanish King's son-in-law, a substantial expansion of his Italian domain and an elevation to the title of King of Etruria. This Treaty of San Ildefonso, signed on October 1, 1800, was both secret and provisional. It was not to go into effect until Napoleon could fulfill his promise to the Spanish Bourbons and until termination of the war with England made it possible for France to take over Louisiana without immediately losing it to England or to the United States.

When other European governments withheld recognition of the proposed Kingdom of Etruria, Spain began to regret its bargain. Napoleon bore the Spanish delays with reasonable patience as long as the continued war in Europe made a showdown unwise, but in the spring of 1802 the situation changed radically. After the signing of the Treaty of Amiens with England, Napoleon found his hands free at last to pursue a policy of expansion in America. Therefore he insisted that Spain carry out its part of the agreement. Reluctantly—since the Parma situation was by no means satisfactorily arranged—the Spanish government agreed to order an early transfer of Louisiana to France. In return, Napoleon gave a new pledge—soon proved worthless—that he would never alienate this American territory to any other power without first giving Spain an opportunity to recover it.

Jefferson and New Orleans

The bargain between Spain and France was a secret so poorly kept that within eight months rumors of the Treaty of San Ildefonso began to percolate into Washington. To an administration predisposed toward friendly relations with France, these reports were disturbing. Secretary of State Madison warned Louis Pichon, French chargé d'affaires, that it would be most unwise for France to take over Louisiana. Americans were used to Spanish rule and could tolerate it despite its absurdities; but if France were to gain control of the mouth of the Mississippi, almost daily clashes would probably result.

To Robert Livingston, the new United States Minister to France, Madison repeated these observations and instructed him to make every effort to dissuade Napoleon from his course. The French ruler should be warned that his acquisition of Louisiana might drive the United States into alliance with England. If Napoleon still persisted in his plan, Livingston was to suggest that France take some step to reconcile American opinion. For instance, if the Spanish cession to France included the Floridas, France should transfer them, or West Florida at least, to the United States. Or, if the cession did not include the Floridas, Napoleon ought to use his good offices to help the United States acquire them from Spain.

This confusion as to whether the deal between Spain and France included merely Louisiana or involved one or both of the Floridas reflected the difficulty encountered by the Jefferson administration in obtaining exact information about the situation. For months France denied the whole Louisiana story, and the American government was compelled to base its policy upon the conflicting reports that reached Washington from Paris, Madrid, and London.

Enough was known by April, 1802, however, to prompt Jefferson to write a strongly worded letter to Livingston. The cession of Louisiana to France "completely reverses all the political relations of the United States," declared the President. Hitherto, he continued, Americans had regarded France as their natural friend, but there was on the globe "one single spot, the possessor of which is our natural and habitual enemy." That spot was New Orleans, through which must pass to market the produce of three-eighths of American territory. Spain might have retained that port quietly for years because her feeble state would induce her to make greater and greater concessions to the United States. But, if it fell into the hands of France, the impetuosity and restlessness of French character would inevitably lead to hostility.

> The day that France takes possession of New Orleans, fixes the sentence which is to restrain her forever within her low-water mark. It seals the union of two nations, who in conjunction, can maintain exclusive possession of the ocean. From that moment, we must marry ourselves to the British fleet and nation.

Were such an Anglo-American alliance formed, Napoleon must expect to lose Louisiana whenever war broke out in Europe. Livingston was instructed to urge these considerations on France in an attempt to deter her from carrying out the treaty with Spain. If Napoleon ignored this remonstrance and acquired Louisiana, the American Minister was to press for a cession of New Orleans and the Floridas.

Nothing more strongly reveals the importance Jefferson attached to New Orleans than this threat to reverse his party's historic foreign policy by allying the United States with Great Britain. To make doubly sure his warning reached the highest level of the French government, the President entrusted its delivery to Pierre Du Pont de Nemours, a distinguished French scholar who had recently moved to the United States. Du Pont was invited to read the dispatch himself and to impress its message on his influential friends in Paris.

Napoleon's first reactions to these American protests were discouraging. Both Livingston and Du Pont reported that he was no longer making any secret of his intention to take over Louisiana and that he was cool to all suggestions that he sell any part of it.

Still worse news arrived from New Orleans. On October 18, 1802, Juan Morales, the Spanish Intendant, issued a brusque proclamation withdrawing the right of deposit. American boats on the Mississippi could no longer store their produce in the warehouses of New Orleans without paying customs duties. Morales justified his action on the ground that the right conferred for three years in the Treaty of San Ildefonso had long since expired and that the state of war which had made it advisable to extend the privilege had now ended. But Americans indignantly rejected this explanation, pointing out that the Treaty of San Lorenzo had stipulated that at the expiration of the three-year term, the right of deposit was to be continued either at New Orleans or at some other suitable place on the lower Mississippi.

Why had this Spanish official taken such arbitrary action? Contemporary American opinion believed he would not have ventured such a step without orders from Madrid and that the new policy must have had its real origin with Napoleon. Historical investigation has confirmed the first of these assumptions, but not the second. Intendant Morales did indeed receive orders from the Spanish home government to revoke the right of deposit—orders so secret that he was forbidden to reveal them even to the Spanish governor at New Orleans. Yet it is by no means certain the French government had directed the change of policy. Spain's real motivation may have been a belated effort to combat smuggling at New Orleans or a perverse attempt to embroil the United States and France in controversy on the eve of the retrocession of Louisiana. On the other hand, subsequent French policy tends to strengthen the suspicion that the French government wanted the right of deposit withdrawn before it assumed control.

Threats of War

Whoever was ultimately responsible for the order revoking the right of deposit, the reaction of the American public was vehement. Newspapers in all sections condemned the new policy as an outrage not to be tolerated. Western legislatures memorialized Congress to take effective action to obtain relief. Even more bellicose than the Westerners were the Eastern Federalists. Alexander Hamilton, writing as "Pericles" in the *New-York Evening Post*, warned that Napoleon's control of Louisiana "threatens the early dismemberment of a large portion of the country." Only two courses of action were possible, he asserted: "First, to negotiate, and endeavor to purchase; and if this fails, to go to war. Secondly, to seize at once on the Floridas and New Orleans, and then negotiate." Hamilton favored the second, more aggressive action.

Hamilton and other Federalist leaders regarded the crisis as a magnificent opportunity to recoup the fortunes of their party. By championing Western interests, they hoped to gain political strength in the sections of the country where they had always been weak. This might pave the way for a Federalist return to office on a popular program of an Anglo-American war against France and Spain. The Federalist minority in Congress found itself in a position to embarrass the administration. Jefferson's message to Congress of December, 1802, was criticized for not dealing in forthright fashion with the current crisis, and the House passed a resolution calling upon the President to submit to Congress all information in his possession concerning the retrocession of Louisiana to France.

The Monroe Mission

Alarmed by Federalist tactics and eager to prove to the West that the administration was doing all it could to protect American rights,

Jefferson decided to send a special envoy to Paris. James Monroe was chosen, both because he was supposed to have unusual influence in France and because he had the reputation of being a particularly zealous champion of Western interests. Confirmed by the Senate on January 12, 1803, despite Federalist opposition, the special envoy was given wide powers. First, he was to attempt, in collaboration with Livingston, to obtain the cession of "New Orleans and of West and East Florida, or as much thereof as the actual proprietor can be prevailed upon to part with" by offering a maximum of 50 million livres ($9,375,000). Monroe was authorized to negotiate with the Spanish government as well as the French. If unsuccessful at both Paris and Madrid, he was to proceed to London to discuss the possibilities of an Anglo-American alliance.

The appointment of Monroe did not halt Federalist attempts to force Jefferson's hand. In February, 1803, Senator James Ross of Pennsylvania offered a resolution authorizing the President to call out 50,000 Western militiamen for an attack upon New Orleans. The Western representatives rejected this bid for their support, and the motion was defeated. Instead, a proadministration resolution authorizing military preparations in less provocative terms was adopted.

Although the war talk of 1803 was largely motivated by politics, it probably had its influence on the French government. Livingston saw to it that news of Ross's motion came to the attention of French officials, and Pichon, the chargé d'affaires, sent solemn dispatches to Paris, warning of the dangerous state of American opinion. Like Pichon, the Marquis de Casa Yrujo, the Spanish Minister at Washington, disapproved the policy of his own government. His protests against the withdrawal of the right of deposit convinced the Madrid government that a mistake had been made, and the disputed right was restored in May, 1803.

Napoleon Decides to Sell

Napoleon's Louisiana policy was closely related to other matters—to the general European situation, for one thing, and to the French position in Santo Domingo, for another. The latter problem was one that had become increasingly acute. This West Indian colony of France had been in a state of turmoil since the early days of the French Revolution. The Negro slaves had risen against their masters, and most of the whites had fled. Order was finally restored by Toussaint l'Ouverture, a great Negro leader whom the government of France had placed in command of the armed forces on the island. Napoleon, however, was unwilling to leave the government of Santo Domingo in the strong hands of Toussaint, whose recognition of French authority was little more than nominal. Therefore early in 1802, Napoleon sent his brother-in-law, General

Charles Leclerc, with a fleet and army of 20,000 men to the West Indies, with orders to restore French rule and reduce the Negroes again to slavery.

The close linkage between French policy in Santo Domingo and in Louisiana was obvious. Napoleon hoped to restore the plantation economy of all the French West Indian possessions—Guadeloupe and Martinique as well as Santo Domingo. These colonies would produce sugar and other tropical commodities and would import lumber and provisions from Lousiana. Essential to these dreams of a revived overseas empire was the continuance of peace in Europe, because these exposed outposts would be easy prizes for the British navy in case of war.

General Leclerc found it no easy task to subdue the rebellious islanders. Toussaint l'Ouverture's armies continued to resist, until the French disposed of the Negro hero through trickery. Promised honorable terms, Toussaint was induced to lay down his arms. In violation of these pledges, the rebel leader was seized and sent to France, where he died in prison in 1803. But the Bonapartist regime gained no permanent advantage from this act of treachery. Leclerc's army melted away during the year 1802, victim of both Negro guerrilla attacks and yellow fever. The general himself died, leaving the command in hopelessly incapable hands. Napoleon tried to retrieve the situation by preparing a new expedition, with orders both to pacify Santo Domingo and to occupy New Orleans. These reinforcements, however, never left the ports of Holland where they were mobilized. Severe winter weather delayed the departure for months. Then an ominous gathering of war clouds in Europe caused Napoleon to countermand the expedition.

Events had been moving irresistibly toward a renewal of war. Napoleon's restless ambition impelled him to use the months of peace to strengthen his domination of neighboring Holland, Switzerland, and Italy. The British, already alarmed by French policy in Santo Domingo and Louisiana, were strongly opposed to Bonaparte's tactics in Europe and therefore refused to carry out their own treaty commitments in matters like the evacuation of Malta. The wily Talleyrand, whom the British had offered to bribe if he could induce Napoleon to keep the peace, attempted to divert the First Consul's attention from Europe to America, but the latter refused to follow his Minister's advice.

On Easter Sunday, April 10, 1803, while Monroe was on the road between Le Havre and Paris, Napoleon abruptly summoned François de Marbois, his Finance Minister, and Admiral Denis Decrès to his palace to advise him on what to do about Louisiana. With war likely to break out at any moment, how could he place this American territory beyond the reach of England? "I am thinking of ceding it to the United States," Napoleon announced. "They ask me only for one city of Louisiana, but

I regard the entire colony as already lost, and it seems to me that in the hands of this new-born power, it will be more useful to the policy and even to the commerce of France, than if I should try to retain it." Both Marbois and Decrès approved this proposal, and the following morning Napoleon ordered Marbois to initiate negotiations with the Americans, stipulating only that hard cash be paid to fill the French war chest. By entrusting the business to his Minister of Finance, Bonaparte was making sure Talleyrand could not sabotage the deal as he had in the XYZ Affair.

The Louisiana Purchase

Talleyrand himself surprised Livingston with a hint of the new policy on April 11 when he inquired abruptly what the United States might be willing to offer for the whole of Louisiana. Serious negotiations did not begin, however, until two days later, when Marbois met the American Minister in a midnight conference. Livingston, who was jealous of Monroe and had been trying to obtain a settlement before the latter's arrival, was at first cautious. He complained that Napoleon's asking price, about 125 million livres (more than 23 million dollars), was more than the United States could pay and repeated that all his country was interested in was New Orleans and the Floridas.

When Livingston and Monroe finally met, they talked over the French proposal and agreed that they should follow it up. For several weeks they tried to have the price further reduced, but finally approved terms suggested by Marbois. For the whole Louisiana Territory the United States was to give 80 million livres (about 15 million dollars). Of this sum, 20 million livres was to be paid by the American government to discharge certain debts for supplies that France had acknowledged in the Convention of 1800. The proceeds of the balance were to be made available to Napoleon through English bankers—a transaction subsequently carried out despite the outbreak of war between France and Britain.

By its other provisions, the Louisiana cession treaty, signed April 30, 1803, stipulated that the inhabitants of the ceded territory were to be "incorporated in the Union of the United States" and admitted as soon as possible to the enjoyment of all the rights of American citizens. French ships bringing French goods and Spanish vessels bringing Spanish goods into New Orleans and other Louisiana ports were given special privileges for a period of twelve years. On the important matter of boundaries, the treaty was indefinite. France ceded to the United States what Spain had granted to her under the Treaty of San Ildefonso; this was described as "the colony or province of Louisiana with the same extent that it now has in the hands of Spain, and that it had when France possessed it. . . ." Did this mean that West Florida was included? Livingston believed it did

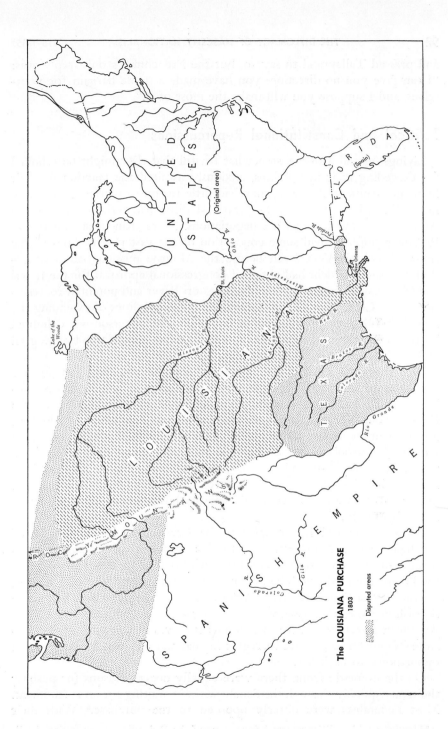

The LOUISIANA PURCHASE
1803

Disputed areas

UNITED STATES
(Original area)

FLORIDA
(Spain)

LOUISIANA

TEXAS

SPANISH EMPIRE

Lake of the Woods

St. Louis

New Orleans

Ohio R.

Mississippi R.

Missouri R.

Arkansas R.

Red R.

Brazos R.

Colorado R.

Rio Grande

Perdido R.

ROCKY MOUNTAINS

Gila R.

Colorado R.

Yellowstone R.

R. Columbia

and pressed Talleyrand to say so, but the Frenchman's only reply was: "I can give you no direction; you have made a noble bargain for yourselves, and I suppose you will make the most of it."

Political and Constitutional Repercussions

Livingston and Monroe, somewhat fearful that they might be rebuked for exceeding their instructions, anxiously awaited the reaction of their home government. Actually, they had little reason to worry. At the first news of Marbois's proposal, Secretary Madison had written to urge the American envoys to press the negotiations. More than most Americans, President Jefferson had some conception of the vast potentialities of the trans-Mississippi West. Even before the Monroe mission had been authorized, the President had obtained congressional approval for the Lewis and Clark expedition to explore the Missouri River and potential routes to the Pacific Coast, as well as to investigate the possibilities of extending the American fur trade into this region. Consequently, Jefferson was delighted by the news that an unexpected diplomatic development was bringing all of Louisiana under the American flag.

The treaty of cession did, however, involve the President in one serious embarrassment. Throughout the Washington and Adams administrations he had been a stern advocate of strict construction of the Constitution. Where in that document was power delegated to the Federal government to acquire territory by purchase and incorporate it into the Union? Jefferson's first reaction was that a constitutional amendment would be required, but his advisers opposed this idea. By resort to the Hamiltonian doctrine of implied powers it was easy to argue that the power to make treaties necessarily involved the power to acquire territory by treaty.

Jefferson allowed his scruples to be overridden for a number of excellent reasons. No one wanted Louisiana more than he, and any untoward delays based on the constitutional issue were likely to result in the loss of the territory. The Spanish government, naturally indignant at the thought of France receiving American money for land over which the Spanish flag was still flying, was protesting shrilly to both the French and American governments. More ominous still was the news from Livingston: Napoleon had begun to regret his bargain and was looking for an opportunity to back out.

On the domestic front, there were equally cogent reasons for pushing the treaty quickly through the Senate without waiting for an amendment. Most Federalists were bitterly opposed to the purchase.[2] With their

[2] Hamilton took a different stand from most of the Federalists. In an unsigned editorial in the *New-York Evening Post*, he declared that the acquisition of Louisiana

strength concentrated in the older states of the Northeast, they could see nothing but trouble for the Federalist party in opening the way for the creation of more Western states.

Under these circumstances, Jefferson readily agreed that Congress be called into special session and that the treaty be approved with as little debate as possible. Although the Federalist senators put up a bitter opposition, the Democratic-Republicans had the votes to win approval by a margin of 24 to 7. Then, in keeping with Jeffersonian principles, since the treaty involved a payment of money, it was also submitted to the House of Representatives, where it was approved by a vote of 90 to 25.

The actual transfer of the territory took place at New Orleans on December 20, 1803. The commissioners representing the United States were William Claiborne, Governor of the Mississippi Territory, and General James Wilkinson, the calculating adventurer who had so long been in the pay of Spain. The retrocession of Louisiana from Spain to France, promised under the Treaty of San Ildefonso, had not actually taken effect until November 30, 1803, and French rule over the territory, therefore, lasted less than a month.

The forgotten people in all these diplomatic intrigues had been the actual inhabitants of the colony—French, Spaniards, Negroes, and Indians. How they felt about the annexation of the Louisiana Territory by the United States was thus described at the time: "The inhabitants, tho' mortified at being put up, in this manner, at auction, are yet well pleased with being transferred to the Americans. Some of them have been calculating, at what rate they were actually sold, & make it amount to about eleven sous pr head, including negroes & cattle." [3]

In this affair, as in the case of the Barbary pirates, the Jefferson administration, aided by good fortune, achieved a striking triumph. The United States was doubled in size as a result of the acquisition of the Louisiana Territory, the troublesome Mississippi question was largely solved, and France did not become a dangerous neighbor. But the renewal of war in Europe inevitably involved the nation again in the old wrangles over neutral rights, and to these problems no such happy and speedy solutions proved possible.

---

should be a cause of exultation to all Americans. He did not concede, however, that any credit was due Jefferson, whose policy he condemned as feeble and pusillanimous in not having seized New Orleans.

[3] Quoted in Arthur P. Whitaker, *The Mississippi Question, 1795–1803: A Study in Trade, Politics, and Diplomacy* (New York: Appleton-Century-Crofts, Inc., 1934; copyright 1934 by the American Historical Association, Washington, D.C.), p. 253.

6

DILEMMA OF A NEUTRAL

Although Thomas Jefferson, like George Washington, had urged that the United States avoid involvement in European wars, the great struggle between England and the Empire of Napoleon made this advice increasingly difficult to follow. American merchant ships, seeking the rich profits from wartime trade, suffered a variety of harassments. England and France, engaged in a struggle to the death, both dealt harshly with neutral rights; England, with her control of the seas, however, antagonized American opinion the more. In the face of these actions by the belligerents, both Jefferson and Madison attempted to obtain respect for American rights and yet avoid war. In the end, this policy of peaceable coercion failed, American sensibilities were rubbed raw, and the War of 1812 resulted. Also contributing to this conflict were American ambition to expand national boundaries to include Canada and Florida and American resentment at British intrigue among the Indians.

Napoleon versus England

By November, 1804, Napoleon Bonaparte had become powerful enough to command the presence of Pope Pius VII at the impressive ceremonies in Notre Dame Cathedral, where he assumed the title of Emperor of the French. The new Emperor's ambition was to dominate Europe, compel other powers to subordinate their policies to his, and open new markets for French manufacturers and merchants.

The British government regarded such policies as dangerous challenges to English interests. Complete French domination of Europe would halt or at least seriously reduce English exports to the Continent, while a revival of French naval and colonial power would threaten English commercial enterprise in other parts of the world. In the effort to thwart the Napoleonic plans, England sometimes had to carry on the battle alone;

at other times she was able to organize coalitions of other European powers to assist her.

Napoleon, for his part, was convinced that his empire would never be secure until stubborn England was humbled. For two years after the renewal of war between France and England in 1803, the Emperor planned to invade and conquer the island kingdom. For this apparent purpose he mobilized a large army and a flotilla of ships and barges along the Channel coast. His hope of strengthening the French navy to a position where it could battle the enemy on even terms was dashed, however, by the great English naval victory at Trafalgar in October, 1805.

Despite this setback, Napoleon's control of Europe became more and more complete. An enemy coalition was shattered when he defeated the Austrians at Austerlitz in 1805 and crushed the Prussians at Jena the following year. Then, in 1807, Napoleon persuaded Tsar Alexander I at Tilsit to sign a treaty of peace and alliance. Thus with the major Continental powers either defeated or outwardly friendly, French dominance of Europe seemed virtually complete.

Under these circumstances, the conflict between France and England became primarily one of economic moves and reprisals. England's policy was to use her naval superiority to prevent her enemy from importing military supplies and provisions, to drive French merchant shipping from the seas, and to cut off all intercourse between France and her colonies. But it was no part of English economic strategy to prohibit all trade between Britain and Europe. On the contrary, the British government endeavored to retain for English merchants as much commerce as possible in the Continental ports that had always constituted her nearest and best markets.

Napoleon naturally sought to defeat these English objectives. Because the enemy's control of the seas made it impossible to depend on French shipping for essential imports, it was necessary to encourage neutral shipping to help supply France and her colonies. At the same time, neutral trade that might benefit England must be suppressed. This economic policy of Napoleon was by no means merely defensive. To try to cripple England and force her government to submit, he developed the so-called "Continental system," under which he sought to close Continental ports to English trade. By so doing, he believed, the despised "nation of shopkeepers" would be forced to come to terms.

Dispute over Impressment

Even after England and France resumed war in 1803, American relations with these belligerents were reasonably satisfactory for a time. American ships carried on a lively trade not only with both countries, but with their West Indian colonies as well, and the two warring nations refrained from harsh measures against such neutral commerce. Indeed, the principal causes of friction between the Jefferson administration and Anthony Merry, British Minister at Washington from 1803 to 1806, were to be found in such inconsequential issues as the seating arrangements at state dinners.

Yet during this period of diplomatic calm, one serious issue continued to cause trouble: the British practice of impressment, or forcing sailors into service on their naval vessels. English highhandedness in this matter is to be explained by the navy's extraordinary importance to British security. To maintain the manpower of the fleet was a matter of national life and death. Because living conditions aboard British men-of-war were notoriously bad and discipline harsh, it was hopeless to depend on voluntary enlistments to keep up the crews. Therefore His Majesty's navy relied on press gangs, which conscripted or shanghaied men with a minimum of ceremony—picking them up on the streets of English towns, from taverns, or off the decks of English merchant ships. Because sailors thus recruited were apt to desert at the first opportunity, the navy was faced with the perennial problem of trying to recover its deserters or to impress new men to fill the vacancies.

Many English sailors, some of them deserters from the navy and others runaways from merchant ships, found employment in the American merchant marine and on American naval vessels. Conditions there, although far from ideal by modern standards, were much better than those on English ships; wages were higher and discipline less rigorous. The British government refused to concede that its subjects could thus escape their obligations. British men-of-war therefore halted American vessels on the high seas, examined the seamen, and removed any alleged to be Englishmen. Whether or not such sailors were actual deserters, they were liable for service in the British navy from the very fact of their English nationality. Many claimed American citizenship on the basis of naturalization, but to do so was of no avail because Britain refused to recognize a change of allegiance.[1]

The United States remonstrated against British impressment practices on two important grounds. In the first place, the Americans denied the right claimed by England to stop and search American ships on the high seas for this purpose. That a neutral ship might be stopped and searched for contraband was conceded, but examination of the crew and removal of sailors, whether English or not, were condemned as violations of American sovereignty. An even more serious grievance was based on the

---

[1] The idea of indelible allegiance was not peculiar to the British at this time. On the contrary, Chief Justice Oliver Ellsworth upheld this principle in a case in the United States Circuit Court in 1799.

contention that many of the impressed seamen were not English subjects, but native-born Americans. It was naturally difficult to distinguish between Englishmen and Americans on the basis of appearance and language, and British captains in need of more hands were far from careful. Indeed, the snap judgments on which impressments were based constituted one of the strongest grounds for American protests. In 1804, for instance, Secretary of State Madison declared that impressment was "peculiarly indefensible, because it deprives the dearest rights of persons of a regular trial, to which the most inconsiderable article of property captured on the high seas is entitled, and leaves their destiny to the will of an officer, sometimes cruel, often ignorant, and generally interested, by his want of mariners, in his own decisions."

To protect themselves from impressment, many sailors carried papers certifying that they were either native-born or naturalized American citizens. Unfortunately, such documents were often fraudulent, being issued by venal American magistrates to anyone who would pay for them and sold by one sailor to another. Under the circumstances, it is not surprising that British officers frequently treated these certificates with contempt.

The impressment issue had first caused serious controversy during the administrations of Washington and John Adams. Indeed, one reason why John Jay had been sent to England in 1794 was to try to persuade Britain to modify this practice, but this and subsequent attempts to settle the problem had failed. Of course, during the period when England and France were at peace, impressment was less urgent, and the Jefferson administration was faced with more important problems. As long as Napoleon persisted in his attempt to take over Louisiana, Jefferson was careful to keep relations with England as cordial as possible. But the purchase of Louisiana freed his hands to deal more vigorously with the impressment issue, while the renewal of the European war raised the problem once more and made a stronger American policy necessary.

Consequently, in January, 1804, Secretary Madison sought a treaty with England dealing with impressment and other issues of neutral rights. The United States insisted upon the principle that no sailor be taken off the ship of one party by the armed vessels of the other upon the high seas. In return for this agreement, Madison suggested an arrangement be made for the mutual surrender of deserters. To refute the English contention that they were impressing only their own nations, Madison asserted that of the 2,059 about which the United States complained between 1797 and 1801, only 102 sailors were actually British subjects, while 1,142 had been released as non-British.

If the Jefferson administration expected Britain seriously to curb impressment, it was soon disillusioned. Lesser English officials particularly opposed giving in to American protests. "If we yield an iota without a real and perfect equivalent," wrote one of Merry's subordinates in the British legation in Washington, "we are lost. Every concession will be, as it has always been, ascribed to our fears; and this country is rising fast, if it be not checked very speedily and effectually, to an importance which will most sensibly annoy us." [2]

Instead of abating, impressment abuses increased. In June, 1804, fourteen men were forcibly removed from a British merchant ship in New York harbor and impressed into the service of two British men-of-war. After this violation of American sovereignty, the British naval vessels moved just off Sandy Hook, where they hovered for weeks, harassing American ships and making additional impressments.

As a warning that the United States would not tolerate impressment in its own territorial waters, Congress authorized the President to forbid the entrance of armed foreign vessels into American ports and to cut off the supplies of ships refusing to depart. Madison continued to promote his "flag-protection doctrine"—the contention that the American flag protected all who sailed under it on the high seas. The British characterized this position as "too extravagant to require any serious refutation," and insisted upon their right to inquire into the citizenship of crews on American ships and to remove any members claimed to be English subjects.

The Essex Case and Its Aftermath

In 1805, the acerbity of Anglo-American relations was intensified by a decision rendered by Sir William Scott, England's most famous admiralty court judge. The issue was significant, relating to the right of American ships to reexport from American ports produce they had brought in from the French West Indies.

The extent to which Americans would be permitted to trade in the products of the French islands had been a matter of controversy since the outbreak of war in 1793. The British based their policy on the so-called Rule of 1756, which stipulated that a belligerent prohibiting its colonial trade to foreign nations in time of peace could not open such trade in time of war. At first the British interpreted this rule to mean that all neutral trade with the French colonies was prohibited. Vehement American protests, however, had caused a modification of British practice in 1794 to permit Americans to carry on trade between the French West

[2] Reprinted by permission of The Bobbs-Merrill Company, Inc., from Irving Brant, *James Madison, Secretary of State, 1800–1809* (Copyright 1953 by The Bobbs-Merrill Company, Inc., Indianapolis), p. 172.

Indies and the United States, although the direct carriage of goods from those French islands to Europe was still prohibited.

Enterprising American ship captains found it highly profitable to bring French West Indian goods into American ports, pay the required duty, and then reexport them to France and other parts of Europe. In such circumstances most of the American duties were refunded. Thus the question arose: did such commodities become American goods as a result of their brief sojourn in American waters, or were they still French colonial products being transported to Europe in violation of British rules of maritime war?

When this issue had first come before Sir William Scott in 1800 in the case of the *Polly*, he had held that the landing of a cargo in an American port and the payment of the necessary duty gave the goods an American character, and thus they were not subject to seizure if subsequently exported to France. But in the *Essex* case of 1805, Scott took a somewhat different position. Developing the so-called "doctrine of continuous voyage," he decided that when a return or drawback of customs duties was allowed on the reexported cargoes, the goods were not to be considered as having been actually imported into the United States. They were therefore subject to seizure by the British navy under the Rule of 1756.

The *Essex* case had immediate consequences. Early in 1806, Minister Monroe complained to the British government that approximately 120 American ships had been seized and detained during the preceding months. Little attention was paid to the remonstrance, for the British Admiralty had the support of a vocal section of English opinion. West Indian planters, ambitious to capture the European market for their own produce, disliked seeing commodities from the French islands find their way to Europe. Also threatened by the growth of American neutral trade were British shipping interests. James Stephen, a Scottish lawyer, revealed this clearly in his pamphlet, *War in Disguise, or, The Frauds of the Neutral Flags* (1805). Warning that American merchants were likely to capture the whole West Indian carrying trade, thus ruining British planters and shippers as well as the colonial market for British manufacturers, Stephen urged a drastic policy to prevent American ships from carrying products from enemy islands to Europe. Such contentions were refuted in an answering American pamphlet, published anonymously but well known to be the work of James Madison. With characteristic thoroughness, the Secretary of States challenged the whole doctrine of the Rule of 1756. He pointed out that the English were twisting international law to serve their own economic advantage. In Madison's words:

> 1st. Whilst Great Britain denies to her enemies a right to relax their laws in favor of neutral commerce, she relaxes her own.

2nd. Whilst she denies to neutrals the right to trade with the colonies of her enemies, she trades herself with her enemies, and invites them to trade with her colonies.[3]

The fact that both England and France permitted their own nationals to trade with the enemy by special license whenever it served their interests, was a continuing grievance to the United States.

The Monroe-Pinkney Mission

When Congress met in December, 1805, discussion centered on recent British seizures of American ships and British intransigence on the impressment issue. Several bills were introduced to deal with these problems; one measure proposed the death penalty for foreign naval officers who illegally impressed American seamen, and another, a ban on the importation of all British goods. In the end, however, a more temperate Nonimportation Act was passed, prohibiting the entry of certain enumerated articles of British manufacture. This law was not to become effective until November 15, 1806—a provision obviously intended to give the British sufficient time to discontinue the practices that had led to the crisis.

Hoping to embarrass President Jefferson, the Federalists then demanded that a special mission be sent to England to deal with outstanding differences. Much to their surprise, the President did not oppose the idea. Indeed, there is reason to believe that Jefferson himself wanted such negotiations and welcomed the pressure from his political opponents. To head the mission the President appointed James Monroe, the American Minister to London, and William Pinkney, an eminent Maryland lawyer and moderate Federalist.

Prospects for an Anglo-American settlement appeared fairly bright when Pinkney arrived in England in June, 1806. William Pitt, the resolute Prime Minister who had insisted on using every weapon to defeat Napoleon, had died in January, and Charles James Fox, long counted a friend of America, was now Foreign Secretary in the cabinet of Lord Grenville. But a friendlier attitude in the British Foreign Office was not enough to assure a settlement. Secretary Madison's instructions to Monroe and Pinkney were strict: the two men were to promise a revocation of the Nonimportation Act only if Britain renounced its asserted right to impress sailors from American ships on the high seas and permitted trade in French West Indian produce reexported from American ports. To concede these principles in the explicit terms of a treaty, however, would have been a humiliating reversal of British policy and would have aroused

[3] Reprinted by permission of The Bobbs-Merrill Company, Inc., *ibid.*, p. 298.

a storm of opposition from the British public. Therefore Fox sought to persuade the American envoys to accept verbal assurances that British practices would be moderated and confine the terms of the proposed treaty to less controversial issues.

Fox's sudden death in September threw the negotiations into the hands of Britons even less willing to concede vital principles in the formal phrases of a treaty. Despairing of their chances to obtain the kind of agreement that Jefferson and Madison had demanded, Monroe and Pinkney at last decided to come to terms on the only basis that appeared feasible. On December 31, 1806, a treaty was signed, dealing with a number of outstanding issues, but saying nothing about impressment. On this issue, however, the Americans were given an informal promise that the worst abuses would be corrected.

The President and the Secretary of State were greatly disappointed in this outcome of the Monroe-Pinkney mission. They regarded the agreement as even less satisfactory than the despised Jay Treaty of 1794. Accordingly, the administration instructed the two envoys to reopen negotiations for better terms. To give diplomacy still more time to find a satisfactory solution, it was decided not to put the Nonimportation Act into effect until December, 1807. As it turned out, the failure of the 1806 negotiations was of crucial importance. During the next twelve months events took place that made the prospects for an Anglo-American settlement increasingly grim.

Orders and Decrees

In the strange contest between the French tiger and the British shark, the two belligerents relied increasingly on the weapons of commercial retaliation. By an order of the Privy Council of May 16, 1806 (called Fox's blockade), the British government declared the entire English Channel–North Sea coast under blockade from Brest to the mouth of the Elbe River. As a concession to neutrals, however, only the Channel ports from the mouth of the Seine to Ostend were placed under absolute blockade; the ports outside that area were open to neutral ships with the exception of those sailing to and from hostile ports. To this pronouncement, the United States entered a mild protest against "paper blockades" —that is, against blockades based simply on decree, which were not actually enforced by naval vessels in the immediate vicinity of the enemy ports. But the Jefferson administration did not press the issue because the concessions to neutrals in Fox's blockade actually favored American trade in reexported West Indian goods.

Glad of an excuse to retaliate against Britain, Napoleon countered with the Berlin Decree of November 21, 1806: the British Isles were declared to be blockaded; all goods of English manufacture were subject to seizure; and all vessels, regardless of nationality, which came directly from England or her colonies or which visited English ports, were to be excluded from areas under French control. Neutral vessels and cargoes entering French ports in violation of this decree were subject to confiscation. If Fox's blockade were in part a paper one, the French countermeasure was entirely so; without a strong navy, Napoleon's only method of enforcement was punitive action against vessels that fell into his hands in Continental ports. The Emperor's obvious purpose was to destroy the European market for English goods, whether carried in English or neutral ships.

England in turn retaliated with the Order in Council of January 7, 1807, prohibiting neutral trade between any two ports controlled by France. This was a serious matter to American ship captains because they had built up a profitable business in plying between the various Continental ports, disposing of their American cargoes, sharing in the European coastal trade, and picking up cargoes for the return trip to America.

When Napoleon and Alexander I of Russia became allies in June, 1807, the Tsar agreed to enforce the French decrees in all parts of his empire and to join Napoleon in imposing the Continental system on all Europe. The Berlin Decree, hitherto largely a dead letter, was now enforced, and numerous seizures of neutral vessels and cargoes followed.

The harassment of neutrals reached its climax with the British Orders in Council of November 11, 1807, and Napoleon's Milan Decree of December 17, 1807. The former prohibited all trade with ports under the control of France and her allies, unless ships first called at an English port, paid duties on their cargoes, and were cleared for sailing to enemy ports. This was an attempt on the part of England to exercise absolute control over neutral trade with Napoleonic Europe; England would decide what goods should be allowed to go through the paper blockade and levy tribute on whatever trade was thus permitted. By the Milan Decree, Napoleon ruled that any neutral vessel that allowed itself to be searched by an English ship, or that called at an English port and paid duty on its cargo, should be treated as a denationalized vessel, subject to seizure by the French.

In theory, all neutral trade with the belligerents was now prohibited. If an American vessel attempted to trade with any part of French-dominated Europe without English permission, it was subject to seizure by the British navy. If such a ship visited England either to deliver a cargo or to receive clearance for a voyage to the Continent, it was subject to seizure by the French. In actual practice, however, the rival blockades were far from absolute. The French lacked the naval strength to interfere seriously with shipping between the United States and various parts of the British Empire. Trade between the United States and the Continent of Europe was more hazardous, it is true, but much of it still continued, some under British license, some without. The main effect of the rival orders and decrees was twofold: the hazards of neutral trade increased the profits of those merchants who successfully completed their voyages; on the other hand, the increasing number of seizures embroiled the American State Department in continuous disputes with the two belligerent governments.

The Chesapeake Affair

On June 22, 1807, the *Chesapeake,* an American naval frigate sailing from Hampton Roads, Virginia, where it had been fitting out for sea, was stopped by the British frigate *Leopard* just outside American territorial waters. When Commodore James Barron refused to allow the *Chesapeake* to be searched for deserters, the *Leopard* fired on it, killing three men and wounding eighteen others. The *Chesapeake,* her decks still littered with gear, was not prepared for action, and her crew managed to fire only one gun for the sake of honor before striking their colors and submitting to search. The British removed four alleged deserters. One of these, a British subject, was found guilty after a trial at Halifax and hanged from the yardarm of a British man-of-war. The other three proved to be United States citizens.[4]

For a British warship to stop an American naval vessel and remove members of its crew was obviously a matter of much greater seriousness than acts of impressment carried out against merchant ships; some Americans even proclaimed it an act of war. Public indignation mounted throughout the country. A mob of angry citizens in Norfolk demonstrated in the streets and assaulted British sailors on shore leave, while the inhabitants of Hampton destroyed hogsheads of water destined for English ships. Public mass meetings in many communities passed resolutions of protest. President Jefferson ordered all British warships to leave American harbors, summoned home the American squadron from the Mediterranean, and sent an American warship to England with a demand not only for formal disavowal of the attack, but also restoration of the impressed sailors.

The new British Foreign Secretary, George Canning, resembled Pitt in his determination to employ British sea power to the fullest. Even he, however, realized that the Royal Navy had gone too far in the *Chesapeake*

---

[4] Two of these men were native-born, the third was naturalized and had run away from British ships after previously being illegally impressed. One of these Americans died in British custody, but the other two were eventually returned—four years later—to the deck of the *Chesapeake.*

affair. Without waiting for the American note of protest, the British government renounced any claim of a right to search neutral naval vessels for deserters. If the United States had been willing to treat the *Chesapeake* affair as an isolated case, satisfactory apologies and reparations would probably have been made. But Jefferson and Madison, believing they had Britain clearly in the wrong, sought to push their advantage to obtain a complete British abandonment of impressment. Canning was by no means ready to make such sweeping concessions. Indeed, when he sent George Rose to Washington to negotiate on the *Chesapeake* affair, he instructed this special envoy to require an order from Jefferson reopening American ports to British warships as a precondition to any settlement at all.

The Embargo

When Congress convened in special session in October, 1807, the danger of war seemed so great that it authorized new fortifications and the building of additional gunboats. The next month's news from Europe was uniformly bad: Canning's policy appeared to make a satisfactory solution of the impressment issue impossible; the Orders in Council of November 11 and Napoleon's tightening Continental system threatened more seizures of American ships.

Despite the pressure of American opinion, Jefferson did not want war. The recent steps to strengthen American defenses could not conceal the fact that the nation—largely because of Jeffersonian economies—was ill-prepared for war. Moreover, since the days of the Washington administration both Jefferson and Madison had believed the United States could obtain respect for its rights without resort to hostilities by the simple method of cutting off trade with offending nations dependent on American supplies. Since diplomacy alone was not enough to gain the national objectives, the administration now decided to formulate a strong policy of commercial coercion to force England and France to end their interference with neutral commerce and the abuses of impressment.

As a first installment, the Nonimportation Act, so long suspended, was put into effect on December 14, 1807. Jefferson believed, however, that more drastic steps of peaceable coercion would be necessary and appealed to Congress for permission to lay "an Embargo on all ships and vessels in the ports and harbors of the United States." More specifically, he sought to prohibit the clearance of any ships within American ports for any foreign countries, except in ballast; ships engaged in the American coastwise trade must furnish bond before sailing to ensure that their cargoes reached their proper destinations. Although bitterly opposed by Federalists as well as by dissident Democratic-Republicans under the leadership of John Randolph, the proposal was quickly enacted into law on December 22, 1807.

This embargo measure proved to be one of the most controversial acts ever passed by Congress. A faction of bitter-end New England Federalists, headed by former Secretary of State Timothy Pickering, carried their opposition almost to the point of sedition. Pickering, for instance, advised George Rose, the special British envoy, that England should make no concessions to the Jefferson administration. The Pickering faction even opened secret discussions with British officials in Canada about the possibility of the secession of New England in case of an Anglo-American war. Not all old-time Federalists, however, were ready to intrigue against the foreign policy of the nation. Former President John Adams disapproved these disloyal activities, and John Quincy Adams, his son, openly broke with the Federalist party on the issue.

There is no doubt the embargo wrought serious hardship to American merchants and shippers, especially in New England, whose major source of livelihood was affected by the ban on shipping. Likewise, thousands of farmers quickly learned they could not dispose of their surplus staples like cotton, tobacco, and grains in the English market. Unemployment mounted, especially in port towns, and protests became vocal in many parts of the country. Merchants, willing to take their chances in the hazardous but extremely profitable neutral trade, contrived to evade the embargo through dozens of ingenious artifices, just as their colonial ancestors had circumvented the British Navigation Acts. Sailors sought employment on English ships and unknowingly helped to ease the impressment issue.

President Jefferson, though admitting the great economic costs of peaceable coercion, still persisted in his policy. In January, 1809, he induced Congress to pass a drastic enforcement act, which required the posting of bonds three times the value of the cargoes by ship captains engaged in the coastal trade. Thus the President hoped to prevent illicit commerce, particularly with Canada and the West Indies. In the public mind, this measure only increased the unpopularity of the embargo.

As far as the British Empire was concerned, the embargo had some effect. Numerous cotton textile factories in England had to shut down because of scarcity of raw materials, and appeals were made to Parliament to rescind the orders in council. Canada and the British West Indies likewise suffered when American victuals were shut off. But the average Englishman, anxious to have his country defeat hated France, willingly underwent temporary hardship and privation. He was aided somewhat by the fact that England raised bumper crops in 1808, so there was less dependence on imports from the United States.

On France the embargo made little impression. The tightening British blockade and control of the seas had largely prevented American ships from reaching French ports in the years preceding the embargo. Moreover, to the extent that the embargo injured England and threatened to embroil that nation in war with the United States, Jefferson's policy seemingly favored French interests. Napoleon even posed as an aide to Jefferson with his Bayonne Decree of April 17, 1808, under which any American ship found in European ports in defiance of the embargo was subject to seizure by the French. It could not be an American ship, argued Napoleon, and therefore must be a British vessel illegally flying the American flag. Under this decree, the French confiscated American property valued in the millions of dollars.

Thus Jefferson's objective was not attained. Neither England nor France showed any indication of relaxing the orders in council or decrees, while the American people were becoming more and more dissatisfied. On March 1, 1809, just three days before Jefferson left the White House, the embargo was terminated.

Because the embargo paralyzed American trade for fourteen months without winning any diplomatic concessions for the United States, it must be considered a failure. Yet it should be pointed out that this was a pioneer effort to find some means other than war to compel recognition of American rights. If the embargo had been loyally supported by all classes in America instead of becoming a political football, it might have been effective in supporting the American contentions on impressment and neutral trade. And if a settlement of these issues had been reached in 1808 or 1809, the War of 1812 might have been avoided. On the brighter side, too, the embargo gained a temporary respite from war, a respite sorely needed. The impressment problem was temporarily eased, and American capital, hitherto invested principally in commerce, began to turn to manufacturing, thereby contributing to a more diversified and self-sufficient national economy.

Madison's Diplomacy

Despite the unpopularity of the embargo, the Democratic-Republicans easily elected James Madison to the Presidency in 1808, along with a secure majority in Congress to support his policies. After eight years of service as Secretary of State, it was scarcely to be expected that Madison would delegate primary responsibility for the nation's foreign relations to the new Secretary of State, Robert Smith of Maryland. For better or worse, leadership in diplomacy rested in the President's hands.

Madison still hoped to win concessions from the belligerents through the weapon of commercial coercion. Therefore, at the same time that the embargo was repealed, the so-called Nonintercourse Act was passed. This measure barred from American waters both English and French naval vessels, closed American ports to British and French merchantmen, prohibited American ships from clearing for belligerent ports, and forbade imports from either of the warring countries. In case either belligerent revoked its obnoxious orders or decrees, the President could reopen trade with that nation. Madison earnestly hoped that both England and France would do so.

Since the Nonintercourse Act repealed the old Nonimportation Act and placed England and France on the same footing, the British objected less to this law than to the earlier one. Indeed, Foreign Secretary Canning gave William Pinkney, now American Minister to England, reason to believe that a settlement might now be possible. The new negotiations were entrusted to David Erskine, the British Minister to Washington. This English diplomat, a Whig with an American wife, disapproved of his government's harsh naval policy and failed to inform Madison and Smith of the serious conditions laid down in Canning's instructions. The Foreign Minister had agreed, it is true, to withdraw the orders in council of January and November, 1807, in return for the reopening of American ports to English trade, but he had made this conditional upon the United States continuing to enforce nonintercourse with France, renouncing its trade in the produce of French colonies, and consenting to British seizure of American ships that attempted to trade with France and her allies in violation of American law.

This lack of candor resulted in a serious misunderstanding. Assured by Erskine that the orders in council would be withdrawn on June 10, 1809, as far as the United States was concerned, President Madison proclaimed that trade with England would again be permitted. As soon as Canning learned that his Minister had failed to exact the conditions of his instructions, he repudiated the arrangement and recalled Erskine. Once again hopes of an Anglo-American accord were shattered, while American opinion found new cause for indignation in Canning's arrogant demands.[5]

To succeed the easygoing Erskine, Canning sent over a Minister with a very different background. Francis James Jackson had recently represented his country at Copenhagen, where he played a part in the high-handed proceedings by which the British navy seized the Danish fleet to prevent its falling under Napoleon's control. "Copenhagen" Jackson was not likely to make excessive concessions on neutral rights. On the

[5] To make matters worse, many American ships, filled with cargoes of foodstuffs and other commodities which England needed, left for the British Isles after Madison's proclamation. Their arrival in England helped that belligerent in many ways and thus eased the pressure for rescinding the orders.

contrary, the new Minister took a decidedly stiff position in the futile exchange of notes through which each of the two governments tried to pin on the other responsibility for the Erskine fiasco. Since Madison and Smith were as unyielding as Jackson, personal relations soon broke down completely. The United States refused to receive further communications from Minister Jackson, and the British government demonstrated its displeasure by delaying the appointment of a successor for almost two years.

Meantime, the Nonintercourse Act had proved of dubious value. Since it permitted trade with all countries except England and France, it escaped the unpopularity of the embargo, but its coercive effect was slight. Evasion was even easier than in the case of the embargo, and an extensive illicit trade with the belligerents grew up again, particularly through neutral ports in the Scandinavian peninsula and the British colonies of Canada and Nova Scotia.

Consequently, early in 1810 the issue of American commercial policy was once again before Congress. The Nonintercourse Act was about to expire, and the legislators had to decide whether to extend its life, allow it to die unconditionally, or substitute some new measure. On May 1, 1810, a clumsy compromise was adopted, known as Macon's Bill No. 2.[6] Under this law, nonintercourse was terminated and Americans could trade with all nations, although British and French naval vessels continued to be excluded from American ports. If, however, either belligerent should revoke its objectionable orders or decrees before March 1, 1811, and the other should not follow suit within three months, the President was authorized to reinstate nonintercourse with the country failing to make concessions.

Napoleon's Trap

Napoleon, still relying upon the Continental system to humble England, weighed every shift of American policy by its effect on the struggle between the two belligerents. The American embargo had pleased him because it created a serious barrier to England, both in obtaining supplies from America and in selling her manufactured goods in the United States. Nonintercourse, on the other hand, had aroused his anger because England had indirectly recovered much of her trade with America, while France had not gained any comparable benefit. The Emperor demon-

[6] Named for Nathaniel Macon of North Carolina, chairman of a special House committee which was considering the problem. Macon's Bill No. 2 was substituted for Macon's Bill No. 1, which would have permitted American ships to trade with England and France, but excluded all ships of those countries from American ports.

strated his displeasure with the Rambouillet Decree of March 23, 1810, which ordered the confiscation of American ships found in French ports.

Since Macon's Bill No. 2 opened the door still more to a revival of Anglo-American trade, Napoleon had reason for greater discontent. However, the French ruler saw in the peculiar provisions of the act an opportunity not only to obtain diplomatic advantage for his country, but also to embroil the United States with England. The trap was set in a letter of August 5, 1810, from the Duc de Cadore, Napoleon's Foreign Minister, to John Armstrong, the American Minister to Paris:

> ... I am authorized to declare to you, sir, that the decrees of Berlin and Milan are revoked, and that after the first of November they will cease to have effect; it being understood that, in consequence of this declaration, the English shall revoke their orders in council, and renounce the new principle of blockade, which they have wished to establish; or that the United States, conformably to the act you have just communicated, shall cause their rights to be respected by the English....

The language of this Cadore letter was ambiguous. Were the French decrees actually revoked, or did Cadore only promise their revocation on condition that England altered her policy?

President Madison, eager to believe that peaceable coercion was at last beginning to pay dividends, took the French assurance at face value. He issued a proclamation on November 2, 1810, which declared that the French decrees had been revoked and that all American restrictions hitherto imposed on French ships were to cease. Unless the British government rescinded its orders within three months, nonintercourse between the United States and England would again be enforced.

Minister Pinkney made every effort to obtain parallel concessions from the British, but the English leaders received with justifiable skepticism the news that Napoleon had revoked his decrees. Once again the diplomats became involved in futile exchange. The Americans insisted that the Cadore letter was adequate evidence that the French decrees were no longer operative; the British contended that there must be more concrete evidence of an actual change of French policy. The resulting deadlock was made worse by British governmental conditions. This was a period of weak ministries, when politicians were reluctant to commit themselves on important issues. Moreover, King George III had become incapacitated by mental illness, and the problem of instituting a regency monopolized attention.

Throughout 1811, therefore, Anglo-American relations became increasingly strained. Disgusted with the procrastination of the London government, Pinkney retired from his post in February, and no new minister was sent over to replace him.[7] On March 2, President Madison signed an act reviving nonintercourse with Britain.

Napoleon had thus achieved a minor diplomatic victory, which promised to become a major one if the bad Anglo-American relations resulted in war. But just how much had the wily Emperor actually conceded to win this advantage? The proof of whether or not the Berlin and Milan decrees had really been revoked was to be found in the conduct of the French authorities, and this turned out to be far from conclusive. American ships continued to be detained in French ports. The disposition of these cases was tiresomely delayed, with the French admiralty courts showing an obvious reluctance to clarify the legal situation. At best, Napoleon appeared determined to grant only limited exemption to American vessels. As far as the Continental system as a whole was concerned, the French ruler was anxious to enforce it still more drastically. American ships that called at English ports before sailing on to Europe were deemed to have violated American law and hence subject to confiscation by the French. The Madison administration was therefore placed in the uncomfortable position of attempting to obtain from Napoleon more satisfactory assurances that his obnoxious decrees had been revoked and at the same time insisting to Britain that the revocation had actually taken place.

The War Hawks

Meanwhile, American diplomacy was being influenced by a significant shift in public opinion. Whereas talk in earlier years had been focused largely on the possibilities of obtaining concessions from the belligerents through peaceful means, popular discussion now frankly accepted the likelihood of war. The belligerent party in Congress, hitherto a minority, became the dominant faction in the session that convened in November, 1811, having been summoned a month earlier by President Madison because of the critical foreign situation.

The new war spirit was particularly strong in the frontier sections— regions remote from the areas most concerned in issues of impressment and neutral trade. This paradox is to be explained by the renewed eruption of frontier grievances against both England and Spain, closely related to events described in earlier chapters.

The suspicion of settlers in the Old Northwest that agents from Canada were forever stirring the Indians to hostility against the Americans had

---

[7] Pinkney had been permitted to take this step at his discretion by the Madison administration, which resented the delay in the appointment of a new British minister to Washington. Ironically, at just about the time of Pinkney's departure, England announced she was sending Augustus J. Foster to the United States.

been temporarily quieted by the Jay Treaty and the evacuation of the Northwest posts. As early as 1807, however, when the *Chesapeake* affair provoked talk of an Anglo-American war, rumors began to circulate about renewed British intrigue. At first these reports occasioned little concern, but as time passed the Westerners became more and more apprehensive. And with the revival of the old fear went a growing conviction that the best way to pacify the Indians was to drive the British completely out of Canada—no difficult task in the opinion of "war hawk" legislators.

In February, 1810, Henry Clay of Kentucky declared in the Senate:

> The conquest of Canada is in your power. I trust I shall not be deemed presumptuous when I state that I verily believe that the militia of Kentucky are alone competent to place Montreal and Upper Canada at your feet. Is it nothing to the British nation; is it nothing to the pride of her Monarch, to have the last of the immense North American possessions held by him in the commencement of his reign wrested from his dominion? Is it nothing to us to extinguish the torch that lights up savage warfare?

The principal reason for growing apprehension about the Indians lay in the rising influence of Tecumseh and his brother, the Prophet. These remarkable leaders, accurately analyzing the reasons for their people's decline, had attempted to preserve Indian independence by opposing the whisky habit, encouraging hard work in the cultivation of the soil, and organizing a great confederacy through which the Indians might negotiate with the whites on equal terms, instead of submitting to piecemeal loss of their lands. British officials in Canada encouraged this reform movement and laid plans for an Indian alliance in case of an Anglo-American war. At the same time, however, they used their influence to restrain their potential allies from premature attacks.

Frontier opinion bitterly resented Tecumseh's activities, and in November, 1811, General William Henry Harrison led an American force against the model Indian village of Tippecanoe, destroying the settlement and killing a number of the braves. This frontier skirmish was magnified into a major battle, Harrison became a popular hero, and anti-British feeling was intensified because some of the Indians were armed with British weapons. "*The blood of our murdered countrymen must be revenged,*" wrote Andrew Jackson of Tennessee. "I do hope that Government will see that it is necessary to act efficiently and that this hostile band which must be excited to war by the secret agents of Great Britain must be destroyed."

In Congress references to the advantages to be gained by going to war with England became increasingly explicit. Representative Felix Grundy of Tennessee declared:

We shall drive the British from our Continent—they will no longer have an opportunity of intriguing with our Indian neighbors, and setting on the ruthless savage to tomahawk our women and children. That nation will lose her Canadian trade, and, by having no resting place in this country, her means of annoying us will be diminished.

Although frontier regions like Georgia and Mississippi Territory had little reason to fear agents from Canada, they did have anxieties of their own. The Louisiana Purchase had ended the threat of French control over New Orleans, but the Spaniards still held the Floridas. To Westerners living in areas where the Mobile River or the Apalachicola provided the natural waterway for moving produce, Spanish control of the Gulf Coast was irksome in the extreme. These frontiersmen, like their brothers to the north, were obsessed by the fear that their foreign neighbors were sitrring up trouble among the Indians.

The Jefferson and Madison administrations placed a high priority on obtaining the Floridas for the United States. By a combination of infiltration through settlement and a synthetic domestic uprising, the United States had obtained effective control of West Florida during the years 1810 and 1811. A similar process appeared likely to wrest East Florida from the feeble hands of the Spaniards despite the Madison administration's embarrassed disavowal of an American agent who went too fast in implicating the United States in the spring of 1812.[8]

The expanionists of the Old Southwest welcomed the gathering war clouds between the United States and Great Britain. They reasoned that the outbreak of an Anglo-American war would almost inevitably be followed by the American occupation of Florida. English troops were fighting in Spain to expel the regime of Joseph Bonaparte on behalf of the exiled Bourbons. This intricate involvement of Britain in Spanish affairs argued that the United States would need to occupy Florida to keep its ports and provisions out of hostile English hands.

Sectional jealousy might have caused Southerners to fear the annexation of Canada and Northerners to oppose the acquisition of Florida had not the anticipated war with England promised to bring prizes to both regions. As the situation developed in the early months of 1812, the war party had enough strength throughout the Western regions, in combination with more scattered support among Eastern Democratic-Republicans, to carry through its drastic program.

The ambition to expel the English and the Spaniards, to subdue the Indians, and to win rich new agricultural lands does not mean that these were the only factors making for war. The Westerners and Southerners were exasperated over the national humiliation involved in the flaunting of American neutral rights at sea. Moreover, both the West and the South

[8] The Florida issue will be discussed in detail in chap. 8.

had suffered directly from English orders in council and French decrees. Foreign markets for American produce had been contracted, prices had fallen, and complaints of hard times were widespread. "We must either prepare to maintain the right to carry our produce to what market we please," asserted Nathaniel Macon of North Carolina, "or to be content without a market."

The Decision for War

Ironically, the war spirit was rising in America at just the time England was showing a greater desire to appease the United States. Although the overextension of Napoleon's efforts into Spain and Russia were destined to involve him in fatal defeats in 1812, the British had little reason to know that they were near decisive victory. On the contrary, the situation looked grim. Napoleon's Continental system and America's commercial restrictions had taken their toll, and English commerce and industry were stagnating.

Through Augustus J. Foster, the new British Minister sent to the United States in 1811, the British government at long last apologized for the *Chesapeake* affair and restored the two surviving sailors to the American warship from which they had been taken so ruthlessly four years earlier.

This conciliatory gesture met with little response. For one thing, Foster had not been authorized to make any concessions on impressment or orders in council—the issues still holding first importance in the eyes of both President Madison and James Monroe, who had succeeded Smith as Secretary of State in April, 1811. Moreover, the *Chesapeake* affair was now ancient history, and public excitement was currently aroused over a recent incident in which the American frigate *President* had become involved in a night battle with a British vessel hovering off the Virginia coast. The American commander, Commodore John Rodgers, was disappointed when daylight revealed that the ship disabled by his fire was only the *Little Belt*, a corvette half the size of the *President*. But the disparity in the size of the two ships did not prevent a new wave of anti-British feeling from sweeping the country. To many hotheaded Americans the crippling of the *Little Belt* was the United States Navy's true revenge for the *Chesapeake* outrage. Also damaging to the chances of conciliation were the numerous impressments and seizures of American vessels carried out off the American coast during the summer and fall of 1811.

When the Twelfth Congress convened in November, 1811, the temper of the legislators was reflected in the election of Henry Clay as Speaker of the House of Representatives. Madison's message contained a grave review of the foreign situation and called upon Congress to put "the United States into an armor and attitude demanded by the crisis, and corresponding with the national spirit and expectations." A special House committee under the chairmanship of Peter B. Porter of western New York brought in a militant report, asserting that it was the "sacred duty of Congress" to call forth the patriotism of the nation and "to procure that redress which has been sought for by justice, by remonstrance, and forbearance in vain." After heated debate, Congress authorized the enlargement of the Army, the arming of merchant vessels, and other preparatory measures. As additional proof of British duplicity, President Madison sent to Congress in March, 1812, the so-called Henry Papers, purchased from a disgruntled British secret agent who had been intriguing among Boston Federalists.

Although President Madison signed these warlike bills, he still tried to hold the door open for negotiations with England. The decisive factor in convincing the President that war was inevitable was a note from the British government in March, apparently finally refusing American demands. On April 4, 1812, Madison signed a bill imposing a ninety-day embargo, whose obvious purpose was to hold American ships in port pending an anticipated outbreak of hostilities.

After two months more of futile diplomatic jockeying, Madison sent a message to Congress on June 1, recommending a declaration of war. The four grievances he stressed were the British practice of impressment, the hovering of British warships off the American coast to harass American trade, British enforcement of paper blockades, and the orders in council. The declaration was bitterly opposed not only by the Federalists, but by many Eastern Democratic-Republicans as well. The final vote in the House was 79 to 49, and in the Senate 19 to 13. On June 18, 1812, President Madison signed this war resolution, and the long struggle to preserve neutrality was terminated.

In those days when news took some three to four weeks to cross the Atlantic, neither Congress nor the President could know that the United States had won a remarkable diplomatic victory only two days before the declaration of war. On June 16, Lord Castlereagh had announced in Parliament his intention to revoke the long-disputed orders in council. To be sure, this did not remove all the American grievances, but the change of policy did indicate a strong desire to avoid war with the United States. Had the decision been made earlier or had the war party not gained ascendancy in America, many lives and much property might have been spared.

As a further irony, the Madison administration was itself compelled to admit that France's violation of American rights had been as flagrant as

England's. In an attempt to obtain a settlement of outstanding grievances with Napoleon, Joel Barlow, the Connecticut poet, had been sent to Paris as United States Minister in September, 1811. At first subjected to intolerable delays and evasions, he finally obtained from the Duc de Bassano, the French Foreign Minister, a confirmation of the revocation of the Berlin and Milan decrees.[9] His attempts to gain a satisfactory commercial treaty and indemnities for illegal seizures, however, were unsuccessful. In Madison's message asking a declaration of war against England, he alluded to the illegal capture of American ships by French privateers and naval vessels, to "the violent and retrospective orders of the French government against the property of our citizens," and to other French violations of American rights. "I abstain at this time," Madison declared, "from recommending to the consideration of Congress definite measures with respect to that nation." [10]

Frustrations of War

The war hawks' rosy dreams of easy conquest were soon shattered in the harsh world of wartime realities. It soon became apparent that mere enthusiasm could not win battles. The War Department was inefficient, and the necessary task of raising, arming, and provisioning troops was badly mismanaged. Most of the ranking Army officers were old and inexperienced, while the soldiers under their command were poorly trained. When one of these unready armies was prematurely sent to invade Canada, the expedition not only failed, but resulted in ignominious surrender at Detroit. Similar, if less humiliating, failures in attempts to invade Canada from New York State in the first year of the war proved that the British, even with their regular troops tied up in Europe and dependent upon Canadian militiamen and their Indian allies, were not going to be easily driven from their North American possessions.

The campaigns of 1813 and 1814 were somewhat better fought, with the Americans winning occasional victories and making short advances into Canada. No sustained offensive could be launched, however, and after Napoleon's defeat in Europe in 1814, it became a serious question whether the tables might not be reversed with substantial British conquests of American territory. Even with their limited resources of the

[9] The form of the Bassano letter was far from satisfactory since it made it obvious the decrees had not actually been revoked at the time Madison asserted they had been in his negotiations with England.

[10] Yet the militant spirit in the United States was so strong that a proposal in the Senate to declare war against France as well as against England was defeated by the close vote of 18 to 14.

early war years, the English managed to occupy a large area of eastern Maine and such strategic points as Fort Niagara in New York State and Mackinac Island between Lake Huron and Lake Michigan.

The Americans found some compensation for the Army's lack of success in the better record of the Navy. In single engagements, such frigates as the *Constitution* ("Old Ironsides") won a series of brilliant victories, but these successes had little influence on the course of the war. The fact of the matter was that the American Navy was very small and the British navy was large and powerful. The English established an effective blockade off the American coast and swept American commerce from the Atlantic. More humiliating still, the British so controlled the seas that they could land troops almost at will to raid and pillage American coastal towns. The most bitter blow to American pride came in the summer of 1814, when President Madison and other government officers had to scramble out of Washington, leaving the city to be occupied and the public buildings to be burned by British forces.

On the inland waters, the Americans did much better, winning such resounding naval victories as those of Perry on Lake Erie in 1813 and of Macdonough on Lake Champlain the following year. Such exploits as these, however, could not shift the balance of the war as a whole.

There was no recess on politics during the war. On the contrary, the Federalists unsparingly condemned what they regarded as the bungling of the Madison administration. Opposed to the war in the first place and embittered by American defeats, the New England Federalist governors refused to cooperate. They attempted to keep their militia on defensive duties within their own state boundaries and threatened to nullify any national conscription law. The most bitter Federalist leaders advocated secession and a separate peace with England. A policy of immediate secession was voted down by the more moderate majority at the Hartford Convention of 1814, but even so there was a threat of eventual disunion unless the Federal Constitution were radically revised.

Confronted with this serious internal dissension and unable to gain decisive victories in the field, the Madison administration was eager to make peace whenever England would agree to honorable terms.

7

PEACE AGAIN

In June, 1812, Congress, exasperated by British impressments and paper blockades and excited by the prospect of American conquest of Canada and Florida, had declared war on Great Britain. In February, 1815, the Senate ratified the Peace Treaty of Ghent, which gave the United States none of the objectives for which she had been fighting—no guarantee of freedom from impressments, no confirmation of neutral rights of trade, and no new territories. To the chagrined Henry Clay, who had helped negotiate the document, it seemed "a damned bad treaty."

Yet the Treaty of Ghent met with a far different reception than that which the Jay Treaty had received in earlier days. Booming cannon and pealing church bells bespoke enthusiastic national approval. The peace treaty, moreover, was only the first step in the establishment of improved relations between the recent enemies. Despite subsequent war scares, the two English-speaking nations were never again to take up arms against each other. To understand how the melancholy story of the War of 1812 had this unexpectedly happy ending, it will be necessary to follow the course of events on both sides of the Atlantic.

Peace Overtures

Almost from the beginning of hostilities, the American and British governments exchanged suggestions on how the struggle might be halted. Just a week after the declaration of war, Secretary of State James Monroe instructed Jonathan Russell, the American chargé d'affaires who was still in London, that the United States would be willing to make peace if the British repealed the orders in council and settled the impressment issue. A month later, when news of the actual repeal of those orders reached Washington, Monroe wrote new instructions, concentrating on impressment. In the fall, the United States learned from Admiral Sir John Warren at Halifax that he was authorized to propose an armistice. Once again Monroe expressed willingness to negotiate, but made his assent contingent on British renunciation of its claim to impress sailors from American ships in return for an American promise not to employ British seamen.

It was obvious from these exchanges that both countries would be happy to make peace if they could do so without humiliating concessions. Britain, deeply involved in the climactic phase of the struggle against Napoleon, had not wanted war in the first place. The United States, its hopes of easy conquest dashed by a series of humiliating defeats and its will to fight paralyzed by internal dissensions, was now looking for an honorable way out of the conflict. The road to peace, however, was blocked by formidable obstacles. The Madison administration could not yet give up its effort to protect American seamen from the hateful practice of impressment; Britain, fighting for survival, could not renounce this policy.

Tsar Alexander I of Russia, mobilizing his defenses against the invasion of Napoleon's Grand Army, was seriously troubled by the knowledge that the war in America was diverting part of the energies of his British ally. A week after Napoleon entered Moscow, the Tsar sounded out John Quincy Adams, the American Minister to Russia, as to whether his country would accept an offer of mediation. Adams replied that he had no instructions on this point, but that he was confident such an offer would be interpreted as evidence of the Tsar's friendship and be carefully considered.

Thus encouraged, Russia presented a formal mediation offer at Washington in March, 1813, which President Madison promptly accepted. The war had been going badly; his Cabinet was divided into hostile factions; and New England's opposition to the war was growing still more bitter. Moreover, by this time the failure of Napoleon's Russian campaign had become known, and the American government feared a turn of events whereby the French might be completely defeated and the United States might feel the lash of England's full military and naval power. The President therefore determined to send abroad a distinguished mission to obtain peace if honorable terms could be gained, or to unify the country behind the war effort if British demands proved excessive.

The American commission that assembled in St. Petersburg in July, 1813, consisted of Minister John Quincy Adams, Secretary of the Treasury Albert Gallatin, and Senator James A. Bayard of Delaware, a Federalist. For six months these gentlemen lingered in the Russian capital while the Tsar carried on desultory exchanges with Britain concerning the proposed mediation. Lord Castlereagh, the English Foreign Secretary, had been placed in a delicate position by the Tsar's offer and its prompt American acceptance. At all costs he wanted to maintain the Anglo-Russian alliance against Napoleon, but at the same time he feared that Russian mediation in the war between England and the United States would result in developments unfavorable to British interests. After all, since the days of Catherine the Great and the Armed Neutrality, the Russian position on neutral trade and maritime law had not been in sympathy with British practices. Were the Russians to propose that the disputed points of international law be submitted to an international conference, England might find herself without support even from her own allies.

Castlereagh eased his way out of this dilemma by rejecting Russian mediation as gently and courteously as possible, and at the same time announcing British willingness to negotiate directly with the United States. A formal offer to this effect reached Washington just before New Year's Day, 1814. The Madison administration promptly accepted and named a commission of Adams, Gallatin, and Bayard, who were still abroad, and two new members: Henry Clay, the Speaker of the House, and Jonathan Russell, a young Massachusetts politician who had had experience in the Paris and London legations before the war.[1]

The Negotiations at Ghent

The choice of meeting place caused some difficulty, but the two governments finally agreed on Ghent. This Belgian city was reasonably close to England and, perhaps more important, was located on the route between London and Vienna, where a great international congress was drawing a new map of Europe in the fall of 1814.

Since Britain was using her ablest diplomats at Vienna, the men selected for the Ghent mission were inferior in prestige and skill to their American counterparts. Lord Gambier, the chief commissioner, was best known as a naval officer; Henry Goulburn was an able civil servant, but very young for so responsible a post; and Dr. William Adams was, in John Adams's phrase, a "blunderbuss of the law"—a supposed authority on international law, but a slow-witted and unimaginative negotiator. As a compensating factor, however, these British envoys could easily communicate with government officials in London or the first-rank diplomats at Vienna for instructions.

President Madison made excellent choices as far as four members of the American delegation were concerned. John Quincy Adams, who headed the mission, had qualities strikingly similar to those of his father, the second President. The son had the same intense patriotism, a patriotism that had caused him to leave the Federalist party when the New England Federalist leaders had flirted with treason in their opposition to Jefferson's

[1] Gallatin and Clay took this occasion to resign from their respective posts as Secretary of the Treasury and Speaker.

embargo. Although he had also the inflexible honesty, the erudition, and the industriousness that had been characteristic of his father, he had inherited the family vices: irascibility, stubbornness, and aloofness. Albert Gallatin was a man of such great prestige that his colleagues often looked to him, rather than to Adams, for leadership. A Swiss by birth, Gallatin had come to America during the Revolution and had made a brilliant record as Congressman from Pennsylvania and then as Secretary of the Treasury under both Jefferson and Madison. Highly educated, cool in temperament, and urbane in manner, he was well equipped to mediate among the more volatile commissioners. Bayard, eloquent, companionable, and gracious, was as typically the Southern gentleman as Adams was the Yankee. Henry Clay, a young Virginian who had followed the frontier into Kentucky, had jumped into national prominence through his patriotic eloquence, his political astuteness, and his commanding personality. Between the pious and abstemious Adams and the whisky-drinking, card-playing Clay, there was a personal gulf as wide as the distance from Massachusetts to Kentucky. Russell, the fifth member of the commission, was a young man of much less prestige than his colleagues. Politically ambitious, he attached himself to Clay in the internal factions within the commission. As a group, the five American envoys were men of strong individuality who might not always agree among themselves, but who would put up a strong front on behalf of American interests.

Although the American mission was ready to begin negotiations as early as June, 1814, the English contrived to postpone the opening talks until August for obvious reasons. The military situation in the summer of 1814 was already favorable to the English and promised to become more so. Despite a number of American victories in single engagements and effective commerce raiding by American privateers off Britain, the Royal Navy dominated the Atlantic. Rarely has a blockade been so effective as the one established off the American coast; commerce between the Atlantic ports and the outside world was almost completely cut off. The British, landing their forces almost at will, raided and pillaged the coastal towns.

On the Canadian frontier, the situation was almost equally discouraging to the United States. Repeated attempts to invade Canada had bogged down, leaving the Americans in control of only a few British posts like Fort Malden on the Detroit River and Fort Erie on the Niagara. Possession of these pawns was overbalanced by British seizure of Fort Mackinac, located in the straits between Lakes Michigan and Huron, and Fort Niagara in western New York, to say nothing of all eastern Maine beyond the Penobscot River. The only bright spot for the Americans was the fact that British supremacy in ocean vessels counted for nought on the Great Lakes. The struggle for control of the inland waters was fought with ships hastily built along the shores, and here the Americans more than held their own. Perry's great victory of September, 1813, had given them control of Lake Erie, while on Lake Ontario they maintained an uneasy balance of power.

Having turned back American attacks with poorly trained Canadian and Indian forces, Britain believed that the termination of hostilities in Europe would inevitably open the way to decisive English victories in America. Following Napoleon's abdication in April, 1814, the British began to transfer seasoned veterans to Canada. By June, 1814, plans were under way to use this formidable army for a decisive invasion of New York by way of the historic Lake Champlain route. Still more threatening were British plans for an assault upon New Orleans that might detach the United States from its prized acquisition, the Louisiana Purchase. By delaying peace negotiations, the English government expected to gain most of the aces in the diplomatic pack.

The severe terms Britain was preparing to impose could scarcely be harsh enough to suit the English press. The London *Times* denounced Madison as a liar, an imposter, and a traitor—as contemptible as Napoleon himself. The President and his associates were depicted as being "struck to the heart with terror for their impending punishment." "Strike!" thundered the *Times*, "chastise the savages, for such they are!" And when the British commissioners departed for Ghent, the same newspaper instructed them: "Our demands may be couched in a single word,—Submission!"

Far from resigning themselves to submission, President Madison and Secretary Monroe still clung to the hope that the British could be persuaded to accept the American position on impressment and neutral rights of trade, and indeed the American commissioners were instructed to be firm on these points. "If this encroachment of Great Britain is not provided against," wrote Monroe in specific reference to impressment, "the United States have appealed to arms in vain. If your efforts to accomplish it should fail, all further negotiations will cease, and you will return home without delay." The instructions also suggested that Britain cede Canada or at least control of the Great Lakes to the United States.

With each government refusing to concede, the negotiations at Ghent appeared destined for failure. At the first meeting on August 8, the British took the offensive. They asserted that a *sine qua non* [2] of peace would be to grant England's Indian allies definite boundaries for their territories. Goulburn, the British spokesman, also warned that a revision of the boundary between the United States and adjacent British colonies would be demanded, while the special fishing privileges granted to Americans under the Treaty of 1783 would not be renewed without an equivalent. The demand that an Indian barrier state be created south of the Great

[2] *Sine qua non* means an indispensable provision or condition.

Lakes was strongly resisted by the American commissioners, who asserted that their country would not accept any interference in dealing with Indian tribes within American territory. When further negotiations revealed that the British also wanted to prohibit the Americans from maintaining naval vessels or forts on the Great Lakes while permitting such rights to themselves, the possibilities of a settlement seemed even more remote. The most the Americans would offer was mutual restoration of territories and the postponement of other issues until after the close of hostilities.

A more experienced cardplayer than his colleagues, Henry Clay believed the British were bluffing and might give up many of their demands if their hand were called. This proved to be the case. Faced with the possibility that the negotiations might break down, Lord Castlereagh was reluctant to have his country appear to be continuing the war merely for territorial objectives. To do so might unite the Americans behind the Madison administration and divide the war-weary English nation. Accordingly, the British representatives were instructed to modify their stand. On September 19, Lord Gambier and his colleagues said the British would give up their demand for exclusive control of the Great Lakes and for a definite Indian territory if the Americans agreed to a much milder proposal to include the Indians in the pacification. Eventually the two sides compromised on a face-saving formula: each promised to make peace with its own Indian allies and to restore to them all the possessions and rights they had enjoyed before the war.

The Madison administration had meanwhile adopted a more realistic position by abandoning its insistence upon the blockade and impressment issues. With the European war about over, these issues no longer had vital importance. Freed by these new instructions, the American commissioners stood a much better chance for success.

Even with these improved prospects, however, the negotiations followed a rocky road. On boundary questions and fishing rights the two governments were far apart. The British insisted that a basis for settlement must be *uti possidetis*, which meant that the British intended to keep the American districts they then occupied, except in cases where they exchanged such places for territory conquered by the Americans or for some other compensating advantage. In specific terms, the British asked for Moose Island, on which the town of Eastport, Maine, was located, for strategic territory in northern Maine (so that a British military road could be constructed from Quebec to the Atlantic), for the district around Fort Niagara in western New York, and for Mackinac Island. In addition, the British sought a settlement of the disputed Northwest boundary that would give them access to the Mississippi River. Severe though these terms were, they would have been still more drastic except for the unexpected defeat of Sir George Prevost's invasion along the Lake Champlain route. Before news of the disastrous Battle of Plattsburgh reached London, the British had intended to demand a large slice of northern New York.

To John Quincy Adams, the negotiations at Ghent had reached a point strongly reminiscent of those at Paris at the end of the Revolutionary War, as he indicated in a letter to his father:

> The situation in which I am placed often brings to mind that in which you were situated in the year 1782. . . . I am called upon to support the same interests, and in many respects, the same identical points and questions. . . . It is the boundary, the fisheries, and the Indian savages.[3]

The American commissioners stubbornly opposed any cession of territory or surrender of rights. They insisted on a return to the *status quo ante bellum*.[4] This position placed England in a difficult predicament. Should it break off negotiations and force its terms upon the United States through unrelenting military pressure? Or should it retreat once more from the diplomatic position it had taken? Humiliating though it was to do the latter, Lord Castlereagh and his associates in the British cabinet eventually chose this path.

The English decision was based on many factors. The military news from America was not so favorable as had been expected. The defeat at Plattsburgh was a stunning blow. While English pride was partially salved by reports of the British capture of Washington and the burning of its public buildings, actually that city was of no strategic value and no attempt was made to hold it. Moreover, English attempts to seize Baltimore, a city of much greater military importance, were repulsed. It was obvious that decisive victory in America could not be achieved without a major effort, and such an effort was more than the British government felt it could ask of the war-weary English nation, already staggering under its heavy burden of taxes.

When the British cabinet sought the opinion of the Duke of Wellington, England's greatest soldier, his answer was blunt:

> In regard to your present negotiations, I confess that I think you have no right, from the state of the war, to demand any concession of territory from America. . . . You have not been able to carry it into the enemy's territory, notwithstanding your military success and now undoubted military superiority, and have not even cleared your own territory on the point of attack. . . . You can get no territory; indeed, the state of your

---

[3] Reprinted by permission of Alfred A. Knopf, Inc., from Samuel Flagg Bemis, *John Quincy Adams and the Foundations of American Foreign Policy* (Copyright 1949 by Alfred A. Knopf, Inc., New York), p. 196.

[4] *Status quo ante bellum* means the state of affairs existing before the war.

military operations, however creditable, does not entitle you to demand any.[5]

An even more urgent reason to avoid further involvement in America was the European situation. France was restless in defeat, and the danger of a Napoleonic restoration and a new outbreak of war was a constant worry to the English. At the Congress of Vienna matters ran far from smoothly because the victorious allies were sharply divided on many important issues. On November 8, 1814, Lord Liverpool, the Prime Minister, wrote to Lord Castlereagh:

> I think we have determined, if all other points can be satisfactorily settled, not to continue the war for the purpose of obtaining or securing any acquisition of territory. We have been led to this determination by the consideration of the unsatisfactory state of the negotiations at Vienna, and by that of the alarming situation of the interior of France. We have also been obliged to pay serious attention to the state of our finances... under such circumstances, it has appeared to us desirable to bring the American war if possible to a conclusion.[6]

While the British government was struggling with these problems, the American commissioners were preparing the draft of a treaty. On one point Adams and Clay found themselves in bitter disagreement. To the Yankee, it was a matter of paramount importance for American fishermen to retain the rights defined in the Treaty of 1783. If the British would concede this, Adams saw no reason to oppose an extension of the clause giving Britain the right to free navigation of the Mississippi. He regarded this provision as harmless because British territory did not border on that river.[7] But Clay, quick to assert the interests of the West, bitterly opposed any explicit renewal of the British right to navigate the river. The other commissioners overrode these objections and proposed to the British that both the disputed rights be recognized in the treaty. The British would not agree, however, because they considered the fishing rights demanded by the Americans far too valuable to be purchased with the right of navigation the British would be unable to exercise. In the end the peace treaty was silent on both issues.

The Treaty of Ghent

On December 14, 1814, the Treaty of Ghent was finally signed. It provided for the cessation of hostilities, the return of all prisoners of war,

[5] *Supplementary Dispatches, Correspondence, and Memoranda of Field Marshal Arthur Duke of Wellington*, edited by his son, the Duke of Wellington (London, 1858–1872), IX, 438.

[6] *Ibid.*, p. 435.

[7] At the time the Treaty of Paris was drawn up, the sources of the Mississippi were assumed to lie in British territory, some 200 miles north of their actual location.

and the restoration of all captured territories. The British agreed to return, or compensate the owners for, all slaves carried off by their forces. The two governments pledged to use their best efforts to abolish the slave trade, to make peace with the Indians, and to restore to the Indians all rights and territories they had held before the war.

The treaty also provided for the establishment of four mixed commissions to decide the ownership of the islands in Passamaquoddy Bay and to determine the rightful boundary along the disputed points from the St. Croix River in the East to the Lake of the Woods in the West.[8] The treaty was silent on the highly disputable question of the northern boundary of the Louisiana Purchase.

The Prince Regent of England approved the agreement at once; President Madison accepted the document as soon as it arrived in Washington, and the Senate gave its unanimous assent on February 17, 1815—just six days after news of Andrew Jackson's great victory at New Orleans reached the capital.

Why was the Treaty of Ghent—silent though it was on the issues of blockade, impressment, and territorial acquisitions—so popular? In part, it was because the American public realized that their negotiators had done well under the circumstances. Since the earlier exchanges of the commissioners at Ghent had been published, Americans knew that the original harsh British peace terms had been successfully resisted by Adams and his colleagues. Moreover, the war had originated from wounded American pride as much as from any other grievance. Despite the many defeats suffered, national pride had been restored by the brave exploits of the *Constitution* and other frigates, by the great victories on Lake Erie and Lake Champlain, and, above all, by the defeat of the British at New Orleans. What did it matter, then, if the British had made no concession to the American position on impressment and neutral trade rights? With Europe again at peace, these issues no longer had practical importance.

The Unguarded Frontier

After the Napoleonic war, Lord Castlereagh based British foreign policy on the principles of appeasement and conciliation. England's security, the great Minister believed, lay in avoiding further conflict and in settling by reasonable compromise issues that might lead to dangerous friction. The British Foreign Secretary's pacific inclinations were matched by James Monroe, who remained Secretary of State until March, 1817,

[8] The mixed commissions successfully divided the eastern islands, alloting three to the United States and the rest to Great Britain. The boundary line between the St. Lawrence River and Lake Huron was also satisfactorily located. For the failure of the other commission efforts, see the discussion of the Northeast boundary controversy in chap. 10.

when he became the fifth President of the United States, and by John Quincy Adams, who served as Minister to England from 1815 to 1817 and then returned to Washington to become Monroe's Secretary of State.

The first indication of this postwar friendship was shown in London, where Albert Gallatin and Henry Clay opened negotiations with Henry Goulburn, Dr. William Adams, and Sir F. J. Robinson for a commercial treaty in the spring of 1815. Although the American envoys failed to persuade the British to approve a ban on impressment, they did reach several agreements. First of all, the United States was to be allowed to trade freely with the British East Indies for four years.[9] Next, neither signatory would levy discriminatory duties upon the commerce of the other. And, finally, provision was made for sending consuls to each other's possessions. Mutual ratification enabled this commercial treaty to become effective on July 3, 1815.

A more important dividend from the mutual investment of good will was the Rush-Bagot Agreement of April, 1817, which provided for limitation of naval vessels on the Great Lakes. This accord put an end to a threatened shipbuilding race on these waters after the War of 1812. When the United States renewed suggestions for disarmament previously made during the peace negotiations of 1782 and the Jay efforts of 1794, Castlereagh gave the idea a sympathetic reception. Subsequent negotiations resulted in an historic exchange of notes between Charles Bagot, the British Minister to Washington, and Richard Rush, acting Secretary of State during Monroe's first months in office. The two governments agreed to restrict their respective naval forces on Lake Champlain to one small vessel carrying a single cannon, to one similar ship on Lake Ontario, and to two ships for all the other Great Lakes. Such armaments were, of course, insignificant for hostile purposes and were only useful to enforce the customs laws.[10]

Britain's alacrity to accept naval disarmament on the Great Lakes is undoubtedly to be explained by her frank recognition that the Americans would hold the advantage in any building race. In the event of future war between England and the United States, Canada would in any case lie largely defenseless against attacks from her rapidly growing neighbor.

The Rush-Bagot Agreement related only to naval vessels, but this accord tended to discourage all kinds of military preparedness along the

[9] This clause was in effect a continuation of the commercial rights provided in the Jay Treaty of 1794, but which had been allowed to expire in 1807.

[10] Since it was based upon a mere exchange of diplomatic notes, the Rush-Bagot Agreement had at first the character of an executive agreement, binding only upon the administration which had signed it. In 1818, however, Monroe gave it a more permanent character by obtaining the advice and consent of the Senate. In its new form, the convention was subject to abrogation by either party upon six months' notice, but it still remains in effect.

Canadian-American border. The old forts were maintained until after the Civil War, but eventually they were allowed to fall into decay with the result that the long boundary became, in all truth, "the unguarded frontier."

The Convention of 1818

Unable to agree upon the troublesome fishery and Northwest boundary problems, the negotiators at Ghent had finally shelved the questions. But the establishment of good relations between the United States and Great Britain required some kind of settlement of these two matters, as well as of other less pressing problems. Some progress toward this end had been made by John Quincy Adams while he was Minister to England, and he continued the negotiations when he became Secretary of State.

Adams, strongly influenced by his father, contended the Americans had a natural and perpetual *right* to fish along the coasts of Newfoundland and Labrador. Since this had been recognized by Britain in the peace treaty of 1783, it could not now be called into question. The British government insisted, on the contrary, that it enjoyed full sovereignty along the coasts of British North America and that the *privileges* granted in 1783 had lapsed with the declaration of war between the two countries in 1812. Once this basic British claim were conceded, Lord Castlereagh offered to define in generous terms just what fishing privileges the Americans would enjoy in the future.

Adams was at first reluctant to compromise. "I am afraid we shall have to fight for this matter, in the end," he told Minister Bagot, "and I am so confident of our right that I am for it." President Monroe, however, exercised a restraining influence on his stubborn Secretary; no longer the rash and impulsive diplomat he had been in the 1790s, Monroe was willing to meet the English halfway in this and in other matters.

The Northwest boundary controversy was a tangled web of several different disputes. In the first place, there was need to repair a defect in the treaty of 1783 stipulating that the boundary should run "on a due west course" from the most northwestern point of the Lake of the Woods to the Mississippi River. Since the Mississippi had its source 152 miles south of this latitude, it was obvious that a line drawn due west would never intersect the river. The British had an easy solution to suggest: they wanted to bridge the gap by a line drawn southerly from the Lake of the Woods to the Mississippi.[11] But the Americans were reluctant to grant access to the great river in any case, and their reluctance had been increased by the Louisiana Purchase. This acquisition opened up new issues

[11] A treaty to this effect, the so-called King-Hawkesbury Convention, had been signed in 1803, but it was rejected by the Senate.

for dispute. How far north did the Louisiana Territory extend? Did it include the Oregon country on the Pacific Coast?

The United States based its claim to Oregon not only on the Louisiana Purchase, but on prior discovery. In 1792, Captain Robert Gray, sailing out of Boston in the *Columbia*, had visited the coast of the Pacific Northwest in search of furs for the China trade. He had discovered the great Columbia River and named it for his vessel. In 1805, the Lewis and Clark expedition had reached this river by an overland route and explored much of its course.

The British countered these claims with the contention that Gray's discovery had been preceded by their own Captain James Cook's voyage to these parts in 1778. They pointed also to the Nootka Sound Convention of 1790 as a Spanish concession of British rights in the area.

Both British and American diplomats valued Oregon almost exclusively in terms of the fur trade. In 1811 the Pacific Fur Trading Company, organized by the American John Jacob Astor, established a trading post at the mouth of the Columbia River. This aroused the jealousy of the North West Company of Canada, which was ambitious to dominate the fur trade of this whole region. During the War of 1812 the North West Company easily eliminated Astor as a competitor in the Columbia River country. Astor's Canadian partners sold out their interests to the British company, and an English warship put in at Astoria to replace the Stars and Stripes with the Union Jack and rename the settlement Fort George. These events left a puzzle for the two governments after the war. Was Astoria one of the places included in the Treaty of Ghent's provision for the restoration of all conquered territories?

Lord Castlereagh, determined to avoid new quarrels with the United States, ordered Fort George to be returned to the United States. On October 6, 1818, the American flag was once again raised at the mouth of the Columbia River. The trading post, however, continued in the possession of the North West Company, and the British insisted that their concession at Fort George did not involve any acknowledgment of American sovereignty over the Oregon country.

Encouraged by the British government to believe the time was ripe for a settlement of all outstanding difficulties, President Monroe appointed Richard Rush, American Minister to England, and Albert Gallatin, Minister to France, as commissioners to meet in London with representatives of England. The result of these discussions was the so-called Convention of 1818, signed on October 20 of that year.

The new agreement carefully defined certain parts of the southern and western Newfoundland coasts, the Labrador coast, and the shores of the Magdalen Islands, where the inhabitants of the United States, in common with British subjects, were to have forever the liberty to take fish

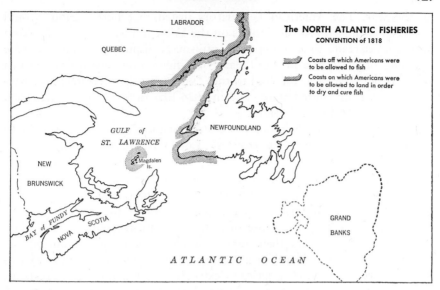

The NORTH ATLANTIC FISHERIES
CONVENTION of 1818

Coasts off which Americans were to be allowed to fish

Coasts on which Americans were to be allowed to land in order to dry and cure fish

of every kind. Additionally, the Americans were to be allowed to dry and cure fish in any of the unsettled bays, harbors, and creeks in designated parts of southern Newfoundland and Labrador. In return for these privileges, the United States renounced any claim to take or dry fish within three miles of the coast of any other British North American possession, although American ships were to be allowed to enter these waters to seek shelter, repair damages, or obtain and purchase wood.

The Northwest boundary from the Lake of the Woods to the Rocky Mountains was fixed at the 49th parallel. Instead of dividing the Oregon Territory, the two parties agreed to joint occupancy for ten years.

The Convention of 1818 also dealt with commercial relations and the return of slaves carried off by the British during the War of 1812. The commercial clauses, for the most part, confirmed principles followed prior

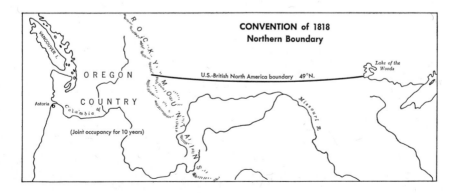

CONVENTION of 1818
Northern Boundary

U.S.-British North America boundary 49°N.

(Joint occupancy for 10 years)

to the war. The American negotiators urged that both nations would profit by lifting British restrictions on the West Indian trade, but England was not yet ready to abandon mercantilism. A dispute regarding the true meaning of the clause in the Treaty of Ghent providing for the return of deported slaves was referred to the Tsar of Russia as arbiter. His decision favored the United States, and in 1826 Britain finally paid $1,204,960 in settlement of all these claims.

Gallatin and Rush made one more attempt during the London talks to settle the old impressment controversy. Lord Castlereagh gave the American proposals surprisingly sympathetic consideration, and for a time it seemed that this question too might be settled by the Convention of 1818. In the end, however, the parties failed to agree, and the new treaty, like its predecessors of 1794 and 1815, was silent on the issue.

Despite this failure, the cause of Anglo-American friendship had been much further advanced than anyone could have imagined during the bitter wartime days when British soldiers were putting the torch to Washington in retaliation for American destruction in Canada. The Treaty of Ghent, the Rush-Bagot Agreement, and the Convention of 1818, taken together, had laid the basis for durable peace between the two nations.

PART TWO

1815 to 1890

Continental Expansion

More than before or after, Americans from 1815 to 1890 were able to turn their backs upon the rest of the world and concentrate their energies on expanding their national boundaries and developing their continental economy. Their relative freedom from European involvements was facilitated by the absence of great wars in which the belligerents interfered with American use of the sea lanes. Under these favoring circumstances, it was relatively easy for American statesmen to maintain a two-world philosophy. One world was that of the Eastern Hemisphere, where decadent monarchism and tyrannical rule prevailed; the other was that of the Western Hemisphere, the stronghold of republican freedom and virtue. The Monroe Doctrine was asserted as a shield to protect the Western Hemisphere from Old World domination, and the converse proposition that the less America had to do with Europe the better was widely held.

Yet this did not mean that the United States had no important dealings with other countries. On the contrary, assertive American nationalism, the frontiersman's appetite for new lands, and the merchant's ambition for more trade combined to bring the nation into fateful contacts with other governments. With Spain the United States debated control of Florida and various sections of the trans-Mississippi region; with England there was a diplomatic struggle over the Pacific Northwest; and with newly independent Mexico there were hot-blooded clashes over Texas, California, and New Mexico.

Widespread faith in "manifest destiny" created a demand for still further annexations. Canada, Mexico, Central America, Cuba, and the islands of the Pacific all appealed to one American group or another. Before the

Civil War further ventures were held in check by the mutual suspicion of Northern and Southern expansionists, each fearful of territorial acquisitions that might strengthen the other party. In regions like Central America, moreover, British sea power was still too formidable for the Americans to challenge.

After the Civil War a few Republican leaders became ardent expansionists. Except for Alaska and Midway, however, the dreams for further annexations went unrealized. Congressional opposition to presidential projects reflected a widespread lack of interest on the part of the general public. National energies found their outlet in the building of railroads, the consolidation of industry, and the exploitation of Western lands and resources. Diplomacy found its most important business not in pushing toward new goals but in settling troublesome disputes.

8

THE FLORIDA QUESTION

Although American expansionists were never to achieve the annexation of Canada, their desire for the Floridas was not long thwarted. Spain, already a declining power before the Napoleonic era, was disastrously crippled during the long European war. From 1808 to 1814, it had two governments: one, the French puppet state headed by Joseph Bonaparte, Napoleon's brother; the other, the Regency, ruling in the name of Ferdinand VII and supported by Spanish patriots and British armies operating in the Peninsula. While Spain was convulsed by civil war at home, she was confronted by surging revolts and demands for independence in her colonies. In such a situation it was inevitable that she should lose control of the Floridas to the powerful young nation neighboring these colonies on the north. The only real questions were when and how the transfer to the United States would be accomplished.

Disputed Boundaries

As a result of the Louisiana Purchase, France had ceded to the United States all the territory acquired from Spain in the Treaty of San Ildefonso. Under the secret agreement, this territory had been vaguely defined as:

> The colony or province of Louisiana, with the same extent that it now has in the hands of Spain, and that it had when France possessed it; and such as it should be after the treaties subsequently entered into between Spain and other states.

What did this language mean? Did the Louisiana Territory include Texas? Did it include the Great Plains east of the Rockies? Did it include part of West Florida?

All of these questions were of eventual importance to the United States, but the issue of greatest immediate concern was whether the Territory extended into West Florida. To American frontiersmen pushing their way into western Georgia and the regions that eventually became the states of Alabama and Mississippi, it was intolerable that the coast of the Gulf of Mexico and the lower courses of the rivers running into it were controlled by Spain. In the negotiations resulting in the Louisiana Purchase, Livingston and Monroe had been instructed to obtain both New Orleans and West Florida, and these diplomats were eager to believe that they had actually done so.

In reality, it was extraordinarily difficult to say whether or not the Louisiana Territory included part of West Florida. In 1719, Spain and France had agreed that the dividing line between Spanish Florida and the French holdings around New Orleans should be the Perdido River, but in 1763 the situation was complicated by the Treaty of Paris, under which France and Spain ceded to Great Britain their possessions east of the Mississippi. The British then organized their newly gained land into two colonies, East Florida and West Florida, separated by the Appalachicola River. At the conclusion of the American Revolution in 1783, however, England gave both Floridas to Spain. Did the Treaty of San Ildefonso mean that Spain was restoring to France the Louisiana of the days prior to 1763 (which had extended to the Perdido River) or that of the period between 1763 and 1783 when it was limited to the region west of the Mississippi? This point had been left deliberately vague to conceal a difference of opinion between the Franco-Spanish negotiators.

Although the American claim to West Florida seems weak to present-day scholars, it was to the advantage of the Jefferson administration to persist in it. That was undoubtedly why Monroe and Livingston insisted that the very words of the Treaty of San Ildefonso be included in the Louisiana Purchase treaty. In order to ensure that the American claim might be respected, Monroe was instructed to go to Madrid to seek an immediate settlement of the Florida problem by offering to buy all Spanish rights in both Floridas for 2.5 million dollars. When Napoleon strongly advised against this mission because of his belief that Spain was still too indignant about France's trickery to accept America's offer, Monroe went to London instead to try to solve the impressment issue.[1]

Pushing American Claims

Hoping that Spain would recognize American claims, Congress passed in 1804 the so-called Mobile Act, which enlarged the Mississippi customs district to include "all the navigable waters, rivers, creeks, bays and inlets lying within the United States, which empty into the Gulf of Mexico east of the River Mississippi." By another provision, the President was

[1] See chap. 6.

given discretionary power to create a separate customs district around Mobile, located in the easternmost part of the disputed territory.

The Mobile Act brought bitter protests from the Spanish Minister in Washington, who demanded repeal of the offensive clauses threatening his country's sovereignty over West Florida. Although both Jefferson and Madison complained to Madrid about the Minister's strong language, they sought to avoid the appearance of force. The President pointed out that creation of a Mobile customs district was merely discretionary and announced that the port of entry on the Mobile River would be at Fort Stoddert, undisputably in American territory.

After the flare of bad tempers over the Mobile Act had died down, Monroe and Charles Pinckney, the American Minister to Spain, spent five months in Madrid during 1805 in a fruitless effort to persuade Pedro de Cevallos, the Spanish Foreign Minister, to come to terms. They sought not only to obtain the eastern boundary of the Louisiana Purchase at the Perdido River, but to acquire the rest of the Floridas for a sum of not more than 2 million dollars, to be used to meet certain American claims against Spain dating back to the period of 1796–1802 when Spain had seized 125 American ships and permitted French vessels to make additional seizures in Spanish waters.[2] Still a third objective was to settle the western boundary of the Louisiana Purchase; although the Jefferson administration claimed all of Texas to the Rio Grande, it was willing to compromise on a line farther east if this would facilitate the Florida settlement.

Unsuccessful in gaining the Floridas by direct negotiations, Jefferson and Madison now attempted more circuitous tactics. They felt that the real key to the situation lay in Paris, where Napoleon and Talleyrand had been attempting to soothe Spain's ruffled feelings over the Louisiana Purchase by supporting her position on the West Florida issue. Now, however, Talleyrand, with his characteristic duplicity, was giving the impression that France might alter this policy. As the Americans nibbled at his hook, the wily Frenchman secretly proposed that France act as mediator in a deal whereby the United States would pay 10 million dollars for both Floridas and agree to have the western boundary of the Louisiana Purchase drawn 250 miles east of the Rio Grande. As the Americans readily guessed, Napoleon's secret intention was to extort the purchase money from feeble Spain for his own purposes.

Although Jefferson was not above playing Talleyrand's game, he thought that 5 million dollars was all that the United States should pay. Even so, the President's attempt to get funds for a little-understood pur-

[2] In 1802, Spain and the United States had provided for the submission of these claims to a mixed commission, but this agreement had never been ratified. At first the United States Senate refused its approval; later, when the Senate reversed its position, the Spanish government declined to ratify in protest against the Louisiana Purchase.

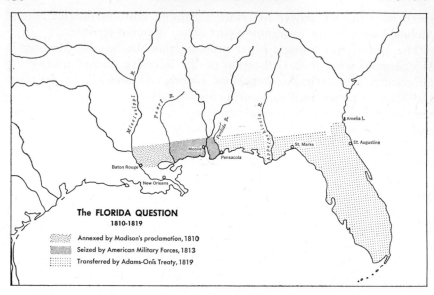

The **FLORIDA QUESTION**
1810-1819

Annexed by Madison's proclamation, 1810
Seized by American Military Forces, 1813
Transferred by Adams-Onís Treaty, 1819

pose aroused bitter opposition in Congress among the groups already suspicious of the pro-French tendencies of the administration. John Randolph broke with Jefferson on the issue, but the President mobilized enough votes to obtain an appropriation of 2 million dollars, which he felt would cover the first installment of the purchase price. Once again the plans went awry. Special commissioners John Armstrong and James Bowdoin, during several months of discussion in 1806, found that Napoleon had grown cool to the Florida deal.

It was not until 1808, when the still-rankling *Chesapeake* affair and the embargo policy made war between the United States and England appear likely, that Napoleon again dangled the Florida bait before Jefferson. If the United States joined the war against Britain, the Emperor promised to use his influence with Spain to help the Americans acquire the coveted territory. Madison's reply was too cautious to suit the Emperor, and the project was dropped.

Annexation of West Florida

Yet in the same year, 1808, the Florida question entered a new phase by the action of Napoleon himself. The Emperor ruthlessly forced the abdication of Ferdinand VII and installed Joseph Bonaparte on the Spanish throne. The unpopularity of this action resulted in a violent civil war, which broadened in scope when British troops intervened to support Ferdinand's faction and Napoleon sent in French soldiers to maintain his brother. These developments influenced the Florida issue in two ways: the United States realized the futility of trying for the present to acquire the Floridas by diplomacy or purchase; on the other hand, the temptation to take advantage of Spain's helplessness was greater than ever.

James Madison, who succeeded Jefferson in the White House in 1809, was now willing to listen to the course of action that William Claiborne and David Holmes, the governors of the Orleans and Mississippi Territories respectively, had been urging for some time. West Florida, they insisted, should be occupied by the United States if a favorable opportunity should arise. What Claiborne in particular wanted was American intervention at the invitation of the inhabitants themselves. "Can no means be devised," asked the Orleans governor of a secret agent, "to obtain such a request?"

In reality, the Spanish position was so weak that active fomentation of revolt was hardly necessary. West Florida had a small but highly heterogeneous population, the result of having been under the French, English, and Spanish flags. By 1810, moreover, these older groups were far outnumbered by Americans who had made their way down to the Gulf from neighboring American territories. Each of these national elements provided the nucleus for political intrigue, and a large slave population and an oversupply of outlaws and refugees added to potential unrest.

Trouble began in July, 1810, when a number of residents in West Florida, most of them Americans, demanded the popular election of a colonial governing council. Carlos de Lassus, the commandant at Baton Rouge who was acting for the absent Spanish governor, cooperated with the agitators in the hope of guiding the movement into support for Ferdinand VII. For a time this objective appeared successful; the newly elected convention for the Baton Rouge district dutifully announced that its purpose was "to promote the safety, honor, and happiness of our beloved king, Ferdinand VII." Despite this initial affirmation of loyalty, however, the convention steadily assumed more and more powers of self-government, thereby reducing the unhappy commandant to little more than a figurehead.

This state of affairs did not continue long. Warned that the returned Governor Vizente Folch was about to lead troops to Baton Rouge to restore full Spanish authority, the convention heads took drastic action. On September 10, 1810, they sent an armed force which overpowered the local Spanish garrison and arrested De Lassus. The convention, under the chairmanship of John Rhea, then formally declared the independence of West Florida and invited annexation by the United States.

President Madison was prompt to respond. On October 27, he issued a proclamation reasserting that West Florida was part of the Louisiana Purchase. Since the present situation was dangerous to American security, he ordered Governor Claiborne to take possession of the territory—an order that was quickly carried out with a small American force.

At first this intervention affected only the western part of the territory in dispute, for Governor Folch was able to retain control of the rest of West Florida. But his policies were vacillating, and he was unable to cope with the marauding outlaw bands now terrorizing the coast. Consequently, Claiborne felt justified in extending American occupation over most of the remaining territory except the district around Mobile by the end of the year.

The Madison administration was now confronted with the problem of justifying its West Florida policy both to its own countrymen and to foreign governments. The Federalists denounced the seizure both as unjust to Spain during its time of trouble and as additional evidence of the administration's willingness to play Napoleon's game. The Democratic-Republicans, however, succeeded in convincing a large part of the public that the occupation of the territory was justified not only in view of American claims under the Louisiana Purchase, but also as a necessary precaution to keep the Gulf Coast out of British hands. In response to vigorous protests from Britain and the Spanish Regency, Secretary of State Monroe defended his government's policy, arguing that the collapse of Spanish authority had necessitated American intervention to restore peace and order. The occupation was merely provisional, he said, and it did not preclude an eventual settlement through direct negotiation between Spain and the United States.

However much Monroe might assert that the West Florida dispute was still within the area of diplomacy, it was inconceivable that the United States would actually give up the territory it had occupied. In April, 1812, when Louisiana was admitted to the Union as a state, its eastern boundary was fixed at the Pearl River, thus including the important Baton Rouge district. The region between the Pearl and Perdido Rivers was formally added to the Mississippi Territory by proclamation of Governor Holmes in August, 1812. The Spanish garrison remained in possession of Mobile until April, 1813, when General Wilkinson demanded its surrender to prevent its use as a British base of operations during the War of 1812. When this last bit of territory passed without bloodshed under American control, the United States completed its effective annexation of West Florida as far east as the Perdido River. The Spanish Regency naturally continued to protest. There was much justice in its contention that the United States had resorted to internal subversion and external pressure to obtain possession of land to which its legal title was dubious.

East Florida—A Troublesome Neighbor

To the Floridas east of the Perdido River, the United States had laid no claim. Even the most exaggerated interpretation of the Louisiana Purchase provided no basis for such an assertion. Nevertheless, the acquisition of East Florida continued to be the persistent goal of the Jefferson and Madison administrations. American monetary claims against Spain were pushed in the hope that this pressure might induce Spain to consent to sell this territory.

New grievances against the Spanish regime accumulated rapidly. The Seminole Indians, who lived in Florida, frequently crossed the border to attack and plunder the Georgia frontier. Such episodes provided legitimate cause for protest, because the Treaty of San Lorenzo (Pinckney's Treaty) of 1795 had stipulated that both parties should restrain the Indians living within their respective boundaries.

The Indian situation inflamed American opinion all the more because the southern tribes were notoriously under the influence of British fur traders who maintained posts in Pensacola, Mobile, and other Spanish towns. The agents of these firms were suspected of supplying arms to the Indians and inciting them to attack the Americans. This intrigue was alleged to extend not only among the Seminoles, but among the Creeks and Cherokees who lived north of the border.

Americans were also indignant over the ease with which their slaves slipped over the Florida boundary and found refuge on foreign soil. In 1797, the Spanish colonial authorities had agreed to return such fugitives, but those officials proved unable or unwilling to fulfill this obligation. Consequently, the sparse population of the Floridas was augmented by an increasing number of runaway Negroes. This element, plus growing gangs of white adventurers and outlaws, gave additional cause for alarm to the American frontier settlements.

The Spanish civil war and the independence movement sweeping through the Spanish colonies added further complications to the situation. A permanently independent Florida, dominated by outlaws and former slaves, would be a most undesirable neighbor. Even more serious would be the threat to American security were this feeble colony to fall under Britain or France.

Under the circumstances, it is hardly surprising that the Madison administration toyed with schemes for bringing East Florida under the American flag in much the same way that this objective had been achieved in West Florida. In January, 1811, Congress authorized the President to take possession of all or any part of the Floridas east of the Perdido River if either the local authorities agreed to such an occupation or any foreign government attempted to seize the colony.

To explore the possibility that the discouraged and isolated Spanish authorities at St. Augustine might be induced to surrender East Florida, the Madison administration appointed as its commissioner General George Mathews, a former governor of Georgia. Mathews reported to Secretary of State Monroe that the East Florida officials were unwilling to make such an agreement, but that the inhabitants of the colony were ripe for revolt. He proposed to help these potential insurrectionists by supplying them with arms and by mobilizing American troops near the Georgia-Florida border, ready to occupy any rebellious districts. Secretary Monroe made no reply to Mathews's suggestions, and the commissioner, taking silence to mean consent, plunged enthusiastically into his subversive work. Since the pro-American faction within Florida was too weak for his purpose, he encouraged Georgia volunteers to cross the frontier to lead the movement.

In March, 1812, Mathews's synthetic insurrection began. With American gunboats hovering off the coast, rebels gained control of Amelia Island, at the mouth of the St. Marys River directly to the south of the Georgia boundary. General Mathews promptly sent waiting American troops to the spot and raised the American flag. Exhilarated by this easy success, Mathews led his combined force of insurrectionists and regular troops against St. Augustine. The Spanish garrison refused to surrender the capital city, however, and Mathews was compelled to lay siege to it.

When the special commissioner brashly reported to Washington that "the constituted authorities of E. Florida"—that is, the insurgents he had recruited—had ceded the entire province to the United States, the Madison administration found itself in an embarrassing position. Mathews had concealed his hand so poorly that the artificial character of the rebellion was clear to all the world, and it was equally obvious that the movement could not have succeeded without the collaboration of the United States Army and Navy.[3] Secretary of State Monroe felt it necessary to disavow Mathews's actions and dismiss him from his post.

It was one thing to repudiate Mathews and quite another to order the prompt evacuation of the occupied section of northeast Florida. Using the excuse that the withdrawal could not take place until the Spanish authorities gave satisfactory assurances that the insurrectionists would not be punished, the Madison administration prolonged the occupation until after the outbreak of the War of 1812. As explained in an earlier chapter, the war hawks eagerly anticipated that the war would result in the conquest of both Canada and Florida.

So far as Florida was concerned, American expansionists were thwarted more by the United States Senate than by any opposition Spain could offer. The House of Representatives passed a bill authorizing the President to occupy both Floridas, but the upper house rejected the measure by the close vote of 14 to 16. The negative votes represented a coalition of Federalists, Northern Democratic-Republicans opposed to southern ex-

---

[3] The Madison administration's embarrassment was intensified by the fact that it was just at this time accusing England of carrying on subversive activities among the New England Federalists. See chap. 6, on the Henry affair.

pansion, and Southern Democratic-Republicans who had quarreled with
the administration on other grounds. Despite this defeat, Madison and
Monroe still hoped to push through their policy. American soldiers,
now under the command of Governor D. B. Mitchell of Georgia, continued to hold the district outside St. Augustine, and General Thomas
Pinckney was ordered to mobilize troops for probable operations in East
Florida, while General Andrew Jackson was directed to prepare forces
farther west for the capture of Pensacola and Mobile. But in January,
1813, the Senate once again vetoed administration plans. The occupation
of West Florida to the Perdido was approved, it is true, but not the
proposed action against the rest of Florida. Pinckney and Jackson were
given new orders, and Mitchell was directed to evacuate the St. Augustine
district as well as Amelia Island.

During the last phase of the War of 1812, events occurred to strengthen
the contention that Spanish control of Florida was a menace to the
United States. When the Creek Indians took to the warpath in August,
1813, and massacred hundreds of men, women, and children in the
frontier settlements, the complicity of English and Spanish agents was
suspected. Whether or not these particular suspicions were justified,
British intervention in other ways was clearly evident. English forces
occupied Pensacola as a base of operations, and Major Edward Nicholls
armed both Indians and Negroes for attacks upon Americans. This was
an early round in the contest for New Orleans and the Mississippi River.

General Jackson reduced this threat for the time being by invading
Spanish territory and driving the British out of Pensacola in November,
1814. Yet one result of the War of 1812 was to strengthen the American
feeling that Spanish control of the Floridas was both a nuisance and a
menace to the United States.

New Negotiations for East Florida

With the defeat of Napoleon and the restoration of Ferdinand VII to
full power at Madrid, the Spanish government hoped to regain the overseas empire that had been slipping from its grasp. During the Anglo-
American peace negotiations at Ghent, Spanish diplomats appealed to
England to make the restoration of West Florida one of the conditions
of peace. Similar pleas were made at the Congress of Vienna, where Spain
sought a return of the Louisiana Purchase. No effective help was forthcoming; England and other allies of Spain had their own interests to
pursue and had nothing to offer King Ferdinand except polite sympathy.

Thus isolated, Spain had no alternative but to reopen negotiations with
the United States through Don Luis de Onís y Gonzales, a wily diplomat
whom the Regency had sent to America as early as 1809, but who had

not been officially received by the Madison administration until December, 1815. On the American side, Secretary of State Monroe had principal responsibility until 1817, when he moved into the White House. Then the negotiations were entrusted to the capable new Secretary of State, John Quincy Adams.

When the postwar discussions began, the two governments were far apart in their ideas. In order to obtain clear title to both Floridas, Secretary Monroe was willing to sacrifice part or all of Texas, but he could scarcely concede Onís's demand that the United States restore the whole Louisiana Purchase to Spain.

Once again events strengthened the American hand. Spain's Latin American colonies had been unwilling to accept the rule of Ferdinand VII and were successfully resisting Spanish attempts to subdue them. Although the United States refrained for the time being from recognizing these new republics, it maintained so tolerant a neutrality that filibustering expeditions were easily organized on American soil. The air was thick with rumors of adventurers' intrigues and plots to seize the Floridas or Texas. The Spanish government realized that unless it bargained soon with the United States, it might have nothing to bargain with. By January, 1818, Spanish diplomats had acquiesced in American possession of the Louisiana Territory, but were trying to keep the western boundary as far east as possible.

The wheels of diplomacy were now moving, but they were grinding slowly and with frequent breakdowns until the headstrong tactics of General Jackson suddenly brought them to painful acceleration.

The Jackson Affair

American frontier settlements in Georgia and Alabama Territory continued to be terrorized by the assaults of Seminole Indians, runaway slaves, and outlaws, operating from Florida hideouts. Spanish colonial officials were accused of doing nothing to repress these attacks, and English fur traders and adventurers were suspected of actively inciting them.

As one measure to meet this border menace, the Monroe administration ordered the reoccupation of Amelia Island, which had become a notorious pirate base. As another, General Jackson was given orders to subdue the Seminoles, pursuing them if necessary into Spanish territory, but respecting Spanish authority "wherever it is maintained." Jackson, long an advocate of more vigorous measures to defend the frontier, received these instructions with enthusiasm and immediately wrote to Washington suggesting even more drastic steps. The whole of East Florida, he declared, should be seized and held as indemnity for "the outrages of Spain upon the property of our Citizens." This could be done without implicating the government. "Let it be signified to me through any channel (say Mr. J. Rhea) that the possession of the Floridas would be desirable to the United States, and in sixty days it will be accomplished."

Just what happened next became a matter of acrimonious controversy. In later years Jackson claimed that President Monroe sent secret orders for the seizure of Florida in a letter written by Rhea and discreetly burned by Jackson. Monroe categorically denied this. On the basis of his earlier handling of the Mathews affair, it seems likely that Monroe made no reply at all, thus leaving the way open to approve or disavow Jackson's actions as the situation might develop.

With or without secret orders, Jackson was soon in effective occupation of the Floridas. Falling upon the Seminoles with a force of 3,000 men, he pursued them eastward as far as the town of St. Marks, 10 miles from Apalachee Bay on the Gulf of Mexico. He occupied this Spanish fort over the protests of the local authorities and then turned west to seize Pensacola, the capital of West Florida. Among the prisoners taken in this vigorous campaign were two English subjects, Captain Robert C. Ambrister and Alexander Arbuthnot. Since the former had been captured arms in hand at the head of a band of Indians, his complicity in the native attacks against the American frontier was scarcely in doubt. The guilt of Arbuthnot, a seventy-year-old fur trader, was not so clear, but damaging letters captured with him indicated that he too had been active in Indian intrigue. A court-martial found both men guilty and sentenced Ambrister to be shot and Arbuthnot to be hanged. Jackson ordered the prompt execution of the condemned men.

The general's headstrong conduct brought down a storm of criticism upon the Monroe administration. From Spain came indignant demands that the invading American troops evacuate the Floridas at once and that Jackson be punished. English public opinion flamed with indignation over the summary execution of British subjects. Within the United States the repercussions of the affair were equally serious. Henry Clay and his followers denounced both the general and the President, who was accused of committing acts of war without authority from Congress.

The Florida issue also divided the Cabinet. Secretary of War Calhoun immediately countermanded Jackson's order for the occupation of St. Augustine and recommended immediate evacuation of St. Marks and Pensacola and the court-martialing of the general. All the other members except Adams favored a similar course. The Secretary of State, however, defended Jackson, arguing that his drastic measures had been justified by the misconduct of the Spanish officials.

President Monroe decided upon a middle course. He wrote a friendly letter to the general, explaining that the latter had exceeded his authority and that the occupied towns would have to be given up. But Jackson was praised for his patriotism and no effort was made to punish or reprimand him. Undoubtedly the general's extraordinary popularity with the American public influenced Monroe in his decision to deal gently with this rash subordinate.

Lord Castlereagh, ignoring the clamor of British public opinion, carefully studied the trial proceedings in the Ambrister and Arbuthnot cases. He came to the conclusion that since the two men had been engaged in unlawful activities, no formal protest against their executions should be lodged. The British Minister's handling of the issue reflected his determination not to jeopardize the improved relations between the two countries symbolized by the Rush-Bagot Agreement and the Convention of 1818.

Secretary of State Adams proved fully capable of dealing with the diplomatic ramifications of the Florida affair. He met Spanish protests with a vigorous counteroffensive. In a strong note of November, 1818, he acknowledged that Jackson had acted upon his own authority in seizing St. Marks and Pensacola, but justified these actions as "necessary measures of self defense." Although the posts were being returned, Spain was sternly warned that, if American security ever again required their occupation, their seizure would probably be permanent. Spain must either garrison the Floridas with enough troops to maintain order or cede them to the United States. Adams's strong language made a deep impression both in Europe and in the United States, where it helped to quiet congressional criticism.

The Adams-Onís Treaty

As Monroe and Adams had hoped, the Jackson affair served as a sharp warning to Spain. Onís stated the situation bluntly in a dispatch to his home government: "If His Majesty can't get the support of any Power, and hasn't sufficient forces to make war on this country, then I think it would be best not to delay making the best settlement possible, seeing that things certainly won't be better for a long time."

Although Spain was now reconciled to the loss of the Floridas, she retreated somewhat more slowly upon other issues involving the boundaries of the Louisiana Purchase. She placed primary importance on the retention of Texas, because Mexico, like most of her other colonies, was in a state of revolt and Spain's only chance to retain control was to keep the American frontier as far east of the Rio Grande as possible.

The Monroe administration's recent negotiations with England over the Northwest boundary had focused attention on the Oregon territory, and Adams was determined that the projected treaty with Spain should

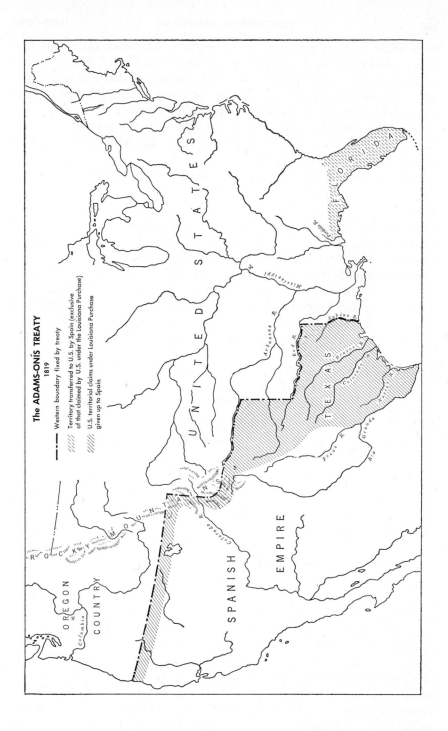

The **ADAMS-ONÍS TREATY**
1819

—··— Western boundary fixed by treaty

///// Territory transferred to U.S. by Spain (exclusive
of that claimed by U.S. under the Louisiana Purchase)

///// U.S. territorial claims under Louisiana Purchase
given up to Spain

OREGON
COUNTRY
Columbia R.

ROCKY MOUNTAINS

UNITED STATES

SPANISH

EMPIRE

Colorado R.

Pecos R.

Rio Grande

TEXAS

Nueces R.

Colorado R.

Brazos R.

Red R.

Sabine R.

Arkansas R.

Mississippi R.

FLORIDA

Perdido R.

be written in such terms as to strengthen American claims to that region. Spain was at first reluctant to admit the United States to any foothold on the Pacific Coast. Forced by Adams's persistence to give up this point, she held out for a line as far north as possible. Eventually the two sides narrowed their differences until they were only two degrees apart: Adams was holding out for a line at the 41st parallel and Onís for the 43rd parallel. The decision to accept the 42nd parallel was a natural compromise.

The long and difficult negotiations finally came to an end with the signing of the Adams-Onís Treaty (sometimes called the Florida or the Transcontinental Treaty) on February 22, 1819. By wording carefully chosen to avoid the issue of whether American occupation of West Florida to the Perdido had been legal, the treaty transferred to the United States all of the King of Spain's territories in East and West Florida "which belong to him." The boundary line between the United States and Spain west of the Mississippi was to start at the mouth of the Sabine River and follow that river northward to the 32nd parallel; then it was to be drawn due north until it intersected the Red River; it was to follow that river west to the 100th degree of west longitude and then due north to the Arkansas River, which it was to follow to the 42nd parallel; it was then to follow that parallel west to the Pacific Ocean. The United States agreed to exonerate Spain from all claims of American citizens up to a total of 5 million dollars. The amount and validity of these claims was to be fixed by an American commission.

Although Adams was later criticized for having sacrificed the claim to Texas, the immediate response to the treaty was entirely favorable. Two days after the agreement was signed the Senate unanimously ratified it. The Floridas were still the primary objective of the expansionists, and the abandonment of the United States' inconclusive title to lands west of the Sabine seemed a small price to pay. Moreover, Adams's success in having the boundary line extended to the Pacific provided an unexpected dividend.

The Madrid government was less happy with the treaty. Onís was criticized for not having obtained pledges that the United States would abstain from recognizing the independence of the Latin American republics or from helping them in other ways. The King postponed ratification and sent a new minister to Washington to seek better terms. This Spanish delay threatened to reopen the whole controversy. Some congressmen urged the immediate occupation not only of the Floridas, but of Texas as well. Cooler counsels prevailed, however, and the Monroe administration was able to prevent such drastic action. The Spanish government, thus warned of the futility and danger of further procrastination, finally consented to ratification, and the Adams-Onís treaty went into effect on February 22, 1821, exactly two years after its signing.

9

THE MONROE DOCTRINE

The confident nationalism reflected in the Monroe administration's Florida policy also controlled its reaction to the great struggle for independence taking place in Latin America. Although Monroe and Adams resisted rash pressures that would have forced them into premature and dangerous measures, they gave the new republics such cautious encouragement as they could and extended diplomatic recognition as soon as it was possible to do so with reasonable safety.

The birth of these new nations centered attention on the whole problem of the relations of the New World to the Old. Could the United States stand idly by if European empires sought new colonies in the Western Hemisphere? What should the national policy be, were the independence of the infant Latin American nations to be threatened by intervention from abroad? President Monroe's strongly phrased answers to these questions constitute the doctrine which has made his name famous in American history.

The Recognition Problem

When Napoleon placed his brother, Joseph Bonaparte, on a shaky throne at Madrid and the patriot faction responded by establishing a rival regency in the name of the legitimate monarch, Ferdinand VII, the consequences were tremendous both for Spain and the Spanish colonies. In the mother country, the two regimes became locked in the terrible Peninsular War, with French troops supporting the Bonapartist cause and British troops that of the Regency. Both governments claimed authority in the colonies, but neither was able to exercise it effectively. The result was a period of great confusion in which troops loyal to Ferdinand struggled with rebel factions eager to throw off the Castilian yoke.

The various colonies made uneven progress in their struggle for independence. The early victories of the insurgents in Venezuela and Chile proved premature, and the royalist factions were able to regain supremacy and to maintain it for several years. In Buenos Aires, on the other hand, the liberal party achieved autonomy as early as 1810 and formally proclaimed independence in 1816. In Mexico, the royalist element was unusually strong and kept control of the situation until 1821. In a situation so kaleidoscopic, the United States found it difficult to formulate a consistent policy.

As early as 1808, President Jefferson expressed keen interest in the prevailing unrest in Latin America. In essence, his position was that, although the United States could not actively help the insurgents, it should welcome their efforts. If royalist Spain proved strong enough to retain the colonies, the United States could not object; but the most desirable outcome of the situation would be the exclusion of all European influence from the Western Hemisphere.

Although Jefferson was thus thinking in terms essentially similar to those of the later Monroe Doctrine, neither he nor Madison made much progress toward this goal. The embargo cut off American commerce with South America just when it was growing to significant proportions. Ironically, as the trade of the United States with the insurgent colonies declined, that of England increased.

So long as Napoleon remained in power, the Spanish Regency enjoyed strong support among many sections of the American public. The struggle of the Spanish patriots to drive out the Bonapartist intruders appeared to be the cause of human freedom. Perhaps even more effective in influencing opinion was the flourishing grain trade American merchants had built up in supplying the Regency and their British allies. Conflicting ties of sentiment and material interest thus resulted in a division of American opinion toward Latin America. Conservative commercial circles tended to be pro-British and pro-Regency; republican agrarian elements sympathized with the rebels.

The War of 1812, even more than the earlier embargo, arrested the growth of American trade with Latin America. To British merchants, excluded from markets in the United States and in Continental Europe, the situation in the Spanish colonies presented golden opportunities. Despite the close alliance between the British government and the Spanish Regency, the English showed few scruples about carrying supplies to rebel ports.

After the war, American interest in Latin America increased. The sympathy the Spanish Regency had enjoyed was speedily forfeited when Ferdinand VII restored reactionary absolutism. Moreover, American merchants were now eager to trade in Latin American ports, and many Army officers and privateersmen were ambitious to sell their services to the rebel forces. Henry Clay, Speaker of the House of Representatives, became the special champion of Latin American independence. "I consider," he declared, "the release of any part of America from the domination of the Old World as adding to the general security of the New."

Both President Madison and President Monroe were convinced that the situation required caution. They believed the Latin American rebels, given a free hand, had a good chance to achieve independence without outside aid. The greatest danger to the patriot cause was that one or more European powers might help Spain reconquer her colonies. Such intervention would be consistent with the principle of legitimacy upon which the Congress of Vienna had based the European peace settlement.

Since England held the preponderant sea power, her attitude toward Latin America was of prime importance. From his observations in London immediately after the War of 1812, John Quincy Adams concluded that the British government favored a restoration of Spanish authority over the colonies, but only under conditions that would keep Latin American ports open to foreign commerce.

Under these circumstances, Madison thought it would be a mistake for the United States to give open help to the Latin American rebels. To do so might provoke the very European intervention the United States wanted to prevent. On September 1, 1815, the President issued a proclamation of neutrality, and by subsequent laws Congress attempted to prevent either the Spanish government or the rebels from gaining exclusive advantages. Neither contestant was happy with this policy. Spain bitterly complained because the insurgents were accorded belligerent rights; the Latin American governments protested the administration's efforts to prevent the outfitting of filibustering expeditions on American soil.

After Monroe became President and Adams Secretary of State, American policy was somewhat modified in accordance with the personal leanings of these two leaders. At heart Monroe, still the idealistic republican who had sympathized so strongly with the French Revolution during the 1790s, was inclined to help the liberal cause in Latin America. Long experience and the responsiblities of office, however, had taught the President the advantages of prudence. He hoped the United States might gain the support of England in recognizing the independence of the new republics. Adams did not share Monroe's enthusiasm for the Latin American patriots, whom he suspected of being mere adventurers without ability to establish stable and responsible governments. Nor did the Secretary of State agree with the President that the British were likely to cooperate with America in these matters.

In 1818 and 1819, steps were taken that reflected Monroe's optimism rather than Adams's skepticism. In May, 1818, Richard Rush, the United

States Minister to England, was instructed to sound out the British government on joint measures that might contribute to "the total independence of the Spanish South American provinces." This overture was rebuffed by Lord Castlereagh, who remarked that the views of the two governments were not identical.

Although England was unwilling to recognize the independence of the new republics, she did not favor foreign intervention to restore Spanish authority. When France and Russia suggested at the Congress of Aix-la-Chapelle (1818) that the European powers propose reasonable terms to the rebellious colonies and then use economic pressure to coerce them into acceptance, England vetoed the plan. This act encouraged the Monroe administration once again to propose collaboration. Lord Castlereagh, however, was still cold to the idea and frankly admitted he hoped for a restoration of Spanish authority under conditions favoring freedom of trade.

Unable to obtain English support, Monroe had to decide whether the United States should go it alone in recognizing Latin American independence or continue the policy of neutrality and watchful waiting. Despite heavy attacks from Clay and the more radical newspapers, the administration continued the policy of delay. To some extent, this caution was dictated by a wish not to antagonize Ferdinand's government while the Adams-Onís Treaty was still awaiting ratification. Even more influential, however, was the trend of events both in Latin America and in Europe.

American commissioners, appointed to investigate Latin American conditions, made conflicting reports in 1818. Although all agreed Spain could not reconquer the Buenos Aires district, they differed in their estimates of the stability of that government and of other revolutionary regimes seeking recognition. Developments during the next two years did little to clear the air. Moreover, the European situation was such that Monroe feared premature recognition might injure, rather than help, the Latin American republics.

By the end of 1820, the proponents of recognition found themselves in a stronger position. The tide of battle, which had flowed first in one direction and then in another, now moved much more strongly in the direction of independence. In Spain, meanwhile, a contest had developed between the absolutists and the constitutionalists. The hope that a more liberal government would abandon the attempt to coerce the colonies proved ill-founded, but political strife at home further weakened the Spanish overseas effort.

These changing conditions were reflected in mounting support in Congress for the Latin American republics. In March, 1818, when Clay tried to force the President's hand by seeking an appropriation for a minister to Buenos Aires, his proposal was defeated in the House by a vote of 115 to 45. Two years later, in May, 1820, a more temperate resolution for the appointment of ministers to any Latin American governments the President might see fit to recognize was carried in the House by a vote of 80 to 75. A year later the House voted 134 to 12 for a resolution expressing strong sympathy for the Latin American patriots in their struggle for independence.

Public interest in the recognition problem was intensified by two widely reported speeches. On May 29, 1821, Henry Clay, who was retiring temporarily from politics, delivered a farewell address to his admirers in Lexington, Kentucky. He criticized the Monroe administration for flaunting public opinion in its delay of recognition; he called for American support of the Latin American cause "by all means short of actual war," and he spoke vaguely of the need for collaboration among all the American republics as a counterpoise to the Holy Alliance.

John Quincy Adams replied to Clay in a Fourth of July oration, delivered in the House of Representatives. Even though he undertook to divest himself of the responsibility of speaking for the government by appearing in the academic gown appropriate to his rank as Boylston Professor of Rhetoric at Harvard College, his audience found it difficult to forget that the man in this professorial disguise was actually the Secretary of State. While much of the speech was devoted to twisting the British lion's tail in traditional Fourth of July fashion, Adams had two highly important points to make about contemporary international relations. One was a condemnation of colonialism: "Colonial establishments," declared Adams, "cannot fulfil the great objects of government in the just purpose of civil society." The second was a plea for isolationism: the United States should avoid involvement in foreign wars, even wars of liberty, because resort to force would tarnish American ideals and encourage the growth of imperialism. The Secretary of State thus announced his sympathy with colonists seeking their independence, but rejected Clay's advice that the United States actively intervene.

The long controversy over recognition was finally settled by the logic of events. By the end of 1821, the reality of Latin American independence could scarcely be doubted. Buenos Aires, Venezuela, Colombia, Peru, Chile, and Mexico were all in varying degrees under patriot control. The success of the rebels meant the time had come for the Monroe administration to take action. To delay recognition longer might forfeit the friendship of these new governments. On March 2, 1822, President Monroe sent a message to Congress specifying the Latin American states he considered entitled to recognition and asking for the necessary appropriations. Congress passed almost unanimously the requested legislation. Even conservative newspapers approved the new policy. Hope of increasing trade with the new states was one motive; natural sympathy with nations following the example of the United States in asserting their independence was another.

The first of the new governments actually to gain recognition was Colombia. On June 19, 1822, the sick and dying Manuel Torres, who had spent many years in the United States in the interests of the Colombian patriots, was received by President Monroe in a brief, but emotion-charged audience. Mexico was formally recognized in December, 1822, and Buenos Aires, Chile, Central America, and Peru within the next four years. The United States also exchanged diplomatic representatives with Brazil, the former Portuguese colony that had recently declared itself an independent monarchy under a branch of the Portuguese royal family.

The Threat of Intervention

The European powers were by no means disposed to follow the lead of the United States, for such a step would violate principles that had dominated the Old World since the overthrow of Napoleon. Except for Brazil and Mexico, where monarchies were temporarily established, the new states were republican in form—something distasteful to all the European governments of the day, England included. Moreover, from the conservative point of view, the new regimes were all illegitimate because they had been established by revolution against Ferdinand VII, the lawful sovereign.

Old World conservatism found its embodiment in what was known as the Holy Alliance. The popular use of this term reflected some confusion between two different groupings of the powers, both formed in 1815. For the purpose of preserving the peace established at the Congress of Vienna, the four nations that had defeated Napoleon—England, Austria, Russia, and Prussia—agreed to continue the Quadruple Alliance for twenty years and to hold periodic conferences to discuss international problems. Not content with this limited alliance, Tsar Alexander I of Russia invited his fellow monarchs to join in a vague and visionary pledge to cooperate with each other as brothers and to rule their subjects in the spirit of Christian charity. All the sovereigns of Europe except the Pope, the Sultan of Turkey, and the Prince Regent of England went along with the Tsar's project, not out of any enthusiasm for it, but out of deference to the Tsar's tremendously powerful position in international politics. The name "Holy Alliance," which applied more properly to the Tsar's Christian fraternity, also became attached in popular usage to the Quadruple Alliance.

The periodic European congresses, provided for by the Quadruple Alliance, supplied the great powers with a mechanism for international cooperation somewhat similar to the later League of Nations or United

Nations, although much more limited in membership and program. At the Congress of Aix-la-Chapelle in 1818, France's good behavior under the restored Louis XVIII was approved and she was admitted to the alliance. Two years later the allies were confronted by the problem of local revolutions that had wrested constitutions from unwilling monarchs in Spain and Naples. At the Congress of Troppau (1821), the powers split, with the three eastern absolutisms—Russia, Prussia, and Austria—upholding the principle that all internal revolutions were dangerous to the *status quo* and there should be suppressed, while England and France opposed this sweeping declaration.

Despite English disapproval, the policy of intervention gained ground. In 1821, Austrian troops marched into Italy to quell popular movements in Naples and Piedmont and to restore the local rulers to absolute power. In 1822, the Congress of Verona, against strong British opposition, accepted France's offer to intervene in Spain. The following year French troops restored Ferdinand to full power, a restoration the stupid king utilized to institute a reign of terror against the constitutional party.

What step of intervention would come next? Ferdinand VII was eager to have the support of the Holy Alliance in regaining control of his American colonies. Would he succeed? Out of such questions as these arose discussions that give birth to the Monroe Doctrine.

Actually, the danger of European intervention against the new republics was not very great. To be sure, reactionary French elements, responsible for the restoration of Spanish absolutism, talked vaguely of completing the task by moving against the former colonies, but in France itself there was wide division of opinion. Liberals had been shocked by the intervention in Spain, and even conservatives were disgusted by Ferdinand's excesses. Any policy of interference overseas would have been strongly opposed also by merchants eager to trade with the new republics.

The most the French government could hope to do, therefore, was to promote some kind of Spanish-American settlement that would preserve the principle of legitimacy without sacrificing French commercial interests or involving the nation in extensive naval and military operations. With foolish optimism, French officials pinned their hopes upon inducing the Latin Americans to substitute monarchical government for the hated republicanism and to accept Spanish Bourbon princes for their kings. To give a strong moral sanction to such a settlement, France tried to promote a new congress of European powers.

Probably the most active champion of the idea that the principle of legitimacy must be extended to the Americas was Count Carlo Pozzo di Borgo, a Corsican who served as Russian Ambassador to France. He worked tirelessly to promote intervention in conferences with French officials, in dispatches to the Tsar, and in advice to Ferdinand VII. Tsar

Alexander I was as eager as his Ambassador to see Spanish royal authority restored, but fortunately he was more moderate in his methods. Fearing British hostility to any drastic measure of intervention, he devoted his efforts to trying to obtain a congress.

With England known to be inimical to the whole idea of intervention and the Holy Alliance powers uncertain and divided as to what should be done, the danger of European ships and troops being used to restore Spain's rule over the colonies did not appear to be ominous. President Monroe would probably not have become sufficiently anxious to employ the strong language of his December, 1823, message to Congress had not new and more disturbing news come to Washington during the summer and fall of 1823.

Russian Expansion on the Pacific Coast

Quite independently of the Latin American problem, a situation had been developing on the Pacific Coast that gave the Monroe administration serious concern. Russia had been interested in this region since 1727, when Vitus Bering discovered the strait that bears his name. Scattered fur-trading posts had been established on the islands off the American coast, and in 1799 the Russian-American Company was organized, with exclusive trading rights and jurisdiction along the coast as far south as the 55th parallel. In reality, Russian traders penetrated far south of this line, even building a post near Bodega Bay, some fifty miles north of San Francisco, on land claimed by Spain.

Although there were occasional clashes between Russian and American traders, the United States government placed no great importance on the issue until it learned of an imperial decree of 1821, in which the Tsar renewed the privileges of the Russian-American Company and extended its jurisdiction south to the 51st parallel. All foreign ships were forbidden to come within 100 Italian miles of the coast, and a Russian warship was sent to enforce this prohibition.

Both Great Britain and the United States protested. The Monroe administration, which had sought to protect American claims to the Oregon Territory by the joint-occupancy agreement with England in 1818 and the Adams-Onís Treaty with Spain the following year, could scarcely allow this Russian assertion of exclusive jurisdiction to go unchallenged. Negotiations between the United States and Russia on this issue plodded along until July, 1823, when Secretary of State John Quincy Adams obtained President Monroe's assent to a significant formulation of policy.

Instead of limiting his protest to Russia's action in extending its claim from the 55th to the 51st parallel, Adams informed the Russian Minister that the United States would "contest the right of Russia to *any* territorial expansion on this continent, and that we should assume distinctly the principle that the American continents are no longer subjects for *any* new European colonial establishments." Adams incorporated similar ideas in instructions to the American Minister to Russia and in suggestions to Monroe for the President's annual message to Congress.

This sweeping assertion that the United States considered the American continents closed to further European colonization was a radical position with little precedent in international law and diplomacy, but Adams's thought had been moving in this direction for some time. In 1819, the Secretary of State had said in a Cabinet meeting that Europe should get used to the idea that the proper dominion of the United States was the entire continent of North America. In conversation with the British Minister to the United States in 1821, Adams had grudgingly conceded that the United States would have to leave the British in possession of the North American colonies it already had. "Keep what is yours," the strongly nationalistic Secretary had declared, "but leave the rest of the continent to us." From these sentiments it was but a short step to the noncolonization principle that became part of the Monroe Doctrine in 1823.

Anglo-American Flirtation

Although both England and the United States were opposed to any European intervention to restore Spanish rule over her former colonies, it was not easy for the two countries to cooperate in their actions. Their traditional mutual distrust had been softened by the Rush-Bagot Agreement and the Convention of 1818, but no real cordiality had developed. Americans still complained they were treated with an attitude of superiority and condescension by the British aristocracy.

When France invaded Spain to restore Ferdinand to absolute power, the Monroe administration feared that an Anglo-French war might result. In such a conflict, what would become of Cuba? Now in possession of both Floridas, the United States was strongly opposed to the transfer of that strategically located island to either France or England. Yet if a great war revolving around the Spanish problem broke out, there was real danger that one of the great powers might somehow acquire this Caribbean prize. American officials considered the advisability of encouraging a Cuban revolution and then annexing the island on the request of the inhabitants, after the fashion of West Florida.

The British government was aware of American nervousness on the Cuban question. Not wanting to see Cuba fall into the hands of either France or the United States, George Canning, who had become British

Foreign Secretary following the suicide of Lord Castlereagh in 1822, gave serious thought to the possibility of coming to a friendly understanding with the United States on the whole Latin American problem.

Canning had some reason to hope for Anglo-American cooperation because of the friendlier feeling developing between the two countries in the spring of 1823. Britain's refusal to approve the schemes of the Holy Alliance had had the effect—so George Canning was informed by his cousin, Stratford Canning, British Minister to Washington—"of making the English almost popular in the United States." Even the frigid Adams had "caught a something of the soft infection." The Secretary of State was indeed on his good behavior, not only because of his approval of the general tendency of Britain's policy toward Latin America, but because he hoped to settle outstanding differences over American commerce with the British colonies and the abolition of the slave trade.

The British Foreign Secretary now began an ardent wooing of the United States. In April, 1823, he amazed Richard Rush, the American Minister to England, by publicly praising Jefferson's doctrines of neutrality; some months later he went out of his way to send President "Munro" and Secretary of State Adams a copy of one of his speeches, corrected in his own handwriting. Having prepared the way by these and other cordial gestures, Canning, with artful casualness, inquired of Rush on August 16 whether the United States might join England in a warning to Europe against interference in Latin America.

On August 20, Canning made his proposal, still "unofficial and confidential," more definite in a private letter to Rush. "Is not the moment come," inquired the Foreign Secretary, "when our Governments might understand each other as to the Spanish American Colonies? And if we arrive at such an understanding, would it not be expedient for ourselves, and beneficial for all the world, that the principles of it should be clearly settled and plainly avowed?" Canning declared that the recovery of the colonies by Spain was hopeless and that the question of their recognition as independent states was "one of time and circumstances." On the other hand, his government would by no means wish to hinder any arrangements which Spain might be able to make with her former colonies by friendly negotiation. The British themselves did not aim at acquiring any portion of the colonies and would oppose the transfer of any of them to any other power. The United States was invited to join with England in a mutual declaration of these principles. "There has seldom, in the history of the world," Canning argued, "occurred an opportunity when so small an effort, of two friendly Governments, might produce so unequivocal a good and prevent such extensive calamities."

For a month Canning continued to press his proposal upon the American Minister in letters and conferences. The Foreign Secretary even carried on his courtship in public. In a speech at Liverpool he lauded the common language, the common spirit of commercial enterprise, and the common regard for liberty shared by the two countries. "The force of blood again prevails, and the daughter and the mother stand together against the world."

Rush's reaction to the Canning proposals was mixed. This sudden display of friendship did not alter his earlier conviction that the British governing classes were at heart anti-American. If joint action with the United States were being urged, Rush believed the reason must be British self-interest. England had broken with the Holy Alliance, not because she really objected to its reactionary principles, but because the extension of Austrian and French influence might endanger her own power. "She at last perceives a crisis likely to come on, bringing with it peril to her own commercial prospects on the other side of the Atlantic, & to her political sway in both hemispheres." Despite his skepticism of British motives, Rush believed it would be to American interest to accept the proposal, provided England would recognize the new Latin American governments without further delay.

While the American Minister was still awaiting his government's response to the British overture, Canning suddenly dropped the whole matter. The Foreign Secretary offered no explanation, but Rush suspected he must have reached an understanding with France—and this proved to be the case. Early in October, Canning warned Prince Jules de Polignac, the French Ambassador to London, that Britain would oppose any European intervention to help Spain reconquer her colonies. The French reply, embodied in the so-called Polignac Memorandum, was completely reassuring: France disclaimed any intention of appropriating any part of the Spanish empire in America and abjured any design of employing force against the colonies.

Thus two months before the famous Monroe Doctrine message was sent to Congress, the actual threat of European intervention in the New World, never great in the first place, had largely evaporated. England had warned France, France had professed the purity of her intentions, and the proposal for joint Anglo-American action was already out of date. As so often in diplomatic history before the days of the Atlantic cable, however, news of the changed situation in Europe did not reach America until after important policy decisions had been made.

Charting a Course

As soon as the Canning proposals arrived in Washington in early October, 1823, President Monroe began to consider carefully what reply should be made. First he turned for counsel to his two predecessors, Jefferson and Madison, and both advised acceptance. Jefferson's letter was particularly impressive, since it dealt with the whole problem of America's relationship with the rest of the world. The first and fundamental maxim, Jefferson advised, should be "never to entangle ourselves in the broils of Europe"; the second, "never to suffer Europe to intermeddle with cis-Atlantic affairs." America, North and South, had interests distinct from those of Europe. "She should therefore have a system of her own, separate and apart from that of Europe. While the last is laboring to become the domicile of despotism, our endeavor should surely be, to make our hemisphere that of freedom." By acceding to the British proposal, the United States would detach England from the Holy Alliance and bring her mighty weight into the scale of free government. "Great Britain is the nation which can do us the most harm of any one, or all on earth; and with her on our side we need not fear the whole world."

The Canning proposals also provided the agenda for a series of grave Cabinet meetings. The danger of European intervention had hitherto not been taken very seriously; now the feeling was that, if England were sufficiently alarmed to propose joint action, the threat must have greater reality. By coincidence, messages from Russia arrived just in time to increase this feeling of apprehension. On October 16, a Russian note announced that the Tsar, "faithful to the political principles which he follows in concert with his Allies," could not under any circumstances recognize the new Latin American governments, born out of revolution. A month later a second note strongly upheld the principle of intervention as it had been carried out in the case of Spain. Although these Russian pronouncements contained no explicit threat of intervention in the New World, their uncompromising avowal of Holy Alliance principles shook the nerves of some members of the Monroe Cabinet. According to Adams, the President was "alarmed far beyond anything that I could have conceived possible," and Secretary of War Calhoun was "perfectly moonstruck."

The Secretary of State was less excited than his colleagues. He still thought intervention very unlikely, but he believed, nevertheless, that the time had come for action. He was reluctant merely to accept the British proposal because he felt that the United States should take the lead in matters concerning the Western Hemisphere. Under the Canning program, England would undoubtedly receive most of the credit for saving Latin America and would reap most of the benefits in the form of commercial advantages. Moreover, Adams feared that England might use an Anglo-American agreement to try to prevent the United States from obtaining such Spanish territory as Texas and California at some future time. Therefore, knowing that the British would support virtually any position the Americans took, the Secretary argued in favor of a strong pronouncement of American policy at once, without waiting for an under-standing with England. "It would be more candid as well as more dig-nified," Adams insisted, "to avow our principles explicitly to Russia and France, than to come in as a cock-boat in the wake of the British man-of-war." To this strategy the Cabinet readily agreed.

The form the pronouncement should take was the next issue. Adams as-sumed it would serve the purpose if he wrote strong replies to the British and Russian governments and then published the documents. The Presi-dent, however, decided to make the announcement in his annual message to Congress. In his first draft, Monroe included a strong condemnation of France's intervention in Spain and a recommendation that the United States recognize the independence of Greece.[1] Adams believed this would be a mistake, since America would be interfering in strictly European questions at the very time she was protesting European interference in the Western Hemisphere. The President accepted this criticism and revised his message to incorporate the principle of the two spheres— a principle that Jefferson had also emphasized.

The Doctrine Announced

In the annual message as finally submitted to Congress on December 2, 1823, what was destined to be known as the Monroe Doctrine was con-tained in two widely separated passages. In a section devoted to foreign affairs near the beginning of the document, President Monroe alluded to Russian claims in the Pacific Northwest and spelled out the noncoloniza-tion principle just as Adams had formulated it:

> ...the American continents, by the free and independent condition which they have assumed and maintained, are henceforth not to be con-sidered as subjects for future colonization by any European powers....

Much later in the message, after an extended discussion of domestic issues, Monroe turned to Latin American affairs. He referred to French intervention in Spain in terms of mild disapprobation, but hastened to add that "in the wars of European powers, in matters relating to them-selves, we have never taken any part, nor does it comport with our policy to do so." The case was different, however, in respect to affairs in the Western Hemisphere. "The political system of the allied powers is essentially different...from that of America." To the defense of liberty the whole United States was devoted.

> We owe it, therefore, to candor and to the amicable relations existing between the United States and those powers [of the Holy Alliance] to declare that we should consider any attempt on their part to extend

[1] The Greeks had been in revolt against Turkish rule since 1821.

their system to any portion of this hemisphere as dangerous to our peace and safety. With the existing colonies or dependencies of any European power we have not interfered and shall not interfere. But with the Governments who have declared their independence and maintained it, and whose independence we have, on great consideration and on just principles, acknowledged, we could not view any interposition for the purpose of oppressing them in any other light than as the manifestation of an unfriendly disposition toward the United States.

Reception of the Doctrine

Monroe's words, published in newspapers throughout the country, were greeted with general enthusiasm. A British diplomat in Washington reported to Canning that it would be difficult in a nation of such great diversity and conflict of opinion to find a "more perfect unanimity" than that supporting this sturdy pronouncement of nationalism. The Briton, however, may have overstated the case. Congress demonstrated a certain coolness to the President's policy. A resolution introduced by Clay, committing the legislative branch to oppose any forcible intervention by the Holy Alliance against the new republics, was allowed to die, and proposals to increase the Navy also failed to carry.

To the reactionary governments of Continental Europe, the Monroe Doctrine seemed a piece of brash impudence. Prince Metternich of Austria lamented that these "indecent declarations" had cast blame and scorn on the "institutions of Europe most worthy of respect" and had lent new strength to the "apostles of sedition." The Tsar declared that Monroe's message contained "views and pretensions so exaggerated" that it merited "only the most profound contempt." Yet the Holy Alliance powers entered no formal protest against the President's language. They attributed Monroe's strange behavior to the mysteries of American politics and formulated their own policies toward Latin America without worrying over the position the United States had taken. This upstart republic, they believed, was powerless to back up its brave words; their only concern was with mighty England.

Reaction to the Monroe Doctrine in British governing circles was decidedly mixed. The President's firm stand pleased Canning in so far as it strengthened the latter's own position of opposing any European intervention to restore Spanish rule over the revolted colonies, but the form of the American declaration and some of the words the President had used were not so welcome. The noncolonization principle was completely unacceptable, and English diplomats bluntly notified the Americans that they considered the unoccupied parts of the Western Hemisphere as much open to colonization as hitherto by Great Britain

and other European powers. Toward the other great principle of the
doctrine—nonintervention—Canning's reaction was not opposition, but
jealousy. He resented the fact that without waiting for further negotiations on the proposed joint Anglo-American action, the United States had
seized the opportunity to make an independent announcement. This
seemed to the Foreign Secretary to be a cheap bid for popularity in Latin
America. The United States was posing as protector of the new governments despite the fact that their real security depended on British sea
power.

The warmth pervading Anglo-American relations during the year 1823
gave way to a decided coolness the following year. When Rush announced
that the American government was now ready to consider collaboration,
Canning brusquely replied that the situation had completely changed.
Nor did the British government respond favorably to Adams's hope for
a general conference on outstanding difficulties. In Latin America, England and the United States became more open rivals for influence.

Clarifying the Doctrine

Although Monroe's words had been firm and brave, they had raised
as many questions as they had settled. Would the United States actually
go to war to protect the independence of its Latin American neighbors?
Would it enter defensive alliances with them? Would the United States
insist that all its new friends adopt a republican form of government?
During the last year of Monroe's term, several episodes occurred to throw
light on these issues.

In July, 1824, José María Salazar, the Colombian Minister to the United
States, called attention to the continued occupation of Spain by French
troops. He believed French influence might result in a new Spanish effort
to reconquer the colonies and asked what the policy of the United States
would be in this event. Or if no attempt to send troops were made,
intervention might take the form of encouraging monarchism in the new
states. Would the United States resist this type of interference, and
would she enter into an alliance with Colombia for this purpose?

Adams's reply to Salazar was cautious. He discounted the likelihood
of European pressure to impose monarchies on Latin America. Whether
or not the United States would go to war under any particular set of
circumstances was, he pointed out, entirely within the power of Congress
to decide. A purely Spanish expedition against one of the former colonies
would not raise the issue; the occasion for action under the Monroe
Doctrine could arise only by "a deliberate and concerted system of the
allied Powers to exercise force against the freedom and Independence of
your Republic." In such an event, the United States could not act with-

out a previous understanding with European powers having interests similar to its own. Only under these circumstances would it consider an alliance with Colombia.

This statement made it obvious that the Monroe administration did not intend to be drawn into any rash adventures. It was limiting its opposition to European intervention to cases in which there should be a flagrant exercise of allied force. And even in these circumstances it was maintaining a free hand in deciding what it should do. It hoped to act only in concert with England and to avoid entangling alliances with the new governments in Latin America.

Although President Monroe, long an ardent champion of republicanism, made no secret of his hope that the new Latin American nations would choose this form of government, he did not insist upon it. The Empire of Brazil, which had selected a member of the royal family of Portugal as emperor, was accorded diplomatic recognition in 1824. Monroe hoped that this tolerance of Latin American monarchies would help reconcile the European powers to his policies.

The Monroe Doctrine received still further clarification in December, 1824, when Monroe sent his final annual message to Congress. While still standing firm upon the ground he had taken the year before, the President emphasized the point that the United States claimed no right to interfere with the internal affairs of its hemisphere neighbors; it believed "that every people have a right to institute for themselves the government which, in their judgment, may suit them best."

The Panama Congress Fiasco

On March 4, 1825, John Quincy Adams became President of the United States. The new Secretary of State was Henry Clay, formerly a severe critic of Adams's foreign policy, but now his political ally. Clay was not only the foremost American champion of the new Latin American governments, but a strong advocate of cooperation among the Western Hemisphere nations. Adams's own inclinations had originally been more isolationist than those of Clay, but the formulation of the Monroe Doctrine and other recent events had influenced him to look with more favor on cooperation.

The initiative for Pan-American collaboration, however, was taken by neither Adams nor Clay, but by Simón Bolívar, the heroic liberator of Colombia and Peru. Having successfully negotiated several bilateral treaties of alliance between Colombia and other Latin American countries, Bolívar proposed a general conference at Panama. The Liberator had not originally included the United States on the invitation list, but Colombian officials, acting on their own responsibility during Bolívar's absence in

Peru, sounded out the Adams administration on the idea. The agenda suggested for the Panama Congress included such matters as the codification of international law, joint measures to enforce the noncolonization principle, abolition of the slave trade, and a common policy toward the Negro republic of Haiti. The Colombian government discreetly omitted mention of certain other proposals it hoped to make at Panama, such as the launching of a joint Mexican-Colombian expedition to overthrow Spanish rule in Cuba and Puerto Rico and the Pan-Americanizing of the Monroe Doctrine through a joint defense treaty.

Adams and Clay, after consultation with the rest of the Cabinet, decided the United States should be represented at the Panama Congress. The President first tried to persuade the distinguished Albert Gallatin to head the American delegation. When Gallatin refused, Adams nominated Richard C. Anderson, the United States Minister to Colombia, and John Sergeant, a well-known Philadelphia lawyer. In a special message to Congress on December 26, 1825, the President asked confirmation of these appointments and an appropriation to pay the expenses of the mission. He promised that the government would not contract alliances nor engage in any project importing hostility to any other nation. Instead, it would confine its efforts to seeking commercial reciprocity, freedom of the seas, and support of the noncolonization principle.

The Panama Congress project encountered suspicion and opposition from Congress. Much of this hostility was purely political. The supporters of Andrew Jackson, embittered by the events that had sent Adams to the White House instead of their own hero, were determined to wreck the administration. Clay, who had acted as kingmaker in the election of 1824, was particularly hated, and any project with which he was closely connected was certain to be defeated. So bitter was the feeling that the vitriolic John Randolph denounced Adams and Clay as a "combination of the Puritan with the black-legg" and a "coalition of Blifil and Black George"—appellations so offensive to Clay that he challenged Randolph to a duel. Fortunately both contestants missed their marks, and Adams was spared the necessity of finding a new Secretary of State.

The Panama Congress plan offended other senators on different grounds. Some of them denounced what they considered a repudiation of the isolationist policies advocated by George Washington and by John Quincy Adams himself in earlier days. Southern legislators, always fearful of a slave insurrection within the United States, were opposed to any international meeting at which Negro representatives from Haiti might be present or through which the Haitian government might obtain diplomatic recognition. On similar grounds, they were against any policy that might result in the establishment of Negro republics in Cuba or

Puerto Rico. They also frowned on a meeting that might favor abolition of slavery.

The opponents of the Panama Congress were strong enough to provoke long debate and to delay action, but in the end the legislators were unwilling to take the responsibility of defeating a mission that might enhance United States prestige in the Western Hemisphere. In March, 1826, the Senate finally approved the mission by a substantial majority, and the House followed suit a month later.

Adams and Clay appeared to have won a decisive victory in this bitter battle with their congressional enemies. The Secretary of State hoped to consolidate this triumph with a bold show of leadership at the Panama Congress. His instructions to Anderson and Sergeant suggested a series of "good neighborhood" treaties, by which the nations of the Western Hemisphere would affirm the principles of foreign policy upon which the United States had already taken its stand: noninvolvement in European wars, opposition to further European colonization in the New World and to European intervention, commercial equality and reciprocity, abolition of privateering, and other reforms in maritime law. On the other hand, Clay made clear the strong opposition of the United States to any Mexican or Colombian expedition against Cuba and Puerto Rico. He was also conservative on the recognition of Haitian independence, claiming that the Negro regime was still partially under French control.

Clay's pronouncements, however, never reached the ears of the Latin American representatives who assembled at Panama on June 22, 1826. Sergeant, fearful of traveling in the pestilential tropics during the summer heat, refused to leave the United States until autumn. Anderson, more courageous but less wise, set out from Bogotá, Colombia, only to be struck down by fever in the port city of Cartagena, where he died on July 24. Although dismayed by these mishaps, President Adams still hoped his country might be represented when the congress reconvened in the more healthful city of Tacubaya, Mexico, to which it had been adjourned after three weeks of deliberation at Panama. He accordingly appointed Joel Poinsett, American Minister to Mexico, to succeed Anderson and ordered the new delegate to proceed to Tacubaya with Sergeant. But ill fortune still pursued the enterprise; only one or two of the Latin American delegates straggled into the Mexican city, and the congress never formally reassembled.

All the effective work of the Panama Congress was therefore accomplished during its three weeks of deliberation in the summer of 1826. The results fell far short of Bolívar's lofty dreams. Only four of the seven well-established Latin American states were represented.[2] None of

[2] The countries which sent delegates to Panama were Colombia, Peru, Central America, and Mexico. The unrepresented states were Argentina, Brazil, and Chile.

the projected treaties of alliance and cooperation became effective. Despite its apparent failure, however, the Panama Congress had profound significance for the future. When the modern movement toward inter-American collaboration began in the late nineteenth century, the statesmen drew inspiration from the brave, but abortive, efforts of 1826.

The Panama Congress episode cost the United States much of the good will that its policy of recognition and the Monroe Doctrine had won for it in Latin America. Taking shrewd advantage of the misadventures that had left the Adams administration unrepresented at Panama, Edward J. Dawkins, the unofficial British delegate, had managed to increase English prestige and undermine that of the United States. By this diplomatic victory, Canning won back most of the ground he had lost when Monroe sent his famous message to Congress in 1823.

As the threat of European intervention evaporated, the Monroe Doctrine seemed to lose whatever importance it had had. The United States turned its back on both Europe and Latin America and devoted its energies to internal development and the acquisition of contiguous territories. The resulting policy of expansion was one much more likely to arouse Latin American fears and jealousies than to lay the basis for a policy of friendly cooperation. The revival of the Monroe Doctrine and increased participation in the affairs of the Western Hemisphere were developments postponed for later periods of American history.

10

REPAIRING RELATIONS WITH
FRANCE AND ENGLAND

The success or failure of American Presidents in the field of foreign policy has often been more influenced by time and circumstance than by their training and experience. Probably no man ever entered the White House with a more impressive record of diplomatic accomplishment than did John Quincy Adams. Yet his Presidential years were marked with frustrations in the foreign field no less painful than those he encountered in domestic politics. On the other hand, from Andrew Jackson's faulty education and his rash aggressiveness in the Florida affair, it might have been expected that his terms in office would be filled with diplomatic storms. Strange to relate, however, Jackson, as President, not only avoided dangerous adventures, but succeeded in solving some of the identical problems that had confounded Adams.

Jackson's successors, the Democrat, Martin Van Buren, and the Whigs, William Henry Harrison and John Tyler, were seldom faced with serious crises in the field of foreign affairs. True, minor irritations with England and France were never lacking, and on several occasions the glowing embers of discord threatened to be fanned into flame by some sudden gust. Any widespread conflagration was prevented from developing, however, because common-sense diplomacy served the vital function of throwing water upon any menacing blaze.

Trade with the West Indies

Jackson chose as his first Secretary of State Martin Van Buren, the shrewd leader of the New York Democracy. Van Buren was totally lacking in diplomatic experience, but he was an able lawyer, calm and unruffled in manner, and well equipped with common sense. A reshuffling of offices in 1831 made Edward Livingston Secretary of State, while in subsequent developments, Louis McLane of Delaware was Secretary from 1833 to 1834, and John Forsyth of Georgia from 1834 to 1837. Despite this bewildering procession through the State Department, Jacksonian foreign policy was not lacking in continuity. The old general continued to be master in his own house, and Van Buren remained his most trusted adviser.

One of the most troublesome problems Jackson and Van Buren inherited from Adams and Clay was that of American commercial rights in the West Indies. It will be recalled that the British West Indies had been the most valuable market for colonial American merchants and that this market had been largely lost when the United States declared its independence. Several attempts had been made to negotiate on this issue, notably during Jay's mission of 1794, but no satisfactory basis for settlement had been discovered.

Although the need for American provisions during the Napoleonic wars had led to partial relaxation of the British Navigation Acts, the old system was reimposed after those hostilities were over. British ports in both the West Indies and North America were closed again to all foreign shipping. English ships were allowed to carry on a limited trade between the British West Indies and the United States, it is true, but American products such as lumber and provisions, that might compete with similar commodities from British North American colonies, were excluded.

The West Indian planters complained of the high cost of provisions and agitated for admission of American ships with their cheaper cargoes. Counterbalancing this pressure, however, was the insistence of Canadian lumbermen and fishermen and British merchants that any relaxation of the mercantile system would ruin them. Caught between these conflicting forces, the British government had to move cautiously. It was willing to discuss concessions to the United States, but demanded reciprocal advantages at every point.

Acting upon the advice of President Monroe and Secretary of State Adams, Congress tried to force the British hand by retaliatory legislation. Through a mild act of 1817 and a more stringent one of 1818, British ships coming from or going to the British West Indies were excluded from American ports. When these measures did not bring satisfactory concessions, Congress passed a still more severe retaliatory law in 1820. The resulting nonintercourse caused great hardship both in the West Indies and in the southern part of the United States, from which many products had hitherto been carried to the islands in English ships. Britain and the United States were like two rough-and-tumble fighters, each grasping the other's throat, waiting for the other to yield.

England made the initial conciliatory move as a result of the demand for a change of policy not only from the West Indian planters, but from moderate Tories who were now advocating some modification of the old mercantilist system. In 1822, Parliament offered to open a limited number of British colonial ports to American ships, but only after carefully enumerating the commodities Americans could take in and out of such ports. Since the British concessions were made contingent upon a comparable relaxation on the American side, Congress passed modifying legislation in 1822 and 1823.

These timid, but wholesome, steps toward reciprocity were halted, however, by a new controversy. Britain persisted in giving preferential tariff rates to her own colonies, while the United States collected higher tonnage taxes and customs duties from English vessels carrying British colonial goods than was charged on similar items brought in by American ships. In 1825 a new act of Parliament brought this issue to a head. The Navigation Acts were again amended, this time in particulars that placed American merchants at a disadvantage in both the West Indies and Latin America. Moreover, this new law carried the threat that American ships would once again be excluded from West Indian ports unless the discriminatory duties on British vessels were removed.

In his reaction to British pressure, President Adams displayed both the nationalism and the stubbornness characteristic of his family. Not only did he oppose any congressional action to meet the British demands, but he delayed further negotiations for many months. It was not until the summer of 1826 that he instructed Albert Gallatin, now Minister to England, to offer concessions—but then it was too late. The British had already taken the final step of closing the West Indies, as well as many other imperial ports to American ships. Adams responded with a proclamation denying British vessels from the West Indies the right to enter ports of the United States.

Although the retaliatory measures of the two governments had now halted all direct trade between the United States and the British West Indies, the results were less damaging than might have been anticipated. American ships were still able to carry on a large indirect trade with the English colonies through the neighboring Danish and French islands. Nevertheless, Adams's policy was bitterly condemned in the agricultural South. The President was denounced by his political opponents for "folly," "impolicy and imbecility," and "pertinacious continuance in error." Such attacks contributed to the growing unpopularity of Adams and his defeat in the election of 1828.

Jackson and Van Buren made the West Indies trade problem one of their first concerns. In instructions to Louis McLane, then Minister to England, the Secretary of State repudiated completely the policy of Adams and Clay. "Their views...," Van Buren wrote, "have been submitted to the people of the United States, and the counsels by which your conduct is now directed are the result of the judgment expressed by the only earthly tribunal to which the late Administration was amenable for its acts." The English government was to be informed that the United States was now willing to accept the conditions laid down in the British act of 1825.

McLane discovered, however, that Lord Aberdeen, the British Foreign Secretary, was not eager to accept the American proposal. British colonial exporters from St. Johns, Halifax, and Montreal had profited by the exclusion of American merchants and demanded that the home government continue to protect their interests.

Jackson, not a patient man, soon began to grumble at the delay and suggested that a prohibition on trade between the United States and Canada might be necessary to bring England to terms. It was decided, however, to postpone further retaliation until still another olive branch had been extended. Therefore in 1830, Congress empowered the President to open American ports to British ships from the West Indies whenever he received satisfactory evidence that those colonial ports had been opened to American vessels.

The British now decided to come to terms, and what was known as the "Reciprocity of 1830" was arranged. This provided a fair compromise of the issues that had so long divided the two countries. American merchants, farmers, fishermen, and lumbermen were benefited by new British regulations allowing American ships to enter British West Indies ports with almost all kinds of American goods. These vessels were also permitted to carry West Indian products both to the United States and to foreign countries, although not to other British Empire ports. At the same time, however, the British were careful to protect the interests of their own colonies and merchants. They maintained their right, which Adams and Clay had disputed, to grant preferential duties to imports into the West Indies from their own colonies. Since this gave an advantage to the British in the carrying trade, much American produce, destined for the West Indies, continued to go through Halifax and other British North American ports.

The privileges extended to the British produced some condemnation of the reciprocity agreement in the commercial centers of the United States. Opponents of the administration also sharply criticized Van Buren's instructions to McLane in 1829. These, declared Daniel Webster, were derogatory to the character and honor of the United States.[1] Nevertheless, Jackson's settlement of the West Indies problem was highly popular

---

[1] Opponents of the administration were able to use these instructions to McLane effectively in blocking Senate confirmation for Jackson's nomination of Van Buren as Minister to England in 1832.

in sections of the country that produced a surplus for export. The President's supporters praised him in lavish terms; "Honor to the President of the people's choice!" proclaimed one election handbill. The trade lost "by the blundering diplomacy of the coalition administration" had been restored "by the upright, able, and honest administration of Andrew Jackson."

Claims against France

A second exasperating problem inherited by Jackson was that of the so-called "spoliation claims" against France, which resulted from damages suffered by American merchants and shipowners through Napoleonic seizures. When the able Albert Gallatin, Minister to France from 1816 to 1823, had pressed these claims upon the government of Louis XVIII, he had met with evasions. Although the restored Bourbons did not deny the illegality of many of Napoleon's acts, they were reluctant to pay for such misdeeds. Indeed, they protested that the nation would be bankrupted were all such foreign demands met.

To counter the spoliation claims, France asserted that the United States owed her money on two old bills. One of these was the troublesome Beaumarchais account, unsettled since Revolutionary War days; [2] the other arose from a disputed interpretation of article 8 of the Louisiana Purchase Treaty of 1803. The stipulation that France was to enjoy in the ports of the ceded territory the commercial privileges of "the most favored nation" was interpreted by France to mean that the United States should automatically extend to her certain concessions allowed to Great Britain on a reciprocal basis in 1815. The United States denied this, contending that France was not entitled to equal treatment with Great Britain unless she made the same or equivalent concessions to the United States. [3]

President Jackson appointed William Rives of Virginia as Minister to France. In dealing with the tangled web of conflicting claims, Rives demonstrated persistence and energy. He had almost brought the Bourbon government to the point of settlement when the Revolution of 1830 swept Charles X from the throne, and he had to begin all over again with the government of Louis Philippe. The new king, who had lived briefly

[2] See chap. 1.

[3] The point, though technical, was important for future reciprocity policy. The United States at this time was insisting upon a "conditional most favored nation" policy—that is, reciprocal concessions made to one nation should not automatically extend to other nations unless those other nations made equivalent concessions to the United States. France was advocating "unconditional most favored nation" policy— that is, automatic extension of concessions made to one nation to all other nations enjoying most favored nation relations with the granting power.

in the United States during his days of exile, professed eagerness for good relations. None too secure on his throne, however, he hesitated to commit his government to agreements that would cost money and necessitate the imposition of new taxes. To help overcome the hesitation of the king and his ministers, Rives recruited the assistance of America's old friend, the Marquis de Lafayette.

At last on July 4, 1831, the two nations concluded a treaty that embodied a sensible financial compromise. France agreed to pay the United States a total of 25 million francs in six annual installments, and the United States promised to pay France 1.5 million francs, to be deducted from the French payments. The United States did not concede the French interpretation of the Louisiana Purchase Treaty, but mollified Gallic complaints with a reduction of tariff rates on French wines.

Congress, well satisfied with the bargain, quickly passed the necessary legislation to implement the treaty. In France, however, the situation was different. The government was sharply criticized for agreeing to pay too much, and the Chamber of Deputies demonstrated strong reluctance to make the needed appropriations.

The first installment fell due on February 2, 1833, a year after the treaty was ratified. When no proffer of money was forthcoming, the Jackson administration attempted to force the issue by drawing a draft upon France for the amount due. The draft was returned unpaid for lack of funds, with resultant hard feelings on both sides. The French government was irritated with the United States for attempting that form of collection; Jackson was angry both with France for failing to pay, and with his old antagonist, the Bank of the United States, for its audacity in charging the government $175,000 in damages and fees on the abortive transaction.

When Edward Livingston arrived in Paris in the autumn of 1833 to succeed Rives as Minister, he was assured by Louis Philippe that the treaty terms would be fulfilled. But the king proved unable to keep his pledge because the Chamber of Deputies refused to make the necessary appropriation. Louis McLane, now Jackson's Secretary of State, urged the President to retaliate by asking Congress for authority to commission privateers against French commerce. Jackson, with his customary belligerency, was eager to act upon this advice, but, thanks to the less warlike influence of Vice President Van Buren and Roger Taney, the Secretary of the Treasury, it was decided to give the French government more time.

A year later the situation remained the same. Louis Philippe still professed his desire to make the required payments, but the Chamber of Deputies still did nothing to help him. A dispatch from Minister Livingston hinted that the royal hand would be strengthened if Jackson's annual message to Congress demonstrated "a strong national feeling on the subject." This was all the encouragement the President needed to include some exceedingly stiff language in his message of December 1, 1834. "It is my conviction," Jackson declared, "that the United States ought to insist on a prompt execution of the treaty, and in case it be refused or longer delayed take redress into their own hands." Appropriate redress, he advised Congress, would be to seize enough French property in the United States, either private or public, to satisfy the debt.

If Louis Philippe's ministers had indeed invited Jackson to exert a degree of pressure upon France, they received more than they wanted. The President's aggressive language, as reported in the Paris press, was so deeply resented that the ministry did not dare ignore it. The Chamber of Deputies appropriated the money due the United States, but directed that payment not be made until an apology was offered for Jackson's unkind references to France.

These developments resulted in a new and more serious deadlock. Jackson took the position that no foreign government could require an apology or explanation for language not addressed to that government at all, but to Congress. The annual message was held to have a purely domestic character, under which the President was simply carrying out his constitutional obligation to give Congress "information of the state of the Union" and to recommend "such measures as he shall judge necessary and expedient." When both France and the United States ordered home their respective ministers, the situation began to resemble that which had preceded the quasi-war of 1798.

Fortunately, however, both governments really desired peace. President Jackson made a conciliatory gesture in his annual message of December 7, 1835. Although he assured Congress that national honor would "never be strained by an apology" from him for "the statement of truth and the performance of duty," he denied that in his earlier words he had intended "to menace or insult the Government of France." In a second message to Congress a month later, he repeated his refusal to apologize, but professed his pacific intentions.

The British government now offered to mediate, and a formula for settlement was soon discovered. The French government sent word that "the frank and honorable manner" in which the President had expressed himself had removed the obstacles in the way of executing a treaty. On May 6, 1836, Jackson was able to inform Congress that four overdue installments had been received and that cordial relations were now restored with France.

Prior to this happy ending, Jackson's handling of the spoliation claims had been under some attack in Congress and elsewhere as unduly belligerent. The final outcome of the affair quieted criticism, however, and added to the President's extraordinary popularity.

Rebellions in Canada

The northern boundary of the United States, so often the area of tension in American diplomatic relations, once again became a sore spot between 1837 and 1842. Troubles began with the outbreak of rebellions across the border in 1837. In Lower Canada (the present-day Province of Quebec), the French leader, Louis Papineau, unsuccessful in obtaining larger powers of self-government for the colonial assembly, incited his followers to revolt. When British authorities speedily suppressed the uprising, Papineau fled to the United States. In Upper Canada (present-day Ontario), conflict arose out of the discontent of recent immigrants from the United States and Great Britain with the oligarchical control of the colonial government by British officials and the old conservative element descended from American Loyalist stock of Revolutionary War days. Rebuffed in their efforts to obtain reforms, the liberals resorted to arms. When the rebels were defeated in an attack upon Toronto, they retreated to Navy Island, a bit of Canadian territory in the Niagara River.

Although William Lyon Mackenzie, the rebel leader, had only about twenty followers with him when he reached the island, he followed a bold course. Running up a flag containing twin stars and a new moon emerging from the clouds, he announced the establishment of a provisional government and invited enlistments in his "army." His stirring proclamations and promises of free land soon attracted a thousand recruits to Navy Island, some from Canada and others from the United States. To command this irregular company, Mackenzie commissioned Rensselaer Van Rensselaer, a member of New York's most famous landholding family.

The explosive possibilities of this situation were obvious. Sympathy for the Canadian rebels ran high in Buffalo and other American border towns, where Mackenzie spoke to crowded public meetings. Arms, provisions, and recruits were easily transported to Navy Island. This dangerous state of excitement on the American side of the line was paralleled in Canada, where indignant British officials and Canadian loyalists blamed the United States not only for the material aid the rebels were obtaining, but also for the dangerous democratic ideas that had provoked this challenge to British authority.

President Van Buren recognized from the beginning the danger of serious trouble. On December 7, 1837, he requested the governors of New York, Vermont, and Michigan to arrest promptly anyone engaged in hostile preparations against Canadian territory. On January 5, 1838, he warned Americans not to give aid to the rebels. United States troops under the command of General Winfield Scott were sent to Buffalo to watch the border, and two steam vessels were hired to patrol Lake Erie and Lake Ontario in order to intercept any American boats attempting to run men and supplies into Canada. These efforts were not at first successful because of widespread American sympathy with the rebels and the ease with which the border could be crossed. Eventually, however, the insurgent cause was doomed. Van Rensselaer and other leaders fell into British hands, while Mackenzie was arrested and imprisoned on one of his recruiting forays into the United States.

The Caroline Affair

During the early days of the insurrection before Van Buren's measures to prevent trouble could become effective, an incident occurred that threatened to have most serious consequences. The *Caroline*, an American-owned steamship, had been hired by the rebels to transport men and supplies to Navy Island. Determined to end this nuisance, the colonel in charge of the loyalist Canadian troops in the area ordered a small naval force to cross the river and destroy the *Caroline*. This mission was carried out with dramatic decisiveness on the night of December 29, 1837. The Canadians caught the offending vessel at a wharf on the American side of the river and overpowered the crew in a scuffle in which one American, Amos Durfee, was killed. Set afire and adrift, the *Caroline* sank to the bottom of the river a mile or two above Niagara Falls.

This audacious deed was vigorously applauded as a justifiable act of self-defense on the Canadian side of the line. Members of the raiding party were feted as heroes, and the commanding officer was knighted by the British government.

Across the river in Buffalo, however, the deed was viewed quite differently. Durfee's body was displayed on the city hall piazza, and placards grimly illustrated with coffins announced his funeral. The excitement spread from one border town to another, as the *Buffalo Daily Star* declared that "the whole frontier from Buffalo to Lake Ontario now bristles with bayonets." Over the next two weeks rebel recruiting activities in the United States reached their peak. Inflamed partisans broke into government arsenals to obtain arms.

The danger that these activities might plunge the United States into war was averted by the countermeasures of the Van Buren administration, the vigorous defense of the frontier by loyal Canadian forces, and the sobering influence of responsible American citizens who condemned dangerous meddling in Canadian affairs. Even so, however, the threat of new incidents continued throughout 1838. So-called "Hunters' Lodges" and other secret societies pledged to help the rebels kept up an incessant agitation. Several attempts to invade Canada were suppressed; one of these occurred in December, 1838, when four hundred "Hunters" marched through the streets of Detroit, shouting "Remember the *Caroline!*" Armed men crossed from Detroit into Windsor, Canada, where they set fire to a Canadian steamer. Several of the raiders were captured by the Canadians and executed.

Meanwhile, the *Caroline* affair had provided plentiful material to keep the diplomats busy. Secretary of State John Forsyth denounced this violation of American sovereignty and demanded both indemnity and pledges that such acts would not be permitted in the future. On the other hand, Lord Palmerston, the British Foreign Secretary, defended the attack as a necessary act of self-defense. Controversy dragged on over the next three years until an incident occurred to bring the issue to a crisis.

The McLeod Affair

In November, 1840, one Alexander McLeod fell under suspicion of being the man who had killed Amos Durfee aboard the *Caroline*. As a consequence, McLeod was arrested, imprisoned at Lockport, New York, and indicted for murder. All the angry excitement of the earlier days was rekindled as this opportunity to avenge Durfee's death presented itself. Upstate New York opinion demanded blood. Even if the unfortunate McLeod escaped legal execution, he was in danger of being lynched by some irate mob.

The British government demanded McLeod's immediate release. The destruction of the *Caroline* was described as a public act carried out under official orders for which individual subordinates could not be held responsible. Moreover, so the British asserted, McLeod had not even been present on the scene. Lord Palmerston, famous for diplomatic vigor, warned the American Minister in London that the execution of the accused man would be the signal for war.

This diplomatic time bomb was left ticking on Washington desks when the Democrats turned over the government to the Whig President-elect, William Henry Harrison. Daniel Webster, the new Secretary of State, sought desperately for some means of detaching the fuse. He sent an emissary to Albany to ask the help of Governor William Seward in having the proceedings against McLeod dismissed. But Seward, fearful of public opinion and jealous of states' rights, insisted that the prisoner be tried. He did confide, however, that strong evidence of McLeod's innocence had been discovered, so a pardon might be expected in case of conviction.

Even this promise by the governor that McLeod would not go to the gallows did not quiet Webster's apprehensions. If the case went to trial, public opinion might become so aroused that an acquittal would be followed by mob action. The United States district attorney was ordered to appear for McLeod in an attempt to have the prisoner released through habeas corpus proceedings, but the New York Supreme Court denied the motion. The situation was a dramatic demonstration of the peculiarities of the American constitutional system. While the Federal government, charged with sole responsibility in foreign affairs, had to deal with all the diplomatic complications created by McLeod's impending trial, the prisoner's fate was entirely in the hands of the New York State authorities. There was no legal means by which the Federal officials could obtain his release.

As the trial date approached, Webster became increasingly apprehensive. To John Tyler, who had succeeded to the Presidency upon the death of Harrison, the Secretary wrote: "It becomes us to take all possible care that no personal violence be used on McLeod. If a mob should kill him, War w'd be inevitable, in ten days. Of this there is no doubt." The feeling of tension was intensified by reports of new border raid plots on the part of the secret societies, the mobilizing of Canadian defense forces, and indications from England that the British navy was being alerted for possible action.

McLeod was finally brought to trial in Utica, New York. The town was filled with strangers, including Mackenzie and other Canadian agitators, but adequate steps had been taken to protect the prisoner and the trial went forward in orderly fashion. A strong defense was presented, based on the alibi and the contention that McLeod had not even participated in the attack on the *Caroline*. On October 12, 1841, the jury brought in a verdict of not guilty, and McLeod was safely escorted across the border, to the intense relief of the statesmen of both countries.

In order to avoid such dangerous situations in the future, Congress enacted a law in 1842, authorizing the Federal courts to issue writs of habeas corpus and discharge from custody any person accused of an unlawful act proved to have been committed under the orders of a foreign government. This would have the effect of transferring such cases to the jurisdiction of the Federal courts.

McLeod's acquittal did not settle the dispute that had arisen out of the *Caroline* affair itself. Webster, like his predecessor, contended that the attack had been an unwarranted violation of American sovereignty. Lord Palmerston insisted it had been a necessary act of self-defense for which Britain would never apologize, and Lord Aberdeen, who succeeded Palmerston in the Foreign Office in 1841, took the same position. Nevertheless, Webster was finally able to reach a satisfactory understanding with Lord Ashburton, whom Lord Aberdeen sent to the United States to deal with various pending controversies. By an informal exchange of notes during the summer of 1842, Ashburton acknowledged that the United States was correct in the general principles of international law involved and that the attack on the *Caroline* was therefore justifiable only on the grounds of overwhelming necessity. "Looking back to what passed at the distance of time," the English diplomat wrote, "what is, perhaps, most to be regretted is that some explanation and apology for this occurrence was not immediately made." Webster closed the book on the episode by replying that the President received this acknowledgment "in the conciliatory spirit which marks your Lordship's letter."

The Northeast Boundary Dispute

Back in 1782 when the American and British commissioners at Paris were attempting to mark the limits of the new nation, it had seemed reasonable to use the "highlands which divide those rivers that empty themselves into the river St. Lawrence from those which fall into the Atlantic Ocean" to define this part of the boundary. To make clear to themselves just what they meant, the negotiators had marked out the line on a map, but this had unfortunately disappeared after the treaty was signed. The result was confusion and dispute.

In the Treaty of Ghent of 1814 several mixed commissions were provided to deal with this and other unsettled boundary questions. From 1816 to 1821 the particular two-man commission charged with locating the elusive watershed between the St. Lawrence and the Atlantic struggled with its assignment. The commissioners were far apart in their ideas. The American contended that the stipulated highlands were the Notre Dame Mountains, which lay far to the north, only 30 or 40 miles below the St. Lawrence. The British commissioner, on the contrary, insisted that the specified highlands lay along the headwaters of the Penobscot and the Kennebec, some hundred miles farther south. Over 12,000 square miles were thus in dispute. Although most of it was desolate country, valuable only for its timber, neither party would recede from its claim. The British contention, somewhat farfetched in that it was based on the theory that the St. John River, emptying into the Bay of Fundy, should not be considered one of the rivers flowing into the Atlantic Ocean, was stubbornly argued for strategic reasons. Only by combatting the American claim could the British keep control over the natural transportation routes between the important cities of Quebec and St. John. On the other hand, the new state of Maine, created by separation from Massachusetts in 1820, was determined to retain as much territory as possible.

In 1822 the mixed commission finally admitted complete inability to fix the line, and the two governments were faced with the problem of what to do next. Already the advancing frontiersmen of Maine and New Brunswick were moving into the disputed territory. The Treaty of Ghent had provided that questions left unsettled by the mixed commissions might be submitted to the arbitration of some friendly sovereign, but the United

States, knowing the proclivity of arbitrators to split the difference rather than determine the merits of a difficult case, was reluctant to use this means of settlement. Unable to reach a decision in direct negotiations the two nations finally agreed in 1827 to submit the dispute to the King of the Netherlands.

American forebodings were realized in the King's decision handed down in 1831. Asserting that it had been impossible to define the line on the basis of the Treaty of 1783, the King recommended a so-called "line of convenience" or compromise line. This would have awarded about two-thirds of the disputed territory to the United States.

When the British government announced its willingness to accept the award, the Jackson administration was confronted with a difficult decision. Since the King of the Netherlands had disregarded the terms of submission by basing his findings upon compromise rather than on an interpretation of the old treaty, the United States did not feel bound to accept the results of the arbitration. Nevertheless, the award was sufficiently favorable so that President Jackson's personal inclination was to accept it as the best way out of a bad situation. Angry protests from Maine and Massachusetts warned the President, however, that this might be highly unpopular, and in the end Jackson shifted the responsibility to the Senate. There a constitutional issue was raised in the claim that Maine could not be deprived of territory without its consent, and the arbitral award was rejected.

Over the next decade the boundary dispute became increasingly bitter, particularly as it was aggravated by wrangling frontiersmen and self-important local officials. When Maine sent a census taker into the disputed territory in 1838, he was arrested and lodged in a New Brunswick jail. The following year the so-called Aroostook War broke out. At the direction of the Maine legislature, land agents, accompanied by two hundred men, went to the Aroostook River with orders to arrest and imprison trespassers. This force found itself outnumbered by a company of three hundred armed New Brunswick men. Fifty of the Maine men were captured and put in jail. The excited Maine legislature now appropriated $800,000 for a military force to defend its borders and called upon the Federal government for aid. Congress responded by an act, passed by a vote of 201 to 6 in the House and unanimously in the Senate, which authorized President Van Buren to use force if necessary to resist any British attempt to establish exclusive jurisdiction over the area in dispute.

Although the Aroostook War had been bloodless up to now, real hostilities seemed inevitable unless means were found to lessen the rising tension. Fortunately on February 27, 1839, the two governments arranged a modus vivendi,[4] providing for the release of the American

---

[4] Literally, a mode of living—hence a temporary arrangement between two governments to avoid clashes pending final settlement of a dispute.

prisoners and a withdrawal of military forces from the disputed territory. An uneasy truce was thereafter maintained.

On this, as on other issues, the United States found Britain difficult to deal with so long as the pugnacious Lord Palmerston remained in the Foreign Office. In the fall of 1841, however, changes of government in both Washington and London provided hope that a fresh effort to settle the dangerous dispute might be made. Daniel Webster, who had become Secretary of State, was the nation's most famous lawyer and orator. As the hero of New England, he could expect to receive much more cooperation from Maine and Massachusetts than that given his Democratic predecessor from Georgia. On the other side of the Atlantic, Palmerston had been succeeded as Foreign Secretary by the more conciliatory Lord Aberdeen.

The Webster-Ashburton Treaty

To seek a settlement of the various outstanding differences between Great Britain and the United States, the London government sent Lord Ashburton to America in 1842. It was an excellent appointment. By birth Lord Ashburton was Alexander Baring, head of one of England's most famous banking firms. As a young man he had lived several years in the United States, managing the affairs of the family firm and marrying an American woman, the daughter of a wealthy United States Senator from Pennsylvania. Webster had met Ashburton on a trip to London in 1839, and the two men had developed a mutual liking. When the special envoy arrived in Washington in April, he immediately became the central figure in a gay round of banquets and parties.

Webster was well aware that his most difficult negotiations might have to be with his fellow New Englanders, rather than with Lord Ashburton. In softening up the state authorities for the compromise he knew would be necessary, the Secretary of State made shrewd use of a secret document placed in his hands by Professor Jared Sparks of Harvard College. During his researches on the history of the American Revolution, Sparks had discovered in French archives an old map of North America with a red line indicating the boundary between Canada and the other colonies. The professor strongly suspected that this was the very map used by Franklin and his fellow diplomats in the negotiations of 1782. If so, the document was extremely damaging to the American case, because it indicated a boundary even farther to the south than the English claimed. Webster secretly showed Sparks's copy of the map to his New England friends to drive home the point that the time had come to make the best deal possible on the disputed boundary. At Webster's request, Maine and Massachusetts sent commissioners to Washington to consult with him during the negotiations.

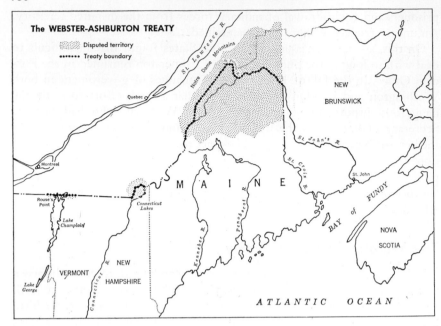

The WEBSTER-ASHBURTON TREATY

Despite the favoring circumstances, the early exchange of notes between Webster and Ashburton demonstrated that the two governments were still far apart in their ideas. It was difficult for the Englishman to understand the peculiarities of the American political system under which, as he said, "the representatives of a state could block the plans of the nation." In the darkest period of the negotiations, President Tyler kept the discussions going by a personal appeal to Lord Ashburton.

After slaving through many weeks of an unusually hot summer, the two diplomats finally agreed to the Webster-Ashburton Treaty of August 9, 1842. Abandoning the attempt to make sense of the old treaty of 1783, the negotiators charted a compromise line, which ran from the source of the St. Croix River due north to the St. John River. It then followed the St. John, the St. Francis, and other waterways to the outlet of Lake Pohenagamook. From this northernmost point the line took a southwesterly course until it intersected the 45th parallel,[5] which it followed to the St. Lawrence River.

Although the line of 1842 awarded the United States slightly less territory than that proposed by the King of the Netherlands in 1831, it was a sensible solution of a troublesome problem. Maine and Massachusetts

[5] Instead of following the true parallel, the line followed the parallel as it had been inaccurately surveyed in 1774. The practical effect of this was to confirm to the United States a fort at Rouses Point, guarding the outlet of Lake Champlain. This strategic point lay to the north of the true parallel. The Webster-Ashburton line also favored the Americans in the region to the north of the Connecticut Lakes.

were still reluctant to accept the boundary, but were induced to do so partly by the adroit use Webster made of the red-line map, and partly because the United States, under a treaty clause, compensated each of them with $150,000 for expenses incurred during the course of the long dispute. An additional concession to Maine was the free use of the St. John River in transporting forest products to the sea.

The treaty also dealt with several other matters. The boundary in the Lake Huron–Lake Superior region and farther west to the Lake of the Woods was now clearly defined. More satisfactory provisions for the extradition of persons indicted for crime were included. Finally, Great Britain and the United States agreed that each maintain a naval squadron off the African coast adequate to enforce their respective laws prohibiting the foreign slave trade. The two squadrons were to operate separately, but their commanders must cooperate with each other.

This last provision was intended to resolve a difficult problem that had arisen from a vigorous British campaign against this inhumane traffic. Since the slave trade was forbidden by the laws of all civilized countries, the English government had successfully persuaded most of the important nations to agree that the naval vessels of any contracting power might search any merchant ships on the high seas. The United States government, extremely sensitive on the subject of visit and search because of the impressment dispute of earlier days, had refused to enter into any such agreement. The result had been a scandalous situation in which scores of foul-smelling slave ships ran up the American flag to protect themselves against British interference. Webster's promise that his country would maintain its own squadron might have ended this abuse if the stipulation had been faithfully carried out. Unfortunately, American enforcement measures continued to be feeble.

Another dispute involving slavery was discussed by Webster and Ashburton, although no formal agreement was reached. The *Creole*, an American ship engaged in the domestic slave trade, had been en route from Hampton Roads, Virginia, to New Orleans in the fall of 1841 when the Negroes mutinied, killed one white passenger, and took the vessel into Nassau in the Bahamas. There the British authorities arrested and hanged the actual murderers, but set the rest of the slaves free on the grounds that human servitude was illegal on British soil. This episode so aroused Southern anger that Webster felt he must make a vigorous demand for either the return of the Negroes or damages. Although Ashburton had no instructions in the matter, he did promise that in the future there would be no "officious interference" with American vessels driven into the British West Indies by accident or violence.[6]

Webster tried to write into the treaty the old American contentions

[6] The *Creole* case was eventually referred to a mixed claims commission in 1853, and the United States was awarded $110,000 in damages.

on impressment. Lord Ashburton was sympathetic, but Lord Aberdeen sternly forbade any retreat from the traditional British position. The Secretary of State did, however, send a strong note, stating the American stand in terms the British government did not attempt to refute.

When the treaty was finally signed and sent to the Senate for approval, Webster had reason to be apprehensive because of the bitter political situation. After the death of Harrison, Tyler had antagonized the powerful Henry Clay by refusing to support Clay's legislative program and had in consequence been read out of the Whig party. All his Cabinet except Webster, who felt duty-bound to complete the current diplomatic negotiations, had resigned. By sticking with Tyler, Webster drew down upon his head much of the political lightning crackling around the President. Even in New England there were angry protest meetings. Since Tyler and Webster were even less popular among the Democrats, they were for the time being at least in the impotent position of politicians without a party.

Much of the prevalent bitterness was reflected in the attacks upon the treaty made by two Democratic senators, James Buchanan of Pennsylvania and Thomas H. Benton of Missouri, but the opposition soon collapsed. The treaty was generally popular throughout the country, and many doubtful senators were convinced by the circulation of the red-line map. On August 20, 1842, the upper house therefore gave its consent by a vote of 39 to 9.

The treaty's popularity in America aroused English suspicion that it was unduly favorable to the United States. There were angry protests from Canada, and Lord Palmerston made the most of the issue in the hope of bringing down the Tory government. Since the story of the red-line map was no longer a secret, Palmerston played it up in an effort to prove that Webster had used unethical tactics. This argument, however, boomeranged in astonishing fashion. During the parliamentary debate it was revealed that the British government had its own secret map, complete with a red line supposedly drawn by George III himself. And this British map, known to Palmerston during his period in office but not disclosed to his Tory successors, strongly supported the American case! In the end, Parliament passed a resolution, thanking Lord Ashburton for his success in negotiating a treaty "alike honorable and advantageous to each of the high contracting parties"—a verdict on the Webster-Ashburton Treaty that may well be adopted by present-day historians.

11

FRONTIER PRESSURES

Although sparks like those given off by the *Caroline* affair or the Aroostook War had sometimes threatened to set off explosions along the northeastern boundary, the really serious threats of war during the 1830s and 1840s developed elsewhere. Throughout these years American frontiersmen were pushing their way west, settling wherever they found inviting prospects. Political boundaries meant little to this restless breed, and they established their new homes as readily in Texas and California under the Mexican flag or in the disputed Oregon country as they did on soil undeniably American. This readiness to accept foreign jurisdiction did not mean the settlers completely adapted themselves to their new status. On the contrary, they were easily provoked to protests and revolts and to demands for annexation by the United States.

American Settlement in Texas

Just a year after the signing of the Adams-Onís Treaty, which confirmed Spain's title to Texas, the Spanish governor of this province was surprised by a visit from one Moses Austin, a Connecticut Yankee who had been living for some twenty years in Missouri. In accordance with the Spanish policy of excluding all foreigners, Austin was at first ordered to leave Texas at once. He talked so persuasively, however, that not only was he allowed to prolong his visit, but he soon influenced the governor to recommend that he be given a large tract of land.

By a decree of January 17, 1821, the Spanish viceroy of Mexico granted Austin permission to settle with three hundred families in Texas—provided they took an oath of allegiance to the King of Spain and professed the Catholic religion. Two considerations probably underlay the remarkable generosity of this grant: 1821 was a year of revolution in the Spanish fatherland, liberal principles were popular, and a relaxation of the rigid colonial system seemed to be in order; secondly, the indulgent viceroy apparently assumed the new settlers would be French and Spanish Catholics discontented with American rule over the Louisiana Territory.

Moses Austin died before he could take advantage of this liberal decree, but his son, Stephen, an able young man of twenty-seven, promptly claimed the same rights. By December, 1821, the first American settlement was established on the fertile lands of the Brazos River Valley in southeastern Texas. Yet recent events in Mexico temporarily obscured the Austin claim. The Mexican people, following the example of those in other Spanish colonies, had just proclaimed their independence, and it was not until 1823 that the new regime confirmed Austin's grant and entrusted him with almost complete powers of government over his fellow settlers. In addition, this colonization act provided both for direct land grants to individual settlers and indirect ones through *empresarios* or contractors who were to obtain substantial bonuses for their own use if they settled two hundred families in Texas. Although this law required the newcomers to be Catholics, it was exceedingly liberal in all other respects.

This act of 1823 was soon supplanted by various measures, but, although the details changed, the philosophy behind them remained the same, at least until 1827. Mexican policy aimed at encouraging immigration, and land-hungry Americans, particularly Southerners seeking cheap land on which to grow cotton, were more than ready to be encouraged. Ambitious *empresarios* recruited companies of settlers, while restless squatters moved into Texas without bothering about legal formalities. The British Minister to Mexico predicted grave dangers ahead in a dispatch of 1825 to his Foreign Office:

> On the most moderate computation six hundred North American families are already established in Texas; their numbers are increasing daily, and though they nominally recognize the authority of the Mexican Government, a very little time will enable them to set at defiance any attempt to enforce it.... In the event of a rupture between this country and the United States, their feelings and earlier connections will naturally lead them to side with the latter; and in time of peace their lawless habits, and dislike of all restraints, will, as naturally, induce them to take advantage of their position which is admirably adapted for a great smuggling trade, and to resist all attempts to suppress it. In short, Mexico, though she may gain in point of numbers, will not, certainly, acquire any real strength, by such an addition to her population.[1]

[1] Reprinted by permission of Charles Scribner's Sons from George L. Rives, *The United States and Mexico, 1821–1848* (Copyright 1913 by Charles Scribner's Sons, New York), vol. I, pp. 153–154.

Growing Friction

As Minister Ward and other observers predicted, the rapidly growing American population in Texas was bound to arouse Mexican apprehensions. Just as inevitably, any Mexican attempt to halt immigration or to curb the activities of the settlers was certain to create serious resentment.

In 1824, the Republic of Mexico had adopted a federal constitution, modeled in some degree upon that of the United States. Although provision was made for a generous degree of states' rights, Texas was merged in the large state of Coahuila-Texas. Under this arrangement, the American settlers were unhappy: the state capital and courts were hundreds of miles away and staffed by Mexicans in whom the Americans had little confidence. Consequently, the Texans substituted where they could informal associations and courts.

So long as the Texans were left to shift for themselves, they were reasonably contented with Mexican rule. This period of salutary neglect lasted for several years because the Mexicans were preoccupied with their own political problems. Under Spanish rule they had had almost no opportunity to govern themselves, and so the new republic was kept in turmoil by tumultous elections, *coups d'état*, military dictatorships, and bitter civil wars.

Nevertheless, Mexican political leaders found time to become increasingly suspicious of the United States. Joel R. Poinsett and Anthony Butler, American Ministers to Mexico during the administrations of Adams and Jackson, helped to initiate this suspicion because they allegedly took sides in Mexican domestic politics and engaged in various forms of intrigue. Their unpopularity increased when Mexico learned that they had been instructed to propose the American purchase of Texas.

Not only was national pride wounded by the easy assumption of Washington politicians that an offer of American gold would induce the young republic to give up some of its territory, but these clumsy efforts to purchase Texas were an important factor in changing the Mexican attitude toward American settlement in Texas. This immigration was now feared as part of an insidious plot to bring the whole territory under the Stars and Stripes. A small revolt in eastern Texas in 1826 so strengthened these fears that during the next two years Mexico issued a series of orders aimed at curbing American immigration. It was much easier to proclaim this policy than to carry it out and the stream of Americans into Texas scarcely lessened. A similar lack of firmness was demonstrated in 1829 when the Mexican government abolished slavery, only to exempt Texas from the ban when loud protests ensued.

In 1830, however, the anti-American policy took more serious form. No foreigner could enter the country without a proper passport, the importation of slaves was forbidden, and all colonization not authorized under existing contracts was banned. In addition, every effort was made to encourage Mexican settlement in Texas, which was garrisoned with convict troops to enforce the new restrictions. Some hotheaded Texans wanted to resist these drastic measures by force, but Stephen Austin counseled moderation and induced the Mexican authorities to allow a somewhat reduced immigration to continue. Thus by 1834 the population of Texas had grown to about 30,000 persons, only one-tenth of whom were Mexicans.

Although serious trouble was for the moment avoided, the growing friction could scarcely be concealed. The Texans were irked by a local situation where only seven municipalities had been organized, where all marriages and baptisms had to wait upon the infrequent visits of Roman Catholic priests, and where schools were privately organized and supported. There were economic grievances as well; facilities for coastwise trade with the rest of Mexico were undeveloped and there were serious disadvantages in selling produce and buying manufactured goods at New Orleans.

Then in 1832 General Antonio López de Santa Anna gained control of the Mexican government. Although at first he made various concessions to the Texans, by 1835 his real intentions had become clear. With the support of the army and the Church, he established what was in effect a military dictatorship. A complaisant congress set aside the constitution of 1824 in favor of a centralist system and abolished the liberal reforms of earlier regimes. The states were reduced to administrative departments, wholly dependent on the central government. Local authorities who tried to resist these changes were ruthlessly crushed as their militias were reduced to one soldier for each five hundred inhabitants and all other persons were ordered to surrender their arms.

In the resulting civil war, conservative Texans tried to preserve a strict neutrality, believing that the opposition to Santa Anna was led by selfish land speculators and merchants. During the summer and fall of 1835, however, public opinion gradually changed as the conviction grew that the new centralized regime was going to subjugate completely all of Texas. On October 2 a group of Texas volunteers did repel an attempted invasion by some of Santa Anna's troops.

The continued menace of invasion caused the Texans to establish a provisional government "in defence of their rights and liberties, which were threatened by the encroachments of military despots, and in defence of the republican principles of the federal constitution of Mexico." Nothing was said about independence; the delegates to the provisional assembly merely hoped that they could rally liberal factions in other parts of Mexico to restore the old constitution.

By this time, however, Santa Anna had so cowed the opposition elsewhere that the Texans found themselves fighting alone. In March, 1836, the situation came to a crisis with the dictator's army poised for invasion at the very moment a newly elected Texas convention was meeting to determine future policy. On March 2 the delegates unanimously adopted a declaration of independence, followed two weeks later by a constitution. The new republic immediately faced a period of fiery trial. On March 6 a hopelessly outnumbered garrison of 188 men was wiped out at the Alamo in San Antonio; less than three weeks later some 350 Texan prisoners of war, taken at Goliad, were shot in cold blood on Santa Anna's orders. The cause of Texas now had its martyrs, and the dictator was hated with greater intensity.

The military situation for the Texas army, commanded by General Sam Houston, a former Governor of Tennessee and an old friend of Andrew Jackson, seemed black as it retreated across Texas. Yet when the pursuing Santa Anna, made careless and confident after his initial victories, mistakenly divided his forces, Houston suddenly attacked at the San Jacinto River and the Texans won a quick and easy victory on April 21. Among their prisoners was none other than Santa Anna.

Although there were widespread demands for the dictator's execution in retaliation for the Goliad massacre, Houston and other cooler heads had better plans for this important captive. The terrified prisoner was more than willing to negotiate with them, and on May 14, 1836, he signed the Treaty of Velasco, providing for the withdrawal of all Mexican troops south of the Rio Grande and safe conduct for Santa Anna back to Mexican soil. Under a secret agreement signed the same day, the Mexican President promised to arrange for the Mexican congress to recognize Texan independence.

While the Texan leaders placed great importance on these treaties, their actual value in international law was small because they had been negotiated by a prisoner of war in fear of his life and were never ratified by the Mexican government. Indeed, the authorities at Mexico City promptly notified the world that they would not consider themselves bound by any agreements made under such circumstances.

As for Santa Anna, popular indignation was too great to permit the Texan government to carry out its pledge to release him. Only after several months of imprisonment was the tarnished Mexican hero allowed to return home, where he promptly repudiated his commitments with the Texans. Although he went into temporary retirement, Santa Anna was singularly indestructible, and again and again took advantage of some domestic crisis to return to power.

After the battle of San Jacinto, the Republic of Texas maintained a *de facto* independence. The Mexican armies did not launch another major invasion because their government was preoccupied with domestic problems. Nevertheless, Mexico continued to claim sovereignty over its lost province and to oppose any diplomatic step that would recognize Texas as independent.

Jackson and the Texas Problem

When the Mexican government spurned the Jackson offer—through Minister Butler—of 5 million dollars for Texas and then in due course Texas proclaimed its independence and applied for annexation by the United States, the sequence of events seemed exceedingly suspicious to many critics. It appeared to be West Florida all over again. Antislavery zealots charged that this was a wicked conspiracy of the slave interests to bring new slave states into the Union. The well-known friendship between Jackson and Houston helped lend credence to this theory. Actually, however, there is little evidence the Jackson administration instigated or improperly aided the Texas revolution. Indeed, when the President received an urgent appeal for help from Stephen Austin, he recorded his reaction in these words:

> The Texians [*sic*] before they took the step to declare themselves Independent, which has aroused and united all Mexico against them ought to have pondered well—it was a rash and premature act, our neutrality must be faithfully maintained.

The faithful maintenance of neutrality was a pious ideal easy to affirm, but difficult to enforce. Americans followed the Texas struggle with excited interest, and Texan agents found an eager response to their appeals for men and supplies. At a public meeting in New Orleans in July, 1835, the chairman urged immediate action in behalf of the suffering people of Texas by "friends of civil and religious freedom." The following October the city raised $7,000 for the good cause and sent two companies of volunteers to the front. Similar groups of armed men poured into Texas from Tennessee, Kentucky, and Alabama. Indeed, four-fifths of the soldiers killed at the Alamo, Goliad, and other disasters during the spring of 1836 are believed to have been volunteers from across the border.

The Jackson administration's halfhearted efforts to stop these violations of neutrality had little success. The laws were lax, and, when prosecutions were attempted, local sympathies were so strongly pro-Texan that convictions were almost impossible. Under the circumstances, it is not surprising that Mexico blamed its difficulties in crushing the revolt upon the United States and that bitter feelings resulted.

Reports of Mexican atrocities raised American sympathy for Texas to a high peak early in 1836, with the result that news of Houston's victory at San Jacinto was received with jubilation. John Quincy Adams, now a Massachusetts congressman, wrote in his diary: "Glorious news from Texas that Santa Anna had been defeated and taken by Houston, and shot, with all his officers," while President Jackson delightedly called for a map on which he futilely tried to locate the San Jacinto River. Memorials from all over the nation poured into Washington urging recognition of Texan independence, and Congress resolved by overwhelming majorities that this should be done when the new republic was "capable of performing the duties and fulfilling the obligations of an independent Power."

The President, however, moved with uncharacteristic caution. In an election year the Texan issue bulged with unexploded dynamite. Although the abolitionists were still a small and unpopular minority, opposition to annexation on political grounds was developing rapidly. For example, before the end of May, Adams had so far forgotten his enthusiasm for the heroes of San Jacinto that he accused the Jackson administration of scheming to involve the United States in war with Mexico to advance the slavery interests.

Thus when Texas sent William F. Wharton to Washington in December, 1836, to seek recognition and annexation, he received a discouraging reception. Jackson had just informed Congress that "it becomes us to beware of a too early movement, as it might subject us, however unjustly, to the imputation of seeking to establish the claim of our neighbors to a territory, with a view to its subsequent acquisition by ourselves."

At heart, however, Jackson had always been pro-Texas, and it is not surprising that before he left the White House he extended recognition to the young republic. Van Buren, who succeeded Jackson on March 4, 1837, dragged his feet momentarily on the new policy but finally received the new Texas Minister, General Memucan Hunt, on July 21, 1837, thus completing the formality of recognition despite bitter Mexican protests.

Annexation Rejected

Following the Texan declaration of independence, the inhabitants almost to a man favored speedy annexation by the United States. In addition to the natural feelings of a population almost all born under the American flag, there were obvious advantages to be gained, the most important being that of defense. Texas had only about 35,000 inhabitants, while across the border were 8 million Mexicans. Obviously, if the latter ever put their political house in order and united on a campaign of reconquest, Texas would be in grave danger. In September, 1836, when the Texan voters were asked to express themselves on the issue, the vote was almost unanimous for annexation. Yet Minister Hunt discovered that the American door was closed to his republic's offer. On August 25, 1837, Secretary of State Forsyth told him that acquisition of Texas would almost inevitably mean war with Mexico.

To be thus rebuffed was galling to Texan pride, and the annexation offer was formally withdrawn in favor of plans for permanent independence. Despite a large debt, an empty treasury, and serious problems of defense, the new republic seemed to have promising prospects. The acquisition of neighboring territory, perhaps as far west as the Pacific, the encouragement of immigration, and the cultivation of close diplomatic and economic ties with England and France were the long-range policies that Texan nationalists counted upon to give their country a glorious future. A Republic of Texas, larger and more powerful than the United States itself, was not beyond the range of possibility.

Tyler and Texas

Through the sinuosities of American politics, the Whigs in 1840 had nominated John Tyler of Virginia as running mate on a ticket headed by General William Henry Harrison of Indiana. When the old general died a month after his inauguration, Tyler became President. The irony of the situation lay in that fact that the new Chief Executive, although an anti-Jackson man, was in all other respects a typical states'-rights Democrat: a firm believer in free trade and the sanctity of the slavery institution.

Inevitably Tyler looked upon the Texas question differently from Van Buren. A few months after he entered the White House he suggested to Daniel Webster, the Secretary of State he had inherited from Harrison, that the acquisition of Texas would throw a "bright lustre" over his administration and would greatly benefit Eastern business interests. Tyler was an ambitious man without a party, who hoped to use the Texas issue to win a personal following and thus snatch away from powerful rivals like Clay and Van Buren either the Whig or Democratic party nomination in 1844.

Webster, however, would not support such a policy. By remaining in his Cabinet post to complete his negotiations with Lord Ashburton, the Secretary of State was already jeopardizing his political future. To aid the President in acquiring Texas would not only be suicidal to his position as leader of the New England Whigs, but would be contrary to his own scruples. Thus when Texas raised the question of annexation again in 1842, Webster gave it no encouragement. Under such circumstances, Tyler had to bide his time.

Although active agitation for annexation had quieted down, even in the South, after 1838, several developments soon revived interest. Rebuffed in

Washington, the new republic sought help from Europe. France responded by extending recognition in 1839, and England the next year. British statesmen opposed American acquisition of Texas because it would increase American domination over the Gulf of Mexico. Therefore they wanted either to leave Texas as a self-governing province under Mexico or to reconcile Mexico to Texas independence. Englishmen saw, moreover, many economic advantages in an independent Texas. The territory had almost unlimited possibilities for cotton growing, and English manufacturers hoped to make it their principal source of supply, particularly if the new republic adopted a policy of free trade. Texas, with a rapidly growing population, would offer a magnificent market for British manufactures. Many of these goods, the English optimistically assumed, would then be smuggled across the long border into the United States.

In return for British assistance in arranging satisfactory peace terms with Mexico, Texas might, it was hoped, abolish slavery. The English interest in this matter was partly humanitarian and partly selfish. By abolishing slavery in their own Empire in 1833, the British had put themselves at a considerable disadvantage because West Indies sugar and cotton had to compete with slave-produced staples of countries like the United States and Texas. Abolition of slavery in other countries would tend to equalize the competition. Moreover, emancipation in Texas would obviously weaken the institution in the United States. With the market for American cotton restricted by Texan competition, the value of slaves would decline and the wide open spaces across the Sabine River would become a haven for runaway Negroes.

Texas shrewdly played Britain and the United States against each other to see which would offer most. To the British envoy President Houston offered words of encouragement, indicating that abolition of slavery was being seriously considered; at the same time Houston saw to it that Tyler and other Southern politicians were kept informed of the English siren song.

Seriously alarmed by these reports, President Tyler and his friends began to try out public opinion on the Texas issue. Thomas W. Gilmer, a Virginia congressman, initiated the campaign in January, 1843, with an open letter warning that Texas must inevitably become part of the United States or fall under British influence. Ex-President Jackson endorsed this thesis and added persuasive reasons of his own: once annexed, Texas could never be used by an unfriendly power as a base for operations against the United States or for inciting Southern slaves to revolt.

As Tyler thus laid the ground for taking up the Texas question, Webster's continued presence in the Cabinet became an embarrassment. In reality, the Secretary of State was as anxious to resign as the President was to have him go, but both men were looking for some face-saving way out of the situation. Webster would have liked to become Minister to England, but Edward Everett, who enjoyed his London post, refused to resign or go on a special mission to China.[2] Finally, on May 8, 1843, the comedy was ended when Webster simply resigned.

He was succeeded by Judge Abel P. Upshur of Virginia, formerly Tyler's Secretary of the Navy, who looked at the Texas problem entirely from the Southern point of view. To John C. Calhoun, temporarily in retirement, Upshur wrote:

> My own mind is very much disturbed on the subject of Texas.... There can be no doubt, I think, that England is determined to abolish slavery throughout the American continent and islands if she can.... I can find no other motive than a desire to find or create markets for her surplus manufactures, and to destroy all competition with the laborers of her colonies.... The present attempt upon Texas is the beginning of her operations upon us.[3]

When Tyler and Upshur tried to open negotiations on a treaty of annexation, they found Isaac Van Zandt, the Texan Minister, unable to act without instructions from his government, and the necessary authority was not immediately forthcoming. Twice rebuffed when they suggested annexation, the Texan authorities were reluctant to reopen the question. Moreover, President Houston and many fellow Texans could now see advantages in continuing independence. After some delay, however, the requisite instructions were sent to Van Zandt.

The Annexation Treaty

On February 28, 1844, Secretary Upshur was a victim of a gun explosion during the trial run of the battleship *Princeton*. To fill the vacant office, John C. Calhoun was named. On April 12, the great South Carolinian completed a treaty of annexation under which Texas ceded to the United States all its territories, Texas citizens were admitted as full American citizens, and the United States assumed the public debt of Texas in an amount not to exceed 10 million dollars.

Even before this treaty was sent to the Senate for approval, Secretary Calhoun tried to explain to Richard Pakenham, the British Minister to the United States, the reason for the American action. Annexation was a necessary act of self-defense to protect the United States against the abolitionist policies of England. If this British purpose were to be achieved,

---

[2] Caleb Cushing, one of Webster's followers, accepted the China post. See chap. 13.

[3] Reprinted by permission of The Bobbs-Merrill Company, Inc., from Charles M. Wiltsie, *John C. Calhoun, Sectionalist, 1840–1850* (Copyright 1951 by The Bobbs-Merrill Company, Inc., Indianapolis), p. 154.

it would involve "the greatest calamity" for the whole country, especially for the Negro race itself.

The treaty reached the Senate at the worst possible time for judicious consideration. The national party conventions were about to meet, and the political pot was boiling vigorously. Both Clay, the leading Whig candidate, and Van Buren, the most likely Democratic nominee, had just written public letters opposing the acquisition of Texas, at least for the time being. Such was the situation on April 27, when the treaty and various supporting documents, including the explosive Pakenham letter, leaked out to the press. William Lloyd Garrison's *Liberator* denounced the transaction as involving "an amount of hypocrisy and villainy, of treachery and oppression, unexampled in the criminal history of any nation, either in ancient or modern times." Horace Greeley's *New York Tribune* was almost as violent, pronouncing this treaty to be an "unprecedented and unwarrantable outrage."

In the Senate, the Whigs lined up almost solidly against the treaty, while the Democrats were badly divided. Senators Robert Walker of Mississippi and James Buchanan of Pennsylvania supported annexation, but the powerful Thomas Hart Benton of Missouri opposed it. From behind the scenes two former Democratic Presidents exerted their influence in opposite directions: Jackson for annexation and Van Buren against. In the end, the treaty was badly defeated, with only 16 senators favoring ratification as against 35 opposed. Although this vote mirrored the sectional division of public opinion, it did not follow these lines completely; several Northern Democrats voted for the treaty, and several Southern Whigs against it. One of the considerations strongly influencing the decision was the belief that annexation might bring immediate war with Mexico. Despite this defeat, the annexation movement was still very much alive, and the election campaign of 1844 provided a perfect opportunity to carry the issue to the country.

The Oregon Question

Also approaching a crisis in 1844 was the problem of the Oregon country. In earlier chapters it has been explained how Great Britain, Russia, Spain, and the United States all laid claims to the Pacific Northwest. By the Adams-Onís Treaty of 1819, Spain had renounced to the United States all its rights north of the 42nd parallel, while Russia had given up claim to any territory south of 54°40′ in treaties with the United States in 1824 and with Britain in 1825. These agreements left the region between 42° and 54°40′ still in dispute between England and the United States. The Convention of 1818 had postponed the issue by stipulating that for ten years the area should be open to trade and settlement by the nationals of both countries.

During the 1820s, Congress displayed a flurry of interest in the problem. In 1824, the House of Representatives approved the so-called Floyd Bill to organize Oregon as a territory. This did not mean that the legislators were convinced that the Pacific Coast area was destined to become part of the American Union. On the contrary, many assumed that this region was too remote ever to become an integral part of the nation and that what was more likely was the establishment of some kind of independent American republic. The essential goal was to keep as much of the region as possible out of British hands. This nationalistic ambition underlay the noncolonization principle of the Monroe Doctrine, which Canning found so exasperating.

Since the 1790s, American sailing vessels had been participating profitably in the China trade, and this economic interest was bound up in the Oregon question. To facilitate it, the Americans needed good Pacific ports along a coast where good harbors were scarce. Even the Columbia River was scarcely an answer to this problem, because its mouth was obstructed by a sand bar. Only the Strait of Juan de Fuca would give access to Puget Sound and the deep-water harbors needed not only by the China traders, but by naval vessels and whalers as well. For this reason the United States held firm to its contention that it would not accept a boundary south of the 49th parallel.

On the British side, interest in the Oregon country increased after 1821, when the old Hudson's Bay Company was merged with the newer North West Company, which had opened up the Oregon fur trade. For the next twenty-five years the reorganized Hudson's Bay Company was the most powerful influence in the region, dominating its commerce and providing it with the essentials of government. Dr. John McLoughlin, the company's chief factor, became the benevolent despot of the whole area. Since the British government in earlier negotiations had already offered to recognize the Columbia River as the boundary between British and American territory, the company confined most of its activities to the region north of that river.

The Hudson's Bay Company was strongly opposed to fixing the boundary at the 49th parallel, because to do so would cut it off not only from the Columbia River, but from the Strait of Juan de Fuca as well. Canning was fully sympathetic with the needs of the company and had his own additional reasons for taking a firm stand on the Oregon problem. Always anti-American except for the brief flirtation preceding the announcement of the Monroe Doctrine, he was particularly reluctant to allow the Americans to gain good ports on the Pacific.

During the winter and spring of 1826–1827, Albert Gallatin, sent to

London on special mission by the Adams administration, had conducted important negotiations on the Oregon question. As a concession to persuade the British to accept the 49th parallel, Gallatin offered to grant the English free navigation of the Columbia; as a counterproposal, the British suggested that the Americans accept the Columbia River boundary and an enclave of territory on Puget Sound, adequate to provide them with a deep-water port. Since neither country would agree to the other's proposals, the negotiators had to content themselves with an arrangement to extend the joint occupation principle for an indefinite period. Either party could terminate it on one year's notice.

Actually, the principle of joint occupation favored the Americans. In 1827, the Hudson's Bay Company was firmly established in Oregon, and American settlement was nonexistent. Postponing the boundary issue allowed the American frontier movement to follow its destined course and exert its weight in the diplomatic balances.

Permanent American settlement in Oregon began about 1834 with the arrival of the first American missionaries. Enthusiastic reports of the region's resources eventually brought out settlers of a different kind, many of them rough and turbulent men from Missouri and other states of the Middle West. In 1843, about a thousand men, women, and children made the arduous 2,000-mile trip over the Oregon Trail, and as many or more took the overland journey each year thereafter. Some emigrants turned south in present-day Idaho and made their way down into California, further complicating the already troubled relations between the United States and Mexico.

Many newcomers entered Oregon with a violent prejudice against the Hudson's Bay Company, fed by false stories that it was molesting the Americans and inciting Indians against them. Actually, the patriarchal McLoughlin treated the emigrants kindly, several times sending them provisions to alleviate shortages. Peaceful relations were facilitated by the circumstance that the Americans found their promised land in the fertile Willamette Valley on the south side of the Columbia River. As late as 1845, there were only eight Americans living north of the Columbia in the territory actually in dispute between the two governments.

Despite the Hudson's Bay Company's still unchallenged reign in its own sphere of influence, the presence of 5,000 American settlers in the Willamette Valley was a matter of concern. Although serious trouble was avoided, irritating incidents did occur, and there was always the danger of a real explosion. As a measure of prudence, the company made preparations as early as 1843 to transfer its main depot from the Columbia River to Vancouver Island, north of the Strait of Juan de Fuca.

The word "Oregon" began to exert an intoxicating influence in American politics. In 1843, Senator Lewis F. Linn of Missouri proposed a bill to provide Oregon with territorial government, fortifications, and land grants. In the Middle West, where this idea gained immediate popularity, public meetings in the principal cities petitioned Congress to take action. Although cooler heads pointed out that the Linn Bill would violate the joint occupancy agreement, the expansionists waved this objection aside, demanding that the United States at once extend its authority over the whole Oregon country. Throughout the next two years, the issue was hotly debated, with the Whigs and Southern Democrats counseling caution and the Western Democrats crying for action.

Missouri politicians embraced the cause with special warmth. "Thirty thousand rifles in Oregon," roared Thomas Hart Benton, "will annihilate the Hudson's Bay Company." "The march of empire is westward," echoed David R. Atchison; "nothing will, nothing can check it."

President Tyler took cautious notice of the new interest in Oregon. Early in his administration he had been more interested in California than in Oregon and had suggested that the United States might accept the Columbia River boundary if Britain would induce Mexico to sell a major part of California to the United States. When this proposal met a cool response both in London and Mexico City, Tyler had quickly reverted to the earlier American policy of insisting upon the 49th parallel. In December, 1843, he recommended that emigrants be protected from the Indians by erecting a string of forts along the Oregon Trail. The President was opposed, however, to any precipitate act that might cause war with England, and in this policy he had the support of Calhoun, who had once defined the proper attitude to be maintained as one of "masterly inactivity."

The Election of 1844

With Southern Democrats anxious to annex Texas immediately and Western Democrats equally fervent to extend American sovereignty over all Oregon, the expansion issue was certain to be raised during the Presidential campaign of 1844. The Whig convention, meeting on May 1, nominated Henry Clay and avoided commitment on the Texas and Oregon questions. On the other hand, the Democrats, who convened later the same month, took a strong position. The Southern wing of the party, never enthusiastic about Van Buren anyway, used his recently announced opposition to the immediate acquisition of Texas to block his nomination. Instead, first place on the ticket went to former Governor James K. Polk of Tennessee, an advocate of annexation.

The Democratic platform combined the demands of both South and West:

Resolved, that our title to the whole of the territory of Oregon is clear and unquestionable; that no portion of the same ought to be ceded to England or to any other power; and that the re-occupation of Oregon and the re-annexation of Texas at the earliest practicable period are great American measures, which this convention recommends to the cordial support of the Democracy of the Union.

In some respects, this wording was extraordinarily clever. The emphasis on *re*-occupation and *re*-annexation suggested that the United States was demanding no more than what had clearly belonged to her before these territories had been lost through the diplomatic mistakes of John Quincy Adams. Moreover, the statement that Texas and Oregon were to be acquired "at the earliest practicable period" could be interpreted in a conservative sense to appease the Van Burenites who opposed any sudden, drastic action on the Texas question.

The most radical aspect of the platform was its uncompromising demand for "the whole of the territory of Oregon." As popularized in the slogan "Fifty-four forty or fight," this was a dangerous appeal to the voters. It ignored the diplomatic facts of life, since all well-informed politicians knew that for twenty years the United States had been ready to accept the 49th parallel and that the only territory really in dispute lay between that line and the Columbia River. To demand more was to invite war with England.

During the campaign, Texas rather than Oregon was the focus of attention. The issue injured the Whigs, because Clay antagonized the extremists on both sides of the question. Alarmed by the reaction in the South to his earlier "Raleigh letter" opposing immediate annexation, the Whig candidate tried to repair the damage with his "Alabama letters." If Texas could be acquired "without national dishonor, without war, with general consent of the States of the Union, and upon fair and reasonable terms," Clay would, he said, "be glad to see it." These words alarmed the abolitionists, many of whom cast their votes for James G. Birney, the Liberty party candidate.

The election of 1844 was by no means a popular referendum on the question of expansion. Clay's equivocation clouded the issue, and the election of Polk could be attributed to such other causes as Whig losses to the Liberty party, foreign-born resentment to the nativist issue, and opposition to the Whig economic program. Party loyalty was often the deciding factor. The Van Burenites supported Polk despite their opposition to annexation, just as most of the Southern Whigs voted for Clay, even though they desired to see Texas in the Union.

Despite all this confusion, the election had results of the most far-reaching character. The victorious Democrats came to power, committed to a strong policy on both the Texas and Oregon questions. To be sure, politicians often treat party platforms more as artful traps to capture votes than as seriously intended programs for future action. Men of this character soon forget their campaign pledges. But James K. Polk, the President-elect, was a statesman of a different stamp. Tremendously serious and hard-working, he entered the White House dedicated to a vision of seeing the American flag wave not only over Texas and Oregon, but over California and New Mexico as well.

12

MANIFEST DESTINY

In the July, 1845, issue of the *Democratic Review,* John L. O'Sullivan, New York editor and enthusiastic expansionist, coined an historic phrase and also defined it. The magic words were "manifest destiny"; the definition was that the United States should "overspread the continent allotted by Providence for the free development of our yearly multiplying millions."

Both the date and the phraseology were significant. The urge to bring new territory under the American flag, still rather weakly supported as late as the spring of 1844, gained startling strength during the next twelve months. The tidal wave of expansionism engulfed Henry Clay and brought James K. Polk to the White House. By this time, the decision to annex Texas had already been made; a new strong policy on the Oregon question was in the process of formulation; and the intoxicating possibilities of acquiring California were being discussed.

More important, the American people, or at least most of them, had gained a mystic sense of national destiny. The rapid growth of the population led to predictions that during the next hundred years, the United States might acquire a population of 300 million. As a contemporary jingle boasted: [1]

> We have, thank heaven! a most prolific brood;
> Look at the census, if you aim to know—
> And then, the foreign influx, bad and good;
> All helps new lands to clear—new seeds to sow;
> We must obey our destiny and blood,
> Though Europe show her bill, and strike her blow.

To support these future generations, it was believed that the United States needed to add still more land to its already vast domain. Acquisition of

[1] *Democratic Review,* XVIII (1846), 92.

new territory would, in Andrew Jackson's words, "extend the area of freedom," would bring the blessings of American democratic institutions to adjacent regions, and save them from the misrule of inferior breeds like the Mexicans or from the despised monarchism of England and France. Eastern merchants also dreamed of glory. By Yankee drive and boldness they hoped to capture more and more of the world's markets—particularly in areas bordering on the broad Pacific. To achieve their own version of manifest destiny they needed seaports on the West Coast.

Annexation of Texas

The expansionists did not wait for Polk's inauguration to gather in the first fruits of their 1844 electoral triumph. Even before the Senate's rejection of the annexation treaty, President Tyler had been calculating the possibilities of acquiring Texas through a joint resolution of Congress, a procedure needing only a simple majority in each House instead of the difficult two-thirds majority in the Senate required for approval of treaties. On June 10, 1844, two days after the final rejection of the treaty, Tyler sent a special message to Congress, recommending this course of action. The President was too unpopular, however, and the political atmosphere was too hot for favorable consideration of the proposal at that time.

When Congress reconvened in December, 1844, a month after the election of Polk, the situation was entirely different. Tyler's recommendation that Texas be offered annexation by joint resolution now gained a serious hearing. Although the die-hard opponents were still vigorously against the proposal, the swing of public opinion in the other direction was very pronounced. Even in Augusta, Maine, the capitol building was not large enough to accommodate the crowd attracted to a proannexation meeting. Senator Thomas Hart Benton of Missouri, one of the most bitter opponents of the earlier treaty, was now searching for some face-saving way to change sides and restore himself to good standing in Democratic party circles.

Even with this favorable political atmosphere, the expansionists found it difficult to phrase a set of resolutions that would command a majority in the two houses. Much political jockeying and compromise were necessary before a joint resolution providing for annexation finally passed on February 27, 1845. In the Senate, the measure just squeezed through by a vote of 27 to 25; in the House, the margin was more decisive—120 to 98. The decision was more political than sectional. All but a handful of Whigs opposed the joint resolution, while most of the Democrats supported it. Many reluctant Northern Democrats cast their votes for annexation out of fear that President-elect Polk would cut them off from the patronage unless they did so. Democratic congressmen from the West were influenced by their interest in the Oregon question, on which they wanted to win Southern support.

Even after the passage of the joint resolution, many months of delicate maneuvering were required to shepherd Texas safely into the fold. The joint resolution specified that the new state was not to be admitted until the existing government of Texas had consented to the election of a constitutional convention, which must approve annexation and draft a new state constitution. Then the people of Texas must ratify this document. Whether annexation could leap these hurdles was by no means certain. For one thing, the Senate's rejection of the treaty, coming on the heels of several earlier rebuffs, had wounded Texan pride and strengthened the determination of many to remain independent. Furthermore, the joint resolution contained conditions unfavorable to Texas. While the new state was to turn over all its public buildings and military establishments to the United States, it was left to shoulder its own large public debt. By stipulating that all boundary questions be adjusted by the United States government, Congress pointedly refused to commit itself on the aggressive Texan claims to the Rio Grande boundary and to large parts of New Mexico.

Fortunately for the incoming Polk administration, Tyler had entrusted American interests in Texas to the capable hands of Major Andrew Jackson Donelson. In addition to his own native shrewdness, this chargé d'affaires had the important advantages of being the nephew and namesake of Andrew Jackson and a close friend of the proud and ambitious Sam Houston, perhaps the most influential citizen of Texas. Donelson still needed to play his cards well, because Houston favored continued Texan independence, while his successor, President Anson Jones, even more strongly opposed annexation.

Donelson's dangerous opponent in the game to control the destiny of Texas was the British chargé, Captain Charles Elliot. English determination to block American annexation had reached a high point the preceding year, while Tyler's treaty was under consideration. Lord Aberdeen had gone so far as to gain the support of France in trying to persuade Mexico to acknowledge the independence of Texas and then to guarantee the independence and territorial integrity of both Mexico and Texas even at the risk of war with the United States.

Fortunately this British policy of all-out opposition had weakened significantly during subsequent months. Mexico's reluctance to admit that Texas was irretrievably lost was one reason; Louis Philippe's sensitivity to charges of undue subservience to England was another. Meantime, British officials had become somewhat hesitant themselves. To push the Aberdeen project too far during the American election might hurt Clay and play into the hands of the Democrats. Then, with the election over, the rise of American expansionism became so menacing that England had to step warily, lest she find herself involved in war.

Despite this greater caution, the British and French governments instructed their representatives in Texas to continue their undercover efforts to block annexation, and this Captain Elliot and his French colleague, the Comte de Saligny, proceeded to do. Before Major Donelson could officially transmit the American offer to the Texan government, Elliot and Saligny were in secret conference with President Jones. The latter was readily persuaded to accept the good offices of England and France in a last effort to obtain a peace treaty with Mexico, and Captain Elliot set off on an ultra-secret mission to the Mexican capital.

José Herrera, who had become President of Mexico in December, 1844, was an honest and intelligent politician who could see the wisdom of following English advice. When, however, he appealed to his congress for authority to conduct the negotiations, he provoked an uproar. Mexican public opinion was still violently anti-Texan, while England and France were suspected of having designs of their own on such Mexican territory as California, Yucatan, and even Texas itself. In the end, Captain Elliot obtained what he wanted—Mexican acceptance of the Texan offer to treat on the basis of permanent Texan independence. The transaction took so many weeks to complete, however, that the British representative did not return to Texas with the news until May 30, 1845.

Had the Mexican decision to recognize Texan independence been made six months earlier, annexation might have been blocked. As it was, however, the move came too late. Although President Jones and his cabinet might prefer the glory of their exalted offices to the more prosaic posts that statehood would provide, the common people of Texas had no such stake in the old order. Most of them had been born under the American flag and had no compulsive loyalty to an independent Texas. Annexation to them was a way out of the region's serious problems of defense and finance. The new proposals from Mexico City aroused only suspicion, because the average Texan trusted neither Mexicans nor Britons.

Major Donelson had seen in this proannexation public opinion his best weapon for overcoming the antiannexation leanings of the Texan officials. Houston was brought into line by hints that a man of his stature might easily become the next President of the United States. Jones was pushed into reluctantly summoning a special session of the Texan congress. Meeting in June, the legislators unanimously approved the proposed constitutional convention and rejected Jones's alternative project of a treaty with Mexico.

The Texas convention acted with equal decisiveness. On July 5, 1845, it approved annexation with only one dissenting vote and then began drafting a state constitution. The new instrument of government was submitted to the Texan voters in October and overwhelmingly approved.

In December, 1845, the United States Congress voted to admit Texas into the Union, and the following February annexation was formally completed in a touching ceremony in which retiring President Jones reverently lowered the Lone Star flag so that the Stars and Stripes might be raised in its place. The Polk administration had thereby achieved its first victory for manifest destiny.

Stalemate on Oregon

In his inaugural address, President Polk declared: "Our title to the country of the Oregon is 'clear and unquestionable.' " He then promised to "assert and maintain by all constitutional means" American rights in the area and declared that American settlers should be brought under the jurisdiction of United States law.

Polk did not specifically say that he was asserting a claim to the whole territory up to 50°40', but his speech was generally so interpreted both in the United States and in England. The London *Times* warned that "the territory of Oregon will never be wrested from the British Crown to which it belongs, but by war," and Lord Aberdeen told Parliament: "We possess rights which, in our opinion, are clear and unquestionable; and, by the blessing of God and with your support, those rights we are fully prepared to maintain."

Despite these rumblings, there seemed a good chance that the two governments might come to a quiet settlement during the summer of 1845. On July 12, the new Secretary of State, James Buchanan of Pennsylvania, addressed a long note to Richard Pakenham, the British Minister at Washington, defending the American claim to all of Oregon, but, nevertheless, offering to compromise on the basis of extending the 49th parallel boundary from the Rockies to the ocean. Great Britain might have the free use of any Vancouver Island ports south of this line that she cared to designate. Buchanan explained the inconsistency of the American offer on the grounds that Polk "felt himself embarrassed, if not committed, by the acts of his predecessors." In other words, the President realized that the Democratic platform of 1844 notwithstanding, he could not ignore the fact that Monroe, Adams, and Tyler had all been willing to accept the 49th parallel.

At the same time Polk was reluctantly renewing the offer of his predecessors, Lord Aberdeen was privately pointing out to his colleagues that a settlement might become advisable on the basis of the 49th parallel, with certain modifications. Indeed, as early as March 4, 1844, Aberdeen had instructed Pakenham to endeavor, without committing himself, "to draw from the American negotiator a proposal to make the 49th degree of latitude the boundary, with the proviso that the ports to the south of that parallel to the Columbia inclusive, shall be free ports to G. Britain." Although Buchanan's note did not quite meet these specifications, it came close enough to make bright the prospects for settlement.

Unfortunately, however, both the British and American governments were so afraid of antagonizing public opinion in their own countries that the negotiations of 1845 broke down. Hoping to obtain further American concessions, Pakenham made the mistake of rejecting Buchanan's offer without even referring it to his home government. Thereupon, President Polk instructed his Secretary of State to withdraw the American offer and to make no new proposal. The President appeared to be relieved rather than distressed by Pakenham's conduct. To Buchanan, Polk confided that, if the American offer had been accepted, the administration would have been severely criticized; "as we came in on Texas the probability was we would have gone out on Oregon."

Polk Reasserts the Monroe Doctrine

President Polk's first annual message to Congress of December 2, 1845, reflected his annoyance with England on both the Texas and Oregon issues. On the latter, he declared that since all attempts at compromise had failed, Congress should consider measures for ensuring the security of American residents in Oregon and maintaining the "just title" of the United States to the territory. For one thing, Congress should authorize the President to give the year's notice necessary for terminating the joint occupancy agreement of 1827. Additionally, immediate action should be taken to extend the protection of American laws to American citizens already living in Oregon. Polk closed this part of his message with a hint of possible war:

> At the end of the year's notice, should Congress think it proper to make provision for giving that notice, we shall have reached a period when the national rights in Oregon must either be abandoned or firmly maintained. That they can not now be abandoned without a sacrifice of both national honor and interest is too clear to admit of doubt....

The President had still more to say about America's relations to Europe. In words that had an obvious reference to Texas and California as well as to Oregon, Polk noted that in some nations the doctrine had lately been advanced that a "balance of power" was desirable to check American growth. He warned that the United States would resist any European interference on the North American continent "at any and all hazards."

Polk then went on to review the principles which Monroe had laid down in his famous message of 1823. He strongly endorsed them all and placed particular emphasis on the noncolonization doctrine, saying:

> This principle will apply with greatly increased force should any European power attempt to establish any new colony in North America.... Existing rights of every European nation should be respected, but it is due alike to our safety and our interests that the efficient protection of our laws should be extended over our whole territorial limits, and that it should be distinctly announced to the world as our settled policy that no future European colony or dominion shall with our consent be planted or established on any part of the North American continent....

The "Polk Doctrine," as this pronouncement has sometimes been called, marked a significant landmark in the evolution of American foreign policy. Despite the stir created by its original pronouncement, the Monroe Doctrine had been scarcely mentioned for twenty years. It was Polk, therefore, who restored the old doctrine to life and gave it the venerated niche it has since continued to occupy.

In restating the Monroe Doctrine, Polk both limited and extended it. The limitation—which proved to be peculiar to Polk himself—was to apply the doctrine only to North America, instead of to the entire Western Hemisphere. The extension was to go beyond Monroe in warning Europe not only against military intervention, but against any kind of "interference."

The Oregon Settlement

Polk's real intentions on the Oregon question were something of a mystery both in England and in America. Had he committed himself in all seriousness to the slogan "fifty-four forty or fight"? Or was he merely exerting pressure on England to obtain the best settlement possible? To a friend, the President merely confided his conviction "that the only way to treat John Bull was to look him straight in the eye"; that he considered "a bold & firm course on our part the pacific one"; and that if Congress faltered or hesitated, "John Bull would immediately become arrogant and more grasping in his demands."

However pacific Polk's intentions really were, there was danger that his aggressive tactics might so excite the more rabid expansionists as to make compromise impossible. In the congressional debate on the bill to terminate joint occupancy, many legislators indulged in wild talk. Senator Lewis Cass of Michigan called for military preparation and declared that it was better "to fight for the first inch of national territory than for the last." Representative Levin of Pennsylvania based the American claim

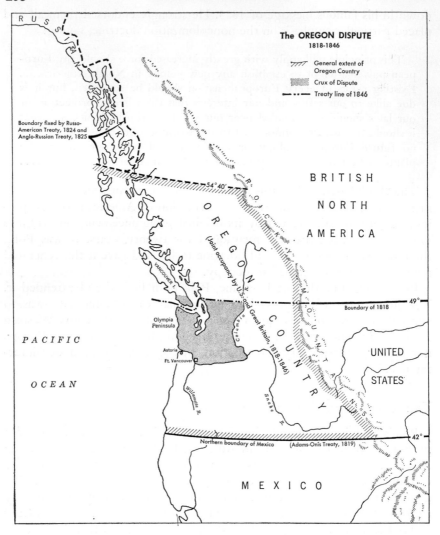

The OREGON DISPUTE
1818-1846

//// General extent of
      Oregon Country
      Crux of Dispute
—··— Treaty line of 1846

R U S S I A

Boundary fixed by Russo-
American Treaty, 1824 and
Anglo-Russian Treaty, 1825

54° 40'

BRITISH

NORTH

AMERICA

O R E G O N

(Joint occupancy by U.S. and Great Britain 1818-1846)

R O C K Y   M O U N T A I N S

Boundary of 1818   49°

VANCOUVER I.

Olympia
Peninsula

Astoria

Ft. Vancouver

PACIFIC

OCEAN

C O U N T R Y

Willamette R.

Snake R.

UNITED

STATES

Northern boundary of Mexico   (Adams-Onís Treaty, 1819)   42°

M E X I C O

to all of Oregon upon the "genius of American institutions" and "the
laws of God"—thus brushing aside the question of whether England or
the United States had the stronger title to the disputed territory. Inflam-
mable talk at Washington had its impact on popular opinion elsewhere.
An observer in Georgia listened to a crowd, "not one of whom knew
on which side of the Rocky Mountains Oregon was, swear that they
would support and fight for Polk *all over the world*, that he was right,
and we would have Oregon and thrash the British into the bargain."

Fortunately, such irresponsible talk was balanced by the prudent advice of many other Americans who urged that the door to compromise

be left open. Within Polk's own official family, Secretary Buchanan and Louis McLane, the American Minister to England, exerted such modifying influence. In the Senate, John C. Calhoun and Daniel Webster both argued for a peaceful course. Even Thomas Hart Benton, who had been one of the most zealous champions of American rights in Oregon, advised that the extreme American claims could not be justified.

In the end, Congress passed a joint resolution on April 23, 1846, which authorized the President, at his discretion, to give the necessary year's notice for the abrogation of the joint occupancy agreement. Much of the measure's sting was removed by its preamble, which stated that the purpose was to encourage the adoption of all proper means for "a speedy and amicable adjustment" of the dispute.

Meanwhile, pacific influences had also been at work in England. The Hudson's Bay Company was no longer unyielding in its demand for the Columbia River boundary. As pointed out in the preceding chapter, the company had transferred its principal depot to Vancouver Island, partly for better security in case of trouble with the American settlers on the Willamette, and partly because of the dwindling fur trade. The British government, however, had good reasons for wanting to eliminate a source of friction and possible war with the United States. Ireland was facing starvation in 1846 because of the failure of the potato crop, and Sir Robert Peel, the Prime Minister, needed imports from America to help alleviate the famine. By first suspending and later repealing the import duties on grain (the so-called corn laws), the British government hoped to serve its immediate needs and at the same time improve Anglo-American relations. "Many things," Lord Aberdeen advised Minister Pakenham, "may shortly occur to improve the prospect of affairs very considerably. The access of American corn to our markets would go far to pacify the warriors of the Western States."

The English wanted to use the repeal of the corn laws to encourage a more general extension of free trade. The United States was one of the most important markets for British manufactures, and English leaders hoped the present Democratic Congress would substantially lower the American tariff. A peaceful solution of the Oregon dispute would contribute to this long-range economic program.

For these and other reasons Lord Aberdeen was ready to accept the 49th parallel, provided Britain's needs for adequate Pacific Coast ports were met. For several months the Foreign Secretary had been subtly preparing English opinion for a retreat on the Oregon issue. Consequently, he was ready to move quickly, and, as soon as word of Congress's action reached England, he instructed Pakenham to make a new proposal, spelling out the kind of sensible terms that reasonable men on both sides of the Atlantic had been privately discussing for some time. The 49th parallel was to be extended from the Rockies to the sea; from this point the line was to follow the middle of the channel of Juan de Fuca Strait, thus leaving Vancouver Island under British sovereignty; the Strait was to be open to the free navigation of both parties; and the Columbia River was to be freely navigated by the Hudson's Bay Company and its customers.

Unwilling to take personal responsibility for abandoning the full American claim, President Polk submitted the British proposal to the Senate. The rabid expansionists still opposed compromise, but by this time they were so outnumbered that the British terms were approved by a vote of 38 to 12. Thereupon, a treaty was signed on June 15, 1846, and the Senate gave it formal approval three days later.

American Interest in California

Soaring American faith in manifest destiny combined with Mexican weakness suggested that Texas might not be the only territorial gain the United States would make in the Southwest. In March, 1845, the *Baltimore American* declared: "The Rio Grande has no more efficacy as a permanent barrier against the extension of Anglo-Saxon power than the Sabine possessed. The process by which Texas was acquired may be repeated over and over again...." The St. Louis *Missourian* expressed the complacent opinion that in any future acquisition of Mexican territory, the American people would merely be "carrying out a decree of the Almighty."

It was particularly easy to believe that manifest destiny was beckoning in the direction of California. The magnificent resources of this region had first been recognized by Spanish Franciscan missionaries in 1769. During the next half century, the California missions enjoyed fabulous prosperity from their great herds of cattle and horses and their thriving vineyards. After Mexico became independent, the missions fell into decay, and the general economic life of the province languished. California was too far from Mexico City to be governed effectively during these years of frequent civil war.

As it became obvious that the Mexican grip on California was far from firm, this fine Pacific territory looked increasingly attractive not only to Americans, but to French and British as well. While Richard Pakenham was British Minister to Mexico (before being transferred to the Washington legation), he informed his government of the resources of California, "its commanding position on the Pacific, its fine harbours, its forests of excellent timber for ship-building." These, he argued, "render it by all means desirable, in a political point of view, that California, once ceasing to belong to Mexico, should not fall into the hands of any Power but England." British creditors, despairing of collecting from the bankrupt

Mexican government, suggested that the debts be discharged by granting them vast tracts of land in the coveted territory.

Although much of this foreign intrigue was behind the scenes, the American newspapers knew enough of what was going on to sound a warning. In February, 1845, the *New York Herald* declared: "Should Texas be annexed, the next movement of Great Britain will probably be to negotiate with Mexico for the purchase of California. . . . In this she will be successful unless intercepted by our government."

The Americans' own interest in California went back to 1822, when Yankee ship captains first visited the coast to obtain hides. This trade, at a peak during the 1830s, became less profitable after 1840, but by this time American merchants were sufficiently familiar with such California harbors as San Diego, Monterey, and San Francisco to recognize their potentialities. In 1842, Secretary of State Webster asserted that "the acquisition of so good a port on the Pacific as San Francisco is a subject well deserving of consideration. It would be useful to the numerous Whale Ships and trading vessels of the United States, which navigate the Pacific, & along the Western Coast of America."

The American Navy's interest in California was embarrassingly revealed by an episode in 1842. In that year Santa Anna's government had attempted to reopen the Texas war with sporadic raids and had issued stern warnings against American interference. News of these Mexican measures reached Commodore Thomas A. C. Jones, commander of the United States Pacific squadron, while he was in a Peruvian port. Rashly concluding that war would soon break out, Jones conceived his mission to be that of seizing the ports of California to keep them out of British hands. He arrived at Monterey on October 19, 1842, easily overawed the local garrison, and raised the American flag. The occupation was no sooner completed than Jones learned it was all a mistake—the expected war had not materialized. The overeager commodore lowered the American flag, saluted that of Mexico, and sailed away. Secretary Webster made the proper apologies for Jones's conduct, but the episode was not easily forgotten, since it provided both Mexico and Europe with a preview of what would inevitably happen if war actually did break out between the United States and its southern neighbor.

During the next three years American interest in California mounted. Richard Henry Dana's *Two Years Before the Mast*, published in 1840, was followed by other widely read accounts of California. Thomas O. Larkin, an influential American merchant in Monterey, began a series of letters to the *New York Herald* in 1843. Captain John C. Frémont, a famous explorer of the Far West, published his *Narrative* in 1845. Not only were many Americans reading about California, but an increasing number of them were crossing the overland trails to settle there. Sutter's Fort, on the site of present Sacramento, was the center of a growing American colony. In 1845, there were only some 10,000 whites in all of California, and about 800 of them were Americans.

Shortly after his inauguration, Polk announced to his close friends that the acquisition of California would be one of his principal goals, and it could be accomplished without war. When Larkin, who had been appointed American consul in Monterey, warned of the suspicious activities of his British and French colleagues, Polk sent him confidential directions on how to handle the situation. He was to "exert the greatest vigilance in discovering and defeating any attempt" of foreign governments to gain control of California. While the President would make no effort "to induce California to become one of the free and independent States of the Union," if the inhabitants themselves should desire this, "they would be received as brethren, whenever this can be done without affording Mexico just cause of complaint." For the present, the best policy was to let events take their course, unless an attempt were made to transfer California to Britain or France. In short, Polk was confident that the westward march of pioneers would settle the California question just as it had that of Texas. He also hoped, as we shall presently see, that Mexico might acquiesce in the inevitable by selling California to the United States.

There was real danger that the plan of making California another Texas might be ruined by premature action of American adventurers. In the early months of 1846, Captain Frémont was again in California with an exploring party. Wrangling with the local Mexican officials, Frémont became a focal point around which the discontent of the American settlers could concentrate. In June, a small group in the Sacramento Valley seized the garrison town of Sonoma, proclaimed an independent republic, and raised a home-made flag upon which the figure of a bear had been crudely drawn. While it is uncertain whether Frémont had instigated the revolt, he and his men soon joined the movement. This unauthorized conduct by a United States Army officer embarrassed Consul Larkin, who had been encouraging the Spanish element in California to assert their independence from Mexico. Just what the future of the Bear Flag Republic would have been is uncertain, because on July 2, 1846, the situation was dramatically changed by the news that Mexico and the United States were at war. This time the report was true.

Background of the Mexican War

The most important cause of the Mexican War was Mexican resentment over the whole Texas episode. In 1843, the Mexican government had bluntly warned that it would consider American annexation of Texas as "equivalent to a declaration of war against the Mexican Republic." As soon as President Tyler signed the joint resolution offering annexation, Juan Almonte, the Mexican Minister, protested strongly to the American government and left the country. In Mexico City, similar steps were taken, thereby breaking off all official diplomatic relations between the two countries. Throughout the summer of 1845, Mexico seemed about to begin hostilities.

In addition to the gaping wound left by the Texas episode, relations between Mexico and the United States had been injured by other grievances that had been piling up over several years. As a result of disturbed political conditions, many American citizens—in common with those of England and France—had suffered losses through illegal Mexican seizures of ships and goods, as well as through other arbitrary acts. The Adams administration had begun to press these claims against Mexico, and the Jackson administration inherited the problem. In 1837, Jackson's impatience with Mexican evasions reached the point where he asked Congress for authority to use the Navy to force a settlement. Congress was unwilling to place this much power in the President's hands, and the claims problem was, therefore, still outstanding when Van Buren became President.

In 1840, after exasperating delays, Mexico and the United States finally submitted the claims to a mixed commission, consisting of two representatives from each nation with an umpire chosen by the King of Prussia. This commission awarded the American claimants 2 million dollars, which Mexico agreed to pay in quarterly instalments over the next five years. After three payments, however, she stopped. Lack of funds was the official reason given, but undoubtedly anger over the Texas question was a contributing factor.

Mexican-American relations were also strained by unsatisfactory commercial relations between the two countries and by fear of American expansionism. California, New Mexico, and even Mexico itself seemed to be in danger. The *New York Herald* stated: "The bastard republic of Mexico appears to be in the last stages of decline; it is a mere skeleton of a nation, and can only be restored to full health by the Anglo-Saxon race, given in suitable doses."

The Slidell Mission

Despite the severance of diplomatic relations in 1845, it still seemed possible that war could be avoided. President Polk, aware that the Oregon question might result in hostilities with England, was anxious to find a peaceful solution to the difficulties with Mexico. Enthusiastic expansionist though he was, he believed that the American frontier movement and the timely offer of American money could bring California under the American flag without the use of force.

In Mexico, meanwhile, even though open preparations for war were being made, pacific influences were also at work. President Herrera was intelligent enough to realize that war was more likely to add to than to solve his country's difficulties. Accordingly, when the American consul asked him whether a new envoy from the United States might be received, the answer was favorable.

Encouraged by this report, Polk appointed John Slidell, a congressman from Louisiana, as Minister to Mexico. His instructions, dated November 10, 1845, were to counteract the influence of foreign powers and to restore "those ancient relations of peace and good will which formerly existed" between the United States and Mexico. Slidell should first deal with the long-accumulated claims of American citizens. Secretary Buchanan conceded that the Mexican government was not in a position to satisfy these with money, but outstanding boundary disputes between the two countries suggested a way to solve the problem. Waiving the Mexican contention that Texas extended no farther than the Nueces River, Slidell was to offer to have the American government assume payment of the claims of its own citizens against Mexico, if the Mexican government would accept the boundary as defined by the Texas Congress in 1836. This would follow the Rio Grande from mouth to source and thence run due north to the 42nd parallel, thus including part of New Mexico. If Mexico would accept either of two other suggested lines somewhat farther to the west and including still more of New Mexico, the United States would be willing to pay an additional 5 million dollars.

The instructions to Slidell also raised the explosive issue of California. After expressing serious apprehension that Great Britain and France had designs upon this weakly held Mexican territory, Buchanan informed Slidell:

> Under these circumstances, it is the desire of the President that you shall use your best efforts to obtain a cession of that province from Mexico to the United States. Could you accomplish this object, you would render immense service to your country, and establish an enviable reputation for yourself. Money would be no object, when compared with the value of the acquisition. Still, the attempt must be made with great prudence and caution, and in such a manner as not to alarm the jealousy of the Mexican government.

For all of California Polk was willing to pay 25 million dollars; for the northern part, to include San Francisco Bay, he would go as high as 20 million dollars. All in all, Slidell's instructions reflected not so much an intention to coerce Mexico as a rather naïve overestimate of what money would do in the way of overcoming the hostility of a proudly nationalistic people.

The mission was a total failure. By the time Slidell reached Mexico, the Herrera administration had come to regret its promise to receive a new envoy. Already under attack for not being firm enough in defense of Mexican rights, the regime readily found an excuse for not accepting Slidell. It objected to the American envoy's commission because he came as a regular minister empowered to deal with a great variety of problems rather than as a special commissioner to treat on the Texas issue alone.

After this initial impasse, the situation rapidly went from bad to worse. The Polk administration, insisting that the annexation of Texas was a completely closed matter, made the satisfaction of American claims the principal issue and refused to change Slidell's commission. In Mexico, the tottering Herrera regime fell in December, 1845, and General Mariano Paredes, supported by a coalition of clerics, militarists, and monarchists, became temporary President of the country. The new administration was even more firmly opposed than its predecessor to negotiating with the Americans. In March, 1846, Slidell made a final effort to carry out his mission, only to be rebuffed in haughty fashion.

In refusing even to treat with the American envoy, the Mexican government was living dangerously. Public opinion had become violently anti-American. Conservatives disliked the democratic ideas and the Protestantism of the northern neighbor, while Mexicans of all classes resented *yanqui* brusqueness and assumptions of superiority. Instead of fearing war with the United States, many Mexicans welcomed the idea. They regarded the Americans as unmilitary, ready to bluff and brag but not to fight. Well aware of Northern opposition to Southern expansion, the Mexicans believed the United States would be too bitterly divided to wage war effectively. Moreover, despite British advice that Mexico follow a more pacific policy, the Paredes government, like its predecessors, counted on aid from across the Atlantic. With the Oregon issue still unsettled in the early months of 1846, these calculations had some rational basis.

On May 8, 1846, Slidell returned to Washington with his report on the futility of further negotiations. The following day the Polk Cabinet made the final decision on the next step to be taken—a step under discussion for several weeks. All agreed that Polk should ask Congress to declare war. On the very night of this decision, news reached the capital that hostilities had already begun two weeks earlier.

Alleged Aggression

Behind the skirmish that brought Mexican and American forces into conflict on April 25, 1846, lay several months of maneuvering on the Texas frontier. As soon as Texas had accepted the American annexation order, the United States government had assumed the responsibility of defending its acquisition from threatened Mexican attack. At the end of July, 1845, General Zachary Taylor had started building up a military force at Corpus Christi on the Gulf Coast. Since this was south of the Nueces River, it lay in territory that Mexico denied was part of Texas. Nevertheless, American penetration into the disputed zone was not deep enough to be highly provocative.

When early reports from Slidell in Mexico made war seem likely, the Polk administration ordered General Taylor on January 13, 1846, to advance to the Rio Grande, but to avoid hostilities unless war were declared or his army were attacked. From Polk's point of view, this was a natural move: if war were inevitable, this was a step to protect what the Americans claimed to be national territory; if war did not materialize, it would increase the diplomatic pressure on Mexico for a settlement. From the Mexican point of view—and from the point of view of Polk's Whig critics —the advance was a deliberate challenge.

At all events, Taylor's arrival on the great river opposite Matamoras was soon followed by fateful action. On April 12, the Mexican general, Pedro Ampudia, ordered the Americans to withdraw north of the Nueces. This demand was refused, and on April 25 hostilities began in a skirmish between a small scouting party of Americans and a larger force of Mexicans who had crossed the Rio Grande. Several Americans were killed and wounded, and the remainder were captured.

This was the news that reached Washington on May 9, just after the Polk administration had already decided to ask Congress for a declaration of war. The President eagerly seized upon the incident to justify his course. In his message to Congress on May 11, he asserted:

> The cup of forbearance had been exhausted even before the recent information from the frontier of the Del Norte. But now, after reiterated menaces, Mexico has passed the boundary of the United States, has invaded our territory and shed American blood upon the American soil. She has proclaimed that hostilities have commenced, and that the two nations are now at war.

For the moment, Polk's charge that American blood had been shed on American soil created a strong impression. The House of Representatives passed the war resolution by a vote of 174 to 14 after only half an hour of debate; the Senate was somewhat more deliberative, but delayed for only a day before assenting by a vote of 42 to 2.

Even in the excitement of the moment, however, Polk's policy did not escape criticism. Congressman Joshua Giddings of Ohio, an ardent opponent of slavery, charged that "the President obviously intended to involve us in a war with Mexico." Congressman Alexander H. Stephens, a Georgia Whig, called the conflict an "Executive war" that had resulted from Polk's "impudence, indiscretion, and mismanagement." Even Senator John C. Calhoun, the veteran South Carolina Democrat, rebelled against voting for a preamble to the war resolution that would have declared that the conflict had begun "by the act of the Republic of Mexico."

As the war dragged on over many months, criticism of the President increased. He was contemptuously referred to as "Polk the Mendacious"— a phrase that implied he had lied in attributing the outbreak of hostilities to an act of Mexican aggression. Almost all the Whigs and many Northern Democrats joined in the attack upon the President. Denying that the war was one of defense, they charged that it was being fought to add new slave states to the Union. In view of Polk's attempts to negotiate and the stubbornness of the Mexican refusals, it was hardly just to charge that the President had deliberately provoked war. A stronger case could be made, however, for criticizing his policy as inept.

The Trist Mission

The military history of the war was an almost monotonous record of American victories. After several sharply fought battles, General Taylor completely controlled northern Mexico. The California ports fell to the American Navy with scarcely any opposition, while an overland expedition, under Colonel Stephen Kearny, captured the important New Mexico trading post of Santa Fé. Kearny then led his forces on to California to complete the American domination of that territory, already far advanced by Frémont's Bear Flag rebellion and by the action of the Navy. Though of minor military significance, these operations were of diplomatic importance because they guaranteed that California and New Mexico, the goals of Polk's ambition, would be in American hands when peace negotiations began.

Since war had come, the President hoped for a short conflict. Taylor was under orders to carry on operations on a limited scale and to attempt to reconcile the Mexican population as he advanced. Polk believed the Mexican government would speedily realize its mistake and agree to negotiate on the basis laid down in the Slidell instructions.

These hopes for a short war and a speedy peace were doomed to disappointment. Polk's first disillusionment came when he attempted to make use of the notorious Santa Anna. This wily politician, living in exile in Havana when hostilities began, managed to get word to Washington that he would be amenable to peace proposals if he could return to power in Mexico. Accordingly, he was quietly passed through the American blockade. He double-crossed Polk by using his return to the presidency of Mexico not to make peace, but to rally his people for further resistance. In a second effort to hasten negotiations, Polk tried to persuade Congress to appropriate 2 million dollars for vaguely defined purposes. Undoubtedly the President wanted this large amount of cash so that he could make an immediate payment to any Mexican government ready to risk the hostility of its own people by ceding territory to the United States. A suspicious Congress refused to pass the bill, and its only result was to introduce into American politics the Wilmot Proviso, a highly controversial proposal to prohibit slavery in any territory acquired as a result of the war.

Thwarted in these attempts to negotiate, Polk tried to intensify pressure upon the Mexicans by ordering Taylor to be more aggressive and by sending General Winfield Scott to make an amphibious attack on Vera Cruz and then to march on Mexico City. Scott's campaign was brilliant and successful, but the ironic result was to throw Mexico into almost hopeless chaos. Santa Anna fled the country again, and it seemed to the perplexed Americans that the making of a peace treaty had become almost impossible because Mexico had no government sufficiently strong and stable to represent the defeated party.

It was in this difficult situation that one of the most curious diplomatic missions in American history was initiated. Soon after Scott invaded Mexico, President Polk sent Nicholas P. Trist, the chief clerk of the State Department, to join him. Trist was under secret instructions to open negotiations with the enemy at the first favorable opportunity, and he was provided with a draft treaty for this purpose. He was to insist upon a cession of California and New Mexico, but was authorized to offer as much as 30 million dollars as compensation, provided Mexico would grant the maximum American demands, which would have included both Upper and Lower California.

Polk, by nature secretive in his methods, had particular reason to cover his movements in view of the bitterly partisan attacks to which his every step was being subjected. Nevertheless, his elaborate precautions to have Trist travel incognito proved futile. Shortly after the envoy's departure, news leaked to the newspapers of his actual instructions, thereby revealing to the country the full extent of the administration's war aims.

Trist was condemned as a nonentity and a Democratic political hack, unequal to the task entrusted to him—a somewhat unjust judgment, since through experience in the State Department and his good knowledge of Spanish he actually possessed useful qualifications. General Scott, a Whig with political ambitions, at first looked upon Trist as a political commissar sent by the Democratic administration to spy upon him and threatened to resign unless his unwelcome guest were recalled. By a curious turn of events, however, the mutual hostility between Scott and Trist soon turned to friendship. The special envoy even sided with Scott in an acrimonious dispute which later broke out between the general and some of his Democratic subordinates.

In the highly charged political atmosphere of the day, the more closely Scott and Trist cooperated, the more both men fell in disfavor with the Polk administration. The President's suspicion reached a climax when he learned that Scott had granted the enemy a temporary armistice in August, 1847, to allow Trist to attempt peace negotiations before the final assault on the capital. Even in its hour of extreme peril, however, the Mexican government would not concede more than the Nueces frontier in Texas and Californian territory around San Francisco. The peace talks therefore speedily broke down, and Scott renewed his offensive. Polk hastily concluded that the armistice had been a mistake and that Trist's bungling efforts might be regarded as a sign of American weakness. Consequently he ordered the discredited envoy to return home at once.

In those days of slow communication, dispatches were likely to arrive long after the situation that had occasioned them had significantly altered. By the time the recall reached Trist, Scott's army had occupied Mexico City, and a new Mexican government under Manuel de la Peña y Peña had come to power, reconciled to the necessity of making peace. The American envoy was faced with a difficult decision. Should he turn his back on the new situation and return to the United States? Or should he disobey his orders and remain in Mexico in a final effort to obtain a treaty? General Scott encouraged him to take the latter course. Both men believed that were the opportunity lost, the Mexican situation might deteriorate to the point where there would be no Mexican government with which to deal.

The Treaty of Guadalupe Hidalgo

On February 2, 1848, Trist and the Mexicans signed the Treaty of Guadalupe Hidalgo, which reestablished peace between the two countries. The new boundary was to be the Rio Grande, the southern boundary of New Mexico, and along the first branch of the Gila River to its juncture with the Rio Colorado, and then along the division line between Upper and Lower California. In practical terms, the United States acquired the Mexican provinces of New Mexico and Upper California, including the valuable ports of San Diego, Monterey, and San Francisco. As compensation, the United States paid Mexico 15 million dollars and assumed payment to its own citizens of the old prewar claims against Mexico. In other clauses, the United States promised to restrain the Indians in the ceded territory from attacks on Mexico, and the two parties agreed to arbitrate any future disputes.

The news that Trist had disobeyed his instructions filled President Polk with indignation. He wrote in his diary: "Trist has proved himself to be an impudent and unqualified scoundrel." Yet the President controlled his anger sufficiently not to disavow the new treaty without careful study.

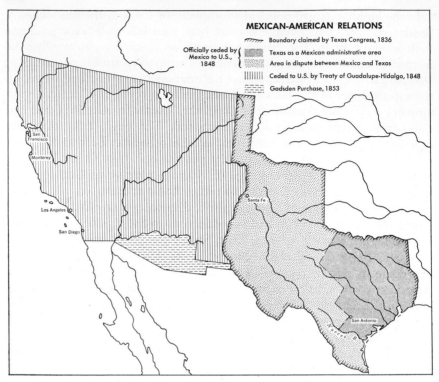

MEXICAN-AMERICAN RELATIONS

Boundary claimed by Texas Congress, 1836

Officially ceded by Mexico to U.S., 1848 { Texas as a Mexican administrative area

Area in dispute between Mexico and Texas

Ceded to U.S. by Treaty of Guadalupe-Hidalgo, 1848

Gadsden Purchase, 1853

When this study revealed that Trist had actually made a good settlement along the lines of his original instructions, the President decided to submit the document to the Senate. Here it encountered an initially hostile reception. All but one member of the Foreign Relations Committee favored rejection as a means of rebuking the disobedient envoy. Polk successfully pointed out, however, that Trist's treaty and not Trist himself was really the issue, and the document was allowed to go before the full Senate for debate.

When the treaty was considered on its merits, some senators opposed it because it added too much territory to the United States, and others because it added too little. Certain Whigs of both the East and the South disliked the annexation of vast new territories because it would precipitate a bitter struggle over the slavery issue. On the other hand, the most radical expansionists among the Democrats criticized the treaty because they sympathized with a war-born popular impulse to demand even more territory.

The movement to annex all or most of Mexico appeared for a time to be formidable. Within Polk's own Cabinet, Secretary of State Buchanan and Secretary of the Treasury Robert Walker gave it encouragement.

But the President, ardent expansionist though he had been, opposed this demand for unlimited aggrandizement. The Treaty of Guadalupe Hidalgo completed the accomplishment of his goals. To annex sparsely settled outlying provinces of Mexico was one thing; to add heavily populated parts of the Mexican homeland would be something quite different and would bring with it the difficult problems of assimilating an alien and hostile people.

Polk's judgment of the situation coincided with that of the great majority of Americans, both in and out of the Senate. Therefore, on March 10, 1848, the treaty was approved by a vote of 38 to 14. Philip Hone, a witty New York Whig, characterized the settlement as one "negotiated by an unauthorized agent, with an unacknowledged government, and submitted by an accidental President to a dissatisfied Senate." The unfortunate Trist was made the scapegoat for these frustrations. For the rest of his life Polk refused to speak to him, and was even so ungenerous as to refuse to approve his salary and expenses for the period following his recall—an injustice Congress did not remedy until 1871.

Wrangles over men and methods, however, could not halt the march of events. The demand of Eastern merchants for ports on the Pacific and the pressure of westward-moving frontiersmen had combined to influence the course of diplomacy and war. Between 1845 and 1848, the United States had acquired the vast territories of Texas, Oregon, California, and New Mexico, thereby increasing its total area by about one-third.

13

LOOKING FOR NEW WORLDS TO CONQUER

The annexation of Texas, Oregon, and California—all within a period of four years—did not sate the appetite of American expansionists. On the contrary, these relatively easy successes contributed to the growth of an assertive nationalism that threatened to lead the country into dangerous adventures.

General Zachary Taylor took with him to the White House in 1849 the brusque forcefulness reflected in his nickname of "Old Rough and Ready." During his fifteen months as President, Taylor, supported by his loyal Secretary of State, John M. Clayton of Delaware, expelled the French Minister over a minor episode and broke off diplomatic relations with Portugal. After the old soldier's death in July, 1850, the Presidency passed into the more cautious hands of Millard Fillmore, who made the experienced Daniel Webster his Secretary of State. Even with this change of personnel, American diplomacy still displayed a high degree of boast and bluster in its defiance of Old World monarchism and advocacy of republicanism.

In this flurry of jingoism, Whig politicians assumed the protective coloration necessary for survival in a day of noisy nationalism, but even so they did not escape Democratic condemnation for lack of spirit. The Clayton-Bulwer Treaty, negotiated to end Anglo-American rivalry in Central America, was denounced as a shameless Whig surrender of national interest. When Franklin K. Pierce became President and William L. Marcy Secretary of State in 1853, the new administration embarked on a vigorous foreign policy intended to bring additional territory under the American flag and greater popularity to the Democratic party.

Fortunately, there was more thunder than lightning in these diplomatic squalls. Whigs and Democrats alike wisely chose the path of compromise when foreign issues became really serious.

The Kossuth Affair

During the year 1848 a tidal wave of revolution swept over Europe, convulsing the politics of France, Germany, Italy, and the Austrian Empire. At first the liberals carried everything before them, but this phase was short-lived, for soon almost all their gains were lost in ensuing counter-revolutions.

Americans did not conceal their strong sympathy for the republican movement abroad. They followed with particular interest developments in Hungary, where revolution ran its full cycle during the years 1848 and 1849. From moderate demands for autonomy and constitutional guarantees, the Hungarians, threatened by restoration of Habsburg absolutism, passed to the radical position of declaring their national independence in April, 1849. As President, they named Louis Kossuth, an eloquent orator and journalist.

President Taylor and Secretary Clayton, eager that the United States be the first to recognize the new republic if it could maintain itself, sent Dudley Mann to Hungary as a special agent to study the situation. Before the American envoy could carry out his mission, Austrian and Russian troops had crushed the Kossuth regime and restored the "legitimate" rule of Emperor Francis Joseph.

Despite the fact that the Mann mission was abortive, the Austrian government unwisely made an issue of President Taylor's conduct. In September, 1850, after Taylor's death, Chevalier J. G. Hülsemann, Austrian Minister to the United States, protested both the Mann mission itself and the language sympathetic to Hungary that the late President had used in his annual message to Congress.

This protest provided Daniel Webster, the new Secretary of State, with a rare opportunity to exercise his patriotic rhetoric. In his famous "Hülsemann letter," Webster made the familiar point that a President's communications to Congress are purely domestic in character and thus not proper subjects for discussion with foreign governments. He defended Mann's fact-finding commission as "wholly unobjectionable and strictly within the rule of the law of nations and the duty of the United States as a neutral power." Having thus rejected the Austrian protest, the Secretary declared that republican movements would always arouse American sympathy:

> Well-known circumstances in their history, indeed their whole history, have made them the representatives of purely popular principles of government. In this light they now stand before the world. They could not, if they would, conceal their character, their condition, their destiny.

Webster boasted that the United States was spread over "one of the richest and most fertile" regions of the globe and that, in comparison, the Habsburg possessions were "but as a patch on the earth's surface." As far as European retaliation was concerned, "the United States are quite willing to take their chances and abide their destiny."

To a friend Webster readily confessed that his note had been "rough and boastful." "My excuse," he said, "is two fold: 1. I thought it well enough to speak out, and tell the people of Europe who and what we are, and awaken them to a just sense of the unparalleled growth of this country. 2. I wished to write a paper which should touch the national pride, and make a man feel *sheepish* and look *silly* who should speak of disunion." As the Secretary well knew, Austria was too far away to make her resentment of his language dangerous.

Habsburg dignity was still further wounded when Kossuth, who had fled to Turkey for refuge, was brought to the United States in an American naval vessel as guest of the nation. The famous rebel, regarded by the American public as a sort of Hungarian George Washington, was given a tumultuous welcome. President Fillmore entertained him at a White House dinner, and senators and representatives of both political parties turned out in force for a congressional banquet in his honor. Webster, hoping for the Whig presidential nomination, used this banquet as an occasion to express eloquent sympathy for "Hungarian independence, Hungarian self-government, Hungarian control of Hungarian destinies." Hülsemann, unwilling to accept Webster's explanation that he had been speaking in "his private capacity," withdrew from Washington until Webster's death made it possible to forget the incident.

The real disillusionment, however, was Kossuth's. The warmth of his reception had kindled hope that the United States would abandon its traditional policy of noninterference in European affairs to join with England in supporting the cause of Hungarian independence. But to all such proposals Webster was determined, as he said, to "have ears more deaf than adders." Other politicians who had wined and dined the Hungarian patriot were equally cool to appeals for material aid. For a time Kossuth had his hopes raised through his friendship with George Sanders, American consul at London and the moving spirit in a Democratic party faction called "Young America," which sought United States leadership in the republican movement throughout the world. The consul's London house became the meeting place for Kossuth, Mazzini, Garibaldi, and other famous European liberals. But the United States Senate, doubtless worried by all this radicalism, refused to confirm Sander's appointment and he had to come home, much to Kossuth's disappointment.

Relations between Austria and the United States were soon ruffled by another episode. The Hungarian patriot, Martin Koszta, who had also participated in the independence attempt of 1849, subsequently established residence in the United States. In 1853, while on a business trip to Smyrna, Turkey, he was seized by a gang, thrown into the harbor, and subsequently picked up and placed in irons aboard an Austrian naval vessel. American diplomatic representatives in Turkey demanded his release, but the Austrians refused. Just as Koszta was about to be taken to Austria, an American naval ship arrived in Smyrna harbor. Intervening on the prisoner's behalf, Captain David Ingraham threatened to use his guns unless Koszta were freed. As a result of this ultimatum, the Austrians turned their prisoner over to the custody of the local French consul.

Chevalier Hülsemann, who had come off second best in his diplomatic duel with Webster, now challenged Secretary Marcy with the demand that Ingraham be censured and Koszta turned over to the Austrian government. Although the Hungarian *émigré* was not actually an American citizen, he had taken the first steps toward naturalization; for this and other reasons, Marcy concluded that he was entitled to protection of the United States government. The Secretary's forceful exposition of his position was widely circulated throughout the country and brought the same enthusiastic response as had Webster's defiance of the Old World. Marcy's note was particularly useful to the Democrats in appealing to the immigrant vote. Koszta's adventures finally ended with his safe return to the United States.

New Interests in the Far East

In 1784, just a year after the close of the American Revolution, the *Empress of China* sailed from New York on the first American voyage to the Far East. She crossed the Atlantic, rounded the Cape of Good Hope, traversed the Indian Ocean, and successfully reached the Chinese port of Canton. A year later she was back in New York with a cargo of tea and other Far Eastern commodities. Other voyages soon followed to China, to India, and to the Dutch East Indies by both the Atlantic and Pacific routes. The latter was particularly important to the American future because it drew American ships to the Pacific Northwest and to the Hawaiian Islands.

Edmund Roberts, a New Hampshire merchant who understood from experience the inconveniences involved in visiting ports of Oriental despots, asked the United States government for authority to negotiate a series of commercial treaties. The Jackson administration gave him a rather halfhearted commission, and in 1833 Roberts made satisfactory agreements with Siam and Muscat.[1] This success encouraged the State

[1] Muscat was in southeastern Arabia. The Sultan of Muscat exercised wide powers in the western part of the Indian Ocean.

Department to send Roberts back to the Far East in 1835 to visit Cochin China and Japan. The envoy's death at Macao the next year brought this second mission to an unhappy termination before it had achieved any of its objectives.

Meanwhile, American merchants were developing a particularly profitable trade with China. The Middle Kingdom, as the Chinese called their vast empire, was proud of its ancient civilization. The Chinese emperor lived in remote splendor in the interior city of Peking and would not receive envoys from the outside world unless they bore tribute and abased themselves in the kowtow, thus acknowledging his suzerainty. Merchants, whether native or foreign, enjoyed little respect, and foreigners, regardless of their profession, were treated with contempt and suspicion.

Trade with the outside world was permitted only at the Portuguese leasehold of Macao and in the great Chinese port of Canton. Foreigners at Canton were required to confine their activities to a limited area outside the city wall and to carry on all their dealings with a few designated Chinese traders called the hong merchants. The latter paid the provincial bureaucracy heavily for their privileges and recouped by extorting from foreigners. Although these exactions were heavy and conditions of trade humiliating, American merchants at Canton made good profits and did not at first request any special protection from their own government.

The Opium War

This *status quo* was disrupted during the late 1830s when the Chinese government sought to stamp out the opium trade. Although the importation of this drug had always been illegal, the connivance of local Chinese officials had made smuggling easy, and thus a large trade in opium had been built. Foreign merchants closed their eyes to the moral issues involved in this demoralizing traffic because opium proved to be one of the few commodities the annoyingly self-sufficient Chinese would accept in exchange for their tea and silks. Americans, like the English and other foreigners, were heavily involved in this drug trade. When the Chinese government abruptly changed its policy and, by harsh and arbitrary measures, attempted to destroy the traffic it had so long tolerated, serious trouble followed. England and China became involved in the so-called Opium War (1839–1842)—somewhat misleadingly named because the real issue was the unsatisfactory system under which China had been conducting all her relations with the rest of the world.

China, unable to resist British coercion, was compelled to sign the Treaty of Nanking (1842), under which the English obtained the island of Hongkong, while four other ports besides Canton were opened to foreign trade.

It was important to the future of the Far East that the British not be granted exclusive privileges in the five ports. Therefore the Chinese government, with British approval, extended equal trading opportunities to all foreigners, thus recognizing the "most favored nation" principle; this, in turn, was the foundation of the Open Door policy of later fame.

Since the Treaty of Nanking brought these automatic advantages to American merchants, the United States was placed in the happy position of having its citizens gain new rights in China without paying the price, either in military expenditures or in Chinese resentment, that the British had. But this achievement did not satisfy American ambition. During the opium crisis in 1839, American merchants at Canton had asked Congress to appoint a commissioner to negotiate a commercial treaty with China. While the Anglo-Chinese War was in progress, American interest in China mounted, as the public, conveniently ignoring its own country's complicity in the opium traffic, self-righteously condemned the British.

The Cushing Mission

On December 30, 1842, after news of the Treaty of Nanking reached Washington, President Tyler sent to Congress a special message, recommending that a permanent commissioner be authorized "to reside in China to exercise a watchful care over the concerns of American citizens." Although the unpopular Tyler administration was unable to obtain the full appropriation it had requested, Congress did approve a special mission. The President appointed to this post Webster's political ally, Caleb Cushing, a Massachusetts lawyer and member of the House Committee on Foreign Affairs. In order to impress the Chinese, Cushing fitted himself with a major general's uniform, braided and embroidered even beyond the custom of the day. More to the point, perhaps, was the arrangement for an escort of a fleet of naval vessels.

By combining genial courtesy with vague hints of unpleasant consequences that might follow failure of his negotiations, Cushing obtained from the Chinese an agreement, in some respects more favorable than the one England had exacted by force of arms. This Treaty of Wanghia, signed July 3, 1844, liberalized the conditions under which merchants could do business in the open ports, permitted foreigners to employ Chinese teachers and to purchase Chinese books, and stipulated that the treaty might be revised after twelve years. More important still, it set forth the principle of extraterritoriality, that is, the right of United States citizens to be tried and punished by their own consuls rather than by Chinese courts. Cushing's treaty provided the model for Chinese treaties subsequently made by France, Norway, and Sweden. The partial opening of China, effected through the Opium War and the subsequent treaties, was important not only in increasing commercial contacts between the Orient and the West, but in encouraging the activities of missionaries.

During the years 1857 to 1860, China's relations with the outside world were once again rudely jolted when she became involved in two new wars with England and France. Russia and the United States remained neutral, but benefited through a new series of treaties exacted from China at Tientsin in 1858. Eleven new treaty ports were opened; foreigners gained the right to travel and trade throughout China; and the various powers were permitted to maintain legations at Peking.

Early American Interest in Japan

Japan's first contacts with the Western world had occurred during the sixteenth century when Portuguese and Spanish traders and missionaries made their way into this remote area. These were later followed by the Dutch and the English. For several decades the foreigners had been well treated, and many Japanese accepted Christianity. Gradually, however, dissensions among the missionaries themselves and fear of their growing influence had brought a drastic reaction. Many foreigners were killed or expelled, the native Christians persecuted out of existence, and practically all contact between Japan and the outside world cut off. No Japanese subject could travel abroad and no foreigner visit Japan. The Japanese were even forbidden to build ships larger than those needed to navigate their own waters. The only foreigners to whom any concessions were made were the Dutch and the Chinese, who were allowed a very limited trade at Nagasaki. The Dutch had to carry on all their transactions on the island of Deshima and were placed under the most humiliating restrictions.

Behind these barriers Japan maintained a picturesque but static civilization, largely derived from the Chinese. The nominal head of the state was the Mikado, regarded as divine and living in seclusion at Kyoto; the effective ruler was the Shogun, who lived in his palace in Yedo (Tokyo). Society was organized along feudal lines, with the daimyos, or nobles, and the samurai, or warriors, as the most respected classes.

In 1798, when the Napoleonic War made the Dutch cautious about sailing ships under their own flag, they chartered an American vessel, the *Eliza*, to make the annual voyage from the East Indies to the trading post at Deshima. American sea captains in Dutch employ visited Japanese waters in several subsequent years, thus planting the seed of American interest in this remote and mysterious kingdom.

During the 1830s and 1840s, Japan grew somewhat more important in the American consciousness. Yankee whaling ships, carrying on their adventurous trade in the northern Pacific, often sighted these islands. From time to time an American whaler or a cargo vessel bound for China would be shipwrecked off the Japanese coast. The more fortunate survivors were well cared for and eventually turned over to the Dutch at Deshima. On a few occasions, however, the castaways were treated as spies and imprisoned for many months before their eventual release. Stories of such cruelties circulated in the maritime districts of the United States and created a demand that the government do something about the situation.

The belief that Japan should be forced to make some kind of commercial treaty was increased by the success of the Roberts and Cushing missions and by the mounting importance placed upon Far Eastern trade after the annexation of Oregon and California. By the 1840s, moreover, steamships had been improved to such an extent that the possibility of establishing steamer lines across the Pacific was being discussed. Coal was essential for this purpose, and Japan was rumored to have valuable deposits. Consequently, Commodore James Biddle visited Japan in 1846 to inquire whether the government would be willing to make a treaty with the United States. The reply was blunt: Biddle was ordered to depart and never to come back.

The Perry Mission

Such was the situation when the Fillmore administration took up the problem. Appropriately, Daniel Webster, who had drafted Cushing's instructions in 1844, was once again Secretary of State when an American naval expedition to Japan was being planned. Webster made the first draft of instructions for the projected mission, but his fatal illness placed the final arrangements in other hands. Commodore Matthew C. Perry, selected to lead the expedition, was allowed a large share in the writing of his own instructions. To Edward Everett, the new Secretary of State, was entrusted the task of composing a properly rhetorical letter from President Fillmore to the Japanese Shogun.

It had originally been planned to send a fleet of eleven or more vessels, but the force that Perry actually took with him to Japan was much smaller, being composed of two side-wheel steamships and two sloops. This flotilla made its appearance in the Bay of Yedo on July 8, 1853, anchoring off Uraga, about 30 miles from the city of Yedo. When local Japanese officials ordered these ships to withdraw to Nagasaki, Perry firmly refused. Japanese guard boats were sternly warned to keep their distance.

Conducting himself with firm courtesy, Commodore Perry sought to impress the Japanese with the importance of his mission. He remained in the seclusion of his own quarters and dealt with local officials only through his subordinates. Unless the Shogun designated a person of suitable rank to receive the President's letter, Perry threatened to land with a sufficient force to deliver it in person. Bowing to the commodore's will, the Japanese made the necessary arrangements, and on July 14 an impressive ceremony took place. While some six thousand Japanese troops, armed with bows, antique muskets, and other weapons, lined the beaches for a mile or more, Perry came ashore, accompanied by a force of about four hundred men, and ceremoniously delivered the President's papers and other communications to two high dignitaries.

After thus notifying the Japanese of the American desire for a treaty, Perry wisely acceded to the Japanese request for ample time to consider their reply. To his hosts' great relief, he announced that he would go away and return in the spring. The American fleet spent the next few months in Asiatic waters and, enlarged to a total of nine ships, came back to Yedo Bay in February, 1854. This time Perry met a friendly reception, and the Japanese announced their decision to negotiate. To symbolize the new relationship, the two parties exchanged elaborate courtesies. The Americans presented the Japanese with such examples of Yankee ingenuity as illustrated books, telegraph instruments, and a miniature steam railroad; the Japanese reciprocated with gifts of silks, lacquerwork, and porcelains.

Perry's treaty, signed March 31, 1854, was something of an anticlimax. As compared with Cushing's treaty, it conceded very little. The Japanese agreed to give proper treatment to shipwrecked seamen and to open two minor ports for the purchase of supplies. The treaty did not give the Americans extraterritorial rights, but it did contain a most favored nation clause, promising that Japan would automatically extend to the United States any privileges granted to other foreign powers.

The commodore's visit to Japan was much more important than this slender treaty would indicate. The American fleet had made its visit at a strategic moment, when the old system of exclusion was under pressure from many quarters. Through their contacts with the Dutch, the Japanese had become aware of the growing material power of the Western world and the unhappy experience of the Chinese in their attempt to resist English demands. They were even more conscious of the imperial expansion of Russia, which had carried Tsarist domination to the coast of Siberia and was threatening Sakhalin and the Kurile Islands. Under these mounting pressures, the Japanese leaders were divided; some wanted to continue the rigid policy of seclusion; others believed Japan must accept contacts with the outside world in order to learn the technological secrets that gave the West such menacing power.

Perry's opening of Japan had its immediate result in encouraging other governments to demand treaties. England, Russia, and the Netherlands all obtained agreements with Japan during 1854 and 1855. In so far as these treaties went beyond Perry's, the new concessions were automatically extended to the United States under the most favored nation principle.

The Accomplishments of Townsend Harris

It remained, however, for another able American to take the next major step toward changing Japan's relations with the outside world. The first consul appointed under the new treaties was Townsend Harris, a New York merchant, whom the Pierce administration chose for this important post in 1855. Taking up his residence at Shimoda the next year, Harris set for himself two immediate objectives: to gain an audience with the Shogun himself and to negotiate a real commercial treaty. In both of these Harris was successful. Although the Japanese resorted to evasion and delay, the politely insistent Harris was eventually presented to the Shogun. While a roomful of Japanese dignitaries prostrated themselves before their ruler, Harris stood proudly erect and made his formal address.

The treaty, signed in 1858, was a document of vital importance. A total of five ports were opened to trade under liberal regulations; in these Americans might lease land and erect buildings; in two other cities, Yedo and Osaka, they received more limited rights of residence. The Americans were to have free exercise of their religion and rights of extraterritoriality. Perhaps most important of all, Japan and the United States recognized the reciprocal right of each to maintain a diplomatic legation at the capital of the other.

Without any threat of force Harris had achieved a great triumph of American diplomacy. The consul's fairness and courtesy made him highly popular among the pro-Western faction of the Japanese. Unfortunately, however, the opening of the nation was bitterly opposed by many conservative nobles. In the early 1860s, when Japan was pressed by the demands of other powers, a wave of antiforeign demonstration swept over the country. The Mikado ordered the outsiders expelled, and a powerful daimyo undertook to close the Straits of Shimonoseki to foreign shipping. This led to punitive action by the Western powers. A United States naval vessel, the *Wyoming*, sank two hostile Japanese ships in 1863, and the following year another American vessel cooperated with British, Dutch, and French ships in an attack on the Shimonoseki ports. An indemnity of 3 million dollars was imposed upon Japan; the American share of $270,000 was eventually returned to Japan in 1883 by congressional order.

These unhappy events were symptomatic of a great internal crisis in Japanese politics. The Shogun's inability to defend the kingdom turned a powerful faction of the daimyos against him. As a result, in 1867 he was compelled to relinquish his powers, and the Mikado thereupon assumed full authority. This "Meiji Restoration" was followed by one of the most remarkable transformations of a nation's government and society in all history.

Other Pacific Interests

As soon as American vessels began to cross the Pacific in the late eighteenth century, the unusual importance of Hawaii became obvious. These islands were ideally located to break the long trans-Pacific passage and to provide water and supplies. A few American traders decided to reside there permanently. An American influence of another kind began in 1820, when a group of Protestant missionaries arrived. As a religious field, Hawaii proved extraordinarily fruitful, for thousands of converts were made, with far-reaching consequences for the native culture. Americans who came to Hawaii to trade or to preach fell in love with the delightful climate and remained to make homes and raise families. For a livelihood, many grew sugar and other semitropical crops. Thus the American colony, composed of merchants, whalers, missionaries, and planters, stead-

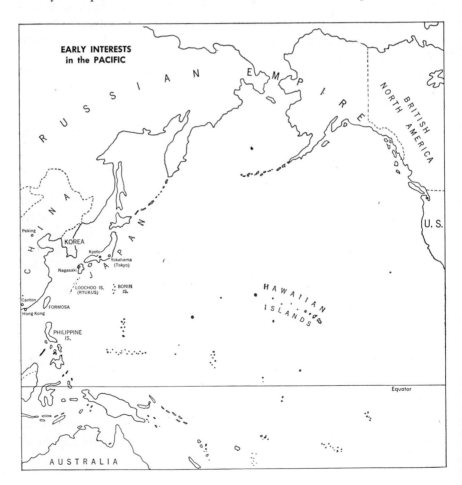

ily increased. This growth, in turn, influenced Hawaiian politics, as the native kings accepted an increasing amount of American advice.

Islands of such obvious strategic importance could not fail to attract the attention of other nations as well, and British and French ships visited frequently. For this reason, President Tyler made an important statement of American policy in 1842—in the same message to Congress in which he proposed the Cushing mission to China. Any attempt by another power to seize or colonize Hawaii, or to subvert its government, Tyler declared, "could not but create dissatisfaction on the part of the United States." He went on to explain that the United States sought no exclusive privileges for itself in the area, "but is content with its independent existence and anxiously wishes for its security and prosperity."

The American pronouncement came none too soon. Within a few months an overzealous British naval officer raised the Union Jack over Hawaii and claimed the islands for his sovereign. Commodore Lawrence Kearny of the United States Navy, returning from a voyage to China, vigorously protested this action. When the State Department followed with a formal remonstrance, the British government promptly disavowed the act. In 1849 a somewhat similar incident occurred when the French seized Honolulu, only to retire when the United States made known its displeasure.

The Hawaiian King, eager to keep his country out of European hands, offered the islands to the United States. No action was taken by the Whigs, but the Democrats were definitely interested in this opportunity to advance the American flag a third of the way across the Pacific. Secretary of State Marcy authorized the negotiation of an annexation treaty. Such a treaty was actually drafted, but President Pierce dropped the matter after receiving a sharp British protest and criticism from Americans opposed to the provision for Hawaiian statehood.

Commodore Perry frankly favored the annexation of Far Eastern bases. While he was sailing on his mission to Japan, he recommended that the United States attempt to gain footholds in the Loochoo Islands (now called the Ryukyu Islands, located south of Japan), the Bonins (east of the Loochoos), and Formosa. Washington looked upon these ambitious proposals with great caution. The Fillmore administration authorized Perry to occupy ports in the Loochoos only if Japan refused to make a treaty; the Pierce administration was even more reluctant to consider annexation unless authorized by Congress. In the end, the success of Perry in obtaining what he asked from Japan decided the question.[2]

[2] Meanwhile, however, America's future interest in Okinawa had been anticipated in the fact that Perry made this island (then called Great Loochoo) the rendezvous for his fleet. He also made an agreement with the king of the Loochoos similar to the treaty he had concluded with Japan. When Japan formally asserted sovereignty over the islands in 1872, she promised to continue these privileges.

In the case of the Bonins, Perry went farther in trying to commit his government to a policy of annexation. At his orders, an American vessel took formal possession of the so-called Baily's Islands in the southern part of the Bonin group. The British entered a counterclaim, but neither government was deeply interested in the question. Thus when Japan asserted sovereignty over the entire Bonin group in 1862, the Western powers readily acquiesced.

To Perry and other early American expansionists, Formosa was particularly inviting because this feebly held Chinese possession had valuable coal deposits. An American firm, dealing in camphor, established a trading post there during the 1850s, and even raised the American flag. Dr. Peter Parker, a medical missionary who was made United States commissioner to China in 1855, strongly recommended that his government retaliate for various Chinese affronts by taking Formosa. But once more the Pierce administration resisted temptation. Parker was bluntly notified in 1857 that the United States was not at war with China, "nor does it seek to enter into that empire for any other purpose than those of lawful commerce, and for the protection of the lives and property of its citizens."

Thus manifest destiny, which had carried the American flag to the Pacific Coast, was not yet extended to the acquisition of distant insular possessions. During the 1850s the Hawaiian Islands were particularly appealing, but even there the annexation movement was premature. The idea of Perry and Parker that the United States should follow the example of England in laying claim to strategic island bases did not gain wide support. Whigs and Democrats alike confined their policy to the extension of opportunities to American merchants and missionaries through such treaties as those made with China and Japan.

The Central American Puzzle

Democratic and Whig administrations from 1845 to 1860 were compelled to pay increasing attention to problems arising out of Anglo-American relations in Central America. The prize at stake was control over any canal that might be built to connect the Atlantic and Pacific Oceans.

Dreams of such a waterway had begun almost as soon as Spanish explorers had learned enough of New World geography to demonstrate that North and South America were connected by a narrow isthmus. After the United States became an independent nation, her statesmen inherited an interest in such a project. In 1826, for example, Clay's instructions to the American delegates to the Panama Congress had referred to the possibility of an isthmian canal. Talk of this kind continued to be casual, however, until the 1840s, when American settlement on the Pacific Coast suddenly made the issue of communication vitally important.

These changed circumstances spurred American leaders to consider seriously affairs in Central America, where the situation was anything but assuring. After the collapse of the Spanish Empire, a Central American federation had been organized, but rivalries among the constituent states had prevented the union from becoming strong. Between Mexico on the north and New Granada (the future Colombia) on the south, five weak republics—Guatemala, Honduras, Salvador, Nicaragua, and Costa Rica—had taken their places on the map.

These weak and divided Central American republics had created a vacuum of effective sovereignty into which British power had been steadily pushing since 1815. The first center of influence was Belize, a coastal district to the north and west of the Bay of Honduras. Buccaneers in search of valuable logwood had been the first Englishmen to visit this region in the seventeenth century. The Spaniards had tried to drive the log cutters out, but the British had persisted in their encroachments and had been able to maintain a number of coastal settlements. In 1786, the situation had been clarified by a treaty in which Spain admitted the right of the British to occupy the coast and carry on their lumbering operations, while the British recognized the sovereignty of Spain over the territory. When the rest of Central America became independent of Spain, the British found it convenient to maintain the fiction that Belize was still under the Spanish crown. This distinguished it from the rest of Central America and gave the British a free hand to transform it gradually into the colony of British Honduras and to enlarge its boundaries.

A second area of British interest lay in the Bay Islands in the Bay of Honduras. Although the Republic of Honduras had attempted to establish its sovereignty over these strategically located bits of territory, British local officials from Belize had forced the Honduran flag to be lowered in 1838 and had raised that of Great Britain.

The third and, in some ways, most critical region over which the English extended their influence was the so-called Mosquito Coast, to the east of Honduras and Nicaragua. This was the home of the Mosquito Indians, a hybrid people descended from aborigines, runaway Negro slaves, and white adventurers. The Mosquitos had resisted effective subjection by the Spaniards through cultivating close relations with the British colony of Jamaica. English traders took up their residence at Bluefields and other Mosquito towns. Here, as in Belize and the Bay Islands, the collapse of the Spanish Empire provided an opportunity for the British to extend their influence. The old alliance with the Mosquitos was transformed into a full protectorate. In 1844, the territory was given the name of Mosquitia and its own flag, closely resembling the Union Jack.

The Bidlack Treaty

How had Washington reacted to these various events? Although the territorial extension of Belize, the occupation of the Bay Islands, and the tightened protectorate over the Mosquito Coast all challenged the non-colonization principle of the Monroe Doctrine, Jackson and Van Buren had made no serious protest. Central America had seemed too remote and too chaotic to arouse any lively American interest.

The first stirring of activity came during the Polk administration. In 1846, an opportunity suddenly arose for the United States to make a countermove. Benjamin Bidlack, the American Minister to New Granada, had been instructed to negotiate a new commercial treaty. At the suggestion of the Foreign Minister of New Granada, the treaty was extended to give the United States and its citizens a right of way across the Isthmus of Panama by any available method of transit. In return, the United States guaranteed neutrality of the isthmus, as well as New Granada's sovereign rights in the territory. Although a canal along this route did not materialize for sixty years, the Bidlack Treaty did facilitate the construction of an American-owned railroad across Panama in 1855.

The aggressive Polk might have been expected to challenge British expansion still more directly, but he was in no hurry to act. The Oregon controversy and the Mexican War made it unwise to look for new troubles. In 1848, however, the British took a step Polk could not afford

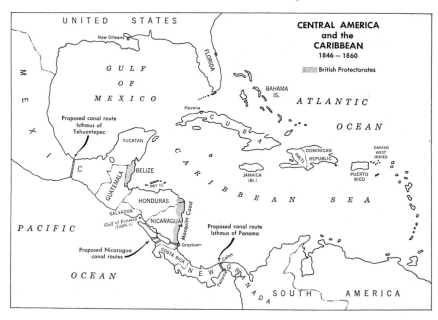

to ignore. Professing to act on behalf of their ally, the Mosquito king, they drove the Nicaraguan garrison from San Juan (called Greytown by the English) and raised the Mosquito flag. This seizure of the mouth of the San Juan River was of great significance because it gave the British control over the Atlantic terminal of one of the most promising canal routes. From the British point of view, this was a defensive step to prevent the expansion-minded Americans from gaining exclusive control over a Nicaraguan canal to the detriment of English shipping.

Although Polk did not reply directly to the Nicaraguan cry for help, he did send Elijah Hise to investigate the situation. Alarmed by evidence of British imperialism, Hise ignored his cautious instructions and negotiated a treaty with Nicaragua, by which the United States would receive exclusive rights to build and fortify a canal or other means of transportation in return for a guarantee of Nicaraguan territory.

Even before the Hise treaty reached the United States, the revolving wheel of politics had placed Taylor in the White House. The Whig administration replaced Hise with Ephraim George Squier, an energetic young man with an interest in archaeology. Squier became involved in a diplomatic duel with Frederick Chatfield, the British consul to Central America. While Squier worked to build a solid Central American front to oppose British expansion, Chatfield countered by playing up pro-English factions in Guatemala and Costa Rica. The latter, indeed, seemed on the road to becoming a British protectorate.

The Squier-Chatfield rivalry focused on the proposed Nicaraguan canal. Through the American envoy's efforts, the Nicaraguan government granted to an American company the right to build a canal by way of the San Juan River and Lake Nicaragua. Squier followed this by negotiating a new treaty, under which the United States and Nicaragua would defend the canal company's enterprise, while the United States would guarantee neutrality of the canal and Nicaragua's sovereignty along the canal route. Chatfield immediately informed Nicaragua that the lower part of the San Juan River belonged to Mosquitia. The British also warned the canal company not to begin construction without Mosquito approval.

Both Squier and Chatfield had their eyes on Tigre Island, a bit of Honduran territory in the Bay of Fonseca at the Pacific end of the projected canal. When Chatfield threatened British seizure of the island to enforce payment of certain claims, Squier induced Honduras to cede the territory to the United States for eighteen months pending future developments. Chatfield promptly ordered a British naval vessel to take possession of Tigre Island. Both envoys had been acting without instructions, and further trouble was avoided when Britain ordered an evacuation. Before English intentions were clear, however, the Tigre Island episode had played its part in antagonizing American public opinion.

The Clayton-Bulwer Treaty

Actually American and British envoys to Central America were playing the diplomatic game more aggressively than their respective governments. In repudiating the Hise treaty, Secretary of State Clayton showed his disapproval of seeking exclusive American control over the proposed canal. His ideal, on the contrary, was a neutralized waterway open to all countries on equal terms. He disliked the Mosquito king's seizure of San Juan, and indeed the whole fiction of an independent Mosquitia as a threat to such a neutralized canal. His objective, therefore, was to negotiate an Anglo-American treaty, under which the British would give up their protectorate and agree that neither nation would seek to control or fortify the projected canal.

Lord Palmerston, the British Foreign Secretary, was sympathetic to the ideal of the neutralized waterway and willing to give assurances that his country would not use its position in Central America to dominate the transit routes, but he opposed any explicit British pledge to give up the Mosquito protectorate. Under these circumstances, the negotiation of a canal treaty was largely a search for words—words that to the American government would convey the impression of a British retreat, but to the British would mean American acquiescence in the *status quo*.

After several months of delicate maneuvering both at London and Washington, Secretary Clayton signed a treaty with Sir Henry Bulwer, the British Minister, on April 19, 1850. In its important first article, the Clayton-Bulwer Treaty declared that neither party would ever "obtain or maintain for itself any exclusive control" over the proposed canal. The signatories further agreed that neither would maintain any fortification commanding the canal, "or occupy, or fortify, or colonize, or assume, or exercise any dominion over Nicaragua, Costa Rica, the Mosquito Coast, or any part of Central America." But what did these words mean? Did the British intend to keep their protectorate over the Mosquitos or to give it up? What was "Central America"? Did it include Belize and the Bay Islands? All these questions were left in doubt.

The rest of the treaty was more explicit. The two governments agreed to use their influence with the various Central American states to facilitate construction of the canal and to establish a free port at each end. They also promised to protect the canal against interruption of transit and to guarantee its neutrality. The principles of the treaty were to apply not only to a Nicaraguan canal, but to any other practicable means of transportation built across the isthmus at Panama, Tehuantepec, or elsewhere.

Although the Senate had a Democratic majority, Clayton gained approval for the treaty through the cooperation of Senator William R. King of Alabama, chairman of the Foreign Relations Committee. King defended the agreement as a victory for the Monroe Doctrine, since it would, he assumed, result in British abandonment of the Mosquito protectorate and a general backtracking elsewhere in the region. Despite the opposition of more partisan Democrats like Senator Stephen Douglas of Illinois, the treaty was approved by a vote of 42 to 11.

Palmerston, fearing the United States might use the Clayton-Bulwer Treaty to dispute the British position in Belize and the Bay Islands, instructed Bulwer to declare that Great Britain did not understand the new treaty "to apply to Her Majesty's settlement at Honduras or to its Dependencies." By "Dependencies" the British clearly meant the Bay Islands. Clayton's counterstatement avoided committing the United States this far, but did acknowledge that the negotiators had not understood the treaty to include British Honduras "nor the small islands in the neighborhood which may be known as its dependencies."

Although this exchange of interpretations was not officially submitted to the Senate, its contents became generally known and added to the unpopularity of the Clayton-Bulwer Treaty. The Democrats became increasingly hostile to the agreement when it became apparent the British did not consider themselves bound to relinquish what they had already taken in Central America, but only to take no more.

For ten years the interpretation of the Clayton-Bulwer Treaty remained a matter of controversy between England and the United States. American public opinion found a new source of grievance when a royal proclamation of 1852 announced the formal organization of the British "Colony of the Bay Islands." There were excited debates in Congress and numerous exchanges of notes between the two governments. The Buchanan administration seriously considered abrogating the treaty and attempting, in the name of the Monroe Doctrine, to force Britain out of all her Central American holdings, Belize included.

In the end, however, conciliatory counsels prevailed. President Buchanan and Secretary of State Lewis Cass promised to abide by the Clayton-Bulwer Treaty, and Britain agreed to acknowledge the sovereignty of Nicaragua over the Mosquito Coast and also to recognize that the Bay Islands belonged to Honduras. Belize, on the other hand, was to be retained as a British dependency, with boundaries to be defined by agreement with Guatemala. These arrangements were carried out in a series of treaties between Great Britain and the separate Central American states concerned. By December, 1860, President Buchanan could therefore announce to Congress:

> Our relations with Great Britain are of the most friendly character. . . .
> The discordant constructions of the Clayton and Bulwer treaty between
> the two Governments, which at different periods of the discussion bore

a threatening aspect, have resulted in a final settlement entirely satisfactory to this government.

The British decision to relinquish the Bay Islands and the Mosquito protectorate ended the first campaign to abrogate the Clayton-Bulwer Treaty. Indeed, it placed that disputed piece of Whig diplomacy in a much more favorable light because the treaty had provided the legal basis for pressing the British into a retreat. The agreement, however, remained unpopular with those Americans who wanted the United States to have exclusive control over any isthmian canal, and this point of view was destined to gain overwhelming strength over the course of the next two generations.

William Walker and the Filibusters

Before England and the United States finally worked out a reconciliation of their Central American policies, regional problems had been multiplied by the prevalence of filibustering during the 1850s. The filibusters were adventurers who organized their own armies and intervened in the unstable politics of Latin America. The United States was a particularly fertile field for recruiting such forces. Mexican War veterans, disappointed prospectors for gold, Southerners yearning for adventure, and restless men without regular employment were all likely prospects for filibustering expeditions. American opinion, particularly in the South, was tolerant of such activities, while the neutrality laws were inadequate and difficult to enforce.

The greatest of the filibusters was William Walker, a Tennessean whose restless ambition had turned successively to the fields of law, medicine, and journalism. In 1850 he moved to California, and three years later he invaded Mexican soil on the first of his expeditions. After some initial success in his attempt to detach Lower California and neighboring districts from the rest of Mexico, he failed and returned to California.

Then in May, 1855, Walker and fifty-six followers embarked for Central America at the invitation of one of the parties in a Nicaraguan civil war. Six months later he was the master of Nicaragua. He and his allies had captured Granada, the capital city, installed their own candidate as provisional president, and made Walker himself commander-in-chief. The next year Walker took over the presidency as well.

The secret of the adventurer's success lay in large part in his relations with the Accessory Transit Company, organized by Commodore Cornelius Vanderbilt to transport California-bound freight and passengers across Nicaragua. Through this connection, Walker not only obtained ships for his operations, but free transportation of volunteers and provisions.

Walker's activities became a matter of domestic controversy within the

United States. Southerners, hopeful of bringing new slave states into the Union, made a hero of Walker and joined his army. Walker in turn bid for their favor by repealing the Nicaraguan laws forbidding slavery. Northerners who opposed the extension of slave territory denounced the government for not acting with more energy to preserve American neutrality. Caught between these two fires, the Pierce administration at first refused to recognize the Walker regime, but then changed its policy in the election year of 1856. On May 20, President Pierce accorded formal recognition, and on June 3 the Democratic party platform expressed sympathy for the efforts to "regenerate" Nicaragua.

American policy toward Walker was influenced not only by domestic politics, but by the jockeying for power between England and the United States. The recognition of Walker was in part a retaliation against Britain for its persistence in holding on to the Mosquito Protectorate and the Bay Islands. The English countered by selling arms to Costa Rica to strengthen its defenses against Walker.

In the end, the Walker rocket fell as rapidly as it had risen. In his complicated dealings with the Transit Company, the filibuster had sided with the rivals of Vanderbilt who were trying to squeeze the commodore out. In retaliation, the commodore's agents were active in building a Central American coalition against Nicaragua. To avoid capture by his enemies, Walker surrendered to an American naval commander in 1857 and returned to the United States.

But the Walker story was not over. After several efforts to organize new expeditions, he finally reached Honduras. There he was arrested by a British naval officer and turned over to the Honduran authorities, at whose hands he was tried and shot in September, 1860. The passing of this colorful troublemaker helped to quiet the mutual suspicions that had hitherto prevented a good understanding between Great Britain and the United States on affairs in Central America.

14

DIPLOMACY AND THE
SLAVERY ISSUE

"The policy of my administration," President Franklin Pierce declared in his inaugural address in 1853, "will not be controlled by any timid forebodings of evil from expansion. Indeed, it is not to be disguised that our attitude as a nation, and our position on the globe render the acquisition of certain possessions, not within our jurisdiction, eminently important for our protection." In this frank commitment to a policy of expansion, Pierce certainly had Cuba in mind and was probably thinking as well of possible American annexations in northern Mexico and Canada.

Except for a small acquisition from Mexico, however, none of these dreams materialized. The policy of expansion could not succeed because it became deeply involved in sectional politics. Whatever had been gained for the cause of national unity by the Compromise of 1850 was lost in the controversy that began with the Kansas-Nebraska Act and continued to mount until it resulted in secession and civil war.

Pearl of the Antilles

The Spanish possession of Cuba lay only 90 miles to the south of Key West, Florida. With its fertile soil and warm climate, it was ideally suited for the growing of sugar. Strategically, it controlled the entrance to the Gulf of Mexico. Havana's fine harbor was a natural port of call for ships plying between the Atlantic and Gulf ports of the United States, and the growing Cuban population offered an inviting market for American trade. From the earliest days of the republic, American statesmen had asked themselves whether an island so close and so desirable was not destined to come eventually under the American flag. During the Jefferson administration the so-called "no-transfer" doctrine was roughed out: so long as Cuba remained under the weak Spanish Empire, the United States would acquiesce; but it would oppose any attempt by England or France to annex the island. Seldom explicitly stated, but generally understood, was the corollary that if the Cubans were to gain their independence and apply for admission to the United States, they would be welcome. Cuba, Jefferson wrote, would be "the most interesting addition which could ever be made to our system of States."

During the years in which Spain was losing control of her mainland colonies, she managed to retain Cuba and Puerto Rico. But the crisis in the Spanish Empire increased the nervousness of the United States lest England or France try to seize this valuable prize. In April, 1823, some eight months before the Monroe Doctrine was announced, Secretary of State John Quincy Adams outlined American policy in an important note to the American Minister in Madrid. He explained the importance of Cuba to the United States and indicated that the government would oppose any English or French attempt at annexation. Looking toward the future, Adams predicted that within fifty years the acquisition of Cuba would prove "indispensable to the continuance and integrity of the Union itself." He acknowledged that the time for American annexation had not yet come, but he went on in vivid language to assert:

> There are laws of political, as well as of physical gravitation, and if an apple, severed by a tempest from its native tree, cannot choose but fall to the ground, Cuba, forcibly disjointed from its own unnatural connection with Spain, and incapable of self-support, can gravitate only toward the North American Union, which, by the same law of nature, cannot cast her off its bosom.

Adams's frank language demonstrates that the Cuban issue was not at this time involved in sectional politics. Northern expansionists were as determined as Southern to keep England and France out of the island and to anticipate the day when the United States would gather in the ripe fruit.

During the 1830s and 1840s, the situation was significantly altered by the slavery issue. Cuban sugar planters owned large numbers of slaves and continued to import still more despite Spain's prohibition of the foreign slave trade in 1820. Great Britain, prompted by the mixture of humanitarian and selfish motives that had been evident in her policy toward Texas, exerted pressure on Spain to cooperate in stamping out the slave trade and to adopt a policy of gradual emancipation. Fear that slavery might be abolished in Cuba and that free Negroes might overthrow Spanish rule and establish a "black republic" like Santo Domingo became a nightmare to Southern spokesmen. Such an "Africanization" of Cuba, they were convinced, would be a terrible threat to the United

States because it might incite a general slave insurrection. Therefore Southern politicians were determined the British should neither annex Cuba for themselves nor use their influence to develop a Spanish policy of emancipation. Eager to add new slave states to the Union, the Southerners impatiently waited for some future storm to sever the Cuban apple, and some of them frankly favored shaking the Spanish tree.

Appropriately, it was the strongly expansionist Polk administration that made the first positive attempt to acquire Cuba. In an instruction of June 18, 1848, to the American Minister to Spain, Secretary of State Buchanan emphasized the strategic danger of allowing the island to fall into British hands. Asserting that the United States would never acquire Cuba "except by the free will of Spain," Buchanan authorized the Minister to offer as much as 100 million dollars for the purchase of the island. Once more, as in his policy toward Mexico, President Polk overestimated what American dollars could buy. The Spanish Foreign Minister replied that his country would prefer seeing Cuba sunk in the ocean than transferred to another power.

The López Mania

Narcisco López, a Venezuelan by birth, had held important posts both in Spain and Cuba. Falling out of favor with Cuban provincial authorities and failing in business, López turned revolutionist. When a plotted uprising miscarried in 1848, the adventurer fled to the United States, where, for the next three years, his efforts to organize filibustering expeditions created a series of problems for the Washington authorities.

The López venture received wide support. In New York there was already an active junta of exiled Cubans receiving financial support from Havana. Although both Jefferson Davis and Robert E. Lee were discreet enough to decline the honor of leading the volunteers who would free Cuba from the Spanish yoke, there were many other Southerners ready to offer their services. López was therefore able to gather some eight hundred men at Round Island in the Mississippi near New Orleans.

The Whig administration made a determined effort to break up the movement. In August, 1849, President Taylor officially denounced illegal activities of this character, and shortly after, a fleet of United States naval vessels dispersed the Round Island forces. Federal action also prevented two ships destined for the filibuster fleet from leaving New York.

Despite these setbacks, López persisted in his efforts. Early in 1850, he sailed from New Orleans with three shiploads of followers, totaling some 750 men, ostensibly for Yucatan. American warships were sent to Cuban waters to intercept the filibusters, but López's principal ship eluded capture and landed at Cárdenas in northern Cuba. There the invaders looted and burned several public buildings, but the expected Cuban uprising failed to materialize and López and his followers had to seek refuge on their ship. They raced into Key West, Florida, just ahead of a pursuing Spanish naval vessel, only to be subsequently arrested by American authorities for violating the neutrality laws. Sympathetic Southern jurors refused to convict López, and he became more of a hero than ever.

The two other ships that had set out for Cuba in 1850 were less fortunate. Captured by the Spaniards, these vessels were taken to Havana, where the American filibusters were tried as pirates. Secretary Clayton, who had attempted to prevent the expedition in the first place, now worked to save the lives of the prisoners. All but three of the men were released for lack of evidence; the others were convicted and sent to a Spanish prison, but were soon pardoned by the Queen "as a new proof of friendship to the United States."

The fiasco of 1850 was scarcely over before López organized a new expedition. Early in August, 1851, he again sailed from New Orleans, this time with the connivance of the collector of the port. With him went a volunteer force of about four hundred men; a few were Cuban exiles and Hungarian refugees, but most were American citizens, often of good Southern families. Prominent among them was Colonel William L. Crittenden, nephew of the Attorney General of the United States. Landing some 60 miles from Havana, the expedition attempted to invade the island, but once again there was no popular uprising to greet the liberators. Separated from the main invasion force, Crittenden and fifty others were captured by the Spaniards and summarily shot as pirates. López and the remainder eluded capture for a few days longer, but ultimately had to surrender. The leader was garroted in the Havana public square, while about 160 of his followers were sent to Spain for penal labor in the mines. They were finally pardoned in 1852, largely through the intercession of the American Minister.

The execution of Crittenden and his fellow Americans deeply shocked public opinion, even in the North. A mob in New Orleans retaliated by sacking the office of a Spanish-language newspaper and by breaking into the office of the Spanish consul, where, in addition to considerable property damage, pictures of the Queen and the Captain General of Cuba were defaced and a Spanish flag torn to bits. In fear for his life, the consul fled to Havana.

Daniel Webster, now Secretary of State, risked his popularity by apologizing to the Spanish government for these "disgraceful acts." He promised a salute to the Spanish flag and proper treatment for any consul who should be sent to New Orleans. Although Webster pointed out that his government did not have the same responsibility toward private Spanish citizens that it did toward the consul, Congress, after the release of the

American prisoners in Spain, did vote $25,000 to compensate the victims of the New Orleans riots.

The López affair had important consequences, both domestic and foreign. In internal politics, the Whig attempts to repress the filibustering expeditions were unpopular throughout the South and in many sections of the North. Whig policy toward Cuba contributed to the victory of Pierce and the Democrats in the election of 1852. On the international scene, the inability of the American authorities to prevent filibustering convinced the British and French governments they should help Spain hold Cuba against rapacious Americans. Consequently, British and French naval vessels were ordered to patrol the waters off the island.

Spain appealed to both powers for an explicit guarantee of her sovereignty over Cuba, but the British government was reluctant to give this unless Spain liberalized its government over the island and effectively repressed the slave trade. In the end, the British and French authorities proposed to the United States a treaty pledging all three nations to respect Spanish sovereignty over Cuba. The Whig administration gave private assurances that it would not interfere in Cuba, but postponed any final answer to the Anglo-French suggestion until after the presidential campaign.

When the election returns seemed to favor the annexation of Cuba, the Fillmore administration tried to cut some of the ground from under the incoming Democrats. Webster was now dead, but his successor, Edward Everett, wrote a long note rejecting the proposed tripartite treaty. Although the President did not covet Cuba for the United States, he considered "the condition of Cuba as mainly an American question." It was only necessary to examine the map, Everett pointed out, to see how remote were the relations of Europe and how intimate those of the United States with this island. Reviewing the whole history of American expansion, the Secretary concluded that it would be as easy to dam up the Gulf Stream as to fix the fortunes of Cuba by a permanent treaty.

This rapping of English and French knuckles met an enthusiastic response in the United States. Senator Stephen A. Douglas, rising leader of the Democratic party, asserted that Everett's note was "applauded by the almost unanimous voice of the American people." In Europe, needless to say, the document was condemned as new evidence of American jingoism.

The Diplomacy of Pierre Soulé

President Pierce chose as his Minister to Spain Senator Pierre Soulé of Louisiana. From the beginning the appointment was a highly controversial

one. Born in the French Pyrenees, Soulé had chosen the law as his profession. His career in France was ruined when he became involved in republican politics during the days of the Bourbon restoration. Convicted
on charges of revolutionary activities, he avoided a prison term by fleeing
the country. After various adventures, he finally found a congenial home
in New Orleans, where his French background and fiery eloquence
brought him success both as lawyer and politician. Elected to the United
States Senate, he became one of the leading spokesmen for the extreme
states' rights faction of the Democratic party. Paradoxically, this zealous
defender of slavery continued to be an apostle of republicanism. He attached himself to Stephen A. Douglas, John L. O'Sullivan, and other leaders of the "Young America" group who favored American expansion, as
well as close ties with Kossuth, Mazzini, and other European revolutionaries. Since this faction of the Democratic party had opposed the naming
of Marcy, an "old-fogy" conservative, as Secretary of State, Soulé's appointment to the Madrid post was Pierce's method of appeasing this powerful group.

To the Spanish government, the naming of Soulé was as provocative
as the waving of a red banner before a bull in a Madrid arena. In addition to his general reputation as a revolutionary republican, the Louisiana
politician had been outspoken in advocating American annexation of
Cuba. He had lauded López and Crittenden as martyrs for freedom. On
the evening before his departure for Spain, Soulé was serenaded at his
New York hotel by five thousand partisans of Cuban freedom and made
an indiscreet speech in reply. The Austrian Minister informed his government that he was "unable to imagine anything more insulting to Spain"
than this incident.

The Spanish government was tempted to refuse to receive Soulé, but
the British and French envoys advised against any such rejection because
it would simply play into the hands of rabid American annexationists.
The Spaniards not only decided to follow this advice, but to place the
delicate responsibility of negotiating with the American in the hands of
a man who knew Soulé well, Don Ángel Calderón de la Barca, Spanish
Minister to Washington now recalled to become Foreign Minister.

After his arrival in Spain, Soulé lurched from crisis to crisis. The first
draft of the speech he intended to make when he was presented to the
Queen was considered so injudicious in its demand that Spain cease taking
advice from England and France and accept an alliance with the United
States that Calderón insisted it be rewritten. When slighting remarks were
made about Mrs. Soulé's gown at a ball given by the French Ambassador,
two duels resulted. Soulé's son engaged in a half-hour's swordplay with
the Duke of Alba, one of Spain's leading aristocrats—fortunately with-

out injury to either party. Soulé himself challenged the host, the Marquis de Turgot, and Madrid was treated to the scandal of the American Minister shooting the French Ambassador in the knee. As a consequence, Soulé suffered a long period of social ostracism.

Fortunately for the American Minister, Queen Isabella and the Queen Mother, Maria Christina, disliked the upstart Emperor Napoleon III of France. Accordingly, they regarded the wounding of the French Ambassador rather cheerfully. Soulé, indeed, became a favorite of the royal ladies, who were intrigued with the Franklin-like costume the American Minister had adopted to advertise his republicanism. The Queen Mother, to whom most of Cuba belonged, even listened with interest to Soulé's arguments that Spain should sell the island to the United States to remove a cause of Spanish-American friction and raise necessary revenue for the kingdom. As an alternative, he implied that the United States might make a loan to Spain, with Cuba as collateral.

The American Minister had to make these suggestions cautiously, because Marcy's original instructions were surprisingly conservative. Soulé was forbidden to renew Polk's offer to purchase Cuba and was required to concentrate on obtaining a commercial treaty to make possible direct dealing with the Captain General of Cuba without going through the time-consuming procedure of referring all questions to Madrid. Pierce and Marcy had limited the envoy's authority in order to allow the uproar caused by the López affair and the appointment of Soulé to subside. It was still the administration's long-range policy to annex the island, but watchful waiting was best for the time being.

In the spring of 1854, Pierce and Marcy decided on a change of policy, apparently as a result of several factors. In the first place, there were Soulé's reports from Spain, describing his friendly relationship with the Queen and the Queen Mother and emphasizing the unstable Spanish political situation that might result in changes in the ministry and new diplomatic opportunities. In the second place, a series of episodes involving the rights of American citizens, culminating in the *Black Warrior* affair presently to be discussed, had strained the patience of the administration. On April 5, 1854, the Secretary of State wrote important new instructions to Soulé. Should circumstances provide a favorable opportunity, he was to renew the attempt to purchase the island; he might offer as much as 130 million dollars—or 30 million dollars more than the Polk administration had bid in 1848. If Spain refused to sell, Marcy continued, "you will then direct your efforts to the next most desirable object which is to detach that island from the Spanish dominion and from all dependence on any European power." This suggestion that it might become necessary to "detach" Cuba from Spain was strong drink to be offered an envoy so easily intoxicated as Soulé.

The Black Warrior Affair

If the Pierce administration wanted a suitable pretext for quarreling with Spain, the highhanded action of the Havana authorities in seizing the *Black Warrior* on February 28, 1854, provided an opportunity. This American-owned side-wheel steamer had been plying between New York and Mobile, with Havana as a port of call. By an informal arrangement with the port authorities, she, like several other ships of her type, had been exempted from the law requiring a manifest of cargo on each visit to Havana. On her eighteenth voyage she unexpectedly ran into trouble. On grounds that her owners had violated the port regulations by not making out a proper manifest, the *Black Warrior* and her cargo, consisting of cotton, specie, and other merchandise bound for New York, were seized and her captain arrested. To have the letter of the law so rigorously applied aroused the deep resentment of the crew. "I do not hesitate to say," the purser asserted, "that we have been subjected to the most villainous and outrageous treatment that has ever been inflicted upon a friendly power, and if we are not protected and redressed in this matter by our Government, the American eagle had better fold its wings forever."

Far from folding its wings, the American eagle began to scream shrilly. The newspapers described this episode as only the latest and most flagrant affront that American citizens had received at Spanish hands and accused England of being behind this insult. Congress asked the President for all available information, and Pierce responded on March 15 with a strong message characterizing Spain's action as "so clear a case of wrong that it would be reasonable to expect full indemnity therefor as soon as this unjustifiable and offensive conduct shall be made known to Her Catholic Majesty's Government." He warned, however, that similar expectations in other cases had not been realized and stressed the inconvenience of having to deal with Madrid on all such issues. If an amicable settlement proved impossible, Pierce promised "to use the authority and means which Congress may grant, to insure the observance of our just rights, to obtain redress for injuries received, and to vindicate the honor of our flag."

Secretary of State Marcy instructed Soulé to demand an indemnity of $300,000, better means of communication between the American consul in Cuba and the Captain General, and punishment of the Cuban officials responsible for the seizure. Soulé was given strict orders on how he was to proceed with the case. He was to make a strong statement of the American position, then refrain from further discussion on the issue, but "obtain as early a reply as practicable to your demand."

In his eagerness to use the situation to promote annexation, Soulé exceeded his instructions. When a prompt reply was not forthcoming to his first note, Soulé, although himself a Catholic, ignored the fact that it was Holy Week when official Madrid was preoccupied with religious activities. On April 11, he addressed a peremptory note to Calderón, renewing the demand for a $300,000 indemnity, specifying that the guilty Havana officials must be dismissed, and requiring an answer within forty-eight hours. Calderón responded to this ultimatum with a note complaining of Soulé's bad manners and insisting the Spanish government needed more time to frame a reply.

Despite the American envoy's fuming, the Spanish government did not make formal answer until May 7. Coached by the British and French envoys, Calderón tried to avert the lightning by conciliatory steps. He pointed out that the *Black Warrior* and its cargo had long since been restored to their owners and that a fine of $6,000 imposed at Havana had now been remitted. He denied, however, there had been any insult to the American flag and therefore refused the demand for indemnity.

By the time the Spanish reply reached Washington, the war fever in America had largely subsided. Northern newspapers like the *New York Times* and the *Philadelphia Public Ledger* were demanding the repudiation and recall of the impetuous Soulé. Northern opinion was also alarmed by reports of new filibustering expeditions being organized in the South. Even more important was the strong antiadministration feeling raised by the Kansas-Nebraska Act. Under these circumstances, Marcy decided to ease up on the *Black Warrior* issue. He wrote to Soulé that, although the Spanish reply was unsatisfactory in many of its contentions, Soulé was not to take any further steps for the present. Instead, Marcy informed the Minister, the United States wanted to try to settle all outstanding questions between the two nations by sending two commissioners to Spain to assist Soulé in new negotiations.

Marcy's reply made Soulé so unhappy that he thought of resigning. In the end, however, he merely displayed his pique by keeping Marcy's note to himself and not revealing its contents to the Spanish government until curtly ordered to do so six months later. The *Black Warrior* case was thus unnecessarily prolonged until June, 1855, when the United States accepted Spain's offer to pay an indemnity of $53,000. By this time Soulé was no longer the American Minister.

During the summer of 1854, when the *Black Warrior* fuse was sputtering out, Soulé became deeply involved in Spanish internal politics. Queen Isabella's notorious immorality, the despotic and corrupt character of the government, discontent in the army, and widespread poverty had all combined to bring the kingdom to the brink of revolution. It was a time of changing ministries, army mutinies, and popular insurrections. In these troubled waters Soulé fished eagerly, without regard for the careful code of conduct that should guide a diplomat accredited to a foreign government. The British Ambassador reported that Soulé was believed to be spending large sums of money from private American sources to aid the revolutionists. Still obsessed with the dream of annexing Cuba, the American Minister hoped either to bribe the Queen into accepting a ministry that would make the cession or to help the republicans establish a government that would accomplish the same purpose. Once again, however, Soulé failed; the Spanish monarchy outrode the storm; and the only result of the envoy's intrigues was to stiffen Spanish determination to retain the coveted island.

The Ostend Manifesto

Secretary Marcy's plan to appoint a special commission to negotiate a general settlement with Spain had to be abandoned. In the first place, the idea was so distasteful to Soulé that he would not cooperate. Secondly, Congress adjourned in 1854 without granting the 10 million dollars Pierce had asked for this purpose. As an alternative, the administration hit upon the idea of having Soulé consult on the Cuban problem with James Buchanan and John Y. Mason, the American Ministers to England and France. The fact that Spain was beset by internal troubles and France and England were involved in the Crimean War seemed to offer an opportunity for some new step, perhaps along lines previously suggested by Buchanan for exerting pressure through international banking houses holding Spanish bonds.

Marcy instructed Soulé to arrange the proposed meeting. The three ministers were "to consult together, to compare opinions as to what may be advisable, and to adopt measures for perfect concert of action" in aid of Soulé's negotiations at Madrid. They were to report their recommendations to the State Department by special messenger as soon as their consultation was over.

Buchanan and Mason were somewhat reluctant to risk antagonizing public opinion by attending such a meeting, but Soulé, who had been unable to win the Cuban pot with the cards in his original hand, drew the new one dealt by Marcy with eagerness. Ruling out Paris and other suggested meeting places, the three ministers finally decided on Ostend, a quiet Belgian port, where they met on October 9. After three days of discussion, they separated and went by different routes to Aix-la-Chapelle in Germany for more talk. Finally, on October 18, 1854, they signed their report to Marcy, which became rather misleadingly known as the "Ostend Manifesto."

The three signatories concluded that "an immediate and earnest effort ought to be made by the government of the United States to purchase

Cuba from Spain." This proposal should be made to the Supreme Constituent Cortes of Spain, which was about to convene. By various ingenious arguments, the ministers attempted to demonstrate that the American purchase would be in the best interests of the United States, Cuba,
and even Spain herself. They then passed to a more controversial issue.
If Spain, "dead to the voice of her own interest, and actuated by stubborn
pride and a false sense of honor," should refuse to sell, what ought to be
the course of the American government? Since self-preservation was "the
first law of nature, with States as well as with individuals," Americans
would be forced to consider whether Cuba, in the possession of Spain,
seriously endangered the internal peace of the United States and "the
existence of our cherished Union."

> Should this question be answered in the affirmative, then, by every law,
> human and divine, we shall be justified in wresting it from Spain if we
> possess the power; and this upon the very same principle that would
> justify an individual in tearing down the burning house of his neighbor
> if there were no other means of preventing the flames from destroying
> his own home. . . . We should . . . be recreant to our duty, be unworthy
> of our gallant forefathers, and commit base treason against our posterity,
> should we permit Cuba to be Africanized and become a second St. Do-
> mingo, with all its attendant horrors to the white race, and suffer the
> flames to extend to our neighboring shores, seriously to endanger or
> actually to consume the fair fabric of our Union. . . .

If the Ostend report is read carefully, it is clear that it was really recommending a new attempt to purchase Cuba. The suggestion that it might
be justifiable to seize the island was hedged with conditions indicating this
was considered a last recourse, to be used only if conditions on the island
became dangerous to the United States. Although the actual authorship
is disputed, the basically conservative hand of Buchanan is evident. Indeed, the more impatient Soulé thought it necessary to send a private
letter to Marcy, frankly advocating the use of force.

The Ostend meeting was one of the worst-kept secrets of the nineteenth
century. Even before the American diplomats gathered in Belgium, newspapers in both Europe and the United States were predicting some kind
of "congress of the American ambassadors." Under these circumstances,
the fact that the three ministers had actually met was widely reported, and
journalists eagerly tried to learn what had been decided. The *New York
Herald*, whose editor, James Gordon Bennett, had a personal grievance
against President Pierce because he had not received a coveted diplomatic
appointment, was particularly persistent in ferreting out the story. Partly
through leaks, partly through shrewd guessing, the *Herald* came close
to the truth in predicting that "the United States will say to the so-called
government of Spain— What we must have is security for the future.

We tender to you twice the amount of its actual value. If you do not accept our proposal, we must take the island."

By the time the Ostend report actually reached Washington, such shrewdly speculative news stories were already seriously embarrassing the administration. Furthermore, the Democrats were smarting from a thorough thrashing in the congressional elections of November, 1854. Marcy took prompt steps to disassociate himself from the more controversial parts of the report. In instructions to Soulé on November 13, the Secretary reiterated the administration's desire to purchase Cuba if an opportunity presented itself. Soulé was forbidden, however, to press the issue upon an unwilling Spanish government and was directed instead to resume negotiations on the *Black Warrior* case and related issues. The President, warned Marcy, "wants all controversial points adjusted by negotiations and not coercion." Although the Secretary conceded that the ministers had not actually recommended "the alternative of cession or seizure," he feared that certain phrases in the report might be thus construed. Therefore, he made it clear that the President was opposed to the use of force and did not consider conditions in Cuba a menace to American security.

Marcy's reply was clearly a rebuke, not so much to the Ostend Manifesto itself, as to the more drastic position Soulé had taken in his private letter. The American Minister to Spain recognized at once that the game was up and promptly resigned. He felt the administration had made him the scapegoat for the failure of its own policy. There was some ground for his resentment, since Marcy's note of April 5 in which the Secretary had directed Soulé to attempt "to detach" Cuba from Spanish dominion certainly seemed to implicate Marcy in the line of thinking reflected by the Ostend Manifesto. Apologists for the administration have claimed, however, that by detaching Cuba, Marcy meant no more than to encourage the Cubans to assert their independence and that this was far different from an American seizure of the island. Furthermore, Pierce and Marcy had good reason to feel Soulé's whole line of conduct abroad had ruined their own prospects for gaining Cuba by peaceful negotiation.

The steps taken to disavow the Ostend Manifesto were not enough to save the Pierce administration from severe criticism. Responding to pressure from Congress and the newspapers, the State Department finally made public the pertinent documents in March, 1855. The correspondence was somewhat expurgated, Marcy's "detach Cuba" instruction being one of the items significantly omitted. Even so, the episode provided abundant ammunition for the enemies of the administration. Horace Greeley in the *New York Tribune* called the Ostend report "The Manifesto of the Brigands" and denounced Soulé and the slavocracy for the infamous "seizure" doctrine. The *New York Herald* asserted that the

Manifesto had been "a faithful and complete embodiment of the Cuban policy of the administration down to that time" and attributed its rejection to "the anti-Nebraska reaction of the October and November elections that frightened off our trembling and shrinking Executive." Across the Atlantic, the great London *Times* declared that American diplomacy was "certainly a very singular profession," which "combines with the utmost publicity the habitual pursuit of dishonourable objects by clandestine means."

The signers of the Ostend report went on to very different destinies. Soulé returned to America to resume his New Orleans law practice and to play a relatively minor role in the Confederacy during the Civil War. Mason, upset by Marcy's disavowal of the report, suffered a stroke of apoplexy and died a few years later. But Buchanan rode out the storm, retained his London post, and was elected President in 1856. He continued to advocate the purchase of Cuba throughout his term in the White House, but the blunders of the Pierce administration had ruined whatever chance there might have been for a transfer of the island to the United States by peaceful means.

Relations with Mexico

The Treaty of Guadalupe Hidalgo had ended the state of war with Mexico, but had not removed all causes of antagonism. On the contrary, the treaty itself provided issues for disagreement. There were disputes over the new boundary and Mexican protests that the United States was not carrying out its promise to restrain Indians living under its jurisdiction from making forays into Mexico. Walker's invasion of Lower California in 1853 was only one of several filibustering expeditions against Mexico organized among the restless Californians.

The Monroe Doctrine, revived by Polk, was regarded with suspicion in Mexico as a potential cloak for American aggression. In 1848, for example, Mexico's southernmost state of Yucatan rebelled against the central government. The rebel regime addressed appeals for help to Great Britain, Spain, and the United States, offering to enter into close relations with whichever power would grant it protection. President Polk felt the danger of foreign intervention was serious enough to lay the issue before Congress. The Senate Foreign Relations Committee recommended temporary military occupation of Yucatan—a step that a few of the more rabid expansionists hoped might lead to annexation. But this proposal met strong opposition from congressional moderates, who regarded intervention in the internal affairs of another country as a perversion of the true Monroe Doctrine. In the end, nothing was done.

Equally disturbing to suspicious Mexicans were American efforts to gain transit rights across the Isthmus of Tehuantepec. Like Panama and Nicaragua, this strip of territory where the Atlantic and Pacific Oceans were only 125 miles apart was regarded as a promising route for either a canal or a railroad. An American company had been organized to build a Tehuantepec railroad, and Secretary of State Webster had sought to make the necessary diplomatic arrangements with the Mexican government. These negotiations broke down in 1852, however, when the Mexican Congress rejected the treaty.

American relations with Mexico were complicated by another troublesome problem. Since 1845 the need for a transcontinental railroad linking the Mississippi Valley with the Pacific Coast had become increasingly apparent. Three possible routes—a northern, a central, and a southern—had been suggested. Because the pattern of settlement and the commercial relations of the new states with the old would be powerfully influenced by the route chosen, the transcontinental railroad question became deeply involved in sectional politics of the day.

In many ways the advocates of a southern route had a good case. Mountain ranges and severe winters were not the obstacles in the Southwest that they were farther north. Moreover, there were more existing settlements to be served in this section of the country. Unfortunately, however, the best southern route lay below the Gila River through territory still belonging to Mexico under the Treaty of Guadalupe Hidalgo. American acquisition of this district became vitally important to the advocates of the southern route.

The Gadsden Purchase

Such were the outstanding problems between the United States and Mexico when Pierce became President in 1853. The administration chose as Minister to Mexico General James Gadsden of South Carolina. Gadsden, an army engineer who had served for ten years as the president of the South Carolina Railroad, was a leading advocate of a southern transcontinental line. His appointment to the Mexican mission had been arranged by Secretary of War Jefferson Davis, strongest spokesman for Southern interests in the Pierce Cabinet.

Santa Anna, the hardy perennial of Mexican politics, had recently returned to the presidency when Gadsden arrived in Mexico City. Naturally Santa Anna had no love for the Americans, but he desperately needed money to carry on his government in the face of an empty treasury. Encouraged to believe that the Mexican leader might be in a mood to sell a large strip of territory, Secretary Marcy authorized Gadsden to offer as much as 50 million dollars for a cession to include all of Lower California and a large section of northern Mexico. President Pierce favored this because it would establish the border along easily defended mountain ranges. The American Minister was instructed to offer proportionately smaller amounts for a number of other suggested boundaries.

Santa Anna was too shrewd a judge of what he could get away with with his own people to transfer that much real estate to the hated *yanquis*. Moreover, he well knew that what the Pierce administration most wanted was to obtain a railroad route. So the Mexican held out for the smallest possible cession and the highest price.

After hard bargaining, the so-called Gadsden Treaty was finally signed on December 30, 1853. This agreement transferred to the United States about 39,000 square miles of barren but strategically located territory south of the Gila River. Additionally, Mexico agreed to release the United States from the obligation to prevent Indian raids into Mexico, but the United States promised to help Mexico defend itself against such Indians. On its part, the United States agreed to pay Mexico 15 million dollars in cash and to assume the claims of American citizens against the Mexican government to the extent of 5 million dollars more.

The Gadsden Treaty went to the Senate at the worst possible time. The Kansas-Nebraska Bill had reopened the whole slavery issue, and the antislavery faction denounced the proposed purchase as a shameless attempt to increase the number of slave states. On the other hand, Senator William M. Gwin of California and a few other legislators opposed the treaty because it did not acquire enough Mexican territory. The deliberations of the Senate were further confused by the feverish activities of rival groups of speculators, seeking to have the treaty amended to protect their various special claims and interests in Mexico.

At first, the confused situation made it appear unlikely the treaty would be ratified. On April 17, 1854, it was actually rejected, but soon afterwards the legislators who wanted some kind of Mexican cession compromised their differences and forced a reconsideration. On April 25 the treaty was finally accepted by a vote of 33 to 12, but in a form radically changed from the original. Through a series of Senate amendments, the cession had been reduced from 39,000 square miles to less than 30,000; the price had been lowered from 15 million to 10 million dollars, with no provision for satisfying the claims of American citizens against Mexico; the American promise to help Mexico against the Indians had been struck out; the United States had been given freedom of transit across the Isthmus of Tehuantepec and the right to intervene if necessary to protect the construction activities of certain American railroad promoters.

It now became the unhappy task of Gadsden to transmit this mutilated treaty to the Mexican government for approval of the amendments. Santa Anna wanted to reject them, but he was in no position to do so because of his desperate need for money. Even after ratification, however, there were difficulties. When the necessary appropriation bill went before the House of Representatives, it was opposed by the formidable Thomas Hart Benton of Missouri, who wanted the transcontinental railroad built along the central route. He described the territory acquired by the Gadsden Purchase as "so utterly desolate, desert and God-forsaken that . . . a wolf could not make his living there." But the administration pushed through the appropriation bill by a vote of 105 to 63.

Further Mexican Complications

The Gadsden Treaty gave the United States its desired railroad route, but it did not bring good relations with Mexico. Political conditions south of the border continued to be chaotic, and Americans doing business there suffered a variety of assaults, arrests, and confiscations that laid the basis for extensive claims against the Mexican government. Since European nations had similar grievances, there was increasing danger of some kind of foreign intervention to challenge the Monroe Doctrine. The situation was further complicated by the tendency of foreign diplomats to meddle in Mexican politics. The French, English, and Spanish ministers supported Santa Anna and other conservatives, while the American envoys aided the Liberals, particularly the great Indian hero, General Benito Juárez, who became a power in Mexican affairs during the 1850s.

President Buchanan initiated an ambitious policy to advance American interests in Mexico. In 1857 he instructed John Forsyth, the American Minister, to attempt to purchase Lower California and a large slice of northern Mexico, as well as to obtain more satisfactory safeguards for the Tehuantepec transit route. Mexican leaders were tempted by the prospect of getting more American money, but they were afraid to flout national pride by ceding further territory.

Thwarted in this endeavor, Buchanan then asked Congress in 1859 for authority to use American military forces in Mexico to restore order and collect indemnity for earlier outrages. His plan was to cooperate with Juárez in establishing a pro-American regime in Mexico City. Congress, preoccupied with the slavery problem, did not even consider the President's recommendation.

Nor did Congress support Buchanan when he sent to the Senate the so-called McLane-Ocampo Treaty, under which the Juárez government, in exchange for a loan of 4 million dollars, would have granted the United States not only a right of way across Tehuantepec, but two other railroad routes across northern Mexico. The United States would have had unusual powers to use military force to protect these routes.

In the end, therefore, eight years of feverish Mexican diplomacy under Pierce and Buchanan produced only the Gadsden Treaty. On the eve of the Civil War, Mexican political anarchy and European impatience were combining to create a situation full of serious implications for the future.

Reciprocity with Canada

If Cuba and northern Mexico were the favorite goals of Southern expansionists, their Northern counterparts continued to hope for acquisition of the Canadian provinces. The question appeared to be moving into the realm of practical politics in 1849, when a substantial Canadian faction urged annexation by the United States because of hostility to British rule. Some members were Tories, disgusted with British reforms that had united Upper and Lower Canada, thereby increasing the influence of the Liberals and the French Canadians. So heated had politics become that a Montreal mob stoned the carriage of Lord Elgin, the Governor General, and set fire to the Parliament buildings. Even more serious a factor in promoting the desire for annexation was the serious depression blamed on the mother country's free-trade policy. Deprived of preference in the English market, the Canadians now found themselves competing with the United States and other producers of raw materials. They desperately needed to sell their goods across the border, but the American tariff was a serious barrier. Annexation by the United States offered a solution.

English public opinion was not unanimously opposed to the loss of Canada. The free-trade movement tended toward anti-imperialism. It was commonly assumed that colonies cost more to administer than they were worth and would inevitably detach themselves from the mother country when they reached maturity. "The whole current of opinion among England's most influential statesmen," declared a Montreal editor in 1849, "is evidently tending toward that point when they will bid adieu to the colonies, with wishes for their prosperity and hopes for continued friendship." This feeling that Canada had become Britain's neglected child helped to create annexation sentiment.

The protest against existing conditions reached a peak in October, 1849, when more than a thousand Canadians signed the so-called "Annexation Manifesto," detailing economic grievances and calling for "a friendly and peaceful separation from the British connection, and a union upon equitable terms with the great North American Confederacy of sovereign States." The publication of this document provoked strong reaction. An antiannexation movement was promptly organized by thousands of Canadians who either still cherished the British connection or disliked the United States. Even William Lyon Mackenzie, who had led the revolt against British rule in 1837, now took the opposite side, declaring: "American democracy as it presented itself in the form of political corruption,

crass materialism and human slavery, filled his soul with righteous indignation."

Even though the Canadians were sharply divided on the matter of annexation, both sides recognized the urgency of the economic problem.
Responding to pleas from the North American colonies, the British Minister at Washington pressed for a reciprocity agreement to encourage
Canadian-American trade. The Polk administration favored this, and in
1848 a reciprocity bill passed the House of Representatives, but was
tabled in the Senate. A similar measure failed the following year. Throughout the Whig administrations of Taylor and Fillmore, the reciprocity
issue was discussed, but without effective action.

Annoyed by this delay, residents of the British maritime colonies retaliated by demanding that American fishing be narrowly confined to the
limits specified in the Anglo-American treaty of 1818.[1] The colonists
accused the Yankee herring and mackerel fishermen of taking their catches
illegally in the bays and inlets of Nova Scotia, Cape Breton, and Prince
Edward Island. In support of these protests, the British sent a fleet of
armed cruisers to police those waters in 1852. This action angered the
Americans, who insisted they were being deprived of rights properly
belonging to them under the treaty. President Fillmore answered by sending a steam frigate under Commodore Perry to protect the Yankee fishermen, and the following year Pierce dispatched a larger naval force. Danger
of a clash was reduced, however, when the English temporarily relaxed
their strict enforcement policy.

The fisheries dispute spurred both sides to seek a general reciprocity
agreement, but two major obstacles had to be overcome. The first was the
difficult problem of reaching a bargain fair to each side; the second was the
still more difficult task of overcoming the opposition certain to be encountered in both Canada and the United States. North of the border, British
modification of the Navigation Laws and other factors had helped to restore
prosperity. As a result, the annexation movement had collapsed, and a
widespread hostility toward the United States was now evident, particularly in the eastern provinces. In the United States, on the other hand,
any proposal involving Canada was likely to arouse dissension between
Northerners who hoped to expand in that direction and Southerners who
opposed this.

The Pierce administration employed Israel D. Andrews, the American
consul at St. John, New Brunswick, as special agent to promote the reciprocity movement among the leaders of New Brunswick and Nova
Scotia. He was allotted the modest sum of $5,000 to carry on his propa-
ganda, but, in his eagerness to succeed, far exceeded his authorization. He

[1] See chap. 7.

gave dinner parties, hired coaches, subsidized newspapers, employed secret agents, contributed to the campaign funds of proreciprocity politicians, and made payments "to officials and to others for whom it was not proper to ask for vouchers." In a subsequent but unsuccessful attempt to obtain reimbursement for these mysterious transactions, Andrews said: "I unhesitatingly declare that the expenditure saved the treaty."

In Washington, the frigidity of certain legislators was melted by the warmth of British hospitality. On May 26, 1854, Lord Elgin arrived in Washington and, during the next week, he and John F. Crampton, the British Minister, tirelessly courted members of the Senate. They lavished their charm particularly on Southern Democrats, who feared reciprocity as a step toward annexation. As guest of honor in Washington homes, Lord Elgin was the life of the party with his witty repartee and racy stories. The round of festivities reached a climax with Crampton's ball in celebration of the Queen's Birthday. In reference to this event, critics later alleged that the reciprocity treaty had been "floated through on champagne."

Whether it was their persuasion or their wine, the English diplomats gave the reciprocity proposal the impetus it needed. On June 5, 1854, the so-called Elgin-Marcy Treaty was signed, and on August 2, the Senate approved it by a vote of 32 to 11. This treaty enlarged the privileges that American fishermen were to enjoy off the British North American coasts and granted reciprocal fishing privileges to British colonial fishermen as far south as Norfolk, Virginia. There was to be free trade in a list of specified commodities that included fish, tobacco, coal, furs, rice, and turpentine. The Canadians were granted free navigation of Lake Michigan in return for American free use of the St. Lawrence, the St. John, and the Canadian canals.

On the American side, the motives underlying acceptance of the reciprocity treaty were mixed. In addition to the immediate advantage to be gained by increased trade, President Pierce and other Northern expansionists hoped that closer Canadian-American accord would smooth the way for eventual annexation. Some Southern extremists opposed the treaty on just this ground, but other Southerners supported reciprocity because they believed it would solve Canadian economic problems and thus prevent a revival of the annexation movement. Southern opposition to the administration's Canada policy was also dulled by the inclusion of tobacco and other Southern commodities on the free list and by gratitude to Pierce for his support of the Kansas-Nebraska Act.

Although the reciprocity agreement appeared to be working to the mutual satisfaction of both countries during the first few years, American opinion gradually turned against the arrangement. Manufactured goods had not been included on the free list, and American manufactures found Canadian tariffs an obstacle to developing the market they had expected. Even more injurious was the anti-British and anti-Canadian feeling created in the United States during the Civil War. The treaty had provided that after ten years the agreement might be terminated upon one year's notice; in 1865, the United States availed itself of this privilege. An interesting experiment in economic cooperation was thus concluded.

Disputes with England

On May 28, 1856—almost two years to the day from the Queen's Birthday celebration at which the American politicians had drunk British champagne so enthusiastically—Secretary of State Marcy dismissed John F. Crampton from his post as British Minister at Washington. The American government's decision that Crampton was no longer welcome climaxed a serious disagreement over British recruiting activities during the Crimean War.

The Crimean War began in March, 1854, when England and France went to the assistance of Turkey to prevent an expansion of Russian power into the Near East. The contest developed into a long campaign by the Allies to capture the Russian Black Sea port of Sebastopol on the Crimean peninsula. English public opinion was sickened by the shocking casualty lists from the front, and the British government made a desperate effort to lighten the burden on English manpower by encouraging the recruitment of a Foreign Legion. In December, 1854, Parliament passed a Foreign Enlistment Act, under which it was hoped soldiers might be obtained from countries like Germany, Switzerland, and the United States.

Prospects for recruiting men in America appeared to be promising. The Mexican War had given thousands of Americans a brief experience of military life and excitement. Many of these veterans were ready for further adventure, as the popularity of filibustering had demonstrated again and again. Other likely prospects were to be found among recent immigrants from the British Isles who still felt the tug of loyalty to the mother country and among the restless unemployed of the cities.

Unfortunately—from the English point of view—recruiting for foreign armies had been strictly prohibited by the Federal Neutrality Act of 1818, passed during the Spanish American wars for independence. It was Minister Crampton's delicate task to reassure Marcy that American law would be respected, while at the same time he was quietly encouraging evasion. Crampton worked through private persons, who set up undercover recruiting offices in such cities as New York, Boston, Philadelphia, and

Baltimore. Here would-be volunteers were given passage money and instructions for reaching Halifax, Nova Scotia, where they were formally enlisted. Although Crampton himself and several British consuls were involved in these activities, they left the handling of funds and other details of organization as much as possible to others. Joseph Howe, a prominent Nova Scotia newspaper editor and politician, made a series of mysterious trips between Halifax and Washington in connection with the recruiting efforts.

Although Marcy at first accepted the sincerity of Crampton's assurances that the British were abiding by the law, the Secretary of State soon suspected that such was not the case. In July, 1855, the United States made its first formal protest, but by this time the London government had already realized that the indiscretions of its envoys might lead to trouble and had ordered the foreign recruitment program abandoned. Crampton either did not receive these orders or disobeyed them because the recruiting campaign in the United States continued until mid-August, almost two months after the London order had been issued.

During the autumn of 1855 the whole story was revealed. Henry Hertz, one of Crampton's agents, was arrested, tried, and convicted for violating the Neutrality Act. His confession and other testimony at the trial implicated the British Minister and two consuls. Another chain of circumstances led to the arrest and indictment of Charles Rowcroft, the British consul at Cincinnati, although the case was dismissed by the President at British request.

The British ministry argued there had been no violation of American law because the actual enlistments had taken place outside of the United States. Secretary Marcy responded, however, that payment of money to potential recruits was both a violation of the statute and an infringement of American sovereignty. Therefore on December 28, 1855, he requested Britain to recall not only Crampton and Rowcroft, but the British consuls at Philadelphia and New York as well. Lord Clarendon, the British Foreign Secretary, still defended the conduct of his subordinates and refused to recall them. Thereupon Marcy dismissed the Minister on May 28, 1856, and revoked the exequaturs[2] of the three consuls.

Although the British government was still unwilling to admit the misconduct of its representatives, it showed no wish to prolong the controversy. It refrained from taking the obvious step of retaliation, which would have been to request the recall of the American Minister at London. The Palmerston ministry was sharply criticized by Gladstone, Disraeli, and other parliamentary leaders for its bungling of the whole foreign recruitment program.

[2] An exequatur is the written authorization of a consular official by the government to which he is accredited.

The Slave-trade Controversy

Another problem plaguing Anglo-American relations during the late 1850s was closely related to the slavery controversy. In an earlier chapter, British efforts to obtain the cooperation of other nations in stamping out the slave trade have been discussed. It will be recalled that American suspicion of England because of the earlier impressment controversy had led the United States to refuse to concede to the British navy a right to visit and search suspected slave ships flying the American flag. Instead, the Webster-Ashburton Treaty of 1842 had stipulated that the United States would maintain its own naval squadron off the African coast to cooperate with the English in trying to stop the illegal trade.[3] Unfortunately, this American pledge had not been adequately carried out, and the scandal of slave traders using the American flag to cover their activities had continued.

After the Crimean War, when the illegal slave trade was on the increase, the British navy resumed its policy of rigorous enforcement. As news reached the United States of the stopping and searching of American merchant ships not only off the African coast but in the Gulf of Mexico as well, the old issues of Jefferson's and Madison's day seemed suddenly to be revived. In June, 1858, the Senate passed a unanimous resolution declaring the "immunity of their merchant vessels upon the high seas will be steadily maintained by the United States under all circumstances as an attribute of their sovereignty never to be abandoned, whatever sacrifices its protection may require." Buchanan's Secretary of State, Lewis Cass, contended for freedom of the seas with the eagerness of a true politician desirous of winning applause by defying the British lion.

The English no longer pretended they had an unlimited right of visit and search, but they did argue that they had a right to visit ships flying the American flag to discover whether they were really American. Cass admitted that a ship illegally flying the flag was entitled to no protection by the United States, but he warned the British that they stopped suspected ships at their own risk. If the vessels were really American, they were entitled to sail the seas without interference. To underline this position, President Buchanan ordered every available naval vessel to the Gulf of Mexico with orders "to protect all vessels of the United States on the high seas from search or detention by the vessels of war of any other nation."

In the face of these measures, which were strongly supported by American public opinion, the British government backed down. It disavowed the conduct of its naval officers and ordered them to cease stop-

[3] See chap. 10.

ping American ships. This diplomatic victory was most welcome to the Buchanan administration, to which victories of any nature were infrequent.

Britain had coupled its conciliatory gesture with an appeal to the United States to cooperate in some acceptable way in wiping out the slave trade. The Buchanan administration took a step in this direction by increasing American naval patrols and agreeing with the British on uniform instructions to its commanders. But really effective measures were not taken until after the outbreak of the Civil War, when in 1862 Secretary of State William Seward signed a treaty with England, providing mutual right of visit and search in certain specified waters and establishing mixed courts to try alleged slave traders.

The Anglo-American flare-up over the slave-trade issue provided an appropriate anticlimax to the diplomatic history of the Pierce and Buchanan administrations, when again and again American foreign relations had been complicated by ramifications of the country's most serious domestic problem.

15

CIVIL WAR DIPLOMACY

With the outbreak of the Civil War in April, 1861, the United States was placed in an unusual position. She was now a belligerent, whereas the powers of Europe were neutral. She was therefore compelled to demand that the rights of a nation at war be respected by countries at peace, instead of the reverse—as she had done during the long Napoleonic struggle. In her new and unfamiliar role as a belligerent, the United States sometimes trod on questionable ground—not that she foreswore her earlier position on neutral rights, but she did provide new interpretations concerning neutral obligations.

Believing that her asserted rights as a state would not be protected under the presidency of a "black" Republican, South Carolina seceded from the Union on December 20, 1860, and, by the following February, six more states, all from the Deep South, had also withdrawn. Thereupon the Confederate States of America was established, with a constitution and a chief executive, Jefferson Davis.

All efforts to compromise the differences and to restore the Union failed. The seceded states began to take over Federal property within their borders, and on April 12, 1861, opened the attack on Fort Sumter in Charleston harbor. Lincoln's answer was to call for 75,000 volunteers on April 15 to quell "combinations ... too powerful to be suppressed by the ordinary course of judicial proceedings." This was no declaration of war in the formal sense; indeed, throughout the four-year struggle, the President refused to admit a war was in progress. To Lincoln, the South was in a state of insurrection, and the United States was using its Army and Navy as a police force to put down a large-scale form of rioting so that the Union could be restored.

To Europe, however, the bloody conflict was more than an insurrection, particularly since the Confederacy now included eleven states and was able to maintain an established government, since so many men were

involved, and since certain methods employed by both groups of participants were those used normally only in wartime.

Among these methods, the issuance of letters of marque [1] by the Confederacy and the proclamation of a blockade by the North were the
most important in their effect on diplomacy. European opinion was also
influenced by Lincoln's pronouncement that the conflict was being waged
by the North not to abolish slavery, but to preserve the Union.

Throughout the war, both the North and the South gave serious attention to Europe. The North's objective was to keep the contest localized;
the South's hope was to obtain European recognition of its asserted independence and, if possible, to gain European allies. In this contest, both
parties concentrated on Great Britain, on the probably correct assumption
that as England went, so would go France and possibly the rest of Europe.

The Position of England

When South Carolina seceded, the diplomatic relations of the United
States with Great Britain were good. The older causes of antagonism
between the two nations apparently had been allayed. The long controversy over impressment had died out with the conclusion of the Napoleonic struggle, and the companion issue concerning expatriation—
"once an Englishman, always an Englishman"—had not been widely
applied by England in many years. Moreover, in 1858 Britain had definitely
renounced the right to search ships of other countries on the high seas
during periods of peace, except when she had treaties specifically allowing
such a practice. British opposition to territorial expansion by the United
States had come to an end with American acquisition of Texas and the
subsequent division of Oregon. The more recent differences in Central
America had been peacefully settled when England accepted the American retroactive definition of the Clayton-Bulwer Treaty of 1850.

From the time of South Carolina's secession until the middle of April,
1861, when actual hostilities broke out, England generally sided with the
Federal government. To the average Englishman, the issue dividing the
North and the South was slavery, and he had little sympathy for the
Southern desire to maintain that institution. The London *Times* of January 4, 1861, probably voiced majority opinion when it stated: "We cannot
disguise from ourselves that, apart from all political complications, there
is a right and a wrong in this question, and that the right belongs, with
all its advantages, to the States of the North."

With the outbreak of hostilities and Lincoln's assertion that his object
was simply to preserve the Union, there was an immediate shift in

[1] Letters of marque were commissions authorizing privateering.

British opinion. The coalition cabinet, headed by Prime Minister Lord Palmerston and containing the powerful Foreign Secretary, Lord Russell, and the sometimes bellicose Chancellor of the Exchequer, William Gladstone, soon showed a certain degree of hope that the Confederacy would succeed, thereby permanently splitting the United States and ending its growing competition with the British Empire. Yet both Palmerston and Russell would not do anything to so antagonize the North that England might be involved in the war. This position was indicated by Palmerston's note to Russell on October 22, 1862: "We must continue to be lookers-on. . . ."

The English nobility sympathized with the Confederacy. To the members of the peerage, the North was little more than a nation of uncouth shopkeepers; the only blue bloods, the closest approach in America to themselves, were to be found in the South. English manufacturers and shippers likewise tended to be pro-Southern, hoping that Confederate success would end the increasing American industrial and mercantile growth. These Britons also looked with favor on the free-trade policy of the Confederacy, which was very different from the high-tariff legislation that Northerners pushed through Congress during the early months of the war. It was these business interests that theoretically dominated the House of Commons, but political differences among them enabled the liberal element, headed by such men as John Bright, Richard Cobden, and William Forster, to prevent Parliament from taking steps leading to British recognition of Southern independence. These champions of the North correctly realized that the preservation of the Union was dependent on the ending of slavery, despite Lincoln's original view of the war. And the English working classes were generally pro-North; to them slavery anywhere was anathema. They were willing to undergo temporary privation and hardship—the result of English mills closing down because of the dearth of American raw materials, if by so doing slavery might be stamped out. Since the English workers wanted more democracy for themselves, they regarded a victory of the democratic North over the aristocratic South as of vital importance.

The British press was likewise divided on the American issue. The London *Times*, shifting its position after Fort Sumter, became the leading supporter of the Confederacy, while the *Spectator* also contained many articles and letters advocating prompt British intervention in favor of the South. On the other hand, the *Daily News* and the *Morning Star* were the most prominent publications supporting the North. In similar fashion, leading English writers were divided in their opinions about the Civil War.

In France, Napoleon III was undoubtedly the greatest advocate of

Southern independence, not that slavery was important to him, but his hopes of building a new colonial empire on a Mexican base [2] rested upon a weakened United States. Foreign Minister Edouard Antoine Thouvenel and Henri Mercier, Minister to the United States, shared their monarch's views. All three men hesitated, however, to take any untoward steps alone. They followed the lead of England, and England would not go beyond a proclamation of neutrality. Perhaps tempering the French position was the inconsistent desire to have a strong and united America to offset the growing power of Britain. Certainly this appeared to be the opinion of the majority of Frenchmen, according to the Confederate agent, Henry Hotze. Especially antagonistic to the views of Napoleon and the diplomatic leaders were the Orleanists and "red republicans," who regarded the breakup of the United States "as destroying a naval power which they had looked upon as a counterpoise to that of Great Britain." Elsewhere in Europe, more attention was paid to domestic and Continental affairs than to the situation in America.

Seward's "Thoughts"

William Seward, Lincoln's Secretary of State, had a high opinion of his own abilities and sometimes indulged in rash talk during times of stress. Yet basically he was an able man who demonstrated courage and skill in steering the United States through troubled waters. He could be belligerent in tone at the outset of some new diplomatic problem, but after the original outburst, he could settle the matter in such a conciliatory way that all parties concerned were satisfied.

Prior to his assignment to the State Department, Seward's public career had been in the field of politics. Indeed, he had sought the presidency in 1860, and he continued to believe he was the ablest man in Washington and thus should be the power behind the Chief Executive. To Seward, the preservation of the Union was all-important, and he tried by many means to prevent the secession of the South between Lincoln's election and the firing on Fort Sumter the following April.

When it became apparent that compromise would not solve the domestic differences, Seward had the wild idea that the situation might be saved by involving the United States in a foreign war. The desire to defeat a common enemy might magically reunite the two sections of the country. The Secretary's chief source of worry was a message he received from C. J. Helms, the American consul general in Cuba, to the effect that on March 29, 1861, Spain had sent two artillery companies aboard a man-of-war to the Dominican Republic, "with a view of taking possession of that island." To Seward this was the first step in a plot en-

[2] See chap. 17.

gineered by Spain, Great Britain, and France to gain Mexico. Consequently he presented to President Lincoln on April 1, 1861, "Thoughts for the President's Consideration," in which he complained that "we are at the end of a month's administration and yet without a policy, domestic or foreign." Then he proposed that the domestic policy should be to "change the question from one upon slavery or about slavery to one upon union or disunion." Much more important, however, was his suggestion for an aggressive foreign policy:

> I would demand explanations from Spain and France, categorically at once. I would seek explanations from Great Britain and Russia, and send agents into Canada, Mexico, and Central America to rouse a vigorous spirit of independence on this continent against European intervention. And if satisfactory explanations are not received from Spain and France, would convene Congress and declare war against them.

Such a contest might result in the capture of Cuba, which might satisfy the South and thereby prevent the secessionist movement from continuing.

These "Thoughts" made little impression upon President Lincoln. Rejecting Seward's uncomplimentary suggestion that the presidency be turned over to a more forceful person (such as Seward himself), Lincoln let his Secretary of State know that he intended to formulate national policy with "the advice of all the cabinet." Despite this early rebuff, Seward did his work well. He insisted upon European respect for the rights of the belligerent North and did not hesitate to threaten the possibility of war to enforce them. The Secretary was successful in keeping England and France outwardly neutral and in preventing them from recognizing the independence of the Confederacy.

Assisting the Secretary of State were Charles Francis Adams (son of John Quincy Adams), who was the Minister to England, and William L. Dayton, the Minister to France. Adams had had more experience in the diplomatic field and played an important role in keeping England neutral. Dayton was a "gentlemanly and dignified" person who performed his work adequately, despite his lack of diplomatic training.

The Confederate Position

The Confederate States of America asserted from the outset that it was an independent nation which should receive both recognition and aid from Europe. The Southern leaders believed they held a full hand of trumps. Ideologically, they were fighting for their freedom, like the American patriots of 1776, and they counted on the strong spirit of nationalism to be found in Europe. Also England would surely like to see its competitor, the United States, weakened by the loss of the Confederacy. The fact that the South was primarily a rural area with a low tariff would make an especial appeal to English commercial interests. And above all, the states that had seceded produced more than 75 per cent of the high-grade cotton used in the textile factories of both England and France; thus "King Cotton" would be a potent factor in influencing those two countries to assist the Confederacy in maintaining its independence.

Shortly after Jefferson Davis was inaugurated as President of the Confederate States of America in February, 1861, he appointed A. Dudley Mann, William L. Yancey, and Pierre A. Rost as commissioners to Europe.[3] These three men, not especially trained in matters diplomatic, were instructed to try to obtain recognition of Southern independence by the major powers, as well as European assistance in breaking the Northern blockade. To accomplish these objectives, the agents were to offer treaties giving favorable commercial rights.

Unfortunately for the Confederacy, these commissioners were never formally received by the governments of the countries they visited, although they did meet unofficially with Lord Russell and Napoleon III. On May 3, 1861, when Rost and Yancey conferred with the English Foreign Minister, they made an earnest plea for recognition of independence, promising in return that the South would never engage in the slave trade. Russell, however, would make no commitments, and he rejected their pleas again on May 9. When Charles Francis Adams arrived a few days later to assume his post as Minister from the United States, he complained about these commissioners, saying in effect that their reception, even unofficially, was tantamount to English recognition of the Confederacy. Secretary Seward shared this view; he informed Adams on May 21 that he must "desist from all intercourse whatever, unofficial as well as official, with the British Government, so long as it shall continue intercourse of either kind with the domestic enemies of this country."

Consequently, Lord Russell told Adams in June that no more interviews, even personal ones, would be held with the Confederate agents. Thus rebuffed, the Southern spokesmen were furious; Yancey reported to his government that England was "truckling" to Minister Adams.

The Proclamations of Neutrality

In spite of this setback, the Confederate commissioners may have accomplished something: both England and France were pushed into issuing

---

[3] Ultimately the Confederacy named diplomatic agents to most of the nations of Europe, as well as to several republics in the Western Hemisphere. In addition, there were many commissioners sent overseas to negotiate for ships, supplies, and loans. Henry Hotze was one of the ablest and might be called the coordinator of Confederate activities.

proclamations of neutrality. President Lincoln, as has been explained, declared from the outset that the Civil War was not a war, but an insurrection. Under such circumstances, foreign nations could not logically intervene in any way nor furnish assistance to the rebellious states. The extent of the contest, however, as well as the early military victories of the South, Davis's issuance of letters of marque, and Lincoln's proclamation of a blockade, made it difficult for Europe to accept Lincoln's position. In England and France, in particular, there was a growing feeling that the struggle in the United States was a full-scale war and should be recognized as such.

On May 3, 1861, the English Attorney General sent a message to Lord Russell concerning the possible recognition of Confederate belligerent status and the subsequent right to grant letters of marque. The Attorney General believed "the best solution would be for the European nations to determine that the war between the two Confederacies shall be carried on on the principles of 'Justum Bellum,' and shall be conducted according to the rules of the Treaty of Paris.[4] Recognize the Southern States as a Belligerent on this condition only."

Before taking action, however, Lord Russell instructed Lord Cowley, the British Minister at Paris, to confer with Thouvenel, the French Foreign Minister, about joint recognition of Confederate belligerency, as well as joint support of the Declaration of Paris, particularly those clauses concerning blockades and privateering. Thouvenel was in complete agreement, even though Napoleon III was reported to have said on May 19 that he hoped for "the perpetuation of the Union of the States."

Encouraged by Lord Cowley's report, the British government proclaimed a policy of neutrality on May 13, 1861. In it, England recognized that a state of war existed between the United States and "states styling themselves the Confederate States of America." Englishmen were ordered not to enlist in the army of either contestant, or to encourage others to enlist, or to equip warships for either. If an attempt were made to equip such vessels in British yards, they would be forfeited to the British government. Were a belligerent warship to enter a British port, it could do so only to obtain food, water, or repairs; it could not change or increase its battle equipment. Finally, any British subject who violated this proclamation would be subject to punishment through British justice and would subsequently forfeit all claims to British protection.

This proclamation was not a recognition of Southern independence. It did deny, however, the Lincoln position by according the status of a belligerent to the Confederacy. To Minister Adams, who had arrived in England the same day, this action was a breach of faith on England's part. His predecessor, George Dallas, had been promised that Britain

---

[4] An agreement of 1856, whereby the principal European powers had defined the rules of maritime warfare and the rights of neutrals.

would not take any step until Adams reached the country;[5] to Adams this meant that he would be given an opportunity to present the Northern side of the case. The new Minister subsequently wrote "that the action ... seemed ... a little more rapid than was absolutely called for by the occasion." To him, the South had not as yet shown either the strength or the ability to maintain its status as a belligerent. Adams continued: "It pronounced the insurgents to be a belligerent State before they had ever shown their capacity to maintain any kind of warfare whatever" and "considered them a marine power before they had ever exhibited a single privateer on the ocean."

On June 10, 1861, France followed the British lead by issuing a more exact and explicit proclamation of neutrality. This action was largely overlooked by the United States, which was still smarting over the English decision.

The Trent Affair

In the fall of 1861, the North increased the ill feeling between itself and Great Britain in the so-called *Trent* affair. Because the three original commissioners had made little progress in Europe, Jefferson Davis named two new ones in October: James M. Mason of Virginia (who may have been a poor choice because he was the author of the Fugitive Slave Act), to go to England, and John Slidell of Louisiana, to France. These envoys sailed from Charleston on October 12, aboard the *Theodora*, reached Cárdenas, Cuba, two days later, and then proceeded by land to Havana. There they boarded the British steamer *Trent* on November 7. The following day, Captain Charles Wilkes of the U.S.S. *San Jacinto* stopped the *Trent* by firing two shots across her bow. After some controversy, including a slight show of force, Mason and Slidell, together with their secretaries, were arrested and removed to the *San Jacinto*. The *Trent* was allowed to continue its trip to England, but the envoys were imprisoned in Fort Warren, located in Boston harbor.

When news of the capture of Mason and Slidell reached the North shortly after the middle of November, there was wide popular enthusiasm. Wilkes was regarded as a national hero who had successfully twisted the British lion's tail, and he was feasted in many cities, including Boston. Congress showed its gratitude by immediately passing a resolution of thanks. The press headlined the event as a glorious action. When soberer minds warned of British protests, the excited patriots argued that the North could defeat England as well as the South.

[5] Lord Russell had informed Dallas that he "acquiesced in the expediency of disregarding mere rumor" and would await "the full knowledge to be brought" by Adams.

In high places, however, the same enthusiasm was not to be found. President Lincoln, though refusing at first to release the envoys, feared they might become "embarrassing prisoners." Postmaster General Montgomery Blair voiced the opinion that Mason and Slidell must be freed, and the same view was echoed by the influential Senator Charles Sumner of Massachusetts. Secretary of State Seward instructed Minister Adams to inform Lord Russell that Captain Wilkes had seized the two Confederates without official orders. And Secretary of the Navy Gideon Welles, while congratulating Wilkes, hoped his action would "not be permitted to constitute a precedent."

In England, news of the *Trent* affair touched off dangerous outbursts of indignation. Although British legal experts were divided on the issue, with some upholding the right of an American warship to remove Confederate agents from an English vessel and some denying it, popular opinion held the Americans to be completely in the wrong. The press was filled with protests against Wilkes's action, and some papers asserted that this insult to the British flag could be wiped out only by war. In the light of this highly inflamed opinion, the government had to formulate its policy with care.

Other powers denounced the seizure of the commissioners. Denmark, Italy, Prussia, and Russia expressed the opinion that the United States was in the wrong. Foreign Minister Thouvenel of France warned its Minister in Washington that unless the United States gave up the prisoners, war would materialize.

Lord Russell drafted an ultimatum demanding that the United States release Mason and Slidell within a week and make immediate apology for their seizure. If this harsh document had gone to Washington in its original form, the outcome of the crisis would probably have been war. Fortunately, however, Prince Albert, Queen Victoria's husband, even though he was a dying man, exerted his influence for peace. Amendments suggested by the Prince Consort removed much of the sting of Russell's note. Though the British government hoped for peace, it recognized that war might come and ordered the dispatch of 8,000 additional troops to Canada and the establishment of a temporary embargo on arms and ammunition.

Time worked to the advantage of the United States. As December progressed, the war spirit in England gradually died down, so that before Christmas the talk was principally about conciliation. John Bright was of considerable help in this respect, for he arranged numerous meetings and made many speeches in which the theme was peace. Thus Thouvenel was led to say: "It seems to me that there is a pacific current in the air and that the English and Americans who are good calculators will think twice before fighting."

In the North, cooler heads also were prevailing. The feeling grew that a mistake had been made. Thus by the time (December 20) that Lord Lyons, the British Minister at Washington, presented the amended Russell ultimatum to Secretary Seward, majority opinion favored releasing Mason and Slidell. Cabinet consideration of the English note was not taken until Christmas day, and, while secrecy shrouded the meeting, Seward's reply of December 26 indicated that most of the Cabinet favored conciliation.

The Seward note was ingenious. Although the Secretary of State shifted his position frequently, particularly in defining the status of Mason and Slidell, he finally concluded that they were "personal contraband." Captain Wilkes had a legal right to search the *Trent* for contraband, and he made his search according to the rules. Having found contraband (Mason and Slidell), he had a right to seize it. Wilkes, however, had made one important error: he had not exercised the proper method of seizure. He should have taken the *Trent* as a prize to an American port for condemnation. Thus, concluded Seward, Wilkes, through his desire not to inconvenience the owners of the *Trent*, had in a sense broken the law. England, in her protest, was now supporting the principles for which the United States had contended prior to the War of 1812.

The release of Mason and Slidell was then ordered, and they were turned over to the British man-of-war *Rinaldo* at Provincetown on January 1, 1862, as "citizens of the United States." After a stormy journey, during the course of which they were transferred to an English packet, the two controversial figures reached Southampton on January 30.

The news of their release ended the tension in both countries. Lord Russell wrote to Lyons on January 10 that England was content with the conclusion of the *Trent* affair, though he himself did not completely agree with Seward's response of December 26. After all, England did not want war; if it had come, she realized the dangerous position of Canada. Moreover, she knew that the United States had done what Britain had been doing for many years.

The Confederacy was disappointed by the peaceful outcome of the *Trent* affair. It had been hoped in the South that the incident would bring England into the contest against the North, or, failing that, would lead to very strained relations. Either occurrence would be beneficial to the Confederacy. But even during the darkest days of the crisis, Lord Russell continued to refuse to receive formally agents Mann or Yancey "in the present state of affairs."

Problems of the Blockade

While the controversies over the proclamations of neutrality and the *Trent* affair were taking place, problems concerning the blockade became serious. When President Lincoln announced a blockade of the Confederacy on April 19, 1861, he provoked numerous diplomatic complications. In the first place, the announcement raised the question in European minds as to whether a blockade was consistent with the theory that the conflict was an insurrection and not a war.

Another problem involved the Declaration of Paris, which many of the European powers had signed in 1856. This declaration had four major parts: (1) privateering must be abolished; (2) a neutral flag covers enemy goods with the exception of contraband of war; (3) neutral-owned goods aboard an enemy ship are not subject to capture, again with the exception of contraband; and (4) blockades, in order to be recognized, must be effective—that is to say, maintained by a force sufficient really to prevent access to the coast of the enemy. At the time, the United States had been asked to adhere, but Secretary of State Marcy, mindful of the service that privateers had rendered in earlier American wars, had refused to commit his country unless the first article were amended by adding: "and that the property of the subjects or citizens of a belligerent on the high seas shall be exempted from seizure by public armed vessels of the other belligerent, except it be contraband."

Now, however, the Declaration of Paris had more appeal. The North wanted to check Confederate privateering and at the same time institute its own blockade. Consequently, on April 24, 1861, Secretary Seward instructed the American ministers to inform the European governments that the United States was willing to approve the original declaration. Both France and Britain were ready to accept the American position, but only if Seward committed the whole United States to adherence, not simply the North. Despite the fact that Seward could not speak for the Confederacy, the North did its best to follow the principles of the declaration, not only because the United States had long supported its general features, but because it fitted in well with the North's current position.

Since privateering had been abolished by the declaration, Lincoln proclaimed on April 19, 1861, that Confederate privateersmen were nothing more than pirates and were subject to immediate execution if captured. This proclamation brought a storm of protest from both England and France, where such treatment was considered inhumane. Indeed, the proclamations of neutrality may have been hastened by the desire of those two European powers to grant the South belligerent status and thereby remove the possible stain of piracy.

The first opportunity to put the Lincoln proclamation into effect came in June, 1861, when the *Savannah* was captured. Her crew members were brought to trial for piracy, but the jury failed to reach a verdict and the culprits were held as mere prisoners of war. The fact that Jefferson Davis threatened to retaliate by hanging Union soldiers captured at the battle of Bull Run may have made some impression on the Northern jury. Shortly after, the *Petrel* fell into Northern hands, and its crew was also tried on piracy charges. Supreme Court Justice Robert C. Grier, who presided at the trial, asserted that it was inconsistent to treat captured Confederate sailors differently from captured Confederate soldiers. Consequently they were remanded as prisoners of war.

While Confederate privateers enjoyed some success against Northern merchantmen during the remainder of 1861, thereafter privateering on the part of the South declined rapidly. A volunteer Confederate navy was substituted. Also contributing to the ending of privateering by the Confederacy was the British decision of June 1, 1861, that the armed ships of neither belligerent could take prizes into British ports. This announcement was a bitter blow to the South because the Northern blockade made it difficult for Confederate privateers to reach Southern harbors and now British ones were also closed.

Britain was more concerned later when President Lincoln was authorized to issue letters of marque to Northern privateers after March 3, 1863. English shipowners realized that such privateers, in the absence of a Southern merchant marine, would operate chiefly against British commerce destined for the South. Actually no letters were issued, but the threat to do so may have contributed to the British seizure of the Laird rams.

Whereas the privateering issue was not of great import in the diplomatic picture, the blockade occasioned considerable controversy. The three original Confederate agents insisted the Northern blockade was not effective. In late November, 1861, they drew up a list of more than four hundred vessels that had run the blockade since the previous April. And when James Mason finally arrived in England early in 1862, he added more than fifty names to the list. The Confederates, backed up by British consular reports, also insisted the blockade was not in operation continuously. Consequently they sought European aid, first of all to deny its legality, and then to break it by force.[6]

In the fall of 1861 Minister Lyons did not know how to answer Lord Russell's query about the effectiveness of the blockade. He admitted that more ships ran it than were captured, but "it is very far from being a mere paper blockade...it is a most serious interruption of trade." Lord Russell, in his reply of February 15, 1862, wrote:

[6] At the outset, the North was unprepared to maintain more than a "paper" blockade. She had only 44 ships to patrol more than 3,500 miles of Confederate coast, and fewer than 7,500 personnel in the Navy. But by purchasing and building, by sinking ships filled with stones in Charleston harbor, by capturing more and more coastal ports, and by checking the iron-clad *Merrimac* (or *Virginia*), the North gradually made the blockade reasonably effective. Thus while the chances of running the

Her Majesty's Government . . . are of opinion that, assuming the blockade is duly notified, and also that a number of ships is stationed and remains at the entrance of a port, sufficient really to prevent access to it or to create an evident danger of entering or leaving it, and that these ships do not voluntarily permit ingress or egress, the fact that various ships may have successfully escaped through it . . . will not of itself prevent the blockade from being an effective one by international law.

And Russell stood by this position throughout the rest of the war. If English exporters wanted to trade with the Confederacy, they must do so at their own risk; they could not expect any help from their government if their ships were captured while trying to run the blockade. Russell's willingness to concede the legality of the blockade probably reflected his concern lest similar British acts of war be hampered in some future conflict.

France was not so eager to take the same position. Henri Mercier informed Thouvenel in the fall of 1861 that he thought the blockade should not be recognized, and at the same time Napoleon III urged Britain to join France in forcibly breaking it. Neither Palmerston nor Russell would agree, believing it unwise to do so "for the sake of cotton." Again in the spring of 1862, Napoleon tried, stating that the restrictions which the blockade imposed on cotton exports were "not justifiable" because they interfered "with the legal commerce of France." Without English help, however, France could not forcibly end the blockade. Therefore, she next tried to persuade the United States to relax the blockade so that French manufacturers could obtain Southern cotton. In a skillful reply Seward argued that France's commercial future lay with the North. If the Union were restored as a result of a Northern victory, the United States would then produce more cotton, as well as foodstuffs and other raw materials, which would be of untold benefit to France thereafter. Thus, if the blockade were relaxed at this time, the North would be hurt, and so would France be in the future. Nothing more was heard from France about the blockade.

The Doctrine of Continuous Voyage

Although the United States had protested the British application of the Rule of 1756 during the Napoleonic wars, the North invoked the successor to this rule during the Civil War. This outgrowth of the rule was the doctrine of continuous voyage or ultimate destination, which legalized the seizure of contraband goods aboard a neutral ship going

---

blockade were nine out of ten in 1861, they were only one out of two in the last year of the war. In all, some 1,500 vessels were captured with cargoes worth more than 30 million dollars.

from one neutral port to another if it could be shown that the ultimate destination of such contraband was enemy territory.

During the war, English shippers connived with Confederate importers to evade the Northern blockade by sending needed supplies in English (neutral) vessels to the British West Indies or Cuba. From Bermuda, Havana, or Nassau, it was much easier to slip small blockade-running ships into Southern ports. In an effort to stop this practice, Northern naval vessels began seizing British ships engaged in this trade, the most notable instances involving the *Bermuda*, the *Dolphin*, and the *Springbok*. When the owners appealed, the United States Supreme Court upheld the seizures of both the ships and their cargoes. Somewhat different was the case of the *Peterhoff*, seized off the Danish West Indies while en route to Matamoras, Mexico. The Supreme Court decided that the contraband aboard was subject to confiscation, but released the ship and the remainder of its cargo because the blockade could not preclude free use of the Rio Grande for commodities legally consigned to a neutral city.

Many Dutch, French, and German legal authorities condemned this application of continuous voyage. Britain, however, lodged no protests, even though it was the property of her subjects that was involved. This position was partly the result of the new benevolent neutrality toward the North, and partly because Britain might benefit in the future from this application of a doctrine originating in England.

The British-built Confederate Cruisers

In 1861, the Confederacy, with few naval vessels, had little hope of either breaking the Northern blockade or injuring Northern commerce. Therefore, it sent to Europe a delegation, headed by Captain James D. Bulloch, to purchase both cruisers and iron-clad ships. The first privately built ship obtained was the *Oreto*, which sailed from Liverpool late in March, 1862, as an unarmed merchant vessel, unequipped for war and under an English captain. Thereby the English sellers hoped to evade their government's Foreign Enlistment Act, which prohibited them from disposing of a warship to a belligerent. When the *Oreto* reached Nassau, Commander J. N. Maffitt of the Confederacy took over the bridge; at the same time cannon, munitions, other naval equipment, and additional crew members were obtained; and the name of the ship was changed to the *Florida*. Maffitt then sailed the *Florida* through the blockade to Mobile, where the change from merchant vessel to warship was completed, after which she started out on her career of destruction of Northern shipping.[7]

[7] The *Florida* did most of her damage in the Atlantic, capturing 34 Northern ships between the vicinity of New York City and Brazil. In October, 1864, she was captured

When in July, 1862, the *Alabama*, originally called "No. 290," was nearing completion in the Laird shipyards outside Liverpool, Charles Francis Adams lodged a protest with the British government, insisting she was actually a cruiser destined for the Confederacy. He also presented what he considered conclusive proof of his charge, substantiated by the opinion of a queen's counsel, Sir Robert Collier, who wrote: "It appears difficult to make a stronger case of infringement of the Foreign Enlistment Act, which, if not enforced on this occasion, is little better than a dead letter." The officials at Liverpool, however, refused to take any action, so Adams forwarded all the accumulated facts to Lord Russell. The Foreign Minister in turn sent them to the Queen's Advocate. By an unfortunate coincidence this official became seriously ill, and the papers remained untouched for five days. When on July 21 they were finally studied by other experts, the conclusion was that the charges by Minister Adams had merit. The government immediately ordered the Liverpool authorities to prevent "No. 290" from leaving port—but too late.

Perhaps there was an information leak somewhere, for two days earlier the ship had left Liverpool, ostensibly on a trial run, and never returned. She took on guns, other naval equipment, and additional crew members —carried there by other British vessels—in the Azores, where Raphael Semmes assumed command in the name of the Confederacy.[8]

Lord Russell publicly refused at the time to admit that his government was in any way culpable for the escape of the *Alabama* from Liverpool, but privately he wrote to Minister Lyons that the subsequent depredations were "a scandal and a reproach." [9]

Shortly after the *Alabama's* escape, the military situation began to change. Starting with the Battle of Antietam (September 17, 1862), the tide slowly turned in favor of the Union armies. Six days later the Emancipation Proclamation was publicly announced, to become effective

---

in Bahia harbor by the U.S.S. *Wachusett*, which towed her to Hampton Roads. The Brazilian government claimed the *Wachusett* had broken international law. Since the United States agreed, the captain of the *Wachusett* was court-martialed and the American consul at Bahia was dismissed. The *Florida* could not be returned as Brazil had demanded, because she sank near Hampton Roads, but her crew was released. The last phase of this incident occurred in July, 1866, when the U.S.S. *Nipsic* fired a salute to the Brazilian flag at Bahia.

[8] Because of the Northern blockade, the "No. 290," now renamed the *Alabama*, never was able to enter a Confederate port. She nevertheless sank more than 60 Northern ships before her career was ended in June, 1864, by the *Kearsarge* outside Cherbourg, France.

[9] Several other British-built ships left England to become Confederate cruisers, notably the *Shenandoah* and the *Georgia*. All told, these cruisers sank more than 250 Northern ships and caused 700 more to be transferred to foreign registry. It has been said that the American merchant marine did not recover from these losses for at least fifty years.

the following January 1. And the British government refused either to recognize the independence of the Confederate States or to offer mediation.

Despite the change in official British attitude as a result of these events and in spite of the protests of Charles Francis Adams, English shipbuilders continued to carry out contracts with the Confederacy. In the spring of 1863, the cruiser *Alexandra* was completed. On March 30, Adams demanded British governmental intervention to prevent her from leaving port. The troubles arising out of the *Alabama* incident prompted Lord Russell to order the seizure of the *Alexandra* on April 5. Her owners took the case to court, where they successfully persuaded the judges she was a merchant ship, and she was released. The government appealed this decision, but again lost; subsequent appeals, however, so tied up the *Alexandra* that she never reached the Confederacy. That this was a definite change of heart may be learned from Russell's note to Lyons on April 7, 1863: "The orders given to watch, and stop when evidence can be procured, vessels apparently for the Confederate service will, it is hoped, allay the strong feelings which have been raised in North America by the escape from justice of the *Oreto* and the *Alabama*."

The Case of the Laird Rams

The sincerity of the British government was further tested in the case of the so-called Laird rams. If these two iron-clad vessels were allowed to reach the Confederacy, the Northern navy of wooden ships would be in extreme danger. Lincoln's Assistant Secretary of the Navy wrote: "We have no defense against them.... It is a question of life and death." Although Adams had repeatedly warned the British government about the rams, the English officials' procrastination threatened to have the same result as in the *Alabama* affair. On September 5, 1863, Adams delivered to Lord Russell a final protest, couched in the strongest possible language. He accused the British government of practically allowing the insurgents a free hand to build a navy. "This is war," Adams sternly asserted. "No matter what may be the theory adopted of neutrality in a struggle, when this process is carried on in the manner indicated, from a territory and with the aid of the subjects of a third party, that third party to all intents and purposes ceases to be neutral."

This time Lord Russell acted with decision. On the very day that he received Adams's note, he ordered the first ram, then approaching completion, to be held until satisfactory evidence could be given of its destination. The Adams documents provided sufficient proof that the ram was being built for the Confederacy, so in October the iron-clad was seized by the British authorities and placed under guard of a British man-of-war.[10] Thereafter, the North no longer had cause to fear that additional cruisers or any iron-clads would reach the Confederacy by way of British shipyards.

French-built Ships

The problem of neutral shipbuilding for the Confederate States was not limited to England, for Napoleon III, anxious to weaken the United States, had encouraged James Bulloch, John Slidell, and other Southern agents to contact French builders. The Emperor insisted the moves must be secret, for he did not wish the destination of the ships to be known.

Therefore, on January 7, 1863, Slidell made arrangements with M. L. Arman, head of the largest shipbuilding firm in France, for the construction of four clipper corvettes similar to the *Alabama*. They agreed to circulate the story that the vessels were to be sold to the Chinese and Japanese governments for use in the trade between Shanghai, Yedo, and San Francisco. In July, 1863, Bulloch completed another contract with Arman for two rams. To speed up the deal, Arman sublet some of the work to the Voruz firm in Nantes.

These vessels were nearing completion before Northern envoys to France learned what was taking place. In September, 1863, an employee of Voruz approached John Bigelow, head of the American consulate in Paris, with papers he had stolen from Voruz's files. These documents proved conclusively that the corvettes and rams were being constructed for the South and that the license for their armaments had been obtained under false pretenses. Bigelow immediately informed Minister Dayton of these facts, and Dayton realized the seriousness of the situation. He wrote to Secretary Seward: "It seems to me that their action on this subject is likely to afford a pretty good test of their future intentions. As to what the law may be, it does not, I apprehend, much matter: if they mean that good relations with our country shall be preserved, they will stop the building of these ships, or at least the arming and delivering of them; if they mean to break with us, they will let them go on." Without waiting for a reply from Seward, Dayton, already convinced that the French government was an accomplice in the fraud involving the armaments license, took the information to the Minister of Marine, Drouyn de Lhuys. The French official denied any complicity in the affair, but a month later he told Dayton the right to arm the ships in question had been withdrawn.

Naturally the Confederate agents were dismayed and irritated. Here was the French government making a virtue out of interfering with an operation that had been initiated at its invitation and carried on with its

[10] Ultimately the rams were purchased from the Laird Company by the Royal Navy in May, 1864.

knowledge. Slidell pushed his complaint to de Lhuys in November, 1863, only to be informed that France would not be pushed into war by allowing armed ships to leave her ports; she must be bound by her proclamation of neutrality. It was not until May, 1864, however, that Minister Dayton was told specifically the rams had been sold to neutral governments and the clippers would never be delivered to the Confederacy. Wary of French promises from past experience, Dayton replied: "Should these vessels pass into the hands of the Confederates, become armed and commence a system of depradation on our commerce, the exasperation would be such that the Government ... could scarcely keep the peace between the two countries."

The Confederate agents, in an attempt to obtain something from the disaster, sold the six ships to neutral countries: two to Peru, three to Prussia, and one to Denmark. But the one designated for Denmark was completed too late for use in the war with Austria and Prussia, so the Danish government refused to accept it. Thereupon, Arman secretly arranged to turn it over to the Confederacy. It became the *Stonewall*, under command of Captain T. Jefferson Page, but the discovery of leaks and necessary repairs prevented the iron-clad from reaching America before the surrender of General Lee at Appomattox, so Page sold the *Stonewall* to the Captain General of Cuba for $16,000. Thus the question of responsibility for the ram entering Confederate hands had no practical importance.

King Cotton Is Dethroned

As explained earlier, the Confederacy believed it had an important diplomatic asset in cotton. Were the textile manufacturers of England and France to be deprived of that necessary raw material, they would demand that their respective governments either forcibly break the Northern blockade or recognize Southern independence and help to maintain it. And to the demands of the manufacturers would be added the cries of impoverished workers, thrown out of work by the idle mills of Lancashire, the textile center of England.

This Southern belief in the importance of "King Cotton" was shattered long before the surrender at Appomattox. In the first place, European manufacturers had built up a large stockpile of cotton by the time of the outbreak of hostilities in America; indeed, they had obtained most of the South's 1860 cotton crop, amounting to approximately two million bales. As a result, in 1861 there was actually a surplus of cotton on the English market. Had the normal Southern exportations continued during the war, the price would have fallen and there might have been an economic crash, "which must sooner or later have caused great suffering in Lancashire," according to the *Morning Post*.

There is no doubt that the blockade did affect the English situation. By the end of 1862, the number of persons on poor relief in Lancashire jumped from less than 50,000 to about 285,000, and later in the war to more than 400,000. Yet neither operators nor employees voiced any widespread demands that the English government try to break the blockade. Even the optimistic James Mason had to admit that in Lancashire "no open demonstration has been made against the blockade." The manufacturers realized that official British aid to the South would mean war, while the workers, influenced by their own sympathies and the propaganda of John Bright and other middle-class liberals, did not wish to hurt the North in its struggle to stamp out slavery.

Contributing to this English opinion was the fact that some cotton was run through the blockade, although not enough to cause a fall in English prices. As Northern armies invaded the Confederacy, they confiscated Southern cotton, some of which was exported. Egypt and India also increased their shipments of cotton. Then too, other English industries were prospering as a result of demands in the North for consumer and wartime goods,[11] while the destruction of Northern shipping by British-built cruisers became a boon to English exporters. This prosperity enabled Englishmen to help more readily those unemployed in the cotton industry. The North, too, aided by sending over fairly large quantities of food to those on relief.

If England suffered from any scarcity, it was a dearth of grains, especially cereals, caused by bad harvests. While Europe had wheat to sell, its cost was high. So it was only natural for England to turn to the United States, where she could obtain the needed wheat, corn, and the like in exchange for war material. Secretary of State Seward and others in the North ably played up the erroneous English belief that Britain was completely dependent on Northern cereals to help keep her neutral. The gist of their propaganda was that Englishmen would starve if their government helped the South, for the North would withhold the needed items. Thus, as some exuberant Americans saw the situation, King Cotton was dead, and Wheat (or Corn, as the English called all grains) was King.

The Question of Recognition

To the Confederacy and to many of its English and French sympathizers, the proclamation of neutrality was not enough; the Confederacy must be recognized as independent. The year 1862 was a critical one, for not only did the continued blockade raise a number of diplomatic

---

[11] The London *Times* of January 7, 1864, reported, for instance: "We are as busy, as rich, and as fortunate in our trade as if the American war had never broken out, and our trade with the States had never been disturbed."

and economic questions, but a series of Northern defeats and growing sufferings resulting from cotton shortages in Europe brought up the query as to whether Europe should not intervene to end the war.

In England, the proposal to intervene was taken up at a cabinet meeting in early August, 1862. The pros and cons were debated fully before a decision was made that "nothing shall be done until both parties are desirous of it." By fall, however, Lord Russell was seriously considering a joint European proposal for a six-month armistice, which would be the prelude to recognition of Confederate independence. Indeed, William Gladstone apparently paved the way for such recognition in a speech at Newcastle on October 7, when he said:

> We may have our own opinions about slavery; we may be for or against the South; but there is no doubt that Jefferson Davis and other leaders of the South have made an army; they are making, it appears, a navy; and they have made what is more than either, they have made a nation.

Gladstone, however, was voicing his own thoughts, not those of his government. The British mediation offer never was made. There were several reasons for this. In the first place, Minister Adams warned that British recognition would mean war with the United States, and war was not popular in England. Secondly, news had just arrived of the Battle of Antietam (September 17). To many a Briton this meant the tide of war was at last turning in favor of the North. Therefore why recognize the independence of the Confederacy when it faced almost certain defeat? Thirdly, the English believed they were dependent on grains which must be obtained from a friendly North. And finally—and very important— Lincoln issued the preliminary Emancipation Proclamation on September 23. This at last made the abolition of slavery a Northern war objective. While the English press regarded the proclamation with a certain degree of derisive contempt and the Confederacy said it would mark the beginning of a war of attrition, the English people accepted it well, saying, for example, that "Mr. Lincoln's cause is holy and just." Under the circumstances, England could not logically recognize a country fighting to preserve an institution it hated.

Thus the cabinet meeting scheduled to debate the question of recognition was never held. Instead, Sir George Lewis, another member of the cabinet, prepared the public for government policy with a speech in which he said that the Confederate states "had not *de facto* established their independence and were not entitled to recognition on any accepted principles of law." This speech was followed by an official statement from the government on November 13, 1862, that there would be no change in policy. This decision was well received throughout England, where the feeling was "almost universal against interference."

From this time on, Britain made no effort to help the South in any way. Indeed, if anything, she seemed to be more friendly toward the North, as indicated by the seizure of the Laird rams and her acceptance of the American interpretation of the doctrine of continuous voyage.

France, on the other hand, was apparently more eager to recognize the Confederacy and to mediate in the conflict. On September 30, 1861, Henri Mercier informed Thouvenel what he thought of the situation. The Minister was of the opinion that his country and England must act in harmony and unison. The blockade must not be legalized, and recognition should be accorded to the Confederacy at the first favorable moment.

France was also more interested in obtaining Southern cotton than was England. There was a serious depression throughout most of the country, which was blamed largely on the falling off of exports to the United States because of the war and the high Morrill Tariff. The French government saw its own revenue declining as tobacco imports slumped. In April, 1862, an attempt was made to obtain cotton. Thouvenel said: "It may not be simply a question of policy abroad that we shall have to deal with, but of *public peace* at home." Napoleon III announced his readiness to dispatch a large naval expedition to force open the mouth of the Mississippi as a cotton outlet, if England would do the same. But England refused to go along with the proposal and the matter was dropped.

Then, late in October, 1862, shortly after the British decision not to recognize the Confederacy, France proposed that England, Russia, and several other European countries join her in insisting upon mediation to end the great bloodshed in America. Once more England rejected the proposed interference, using the excuse that Russia would not cooperate.

The final effort of France was made early in February, 1863, when Henri Mercier, acting on instructions from Napoleon III, proposed directly to Secretary Seward that there be mediation. On February 6, Seward definitely rejected the offer, and Congress supported him by characterizing it as unwarranted "foreign intervention." France at the same time again tried to persuade Britain to go in with her, but Lord Russell replied: "Her Majesty's Government have no wish to interfere at present in any way in the Civil War. If France were to offer good offices or mediation, Her Majesty's Government would feel no repugnance to such a course on the part of France alone." But France could not act by herself, even to cover up her actions in Mexico, and so the efforts to mediate and recognize were given up.

The Position of Russia

Of the major European powers, Russia was the only one to be consistently friendly toward the North. Perhaps it was not friendship for friendship's sake that caused this, but Russian apprehension about the European situation. She had been defeated by England and France in the Crimean War, and she was concerned lest another conflict develop. Therefore she naturally took a position opposite that of her recent—and possibly future—enemies.

The first indication of the Russian attitude was early in the Civil War when Tsar Alexander II, having recently liberated some of his country's serfs, extended a message of sympathy to President Lincoln in his attempt to destroy slavery in the United States. Another sign of Russia's friendship came in 1863, when she refused to cooperate with France in the attempt to end the Civil War by mediation.

A much misunderstood example of Russia's friendship involved the visit of the Russian fleet to the ports of New York and San Francisco in the fall of 1863. This visit was widely interpreted in the North, as well as in Europe, as a warning to England and France that if they recognized the Confederacy and entered the war on the side of the South, they could expect Russian aid to the North. Actually, however, there was an entirely different reason for the visit.

Russia was having trouble with rebellious subjects in the area seized from Poland. In the spring of 1863, Austria, England, and France protested against what they deemed inhumane Russian efforts to suppress the insurrection. The United States would not cooperate in their threatened intervention, not so much because of lack of sympathy for the Polish rebels, but because such a position would strengthen the North's stand against interference in the Civil War. If the protests of France and her allies proved to be the prelude to another European war, Russia did not wish to have her fleet in the Baltic, where it might be trapped by the British navy. To forestall such a disaster, she sent her fleet to sea, and where was better refuge to be found than in the ports of a friendly United States? Moreover, if that expected European conflict should materialize, the fleet would be in a strategic position to attack enemy commerce and colonial territories; or, on the other hand, the very threat of the Russian fleet might make England think twice before entering a new alliance against the Tsar.

Although well-informed Americans at the time were aware that the Russian visit was largely for selfish reasons, this did not prevent the officers and sailors from receiving the warmest possible welcome. Secretary Seward greeted the commanding admiral in his own Washington home, and both high and low society in New York and San Francisco outdid themselves in entertaining the popular visitors. Whatever its motivation, the appearance of the Russian fleet in American waters in 1863 gave a tremendous lift to jaded spirits in the North and also served to counterbalance the pro-Southern gestures of the British and French governments in the scales of diplomacy. A tradition of Russian-American friendship—somewhat difficult to understand in view of the ideological gap between autocracy and democracy—was strengthened, and the ground was laid for the postwar purchase of Alaska.

From the middle of 1863 until the end of the Civil War, the North had nothing to worry about from Europe. Continued successes on the field of battle, culminating in General Lee's surrender in April, 1865, ended any thought that the Confederacy would succeed. The English government certainly did not want to support a losing cause, the English people were satisfied the United States was fighting slavery, and France could not and would not act alone. Naturally the South was chagrined about her failure to obtain the expected aid from abroad. Even the most optimistic Confederates were compelled to admit by the middle of 1863 that they had failed in their diplomatic endeavors. Judah P. Benjamin, the Secretary of State of the Confederacy, summed up the situation in June, 1863:

> It is impossible not to admit the sagacity with which Mr. Seward penetrated into the secret feelings of the British Cabinet, and the success of his policy of intimidation which the world at large supposed would be met with prompt resentment, but which he with deeper insight into the real policy of that Cabinet foresaw would be followed by submissive acquiescence in his demands.

16

POST–CIVIL WAR EXPANSIONISTS

The final surrender of the Confederate armies in the spring of 1865 brought to an end the military aspects of the Civil War, but there were still ramifications of that struggle with which the United States had to deal. Among these was an enlarged spirit of nationalism expressing itself in two ways. One was a renewed interest in manifest destiny, which took the form of attempted territorial expansion in various parts of the world. Closely coupled with this trend was a desire to provide better national defense.

Manifest destiny was nothing new in American history. From the time the first permanent English settlers landed at Jamestown in 1607, there had been a quest for more land, principally for agriculture. Even before the United States had been established, venturesome colonists had pushed first to the fall line and then into the piedmont, while still more hardy souls found their way beyond the Appalachians. Following the adoption of the Constitution in 1788, land hunger resulted in the Louisiana Purchase, the gaining of the Floridas, the acquisition of Texas, the annexation of the lower half of Oregon, and the conquest of New Mexico and California. Thus by the opening of the Civil War, the United States had reached its present continental limits. More than agrarian expansionist desires had been expressed prior to 1860; proslavery forces had sought Cuba, while commercial and religious interests had combined to advocate American control over islands in the Pacific.

After 1865, expansionists were motivated by a variety of new factors. Naval bases and coaling stations were sought because the Civil War had shown their need. No longer could the growing nation rely tenuously upon the supply stations of foreign countries. In promoting this postwar aspect of manifest destiny, the United States had an energetic protagonist in Secretary of State Seward, an intensely patriotic American who believed territorial expansion to be a necessary concomitant to national strength and greatness. Naturally he had the support of the Navy Department, as evidenced by its annual report of 1865. After showing how American commerce had increased in recent years, the report continued:

> There are circumstances which render it necessary that a commercial and naval people should have coaling stations and ports for supplies at one or more important points on those seas and oceans where there are important interests to be protected, or naval power is to be maintained. . . . A prudent regard for our future interests and welfare would seem to dictate the expediency of securing some eligible location for the purposes indicated.

President Johnson supported the expansionist program, and this was also backed by Americans who were looking forward to the broader industrial and commercial opportunities that new possessions might furnish.

On the other hand, Seward's expansionist plans encountered strong resistance, not only in a Congress dominated by Radical Republicans, but in public opinion as well. The congressional opposition, especially in the upper house, stemmed partly from a dislike of Johnson, who differed politically with the majority and who disagreed with the Radical program for Southern reconstruction, and partly from a struggle between the executive and legislative branches as to their respective powers. The American public, burdened by heavy wartime taxes, viewed the additional expenditures that territorial acquisitions would entail with jaundiced eyes. Moreover, the majority of the people were more concerned about domestic problems: the South, the development of the West, the growth of industry, and the monetary issue, to mention some of the most important.

As a result of this opposition, Seward failed in most of his efforts to acquire additional territory for the United States. His successor during the Grant administration, Hamilton Fish, tried to carry on some of Seward's unfinished work, but was no more successful, despite the active support of President Grant. The American people were not yet ready for any large-scale expansion outside the United States.

The Purchase of Alaska

The only major success achieved by Secretary of State Seward's policy of expansion was the purchase of Alaska. Following the treaty of 1824 which ended Russian encroachment into the Oregon country,[1] relations between the United States and Russia concerning the Pacific Northwest had been quite friendly. True, in the middle 1830s there had been some

[1] See chap. 11.

controversy over Russia's refusal to extend the provisions of article 4 of that treaty, which allowed mutual rights to trade and fish in each other's territory "without any hindrance whatever." Consequently, the Van Buren administration was supposed to have made the first American offer to purchase Alaska, but to no avail.[2]

Shortly after this supposed offer, the Russian-American Company,[3] which had been established in 1799 to administer Alaska in somewhat the same fashion the British East India Company had governed India, began to suffer economic hardship. About 1840, it leased a narrow area along the coast to the Hudson's Bay Company, hoping that the rental would prevent bankruptcy. In turn, that lease to a British company aroused fear in the United States of a possible extension of British control in the Northwest. Consequently, Robert J. Walker, Polk's Secretary of the Treasury and an ardent expansionist, reportedly advocated buying Alaska. Nothing came of this proposal because Polk was much too concerned about Oregon, Texas, and California.

The next step in the Alaska story was taken during the Crimean War, when Russia feared the territory might be captured by England. With the authorization of his government, Baron Edouard de Stoeckl, the Russian Minister at Washington, conferred with Secretary of State Marcy and Senator William Gwin of California about possible American acquisition of Alaska. This might be done by having the territory purchased by the American Russian Commercial Company (established in 1853), consisting mainly of American stockholders in and around San Francisco. The avowed objective of this new firm was to cut ice along the northern Pacific Coast, and possibly to engage in the lumber and fur trade; actually, however, it was organized to provide Alaskans with food and other necessities of life in case the territory became isolated from Russia during the Crimean War. The conferees, after a lengthy survey of the situation, concluded that Britain would not respect the transfer as valid, and thus Alaska might still be a battleground.

Fortunately for Russia, the Hudson's Bay Company realized that if Russia disposed of Alaska, the 1840 lease to the coastal strip would be terminated. Therefore the company persuaded the British government to place Alaska outside the war theater. Since this meant Russia would not lose it in the conflict, she temporarily gave up her idea of selling it.

Yet Stoeckl's original proposal had fallen on receptive ears. The Cal-

---

[2] Nathaniel Banks, chairman of the House Committee on Foreign Relations during the Johnson administration, made this assertion in 1867. No evidence has been unearthed to substantiate his statement.

[3] Shares in this company were purchased by the Tsar, as well as by many Russian nobles. As a result of this financial support and the political influence these stockholders enjoyed, the company was granted many privileges in Alaska.

ifornians became more and more anxious to expand their fur and lumber trade in the Pacific, and the acquisition of Alaska offered a partial answer. Consequently Gwin prevailed upon Secretary Marcy to say to Stoeckl, "If Russia wishes to sell, the United States may be in the market." The Russian Minister could only reply, however, that his government had changed its mind.

But Stoeckl still believed Alaska was a nuisance. As early as 1860, he tried to impress the Russian leaders with the heavy responsibilities of trying to administer the colony without adequate return. He was helped somewhat by the fact that in 1862 the charter of the Russian-American Company expired. The new document offered by the government was less advantageous, so the company would not accept it. In the absence of other means of administering the territory, the company, still losing money, was allowed to continue on practically a day-to-day basis. Obviously something had to be done.

By 1866, the Russian government was convinced that selling was the only solution. The company was closer to bankruptcy than ever before; its stock had declined in value more than 400 per cent in the previous six years. The recent discovery of gold would only complicate the situation, since it would attract to Alaska a heterogeneous and lawless element, chiefly non-Russian. Not only would Russia be disposing of a territory that was growing more unprofitable to govern, but the money received would help her satisfy the company's creditors. Influencing the government toward such a conclusion was Grand Duke Constantine, the brother of the Tsar and also chief of the Admiralty. He believed the cost of defending Alaska, separated as it was from Russia, would be prohibitive. In addition, the Grand Duke was of the opinion that the colony was of no value. By selling Alaska to the United States, Russia could concentrate on the Amur area, which not only had greater natural resources, but was contiguous to the empire. The Minister of Foreign Affairs, Alexander Gortchakov, who previously had been only lukewarm toward disposing of Alaska, now became an ardent advocate, as did also Minister of Finance Reutern.

The most active promoter of the sale, however, was still Minister Stoeckl, who argued that Alaska could not be defended in time of war, and even in time of peace it was constantly being trespassed upon by American hunters and fishermen. He had frequently taken up the latter problem with the American State Department, only to be informed that it was Russia's duty to guard her own shores. Continued complications of this nature might end the good relations between the two nations. To do so would be all the worse because the United States had shown a definite desire earlier to purchase Alaska, and probably was still interested. Moreover, it would be better to have the friendly United States at Russia's back door than a potential enemy. Under the circumstances, Stoeckl cautioned his government not to make any commitments to other countries, so that when the United States renewed its offer, Russia would be free to act.

Thus by the end of 1866, just at the time the Johnson administration was embarking on a policy of expansion, a combination of other interests, worries about defense, and the high cost of administering Alaska caused the Russian government to decide to sell the territory. Stoeckl was therefore instructed to try to persuade the United States to pay a minimum of 5 million dollars for Alaska—this to include the Aleutian Islands, but not the Kuriles. The Minister must insist, however, that the Russian inhabitants who decided to stay in Alaska be fully protected in their property rights and religious freedom. Also, the United States must fulfill any commitments the Russian-American Company had made to both the Hudson's Bay Company and the American Russian Commercial Company.

Stoeckl went about his task in unassuming fashion, trying not to appear eager to sell, since if Secretary Seward could be persuaded to take the initiative, Russia might be able to drive a better bargain. This was a comparatively easy course. The Secretary of State was interested in expansion, and he was already being asked by other Americans to buy Alaska. For instance, in February, 1866, the legislature of Washington Territory petitioned the Federal government to have Russia open Alaskan fisheries to American citizens; and, about the same time, a group of Californians, headed by Senator Cornelius Cole, sought to obtain from the practically defunct Russian-American Company the lease to the coastal strip given to the Hudson's Bay Company in 1840.

Thus with both parties interested, early in March, 1867, the Secretary queried Stoeckl as to the possibility of allowing American fishermen to ply their trade off the Alaskan coast. The Russian Minister replied he was certain his government would not grant such a privilege. Then Seward was jockeyed into the position of asking whether Russia would sell the whole territory. After some discussion, the two men agreed that both countries would benefit from such a deal, but Seward said he could not proceed further until he had the approval of President Johnson. Evidently that consent was obtained, for on March 15, the Cabinet went on record as favoring the acquisition of Alaska.

With this support, Seward resumed his talks with the Russian Minister. The Secretary thought 5 million dollars would be a suitable price; Stoeckl countered by asking twice that amount, thinking he might get at least 6.5 million dollars. After considerable bargaining, they agreed on 7 million dollars; then Stoeckl prevailed on Seward to assume the responsibility of paying the obligations of the Russian-American Company, estimated at $200,000.

There were numerous other details to be arranged concerning the rights of the Russian inhabitants of Alaska. To iron them out, Stoeckl called at Seward's home on the evening of March 29, 1867, while the Secretary was seeking relaxation from the cares of office in a game of whist. Stoeckl suggested that they conclude the work the next day, but Seward, eager to complete the matter about which he was now so enthusiastic, replied that there was no time like the present. After hurriedly calling in Charles Sumner, chairman of the Senate Foreign Relations Committee, the three men sat down to their task. By four o'clock on the morning of March 30 the treaty was finished, and before the day was over, it was in the hands of the Senate with the blessing of the Johnson administration.

So rapid and secret had been the negotiations that not until then did the nation learn of the affair. Because of the President's unpopularity, there was immediate criticism of the treaty. Some newspapers wanted to know why the United States should buy a "barren region" inhabited only "by Siberian malefactors," a territory that was "short of rations" and where there were "long twilights." Everywhere there was talk about "Seward's Folly" and "Seward's Icebox." Such attacks, however, elicited prompt support for the administration. One prominent builder of transcontinental telegraph lines insisted that, under American jurisdiction, the Alaskan population would grow rapidly to develop the commerce and fisheries of that area; as a result, "at no distant day," Alaska would "rival that of Newfoundland and the coast of the Atlantic east of Cape Cod." Others were certain that the acquisition of the territory would give the United States supremacy in the Pacific.

In the Senate there were many who voiced complaints about the money to be spent for a worthless land, so far removed from the United States proper. Others were against the agreement because of their dislike of President Johnson and Secretary Seward. Predictions were rife that the treaty would not be ratified. Such pessimism failed to take into consideration, however, the persuasive powers of both Seward and Sumner. The former, in private talks with key senators, played up the supposed moral support which Russia had given the United States during the latter half of the Civil War,[4] while Sumner made a long and fervent speech in the upper house, pointing out the importance to the nation of acquiring Alaska: the abundance of natural resources, the commercial advantages, and the opportunity to thwart the aspirations of England and to drive another European monarchy from the hemisphere. Consequently, on April 9, 1867, the Senate approved the treaty by the one-sided vote of 37 to 2. The Russian government endorsed the document by the middle of May.

[4] See chap. 15.

Even though Congress had as yet made no provision for paying the $7,200,000 for the territory, Russia showed her good will by allowing American ships to enter Alaskan waters before the end of May. At this time neither Seward nor Stoeckl foresaw any obstacles, but there soon developed a staunch opposition in the House to the appropriation for which President Johnson asked on July 6. Instead of acting on this bill, the national legislature adjourned for the summer. Much concerned by this delay, Stoeckl tried to speed American action by persuading his government to approve the actual transfer of Alaska to the United States. Thus, on October 18, 1867, Brigadier General Lovell Rousseau, acting for the United States, supervised the raising of the American flag at Fort Sitka.

When Congress reconvened in November, its major interest was the impeachment charges against President Johnson. Therefore it was not until the late spring of 1868 that the Alaskan Appropriation Bill was given consideration. On May 18, the House Foreign Relations Committee at last reported favorably on this measure. Even then almost another two months elapsed before it came to a vote. All the old arguments against expansion in general and against Alaska in particular were voiced during the debate, and several new protests were added.[5] Stoeckl spent money freely to obtain a favorable press, and it has also been alleged that he bribed some congressmen to change their minds. At last, early in July the expansionist forces won by a vote of 113 to 43, but only at the price of agreeing to a rider:

> No purchase . . . of foreign territory shall be hereafter made until after provision by law for its payment. And it is hereby declared that all powers vested by the Constitution in the President and Senate to enter into treaties with foreign Governments do not include the power to complete the purchase of foreign territory before the necessary appropriations shall be made therefore by act of Congress.

The upper house refused to approve this important limitation on the treaty-making power, and passed the appropriation bill in its initial form on July 17. The House accepted this Senate version six days later by a vote of 91 to 48, with 77 members refusing to commit themselves on the controversial issue. On July 27, 1868, President Johnson affixed his signature and the acquisition of Alaska was complete.

[5] Some in the House believed Russia should pay the so-called Perkins claim. Benjamin Perkins claimed that during the Crimean War he had contracted with Stoeckl and another Russian, Rakielevicz (who purported to be connected with the Russian Embassy), to deliver ammunition and other supplies to the Russian armies. When Stoeckl refused to pay Perkins and denied that he knew Rakielevicz, the claimant took his case to court, which threw out his suit for damages. Perkins then promised to drop the case, but his heirs, learning of the Alaskan negotiations, demanded $800,000 from the money Russia would receive. A number of congressmen supported the heirs, but nothing came of the issue.

The Midway Islands

While the Alaskan negotiations were hanging fire, the United States, more by a stroke of good luck than anything else, gained its first possession in the Pacific. The China Mail Steamship Company, regularly plying between the United States and the Far East, informed the Navy Department that the Brooks Islands, mere specks in the vast ocean, were unclaimed by any nation and might be had for the taking. Consequently, Captain William Reynolds of the U.S.S. *Lackawanna* was ordered by his superiors to proceed at once to those islands, over which he raised the American flag on August 28, 1867. Just about a month later, Congress endorsed this action and renamed the group the Midway Islands because they were approximately halfway between the West Coast and Japan.

For a number of years, the Midway Islands were not important as either a naval base or a coaling station, since the major harbor was blocked by a sand bar. The necessary dredging was deemed too costly. Thus the only importance of this acquisition at the time was to promote greater interest on the part of Seward and his fellow expansionists in Hawaii and possibly in Samoa.

Failure to Annex the Dominican Republic

Seward's major interest, however, was in the Caribbean area, with particular attention to the Dominican Republic. That country, located on the eastern end of the island of Haiti, had declared itself independent of its stronger neighbor, Haiti, in 1844. Independence did not bring the desired peace, as internal dissension and continued fear of Haitian attacks led to years of trouble and worry. An early Dominican president, Pedro Santana, concluded that the only salvation was to place his country under the protection of some strong nation. For historical reasons, France seemed the logical guardian, but King Louis Philippe refused "to mix in the affairs" of the explosive young republic. Next, Santana approached Spain, only to learn that warnings from Britain and the United States had dissuaded her from accepting the responsibility. Buenaventura Baéz, who alternated with Santana in the presidency, went even further in 1849, when he informed France, England, and the United States that annexation of his country would be preferable to a protectorate. Nothing was accomplished except to have those three powers warn Haiti that they frowned on its aggressions upon its weaker neighbor.

Then came the Crimean War, which involved both France and England and gave Haiti another opportunity to attack the Dominican Republic. The Dominicans would not seek help from the United States because of the slavery issue there; to them the restoration of a slave economy would be just as bad as conquest by Haiti. Fortunately the Haitians were driven out, but the situation became so critical in 1858 that the United States was forced to intervene to restore domestic peace. Baéz was then replaced by Santana early the following year.

Just about this time, Secretary of State Lewis Cass was looking for potential bases and coaling stations. In March, 1859, he was informed by Jonathan Elliot, the American commercial agent in the Dominican Republic, that Santana, pleased by American support, was ready to recip-rocate by granting the United States "a good station for our Navy and depots for our steamers" somewhere along the Dominican coast. Seeking to take prompt advantage of Elliot's information, Cass sent William Cazneau, who was also desirous of expanding his nation's trade and terri-tory, as a special agent. Cazneau was of the opinion that the logical base was Samaná Bay, an excellent natural harbor in the northeastern part of the island; but before anything could be done to obtain a lease for that strategic area, the special agent learned early in March, 1860, that Spain had designs on the Dominican Republic. While there were many Domin-icans not averse to the change, Cazneau warned Cass that an immediate "public demonstration of kindly interest" by the Buchanan administration might induce the Dominicans to fight for their continued independence. Both Buchanan and Cass were too concerned with sectional troubles at home to pay the required attention to external matters. Therefore Spanish influence mounted in direct ratio to the diminution of American interest.

Spain, witnessing the internal schism developing in the United States, worried less about intervening in the Western Hemisphere. Therefore Madrid answered Santana's appeal by sending troops to the Dominican Republic in 1860. The thankful Dominican President then proclaimed on March 18, 1861, that Spain was ready to annex his country.

Just two weeks before Santana's statement, Abraham Lincoln became President. His Secretary of State, William Seward, at once recognized the anticipated Spanish acquisition as a threat to this hemisphere. Here might be the opportunity to prevent the Civil War by engaging in a for-eign conflict. His "Thoughts" gave the general outline,[6] but he was re-buffed by President Lincoln. Therefore all Seward could do about the situation was to inform Gabriel Tassara, the Spanish Minister at Wash-ington, on April 2, 1861, that Madrid's projected action would be re-garded "as manifesting an unfriendly spirit towards the United States." Moreover, any further effort on Spain's part to move into "either the Dominican Republic or any part of the American continent or islands" would be met "with a prompt, persistent, and, if possible, effective re-sistance." A week later, William Preston, the American Minister at

[6] See chap. 15.

Madrid, delivered to the Spanish government Seward's note, which further emphasized the principles of the Monroe Doctrine.

The advent of the Civil War, however, made it impossible for the United States to push the issue, and Spain, casting aside its original reluctance, assumed jurisdiction over Santo Domingo. Seward, with so many other problems on his hands, became less belligerent and more cautious. On August 14, 1861, Carl Schurz, who had replaced Preston at Madrid, was informed that Congress would soon take up the problem, but that body, concentrating on military matters, did nothing. Indeed, throughout the rest of the war, the United States took little if any note of the Spanish intervention.

Yet Spanish control did not afford the Dominicans the expected relief from domestic disorders. Santana, the first captain general, ruled with an iron hand. Then gradually Spain replaced native officials with Spanish ones and set up the same type of unenlightened government that had caused her other colonies to revolt earlier in the century. The Catholic Church resorted to methods similar to those of the old Inquisition. Taxes to support the new regime became heavier and heavier.

Cazneau and some other Americans, notably James Fabens, who were desirous of reviving American interest in Santo Domingo, formed the American West India Company in 1862, with a capital of about a million dollars. This company resorted to all types of propaganda to stress the economic, commercial, and strategic potentialities of that island country. Nothing could be done, however, as long as Spanish rule prevailed, so Cazneau and his associates also encouraged the Dominicans to revolt— not a particularly difficult task. Consequently, in 1863 began the War of the Restoration to reestablish the republic. Aided by Haitians, yellow fever, an inefficient if not corrupt Spanish home government, and resulting popular opposition in Spain to whatever the hated Queen did, the rebels gradually obtained the upper hand. By late 1864, Spain saw the futility of attempting to maintain her control, especially since the end of the Civil War was in sight and the United States would be able to renew and enforce her earlier protest. A belated effort to reach a compromise with the Dominicans having failed, Spain withdrew all of her troops from the country by July, 1865.

During the course of the War of the Restoration, the Dominicans had established a provisional government, which sent Pablo Pujol to Washington for aid. Pujol's appearance placed Seward in a quandary. He wanted to furnish help, but at the same time he could not consistently do so when he was struggling to prevent European intervention on behalf of the Confederacy. Consequently, he had to refuse to receive the Dominican envoy.

The restored republic was in a critical situation. Years of domestic

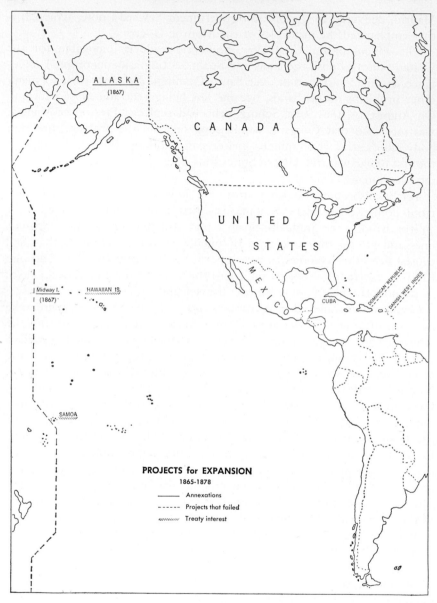

PROJECTS for EXPANSION
1865-1878

—————— Annexations

- - - - - Projects that failed

//////// Treaty interest

turmoil and the recent war against Spain had left it virtually bankrupt. The political situation was little better, for Baéz and José Cabral were constantly struggling for the presidency. The answer to the problem seemed to be help from the United States, no longer under suspicion because it had abolished slavery. Therefore, in the fall of 1865, President Cabral broached the subject of a loan of a million dollars to J. Somers

Smith, the new American commercial agent. When Seward was informed of this request, he suggested that the proper collateral should be the lease of Samaná Bay as a naval base, or, much to be preferred, the sale of that strategic harbor to the United States. Cabral's original reply to the latter proposition was that the Dominican constitution forbade the sale of any territory.

Throughout 1866 and 1867 the deal hung fire. As the Dominican Republic's problems became more critical, Cabral had to change his mind by offering to accept annexation. Several times it appeared as though annexation, purchase, or lease might be consummated, only to have some obstacle appear. Then Baéz, returning to power in 1868, was persuaded, possibly by Fabens, to obtain a loan of £420,000 from the English banking firm of Hartmont and Company. When Hartmont reneged on the deal, the government was in worse financial condition than before.[7]

The desperate Baéz had to turn to the United States for help. The only solution was annexation under any terms America might make. Seward, troubled by mounting opposition in the Senate to his expansionist plans, replied that only Congress could take the necessary step. With the help of President Johnson, whose annual message of December 9, 1868, urged not only the annexation of the Dominican Republic, but of Haiti as well—even though Haiti had not sought this—Seward persuaded Nathaniel Banks, the chairman of the House Foreign Relations Committee, to introduce a resolution on January 13, 1869, providing that American protection be extended over both countries if they desired it. The President must inform Congress, however, before such protectorates were established; and if such action required the expenditure of money, congressional approval must be obtained beforehand. The general feeling against the meddling of the executive branch was so great that the Banks Resolution was overwhelmingly defeated, 126 to 36. Shortly after, Representative Godlove Orth of Indiana introduced another administration-backed measure: if the Dominicans established a satisfactory territorial government, their country should be admitted into the Union as a state. This proposal shared the same fate, being rejected by a vote of 110 to 63.

Thus the Dominican issue was stalemated when Ulysses S. Grant took office in March, 1869. As a military man, Grant realized the strategic importance of insular bases and consequently was ready to carry on to

[7] Hartmont agreed to lend £420,000, but he subtracted immediately a commission of £100,000. The full amount was to be amortized in twenty-five years, with Dominican customs receipts and the mines and forests of the Samaná area as collateral. Hartmont placed on the market £750,000 worth of Dominican bonds at 70, and then failed to carry out other parts of the agreement. Needless to say, the government was left with a much heavier debt (it was responsible for redeeming the bonds at par) and yet had received little capital in return.

fulfillment the work of his predecessor. His Secretary of State,[8] Hamilton Fish of New York, had accepted the post "with a heavy heart and with unnumbered misgivings," for he believed he was not fitted for the position. Unlike Seward and Grant, the new Secretary was not primarily interested in colonial expansion; his major concern was to settle American diplomatic problems by peaceful means and to keep the nation out of trouble. Fish, with his broad outlook, proved an exceptionally competent head of the State Department for eight years.

Fish was not an advocate of the annexation of the Dominican Republic, but he realized that the issue might afford him the opportunity to settle satisfactorily the several controversies with Great Britain—his main objective. President Grant and Charles Sumner, chairman of the powerful Senate Foreign Relations Committee, agreed with each other in favoring firmness and even hostility toward Britain on the *Alabama* claims affair, but were not in accord about the Dominican Republic. Were he able to widen the breach between the President and the Senator on the matter of annexation, Fish might extend the differences to include the problems with England and be able to settle them in conciliatory fashion.

Therefore when Grant started pushing the Dominican annexation issue, Fish hesitatingly went along with him. The President's first step was to send General Orville Babcock, his military secretary, to the republic in July, 1869, as a special envoy. He was warmly welcomed by the shaky Baéz administration, and on September 4 he signed a tentative agreement with Foreign Minister Manuel Gautier for a treaty of annexation and an American loan of 1.5 million dollars. Were the Senate to reject the treaty, the United States would purchase Samaná Bay for 2 million dollars and turn over to the Baéz government additional cash and arms so it could remain in office.

When the Babcock proposal was submitted to the Cabinet, Secretary Fish would not support it. He felt the Cazneau-Fabens group had played too important a role in a scheme that would enrich the American investors, rather than help the United States. As a result of Fish's arguments, the other Cabinet officers rejected the plan unanimously. Thereupon sent by President Grant to the Dominican Republic a second time, Babcock drew up two treaties. The first provided for the annexation of the republic as an American territory, for a loan by the United States of 1.5 million dollars to help pay off the Dominican debt, and for a Dominican promise not to incur any further financial obligations. The other treaty, to be attempted in case the first failed, allowed the United States to lease Samaná Bay area for ninety-nine years at an annual rental to be subsequently determined; furthermore, any time during the leasing period the United States might buy the naval station for 2 million dollars.

[8] Grant had first named Elihu Washburne of Illinois as Secretary, but political complications led to the substitution of Fish on March 11, 1869.

Grant was pleased with these two documents, which he sent to the Senate for ratification in early January, 1870. To make doubly sure that one or the other was approved, the President used all the political pressure at his command and also insisted that a plebiscite be held by the Dominicans to ascertain their opinion about the proposed change in government.[9]

The Foreign Relations Committee, dominated by Sumner, was vehemently against both treaties and reported adversely upon them on March 15, 1870. Sumner followed up his report with a denunciatory Senate speech in which he referred to the Dominican Republic as "Naboth's Vineyard." [10] The adverse report of the committee, Sumner's speech, the continued congressional opposition to executive interference, and the feeling that a corrupt or unfair deal was being made all contributed to a definite swing in the Senate against the treaties. Grant, seeing the turn of affairs, tried mightily to reverse the trend by arguing that ratification of the treaties would indicate "an adherence to the Monroe Doctrine." In support of this contention, he asserted that he had reliable information that a European nation was already offering 2 million dollars for Samaná Bay. Consequently, if the United States refused the Dominican offer to purchase that area, "with what grace can we prevent a foreign power from attempting to secure the prize?" Whereupon he specifically promulgated a corollary to the doctrine: "Hereafter no territory on this continent shall be regarded as subject of transfer to a European power."

The President's efforts were of no avail, for on June 30 the Senate voted 28 to 28 on the issue, far short of the required two-thirds majority needed for ratification. This was a bitter pill for Grant, who had placed so much political emphasis upon having the treaties adopted. Still convinced he was right, he persuaded Congress to send a committee to study the situation again. This committee of inquiry spent several months in the Dominican Republic in 1871 before returning with a report favoring annexation. The senatorial opponents of expansion were much stronger, however, and the American public showed no real interest in the project, so the whole matter died of inertia.[11]

[9] The plebiscite was held in February, 1870. The proponents of annexation, led by the Dominican President and the American investors, used all types of propaganda and pressure upon the Dominican voters. The result was: for annexation by the United States, 15,169; against, 11. According to reports, the eleven adverse votes were to "preserve appearances."

[10] Naboth's Vineyard had reference to the Biblical story in which the aggressive King Ahab took a valuable vineyard away by force from the weaker Naboth.

[11] Grant, angered by the outcome, tended to place most of the blame for the failure to ratify the treaties upon Charles Sumner. Therefore he used his influence in the Senate to have Sumner deposed as chairman of the Foreign Relations Committee on March 9, 1871. In addition, Attorney General Ebenezer R. Hoar, a vociferous critic of Grant's policy in the Cabinet, was compelled to resign. Fish was of course pleased by the action against Sumner, for it made easier the Secretary's solution of the controversies with Great Britain. See chap. 17.

Meantime, Secretary Fish reiterated Grant's "no-transfer" corollary in more forceful terms on July 14, 1870. In this statement he declared:

> This is not a policy of aggression; but it opposes the creation of European dominion on American soil, or its transfer to other European powers, and it looks hopefully to the time when, by the voluntary departure of European governments from this continent and adjacent islands, America should be wholly American. It does not contemplate forcible intervention in any legitimate contest; but it protests against permitting such a contest to result in the increase of European power or influence; and it even impels this government, as in the late contest between the South American republics and Spain, to interpose its good offices to secure an honorable peace.

Although little attention was paid to this broader interpretation to the Monroe Doctrine at that time, it did provide an important foundation for American foreign policy in the future.

The final act in the Dominican episode came when Baéz, still in financial difficulties, signed a contract with an American firm to lease Samaná Bay to it for ninety-nine years at a rental of $150,000 annually. Before the first payment was made, however, Baéz was turned out of office in 1873, and his successor canceled the agreement.

Unsuccessful Efforts to Purchase the Danish West Indies

Closely associated with the interest in the Dominican Republic was the effort of Seward to purchase the Danish West Indies, especially the islands of St. Thomas and St. John.[12] These would be valuable as potential bases for the United States, and at the same time an American purchase would prevent them from falling into the hands of a strong European power. This worry increased after 1864; Prussia had just seized Schleswig-Holstein from Denmark, and Austria might seek compensation by demanding the Danish West Indies. Nothing could be done by the United States to forestall such an event until after its victory over the Confederacy was assured. Consequently it was not until a New Year's (1865) gathering at the White House that Seward, with Lincoln's full approval, greeted General Waldemar Raasloff, the Danish Minister, "with unusual friendliness."

About a week later, Seward secretly informed Raasloff that the United States needed a base in the West Indies. The people of any island acquired for that purpose would enjoy a number of advantages, especially economic, from the change in rule. The Danish government, however, was not ready to sell the islands; any additional loss of territory might bring

---

[12] The third major island, Santa Cruz (or St. Croix), was not under consideration because Denmark believed she was committed to obtain the approval of France before any alienation could take place.

political chaos at home. Nevertheless, Denmark indicated that it might be receptive in the future.

Seward's injuries [13] and Lincoln's assassination prevented any further serious consideration of the issue until near the close of 1865, when the Danish Foreign Office told Raasloff to persuade Seward "to make a definite offer" for the islands.

The Secretary was pleased by this request, but it was not until late January, 1866, that he was ready to broach the matter with President Johnson and the other Cabinet members. He deemed it wise, however, to reach a logical and fair price—using the amounts paid for Louisiana and Florida as examples—before taking any definite steps. Raasloff did not know exactly what his government would ask, but he personally believed that 25 million dollars would be "a reasonable price."

Since this seemed exorbitant to Seward, again there was delay. Moreover, he was being criticized by the advocates of the acquisition of the Dominican Republic for attempting too much, and the Danish Foreign Minister was trying to allay the concern of both England and France over the possible sale. Lord Russell was fairly certain that Denmark would sell "if Seward offers a good price" and so paid little attention to the Danish assertion that there was not "the slightest intention at the time of getting rid of any of her colonies."

Under such circumstances, secret negotiations between Seward and Raasloff continued throughout the remainder of 1866 and 1867. Both men were coy. Seward would ask how much Denmark wanted for the islands without revealing how much he would pay, while Raasloff would ask how much the United States would give without committing himself on his sale price. Finally, on October 24, 1867, Denmark, beset with financial troubles, agreed to a treaty under which she would sell St. Thomas and St. John for 7.5 million dollars, provided the islanders approved the transfer. The Danish legislature quickly ratified this agreement, as did the King. Early in 1868 the plebiscite was held, with results overwhelmingly in favor of American acquisition.[14]

In the United States, on the other hand, there were innumerable obstacles. Seward's optimistic prediction that Congress would go along with the administration's wishes proved false. The Senate kept delaying any decision on the so-called Danish Treaty, and the lower house delivered an unexpected blow to the expansionists on November 25, 1867, when by an overwhelming majority it declared that it was not under any compulsion "to vote money for any such purchase unless there is greater necessity for the same than now exists."

---

[13] Seward had broken his jaw in a carriage accident, and before he recovered from this mishap, he was seriously wounded by one of the conspirators in the Lincoln assassination plot.

[14] The vote in St. Thomas was 1,039 to 22; in St. John, 205 to 0.

Still another blow was delivered the same month when, on successive days, the islands were subjected to an earthquake, a tidal wave, and a hurricane. The resulting damage was great, particularly to the fields of cotton and sugar cane. The American public, which was much more interested in building up the new West and in reconstructing the South than in annexations, was loath to pay 7.5 million dollars for islands subject to such whims of nature. Adding to this opposition was the fact that Alaska had recently been purchased, and any further expenditures would be felt in the form of increased taxes. Nor did the people take seriously the Seward-Navy thesis about national defense. To them there was no imminent danger from abroad, and it did not seem consistent to acquire more bases while the wartime fleets were being cut.

The American press contributed to this popular opposition. The *New York Tribune* of December 19, 1867, was especially critical of the high price for a mere dot on the globe; it also found fault with Seward's failure to seek the "advice and consent" of Congress while the treaty negotiations were under way. The New York *Nation* added its objection on January 2, 1868, when it asserted that if all of Seward's expansionist schemes succeeded, the great danger would be "not for want of territory but from excess of it."

Continued delays prevented further action until Grant became President. Secretary Fish brought up the matter before the new Cabinet on March 23, 1869, only to find the same antipathy as before. The Danish chargé d'affaires tried to force the issue by stressing that American honor was at stake: the United States had initiated the movement for annexation; it would be dishonorable for her to back out of the bargain. Minister Raasloff did his part by resorting to all types of propaganda to turn the tide. Instead of accomplishing this objective, the propaganda served to arouse more strenuous opposition from American periodicals. The *Nation*, for instance, stated on April 1, 1869, that "If there be any species of treaty which enterprising Presidents and Secretaries of State need to be warned not to make lightly, it is treaties for the purchase of new territories." This article then continued: "We do not want to wake up in the morning and find that the Secretary of State has overnight bought us two or three millions of fellow-citizens to be paid for out of our earnings, and provide work for forty or fifty thousand soldiers."

The discouraged Danes made one more attempt to close the deal by offering to sell St. Croix along with the other two islands for just a small additional amount. This added inducement failed to change the senatorial minds. As a result, early in 1870 the Foreign Relations Committee reported unfavorably on the Danish Treaty, which never came to a vote in the upper house. Thus the second major effort of William Seward to obtain Caribbean bases failed.

The Pacific Attraction

Meanwhile, the annexation of Alaska and the Midway Islands had revived American interest in the Pacific area. Particularly exciting to expansionist imagination were the strategically located Hawaiian Islands, where a numerous and influential group of Americans already resided.

In an earlier chapter the abortive effort of the Pierce administration to annex Hawaii has been described.[15] After this project collapsed, Secretary of State Marcy had negotiated a reciprocity treaty with the islands in 1855, but this agreement was rejected by the Senate, largely because of the opposition of the Louisiana sugar growers, who feared Hawaiian competition. In 1867 Secretary Seward revived the reciprocity project. In so doing he was frankly attempting to prepare the way for expansion. To the American Minister at Honolulu Seward wrote that:

> ... a lawful and peaceful annexation of the islands to the United States with the consent of the people of Hawaii ... is deemed desirable by this Government; and that if the policy of annexation should really conflict with the policy of reciprocity, annexation is in every case to be preferred.

The reciprocity treaty of 1867 was defeated in the Senate—in part because some expansionist senators feared reciprocity might prove a barrier to future annexation. Not until near the close of Grant's second term was attention turned again to Hawaii. As so often in the history of American expansion, fear of Britain spurred the nation to action. Hawaii, grievously injured by the decline of the whaling trade, sought to expand the market for its sugar. The islanders threatened to do most of their business with the British Empire if the United States again rejected their request for reciprocity.

In 1875 Secretary of State Hamilton Fish successfully obtained the ratification of a treaty that not only provided for reciprocity, but contained a Hawaiian pledge not to grant similar concessions to any other country. Even more important to American expansionists was the clause in which Hawaii promised not to turn over any territory whatsoever to a third nation. Senator John T. Morgan of Alabama interpreted this agreement thus:

> The Hawaiian treaty was negotiated for the purpose of securing political control of those islands, making them industrially and commercially a part of the United States, and preventing any other great power from acquiring a foothold there, which might be adverse to the welfare and safety of our Pacific coast in time of war.

[15] See chap. 13.

Interest in Samoa

Although the islands of the Samoan group had a total area scarcely greater than that of Rhode Island, they came to have an importance in European and American eyes disproportionate with their size. In the first place, Samoa was on the direct shipping route between Hawaii and Australia, approximately midway between the two. The port of Apia became a natural stopover point for whaling vessels and trading craft. Moreover, Samoa's soil and climate were ideal for coconut trees. Merchants in search of copra, the oil-rich meal derived from coconuts, were drawn to the islands, and many foreign-owned plantations were developed.

Up to about 1850 the English far outnumbered all other foreigners in Samoa. British missionaries gained such influence over the native chiefs that British annexation would have been easy, but the home government was in an anti-imperialistic phase that made it reluctant to take on new responsibilities. During the 1850s the German trading firm of Godeffroy & Son began to operate in the islands so successfully that within thirty years it held much of the land and dominated the Samoan export trade.

Meanwhile, Americans had exhibited a sporadic interest in Samoa. American whaling vessels regularly visited Apia, and in 1839 the United States Exploring Expedition under Lieutenant Charles Wilkes carefully surveyed the inviting harbor of Pago Pago on the island of Tutuila. Thirty-three years later the attention of the expansionist-minded Grant administration was directed to Samoa in connection with the ambitious plans of William H. Webb of New York for a steamship line between San Francisco and Australia. One of Webb's agents reported that Pago Pago was "the most perfectly land-locked harbor that exists in the Pacific," but that all Samoa stood in danger of becoming a German protectorate.

In 1872, just when the Grant administration was pondering the Samoan problem, Commander R. W. Meade of the U.S.S. *Narragansett*, quite on his own responsibility, signed a treaty with a native chief on Tutuila. In return for a promise that the chief was to have the protection of the United States, the Americans were given the exclusive privilege of establishing a naval station at Pago Pago. President Grant accepted the handiwork of this zealous naval officer, but the Senate declined to approve the agreement.

Still eager to support Webb's steamship plans, Grant sent Colonel A. B. Steinberger as a special agent to investigate the Samoan situation. Practically all foreigners who went to Samoa seem to have been tempted to plunge into native politics, and Steinberger was no exception. Within a short time the American agent had installed his own candidate as native king and was himself serving as prime minister. Steinberger's activities brought him into conflict with the British consul, and the American government finally had to repudiate him. Even with this troublemaker gone, a ceaseless jockeying among the rival consuls continued. The natives more than once offered to accept an American protectorate as a way out of their difficulties, but the American government was not ready to promise this.

In 1878, however, the Hayes administration was able to obtain Senate approval for a treaty providing that the United States should have the right to maintain a naval station at Pago Pago and that, in return, the American government would use its good offices to attempt a friendly settlement of any difficulty arising between Samoa and a foreign nation. This agreement was much weaker than that negotiated by Commander Meade in 1872, since it did not give the United States exclusive use of the port or promise American protection.

Britain and Germany also made treaties with the native king, and the British, German, and American consuls agreed among themselves to neutralize the port of Apia and maintain joint control of the municipal government. On this basis, an uneasy peace was maintained in the islands for several years, although not without chronic complaint on the part of British and American residents against the domineering Germans.

Except in the case of Alaska and the Midway Islands, the post–Civil War expansionist movement could not be called successful. There was too much partisan opposition within Congress and too much jealousy between the executive and legislative branches of the government. Moreover, the American people, burdened with heavy taxes and more concerned with domestic matters, were not as yet ready to support the ambitious schemes of Secretary of State Seward and his fellow imperialists. Not until after 1890 were the dreams of the expansionists to be renewed and partially fulfilled.

17

WAR SCARES AND PEACEFUL SETTLEMENTS

The issue of manifest destiny was one of considerable interest to the United States in the period immediately after the Civil War, even though not much was obtained. Just as important in the story of American diplomacy, however, was the solution of several incidents that had developed during the war, but that could not be settled until the Confederacy had surrendered. The two most significant matters that had to await conclusion of domestic hostilities were the French intervention in Mexico, with its resulting Maximilian affair, and several differences with Great Britain, the most controversial of which arose from the so-called *Alabama* claims. The first incident basically concerned the Monroe Doctrine, even though Secretary of State Seward never specifically mentioned it during the negotiations. The second had to do with the responsibilities of a neutral in wartime, and in turn had indirect ramifications involving the United States in dispute with Spain over Cuba.

In dealing with these major problems, together with several minor ones, the United States showed it was becoming a more effective power in international diplomacy. It was ready to use force in the Maximilian affair, and several American jingoists urged the seizure of Canada to compensate for American losses at the hands of British-built cruisers. Yet in the end it was primarily peaceful arbitration and mediation that won European recognition of the position of the United States.

Troubled Mexico

The background of the French intervention was to be found in the troubled situation in Mexico since her war with the United States. Dissatisfaction with the autocratic rule of men like Santa Anna led to a reform movement in the 1850s headed by two outstanding liberals: Benito Juárez and Miguel Lerdo. A particular objective was to decrease the power and influence of the Catholic Church and the army. The liberals succeeded in forcing through a new constitution in 1857, which provided for a number of civil rights, destroyed the special courts for clerical and military culprits, prohibited the Church from holding land not specifically used for religious purposes, and separated state and church. The conservatives objected strenuously to these changes, and the bloody War of Reform followed in 1858. The liberals gained the upper hand and finally made Juárez president in June, 1861.

The efforts of Juárez to effect the recent constitutional reforms were largely thwarted by two groups: on the one hand the local clergy and the military, who stirred up domestic opposition to the changes; and on the other the European creditors, who demanded payment of interest—and, in some cases, principal—on the money which earlier Mexican administrations had borrowed to stay in power. The years of strife had pushed Mexico to the brink of bankruptcy, however, so Juárez, while admitting his country's responsibility for the financial obligations, persuaded the legislature in July, 1861, to approve a two-year moratorium on debt payments. While this decision proved unwise diplomatically, it was the only step Mexico could take to prevent financial chaos and further civil war.

The three major creditors of Mexico were England, Spain, and France. Even before they learned of the moratorium, they were showing unusual concern at what was going on in Mexico. Spain was the first to raise the issue. As early as November, 1859, the Spanish Ambassador at Paris, Alexander Mon, talked of the possible need of setting up a monarchy in Mexico as the only method of providing an effective and lasting government. Were the present civil war to continue, Mon believed that the United States might step in and annex its troublesome neighbor.

To forestall such an eventuality, Spain suggested to France and Britain in January, 1860, that the three powers unite to uphold the political independence and territorial integrity of Mexico. Nothing came of this proposal, but the following fall Spain appeared ready to act alone to oppose the growing strength of Juárez, who was regarded as a menace to the Church and as a puppet of the United States. Orders were sent to Francisco Serrano, Captain General of Cuba, to dispatch a fleet to blockade Vera Cruz; but Serrano, closer to the arena, realized the danger and futility of such an expedition and refused to comply. Had he done so, the United States might have been involved—despite the imminent Civil War.

With the situation worsening in 1861, Spain informed Mexico in April that she must put her house in order, or Spain would step in and do so. A crisis seemed at hand in July, when Juárez, already hated by Spain, dismissed the Spanish Minister, J. F. Pachecho, because he had supported the conservatives. Again Spain was on the verge of blockading Vera Cruz.

Britain also had her grievances against Mexico. The constant broken promises of earlier Mexican administrations to pay English creditors was causing England to conclude that she must adopt a more forceful policy. All parties in the Mexican civil war were antagonizing her by 1861. For example, supporters of Juárez robbed a load of British specie en route from Mexico City to the coast, while backers of a political opponent of Juárez stole more than $600,000 from the British Embassy. Moreover, the vice consul at Tasco was killed during the troublesome times. Sir Charles Wyke, on becoming Minister to Mexico in March, 1861, was instructed by Lord Russell to insist upon compensation for all British losses. Were Mexico to fail to give satisfaction, the Royal Navy might be sent to obtain it by force. When news of the moratorium reached London, the Foreign Minister advocated British seizure of the Mexican customs houses.

Although the French had few monetary claims—about 40 million francs —as compared with the British and the Spanish, and fewer grievances generally, France led the way to actual intervention. Napoleon III was faced by numerous domestic troubles. The French people were unhappy with his rule, which they claimed brought little but economic hardship. Moreover, they were worried about the growing might of Prussia, and they blamed their Emperor for his failure to strengthen the national bulwarks against this aggressive neighbor. In an effort to make his subjects forget their own woes, Napoleon decided upon a typical European plan: when domestic trouble brews, engage in a foreign enterprise. Why not embark on a project which would lead to the establishment of another New France? To do so would increase his prestige both at home and abroad. Mexico, weak and unstable, would be the logical place to start this empire.[1] The time was ripe, too, because the United States, embroiled in domestic conflict, would be unable to make effective protest.

The main obstacles were to be found on France's side of the Atlantic. With Europe a virtual tinderbox, any open aggression on Napoleon's part might be the signal for a general war. Therefore, thought the French Emperor, why not use the excuse of the Mexican moratorium to unite the European creditors in a movement to collect the obligations by force? An additional incentive for such united action grew from the mistreatment of foreign nationals in Mexico. Such intervention would give France

[1] Napoleon's interest in Mexico may have been inspired by Miguel Miramón, who had been driven from the Mexican presidency by Juárez. Miramón then went to France, where he conspired with the Duc de Morny, the unscrupulous adviser of Napoleon III, to promote an alliance between France and the conservative Mexicans who opposed the recent reforms. Yet there is some evidence that several years before the deposition of Miramón, Mexican conservatives, desirous of establishing a monarchy, were conspiring with prominent Frenchmen, possibly even Napoleon, to make a Spanish prince the emperor.

the opportunity to gain a foothold which she could ultimately use to gain her major objective.

United States Moves against Intervention

Rumors of possible European intervention quickly reached the United States. In December, 1860, Robert McLane, American Minister to Mexico, notified the other diplomatic representatives at Mexico City that his government

> does not deny to the European powers the right to wage honorable warfare for a sufficient cause, anywhere, or against any nation; nor does it deny their right to demand redress for injuries inflicted on their respective subjects... but it does deny them the right to interfere, directly or indirectly, with the political independence of the republic of Mexico, and it will, to the extent of its power, defend the nationality and independence of said republic.

The United States held to this position throughout the whole affair. As the threat of intervention grew in 1861, there began a series of incidents which were to be a serious irritant to Franco-American relations throughout the Civil War and after.

Secretary of State Seward, with full approval of President Lincoln, opposed the European attempts to intervene in the political affairs of Mexico, not only because it was contrary to the principles of the Monroe Doctrine, which was not mentioned by name, but also because the United States had recognized the Juárez regime and wished it kept in power. Seward realized, however, that the wretched condition of Mexico's finances and her inability to protect foreigners provided a legitimate reason for European complaint. Therefore, with the help of Thomas Corwin, the able new American Minister to Mexico, the Secretary of State proposed a treaty under which the United States would pay 3 per cent interest on Mexico's debt for the next five years if the European creditor nations agreed not to take hostile action against Mexico during that period. As collateral for the loan, Mexico would grant the United States a security lien on public lands and mineral rights in the northern states of Mexico. If Mexico did not repay this interest in six years, those states would become American property.

This effort to forestall intervention failed. The United States Senate rejected the treaty proposition, and the creditor nations viewed it coolly. The British government believed it would not take care of existing grievances and would only serve as "the preliminary to an entry [by the United States] for inevitable foreclosure." At best, the treaty would take care of only financial claims; it did not reach the heart of the causes which had led to foreign complaints. Yet it was the origin of the American policy which was to be put into effect under President Theodore Roosevelt in the twentieth century: the extension of financial aid and protection to backward Western Hemisphere republics to prevent European intervention.

Not wholly discouraged by this failure, Seward next instructed Minister Dayton to approach French Foreign Minister Thouvenel to find out whether Napoleon would call off the projected intervention if Mexico paid the interest on her obligations. On September 27, 1861, France replied that the principal must be paid as well, even if Mexican ports had to be seized and the customs houses taken over to accomplish this. About the same time, Charles Francis Adams informed Seward that Lord Russell had told him England was not in favor of intervention. Adams believed, however, that the British were evading the question; the London *Times* of September 10 had already declared that English and French cooperation to collect the debts was inevitable. And Carl Schurz, reporting from Madrid, informed the State Department that rumors were rife that a Spanish prince was going to be asked to become emperor of Mexico.

The Convention of London

The truth of these reports was learned when news reached Washington that on October 31, 1861, England, France, and Spain had signed the Convention of London. In it, the signatories agreed to demand from Mexico "more efficacious protection for the persons and properties of their subjects, as well as a fulfillment of the obligations contracted toward their Majesties." The second article of the convention stated that

> the high contracting parties engage not to seek for themselves, in the employment of the coercive measures contemplated by the present convention, any acquisition of territory nor any special advantage, and not to exercise in the internal affairs of Mexico any influence of a nature to prejudice the right of the Mexican nation to choose and to constitute freely the form of its government.

Although the United States was invited to participate, Seward replied on December 4, 1861, that President Lincoln did not question the right of the creditor nations to determine that they had grievances against Mexico and whether those grievances constituted a need for war; but the United States was concerned lest those nations use the grievances as an excuse to obtain Mexican territory or to interfere with the right of the Mexican people to choose their own form of government. Seward admitted that the Convention of London foreswore any such intentions. Yet the United States must decline the invitation to cooperate; to enter such an agreement would be contrary to the traditional policy which abjured foreign alliances, and, in addition, it might injure the good will for the Republic of Mexico, "being a neighbor of the United States on this continent, and possessing a form of government similar to our own. . . ." In conclusion, Seward stated that even though there were valid claims against Mexico, he hoped that "the sovereigns by whom the convention has been concluded shall not seek or obtain any acquisition of territory or any peculiar advantage to itself. . . ."

The signers of the convention went ahead with their plans. A Spanish fleet captured Vera Cruz before the end of 1861 and shortly after was reinforced with French and English troops.[2] Juárez immediately sought a peaceful solution to the differences, and to show his good faith, he allowed the allied invaders to move farther inland to avoid possible fever in the coastal area. Spain, now more interested in Santo Domingo, and Britain, possibly suspicious of French moves, quickly made arrangements with the Mexican President for eventual payment of the debts and for compensation for lives and property lost. France, however, demanded not only that Mexico settle promptly for principal and interest, but insisted that the so-called Jecker claims be paid in full.[3] Britain and Spain refused to back these exorbitant demands and concluded that they had been lured into a French trap. Consequently, by the middle of April, 1862, they withdrew their troops, leaving the Mexican field to France.

By this time the United States had become worried about the trend of affairs. The State Department was hearing more and more rumors of a plan to establish a Mexican monarchy, with Maximilian of Austria as the Emperor. In a circular message to the several American ministers in Europe on March 3, 1862, Seward expressed concern about "the demonstrations . . . against Mexico . . . which will bring in a monarchical government there, in which the crown will be assumed by some foreign prince." The Secretary believed that such a monarchy would have no "prospect of security or permanency," especially "if the throne should be assigned to any person not of Mexican nativity." Only the presence of European troops could maintain such a government. Their presence "would, in fact, make it the beginning of a permanent policy of armed European monarchical intervention injurious and practically hostile to the most general system of government on the continent of America, and this would be the beginning rather than the ending of the revolution in Mexico." While

[2] The English troops had originally been ordered to Canada during the early stages of the *Trent* controversy. Before they reached their destination, they were instructed to change their course to Vera Cruz.

[3] President Miramón, just before he was deposed by Juárez, had approved a bond issue of 16.8 million dollars by Jecker and Company, a Swiss banking firm. Mexico had received but little of the proceeds. After Jecker, under most unusual and questionable circumstances, became a French citizen, the French government supported his claims.

Seward did not mention the Monroe Doctrine specifically, there was no doubt that his position was based on its thesis.

The American public—or at least Northern opinion—generally supported the State Department in its opposition to the proposed monarchy, but some of the newspapers, notably the *New York Tribune* and the *New York Herald*, asserted that the tripartite action against Mexico might do that country some good; it had been a little too obnoxious.

France paid little attention to the promises she had made in the Convention of London; instead, her troops started out for Mexico City. Early in May, 1862, they were defeated in the battle of Puebla. Not until a year later, when General Elie Forey arrived to command a French army that had been increased to nearly 30,000, did Puebla finally fall, followed in June, 1863, by the capture of Mexico City. A French hand-picked junta of Mexican conservatives then selected an assembly of notables, which in turn proclaimed a monarchy in Mexico on July 8, 1863, with the throne to be offered to Maximilian or any other Catholic prince selected by Napoleon. While awaiting the Emperor's decision, Mexico was placed in the hands of a provisional government, headed by General Juan Altamonte, a Mexican conservative. Actually, however, Altamonte's jurisdiction did not extend beyond the comparatively small area around Mexico City controlled by French troops. Elsewhere, the Juárez backers and even conservatives disgruntled with Napoleon's domination of their country were rallying anti-intervention armies.

Maximilian, the younger brother of Emperor Francis Joseph of Austria, was a well-educated prince with some liberal tendencies. As a result of the pressure from his wife, Carlota of Belgium, and from Napoleon, Maximilian promised to assume the Mexican throne, but only if the Mexican people wanted him. The requested plebiscite was held, not throughout Mexico, but only in French-dominated sections where Napoleon's soldiers saw to it that only the right persons voted. Naturally the result was overwhelmingly in favor of Maximilian, who reached Mexico City in June, 1864.

The Position of the United States

Meantime the United States was powerless to act because of the Civil War, but did resort to verbal protests. In 1862, following the French advance into the interior, Seward informed Minister Dayton that all sorts of rumors had reached Washington about Napoleon's intentions. Since these were still only rumors, the Lincoln administration "would in any case be bound to wait for, and not anticipate, a violation" of French promises. Foreign Minister Thouvenel assured Dayton in August, 1862, that his country "did not mean to appropriate permanently any part" of

Mexico, and that her troops would be withdrawn "as soon as her griefs were satisfied." And when those troops had departed, no puppet ruler would be on the Mexican throne. This statement was another phase of French duplicity, for even before the Convention of London, Thouvenel had suggested the naming of a member of European royalty as Mexican emperor, and about the same time (October 9, 1861) Napoleon had written to his Minister in London that Maximilian would probably be selected.

When it became apparent that France was breaking her agreement and defying the Monroe Doctrine, Seward, backed by the military, could do nothing more than warn Napoleon that as soon as the Civil War was over, French troops must be withdrawn. The Secretary of State realized that a belligerent attitude on the part of his country at this time might cause France to ally with the Confederacy—something he wanted to avoid at all costs.[4]

Throughout the rest of the war, Congress showed interest in what was going on south of the Rio Grande. In January, 1863, for instance, John MacDougal, a Democratic senator from California, resolved that the United States should provide Mexico with whatever military and monetary aid she might need "to prevent the forcible interposition of any of the states of Europe in the political affairs of that republic." While the Senate discussed this resolution, most members realized that help for Mexico was merely wishful thinking at the time, and no vote was taken. As to the Northern public, it could read the flood of books and pamphlets which stressed the importance of the Monroe Doctrine and implied that it was being threatened in Mexico.

In 1864, with the war drawing to a close and a political campaign in progress, interest in the Mexican situation was accentuated. In April, Henry W. Davis, head of the Foreign Relations Committee of the House, introduced a resolution declaring that the legislators "are unwilling by silence to have the nations of the world under the impression that they are indifferent spectators of the deplorable events now transpiring" in Mexico. This resolution was passed by a vote of 109 to 0. The major parties in the campaign of 1864 adopted the gist of this resolution as one of their planks. Yet the Northern public did not wish to become too belligerent until victory at home was assured, and this was the position taken by Lincoln and Seward. A few newspapers, such as the *New York Herald* and the *National Intelligencer*, appeared to approve what France was doing; this position, however, was more to embarrass the Lincoln administration than to support Napoleon.

About the same time as the Davis Resolution of April, 1864, Maximilian formally accepted the Mexican throne and signed at his Austrian home

[4] See chap. 15 for an account of Napoleon's pro-South sympathies.

the Convention of Miramar. On the surface, this agreement with Napoleon provided for the reduction of French forces in Mexico to 25,000 as soon as possible; a secret clause, however, stated that the number should be 38,000 throughout the rest of 1864, 28,000 in 1865, 25,000 in 1866, and 20,000 in 1867. As to the financial side of the convention, Mexico must pay France 270 million francs for expenses incurred up to the middle of 1864, and 100 francs per year for each French soldier in Mexico after that time. As a means of payment, Mexico was to float a loan, from which France was to obtain 66 million francs at once.[5]

The Convention of Miramar was a final desperate effort on Napoleon's part to salvage something from what he now realized was a disaster. The Mexican people were not rallying to the monarchy, and keeping a large force overseas was weakening France at home. As early as November, 1863, Napoleon had told Sir Charles Wyke: "I realize that I have got myself into a tight place, but the affair has got to be liquidated." More and more Frenchmen were outspoken in their criticism of government policy, criticisms sharpened by the fact that the North was on the verge of victory. An influential politician and writer said: "In attempting to found an empire in Mexico, it is unfortunately true that we are creating gratuitously an antagonism between American patriotism and France." This opinion grew, as indicated by an article in *Revue des Deux Mondes:* "Once the Civil War is over, the perils of our enterprise are obvious. ...there will be a host of generals and officers without employment; a thousand influences will press the government to vindicate the Monroe Doctrine by force of arms." And, the article continued, if the United States took no action, "the figure of the American filibuster will make his appearance, as he has made it before, to undertake a similar enterprise."

The Fall of Maximilian

With the surrender of the Confederacy in the spring of 1865, Seward's hands were freed. With the United States once more at peace and with a veteran army of nearly a million men available to back up any demands he might make, the Secretary of State could now push Napoleon harder. He consistently refused to confer with Maximilian and just as consistently continued to recognize Juárez as the legitimate head of the Republic of Mexico.

Two courses were open. One was to use force to drive the French troops from Mexican soil and to restore Juárez to the presidency. The other was to continue diplomatic efforts to persuade Napoleon to remove his armies and then count on the Mexican people to overthrow Maximilian.

[5] Maximilian refused France the right to exploit the valuable mines of Sonora or to maintain troops in that state.

The first course was supported for a time by President Andrew Johnson, whose views on Mexico had been expressed during the political campaign of 1864:

> The day of reckoning is approaching. It will not be long before the Rebellion is put down.... And then we will attend to the Mexican affair.... An expedition into Mexico would be a sort of recreation to the brave soldiers who are now fighting the battles of the Union, and the French concern would be quickly wiped out.

General Ulysses S. Grant shared the same view and took prompt steps to prepare for action. He gave General John M. Schofield a year's leave of absence to go to Mexico, where, with the approval of Juárez, he would organize an army of volunteers from the United States. General Philip Sheridan and a force of more than 50,000 men were ordered to Texas to be ready to invade Mexico and to provide arms, ammunition, and equipment to Schofield's volunteers.

Seward, however, was more disposed to follow the second course. Despite the war talk of certain militarists and journalists, the Secretary of State realized that the nation was tired of conflict, and he won Johnson over to his way of thinking. Seward convinced Schofield that he could do more in Paris than in Mexico—that diplomacy was better than the sword. Through John Bigelow, the American consul in Paris, the Secretary began in September, 1865, to advise the French Foreign Office that the best way to prevent war was to end the intervention voluntarily. Each new message was a little more forceful. For example, in December he stated that while the United States wished to remain on friendly terms with France, such a position "would be brought into imminent jeopardy unless France could deem it consistent with her interest and honor to desist from the prosecution of armed intervention in Mexico." The following February 12, 1866, Seward asserted that the continued presence of French troops in Mexico in support of "a European prince ... without her consent and against her will, is deemed a source of apprehension and danger" to the United States. He therefore asked Napoleon to give "definite information of the time when French military operations may be expected to cease in Mexico." The Secretary ended this brusque demand with a face-saving opportunity for the French Emperor: once the French army had left, the United States would not interfere in Mexican affairs. In other words, if Maximilian could maintain his throne, the United States would not challenge his right to do so.

Napoleon, however, had already awakened from his dream of another New France. Before the end of 1865 he had informed Marshal François Bazaine (Forey's successor as commander of the French army in Mexico) that a terminal date must be fixed for the withdrawal of his forces. The motivating factors behind this decision were not so much fear of what the United States might do as concern over the turn of events in Europe. At home, Napoleon was facing increasing political and economic unrest that threatened his throne. To the east, Prussia, dominated by the forceful Prince Otto von Bismarck, had already initiated its program of expansion to make it the most powerful state on the Continent. Under the circumstances, Napoleon became convinced that he must consolidate his forces in Europe. Thus he informed Seward that Bazaine's men would be removed from Mexico in three operations: one-third in November, 1866; one-third in March, 1867; and the remainder in November, 1867. Actually, however, the growing tension in Europe caused the last of the French troops to embark for home in March, 1867.

Maximilian was advised to depart with his protectors, but the Emperor believed that it was his duty to remain at his post. Scarcely had the French troops withdrawn before armies of Juárez and other nationalist leaders closed in on the unhappy Austrian. He was captured in May, 1867, and immediately brought before a court-martial, found guilty of treason, and condemned to death. Juárez, deaf to the many pleas from European capitals and from Washington, refused to commute this penalty, and Maximilian fell before a firing squad on June 19, 1867.[6] Actually, Juárez could not do differently. His countrymen were so incensed by the whole affair that a pardon for Maximilian would have stirred up once more domestic strife.

As far as the United States was concerned, the bloodless victory over the greatest challenge that had ever been offered to the Monroe Doctrine was an indication of the growing strength of America and the increasing respect which European nations had for a policy which had finally come of age. The successful solution of this Maximilian affair also resulted in better relations with the republics of the hemisphere. Temporarily forgotten was the aggressive attitude of the United States in its quest for manifest destiny.

Anglo-American Differences

Even more of a problem than the Maximilian affair and of longer duration were the efforts to settle a variety of differences with Great Britain, the most serious of which were the *Alabama* claims. Of lesser importance, but nevertheless arousing considerable bitterness, were complications with

[6] Carlota, who had escaped, failed in her efforts to persuade Napoleon to intervene with military aid, and her pleas to the Pope were answered with the statement that he could do nothing. She became insane and lived the rest of her life (until 1927) in the belief that she was still Empress of Mexico.

Canada over such varied matters as fisheries, boundary disputes, the Fenian raids, and Confederate attacks from Canada upon the United States.

Secretary of State Seward, with the able support of Minister Charles Francis Adams, tried to solve these issues in peaceful fashion, but he was thwarted in his efforts by Senator Charles Sumner of Massachusetts, an ardent expansionist in the international field and a firm advocate of punishment for the South in domestic politics. Sumner and his Radical Republican cohorts took full advantage of the controversies with Britain to challenge the objectives of the Johnson administration, which represented everything to which they were opposed. Sumner was inconsistent in many ways, notably in desiring to annex Canada but opposing territorial expansion in the West Indies. Likewise detrimental to the Seward diplomacy was the stubbornness of the English ministry, dominated by Lord Russell, who would not admit his country's responsibility for the destruction caused by the cruisers delivered to the Confederacy from British shipyards.

Even before the Civil War was over, Adams had suggested in October, 1863, that the claims arising from that contest be compromised, and at that time the United States might have been content with modest compensation. Lord Russell, however, considered the proposal by Adams as "most burdensome, and indeed, most dangerous."

Yet in 1866, the possibility of settlement appeared bright. In the first place, England was worried about becoming involved in another European war. In such a conflict, the United States and other neutral countries might help Britain's enemies by providing them with armed ships. England could not logically object unless she admitted that she had been wrong in her own actions during the Civil War. As a sign of what might happen, the House of Representatives unanimously voted to amend the Neutrality Act of 1818 to permit American sale of armed vessels to nations at war. While it is true the Senate took no action, Britain foresaw trouble ahead. Another bright spot was a change of ministry in England in 1866, which brought to the Foreign Office the more conciliatory Lord Stanley, who promptly announced his readiness to arbitrate the *Alabama* claims. Seward, however, insisted that the matter of British recognition of the belligerent status of the Confederacy was also involved, for to the Secretary of State this premature recognition was nothing more than "wrongful intervention." Stanley would not approve consideration of this subject, which he believed was the work of "malignant enemies of Great Britain," who were forcing their wishes upon the Secretary of State. Thus the first hopeful attempt at reconciliation failed.

The issue was then formally dropped until 1868, by England, because of the belief that she should not yield to the broad American demands;

by the United States, because of partisan opposition to President Johnson, which made Seward realize the futility of obtaining senatorial ratification for any controversial treaty. Consequently, the Secretary of State turned his major attention to territorial expansion.

In 1868, Charles Francis Adams ended his long period of service in the London legation, and Reverdy Johnson took his place. Johnson, a Maryland lawyer, tried his best to promote arbitration, but his effusive efforts to court good will with flowery oratory made him the butt of criticism in both England and the United States. The *New York Tribune* was especially critical of his speeches, which were characterized as "successive sins," while James Russell Lowell asserted that they were filled with "maudlin blarney."

Despite this unfortunate beginning, the new American Minister continued his efforts and concluded a treaty—a treaty which did not even scratch the surface of the disagreements, however. Even though Seward refused to consider the document, he was encouraged by this initial progress to pursue his objective.

The Johnson-Clarendon Convention

When the Tory Disraeli ministry gave way to the more conciliatory Liberal Gladstone ministry, Seward sent Reverdy Johnson detailed instructions on what should be included in the desired treaty. The result was the Johnson-Clarendon Convention of January 14, 1869. This agreement provided for the arbitration of all claims between the two countries which had arisen since July, 1853, though it did not specifically mention the direct or indirect *Alabama* claims or provide for an expression of regret by England for the incidents.

This convention might have been the basis for a settlement had it been drawn up immediately after the cessation of the Civil War, when the American people were tired of hostilities and would have been willing to agree to almost anything in order to dispose of existing controversies. Even its severest critic, Charles Sumner, admitted later to John Bright that if it had been concluded earlier, the convention would have been ratified. But early in 1869 it had no chance. The Johnson administration, soon to come to an end, had lost what little prestige it had ever enjoyed. The American public, now recovered from its war weariness, was in no mood to be lenient, especially with England, a country regarded as being responsible for numerous injuries and insults to the United States.

Even when the Grant administration came to power, the convention was doomed to failure. The new Secretary of State was Hamilton Fish, already a bitter opponent of Charles Sumner, the powerful chairman of the Senate Foreign Relations Committee. Moreover, there was the feeling in the Senate that the Johnson-Clarendon agreement did not reach the heart of the matter. Without a British admission of guilt or responsibility, ruffled American feelings could not be appeased. Sumner, in a speech against the convention on April 13, 1869, opened his scathing denunciation of Britain by stating: "We begin today an international debate, the greatest in our history, and before it is finished, in all probability the greatest of all history." The Senator stressed three major points. In the first place, England rightfully owed the United States 15 million dollars for actual sinkings by the cruisers built in English yards. Secondly, there were losses of at least 110 million dollars to Americans as a result of exporters fearing to ship goods, changes in ship registrations to neutral flags, and increased maritime insurance. And, finally, British recognition of Confederate belligerency and subsequent aid to the South had prolonged the Civil War at least two years at a cost of some 2 billion dollars to the North. If Britain were unable to pay these direct and indirect claims in cash, the United States would be willing to accept Canada in lieu of money.

Nor did the convention have President Grant's support, for he believed that it was "inadequate in its provisions." Congressman James G. Blaine of Maine, a rising figure in Republican political circles, was among the opponents because he said the agreement "overlooked, and yet by cunning phrase condoned, every unfriendly act of England during the Civil War." Most of the American press attacked the convention; an exception was the New York *Nation*, but even that periodical had reservations about it: "Some of the most foolish and immoral men have produced or advocated excellent lines of policy." As far as the American public was concerned, there were many who earnestly desired the restoration of better relations with England, but who believed the Johnson-Clarendon Convention was not the answer to the problem. Thus the Senate overwhelmingly rejected the convention in mid-April by a vote of 54 to 1.

Sumner continued to demand that Great Britain pay the full bill. Hamilton Fish, on the other hand, wanted above everything a peaceful settlement and feared that Sumner's excessive demands might prevent it. Moreover, the Ten Years' War in Cuba [7] was already raising the question of whether the United States should recognize the belligerency of the Cuban rebels. Were the United States to deny England's right in connection with the Confederacy, it could not consistently act in the Cuban uprising.

After protracted debate, a compromise position was finally taken as the basis for the instructions to John Lothrop Motley, about to succeed Reverdy Johnson as Minister to England. Every nation, Fish asserted, had the right "when a civil contest has arisen within another state, and has attained a sufficient complexity, magnitude, and completeness, to define its own relations and those of its citizens and subjects toward the parties

[7] See pp. 327–330.

to the conflict, so far as their rights and interests are necessarily affected by the conflict." Thereby the door for recognizing the belligerency of the Cubans was left ajar. But to give partial lip service to the Sumner position, the instructions to Motley continued: "The necessity and the propriety of the original concession of belligerency by Great Britain at the time it was made have been contested and are not admitted." Yet unlike the Sumner stand, which insisted that the recognition of the Confederacy was the beginning of all the trouble, the instructions went on to say that British recognition was a part of the case "only so far as it shows the beginning ... of that course of conduct which resulted so disastrously to the United States." By shifting the core of the disagreement to the "acts causing direct damage," Fish narrowed the issues. Yet he wanted a definition of neutral rights and duties to be included in the final settlement.

Minister Motley paid little attention to these instructions when he reopened the talks in London. Instead, he tended to follow the course initiated by Sumner. Both Grant and Seward were angered by his actions because of the Cuban situation. The President was all for recalling Motley immediately, but the more conciliatory Fish persuaded him that a rebuke was sufficient punishment. The Secretary of State concluded, however, that in light of the shortcomings of both Reverdy Johnson and Motley, future negotiations should be conducted in Washington. And with Fish in charge of the operations, the way was paved more rapidly for the ultimate settlement.

Canadian-American Conflicts

Meantime, relations with Canada were undergoing severe strain. The close of the Civil War found the two neighbors at odds on a number of points. The United States blamed the Canadian government for laxity in allowing Confederate prisoners who had escaped into Canada to recross the border to attack Northern towns.[8]

Canada reciprocated by charging the United States with responsibility for Fenian raids into her territory. The Fenian Brotherhood was organized by John O'Mahoney in the 1850s to unite the Irish in America and other countries in support of the cause of Irish independence. Among the many plans, one called for an Irish invasion of Canada. Such an attack would divert English military forces and improve prospects for a Fenian uprising in Ireland. Some Fenians hoped that their activities would involve the

---

[8] The most notable incident took place in October, 1864, when a group of Confederates looted three banks in St. Albans, Vermont, of about $200,000, killed one resident, and almost burned the town to the ground. The raiders successfully returned to Canada, where the local authorities arrested about half of them, but freed them within two months.

United States and Britain in war, a contest which would increase the chances of Irish freedom. During the Civil War the Fenians had made a bid for sympathy by enlisting in the Union army, but their battle songs were dedicated more to independence for Ireland than to Northern success.

With the restoration of peace, the Fenians redoubled their efforts, and their membership grew to possibly 250,000—a growth aided by American hostility to both Great Britain and Canada and by the large number of unemployed Northern veterans. Some of the more vigorous Fenian leaders, referring to themselves as "men of action," were not content with mere talk and drills, but decided on active hostilities. In the late spring of 1866 they openly advertised in American newspapers for volunteers, offering bounties of as much as £100 in cash and 200 acres of Canadian land to those who would serve. The response could not have been great, for on June 1, 1866, a few hundred crossed the Niagara River into Canada, where they captured Fort Erie, only to be overwhelmingly driven back by Canadian militia at Limestone Ridge. The remnants limped back to Buffalo.

Considering the open drilling of the Fenians on American soil and the newspaper advertisements, the United States was somewhat dilatory in its actions. Not until June 6 did President Johnson issue an order insisting upon full enforcement of the Neutrality Act of 1818. This belated action nevertheless won from Britain, through Minister Thornton, a "warm acknowledgment," and from the London *Times* a statement in its columns that "this energetic act of genuine friendship will be long and cordially remembered." Other voices were more critical. The Canadian officials believed that the United States was lax, and some American newspapers made the same charge.

Americans were divided on the issue of the Fenian movement. Some were still angered by the Confederate raids from Canada; others were glad of anything that might weaken England, the traditional enemy. Politicians were eager to obtain the Irish vote. Yet the *New York Times* asserted that the Fenians were "a perpetual social and political scourge upon the American people," while the *Atlantic Monthly* declared that whenever the Irish gained a majority, "government has shown a marked tendency to sink to a savage level."

The American and Canadian authorities combined to prevent most of the subsequent raids which were attempted intermittently until 1871,[9] when the remnants of the "Irish Republican Army" were defeated or captured in their attempt to overrun Manitoba. Even though they did not accomplish anything, the Fenian raids injured Canadian-American relations. American laxity, according to the Canadians, had made such activities possible. This feeling was accentuated when reports circulated that both President Grant and Vice President Schuyler Colfax had been

[9] Most of the raids were organized in upper New York State and in Vermont.

present at Fenian meetings, and that a resolution of Benjamin Butler of Massachusetts to extend welcome to exiled Irishmen had been overwhelmingly endorsed by the lower house. The United States, on its part, protested because Canadian authorities refused to recognize the American citizenship of some of the captured Fenians.

The Fisheries Controversy

Another sign of bitterness came in March, 1865, with the formal notice by the United States that after one year the Marcy-Elgin Treaty of 1854 would be terminated. One important factor in this decision was the hostility developing from the Confederate raids; a second, that the treaty was more favorable to Canada than to the United States; and a third, that the abrogation of the treaty would deal a sharp blow to the Canadian economy and create a desire for annexation to the United States. This idea received additional support when, in July, 1866, just a few months after the abrogation became effective, the House of Representatives passed a bill providing for the potential admission of Canada into the United States.

Great Britain, worried about the turn of events, hastened to take countersteps. While she probably would not have stood in the way of a voluntary withdrawal of Canada from the empire, she could not lose face by allowing it to be forcibly taken from her either by a group of Irish rebels or by the United States. Consequently, Parliament finally approved the British North America Act in July, 1867, which united the provinces under a federal constitution and granted "dominion status"— practically complete self-government. The United States House of Representatives had vainly tried to halt this development by a resolution in March, 1867, contending that any strengthening of monarchical government in the Western Hemisphere would be contrary to the Monroe Doctrine. As far as the majority of Canadians was concerned, the British North America Act stifled any inclination to break away from the empire and join the United States. The idea had never been strong anyway, except in British Columbia.

Likewise contributing to an anti-United States feeling was the issue of the fisheries—a source of controversy since the conclusion of the American Revolution. The inhabitants of the Maritime Provinces had always been jealous of the privileges granted American fishermen and had not liked the rights given in the Marcy-Elgin Treaty, believing England had surrendered "to foreigners the reserved fisheries on our seacoasts" in return for questionable trade advantages. The *Halifax Chronicle* announced at the time: "Our most valuable rights have been swept away by the dash of the Colonial Secretary's pen."

This was the situation at the close of the Civil War when the United States abrogated the reciprocity treaty. As a result, American fishing rights reverted to those granted under the Convention of 1818. Thereafter, Canada allowed Americans to fish in her waters only under license, for which the fee was steadily raised. Since the eventual $2-a-ton rate was considered prohibitive, the larger American fishing boats preferred to take their chances in fishing illegally.

But the Canadians, gradually feeling the adverse effects of the loss of free trade in many commodities with the United States, began to link the fisheries with the broader question of reciprocal trade. The general belief grew that only a revival of the Treaty of 1854 would restore harmony between the two neighbors. Since the United States was adamant in continuing its high wartime tariff, Canada decided to be just as stubborn. As a means of showing the United States that two could play the same game, she passed a measure to keep American fishing boats outside her 3-mile limit and added a strict enforcement act in 1870. Six cruisers were obtained at a cost of a million dollars to police Canadian waters, and it was reported that they seized some four hundred American fishing craft during the first three months of the measure's operation. Naturally such captures only served to widen the breach between the two countries.

Indeed, the *New York Times* believed there might be hostilities before the year was over, and Minister Thornton anticipated retaliation on the part of the United States. On the other hand, Robert C. Schenck, American Minister to England, regarded the Canadian position as both "churlish and offensive." Yet both sides tried to prevent further trouble. The British Minister intimated that if the United States did not agree to renew reciprocity, Canada might be willing to allow Americans to fish off her shores for an annual payment. Certainly Canada would not grant such concessions "without obtaining an equivalent." Secretary of State Fish, although declaring that Canadian seizures jeopardized the cause of conciliation, did not rule out the possibility of his country restoring reciprocity or paying the proposed fee. He tried, however, not to become involved in the controversy because he believed that "it is a matter which wholly concerns Canada." Were Canada not to have wholehearted backing from the mother country, she might be willing to accept a compromise. But by the end of 1870 the issue was still unsolved.

A final source of controversy grew out of the treaty of 1846 involving the division of Oregon. One clause stated that the boundary in Puget Sound was "the channel which separates the continent from Vancouver's Island." That definition seemed clear enough to the negotiators, but actually there were two channels: Haro Strait, claimed as the proper one by the United States; and Rosario Strait, to the east, the boundary claimed by Britain. There were several islands between these two channels, the largest of which was San Juan. To quiet the dispute over ownership, England and the United States had agreed to occupy San Juan jointly in 1860. Since that time, however, the residents of British Columbia had become convinced that it rightfully belonged to them, a belief accentuated by San Juan's strategic importance in commanding the water entrance to that province. The United States countered by insisting that the presence of a large number of American colonists made the island American territory.

The Treaty of Washington

Despite the rejection of the Johnson-Clarendon Convention and the unfriendly attitude of Canada, Hamilton Fish continued to press for a peaceful solution of Anglo-American differences. In this quest he was aided by several developments. One was the removal of Charles Sumner from the chairmanship of the Senate Foreign Relations Committee because of his opposition to Grant in the Dominican diplomacy. Another was British concern lest the Franco-Prussian War broaden to involve England. A third was the Russian decision to abrogate the Black Sea Treaty of 1856; England's denial of Russia's right to do so brought the possibility of war in another arena. Moreover, an increasing number of Americans realized that Canada could never be annexed by peaceful means and did not believe that it was worth a war. Then, too, President Grant, who had earlier been an advocate of the acquisition of Canada, had now turned his attention to problems in the West Indies. Therefore he was no longer an obstacle in the peaceful path Fish wished to follow. And on the other side of the Atlantic, Britain was also doing her part. In 1870 Parliament passed a statute which precluded the possibility of her being involved in any more *Alabama* incidents by prohibiting construction of warships for belligerents. Then the very conciliatory Lord Granville was named Foreign Secretary in the Liberal Gladstone ministry. A number of peace societies in England were also promoting the cause of better relations with the United States.

Climaxing all these developments was the introduction of Sir John Rose to Fish. Rose, a Scot by birth, had become an influential figure in Canadian politics and business. He suggested to the Secretary of State that the time was ripe to discuss Anglo-American differences. After a long series of conferences among Fish, Rose, and Minister Thornton, it was finally agreed in January, 1871, that all controversies be submitted to a Joint High Commission.

The Joint High Commission, composed of eminent men from both sides,[10] opened its sessions on February 27, 1871. An early avowal by the British of "the regret felt by Her Majesty's Government for the escape, under whatever circumstances, of the *Alabama* and other vessels from British ports, and for the depredations committed by those vessels," paved the way for a speedy settlement and resulted in the signing of the Treaty of Washington on May 8. By this famous agreement the *Alabama* claims were submitted to a tribunal of five judges to be appointed by the United States, Britain, Brazil, Italy, and Switzerland, which would meet at Geneva. The arbiters were to be governed by three important rules:

> A neutral Government is bound—
> First, to use due diligence to prevent the fitting out, arming, or equipping, within its jurisdiction, of any vessel which it has reasonable ground to believe is intended to cruise or carry on war against a Power with which it is at peace; and also to use like diligence to prevent the departure from its jurisdiction of any vessel intended to cruise or carry on war as above, such vessel having been specially adapted, in whole or in part, within such jurisdiction.
> Second, not to permit or suffer either belligerent to make use of its ports or waters as the base of naval operations against the other, or for the purpose of the renewal or augmentation of military supplies or arms, or the recruitment of men.
> Thirdly, to exercise due diligence in its own ports or waters, and as to all persons within its jurisdiction, to prevent any violation of the foregoing obligations and duties.

Although England did not concede that these rules had been part of international law during the Civil War, she agreed to allow her conduct to be judged by them. The United States and England both promised "to observe these rules as between themselves in the future," and also to try to have other nations "accede to them."

The Treaty of Washington then went on to provide the means for settling other controversies. A modus vivendi was arranged by which Canada once again allowed Americans inshore fishing privileges for at least ten years, and the United States in turn agreed to admit Canadian fish and fish oil duty free and to allow Canadians to fish in American waters north of the 39th line. If these advantages proved unequal in

---

[10] Representing the United States were Secretary Fish, Supreme Court Justice Nelson, former Attorney General Ebenezer Hoar, Robert C. Schenck, the new Minister to England, and Senator George H. Williams of Oregon. The British members were Earl de Grey of the Gladstone ministry, Minister Thornton, Sir Stafford Northcote, a powerful Conservative who was an important figure in the Hudson's Bay Company, Sir John Macdonald, Prime Minister of Canada (and the only Canadian represented), and Professor Mountague Bernard, an authority on international law. Both delegations represented the varied political and sectional views of their respective nations.

value, a mixed commission would determine how much should be paid by the favored party.

The San Juan dispute was to be settled by a single arbiter, the recently crowned Emperor of Germany. Finally, the treaty opened the waterways bordering Canada and the United States, such as the St. Lawrence, the Yukon, and Lake Michigan, to mutually free navigation, and for free transportation across each other's territory. Specific claims for the Confederate raids from Canada and for the Fenian forays from the United States were dismissed without mention.

That it was a good treaty was shown by the fact that it encountered little opposition in the Senate, where it was speedily ratified on May 24, 1871, by a vote of 50 to 12. Even Sumner, who had long fought any agreement that did not give Canada to the United States, cast an affirmative vote.

Now the major attention was turned to Geneva, where the *Alabama* claims were to be adjudicated. The judge named by the United States was the able and respected Charles Francis Adams, while Assistant Secretary of State J. C. Bancroft Davis was selected to argue the American case. Both sides presented their original briefs to the august tribunal in December, 1871. Unfortunately, Davis's arguments tended to follow the original Sumner line, blaming England among other things for prolonging the Civil War and demanding indirect damages to the tune of about 2 billion dollars. When this demand created such a furor in England that the whole arbitration effort was threatened, the judges prudently ruled that the indirect claims did "not constitute, upon the principles of international law applicable to such cases, good foundation for an award of compensation or computation of damages between nations." Fish instructed Davis to accept this decision. With this major obstacle out of the way, the path to a settlement was eased. In mid-September the international judges decided that since Britain "by omission" had failed to live up to the rules defined in the Treaty of Washington, she must pay the United States 15.5 million dollars in gold.[11] Although the English judge, Sir Alexander Cockburn, dissented, his government approved the decision and ultimately paid the United States, considering the sum reasonable in the face of future fears.

The dispute in the Northwest resulted in victory for the United States when the Kaiser decided that San Juan and several smaller nearby islands were American property. A mixed commission, sitting in Washington, found that the illegal blockade actions of the United States during the Civil War entitled Britons to damages of nearly 2 million dollars, while

[11] Previously, the United States had assumed responsibility for collecting the claims of its citizens. After the award was made, it settled these private claims to the best of its ability.

American claims against England were unwarranted. Another commission, subsequently meeting at Halifax in 1877 to consider the mutual advantages obtained through the fisheries modus vivendi, determined that Americans profited more; therefore the United States must pay 5.5 million dollars. The American commissioner refused to sign this award, but Congress appropriated the money anyway.

The Treaty of Washington proved a triumph for the cause of peaceful settlement of differences between the United States and Great Britain, thereby continuing a policy that had started shortly after the conclusion of the War of 1812. England, despite the heavy bill for damages, gained by being relieved of fear that the United States might build warships for her potential enemies. American happiness with the results was reflected in President Grant's statement in his annual message to Congress in December, 1871, that the treaty "leaves these two Governments without a shadow on the friendly relations which it is my sincere hope may forever remain unclouded."

The Ten Years' War in Cuba

Even while the State Department was trying to solve the differences with Great Britain, the Cubans, still unhappy with Spanish rule, revolted in 1868 to start what was known as the Ten Years' War. In the beginning it appeared as though this would be another ephemeral uprising, to be crushed easily by the Spanish forces. The rebels, however, had good leaders, especially Carlos Manuel de Céspedes, a wealthy Cuban aristocrat with liberal views, and ultimately Máximo Gómez, a hero of the lower classes. The growing strength of the insurrectionists was such that the Spanish Captain General offered to try to satisfy their complaints, but the rebels refused the offer and instead established a provisional government, with Céspedes as President. Both sides then resorted to acts of destruction against lives and property alike.

Such was the situation when President Grant took office. Secretary of State Hamilton Fish realized that if the civil strife continued, it might become exceedingly embarrassing to the United States. Consequently, he instructed Daniel Sickles, a former general and now Minister to Spain, to offer the good offices of the United States to mediate the differences. Fish believed that a good basis for compromise would be for Spain to offer the Cubans a greater degree of autonomy and promise to abolish slavery on the island. As a method of speeding this solution, Fish had Sickles conclude the suggestion with a veiled threat: if the Cuban hostilities were not ended quickly, "an early recognition of belligerent rights is the logical deduction from the present proposals."

The Spanish government was agreeable to an early settlement, but only on Spanish terms. The first prerequisite for an armistice must be for the rebels to lay down their arms; only after that would Spain consider a greater degree of self-government in Cuba—self-government that must be approved in a Cuban referendum. But the Cubans, regarding the proposed laying down of arms as a Spanish trick, rejected the proposal, and the destructive civil war continued.

Under the circumstances, what course should the United States follow? Obviously the Céspedes government had not yet thrown off the Spanish yoke, so Grant and his advisers could not consider recognizing the independence of Cuba. Even if this were the proper ultimate step, the time was not then ripe. Yet the Cuban situation could not be thus easily dismissed, for soon the next problem—that of whether to recognize the belligerent status of the rebels—had to be faced. Charles Sumner, still chairman of the powerful Senate Foreign Relations Committee, vigorously opposed such a move at any time. Secretary of War John Rawlins believed American intervention on behalf of the rebels was the only solution. President Grant saw in eventual Cuban independence a possible aid to his general expansion program in the Caribbean. Consequently, he actually signed a proclamation recognizing Cuban belligerency. Secretary of State Fish, however, considered this action to be ill-advised and ill-timed. As has been recounted, he was already negotiating with Great Britain on the *Alabama* claims and other controversies. If the United States now did for the Cuban rebels one of the very things it had objected to England's doing for the Confederacy, the ground might be cut from under him in his dealings with England. Therefore Fish pigeonholed the presidential proclamation.[12]

The opposition of the Secretary of State to recognizing Cuban belligerency did not mean he was unsympathetic to the rebel cause. On the contrary, he continued to hold the threat of either intervention or belligerency recognition over Spain's head to try to make her grant the reforms the Cubans were demanding.

The Virginius Affair

Having decided against recognizing either Cuban independence or belligerency, the administration tried to adhere to a policy of strict neutrality. This was easier said than done, for American public opinion was overwhelmingly in favor of the rebel cause. This pro-Cuban sympathy led to numerous filibustering attempts to supply the insurrectionists

---

[12] Normally Grant would have resented his Secretary's action, but the turn of events made the President happy over what Fish had done. He subsequently complimented Fish by saying: "Your steadiness and wisdom have kept me from mistakes into which I should have fallen."

with volunteers, arms, and supplies. While many such expeditions were stopped by the American Navy and Coast Guard, the long coast line made it next to impossible to close the door completely.

The most conspicuous defier of the neutrality laws was a Cuban junta in New York, which, financed by sympathetic Americans, obtained the ship *Virginius* to engage in filibustering efforts. Registered in the United States as American-owned and with a crew mainly American, it had been operating in Caribbean waters since 1871, carrying arms both to Venezuela and to Cuba.

On October 31, 1873, the *Virginius* was finally seized by a Spanish gunboat between Jamaica and Cuba. Minister Sickles, on orders from Washington, immediately demanded that the Spanish government not impose any death sentences upon the passengers or crew. For some reason these instructions were delayed in reaching Cuba, and on November 7 and 8 a secret summary court-martial was held. It found fifty-three passengers and crewmen guilty of piracy, and their execution speedily followed.

The American people were shocked by these events, and demands for retaliation, even to the point of war, filled the newspapers. On November 12, Secretary Fish, in a note to the Spanish government, characterized the executions as "butchery and murder." He continued with the assertion that his government would "demand the most ample reparation of any wrong which may have been committed upon any of its citizens or upon its flag." Two days later he instructed Minister Sickles to make three demands on the Spanish government: the release of the *Virginius* and its survivors, a salute to the American flag, and prompt punishment of the Spanish officials responsible for the executions. Were Spain not to comply within twelve days, the Minister should return home. And on November 15, the Fish message was even more belligerent: "If Spain cannot redress the outrages perpetrated in her name in Cuba, the United States will." Yet the Secretary of State cautioned Sickles to avoid "all appearance of menace" when he presented any of these notes to the Spanish Foreign Office, for rumors were already circulating in the United States that the *Virginius* was illegally flying the American flag. But the American Minister, probably welcoming the possibility of war, tactlessly refused to show this restraint.

The Spanish reply of November 18 was unsatisfactory, for she refused to take any action until the *Virginius* was proved to be an American ship. This answer, plus the belligerence of Minister Sickles, persuaded Fish that the negotiations could be conducted more effectively under his watchful care in Washington. There, on November 26, the Spanish Minister promised to deliver the ship and its survivors to the United States. The salute to the American flag, however, was contingent upon the United States proving by December 25 that the *Virginius* was legally registered.

As for the punishment of the local Spanish officials, this would be done only if they were convicted of violating any treaties or laws.

This compromise was satisfactory to the Grant administration and to the American people, who, after the first outburst of indignation, realized that the incident was not worth a war. The *Virginius* was released,[13] and the Spanish government appropriated $80,000 for the families of the men executed. The salute to the flag was never given because of conclusive proof of illegal registry, and the punishment of the local Spanish official took the form of a promotion. Thus the embarrassing *Virginius* affair came to a peaceful end.

Yet the civil war in Cuba still raged, with its threat of more incidents. Consequently Secretary Fish tried to persuade several European powers to cooperate with the United States in negotiating an armistice. He was widely criticized in the United States for breaking the spirit of the Monroe Doctrine, that is, for attempting to bring Europe into a purely Western Hemisphere problem. But the Ten Years' War was near its conclusion. Spain in the long run was too powerful to be defeated by the rebels, who were compelled to agree to peace in February, 1878. The reforms subsequently introduced were not sufficient to keep the Cubans satisfied, and ultimately another uprising in 1895 brought the United States actively into the conflict and resulted in Cuban independence.[14]

Although the United States could easily have intervened in the Ten Years' War, especially at the time of the *Virginius* affair, it kept its hands off and resorted instead to peaceful diplomatic action. By refusing to recognize either the independence or the belligerency of the Cuban rebels, the American government, largely through the wisdom of Hamilton Fish, held firmly to the position it had taken during the American Civil War.

[13] The *Virginus* never did reach the United States. It sank off Cape Hatteras on its way back.
[14] See chap. 20.

18

DIPLOMACY IN LOW GEAR

Except for the more or less abortive expansionist efforts and the settlement of issues arising directly or indirectly out of the Civil War, the quarter century after 1865 was not featured by any earth-shaking diplomatic incidents involving the United States. Perhaps this was because the European scene, following the Franco-Prussian War (1870–1871), was comparatively quiet. Or perhaps it was because American energies were concentrated on domestic problems like the reconstruction of the South, the building up of the West, and the rise of industrialism.

Yet the paucity of major incidents did not mean that the United States withdrew completely within a shell of isolation. It did become involved in a number of minor international problems, many of which scarcely deserve mention. Some incidents, however, raised temporary flurries of excitement and therefore will be considered at some length in tracing the story of that otherwise drab diplomatic era.

The Burlingame Treaty

Secretary of State Seward, despite his many other concerns in the diplomatic field, found time and opportunity to extend the interests of the United States in the Far East, especially in China. In this field he had the able assistance of Anson Burlingame, a man of considerable charm and magnetism. During the Presidential campaign of 1860, Burlingame, then a member of Congress from Massachusetts, had made influential speeches in support of candidate Lincoln. As a reward for his services in a winning cause, he was appointed Minister to China, even though he had had no diplomatic experience.

In his new post, Burlingame faced many problems. In the first place, China was in a state of turmoil. The central government was too weak to keep the several provinces under control. This weakness in turn made it virtually impossible to enforce the various treaties wrung from her in 1858.[1] In consequence, the foreign merchants were complaining about their mistreatment and were demanding even more privileges than existing treaties afforded them.

Despite his inexperience, Burlingame was soon able to assume the leadership among the foreign diplomats at Peking through his conciliatory attitude. Thus the merchants were prevented from pushing their extreme demands and the other diplomats were dissuaded from suggesting to their respective governments that the only solution to Chinese unrest was a partitioning of the country. This change of heart, according to Burlingame's report to Secretary Seward, "is a guarantee of the territorial integrity of the Chinese Empire." Naturally the Chinese government was grateful and reciprocated with an order that no assistance of any type be given the Confederate cruiser *Alabama*, then operating in Far Eastern waters.

The American Minister concluded that Chinese troubles might be somewhat alleviated if the government broke out of its isolationist shell to the extent of sending diplomatic envoys to Western countries. Thus when Burlingame was about to give up his post and return home in 1867, the Chinese authorities asked him to become a member of a three-man commission to visit other countries, explain China's problems, and perhaps obtain new and more satisfactory treaties. Even though Burlingame did not head this commission—although he sometimes gave the impression he did—his selection was a remarkable tribute to the faith China had in him.

The first major stop for this commission was Washington, where it was greeted with enthusiasm. Burlingame made a number of speeches picturing China as a thriving, prosperous country. After many conferences with Secretary Seward, he signed the Burlingame Treaty of 1868. In its commercial clauses, this broadened the Treaty of Tientsin of 1858. Two new articles deserve special mention. One provided for most favored nation privileges for Chinese residing in or visiting the United States. All evidence points to the fact that it was Seward, not Burlingame, who was responsible for this provision; the Secretary of State was desirous of ensuring unlimited cheap coolie labor for the builders of the transcontinental railroads. The second article, on the other hand, stated that the Chinese would not be allowed to become naturalized American citizens.[2] Despite this stipulation, the Burlingame Treaty was lauded in both countries as evidence of improved relations.[3]

---

[1] See chap. 13.

[2] Shortly after this treaty went into effect, Congress passed a law limiting the privilege of naturalization to those of white descent and to those of African origin.

[3] The Chinese mission then went on to Europe, where several other treaties were signed. Burlingame never returned home, dying in Russia in 1870.

The Chinese Must Go

Scarcely was the ink dry on the Burlingame Treaty before a series of events began that eventually forced radical changes in that agreement. To understand those events, it is necessary to go back to gold-rush days in California. In 1848–1849, when the West Coast greatly needed cheap labor, the first Chinese immigrants were welcomed. These Orientals were willing to work long hours for less pay than the average white person at almost any occupation—cooking, laundering, mining, and the like. By 1852 the number of Chinese in California has been estimated at between 10,000 and 18,000. The real immigration boom, however, came after the Civil War with the beginning of the construction of the Central Pacific Railroad. The builders sought cheap labor, and Chinese coolies were largely the answer. Thus during the 1860s an annual average of 16,000 entered the United States. In addition to filling the labor shortage, they were highly regarded for their cleanliness, dignity, and orderliness; when Burlingame was back in China in 1869, he enthusiastically reported to the authorities that there was "room for a million Chinese laborers on the Pacific coast."

Although the flow of these immigrants continued, the attitude of American whites soon changed toward the coolies. The Central Pacific was completed in 1869, thereby throwing thousands of workers into the now overcrowded market. Some complained that there were three persons for every job. Four years later came the Panic of 1873, and with it more unemployment, while the resulting depression, lasting throughout the rest of the 1870s, added to the economic woes. The unemployed whites began to blame the Chinese for their inability to find work, for the Chinese, with their lower standard of living, would accept jobs at low wages.

Particular trouble centers were San Francisco and Los Angeles, where race prejudice reared its ugly head. As early as 1871 a white mob of some 20,000 attacked the Chinese quarter in Los Angeles, hanging fifteen coolies and shooting six others. A few years later a similar mob set upon the Chinese section of San Francisco to kill and destroy property. Contributing to the trouble was the rise of the American labor movement. In 1877 Denis Kearney established a local branch of the Workingmen's party in California; among the objectives of this organization was the elimination of competition from Chinese coolie labor. Kearney, a vigorous rabble rouser, not only kept the white labor element inflamed, but extended the anti-Chinese movement into the political field. The slogan "The Chinese must go" became so popular that in 1879 this labor element elected some fifty delegates to the California constitutional convention, which advocated a number of measures discriminating against the Chinese. Both major parties in California, in their quest for the labor vote, resorted to attacking the Orientals.

Meantime the movement reached Congress, where in both houses the Burlingame Treaty was attacked. A special committee was appointed in 1877 to investigate the West Coast situation and eventually reported that Chinese immigration into the United States was harmful in many respects. Despite opposition from the more liberal members, Congress consequently passed in January, 1879, the so-called "Fifteen-passenger Bill," under which a captain whose ship brought over more than fifteen Chinese on any one trip would be subject to a fine of $100 for each over that number, plus six months in jail. Senator James G. Blaine attacked the Chinese on several grounds: their "blighting system of labor," their refusal to become assimilated, their heathen faith, and even their "impure and lewd" women. He asserted that the United States should change the Burlingame Treaty because China had already violated its spirit by allowing an unlimited number of coolies to sail for the United States; "we have this day to choose whether we will have for the Pacific Coast the civilization of Christ or the civilization of Confucius."

President Hayes, supported by Secretary of State William Evarts, refused to sign the bill because it conflicted with the Burlingame Treaty, and Congress upheld his veto. Yet tempers were such that this could not be the final solution. Somehow the treaty would have to be amended.

To the Hayes administration, the only proper way out was to persuade China to agree to a change in the treaty. Therefore Secretary Evarts instructed George Seward, the Minister to China and son of former Secretary of State Seward, to open negotiations for that purpose. The Minister, however, was opposed to change and did his best to sabotage the effort. Consequently, Evarts sent a special three-man commission to complete the work.[4] After considerable give and take, this so-called Angell Commission prevailed upon the Chinese government to sign a new treaty on November 7, 1880, under which, "whenever in the opinion of the United States" the immigration of Chinese workers were to "affect or threaten to affect" American interests, the United States could *reasonably* "regulate, limit, or suspend" such immigration, but not absolutely prohibit it. Exempted from such limitation were "teachers, students, merchants, or travellers from curiosity," who were still to be protected under the most favored nation privileges of the Burlingame Treaty. Finally, if any future American laws caused hardship, both parties would

---

[4] The members were James Angell, president of the University of Michigan, William H. Trescot, a career diplomat, and John F. Swift, an outstanding California lawyer. The *New York Times* referred to the appointment of Swift as an "act of deference to the senseless clamor of a small section of the country."

meet to consider how to alleviate it. Newspapers on the West Coast vigorously denounced this document because it failed to provide for complete exclusion. Elsewhere, however, the treaty was well received; the *New York Herald*, for example, announced that the new agreement settled "one of the gravest questions that ever menaced our civilization."

The Angell Commission also negotiated a new commercial treaty. Among other things, the United States promised to do its best to prohibit the opium trade, while China agreed to allow extraterritorial courts to be established in her territory for the trial of American citizens.

There was too little time remaining to the Hayes administration to clarify the immigration laws, but shortly after Chester A. Arthur entered the White House on the death of President Garfield, Congress went to work on such a measure. The resulting Chinese Exclusion Act of 1882 limited coolie immigration for ten years. On the expiration of this law, Congress extended its life for a similar period. Then in 1904, over Chinese protests, exclusion was made permanent. Naturally this discrimination brought resentment in China, while in the United States anti-Chinese prejudice was intensified by reports of the mistreatment of American missionaries. This mutual ill feeling, plus cordial relations between the United States and Japan, helps to account for American moral support of Japan in her war with China in 1895.

The Birth of Modern Pan-Americanism

The most active and energetic Secretary of State after Hamilton Fish was James G. Blaine of Maine. His earlier political career left much to be desired, for his name was linked with some questionable railroad dealings, as well as with the big-business element of the Republican party. More-over, his elevation to the headship of the State Department by President Garfield was occasioned by his influence in the party rather than because of any practical experience in the diplomatic field. Blaine brought to the State Department certain weaknesses and certain strengths. In addition to his lack of diplomatic experience, he frequently resorted to bluster, probably a carry-over from his days as a journalist and politician. Further-more, he sometimes blundered by jumping into problems of which he had little knowledge. Contributing to these missteps were some of his appointees to diplomatic posts, who were named more for partisan loyalty than understanding of foreign affairs. On the other side of the ledger, Blaine had a keen knowledge of American domestic problems, together with a considerable amount of personal magnetism. And, finally, he learned quickly, with the result that when he again was named to the State Department by President Benjamin Harrison in 1889, he did a much better job, particularly as a strong and able advocate of American rights.

Blaine's great claim to fame as Secretary of State was his advocacy of Pan-Americanism, a movement that had been gathering dust since the days when Henry Clay was head of the State Department in the 1820s.[5] In order to make his program effective, Blaine assumed first of all that European influence in the Western Hemisphere must be kept at a minimum. Therefore, during his early days as Secretary, he attempted to weaken British influence in Central America by trying to modify the Clayton-Bulwer Treaty of 1850.[6] The impetus had already been furnished by President Hayes, who, worried about French canal projects, notified Congress in March, 1880:

> The policy of this country is a canal under American control.... No contract could ever be entered into between private projectors and the Government of Colombia except in contemplation of this position. ... The United States cannot consent to the surrender of this control to any European power.... An interoceanic canal ... will be ... virtually part of the coast line of the United States.

Since the Clayton-Bulwer Treaty stood in the way of such American control, the House of Representatives authorized the President in April, 1880, to "take immediate steps for the formal and final abrogation" of that document. Neither Hayes nor Secretary Evarts, who had made a close study of the situation, had sufficient time to follow through, so the matter was dumped in Blaine's lap.

The new Secretary of State, upon learning that Colombia was negotiating with several European powers for an international guarantee of the neutrality of a French-built canal across Panama, tried to change the 1850 agreement with England. On June 24, 1881, he sent a note to Lord Granville, the British Foreign Secretary, in which he pointed out that conditions had materially changed since Clayton and Bulwer had completed their treaty. Now the United States had "paramount interests" in the Western Hemisphere that could only be upheld if it alone built and fortified a canal. Replying in November, the Foreign Secretary brushed aside Blaine's arguments and insisted upon the sanctity of the old treaty. Although the Secretary of State failed to win his point, he did promote views that were to gain more and more support in the United States. Furthermore, the Blaine contentions gave British statesmen cause to ponder; in the end, as a result of changing world conditions, they eventually yielded to the American position.[7]

Blaine's successor in the State Department, Frederick Frelinghuysen, tried to circumvent the British by reviving efforts made by Secretaries

[5] See chap. 9.
[3] See chap. 13.
[7] See chap. 22.

Seward and Fish.[8] He negotiated a treaty with Nicaragua through its special agent, Joaquín Zavala, in 1884, which provided that a canal through Nicaragua "shall be built by the United States . . . and owned by them and the Republic of Nicaragua." In addition, there was to be a perpetual alliance between the two countries, with the United States promising to protect the smaller nation's territorial integrity.

Even though President Arthur approved this Frelinghuysen-Zavala Convention, many senators realized that its ratification would violate the terms of the Clayton-Bulwer Treaty and lead to serious trouble with Great Britain. Therefore the upper house turned it down by a vote of 32 to 23—five less than the required two-thirds. And Grover Cleveland, after he became President, refused to try to change this verdict. Although unratified, the convention for the first time brought into debate the principle of public ownership, construction, and operation of the desired canal.

Meantime, Blaine was working on the two main features of his concept of Pan-Americanism. The first of these was, in the Secretary's words, "to bring about peace and prevent future wars in North and South America." This objective could only be achieved through a permanent and comprehensive program of cooperation and good will among the several republics of the hemisphere. Dependent on the success of the first was the second: "to cultivate such friendly commercial relations with all American countries as would lead to a large increase in the export trade of the United States, by supplying fabrics in which we are abundantly able to compete with the manufacturing nations of Europe."

In attempting to put this plan into operation, Secretary Blaine tried not only to diminish European influence, but to end the current strife and threats of strife in the hemisphere. His initial effort was to offer mediation in the War of the Pacific between Chile on the one hand and Peru and Bolivia on the other. Unfortunately the Secretary of State replaced the able American ministers to those countries with tactless, partisan, and less experienced envoys who made any hope of conciliation impossible. After the sudden death of both of these fumbling agents, Blaine tried to undo their errors by sending the experienced and competent William H. Trescot as Minister Plenipotentiary to these three warring countries with instructions broad enough possibly to solve their differences. But the assassination of President Garfield and the succession of Frederick

[8] In June, 1867, Seward had completed the Dickinson-Ayón Treaty with Nicaragua, under which the United States guaranteed the neutrality of a canal through Nicaragua, but did not claim exclusive transit rights in line with the Clayton-Bulwer Treaty. In 1876, Secretary Fish broached the subject of modifying the Clayton-Bulwer Treaty, but when England showed no interest, he quickly dropped the matter. In the same year he also tried to obtain more rights from Nicaragua than the Dickinson-Ayón Treaty granted, but Nicaragua demanded too much in return.

Frelinghuysen to the State Department under President Arthur ended any prospect for peace. In similar fashion, Blaine only made matters worse in his ineffectual efforts to settle disputes between Mexico and Guatemala and between Costa Rica and Colombia.

In spite of his dismal beginning, Blaine went ahead with his plans. With full administration approval, in November, 1881, the Secretary invited the governments of the other eighteen hemisphere republics to send delegates to a conference at Washington the following November. The major objective of the meeting would be "to seek a way of permanently averting the horrors of cruel and bloody combat between countries" of the hemisphere, "oftenest of one blood and speech, or even the worst calamity of internal commotion and civil strife." Inasmuch as three countries on the invitation list—Bolivia, Chile, and Peru—were still theoretically at war, the invitation promised that they would "enter the deliberations" of the meeting "on the same footing as the other powers represented." Despite the fact that nine acceptances were promptly forthcoming, the proposed Pan-American session did not materialize.

Just about three weeks after the invitations were sent out, President Arthur let it be known that he wanted his own official family, not the one he had inherited from Garfield. Under the circumstances, Blaine handed in his resignation, and the State Department was placed in the hands of Frederick Frelinghuysen of New Jersey, a man very different in background and temperament. Whereas Blaine frequently rushed in where others feared to tread, the new incumbent sought to avoid adventure; if trouble loomed, he would do nothing to antagonize the opponent.

To Frelinghuysen, the projected Pan-American meeting spelled trouble. He believed that the United States should not "enter into negotiations and consultation for the promotion of peace with selected friendly nationalities, without extending a like confidence to other peoples with whom the United States is on equally friendly terms." The Secretary's critics inferred from this that he did not wish to antagonize England. But whatever the underlying cause, Frelinghuysen, with President Arthur's approval, withdrew the invitations over Blaine's vehement protests.

There the matter rested until May, 1888, when Congress, disturbed by growing tensions in the hemisphere, requested President Cleveland to call a conference of American republics to discuss ways and means of promoting hemisphere peace and prosperity. The President was receptive to the idea and instructed Secretary of State Bayard to issue the necessary invitations for a meeting to convene in October, 1889.

Appropriately enough, Blaine was once again Secretary of State when the First International American Conference was called to order on October 2, 1889. Except for the Dominican Republic, all the Latin

American states were represented. On the agenda were many items: a proposal for a general arbitration treaty; the formation of an American customs union; uniform customs regulations, weights and measures, and patent and coypright laws; the minting of a common silver trade dollar; similar laws for the protection of property; and the establishment of steamship lines to connect the leading ports of the hemisphere.

The high hopes of Secretary Blaine for success were soon rudely dashed. General suspicion of the motives of the United States and mutual fears and jealousies among the Latin American delegations were too strong to permit agreement. While many economic proposals were made, they were either rejected completely or no positive action was taken. As to the major topic, peace, a treaty under which the several countries would submit to arbitration all controversies except those which might compromise their independence was approved by a majority of the delegations, but only a few of their respective governments consented to ratify it. The same thing happened to a resolution opposing recognition of future territorial acquisitions by conquest.

Yet Blaine's efforts did not go entirely for nought. There was soon established at Washington the International Bureau of American Republics. This agency, whose name was eventually changed to the Pan American Union, became a clearinghouse for the exchange of cultural, economic, and scientific information among the hemisphere republics that did much to break down the barriers standing in the way of accord in 1889. And, just as important, this first meeting, even though accomplishing nothing tangible, established a precedent and made possible regular conferences in the twentieth century.

Broadening the Monroe Doctrine

Another ramification of the interest in problems of the Western Hemisphere was the extension or modification of the Monroe Doctrine during the quarter century following the Civil War. Mention has already been made of the doctrine becoming of age during the Maximilian affair in Mexico, as well as of President Grant's specific nontransfer corollary in the case of the Dominican Republic. Likewise, when President Hayes insisted upon an American canal which would be "virtually part of the coastline of the United States," he was extending the original objective of the doctrine.

In addition, in 1867, Nathaniel Banks, chairman of the House Foreign Affairs Committee, succeeded in having approved a resolution that condemned the British formation of the Dominion of Canada as a violation of the Monroe Doctrine. His argument was based on the premise that the new type of Canadian government would prevent American expansion northward. This resolution had little effect, however, on administration policy.

The following year President Johnson, in his annual message to Congress, reiterated the expansionist principle when he said:

> Comprehensive national policy would seem to sanction the acquisition and incorporation into our Federal Union of the several adjacent continental and insular communities as speedily as it can be done peacefully, lawfully, and without violation of national justice, faith, or honor.

In several other instances during the post–Civil War period American Presidents repeated in different ways the Grant no-transfer thesis. Perhaps the most notable was during the administration of Chester A. Arthur, when Secretary of State Frelinghuysen warned the French Foreign Office in 1885 "that the acquisition of Haitian territory by France would conflict with the principles of our public policy known as the Monroe Doctrine."

While none of these pronouncements aroused much interest or support from an American public more concerned with other matters, they at least indicated that the Monroe Doctrine was still a basic influence in American diplomacy and that attempts were being made in administration circles to interpret it in terms of post–Civil War policy.

A Minister Writes a Letter

Generally speaking, the relations between the United States and Great Britain were cordial during the first administration of Grover Cleveland. The new President's refusal to press the Frelinghuysen-Zavala Canal Treaty was the first indication of that friendly feeling. Although the fisheries problem arose once again, the conciliatory Secretary of State, Thomas Bayard, was able to effect a satisfactory compromise that began with the Bayard-Chamberlain Convention of February, 1888.[9] In addition, Cleveland's active struggle to lower American tariff rates was well regarded in England, a free-trade country.

As the presidential election of 1888 approached, the Republicans were seeking a winning issue. Would it not be smart to charge Cleveland with "truckling" to Great Britain? To do so might swing the so-called Irish vote to Republican candidate Harrison. It might be difficult, however, to support such a contention in view of Cleveland's recent threat of retaliation against Canada if the fisheries agreement were not lived up to.

[9] Although the Senate refused to ratify this convention, Bayard, with Cleveland's approval, worked out a modus vivendi that was satisfactory to both parties.

Fortunately for the Republicans, Lord Sackville-West (the former Sir Lionel Sackville-West), the British Minister to Washington, came to their rescue in unknowing fashion. In September, 1888, he had received a letter from a man who said his name was Charles Murchison and who described himself as of English birth but now an American citizen.[10] Since he still held an affection for his native land, he asked Lord Sackville-West how to vote in the forthcoming election to promote English interests. Without investigating in any way "Murchison's" background, the gullible Briton replied that he believed the reelection of President Cleveland would be for the best.

Republican party officials gleefully seized upon this reply as the proof they had been seeking. Wisely waiting until a couple of weeks before the election to give their opponents less time for rebuttal, they released the Sackville-West letter to the newspapers. Sensational headlines aroused the old anti-British feeling, especially among the Irish-Americans.

President Cleveland gave the British Minister an opportunity to defend himself for thus breaking the rules of diplomatic good behavior by interfering in domestic affairs, but Lord Sackville-West only made matters worse by his statements to reporters. On October 26, 1888, Secretary Bayard then informed Edward Phelps, the American Minister to England, that Sackville-West's "usefulness in this country is at an end." Four days later Bayard went even further, saying that the British Minister "is no longer acceptable to this Government"; consequently he had been handed his passport to "facilitate his withdrawal."

Lord Salisbury, the British Foreign Minister, refused to call his Minister home without giving him "an opportunity for explanation or disavowal." Then, after learning more about the incident, Salisbury insisted that Sackville-West's reply had been in the form of a private letter and therefore could not be considered grounds for recall. While the Foreign Minister admitted that any government could demand the removal of an accredited envoy, the envoy's country did not have to concur in the action "unless satisfied by the reasons, duly produced, of the justice of the grounds on which the demands were made."

There was only one way for Cleveland to break this diplomatic stalemate: he dismissed Lord Sackville-West. Yet the damage had already been done, for this so-called Murchison-letter incident was assuredly one of the factors contributing to Cleveland's defeat in the election of 1888. Lord Salisbury, in line with hostile British opinion, refused to replace Lord Sackville-West until after Cleveland left office, while Secretary Bayard, displaying a truculence unusual for him, announced in no uncertain terms that the Democratic party was not beholden in any

[10] Actually the author was a George Osgoodby, a native Californian, who may possibly have been in Republican party employ.

way to any foreign power. Thus the cordiality between the two Anglo-Saxon countries, which had grown during Cleveland's first administration, was marred by an incident in which domestic political advantage was deemed more important than friendly relations with Great Britain.

The Bering Sea Seal Controversy

An unexpected dividend from the purchase of Alaska was the gaining of the Pribilof Islands, the breeding grounds of fur seals. There seals gathered in late spring and early summer, the females to have their young. With the coming of autumn, both males and females moved south to warmer climates, migrating as far as the waters off Mexico.

Shortly after the purchase, the United States granted the Alaska Commercial Company, consisting of American investors, a twenty-year monopoly to kill seals on the Pribilof Islands in return for annual monetary payments, plus so much for each seal. The profits from sealing were so large that sealers from Canada, Mexico, Japan, and Russia began to compete with the Alaska Commercial Company. Instead of limiting the killing to land, these competitors engaged in pelagic sealing, that is, hunting seals in the open sea. There the sealers could not distinguish—or perhaps did not attempt to distinguish—between male and female seals. When a female was killed, it meant the additional loss of her unborn pup as well as starvation for her baby on shore. Furthermore, the sealers seldom were able to recover more than 20 per cent of the seals killed in open water.

Dismayed by the threatened extermination of the whole seal herd, the United States, long the defender of freedom of the seas, determined to close the whole Bering Sea area to indiscriminate sealers. As early as 1886, an American revenue cutter seized three sealing vessels from British Columbia at least 70 miles from land on charges of "killing fur seal within the limits of Alaska Territory." When Sir Lionel Sackville-West protested, Secretary of State Bayard persuaded the Treasury Department to release the Canadian ships. Yet no attempt was made at the time to settle the basic issues involved. The following year six more ships were seized; this time a Federal district judge ordered them confiscated on the ground that the whole Bering Sea was a mare clausum, completely under the jurisdiction of the United States. Once again Sackville-West objected and insisted that compensation be paid to the owners and their crews.

Secretary Bayard, realizing the potential gravity of the situation, tried to prevent future controversies and at the same time end pelagic sealing by sending similar notes in August, 1887, to the several nations concerned. In these messages he sought their cooperation in preventing the indiscriminate killing of seals by their citizens. The several replies were favorable and the way was apparently clear for an international convention. But this hope was dashed when Canada objected to any restrictions, thus making it impossible for Sackville-West to commit the British Empire. Edward Phelps, the American Minister to the Court of St. James, urged Secretary Bayard to force the issue. As far as Phelps was concerned, Canada had been interfering with American fisheries for years without regard to international law; therefore the United States should do its best "to put an end to a pursuit of the seal by Canadian ships which is unjustifiable and illegitimate." American opinion, as expressed in newspapers throughout the country, tended to support drastic measures, and the House of Representatives even passed a bill which declared that the United States had complete jurisdiction over Bering Sea. The upper house, however, refused to fall in line because the proposal "involved serious matters of international law." Secretary Bayard shared the Senate's doubts, and nothing further was done during the remainder of President Cleveland's first term.

Such was the situation when James G. Blaine again became Secretary of State, this time under President Benjamin Harrison. Soon it became more acute when, in the summer of 1889, American revenue cutters, seeking to prevent pelagic sealing,[11] seized several more Canadian schooners in Bering Sea outside the 3-mile limit. When the London government again protested, Secretary Blaine sent a long reply in January, 1890, justifying the stand of the United States. First of all, he upheld the seizures, not under the former argument of mare clausum, but on the grounds that the Canadian ships "were engaged in a pursuit that was in itself *contra bonos mores*."[12] The best way to save seals from extinction was to insist that they be killed on land only, where the sealers could distinguish between male and female and where all the furs of those killed could be collected. Thus "nations not possessing the territory upon which seals can increase their numbers by natural growth, and thus afford an annual supply of skins for the use of mankind, should refrain from the slaughter in open sea, where the extinction of the species is sure and swift."

Secondly, Blaine challenged the British argument that there could be no control of the seas beyond the 3-mile limit. "The law of the sea is not lawlessness," the Secretary asserted; it could prevent a few persons from exterminating seals for their own private gain to the detriment of mankind as a whole. Britain herself had long since upheld this theory by claiming and enforcing control of the fisheries off the Grand Banks and

[11] On March 2, 1889, Congress had authorized the President to protect the sealing rights of the United States and to declare the Bering Sea in effect an American ocean.

[12] Literally, against good morals.

the pearl beds off Ceylon far beyond the normal mileage. And thirdly, custom was on the side of the United States. First Russia and then the United States since 1867 had enjoyed for a total of a hundred years the exclusive right, unchallenged during that century by other nations, to control seal fisheries in Bering Sea. Then Blaine asked two important questions: "Whence did the ships of Canada derive the right to do that which they had refrained from doing for more than ninety years?" and "Upon what grounds did Her Majesty's Government defend in the year 1886, a course of conduct in the Bering Sea which she had carefully avoided since the discovery of that sea?"

Despite the vigor of his arguments, Blaine concluded with the statement that the door was not closed to compromise and that he was ready to listen to any adequate solution Britain might offer. The only thing he insisted upon was "that all friendly nations will concede to the United States, the same rights and privileges on the lands and in the waters of Alaska, which the same friendly nations conceded to the Empire of Russia."

Lord Salisbury did not reply until June, 1890. While he admitted that the Canadian sealers might be involved in inhumane actions, there was nothing in international commitments which made their actions illegal. On the other hand, the United States was breaking the rules when, while at peace, it seized foreign vessels on the high seas on charges other than for breaking an international agreement or for piracy. With the controversy still unsettled, Salisbury subsequently threw down the gauntlet by informing Blaine that his government "must hold the Government of the United States responsible for the consequences which may ensue from acts which are contrary to the established principles of international law."

This virtual ultimatum naturally stirred war talk in some parts of the United States, particularly after rumors began to circulate that British warships had been seen in the vicinity of Bering Sea. Fortunately, however, cooler minds prevailed on both sides of the Atlantic. Several conferences were held among representatives of the United States, England, Canada, and Russia, and these resulted in February, 1892, in a treaty providing that a tribunal, meeting in Paris, should arbitrate the following questions: (1) What exclusive rights did Russia have over the Bering Sea seal fisheries before 1867? (2) Did Britain recognize those rights? (3) Did the Treaty of 1825 between England and Russia place the Bering Sea in the Pacific Ocean and did Russia exercise any exclusive rights in Bering Sea after that treaty went into effect? (4) Did whatever rights Russia enjoyed pass on to the United States after 1867? and (5) Did the United States have the right to protect seals in Bering Sea outside the 3-mile limit?

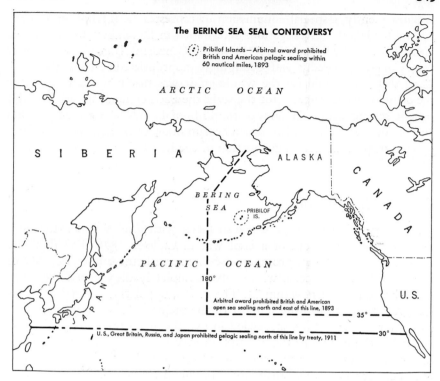

The BERING SEA SEAL CONTROVERSY

Pribilof Islands — Arbitral award prohibited British and American pelagic sealing within 60 nautical miles, 1893

ARCTIC OCEAN

SIBERIA

ALASKA

CANADA

BERING SEA

PRIBILOF IS.

PACIFIC OCEAN

180°

U. S.

Arbitral award prohibited British and American open sea sealing north and east of this line, 1893

35°

30°

U. S., Great Britain, Russia, and Japan prohibited pelagic sealing north of this line by treaty, 1911

JAPAN

Blaine, who had done so much to arrange this arbitration, was not in the State Department when the arbitral decision was reached. He had resigned suddenly and unexpectedly in June, 1892, to be succeeded by John W. Foster, who had recently been serving as agent in charge of preparing the United States case for presentation to the tribunal. Foster's excellent work was all in vain, however, because the American position was basically unsound and because of an Anglo-Russian agreement which hurt the American cause.

On August 15, 1893, the arbitral commission, consisting of judges named by France, Italy, and Sweden, handed down a decision against the United States on all five counts. Since this decision meant that the United States was liable for damages as a result of seizing Canadian sealing schooners outside the 3-mile limit, President Cleveland's Secretary of State, Walter Q. Gresham, immediately offered Britain $425,000 in settlement. Despite the fact that the Canadian claimants had sought slightly more than $540,000, Sir Julian Pauncefote, the British Minister, agreed to accept the American offer, but Congress, bitterly antiadministration because of Cleveland's domestic policies, refused to appropriate the necessary money.

Subsequently, a special commission of representatives from both countries, after lengthy investigation, determined in December, 1897, that the United States should pay $473,151 to the Canadian claimants, an amount that Congess belatedly and grudgingly appropriated. About the only thing that can be said for the whole affair was that it was a victory for the cause of arbitration. As for the seals, the Paris commission did prohibit pelagic sealing within 60 miles of the Pribilof Islands between May 1 and July 31 of each year and laid down certain other rules, but these were not enough to prevent serious decimation of the herds. In 1911, Russia, Japan, Great Britain, and the United States finally agreed on adequate regulations.

Chilean Complications

Secretary of State Blaine was also faced with serious diplomatic controversies that grew out of a civil war in Chile in 1891. The domestic upheaval resulted from growing discontent with the autocratic rule of President José Balmaceda, who almost completely disregarded the legislative branch of the government. The rebels, popularly referred to as the *Congressionalistas*, had the support of the majority of the Chilean people and, after some fighting, succeeded in overthrowing the *Balmacedistas*.

During the course of this revolution several incidents strained United States–Chilean relations and, according to some authorities, led the United States closer to open war than any other incident involving South America. Trouble originated in the attitude of Patrick Egan, the American Minister to Chile and a protégé of Blaine, who not only took sides in the civil war, but made a number of indiscreet statements in favor of the *Balmacedistas*. The victorious *Congressionalistas* resented this as an intolerable interference by a foreign diplomat in Chile's domestic affairs. To make matters worse, Egan allowed some of the *Balmacedistas* to gain asylum in the American legation. While under normal circumstances this was customary practice, Egan was severely criticized by the *Congressionalistas* for his partisanship.

A third incident resulted from the quest of the rebels for arms and other necessities to carry on their fight. They sent the *Itata* to San Diego, California, for military supplies. On the suspicion the ship might be violating the United States neutrality laws, a Federal marshal was stationed on board to ensure that the *Itata* would not leave port until its status was clarified. Despite this injunction, the ship escaped, picked up the arms at nearby Catalina Island, and set out on its return voyage pursued by two United States warships. When the *Itata* reached Iquique, which had been seized by the *Congressionalistas*, an American officer demanded that both ship and cargo be given up and returned to San Diego for trial. The rebels either had to comply or face a possible attack by American forces. Since they were not as yet completely victorious in their civil war, they discreetly surrendered the *Itata*. Subsequently, the United States authorities decided that no American laws had been broken—a decision more easily reached because by this time the *Congressionalistas* had established a *de facto* government in Chile.

Needless to say, the *Itata* affair did nothing to improve relations between the two countries. And even before the United States released the ship, another incident had widened the breach. When the civil war broke out, the United States had sent three naval vessels to Chilean waters to protect American interests. One of these was the *Baltimore,* commanded by Captain Winfield S. Schley. Despite the known hostility of the Chilean masses, the captain granted more than a hundred of his crew shore leave at Valparaiso on October 16, 1891. Toward nightfall irate mobs of Chilean longshoremen, sailors, and citizens attacked the unarmed American tars with a variety of weapons. Two sailors were killed in the melee, numerous others were wounded, and thirty-six were marched off to jail. Accounts of the causes of the affray varied. Some stated that the sailors had done nothing to warrant the unprovoked attack; others asserted that they had imbibed too freely and had become obnoxious and insulting. All agreed, however, that the local police did little or nothing to quell the mobs, and, in fact, some reports had it that the police even participated in the attacks. The Chilean authorities made a thorough investigation and found no basis for bringing charges against the imprisoned sailors, who were promptly released.

To the United States government, however, the incident was not to be dismissed so easily. It was considered to be not the usual type of brawl in which American sailors became involved in foreign ports, but a premeditated attack on wearers of the American uniform and consequently something for which the United States should demand compensation.

But the victorious *Congressionalistas* had not yet established a formal government, and, while the provisional authorities promised to do something about the American demand, they continued to delay. Consequently, President Harrison, in his annual message to Congress in December, 1891, declared: "If these just expectations should be disappointed or further needless delay intervene, I will by a special message bring this matter again to the attention of Congress for such action as may be necessary."

Señor Matta, the provisional Minister of Foreign Affairs of Chile, wrote a public letter on December 11 describing the contents of Harrison's report as inexact and insincere—a diplomatic way of saying the President had lied. This insult aroused a belligerent spirit in the United States, and on January 25, 1892, President Harrison practically asked Congress to approve a declaration of war.

Between the time of the Matta letter and the middle of January, events had moved swiftly in Chile. The provisional government had been succeeded by a new constitutional regime under President Jorge Montt. While antipathy toward the United States still ran strong, the Montt administration realized the futility of antagonizing the United States to the point of war; in spite of an excessive spirit of nationalism, even the most patriotic Chileans knew their nation could not cope with the stronger United States. Consequently, the new Minister of Foreign Affairs, Luis Pereira, apologized for his predecessor's tactless letter and promised that compensation for those killed and injured in the *Baltimore* incident would soon be made. On January 30, 1892, Secretary Blaine instructed Egan to inform the Chilean government that the United States accepted the apology and that the way was now paved for a peaceful settlement of the differences.

Before the year was over outwardly friendly relations were restored, so that President Harrison could inform Congress on December 6, 1892:

> It gives me now great gratification to report that the Chilean Government, in a most friendly and honorable spirit, has tendered and paid as an indemnity to the families of the sailors of the *Baltimore* who were killed and to those who were injured ... the sum of $75,000. This has been accepted, not only as an indemnity for a wrong done, but as a most gratifying evidence that the Government of Chile rightly appreciated the disposition of this Government to act in a spirit of the most absolute fairness and friendliness in our intercourse with that brave people....

Outside of the strain the controversies with Chile placed upon Pan-American relations, the incidents helped to make the United States aware of its weakness in sea power, thereby strengthening the movement to build a bigger and better navy.

Italy and the Mafia Incident

Even while Secretary Blaine was vigorously prosecuting the case against Chile in the *Baltimore* affair, he was engaged in defending his country in a controversy with Italy that grew out of similar mob action in New Orleans. That Louisiana port had long attracted many immigrants, especially Italians. These newcomers were blamed for the extreme lawlessness that pervaded the city, with particular responsibility placed on the Mafia or Black Hand Society. Murders often went unpunished; even when evidence of guilt seemed strong, defendants escaped through fictitious alibis and other forms of perjury.

Local indignation became so vehement that the popular chief of police, David Hennessy, began a personal investigation of the Mafia and its purported members. While so engaged, he was murdered on October 15, 1890, by person or persons unknown. To the enraged populace, however, there was no doubt that the Black Hand was responsible, and a number of suspected members, all of Italian birth, were arrested. As in the past, the resulting trial brought acquittal, though it was once again evident that perjury—and this time bribery and threats as well—played an important part in the verdict. But local anger was now so strong that on March 14, 1891, a mob of several thousand, representing virtually every walk of life, stormed the city jail and lynched eleven suspected culprits.[13]

When Baron Fava, the Italian Minister at Washington, reported this incident to his home government, he was instructed by Marquis Rudini, the Minister of Foreign Affairs, to demand immediate protection of Italians in New Orleans by the United States government and punishment of those responsible for the lynching. Fava followed up this demand with a message to Blaine, in which he decried the attitude of the New Orleans authorities in standing passively by while the lynchings occurred.

Blaine promptly informed Governor F. T. Nicholls of Louisiana of the existing Italo-American treaty that promised "the most constant protection and security" for Italian subjects living in the United States, as well as for their property. To uphold the honor of the United States, Nicholls must therefore cooperate with the Federal government in guaranteeing the treaty provision. The Governor replied that everything was now under control in New Orleans, an investigation was being made, and, from what he had thus learned, the mobs had acted against supposed murderers, not against those of a particular nationality.

To the Italian government, this was not enough. Foreign Minister Rudini demanded official assurance that the guilty ones "have been brought to justice" and immediate indemnity to the families of the lynched men. "A simple declaration, though cordial and friendly," asserted Rudini, "is not sufficient; we want positive facts." When Minister Fava transmitted this message, he emphasized that his government impatiently awaited a reply. Blaine answered that he could do nothing until he obtained all the facts in the case. During the course of subsequent correspondence, Minister Fava was called home in what was virtually, though not officially, a severance of diplomatic relations.

Even though there was talk of war, the situation never reached such a critical stage. The Italian government quickly realized that its initial demands for immediate action had been too strong. Therefore, it shifted to the more reasonable request that the United States merely see that the guilty were tried and that an indemnity be paid as a matter of principle.

[13] Five of the victims were still awaiting trial, three were being held for new trials, and the remaining three had been acquitted but not released.

Blaine's subsequent handling of the case was calm and collected, firm yet conciliatory. He pointed out how the American Constitution operated and stressed the system of American justice. If a wrong had been done, the United States would do its best to correct it. Tempers on both sides cooled as quickly as they had originally flared. The issue was peacefully terminated in April, 1892, when Italy was informed that eight of those lynched were naturalized American citizens, when the Federal government paid $25,000 in indemnity, and when the Italian Minister returned to Washington. Yet the incident, like the earlier McLeod affair,[14] revealed a weakness of the American form of government—the inability of the Federal government to intervene in matters reserved to the states, even when the rights of foreign nationals were involved.

All the diplomatic incidents of this period showed a certain ardor in promoting American rights and American interests. While it is true that these incidents were not of major significance, they were indications of a spirit that was soon to become an important aspect of the rise of the United States to a position of world power.

[14] See chap. 10.

PART THREE

1890 TO 1917

The Age of Imperialism

Between 1890 and 1917 the United States annexed Puerto Rico and the Virgin Islands in the Caribbean, and Hawaii, the Philippines, Guam, and part of the Samoan group in the Pacific. It built the Panama Canal through a leased zone in which it exercised essentially sovereign powers and maintained protectorates over Cuba, Haiti, the Dominican Republic, Nicaragua, and Panama. It vigorously upheld the Monroe Doctrine in Latin America and exhorted the other powers to maintain the Open Door and respect the independence and territorial integrity of China. It played the role of peacemaker between Russia and Japan and helped avert a threatened war between France and Germany over North Africa.

America's more active role in world affairs resulted from many factors. The quickening of European imperialism served as both example and warning. The United States faced the apparent alternatives of either playing the game or sitting on the sidelines while the other powers divided the prizes. For vigorous and ambitious young politicians like Theodore Roosevelt and Henry Cabot Lodge the answer was simple: the United States should build up its Navy and extend its influence. They eagerly accepted and popularized Captain Alfred Thayer Mahan's teaching that control of the seas was essential to national greatness. Industrialists and bankers played a mixed role in the new imperialism: they welcomed new markets and new opportunities for investment, but they feared war and costly adventures.

Missionaries and publicists helped to convince large sections of the public that the nation had a sacred duty to carry Christian civilization and Anglo-Saxon principles of government to backward countries. It was not mere coincidence that the age of imperialism in foreign affairs overlapped the age of progressivism in domestic politics. Although not all crusaders for reform were expansionists, many of them were—and for an obvious reason. Dedicated to correcting abuses and expanding democracy at home, they became readily convinced that the United States had a mission to deliver Cuba and the Philippines from Spanish misgovernment and to teach the ways of democracy to the Mexicans and to other unruly breeds to the South. Sometimes—as in the case of Theodore Roosevelt and Albert Beveridge—the progressives were open and avowed imperialists; sometimes—as in the case of Woodrow Wilson and William Jennings Bryan—they thought of themselves as anti-imperialists. Yet in actual practice the moral fervor of both groups was likely to point in the same direction, toward extending American influence beyond the American borders.

Strong though the forces were that pushed the nation into imperial ventures, the counterforces were never negligible. Many Americans deplored the imposition of American rule upon foreign populations and the use of American marines to police the Caribbean. Moreover, American expansion threatened to be self-defeating, even from the imperialist point of view. The more the North American giant brandished the big stick, the more difficult it became for him to win the real friendship and trust of sensitive and suspicious neighbors. Much of the supposed necessity for American intervention was removed by World War I, which resulted in the destruction of the German navy and relieved the United States of its earlier worries that foreign nations might establish new naval bases in the Caribbean. America's brief experiment with direct imperialism had largely spent its force by 1917.

19

THE NEW IMPERIALISM

The slogan "manifest destiny," which had stirred Americans so deeply in the 1840s and then had lost much of its potency for half a century, once again began to exert a powerful influence during the 1890s. Champions of a "strong" policy demanded a modern navy, annexation of island bases in the Caribbean and the Pacific, an American-controlled isthmian canal, and recognition of the United States as the paramount nation in the Western Hemisphere. Although Harrison sympathized with the new imperialism and Cleveland resisted it, both Presidents felt its influence in dealing with the practical problems of their administrations.

European Expansion

Public opinion in the United States was strongly influenced by developments abroad. One European nation after another embarked upon a vigorously imperialistic policy during the last quarter of the nineteenth century. The advocates of "Little England" had had their day and had now been supplanted in influence by unabashed champions of expansion like Benjamin Disraeli and Joseph Chamberlain. Meanwhile, France found compensation for its wounded pride after the Franco-Prussian War by extending its rule over large parts of Africa and Southeast Asia. Germany entered the colonial race a little late, but was pushing vigorously ahead during the 1880s. The vast Russian Empire was growing along its edges, restlessly striving to extend its domination in the Near, the Middle, and the Far East. Even weaker states like Italy and Belgium were seeking a share in the partition of Africa.

European expansion was defended by a variety of rationalizations—most of which were echoed by American expansionists. Rapid industrialization led to a demand for new markets and sources of raw materials. To protect vital commerce, there was pressure for larger navies and more naval bases. Capitalists, seeking profitable employment for their surplus funds, loaned money for the development of backward nations and then called upon their governments to protect these investments. Zealous Christians regarded Africa and Asia as fields ripe for missionary harvest. Racial theorists, confident in the superiority of their own kind, proclaimed that it was "the white man's burden" to undertake the rule of the black and brown men of other continents.

These European developments influenced Americans in different ways. Some regarded the growth of colonialism as evidence of the onward march of civilization and believed the United States must share these new responsibilities. To emulate the European powers by acquiring overseas colonies was considered essential to the nation's recognition as a world power. Others reacted not so much in admiration as in fear of European imperialism. Would the European powers be content to extend their domination merely over Asia and Africa? Would they not also seek to interfere in areas like South America, the Caribbean Sea, and the eastern Pacific? American expansion was urged as a defensive policy to forestall the movement of European nations into places that might menace American security. On the other hand, many Americans opposed the whole spirit of imperialism as clashing with the ideal of government by the consent of the governed.

Impact of Industrialism

During the fifty years between the 1840s and the 1890s, the United States had gone through a period of significant economic change. In earlier days the nation had been predominantly agricultural, and the impulse that had carried frontiersmen into Texas and Oregon had been primarily land hunger. During the ensuing years the country had become heavily industrialized. Between 1850 and 1889 the annual value of products manufactured in the United States had increased from about 1 billion to over 9 billion dollars. In 1894 the United States achieved the rank of first among the industrial nations of the world.

As national productivity increased, the character of foreign trade was altered. The change was gradual rather than dramatic. In 1890, almost four-fifths of American exports were still raw materials and foodstuffs; cotton, meat, and wheat were the big three, accounting for almost 60 per cent of the total. But manufactured goods like petroleum products, steel, and textiles were becoming more important on the export list. On the import side of the ledger, the United States was taking relatively less in foreign manufactured goods, but more foods and raw materials like sugar, coffee, wool, silk, and rubber.

Many American businessmen, noting these economic trends, demanded a more active foreign policy that would open up foreign markets and assure access to essential raw materials. They wanted favorable commercial treaties, better consular service, subsidies for shipping, equal opportunities in foreign ports, and protection for American investments abroad. They regarded a stronger American navy as essential to gaining respect for American interests.

Yet the relation between the growth of American capitalism and the resurgence of American imperialism was not so close as Marxist interpreters would like to believe. American manufacturers still saw in the large and growing American population their most promising market, and most of the energy of the captains of industry was devoted to outwitting their domestic competitors. Many businessmen feared the cruder forms of imperialism that might involve the nation in war and high taxes.

In so far as an aggressive policy of expansion might bring the United States into conflict with Great Britain, conservative Americans were particularly cautious. They regarded the economic ties between the two countries as far more important than any prizes that might be won in a race for colonies. In 1895, some 58 per cent of American exports were going to the British Empire, as contrasted with only 4 per cent and 1½ per cent that went to South America and Asia respectively. British capital was heavily invested in American railroads and other enterprises.

In the contest that developed between the imperialists and the anti-imperialists, American businessmen were, therefore, to be found on both sides. They gave strong support to some items in the imperialist program, but opposed others. On the whole, it was the politicians and the publicists, rather than the capitalists, who took the most active role in promoting the new imperialism.

Prophets of Empire

Charles Darwin's theory of evolution through natural selection provided the nineteenth century with its most intriguing idea. Scores of social thinkers set themselves the task of translating the Darwinian hypothesis from the zoological world for which it had been originally formulated to the world of business and government. "Survival of the fittest" provided a convenient phrase to justify everything from the wealth of John D. Rockefeller to the British system of government.

Social Darwinisn supplied particularly persuasive arguments for imperialism. In 1885, John Fiske, the foremost popularizer of the evolutionary theory in America, wrote an article for *Harper's Magazine* entitled "Manifest Destiny," in which he undertook to demonstrate that the "English race" with its superior civilization was destined to extend its power and influence until "four-fifths of the human race will trace its pedigree to English forefathers." The United States, Fiske believed, had an important role to play in this extension of English civilization. Josiah Strong, an influential Congregational minister, saw in the struggle for survival a means by which God worked out his purposes in the world. In *Our Country: Its Possible Future and Its Present Crisis*, Strong exalted the Anglo-Saxon race as "the representative ... of the largest liberty, the purest Christianity, the highest civilization."

> If I read not amiss, this powerful race will move down upon Mexico, down upon Central and South America, out upon the islands of the sea, over upon Africa and beyond. And can any one doubt that the result of this competition of races will be the "survival of the fittest"?

Professor John W. Burgess of Columbia University, probably the most respected political scientist of the day, taught that only the Teutonic nations possessed in the fullest degree "the capacity for establishing nation states." Therefore they were "called to carry the political civilization of the modern world into those parts of the world inhabited by unpolitical and barbaric races; i.e., they must have a colonial policy." Professor Burgess was impatient with the reluctance of some of his countrymen to see the United States interfere in the affairs of backward states. Not only was such interference justified, but it was a duty to world civilization.

The New Navy

During the 1880s there was growing concern over the decrepit condition of the American Navy. After the Civil War, the government had economized by dismantling its wartime fleet with blind haste and thoroughness. The Navy of 1880 was composed of a miscellaneous aggregation of museum pieces, some of them built during the presidency of John Adams. The American Navy had been standing still during years when the European nations were experimenting with armored ships, rifled guns, torpedoes, and the use of steam.

This situation was particularly alarming to statesmen who wanted to see the United States enjoy the respect that they believed to be due a great power. In 1880, Representative Washington C. Whitthorne of Tennessee argued that commerce required a strong navy. Anticipating Mahan by ten years, he drew from history the lesson that "those nations which have attained the highest rank in dominion, power and civilization" were those which had powerful navies and a large merchant marine. Four years later, Senator John T. Morgan of Alabama asserted that he could cite "instance after instance ... where the policy of the United States Government has been one of a hesitating and lame character because we were

known not to possess the available power that a great fleet would give us."
Admiral David Porter contended that a small navy could not be an effective one. "A navy must be large in proportion to what will be required
of it—protection to commerce in all quarters, and strong enough to take
the initiative. . . ."

Goaded by such men and by a succession of conscientious secretaries
of the Navy, Congress began to appropriate money for building modern
steel ships. Four cruisers were authorized in 1883, and thirty other vessels
between 1885 and 1889. In 1890, the first true American battleship was
ordered. The threat of war with Chile over the *Baltimore* affair in 1891
strengthened the movement for the new fleet.

Interest in the navy was powerfully stimulated after 1890 by the writings of Captain Alfred Thayer Mahan. This scholarly professional sailor,
the superintendent of the Naval War College at Newport, Rhode Island,
gained sudden fame with the publication of *The Influence of Sea Power
upon History, 1660–1783* (1890). Although primarily a study in British
naval history, Captain Mahan's book was studded with general reflections
upon the influence of sea power in determining the strength and destiny
of nations. National greatness required commerce, and commerce required the protection of a powerful navy. Effective sea power also demanded a large merchant marine and colonies to serve both as a stimulus
to trade and as naval bases.

Mahan's theories were eagerly taken up abroad. The English, naturally
flattered by the praise the American officer had lavished on their historic
policy, honored him with Oxford and Cambridge degrees and a round
of naval banquets. Kaiser William II of Germany placed Mahan's book in
the hands of all his naval officers. In Japan the famous treatise also made a
profound impression.

Pleased though Mahan was by this foreign recognition, his great aspiration was to influence the policy of his own country. From his point of
view, the United States was almost completely deficient in all the elements
of effective sea power. Its Navy was pathetically small and committed to
a single-ship, commerce-raiding concept that Mahan believed to be hopelessly out of date. He taught that a modern navy derived its strength
primarily from capital ships concentrated and maneuvering as a fleet. To
him the building of the right kind of navy would be only the beginning.
The United States would need as well an isthmian canal under its own
control, naval bases in the Caribbean and the Pacific, and an adequate
merchant marine. A steady stream of books and magazine articles flowed
from Mahan's tireless pen.

Mahan's gospel found eager listeners among a group of young Americans already strongly expansionist in their sympathies. Two most ardent
disciples were Henry Cabot Lodge, congressman and later senator from

Massachusetts, and Theodore Roosevelt, just beginning his rocketlike rise in politics. Whitelaw Reid, publisher of the *New York Tribune* and influential Republican, was another.

Excitement over Samoa

The new imperialism found an early focus in Samoa. The various agreements of the late 1870s had brought a temporary lull in the rivalry among the German, English, and American residents of the islands, but in 1884 there was alarming evidence of a hardening in German policy. Chancellor Bismarck, who had hitherto opposed German expansion overseas, became a convert to colonialism, and it soon became obvious that Samoa stood high on the list of German ambitions.

In November, 1884, the German consul at Apia used the pretext of the native government's inadequate protection of German property to force a new treaty on Malietoa, the Samoan king. In all matters affecting the German residents, Malietoa had to promise to accept the decisions of a German-dominated council. When the king secretly asked Britain to establish a protectorate, the German consul retaliated by raising the German flag over Apia and taking over the municipal government despite protests from the British and American consuls. The Germans also encouraged Tamasese, who had been serving as vice king, to revolt against Malietoa and claim the throne for himself.

In the confused events that followed the adoption of this aggressive German policy, it is clear that Bismarck was attempting to annex the islands. But since the Chancellor did not want serious trouble with England and the United States, he was careful to restrain his subordinates when they carried things too far. He therefore disavowed his consul's action in trying to establish exclusive German jurisdiction over Apia. At the same time, however, Bismarck conveyed to both the British and American governments his belief that the natives were incompetent to rule the islands without help and that the country with the largest trade in the islands—Germany, of course—should provide guidance. Cleveland's Secretary of State, Thomas F. Bayard, refused to concede that a German protectorate was necessary; instead he proposed a three-power conference on the Samoan problem.

Bismarck accepted Bayard's proposal in principle, but suggested that any such meeting should be postponed until the three nations had sent commissioners to Samoa for a firsthand investigation. Accordingly, President Cleveland appointed George H. Bates of Delaware to visit Samoa in 1886. Bates's report supported the idea that the natives were incapable of complete independence, but argued that the United States, rather than Germany, should be the protector. Bates discussed the possibility that an isthmian canal would soon be built; if that were the case, American trade in the Pacific would greatly increase. Therefore, he suggested, it would be logical to extend the Monroe Doctrine to a larger area—certainly to Hawaii and probably to Samoa as well.

Bismarck found Britain much more sympathetic than the United States to the idea of a German protectorate. When the German Ambassador at London pointed out that England could not expect to have German support for her action in Egypt unless the British cooperated with German policy in Samoa, Lord Salisbury, the British Prime Minister, quickly got the point. Salisbury stated his own preference for a colonial division that would give Samoa to Germany, the Friendly Islands to Britain, and Hawaii to the United States, but he warned that Australian fear of German expansion would force him to go slowly. The German Ambassador argued "that the Americans would have to be restrained in every possible way," because they now appeared "to interpret the Monroe Doctrine, as though the Pacific Ocean were to be treated as an American Lake."

This behind-the-scenes diplomacy explains why Secretary Bayard found it difficult to achieve his goals when he met with the English and German ministers on the Samoan problem in July, 1887. This Washington Conference adjourned in failure after it became obvious that Bayard's policy of preserving Samoan independence and autonomy, with equal rights to the treaty powers, was in direct conflict with the German determination to dominate the islands. England supported Germany in these discussions.

Following the failure of the Washington Conference, Germany once again resorted to drastic measures in Samoa. Alleging that King Malietoa had permitted pilfering from German plantations and insults to the German Emperor, the Germans declared war on the native regime. After German marines had occupied Apia, Tamasese was recognized as king and Malietoa was transported to a distant island, where he lived in exile for the next few years. These highhanded proceedings brought indignant protests from Harold M. Sewall, the American consul. The pro-German Tamasese soon found himself faced with a formidable rebellion led by Mataafa, another prominent chief. When a German attempt to capture the rebel was repulsed with heavy losses, German warships retaliated by shelling undefended native villages.

The news from Samoa was highly disturbing to American public opinion. The *New York Sun* condemned Cleveland's handling of the situation as "unfortunate, if not humiliating." The *San Francisco Examiner* said Germany had been simply a "highwayman." The *New York Herald* thought that war was imminent and that American naval officers were "sniffing the battle." Congress responded to the excitement by voting $500,000 for the protection of American rights in Samoa and another

$100,000 for the improvement of Pago Pago harbor. More sober citizens were disturbed by the growing talk of war. A naval authority believed that in case of hostilities, nothing would prevent the German navy from sailing into New York harbor and threatening to destroy the city unless ransom were paid.

The Samoan situation moved toward a crisis in the early months of 1889. Although Bayard still hoped for a peaceful solution, he went along with a decision to send additional naval vessels to the islands to protect American interests. On March 16, 1889, six warships—three American, two German, and one English—were anchored in Apia harbor, nervously awaiting developments. What happened, however, was not the anticipated incident that might result in war, but a great display of the force of nature. A hurricane and tidal wave bore down on the rival ships, wrecking with considerable loss of life all but the English vessel, which managed to ride out the storm. The shock of this disaster temporarily quieted the bickering factionalism in the islands.

The Tripartite Treaty

Meanwhile, quite independently of this development, the diplomats had recognized the folly of risking war over these distant bits of territory and had started the machinery running toward settlement. Chancellor Bismarck invited Britain and the United States to resume the discussions broken off in 1887. The new conference, held at Berlin, finally resulted in the Tripartite Treaty of June 14, 1889.

In its first article, the agreement appeared to support the principles for which the United States had been contending: Samoa was to be neutral territory in which the subjects of the three signatory powers were to have "equal rights of residence, trade and personal protection"; the natives were freely to elect their own king; and none of the powers was to exercise any separate control over the islands or the Samoan government. But the independence seemingly recognized in the first article was taken away by subsequent provision for a foreign-appointed chief justice, who was to exercise jurisdiction over all important disputes, even those involving the election of the king and the definition of his powers.

In reality, the Tripartite Treaty established a joint protectorate of Germany, England, and the United States over Samoa. Anti-imperialists in the United States shook their heads over this "entangling alliance." Democrats and Republicans were equally involved in this departure from precedent. Bayard had initiated the negotiations that led to the agreement; Secretary of State Blaine, his Republican successor, had carried them through.

As a practical solution of the Samoan problem, the Tripartite Treaty proved a failure. Bickering among the rival foreign factions continued until the islands were finally partitioned between Germany and the United States in 1899.[1]

Strange Interlude in Hawaii

By permitting Hawaiian sugar to enter the United States duty-free, the Hawaiian-American reciprocity treaty of 1875 [2] brought prosperity to the islands. Between 1877 and 1887 Hawaiian sugar production increased fivefold. On the American side, the port of San Francisco and the California sugar refineries both benefited greatly. In 1887, the reciprocity agreement was extended for seven more years, but not before the Senate, now more sensitive to the needs of the Navy, had exacted a new condition. The United States was granted the exclusive right to utilize Pearl Harbor as a coaling and repair station for its ships.

The more closely Hawaii was bound to the United States by these economic ties, the more alarmed the sugar planters became at any threat of change in the relationship. Although the Democratic-sponsored Mills Bill failed to pass Congress in 1888, its proposal to put sugar on the free list disturbed Hawaii. What advantage would the islands hold if all foreign sugar could enter the American market on equal terms? In 1889, the Hawaiian government proposed to Secretary of State Blaine a new treaty that would provide for complete free trade between the two countries, reciprocal extension of any bounties or special privileges granted to domestic producers, and an American guarantee of Hawaiian independence. But these proposals went too far to suit the more nationalistic elements among the Hawaiian natives, and the negotiations had to be dropped.

In 1890, the blow the Hawaiian planters had feared finally fell. The McKinley Tariff not only placed sugar on the free list, but, worse still from the Hawaiian point of view, granted a bounty of 2 cents a pound to domestic producers. Hawaiian sugar now entered the United States under a serious disadvantage in competing with the American-grown product. The price of sugar in Honolulu dropped from $100 a ton to $60, and the planters' properties depreciated in value an estimated 12 million dollars.

The Hawaiian government now revived its proposal for a free-trade treaty, but President Harrison refused to go along because he considered the project inconsistent with the Republican gospel of protection. With this door closed, some sugar planters viewed annexation by the United States as the only means to restore and extend Hawaiian prosperity.

The desirability of annexation was, however, a question on which the

[1] See chap. 20.
[2] See chap. 16.

islanders were sharply divided. The plantation economy had given Hawaii a peculiar social structure. The sugar properties and other key resources were owned by companies composed almost exclusively of nonnative stockholders. Americans held the largest share, but British and Germans were also heavy investors. To provide the necessary labor for the plantations, thousands of Chinese and Japanese workers had been brought into the islands under contract. Many of the wealthiest planters were reluctant to come under the American flag, since annexation would presumably extend to Hawaii the American prohibitions against immigration of contract laborers in general and Chinese workers in particular.

Also involved in the division of Hawaiian sentiment on the annexation question was the confused condition of Hawaiian politics. In 1887, the white business and missionary elements, disgusted with the corrupt and capricious rule of King Kalakaua, forced the so-called "bayonet constitution" upon the unwilling monarch. This document purported to establish a constitutional monarchy and parliamentary government; in reality, however, property qualifications and other safeguards gave the white minority the upper hand against the more numerous native and Oriental elements in the population.

Even after their victory in 1887, the whites felt they were in a precarious position. A native Hawaiian faction, secretly encouraged from the royal palace, agitated incessantly against the constitution. After Kalakaua died in 1891, his sister, Liliuokalani, became Queen and focal center of native resentment against white domination. Some kind of coup under which the Queen would abrogate the constitution and restore personal government was feared.

The Annexation Movement

A small group of businessmen, particularly suspicious of the Queen's intentions, formed a secret Annexation Club. The most active member was Lorrin A. Thurston, an American lawyer and investor long active in Hawaiian politics. In the spring of 1892, Thurston visited Washington, where he called upon Secretary Blaine and other influential political leaders to sound them out on the probable American reaction in case the Hawaiian government should ask for annexation. Finding an encouraging response, Thurston submitted a blueprint of the manner in which the Hawaiian annexationists hoped to achieve their goal. In brief, they planned to promote annexation sentiment among the general Hawaiian public, offer inducements to some native politicians to win their support, and gain the appointment of a proannexation cabinet that would push the necessary measures through the Hawaiian legislature. Thurston hoped the Queen could be induced "to retire peaceably upon a liberal pension." If she made trouble, it might be necessary to remove her forcibly.

It is uncertain whether either Blaine or John W. Foster, who succeeded him as Secretary of State in June, 1892, ever actually saw Thurston's bold program. The authorities at Washington followed the policy of listening sympathetically to the overtures of the Hawaiian annexationists, but avoiding any overt complicity with the faction plotting to remove Liliuokalani from her throne.

John L. Stevens, the United States Minister to Honolulu, was not so careful. From the time of his arrival in the islands in September, 1889, he filled his dispatches to Washington with alarming reports of political unrest in Hawaii, of the shortcomings of the monarchy, of the intrigue of foreign governments, and of the desirability of annexation by the United States. In November, 1892, he wrote:

> Destiny and the vast future interests of the United States in the Pacific clearly indicate who, at no distant day, must be responsible for the government of these islands.... Hawaii has reached the parting of the ways. She must now take the road that leads to Asia, or the other, which outlets her in America, gives her an American civilization and binds her to the care of destiny.

Not content with pointing out the path of destiny to his own government, Stevens did what he could to hasten Hawaii along the road. He fraternized openly with the Annexation Club and publicly criticized the monarch to whom he was accredited. The Minister's well-known sympathies encouraged the annexationists to continue with their intrigues and gave Liliuokalani good cause for alarm.

The Queen's desperation led her to take a false step that played directly into the hands of her enemies. Taking advantage of a split between white and native factions in the legislature and the resulting fall of the pro-annexationist ministry, Liliuokalani appointed a new cabinet more likely to acquiesce in her wishes. Then, on January 14, 1893, she attempted to proclaim a new constitution that would weaken the privileged position of the whites and greatly enhance her own power.

Her efforts were frustrated by the timidity of her own ministers. Fearful of serious trouble if they countersigned the new document, they sought counsel from Thurston and his friends as to what they should do. They were advised to refuse to sign—advice which they promptly followed. Consequently, when a large crowd of natives gathered before the royal palace to receive the expected constitution, Liliuokalani had to announce the postponement of the document.

This royal retreat did not save the throne. The Annexation Club realized the time was ripe to achieve its goal. The Committee of Safety, composed of thirteen club members, assumed direction of the developing revolution. A number of conservatives, not hitherto committed to annexation, were won over with the argument that the Queen's recent conduct demonstrated the need of governmental change. Among the converts was the highly respected Sanford B. Dole, associate justice of the Hawaiian Supreme Court.

During the next three days the revolutionary party pushed its preparations for establishing a provisional government. Liliuokalani offered numerous concessions, but her opponents were past compromise. The Committee of Safety appealed to Minister Stevens to have troops from the U.S.S. *Boston*, conveniently anchored in Honolulu harbor, landed to protect American lives and property. Stevens readily complied, and, on the afternoon of January 16, 1893, a force of some 160 sailors and marines with two light cannon marched through the streets of the city. They took up positions at strategic points, some at the legation and the consulate, others in a vacant building close to the Government Building and the royal palace.

Revolution in Hawaii

With all in readiness, the actual revolution proceeded like clockwork. On the afternoon of January 17, a member of the Committee of Safety mounted the steps of the Government Building and read a proclamation abrogating the monarchy and instituting a provisional government headed by Judge Dole. Minister Stevens immediately announced American recognition of the new regime. Although Liliuokalani was reluctant to surrender, her ministers advised her to do so to avoid bloodshed. Consequently she signed a declaration, which stated that she yielded

> to the superior force of the United States of America, whose minister plenipotentiary ... has caused the United States troops to be landed at Honolulu, and declared that he would support the ... Provisional Government.
>
> Now, to avoid any collision of armed forces and perhaps the loss of life, I do, under this protest, and impelled by said force, yield my authority until such time as the Government of the United States shall ... undo the action of its representative and reinstate me in the authority which I claim as the constitutional sovereign of the Hawaiian Islands.

In the excitement of the day one shot had been fired and one native policeman, loyal to the Queen, wounded. Except for this, the fall of the old regime had been bloodless. Other foreign diplomats quickly followed the lead of Stevens in recognizing the new government.

Cleveland Says No

The Dole government had from the beginning frankly asserted that its objective was to arrange, as quickly as possible, for annexation of Hawaii by the United States. Two days after the revolution, Thurston and four other commissioners embarked for Washington to negotiate an appropriate treaty.

They arrived in San Francisco simultaneously with the first news of the overthrow of the Hawaiian monarchy. The expansionist press was delighted with these developments. According to the *New York Tribune*, the popular verdict was "clear, unequivocal, and practically unanimous. Hawaii is welcome." The *Washington Post* warned that any hesitation would play into the hands of the intriguing British. On the other hand, certain newspapers had serious misgivings. The *New York Times* asserted:

> We should annex Hawaii, if at all, as we should buy a ham. Let us first determine whether we want it or have any use for it; then whether it is worth the price, and thirdly whether the pretended owners are the real owners and can deliver the goods. We have serious doubts on all these points.

The Harrison administration strongly supported Minister Stevens in most of the steps he had taken. Secretary of State Foster's only rebuke was in connection with the Minister's action of February 1, when he had announced that Hawaii was under United States protection and ordered the American flag raised over the Government Building. This step was approved by Foster in so far as it pledged American cooperation with the provisional government in maintaining order, but it was disavowed as an act implying that a formal United States protectorate had been established.

Secretary Foster promptly sounded out foreign governments on the Hawaiian situation. He encountered no opposition to the idea of American annexation—not even from Great Britain or Japan, from whom some hostility might have been anticipated. With the diplomatic situation thus prepared, the Hawaiian commissioners and the friendly Harrison administration found little difficulty in reaching an agreement. A treaty, signed February 14, 1893, provided for annexation of the islands as "an integral part of the territory of the United States" and the payment of an annuity of $20,000 a year to Liliuokalani for life.

The treaty was promptly submitted to the Senate, where it was approved by the Foreign Relations Committee. After this preliminary victory, however, the annexation bandwagon broke down. Republican hopes for sufficient Democratic support to ratify the treaty while Harrison was still in office proved empty. When Democratic senators looked to Cleveland for guidance, the President-elect let it be known that he wished the question postponed until after Inauguration Day.

On March 4, 1893, the second Cleveland administration took office in a mood of hostility toward the whole imperialistic trend in American foreign policy. Walter Q. Gresham of Indiana, the new Secretary of State, had been a prominent Republican and Cabinet officer under Arthur, but had broken with the party and supported the Democrats in the 1892 election. A long-time rival of Harrison in Indiana politics, he could be expected to regard with suspicion the actions of the outgoing administration.

Under the circumstances, it is not surprising that one of Cleveland's early acts was to withdraw the annexation treaty from the Senate and to appoint James H. Blount of Georgia, a former chairman of the House Foreign Relations Committee, as special commissioner to investigate the whole Hawaiian situation. Blount arrived in Honolulu on March 29 and immediately demonstrated that annexation was no longer a foregone conclusion. He ordered the American flag hauled down and the marines and sailors to return to their ship. Next, Blount heard testimony from all Hawaiian factions on the background of the revolution, the exact part played by Minister Stevens and the Navy in the Queen's overthrow, and the wishes of the population for the future.

Blount's long report, dated July 17, 1893, constituted a severe indictment. He concluded that the annexationists would not have acted as they did except for Stevens's promise to protect them. It was the landing of American troops that had emboldened the Committee of Safety to proclaim a new government and had intimidated the Queen into surrendering her authority. The Commissioner was convinced that any fair plebiscite would result in a five to one majority against annexation. He summed up the situation in these words:

> The undoubted sentiment of the people is for the Queen, against the Provisional Government, and against annexation. A majority of the whites, especially Americans, are for annexation.

If the United States refrained from annexing the islands, the commissioner predicted the unpopular provisional government would soon fall.

The Blount report, fortifying as it did the prior inclinations of President Cleveland and Secretary Gresham, killed any prospect for immediate annexation. So much was clear. But did the United States have a moral responsibility to undo the wrong done by its agents? Should it attempt to restore Liliuokalani to her throne? Such a course appealed to the chivalrous Gresham, who was shocked that a woman had been so shamefully treated. Attorney General Richard Olney, more hardheaded by temperament, conceded that ethical considerations demanded the Queen's restoration, but he warned that the United States also had responsibilities toward the Dole government, which had come into power under American protection. Any American use of force against the provisional government would be unjust, as would any action placing the revolutionists at the mercy of a restored and vengeful Queen.

Seeking a way out of this troublesome dilemma, President Cleveland sent a new Minister, Albert S. Willis, to Hawaii with instructions to convey to Liliuokalani the President's regret at the "flagrant wrong" done her and his request for a pledge of full amnesty to the revolutionists if she were restored to power. Once this assurance was given, Willis was to have the even more delicate task of convincing the Dole government to step aside peacefully.

The Cleveland program tripped over the first hurdle. Pressed by Minister Willis to indicate how she would treat her enemies, Liliuokalani was reported to have replied: "There are certain laws of my Government by which I shall abide. My decision would be, as the law directs, that such persons should be beheaded and their property confiscated to the Government." At the urging of Gresham, Willis then pressed the Queen for a more satisfactory reply and eventually obtained the required assurances. But the offer of amnesty did not tempt the provisional government; on December 23, Dole firmly rejected Willis's request that the monarchy be restored.

Even before Cleveland ran into this last barrier, he had confessed the failure of his policy. In a special message to Congress on December 18, 1893, the President reviewed the whole story. He strongly condemned "the notorious predilections" of Minister Stevens for annexation, the "lawless occupation of Honolulu under false pretexts by United States forces," and the premature recognition of the provisional government. He reported his own efforts to restore the Queen and the frustrations he had encountered. Finally, he commended the subject to the consideration of Congress and promised to cooperate in "any legislative plan which may be devised for the solution of the problem before us which is consistent with American honor, integrity, and morality."

Given Cleveland's premises, no satisfactory solution to the Hawaiian question was possible, whether by presidential or congressional action. Cleveland could only wash his hands of the whole business and await developments. These did not take the course Blount had predicted. Instead of falling, the Dole government steadily entrenched itself in power. In 1894, a constitutional convention, carefully manipulated by the dominant faction, drafted a new constitution, providing for a republican form of government with a president and a two-house legislature. Literacy and property qualifications were so drafted as to place control in the hands of the whites. The next year Dole decisively defeated an incipient native revolt. Liliuokalani and other suspected conspirators were sentenced to fines and prison terms.

Cleveland's whole course of action was bitterly condemned by the expansionists. Senator Shelby Cullom of Illinois said that Blount's hauling down of the flag in Hawaii was as infamous as the acts of rebels and traitors during the Civil War. The *Independent* declared that the effort to restore the Hawaiian Queen "is properly called a policy of infamy." Naturally, the criticism came mostly from Republican sources, but Democrats also showed some distress. The *New York World* thought Cleveland's concern for "right and justice" might apply in utopia, but was not applicable "to the affairs of nations in this hardheaded, workaday world."

The Venezuelan Boundary Dispute

Charges that Cleveland was indifferent to national interests found a new focus in the Venezuelan boundary dispute. The administration, it was alleged, was allowing England to extend her imperial holdings in South America under cover of a disputed boundary between British Guiana and Venezuela.

The frontier in question had been a matter of controversy for decades. Both Great Britain and Venezuela were the heirs to earlier regimes in the area: the English had taken British Guiana from the Dutch; the Venezuelans had won their independence from Spain. The boundary depended on the interpretation of ancient treaties and involved the historical problem of just where the Dutch and Spaniards had settled and exercised jurisdiction. In 1841, Sir Robert Schomburgk, employed by the British, had surveyed a line that the English regarded as a minimum frontier, although they claimed land to the west of this as well. The Venezuelans never recognized the Schomburgk line; they claimed on the contrary a vast area extending east to the Essequibo River. Little value was attached to the wilderness involved in these rival claims until after 1880, when gold mining began there. This new circumstance served to stiffen the attitude of both governments. Venezuelan diplomats sought the assistance of the United States, and the American State Department suggested submitting the whole matter to arbitration—a course of action Venezuela had already proposed. The British were against unlimited arbitration, although they offered other compromises to end the deadlock.

In Cleveland's annual message of December, 1894, he repeated the wish that the dispute might be arbitrated. The British government now indicated willingness to submit its claims to lands lying west of the Schomburgk line, but refused to permit arbitration of the whole dispute. The situation was becoming dangerous; there had been no diplomatic relations between Great Britain and Venezuela since 1887; extensive mining concessions were being granted in the disputed area; and Venezuelan police had been arresting British subjects near the Schomburgk line. Most serious of all, the controversy was becoming a subject of excited discussion by American politicians and editors.

Much of the sudden burst of talk and print about the dispute resulted from the propagandist activities of William L. Scruggs. After serving as Minister to Venezuela under Harrison, he had returned to the United States as a special agent of the Venezuelan government. In the fall of 1894, Scruggs had written a widely distributed pamphlet with the arresting title: *British Aggressions in Venezuela, or the Monroe Doctrine on Trial*. From his base in Washington, he supplied copious material to jingo journalists and influential legislators. He also took the Venezuelan case directly to President Cleveland and Secretary Gresham.

There was, of course, another side to the affair. England was not greatly at fault for failing to settle the boundary dispute. The Venezuelan government had been unstable, arrogant, and generally difficult to deal with. The full Venezuelan claim was regarded by well-informed experts as so unreasonable that the principle of unlimited arbitration could hardly be applied. Regardless of the merits of the case, many sober scholars doubted whether the issue came within the proper scope of the Monroe Doctrine, or whether there were real grounds for intervention by the United States.

Such misgivings, however, troubled few newspaper men. To the *New York Tribune* the case was "perfectly simple": Venezuela owned the land; Great Britain coveted it and was trying to grab it—by guile if she could, by force if she had to. The *New York Sun* asserted that unless the Cleveland administration were prepared to abjure the Monroe Doctrine, it must make a peremptory demand that the dispute be arbitrated. Should the demand be refused, the Venezuelans would have to fight for their rights and it would be the duty of American citizens to support them.

Criticism of the administration's foreign policy reached a crescendo in the spring of 1895, when the British coerced Nicaragua into settling a minor dispute by temporarily occupying the port of Corinto. Cleveland and Gresham were widely condemned for not protesting this action. "Are we going to stand idly by," asked the *Boston Journal*, "and permit the story of India and Egypt to be repeated on the American continent?" It was widely assumed that, having forced its will upon Nicaragua, England would not hesitate to use similar tactics with Venezuela.

Such was the situation when Secretary Gresham died in May, 1895. To fill the vacancy, the President promoted his Attorney General, Richard Olney. The new Secretary of State was an austere Boston lawyer; even within his own family he preserved a stern dignity, and in his conduct

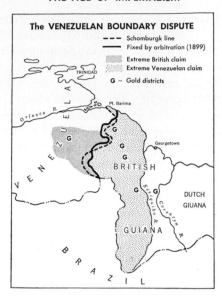

The VENEZUELAN BOUNDARY DISPUTE

of foreign affairs he was reserved in bearing and extremely tenacious on every point. That the hard-bitten Olney would deal with the Venezuelan matter very differently from the gentle Gresham was to be expected.

The Olney Doctrine

During the next few weeks a long dispatch on the Venezuelan affair was prepared with the enthusiastic approval of the President. Olney's note of July 20, 1895, has become famous both for its brusque phrasing and for the extensive character of the interests claimed for the United States. It consisted of two parts: the first, a review of the Venezuelan dispute itself; the second, a discussion of the Monroe Doctrine designed to prove that, since any attempt of Great Britain to extend its territory in South America under cover of a boundary dispute threatened American interests, the United States had a right to ask that such a question be arbitrated. Olney's discussion of the Monroe Doctrine was couched in language so blunt it could hardly fail to offend the English. At one point he stated that "distance and three thousand miles of intervening ocean make any permanent political union between an European and American state unnatural and inexpedient." A little later he asserted: "Today the United States is practically sovereign on this continent, and its fiat is law upon the subjects to which it confines its interposition." The eagle was screaming from the peace-loving Cleveland's own nest.

The dispatch to England was sent with the utmost secrecy. Even in the State Department only a few trusted subordinates knew what was happening. Cleveland and Olney hoped to press their case vigorously enough to achieve diplomatic victory by the time Congress convened in December. The political importance of this became more and more obvious as the expansionist attacks upon the administration grew bolder. Senator Lodge championed the cause of Venezuela in a widely read magazine article and confided to a friend that at the next session of Congress he intended to reassert the Monroe Doctrine in a way to "make some of the brethren sit up and take notice." Republican Senator William E. Chandler of New Hampshire wrote an editorial for a local paper entitled: "Our Coming War with England—a Prediction." The mail brought to the President and the Secretary of State beseeching letters from local Democratic politicians, fearful lest the Republicans convince the country that they were the only patriotic party.

Much to Cleveland's annoyance, the British reply had not been received when Congress met. All the anticipated trouble materialized as Senators Lodge and Cullom introduced resolutions affirming the Monroe Doctrine, while other senators indulged in miscellaneous denunciations of British imperialism and the spinelessness of the administration. Most alarming of all was the attempt of Representative Leonidas Livingston of Georgia to have Congress authorize a special committee to examine the boundary dispute and recommend a course of action. Unless Cleveland acted decisively, he was in danger of losing the initiative to a rebellious legislature.

With such a possibility to worry about, the President was far from happy with the British replies that finally arrived. In one note Lord Salisbury, the Prime Minister and Foreign Secretary, flatly denied that the Monroe Doctrine had any standing in international law or that the United States had any basis for intervention in the Anglo-Venezuelan dispute. In a second dispatch, Salisbury reviewed the boundary controversy and rejected all Venezuelan claims east of the Schomburgk line. Cleveland forthwith prepared a stern special message to Congress based on a draft by Olney.

This message was read on December 17, 1895, amid scenes of wild enthusiasm. The boundary differences were discussed in terms that left no doubt of Cleveland's belief that Venezuela was being badly used, and the principle was set forth that any extension of British territory in violation of Venezuela's rights would be contrary to the Monroe Doctrine. Since Great Britain refused to arbitrate the whole issue, Cleveland sought congressional authorization to appoint a commission to decide the true divisional line. When this was done, it would be the duty of the United States to resist British seizure of any territory belonging rightfully to Venezuela.

What had prompted the ordinarily pacific Cleveland to adopt so belligerent a policy? English opinion was quick to conclude that it was a cheap political trick to obtain a third term for himself, but this was hardly just. The President's stern words reflected his conviction that important American interests were involved in this distant boundary dispute. There was a quickening spirit of nationalism throughout the country, and Cleveland could not entirely escape its influence.

The War Scare

The administration's course was one to which public opinion reacted strongly. During the next two weeks praise was lavished and denunciation heaped upon Cleveland and Olney in a flood of letters, editorials, interviews, speeches, and public meetings. The politicians supported the President almost unanimously. Senator Lodge, hitherto one of Cleveland's most bitter critics, was enthusiastic; Senator John Sherman of Ohio endorsed every word. The silver advocates hoped America would now escape the domination of the British money power. "I am for war and free silver," asserted Senator Pugh of Alabama, while Stewart of Nevada said: "War is a good thing even if we get licked. If it comes to serious trouble between the two countries we'll have an opportunity to get even with Great Britain for its international policy."

The great bulk of the press made the President's stand its own and frequently outdid him in aggressiveness. The possibility of war was exciting. Enterprising reporters sought interviews with professional and amateur military experts. General Lew Wallace, the author of *Ben Hur*, predicted the probable course of an Anglo-American war. "It would go hard with us at first," he admitted, "but we would not be idle. Before a year there would be no British commerce . . . and at the end, as I see it, we would own everything on this side of the globe from the Gulf of Mexico to the North Pole." Theodore Roosevelt was strongly moved. "I do hope there will not be any back down among our people," he wrote to Lodge. "Let the fight come if it must; I don't care whether our sea coast cities are bombarded or not; we would take Canada."

Congress provided impressive evidence that Cleveland had the support of the nation. The day after the delivery of the special message, the House unanimously authorized the President to appoint the commission he had requested, and three days later the Senate likewise approved.[3] Politically speaking, Cleveland's policy had no opposition.

The danger of war was also increased by the tone of the English press. The London *Times* haughtily insisted that "the concessions that this country is imperiously summoned to make are such as no self-respecting

[3] Cleveland appointed five distinguished jurists and educators to the commission. They conducted a painstaking investigation, but were relieved of the necessity of reporting because the dispute was settled through other channels.

nation, and, least of all, one ruling an empire that has roots in every quarter of the globe, could possibly submit to." The *Pall Mall Gazette* professed not to be angry; it was partly astonished, partly amused, and also somewhat embarrassed as when someone else has committed a breach of decorum in public. "We know it is not our fault, yet we feel awkward and are disposed to blush."

In both countries there were a few independent souls brave enough to rebuke the jingoes. Edwin L. Godkin, editor of both the *New York Evening Post* and the *Nation*, strongly criticized Cleveland's action, as did also Joseph Pulitzer, the influential publisher of the *New York World*. Pulitzer's campaign to preserve peace came to a climax just before Christmas. In answer to cablegrams asking for expressions of opinion on the crisis, an impressive list of English statesmen and churchmen responded with declarations of friendship for the United States and expressions of horror at the very thought of war. The greatest sensation was reserved for Christmas Day, when most of the *World's* front page was filled with facsimiles of cablegrams sent by the Prince of Wales and the Duke of York. Cleveland's policy was also strongly condemned by many Eastern college professors, clergymen, and business leaders. Wall Street's nervousness was reflected by a break in the stock market.

Although war talk had largely subsided by the end of the year, the situation was still potentially dangerous. Much more was at stake than the possession of a stretch of South American wilderness. Rightly or wrongly, American statesmen regarded the affair as a test of British intentions in the vital Caribbean zone. Cleveland had taken a stand from which he was not likely to be moved, nor was there the least possibility that Congress would repudiate his policy. The indispensable prelude to restored Anglo-American amity would have to be a change of heart by Britain.

For a time Englishmen did not realize this. They thought Cleveland had taken an unreasonable position from which he would be compelled to retreat. The British public had been left dangerously in the dark as to the seriousness with which Americans regarded the Venezuelan issue. The London *Chronicle* took the lead in rectifying this situation by sending a special correspondent to the United States to get the American point of view. Later, another English paper gave an entertaining summary of this journalistic adventure: [4]

> It was the period when the Monroe Doctrine was running rampant along the shores of Columbia and the American eagle was sitting on the Statue of Liberty at the entrance of New York Harbor shrieking for the blood of English tyrants. Into the haunt of these ravenous beasts our contemporary dispatched a special correspondent with instructions to make his way into the savage interior of the United States, and, if

[4] Reprinted in the *Chicago Tribune*, Nov. 15, 1896.

possible, reach the fabled city of Washington. The gallant envoy accomplished the task, and not only reached the goal of his enterprise,
but succeeded in bringing away an interview with the wild Senators and
valuable specimens of the Anglophobus Americanus.

At first, the inclination of Lord Salisbury and his colleagues was to
stand firm. Tory displeasure with America, however, was soon diluted
by concern over imperial interests in other quarters. Two weeks after the
Cleveland bombshell, the British world was startled by news of the
Jameson raid. One of the close associates of Cecil Rhodes had led an army
of English freebooters into the Transvaal Republic in South Africa. The
raid failed ludicrously, and British opinion would have condemned the
whole incident had not the German Emperor interfered by cabling to
President Kruger a congratulatory message couched in terms regarded
as deliberating insulting to the British. It was significant that whereas
Cleveland's unkind words had provoked little more English reaction than
hurt surprise, those of William II were greeted with loud demonstrations
of John Bull wrath.

Soon after the news of the Kruger telegram, Joseph Chamberlain, the
Colonial Secretary, wrote to Lord Salisbury: "I think that what is called
an 'Act of Vigour' is required to soothe the wounded vanity of the nation. It does not much matter which of our numerous foes we defy, but
we ought to defy someone." Specifically, he recommended defying Germany and the Boers, while conciliating America. By the middle of January, 1896, Salisbury and Olney had begun to exchange unofficially ideas
upon how the controversy might be settled.

The Tory ministers now made valiant efforts to appease American public opinion. In public speeches, Lord Salisbury and his colleagues denied
any intention to violate the Monroe Doctrine. Commenting on Venezuela's position on the Caribbean Sea, the Prime Minister conceded that "it
was no more unnatural that the United States should take an interest in
it than we should feel an interest in Holland and Belgium." These were
soft words that turned away wrath. The *New York Tribune* rejoiced that
the British government had recognized the legitimate interests of the
United States "in the most direct and unmistakable manner."

Even after this clearing of the storm clouds, several months of higgling
were required to reach a settlement. In November, 1896, Olney and Lord
Salisbury finally arrived at a compromise that combined the principle of
unlimited arbitration demanded by the United States with face-saving
conditions to satisfy England. Three months more were needed to draft
an Anglo-Venezuelan treaty and to obtain Venezuelan assent to the arrangement. The document, signed on February 2, 1897, provided that the
parties submit the entire boundary dispute to arbitration, but that the
arbiters should recognize fifty years of occupation as giving title.

The settlement cost England very little in territory. Although the boundary established by the arbitral tribunal did not follow the original Schomburgk line, it was almost as favorable from the English point of view. But the final establishment of the boundary was, after all, not the most important matter. English newspapers at once pointed out the more significant aspects of the affair. The London *Times* observed that the settlement amounted to recognition of a general protectorate by the United States over Latin America, yet it made no complaint. The *St. James Gazette* said:

> Lord Salisbury's great admission of the principle that the United States have the right to intervene in frontier disputes of the American powers and to compel the disputants to arbitrate altogether transcends in importance the question of the Guiana boundary. It is a formal recognition of the influence of the United States on the American continent, and gives the President a position in the New World which the Medieval Popes and Emperors tried vainly to claim in Europe.

Lord Salisbury had virtually surrendered to Cleveland and Olney. Yet, paradoxically, it was one of the most profitable decisions ever made by a British statesman. Americans had now been given impressive evidence that England valued good relations with the United States far above any other interest in the Western Hemisphere. The essential condition for good understanding between England and the United States—destined to be so important in the twentieth century—had been laid. And, ironically, the new imperialism had gained one of its most impressive victories through the diplomacy of the anti-imperialist, Grover Cleveland.

20

THE UNITED STATES EMERGES AS A
WORLD POWER

The new imperialism, partially held in leash by the stubborn Cleveland, broke its bonds after the more pliant McKinley became President. Jingoism found an exciting focus in the bitter struggle between Spain and her rebellious Cuban colony. The explosive pressure, built up by politicians, publicists, and newspapermen, finally burst through all barriers. Although petty as a military contest, the Spanish-American War had widespread consequences. Before the fateful year 1898 was over, Puerto Rico, the Philippines, and Guam had all been brought under the American flag as a result of conquest from Spain, and both Hawaii and Wake had been annexed in large part as a result of the imperialism engendered by the war. The following year Tutuila in the Samoan group was added to the American empire. More important than the territorial acquisitions themselves were the new responsibilities thrust upon a nation with colonial possessions thus spread across the globe.

Insurrection in Cuba

After the protracted Cuban revolt known as the Ten Years' War finally came to an end in 1878, economic and social changes of a fundamental character took place on the island. American and European capitalists invested heavily in the sugar industry, introducing new methods that gradually upset the traditional pattern established by the older planters. The gradual emancipation of the slaves, completed in 1886, and the transition to a free labor system employing both white and Negro workers, added to the colony's economic problems.

When the rebels agreed to lay down their arms in 1878, the Spanish government made vague promises of political reform. Some decentralization of authority and greater participation of the islanders in local government did in fact follow, but Cuban liberals complained that the colonial administration was still arbitrary and corrupt. A standard grievance was that the best opportunities, both political and commercial, were reserved for those of Spanish birth. A majority of the islanders would have been content with self-government under the Spanish flag, but a more radical faction, encouraged by Cuban firebrands living in the United States, aspired to full independence.

Economic conditions played into the hands of the revolutionists. The American Panic of 1893 was part of a much wider economic depression that demoralized the world market for sugar, tobacco, and other Cuban exports. Another serious blow came in 1894 when the Wilson-Gorman Tariff, passed by a Democratic Congress, removed sugar from the free list, where it had been placed by the Republican McKinley Tariff of 1890. American legislators, playing politics with the tariff issue, were unsettling the economy of Cuba, just as they had that of Hawaii.

As falling prices and unemployment scourged the island, mounting unrest led to a new insurrection in February, 1895. The first rebel leader was José Martí, an *émigré* who for several years had been actively organizing the independence movement in the United States. He was killed soon after his return to Cuba, but the leadership passed into the willing hands of Máximo Gómez. A Dominican by birth, Gómez was a tough old guerrilla fighter who had commanded the rebels during the Ten Years' War. Believing that the earlier revolt had failed because it was confined to the sparsely settled eastern part of the island, Gómez was now determined to carry the struggle into the heavily populated western part. He did not have sufficient manpower to put a disciplined, uniformed army into the field, but he could send out small companies of men, many of them mounted, to attack isolated Spanish garrisons and troops on the march.

Gómez depended still more on the strategy of destruction. By burning cane fields, ranch houses, and other properties, he aimed to paralyze the economic life of the island. This, he believed, would serve the rebel cause in several ways. The government would be deprived of tax revenues, and the unemployed laborers would be forced into the ranks of the insurrectionists. Since American-owned property would go up in flames along with the rest, the United States would become involved in claims disputes and would eventually intervene.

As was inevitable, rebel terrorism provoked the Spaniards into increasingly harsh countermeasures. When General Martínez Campos, the aged Captain General who had crushed the Ten Years' revolt, discovered his policy of concession and moderation would not work, he resigned his post and recommended as his successor General Don Valeriano Weyler y Nicolau. Arriving in Cuba in February, 1896, General Weyler initiated a vigorous policy that soon earned him the title of "The Butcher" in the reports of unfriendly American newspapermen. Especially denounced was his "reconcentration" policy, under which the noncombatant population was ordered into concentration camps within the Spanish lines. All persons found in the cleared districts were to be considered as rebels liable to summary punishment. Since the Spaniards were confronted by an enemy likely to fight by night and to conceal itself among the civilian populace by day, the reconcentration order was not unreasonable, but it did add to the economic chaos already created by rebel devastation. The crowded concentration camps were quickly afflicted with malnutrition and disease, with resulting high mortality among the civilian occupants.

The situation in Cuba was bad enough in sober fact, but its horrors were grossly exaggerated in the columns of American newspapers. Unhappily, the conflict in Cuba coincided with one of the most bitter rivalries in the history of American journalism: William Randolph Hearst's *New York Journal* was attempting to capture circulation from Joseph Pulitzer's well-established *New York World*. Eager for sensational headlines, the two papers specialized in Cuban atrocity stories. In February, 1897, for example, the *Journal* titillated its readers with a half-page drawing by the famous Frederic Remington, which depicted a nude woman surrounded by Spanish police officers under the provocative caption "Spaniards Search Women on American Ships." The accompanying story was written by Richard Harding Davis, the most famous American reporter of the day. In this case, it was subsequently revealed that the young lady in question had actually been searched in the privacy of her cabin by a police matron; but the truth rarely caught up with the fiction in these stories. Consequently, the American public gained a distorted picture of the Cuban struggle in which skirmishes were magnified into battles and the insurgents won a series of imaginary victories. The Spaniards were always depicted as arbitrary and cruel, while a veil was discreetly drawn over the terroristic activities of the rebels.

Although not all newspapers exploited the situation as shamelessly as did the *Journal* and the *World*, even the more sober papers conveyed a disquieting picture. In any struggle for independence, American sympathies were almost always strongly drawn to the side fighting for freedom. This natural interest was intensified by the fact that the struggle was taking place on a nearby island, strategically located in relation to the Caribbean Sea and to any future isthmian canal. Add to this, the fact that during 1895 and 1896 the politicians were eagerly seeking whatever issues might serve them in the approaching presidential campaign, and it becomes easy to understand why Cuba became a subject of constant agitation.

Cleveland and the Cuban Problem

For two years the Cuban problem was one more burden piled upon the already heavily laden shoulders of Grover Cleveland. The President's policy of maintaining American neutrality and avoiding intervention was characteristically cautious, but these ideals were more easily pronounced than made effective. Complications arose out of the large Cuban-born population living in the United States, especially in New York City, New Orleans, and Florida. The New York junta, organized by Martí, maintained close contacts with all these groups. Once the insurrection began, these Cuban-Americans supplied propaganda to cooperative journalists and forwarded money, arms, and volunteers to the rebels. The Cleveland administration was able to halt almost half of the 71 shipments known to have been attempted, while the English and Spaniards intercepted a few more; but the 27 shipments that did get through were enough to provoke serious complaint from the Spanish authorities.

Before the insurrection was two weeks old, Spanish nervousness resulted in an unhappy incident. The American mail steamer, *Alliança*, sailing between Colón and New York, was fired upon by a Spanish gunboat six miles off the eastern coast of Cuba. Although the ship was not hit, senatorial fireworks began at once. Senator John T. Morgan of Alabama, a leading Democratic expansionist, favored sending an American fleet to Havana, frankly disclosing his feeling that Cuba should become an American colony; Senator Shelby Cullom of Illinois, his Republican colleague, believed it was time "that some one woke up and realized the necessity of annexing some property." The Spanish government made a somewhat belated apology for the *Alliança* incident and promised the offense would not be repeated.

More serious was a growing list of grievances arising out of losses or injuries to American citizens. Under international law, the Spanish government was responsible for destruction of property wrought both by its own troops and the insurgents. A number of persons arrested by the Spanish authorities claimed American citizenship despite their Spanish-sounding names. Some of these had really been born or legally naturalized in the United States; others, however, possessed fraudulent papers. The Cleveland administration found it difficult to decide who was and who was not entitled to American protection.

The President's troubles were increased by congressional interference. In April, 1896, after a debate characterized by vigorous denunciations of Spanish barbarism, both houses overwhelmingly passed a set of resolutions declaring that a state of war existed in Cuba, that the insurgents were entitled to belligerent rights, and that the United States should maintain a strict neutrality, but at the same time use its good offices to obtain Spanish recognition of Cuban independence. These resolutions were not binding upon the President and did not influence him to change his policy.

Yet quite apart from this congressional action, the administration had decided to try to mediate between Spain and the Cuban rebels. In a note of April 4, 1896, to Enrique Dupuy de Lôme, the Spanish Minister to the United States, Secretary of State Olney described the concern felt by the American people over the Cuban situation. He went on to warn: "That the United States cannot contemplate with complacency another ten years of Cuban insurrection, with all its injurious and distressing incidents, may certainly be taken for granted." The object of his note, however, was "not to discuss intervention, nor to propose intervention, nor to pave the way for intervention." Its purpose was exactly the reverse: "to suggest whether a solution of present troubles cannot be found which will prevent all thought of intervention by rendering it unnecessary." To secure the immediate pacification of Cuba, the United States wished to cooperate with Spain on a plan that, "leaving Spain her rights of sovereignty, shall yet secure to the people of the island all such rights and powers of local self-government as they can reasonably ask." It was up to Spain to decide what reforms she could offer, but if they were such that the United States could support, the American government would exert its influence to have them accepted by the insurgents.

It would have spared Spain much future humiliation had she accepted Cleveland's friendly offer. Some responsible Spanish officials urged that this be done, but in the end other counsels prevailed. The Spanish reply called attention to vague reforms already promised, but proudly rejected American mediation. Any such interference would jeopardize Spain's future authority, detract from her national dignity, and impair her independence. "In brief," De Lôme wrote, "there is no effectual way to pacify Cuba unless it begins with the actual submission of the armed rebels to the mother country." The Spanish Minister pointed out what was probably true—that the insurgents themselves would spurn the autonomy which Cleveland was urging the mother country to offer.

The Republican party platform of June, 1896, asserted: "We watch with deep and abiding interest the heroic battles of the Cuban patriots against cruelty and oppression. . . . We believe that the government of the United States should actively use its influence and good offices to restore peace and give independence to the islands." The Democrats were more cautious, confining themselves to an expression of sympathy for the people of Cuba "in their heroic struggle for liberty and independence." Actually, however, the presidential campaign involved the foreign policy issue much less than had been expected. The nomination of Bryan transformed the contest into a bitter struggle between crusading free silver advocates and defenders of the gold standard.

After the Republican victory, the Cuban question again gained prominence. In his last annual message, President Cleveland once more urged the importance of American neutrality, while expressing the opinion that a Spanish grant of genuine autonomy might pacify the island. But he issued a significant warning:

> It should be added that it can not be reasonably assumed that the hitherto expectant attitude of the United States will be indefinitely maintained. . . .
>
> When the inability of Spain to deal successfully with the insurrection has become manifest, and it is demonstrated that her sovereignty is extinct in Cuba for all purposes of its rightful existence, and when a hopeless struggle for its reestablishment has degenerated into a strife which means nothing more than the useless sacrifice of human life and the utter destruction of the very subject-matter of the conflict, a situation will be presented in which our obligations to the sovereignty of Spain will be superseded by higher obligations, which we can hardly hesitate to recognize and discharge. . . .

The Republican expansionists in Congress made a new attempt to force the administration into action. Awake to the political danger of involving the country in war after the party came to power, the Republican strategists hoped to push the Cuban situation to a showdown while Cleveland was still in the White House. Senator Don Cameron of Pennsylvania introduced a resolution recognizing the independence of the Cuban republic. When it appeared this hostile gesture toward Spain might actually pass, Secretary Olney squelched it with a strong public statement which pointed out that congressional recognition of Cuban independence would not bind the executive and would only serve to "inflame popular passions, both in this country and elsewhere," thereby imperiling Americans living or traveling abroad.

McKinley Attempts Diplomacy

Despite Republican criticism of Cleveland's Cuban policy, McKinley's inauguration on March 4, 1897, brought no immediate changes. The new President's strong wish was to avoid war and to work for a revival of domestic prosperity. In this cautious program he had the strong support of Mark Hanna, his millionaire friend and adviser, and of other conservative businessmen.

In order to make a Senate seat for Hanna, McKinley had induced

Senator John Sherman of Ohio to accept appointment as Secretary of State. Since Sherman had long been a distinguished legislator and party leader, he might have been expected to perform brilliantly in this new post. Unfortunately, however, the seventy-three-year-old appointee was past his prime. Failing memory and other infirmities made Sherman unequal to his heavy duties. The Assistant Secretary of State, upon whom much responsibility consequently fell, was Judge William R. Day, a lawyer from Canton, Ohio, the President's home town. Day was conscientious but inexperienced. As a result of this situation, McKinley had to feel his way through the Cuban imbroglio without the help he might have received from a strong State Department.

At first the prospects for a peaceful outcome appeared promising. Just before McKinley took office, the Spaniards announced a program of limited reform. On the American side, a clarification of the neutrality laws by the Supreme Court had been followed by more effective steps to combat filibustering. Despite these favorable developments, Weyler's reconcentration policy continued to shock American public opinion. Terrible reports of starvation and death appealed to the humanitarian impulses of the people. Although the destructive activities of the rebels were equally responsible for these sufferings, it was the Spaniards who were blamed.

Like Cleveland, McKinley knew the best hope for avoiding eventual American involvement lay in convincing the Spanish government that it must alter its policies. In July, 1897, a new minister, General Stewart L. Woodford, was sent to Spain with instructions to inquire "whether the time has not arrived when Spain, of her own volition ... will put a stop to this destructive war and make proposals of settlement honorable to herself and just to her Cuban colony and to mankind." The United States stood ready to tender its good offices.

Soon after Woodford's arrival in Madrid, a turnover in the Spanish government appeared greatly to improve the chances for his mission's success. In August Premier Antonio Canovas had been assassinated by an Italian anarchist, and a month later the Conservative cabinet, which had attempted to carry on after his death, resigned. This brought to power a Liberal ministry headed by Praxedes Sagasta. Since Sagasta had been a bitter critic of the Conservatives' Cuban policy, a genuine new departure might now be expected. General Weyler was promptly recalled, and General Ramón Blanco became Captain General of Cuba.

On October 23, 1897, the Sagasta government replied to McKinley's offer of mediation. Foreign Minister Pío Gullón declared that Spain was preparing to grant autonomy to Cuba in all matters except foreign affairs, defense, and the administration of justice. The good offices of the United States were appreciated, but were not needed at this time. The American government could best help the Spaniards to pacify the island by stricter enforcement of its neutrality laws to suppress filibustering.

During November and December, the Spanish government started carrying out its new policy. Although General Blanco continued military operations against the insurgents, he modified some of the harsher features of the reconcentration policy. On November 25, the royal decrees granting autonomy were issued, and Blanco began to carry them out at Havana.

President McKinley showed cautious optimism in his annual message to Congress in December. He repeated the familiar indictment of earlier Spanish misgovernment in Cuba and condemned the harshness of the Weyler regime, but he praised the "hopeful change" that had apparently taken place in the Spanish government. "I shall not impugn its sincerity," the President declared, "nor should impatience be suffered to embarrass it in the task it has undertaken."

The need for patience was indeed great if the policy of autonomy were to have any chance to succeed. In Cuba itself opinion was dangerously divided. Although a large faction of moderates was ready to cooperate, the whole idea of autonomy was hateful to extremists of both the right and the left. The so-called "Peninsula Spaniards," who had prospered under the old regime, scorned the new reforms as an evidence of weakness and a threat to their privileges. Antiautonomy sentiment in Havana was expressed in hostile demonstrations, which were promptly reported to Washington by Fitzhugh Lee, the American consul general. Lee was convinced that autonomy would not work; it would only lead to disorders jeopardizing American lives and property. He warned that it might become necessary to send a warship to Havana to protect United States citizens.

Even more hostile to autonomy were the insurgents, who would be satisfied with nothing less than full independence. The Cuban junta in the United States provided a steady flow of antiautonomy propaganda, which ridiculed the Spanish concessions as meaningless. Not only were the most important areas of government reserved to the mother country, but the captain general was still to be appointed from Spain and no measures of the Cuban legislature were to become law without his approval. Spanish trade and manufactures were to be protected by preferential duties. Behind this controversy lay the simple fact that the word "autonomy" meant different things to different people. From the Spanish point of view, the concession of local self-government was generous; from the American point of view, genuine autonomy would have given Cuba quasi-independence like that enjoyed by Canada under the British crown.

The De Lôme Letter

As the critical year 1898 began, both McKinley and Sagasta had high hopes for peace. According to the Spaniards, time was what was most needed—time for the proposed Cuban legislature to convene and complete the organization of the new government and time for Blanco to suppress the guerrillas and restore order to the island. From McKinley's point of view, time was very short. He had on his hands a restless Congress, mistrustful of Spanish good faith and eager to force a stronger policy upon the executive.

Unfortunately for the moderates, two events played straight into the hand of the interventionists. The first of these episodes involved De Lôme, the Spanish Minister in Washington. This diplomat was hated by the Cuban junta for his success in dealing with the Cleveland and McKinley administrations and in countering the activities of the revolutionary party. In December, 1897, a Cuban spy stole from the Havana post office a private letter from De Lôme to a friend in Cuba. This epistle made its way into the hands of the New York junta, which turned it over to Hearst's eager New York Journal.

On February 9, 1898, a facsimile of the De Lôme letter was published in the Journal, together with a rough translation of the diplomat's very undiplomatic language. President McKinley was described as "weak and a bidder for the admiration of the crowd, besides being a common politician who tries to leave a door open behind himself while keeping on good terms with the jingoes of his party." In addition to its slurs upon the President, the letter referred in somewhat cynical terms to the autonomy experiment and suggested that it would be very advantageous to Spain to take up, "even if only for effect," the question of commercial relations so that some prominent man might be sent to the United States whom De Lôme could "make use of ... here to carry on a propaganda among the Senators."

On the surface, the De Lôme blunder was soon patched up. The Spanish Minister made no effort to deny his authorship of the letter, and the State Department at once asked for his recall. The Spanish government replied it had already accepted the Minister's resignation [1] and appointed a chargé to relieve him. Although Gullón expressed regret for De Lôme's indiscretion, the widely publicized letter had done damage not easily

[1] De Lôme, forewarned that the letter was going to be published, offered his resignation to his home government on February 8. He did not remember exactly what he had written, but he was sure that the disclosure would end his usefulness in the United States.

repaired. It supported the suspicion of many Americans that Spain was cynical and insincere in its new policy.

The Loss of the Maine

Less than a week after the publication of the De Lôme letter, Spanish-American relations suffered a much more serious blow. On January 25, 1898, the United States battleship *Maine* had steamed into Havana harbor. Behind her arrival lay a somewhat confused story. On the basis of Consul General Lee's warnings that anti-American demonstrations might break out, the *Maine* had been anchored for several weeks at Key West, Florida, ready to move to Havana on short notice. Even though Lee's subsequent reports were less alarming, the McKinley administration decided to send the *Maine* anyway as evidence of a new policy of resuming "friendly naval visits at Cuban ports." Lee, fearful lest the "friendly" character of this visitation might not be apparent to the Spaniards, advised postponement—but too late.

The Spanish government accepted the American assurance that the *Maine's* mission was friendly and promised to reciprocate by sending one of its warships to visit New York. Although some elements in Havana did not conceal their resentment, the local Spanish officials were punctilious in extending every courtesy to their self-invited guests. After the *Maine* had been at Havana for ten days, Washington cabled Lee about the advisability of moving the ship out to sea to protect her crew from disease. The nervous consul general believed it would be unwise to do so until another ship were sent to replace her.

Thus it was that the *Maine* was peacefully riding at anchor on the night of February 15, 1898, when she was suddenly destroyed by an explosion. Sinking rapidly, the battleship carried to the bottom of Havana harbor most of her sleeping crew. Out of a complement of 353 officers and men, 266 lost their lives. The city of Havana exhibited a grief that appeared wholly sincere. Spanish boats hurried to the scene to help rescue the survivors; the wounded men were given the best of care; and the bodies of the dead were recovered and reverently buried after an elaborate funeral ceremony in the Havana cathedral.

The real cause of the destruction of the *Maine* constitutes one of the mysteries of history. The Spaniards believed the explosion was internal, caused by an accidental igniting of the ship's magazine. After a month of study and deliberation, a United States naval court of inquiry came to a contrary conclusion; the sinking, it reported, was caused by "a heavy external explosion as by a mine, which drove the bowplates inward" and was followed by the explosion of the forward magazine. This finding was reaffirmed in 1911 when the hulk was raised, although some experts remained unconvinced. In any case, the most important question still remained unanswered. Was the disaster purely accidental, or had some individual or group been guilty? Since the incident might so easily lead to war, it was difficult to believe that any important Spanish official was involved; but might not some hot-headed minor officer have found outlet for his anti-Americanism in this terrible way? Or, on the other hand, might it not have been the work of some Cuban rebel, seeking to involve Spain in war with the United States? The answers to these questions will, in all probability, never be known.

President McKinley, although shocked by the *Maine* disaster, still tried to prevent rash action. As a visiting senator remembered it, the President said:

> I don't propose to be swept off my feet by the catastrophe. My duty is plain. We must learn the truth and endeavor, if possible, to fix the responsibility. The country can afford to withhold its judgment and not strike an avenging blow until the truth is known.

The Jingoists Gain Control

It was not to be expected that the jingo press would follow the President's example. *New York Journal* headlines shouted: THE WAR SHIP MAINE WAS SPLIT IN TWO BY AN ENEMY'S SECRET INFERNAL MACHINE. Drawings were published to show just how the diabolical Spaniards must have placed a torpedo under the ship and detonated it from the shore. Excited citizens organized volunteer regiments for the expected conflict. Even were Spanish complicity never proved, many Americans argued that the explosion had demonstrated Spain's inability to protect foreign lives and property in Cuba. Did the United States not therefore have an obligation to intervene on behalf of the civilized world?

Even while the naval court of inquiry was still working on its assignment, official Washington was showing more and more of the war spirit. With McKinley's approval, Congress rushed through without a dissenting vote a 50-million-dollar appropriation for national defense. On March 17, Senator Redfield Proctor of Vermont related in the upper house what he had seen on a recent trip to Cuba. Describing the plight of victims of the reconcentration policy, he declared:

> Torn from their homes, with foul earth, foul air, foul water and foul food or none, what wonder that one half have died and that one quarter of the living are so diseased that they cannot be saved? ... To me, the strongest appeal is not the barbarity practiced by Weyler nor the loss of the *Maine* ... but the spectacle of a million and a half people, the

entire native population of Cuba, struggling for freedom and deliverance from the worst misgovernment of which I ever had knowledge.

Proctor's somber words had an immense effect upon the country because he had the reputation of being a conservative legislator, untouched by blatant jingoism.

The pressures now building up around President McKinley would have been difficult for any man to withstand. Among other things, he had to worry about the political consequences that might follow longer delay. The Free-silver Democrats and the Populists were now embracing the cause of suffering Cuba with alarming ardor, and congressional elections were coming up in November. The harrassed President still hoped to avoid war, but he knew this could only be done if he could get the Spaniards out of Cuba.

Desperate Diplomacy

McKinley was not the only statesman who felt his freedom of action constrained by public opinion. On February 26, 1898, General Woodford reported that the Sagasta government believed Cuban autonomy was the utmost concession that could be made without provoking the Spanish people themselves to revolution. "They want peace," explained the Minister, "if they can keep peace and save the dynasty. They prefer the chances of war, with the certain loss of Cuba, to the overthrow of the dynasty."

General Woodford believed American purchase of Cuba would be the only way to preserve peace. This door, however, was slammed shut from both directions. Rather than sell the island, Woodford was informed, "the Queen would prefer to abdicate her regency and return to her Austrian home." And from the State Department came the blunt statement: "We do not want Cuba."

As usual, Spain was pleading for time. She would place the problem of working out a satisfactory settlement in the hands of the Cuban congress, which was to convene on May 4. Meantime, she would grant an armistice if the United States would undertake to obtain the compliance of the rebels. The State Department replied that peace might be possible if Spain revoked its reconcentration policy and offered the Cubans "full self-government, with reasonable indemnity." Pressed by Woodford as to what this meant, the Department cabled back: "Cuban independence."

Since Sagasta had already indicated that Spain would risk defeat in war rather than endanger the dynasty, McKinley's insistence on Cuban independence made a peaceful solution of the crisis almost impossible. Yet still the diplomatic fencing continued. On March 27, the United States made three specific proposals. First, there should be an armistice until October 1, while peace negotiations were conducted with the United States acting as mediator. Second, there should be an immediate revocation of the reconcentration order and prompt steps taken to relieve suffering with American help. Third (to be added if possible), the President of the United States should be the final arbiter in case Spain and the insurgents had not come to terms by October 1.

The Spanish reply was handed to Woodford on March 31. It stated that the future form of government was for the Cuban congress to decide, but it must not diminish the powers reserved to the central government under the autonomy decrees. An armistice would be granted, but only if the insurgents asked for it. Woodford sorrowfully described Sagasta's predicament: "Spanish pride will not permit the ministry to propose and offer an armistice, which they really desire. . . . I am told confidentially that an offer of armistice by the Spanish Government would cause revolution here."

On receipt of this dispatch, President McKinley gave up hope for a diplomatic solution to the situation and began preparing a special message to Congress. At first it was planned to present this on April 4, but the need to remove American citizens from the danger zones resulted in a week's delay. During this period of grace, several other futile attempts were made to break the diplomatic log jam.

Attempts at Foreign Mediation

Ever since the danger of American interference in Cuba had first become serious in 1896, María Cristina, the Spanish Queen Regent, and her ministers had clung to the hope that the great European powers would combine to protect Spain. The idea had received encouragement in various capitals. The Austrian Emperor sympathized deeply with the Queen Regent on dynastic grounds; the German Kaiser, believing the monarchical principle to be at stake, was eager to do something; and French statesmen were influenced by large French investments in Spain. Even with these governments, however, the Spanish diplomats found more sympathy than readiness for action. Each would welcome an intervention, but each feared to take the initiative.

Of critical importance was the attitude of Great Britain. At first the English sided with Spain. In May, 1896, while the Venezuelan boundary dispute was still in a critical stage, Lord Salisbury had advised the Spanish government to reject Cleveland's mediation offer and promised to give Spain every possible assistance it could without a breach of neutrality. During the next three months, however, the British position changed completely. Having decided to meet American wishes on the boundary dispute, Lord Salisbury determined to go all the way in promoting good relations. In August, 1896, the British helped the Americans to thwart a Spanish attempt to line up the European powers in a common front to oppose American intervention. Thereafter, the British government consistently sided with the United States on the Cuban question.

British policy is to be explained largely in terms of world politics. England, with colonial and commercial interests in every quarter of the globe, felt dangerously isolated. This was particularly true in the Far East, where the scramble of the European powers for concessions and spheres of influence threatened to close much of the Chinese market to British merchants. Hoping to win support for the Open Door, the British were eager to earn American gratitude by cooperation on the Cuban question. This did not mean that England wanted a Spanish-American War. The contrary was true, because a peaceful solution of the Cuban question would permit the United States to pay more attention to the China problem. By giving McKinley diplomatic support, the British hoped to induce Spain to make the sweeping concessions needed to prevent hostilities.

British Empire opinion was not invariably sympathetic to the United States. In the *Toronto Mail and Express*, for example, the following appeared:

> No doubt if we knew what exactly is true
> You're anxious for Cuba, not Cuba for you.
> I am sure that you wish it, would think it quite grand
> To have the whole continent at your command.

Despite dissenting voices, however, the English press as a whole was much more willing than other European commentators to credit the United States with humanitarian motives. Near the end of March, as the Cuban crisis approached a climax, the London *Times* published a warmly pro-American poem by Alfred Austin, the poet laureate:

> Yes, this is the voice of the bluff March gale;
>   We severed have been too long;
> But now we have done with a worn-out tale
>   The tale of an ancient wrong—
> And our friendship shall last as love doth last
>   And be stronger than death is strong.

During the first week of April when it became obvious no really vigorous action could be taken in the name of Europe as a whole, the German government suggested that the Pope's aid be solicited. It was believed a grant of Cuban independence through papal arbitration might satisfy both America and the Spanish people. This was a promising idea and the Vatican was willing to cooperate, but Madrid balked at an arbitration that would result in the complete loss of her colony. The

Pope's efforts did contribute largely to the decision of the Spanish government to declare an armistice, but this concession came too late.

Meanwhile, the Austro-Hungarian government took the initiative in proposing that the Washington representatives of the six European powers express collectively their hope for the preservation of peace. The British government gave cautious assent, both because it genuinely wished for peace and because it did not care to add to British isolation by remaining aloof. But Lord Salisbury carefully warned Sir Julian Pauncefote, the British Ambassador, that he should do nothing in the matter except what was agreeable to President McKinley.

The upshot of all this was a bit of pageantry. On April 7, representatives of the six powers called in a body on the President and presented a mild note expressing hope that further negotiations between the United States and Spain would end the crisis. McKinley acknowledged the disinterested character of this communication, but expressed confidence that equal appreciation would be shown for the American endeavor to fulfill a duty to humanity by ending an insufferable condition. All sting was removed from the collective action by the fact that Pauncefote had not only made certain the American government would not object to the presentation of the note, but had even submitted the text in advance to the State Department.

Tobogganing into War

Although McKinley's war message was already prepared and resting in the White House safe, Minister Woodford had not given up hope he might achieve the independence of Cuba through diplomacy. On April 10, he believed the victory was won. Bowing to pressure from the Vatican and the European powers, the Spanish government authorized the Captain General of Cuba to declare a suspension of hostilities. Since the reconcentration order had also been revoked, Spain seemed now to have yielded to all the American demands.

President McKinley, however, had gone too far to turn back. On April 11, he sent his message to Congress just as he had written it, except for two brief concluding paragraphs in which he referred to the armistice declaration and commended this new circumstance to Congress's "just and careful attention." In the main body of his message he reviewed the whole situation and made his momentous recommendation:

> In the name of humanity, in the name of civilization, in behalf of endangered American interests which give us the right and the duty to speak and to act, the war in Cuba must stop.... I ask the Congress to authorize and empower the President to take measures to secure a full and final termination of hostilities between the Government of Spain and the people of Cuba, and to secure in the island the establish-

ment of a stable government, capable of maintaining order and observing its international obligations, insuring peace and tranquility and the security of its citizens as well as our own, and to use the military and naval forces of the United States as may be necessary for these purposes.

If the President could thus shrug off the Spanish concessions, it is little wonder they were dismissed by the rest of the country as insincere and worthless. With the receipt of McKinley's message, Congress abandoned itself completely to the war spirit. Democrats competed with Republicans in violent abuse of Spain. The only dispute was over just what form the authorization for the use of force should take and the degree of recognition to be given to the insurgent government. After a week of excited debate, Congress finally passed and the President signed on April 20, 1898, a set of resolutions declaring that the Cuban people "are, and of right ought to be, free and independent"; that the United States had the duty to demand that Spain relinquish its authority and withdraw its armed forces from the island; and that the President was empowered to use the entire armed force of the United States to carry out these resolutions. To remove any imputation of selfish imperialism, Congress accepted without opposition a fourth resolution proposed by Senator Henry M. Teller of Colorado:

> That the United States hereby disclaims any disposition or intention to exercise sovereignty, jurisdiction, or control over said Island except for the pacification thereof, and asserts its determination, when that is accomplished, to leave the government and control of the Island to its people.

Although Spain had little but Castilian pride with which to defend its empire, she had no intention of submitting without a fight. On April 21, the Spanish government broke off diplomatic relations, and the next day President McKinley proclaimed a blockade of Cuban ports. Finally, on April 25, Congress formally declared the existence of a state of war.

Relations with Europe

Even in England, McKinley's refusal to consider the final Spanish concessions and Congress's noisy surrender to jingoism created a very bad impression. Queen Victoria wrote in her diary: "War seems hopelessly declared.... It is monstrous of America," while the *Saturday Review*, in an editorial headed "America the Bully," declared the United States had been guilty of "a crime against humanity."

Although the story did not come out until long after the war, Sir Julian Pauncefote had participated with his fellow diplomats in drafting a condemnation of American action. On April 14, while Congress was still debating McKinley's message, the ambassadors met at the British Embassy and agreed to propose to their home governments a joint declaration that American intervention in Cuba would "not be justified" in view of the Spanish concessions of April 10. Fortunately for Anglo-American relations, the London government vetoed a step recognized to be both futile and certain to antagonize American opinion. Most of the other European governments took a similar position, and the plan for a joint protest fell through.

English criticism soon died down. As a whole, the British press was remarkably pro-American throughout the conflict, and the Salisbury government supported the United States in every way a neutral could. In a letter to Queen Victoria, the Spanish Queen Regent complained that American ships were obtaining coal from English ports while this was being denied to Spanish vessels, and that the Philippine insurgents had been permitted to organize an expedition against Manila in the British colony of Hong Kong.

Joseph Chamberlain, the British Colonial Secretary, openly advocated an Anglo-American alliance. In a speech at Birmingham on May 13, 1898, he declared: [2]

> I do not know what the future has in store for us, I do not know what arrangements may be possible with the United States, but this I know and feel—that the closer, the more cordial, the fuller and the more definite, these arrangements are with the consent of both people, the better it will be for both and for the world.... And I even go so far as to say that, terrible as war may be, even war itself would be cheaply purchased if in a great and noble cause the Stars and Stripes and the Union Jack should wave together [*loud and prolonged cheers*] over an Anglo-Saxon alliance.

Although most Americans were not ready to go this far, English friendship was highly valued because Continental European opinion was, for the most part, bitterly anti-American. The Paris *Temps* asserted the great powers were "awaiting the proper moment for effective intervention." In several countries, traveling Americans were treated with such discourtesy that they returned home. Rightly or wrongly, the Germans were believed to be particularly hostile.

The War with Spain

As a military and naval conflict, the Spanish-American War was not a major struggle. Neither contestant was well prepared, but, fortunately for the United States, Spain, wearied by three years of effort to quell

[2] Reprinted by permission of St. Martin's Press, Inc., from J. L. Garvin and Julian Amery, eds., *The Life of Joseph Chamberlain* (Copyright 1932–1951 by St. Martin's Press, Inc., New York), vol. III, pp. 301–302.

colonial revolts and troubled by problems of logistics and morale, was in the worse position.

The actual fighting began, strangely enough, in the Philippines on May 1, 1898, and was practically over by the end of July. This "splendid little war," as John Hay, then Ambassador to London, termed it, found the Americans overwhelmingly victorious on land and sea along the three fronts: Cuba, Puerto Rico, and the Philippines. On July 22, the Duke de Almodóvar del Río, the new Spanish Foreign Minister, inquired of President McKinley what might be done to spare Cuba the horrors of further war. This peace overture was delivered to the American government four days later through Jules Cambon, the French Ambassador at Washington. On July 30, Secretary of State William R. Day [3] gave the American reply. As preliminary terms of peace, the United States demanded that Spain relinquish sovereignty over Cuba, cede Puerto Rico and one of the Ladrone Islands to the United States, and consent to American occupation of Manila "pending the conclusion of a treaty of peace which shall determine the control, disposition and government of the Philippines." Spain tried to obtain some assurance that the Philippines would remain under her sovereignty, but the United States insisted upon a completely free hand at the peace conference. On August 12, Ambassador Cambon, acting for the Spanish government, signed a protocol embodying the American terms without substantial modification. President McKinley thereupon ordered an immediate suspension of hostilities.

Problems of Peacemaking

To represent the United States at the peace conference, which, under the terms of the protocol, was to meet at Paris before October 1, 1898, President McKinley appointed four Republicans: Day,[4] Whitelaw Reid, publisher of the *New York Tribune*, and Senators Cushman K. Davis of Minnesota and William P. Frye of Maine; and one Democrat, Senator George Gray of Delaware.

At Paris, agreement was easily reached on several matters: the ending of Spanish sovereignty over Cuba, the cession of Puerto Rico to the United States, and the decision about which Ladrone island the United States was to acquire—Guam. There were, however, two major points of controversy: who should pay off the so-called Cuban debt of about 400 million dollars, and what should happen to the Philippines. In determining what position to take on these moot matters, the American delegation was in constant cable communication with the administration in Washington. In this respect, the members differed from the envoys

[3] Day had succeeded the ailing John Sherman on Apr. 25, 1898.
[4] In order to take up this new assignment, Day resigned as Secretary of State. He was succeeded by John Hay, who had been Ambassador at London since 1897.

who had negotiated earlier peace treaties involving the United States. Prior to 1898, such delegations had been left largely to their own devices, and the government at Washington did not know the final terms until the completed treaty was brought home. In the negotiations at Paris in 1898, however, both the government and the American people learned what steps were taken almost as soon as a compromise was reached, and, indeed, some of the terms were actually dictated from Washington.

On the controversial debt question, the American commissioners successfully insisted that Spain be responsible for paying the Cuban debt. This position was based on the belief that Cuba would be in a difficult situation if she began her independent career with a heavy financial burden.

Spotlight on the Philippines

It was the Philippine problem, however, which aroused the greatest controversy, not only at the peace table, but in the United States as well, for it brought to the fore the whole question of imperialism. Before 1898, most Americans had scarcely known where the Philippines were located. The situation had been different, however, with avowed expansionists like Mahan and his disciples. Theodore Roosevelt, whom McKinley had appointed Assistant Secretary of the Navy, had decided as early as September, 1897, that in case of war with Spain—something he ardently favored—a blow should be struck against this Spanish Far Eastern colony. He had pulled political wires to have Commodore George Dewey appointed to the Asiatic command over the heads of older officers. Then, on a fateful February day in 1898, Roosevelt had brashly taken advantage of Secretary of the Navy Long's brief absence from his desk to send the following order:

> Dewey, Hong Kong:
>   Secret and confidential. Order the squadron . . . to Hong Kong. Keep full of coal. In the event of declaration of war with Spain, your duty will be to see that the Spanish squadron does not leave the Asiatic coast, and then offensive operations in Philippine Islands. . . .
>   Roosevelt

The Assistant Secretary's plans had worked out perfectly. To the amazement of the American public, on May 1, 1898—within a week after the declaration of war, Commodore Dewey had engaged and destroyed the Spanish fleet in Manila Bay. Manifest destiny had suddenly beckoned in an unexpected quarter of the globe.

The sequel to this naval battle had been a difficult situation. The Spanish fleet had been liquidated, but for weeks the Americans had not had sufficient ships and troops to destroy the land fortifications of Manila or to force the surrender of the Spanish garrison. While awaiting reinforcements, Dewey had maintained a blockade and given support to Filipino insurgents led by Emilio Aguinaldo. Within a few weeks, British, French, Japanese, and German warships had arrived to watch the situation and protect their countries' nationals.

Troublesome problems had arisen from the blockade. Captain Chichester of the British navy had cooperated thoroughly with the American regulations, but there had been disagreements between Dewey and Vice Admiral von Diederichs, the German commander. To make matters worse, Diederichs's squadron had been more powerful than Dewey's. Dewey had been convinced that the unfriendly Germans were deliberately flouting his regulations. Matters had come to a crisis in July, when Dewey had angrily threatened war unless the German ships complied with his orders to stop and allow their identity to be established. Relations had improved after this outburst, but until the final fall of Manila on August 13, friction between the two commanders had continued. The friendliness of the British had been in such marked contrast to the attitude of the Germans that all manner of legends sprang up after the war. Many Americans came to believe that only the decisive action of the British had saved Dewey's fleet from a German attack during the final assault on Manila.

Not only had the English applauded Dewey's victories in the Philippines, but they had urged the United States to keep the islands. Early in May—long before American opinion had had a chance to crystallize, the London *Times* had said that, if the United States would undertake the responsibility of ruling the Philippines, "we should welcome that as the best solution of the problem for all parties concerned." The *Times* had been particularly anxious that Germany, France, or Russia not be given an opportunity to obtain the islands.

Even before the war was over, American public opinion divided sharply on the question of whether the United States should annex all or even part of the Philippines. Within the business world the idea soon gained strong support. With a population of some 7.5 million, the islands offered attractive possibilities for American trade. Even more important in the eyes of many businessmen was their proximity to China. Annexation would give leverage to American diplomacy in insisting upon equality of opportunity in the great Asiatic mainland markets.

American acquisition of the Philippines also appealed strongly to many church leaders. Interest in foreign missions was running high, and it was therefore easy to see God's will in Dewey's dramatic victory. The fact that many Filipinos had been converted to Catholicism under Spanish rule merely increased the desire of the more aggressive Protestants to enter this mission field. Reminding its readers that Spain had excluded American missionaries from the Philippines, the *Christian and Missionary Alliance* rejoiced that "God has interposed, and a brighter dawn has come." The *Baptist Union* defined the American obligation thus: "We must give to these islands which we have delivered the Gospel whose principles are the only true foundation and guarantee of liberty. The conquest by force of arms must be followed up by conquest for Christ." This Protestant assumption of superior virtue naturally annoyed the Catholics, but even many of the latter favored annexation. They scoffed at the idea that the Protestants would succeed in their proselytizing efforts and stressed the advantages of sending American priests into the islands.

Despite the persuasive arguments of the expansionists, the annexation of distant territories was strongly opposed by many Americans. A few of the anti-imperialists were persons connected with the domestic production of cane or beet sugar, who stood to lose by American acquisition of sugar-producing islands; but most of them had no such material interest. They disliked imperialism because it involved the imposition of American rule over native populations without the consent of the governed. From the anti-imperialist point of view, this violated the ideals of the Declaration of Independence and the whole philosophy on which the United States based its nationhood. This dislike for colonialism was shared by a curious assortment of prominent Americans: Mugwump reformers like Carl Schurz and Charles Francis Adams; old-line Republicans like Senator George F. Hoar of Massachusetts and former President Benjamin Harrison; Gold Democrats like former President Grover Cleveland and Richard Olney; and Free-silver Democrats like William Jennings Bryan and Senator Benjamin Tillman of South Carolina. The anti-imperialist group included many distinguished names, but it lacked homogeneity and leadership. Even more important, it was attempting to oppose the expansionist movement at a time when patriotic nationalism had been deeply stirred by American military and naval victories.

Even among the peace envoys there was difference of opinion. Reid, Davis, and Frye inclined strongly toward the expansionist position, while Gray was antiexpansionist and Day took the moderate stand that the United States should keep only a coaling station in the Philippines.

The Spanish diplomats at Paris took the stand that the Philippines were not an issue in the war. Moreover, American occupation of the region around Manila certainly did not constitute conquest of the whole island group.

Under the circumstances, President McKinley was frankly troubled by the issue. On September 16, 1898, when he sent his first instructions to the peace commissioners, he insisted only upon the island of Luzon. His final decision was reached over a month later on October 26, when he wrote that the United States, "whatever it might prefer as to the Philippines, is in a situation where it cannot let go." He had therefore concluded that "duty requires we should take the archipelago."

Why had the President now been converted to the position of the extreme expansionists? One factor that had apparently weighed heavily was the seeming absence of an acceptable alternative. To turn the Philippines back to Spain was a course unpalatable to American public opinion, now thoroughly convinced of Spanish inability to govern her colonies. To allow the Filipinos to assume responsibility for their own government might appeal to idealists, but reports on the political capabilities of Aguinaldo and his followers were not encouraging. Philippine independence, it was widely believed, would simply open the door to civil war and speedy conquest by some foreign power. If the United States abstained from annexation, Germany would be likely to move in. England and even Japan urged American annexation as the best solution.

McKinley was also strongly influenced by at least three other factors: increased business support for expansion, the rising popularity of empire among the voters, and the humanitarian arguments of the church group. To a party of Methodist ministers, the President confided that he had walked the floor of the White House night after night and gone on his knees in prayer for light and guidance. Late one night it had come to him "that there was nothing left for us to do but take them all, and to educate the Filipinos and uplift and civilize and Christianize them, and by God's grace do the very best we could by them, as our fellow-men for whom Christ also died."

Once the President's mind was made up, he persisted in demanding all the Philippines, even after the peace commissioners suggested compromise to overcome Spanish opposition. In view of the circumstances, Spain had finally to yield, and on December 10, 1898, the peace treaty was signed. Spain agreed to relinquish all sovereignty over Cuba, for whose government the United States would assume temporary responsibility, and Spain would pay the Cuban debt. Spain also ceded to the United States Puerto Rico, Guam, and the Philippines. To assuage the Spanish loss of the latter, the United States gave the vanquished nation 20 million dollars, the estimated value of the nonmilitary improvements Spain had constructed in the islands. In other provisions, the treaty promised freedom of religion to the inhabitants of the ceded islands and assured Spain equality of trading privileges in the Philippines for ten years.

The anti-imperialists, led by Senator Hoar, put up a stiff battle in the Senate, but the treaty was eventually approved on February 6, 1899, by the close vote of 57 to 27—just one vote more than the necessary two-thirds. Even this narrow victory could probably not have been achieved had not Bryan passed down the word that he believed the Democrats should allow the treaty to go into effect and then make anti-imperialism and Philippine independence the leading issue in the next presidential election.[5]

Annexation of Hawaii

The exciting events of 1898 focused attention on the whole Pacific area, and the expansionists, now in the driver's seat, gathered in their first fruits even before the war was over. The annexation of Hawaii, which Cleveland had blocked in 1893, was easily accomplished under the new circumstances of 1898.

President McKinley, although not an ardent expansionist, had been won over to the Hawaiian project during his early months in the White House. On June 16, 1897, a new annexation treaty, similar to that of 1893 except that it provided no compensation for the deposed royal family, was signed and sent to the Senate. The Japanese government was concerned by this development because recent immigration had made the Japanese the most numerous element in the islands—outnumbering the native Hawaiians two to one and Americans and Europeans six to one. From the Japanese point of view, American annexation was deplored because it might jeopardize the rights of these Japanese nationals and threaten the security of the Japanese homeland.

News that Japan had formally protested against the treaty excited the American expansionists. Assistant Secretary of the Navy Theodore Roosevelt warned in a public speech: "The United States is not in a position which requires her to ask Japan or any other foreign Power what territory it shall or shall not acquire." He was reprimanded by his superiors for this belligerence, and the State Department sought to mollify Japan by promising that all her legitimate interests would be respected. In December, 1897, Japan accepted these assurances and withdrew her protests; but the storm clouds that had momentarily appeared on the horizon of Japanese-American relations were ominous for the future.

The annexation treaty required sixty favorable Senate votes, which were more than the expansionists could muster against the opposition of the domestic sugar faction and the anti-imperialists. In March, 1898, the proponents of annexation gave up on the treaty and initiated steps to acquire Hawaii by joint resolution, following the precedent of Texas in 1845.[6]

Although the new strategy required only a simple majority in both houses, it still faced formidable obstacles. House Speaker Thomas Brackett

---

[5] A resolution promising eventual independence for the Philippines was defeated only by the vote of Vice President Garret A. Hobart.

[6] See chap. 12.

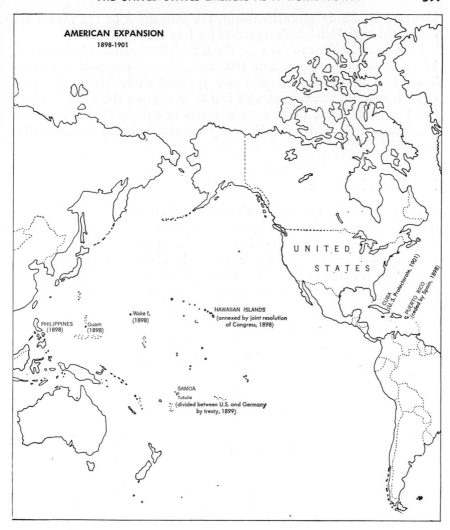

AMERICAN EXPANSION
1898-1901

UNITED STATES

PHILIPPINES
(1898)

Guam
(1898)

Wake I.
(1898)

HAWAIIAN ISLANDS
(annexed by joint resolution
of Congress, 1898)

SAMOA
Tutuila
(divided between U.S. and Germany
by treaty, 1899)

CUBA
(U.S. Protectorate, 1901)

PUERTO RICO
(Ceded by Spain, 1898)

Reed was a staunch anti-imperialist, ready to use his strong powers to prevent the joint resolution from coming to a vote. But the outbreak of war and the Battle of Manila Bay gave the expansionist cause an irresistible impetus. Even amateur naval strategists could understand the importance of Hawaii to protect American communications in the Pacific and to defend the West Coast of continental United States. The recent unpleasantness with Japan made this argument all the more impelling.

Under these new pressures, Reed and other conservatives had to yield. On June 15, 1898, the House passed the resolution by a vote of 209 to 91, and three weeks later the Senate fell into line by a vote of 42 to 21. Since

Hawaii had already given its assent, the annexation of the islands was completed with McKinley's signature on July 7.

Next, as an incident to the war, the United States annexed unoccupied Wake Island in the summer of 1898 and formally occupied it in 1900. This island was chiefly valuable as a potential cable station. American expansionists and missionaries also had their eyes on the Spanish-owned Caroline Islands. The peace commissioners at Paris proposed American purchase of those islands, but Germany induced Spain to sell them to her instead.

Partition of Samoa

The condominium of 1889 under which Germany, Great Britain, and the United States had assumed joint responsibility for the government of the Samoan Islands had never been popular in America, where it was regarded as an entangling alliance. Germany also hoped for some more satisfactory solution of the problem. In 1899, the death of the native king and a renewal of factionalism among the foreign elements in the islands offered an opportunity to reopen the question. The German government, alarmed by the rise of anti-German and pro-English sentiment in the United States during the Spanish-American War, was eager to arrange an amicable partition of the Samoan group. England was ready to bow out if she could obtain compensation elsewhere.

Under this combination of favorable circumstances, a satisfactory settlement was not difficult to achieve. By a treaty of December 2, 1899, Germany and the United States divided the islands. Germany acquired the western islands; the United States, the eastern.[7] Although the two largest islands were included in Germany's share, the Americans gained Tutuila with its excellent harbor of Pago Pago.

By 1900 the new imperialism was well established. McKinley's easy reelection victory over the anti-imperialist Bryan seemed to place the seal of popular approval on what Senator Lodge had appropriately named "the large policy" of 1898.

[7] Great Britain and Germany had already signed an agreement (Nov. 14, 1899), under which the British withdrew entirely from Samoa and as compensation received the Tonga Islands, some of the Solomon group, and concessions in West Africa.

21

JOHN HAY AND THE OPEN DOOR

American expansionists had gained much by the acquisitions of 1898 and 1899, but some cherished prizes still remained to be won. Two immediate goals were to assert in a more vigorous way the right of American merchants to trade in a China threatened with partition among the European powers and to gain the right to build an American-controlled canal to link the Atlantic and Pacific Oceans. Although the McKinley administration took up both problems, circumstances dictated that the China issue be first to result in important steps.

In charge of the State Department during these momentous times was John Hay, Secretary from 1898 to 1905. Hay had had an extraordinary life. During the Civil War he and John Nicolay had lived in the White House as Abraham Lincoln's personal secretaries. The President had treated the two young men almost as sons, and they had testified to their filial affection in a ten-volume biography published twenty years later. Besides this vast venture in historical writing, Hay had gained a reputation as a novelist, poet, and journalist. Successful in both literature and finance, he had for many years lived as a gentleman of leisure. He and his intimate friend and next-door neighbor, Henry Adams, had made their homes oases of culture in Washington's excessively political society. It was from this pleasant world that President McKinley had summoned Hay, first to be Ambassador to England and then to head the State Department.

Hay had many assets. He was a man of unusual intelligence, with a wide knowledge of world affairs. His wit and charm had won him friends among the leading public figures of both the United States and England. But Hay also had handicaps. Plagued by poor health and an inability to get along with politicians, the Secretary's relations with the Senate were frequently unhappy. So long as his fellow Ohioan, McKinley, was in the White House, Hay had practically a free hand. When McKinley's assassination in 1901 brought Theodore Roosevelt to the Presidency, Hay's influence diminished because Roosevelt dearly loved to steer his own ship through the diplomatic seas.

Anglo-American Understanding

The cornerstone of John Hay's foreign policy was close cooperation between the United States and England. The new Secretary's natural affection for Great Britain had been strengthened during the year he spent in London as Ambassador. The English had given him a hearty welcome not only because they admired his literary achievements, but also because they were well disposed toward President McKinley. Usually they felt happier with low-tariff Democrats in power than with protectionist Republicans, but Bryan's free-silver heresy had frightened financial London, and the victory of the conservative McKinley had been greeted with enthusiasm.

During 1898 the two countries seemed to be moving into an ever-closer relationship. Britain, feeling the dangers of isolation, was eager for American diplomatic support, particularly in the Far East, while the United States welcomed sympathy for its Cuban policy. Some Americans were ready to follow wherever this new friendship might lead. To the *Outlook*, it appeared that the Spanish-American War's most important result might be "the creation of a good understanding between England and the United States, leading eventually to a real and definite alliance between them in the interest of the world's civilization." Many advocated what they called "race patriotism," by which they meant a sense of Anglo-Saxon solidarity. In 1898 and 1899 no fewer than six books and fifty-six magazine articles dealing with this subject were published in the United States, Great Britain, and Canada. Many of the authors were open and avowed advocates of an Anglo-American alliance.

Joseph Chamberlain, the British Colonial Secretary, effervesced with enthusiasm for such a project. "Shoulder to shoulder," he told Ambassador Hay in April, 1898, "we could command peace the world over. . . . I should rejoice in an occasion in which we could fight side by side. The good effect of it would last for generations." Aware of the American tradition against foreign entanglements, Hay had been cautious, but he gave the idea as much support as he thought safe. For his most important speech in London, he chose the significant subject: "A Partnership in Beneficence."

When Chamberlain suggested the possibility of an Anglo-American alliance in a public speech, his words received a surprisingly favorable reception in the United States. "Mr. Chamberlain may have been dreaming," asserted the *New York Herald*, "but it would be the consummation of the most momentous event since the Christian era if the dream came true." This feeling of mutual interest lay behind England's urging that the United States annex the Philippines. British imperialists believed that Americans, hitherto critical of colonialism, might be more sympathetic toward the British Empire if the United States assumed this new responsibility. In January, 1899, Chamberlain told a Birmingham audience that Providence intended Great Britain to be a great governing power, but that she would no longer be alone since the United States was beginning to share the task. The first business of the Salisbury government was "to draw closer the bonds which united us to the other members of the English-speaking race and to promote their co-operation in the great work of civilization which appears to be the mission of the Anglo-Saxon race."

The McKinley administration had an opportunity to demonstrate its friendship during the Boer War (1899–1902). At a time when most of Europe was strongly anti-British, the United States maintained its traditional neutrality, but avoided any action that might hamper the English war effort. When British ships stopped American vessels carrying supplies to the Boers, Hay was satisfied with British offers to purchase the confiscated goods. When the Boers protested against British army purchases of horses and mules, the American government refused to interfere with a trade permissible under international law.

The expansionists undertook to defend British action as necessary to the progress of civilization. Hay, although correct enough in his public statements, was savagely anti-Boer in private conversation. Admiral Mahan wrote magazine articles upholding the British side, and Theodore Roosevelt told a German friend: "I have great sympathy for the Boers and great respect and liking for them, but I think they are battling on the wrong side in the fight for civilization and will have to go under." The *Cleveland Plain Dealer* pointed out that England's troubles in South Africa were not dissimilar from American difficulties with the insurgent Filipinos. "We are both in the same boat, more's the pity for both."

The McKinley administration's pro-British leanings were unpopular with large sections of the American public. To sympathize with small nations attempting to maintain their independence was as natural as breathing for most Americans. Citizens of Irish and German ancestry were particularly vocal in their pro-Boer feelings. Irish-American newspapers published directions on how to reach the Transvaal—obviously for the benefit of Americans who wanted to volunteer in the Boer army. In February, 1900, an Irish ambulance corps paraded down Fifth Avenue prior to embarking for South Africa. Many pro-Boer rallies were organized, and United States senators and representatives were usually available as speakers, particularly as the election of 1900 approached. At one such meeting in Washington, Senator William V. Allen, a Nebraska Populist, charged: [1]

> There is no doubt that the shadow of England's hand falls across the path of the present administration. When I go up to the Capitol and also to the Treasury Department, I actually feel that I am trespassing on John Bull's territory.

The Boer War sharpened a controversy that had already begun. The idea of some kind of Anglo-American alliance, so frequently expressed in 1898 and 1899, had from the start been violently resented by many Americans. The anti-imperialists distrusted any tie with England that might involve the United States in foreign adventures. The Irish, in particular, had a long tradition of hostility to Britain. Even during Spanish-American War days, Irish marchers had paraded through the streets of Philadelphia carrying slogans that read: "England Sent Small-Pox Infested Rags to New York in 1862," "George Washington Would Never Trust England," and "Has McKinley Forgotten the *Alabama* Affair?"

German-Americans also hated Anglo-Saxon alliance talk. They resented the anti-German tone of the American press in 1898, especially the frequent quotation of unfriendly comments from German newspapers. They became convinced that an unholy alliance involving British bankers and the great news services was attempting to create bad feeling between Germany and the United States. This German-American protest movement was very welcome to the German government, which was seriously concerned over its unsatisfactory relations with the United States. The German-American vote was believed to be of such importance to the Republicans that the McKinley administration would be compelled to repudiate the Anglo-Saxon alliance idea. Well remembering the fate of Lord Sackville-West, German Ambassador Theodor von Holleben was careful not to become too deeply involved, but even without direction from the Embassy, German-American protest against the alliance was vociferous.

In American politics, the charge of pro-British leanings had always been damaging. By the fall of 1899, Republican chieftains were seriously worried. The issue came to a head during the off-year election campaign in Ohio, a state where more than one-fifth of the population was of immediate German and Irish stock and where the Democrats were denouncing "the secret and vicious alliance now in evidence between England and the Republican Administration." Beseeched by the politicians to save President McKinley from the humiliation of a Democratic victory in his own state, Secretary Hay wrote an open letter to the chairman of the Republican state committee: [2]

[1] *Irish World*, Jan. 27, 1900.
[2] London *Times*, Sept. 14, 1899.

There is no alliance with England or with any Power under heaven, except those known or published to the world.... No treaty other than these exists; none has been suggested on either side; none is in contemplation. It has never entered into the mind of the President or any member of the government to forsake, under any inducement, the wise precept and example of the fathers which forbade entangling alliances with European powers.

Hay's skillful pen turned the trick. A million copies of the letter were distributed as campaign literature, and the Republicans won a smashing victory in the Ohio election. This episode, however, gave Hay a sense of the realities of the situation; he confided to Henry White in the London Embassy: [3]

The fact is a treaty of alliance is impossible. It would never get through the Senate. As long as I stay here no action shall be taken contrary to my conviction that the one indispensable feature of our foreign policy should be a friendly understanding with England. But an alliance must remain in the present shape of things an unattainable dream.

By the end of 1899, the first wave of Anglo-American affection born of the events of 1898 had spent itself. The United States was still grateful; England still friendly. But talk of an Anglo-Saxon alliance became less frequent; to maintain the good understanding seemed problem enough. Nevertheless, the close relations between Washington and London played an important part in Hay's diplomacy as he took up the problems of China and the isthmian canal.

The China Problem

The Sino-Japanese War (1894–1895) marked the opening of a new phase in the history of the Far East. Japan's decisive victory dramatized two facts, both of immense importance for the future. First, Japan had come of age from the standpoint of Western technology and military power; she was now a force to be reckoned with in world politics. Second, China was a helpless giant, unable to defend herself. For the next five years the Chinese were to suffer a series of diplomatic humiliations.

Japan's dividends from the war included the strategic island of Formosa, an indemnity, and commercial concessions. China was compelled to surrender her claim of suzerainty over Korea, leaving that country nominally independent, but actually wide open to Japanese penetration. Valuable though these prizes were, Japan had tried to get still more; the original

[3] Reprinted by permission of the publisher from Tyler Dennett, *John Hay: From Poetry to Politics* (Copyright 1933 by Dodd, Mead & Company, Inc., New York), p. 221.

peace treaty had included a cession of the Liaotung Peninsula, the gateway to Manchuria. Here, however, Japan had been blocked by the combined opposition of Russia, France, and Germany; under this European pressure, the peninsula had been left to China. Greatly to Japanese indignation, Russia obtained a twenty-five year lease to the Liaotung region only three years later. By developing a base at Port Arthur and exploiting railroad concessions, Russian influence became dominant throughout Manchuria.

Meantime, Germany and France had also been dipping into the China pie. The murder of two German missionaries offered the Kaiser a convenient occasion for exacting a lease of Kiaochow and important privileges in the rest of the Shantung Peninsula. France extended its influence in southern China by obtaining a lease of Kwangchow.

As for England, a cynic might say—as was said of the Austrian Empress, Maria Theresa, during the partition of Poland—that she wept and took her share. Claiming that it was necessary to preserve the Far Eastern balance of power, Britain leased Weihaiwei in northern China and acquired additional territory behind Kowloon, on the Chinese mainland opposite Hong Kong.

An even greater threat to China's independence grew out of so-called "spheres of influence." Lacking capital, the Chinese had to depend on foreign businessmen for the development of much-needed railroads and mines. By 1898, these economic interests had become localized in different parts of China. By various treaties, Russia had gained a paramount position in Manchuria, France in southern China, Germany in the Shantung Peninsula, and England in the important Yangtze River Valley. To many observers, this seemed to be earmarking Chinese territory for future partition.

England Revives the Open Door

England's protests that she did not like this trend of events were by no means hypocritical. Under the Open Door policy whereby Chinese ports had been open to all merchants on a basis of equality, the English had done extremely well. Their share in China's total foreign trade was about 65 per cent; their domination of the carrying trade in and out of Chinese ports was even greater, amounting to about 85 per cent. If the empire were partitioned among the powers, no share that England might acquire could compensate her for exclusion from the rest. England's sincerity in advocating continuance of the Open Door policy could therefore scarcely be doubted. Yet the problem was far from simple. To insist on trading equality even to the point of war was fraught with danger unless Great Britain could count upon the support of some other nation. Chamberlain's ardent wooing of the United States during 1898 and 1899 was part of a larger British effort in which the possibilities of alliance with Russia, the United States, Japan, and Germany were successively explored. At the same time, England was playing the balance-of-power game by extending its own leaseholds and spheres of influence.

Did the United States have anything to lose in this Far Eastern scramble? Very little, most Americans would have replied before the Spanish-American War. The trade statistics were far from impressive. Only about 2 per cent of the total American foreign trade was with China, while an additional 2 per cent was with Japan. These Far Eastern markets seemed of little importance to the United States when compared with those in Canada and Europe.

Yet these figures were somewhat misleading. American businessmen who had been studying the China market could see great potentialities for the future. As the Asiatic demand for Western goods increased, the possibilities for trade expansion seemed almost limitless. Given a fair competitive opportunity, American industrialists believed they had an excellent opportunity to outsell their foreign rivals. Textile manufacturers were particularly eager to develop the China market, where their sales had shown an exciting increase during the 1890s. Also greatly interested were the oil and steel companies. In 1895, a number of bankers and industrialists had organized the American-China Development Company to seek railroad concessions.

Despite its supposedly close alliance with business, the McKinley administration displayed surprisingly little concern at first with the China situation. In fact, Secretary of State John Sherman was less responsive to suggestions from the business groups wishing to expand their Far Eastern markets than Olney, his Democratic predecessor, had been. "The noncommittal attitude of the administration toward the present situation in China," complained the New York *Journal of Commerce*, "is not at all satisfactory to the representatives of large mercantile interests in this city who are familiar with the possibilities of American trade with the Far East." In letters to the *New York Evening Post* and in an article in the *North American Review*, Charles Denby, Jr., called attention to the fact that American trade was second only to that of England. From whatever nation dominated Chinese soil the United States should therefore demand tariff equality. Since Denby was the son of the American Minister to China and had himself been secretary of legation at Peking, his pronouncements attracted considerable attention.

This flurry of interest in the China situation resulted in unusually strong expressions of pro-British opinion. In February, 1898, the *Review of Reviews* stated bluntly: "English influence in China makes for the open and liberal policy that is most favorable for the United States. So far, therefore, as our sympathies are allowed to be governed by our interests, it is plain that we should incline toward the continuance of further development of England's influence and power everywhere in Asia." Senator Henry Cabot Lodge, often a critic of the British, wrote to his friend Henry White, secretary of the United States Legation in London: [4]

> If I had my way I should be glad to have the United States say to England that we would stand by her in her declaration that the ports of China must be opened to all nations equally or to none, and if England takes that attitude firmly I am in hopes that this may come about, although our foreign policy is always more haphazard than I like to see it.

All this discussion of the Chinese situation resulted in a direct, though unofficial, British approach to the United States. In a memorandum of March 8, 1898, Lord Pauncefote inquired whether the British government could count on the cooperation of the United States in opposing action by foreign powers that might tend to restrict freedom of commerce in China. The American reply was a polite refusal. Secretary Sherman said no change of policy was necessary because the United States had no information indicating that trade would be restricted through foreign occupation of Chinese ports. Undoubtedly the administration's preoccupation with Cuba made it unwilling to look for trouble in the Pacific. It seemed expedient to accept at face value German and Russian assurances that exclusive privileges were not being sought, even though the American Minister to China, the senior Charles Denby, was advising the State Department that the situation was serious.

The American rebuff was not severe enough to discourage the British government from hoping that the United States might soon take a more pronounced stand. It was this consideration that dominated English policy toward the Spanish-American War and the Philippines question. In January, 1899, Pauncefote again suggested joint Anglo-American action in the Far East. By this time the Secretary of State was John Hay, a man much more likely to be attracted to such a proposal than John Sherman. Nevertheless, Hay, fearful of the Senate, regretfully brushed off the overture.

Despite this apparent stalemate, several forces were pushing the United States toward a more positive policy. Annexation of the Philippines resulted in much greater interest in the whole Far Eastern situation. In June, 1898, the American Asiatic Association was organized, through which pressure was repeatedly exerted on the government. In January, 1899, the State Department received a memorial from textile manufac-

---

[4] Reprinted by permission of the publisher from Allan Nevins, *Henry White: Thirty Years of American Diplomacy* (Copyright 1930 by Harper & Brothers, New York), p. 166.

turers, warning that the China market would be lost to American cotton exports "unless a vigorous policy is pursued on the part of the . . . Government." Hay was sufficiently impressed to instruct American diplomats at St. Petersburg and Peking to be vigilant in upholding American rights. The State Department was also under pressure to give greater protection to the more than a thousand American missionaries in China.

The Far Eastern situation gained still more attention during Lord Charles Beresford's visit to the United States in February, 1899. Beresford was a British admiral whose naval exploits had made him a popular hero. Sent on a mission to China by the British Associated Chambers of Commerce, he made an almost regal progress through the Orient. Consequently, when he arrived in San Francisco and set across the country on his way back to England, he became the social lion of the day. Chambers of commerce in the principal American cities arranged banquets in his honor, and Secretary Hay entertained him in Washington. Colorful and talkative, Beresford was a persuasive salesman for the idea of Anglo-American cooperation in support of the Open Door. Commenting on the doughty sea dog's visit, the *New York Herald* reported that he had addressed "the most influential merchants and bankers of the city." "So far as this country . . . is concerned," concluded the *Herald*, "his mission has been a phenomenal success." After his return home, Beresford continued to press his case in a widely read book, *The Break-up of China*.

The Open Door Notes

Highly influential in finally convincing Hay that he should take some vigorous step were two men little known to the general public: William W. Rockhill and Alfred E. Hippisley. Rockhill was an American who, after serving in a variety of diplomatic posts and traveling widely in the Orient, had been appointed to a position in Washington where Secretary Hay could benefit by his advice on Far Eastern affairs. Hippisley, an Englishman, had served many years as a member of the Chinese Imperial Maritime Customs Service. He and Rockhill had become close friends during their service in China. Hippisley was visiting his American wife's family in Baltimore during the summer of 1899 when the China problem was attracting such wide attention. Naturally he confided to Rockhill his concern over the trend of events and his belief that the United States should take a strong position; as naturally, Rockhill transmitted these ideas to Secretary Hay.

At first Hay was reluctant to act, recognizing the political danger of flouting the nation's isolationist traditions. President McKinley was even more opposed to any adventurous step. In the middle of August, however, the administration rather suddenly came around to the Hippisley-Rockhill point of view. In part, the administration was probably influenced by the opinion of Dr. Jacob Gould Schurman, president of Cornell University, who had just returned from an official fact-finding mission to the Philippines. In a widely publicized interview, Schurman discussed the China situation in alarming terms, warning that Russia was likely to take over more and more Chinese provinces, "and when it gets them it will do as that country has done hitherto—put a duty on all foreign goods." Another new development was a Russian decree declaring Talienwan on the Liaotung Peninsula an open port for the period of the Russian lease. This reassuring news might seem to make American action unnecessary, but Hippisley argued that it presented Hay with a golden opportunity to enlist Russia's support in a general affirmation of the Open Door.

In August, 1899, Secretary Hay, vacationing in New Hampshire, wrote to Rockhill, requesting him to draft a dispatch to be sent to the appropriate foreign capitals. This was the official blessing that Rockhill had been hoping for, and he lost no time in complying. Less than two weeks later, on September 6, 1899, the famous Open Door notes were sent to Germany, Russia, and England, and within the next few months similar notes went out to Japan, Italy, and France.

The notes asked each government to give formal assurances for itself, and lend its cooperation in obtaining like assurances from the other interested powers, "that each, within its respective sphere of whatever influence—"

> *First.* Will in no way interfere with any treaty port or any vested interest within any so-called "sphere of interest"...or leased territory it may have in China.
>
> *Second.* That the Chinese treaty tariff...shall apply to merchandise landed or shipped to all such ports as are within said "sphere of interest" ...no matter to what nationality it may belong, and that duties so leviable shall be collected by the Chinese Government.
>
> *Third.* That it will levy no higher harbor dues on vessels of another nationality frequenting any port in such "sphere" than shall be levied on vessels of its own nationality, and no higher railroad charges over lines built, controlled, or operated within its "sphere" on merchandise belonging to citizens or subjects of other nationalities transported through such "sphere" than shall be levied on similar merchandise belonging to its own nationals transported over equal distance.

Like the famous Monroe Doctrine of an earlier day, the Open Door notes have often been misunderstood. As to authorship, it is clear that only by adoption was Secretary Hay the father of the policy. In general terms, the Open Door was at least as old as the "most favored nation" treaties of 1842. So far as the documents of 1899 were concerned, the name at the bottom was Hay's, but the ideas were largely those of Hippisley, while the actual wording was that of Rockhill.

On the other hand, the fact that Hippisley was an Englishman has sometimes given the impression that the United States had become nothing but the pawn of British diplomacy in the Open Door notes. This is misleading, because subsequent events proved that the British government was somewhat embarrassed by the form of Hay's diplomacy. Hippisley's ideas represented not so much the ideas of the Salisbury cabinet as those of the Chinese Imperial Maritime Customs Service, an organization staffed with Englishmen but working for the Chinese government. The customs service was upset by a recent event, described by Hippisley as "the narrow, unjust, and shortsighted policy of Gt. Britain in expelling the Chinese Customs-house from the Kowloon extension," thereby bringing about an "enormous increase of smuggling." Hippisley obviously wanted the United States to gain a pledge of good behavior not only from other powers, but from Great Britain herself.

The original Open Door notes made no attempt to halt the encroachments upon Chinese sovereignty. On the contrary, they assumed the inevitability of spheres of influence and confined themselves to an attempt to preserve certain carefully defined treaty rights, under whatever sovereignty the ports of China might fall. Since the United States had neither the power nor the disposition to back the Open Door by force, Hay's diplomacy was merely an appeal to the honor of the various governments.

The replies Hay received were cautious and evasive. Great Britain was willing to give assurances that the Secretary's three principles would be recognized in Weihaiwei and most other ports within her sphere, but made an exception of Kowloon. Furthermore, even this limited assent was contingent upon similar declarations being made by the other powers. Since they also gave only conditional approval, the chain Hay was trying to forge was no stronger than its weakest link. In the case of Russia, this link was weak indeed, for her reply was so hedged by conditions as to make it almost a refusal.

Instead of pressing for more meaningful pledges, Secretary Hay brought the episode to a conclusion by sending out a circular dispatch on March 20, 1900, in which he asserted that all the powers had assented to his proposal and that in each case he considered the assent "final and definitive." As diplomacy, this was a shrewd maneuver, since it left to foreign governments the onus of disputing him and protesting that they had *not* accepted the Open Door policy. Whether Hay's conduct was equally commendable in terms of giving accurate information to his own people was less certain. The American public jumped to the conclusion that Hay had achieved much more than he actually had.

The Boxer Rebellion

Hay's policy of protecting American commercial interests in China through international cooperation was soon put to a severe test. In June, 1900, Chinese resentment at high taxes, drought, and diplomatic humiliation boiled over in antiforeign riots. Popular frenzy had been whipped up by a secret patriotic society known as the "Fists of Righteous Harmony" or "Boxers." The murder of Christian missionaries and their Chinese converts was followed by an attack upon the foreign diplomatic corps at Peking. The German Minister and the secretary of the Japanese Legation were killed, and most of the other diplomats and their families took refuge in the British Legation, where Chinese zealots kept them under siege for weeks. Since the Boxers had also torn up railroad tracks and telegraph lines connecting Peking with the coast, the world was without news from the Chinese capital. While reports circulated that the whole foreign colony had been massacred, an international relief force was mobilized at Tientsin. Hay added to his reputation for cleverness by utilizing circuitous Chinese routes to learn that the diplomats were still alive. Finally, on August 14, 1900, the relief expedition reached Peking and rescued the legations, weary but unharmed after eight weeks of siege.

The ability of the diplomats to hold out was a tribute to their heroism, but it was also evidence that the Chinese never made the final mass attack that would have overpowered them. What stayed the Boxers' hands? One answer to the problem probably lies in the rather ambiguous relation of the Chinese government to the rebellion. Ostensibly the riots had been spontaneous outbreaks, which the Chinese authorities were unable to quell. Yet it was notorious that the Empress Dowager, a much more powerful figure than the weakling Emperor, secretly sympathized with the Boxers. Indeed, the story is told that the shelling of the French Cathedral was suspended for a few hours one afternoon out of deference to the Empress, who was picnicking with her ladies on the palace grounds and complained that the noise gave her a headache. There is, therefore, a strong probability that the Chinese government, fearful of the consequences that might follow the shedding of more diplomatic blood, had used its influence to restrain the rebels. John Hay's biographer suggests, moreover, that the conciliatory policy of the American Secretary of State may have been the decisive factor in inducing the Chinese to spare these foreigners.[5]

That China would be punished for the foreigners' losses of life and property was inevitable, but what form would the punishment take? Even

[5] Dennett, *John Hay*, pp. 306–307.

while the fate of the legations was still in doubt, Secretary Hay tried to forestall demands that would result in the partition of the empire. On July 3, 1900, he defined American policy in a circular telegram to the other powers. Although the United States would hold the actual culprits "to the uttermost accountability," it would continue to recognize all Chinese officials who would endeavor in good faith to protect foreign rights. With the Chinese people generally the United States sought "to remain in peace and friendship." Hay then went on to say:

> ...the policy of the Government of the United States is to seek a solution which may bring about permanent safety and peace to China, preserve Chinese territorial and administrative entity, protect all rights guaranteed to friendly powers by treaty and international law, and safeguard for the world the principle of equal and impartial trade with all parts of the Chinese Empire....

This important dispatch went significantly beyond the Open Door notes of 1899. Whereas the earlier document had appeared to acquiesce in the partition of China, Hay now asserted that American policy was to preserve Chinese territorial integrity and independence. Even the reiteration of the Open Door principle was more forceful. Whereas the 1899 notes had defined American rights rather narrowly and legalistically, this one called for "equal and impartial trade" with all parts of China.

Although Hay did not request replies from the other governments, he would have been glad to receive reassuring statements. All that was forthcoming, however, were a few indirect and vague concurring comments. As in 1899, Hay tried to make the most of these. Making public the text of his circular, he reported optimistically that the other powers had been giving "favorable consideration" to the American views. Once again the American public received the somewhat erroneous impression that Hay had scored a striking diplomatic victory.

The truth was that the Far Eastern situation was responding much more to the hard realities of power politics than to the moral pronouncements of the American State Department. To counter the growing Russian threat to Manchuria, England took two significant steps. One was to come to an agreement with Germany for the mutual recognition of the Open Door in their respective spheres of influence; the other was to move closer to Japan—thus making the first move toward a policy destined to lead to the Anglo-Japanese Alliance and the Russo-Japanese War. For the moment, a precarious balance of power was established that saved China from further losses of territory.

Even so, China's punishment was severe. Foreign troops both in Peking and elsewhere looted and murdered in a fashion that made a mockery of their claims to be the avenging angels of Western civilization. The formal terms imposed upon China were embodied in a peace protocol signed at Peking on September 7, 1901. An indemnity of 333 million dollars was levied; guilty officials were to be punished; communications between the Peking legations and the sea were to be made secure through foreign garrisons; additional commercial privileges were to be granted. The United States had tried to keep the indemnity within reasonable limits; for itself it took only 25 million dollars. Much of this was eventually returned to China, which used it for the education of Chinese students in the United States.

Even Secretary Hay himself had not been entirely consistent in his China policy. In November, 1900, he instructed the American Minister to China to try to obtain an American naval base at Samsah Bay in Fukien Province. This secret move, made in response to pressure from the War and Navy Departments, was thwarted by Japan, which claimed a sphere of influence in Fukien and gently rebuked Hay for departing from the principles he himself had laid down in the July 3 circular.

Although the American public exaggerated his role in saving China from partition and averting war in the Far East, Hay's diplomacy of 1899 and 1900 was of vast importance for the future. Like Monroe in 1823, he had laid down certain principles, to which subsequent secretaries of state again and again recurred. American persistence in holding to the Hay policy contributed to the crisis that reached its climax when Japanese planes swooped down on Pearl Harbor in 1941.

22

ROOSEVELT GETS HIS CANAL

No item on the imperialist program had greater priority than the building of an American-controlled canal to link the Atlantic and Pacific Oceans. All the exciting events of 1898—the battleship *Oregon's* dramatic voyage around Cape Horn; the Navy's operations in the Caribbean and the Far Pacific; the annexation of Puerto Rico, Hawaii, and the Philippines—had underlined the necessity of speedy communications between the two oceans.

Post–Civil War Developments

The principal difficulties in the way of canal construction were not financial or technical, but diplomatic. American public opinion had long since turned strongly against the limitations embodied in the Clayton-Bulwer Treaty of 1850,[1] under which Great Britain and the United States had pledged that neither would exercise "exclusive control" over an isthmian waterway. As early as 1869, President Grant insisted that the canal should be built and operated under the exclusive control of the United States. Ten years later, this position had been even more forcefully stated by President Hayes. During the Garfield and Arthur administrations, the State Department had first appealed to England for a revision of the Clayton-Bulwer Treaty and later, after this move failed, had negotiated the Frelinghuysen-Zavala Treaty with Nicaragua. This effort to get rid of the old treaty by acting as though it were dead failed through Senate opposition and the disapproval of the incoming President Cleveland.[2]

Meantime, Americans were watching the birth of a project of a different character. In 1879, Ferdinand de Lesseps, the famous French engineer

[1] See chap. 13.
[2] See chap. 18.

who had built the Suez Canal, organized the *Compagnie Universelle du Canal Interocéanique* to construct a waterway across the Panama Isthmus. The company purchased the so-called Wyse canal concession that the Colombian government had granted in 1878, sold large quantities of stock, mainly to the French public, and began excavating. After this promising beginning, however, the De Lesseps project became mired in a hopeless morass of financial, technical, and political disasters. In 1889, when about two-fifths of the digging was completed, the company went into bankruptcy amid ugly charges of graft and mismanagement. An attempt to revive the project was made in 1894, when the New Panama Canal Company was organized. Once again, however, it became apparent that the task was too big to be done by private enterprise. By 1898, it had become obvious that the new company's best hope of salvaging something from the wreck was to sell the unfinished canal and its valuable rights under the Wyse concession to the United States.

England's Change of Heart

Even before the Spanish-American War, the British government decided that a dog-in-the-manger policy would simply postpone the building of a waterway needed as much by British commerce as by American. Moreover, nothing would contribute more to improving Anglo-American relations than a graceful retreat on this issue. A hint to this effect had been dropped to the American State Department while Olney was still Secretary. Consequently, when John Hay suggested in 1898 that the two governments consider a revision of the old Clayton-Bulwer Treaty, Lord Salisbury cheerfully agreed.

Hay had little difficulty in working out details with Lord Pauncefote, the British Ambassador, and he had every expectation that the British government would promptly approve the draft treaty sent to London in January, 1899. At this point, however, the first of a series of frustrating delays occurred. Canada and the United States had been disagreeing over a wide variety of issues, including the Newfoundland fisheries, the Bering Sea seals, and the Alaska boundary. Eager to keep Canada happy, the British government hoped to induce the United States to make some concessions to its northern neighbor in return for the canal treaty, but months of tedious negotiations failed to result in a Canadian-American settlement.

Meantime, Congress was becoming dangerously restless on the canal issue. Bills were introduced that would have required the President to ignore the Clayton-Bulwer Treaty and proceed at once with plans for building a fortified canal. In a private letter of January, 1900, Hay urged Ambassador Joseph H. Choate to impress upon the British government the seriousness of the situation and the importance of speedy action. "I think we ought to make an effort to arrange the matter through diplomatic channels, so that at least the administration would have its skirts clear of any complicity in a violent and one-sided abrogation of the Clayton-Bulwer Treaty."

The First Hay-Pauncefote Treaty

The British government, not wanting to injure Anglo-American relations during the Boer War and worried lest the Anglophile Hay resign his post, took speedy action. On February 3, 1900, Hay and Pauncefote signed a treaty embodying the exact terms that the two had drafted a year earlier. This so-called First Hay-Pauncefote Treaty provided that the United States might construct a canal and enjoy exclusive control of its management. The waterway was to be neutralized under rules substantially like those embodied in the Suez Canal Convention of 1888. One rule stipulated that the canal should be free and open, both in war and peace, to all nations on terms of equality; another permitted the United States to maintain a police force in the canal zone, but prohibited fortifications. Finally, the treaty provided that other nations be invited to adhere to these stipulations. All in all, the new agreement constituted an important revision of the Clayton-Bulwer Treaty, but left the older document still in force.

By gaining the support of Democratic Senator John T. Morgan of Alabama, leading champion of a Nicaraguan canal, Hay hoped to pave the way for Senate approval, but, as he wrote to Choate, he realized that the treaty would be opposed by politicians who believed "that we are derelict in our duty in having got a whole loaf and not having demanded two."

Hay's gloomy predictions were more than fulfilled. Although the treaty was supposed to be secret until the Senate had acted, the *New York Sun* obtained a copy and began a savage attack upon it. Irish reaction was summed up in the scare headlines of the *Irish World:* BETRAYAL OF AMERICAN INTERESTS. THE CANAL TREATY SURRENDERS EVERYTHING TO GREAT BRITAIN AND ABANDONS THE MONROE DOCTRINE. IT IS AN ANGLO-AMERICAN ALLIANCE. REAFFIRMS THE DEAD CLAYTON-BULWER TREATY. MAKES ENGLAND MASTER OF THE CANAL, AND EXPOSES OUR PACIFIC COAST TO ENGLISH ATTACK IN CASE OF WAR.

For such assaults Hay was prepared. Much more dangerous was the blow struck from an unexpected quarter. Soon after the text of the treaty leaked out to the press, a little group of prominent Eastern Republicans, including President Nicholas Murray Butler of Columbia University,

Albert Shaw, editor of the *Review of Reviews*, David Jayne Hill, an Assistant Secretary of State, and Theodore Roosevelt, now Governor of New York, met to discuss the matter. This conclave resulted in a public statement by Roosevelt expressing hope that the treaty would be rejected "unless amended so as to provide that the canal, when built, shall be wholly under the control of the United States, alike in peace and war." This was vital, the Governor argued, "no less from the standpoint of our sea power than from the standpoint of the Monroe Doctrine." When Hay wrote in hurt surprise to ask: "Cannot you leave a few things to the President and the Senate, who are charged with them by the Constitution?" Roosevelt elaborated upon his objections. An unfortified canal, open even to enemies in wartime, would expose the Pacific Coast to attacks from powers like Germany or France. Even more objectionable was the provision for inviting other nations to join in guaranteeing the canal's neutrality. Such a precedent would lead to European involvement in all kinds of Western Hemisphere business.

Since the free-silver Democrats and Populists were always opposed to closer Anglo-American relations, the defection of the more aggressive Republican expansionists ruled out unqualified Senate approval of the treaty. Roosevelt's friend, Senator Lodge, took a leading part in attacking the document, but the issue was so loaded with political dynamite that no action at all was taken until after McKinley was safely reelected. Then in December, 1900, the treaty was finally approved, but not until three significant amendments had been added. One provided for the definite suspension of the Clayton-Bulwer Treaty; the second, while allowing the principle of neutralization and nonfortification to stand, reserved for the United States the right to take measures necessary for national defense and the maintenance of order; the third eliminated the invitation to other powers to join in guaranteeing the canal's neutrality.

In a private letter to Ambassador Choate, Hay bitterly blamed Democratic malice and Republican timidity for mutilating his handiwork. Of the amendments he said: "They deform and disfigure the Treaty; they take much from the grace and value of the concession which Great Britain has made us; but beyond the matter of taste and good manners, I consider them of little moment. They give no additional advantage to us; they demand no sacrifice from Great Britain." He therefore hoped Lord Salisbury would accept the amended treaty, saying: "Take your treaty, Brother Jonathan, and God send you better manners." [3]

Choate did what he could to sell this point of view to the British government, but to no avail. Piqued by the way the Senate had acted, the Salisbury government rejected the Senate amendments.

[3] Hay to Choate, Dec. 21, 1900, Joseph H. Choate Papers, Library of Congress.

The Second Hay-Pauncefote Treaty

Although the failure of the First Hay-Pauncefote Treaty caused a temporary coolness in Anglo-American relations, the eventual outcome was good. Realizing that haste would be necessary if an impatient Congress were to be prevented from simply tearing up the Clayton-Bulwer Treaty, the diplomats went promptly to work on a new agreement.

Learning from his mistakes, Hay kept the Republican expansionists well informed on the negotiations. He was particularly careful to enlist the help of Lodge and Roosevelt. The Massachusetts Senator was encouraged to meet leading English public figures on a London trip during the summer of 1901. As Hay gleefully explained, he had annexed Lodge to the Embassy "so that if he kicks at the treaty this winter he will be kicking his own shins." Hay's careful handling of Roosevelt became especially important because, by the time the new agreement was ready for signature, the Rough Rider had become President of the United States.

The Second Hay-Pauncefote Treaty, signed November 18, 1901, resembled its rejected predecessor in providing that the United States might construct a canal and enjoy exclusive control over its management. Provisions for neutralization included a pledge that the canal should be free and open to both merchant vessels and warships of all nations on terms of entire equality. Unlike the earlier agreement, however, this one specifically superseded the Clayton-Bulwer Treaty, permitted the United States to maintain military police along the canal, and omitted any provision for an international guarantee. Most important of all, the earlier prohibition against American fortification was omitted. In this particular, the second treaty went even beyond the Senate amendments to the first treaty.

Although Senator Joseph W. Bailey of Texas complained that "the new treaty takes Great Britain into partnership with us, and that is something the American people will not stand," the great majority of senators were well pleased with Hay's achievement. The vote for approval was 72 to 6.

Battle of the Routes

With his strong interest in American sea power, Theodore Roosevelt was determined to make the building of a waterway between the Atlantic and the Pacific his principal accomplishment. As he wrote to Secretary Hay on July 1, 1902: "The great bit of work of my administration, and from the material and constructive standpoint one of the greatest bits of work that the twentieth century will see, is the Isthmian Canal."

By the ratification of the Hay-Pauncefote Treaty the first barrier in the path had been cleared. The next steps were destined to be more difficult. Since the 1850s, most Americans had concentrated their thinking on the Nicaraguan route. The Panama alternative, shorter and more feasible from the engineering point of view, had received less attention than it deserved. During the first six months of 1902, however, opinion took a remarkable shift.

The chain of circumstances leading to the victory of the Panama route was briefly this. In November, 1901, the Walker Commission, which had been studying the problem for more than two years, reported that actual construction costs of the two alternatives would be: Nicaragua route, $189,864,062; Panama route, $144,233,358. However, in order to use the Panama route, the United States would have to purchase the rights and property of the New Panama Canal Company. The company had refused to fix a price for these rights, but had suggested that their value lay in the neighborhood of 109 million dollars. Therefore the commission unanimously recommended the Nicaraguan project.

Warned by this report that, if it were too greedy, it might get nothing at all, the New Panama Canal Company speedily offered to sell for 40 million dollars—the sum suggested by the Walker Commission as fair value for the property. President Roosevelt, a recent convert to the Panama route, urged the Walker Commission to reconsider its findings in view of the company offer. This the commission promptly did, and on January 18, 1902, it issued an important supplementary report recommending Panama as "the most practicable and feasible route."

Even with this tactical victory, the Panama faction had a stiff fight on its hands. On January 9, 1902, the House of Representatives had passed by the impressive margin of 308 to 2 the Hepburn Bill, providing that the canal be built through Nicaragua. To block the Hepburn Bill in the Senate required all the ingenuity of three able men: William Nelson Cromwell, Philippe Bunau-Varilla, and Mark Hanna. Cromwell, American attorney for the New Panama Canal Company, was a clever New York corporation lawyer with all the Washington connections to make him a skillful lobbyist. Bunau-Varilla, a French engineer and former associate of De Lesseps, had come to America in 1901 to write and speak in favor of the Panama route. His master inspiration as a propagandist was to place on each senator's desk a mounted Nicaraguan postage stamp showing a steaming volcano— grim warning of the volcanic hazards that were alleged to threaten the Nicaraguan route. Unkind rumor had it that Mark Hanna's help was gained by a $60,000 contribution from Panama Company funds to the Republican campaign chest of 1900. A more probable explanation would be that the Ohio Senator preferred the Panama route because of his businessman's estimate of comparative costs and engineering difficulties.

At all events, six months of complicated legislative maneuvering and debate finally resulted in the so-called Spooner Act, which received Roosevelt's signature on June 28, 1902. By this the President was authorized to acquire for the United States, at a cost not to exceed 40 million dollars, all the isthmian rights and property of the New Panama Canal Company; he was further empowered to obtain from Colombia on such terms as he deemed reasonable a canal zone at least 6 miles wide and such other territory as might be required. These things done, he was to proceed to build the canal. If it proved impossible within a "reasonable time" to acquire the necessary rights in Panama, he was to go ahead with the alternative Nicaraguan project.

The Colombian Obstacle

The Spooner Act enjoined upon President Roosevelt the responsibility of coming to a speedy agreement with Colombia, but Vice President José Marroquín, a teacher and writer who had been thrust into the uncomfortable position of Colombian strong man, was hardly in a position to follow a clear-cut policy in the negotiations. Marroquín's Conservative regime was hated by the Liberals, and the country was convulsed by civil war during most of 1901 and 1902. The Vice President would have greatly preferred to postpone all canal negotiations until after he had crushed his rivals at home. Compelled by circumstances to go through the motions of diplomacy, he dragged his feet, exasperating both the American government and his own diplomatic agents by his delays and contradictory policies.

Marroquín's fumbling reflected the conflicting impulses he felt in his own thinking. He wanted the canal to be built and desperately needed whatever revenue Colombia might derive from the project. At the same time he disliked letting the American camel get a nose into the Colombian tent and feared that if he gave away too much he would weaken his own political position. In a letter written in July, 1902, the Vice President described his predicament: [4]

> Concerning the canal question, I find myself in a horrible perplexity; in order that the North Americans may complete the work... it is necessary to make concessions of territory, of sovereignty, and of jurisdiction, which the Executive Power has not the power of yielding; and if we do not yield them and the North Americans determine to build the canal, they will open it without stopping at trifles, and then we

[4] Reprinted by permission of the publisher from Dwight C. Miner, *The Fight for the Panama Route* (Copyright 1940 by Columbia University Press, New York), p. 233.

will lose more sovereignty than we should lose by making the concessions they seek.

History will say of me that I ruined the Isthmus and all Colombia
by not permitting the opening of the Panama Canal, or that I permitted
it to be done, scandalously injuring the rights of my country.

I would only be able to free myself of my responsibilities if I should
succeed in transferring them to the congress....

If Colombia must give up some of its cherished sovereignty, she hoped
at least to be amply compensated both by the United States and by the
New Panama Canal Company, since the latter's 40-million-dollar deal
could not be consummated without Colombia's consent. When Tomás
Herrán became chargé d'affaires at Washington in December, 1902, he
was instructed to demand a 10-million-dollar indemnity, plus an annual
payment of $600,000. Hay was ready to offer the 10 million, but wanted
to limit the annuity to $100,000. Attorney Cromwell, eager to promote
the New Panama Canal Company's interest, acted as mediator in arranging a compromise annuity of $250,000.

Reluctantly, because he feared Colombian public opinion would be
disappointed with the bargain, Herrán signed the so-called Hay-Herrán
Treaty of January 22, 1903. By this agreement Colombia was to authorize
the New Panama Canal Company to sell its isthmian rights and property
to the United States; the United States was to have the exclusive right for
one hundred years—to be renewed for similar periods for as long as the
United States might desire—to construct, maintain, and protect a canal;
for the same period the United States was to have control over a canal
zone 6 miles wide; within the canal zone the United States was to enjoy
certain extraterritorial rights; Colombia was to receive 10 million dollars
upon the exchange of ratifications, and annual payments of $250,000 be-
ginning nine years later.

Approved without amendment by the United States Senate, although not
without bitter opposition from the faction favoring the Nicaraguan route,
the Hay-Herrán Treaty needed only the approbation of the Colombian
government to go into effect. At this point, however, John Hay's diplomacy suffered another defeat. The Colombian congress, elected according to an agreement terminating the civil war, convened at Bogotá in
June, 1903. On August 12, after several weeks of excited debate, the treaty
was rejected by the almost unanimous vote of the Colombian senate.

The situation that brought about this unhappy result was complicated
beyond the ability of most North Americans to understand. In the first
place, Marroquín was not the all-powerful dictator that outsiders believed. In the new congress he was confronted not only by the Liberals,
but by rival factions within his own Conservative party. Marroquín's

enemies saw in the unpopular treaty an opportunity to assail the patriotism of his regime.

In order to strengthen his position, Marroquín tried desperately to obtain further concessions from the United States. The first major grievance against the treaty was the matter of Colombian sovereignty, which seemed to be undermined by the perpetual lease, the provisions for extraterritoriality, and other treaty clauses. The second sore point was the amount of compensation. Most Colombians, regardless of party, thought the United States had driven a hard bargain. Two possibilities for extra compensation suggested themselves. One was to induce the United States to make a larger direct payment; the other was to insist that the New Panama Canal Company hand over to Colombia perhaps one-quarter of its 40 million dollars in return for Colombia's consent to the transfer of the company's rights.

The Roosevelt administration did nothing to help Marroquín in his predicament. Instead, there was an effort at big-stick diplomacy, a brusque insistence that Colombia accept the treaty exactly as written. In his tenderness for the interests of the New Panama Canal Company, Hay even allowed Cromwell to draft State Department dispatches.

Caught in this squeeze between his domestic enemies and the unsympathetic North Americans, Marroquín abandoned the fight to obtain congressional approval. He still hoped the canal would be built through Colombian territory, but he believed that only the shock of the treaty's rejection could bring about, both in Colombia and in the United States, the reaction necessary for a final settlement.

Revolution in Panama

In view of the many occasions on which the United States Senate had refused to approve treaties òr had amended them past recognition, the politicians at Washington might have been expected to understand the conduct of their opposite numbers at Bogotá. But President Roosevelt was a man of strong will, given to oversimplifying complex situations and classifying men who opposed him as wicked. In his blunt analysis, Marroquín was a dictator who had given a promise and then had failed to keep it. Roosevelt regarded the summoning of the Colombian congress, which had not met since 1898, as simply a bit of window dressing to cloak blackmailing attempts against the United States and the New Panama Canal Company. The President and the Secretary of State competed with each other in coining uncomplimentary epithets for the Colombian politicians. Roosevelt alluded to "contemptible little creatures," "jack-rabbits," and "foolish and homicidal corruptionists," while Hay called them "greedy little anthropoids."

A more patient man than the President would have moved slowly, for a few face-saving concessions might still have gained Colombian consent. Moreover, Roosevelt had a winning card in the alternative Nicaraguan route. He could have taken up this familiar project, either with the serious purpose of carrying it through or as a warning to Colombia to adopt a more reasonable attitude.

But Roosevelt was now determined to use the Panama route with or without Colombian consent. One small nation, unable to rule itself efficiently, must not, he argued, be permitted to thwart a project beneficial to the whole civilized world. Even before the Colombian congress finally rejected the treaty, the President had begun considering what his course should be in case this happened. He was particularly impressed by a memorandum prepared by John Bassett Moore, formerly a State Department official and now professor of international law at Columbia University. Moore argued that the United States already had important rights under the old Bidlack Treaty of 1846.[5] In return for a pledge "that the right of way or transit across the Isthmus of Panama upon any modes of communication that now exist, or may be hereafter constructed, shall be free and open to the Government and citizens of the United States,"

[5] See chap. 13.

the United States had guaranteed the neutrality of the isthmus "with the view that the free transit from one to the other side may not be interrupted." Under this provision Colombia had benefited; not only had foreign powers been warned against encroaching upon her sovereignty, but American forces had several times intervened to prevent rebels from using the Panama Railroad against the Colombian government. To Moore's legal mind, this imposed an obligation upon Colombia not to obstruct the building of the canal contemplated in the Bidlack Treaty. In October, 1903, Roosevelt was working upon the draft of a message to Congress, requesting authority to dig the canal without further negotiations with Colombia.

In the end, however, events took a different course. The state of Panama, remote from the rest of Colombia and without good communications except by sea, had already shown separatist tendencies. The residents of the district were eager for the material benefits that would flow from the canal, and it had frequently been predicted that if Bogotá failed in the negotiations, the Panamanians might attempt to secede and deal directly with the United States. A small group on the isthmus began to formulate definite plans for such an uprising in May, 1903, even before the Colombian congress convened, with quiet encouragement from officials of the Panama Railroad Company and the New Panama Canal Company. Despite these favoring factors, the conspirators were rather discouraged with their progress until the energetic Philippe Bunau-Varilla reappeared upon the American scene in September.

The would-be revolutionists were prudent men. Before they risked their lives, they wanted to know what the United States government was likely to do. If, as on earlier occasions, American intervention in Panama took a form that favored the Colombian government in power, the rebellion would fail. If, on the contrary, the United States used the guarantee of uninterrupted transit across the isthmus to prevent Colombian forces from operating against the rebels, the latter were sure to win.

To try to obtain an answer to this all-important question, Bunau-Varilla interviewed both the President and the Secretary of State. The two listened with interest to the Frenchman's warning that a Panama revolution was likely to occur and that the administration should be prepared for such an event. Although Roosevelt and Hay apparently gave no explicit promise that the rebels would have American protection, they listened with such obvious sympathy that Bunau-Varilla was able to guess that this would be the case.

Certainly the arrival of the U.S.S. *Nashville* at Colón, the Atlantic terminal of the Panama Railroad, on November 2, 1903, was no accident. Some two weeks earlier the Navy Department had ordered several American warships to move to the expected trouble spot. On the evening of

November 3 the conspirators made their move in Panama City. Arresting a few loyal Colombian army officers, they easily gained control. A Colombian warship in the harbor opened up a brief bombardment, killing one unfortunate Chinese and wounding an ass in the slaughterhouse, but this was the only resistance to the revolution on the Pacific coast.

The situation at Colón was less favorable, because a force of some four hundred Colombian troops had recently arrived at the scene—enough men to suppress the whole rebellion if they were allowed to use the Panama Railroad. This, however, was prevented, first by subterfuges practiced by the railroad officials, and then by direct order of the United States Navy. When the Colombians threatened to fight, the decks of the *Nashville* were cleared for action. Seeing the hopelessness of his position, the Colombian commander accepted a Panamanian bribe of $8,000 and two cases of champagne to evacuate the city. By November 5 the rebels were in control of the whole isthmus. Any chance for the Colombian government to reconquer its territory was ended by the blunt warning that American naval vessels now guarding both the Atlantic and Pacific approaches would prevent the landing of Colombian forces.

On November 6, 1903, Secretary Hay recognized the new Republic of Panama, and on November 19, the Secretary and Bunau-Varilla, now acting as Minister Plenipotentiary for the new nation, affixed their signatures to the Hay-Bunau-Varilla Treaty. By this agreement, Panama received the 10-million-dollar indemnity and $250,000 annual payment that had been offered to Colombia. The United States gained more than it would have under the rejected treaty: the canal zone was to be 10 miles wide instead of 6; within the zone the United States was to exercise all powers of government rather than the more limited powers defined in the Hay-Herrán Treaty; and the grant was "in perpetuity." In conclusion, the United States guaranteed and promised to maintain the independence of the new republic.

Although the Senate approved the Hay-Bunau-Varilla Treaty by the decisive vote of 66 to 14, Roosevelt's policy did not escape bitter criticism from the Democrats and from many newspapers. Even though the whole story of the Panama revolution was not known, some things were disturbingly obvious. The arrival of the *Nashville* on the eve of the uprising, the one-sided intervention that protected the rebels and made it impossible for the Colombians to move their forces, the speed with which the Roosevelt administration recognized the new republic and negotiated a highly advantageous treaty—all these circumstances made it appear that the United States had been guilty of seizing a weaker nation's territory under a flimsy camouflage. Both the legalistic justification based upon the Bidlack Treaty and the President's highly moralistic pronouncements about Colombia's duplicity and the American duty to act on behalf of civilization had a somewhat hollow ring. Indeed, in later years Roosevelt stated his case more candidly in a public address: [6]

> I am interested in the Panama Canal because I started it. If I had followed traditional, conservative methods I should have submitted a dignified State paper of probably two hundred pages to Congress, and the debate on it would be going on yet; but *I took the Canal Zone* and let Congress debate and while the debate goes on the Canal does also.

By thus "taking" the Canal Zone, Roosevelt cut the Gordian knot that had held up construction of the all-important waterway, but the incident cost the United States a heavy price in Latin-American good will. Throughout Central and South America the Panama episode brought dislike and fear of the "Colossus of the North," whose aggressive policies seemed to threaten the independence of smaller neighbors. Many years were to elapse before the United States would win again the trust it had forfeited. A different course on Roosevelt's part might have cost the United States more in dollars, but less in Western Hemisphere esteem.

The New Balance of Naval Power

Although the way in which it had gained control of the Canal Zone put a serious strain on the relations of the United States with its neighbors to the south, the waterway itself was a major contribution to American commercial and naval strength. Relieved of the necessity for the long, dangerous voyage around Cape Horn, American ships sailing from East Coast ports were now in a position to expand their trade in the Pacific. The once-remote countries along the west coast of South America, with their valuable copper and nitrates, were now readily accessible. The American Navy greatly increased its effective power by gaining the means to shift units quickly from one ocean to another.

Well before the Panama Canal was ready for use in 1914, the United States had gained naval supremacy in the Caribbean Sea. Great Britain, long the dominant power in that region, gracefully retreated, cutting its Caribbean fleet to a minimum. In part, the new British policy reflected the striking improvement in Anglo-American relations. As soon as it became obvious that England and the United States were more likely to be allies than enemies in any future conflict, a redeployment of British naval power became natural. English statesmen, however, were influenced even more by the European situation. Kaiser William II, who had been the dominant figure in the German government since the resignation of Chancellor Bismarck in 1890, was an impulsive and strong-willed monarch, given to sword-rattling oratory. How much real menace lay behind the

[6] *New York Times*, Mar. 25, 1911. The italics are added.

Kaiser's talk was difficult to measure, but the British were unhappy over Germany's aggressive trade expansion, its growing colonial ambitions, and, above all, its extensive naval building program. The withdrawal from the Caribbean and the concentration of the British fleet in European waters reflected these English fears.

American statesmen also kept a suspicious eye on Germany. The unpleasant episodes during the Samoan crisis and the Spanish-American War encouraged anti-German feeling, particularly in Navy circles. The British naturally played upon these American suspicions and dropped frequent warnings against Germany's supposed ambitions. Many Americans became convinced that Germany resented the Monroe Doctrine and was only waiting an opportunity to gain a foothold in the Western Hemisphere. Subsequent research in the German archives has revealed that these fears were greatly exaggerated. Whatever their ambitions in the rest of the world, most Germans were sufficiently realistic to understand that British naval supremacy in the eastern Atlantic and American in the western would make any imperialistic German venture in Latin America a losing game.

Yet American statesmen refused to draw comfort from the map. The defense of the Panama Canal became one of the most powerful factors in shaping American foreign policy. Again and again the United States was destined to take preventive steps to make doubly sure that neither Germany nor any other great power gained a base within the vital Caribbean zone.

Protectorate over Cuba

American sensitivity over the Caribbean area was reflected in policy toward Cuba. Although the pledge of 1898 was respected by an early recognition of Cuban independence, the United States kept a nervous eye on developments in the nearby island. In 1901, when the Cubans were drafting a constitution under the tutelage of General Leonard Wood, the United States Congress responded to a suggestion of the War Department by enacting the Platt Amendment—originally a rider to the Army Appropriation Act of that year. This stipulated that American military withdrawal from the island should be conditional upon the incorporation of seven provisions into the Cuban constitution. The most important of these pledged Cuba never to enter into any treaty which would impair her independence or result in a transfer of territory, never to contract any debt beyond her ability to pay out of ordinary revenue, to recognize that the United States might intervene for the maintenance of Cuban independence and order, and to promise to lease coaling and naval bases to the United States. The Cuban constitutional convention at first overwhelmingly rejected the Platt proposals. Since there was no other way to achieve independence, however, the Cubans eventually wrote the required provisions into their constitution. To shackle the island republic still more tightly, the United States insisted on incorporating the Platt Amendment into a formal treaty between the two countries in 1903.

After the withdrawal of American forces in 1902, President Tomás Estrada Palma at first governed Cuba without serious trouble. Soon after his reelection in 1905, however, strife and bloodshed broke out between the President and his opponents, who accused him of dictatorial designs. Roosevelt delayed American intervention until he became convinced that Palma could not restore order. Then a small military force was ordered to the island and American supervision of the government restored. In dealing with this unhappy situation, Roosevelt showed more than his usual restraint. He ignored demands of American expansionists for annexation and concentrated upon economic and political reform. "I am doing my best," he wrote to a friend, "to persuade the Cubans that if only they will be good they will be happy; I am seeking the very minimum of interference necessary to make them good." Naturally many Cubans refused to acknowledge the necessity of this paternalistic policy, but there was no serious resistance to American rule and, in January, 1909, American forces were again withdrawn, leaving the Cubans to govern themselves.

Debt Collecting in Venezuela

Even before the Panama revolution, American attention had been drawn to the problems involved in European intervention in the Caribbean Sea region. Late in 1902, Germany, England, and Italy began a joint blockade of Venezuelan ports to compel dictator Cipriano Castro to pay numerous obligations due to foreign bondholders and other private creditors. Castro's highhandedness in these matters had become so notorious that a showdown had long been expected.

As early as July, 1901, Roosevelt had written in an unofficial letter to a German friend: "If any South American state misbehaves toward any European country, spank it." The President expressed much the same idea in his message to Congress in December, 1901, when he asserted that the Monroe Doctrine did not guarantee any American state against punishment for misconduct, provided this did not result in the acquisition of territory by any non-American power. Soon after, German Ambassador Theodor von Holleben formally notified the American government that Castro's attitude might make it necessary for Germany to take coercive steps: first, in the form of a blockade of Venezuelan harbors; then, if that failed, by the temporary occupation of Venezuelan ports and the collection of customs. This document brought no protest from Washington.

In a formal reply Secretary Hay expressed confidence that German pledges against permanent occupation of American territory would be faithfully kept.

In November, 1902, when informed by the British Ambassador that his country was also contemplating action against Venezuela, Hay declared that although the United States regretted the use of European force against Latin-American countries, it could not object to Europe taking steps to obtain redress for injuries suffered by European subjects, provided no acquisition of territory was contemplated.

Although Roosevelt seemed almost to encourage Castro's spanking, he was not without misgivings about the situation. Suspicion of Germany had pervaded Navy circles since the Spanish-American War. Many admirals were convinced that the Kaiser was maneuvering to obtain a naval base in American waters and that the projected debt-collecting expedition against Venezuela was a key move in the game. In November, 1902, Admiral H. C. Taylor, chief of the Bureau of Navigation, warned that any German attempt to occupy Venezuelan customs houses would lead to a war in which Venezuela would be defeated and subjected to German demands for indemnity. Unable to pay, Venezuela would either have to give up territory or mortgage her revenue in such a way as to place her in political dependence to Germany. Since neither of these things must be allowed to happen, Taylor advised that the United States keep at all times a force at Puerto Rico equal or superior to the whole German fleet in the Caribbean. "Our aim must be at all times to be in a better state of preparation for war than Germany is, and her every movement must be met by corresponding preparatory action on our part."

The Navy probably misjudged German intentions, and there is no reason to believe that the President was equally alarmed. Nevertheless, he took care to be prepared for any contingency. On several occasions Roosevelt stressed the point that the Monroe Doctrine could be maintained only if the Navy were kept in fighting trim. Moreover, he ordered the ships of the European, North Atlantic, and South Atlantic squadrons to concentrate at Puerto Rico for the most ambitious maneuvers that the American Navy had ever attempted in peacetime. Admiral Dewey was to be in personal command; this, Roosevelt thought, would have a "very beneficial" effect abroad as well as at home.[7]

It was scarcely coincidence, therefore, that, when the German and British fleets began the coercion of Venezuela with the seizure and sinking of Venezuelan gunboats on December 9, 1902, the American Navy was poised at Puerto Rico ready for whatever action might be necessary.

[7] Roosevelt to Admiral Dewey, June 14, 1902, Roosevelt Letter Books, Library of Congress.

A cartoon in the Chicago *Inter-Ocean* showed Uncle Sam looking out from the prow of a battleship which dwarfed the nearby German and English boats. "Collect your money," the caption read, "but don't forget the Monroe Doctrine."

American newspapers made much of the sinking of Venezuelan ships and the bombing of Venezuelan towns. The *St. Louis Globe-Democrat* admitted the villainy of Castro, but asserted that nothing that the Venezuelan dictator had done "afforded the shadow of a provocation for the buccaneer raid which has been made upon his country under the pretext of a desire to collect debts due to private individuals who were well aware of the risks they were running when they invested their money and their labor in Venezuela." All the leading New York newspapers agreed that the sinking of Venezuelan ships had been unjustified. The *Brooklyn Daily Eagle* regarded the European action as equivalent to an undeclared war against Venezuela, which "engenders the suspicion that not the debts but other things are the object." Senators and representatives were described as upset by the situation and fearful that the President was not taking adequate steps to protect the Monroe Doctrine.

Significantly, it was Germany rather than Britain that drew most of the American anger. The *New York Herald* declared that it was plain to every American that Venezuela was "but a pretext for an insidious attempt to break down the Monroe Doctrine" and warned: "There is no room for the German Emperor on the Western Hemisphere." According to the *Brooklyn Daily Eagle*, Great Britain was well-meaning though weak, but Germany must be regarded with grave suspicion. A German newspaper correspondent, reporting from New York, complained: "The greatest excitement prevails here. The entire press holds Germany responsible for the present stiuation. Germany is attacked in hostile articles, while Great Britain is praised."

The distinction the American press drew between England and Germany was probably unjust, because the policy of joint coercion was as much British as German in origin. Nevertheless, once it became evident that the blockade was highly unpopular in the United States, the British press began to join in criticism, and the British government was soon eager to find a way out. Although the German government was not under similar attack at home, it was dismayed by the American and British popular reaction.

As soon as Castro found himself in serious trouble, he offered on December 13, 1902, to submit the claims to arbitration. Fearful that the wily Venezuelan was merely temporizing, the British and German governments at first hesitated, but as disturbing news of American public opinion arrived they modified their policy. On December 16, the British cabinet decided to accept the idea of arbitration; the next day the German government also agreed; and on the 18th the decision was transmitted to Washington.

Although the tension was momentarily relaxed, the episode was by no means closed. Until the actual details of the arbitration agreement could be arranged, the British and Germans were determined to continue the blockade. A first problem was that of choosing an arbiter. Roosevelt himself was invited to assume this responsibility, but he refused, suggesting as an alternative that the dispute be submitted to the Hague Tribunal.[8] Then a long delay was caused by the question of whether the nationals of the blockading powers should be entitled to a preferential position among the creditors and by other questions of procedure. In January, 1903, the German fleet provoked still more American resentment by bombarding Venezuelan forts and ships. Under the circumstances there was great relief in Washington when arrangements for arbitration were finally completed on February 9, and the irritating blockade was terminated.

A tantalizing historical puzzle is involved in the debt controversy. As early as 1905, Roosevelt began to relate how he had forced an unwilling German Emperor to accept arbitration by threatening to send Dewey's fleet to the scene. In subsequent versions the story became more and more dramatic until it reached its final form in a letter which Roosevelt wrote in 1916 to William Roscoe Thayer, the biographer of John Hay. Since competent historians have been unable to find in the German archives any evidence of such an ultimatum, many authorities have dismissed the story as a legend, originating in Roosevelt's imagination and love of self.[9] On the other hand, a later study of the problem concludes that Roosevelt probably did transmit certain warnings to the German government, although of a less blunt and unpleasant character than his later accounts would suggest.[10]

Despite the dispute over Roosevelt's exact role, there can be no doubt that the German government was dismayed by the unexpected torrent of abuse from the American press. Convinced that it had been badly informed on probable American reaction, the German government abruptly dismissed Ambassador Holleben and appointed in his place Roosevelt's close friend, Baron Speck von Sternberg.

[8] See chap. 26 for the establishment of the Hague Tribunal.
[9] See especially Dexter Perkins, *The Monroe Doctrine, 1867–1907* (Baltimore: Johns Hopkins Press, 1937), pp. 319–395.
[10] Howard K. Beale, *Theodore Roosevelt and the Rise of America to World Power* (Baltimore: Johns Hopkins Press, 1956), pp. 395–431.

The Roosevelt Corollary

While the American press was lamenting the coercion of Venezuela, English newspapers and political leaders pointed out that, if the Americans objected to European punishment of misbehaving Latin-American neighbors, the United States itself would have to assume responsibility for disciplining them. Similar suggestions had come from Europe on earlier occasions. President Roosevelt quickly adopted this point of view, which was thoroughly consistent with his own belief that the civilized nations had an obligation to impose good behavior upon the more "backward" peoples. Revealing in a private letter how he really felt about Latin America, he disclosed his determination to show "those Dagoes that they will have to behave decently."

Events in the Dominican Republic soon provided an occasion for publicly announcing that the United States had assumed the role of policeman for the Western Hemisphere. Because of obligations long overdue both the American and European claimants, the Dominican Republic was in danger not only of provoking action similar to that taken against Venezuela, but of having to surrender control of its customs houses to outside powers. Moreover, the possibility of European intervention had recently been increased as a result of the Hague Court's decision [11] giving preference to the claims of the blockading powers in the Venezuelan debt case. It was feared that this might encourage the further use of force and hurt the position of American creditors.

In May, 1904, Roosevelt gave a preview of his new policy in a letter read by Elihu Root at a Cuban anniversary dinner. "Brutal wrongdoing, or an impotence which results in a general loosening of the ties of civilized society," the President asserted, "may finally require intervention by some civilized nation, and in the Western Hemisphere the United States cannot ignore this duty."

Although this Rooseveltian pronouncement was criticized in some quarters as jingoistic, the President persisted on his new course. In his annual message to Congress in December, 1904, he denied that the United States had any aggressive designs toward other Western Hemisphere countries. "All that this country desires is to see neighboring countries stable, orderly, and prosperous. ... If a nation shows that it knows how to act with reasonable efficiency and decency in social and political matters, if it keeps order and pays its obligations, it need fear no interference from the United States." However, "chronic wrongdoing" or "impotence" might ultimately require intervention by some civilized nation, "and in the Western Hemisphere the adherence of the United

[11] See chap. 26 for the establishment of this court.

States to the Monroe Doctrine may force the United States, however reluctantly, in flagrant cases of such wrongdoing or impotence to the exercise of an international police power."

In simple terms, this so-called Roosevelt Corollary asserted that in order to prevent European interventions with possible transfers of territory, the United States would itself force reform upon misbehaving Latin-American countries. Since the original Monroe Doctrine had never claimed any right of the United States to interfere in the internal affairs of other countries, this was a radical departure.

The Corollary Applied

Even before Roosevelt's message to Congress, affairs in the Dominican Republic were leading to increased American involvement. Under an arbitral award of 1904 one of the Dominican customs houses had been placed under a financial agent of the United States to assure the payment of obligations due to the Santo Domingo Development Company, an American-owned enterprise. France and Belgium were arguing that they should control other customs houses to protect the interest of their nationals, and Dominican President Carlos Morales was appealing to Washington for help. Under these circumstances, it required very little urging from the American State Department to induce Morales to request that the United States take over the entire customs collection. On February 7, 1905, the two governments signed a protocol providing that an American collector of customs should assume the responsibility for collecting and distributing these revenues, with 45 per cent to be turned over to the Dominican government and the balance to be divided equitably among the foreign creditors.

When the President submitted this protocol to the Senate, his policy encountered so much opposition that no action could be taken before Congress adjourned in March. Unwilling to delay the project, Roosevelt arranged a modus vivendi under which the American financial receivership went into operation. Annoyed by this action, the Senate continued to withhold approval of the treaty for two years. On his side, Roosevelt proceeded under the existing executive agreement to reorganize Dominican finances. From the technical point of view, the receivership was highly successful. Honestly and efficiently collected, the revenues rapidly increased to the mutual advantage of the foreign creditors and the Dominican government. To consolidate these gains, the American banking firm of Kuhn, Loeb and Company agreed to liquidate the old obligations with a new bond issue.

These latest arrangements made it imperative that the Senate give the financial protectorate its blessing. Secretary of State Elihu Root, who had succeeded John Hay in July, 1905, negotiated a new treaty, much like the original one but with a few minor changes to meet senatorial objections. Root, who was generally much more successful than Hay in handling politicians, finally obtained Senate approval in February, 1907.

Dr. Root Applies the Salve

Roosevelt's highanded action in Panama and, to a lesser extent, his pronouncement of the Roosevelt Corollary and his intervention in the Dominican Republic and Cuba, had placed a serious strain on American relations with Latin America. Fear of the Colossus of the North was inevitable, even though the energetic President again and again declared that the southern neighbors had nothing to fear if they behaved themselves.

Fortunately, Secretary Root recognized the need for countermeasures. Although he was as determined as the President to maintain order and prevent European interventions in the vicinity of the Panama Canal, he believed that American interests required more friendly relations with the Western Hemisphere states. "The South Americans now hate us," Root wrote to a Democratic senator, "largely because they think we despise them and try to bully them. I really like them and intend to show it. I think their friendship is really important to the United States, and that the best way to secure it is by treating them like gentlemen. If you want to make a man your friend, it does not pay to treat him like a yellow dog." [12]

Root's most effective gesture of friendship was to attend in person the Pan-American Conference of 1906 at Rio de Janeiro. In an impressive speech he told the delegates: "We wish for no victories but those of peace; for no territory except our own; for no sovereignty except the sovereignty over ourselves. . . . We neither claim nor desire any rights, or privileges, or powers that we do not freely concede to every American republic." [13] After leaving Rio, Root visited seven other Latin-American countries. For the sake of improved relations between the United States and her southern neighbors, he attended a succession of receptions, lunches, and dinners; made and heard dozens of speeches; and drank innumerable toasts in warm, sweet champagne. Although Latin Americans were not entirely won over, Root had a generally friendly reception. In the judgment of Senator Henry Cabot Lodge, Root had "done more to advance our good relations with South America & to assure our

[12] Reprinted by permission of the publisher from Philip C. Jessup, *Elihu Root* (Copyright 1938 by Dodd, Mead & Company, Inc., New York), vol. I, p. 469.

[13] *Speeches Incident to the Visit of Secretary Root to South America* (Washington: Government Printing Office, 1906), p. 12.

moral supremacy in this hemisphere than has been effected in all the years since Henry Clay began it."

In dealing with certain specific issues, Root was less successful. Since 1902 the Argentine government had been pressing for a principle originally formulated by the famous Argentine Foreign Minister, Luis M. Drago. The Drago Doctrine would deny the right of a European power to use armed force against any American state for the purpose of collecting debts owed to foreign nationals. At the Rio Conference and during his visit to Argentina, Secretary Root announced his sympathy with this position; and, faithful to a pledge made at the conference, the United States had the issue placed on the agenda of the Second Hague Conference in 1907. Unwilling to go as far as Argentina wanted, the American delegation supported a compromise under which the forcible collection of debts was condemned, but an exception was allowed in cases where the debtor state had either refused to submit the claims to arbitration or had failed to carry out an arbitral award. Disappointed that the Drago Doctrine, pure and unadulterated, had not been adopted, the Latin-American countries refused to accept the compromise convention.

By the time Theodore Roosevelt left the White House, the diplomatic obstacles to an isthmian canal had been removed and the actual construction of the great waterway had begun. Since protection of the canal had become one of the principal objects of American foreign policy, the United States had taken strong action to remove excuses for any European intervention in the region. The "big-stick" diplomacy of these years had cost the United States rather heavily in Latin-American trust, but Elihu Root's tactful diplomacy had repaired a good part of the damage.

23

ROOSEVELT AND WORLD POLITICS

The involvement of the United States in world politics, initiated with the annexation of the Philippines and the formulation of Hay's China policy, became firmly established during the Presidency of Theodore Roosevelt. The European powers recognized American strength and competed for American friendship, while Roosevelt took a keen interest in world affairs and loved to have a part in the game. Within the domestic field there was no issue critical enough to absorb all the restless energy of the youthful President; only in foreign relations did he find full scope for his ambition to play the role of major statesman.

European Overtures

Roosevelt occupied the White House during a period of vast significance in European diplomacy. This was the time when the division of Europe into rival armed camps was completed, and only the Sarajevo spark was needed to set off the World War I explosion. Roosevelt saw and deplored the trend of events, but was unsuccessful in altering it.

In September, 1901, when Roosevelt became President, the alliance system was still in the process of evolution. Germany and Austria had been linked in 1879; three years later Italy had been added as a somewhat shaky member of what then became the Triple Alliance. In opposition to this grouping, tsarist Russia and republican France had submerged their ideological differences to become allies in 1894. At first Britain tried to remain aloof from these combinations, but by the end of the nineteenth century splendid isolation no longer seemed a safe policy. With her world-girdling empire and trade interests Britain needed friends. The Boer War provided final proof that a fundamental revolution in British foreign policy had become necessary.

From 1899 to 1904 Britain was in the market for allies. As we have already seen, the possibilities of an Anglo-American alliance were frequently discussed, but any such link was too drastic a break with American tradition to be really feasible. To many English leaders, Germany seemed the most desirable ally, but negotiations between the two countries broke down. The German ambition to have a modern navy, to acquire colonies, and to expand overseas trade contributed instead to a growing suspicion and hostility between the two nations. Eventually, therefore, Britain found her friends elsewhere: the Anglo-Japanese alliance was signed in 1902; the Entente Cordiale with France was arranged in 1904; and a settlement with Russia was reached in 1907.

As the rivalry between the emerging European camps intensified, each side made feverish efforts to gain the moral support of the United States. Germany, in particular, wished to counteract the hostility which had developed toward her as a result of the Samoan affair and the Spanish-American War. By rather clumsy efforts to influence the American press, by sending Prince Henry, the Kaiser's brother, on a good-will visit in 1902, and by the well-publicized gift of a statue of Frederick the Great, William II and his ministers tried to quiet American suspicions and lay the foundations for German-American friendship. Alarmed by this campaign, British, French, and Russian diplomats took every opportunity to plant anti-German stories in the newspapers and to promote their own interests.

Because Theodore Roosevelt had a taste for personal diplomacy and loved to operate on a confidential man-to-man basis, the European governments took pains to send to Washington ambassadors whom the President would like. One of England's initial advantages was the presence on the scene of the experienced and thoroughly trusted Lord Pauncefote. When Pauncefote died in 1902, the British sent over as his successor Sir Michael Herbert, with whom Roosevelt had maintained a close friendship since the days when both men had been in Washington during Roosevelt's period of service as Civil Service Commissioner. Alarmed at this development, the Kaiser countered by appointing to the German Embassy another close chum of the President's, Baron Hermann Speck von Sternberg. Of him Roosevelt once wrote: "I have never met a man for whom I had a higher respect or regard." Unfortunately for the British, Sir Michael died in 1903, and England was not again represented by an ambassador whom Roosevelt really liked until James Bryce was appointed to the post late in 1906. Sternberg, however, found a formidable rival in Jean Jules Jusserand, who became French Ambassador to the United States in 1903. A scholar and a wit, Jusserand became one of Roosevelt's favorite companions on hikes through Rock Creek Park and on the White House tennis courts.

The strongly personal flavor of Roosevelt's diplomacy is also illustrated by the long-distance friendships he maintained with European rulers. As Jusserand uneasily noted, the American President and the German Emperor had many characteristics in common: both were impulsive, had fixed moral and religious ideas, and were fascinated by military affairs. Roosevelt credited William with many qualities that he admired—intelligence, vigor, and masterfulness—but he disliked certain other traits of the imperial personality, such as vanity, boastfulness, and suspiciousness. Nevertheless, the President and the Kaiser frequently sent messages to each other. Balancing this was the rather unusual friendship that grew up between Roosevelt and King Edward VII of England.

Roosevelt's initial preference had been for maintaining close relations with both Britain and Germany. Before he became President he wrote to his friend, Sternberg: "As you know, I have a very strong hope that Germany, England and the United States will more and more be able to act together." In 1905 he was still talking in these terms; he deplored the growing rift between Germany and Britain and tried to bridge it. But the rivalry was too deep-seated to be eradicated, and when a showdown came, Roosevelt sided with England and France. Despite his affection for Sternberg, the President, in common with many Americans, distrusted the Kaiser and was unwilling to see Germany become the dominant world power.

The Russo-Japanese War

The tensions that led to an outbreak of war between Russia and Japan had been building up since the end of the Sino-Japanese War in 1895. Russia had antagonized the Japanese, first by combining with France and Germany to deprive Japan of some of the fruits of her victory, and then by acquiring for herself some of the same prizes. Step by step Russia had brought Manchuria under her domination. This the Japanese might have put up with, had Russia not also extended her intrigues into nominally independent Korea, where Japan herself wanted the dominant influence.

Japan's determination to resist further Russian expansion led to the negotiation of the Anglo-Japanese alliance in 1902. The Roosevelt administration welcomed this because it promised to create a counterweight to Russia. American commercial firms regarded Manchuria as a particularly promising market and were convinced that Russia was trying to keep them out. "I have not the slightest objection to the Russians knowing that I feel thoroughly aroused and irritated at their conduct in Manchuria," Roosevelt wrote to Hay in 1903, "that I don't intend to give way and that I am year by year growing more confident that this country would back me in going to an extreme in the matter."

Although Roosevelt did not really want the United States to fight for the Open Door in Manchuria, he was certainly not adverse to Japan's doing so. In January, 1904, the American government assured the Japanese that, in the event of a Russo-Japanese war, "the American policy would be benevolent toward Japan." When hostilities actually began on February 8, 1904, with a Japanese surprise attack upon Port Arthur, the island kingdom's act of aggression provoked no condemnation from either the American press or the government. "Was not the way the Japs began the fight bully?" Elihu Root wrote Roosevelt, and there is no doubt the President agreed.

Officially, the United States limited its reaction to a proclamation of neutrality and an effort to commit the belligerents "to respect the neutrality of China and in all practicable ways her administrative entity." The phrase "administrative entity" was intended to guarantee a continuance of Chinese sovereignty over Manchuria after the war. As Roosevelt later explained the issue: [1]

> Yes, it was on the suggestion of "Bill the Kaiser" that we sent out the note on the neutrality of China. But the insertion of the word "entity" was ours. His suggestion originally was in untenable form; that is, he wanted us to guarantee the integrity of China south of the latitude of the Great Wall, which would have left Russia free to gobble up what she really wanted.

But the maneuver was unsuccessful; with German support Russia carefully excluded Manchuria from her pledge.

Roosevelt later described another step which, if he really took it, was highly significant: [2]

> As soon as this war broke out, I notified Germany and France in the most polite and discreet fashion that in event of a combination against Japan to do what Russia, Germany, and France did to her in 1894, I should promptly side with Japan and proceed to whatever length was necessary on her behalf.

Since the archives have disclosed no supporting evidence, this story, like that of the ultimatum to the Kaiser on the Venezuelan debt issue, has been regarded with great skepticism by most historians.

From the beginning Roosevelt aspired to the role of peacemaker. In 1904 and 1905 Ambassador Sternberg was at the height of his influence

---

[1] Roosevelt to Root, Feb. 16, 1904. Reprinted by permission of the publisher from E. E. Morison, ed., *Letters of Theodore Roosevelt* (Copyright 1951 by Harvard University Press, Cambridge), vol. IV, p. 731.

[2] Reprinted by permission of the publisher from Tyler Dennett, *Roosevelt and the Russo-Japanese War* (Copyright 1925 by Doubleday & Company, Inc., New York), p. 2.

with Roosevelt, and through Sternberg the American President and the German Emperor exchanged ideas about desirable peace terms. In December, 1904, Roosevelt impressed upon Sternberg that "it was equally to the advantage of Germany and America that Japan should succeed, but not too overwhelmingly—that Manchuria should be restored to the Chinese, with the open door—but that there should [be] sufficient strength left on both sides to guarantee fair treatment to other nations."

On his side, the Kaiser was playing a complicated game. Hopeful for a time that the Tsar's troubles in the Far East might play into Germany's hands and result in a Russo-German alliance, William gave at first little encouragement to American mediation overtures. But as Russia's troubles multiplied on the battlefield and at home, Germany concluded that the restoration of peace was imperative. Suspicious of the growing intimacy of Britain and France and fearful that the Far Eastern question might be submitted to a congress of powers in which German interests would be slighted, William began to display real eagerness for an American mediation. Although Roosevelt ridiculed the more extreme suspicions of the Kaiser—"What a jumpy creature he is, anyhow!"—he too opposed a general international conference, much preferring that Japan and Russia should negotiate with each other directly.

Such was the situation when in April, 1905, the Japanese government turned to Roosevelt for advice upon how peace negotiations might be set in motion. The extreme secrecy of the Japanese move reflected not only an unwillingness to show any weakness in the eyes of the world, but also a fear of provoking hostile demonstrations at home. Behind the scenes conflicting factions were struggling for control of Japanese policy. A war party, including most of the military leaders, wanted to continue hostilities to assure the collection of a stiff indemnity and large annexations, but a more moderate group, worried by the war's heavy cost in money and manpower, desired an early peace.

For a month the Japanese government hesitated. But on May 27 and 28, 1905, the Japanese destroyed the Russian fleet in the great Battle of Tsushima, and this victory emboldened the Japanese Foreign Minister to suggest that Roosevelt invite the two belligerents to meet in direct negotiations. Thus secretly assured that Japan would welcome a peace conference, the President began to press Russia for a similar promise. This was not easy to get, because die-hards in the Russian government, willing to risk complete disaster rather than acknowledge defeat, tried to keep the American Ambassador from talking privately to the Tsar. On June 7, however, the American diplomat had an opportunity to urge his case, and the Tsar finally agreed—influenced in part by the threatening Russian domestic situation and by secret letters he had been receiving from his cousin, the Kaiser.

On June 10, 1905, President Roosevelt issued public invitations to Russia and Japan, and the promised acceptances were promptly forthcoming. Even so, however, it proved difficult to arrange the details. "Oh, Lord!" the exasperated peacemaker wrote, "I have been going nearly mad in the effort to get Russia and Japan together. The more I see of the Czar, the Kaiser, and the Mikado the better I am content with democracy, even if we have to include the American newspaper as one of its assets." Although Russia would have preferred a European conference site and Japan an Asiatic one, the two compromised on Washington. At the suggestion of Roosevelt, who had good reason to know that Washington in August was not a pleasant place to do business, the meeting was finally planned for the Portsmouth, New Hampshire, navy yard.

The Portsmouth Conference opened on August 9 with the President graciously playing the role of host at a luncheon aboard his Presidential yacht. When the proper ceremonies had been completed, Roosevelt left the delegates to carry on their own discussions and retired to his summer home at Oyster Bay, Long Island. Even at long distance, however, the President kept a finger on the pulse of the conference, offering advice and inviting the diplomats to consult privately with him when the negotiations threatened to break down. At first Roosevelt urged the Russians to accept the full Japanese demands, including an indemnity and the cession of the island of Sakhalin, but the Russian chief delegate, Count Serge Witte, was a shrewd and courageous statesman. In Russia he had advocated peace in opposition to the warmongers; now at Portsmouth he resisted the extreme Japanese demands and maneuvered skillfully to reverse the hitherto anti-Russian sentiment of the American press. In the end, Roosevelt felt obliged to warn his Japanese friends not to antagonize world opinion. "Every interest of civilization and humanity," the President advised, "forbids the continuance of the war merely for a large indemnity."

The conference came to a dramatic climax on August 29, 1905, when the Japanese finally gave in and accepted a compromise. Although the Treaty of Portsmouth, signed September 5, provided no indemnity and gave Japan only the southern half of Sakhalin, its other terms were highly favorable to the victor. Russia conceded Japan's paramount interest in Korea and transferred to her the Port Arthur and Liaotung leaseholds as well as control of the railroads in southern Manchuria.

To Roosevelt now fell the congenial task of reading congratulatory telegrams and press clippings from all over the world. The Russian Tsar and the Japanese Emperor sent their fervent thanks; the German Emperor was effusive in his praise. After surveying the press comment, the American magazine, *Public Opinion*, concluded that the President was "the most popular man in the world" and "an international asset." The applause reached its culmination when Roosevelt was awarded the Nobel Peace Prize for his efforts.

Roosevelt's mediation had been motivated, not by an abstract passion for peace, but by an attempt to calculate American national advantage. American interests, particularly her promising trade in Manchuria, appeared to require a balance of power in the Far East. Since Russia had threatened that balance, Roosevelt had strongly supported Japan. Yet Roosevelt's confidence that the United States could rely on Japanese friendship was soon shaken.

Even before the Russo-Japanese War was over, Roosevelt heard disquieting news. In a note to Hay in December, 1904, the President referred to reports from American military attachés describing the growth of a violent antiforeign spirit in the Japanese army and among the Japanese masses. "Not only is this feeling manifested against all foreigners, but what I was surprised to hear, it appears to be particularly violent against Americans." [3] To another diplomat, Roosevelt confided that he was prepared to see Japan get "puffed up with pride ... and turn against us." The most serious warning of potential trouble was the outbreak of anti-American riots in Tokyo when the terms of the Treaty of Portsmouth were revealed. Ignorant of the fact that their own government had asked Roosevelt to arrange the peace conference, the Japanese mob blamed Japan's failure to make Russia pay the costs of the war and give up more territory upon American interference. "The outbreak in Tokio," the President wrote to Senator Lodge, "is unpleasant evidence that the Japanese mob—I hope not the Japanese people—had had its head completely turned; the peace is evidently a wise one from *our* standpoint too." [4]

The Taft-Katsura Memorandum

Sporadic anti-American outbreaks did not seriously worry Roosevelt because he was confident that the basis for close relations between the Japanese and American governments had been laid by secret diplomacy during the summer of 1905.

Sure of Roosevelt's sympathy, the Japanese and British governments kept him fully informed of the negotiations by which they proposed to renew their alliance. Roosevelt not only gave this project his blessing, but expressed the wish that it were possible for the United States to join too. In view of the Senate's attitude toward alliances, however, the President complained he "might just as well strive for the moon as for such a policy." Yet if to join the Anglo-Japanese alliance was impossible,

[3] Roosevelt to Hay, Dec. 23, 1904, Roosevelt Letter Books, Library of Congress.
[4] Roosevelt to Lodge, Sept. 6, 1905, *ibid.*

Roosevelt did what was, from his point of view, the next best thing by giving secret assurances to both England and Japan. Not trusting the bumbling English Ambassador, Sir Mortimer Durand, for such delicate negotiations, the President arranged to have his old friend, Sir Cecil Spring-Rice, visit Washington early in 1905 and carry back highly confidential assurances to the British government. Further communications were carried to London by Senator Lodge on a visit in June, 1905.

A confidential channel to the Japanese government was provided when Secretary of War Taft visited Tokyo on a good-will trip in July, 1905. On the 27th of that month, Taft and Count Taro Katsura, the Japanese Foreign Minister, had one of the most extraordinary conversations in the history of American diplomacy. Katsura first assured Taft that "Japan does not harbor any aggressive designs whatever on the Philippines," and then observed that the fundamental principle of Japan's policy was the maintenance of general peace in the Far East. The only means for accomplishing this would be to form a "good understanding between the three governments of Japan, the United States and Great Britain." Finally, the Japanese Minister turned to the most delicate issue, that of Korea. Unless Japan took some positive action to prevent it, Korea would revert to her old game of playing one power against another and would thereby become the cause of new wars. Taft's reply must have warmed his host's heart: [5]

> Secretary Taft fully admitted the justness of the Count's observations and remarked to the effect that, in his personal opinion, the establishment by Japanese troops of a suzerainty over Korea to the extent of requiring that Korea enter into no foreign treaties without the consent of Japan was the logical result of the present war and would directly contribute to permanent peace in the East. His judgment was that President Roosevelt would concur in his views in this regard, although he had no authority to give assurance of this. . . .

When an "agreed memorandum" of the Taft-Katsura conversation was submitted to Roosevelt, he at once cabled Taft that the latter had been "absolutely correct in every respect. Wish you would state to Katsura that I confirm every word you have said."

Why had the President given Japan a blank check to do whatever she wished in Korea, when the American policy on China was based on such different principles? In part, the answer lies in the special circumstances of the Korean case. The Korean Emperor's reputation for intrigue and corruption and his military helplessness all combined to harden Roosevelt against him. "We can not possibly interfere for the Koreans against Japan," the President wrote to Hay in January, 1905. "They could not strike one blow in their own defense." Even if the case had been other-

[5] *Miscellaneous Letters of the State Department*, part III, July, 1905.

wise, however, the President was realist enough to know that it was hopeless to oppose Japan's policy in this area for which she had already fought wars against China and Russia. Since this was so, Korea seemed a cheap price to pay for Japan's promise to leave the Philippines alone and for the more general prospect of good Japanese-American relations.

In the sequel, Korea felt the full impact of Japanese imperialism. Two months after the Treaty of Portsmouth the Korean Emperor was compelled to sign an agreement under which his kingdom became a Japanese protectorate, and in 1910 Japan formally annexed the country. American opinion was subsequently shocked by reports of the harshness of Japanese rule.

The Morocco Crisis

During the year 1905 Ambassador Sternberg appeared to be highly successful in cultivating a close collaboration between the Kaiser and Roosevelt. The President particularly appreciated William's assistance in inducing the Tsar to accept the Portsmouth Conference. "In my letters to you I have sometimes spoken sharply of the Kaiser," Roosevelt wrote to his English friend, Spring-Rice. "I want to say now that in these peace negotiations he has acted like a trump. He has done everything he could to make the Czar yield and has backed me up in every way, and I thoroughly appreciated how he has behaved." [6] Roosevelt criticized the British for not having cooperated in his Far Eastern peacemaking to the same degree.

Having collaborated with the United States in the Far East, the German government hoped to gain American support for the German position on other issues. Thus it was that in March, 1905, Sternberg became the bearer of a letter from William complaining of French policy in Morocco. Roosevelt at first made light of the matter: "I wish to Heaven our excellent friend, the Kaiser, was not so jumpy and did not have so many pipe dreams."

But the Franco-German rivalry over Morocco was in reality a highly serious business. As part of the Entente Cordiale of 1904, England had granted France a free hand in Morocco in return for French recognition of England's paramount interest in Egypt. Strengthened by this deal and by similar ones with Italy and Spain, the French Foreign Minister, Théophile Delcassé, began to press the Sultan of Morocco for "reforms" that would make him dependent upon France. The German Foreign Office was determined to resist this policy, which it believed to be a threat to German commercial interests. This led, for one thing, to the

---

[6] Roosevelt to Spring-Rice, Sept. 1, 1905, Roosevelt Letter Books, Library of Congress.

appeal to Roosevelt, and, for a second, to the provocative visit the Kaiser —against his personal wishes—made to Tangier, Morocco, on March 31, 1905. In a belligerent speech the Emperor championed the freedom and independence of the Sultan and warned that Germany would insist upon an equality of rights with other powers.

Quite apart from Germany's material stakes in the Morocco question was the larger issue of the European balance of power. By forcing the Morocco question to a showdown, Germany hoped to humiliate France, while her ally, Russia, was tied up in the Far East. England, the Germans believed, would not support France to the point of war, and France would therefore have to back down. The crucial issue became the German demand for an international conference to discuss the Morocco question. Determined not to allow the Entente Cordiale to be shattered by its first real testing, the British urged the French to decline the German proposal. As the danger of war increased, Ambassador Sternberg transmitted more and more letters from the Kaiser to the President. The Germans made much of the fact that they were contending for the same Open Door policy in Morocco that the United States upheld in China. If only Roosevelt would use his influence, the Kaiser urged, England would drop her opposition to a conference and peace would be assured.

The President tried to avoid involvement at first. Although the United States was a party to the Treaty of Madrid of 1880, by which the rights of foreigners in Morocco were defined, the actual American stake in Moroccan trade was very small. Furthermore, Roosevelt was fully aware of the danger that the Germans might try to use him for purposes of their own. By June, however, the situation had become so serious that the President felt he should do something. In confidential talks with Sternberg and Jusserand he became convinced that each Ambassador was a little ashamed of the intransigence of his own government. In France, moreover, the chances for moderation had increased when Premier Pierre-Maurice Rouvier forced the resignation of the anti-German Delcassé.

Roosevelt now began to urge France to consent to the conference. "I know your government will consider that I am meddling in its affairs," he told Jusserand, "but since the Moroccan question threatens a war between Germany and France that would destroy world peace, I feel justified." Shrewdly Roosevelt confided in the French Ambassador that the real difficulty was "the immeasurable vanity of William II," and that France ought "to help him save face if thereby one can avert a war."

When the French finally agreed to a conference, Roosevelt turned his blandishments upon the Kaiser, praising him for the great diplomatic victory he had already won and advising him not to endanger his gains by bickering over details. Sternberg took the extraordinary step of placing the German fate in Roosevelt's hands. "In case during the coming conference differences of opinion should arise between France and Germany," the Ambassador promised, the Kaiser, "in every case, will be ready to back up the decision which you consider to be the most fair and practical." When this pledge later proved embarrassing, the Foreign Office criticized Sternberg for having exceeded his instructions, but the assurance had at least been successful in quieting the last French objections to the conference.

The Kaiser's confidence that Roosevelt sympathized with the German position was ill-founded. On the contrary, the President was coming to look at the Morocco question more and more from the French point of view. Warned by Jusserand of reports that, in case of war with France, Germany might invade neutral Holland, Roosevelt confided that in such a case he would send American naval vessels to see that the Germans did not take over Dutch colonies in the Caribbean and the East Indies. The President also coached the French on how to handle the Kaiser on the basis of his own experience in the Venezuelan debt affair. The point was not to drive William into a corner, but always to leave him room for an honorable exit.

Despite some congressional criticism, the President sent the highly competent Henry White to represent the United States at the Algeciras Conference of 1906. Although White's public role was a modest one, Germany and France kept up their behind-the-scenes efforts to swing American support to their side. When the conference was threatened with deadlock, Roosevelt suggested a compromise that paid lip service to the principle of the Open Door, but permitted France and Spain to control the Moroccan police. Although Germany was reluctant to concede this vital point, she finally gave in after Roosevelt referred to Sternberg's pledge that the Kaiser would accept the President's decision. "In this Algeciras business," Roosevelt confided to a friend, "you will notice that while I was most suave and pleasant with the Emperor, yet when it became necessary at the end I stood him on his head with great decision."

Convinced that vanity was the key to the Kaiser's character, the President took pains to give William credit for the settlement. Shortly after the conference, Roosevelt received a group of German war veterans and read a little speech praising the Kaiser's great contribution to peace. The President's flattery helped to reconcile Germany to accepting with good grace what was in reality a diplomatic defeat, since the conference had resulted not only in confirming France's special position in Morocco but in strengthening the Entente Cordiale.

San Francisco Offends Japan

By a strange quirk of history, Theodore Roosevelt's whole policy of cultivating close relations with Japan was placed in jeopardy by a local school board order, at first considered so unimportant that even the local press relegated the news to a back page.

Starting in the 1890s, Japanese laborers had migrated to the West Coast in increasing numbers. By 1900, when the annual influx rose to about twelve thousand, Californians had become seriously concerned. To quiet these apprehensions, the Japanese government voluntarily announced in August, 1900, that it would no longer grant passports to laborers desirous of going to the United States mainland. Although this policy—sometimes called the first Gentleman's Agreement—cut by half the number of coolies entering in 1901, it did not solve the problem from the Californian point of view. For one thing, the passport restrictions were not adequately enforced. For another, Japanese laborers in large numbers entered Hawaii and Mexico, which were not covered by the restrictive policy. Once admitted to those places, there was no bar to their moving to the United States.

California labor unions, which had been vigorously anti-Chinese in an earlier generation, now led the demand for Federal legislation to exclude the Japanese. The exclusion request took a more insistent form in 1905 when the San Francisco newspapers took up the cause. On February 23 the usually conservative *San Francisco Chronicle* began a sensational series of articles on the alleged Japanese menace. California politicians quickly responded to the call, and within a week the state legislature unanimously passed resolutions calling upon President Roosevelt to halt the Japanese flood, either by treaty or by some other means.

In May, 1905, the San Francisco labor unions sponsored a mass meeting which launched the Japanese and Korean Exclusion League. This trouble-making organization, which a year later boasted a membership of nearly 80,000, agitated not only to exclude Japanese immigrants, but to boycott Japanese business establishments and to segregate Japanese school children.

However California might feel on the immigration question, the prospects for congressional action were poor. In the East there was a widespread feeling that the Chinese exclusion acts had been unduly harsh and that the error should not be repeated with the Japanese. President Roosevelt was especially opposed to any such affront to Japanese pride. He confided to Senator Lodge that the West Coast agitation "utterly disgusted" him. The fact that the legislators from this section were luke-warm toward naval expansion compounded their folly. "It gives me a feeling of disgust to see them challenge Japanese hostility and justify by their actions any feeling the Japanese have against us, while at the same time refusing to take steps to defend themselves against the formidable foe whom they are ready with such careless insolence to antagonize." [7] In his annual messages of 1904 and 1905 the President advised against discriminatory immigration legislation.

The terrible San Francisco earthquake and fire of April, 1906, intensified the anti-Japanese movement. Despite the fact that Japan contributed more to the relief of this disaster than all other foreign nations combined, the widespread destruction disrupted normal housing patterns and led to charges that the Japanese were encroaching upon white residential districts. The unsettled condition of the city led to an increase in crime and assaults, in which the Japanese were often the victims. Labor unions picketed Japanese restaurants, ostensibly because the establishments were nonunion, but also out of prejudice against their owners.

Against this background the San Francisco School Board on October 11, 1906, passed a resolution ordering all Japanese, Chinese, and Korean children to attend a special segregated school. Among the excuses offered for this policy were the crowded conditions in the regular schools, the fact that some Japanese pupils were as much as twenty years old, and the charge that they were of inferior morals. According to the *San Francisco Chronicle:*

> Whatever the status of the Japanese children while still young and uncontaminated, as they grow older they acquire the distinctive character, habits, and moral standards of their race, which are abhorrent to our people. We object to them in the familiar intercourse of common school life as we would object to any other moral poison.

These allegations largely collapse when critically examined. Since only 93 Japanese children were involved and these had hitherto attended 23 different schools, they could not have contributed materially to the over-crowding. Of these 93 pupils, only 33 were over 15 years of age and only 2 were 20 years old. Rather than being dirty and vicious, the Japanese children had the reputation of being exceptionally clean and well behaved—model pupils whom the white children might well have emulated. The school order was in reality a petty act of discrimination, motivated by race prejudice, economic jealousy, and resentment at Federal complacency on the immigration question.

The San Francisco authorities were quite unprepared for the storm their action provoked. The Japanese consul at San Francisco entered a formal protest and advised Japanese children not to attend the special

---

[7] Reprinted by permission of the publisher from Roosevelt to Lodge, May 15, 1905, *Selections from the Correspondence of Theodore Roosevelt and Henry Cabot Lodge, 1884–1918* (Copyright 1925 by Charles Scribner's Sons, New York), vol. II, p. 122.

school. Some 2,500 Japanese held a mass meeting at San Francisco, where the segregation order was denounced and plans made for opposing the policy in the courts. When the news reached Japan, it created widespread indignation, intensified by the erroneous idea that the children had been completely excluded. One Tokyo newspaper raged:

> Stand up, Japanese nation! Our countrymen have been HUMILI-ATED on the other side of the Pacific. Our poor boys and girls have been expelled from the public schools by the rascals of the United States, cruel and merciless like demons.
> At this time we should be ready to give a blow to the United States. Yes, we should be ready to strike the Devil's head with an iron hammer for the sake of the world's civilization.... Why do we not insist on sending ships?

Fortunately, such passionate outbursts as this were rare. Although expressing hurt surprise, most Japanese newspapers tried to exert a conservative influence. Undoubtedly, confidence in the friendship of President Roosevelt helped to dilute Japanese anger once the first shock of the news wore off. Nevertheless, the situation was serious. To be lumped together with the Chinese and Koreans as inferior "Mongolians" was a humiliation deeply galling to Japanese pride in those days so soon after victory over mighty Russia. As the Japanese Ambassador emphasized in his formal protest to Secretary of State Root: "The exclusion of children from ordinary public schools, because of their Japanese origin, is based on racial distinction and is as such resented by the Japanese people as derogatory to their dignity."

Roosevelt's alarm at what had happened was reflected in a letter to his son: "I am being horribly bothered about the Japanese business. The infernal fools in California...insult the Japanese recklessly and in the event of war it will be the Nation as a whole which will pay the consequences." The administration dumped oil on the troubled waters as promptly as it could. Secretary Root sent a mollifying message to Japan, deprecating the San Francisco action and promising that the Justice Department was exploring the situation to see what might be done. Secretary of Commerce and Labor Victor Metcalf, himself a Californian, was dispatched to San Francisco for an on-the-spot investigation. And, finally, the President himself took up the issue in his annual message to Congress of December 4, 1906. Vigorously condemning the San Francisco action as a "wicked absurdity," Roosevelt appealed for the fair treatment of the Japanese, since "good manners should be an international not less than an individual attribute." He urged Congress to pass legislation that would permit the Japanese to become naturalized and that would strengthen the President's powers to enforce the rights of aliens under treaties. By pledging that "all the forces, military and civil, of the

United States which I may lawfully employ will be employed," Roosevelt seemed to be threatening to use the Army to oppose the segregation order. This, however, was not his intention; his private correspondence shows that he meant only that he would, if necessary, protect the Japanese against mob violence.

In Japan the President's strong language had an almost miraculous success in quieting anti-American feeling, but in California it had the opposite effect. Much of the resentment hitherto focused on the Japanese was now directed against Roosevelt. "As for the ninety-three Japanese," the *San Francisco Examiner* asserted, "they ... will be forgotten as soon as President Roosevelt lays aside his pewter sword, sheathes his fire-belching tongue and ceases his tin-soldier yawp about leading the army and navy against our schoolhouses." California Governor George Pardee, a Republican, strongly condemned the President's message, and the California legislature began to consider bills that would further restrict the Orientals.

Realizing that he had only made the situation worse by appearing to side with the Japanese, Roosevelt began a discreet retreat. In submitting Secretary Metcalf's report to Congress, the President conceded that the San Francisco authorities might be within their rights if they kept all children above a certain age out of the schools. More important, he held several conferences with California senators and representatives, out of which evolved the project of inviting the San Francisco authorities to come to Washington for consultation. Early in February, 1907, therefore, Mayor Eugene Schmitz (then under indictment for graft), the superintendent of schools, the city attorney, and the entire school board crossed the continent to attend a series of White House meetings. Roosevelt and Root finally convinced the reluctant San Francisco visitors that the only way that Japan could be induced to curb the emigration of Japanese laborers would be for the hateful school order to be rescinded. The school board's surrender was not complete: it still insisted on rules that would exclude from the regular schools alien children over the age of sixteen and those without a satisfactory command of English. But Japanese pride was salved; segregation was no longer based on race.

Gentleman's Agreement of 1907

From the beginning, Roosevelt had realized that the heart of the problem was West Coast antagonism to the immigration of Japanese laborers. As one means of dealing with the problem, Congress rushed through a law under which, whenever the President believed that passports issued by any foreign government were being used "for the purpose of enabling holders to come to the continental territory of the United States to the detriment of labor conditions therein," he might refuse to allow these aliens to enter continental United States. Although vaguely phrased, the law was clearly intended to keep out Japanese laborers who tried to move to the United States after stopovers in Hawaii or Mexico.

But the most acceptable solution, Roosevelt was sure, was to induce Japan to halt the immigration at its source. For a time Secretary Root tried to accomplish this by treaty. Since there were no American workers who wanted to go to Japan, however, such an agreement would obviously be one-sided unless the Japanese were given some face-saving concession, such as the right of naturalization. This, however, would require congressional legislation—obviously an impossibility in the heated atmosphere of 1907.

In the end, therefore, the United States and Japan had to fall back upon a new Gentleman's Agreement to plug the loopholes left by the understanding of 1900. Japan undertook to deny passports to Japanese laborers for the American mainland except to those who had previously resided there and to the parents, wives, and children of Japanese residents. Farmers, students, merchants, and tourists might be granted passports, but under careful restrictions. Japan also promised to establish curbs on immigration of laborers to Hawaii and to countries adjacent to the United States.

The Gentleman's Agreement did not achieve dramatic results, but over the course of time Japanese immigration to the United States showed a marked reduction. Whereas in January, 1907, more than 1,300 Japanese had arrived on the American mainland, only 495 came in January, 1908, and only 126 the following December. Yet the Gentleman's Agreement was not sufficiently well understood by the American public to silence sporadic demands for outright exclusion. Consequently the immigration question continued to plague Japanese-American relations over the next two decades.

The Great Naval Demonstration

The rescinding of the San Francisco school order and the negotiation of the Gentleman's Agreement did not bring immediate improvement in Japanese-American relations. On the contrary, the most serious war scare occurred during the summer of 1907. San Francisco continued to be a danger spot. In May, a mob wrecked a Japanese restaurant and bath house; in June, the local authorities denied licenses to Japanese employment agencies. These provocations led to new condemnations of America in the Japanese press, while on the American side the sensational newspapers freely predicted war.

In Europe a Japanese-American war seemed so likely that British and German officials began calculating on the probable outcome of such a contest. According to reports relayed to Washington, London and Berlin thought the odds favored Japan by some 5 to 4. The Kaiser was particularly solicitous that his friend, Roosevelt, should know of mysterious Japanese activities in Mexico and elsewhere.

Although the President refused to believe Japan had any real intention of attacking, he impressed upon the Army and Navy the importance of being prepared for any emergency. Moreover, he began to worry lest Japan consider his hitherto conciliatory policy an evidence of weakness. "I am exceedingly anxious to impress upon the Japanese that I have nothing but the friendliest possible intentions toward them," Roosevelt wrote to a friend, "but I am none the less anxious that they should realize that I am not afraid of them and that the United States will no more submit to bullying than it will bully." [8]

Early in July, 1907, it was announced that the American battleship fleet would take a long practice cruise to the West Coast. This move was not a sudden improvisation but the culmination of two years of planning. Indeed, the cruise would probably have been attempted earlier had not the school crisis occurred when it did. Having first postponed the maneuver because of the delicate international situation, the Roosevelt administration now reversed itself and concluded that a demonstration of naval strength would be helpful.

The announcement that the fleet would go to the Pacific aroused concern and opposition among many Easterners, who feared the maneuver would dangerously weaken Atlantic Coast defenses, cost too much money, or even provoke war. Senator Eugene Hale, chairman of the Naval Affairs Committee, warned that Congress would refuse to make the necessary appropriations, but the President retorted that he had enough funds to send the fleet to the Pacific and there it could stay if Congress did not care to vote the money to bring it back.

Domestic opposition soon subsided as the first stage of the historic cruise was successfully accomplished. Leaving Hampton Roads, Virginia, on December 16, 1907, sixteen battleships steamed south, passed through the Straits of Magellan, and arrived safely in San Francisco on May 6, 1908. En route, the fleet called at several Latin-American ports, where it received a reception even more effusive than that given to Secretary Root two years earlier.

Although rumors that the fleet intended to extend its cruise around the world had been circulating for months, the official announcement was not made until March 13, 1908. Five days later the Japanese government

[8] Roosevelt to Henry White, July 30, 1907. Reprinted by permission of the publisher from Allan Nevins, *Henry White: Thirty Years of American Diplomacy* (Copyright 1930 by Harper & Brothers, New York), pp. 292–293.

formally invited the fleet to include Japan on its itinerary. The invitation was quickly accepted, and, after stopovers at Hawaii and Australia, the battleships arrived at Yokohama on October 18, 1908. Although both the Japanese officials and the naval officers had felt uneasiness lest some drunken American sailor or some rabid Japanese nationalist provoke an incident that would lead to serious trouble, the visit was a great success.

From Japan the fleet visited China and the Philippines, then crossed the Indian Ocean and passed through the Suez Canal into the Mediterranean. On February 22, 1909, less than two weeks before Roosevelt left the White House, the great cruise was completed with the safe return of the battleships to Hampton Roads. Although not all Americans thought that this display of armed might had been admirable, the President had no misgivings. Discussing the matter in his *Autobiography*, he declared that "the two American achievements that really impressed foreign peoples during the first dozen years of this century were the digging of the Panama Canal and the cruise of the battle fleet around the world." And he added that the latter was "the most important service that I rendered to peace."

The Root-Takahira Agreement

As one dividend from improved Japanese-American relations, the two governments reached an important agreement upon the Far Eastern situation. The initiative for these discussions came from Japan the day after the battle fleet left Yokohama. After a few weeks of negotiation, the agreed wording was finally embodied in a note from Ambassador Takahira to Secretary Root, dated November 30, 1908.

Denying "any aggressive tendencies," the two governments defined their policy as "the maintenance of the existing *status quo*" in the Pacific area and "the defense of the principle of equal opportunity for commerce and industry in China." Accordingly, they resolved "reciprocally to respect the territorial possessions belonging to each other." Moreover, they stated their determination to support "by all pacific means at their disposal the independence and integrity of China and the principle of equal opportunity for commerce and industry of all nations in the Empire." In the event of any threat to the *status quo* or the Open Door, the two governments promised to consult with each other.

Unlike the Agreed Memorandum of 1905, the Root-Takahira Agreement was immediately made public. The American press was enthusiastic in its praise. In obtaining a Japanese pledge to respect not only American possessions and the principle of the Open Door but also the "independence and integrity of China," Root was believed to have achieved a triumph of American foreign policy comparable with John Hay's.

Yet diplomatic bargains are not arranged merely for the benefit of one side. What had Japan intended to get for herself from these pious pronouncements? Undoubtedly a free hand in southern Manchuria. The Japanese made no secret of the fact that they considered Manchuria a special area, not properly a part of China at all, in which they had special interests. The Chinese government, convinced that the Japanese-American agreement weakened rather than strengthened its security, protested feebly, but Roosevelt continued to believe that China was too weak to defend herself and that the only chance for real stability in the Far East lay in a balance of power and in friendly Japanese-American relations.

Roosevelt left the White House convinced that his Pacific policy had been a great success. Subsequent events proved that he had not built as firmly as he believed. As early as 1907 Russia and Japan made a secret treaty defining spheres of influence in Korea, Manchuria, and Mongolia. The balance of power upon which Roosevelt counted had, therefore, already been dangerously undermined while he was still President. Another weak point in Roosevelt's policy was the assumption that by fair but firm treatment he could keep the friendship of Japan. Actually, Japan was perilously divided between pro-American and anti-American factions. In the long run, the anti-American element won out, and there is some evidence that the famous battleship cruise played into the hands of the Japanese militarists who wanted to build up the navy and follow a more aggressive course.

Roosevelt's active participation in world politics was based on a strong desire to preserve world peace. As a younger man, he had often seemed to glorify war and to despise pacifism. As President, his efforts to strengthen the Navy and to brandish the big stick testified to his continued belief that an ability and willingness to use force had to be the ultimate security of the nation. Yet residence in the White House was a maturing experience. Roosevelt could see that a great war which diverted the powers from their civilizing mission to fighting against each other would be a terrible catastrophe. By cultivating close personal relations with foreign ambassadors and rulers, by mediating between Japan and Russia, and by attempting to remove sources of friction between Japan and the United States, Roosevelt tried to reduce the dangerous tensions then building up in the world. In the short run, his policies succeeded; in the long run, they failed. But the failure is more to be blamed on the massive forces that were driving the twentieth century toward World War I and World War II than on Roosevelt's mistakes of policy. At least, he perceived that the United States, whether it liked it or not, could no longer remain isolated from the world's troubles.

Diplomacy Becomes Professionalized

The growing involvement of the United States in world politics demanded a thoroughgoing reform of the whole diplomatic establishment. Throughout the nineteenth century the State Department had undergone a leisurely and unplanned growth. Before 1830 the department had been almost a one-man show run by the secretary of state with a handful of clerks. In 1833, Jackson's Secretary of State, Louis McLane, had organized his Washington office in eight bureaus dealing not only with diplomatic correspondence but with such miscellaneous domestic matters as patents, copyrights, pardons, and public archives. With minor changes McLane's organization had been kept until 1870, when Grant's Secretary of State, Hamilton Fish, had overhauled it in radical fashion. In a somewhat bewildering allocation of functions, Fish assigned to the First Diplomatic Bureau, under the first assistant secretary of state, supervision of the diplomatic correspondence with Western Europe, China, and Japan; and to the Second Diplomatic Bureau, under the second assistant secretary of state, responsibility for the Near East, Russia, Latin America, Liberia, and the Hawaiian Islands.

Despite the able services of a few conscientious ministers, the general level of American representation abroad was shockingly low. Since Congress was niggardly in providing for both salaries and expenses, most of the minor diplomatic posts and consulates were held by political hacks willing to accept the least desirable party spoils. The appointments of greater prestige to the major capitals attracted a higher type of office seeker, but here the expense was so great that only men of independent means could afford the honor. Perhaps the best that could be said for the old system was that it occasionally provided American literary men like Washington Irving, Nathaniel Hawthorne, and James Russell Lowell with welcome opportunities to live abroad.

In 1856 Congress attempted a halfhearted reform of the diplomatic service through a law establishing a salary scale and defining the duties of the various ranks. But conditions were still notoriously bad a generation later when the conscientious President Cleveland attempted to clean house through executive orders. An important landmark was achieved in 1893 when Congress authorized the President to promote the most important ministers abroad to the hitherto unused rank of ambassador. Cleveland promptly appointed ambassadors to London, Paris, Berlin, St. Petersburg, and Rome, and these capitals reciprocated by raising the ranks of their own representatives in Washington.

It remained for President Roosevelt to push for more fundamental changes with the enthusiastic support of Secretaries Hay and Root. The

President chose his ambassadors and ministers with great care, and by 1905 he had placed the whole consular service on a merit basis. In 1906 Congress responded to the new spirit by completely reorganizing the consular branch and providing a better salary schedule.

President Taft not only held the ground that Roosevelt had gained, but made significant contributions of his own, especially in the reorganization of the State Department. Under Secretary Knox the nation's world-wide interests at last achieved realistic recognition. To the Division of Far Eastern Affairs, previously set up by Root in 1908, Knox added in 1909 three other regional divisions dealing with Latin America, Western Europe, and the Near East.

24

DOLLAR DIPLOMACY

During the four years of William Howard Taft's Presidency the State Department gained the reputation of being extraordinarily sensitive to the interests of American bankers and traders. Critics, both at home and abroad, condemned this trend to what was called "dollar diplomacy." Yet the forces influencing American policy were too complex to be explained as merely the machinations of capitalist imperialism. A determination to forestall any possible foreign intervention in the vicinity of the Panama Canal, a continued devotion to the ideals of the Open Door and the independence of China, and a sense of mission to promote democracy and progress played roles fully as significant as the desire to provide profitable opportunities for American trade and investment. If Taft's concepts of foreign policy tended to blend equal measures of materialism and idealism, so too did those of Philander C. Knox, the new Secretary of State. Before entering government service as Roosevelt's Attorney General, Knox had been a leading Pennsylvania corporation lawyer. To him as to Taft, bankers and businessmen seemed natural allies in the conduct of American foreign affairs.

The Problem of Central America

In Central America Taft and Knox had to deal with a situation that had caused increasing anxiety to the State Department during the later years of the Roosevelt administration. The five Central American republics—Guatemala, Salvador, Honduras, Nicaragua, and Costa Rica—had long been notorious for violent conduct, both in their internal politics and in their relations with each other. In most of these countries corrupt and dictatorial governments were usually in power, elections were meaningless, and revolutions were periodic. Insurrectionary movements were often organized on adjoining soil by political *émigrés* who had found asylum there; frequently such plots were not only tolerated but encouraged, since each regime was under constant temptation to intrigue in the politics of its neighbors. Naturally, wars and threats of war were frequent. In earlier days a Central American federation had been attempted, but petty nationalism had defeated both the initial attempt and subsequent proposals for its revival. From 1893 to 1909 the most powerful figure in the region was José Zelaya, President of Nicaragua, who yearned to extend his rule over the whole area.

Although to most Americans these countries seemed remote and insignificant, there were sizable stakes involved. In Costa Rica, for example, a little-known American, Minor Keith, had begun building railroads in the 1870s and had promoted banana culture to provide freight for his lines; in 1899 the United Fruit Company had been organized to develop the banana trade in the whole region. Other American syndicates had been formed to build railroads and exploit mines. The dollars involved in these rather risky investments had come not from the conservative banking houses but from more speculative sources.

The State Department's increased interest in Central America was motivated only to a limited extent by a concern to protect these financial ventures. Much more important was the determination to prevent trouble in the vicinity of the Panama Canal. In Elihu Root's words, the building of the great waterway put these countries into "the front yard of the United States."

During the years when Theodore Roosevelt was President and Root Secretary of State, they were able to exert influence in Central America without provoking the Latin-American resentment that would have been caused by direct American intervention. This involved close collaboration between the United States and Mexico, then under the firm and conservative rule of President Porfirio Díaz. In 1906, when hostilities broke out between Salvador and Honduras on one side and Guatemala on the other, Roosevelt and Díaz sent carefully timed telegrams offering their mediation. The U.S.S. *Marblehead* was accepted as the meeting place, and under the friendly supervision of American and Mexican diplomats, the representatives of the quarreling states arranged an armistice—hastened, according to rumor, by the circumstance that the sea was rough and the negotiators were poor sailors. A subsequent Central American conference at San José, Costa Rica, resulted in agreements for closer collaboration by all except aggressive Nicaragua.

This precarious settlement was challenged in 1907 when Zelaya, after engineering a political overturn in Honduras, invaded that country and threatened to attack Salvador as well. Again Roosevelt and Díaz offered their good offices, and Zelaya, sobered by the threat that all the other Central American states might combine against him, accepted.

These events were followed by an important Central American conference at Washington in late 1907. Mexican-American collaboration was again evident, as Secretary Root and the Mexican Ambassador to the United States made the opening addresses. Although the delegates could not agree on a federation, they did negotiate eight treaties intended to initiate a new era of peaceful cooperation. In one of these, each signatory promised not "to recognize any other Government which may come into power in any of the five Republics as a consequence of a *coup d'état,* or of a revolution against the recognized Government, so long as the freely elected representatives of the people thereof have not constitutionally reorganized the country." Each also promised not to permit its territory to be used for organizing revolutionary movements against its neighbors.

By other agreements, the five republics promised to establish an International Central American Bureau and a Central American Court of Justice. The latter project was of particular interest to Secretary Root because it provided a limited experiment along lines that the United States had unsuccessfully sought at the Hague Conference of 1907.[1]

Intervention in Nicaragua

Nicaraguan President Zelaya's cooperation in the effort to establish harmony in Central America was short-lived. Still ambitious to extend his own influence over the region, Zelaya looked with jealous hostility upon the activities of Mexico and the United States. Into the American State Department poured a steady flow of complaints about Nicaraguan policy. Zelaya was accused of seeking to cancel the rights of American concessionaires in order to sell the same privileges to other people; he was suspected of intriguing with Japan for the construction of an isthmian canal independent of American control; and he was known to have borrowed money from a London banking firm to strengthen his regime.

Hated at Washington and Mexico City and also in the capitals of his nearer neighbors, Zelaya was obviously living dangerously. When a revolution against the dictator began on the eastern coast of Nicaragua, the insurrectionary faction quickly received the moral support of the United States. The anti-Zelaya inclinations of the American State Department were intensified when two American soldiers of fortune who had taken commissions in the revolutionary army were captured and executed. On December 1, 1909, Secretary Knox broke off diplomatic relations with Nicaragua in a stern note, in which he asserted: [2]

---

[1] See chap. 26.

[2] *Papers Relating to the Foreign Relations of the United States, 1909* (Washington: Government Printing Office, 1914), pp. 455–457.

The Government of the United States is convinced that the revolution represents the ideals and the will of a majority of the Nicaraguan people more faithfully than does the Government of President Zelaya, and that its peaceable control is well-nigh as extensive as that hitherto attempted by the Government at Managua.

Recognizing that the game was up, Zelaya fled to Mexico, leaving one José Madriz in authority at Managua. The new chief executive took the offensive against the insurrectionists and for a time seemed to be gaining the upper hand. But when the Madriz forces laid siege to the port of Bluefields, where the enemy was bottled up, the United States intervened directly by proclaiming Bluefields a neutral city—ostensibly to protect the lives and property of foreign residents. Prevented by a United States naval vessel from assaulting the port, the Madriz army presently abandoned the unhealthful coast and retired to the interior. This was the turning point in the civil war. The insurrectionists resumed the offensive, new revolts broke out, and in August, 1910, Madriz had to turn over the government to the rival faction.

The victors were confronted with many vexations. By recklessly selling concessions and special privileges to foreigners, the earlier governments had created an almost impossible legal tangle; government finances were in deplorable condition; and the insurgent leaders were soon quarreling among themselves over the political prizes. By no means disposed to follow a hands-off policy, the American State Department took action to bring order out of the Nicaraguan chaos. The American Minister to Panama, Thomas Dawson, was sent to Managua, where he played a vigorous role. By the so-called Dawson agreements, the Nicaraguan leaders promised to establish a provisional government, to submit all unsettled claims to a mixed commission of two Americans and one Nicaraguan, and to seek an American loan.

To accomplish the last of these objectives, Secretary Knox and Nicaraguan Minister, Salvadore Castrillo, signed a treaty on June 6, 1911. In return for support in obtaining a loan from American bankers, Nicaragua promised to place its customs administration under a collector general approved by both the American State Department and the bankers. In submitting the Knox-Castrillo Treaty to the Senate, President Taft stated that it should be the policy of the United States, "especially with respect to countries in geographical proximity to the Canal Zone, to give to them when requested all proper assistance . . . in the promotion of peace, in the development of their resources, and in a sound reorganization of their fiscal systems. . . ." But the Senate, which had for so long refused to give its blessing to Roosevelt's financial protectorate over the Dominican Republic, never did approve Taft's similar arrangements for Nicaragua.

Although the failure of the Knox-Castrillo Treaty prevented Nicaragua from obtaining the full 15 million dollars which she needed, she did get 1.5 million dollars. This loan was accompanied by a series of private contracts with the American bankers, under which Nicaragua agreed to appoint an American collector of customs and to turn over to the bankers a majority of the stock in the Nicaraguan national bank and the national railroad. The contracts stipulated that in case of trouble, the bankers could appeal to the United States government for protection and that the American Secretary of State would be the final arbiter in any dispute arising out of the loan.

The extent of American involvement in Nicaraguan affairs became evident in 1912, when General Luis Mena, the Minister of War, rebelled against President Adolpho Díaz, whom Mena accused of being the tool of American capitalists. The insurrectionary might well have succeeded had not President Díaz promptly requested and received American military help. Professing to act for the protection of American lives and the American-controlled railroad, some 2,700 marines were sent to the trouble spots. The American forces soon broke the back of the rebellion and forced the rebel leader to surrender—although not without the loss of seven American and an unrecorded number of Nicaraguan lives. With order restored, most of the American force was withdrawn, but a corps of 100 marines was left to guard the American legation and to impress the Nicaraguans with the futility of further revolt.

When Taft left the White House in March, 1913, the Nicaraguan situation was far from satisfactory. Díaz had been successful in a recent presidential election, but the results spoke more for the power of the United States than for the President's success or popularity. Nicaraguan finances were still in bad condition, necessitating more loans from the American bankers and more limitations upon Nicaraguan sovereignty. In an attempt to throw a lifeline to the struggling Díaz regime, Secretary Knox negotiated a new treaty, under which Nicaragua would grant the United States canal rights across her territory and the right to construct naval bases in return for a payment of 3 million dollars. Before the Senate could act upon this project, however, Knox had to give up his post to his Democratic successor, William Jennings Bryan.

Meanwhile, the Taft administration had been following similar policies elsewhere in the Caribbean region. In January, 1911, the President had submitted to the Senate a treaty providing for an American-nominated collector of customs in Honduras to protect the interests of American bankers, but this agreement suffered the same fate as the Knox-Castrillo one. The sequel was also the same, since the bankers were encouraged to make their own private contracts with the Honduran government. In Haiti, where French capital had hitherto been much more influential than American, the State Department encouraged four American banks to acquire 20 per cent of the stock of the national bank—an investment that was soon placed in jeopardy by Haitian political anarchy.

In the Dominican Republic, the previously established American financial protectorate worked with reasonable smoothness until 1911, when a new cycle of political assassinations and civil strife began. The Taft administration reacted with stern advice and a display of naval force, but the situation continued to deteriorate, thereby adding one more wailing baby to the several others deposited on Wilson's doorstep by the retiring Republican administration.

The Lodge Corollary

In 1911, Americans, nervous over the security of the Panama Canal and suspicious of Japanese imperialism, became excited over rumors that a Japanese syndicate was trying to purchase 400,000 acres in the Magdalena Bay region of Lower California. This was suspected of being a sinister device for establishing a Japanese naval base on Mexican soil. Though both the Japanese and Mexican governments denied that any such plot was afoot, and President Taft was not alarmed, Senator Henry Cabot Lodge and other ultranationalists persisted in taking the Magdalena Bay reports seriously.

In August, 1912, the Senate, by a vote of 51 to 4, approved a Lodge-sponsored resolution, which declared:

> ... when any harbor or other place in the American continents is so situated that the occupation thereof for naval or military purposes might threaten the communications or the safety of the United States, the Government of the United States could not see without grave concern the actual or potential possession of such harbor or other place by any Government, not American, as to give that Government practical power of control for naval or military purposes.

Thus was born the so-called Lodge Corollary to the Monroe Doctrine —a pronouncement of limited significance because it had originated in the legislative rather than the executive branch. In a private letter President Taft said: "I don't regard the Lodge resolution as very important. ... The Senate cannot declare the policy of this government, ... because it cannot make it. It is only part of the treaty-making power. ... I should not feel under any obligation to follow a resolution like this." [3] Yet whether Taft thought the Lodge Corollary necessary or not, the Senate's action demonstrated in still another way the extreme American sensitivity over the security of the Panama Canal.

[3] Reprinted by permission of Charles P. Taft from Henry F. Pringle, *The Life and Times of William Howard Taft* (New York: Rinehart & Company, Inc., 1939), vol. II, pp. 714–715.

Attempted Reciprocity with Canada

The Taft administration—well intentioned but blundering in its diplomacy—hoped to promote the closest possible economic ties between the United States and Canada. The great northern dominion was developing rapidly; already she provided one of the best markets for American manufactures, and future prospects were even brighter. Threatening this growth of trade was the possibility of a tariff war. In 1907 Canada had negotiated a tariff agreement under which certain French products were allowed to enter the country at lower rates than American; in retaliation the United States threatened in 1910 to impose the maximum Payne-Aldrich tariff rates on imports from Canada. After mutual concessions had eased this conflict, the American and Canadian governments widened their negotiations in an attempt to reach a general reciprocity agreement.

Warned by the short life of the Elgin-Marcy Treaty of 1854 [4] that reciprocity must offer equal advantages to both parties, the negotiators moved carefully. On January 21, 1911, the two governments agreed that they would proceed, not by treaty, but by concurrent legislation of the United States Congress and the Canadian Parliament. This would facilitate approval and allay suspicion, since the experiment could be speedily terminated if either side found it disadvantageous. An extensive free list would include lumber, nearly all agricultural products except wool, certain minerals and certain iron and steel products, and—highly important to Canada—wood pulp and paper. In addition, the tariffs of both countries would be reduced on a long list of other commodities, including meat, flour, maple sugar, farm machinery, and automobiles.

After a hard fight the Taft administration obtained the necessary congressional action. The political alignment was unusual. Supporting Taft were most of the Democrats plus a few standpat Republicans who sided with the President partly out of loyalty and partly out of hope that reciprocity would bring benefits to American manufacturers. In opposition were many rank-and-file Republicans suspicious of any breach in the tariff walls and most of the Middle Western progressives who accused the administration of selling out the farmers to win advantages for Eastern businessmen. In the final Senate vote in July, 1911, 31 Democrats and 22 Republicans favored reciprocity, while 24 Republicans and 3 Democrats opposed it.

Unfortunately, in the heat of the battle, the champions of reciprocity used arguments that were certain to be more popular south of the Canadian border than they would be north of it. Champ Clark of Missouri, the Democratic Speaker of the House, asserted that he favored reciprocity

[4] See chap. 14.

"because I hope to see the day when the American flag will float over every square foot of the British North American possessions clear to the North Pole." In his private correspondence, President Taft was almost as rash. To Theodore Roosevelt he confided that the volume of trade resulting from reciprocity would make Canada "only an adjunct of the United States." In his public speeches Taft was more discreet, but even here he blundered. By stressing that Canada was "at the parting of the ways," he provided Canadian nationalists with a convenient slogan to convince the voters that reciprocity was a diabolical Yankee trick to bring about eventual annexation.

Reciprocity was the principle issue in the Canadian general election of September, 1911. Liberal Premier Sir Wilfrid Laurier made a spirited campaign for the new policy; Sir Robert Borden and the Conservatives bitterly attacked it as endangering the Canadian tie with the British Empire, risking the absorption of the Dominion by the United States, and threatening Canadian manufacturers with ruin. The election returns spelled defeat for both Laurier and reciprocity—much to Taft's disappointment.

Frustration in the Far East

The generally pro-Japanese policy of Theodore Roosevelt was reversed under President Taft. By means of dollar diplomacy Secretary of State Knox undertook to check Japanese and Russian imperialism in Manchuria and to prevent the enlargement of European spheres of influence over China proper. This return to an emphasis upon the Open Door and the territorial and administrative integrity of China resulted in part from the policy recommendations of the Far Eastern Division, one of the special geographical sections recently established in the State Department.

When Taft became President, the acting chief of the Far Eastern Division was Willard Straight, a brilliant and versatile Cornell graduate who had gone to the Far East to work for the Chinese customs service and had subsequently served as a war correspondent during the Russo-Japanese conflict, as American vice consul in Korea, and as American consul in Mukden, Manchuria. Convinced that there was too little American investment in China and therefore too little American influence there, Straight had encouraged Edward H. Harriman, the Napoleon of the American railroad world, in his schemes to purchase the Manchurian railroads as one vital link in a Harriman-controlled round-the-world transportation system.

Through Straight's activities the American State Department became strongly committed to the idea of encouraging American investment in China. With the blessing of the Taft administration, a coalition for this purpose was organized, composed of Harriman himself and his traditional ally, Kuhn, Loeb and Company, and also J. P. Morgan and Company, the First National Bank, and the National City Bank. This group induced Straight to give up his government post and travel abroad as its representative.

Although Straight had initiated the new American policy, Secretary Knox gave enthusiastic support. As a State Department memorandum of September 30, 1909, explained:

> The nations that finance the great Chinese railways and other enterprises will be foremost in the affairs of China and the participation of American capital in these investments will give the voice of the U.S. more authority in political controversies in that country which will go far toward guaranteeing the preservation of the administrative entity of China.

In their effort to counter Japanese and Russian influence, Taft and Knox hoped for the support of England. But this support was never wholeheartedly given. London's paramount interest was to protect the precarious security of the British Empire. So far as Asia was concerned, the British were relying heavily upon the Anglo-Japanese alliance and could not, therefore, risk antagonizing Japan on the Manchurian issue. Since Great Britain was also linked with Russia in the nebulous but important Triple Entente, English policy called for mediating between Russia and Japan and encouraging those recent enemies to follow a policy of collaboration rather than rivalry in Manchuria. Against these hard facts of world politics the Taft-Knox policy had no chance of success.

During the summer of 1909 Harriman and Straight were in Europe trying to purchase the Russian-owned Chinese Eastern Railroad that ran across northern Manchuria. If successful, they planned to use this victory to force Japan to sell them the South Manchurian Railroad as well. Harriman's death in September, 1909, disrupted this project and threatened to halt the whole campaign to employ dollar diplomacy in the Far East.

But Secretary Knox was ready to plunge ahead even when the bankers hesitated. In November, 1909, he attempted a bold maneuver to achieve the neutralization of the Manchurian railroads. China was to be assisted in buying these lines through a loan advanced by an international syndicate in which American bankers, along with those of Russia, Japan, Great Britain, France, and Germany, would participate. By first submitting his plan to England, Knox hoped to gain the diplomatic support that would help him win over the other powers. But Foreign Secretary Sir Edward Grey's reply clearly showed English unwillingness to do anything displeasing to the Japanese allies.

Attempting to copy John Hay's famous tactics, Knox then presented his plan to the other powers with the assurance that England had already accepted it in principle; but the trick did not work. Russia and Japan rejected the neutralization proposals and warned China not to proceed against their wishes. Since France also opposed the Knox program, the United States found its only support from Germany, who was for her own reasons unhappy with the Far Eastern state of affairs. The only practical result of Knox's effort was to push Russia and Japan into a new treaty, redefining their special interests and thereby weakening instead of strengthening China's position.

On the so-called Hukuang railways project, Knox had greater apparent success. In May, 1909, while Straight was still in charge of the Far Eastern Division, he had induced the State Department to send a telegram to Peking, demanding for the American banking group a share in the loan which China had already arranged with a syndicate of British, French, and German bankers for the construction of railroads to link Hankow in central China with the western and southern provinces. Contending that these arrangements violated a promise made by China in 1903 to admit American capital on equal terms with European in any future loans, the Taft administration threatened to reverse the American decision to remit most of the Boxer indemnity. When the Chinese government appeared reluctant to yield to the American demand, President Taft took the unusual step of wiring directly to Prince Chun, the regent of China, on behalf of the American proposal. "I have an intense personal interest in making the use of American capital in the development of China an instrument for the promotion of the welfare of China," he argued, "and an increase in her material prosperity without entanglements or creating embarrassments affecting the growth of her independent political power and the preservation of her territorial integrity."

Despite many months of delay, arising first out of British, then out of Chinese objections, American wishes finally prevailed. In 1911 the Chinese government completed arrangements to make the Hukuang loan from a four-power consortium of British, French, German, and American bankers. Yet Knox's victory was a hollow one; the European partners resented the way the United States had muscled in; the Hukuang loan was so unpopular with the Chinese public that it helped bring on the revolution of 1911; and American capitalists showed little enthusiasm for putting up the money they had promised.

The administration—with the unenthusiastic cooperation of the bankers—held stubbornly to its course. In 1911 a four-power loan to rehabilitate the Chinese currency was arranged, but the money was never actually raised—first because of Russian and Japanese opposition, and second because of the overthrow of the Manchu dynasty. In 1912 when the new government was in need of funds to reorganize its finances, the four-power consortium was enlarged to a six-power one by admitting the bankers of Russia and Japan.

By this time the American bankers were demonstrating even less ardor than in their earlier courtship of China. The reorganization loan was still in the discussion stage when Woodrow Wilson succeeded Taft in the White House. One of the first questions put to the new administration concerned its attitude toward the consortium: the American bankers emphasized that they would not be satisfied with mere State Department approval; if they were going to participate in the proposed loan, they must be asked to do so by the American government.

Woodrow Wilson and his Secretary of State, William Jennings Bryan, were in no mood to continue the alliance between Wall Street and the State Department. Discussing the matter with his Cabinet, the new President said that "we ought to help China in some better way." In a public statement on March 18, 1913, Wilson refused to ask the bankers to seek a share in the reorganization loan. The conditions attached to the loan, Wilson declared, seemed "to touch very nearly the administrative independence of China itself, and this administration does not feel that it ought, even by implication, to be a party to those conditions."

Dollar Diplomacy Attacked and Defended

The promptness with which Wilson and Bryan repudiated the six-power consortium showed that the new President and Secretary of State shared with many other Americans a deep suspicion of dollar diplomacy. How Bryan regarded the matter is well revealed in a letter he wrote to Wilson a few months later. It was "pathetic," he said, "to see Nicaragua struggling in the grip of oppressive financial agreements. . . . We see in these transactions a perfect picture of dollar diplomacy. The financiers charge excessive rates on the ground that they must be *paid* for the risk that they take and as soon as they collect their pay for that risk, they then proceed to demand of the respective governments that the *risk* shall be *eliminated* by governmental coercion. No wonder the people of these little republics are aroused to revolution by what they regard as a sacrifice of their interests." [5]

Similar criticism had been frequent while Taft was still in the White House. Accusing the State Department of acting the part of salesman for American munitions and shipbuilding firms, *La Follette's Weekly Magazine* had denounced the trading of the Navy's secrets for the benefit of financiers like the steelmaker, Charles M. Schwab. "Is there anything,"

[5] Reprinted by permission of the publisher from Ray Stannard Baker, *Woodrow Wilson: Life and Letters* (Copyright 1927–1939 by Doubleday & Company, Inc., New York), vol. IV, pp. 437–438.

the paper asked in 1911, "which Mr. Knox and President Taft will not give to foreign nations in exchange for 'business' desired by their friends in Wall Street?"

Instead of hanging their heads in shame, Taft and Knox defended their policies vigorously. "There is nothing inconsistent," declared the President, "in the promotion of peaceful relations and the promotion of trade relations, and if the protection which the United States shall assure to her citizens in the assertion of just rights under investments made in foreign countries shall promote the amount of such trade, it is a result to be commended. To call such diplomacy 'dollar diplomacy' ... is to ignore entirely a most useful office to be performed by a government in its dealings with foreign governments."

Secretary Knox was even more explicit in his philosophy. "If the American dollar," he asserted, "can aid suffering humanity and lift the burden of financial difficulty from states with which we live on terms of intimate intercourse and earnest friendship ... all I can say is that it would be hard to find better employment."

Whatever the abstract merits of dollar diplomacy might be, Wilson and Bryan soon found that the increasing American involvement in the Caribbean region and elsewhere was a trend too strong to be easily reversed.

25

THE DIPLOMACY OF MORALITY

When Woodrow Wilson appointed William Jennings Bryan Secretary of State, he was recognizing Bryan's unusual eminence in the Democratic party. Since Wilson had in earlier years expressed a wish that the Great Commoner might be knocked into a cocked hat, their new relationship might appear to have been a marriage of convenience rather than of love. Yet though the differences between Wilson's frosty intellectualism and Bryan's genial simplicity were obvious, the two men really had much in common. Both were deeply sincere in their religious convictions; both had strong feelings about right and wrong; both believed that America's mission was to set an example of humane democracy in her relations with the rest of the world; both were natural orators who loved to clothe their policies in stirring rhetoric. Wilsonian diplomacy was destined, therefore, to be highly moralistic in statement and intent. Ironically, however, the hard realities of foreign relations sometimes led Wilson and Bryan into courses of action that seemed to belie their ideals.

The actual record of Wilsonian diplomacy also sometimes suffered because of the imperfect human instruments through which it had to operate. For one thing, Wilson and Bryan both distrusted professional diplomats and demonstrated a preference for appointing inexperienced men to regulate State Department posts and for using unofficial agents operating outside State Department channels. For another, Bryan was a politician to the core, with a deep sense of loyalty to those who had worked for him in earlier party battles. Consequently he felt no hesitation in loading the diplomatic service with those who were in his own phrase "deserving Democrats." Although the Republicans of earlier years had doled out patronage with equal heartiness, Bryan's policy did represent a backward step from recent efforts of Theodore Roosevelt and Elihu Root to extend the merit principle within the State Department and particularly to reform the consular service.

Although Bryan may be justly blamed for certain bad appointments that caused subsequent embarrassment to the administration, he did not deserve the ridicule showered upon him by partisan newspapers. His refusal to serve wine at diplomatic dinners was at most a venial fault; his continuance as lecturer on the Chautauqua circuit provided him with cash to augment his slender income. On more important matters he proved to be a valuable Cabinet member. Although inexperienced in foreign affairs, he had a strong sense of justice and a fund of common sense that Wilson learned to value. It was inherent in Wilson's conception of the Presidency that he was, on all important issues, his own Secretary of State, yet Bryan cheerfully served as loyal lieutenant until the two men finally came to a parting of the ways on the *Lusitania* issue in June, 1915.[1] Bryan's successor, Robert Lansing, was a man of different qualities—cool, realistic, and highly trained in international law. Wilson found his talents useful, but carefully kept the making of policy in his own hands.

Moral Words and Moral Deeds

On March 12, 1913—just eight days after his inauguration—Wilson released a statement to the newspapers emphasizing that "one of the chief objects" of his administration would be "to cultivate the friendship and deserve the confidence of our sister republics in Central and South America." Cooperation was possible only when supported by "the orderly processes of just government based upon law, not upon arbitrary or irregular force." He added a disclaimer of any selfish purpose on the part of the United States, which had nothing to seek except the mutual interests of the two continents and the security of governments "intended for the people and for no special group or interest."

Wilson's words were intended as a warning both to South American revolutionaries who might be plotting trouble and to American bankers who might expect their privileged position under Taft to be continued. The President's condemnation of dollar diplomacy was spelled out more clearly on March 18, 1913, when he withdrew official support from the six-power consortium in China.[2] Both Presidential announcements were made without consultation with the State Department—greatly to the distress of the professional diplomats.

Wilson expressed the ideals of his "new diplomacy" still more vigorously in an address at Mobile, Alabama, on October 27, 1913. To a Southern Commercial Congress that included many Latin Americans, the Presi-

---

[1] Much of Bryan's personal leadership was exercised in negotiating "cooling-off treaties," described in chap. 26. In this endeavor Wilson gave Bryan his enthusiastic support.

[2] See chap. 24.

dent condemned the hard terms imposed by the bankers upon Latin-American states: "Interest has been exacted of them that was not exacted of anybody else, because the risk was said to be greater; and then securities were taken that destroyed the risk—an admirable arrangement for those who were forcing the terms! I rejoice in nothing so much as in the prospect that they will now be emancipated from these conditions. . . ." To reassure the southern neighbors, Wilson gave an impressive pledge: "I want to take this occasion to say that the United States will never again seek one additional foot of territory by conquest." America's fundamental motive in her foreign relations was "the development of constitutional liberty in the world."

On a few issues Wilsonian morality could be applied simply and directly. One of these involved the Panama Canal. In a law of 1912, Congress had exempted from tolls American-owned ships passing from one American port to another. England protested that this exemption violated the Hay-Pauncefote Treaty of 1901, under which the United States had promised that the waterway would be open to the ships of all nations "on terms of entire equality" without discrimination in respect to "the conditions or charges of traffic."

The legal issue involved was not altogether clear. President Taft and other good lawyers in his Cabinet had believed that for the United States to favor its own coastwise shipping was not a violation of the treaty; other lawyers, equally good and equally Republican, like Elihu Root and Joseph H. Choate, believed the British protest was fully justified. British Ambassador James Bryce suggested that the question be submitted to arbitration, but there was strong congressional opposition to such a course of action.

Although the Republican platform of 1912 had avoided the tolls issue, the Democratic and Progressive platforms had both strongly favored exemption. During the campaign Wilson paid almost no attention to the matter, but did support exemption in one speech—largely as an anti-monopoly device to help the American merchant marine compete with transcontinental railroads.

After the election, Root, Choate, and others, ashamed to have the United States go back on its word, undertook to educate Wilson on the moral issues involved. This seed fell on fertile soil, and even before he entered the White House, the new President became convinced that he and his party had been wrong in the stand taken during the campaign. Despite this early conversion Wilson had to proceed very cautiously. The Democratic congressional leaders were strong for the exemption principle, and Bryan also leaned in this direction. Wilson therefore refrained from raising the issue during the months when a maximum of party harmony was vital to the success of his domestic program.

By the fall of 1913 Wilson became deeply concerned in gaining England's support for his policy toward Mexico. Although no explicit deal was made, a British about-face on Mexico in November was significantly followed by a Wilsonian move on the tolls issue two months later. In a White House meeting with the Senate Foreign Relations Committee on January 26, 1914, the President expressed his now strong conviction that the exemption law was a plain violation of the Hay-Pauncefote Treaty. A week and a half later he came out publicly for repeal.

Wilson had to fight hard to gain his goal. Any appearance of knuckling under to John Bull was unpopular not only in Irish-American circles, but also in the old Populist strongholds of the Middle West and the South. Confronted with the opposition of Democratic leaders like Speaker Champ Clark and Representative Oscar Underwood, the President welcomed the support of such Eastern Republicans as Senators Henry Cabot Lodge and Elihu Root. Converted to repeal, Secretary Bryan teamed with Postmaster General Burleson to line up the Democratic rank and file. Influential newspapers like the *New York Times,* the *New York World,* and the *Baltimore Sun* came out strongly for the President's proposal.

Even after a month of preparation the issue was uncertain when Wilson made a personal appearance before Congress on March 5, 1914. Although he expressed his own strong conviction that tolls exemption was "in plain contravention" of the Hay-Pauncefote Treaty, he based his plea for repeal largely on the need for removing the foreign impression that the United States had broken its promise. "The large thing to do is the only thing we can afford to do, a voluntary withdrawal from a position everywhere questioned and misunderstood." The President concluded on a cryptic note:

> I ask this of you in support of the foreign policy of the administration. I shall not know how to deal with other matters of even greater delicacy and nearer consequence if you do not grant it to me in ungrudging measure.

To many listeners this appeared to be a reference to the tangled Mexican situation, but Wilson explained later that what he had in mind was the general moral prestige of the United States in its relations with Latin America.

The President had by no means convinced all his audience. Indeed, Speaker Clark took the floor to lead the opposition in the House, and in the Senate the debate was torrid, with party lines meaning little. In the end, however, the repeal bill was passed by votes of 247 to 162 in the House and 50 to 35 in the Senate.

Wilson's exultation was expressed in a letter to his brother-in-law: [3]

[3] Reprinted by permission of the publisher from Ray Stannard Baker, *Woodrow Wilson: Life and Letters* (Copyright 1927–1939 by Doubleday & Company, Inc., New York), vol. IV, p. 421.

If everything else in connection with this administration is forgotten, the action in regard to Panama will be remembered because it is a long forward step in putting the relationships of nations and the dealings of one nation with another on a par with the dealings of honourable men, one with another.

The English press lavishly praised the President's courage and leadership.

On another issue related to the Panama Canal, Wilson and Bryan undertook to make a similar demonstration of high-mindedness, but here they were thwarted. In June, 1914, the President sent to the Senate a treaty under which Colombia acknowledged the complete title of the United States to the canal and, in return, was promised equal rights in its use and a payment of 25 million dollars. The United States expressed, moreover, "sincere regret that anything should have occurred to interrupt or to mar the relations of cordial friendship that had so long subsisted between the two nations."

Theodore Roosevelt learned with indignation of Wilson's intention to pay compensation and to apologize for his highhanded action in 1903. This, he said, was "an outrage on the honour and a blow to the interests of the American people.... An administration that will conclude such a treaty as this treaty for the payment of blackmail to Colombia has forfeited all right to the respect of the people of the United States." Lodge and others blocked approval of the treaty as long as Roosevelt lived. Not until 1921 did the Senate finally take favorable action—but only after the humiliating expression of regret was omitted.

Even though the Colombian treaty was not ratified during Wilson's Presidency, his attempts to do right brought warm applause in Latin America. This deposit in the bank of good will was highly important, because the President had many checks to draw against it in his dealings with Mexico and the Caribbean countries.

The Problem of Mexico

When Taft turned the burdens of the Presidency over to Wilson, Mexico was in the midst of tumultuous change. Porfirio Díaz, President most of the time from 1876 to 1911, had been an excellent ruler from the standpoint of the Mexican upper classes and foreign businessmen. He had maintained order, repressed troublemakers, and encouraged the investment of outside capital. "My own impression has been," Taft wrote to his brother, "that Díaz has done more for the people of Mexico than any other Latin American has done for any of his people."

Yet beneath the placid surface of Mexican life, explosive discontent had been building up. The landless peons and underpaid workers who composed some 90 per cent of the Mexican population hated the old regime and readily responded to the reformist slogans of Francisco Madero. Increasing disorder in the provinces was followed by street demonstrations in the capital. Finally in May, 1911, Díaz resigned and fled to Europe.

The triumphant Madero served as provisional President for some months and then was duly elected to office according to the forms of the Mexican constitution. As often happens, however, a leader well endorsed to promote a revolution proved ineffective as a responsible statesman. Although honest and sincere in his passion to reform Mexican society, Madero lacked the firmness necessary to deal with the chaos created by the sudden removal of Díaz's iron hand. Property owners trembled as the government proved unable to cope with the assaults, murders, and pillage of marauding bandits, and as ambitious local generals raised banners of revolt.

The Taft administration had been deeply troubled by these developments. Some 1 billion dollars in American investments—mostly in railroads, mines, and plantations, with a small but growing amount in oil—had been put in jeopardy by the Mexican revolution, as had the lives of some 40,000 American citizens living south of the border. Despite this large stake, President Taft had followed a patient policy. He had recognized the Madero government and had strengthened its hand against the rebels by using powers granted to him by Congress to impose an embargo on shipments of American arms to anyone but the legal Mexican government. To enforce this policy and to prevent incursions onto American soil, Taft had mobilized 100,000 American troops along the Mexican border.

From the beginning, Henry Lane Wilson, Taft's Ambassador to Mexico, had had little respect for the gentle but ineffective Madero and had urged Washington to show its teeth in demanding protection for American rights. Ambassador Wilson did not, therefore, hide his satisfaction when in February, 1913, Madero was deposed and imprisoned by one of his own subordinates, General Victoriano Huerta. A few days later Madero was killed—supposedly while trying to escape.

Even though Huerta was suspected of complicity in this murder, the large European powers promptly recognized him as *de facto* ruler. The Taft administration would undoubtedly have done the same had not Wilson's inauguration been so near at hand.

Nonrecognition

When Wilson and Bryan took over the problem, they were not without a host of advisers to tell them what they should do. Ambassador Wilson and other American residents of Mexico City urged prompt recognition of Huerta, as did many American businessmen who counted on the new strong man to rule in the Díaz tradition. But President Wilson regarded with deep repugnance the man who had seized power by such shocking means. "I will not," he said privately, "recognize a government of butchers."

The President soon recalled Ambassador Wilson, whom he thoroughly distrusted and may have suspected of complicity in the Huerta coup. Instead of appointing an official successor, the President sent an unofficial envoy, John Lind, a former Governor of Minnesota and a close friend of Bryan's. The fact that Lind was without diplomatic experience was regarded as an asset rather than a liability.

Lind took with him Wilson's concrete proposals for restoring order in Mexico: (1) all parties should agree to an armistice; (2) there should be an early, free election in which all parties would participate; (3) Huerta should promise not to be a presidential candidate; and (4) all factions should agree to abide by the election results. Although to a former political science professor this seemed a program based on simple common sense, Huerta indignantly rejected what he regarded as intolerable meddling in Mexico's internal affairs. Reporting the results of the Lind mission to Congress on August 27, 1913, President Wilson regretted that Mexico had not chosen the path of "honest constitutional government," but he argued for a policy of patience.

By refusing to recognize Huerta, Wilson hoped to cripple the Mexican's ability to borrow money—at least in the United States—and eventually to bring about his downfall. This denial of recognition to a *de facto* government was contrary to American tradition. Since the days when Secretary of State Thomas Jefferson had had to deal with the problems created by the French Revolution, the practice of the United States had been to recognize any government able to maintain itself in power, protect foreigners, and carry out its international obligations. Because recognition did not imply approval, the United States felt it unnecessary to scrutinize the circumstances that had brought each new regime to power. Yet Wilson's insistence that only governments chosen in honest elections should be recognized was not entirely novel. The Central American pacts of 1907, for example, had affirmed this principle, as had certain Latin-American publicists. Such precedents, however, were much less important to Wilson than his own strong belief that Latin America would never adopt truly democratic and constitutional government unless the United States used its moral influence to bring this about.

Unseating Huerta

In one of his famous phrases Wilson defined his Mexican policy of 1913 as "watchful waiting." By maintaining a strict neutrality and by forbidding American arms shipments to either Huerta or his enemies, the President hoped to bring about the dictator's downfall without active intervention.

To Wilson's disgust, however, Huerta grew stronger rather than weaker. In October, 1913, the general dealt his opponents a stunning blow by arresting 110 members of the Mexican Congress and compelling the cowed remnant to endow him with supreme legislative and judicial power. On October 26 his position as President was confirmed in a rigged election.

To a man of Wilson's scruples, the Mexican dictator's latest tricks provided additional reasons for opposing him. The President was particularly annoyed by the open support given Huerta by the British Ambassador to Mexico, the reputed ally of certain British oil interests. Making his displeasure known to the London government, Wilson pressed strongly for British cooperation with his own anti-Huerta policy. The British, always mindful of the danger of war with Germany and realizing that in such a crisis American friendship would be more vital than Mexican, deferred to Wilson's wishes and withdrew their recognition of Huerta. This change in British policy was closely followed by Wilson's conciliatory action on the Panama tolls controversy.

Even more important as an anti-Huerta measure was Wilson's decision on February 3, 1914, to allow the dictator's enemies to purchase arms in the United States. This step was intended to help Venustiano Carranza and the so-called Constitutionalists who had been challenging Huerta's authority in the northern provinces for many months.

As Wilson moved from passive hostility to a more active policy, Mexican antagonism toward the United States resulted in a number of incidents. The most serious of these occurred on April 9, 1914, when some American sailors loading supplies at Tampico were arrested and marched off to jail. As soon as the local Huertist general heard what had happened, he ordered the men released and sent his personal apologies to Admiral Henry T. Mayo, commander of the American fleet. But Mayo decided the affront had been so flagrant that a formal twenty-one-gun salute to the American flag should be required. President Wilson—with dubious wisdom—backed up this crusty demand with an official ultimatum. Huerta refused to comply unless the American Navy would agree to return the salute, but Wilson would permit no act implying recognition.

The President made arrangements to go before Congress on April 21 to ask for authority to back up his demand with force, but before he could do so the arrival at Vera Cruz of a German arms shipment for Huerta impelled him to move without waiting for congressional sanction. On the morning of the 21st, the United States Navy, acting under Presidential orders, began to occupy the port. Despite sharp resistance that resulted in the death of 126 Mexicans and 19 Americans, Vera Cruz was securely in American hands by the end of the next day.

Meanwhile, Wilson had made his scheduled appearance before Congress, asking not for a declaration of war but for authority to "use the armed forces of the United States in such ways and to such an extent as may be necessary to obtain from General Huerta and his adherents the fullest recognition of the rights and dignity of the United States." He still insisted that he did not want to control "in any degree" the affairs of the sister republic. "The people of Mexico are entitled to settle their own domestic affairs in their own way, and we sincerely desire to respect their right." By overwhelming votes in both houses the President received the powers he sought.

Although the occupation of Vera Cruz was intended as one more blow to dislodge Huerta without resorting to full-scale intervention, its immediate result was quite the opposite. In the United States it played into the hands of the jingoes who were demanding that the United States assume full responsibility for restoring order in Mexico. Across the border, on the other hand, Wilson's professions of disinterested concern for Mexican welfare were regarded as mere hypocrisy, not only by the Huerta faction but by the Constitutionalists as well. An upsurge of Mexican nationalism threatened to plunge the two countries into war.

A timely offer of mediation by the ABC powers—Argentina, Brazil, and Chile—provided a solution to this unhapy situation. Wilson's prompt acceptance convinced many doubtful Latin Americans of his good will, even though the resulting conference of delegates from the United States, Mexico, and the ABC powers at Niagara Falls, Canada, had no conclusive results. Ironically, Huerta was now willing to accept the proposed armistice, but Carranza was not.

Carranza's cold response reflected his brightening hopes for complete victory. Having defeated the Huertistas in the North, the Constitutionalist armies were now driving upon Mexico City itself, and Carranza was determined to win the presidency by his own efforts rather than through foreign mediation. On July 15, 1914, Huerta turned over his powers to an interim government, and a month later the triumphant Carranza with his conquering armies entered the capital. On November 23 the American Navy evacuated Vera Cruz. The demanded salute had never been given, but the issue was no longer important after Huerta's downfall.

Carranza and Villa

Huerta's eclipse brought no end to the worries of either Mexico City or Washington. Carranza's announcement that the revolution was over and that the Mexicans should now respect his authority was treated with contempt by other aspirants for power. The forces that had combined to bring down Huerta now split; Francisco ("Pancho") Villa, hitherto Carranza's most effective ally, became his principal opponent.

In view of the complexity of the Mexican situation, Wilson withheld recognition of Carranza for many months. For some time, indeed, the American government gave its moral support to Villa, believing that this convivial chieftain might be more deferential to American influence than the white-bearded Carranza, whose iron stubbornness matched that of Wilson himself. Certain American newspaper correspondents had taken a fancy to the colorful Villa, whom they glamorized as a sort of Mexican Robin Hood, robbing the rich for the benefit of the poor. For a time in 1914, Villa seemed a likely winner, and he even occupied Mexico City briefly. But Carranza, supported by the ablest Mexican general of the day, Alvaro Obregón, turned the tide of battle and soon drove the Villa armies out of all Mexico except the northern deserts.

The continuance of Mexican strife naturally added to the troubles of the Wilson administration. William Randolph Hearst, the holder of vast Mexican properties, used his newspapers to clamor for full-scale military intervention, while Theodore Roosevelt and his friends were denouncing Wilson's weakness in dealing with the situation. Roman Catholic spokesmen expressed alarm at the anticlerical tendencies of the continuing Mexican revolution and urged the United States to intervene.

After Lansing succeeded Bryan as Secretary of State, the Wilson administration reviewed its Mexican policy in conference with the ABC powers. Unsuccessful in inducing Carranza to surrender power to a new provisional government, the conferees finally decided to accept the realities of the Mexican situation and grant *de facto* recognition to Carranza.

This step, taken in October, 1915, antagonized Villa, who now deliberately set out to provoke American intervention—having convinced himself that this would discredit Carranza and open the way for his own seizure of power. The first shocking action came in January, 1916, when a Villa gang stopped a train at Santa Ysabel in northern Mexico and killed sixteen members of an American engineering party. While American indignation at this massacre was still flaming, Villa struck again—this time by sending a marauding band across the border to shoot up the town of Columbus, New Mexico. This foray of March 9, 1916, resulted in the death of nineteen Americans and spurred the Wilson administration to speedy action. General John J. Pershing was ordered to lead a cavalry force into Mexico and bring back the now-hated Villa, dead or alive.

Wilson still hoped to hold the American expedition to its limited mission and to avoid trouble with Carranza. An agreement between Washington and Mexico City stipulated that each government should have the right to pursue marauding bandits across the other's border. But Carranza resented the fact that Pershing had begun his hot pursuit without waiting for this agreement to be ratified and that the American force, finding Villa unexpectedly elusive, penetrated deeper and deeper into Mexico. Carranza sent his own troops to the scene, ostensibly to look for Villa, but really to keep an eye on Pershing. On June 12, 1916, a rather serious clash near Carrizal cost the lives of twelve Americans and twenty-nine of the Carranza forces. Once again the two countries seemed to be teetering on the brink of all-out war, but a prudent restraint on both sides prevented that disaster. Nevertheless, the frustrating pursuit of Villa and Carranza's sullen hostility provided Republican orators with effective ammunition to use against Wilson in the 1916 Presidential campaign.

In the end, growing Mexican antagonism and the disadvantage of having American troops tied down in Mexico at a time of critical relations with Germany convinced the Wilson administration that it should back down. Since Villa was still at large when the withdrawal of American troops began on January 27, 1917, Wilson had obviously failed in his objective. But at least there were no more border raids, and the acute phase of Mexican-American tension proved to be over.

In early 1917, a Mexican constituent assembly adopted a new progressive constitution, under which Carranza was duly elected to the presidency. On March 13, 1917, the United States granted him *de jure* recognition. But even after this step the two governments wrangled over compensation claimed for losses of American life and property during the revolution [4] and disputed over Mexican attempts to tax American oil companies. In 1920 another outburst of civil strife resulted in the assassination of Carranza and the assumption of the presidency by General Obregón. The new regime was much more thorough in carrying out the revolutionary property laws than the old had been, and another cycle of Mexican-American disputes therefore began. [5]

Wilson's intentions toward Mexico were highly honorable: to rebuke violence and encourage constitutionalism, to encourage the Mexican people in their hopes for agrarian reform and other social changes, and to give reasonable protection to American lives and property without resorting to full-scale military intervention. Nevertheless, almost all Mexicans resented the President's assumption of moral superiority, his insistence on telling them what they ought to do, and his meddling in the hurly-burly of Mexican politics. Observers in other Latin-American countries

[4] According to one calculation, 397 American civilians were killed in Mexico between 1910 and 1920; other losses included: 58 American civilians killed along the border; 64 United States soldiers killed in Mexico and 68 along the border. Shocking though these figures are, it should be remembered that Mexicans residing in the United States were none too secure either; 92 were reported to have suffered violent deaths on American soil in the three years 1913 to 1915.

[5] See chap. 30.

judged Wilson's conduct less harshly. They saw the shortcomings of his Mexican policy, but at the same time they gave him credit for resisting the pressure of American interventionists and for advancing the cause of friendly consultation among the Western Hemisphere nations.

Intervention in Haiti

Midway between Cuba and Puerto Rico lies the island of Hispaniola, with the Republic of Haiti occupying the western part and the Dominican Republic the rest. Achieving its independence from France in 1804 after a bloody upheaval, Haiti entered upon a chaotic history that began with the tyrannical dictatorships of Henri Christophe and Jean Boyer and degenerated into a burdensome succession of short-lived regimes thereafter. Between 1879 and 1915 eleven different Haitian generals fought their way to power, only to be overthrown and sometimes killed by rival chieftains. This chronic civil war burdened the Haitian people with heavy taxes and military obligations, a devastated economy, and widespread disease. No matter who held power, the Haitian government was plagued by corruption and debt.

Haiti's strongest economic and cultural ties had always been with France. French was the official language, and French investors were the largest holders of Haitian government bonds and the securities of the National Railroad, the National Bank, and other concessions. There were, however, smaller investments by German, English, and American interests. In 1910 the National City Bank of New York had joined with three other American banks in acquiring—at the suggestion of the State Department —20 per cent of the stock of the National Bank of Haiti.

That bank was uncomfortably involved in Haitian civil strife. The politicians harassed it with demands for new issues of currency, and in resisting these the bank had the support of the American State Department. In December, 1914, American marines supervised the transfer of some of the bank's funds to the American gunboat *Machias*, which then carried them to New York for safekeeping. Secretary Bryan's uncharacteristic tenderness for banking interests reflected more than a desire to protect the French and American investors. His principal concern was to uphold the National Bank of Haiti as the financial agent responsible for receiving the customs revenues and making payments on the foreign debt.

Bryan's earliest interest in Haiti had been stimulated by rumors that German shipping concerns were attempting to lease Mole St. Nicholas, strategically located on the Windward Passage facing Cuba. Troubled by the perennial bugbear of a possible European naval base in the Caribbean, Bryan sent agents to sound out the Haitian government on whether it might be willing to sell this site for an American naval base. These overtures received no encouragement, and early in 1914 the United States abandoned this effort and sought instead a Haitian promise not to lease territory to any European government.

Throughout 1914 the State Department considered ways and means by which the Haitians might be induced to accept an American financial protectorate similar to that exercised in the Dominican Republic. Negotiations with President Orestes Zamor were carried on by Roger L. Farnham, the agent of the National City Bank. Before the deal could be completed, Zamor had been overthrown by General Davilmar Théodore. Wilson and Bryan appointed a commission to deal with the new regime, but once again revolution intervened and still another Haitian general, Vilbrun Sam, seized the presidency. Sam stubbornly refused to negotiate and, because Bryan was reluctant to force a treaty upon him, the situation came to a temporary stalemate.

But a resort to force came soon after Bryan resigned the secretaryship in June, 1915. Late in July the Haitian political storm reached a violent climax. With Port-au-Prince, the capital, beset by rival armies, the Sam regime rashly executed 167 political prisoners, including former President Zamor. Enraged by this massacre, a mob broke into the French legation where Sam had taken refuge, seized the President, and then proceeded to tear him literally limb from limb. The avengers paraded through the streets, waving the bloody fragments of Sam's body.

This orgy of violence took place on the afternoon of July 28, 1915, just as Admiral William B. Caperton was entering the harbor of Port-au-Prince aboard an American cruiser. Acting promptly on orders from Washington, Caperton landed sailors and marines to restore order and protect foreigners. The Haitians—except for the professional politicians and the *cacos*, or hired soldiers—accepted the intervention, for the moment at least, with relief. Once firmly in control of the capital, the American authorities left no doubt of their determination not to withdraw until a stable government had been established.

After interviewing rival candidates for the presidency, the naval officers reported to Washington that one of these was more deferential to American advice than the other, and the Navy Department promptly wired back: "Allow election of President to take place whenever Haitians wish. The United States prefers election of Dartiguenave." Admiral Caperton acted efficiently to achieve the American goal. Using marines to protect the National Assembly against the disappointed faction, he readily obtained the election of President Sudre Dartiguenave on August 12, 1915.

Secretary of State Lansing instructed the American chargé at Port-au-Prince to recognize the new government only after the latter had signed a treaty with the United States, based upon the American proposals of the preceding year. President Dartiguenave, caught between American

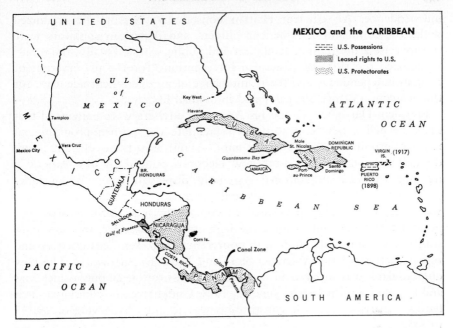

pressure on one side and the rising hostility of the professional politicians and *cacos* on the other, was reluctant to compromise Haitian sovereignty, but finally permitted a treaty to be signed on September 16. Although the Haitian lower house approved the agreement with reasonable promptness, the senate resorted to obstructionism. The American Navy Department impatiently instructed Admiral Caperton to warn the Haitian government that the United States intended "to retain control in Haiti until the desired end is accomplished." The Dartiguenave regime would be supported, but "those offering opposition can only expect such treatment as their conduct merits." Having brandished the stick, the Navy quickly offered the carrot: ratification of the treaty would be followed by measures that would provide employment for "as many Haitians as possible." The Haitian senate sensibly chose the carrot; the treaty was approved on November 11, 1915, and given immediate effect by a modus vivendi signed on November 29. Thereupon the Haitian government was promptly rewarded for its good conduct by receiving $100,000 of its customs revenues.

The treaty of 1916 provided that the Haitian President should appoint a general receiver of the customs and a financial adviser, upon nomination by the President of the United States. Haiti was obligated not to increase its debt without American consent or without providing means for payment and not to sell or lease its territory to any foreign government nor to enter into any foreign treaty that would impair Haitian independence. An efficient Haitian constabulary was to be organized under the command of American officers, and American engineers were to supervise a program of sanitation and public works. Finally, the treaty recognized the right of American intervention "for the preservation of Haitian independence and the maintenance of a government adequate for the protection of life, property and individual liberty."

President Dartiguenave and his American advisers were convinced that Haiti needed a new constitution to facilitate the reform program and remove prohibitions on foreign landholding. But these changes were difficult to obtain. Even after new elections policed by the American marines, the Haitian National Assembly displayed an annoying independence in discussing constitutional proposals. The Haitian President was, therefore, readily persuaded to comply with a Marine Corps suggestion that he should dissolve the legislature. Thereafter, the new constitution was amicably drafted in conferences between Dartiguenave and representatives of the American State and Navy Departments.[6] The new constabulary was ordered to explain the constitution at public meetings and to police a plebiscite on June 12, 1918. Under these circumstances it is hardly surprising that the constitution was adopted by a vote of 69,337 to 335.

Although the Wilson administration insisted that its only desire was to act for the Haitians' own good, it became involved in an increasingly coercive policy. Even during the early days of the intervention, Secretary of the Navy Daniels was shocked to learn that American marines had thought it necessary to shoot down Haitian troublemakers. The Secretary forbade "offensive action against Haitians without first consulting the Navy Department unless absolutely necessary to prevent loss of life or property." In 1918, the imposition of forced labor upon road-building projects and other grievances resulted in a serious insurrection. When the constabulary proved unable to handle the situation, American marines subdued the rebels in a series of operations that cost the lives of some 2,000 Haitians. Even the complaisant Dartiguenave government occasionally got its back up, and in 1920 the American authorities had to stop the salaries of the Haitian puppets in order to get some requested changes in Haitian laws.

Although the intervention brought certain obvious benefits like stable government, better roads, and more adequate sanitary measures, American

[6] Franklin D. Roosevelt, Assistant Secretary of the Navy, boasted in a campaign speech in 1920: "You know, I have had something to do with the running of a couple of little republics. The facts are that I wrote Haiti's constitution myself, and if I do say it I think it is a very good constitution." Sober scholarship suggests that Roosevelt greatly exaggerated his personal role, but undoubtedly the Navy Department was unusually active throughout the whole intervention.

interference encountered increasing antagonism, especially among the Haitian elite who missed the plums they had enjoyed under the old regime. The excitement of World War I for a long time diverted American attention from the Haitian problem, but by 1920 many senators and private commentators were severely criticizing the government's policy.

More Caribbean Involvements

In 1916 Admiral Caperton, fresh from his pacification of Haiti, was ordered to carry out a similar policy in the neighboring Dominican Republic. Military intervention came as the final result of unfortunate developments over the preceding several years. Secretary Bryan had contributed to this situation by appointing as American Minister to the Dominican Republic in 1913 a supposedly "deserving Democrat" named James M. Sullivan. Sullivan, a former prize-fight promoter and lawyer of shady reputation, proceeded to support President José Bordas Valdés against his rivals, gaining in return contracts and concessions for his relatives and friends. Opposition to Bordas erupted in civil war in 1914, and Wilson belatedly took steps to undo the damage Sullivan had done. The Minister was dismissed, and an American commission was sent to the island to mediate among the warring factions.

The election of Juan Y. Jiménez to the presidency quieted the situation temporarily, but the executive's advanced age and feebleness soon resulted in civil strife. In 1915 the American State Department proposed a new treaty similar to that just imposed upon Haiti, but Jiménez rejected terms that threatened Dominican sovereignty. The situation reached a crisis early in May, 1916, when the bitterly anti-American Desiderio Arias led an insurrection that forced out Jiménez. The Wilson administration, determined to keep power from Arias, who was also blamed for many of the difficulties in Haiti, ordered Admiral Caperton to occupy the Dominican capital city on May 15.

Unable to establish a satisfactory regime and fearing that popular elections would result in victory for Arias, Secretary Lansing recommended to President Wilson that the republic be placed under American military control. The unhappy moralist replied: "It is with the deepest reluctance that I approve and authorize the course here proposed, but I am convinced that it is the least of the evils in sight in this very perplexing situation."

Accordingly, on November 29, 1916, the United States proclaimed the establishment of American military government in the Dominican Republic, basing its action upon the contention that the Dominican government had increased its debt in violation of the treaty of 1907. "This military occupation," the proclamation declared, "is undertaken with no immediate or ulterior object of destroying the sovereignty of the Republic of

Santo Domingo. . . ." Its object was to aid in establishing order and to ensure observance of the treaty and the duties of the republic "as one of the family of nations." During the period of military rule, which lasted until 1924, the Dominicans benefited by the cessation of civil strife and by American-directed road building, sanitary reforms, and educational progress. But the affront to Dominican sovereignty was, nevertheless, bitterly resented.

Wilson's ambition to impose good government upon the Caribbean countries led him into new involvements in Nicaragua as well. It will be recalled that Taft and Knox had employed both dollar diplomacy and military intervention to maintain President Adolpho Díaz in power. When Bryan took over the State Department, he had to decide whether to risk a revival of civil war in a region uncomfortably close to the Panama Canal or to continue to support the unpopular Díaz. Choosing the second alternative, Bryan not only completed negotiations for Knox's new treaty, but added a highly controversial "protector" clause, stipulating that Nicaragua was not to declare war without the consent of the United States nor to enter into treaties that would effect its independence or territorial integrity, and that the United States could intervene whenever necessary to preserve Nicaragua's independence or to protect life and property. The proposal that Nicaragua accept a relationship to the United States similar to that of Cuba under the Platt Amendment had come from Díaz himself—in an obvious attempt to keep himself in office with the weapon of American intervention.

The protector clause provoked strong opposition both in Central America and in the United States Senate. Finding himself opposed by the Democratic members of the Foreign Relations Committee, Bryan drafted a new treaty omitting this article. In its final form the Bryan-Chamorro Treaty, signed in August, 1914, and approved by the Senate two years later, provided for an American payment of 3 million dollars in return for the exclusive right to build a canal across Nicaraguan territory. The United States was also to receive a renewable ninety-nine-year lease of the Great Corn and Little Corn Islands in the Gulf of Mexico and a similar right to maintain a naval base on the Gulf of Fonseca on the Pacific Coast.

An unfortunate consequence of the Bryan-Chamorro Treaty was the torpedoing of the Central American Court of Justice, which had been established with Secretary Root's blessing in 1907. Salvador and Costa Rica both objected to certain treaty provisions as conflicting with earlier agreements between Nicaragua and her Central American neighbors. The court upheld these contentions, but Nicaragua ignored the decision. Although the United States was not a member of the court and therefore not subject to its jurisdiction, Wilson and Lansing missed an opportunity to strengthen the machinery for judicial settlement of disputes by not advising Nicaragua to comply. From the American point of view, however, the decision in this case confirmed a suspicion that the court had been acting on political rather than legal grounds, and no effort was made to save the unhappy tribunal.

Under the watchful eye of the United States, Nicaragua remained for the moment quiet and orderly. The pro-American Conservative party continued in power with Emiliano Chamorro elected to the presidency in 1916, and his uncle, Diego Chamorro, in 1920. Although American bankers continued to have great influence, Wilson's diplomacy was less deferential to their interests than Taft's had been. The State Department opposed the preferential claims of the bankers upon the 3 million dollars paid under the Bryan-Chamorro Treaty and brought about a distribution that not only recognized the interests of other claimants, but even provided $500,000 for the Nicaraguan government itself. More important was the establishment of a Joint High Financial Commission in 1917. This body succeeded not only in strengthening government finances and reducing the debt, but in helping the Nicaraguan government to buy back from the bankers the control of the National Bank and the Pacific Railroad.

The Purchase of the Danish West Indies

Still another significant extension of American influence came in 1917 with the purchase of the Danish West Indies, soon renamed the Virgin Islands. Located to the east of Puerto Rico and commanding one of the important sea lanes leading to the Panama Canal, the Danish colony had long been an objective of American diplomacy. During Grant's administration an annexation treaty had been rejected by the United States Senate;[7] in 1902 a similar treaty negotiated by the Roosevelt administration had been approved by the American Senate, only to be rejected by a single vote in the Danish upper house. The outbreak of World War I aroused fears that Germany might conquer Denmark and force her to hand over this strategic territory. Rather than see this happen, Secretary Lansing informed Denmark, the United States would take possession herself. American eagerness to buy gave the Danes a golden opportunity to sell; the treaty, signed on August 4, 1916, set the price at 25 million dollars—five times the sum stipulated in the treaty of 1902. Although the Virgin Islands have been acidly described as "a poorhouse surrounded by salt water," their strategic value resulted in speedy Senate approval of the treaty. The Danish Parliament insisted on submitting the issue to a vote of the Danish people; after a favorable decision, the transfer was finally completed on March 31, 1917.

[7] See chap. 16.

By the end of Wilson's Presidency, the ironic results of his supposedly anti-imperialist policies were clear. Not only had there been no backward step from earlier Republican policies, which had brought Puerto Rico under the American flag, established Cuba as an American protectorate, and acquired a vital interest in Panama, but the American empire had now been rounded out with the annexation of the Virgin Islands and measures reducing Haiti, the Dominican Republic, and Nicaragua to little more than American protectorates.

PART FOUR

1917 to 1945

The Search for World Order

In April, 1917, Woodrow Wilson summoned the American nation to fight "for a universal dominion of right by such a concert of free peoples as shall bring peace and safety to all nations and make the world itself at last free." Twenty-four years later, in December, 1941, Franklin D. Roosevelt declared: "We are now in the midst of a war, not for conquest, not for vengeance, but for a world in which this Nation, and all that this Nation represents, will be safe for our children."

This hope for a safe world in which men could live without fear of violent destruction dominated the discussion of American foreign policy from 1917 to 1945. Isolationists and internationalists disagreed violently about what the nation should do, but professed the same goal—the ultimate establishment of peace and international justice.

Although the horrors of World Wars I and II gave a terrible urgency to this quest for peace, the aspiration itself was by no means new. Before 1914 the United States had been prominent in attempts to devise peaceful means for settling disputes among nations. It had made conciliation and arbitration treaties and urged the establishment of a world court. The outbreak of World War I demonstrated the inadequacy of these measures. Wilson's attempt to maintain the nation's neutrality broke down as he became convinced that Germany's resort to ruthless submarine warfare violated both the letter and the spirit of international law and was indeed "a warfare against mankind."

Wilson believed he had laid the foundation for world order in his League of Nations and died brokenhearted because the nation failed to support him. Yet if the Wilsonian method of preserving peace was rejected, the goal itself was not. Republican diplomacy of the 1920s sought to move forward through disarmament agreements, the outlawry of war, and multilateral pledges to preserve the *status quo* in the Far East.

Attitudes toward foreign policy were closely related to domestic political trends. During the prosperous 1920s close relations with Europe —at least through loans and investments and nonpolitical cooperation— appealed to many Easterners and Southerners, who accepted such ties as part of the twentieth-century way of life. But politicians who sprang out of the tradition of Western agrarian radicalism—men like La Follette of Wisconsin, Borah of Idaho, and Johnson of California—continued to look on European affairs with distaste and to see the sinister hands of London and New York bankers in every proposal for closer international relations.

The dominant Republican party compromised as best it could the internationalist learnings of men like Charles Evans Hughes and Henry Stimson with the anti-internationalism of Borah and Johnson. An area of agreement was found for such goals as disarmament and the outlawry of war—and this emphasis was highly congenial to the economy-minded Coolidge and Hoover administrations for fiscal reasons.

The return of the Democrats to power in 1933 was no guarantee that the nation would swing toward internationalism. For one thing, the party had its own isolationist cores centered around Irish-American politicians like Senator David L. Walsh of Massachusetts and Western radicals like Senator Burton Wheeler of Montana. Moreover, the grim domestic crisis tended to restrain the latent internationalism of Franklin D. Roosevelt himself. With the whole world rocked by economic storm, each nation sought to save itself as best it could. Economists might argue that economic nationalism was folly, yet it was a highly tempting folly. On the intellectual side, new arguments for avoiding involvements in the world's difficulties and concentrating on an "open door at home" were offered by the historian Charles A. Beard and other "continentalists."

Yet however inviting it was for the nation to mind its own business without looking for trouble abroad, the situation eventually became so serious that Americans were compelled to reconsider their position. The dream of a stable world order, cherished by internationalists and isolationists alike, was shattered after 1931. Although England, France, and the United States were powers well satisfied with their existing boundaries and possessions, Germany, Italy, Japan, and Russia were not. Each for its own reasons found the *status quo* unsatisfactory and cherished ambitions of extending its power and influence. Long before World War II broke out in full fury, peace had been violated in Manchuria, Ethiopia, and Czechoslovakia. What to do about this growing aggression became one of the most hotly controverted questions in the history of American foreign policy. The isolationists sought to insulate the nation from the world's troubles by banning all arms sales and loans to belligerents and by renouncing traditional neutral rights. The internationalists protested that such policies played into the hands of the aggressors; they called instead for timely help to nations that would stand up to the totalitarian challenge. Once World War II began, the isolationists steadily lost ground, and Pearl Harbor settled the issue for the time being.

The improved weapons of World War II posed a warning for the American future. From one point of view, the ghosts of Mahan and Theodore Roosevelt must have exulted as the American Navy fought its way across the Pacific to the outskirts of Japan and as amphibious operations opened up North Africa, Sicily, Italy, and France to invasion. Yet if sea power were winning mighty victories, it was only because it used air power as its striking arm. By the end of the war, the decisive instruments of power had become planes and air bases. As the range of bombers became greater and greater, the Atlantic and Pacific Oceans shrank, and it became clear that this would be the last great conflict in which American civilians could hope for immunity from attack.

But need there be another great war? Throughout World War II mankind clung to the hope that this time the victorious powers would establish a just world order. Chastened by experience, Americans took a recess on partisan politics in 1945 and approved almost unanimously American membership in the United Nations. Yet to accept the machinery of world organization was only a first step. The United Nations could only be effective if the still sovereign powers compromised their differences and worked together in cooperation. This was by no means assured in 1945. The United States, Great Britain, and the Soviet Union had collaborated to win a great victory over the Axis, but there was grave reason to fear that the postwar dreams of Joseph Stalin were not identical with those of Winston Churchill and Franklin Roosevelt.

26

THE IDEAL OF PEACE

World War I came as a deep disappointment to millions of peace-aspiring people who had hoped that the trend of history was in the opposite direction. Idealists found it rational to believe the great powers had become so closely interdependent through trade and investment that another major war would be impossible.

In the peace movement of these years the United States played the role of both hero and villain. All the Presidents from Cleveland through Wilson gave strong support to proposed treaties for the peaceful settlement of disputes, and many Americans became earnest advocates of such projects. Yet the United States again and again disappointed the crusaders for peace either through Senate rejection of some hopeful treaty or by some willful display of national sovereignty.

Background of the Peace Movement

The threads that were woven together into the nineteenth-century peace movement ran back into early history. The Greek city states had sometimes avoided war by submitting their disputes to arbitration; wrangling Roman satellites were bound by the decisions of the Roman Senate; medieval rulers often accepted the mediation of the Pope. Again and again political thinkers sketched utopian schemes for international tribunals that would settle disputes among nations on the basis of law and justice. The poet Dante had this dream in the thirteenth century; the statesman Sully and the Quaker William Penn in the seventeenth; the philosophers Kant and Rousseau in the eighteenth; and the utilitarian Jeremy Bentham in the nineteenth. William Ladd, who founded the American Peace Society in 1828, was the tireless advocate of "a congress of the nations for the prevention of war."

Largely independent of this philosophic thread was the work of the great jurists who had attempted to codify legal principles recognized by civilized nations in their relations with each other. The father of international law was the Dutch Hugo Grotius (1583–1645); later thinkers in the field were the German Samuel Pufendorf (1632–1694) and the Swiss Emeric de Vattel (1714–1767). International congresses during the nineteenth century attempted to gain formal recognition for certain principles of international law: the Conference of Paris in 1856 defined the rights of belligerents and neutrals in maritime warfare; the Geneva Conference of 1864 dealt with the humane treatment of sick and wounded soldiers and prisoners of war.

By a third hopeful line of development several international organizations had been created during the nineteenth century to facilitate co-operation for specific purposes. Thus a Universal Postal Union had been founded in 1875, and similar bodies had been set up to deal with telegraphic communication, weights and measures, and several other matters.

A fourth and particularly heartening thread of progress lay in the pacific settlement of disputes. Here the United States and England had made a particularly notable record that dated back to the Jay Treaty of 1794 and included such later landmarks as the Treaty of Ghent (1814), the Treaty of Washington (1871), and the Bering Sea Convention (1892).

Drawing hope from all these developments, a number of peace societies were organized during the nineteenth century. Different in composition and program, they shared a common enthusiasm for general arbitration treaties, whereby nations would promise in advance to avoid war by submitting their disputes to peaceful settlement.

Discussion of actual efforts to establish such machinery will be clarified by explaining the technical meaning of certain terms. If two nations are involved in controversy or war, they will, in the first place, usually seek a settlement through *direct negotiations* carried on through ambassadors, ministers, or special agents under the direction of the foreign offices of the two governments. If the issues are too difficult or complicated to be handled through regular diplomatic channels, they may be submitted to *mixed commissions*, consisting of an equal number of experts from each country without any outside or neutral party. Such commissions were established under both the Jay Treaty and the Treaty of Ghent. Although mixed commissions have often been highly successful, they face the danger of splitting along national lines. To prevent this, the disputing nations may agree to submit their difference to the decision of some neutral third party or parties—as was done with the *Alabama* claims. This is the only procedure properly called *arbitration*. As a step short of arbitration, the two disputants may agree to a *commission of inquiry;* this establishes an impartial body to ascertain the facts about a disputed situation but leaves the final solution to the parties themselves.

Less formal procedures are *good offices* and *mediation*. In the former case a friendly nation offers its services not to settle the controversy, but to bring the quarreling parties into communication so they can settle it themselves—as, for example, when the Tsar of Russia used his good offices during the War of 1812 to bring the United States and England into peace negotiations. In mediation the third power takes a somewhat more active role, acting not only as go-between, but sometimes suggesting compromises that will resolve the difficulties. Thus Theodore Roosevelt acted as mediator in the Russo-Japanese War.

The Olney-Pauncefote Treaty

Agitation for a general arbitration treaty between England and the United States began in 1887 when Randolph Cremer, a Member of Parliament and peace crusader, obtained signatures from 234 members of the House of Commons, memorializing the two governments to make such an agreement. An English delegation crossed the Atlantic to present this petition to President Cleveland. Thus launched, the movement made slow but undramatic progress over the next several years. In 1890 Congress unanimously passed a resolution requesting the President to negotiate a general arbitration treaty with any government with which the United States had diplomatic relations. By a similar unanimous vote the House of Commons passed an encouraging resolution in 1893.

In 1895 Cremer tried to get concrete action by bringing a second petition to America. The slow-moving Cleveland now showed a livelier interest in the project, and promising negotiations between the two governments began. These bright hopes were temporarily wrecked when the Venezuelan boundary dispute blew up a sudden storm in Anglo-American relations. In the long run, however, the war scare of December, 1895, helped rather than hindered the arbitration movement. Peace-loving elements in both countries were stirred to greater activity, and the two governments soon became involved in parallel negotiations, one dealing with the Venezuelan boundary issue, the other with a general arbitration treaty.

President Cleveland and Secretary Olney wanted a strong treaty, obligating the two countries to submit all disputes to arbitration unless Congress or Parliament should declare that the issue was one involving national honor or integrity. They asserted also that the arbitral decisions should be final. Lord Salisbury, the British Prime Minister and Foreign Secretary, was much more cautious. Fearing that the precedent of obligatory arbitration would encourage the trumping up of territorial claims against the British Empire in all parts of the world, he wanted carefully to restrict the principle.

In the end Cleveland and Olney enjoyed a substantial victory. The Olney-Pauncefote Treaty, signed January 11, 1897, covered all types of controversies and provided a final decision in most of them. Money claims not exceeding £100,000 were to be subject to the final decision of a tribunal composed of one arbiter from each country and an umpire chosen by these two; all larger money claims and other disputes except those involving territory were to be submitted to a tribunal of three, but unless the decision were unanimous an appeal might be taken to a second tribunal of five—two from each country plus an umpire chosen by the four. In cases where there was disagreement over the choice of an umpire, he was to be named by the King of Sweden. Territorial claims were reserved for a tribunal of six members—three from each side with no umpire—and were not to be final unless agreed to by at least five of the arbiters; this last, of course, was not really an arbitral body at all but a mixed commission—an important concession to Lord Salisbury.

Churches and peace societies greeted the treaty with jubilation. Public meetings were held, and the legislatures of seven states passed resolutions favoring ratification of the agreement. On the other hand, nationalistic newspapers like the *Chicago Tribune* and Hearst's *New York Journal* denounced the treaty as a dangerous limitation upon American sovereignty, while Irish-American nationalist groups persisted in describing it as an Anglo-American alliance.

When Cleveland turned over the Presidency to McKinley on March 4, 1897, the Senate had not yet acted upon the Olney-Pauncefote Treaty. In his inaugural address the new President warmly favored ratification. Despite this bipartisan support, Senate opposition to the document was strong. Following a procedure destined to be repeated on several later occasions, Senator Henry Cabot Lodge and his Massachusetts colleague, George F. Hoar, led a fight to mutilate the treaty by amendment. They made a vote of two-thirds of the Senate necessary to submit any particular dispute to arbitration; they eliminated the role of the King of Sweden; they excluded from arbitration issues involving not only the nation's honor and territorial integrity but many other matters. Of the treaty's fifteen articles, two were repudiated completely and five others radically altered.

When the Senate took its final vote on May 5, 1897, the treaty had been so amended that it scarcely obligated the United States to do anything. The issue was now not general arbitration at all; the Senate was asked merely to approve a harmless gesture of good will toward England. Even so, however, the treaty failed by three votes to get the two-thirds majority necessary for ratification. The stubborn minority that sent the agreement down to defeat was composed of silver advocates hostile to Cleveland, McKinley, and England; expansionists who feared that arbitration might hamper the nation's new manifest destiny; legislators fearful of the Irish vote; and senators jealous of the executive branch of the government.

The First Hague Conference

On August 24, 1898, the Russian Foreign Office proposed a conference to consider "the most effective means of ensuring to all peoples the benefits of a real and lasting peace, and above all of limiting the progressive development of existing armaments." Why had the Tsar taken this unexpected step? Nicholas II was a man of generous impulses, who had probably been impressed by the organized peace agitation of the 1890s. More important, perhaps, was the encouragement of his shrewd Finance Minister, Count Witte, who was alarmed at the heavy drain of mounting armaments upon the shaky Russian economy. Although skeptical that a peace conference could reduce international tensions, Witte was in a mood to try anything.

Most world leaders regarded the Tsar's idea as visionary, but none of them wanted to bear the onus of refusing to accept his invitation. Twenty-six countries were, therefore, represented at the First Hague Peace Conference, which met in the Dutch capital from May 18 to July 29, 1899. President McKinley sent an American delegation headed by Andrew D. White, former president of Cornell University and at this time Ambassador to Germany.

Although the delegates soon discovered insuperable obstacles to achieving arms reduction, they did find it possible to take a few cautious steps toward international order. They clarified some of the rules of warfare and drafted a Convention for the Peaceful Adjustment of International Differences. The latter agreement asserted the duty of states before resorting to war "to have recourse, as far as circumstances will allow, to the good offices or mediation of one or more friendly Powers," and set forth the right of third parties to offer their mediation, even when uninvited. Another clause of the treaty provided for the appointment of international commissions of inquiry under certain circumstances.

The most hopeful provision was for the establishment of a "Permanent Court of Arbitration." The name of the new tribunal was misleading because neither was it a court in the usual sense of the word, nor did it have a permanent personnel. Instead, each signatory nation was to appoint four eminent jurists to a list of potential arbitrators, leaving the choice of judges for any particular dispute to the nations involved. However, the existence of the panel would, it was hoped, encourage resort to arbitration, while the establishment of an international bureau and a permanent administrative council would facilitate the technical arrangements.

Although conceding that nations could not be required to arbitrate disputes involving their vital interests or national honor, the Russians had proposed a list of minor subjects on which arbitration would be obligatory. Germany, cool to the whole idea of arbitration, strongly opposed any compulsory feature. In the end, the conferees agreed that arbitration should be entirely voluntary. The American and British delegations cooperated closely at the conference, usually exerting their influence to strengthen, not weaken, the arbitration machinery. Nevertheless, the United States did consider it necessary to make a formal reservation against any construction of the Arbitration Convention that would require it "to depart from its traditional policy of not entering upon, interfering with, or entangling itself in the political questions or internal administration of any foreign state, nor shall anything contained in the said Convention be so construed as to require the relinquishment by the United States of America, of its traditional attitude toward purely American questions." Satisfied that American sovereignty and the sacred Monroe Doctrine had thus been safeguarded, the Senate approved all three Hague agreements without change.

To demonstrate its support, the Roosevelt administration provided the Hague Court with its first case—that of the so-called Pious Fund. This involved an American claim against Mexico that dated from the American annexation of California in 1848. Following this transfer, Catholic bishops in California asserted that certain funds, originally set aside for the conversion of California Indians in the seventeenth century and successively administered by the Jesuits, the King of Spain, and the Mexican Republic, should be turned over to them. To settle the long-standing dispute, the United States and Mexico agreed to abide by the decision of arbitrators chosen from the Hague Court panel. The award, which favored the American bishops, was made in 1902, and Mexico promptly complied. A more important case was referred to the Court in 1903, when Germany, Great Britain, Italy, and Venezuela agreed to submit the issue of whether nationals of the blockading powers should have preferential treatment in the payment of the Venezuelan foreign debt.[1]

The Hay and Root Treaties

The convention establishing the Hague Court had not included obligatory arbitration, but it had stipulated that the member nations might agree among themselves to recognize this principle for certain kinds of

[1] See chap. 22.

disputes. Although pessimistic about the chances of getting any general arbitration agreement through the Senate, Secretary Hay finally negotiated treaties with fourteen different nations, including Great Britain, France, and Germany. Sent to the Senate in December, 1904, these were cautiously phrased documents, in which obligatory arbitration was limited to "differences which may arise of a legal nature, or relating to the interpretation of treaties existing between the two contracting parties, and which it may not have been possible to settle by diplomacy," with the additional proviso that such differences did not affect "the vital interests, the independence or the honor of the two contracting states" and did not concern the interest of third parties.

Despite Roosevelt's strong support, the Hay treaties ran into the same kind of trouble the Olney-Pauncefote Treaty had encountered. In a private letter, the President attributed the difficulty to "the idiotic jealousy of the Executive which tends to make the Senate reduce the Executive to impotency." By amending the treaties to require a Senate-approved agreement before any particular issue could be referred to arbitration, the upper house effectively emasculated the obligatory principle. The disgusted President put an end to the matter in the following memorandum: "These arbitration treaties are to be kept in the State Department, and no further steps taken in connection with them. The form in which they were ratified was equivalent to rejection, and will be so treated by the Executive."

After Root succeeded Hay in the State Department, he revived the project. More patient with senatorial scruples than his predecessor had been, the new Secretary thought it worth while to support the arbitration principle with a series of treaties even if the principle of senatorial consent in each particular case had to be included. Accordingly, he negotiated twenty-five such agreements in 1908 and obtained their approval.

The Second Hague Conference

Meanwhile, Root had attempted to strengthen the general cause of international cooperation at the Second Hague Peace Conference in 1907. The American government had strongly backed the idea of a second meeting in notes to the various countries in 1904, but the project had had to be dropped until after the Russo-Japanese War. In 1905, the Russian Ambassador confided to the President that the Hague Conference was a pet project of the Tsar's and that the Tsar would, therefore, like to appear as sponsor of the new meeting. Roosevelt gladly fell in with this suggestion, because, as he wrote to Root: "I particularly do *not* want to appear as a professional peace advocate—a kind of sublimated being of the Godkin or Schurz variety—and it gives us a freer hand in every way to have the Czar make the movement."

Delayed for a variety of reasons, the Second Hague Conference finally convened in June, 1907. Forty-four countries were represented, as compared with twenty-six at the 1899 meeting; prominent among the newcomers were the Latin-American states, invited at the insistence of the United States. The American delegation was headed by Joseph H. Choate, Ambassador to London and a strong advocate of international cooperation.

The Tsar, who had so strongly emphasized disarmament in calling the First Conference, did not even include this subject on the agenda for the Second. England, anxious over the growing German navy, raised the issue, and the United States supported her, but the opposition of the Continental European powers made any arms limitation impossible.

Roosevelt and Root pinned their greatest hopes on strengthening the machinery for the peaceful settlement of disputes. The Secretary believed that what was most needed was a real world court "composed of judges who are judicial officers and nothing else, who are paid adequate salaries, who have no other occupation, and who will devote their entire time to the trial and decision of international causes by judicial methods and under a sense of judicial responsibility." Only in this way, Root believed, could the principle of judicial settlement based strictly upon the merits of the case be established; the trouble with old-fashioned arbitration was the tendency of the arbiters simply to split the difference between the parties. The Conference approved a draft treaty providing for such a court, but the project had to go on the shelf because of disagreement over the method of electing judges. Root's effort bore eventual fruit in the World Court established in 1920, in which, by one of history's ironies, the Senate would not allow the United States to participate.[2]

Similar frustrations dogged most of the other deliberations of the Second Hague Conference. Root instructed the American delegates to work for the principle of obligatory arbitration for certain categories of disputes—always reserving the Senate's jealously guarded prerogative. Once again, however, Germany proved a stumbling block, supporting the principle of general arbitration but raising insuperable difficulties on details. Germany, England, and the United States did agree that an International Prize Court should be established to pass upon the seizure of merchant ships and cargoes during war, but the actual creation of such a tribunal proved impossible. Britain insisted that it was necessary first to define the principles of international law which such a court would apply. The London Naval Conference of 1908–1909 attempted to do this, and the United States Senate approved the resulting Declaration of Lon-

[2] See chap. 29.

don in 1912. The British Parliament, however, was fearful of losing the advantage of Britain's naval supremacy and refused to give its consent, thereby leaving the rules of maritime warfare still much in doubt during World War I.

The adoption of the Drago Doctrine in modified form was one minor achievement of the conference, but even this fruit was embittered by the refusal of the Latin-American countries to approve.[3] Although the Second Hague Conference was generally judged to be a failure—even by the modest standards established by the First—optimists took some comfort in the thought that many significant problems had been discussed and that more definitive results might follow subsequent international meetings.

The Alaska Boundary Dispute

Any easy assumption that arbitration was the answer to all international controversies was refuted by the strange story of the dispute between the United States and Canada over the Alaska boundary. This issue suddenly became urgent in 1898 as a result of the discovery of gold in the Canadian Klondike two years earlier. The Canadians desperately wanted access to the new treasure trove by sea; the Americans insisted that their purchase of Alaska from Russia had given them complete control of the coast. By a treaty of 1825 Great Britain and Russia had agreed that the boundary of southern Alaska should follow the summit of the mountains parallel to the coast except where the mountains were more than ten marine leagues distant from the ocean; then the boundary should be formed by a line parallel to the windings of the coast and never more than ten marine leagues away. The Canadians claimed that this distance should be measured from the mouths of the numerous inlets that broke the coast; the Americans maintained that the boundary should follow the sinuosities of the shore line. Vital stakes were the boom seaports of Skagway, Dyea, and Pyramid Harbor.

Unfortunately for Canada, the United States was in actual possession of practically all the disputed territory. For seventy years the Russian and American assumptions had gone virtually unchallenged; British as well as Russian and American maps indicated the boundary as running around the heads of the inlets. It was, therefore, difficult for the Americans to regard with patience belated attempts of the Canadians to read an entirely different meaning into the treaty. Sir Wilfrid Laurier, the Canadian Prime Minister, sized up the situation thus: "Our American friends have very many qualities, but what they have they keep, and

[3] See chap. 22.

what they have not they want. Perhaps we, too, are built up the same way."

Despite the weakness of the Canadian case, the American government was eager to obtain a friendly settlement of all outstanding disagreements with the British Empire. By so doing, it was hoped, the way would be paved for the United States to gain what it then most wanted— a free hand to build an isthmian canal.[4] In January, 1899, therefore, a deal was tentatively arranged, under which, without admitting Canadian territorial sovereignty, the United States would permit Pyramid Harbor to become a free port under Canadian administration. Such a settlement —so desirable on grounds of good neighborliness—was killed by a storm of condemnation raised against the proposal on the Pacific Coast. Merchants and shipping companies of Washington and Oregon were exploiting a valuable monopoly through American control of all ports leading into the gold country, and they were determined to block any measure whereby the Canadians would gain a foothold on the coast.

Canada now demanded that the boundary question be submitted to arbitration. Coming so soon after the United States had insisted that Great Britain arbitrate the Venezuelan boundary dispute, this proposal appeared logical and reasonable. But the American government was deterred by the knowledge that arbitral tribunals almost always compromise, and on the main issue in this dispute the United States felt itself to be entirely in the right. Therefore Secretary Hay refused to consider any form of arbitration involving a foreign umpire; instead he proposed a tribunal in which three Americans and three British arbiters would decide by a majority vote, thus making a decision impossible unless at least one member of the tribunal voted against his own country. Although this was similar to the form of settlement Lord Salisbury had insisted upon for territorial questions in the abortive Olney-Pauncefote Treaty, Canada refused to go along unless a seventh neutral arbiter were provided. Since neither side would budge, a modus vivendi, or temporary arrangement, was signed to prevent serious conflicts of authority, and the final disposition of the dispute was left for later negotiation.

Secretary Hay continued to hope the boundary could be settled on the basis of his proposals of 1899, but Theodore Roosevelt, who became President in 1901, was at first reluctant to go along with this cautious procedure. "Let sleeping dogs lie," was his admonition to the State Department early in 1902. By the end of the year, however, the ice was ready to thaw. Sir Michael Herbert, the new British Ambassador to the United States, was eager to take some positive step toward improving Anglo-American relations; Roosevelt, a close personal friend of Herbert's,

[4] See chap. 22.

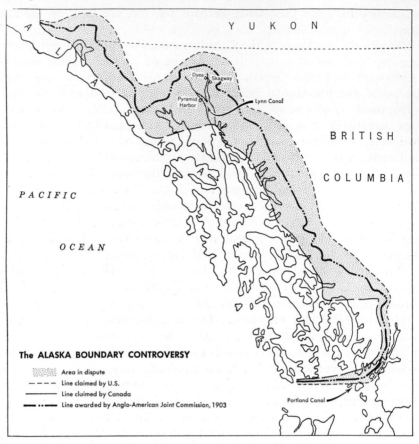

The ALASKA BOUNDARY CONTROVERSY

Area in dispute
- - - - Line claimed by U.S.
——— Line claimed by Canada
—··—·— Line awarded by Anglo-American Joint Commission, 1903

wanted to help him; and the Canadians, realizing the Americans would not yield further, were now reconciled to referring the dispute to a mixed commission. A treaty to this effect was signed on January 23, 1903.

Roosevelt appointed as the three American commissioners Senator Henry Cabot Lodge, former Senator George Turner of Washington, and Secretary of War Elihu Root. The Canadians protested that these were not "impartial jurists of repute" as stipulated in the treaty, but the President stuck to his position. In his view the United States was completely in the right on the boundary issue; the mixed commission was simply a device to enable the British to save face, a graceful gesture to Sir Michael Herbert. He continued to push the business through without regard for Canadian feelings. He sent letters to the American commissioners urging them to press for a speedy decision and threatening to run the boundary line by unilateral action if there were any delay. He even exerted pressure through the British government on the British commissioner, Lord Alverstone, to get him to cast his vote with the Americans against the two Canadians. Not surprisingly, therefore, the commission, by a 4-to-2 vote, decided in favor of the American case on the main points in dispute, although conceding to Canada two islands in the Portland Canal—a bit of sugar coating to which the President had secretly given his blessing.

As might be expected, the Canadians considered this episode a very dubious contribution either to the cause of arbitration or to Anglo-American friendship. But Roosevelt saw the matter quite differently. To an English friend he explained: "I feel that England and the United States, beyond any other two powers, should be friendly with one another, and what I can legitimately do to increase this friendliness will be done. One of the best manifestations of it, by the way, was my insisting upon having the Alaskan boundary settled right, and taking sufficiently active steps to make the British Government understand the seriousness of the situation." [5]

The Newfoundland Fisheries Question

Whereas the Alaska boundary case had demonstrated how *not* to arbitrate a question, the Newfoundland fisheries case showed how an honest resort to arbitration could be rewarded by the fair settlement of a difficult question. The earlier history of the fisheries question has been traced. It will be recalled how the Treaty of Paris of 1783 had given American fishermen a "liberty" but not a right to fish in Newfoundland waters and to dry and cure fish on certain coasts; England claimed that these liberties had been terminated by the War of 1812, but granted them in somewhat more restricted form in the Convention of 1818. [6]

The British interpreted the old treaty to mean that Americans fishing in the permitted waters were subject to the same regulations as Newfoundland fishermen. Although this seemed reasonable enough, such rules often discriminated in practice against the Americans. For example, a prohibition against Sunday fishing was not very serious for men fishing in their home waters, but was expensive and burdensome to fleets that had come up from Gloucester or other New England ports. The Americans complained that the Newfoundland parliament was deliberately trying to injure them. Equally troublesome was the question of just where the Americans did have the liberty to fish. Except in specified areas they were forbidden to take fish within 3 marine miles of any coasts, bays,

[5] Reprinted by permission of the publisher from Roosevelt to Spring Rice, Nov. 1, 1905, *Letters of Theodore Roosevelt*, ed. by E. E. Morison (Copyright 1951 by Harvard University Press, Cambridge, Mass.), vol. V, p. 61.
[6] See chaps. 2 and 7.

creeks, or harbors. The British claimed that this meant 3 miles outside
a line drawn from headland to headland; the Americans argued that the
line should follow the sinuosities of the coast, thus admitting them into
the larger bays.

Secretary Root made the settlement of this ancient controversy one of
his main objectives. In the summer of 1905 he took a vacation trip to
Newfoundland, where he carefully studied the problem on the spot.
After his return he took advantage of the first opportunity, presented by
an alleged act of highhandedness by the Newfoundland authorities, to
reopen the whole issue. After many months of diplomatic jockeying,
England and the United States signed a treaty on January 27, 1909—
Root's last day as Secretary of State—providing that the whole fisheries
question be submitted to a tribunal chosen from the Hague Court panel.

The arbitration proceedings took place at The Hague during the summer of 1910, with Elihu Root serving as chief counsel for the United
States. Although the award favored the British contentions on most
points, the Americans were satisfied because the tribunal held that, while
Newfoundland had the right to regulate the fisheries, her regulations must
be reasonable, and in cases where there was question about this, the
regulations must be reviewed by an arbitral body. "We came out very
well at The Hague, everything considered," wrote Root, "and practically
got substantially all that we were entitled to." An English commentator
summed up the situation thus: "The award ... differs from every other
award that I remember in having been received with equal enthusiasm
by both disputants.[7]

Taft and Arbitration

Both as optimist and former judge, President Taft hoped the rational
procedures of the courtroom might be substituted for the use of force in
international affairs. When Theodore Marburg, a Baltimore publicist,
organized the American Society for the Judicial Settlement of International Disputes in February, 1910, Taft gladly accepted the honorary
presidency. Speaking in March and again in December, the President
supported the movement in sweeping terms. In the latter speech he said:

> If we can now negotiate and put through an agreement with some
> great nation to abide the adjudication of an international arbitral court
> in every issue which cannot be settled by negotiation, no matter what it
> involves, whether honor, territory or money, we shall have made a long
> step forward ... the establishment of a general arbitral court for all
> nations is no longer the figment of the brain of a dreamy enthusiast.

[7] W. T. Stead, "The Fisheries Award," *Independent*, vol. LXIX, Sept. 29, 1910, p. 699.

As the President sat down, French Ambassador Jules Jusserand said to him: "We will make such a treaty with you, if you will make it with us," and Taft happily replied: "I'm your man."

Secretary Knox willingly cooperated with Taft's plan, and on August 3, 1911, treaties were signed with France and Great Britain. The new agreements, going well beyond the cautious Root treaties of 1908, covered all disputes that were "justiciable in their nature by reason of being susceptible of decision by the application of the principles of law or equity." The important question of whether a particular dispute was "justiciable" would be determined by a joint mixed commission to which all disputes not settled by direct diplomacy would be referred. If at least five of the six commissioners decided that the issue was justiciable, the case would go to the Hague Court or some other tribunal.

In a brave argument for the treaties, Taft said:

> We now have treaties of arbitration in which we agree to submit all questions that do not affect our national honor and do not affect our vital interest. Well, that seems to me to be an agreement to arbitrate everything that is highly unimportant. We leave out the questions which when they arise are likely to lead to war. If arbitration is worth anything it is an instrumentality for avoiding war. But, it is asked, would you arbitrate a question of national honor? I am not afraid of that question. Of course I would.

But many other Americans still clung to the notion that national honor was too sacred to be jeopardized through arbitration. One of these was Theodore Roosevelt, whose magazine articles opposing the new treaties were particularly damaging to Taft's project. Following the tactics that had killed the Hay treaties of 1904, the Senate mutilated the Taft ones by amendments: questions involving the admission of immigrants or the rights of aliens in the schools or relating to state debts or to the Monroe Doctrine were excluded from arbitration, and Senate consent to the submission of any particular dispute to arbitration was required.

Although the Senate finally approved the amended treaties by a vote of 76 to 3 in March, 1912, the project was dead. Still clinging to his dream, Taft hoped to negotiate new treaties or to induce the Senate to reconsider its action, but this door was closed by the President's defeat for reelection. As he good-naturedly recalled in later years, he put the treaties "on the shelf and let the dust accumulate on them in the hope that the senators might change their minds, or that the people might change the Senate; instead of which they changed me." [8]

[8] Reprinted by permission of Charles L. Marburg from Theodore Marburg and H. E. Flack, eds., *Taft Papers on the League of Nations* (Copyright 1920 by The Macmillan Company, New York), p. 179.

Bryan and the Peace Movement

Strong partisan though he was on most issues, William Jennings Bryan had given generous support to the Taft arbitration treaties. When the Commoner became Wilson's Secretary of State, he took up the peace crusade where Taft had left off. Bryan hoped to avoid earlier difficulties by proposing a different type of treaty—a type he had been eloquently urging since 1905. Instead of requiring obligatory arbitration, Bryan's model would attempt to avoid war by encouraging delay and conciliation.

Specifically, the Bryan conciliation treaties—often called "cooling-off" treaties—provided that "all disputes . . . of every nature whatsoever, which diplomacy shall fail to adjust" would be submitted to an international commission,[9] which would investigate and report on the controversy. The signatories were not required to accept the commission's recommendations, but they did promise "not to declare war or begin hostilities" until the commission completed its work. The commission was required to report within one year, unless the parties to the dispute agreed on an extension of time. Bryan's principle was simple: just as a man who counts to ten before he strikes a blow usually does not fight at all, so countries that resorted to a cooling-off period would not be likely to declare war. "When men are mad," the Secretary explained, "they talk about what they can do. When they are calm they talk about what they ought to do. And it is the purpose of this plan to provide a time for passion to subside, for reason to regain its throne."

Both the innocuousness of the plan itself and Bryan's skill as a politician prevented any serious trouble with the Senate. Such ratification difficulties as were encountered were usually on the side of the other country involved. In all, Bryan was able to negotiate thirty of his conciliation treaties; twenty-one of them eventually went into force. Great Britain, France, and Italy were among the countries agreeing to the plan; Germany was one of those rejecting it. The Germans professed to believe that such an arrangement between the United States and Germany would be unobjectionable, but that other countries would request similar treaties and Germany would thereby lose the advantage of her superior military preparation.

Although the peace-loving Bryan considered these treaties to be among

[9] These commissions were to be permanent in character—one for each country with which the United States had such a treaty. There were to be five members: each signatory was to appoint one of its own nationals and a second person from some other country. The fifth member was to be chosen by agreement of the two governments.

the greatest achievements of his life, their practical importance was small. The machinery Bryan devised was never actually put to work in specific cases, and vacancies in the permanent commissions were not always filled. The Bryan treaties did, however, suggest some of the procedures for the peaceful settlement of international disputes later written into the Covenant of the League of Nations and the Charter of the United Nations.

An even more important precedent for later international organization was the Pan-American Pact proposal, which the Wilson administration was pushing in 1915 and 1916. Well aware that the Monroe Doctrine was disliked in Latin America as a policy whereby the United States alone decided when and how European threats against the Western Hemisphere would be opposed, certain Americans had been advocating that the Monroe Doctrine be made multilateral, that is, that the Western Hemisphere nations should agree to protect their independence and territorial integrity by mutual action. Representative James L. Slayden of Texas had urged such an arrangement in 1910 and 1911, and Colombia had made a formal proposal in 1912.

The Taft administration had looked with suspicion upon the suggested pact, but Colonel House became an enthusiastic convert, and he in turn excited President Wilson with the possibilities of the idea. Wilson himself wrote the first draft of a possible treaty in December, 1914. After several revisions, the final proposal was for a treaty that would bind the signatories to "a common and mutual guaranty of territorial integrity and political independence under republican forms of government." Additionally, they would agree to settle all disputes by peaceful means and to refrain from assisting the enemies of any signatory government.

Although Bryan, preoccupied with his own conciliation treaties, had had no part in the drafting of the Pan-American Pact, he readily supported the proposal and continued to press it so long as he remained in the State Department. After his resignation, Lansing continued the negotiations.

Despite enthusiastic acceptance of the idea by Argentina and Brazil, Chile was opposed to guaranteeing existing boundaries because of her long-standing dispute with Peru. This obstacle and revived fears of *yanqui* imperialism caused by Wilsonian interventions in Mexico and the Caribbean republics finally combined to prevent acceptance of the Pan-American Pact. Undoubtedly, however, Wilson's thought about this problem strongly influenced his more ambitious dream of a league of nations. Indeed, it was this opportunity to provide in the Western Hemisphere a model to be followed by the rest of the world that particularly stirred Wilson's imagination.

Although the advocates of peace were cruelly disappointed by the outbreak of World War I, they soon redoubled their efforts. The sickening casualties of the European battlefields gave the peace movement after 1914 an urgency that had been lacking in the more academic discussions of earlier years. The new goals were a just peace treaty and the creation of an international organization to prevent wars in the future.

27

WORLD WAR I: THE TRIALS
OF A NEUTRAL

Lulled into a false security by the peace efforts of American diplomats during the two previous decades, the American people were distinctly shocked by the outbreak of war in Europe in August, 1914. Believing that the rising peace movement and the economic interdependence of the world would prevent any major hostilities, they had tended to overlook the division of the great powers of Europe into two rival camps, a division that had brought Europe almost to the brink of war in 1906–1907 over the Morocco incident.[1] To many Americans the peaceful solution of that crisis seemed proof positive that arbitration and mediation had outmoded armed force in settling international disputes. Consequently, events in Europe during the years preceding 1914 were overshadowed in the American mind by domestic matters, particularly those concerned with progressive reforms. If the average American worried about international affairs, it was the Mexican situation that troubled him most.

Yet war did come, and on a broader scale than any since the time of Napoleon a century earlier. President Wilson tried his best to keep the United States out of the struggle, first by a regular proclamation of neutrality, then by requesting the American people to remain impartial in thought as well as in action. The President, still adhering to his earlier views, believed that his offers of mediation would bring the war to an early conclusion. With the passage of time, however, the European conflict affected the United States more and more, both diplomatically and economically. Both groups of belligerents flaunted the American conception of neutral rights, Germany ultimately being deemed the greater transgressor. Finally, in April, 1917, when all mediation efforts had failed, and when Germany had embarked on a policy of unlimited sub-

[1] See chap. 23.

marine warfare, the Wilson administration regretfully concluded that the only way to save the world for democracy appeared to be for the United States to enter on the Allied side.

The European Background

Although the assassination of Austrian Archduke Francis Ferdinand at Sarajevo, the capital of the Austrian province of Bosnia, on June 28, 1914, was the immediate spark that touched off the European powder keg, it was not the main cause for World War I. As has been described earlier, Germany, Austria, and Italy had formed a pact in 1882, followed by a rival Franco-Russian alliance. By the time of the Morocco incident, Great Britain had reached an understanding with the latter allies, largely because of her concern about the growing military and economic strength of Germany. Over the years a combination of nationalism, commercial rivalry, struggle for spheres of influence in Africa and Asia, and concern over balance of power brought the two rival alliances to the verge of war. Blaming the assassination on unbridled Serbian nationalism, Austria served an ultimatum on Serbia, which the latter, with the support of Russia, rejected. Austria, backed by Germany, severed relations with her small Balkan neighbor on July 26, 1914, and within a week war came, to involve eventually Belgium, France, Great Britain, Russia, and Italy as the major countries on the Allied side and Germany, Austria, Bulgaria, and Turkey as the Central Powers. No one country was responsible for bringing on World War I; determination not to let down one's allies involved one nation after another in the widening conflict.

Few Americans had paid much attention to the growing spirit of antagonism that brought on this struggle. Had not Secretary of State Bryan, with President Wilson's approval, named "deserving" Democrats to key diplomatic posts in Europe, the administration might have been better informed of the course of events. But the majority of ambassadors recently sent to represent the United States in the capitals of Europe were largely untrained in diplomacy. Mostly they were men with an intellectual background and liberal views who had supported Wilson's New Freedom.[2] To make matters worse, the ambassadors in the two key

[2] Walter Hines Page, sent to the Court of St. James, had been an editor and publisher more concerned with progressivism at home than diplomatic events abroad. Henry van Dyke, representing the United States in the Netherlands, was a teacher, poet, and clergyman; Thomas N. Page, the envoy to Italy, was best known for his writings; Brand Whitlock, in Belgium, had a political background as a reform mayor of Toledo, Ohio, though he was perhaps better known as a novelist. Myron T. Herrick, originally appointed to the Paris post by President Taft, had not taken advantage of his experience to become fully acquainted with the European scene. Frederick C. Penfield, the Ambassador to Austria, was the nearest approach to a career man.

posts, London and Berlin, took partisan positions. Page became more and more pro-English, appearing to be more of a British apologist than a representative of the United States. This was indicated when he delivered notes of protest from the State Department to Foreign Minister Sir Edward Grey; he frequently stated that they really did not mean what they said, but were written more for home consumption. On the other hand, Gerard was quite definitely anti-German and showed an increasingly critical attitude toward Germany and all that the imperial government stood for. Such bias prevented these two men from sending objective reports to Washington.

President Wilson's advisers at home, both official and unofficial, could not be called impartial, with the possible exception of Secretary of State Bryan. Certainly Robert Lansing, who succeeded him in June, 1915, became increasingly pro-Ally; in fact he stated later that he had not been neutral since the outset of war. Practically the same thing might be said of Colonel House. As to the President himself, despite his initial lofty expressions about impartiality in thought, he veered toward the Allied cause, though not as consistently as did his advisers.

Wilson Proclaims Neutrality

When news reached Washington that the European holocaust had begun, President Wilson immediately issued a routine proclamation of neutrality on August 4. Few Americans doubted the wisdom of this more or less traditional step. Even though there were differences of opinion among well-read Americans and among the American press as to what nation or group of nations was primarily responsible for starting this conflict, there was practically unanimous agreement that the United States should not be drawn into the struggle.

Two weeks later the idealistic President went a step further. Realizing that more than one-third of the American populace had direct or indirect foreign ties,[3] Wilson made an unusual appeal on August 19. After asking "what influence the European war may exert upon the United States," he indicated that it depended "upon what American citizens say and do." Because of their background, "some will wish one nation, others another, to succeed in the momentous struggle. It will be easy to excite

---

Perhaps the weakest appointment was that of James Gerard, a wealthy socialite and Tammany judge, to the Embassy in Berlin.

[3] The Census of 1910 revealed that there were approximately 92 million people in the United States. Of these, nearly 13.4 million were foreign-born; some 13 million more were American-born, with both parents of foreign birth; and about 6 million had one parent foreign-born. Of this total of more than 32 million, 11.6 million had been born in countries on the Allied side and 11 million in Central Power nations.

passion and difficult to allay it." The President believed that "such divisions amongst us ... might seriously stand in the way of the proper performance of our duty as the one great nation at peace." Therefore he urged the people against "passionately taking sides." In order to "be neutral in fact as well as in name," they "must be impartial in thought as well as in action."

The majority of the American people, anxious to avoid being drawn actively into the war, at first did their best to conform to the President's request. As the conflict continued, however, they found it increasingly difficult to preserve an impartiality in thought. Several factors contributed to the swing away from complete neutrality. One strong force was propaganda. Another was trade, which tended to link American interests closely with the Allies. A third resulted from American reaction to German sabotage. And a fourth grew out of the struggle for neutral rights, a struggle in which Germany came to be regarded as the greater culprit.

Effect of Propaganda

Both warring alliances resorted from the very outset to the use of propaganda in support of their cause. As the most important neutral, the United States was literally bombarded with partisan materials in newspapers, books, pamphlets, and speeches. The English and the Germans were particularly active in spending millions of dollars to persuade the American people that their respective sides were waging a just war against vicious and inhumane enemies.

For many years it was believed that a pro-Ally sympathy in the United States resulted from a devilishly clever British propaganda machine operated through a central agency known as Wellington House, and that German efforts, on the other hand, were bungling and inept. Recent studies of this subject, however, show that long before Wellington House began to function smoothly, before the sabotage efforts of the Central Powers were brought to light, and before American lives were lost at sea as a result of German submarine attacks, many Americans had already concluded that the Allies must win. Also those studies reveal that German propaganda was at times skillful and competent, particularly when it hit at Russia, with its despotic government, its aspirations for world power, and its mistreatment of Jews.

What then predisposed so many Americans to the Allied cause? In the first place, since about 1898, diplomatic relations with Britain had steadily improved, while those with Germany had materially worsened. Furthermore, the cultural ties with France had always been strong, and those with England had shown marked improvement in recent decades. Economically, there was a close affinity between Anglo-American bankers and businessmen.

Likewise contributing to the swing of opinion in favor of an Allied victory were the initial actions of Germany herself. To an American majority, Germany appeared to be the first country ready for war—the first nation to welcome hostilities. This belief, plus the fact that she was one of the first to declare war, made it seem that she was the aggressor. The violation of the Belgian neutrality treaty, termed by Germany as a mere scrap of paper, the ruthless rape of Belgium, and the swift overrunning of northern France caused otherwise impartial Americans to sympathize more and more with the apparent Allied underdog.

Prior to 1917, this sympathy did not extend to a wish that the United States enter the war, but it did increase sufficiently to cause a growing hope for Allied victory.

The Economic Impact

Even though President Wilson frequently referred to the conflict in Europe as a war that would not touch the United States, the economic impact was felt in America even before the initial shot was fired. First to feel this impact was the New York Stock Exchange; on July 30, 1914, war rumors had a bearish effect that sent averages down some five points. Within twenty-four hours the Exchange closed its doors—not to reopen until December 12—to prevent a panic that might be brought on by efforts of European countries to liquidate quickly their American securities. There were two important sequels to this closing: the prices of stocks and bonds were frozen at practically prewar levels, and Secretary of the Treasury William G. McAdoo came to the relief of American business by issuing within the next six weeks more than 250 million dollars in emergency currency.

The advent of war likewise had an immediate effect on American exports. Perhaps in an effort to build up stockpiles in anticipation of conflict, Europe had generously purchased American goods, especially farm produce, in 1913. As a result, American farmers had increased their crop yield for 1914, only to discover that the demand declined considerably after August, especially for wheat and cotton, and along with the drop in exports came a falling off of prices. Steel and copper sales also decreased, while the textile industry was dealt a blow when the British blockade cut off the supply of German dyes. Business confidence reached such a low ebb that a panic appeared inevitable.

Such a disaster was averted, however, and early in 1915 a boom was definitely under way. Britain especially realized that the war would be long and consequently she would need a larger stockpile. With her manpower diverted to military service, she must buy more and more of her military and civilian necessities from abroad, and the United States was the natural market. And the United States, despite its proclamation of neutrality and Wilson's efforts to prevent the war from touching the country, was ready to sell. On August 6, 1914, Secretary Bryan was instructed to inform the belligerent governments that "neither the neutrality laws of the United States nor the proclamation of the President make it unlawful to export contraband of war in the ordinary course of commerce." This "business as usual" position was well received by the American people, as indicated by a poll conducted by the *Literary Digest* in January, 1915.

As a result, an increasing flow of weapons, planes, munitions, iron and steel products, and the like were sold to the Allies. The value of these "war babies" between August, 1914, and the entrance of the United States into the war in April, 1917, was more than 6 billion dollars.

American manufacturers would undoubtedly have sold similar material to the Central Powers, but British control of the seas prevented those countries from obtaining delivery of any items they might have ordered. Sales to the Central Powers dropped off sharply from 170 million dollars in 1914 to 1.1 million dollars in 1916. Under the circumstances, Germany felt that the United States was unneutral in supplying one side and not the other. To the Wilson administration, however, it was no fault of the United States that Great Britain could obtain such commodities and Germany could not. According to Secretary Bryan, for his country to change policy would be "an unjustifiable departure from the principle of strict neutrality." And German Ambassador Bernstorff had to admit that the United States had a right to sell arms to belligerents, even though the one-sidedness of the trade did cause considerable ill feeling in his country.

Closely associated with the export of war goods was the problem of payment for them. Britain did not want to ship all her gold across the Atlantic, and the United States did not want her to because the economy of both countries might be dislocated. Therefore as early as mid-August, 1914, the question of loans was raised by J. P. Morgan. Secretary Bryan felt that "loans by American bankers to any European nation which is at war" would be "inconsistent with the true spirit of neutrality." Morgan and his fellow bankers regarded this opinion as official and refused to float the loan the Allies requested.

By October, 1914, however, it was becoming apparent that American trade might be adversely affected by the Bryan thesis. Therefore President Wilson announced that the extension of credit to the Allies would not interfere with America's neutral position, for Americans would not be aiding in the financing of the war for one side, but would be merely facilitating the commerce of the United States. Nearly a year later, the administration, more pro-Ally than previously, relaxed its policy further, deciding that the floating of bond issues by belligerents in the United States not only would be proper, but would help solve the trade problem. Morgan thereupon established a banking syndicate subsequently responsible for subscribing to some 2.3 billion dollars in Allied bonds.[4]

The growth of these economic ties with the Allies in the form of sales of war goods, credit extensions, and bond flotations led to charges, particularly in the 1930s, that American bankers and munitions makers were largely responsible for bringing the United States into World War I in order to protect their investments.[5] Such charges tend to ignore the fact that President Wilson was not at all likely to allow his policy to be dictated by powerful financial groups. Always suspicious of the lobbying of special interests, Wilson would have repudiated any direct suggestion that the nation should go to war to save the pocketbooks of bankers and industrialists. On the other hand, it is undoubtedly true that wartime trade and private lending contributed heavily to growing pro-Ally feeling—particularly in the East and South.

Altercations with the Allies

Despite the definite swing of American opinion in favor of the Allies, there were at first more causes for complaints about British infringements of neutral rights than there were about German. The struggle for neutral rights from 1914 to 1917 was in many ways reminiscent of the struggle more than a century earlier when Jefferson and Madison were trying to persuade or compel England and France to respect the American position.[6] Once again, as during the Napoleonic period, England controlled the seas and would not recognize the stand the neutral United States had taken. Now it was primarily Germany, not France, which was blockaded and using various means, also contrary to American neutral standards, to break the British stranglehold. There was this major difference: in the period prior to the War of 1812 the official American attitude was generally anti-British; in the period from 1914 to 1917 it became increasingly pro-British.

The complaints of the United States against Great Britain largely centered around the interpretation of what was international law. The United States would have preferred that of the Declaration of London,

---

[4] On the other hand, the Central Powers were able to dispose of only some 20 million dollars in short-term bonds, mainly in the early years of the war.

[5] See chap. 31.

[6] See chap. 6.

the codification of maritime law drawn up by a special subcommittee of the Second Hague Conference. But England had never ratified that declaration, and without her approval it was questionable whether it was actually part of international law. Failing to obtain recognition of this declaration, the United States considered falling back on the Declaration of Paris of 1856, which contained a series of provisions that might have been adequate for the middle of the nineteenth century, but not for the twentieth.

Therefore the Wilson administration tried to have the belligerent nations accept as much from both declarations as possible. England, with the largest navy, was just as determined to make her own rules on the high seas; only through this means could she weaken her enemies and thereby win the war. Germany, like France a century before, was the military power on the Continent. In eventual need of all types of supplies, she was ready to support Wilson's position on many points, yet at the same time she was determined to go to any lengths to end the British blockade. In this aspect of the war it was the neutral countries that felt the effects of this maritime struggle, with the United States, the most important neutral, suffering most.

The first Anglo-American controversy arose over what was contraband.[7] Shortly after the outbreak of hostilities, President Wilson sought assurance from both warring parties that the Declaration of London concept would be respected. The initial replies were apparently satisfactory, but, with the passage of time, the Allies gradually added more and more items to the absolute contraband list. Finally, on April 13, 1916, Britain announced that because of the "peculiar circumstances" of the war, she would cease making distinctions between absolute and conditional contraband. Numerous notes of protest from the United States failed to change this decision. American exporters did not, however, complain too much because they were usually compensated for their confiscated cargoes.

A second major controversy involved visit and search. Because of the growing submarine menace, British destroyers took more and more American merchantmen into English ports to be searched instead of conducting their investigation on the high seas. This practice frequently resulted in delays of several weeks. Also, after the Germans sowed mines in the North Sea, England, using the excuse that neutral ships needed English pilots to get through the mine fields safely, lured such vessels

[7] The Declaration of London had divided cargoes into three categories: (1) absolute contraband, consisting of direct implements of war, which was subject to seizure without compensation by a belligerent from any neutral ship; (2) conditional contraband—items that might be used not only by a belligerent army or navy, but also by noncombatants; such commodities were seizable only if proved that they were for enemy armed forces; and (3) free goods or noncontraband, that were not to be disturbed; traditionally food was included in this category.

into British harbors, where they could be searched. Again American objections did not cause England to modify her actions.

The British blockade, enforced hundreds of miles from German ports, also led to notes of protest because it did not conform to American principles. It likewise enabled England to put into practice the doctrine of continuous voyage—definitely forbidden by the Declaration of London— thereby restricting American trade with the neutral countries of Europe. England answered that she had allowed the North to resort to this doctrine during the Civil War so she expected reciprocation now.

Additional causes for complaint in the early stages of the war were numerous. It was, for example, an accepted practice for a belligerent-owned ship to raise a neutral flag as a *ruse de guerre* when an enemy naval vessel was in the vicinity, but British ships often used the American flag for the greater part of the Atlantic crossing. This indiscriminate flying of the American flag by British passenger ships and merchantmen not only was contrary to international law, but gave Germany an excuse for torpedoing such ships. Secretary Bryan sent a vigorous protest to Britain on February 10, 1915, in which he decried "an explicit sanction by a belligerent government for its merchant ships generally to fly the flag of a neutral power within certain portions of the high seas which are presumed to be frequented with hostile warships." To him the "general misuse of a neutral's flag jeopardizes the vessels of a neutral visiting those waters."

Lord Grey defended his country's action by saying it conformed with common usage. He also pointed out that the United States had frequently resorted to the use of neutral flags during the Civil War without British protest. The Wilson administration did not press the issue further.

The censoring of mail was another source of annoyance. Not only did Americans claim that Britons obtained American trade secrets and delayed the arrival of bids on contracts, but the State Department sent a firm note to Ambassador Spring-Rice deploring such a "lawless practice." According to Secretary of State Lansing, if the United States countenanced it, it "would open the door to repeated violations of international law by the belligerent powers." As in other cases, however, England paid but scant attention to the American objection.

President Wilson has been charged with lack of forcefulness and consistency in his controversies with England over neutral rights. Yet, as during the Napoleonic War, it is difficult to determine just what could have been done to bring England to account. An embargo would have been neither feasible nor popular, and coercion was out of the question for a man interested in the cause of peace. So long as British infringements of neutral rights involved only inconveniences and not loss of life, the Wilson administration seemed content simply to protest. Moreover, as the pro-Ally sympathy grew in the United States, fear developed that England would be weakened if she were compelled to conform to the Wilsonian version of neutral rights.

Sabotage

During the course of these Anglo-American differences over neutral rights, Germany was complaining about the unneutrality of the United States, particularly in connection with its increasing trade in war materials with the Allies. As one means of retaliating, Germany embarked on a program of sabotage in order both to cut down on the manufacture of those commodities and to prevent their shipment to England. German agents attempted to foment strikes in munitions plants, to destroy factories and piers by arson or bombs, and to blow up the ships carrying contraband to the enemy.

Most of the efforts failed,[8] but the American fears of fires, explosions, and even death at the hands of saboteurs led to a revulsion of feeling against the Central Powers. This was particularly true in the summer of 1915, when the United States secret service released to the press some of the information discovered in the briefcase of a German agent, Dr. Heinrich Albert. This showed conclusively that Germany was actively engaged in efforts to sabotage American industry. Among those who were handed their passports as a result of such actions were Austrian Ambassador Dumba, Captain Franz von Papen, the German military attaché, and Captain Karl Boy-Ed, the naval attaché.

Submarine Warfare

Much more important than sabotage in turning American opinion more and more against Germany was her submarine warfare. The original reason for resort to such warfare was that Germany felt compelled to use retaliatory steps against England to prevent further weakening through Britain's "food" or "hunger" blockade. This referred to the fact that in January, 1915, England had placed certain cereals and flour on the contraband list. England's excuse was that the German officials had commandeered large supplies for their army and thus food became a contraband item. Therefore, on February 4, 1915, Germany declared that the waters around the British Isles were to be a war zone. On and after February 18, all enemy ships sighted within that zone would be sunk on sight. Neutral vessels entering the area would do so at their own risk, not that

---

[8] The major exception was the so-called Black Tom (New Jersey) explosion on July 30, 1916, which wrecked the docks of the Lehigh Valley Railroad, causing the death of two persons and property damage to the value of 22 million dollars.

German U-boats would knowingly attack them, but because they might not be identifiable. The inability to identify their neutral status might be the result of two factors: the difficulty of recognition through a periscope and the fact that British merchant ships were flying neutral flags.

To President Wilson this German proposal posed threats very different from British infringements of international law. The use of the submarine as a naval weapon might endanger American lives and property because it would be difficult for such a craft to comply with the rules of international law concerning visit and search, warning, and taking care of the safety of passengers and crews. Consequently, in his note of February 10, Wilson denounced submarine warfare as "unprecedented." Were American lives and property lost as a result of submarine attacks, Germany would be held to "strict accountability." The majority of the American people backed the President in his position on this issue. Some authorities nevertheless questioned the legality of Wilson's position. No international conference had as yet ruled on the use of submarines in wartime. They said, therefore, that Wilson was setting up one set of international standards for Britain and another for Germany.

And what was behind the Wilsonian position? In the first place he still adhered to the principle of freedom of the seas. American citizens had the right to travel on the high seas, even on a belligerent-owned merchant or passenger ship, with every expectation of reaching their destinations safely. If such a ship were to be sunk, the attacking vessel, whether it be a surface craft or a submarine, must give warning and see that the passengers and crew were safely disembarked before the fatal sinking. In the ensuing diplomatic discussions over this thesis, Germany at first denied that existing rules of international law specifically covered submarine activities. To the President, however, the maritime code covered all naval vessels. When Germany tacitly admitted that this was probably true, she asserted that the submarine could not conform to the rules. Small in size and poorly armed, the U-boat could not compete on the surface with enemy cruisers, destroyers, or even armed merchantmen. To come to the surface to give warning might be disastrous. Furthermore, an attacking submarine could not take aboard the passengers of a merchantman about to be sunk. To Wilson this was no excuse; if submarines could not operate according to the rules, they should not be used.

Secretary Bryan was correct in his conclusion that incidents would develop, for on March 28, 1915, the British steamer *Falaba* was sunk off the coast of Ireland; among the casualties was one American, Leon Thrasher. Then on May 1, the first American ship, the tanker *Gulflight*, was attacked. Although the ship did not sink, the torpedo explosion killed two crewmen and the captain died of heart failure. American opinion was highly incensed by these two incidents, probably reaching the highest anti-German pitch since the rape of Belgium. While it is true there were no outspoken demands for war, most people felt that unless Germany apologized and offered compensation for the losses, some form of retaliation must be taken.

German reaction to the *Falaba* incident was most unsatisfactory. In early April, Ambassador Bernstorff informed the State Department that his government considered the United States unneutral because it continued to allow the Allies to obtain war materials from American firms and also because it did not insist that Britain observe the rules of maritime law. A few days later Bernstorff stated that Germany would no longer accept responsibility for the safety of citizens of a neutral country sailing on Allied ships. This was scarcely an answer to the administration's charge that the sinking of the *Falaba* was both illegal and "revoltingly inhuman."

Yet Wilson took no formal action since his advisers differed as to the course to follow. Because of the high feeling over the *Falaba* incident and because the American government still refused to stop its citizens from sailing on belligerent-owned vessels, the German Embassy tried to prevent future incidents by warning, through newspaper statements, that prospective American travelers "sailing in the war zone on ships of Great Britain or her allies do so at their own risk."

Sinking of the Lusitania

When the British liner *Lusitania* was sunk off the coast of Ireland on May 7, 1915, with the loss of 1,198 lives, of which 128 were American, opinion in the United States regarded it as a planned mass murder. The horror and shock that followed news of the sinking were not enough to cause a general demand for war, although a few Americans, notably Theodore Roosevelt, believed that this "murder on the high seas" warranted firm American retaliation. The ex-President wanted an immediate embargo established on all trade with Germany, as well as seizure of any German ships in American ports. To him "the firm assertion of our rights" did not necessarily mean war, "but, in any event, it is well to remember there are things worse than war." From across the Atlantic Ambassador Page sent word that the United States would certainly lose face in England if it did not immediately declare war on Germany.

President Wilson was not swayed by such belligerent statements; instead he undoubtedly voiced American majority opinion in his address to several thousand recently naturalized Americans on May 10:

> The example of America must be a special example. The example of America must be the example not merely of peace because it will not fight, but of peace because peace is the healing and elevating influence

of the world and strife is not. There is such a thing as a man being too proud to fight. There is such a thing as a nation being so right that it does not need to convince others by force that it is right.

While the nation might be "too proud to fight," it must do something to prevent future incidents of a similar nature. There was considerable disagreement, however, as to the course to be taken. Secretary Bryan thought that the *Lusitania* incident had been brought on largely by Wilson's continued refusal to warn Americans against traveling on belligerent ships. Furthermore, he believed Britain was as much at fault as Germany because she was arming her merchantmen. Thus, in all justice, both parties should be warned to mend their ways. Counselor Lansing, on the other hand, was of the opinion that Germany must be brought to account in a severe note. Reflecting Lansing's views, the first *Lusitania* note of May 13 stressed the President's version of neutral rights, which were being challenged by Germany's submarine warfare that ran counter to "those rules of fairness, reason, justice, and humanity which all modern opinion regards as imperative." The message concluded:

> Expressions of regret and offers of reparation in case of the destruction of neutral ships sunk by mistake, while they may satisfy international obligations, if no loss of life results, can not justify or excuse a practice, the natural and necessary effect of which is to subject neutral nations and neutral persons to new and immeasurable risks.

Consequently, "the recurrence of anything so obviously subversive to the principles of warfare" must be prevented at all costs.

The American press, particularly in New York, Boston, Baltimore, Washington, and Chicago, gave wholehearted backing to the administration. The *New York Times* expressed the feeling well when it stated that Wilson had "the united support of the American people."

Germany's reply was anything but satisfactory. Instead of admitting the validity of the American position, she asserted that the *Lusitania* was an armed auxiliary naval vessel carrying munitions.[9] Under the circumstances Germany felt justified in the sinking. This reply had just as firm support from the German press as the American note enjoyed in the United States. The general tenor of many articles was that the United States was trying to protect enemy shipping by having its citizens travel aboard British vessels.

Unfortunately for Wilson's position on neutral rights, Secretary Bryan

---

[9] All recent research shows, however, that the *Lusitania* was not armed, nor could it be considered a naval auxiliary. The munitions it carried formed only a small part of its cargo. Moreover, the submarine captain did not know what ship he was torpedoing, merely that it was a large liner. Therefore he should have given warning.

helped to cut the ground from under him by informing Ambassador Dumba not to take the contents of the note too seriously because, whatever happened, the United States would not go to war. News of what Bryan had done leaked out and President Wilson was greatly angered. The Secretary of State's usefulness was at an end, though his resignation shortly after was supposedly for other reasons. Yet the first note to Germany did accomplish something. Its severity, plus the furor developing in the United States, helped to cause the German government, after bitter behind-the-scenes controversy, to order submarine captains on June 6 not to attack the larger enemy passenger ships.

Meantime, Wilson and his advisers were working on the second note. When the President supported Lansing's wish for firmness, Bryan found the excuse to resign. Therefore it was his successor, Lansing, who sent the message of June 9. This denied categorically that the *Lusitania* was armed. Nor would the United States admit "that the proclamation of a war zone from which neutral ships have been warned to keep away may be made to operate as in any degree an abbreviation of the rights either of American ship masters or of American citizens bound on lawful errands on merchant ships of belligerent nationality." This second warning to Germany ended: "Lives of non-combatants cannot lawfully or rightfully be put in jeopardy by the capture or destruction of an unresisting merchantman" whether armed or not.

The German reply was slow in forthcoming, not being received until July 8. In conformity with the instructions to submarine captains of June 6, it announced that there would be "free and safe passage" of liners. There were, however, certain strings attached: the vessels should be specially marked, they should carry no contraband, and Germany should be given reasonable notice about the sailings. The United States was asked in conclusion to increase its merchant marine. By so doing, the number of American citizens traveling on British liners would decrease, and along with this fewer incidents would take place.

Despite the more conciliatory tone of this note, Germany had not disavowed its actions that were contrary to the American conception of neutral rights. The third American note, sent on July 21, therefore concentrated on this aspect, as well as trying to obtain a German promise to cooperate in preserving freedom of the seas. Were Germany to refuse either, she would be considered "deliberately unfriendly" toward the United States. It was not until February 4, 1916, that Germany finally expressed regret for the sinking of the *Lusitania* and promised to indemnify for the losses of American lives. The Wilson administration deemed this satisfactory, even though Germany did not wholly agree to the American version of freedom of the seas.

The Arabic Pledge

The *Lusitania* controversy had not been settled when another incident heightened American animosity. On August 19, 1915, the British 16,500-ton liner *Arabic* was sunk without warning off the Irish coast; among the resulting casualties were two Americans. President Wilson was greatly disturbed by the news, and while not ready to demand war, he was insistent upon obtaining complete satisfaction. Ambassador Bernstorff, considerably worried about American opinion, informed his government that unless it pursued a conciliatory course, the United States would probably sever diplomatic relations.

And in German official circles the gravity of the situation led to a change of policy. The order of June 6 to submarine captains was broadened to include all passenger ships, instead of being limited to the larger liners. By the time Bernstorff was informed of this change, he had already promised on his own responsibility that Germany would indemnify the United States for the *Arabic* losses. Since this promise did not ameliorate American hostility, the German Ambassador, again on his own, submitted to the State Department the so-called *Arabic* Pledge: "Liners will not be sunk by our submarines without warning and without safety for the lives of noncombatants, provided that the liners do not try to escape or offer resistance."

Bernstorff was reprimanded by his government for acting without authority, but Germany conformed both to this pledge and to the broadened instructions to submarine captains for the next half year. Moreover, in October, 1915, Chancellor Bethmann-Hollweg, after lengthy correspondence with the State Department as to whether the sinking of the *Arabic* was justified, finally sent a message regretting the incident, promising compensation, and assuring that "a recurrence of incidents similar to the *Arabic* case is considered out of the question."

President Wilson believed that the partial German change of heart was an important victory for his diplomacy. The furor of American opinion gradually died down, and even some of the most vehement critics of the administration, including Theodore Roosevelt, admitted that Wilson had done a "most gratifying" job. Yet there was the feeling in some quarters that the President's victory was not complete because such troublesome questions as those of visit and search, of merchant ships, of armed liners, and of responsibility for the sinking of the *Lusitania* were still unanswered. The air had been cleared for the time being, to be sure—but for how long no one knew.

Early Mediation Efforts

President Wilson, perhaps not realizing the depth of bitterness between the two rival groups and still imbued with the belief that mediation could stem the war, promptly sent notes on August 4, 1914, to the several belligerent governments in which he offered his good services "in the interest of European peace, either now or at any time that might be thought more suitable." From the administration's point of view the replies were anything but satisfactory. They all vigorously disclaimed any responsibility for starting the conflict and showed no particular desire for a speedy peace.

During the remaining months of 1914, however, rumors persisted that the warring powers were ready to discuss peace terms. Consequently, in December President Wilson requested Colonel House to broach the subject with Johann von Bernstorff and Sir Cecil Spring-Rice, the respective Ambassadors from Germany and England. Bernstorff was fairly optimistic about his government's willingness to retire from Belgium and possibly indemnify the Belgian people if such steps would facilitate peace talks. The British diplomat seemed quite sure that neither his country nor France would reject any reasonable offer Germany might make.

Following House's enthusiastic reports of these conversations, Wilson sent the colonel to Europe at the end of January, 1915. At his first stop in London, he found several obstacles in his path. Germany had initiated submarine attacks that must be stopped. Britain was considering retaliatory steps. Under the circumstances, English leaders were in no mood to talk about peace as long as the new submarine menace was present. Colonel House tried to prevail upon the cabinet members to consider the possibility of a general agreement on European disarmament, to be followed by the establishment of some type of world organization to effect and maintain peace, but to no avail. In Paris, where the threat of German attack was still ominous, the colonel encountered similar opposition. Proceeding to Berlin, he suggested a compromise: Germany should offer to evacuate Belgium, along with adequate indemnity, if Britain would agree to freedom of the seas. But Foreign Minister Gottlieb von Jagow told House that his government would insist on retaining several important Belgian towns and river valleys as its price for peace, along with part of the Belgian Congo and a large indemnity from France. When House presented these terms to French officials, they declared that only a German victory would achieve them. Back in London again, House did obtain a slight concession: if Germany supported a general disarmament agreement, Britain would relax her control of the seas. Scarcely had Britain made this concession than she learned of the sinking of the *Lusitania*.

This act of violence ended all hope of reaching a common ground. Thus House returned home in June, 1915, convinced that the war would be waged until one side had gained by force what it could not win by negotiation and that the United States would soon be drawn into the all-out struggle.

House-Grey Memorandum

The initial failure of his mediation efforts did not discourage President Wilson, who still hoped to bring the war to an early conclusion. With Colonel House as the correspondent, he kept in touch with Sir Edward Grey throughout the spring and summer of 1915, and the British Foreign Minister showed an increasing interest in the cause of peace. Consequently, House was sent again to Europe in December, 1915, to confer directly with the leaders of the belligerent governments about the possibility of a conference to deal with a conclusion of hostilities, the restoration of pre-war boundaries, and the preservation of future peace by limiting armaments and establishing an association of nations.

In both Paris and Berlin, House made little progress, but in London on February 22, 1916, he reached a secret accord known as the House-Grey Memorandum. The gist of the agreement was that

> President Wilson was ready, on hearing from France and England that the moment was opportune, to propose that a Conference should be summoned to put an end to the war. Should the Allies accept this proposal, and should Germany refuse it, the United States would probably enter the war against Germany.
>
> ... if such a Conference met, it would secure peace on terms not unfavorable to the Allies; and, if it failed to secure peace, the United States would leave the Conference as a belligerent on the side of the Allies, if Germany were unreasonable. ...

President Wilson approved this memorandum after adding a second "probably" to qualify the phrase about the United States leaving the conference as a belligerent. Whether the President did so because of his desire to keep the United States out of the war or because of a realization of constitutional limitations on the Chief Executive to declare war is still a matter of controversy.

At any event, when Wilson began to press for British support in calling the proposed conference, he found Grey reluctant. This hesitancy may have been because of the insertion of "probably." It may have been because a prerequisite for the meeting was a clarification of war aims, and the British objective might not conform to Wilson's ideals, thereby losing for England America's moral support. A third possibility was that the presidential campaign of 1916 had started in the United States; if the nation entered the war during its course, Wilson might not be reelected. Thus the Entente would lose a good friend and helper, likely to become an ally. Consequently, this mediation effort also failed. It had certain results however; Wilsonian approval of the House-Grey Memorandum, even with the "probably" reservation, encouraged the British to take a more inflexible position on the blockade and armed ship issues.

The Armed-ship Dilemma

Even while Colonel House was visiting European capitals on another "great adventure" for peace, the administration in Washington was faced with the problem of armed Allied merchantmen. Shortly after the opening of hostilities, the United States announced that it would regard belligerent-owned merchant vessels armed only for defensive purposes as peaceful ships. Not until the fall of 1915, when the British, worried about the increasing submarine menace, began to arm more and more passenger ships and merchantmen, did the matter come to the fore. The immediate issue involved the liner *Persia*, which was torpedoed without warning in the Mediterranean at the end of December with the loss of nearly 350 lives, of which 2 were American. At about the same time armed Allied ships, mainly Italian, were reaching American ports.

Secretary Lansing became troubled by the possible ramifications of this turn of events, which might threaten America's position both on neutral rights and as a neutral. Early in January, 1916, he therefore laid the problem before the President. Did the increase in armaments change the status of such ships from defensive to offensive? If so, would that place them in the category of war vessels? And if they were considered as naval ships, was the United States breaking its neutrality by allowing them to enter American ports? Could the United States complain when they were sunk without warning? And could American citizens properly travel on them?

After considerable discussion without reaching an answer to these questions, the Secretary of State then posed another question: Could the American position on these issues be used to persuade both sides to effect a compromise? England might be prevailed upon to stop arming her merchant ships, and Germany in turn would promise not to sink such ships without warning.

With Wilson's approval, Lansing opened negotiations with the British on January 18, 1916, by saying that the United States might regard armed ships as naval auxiliaries, which could be sunk without warning. The British protested that such a stand would be unneutral because the United States would be changing its definition of international law after the war started, thereby greatly aiding Britain's enemies. In addition, the issue had been raised at a most unpropitious time: Colonel House was even then in Europe trying to promote mediation. Yet his government was placing England in the unhappy position of either seeing its merchant marine sunk or risking a break with the United States by refusing to accept the new American conception.

On the other hand, Germany welcomed the proposed change. Here was an opportunity to force an issue favorable to the cause of the Central Powers. Consequently, both Germany and Austria announced early in February that armed enemy merchant ships would be sunk on sight after the end of the month. Under the circumstances, the American press foresaw a Wilsonian warning against American citizens sailing on such vessels.

Yet after all the furor and conjecture raised by Lansing's proposed modus vivendi, the Wilson administration unexpectedly pulled in its horns. In a sudden reversal of anticipated policy, the Secretary of State informed the press on February 15 that while the government continued to believe that the disarming of British liners and merchant craft would benefit "the interests of humanity," it would not demand observance of the proposed change in international law if Britain refused to accept. Neither would the government warn Americans not to sail on such ships.

It is difficult to determine why Wilson and Lansing proposed the change of policy in the first place, or why the change of heart occurred at the last moment. One explanation is that the administration hoped it would facilitate the conclusion of the *Lusitania* controversy with Germany. The sudden withdrawal of the proposal was probably the result of Wilson's realization that a change would seriously undermine his peace efforts. How could the British look upon him as an unprejudiced mediator if he persisted in supporting the January 18 proposal? And the President subsequently informed his friends that he had erred in the whole affair—an admission quite difficult for Wilson to make.

The Gore-McLemore Resolutions

While the abortive attempts to persuade Britain and Germany to approve Lansing's modus vivendi were going on, some members of Congress, chiefly Democrats from the Middle West, became convinced that the President was leading the United States closer to war. Unaware that Colonel House was even then trying to negotiate for a general peace conference, those men were certain that Wilson's speeches in favor of American preparedness, together with a more vigorous policy toward Germany, were signs of approaching conflict. Therefore they decided to force Wilson's hand by bringing into the open the administration's foreign policy. With the presidential election in the offing, they might thwart

Wilson's renomination by showing the voters where he stood. If he were contemplating war, they believed, he would surely lose ground among the electorate; if he wanted to win the election, he would be forced to take a firmer stand for neutrality.

The particular worry among the isolationists was the fear that the failure of the administration to take a firm stand on the armed-ship issue would lead to more incidents involving the loss of American lives. In turn such incidents would arouse public opinion to demand retaliation, even to the point of war against Germany—something the isolationists wished to avoid at any cost. To them the solution was clear: Americans must be prevented from traveling on armed belligerent ships.

The opening round of the fight to force the President's hand came in December, 1915, with the introduction of a series of resolutions aimed at regulating American production of munitions and prohibiting their export. Bowing to administration pressure, Congress refused to support these proposals. After the sinking of the *Persia*, however, the isolationists redoubled their efforts. On January 5, 1916, Senator Thomas Gore, an Oklahoma Democrat, introduced a bill to deny passports to Americans planning to sail on belligerent-owned ships. A few days later he also proposed that greater protection be given to American noncontraband cargoes against illegal Allied seizures. Shortly after, Jeff McLemore of Texas indicated that he would soon sponsor a measure to prevent American citizens from crossing the Atlantic on armed ships of warring countries.

These Gore-McLemore proposals worried the President. Were he to put his stamp of approval on them he would be abandoning the whole principle of neutral rights that had guided his policy from the beginning of World War I; were he openly to oppose them, his party might be disastrously split, thereby bringing repudiation to himself and his administration. Consequently, he tried his best to work behind the scenes with congressional Democratic leaders to persuade them to prevent either set of resolutions from being introduced. When Germany announced on February 19, however, that armed enemy ships would be considered as naval vessels, the Gore-McLemore bills were promptly brought before Congress, with every expectation of being passed by overwhelming majorities. Thereupon the President redoubled his efforts in special conferences and through numerous letters. Perhaps the most important was the message of February 24 to William Stone, Democratic chairman of the Senate Foreign Relations Committee. After promising to do everything in his power to keep the country out of war, he said:

> For my part, I can not consent to any abridgment of the rights of American citizens in any respect. The honor and self-respect of the nation is involved. We covet peace and shall preserve it at any cost

but the loss of honor. To forbid our people to exercise their rights...
would make everything this Government has attempted and everything
that it has achieved during this terrible struggle meaningless and futile.

Newspapers in all parts of the country threw their support behind the
President; the *New York World* voiced majority journalistic opinion
when it stated on March 3, 1916, that "Whoever defends these resolutions
defends German lawlessness against American rights and American
honor." Undoubtedly most of the American people outside of the Middle
West shared this view. As a result the Senate tabled the resolutions on
March 3, while the House, after a bitter fight, turned them down by the
overwhelming vote of 276 to 142 four days later.

The Sussex Pledge

Encouraged by this victory for his theory of neutral rights, Wilson
was confronted with considerable pressure, particularly from Secretary
Lansing, to compel Germany to revoke her recent decision to regard
armed enemy merchant ships as naval vessels. He refused to be pushed
into a severance of diplomatic relations; such a step would end all possibility of carrying through the mediation recently discussed by House
and Grey.

But Wilson's position was considerably weakened when a German
submarine attacked without warning the unarmed French *Sussex* in the
English Channel on March 24. Although the *Sussex* managed to reach
port, the casualties among the passengers numbered about eighty. News
of this disaster prompted Lansing to redouble his efforts to sever relations
with Germany. The President realized some forceful action was necessary,
but he still would not take the step that might be the prelude to war.
The most he would do was to warn Ambassador Bernstorff that the
United States would break off diplomatic relations with Germany unless
the latter curbed her submarine campaign.

Germany attempted to close the incident by announcing that the
Sussex was a naval ship, only to be charged by Wilson with a "direct
untruth." The first note sent by the State Department on April 19 was
a vigorous warning that if Germany did not immediately cease "its present
methods of submarine warfare against passenger and freight carrying
vessels," which the United States regarded as the "most terrible example
of ... inhumanity," the United States must conclude all diplomatic relations with her.

Many Americans believed diplomatic severance would mean war.
Easterners were mostly ready to take the fateful plunge, but Middle
Westerners thought that the *Sussex* affair did not justify hostilities. The
English government, anticipating an American-German break, made be-

lated apologies for some of its country's protested actions on the high seas. Germany likewise believed that war might materialize and instructed Bernstorff to order German crews to sabotage their ships in American ports.

Yet the German government did not want war with the United States and so sent a conciliatory reply to Wilson. By the so-called *Sussex* Pledge, German submarines would not sink any merchantmen without warning or without trying to save the lives of passengers and crews unless resistance were offered or an attempt made to escape. This pledge, however, was made contingent upon the United States insisting that Britain also adhere to the rules of international law. Were Britain to refuse, then Germany "must reserve itself complete liberty of conscience."

Wilson was pleased with the first part of the German reply, but he refused to be bound by the German threat not to adhere to the pledge if Britain continued to restrict the rights of neutrals. The President's answer stressed the fact that "responsibility in such matters is single, not joint; absolute, not relative"; consequently Germany must respect neutral rights even if other belligerents did not.

Since Germany, by not replying, apparently accepted the Wilsonian version of the pledge, this proved another victory for the President's diplomacy, particularly since there were no more sinkings without warning before February, 1917.

Renewed Troubles with the Allies

On the other hand, relations with Britain reached a low ebb during the spring and summer of 1916. One reason was her refusal to continue the peace talks that the House-Grey Memorandum had supposedly initiated. Another was the furor created in the United States by the severe repression of the Easter Week rebellion in Ireland. Many Americans, particularly those of Irish extraction, condemned the English for atrocities alleged to be worse than those charged against the Germans. Senator William Borah of Idaho made a strong anti-British speech in Congress, and the Senate expressed the wish that all the Irish prisoners be released. American newspapers that normally supported the Allied cause denounced the British executions of the Irish rebel leaders as sheer stupidity.

At about the same time (April) Britain announced that henceforth she would make no distinction between conditional and absolute contraband on the high seas, justifying her decision on the basis of the "peculiar circumstances" of World War I. To President Wilson this was a grievous blow to his neutral rights position.

The climax of ill feeling came on July 14, when England published a list of more than 400 firms located in the Western Hemisphere (of which 87 were in the United States) which were charged with giving aid and comfort to her enemies. Consequently no loyal Briton could do any business with them. Wilson was greatly angered by this so-called blacklist. He objected not only to this extension of the economic war into neutral countries, but to the fact that many American firms on the list were there only because they had German-sounding names. Moreover, neutral companies not on the list would be afraid of doing business with firms that were blacklisted lest their names be added. This blacklist, coming on the heels of the other recent incidents, brought Wilson to "the end of my patience with Great Britain and the Allies." To him the British leaders responsible for issuing the blacklist were little more than "poor boobs." Privately he told his advisers that he was ready to ask Congress for authority to place an embargo on shipments to the Allies and to put an end to all loans.

Despite his ire, Wilson's note of July 26 did not go so far as his private statements would indicate, although it was more harsh and threatening than earlier ones. It merely stated that Britain might expect severe retaliation if it persisted in interfering with American commerce. When Britain failed either to send a prompt reply or to rescind the blacklist, Congress, by amending existing laws, authorized Wilson to refuse the use of American ports to ships of countries interfering with American commerce. Fortunately for Anglo-American relations, however, the President made no use of this power, which would have injured both American and British economy. Yet these controversies with England may have been a factor in Wilson's decision to sign a naval appropriation bill in the summer of 1916 that provided for an increase in the number of battleships; the President said in that connection: "Let us build a navy bigger than hers and do as we please."

Preparedness and Politics

This statement about a bigger navy was indicative of Wilson's change of position. Certainly until the fall of 1915 he had been vigorously opposed to American military preparedness because it might lead the nation closer to the war he was trying to mediate. But the continuation of that conflict and the failure of the belligerents to recognize neutral rights gradually made the President realize that a stronger United States might be able to present a better case.

Early in 1916 he toured the Middle West, where his speeches included appeals for steps to prepare the nation "not for war . . . but for adequate national defense." The public enthusiastically supported this change of heart, setting the stage during the summer of 1916 for Congress to enact such measures as the Hay Act, which provided for a larger army; the Naval Construction Act, which appropriated more than $500 million dollars for a bigger navy; and the Adamson Act, which prevented a railroad strike that might have crippled the transportation system to the detriment of the preparedness program. A Council of National Defense was also established to coordinate the various phases of preparedness efforts.

While this program was being formulated, the presidential campaign of 1916 was getting into full swing. The Democrats renominated Wilson on a platform that praised both his domestic reforms and his policy of neutrality. While Wilson would have preferred to wage his campaign principally on the issue of disloyalty in the United States, or "hyphenism" as he called it, he soon discovered that the most popular slogan was: "He kept us out of war." His Republican opponent, Charles Evans Hughes, was inept in his criticism of the Wilson administration and offered little in the way of a constructive program. In a very close election, the President was returned to the White House for four more years. Many voters undoubtedly cast their ballots for him because of the implied promise that the country would remain at peace. But even Wilson did not think this possible, for he had already said to a friend: "I can't keep the country out of war. . . . Any little German lieutenant can put us into war at any time by some calculated outrage."

Mediation Revived

While the presidential campaign was in progress, Germany unexpectedly professed an interest in peace. Chancellor Bethmann-Hollweg instructed Bernstorff in the summer of 1916 to inform the Wilson administration that his country was willing to accept the President as the mediator at a formal conference. From the German point of view, the strong positions held by their armies on both the western and eastern fronts offered promise of negotiating a favorable settlement. The German Ambassador approached Colonel House on the subject, only to be informed that Wilson would not be able to pursue the matter until his election had been decided. Another reason for this decision may have been House's opposition to such a move without the prior approval of both England and France.

Safely reelected, Wilson turned his attention again to the cause of mediation. The continued conflict, he realized, made American neutrality all the more difficult; the President had already said during the political campaign "that war now has such a scale that the position of neutrals sooner or later becomes intolerable." Sooner or later Germany would resume unlimited submarine warfare; when that happened, the United States must "inevitably drift into war" with her.

But before Wilson was ready to act, Germany took the lead by announcing on December 12, 1916, her willingness to enter a peace conference. The Allies, of course, regarded this gesture with suspicion, and

Wilson at once concluded that no general meeting would succeed unless both groups of belligerents stated their objectives in advance and agreed to a security organization to ensure future peace. Although his advisers were not in full sympathy with his project, Wilson dispatched similar messages to all the warring countries on December 18, incorporating his proposals.

The replies left much to be desired. Great Britain, which had shown an interest earlier in the year, had recently changed governments. Now David Lloyd George was Prime Minister, and his conception of a just peace was one made after Germany had been dealt a "knockout blow." The other Allies agreed with him, so that the answer to Wilson from the Entente was that there could be no just peace until the lands Germany had conquered were wrung from her, their peoples liberated, an indemnity paid for the destruction her armies had wrought, and Europe protected from such "brutal covetousness" in the future.

Germany at first refused to state any concrete terms, although she undoubtedly intended to make annexations of strategic territory. Surely with the President serving as mediator, Germany could not hope to emerge from a peace conference with such gains. Moreover, she was of the opinion that the meeting among the belligerents that she had proposed on December 12 would accomplish much more because it would not bog down as a result of "American indiscreetness and intermeddling."

Realizing that the failure of these attempts to mediate would probably lead to serious consequences—resumption of unrestricted submarine warfare by Germany, losses of more American lives, severance of diplomatic relations by the United States, and then war—the President decided to make a last-ditch effort to avoid the involvement of his country in hostilities, which to him would be a "crime against civilization." His method would be an appeal to the peoples of the nations at war, in somewhat the same fashion as he had "gone to the country" when Congress had turned him down on matters of domestic importance. The means would be an address to the Senate, which would be widely publicized.

In this speech of January 22, 1917, Wilson depicted both the kind of peace the United States desired and the type of postwar world that would avoid future conflicts. To him "peace without victory" was the prime prerequisite for a durable peace.

> Victory would mean peace forced upon the loser, a victor's peace forced upon the vanquished. It would be accepted in humiliation, under duress, at an intolerable sacrifice, and would leave a sting, a resentment, a bitter memory upon which terms of peace would rest, not permanently, but only as upon quicksand. Only a peace between equals can last.

To Wilson other essential conditions to a lasting peace would be freedom of trade, freedom of the seas, the ending of entangling alliances, government by the consent of the governed, and limitation of armaments. Most important of all, such a peace "must be followed by some definite concert of power which will make it virtually impossible that any such catastrophe" as World War I "should ever overwhelm us again." And such a concert must include the United States and other nations of the Western Hemisphere.

Were all these steps taken, there would be created "a peace that is worth guaranteeing, a peace that will win the approval of mankind, not merely a peace that will serve the several interests and immediate aims of the nations engaged."

Wilson's advocacy of "peace without victory" was a bitter blow to the Allies, who accused the President of failing to recognize the high goals for which they were fighting.

Approaching the Brink

The President's "peace without victory" speech was shortly followed by two notes from Germany that made such a peace virtually impossible. The first of these, delivered by Bernstorff on January 31, 1917, contained the terms upon which Germany was willing to negotiate. They included not only the return of her seized colonies, but additional ones as well; the restoration of Belgium, though only after future German safety was assured; the return to France of territory Germany had captured, but with revised boundaries to protect Germany economically and strategically; in similar fashion, her boundaries on the east would have to be redrawn to safeguard Germany against Russia; freedom of the seas must be assured; and German citizens and businesses injured by the Allies must receive adequate compensation. To President Wilson no peace could be made on such a foundation; the Allies certainly would reject a meeting that even considered such terms.

Much more staggering to the President's hopes was the second note, in which Germany changed her position completely. On and after February 1, German submarines were ordered to sink on sight all ships, neutral as well as belligerent, discovered in the waters around Germany's enemies. As a concession to the United States, however, it would be allowed to send one ship a week between New York and Falmouth, provided this vessel followed a course prescribed by Germany, carried no contraband, flew a red and white checkered flag, and had its hull striped red and white.

This decision to break the *Sussex* Pledge and to flaunt Wilson's conception of neutral rights had not been reached without a struggle. The German Admiralty had long pressed for unrestricted submarine warfare as the only means of victory, which depended on isolating Britain from all commerce, neutral as well as Allied. The naval leaders, after much

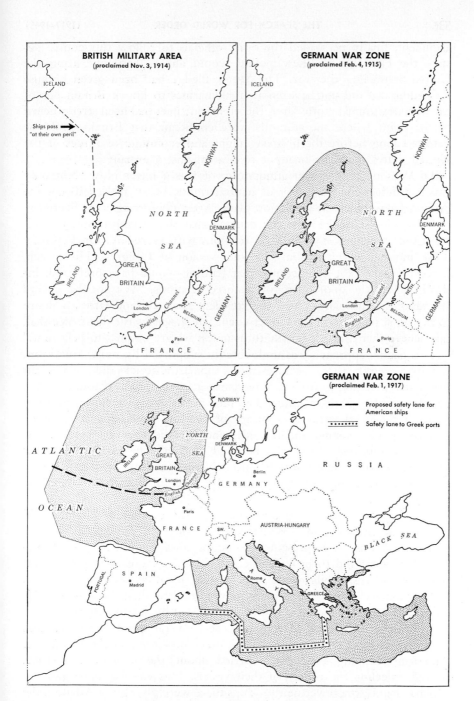

argument, finally persuaded the other officials to follow this course despite the fact that the new policy would almost certainly bring the United States into the war. The *Sussex* Pledge had been given because the Admiralty did not have enough submarines to knock Britain out of the war; now, nine months later, the submarine fleet had been strengthened to the point where the admirals were confident that Britain could be defeated long before the military might and economic resources of the United States could be brought to bear against Germany.

To Wilson this German announcement was a bitter blow. Not only was it a defeat for his policy of neutral rights, but it tended to cut the ground from under his mediation plans. After conferring with Secretary Lansing and Colonel House, he decided that the circumstances necessitated the severance of diplomatic relations with Germany. On February 3, he announced this action to a joint session of Congress. His speech, however, lacked the belligerence that Lansing would have preferred; instead, it held the door open for restored relations. "We are the sincere friends of the German people," the President asserted, "and earnestly desire to remain at peace with the Government which speaks for them. We shall not believe that they are hostile to us unless we are obliged to believe it."

This pacific approach was undoubtedly supported by most Americans, to whom even the threat of unrestricted submarine attacks did not warrant bringing the nation into war. Attendance at peace rallies throughout the country testified to this attitude. The antiwar zealots called for an embargo or even a general strike as a means of averting hostilities. New peace societies quickly sprang up, and older ones showed renewed signs of life. Not to be outdone, those who believed in American entrance into the war on the Allied side insisted, especially through the American Rights Committee, that the President take more forceful action to defend the national honor.

Despite the apparent belief that war might still be avoided no one could doubt that the situation was extremely critical. In anticipation of the worst, the House of Representatives began consideration of a bill to enlarge the Navy and to provide for presidential seizure of shipyards and munitions plants, while work was started on a conscription measure. Little publicity was given to these moves; the President did not wish his continued plans for mediation to be jeopardized by warlike steps.

Before the middle of March, however, several events occurred that helped to swing the pendulum in the other direction. In the first place, American shipping concerns, worried about the submarine menace, started canceling the sailings of their vessels. This was playing right into German hands; the fewer neutral ships there were plying the Atlantic, the fewer supplies England would receive. Moreover, the cutting down of exports threatened the American economy. A possible answer to the problem was to have the Navy convoy the merchantmen; to this suggestion the President turned a completely deaf ear. A second answer was that the merchant vessels be armed for self-defense. Despite the insistence of nearly half the Cabinet members that this be done, Wilson refused on February 23 to be coerced into a move that could easily lead to war.

Most important of all in swinging the pendulum was the unexpected and shocking information that Wilson received from Ambassador Page on February 25 about the so-called Zimmermann telegram. This message had been written by Alfred Zimmermann, the German Minister of Foreign Affairs, to Minister von Eckhardt in Mexico City on January 16. It was sent in code over the American cable to the State Department, which in turn would give it to Bernstorff for delivery to Eckhardt. The British intercepted this message and were able to decode it, but did not reveal its contents to Page until February 23.

The telegram read:

> We intend to begin unrestricted submarine warfare on the first of February. We shall endeavor in spite of this to keep the United States neutral. In the event of this not succeeding, we make Mexico a proposal of alliance on the following basis: Make war together, make peace together, generous financial support, and an understanding on our part that Mexico is to reconquer the lost territory in Texas, New Mexico, and Arizona. The settlement in detail is left to you.
>
> You will inform the President [of Mexico] of the above most secretly as soon as the outbreak of war with the United States is certain and add the suggestion that he should, on his own initiative, invite Japan to immediate adherence and at the same time mediate between Japan and Germany.
>
> Please call the President's attention to the fact that the unrestricted employment of our submarine now offers the prospect of compelling England to make peace within a few months. Acknowledge receipt.

To Wilson, knowledge of this telegram helped to clarify the situation. He now knew that even while Germany was outwardly talking about peace terms, she was not only planning her unrestricted submarine warfare but also a stab in the back for the United States. Even though he still believed that American entrance into the war could be averted, he could not ignore this German duplicity. Consequently, on February 26 he sought congressional authority to arm American merchantmen and, what was more important, the right to "employ any other instrumentalities or methods that may be necessary and adequate to protect our ships and our people in their legitimate and peaceful pursuits on the seas."

Speedy action was necessary, the President realized, because the present Congress would come to an end on March 3. But the legislators were not all of one mind. The isolationists did not all oppose the President's request to arm merchant ships; this was certainly better than full-scale war. Yet most of them did oppose giving Wilson blanket authority, and in this stand they had the support of many interventionists who, while not against the basic purpose of either part of the President's request, wanted Congress in session to check Wilson's possible use of the wide authority he sought.

When it became apparent that his proposals would encounter stormy opposition, Wilson, to help his cause, finally played what he hoped would be his trump card: he released the contents of the Zimmermann telegram to the press, which in turned headlined it throughout the nation on March 1. The isolationists suddenly found themselves on the defensive as the public at last realized the full implication of what Germany was planning. The armed-ship bill, minus the blanket authority, promptly passed the House by the overwhelming vote of 403 to 13. In the Senate, on the other hand, Robert La Follette and George Norris led a dozen arch-isolationists in an opposition filibuster that lasted until the Sixty-fourth Congress came to an end. The irate Wilson vehemently denounced this "little group of willful men, representing no opinion but their own" who had "rendered the great Government of the United States helpless and contemptible," while the majority of the American press supported him by calling the filibusters "Benedict Arnolds" and "Iscariots."

This filibuster delayed the arming of American ships only briefly. The President, still angry at the isolationists, now sought other authority. Both Secretary Lansing and Attorney General Gregory assured him that he had the right to issue the order on the basis of a statute still on the books from the days of the undeclared war against France during the administration of John Adams,[10] as well as a measure of 1819 designed to end piracy on the high seas. Therefore, on March 9 Wilson informed the nation that guns would be mounted on American ships and be manned by naval gunners. And the order came none too soon, for within two weeks German submarines sank several unarmed American merchantmen with a heavy toll of life. The first effect of unrestricted submarine warfare had finally been felt—to provide the overt acts that Wilson had tried so hard to avoid.

And at just about the time of those sinkings the news came of the Russian uprising of March 12, 1917, which overthrew the tsarist regime. Now the great barrier to the American belief that the Allied cause was that of democracy was wiped away. Wilson undoubtedly voiced majority opinion when he said: "If our entering the war would hasten and fix the movements in Russia and Germany, it would be a marked gain to the world and would tend to give additional justification to the whole struggle."

[10] See chap. 4.

Wilson was still struggling with his conscience. He had worked long for mediation, but the events of the past two months had caused him to doubt whether the Central Powers really wanted the kind of peaceful world for which he was striving. Perhaps the only answer was for the United States to enter the war on the Allied side to ensure the establishment of the future conditions he believed the peoples of the world desired. Not wishing to take the fatal step without support, he held a Cabinet meeting on March 20 at which he sought the members' opinion about the course to follow. The prompt reply was to ask Congress to declare war against Germany.

The Declaration of War

Thereupon the President called the newly elected Congress into special session to deal with "grave questions of national policy." Considering the recent events, this could mean only a request for a declaration of war. Thus the chamber of the House of Representatives was filled to overflowing when Wilson began his address on the evening of April 2. First of all he described the effects of unrestricted submarine warfare, under which the Imperial German government had "put aside all restraints of law or of humanity," thereby bringing about "the wanton and wholesale destruction of the lives of non-combatants, men, women, and children, engaged in pursuits which have always, even in the darkest periods of modern history, been deemed innocent and legitimate." Such warfare, Wilson asserted, was against mankind. Diplomacy had failed to stop such warfare; armed neutrality was "ineffectual enough at best." The United States could not "choose the path of submission and suffer the most sacred rights of our Nation and our people to be ignored or violated." The only solution was for Congress to "declare the recent course of the Imperial German Government to be in fact nothing less than war against the government and the people of the United States" and to use all the power and resources of the United States "to bring the Government of the German Empire to terms to end the war."

Then Wilson stated the nation's objectives in going to war:

> There are, it may be, many months of fiery trial and sacrifice ahead of us. It is a fearful thing to lead this great peaceful people into war, into the most terrible and disastrous of all wars, civilization itself seeming to be in the balance. But the right is more precious than peace, and we shall fight for the things which we have always carried nearest our hearts,—for democracy, for the right of those who submit to authority to have a voice in their own Governments, for a universal dominion of right by such a concert of free peoples as shall bring peace and safety to all nations and make the world itself at last free. To such

a task we dedicate our lives and our fortunes, everything that we are and everything that we have, with the pride of those who know that the day has come when America is privileged to spend her blood and her might for the principles that gave her birth and happiness and the peace which she has treasured. God helping her, she can do no other.

The tumultous applause that greeted this speech drowned the protests of the minority led by such men as La Follette and Norris. Even earlier administration critics like Theodore Roosevelt and Henry Cabot Lodge were forced to admit that Wilson had stated the case of the United States most eloquently. Congress was quick to act on the President's request. On April 4 the Senate passed the war resolution by a vote of 82 to 6, and the House concurred two days later, 373 to 50. When President Wilson affixed his signature to this resolution on the afternoon of April 6, 1917, the United States became a belligerent in the great world conflict.

The collapse of the antiwar faction in Congress reflected the final swing of American public opinion. The wish to keep out of the great conflict—so strongly evident during the recent election—had been overwhelmed by the flood of events during the ensuing months. If Wilson's fateful stand on the submarine issue seems in retrospect to have been somewhat stiff and legalistic, particularly in view of America's own use of this weapon during World War II, it must be remembered that unrestricted submarine warfare stood as a symbol for something much more serious: Germany's general reputation for ruthlessness and dangerous yearning for world power. American distrust for Germany had been rising since American and German fleets had brushed shoulders in Samoa and the Philippines late in the nineteenth century. Although they probably exaggerated the scope of German ambitions, American leaders developed suspicions that were confirmed by German conduct in Belgium and France, as well as on the high seas.

To Wilson the challenge in 1917 was, in large part, a moral one. The peaceful and democratic world for which he yearned could not be achieved until Germany's false gospel that might made right was struck down. Probably the President also sensed that the nation's material interests were deeply involved. Certainly from the standpoint of practical men the real issue involved the world balance of power. Throughout American history, the supremacy of British sea power had been one of the facts of life. For decades the United States had resented this, but the old antagonism had largely disappeared by 1914, largely because the British had wisely recognized the Yankee cousin's paramount influence in the Western Hemisphere. If Britain and her allies were now to go down in defeat, who could say what problems would confront the United States in so strange a future?

28

THE LIGHT THAT FAILED

Between 1917 and 1921 the United States fought its way into a position of unprecedented power and influence in the world, only to turn its back on its new responsibilities and return to a policy of isolation. In personal terms this is the story of the triumph and tragedy of Woodrow Wilson; in terms of history it is the story of how millions of men and women in every quarter of the globe were stirred to hope for a new day of liberty and peace, only to have these dreams shattered by the clashing ambitions, both personal and national, of the postwar world.

Wartime Association

When Congress declared the existence of a state of war with Germany on April 6, 1917, the United States was far from ready to fight. Earlier measures had set in motion a vast naval building program and an expansion of the Armed Forces, but much remained to be done. The conscription and training of a huge citizen army was undertaken, together with a mobilization of industry to equip these forces. Although the United States Navy began effective antisubmarine operations in collaboration with the British in May, 1917, it was not until a year later that American troops began to go into action on French battlefields.

During the months in which the United States was completing its preparations, it helped the Allies mostly with food and supplies. Hitherto American support had taken the limited form of bankers' loans; now the near exhaustion of British and French assets made more direct aid necessary. On April 24, 1917, Congress authorized the President to loan up to 3 billion dollars of the proceeds of the First Liberty Loan to nations "engaged in war with the enemies of the United States." The first advances to Britain and France were made the following day.

Eager to avail themselves of these resources, the British and French governments sent war missions to the United States to explain their needs. Similar missions from other countries soon followed. Over the next eighteen months the United States loaned more than 7 billion dollars to Great Britain, France, Italy, Russia, Belgium, Yugoslavia, and Cuba. About nine-tenths of this was spent in the United States for munitions, food, and other supplies.

This close cooperation in financing the war was paralleled in many other fields, especially in the joint operations of the American and British navies. The exact role the American Army would play was not so easily decided. The French and the British were eager to use American troops as replacements in their own battered forces, but General John J. Pershing, the American commander, was insistent that he should have his own American army, fighting on a separate sector of the front. While this disagreement continued, the British were reluctant to divert their cargo ships to ferrying American troops across the Atlantic. This stalemate was broken in March and April, 1918, when the Allied front came under dangerous pressure from the great German spring offensive. The separate peace recently arranged between Germany and Bolshevik Russia made it possible for the Germans to strengthen their drive with many divisions transferred from the eastern front. To meet this threat, British, French, and American authorities at long last decided on a unified command under the French Generalissimo Ferdinand Foch; Pershing at the same time agreed to the emergency use of American divisions to bolster the sagging Allied lines, and the British turned over as much shipping as possible to bring over American troops.

These decisions were made none too soon, because the war was now at its most critical stage. In July, 1918, the Allies stopped the final German drive at the Marne, and in August and September Foch was able to start a vast counteroffensive. At last obtaining command of his own army, Pershing won bitterly fought battles at Saint-Mihiel and in the Argonne Forest. By the end of October the Germans were in desperate retreat.

The Problem of War Aims

Although the word "Allies" was sometimes loosely used to include the United States, President Wilson always carefully emphasized that his nation was merely the *associate* of the other countries fighting the Central Powers. No treaty pledging the United States to make war and peace together with its cobelligerents—the usual form of an alliance—was ever signed.

This distinction is significant, because Wilson regarded the United States as uncommitted by the various treaties and agreements that had been made among the Allies before America declared war. When Foreign

Secretary Arthur Balfour visited America in 1917 as head of the British War Mission, he brought with him copies of these secret treaties. But he found Wilson much more concerned in problems of wartime collaboration than in receiving instruction in this phase of recent diplomatic history. The President's attitude was well illustrated in Taft's report of an interview at the White House in December, 1917. Opposing Taft's proposed visit to England in the interests of closer Anglo-American ties, Wilson questioned the desirability of drawing the two countries more closely together. They had divergent purposes, he said, and the United States must not be placed in a position of seeming, in any way, to be involved in British policy. Wilson cited the secret treaty between Britain and Italy as one example of a British governmental policy of which he heartily disapproved. Although Wilson thus kept a free hand, he might possibly have done better to have accepted a frank discussion of war aims at this time. Desperately needing American aid, the Allies might have conceded much more to the Wilsonian idealism in 1917 than they were willing to in 1919 after victory was won.

The President's unwillingness to participate in the arrangements for partitioning enemy territories was consistent with the position he had assumed long before the United States became a belligerent. Wilson clung as long as possible to a policy of American neutrality because he wanted to act as mediator in arranging a just peace settlement. In his war message of April 2, 1917, he of course dropped the "peace without victory" idea, but he emphasized the unselfishness of American war aims and called for "a universal dominion of right by such a concert of free peoples as shall bring peace and safety to all nations and make the world itself at last free."

By the "concert of free peoples," Wilson undoubtedly meant an association of nations—an ideal that had become more and more prominent in his thoughts. The idea of such a league was by no means original with the President. In a speech accepting the Nobel Peace Prize in 1910, Theodore Roosevelt had advocated "a League for Peace, not only to keep the peace among themselves, but to prevent, by force, if necessary, its being broken by others." Still advocating such a league in 1915, he asserted: "If it is a Utopia, it is a Utopia of a very practical kind." William Howard Taft became president of the League to Enforce Peace, established in 1915 to urge a world organization that would use military or economic measures against any nation that went to war without submitting its grievances either to judicial settlement or to a commission of inquiry. In May, 1916, President Wilson and Senator Henry Cabot Lodge both attended a banquet sponsored by the League to Enforce Peace and delivered eloquent addresses, endorsing in general terms the idea of a postwar association of nations.

A proposal praised by Roosevelt, Taft, Wilson, and Lodge, as well as by scores of other prominent Americans, might seem to have been certain of adoption. Unfortunately, however, suspicions and jealousies splintered the internationalist movement. Roosevelt, still angry with Taft because of the 1912 political campaign, denounced the League to Enforce Peace as tending toward a dangerous disarmament of the "righteous" powers. The league he wanted was one based upon complete victory for the Allies and the imposition of stern justice upon the Central Powers. Despite many points of agreement between Taft and Wilson, the two men disliked each other and cooperated only now and again. As for Lodge, his flirtation with the project was short-lived. Always a strong nationalist and suspicious of arbitration proposals, Lodge soon regretted his endorsement of the League to Enforce Peace. The more definitely Wilson committed himself to the league idea, moreover, the more disposed was Lodge to find sinister dangers in it. The two men, never more than formally polite in their personal relations, became bitter personal enemies during the campaign of 1916, when Lodge accused Wilson of duplicity in the *Lusitania* negotiations and the President retaliated by practically calling the Senator a liar. On February 1, 1917, Lodge delivered a long speech on the Senate floor, warning of the pitfalls in any such "league for peace" as Wilson had advocated in his "peace without victory" message only ten days earlier.

Although preoccupied with immediate problems for several months after the United States entered the war, Wilson returned to a consideration of war aims in the fall of 1917. The problem became suddenly urgent in November when the Bolsheviks seized control of Russia and almost immediately appealed to the Allies to open peace negotiations with Germany on the basis of no annexations and no indemnities. Implicit was the threat that if the Allies refused to do so, the new Russian government would denounce the war as a wicked capitalist conflict and get out. This would not only destroy the eastern front, but might weaken the western one as well, particularly if the Allied populations became convinced that their governments were fighting for purely selfish ends. Certain that a liberal peace program was essential to winning the war, Wilson sought to persuade England and France to join the United States in formulating a declaration. This proved impossible to achieve, although British Prime Minister Lloyd George did state the war aims of his government in somewhat idealistic terms on January 5, 1918.

Wilson's own program was incorporated in a speech before a joint session of Congress on January 8, 1918. As the first of his famous Fourteen Points, Wilson implicitly criticized the secret diplomacy of the past and called for "open covenants of peace, openly arrived at, after which there shall be no private international understandings of any kind but diplomacy shall proceed always frankly and in the public view." Points 2 through 5 dealt with freedom of the seas, removal of economic barriers, reduction of armaments, and a "free, open-minded, and absolutely impartial adjustment of all colonial claims" that would give equal weight to "the interest of the populations concerned" and to "the equitable claims of the government whose title is to be determined." Points 6 through 13 dealt with specific European problems,[1] but point 14—the most important of all—stated: "A general association of nations must be formed under specific covenants for the purpose of affording mutual guarantees of political independence and territorial integrity to great and small states alike."

During the next several months the President returned again and again to the subject of war aims. In a speech on February 11, 1918, he defined the "four principles" on which peace should be based: each part of the settlement should be based upon the justice of that particular case; people should not be bartered about as if they were mere pawns in a game; every territorial settlement should be made in the interest of the populations concerned; and all well-defined national aspirations should be accorded the utmost satisfaction possible without endangering future peace. On still later occasions Wilson added what came to be known as the "four ends" and the "five particulars."

This series of speeches made a great impression, not because Wilson's ideas were particularly original, but because he expressed so well the liberal aspirations of millions of people on both sides of the battle line. The Committee on Public Information, the war agency created to publicize the American cause, found that the Wilson speeches had tremendous propaganda appeal. Translated into several foreign languages, they were widely distributed in Allied and neutral countries. Thousands of pamphlets were also dropped from airplanes or smuggled into the enemy countries.

The Armistice

At the beginning of October, 1918, the German High Command, realizing that German victory was no longer possible, advised its government to avoid catastrophe by seeking an armistice. In this threatened shipwreck, the German Chancellor, Prince Max of Baden, reached for the life preserver seemingly offered by Wilson's peace program. Addressing a

---

[1] They included the German evacuation of Russian, Belgian, and French territory, the restoration of Alsace-Lorraine to France, the readjustment of Italian frontiers "along clearly recognizable lines of nationality," the restoration of a free Poland, autonomous development for the peoples of Austria-Hungary, and reorganization of the Balkan states "along historically established lines of allegiance and nationality...."

note to the President on October 3, Prince Max proposed an armistice and declared significantly: "The German Government accepts, as a basis for the peace negotiations, the program laid down by the President of the United States in his message to Congress of January 8, 1918, and in his subsequent pronouncements. . . ."

Many zealots for the Allied cause regarded the German note as a trap. "Let us dictate peace by the hammering guns," declared Theodore Roosevelt, "and not chat about peace to the accompaniment of the clicking typewriters." The *Cleveland Plain Dealer* echoed this: "Our answer to the Hun twaddle shall be more war."

Despite these warnings, Wilson did not want to close the door against the possibility of shortening the war and saving lives. Cautiously the President sounded out the defeated enemy, exacting an unequivocal acceptance of the Fourteen Points and other evidences of good faith. So obvious was Wilson's distrust of the Kaiser's government that the German people, now desperate for peace, interpreted the President's delay as an invitation to revolution. The protracted armistice negotiations helped to provoke the disorders that led to the Kaiser's abdication and the proclamation of a republic on November 9.

Meanwhile, Wilson had become sufficiently impressed by German sincerity to transmit the armistice request to the Allied leaders. Since the latter had never accepted the Fourteen Points, Colonel House spent several days explaining the Wilsonian program to them, using as the official interpretation a commentary drawn up for him by Walter Lippmann and Frank Cobb, two prominent American newspapermen. Despite some initial hesitation, the Allied leaders gave a qualified assent. Fearful lest Wilson's freedom of the seas might shackle British sea power, England reserved the right to discuss point 2 at the peace conference. Similarly France insisted upon an "elucidation" of point 8, which stated: "All French soil should be freed and the invaded portions restored. . . ." This, according to the French, meant the Germans should pay "compensation" for "all damage done to the civilian population of the Allies and their property," or, in other words, reparations. Wilson then submitted these revised Fourteen Points to Germany and received her approval. This exchange of notes—known as the Prearmistice Agreement—established the foundation on which the eventual peace treaty was supposed to be based.

The armistice itself consisted of military terms drafted by the Allied High Command. Although General Pershing would have preferred unconditional surrender, General Foch and the other Allied leaders believed it would be enough to lay down such strict terms that the enemy would be unable to renew the war effectively. Accordingly, the armistice, which became effective November 11, 1918, provided for an immediate cease-fire to be followed by heavy deliveries of German arms. The Germans were to evacuate all non-German territory, and the victorious powers were to occupy both banks of the Rhine.

For the moment all factionalism was forgotten as milling crowds in every American city and town celebrated the end of hostilities. "Everything for which America fought has been accomplished," Wilson happily announced. "It will now be our fortunate duty to assist by example, by sober friendly counsel and by material aid in the establishment of a just democracy throughout the world."

Storm Clouds

But Wilson's hour of triumph had already been sullied by a serious political setback. On November 5, congressional elections had given the Republicans a substantial majority in the House and a two-vote margin in the Senate. Since the party that controls the White House often suffers this kind of check in midterm elections, this opposition victory would not have been particularly significant except for two circumstances.

One factor injuring the President was that he had asked for a vote of confidence. At the behest of the Democratic campaign managers, Wilson had issued an appeal on October 24, stating: "If you have approved of my leadership and wish me to continue to be your unembarrassed spokesman in affairs at home and abroad, I earnestly beg that you will express yourselves unmistakably to that effect by returning a Democratic majority to both the Senate and the House of Representatives. . . . The return of a Republican majority to either house of the Congress would . . . be interpreted on the other side of the water as a repudiation of my leadership." Although President McKinley had done something similar in 1898, the Republicans denounced Wilson's appeal as a slur upon their patriotism. They were, therefore, quick to interpret their victory in Wilson's own phrase as a "repudiation" of his leadership.

Even more dangerous to the President's position was the opportunity that victory gave to the Republicans to organize the new Congress. Henry Cabot Lodge, one of Wilson's most implacable foes, would now become chairman of the powerful Senate Foreign Relations Committee.

The revival of partisanship was also reflected in criticism of the President's every move in peacemaking. When it was announced that Wilson intended to lead the American delegation in person to the Paris Peace Conference, this departure from precedent was denounced as evidence of the President's love of glory and his "Messiah complex." The other appointments to the Peace Commission were criticized even more sharply. Secretary of State Lansing, Colonel House, military expert General Tasker H. Bliss, and experienced diplomat Henry White were capable men, but the President's failure to name any senators or leading Republicans[2] opened the door to strong attack. Wilson's reluctance to take senators with him is easily understood, because he could hardly have appointed any senators at all without including the troublemaking Lodge. But the President had much less excuse for ignoring other Republican leaders. Either Taft or Root would have been excellent appointments: both were men of wide experience and sincere interest in international affairs whose advice at Paris would have been very useful; both would have given the peace settlement a bipartisan sanction that would almost certainly have ensured Senate approval.

By failing to make the Republicans share peacemaking responsibility, Wilson left them free to intrigue against him. By a strange irony, the President was enjoying the greatest acclaim of his career at the very time when his opponents were plotting his humiliation. Between December 13, 1918, when he landed in France, and January 18, 1919, when the Peace Conference opened, Wilson visited Paris, London, and Rome, receiving some of the most fervent welcomes recorded in history. Cheering crowds testified to the extraordinary hopes being pinned on Wilson to make all dreams come true.

In America, meanwhile, the opposition was planning its strategy. Lodge had urged White to go behind Wilson's back to encourage the Allied leaders to hold out for harsher terms, but White honorably refrained from such a course. Lodge also called several times on Theodore Roosevelt, who was desperately ill in a New York hospital, and the two leaders grimly planned reservations that might be useful in emasculating the still unwritten League of Nations Charter. Although Roosevelt died on January 6, 1919, he had already laid the basis for posthumous revenge against the man whom he hated for many reasons, but especially for thwarting his ambition to raise and command a volunteer American division.[3]

Lodge was highly competent to carry on the fight. On December 21, 1918, the Senator attacked Wilson's ideas on the Senate floor. "Are we prepared," he asked, "to allow any association of nations by a majority vote to order the troops and the ships of the United States to go to war?" One after another, he raised the bogeys that were to be used to scare the nation: that the British Empire would have more votes than the United States, that the Monroe Doctrine would be abandoned, that the League would interfere with the American tariff system and with immigration policy. The next day Lodge discussed his strategy with

[2] White was a Republican, but had not been active in politics.
[3] The actual decision against commissioning Roosevelt was made by General Pershing and other professional army men, although Wilson and Secretary of War Baker readily concurred.

Senator James E. Watson of Indiana. Watson did not see how the League could be defeated, because some 80 per cent of the people apparently favored the idea; Lodge explained that he did not propose to beat it by direct frontal attack but by "the indirect method of reservations."

The First Round at Paris

Just as Wilson, confident he had the support of men of good will everywhere, dangerously underestimated the shrewdness and determination of his American opponents, so too he minimized other practical obstacles to his program. For one thing, he continued to ignore the secret treaties by which the Allies had agreed to a division of enemy territory in various parts of the world. For another, he gave less weight than he should have to the bitterness against Germany that was the inevitable result of four years of war. In a postarmistice British election Lloyd George's coalition had been confirmed in power after a campaign in which popular slogans had been "Hang the Kaiser," and "Squeeze the Germans until the pips squeak!" French opinion was still more demanding of harsh revenge, while even in America there was widespread belief that Germany must be severely punished for her crimes. To draft a peace of justice in such a climate of opinion would be extremely difficult.

Although thirty-two nations were represented at the Paris Peace Conference, the key decisions were made by a handful of men. Pleading the necessity of working through committees of manageable size, the conferees first set up a Council of Ten, consisting of the two principal delegates from the United States, Great Britain, France, Italy, and Japan. When this group was also found too large for informal discussion, the chiefs of state began meeting by themselves. Since Japan was only interested in Asiatic questions, the dominant group now became the Big Four —President Wilson, English Prime Minister David Lloyd George, French Premier Georges Clemenceau, and Italian Premier Vittorio Orlando. The leaders' decisions were eventually ratified in plenary sessions of the entire conference, but these meetings were few in number and purely formal in character. Germany and the other defeated powers had no voice; not until the treaties had been completely drafted were they submitted to the enemy governments, and then only minor revisions were permitted.

The newspaper reporters who had swarmed to Paris were indignant to find the conference work proceeding behind closed doors. They complained that this violated the first of Wilson's Fourteen Points: open covenants of peace openly arrived at. Wilson explained he had meant only that the final results should be made public; he had taken it for granted that delicate negotiations would have to proceed in private, lest every difference of opinion be exacerbated by premature publicity. Even so, the American President favored greater privileges for the journalists than the other Allied leaders would allow.

Early in the conference Wilson won two important points. Over the opposition of the other leaders, he blocked the outright annexation of the former German colonies and the Arab countries under Turkish rule. Instead, these regions were designated as "mandates," to be administered by various nations for the benefit of the native populations and of the world, under the supervision of the League of Nations. The more advanced mandates were to be prepared for independence.

Wilson's second victory was in establishing the principle that the League of Nations be incorporated as an integral part of the peace settlement. Some of the other leaders wanted to postpone this issue, but Wilson believed the best chance of establishing the League would be lost if immediate action were not taken. Moreover, many other problems of the Peace Conference could be dealt with more easily if new international machinery were available.

Wilson himself served as chairman of the commission to frame the League of Nations Covenant. In several earlier drafts prepared by British, French, and American experts, two sharply divergent concepts had appeared. The French idea was for a league of victors with an international army and general staff, whose primary purpose would be to prevent a revival of German militarism. The opposing idea, to which Wilson was strongly attached, was for a league to which all nations, the vanquished along with the victors, would eventually belong. Instead of superseding national sovereignty, this association would rely for its effectiveness upon the cooperation of governments and the organized opinion of mankind.

As presented to a plenary session on February 14, 1919, the Covenant of the League bore the Wilsonian stamp from beginning to end. The League was to function through an Assembly, in which each member state would have one vote, and a Council, where the five principal powers —the United States, Britain, France, Italy, and Japan—would hold permanent seats and the other countries would be represented by four temporary seats. A Secretariat would assemble information for the use of the League and publish the texts of treaties registered by the member states. Among the functions assigned to the League were the establishment of a Permanent Court of International Justice, the formulation of disarmament plans, the supervision of mandates, and the promotion of health and the interests of labor. The League's most important responsibility was to preserve peace. Members agreed to submit any controversy likely to lead to war either to arbitration or to inquiry by the Council, and not to go to war until three months after an award or report had been made. They also promised not to go to war against nations complying with the recommendations of the League. The Council might recommend economic or military sanctions against nations resorting to war in violation of these pledges. What Wilson considered to be "the heart of the Covenant" was Article 10, which read:

> The Members of the League undertake to respect and preserve as against external aggression the territorial integrity and existing political independence of all Members of the League. In case of any such aggression or in case of any threat or danger of such aggression the Council shall advise upon the means by which the obligation shall be fulfilled.

In this way the principle that Wilson had tried to establish for the Western Hemisphere in the proposed Pan-American Pact[4] was to be made the basis for international order throughout the world.

Revisions in the League

The day after the proposed Covenant was presented, Wilson left Europe to return temporarily to Washington, where the approaching adjournment of Congress and other accumulated business required his attention. Inevitably, the League of Nations dominated the stage during the President's reappearance on the home scene. Indeed, the debate began even before Wilson touched land. Two Republican Senators, Borah of Idaho and Poindexter of Washington, and one Democrat, Reed of Missouri, bitterly attacked the Covenant, while Taft came generously to Wilson's defense. "It would be a great tragedy to the history of civilization," the former President said, "if the Senate can be induced by the protests and narrow views of a small number of Senators who have expressed themselves to defeat this grand covenant of peace. . . ." Wilson fired his opening salvo for the League in Lodge's own political stronghold. Landing at Boston, he made a stirring speech in which he declared: "I have fighting blood in me, and it is sometimes a delight to let it have scope."

Wilson took a less aggressive position, however, in a long conference at the White House on the evening of February 26. Entertaining both the Senate and House foreign relations committees at dinner, the President undertook to explain the Covenant to his guests and to answer their questions. But the affair was not a success. Although the Democrats came away feeling Wilson had answered every reasonable objection, the Republicans were only confirmed in their suspicions. Senator Frank Brandegee of Connecticut was reported to have cross-examined the President as sharply as a district attorney.

[4] See chap. 26.

It was Brandegee who suggested to Lodge a few days later the idea of a "round robin," by which as many senators as possible would be put on record as opposed to Wilson's project. Thirty-nine Republican senators and senators-elect signed a declaration asserting that "the constitution of the League of Nations in the form now proposed" should not be accepted by the United States and that the project should be postponed until after peace was made with Germany. A superb tactician, Lodge proposed this declaration as a Senate resolution during the closing hours of the session. Had it come to a vote, it would surely have gone down to defeat, but, when a Democratic Senator made the mistake of objecting to a suspension of the rules, Lodge achieved his real purpose by reading into the record the names of those who would have voted for the resolution if given the opportunity. Thus dramatically announced, the round robin was intended to prove to the country that the Wilsonian League could not achieve the necessary two-thirds majority.

Less spectacular but equally effective as an anti-League stratagem was a filibuster, through which the Republicans blocked the passage of important appropriation bills. This meant Wilson would have to call the new Congress into special session. Once this was done, the anti-League leaders would be in a position to continue their campaign against the Paris treaties.

Never one to retreat under fire, Wilson responded to these attacks with a ringing assertion of his determination to continue on his course. In a speech at the Metropolitan Opera House in New York City, the President declared:

> When the treaty comes back, gentlemen on this side will find the Covenant not only in it, but so many threads of the treaty tied to the Covenant that you cannot dissect the Covenant from the treaty without destroying the whole vital structure. The structure of peace will not be vital without the League of Nations, and no man is going to bring back a cadaver with him.

Wilson's confidence that he could override the opposition was based not only on the conviction that he was in the right, but that the great majority of the American people stood with him. Of this there seemed ample evidence in the enthusiastic applause given his speeches, in the widespread support for the League in the newspapers, in educational circles, and in the churches. Even among the Republicans there was strong pro-League sentiment. Appearing on the same platform with Wilson in New York, Taft said: "Our profound sympathy in his purpose and our prayers for his success should go with him in his great mission." After returning to Paris, Wilson worked to amend the Covenant in

a few significant particulars. As Taft analyzed the situation in a letter
to Wilson: [5]

> If you bring back the treaty with the League of Nations in it, and
> make more specific reservation of the Monroe Doctrine, require ex-
> pressly unanimity of action in the Executive Council and Body of
> Delegates ... and add to Article XV a provision that where the Executive
> Council or the Body of Delegates finds the difference to grow out of an
> exclusively domestic policy, it shall recommend no settlement, the
> ground will be completely cut from under the opponents of the league
> in the Senate.

In charting his course, Wilson studied carefully not only the suggestions offered by Taft, but others submitted by Hughes and Root as
well as by certain Democrats. Lodge was invited by Henry White to
draft amendments, but refused on the ground that Wilson's proper course
should be to have the Senate advise him. Eventually Wilson obtained the
consent of the other leaders at Paris to a series of changes he hoped would
disarm his American opponents: the revised Covenant now recognized
the right of member nations to withdraw from the League upon two
years' notice, permitted them to refuse to accept colonial mandates,
exempted domestic questions from the jurisdiction of the League, and
specified that: "Nothing in this Covenant shall be deemed to affect the
validity of international engagements, such as treaties of arbitration or
regional understandings like the Monroe Doctrine, for securing the
maintenance of peace."

Completing the Treaty

The weeks between March 13, when Wilson arrived back in France,
and June 28, when he left again for home, constituted a period of intense
diplomatic activity. Before the treaty was ready for Germany, a score
of difficult issues had to be dealt with, and on many of them the President
found himself in opposition to some or most of his colleagues. Despite
his distaste for compromise, Wilson had to give way on many issues in
order to reach a settlement. Ironically, some of Wilson's concessions
were the price he had to pay for the American-demanded changes in
the League Covenant.

Twice invaded by Germany within living men's memory, France
sought to cripple the ancient enemy by detaching the vital Rhineland

[5] Reprinted by permission of Charles P. Taft from Henry F. Pringle, *The Life and
Times of William Howard Taft* (New York: Rinehart & Company, Inc., 1939), vol.
II, p. 945.

and organizing it as a French-dominated buffer state. Wilson and Lloyd George opposed this as certain to create future conflicts when millions of resentful Germans would seek to reunify the fatherland. In the end, France had to be satisfied with the recovery of Alsace-Lorraine, League control over the coal-rich Saar Basin with a plebiscite after fifteen years, Allied occupation of the Rhineland for fifteen years, and permanent demilitarization of both banks of the Rhine. As a further concession to French security, England and the United States signed a special treaty —never ratified—promising to aid France in case of German attack.

Wilson and his American advisers were convinced of the futility of demanding reparations beyond the capacity of Germany to pay. On the other hand, France, devastated by war and embittered against the enemy, wanted to collect as much as possible. Lloyd George, torn between recent election pledges to make Germany pay for the war and sober thoughts about the need to restore Anglo-German trade, vacillated on the issue. The final settlement placed the fixing of the reparations bill in the hands of a Reparations Commission, but, by including Allied pensions as one of the categories of damage, opened the way to claims upon Germany far beyond what she could or would pay.[6]

Territorial problems involved Wilson in bitter controversies with Italy and Japan. The President wanted the Adriatic boundary between Italy and the new state of Yugoslavia to be so drawn as to accommodate both the principle of nationality and the needs of Yugoslavia for a seaport. Italy, on the other hand, demanded not only all she had been promised by the secret Treaty of London of 1915, but even more. Especially heated was the controversy over the port of Fiume. When Wilson appealed to the Italian people over the head of Orlando, the latter temporarily quit the conference as a gesture of protest. In the showdown the Italian people supported their own government, but Wilson continued to resist the full Italian demands. In the end, the Fiume question had to be postponed for later settlement.[7]

Soon after Japan entered World War I as the ally of Great Britain, she seized the German Pacific islands north of the equator and also the German leasehold on the Shantung Peninsula in China. By subsequent diplomacy she tried to tighten her grip on these spoils of war. Under heavy pressure China signed treaties transferring to Japan all the economic and political rights the Germans had held in Shantung, while England, France, and Russia assented to the Japanese acquisitions in a series of secret treaties. Despite Japan's strong bargaining position, Wilson made

[6] In 1921 the Reparations Commission fixed the amount of Germany's obligation at 33 billion dollars.

[7] In 1924 Yugoslavia consented to Italian annexation of Fiume in return for port facilities and an outlet to the sea.

a determined effort to help China regain full sovereignty over Shantung. Japan was adamant, however, in her refusal to sign the treaty unless her demands were met, and in the end Wilson had to give in. The treaty assigned Germany's economic rights in Shantung to Japan, but the latter made a verbal promise to withdraw her troops and restore political sovereignty eventually to China. Despite this sugar coating, China was bitterly disappointed and refused to sign the treaty.

The fact that Russia was unrepresented handicapped the Peace Conference, especially in dealing with the problems of eastern Europe. After the Soviet government had made its separate peace with Germany in March, 1918, Allied expeditionary forces had gone into Russia to prevent military supplies from falling into German hands. American troops had participated in these interventions, both around Archangel and Murmansk in northern Russia and in eastern Siberia. When civil war between White and Red armies broke out on many local fronts, the Allied forces became involved as virtual allies of the anti-Communists. This was the situation when the Peace Conference convened; what to do next was a serious problem. Clemenceau wanted an all-out campaign to suppress the Bolsheviks; Lloyd George and Wilson hoped to mediate between the Communists and anti-Communists and thereby establish a government that could speak for Russia as a whole.[8] In the end nothing effective was done; the civil war continued until the Soviet government finally crushed all its enemies; Allied intervention confirmed the anti-Western hostility of Moscow but was never large enough to bring victory to the Whites, who in any case were fatally lacking in support among the Russian people. Realizing the bankruptcy of intervention earlier than did the Allied leaders, Wilson ordered American troops to withdraw from northern Russia in May, 1919, and from Siberia in January, 1920.

When the Paris diplomats had finally compromised their differences sufficiently to complete the draft treaty, they submitted their terms to Germany. Not allowed to negotiate verbally, the Germans submitted an elaborate analysis of the proposed treaty, objecting to many of its terms. Only a few minor revisions were permitted before Germany was confronted with the alternatives of signing or suffering Allied invasion. Bowing to this ultimatum, the German delegates signed the treaty in the Hall of Mirrors in the historic palace at Versailles on June 28, 1919.

The Treaty of Versailles has been severely criticized both by those

[8] One of the minor sensations of the Peace Conference was the confidential mission to Moscow undertaken by William C. Bullitt, a young American diplomat. Bullitt brought back to Paris a Bolshevik offer to make an armistice, come to a conference, and acknowledge Russian debts to the Allies, if the latter would restore diplomatic relations and terminate their intervention. When news of these negotiations leaked out, there was such loud condemnation that the whole matter was dropped.

who think it was too lenient and by those who are convinced it was too severe. Some regret that Wilson interfered with Clemenceau's program for completely crippling the enemy; others denounce the President for not having used Europe's need for American postwar loans to force the Allied leaders to accept his complete program. To the first line of criticism, it may be pointed out that France and the rest of Europe should have found ample security in the treaty provisions almost completely disarming Germany and forbidding the fortification of the Rhineland upon which Germany's own defenses depended. The German aggressions of the 1930s were possible only because the rest of Europe stood by, divided and irresolute, while Hitler rearmed and remilitarized the Rhineland in defiance of the treaty.

Much more serious is the charge that in its severity the Treaty of Versailles violated the Prearmistice Agreement, under which all parties had promised to base the peace settlement upon the Wilsonian principles. The final treaty sinned against the spirit if not the letter of the Fourteen Points. Although most of the points were carried out in some degree, the terms imposed upon Germany were harsh in their total impact. She was stripped of her entire colonial empire and sizeable areas within Europe; she lost important economic resources at the same time that she was saddled with a crushing reparations burden; she had to accept a war-guilt clause and limitations upon her sovereignty that were particularly galling to national pride. This severity had deplorable results both within Germany and outside. Believing the treaty was unfair, the Germans felt no obligation to comply with the hateful *Diktat*. On the other hand, liberal opinion, particularly in England and the United States, became so obsessed with a sense of guilt that German violations of the treaty met no effective opposition until Nazi Germany grew too strong to be held in check without a great war. But if the treaty were too harsh, it should not be forgotten that it would have been harsher still if Wilson had not fought for his principles at Paris.

The treaty had many good features to compensate for its shortcomings. In conformity with Wilson's principle of self-determination, the Czechs, the Poles, and many other nationalities gained recognition of their independence. Moreover, the League of Nations offered a unique opportunity for future international cooperation. In practice, the League fell far short of its objectives. Although it provided the machinery for useful cooperation in nonpolitical matters and dealt effectively with several disputes among the smaller nations, it was timid and hesitant in the face of warlike moves by the major powers. Some of the League's failures were inherent in its structure, but its record would certainly have been much better if the United States had taken its expected place as a leading member.

Stalemate

On July 10, 1919, President Wilson appeared before the Senate to urge approval of the Treaty of Versailles. Describing the League Covenant as the treaty's most important part, he asked: "Shall we or any other free people hesitate to accept this great duty? Dare we reject it and break the heart of the world?"

This emotional appeal did not move Senator Lodge, who had been laying his plans carefully. As majority leader in the Senate, Lodge's position was far from easy. Some fourteen of his Republican colleagues, including such able orators as William E. Borah of Idaho and Hiram Johnson of California, were "irreconcilables" or "bitter enders," who opposed American participation in any association of nations. At the other pole were some twelve Republicans who strongly favored the League but wanted "mild reservations" to protect or clarify the American position. Between the two were the party rank and file, headed by Lodge himself. Highly suspicious of the League, they wanted "strong reservations" that would materially reduce American commitments to any such world organization. To weld these divergent factions into a working unit was a difficult task, yet Lodge, as will be seen, was able to achieve this goal at critical junctures.

Wilson, on the other hand, refused to face up to the realities of the situation. Within his own party his position was strong: of 47 Democratic senators, only 4 opposed the treaty; the other 43 stood loyally behind the President, even though some of them may have had private misgivings. But even with this faithful phalanx, Wilson was far short of the required two-thirds majority; to win his fight he obviously needed an alliance with the more moderate Republicans. Since the President was not adverse to interpretive amendments that would clarify the treaty without changing its meaning or requiring the consent of other nations, it should have been possible to find some common ground between the Wilsonian Democrats and the mild reservationist Republicans. Yet this necessary alliance was never made—largely because of Wilson's reluctance to risk a weakening of the League. Having sacrificed much to gain the consent of his Paris colleagues to revisions of the Covenant, Wilson wanted to stand firm on the treaty as finally signed. By opposing mild reservations as well as strong, the President played into Lodge's hands.

Both Wilson and Lodge counted on public opinion to sway the result. Aware that the treaty had widespread initial support, Lodge played for time by reading the long document to the Senate Foreign Relations Committee and then opening up the committee hearings to every group with a grievance against the Peace Conference. Italians, Chinese, Irish, Egyptians, Hindus, Persians, and Ukrainians all welcomed this opportunity to proclaim their national aspirations.

Lodge requested the President to turn over to the committee all his records of the Paris conference; Wilson, in keeping with precedent, refused—thereby provoking new charges of secret diplomacy. The President did submit to committee questioning at the White House, but he was no more successful in convincing the doubters than he had been in February. Quizzed on the controversial Article 10, Wilson explained that the pledge to protect the territorial integrity and political independence of member states constituted a "moral" rather than a "legal" obligation. The advice of the Council on how the pledge should be carried out in any particular case would require the assent of the United States; and even after such advice was given, Congress retained its constitutional power to act or not to act.

Meanwhile, opponents of the League were able to stir up formidable hostility to the treaty by playing upon the fears of various groups. Ironically, the peace settlement was attacked both by ultranationalist newspapers like the *Chicago Tribune* and the Hearst papers and by reformist journals like the *Nation* and the *New Republic*. The influential publisher, Colonel George Harvey, served the anti-League cause not only with slashing attacks in *Harvey's Weekly*, but by soliciting funds from the conservative millionaires, Henry C. Frick and Andrew D. Mellon. The anti-Japanese prejudices of the West Coast were turned against the League, as were the anti-British sentiments of other sections. The Friends of Irish Freedom, an Irish-American organization formed to promote the cause of an independent Republic of Ireland, was fanatically anti-League; Article 10 was denounced as a diabolical device to use American troops to suppress rebellions against the British Empire.

Despite the clamor of the opposition, Wilson was so confident that the great majority of Americans favored the League that in September he undertook a gigantic speaking tour to mobilize this opinion. Traveling more than 8,000 miles through the Middle West, the Pacific Coast, and the Rocky Mountain states, he made some forty speeches over a period of twenty-two days. Enthusiastic crowds cheered the President wherever he went, and he responded with much of his old-time eloquence and power. Even so, however, the trip was of doubtful wisdom; anti-League senators like Borah and Johnson dogged the President's trail, and their counterattack partially erased his gains. More important was the fact that Wilson was prodigally spending the precious energies he needed for the main struggle in Washington. Following a speech at Pueblo, Colorado, on September 25, he became so ill that he had to cancel the rest of his itinerary and hurry back to the White House.

A few days later Wilson suffered a stroke that incapacitated him for many weeks and from which he never fully recovered. Just when his leadership was most needed, he was too sick to hear more than brief summaries of the Senate situation, carefully censored by his wife and his doctor. The messages he occasionally sent to the Senate Democrats were not those of a practical politician counting votes, but the petulant demands of a sick and weary man.

In the Senate, events moved slowly toward a stalemate. When the Foreign Relations Committee finally reported in September, a majority, composed of nine Republicans, recommended no fewer than forty-five amendments and four reservations to the treaty. Two minority reports were submitted: one, signed by the six Democrats of the committee, favored ratification without change; the other, offered by the independent Republican McCumber, suggested six mild reservations. In the first showdown on the Senate floor, the Democrats and the moderate Republicans combined to defeat the amendments that would have required renegotiation of the treaty, but this promising alliance broke down when the Senate turned to the reservations.

The original four reservations proposed by the Foreign Relations Committee were now expanded to fourteen. Several of these so-called Lodge reservations were assertions of American sovereignty: the United States, for example, would retain complete freedom to declare an issue domestic, and as such excluded from League jurisdiction, and the sole right to interpret the Monroe Doctrine. By other reservations the United States would withhold assent from the Shantung settlement and refuse to be bound by any League decision in which member states of the British Commonwealth cast in the aggregate more than one vote. Still other reservations jealously guarded the powers of Congress: the United States could withdraw from the League by concurrent resolution, which would not require presidential approval, and Congress would have to assent to any American mandate. The most important reservation erased the moral obligation of Article 10: the United States would assume "no obligation to preserve the territorial integrity or political independence of any other country" unless Congress decided to act. By an important preamble, the Lodge reservations provided that ratification of the treaty could not be completed until at least three of the four Allied and Associated Powers (Great Britain, France, Italy, and Japan) accepted the American reservations in writing.

Lodge skillfully rounded up a majority for all his reservations. The irreconcilables voted yes because each additional reservation weakened the American commitment and still left them free to vote against the treaty as a whole. The mild reservationists voted for stronger reservations than they believed really necessary in order to make final ratification more likely. The outgeneraled Democrats cast most of their votes against the Lodge reservations, but were unable to defeat them.

The next issue was whether to give final approval to the treaty with these Lodge reservations. From the White House came word that the President hoped friends of the treaty would vote no, since in this form the resolution provided not for ratification but "rather for nullifaction of the treaty." Bowing to this advice, 42 Democratic senators joined 13 Republican irreconcilables in voting against the treaty with the Lodge reservations. When the fateful roll call was taken on November 19, 1919, ratification with reservations was voted down 39 to 55. The Senate then voted on approving the treaty without reservations, but this proposal was defeated by a vote of 38 to 53, with the reservationists and ir-reconcilables now joining ranks. Only one Republican, McCumber, voted for the treaty in this form, while seven Democrats voted against it.

To partisans of the League the situation was frustrating. Of the 96 senators, at least 80 professed to want the United States to join the new world organization on some basis, and yet it had proved impossible to ratify the treaty either with or without reservations. Moderates tried to work out some acceptable compromise, but this was not easy. Ex-President Taft and the League to Enforce Peace reconciled themselves to the idea that the Lodge reservations would be acceptable, provided the offensive preamble was dropped in favor of one allowing the other powers to acquiesce through silence rather than requiring their written acceptance. There were indications that such acquiescence would prob-ably be forthcoming; statements by prominent British statesmen and official French newspapers indicated a desire to see the United States join the League on almost any terms.

But even before the British and French position had been made plain, the best chance for constructive compromise had been lost. For two weeks in January, 1920, a bipartisan conference of five Democrats and four Republicans had explored the possibility of drafting a set of reservations acceptable to both sides. Alarmed by reports that Senator Lodge might give ground on Article 10, the irreconcilables issued a sharp warning: unless he stood firm they would revolt against his leadership. Shortly after this incident the bipartisan conference broke down in failure.

The Senate reconsidered the treaty in February and March, 1920. The fourteen Lodge reservations—some softened a bit to meet Democratic objections, but others strengthened—were passed again with larger majorities than the previous year. A fifteenth and irrelevant reservation expressing American sympathy for Irish freedom originated with the Democrats themselves—partly as a bid for the Irish vote in the approach-ing election, partly as a device to make the whole reservation idea ridiculous. On March 19, when the Senate took its final roll call on approving the treaty with these fifteen reservations, the vote was 49 in favor to 35 opposed. Believing half a loaf was better than none, 21 Democrats voted for ratification, but 23 others, still following Wilson's wishes, voted nay along with 12 irreconcilable Republicans. Even though a majority now favored ratification with reservations, the treaty was seven votes short of the necessary two-thirds.

The Aftermath

In May, 1920, the Republican-controlled Congress rushed through a resolution drafted by Senator Philander Knox of Pennsylvania, once Taft's Secretary of State and more recently a leading irreconcilable. The Knox resolution would bring the state of war to an end by merely repealing the war declarations of 1917, while reserving for the United States all the advantages that would have accrued to it had it ratified the Treaty of Versailles. The Republicans had two objectives in mind. If Wilson approved the resolution, the country would be at peace and many unpopular wartime laws and restrictions would come to an end. If, on the other hand, Wilson did what was expected and vetoed the resolution, the Republicans could accuse the stubborn President of prolonging the state of war. Wilson did not hesitate. In a stinging veto message he asserted that for the nation to act thus, claiming all the advantages and none of the obligations of the treaty, "would place ineffaceable stain upon the gallantry and honor of the United States."

The President was not only willing but eager to have his whole peace program go before the voters as the principal issue in the 1920 presidential campaign. Always an admirer of the English system under which a ministry could call a general election and appeal to the people, Wilson had written in a Jackson Day message in January, 1920:

> If there is any doubt as to what the people of the country think on this vital matter, the clear and single way out is to submit it for determination at the next election to the voters of the nation, to give the next election the form of a great and solemn referendum. . . .

This dream of a solemn referendum goes far to explain Wilson's refusal to accept the Lodge reservations in March, 1920. By refusing to surrender to what he regarded as a fatal weakening of the League, the President did not realize he was killing the last chance for the United States to join on any terms; instead, he believed he was protecting his ideal until the sovereign people could speak. The situation is all the more tragic because Wilson apparently dreamed of being himself the Democratic candidate in 1920, even though practical politicians knew it would be impossible for a man of broken health and many enemies to defy the no-third-term tradition. In thus counting upon vindication in the forth-coming election, Wilson was exposing himself to one more cruel disappointment.

Developments at the party conventions soon showed how little chance there was the election would provide a meaningful referendum. The Republican party platform was completely equivocal on the League issue, the Democratic one slightly so. Although some responsible Republican leaders wanted a clear-cut pledge to ratify the Treaty of Versailles with the Lodge reservations, Johnson and Borah threatened to bolt the party if this were done. Lodge, therefore, turned his back on his own reservations, threatening to lead a floor fight against committing the party to them. Seeking to preserve party harmony, the senatorial clique dominating the convention pushed through a plank denouncing the Treaty of Versailles, but favoring "agreement among the nations to preserve the peace of the world" through some kind of "international association." In contrast with these words artfully designed to mean different things to different people, the Democratic plank was relatively straightforward in that it advocated "immediate ratification of the treaty without reservations which would impair its essential integrity," but it still wobbled a little by adding that the party did not oppose "reservations making clearer or more specific the obligations of the United States to the League Associates."

As the campaign developed, the League issue became further confused. Touched by a personal appeal from Wilson, James M. Cox and Franklin D. Roosevelt, the Democratic presidential and vice-presidential candidates, promised to base their campaign squarely on the League. On the whole they did so, but, in the final scramble for votes, Cox qualified his stand, taking a position on Article 10 not unlike that in the Lodge reservations.

Cox's concession, however, was a minor equivocation compared to the meandering campaign oratory of Warren G. Harding. In one speech the Republican candidate would appeal to the pro-League vote by talking loftily of the "Association of Nations," which Republican statesmanship would substitute for Wilson's defective League, and in the next he would mollify the irreconcilables by appearing to oppose the whole idea. Thirty-one prominent Republicans, including Root, Hughes, and Hoover, issued an appeal to the voters based upon the contention that a vote for the Republicans was a vote for American membership in the League of Nations with reservations.

When the ballots were counted, one thing was indisputable. The Republicans had won the most decisive victory of their party history. The electoral vote was 404 for Harding to 127 for Cox; in the popular vote the Republican candidate received 16 million ballots to his opponent's

9 million. The results in Senate and House contests were equally decisive.

What did the Republican landslide mean? Harding interpreted it as a decisive vote against the treaty and announced promptly that the League was "now deceased." Yet this was far too simple an explanation. Many supporters of the League had voted for the Republicans because they blamed Democratic stubbornness for blocking ratification of the treaty with reservations and hoped to place the government in more reasonable hands. Probably a large portion of the electorate voted neither for nor against the League because they were weary of the whole long wrangle. Wartime frustrations and postwar tensions had accumulated to the point where the voters needed scapegoats, and the hapless Democrats proved the most convenient victims. Above all, there had been a powerful re-action against Wilson as a person and against the kind of crusading idealism he stood for.

Whatever the voters thought they were doing, American membership in the League of Nations never again became a matter of practical politics. Whatever prestige and strength the infant organization might have gained by active American participation was lost. Instead of as-suming leadership in world affairs during the 1920s, the United States withdrew into its isolationist shell, emerging only on special occasions.

Who was responsible for this deplorable outcome of the League fight? The Democrats denounced the petty partisanship of the Republicans; the Republicans blamed everything on the stubbornness of Wilson. In retrospect, both sides must be given a share of the responsibility. Lodge was guilty of allowing his hatred of Wilson to dominate his conduct. Even before the League Covenant was drafted, he had schemed to mutilate it by amendments and reservations. What was his ultimate objective? Did he really favor United States membership in the League, once the American commitment had been limited by Senate reservations? Or was he at heart an irreconcilable, scheming to block American membership by framing reservations so distasteful to Wilson that he would disavow his own treaty—just as Roosevelt and Taft had disavowed the Senate-mutilated arbitration treaties of 1905 and 1911? Perhaps Lodge himself was not sure of what he really wanted. As we have seen, the ideal of international organization had once appealed to him, and he sometimes acted as though his reservations were intended to promote this goal; yet a stronger impulse seemed to drive him to fear and suspect not just Wilson's League, but all such plans. Certainly Lodge's influence on the Republican Convention of 1920 and in Congress during the Harding administration pointed strongly toward isolation.

But if Lodge were wrong, this did not necessarily make Wilson right. By slighting the Senate and the Republican party in choosing his peace commissioners, Wilson created resentments that were fed by his subsequent conduct. In dealing with the Senate, Wilson erred in not making a stronger effort to win over the Republican moderates instead of antagonizing them and leaving them to follow Lodge. And, finally, when the impossibility of getting the treaty otherwise had been demonstrated, Wilson probably erred again in not swallowing the Lodge reservations. Even though they might have weakened the Covenant, they could not have injured the League as much as did total American abstention.

The tragedy revealed not only human stubbornness and pride, but certain weak spots in the American constitutional system, which gives to American Presidents exceedingly broad power in the conduct of foreign relations, yet allows treaties to be defeated by one-third plus one of the senators.

29

REPUBLICAN PEACE EFFORTS

When Woodrow Wilson, broken in body though not in spirit, vacated the White House in March, 1921, the Republicans assumed responsibility for defining America's relations with the outside world. The Harding and Coolidge administrations had difficult decisions to make. What should be done about the League of Nations? If the United States did not join, should it cooperate in League-sponsored activities? If the path were to be that of isolation, must the nation spend unprecedented sums on armaments? If it did not, could it hope to maintain its traditional Far Eastern policy in the face of rising Japanese imperialism?

For better or worse, the Republican administrations of the twenties worked out their answers to these problems. Compared either to Wilson or to Roosevelt and Taft, Harding and Coolidge were isolationists. Yet their suspicion of European involvements did not prevent the United States from assuming leadership in at least two fields: naval disarmament and the formal renunciation of war as an instrument of national policy.

Back Door to Peace

In December, 1920, Charles Evans Hughes accepted President-elect Harding's invitation to be his Secretary of State. Rumors of the appointment provoked wrathful comments among Republican isolationists. During the treaty fight Hughes had strongly supported the League of Nations. Although he opposed Article 10 and a few other details, he clearly belonged to the mild reservationist camp. He was one of the illustrious "Thirty-one" who had declared that a vote for Harding was a vote for the League with reservations.

Hughes's internationalist learnings were not the only reason why some Republicans sneered at him as the "whiskered Wilson." Throughout a distinguished career as crusading investigator of insurance scandals, Governor of New York, Supreme Court justice, and presidential candidate, Hughes had demonstrated dignity and high-mindedness. Although kindly in his personal relationships, he had a perhaps undeserved reputation for coldness and aloofness as a public figure—a man widely respected but little loved.

That the genial and convivial Harding should have chosen a Secretary of State so unlike himself may seem strange, but it reflected a certain humility on the part of the Ohio politician elected to an office that he himself admitted was too big for him. Announcing his intention to recruit the best minds of the country, Harding gave Cabinet posts not only to Hughes, but to such other respected men as Herbert Hoover and Andrew W. Mellon. Unfortunately, he then proceeded to spoil what might have been an outstanding group by giving other posts to shockingly unqualified cronies.

Hughes belongs to the relatively short list of Secretaries of State who have shaped American foreign policy with little guidance from the White House. Cheerfully admitting his own ignorance of diplomacy, Harding allowed Hughes a free hand except in cases where the President feared trouble in the Senate. Unaware of the rascality that was to disgrace the administration, Hughes gave the President credit for good-heartedness, while Harding regarded his dignified Secretary with a mixture of respect and awe.

Despite strong support from the White House, Hughes soon learned that some things he would have liked to do were politically impossible. When he entered office, he still hoped the United States might join the League of Nations with reservations, but the isolationists would permit no compromise. On April 12, 1921, Harding put the issue at rest by asserting in a message to Congress: "... there will be no betrayal of the deliberate expression of the American people in the recent election ... the League Covenant can have no sanction by us."

Although in its last month the Wilson administration had initiated a policy of complete dissociation from the League, even to the extent of not answering its communications, Hughes tried to modify this by sending "unofficial representatives" to various commissions established by the Treaty of Versailles. But the irreconcilables opposed even this limited cooperation, and Hughes had to proceed very cautiously during his early months in office. Eventually, however, he was able to revive the use of unofficial observers so that the United States could participate in such noncontroversial League activities as control of the opium trade, public health, and relief.

When Harding took office, the United States was still technically at war with Germany. On July 2, 1921, Congress repassed the Knox resolution, which Wilson had vetoed a year earlier.[1] Even though Harding gladly signed this simple declaration ending the war and reserving for the United States all rights to which it would have been entitled under the Treaty of Versailles, the legalistic Hughes was far from satisfied with this solution. Despite the ingenuity with which Wilson had linked the Treaty of Versailles and the League Covenant, Hughes believed that these siamese twins could be separated. By now, however, the very name "Treaty of Versailles" was so hated on Capitol Hill that the Secretary had to drop his plan for ratifying the treaty without the Covenant. Instead, Hughes negotiated the Treaty of Berlin, signed August 25, 1921, by which Germany granted to the United States all the benefits it would have enjoyed under the Treaty of Versailles without imposing any responsibilities. Hughes was evidently a little ashamed of this course of action, but he defended himself in a letter to his son: "This gives us a footing that is practically unassailable, and while it may be swallowed with a wry face, it is privately recognized by all those who have sense enough to appreciate the facts that it is the best that could be done." [2] Similar treaties were subsequently negotiated with Austria and Hungary.

Threatened Naval Race

In 1916, after Wilson's conversion to preparedness, Congress had passed a giant naval construction act, providing for 156 vessels over a three-year period. American involvement in the war delayed the project, but in December, 1918, Wilson asked Congress both for funds to complete the first three-year program and for approval of a second three-year one as well. The President's purpose was to strengthen his bargaining position at the Paris Peace Conference so that he could force the other powers into a League of Nations and ultimate disarmament. When England agreed to the League, Wilson dropped his demand for the second three-year program, but continued to seek heavy appropriations for completing the first one. After the Senate's failure to approve the Treaty of Versailles, administration pressure for a strong navy increased. In Wilson's logic, the alternatives before the country were, on the one hand, cooperation with the League of Nations and an orderly reduction of armaments, or, on the other, isolation and reliance upon a navy "second to none."

Congress and the country were divided on the big-navy issue. Some bellicose nationalists clamored for a huge building program, but peace-loving groups opposed the idea. Many legislators were particularly im-

[1] See chap. 28.
[2] Reprinted by permission of the publisher from Merlo J. Pusey, *Charles Evans Hughes* (Copyright 1951 by The Macmillan Company, New York), vol. II, p. 442.

pressed by heavy postwar taxes and the need for economy. The Republican-controlled Congress took a middle path by providing funds for continuing the 1916 program, but rejecting Wilson's recommendations for the future. Just how the Harding administration would deal with the problem remained to be seen.

Meanwhile, Britain and Japan were also shaping their postwar naval policies. Both countries felt impelled to embark upon more ambitious construction programs to avoid being outclassed by the United States. Yet both found the mounting expense of the armament race a heavy burden to bear.

Rather than load the taxpayers of three countries with the yoke of competitive armaments, common sense seemed to demand some international agreement on the naval problem. And to achieve this, was it really necessary to work through the League of Nations? Significantly, one of the strongest foes of American membership in the League took the lead in demanding an alternative road to arms limitation. On December 14, 1920, Senator Borah introduced a resolution authorizing the President to invite Great Britain and Japan to a conference to discuss a five-year reduction in naval building. Although the Hearst chain and a few other jingoist papers opposed the naval holiday plan, the great majority of the press gave it enthusiastic support, as did also many influential individuals. Snowballing sentiment for disarmament resulted in the incorporation of the Borah resolution as an amendment to the naval appropriation bill in February, 1921.

In his inaugural address President Harding seemed to endorse the idea of a conference. "We are," he said in characteristically fuzzy prose, "ready to associate ourselves with the nations of the world, great and small, for conference, for counsel, to seek the expressed views of world opinion, to recommend a way to approximate disarmament and relieve the crushing burden of military and naval establishment." Yet Harding appeared reluctant to be hurried into action. He opposed the Borah resolution and tried to persuade Congress to grant large naval appropriations to use for bargaining purposes. Not until a new wave of support for a conference developed did the administration permit a moderate appropriation bill containing the Borah resolution to become law in July, 1921.

The American demand for a naval holiday found a sympathetic echo in debt-laden England. Even before the Borah resolution was introduced, Lloyd George had announced a cut in the British naval plans, and in March, 1921, Lord Lee, First Lord of the British Admiralty, declared that his government would gladly agree to parity between the British and American fleets. In unofficial talks with Adolph Ochs, publisher of the *New York Times*, Lord Lee suggested that the British might concentrate their strength in the Atlantic Ocean and leave the Pacific to the United States. Ochs transmitted this information to the American government, where it met encouraging response.

Convinced by events both in Congress and in London that he would have to act quickly if he wanted to hold the initiative, Secretary Hughes sent out notes on July 8, 1921, inquiring whether the British, French, Italian, and Japanese governments would participate in a conference on limitation of armaments to be held at Washington. By an impressive coincidence the Hughes notes left Washington only a few hours before the arrival of a British note, suggesting that President Harding sponsor an international conference to deal with both the armament problem and questions relating to the Far East.

Far Eastern Danger Spots

To understand why the naval question became linked with Pacific area problems requires a discussion of certain earlier developments. The involvement of the European powers in World War I had provided Japan with a golden opportunity to extend her influence in China—much to the alarm of the United States. It has already been noted that Japan declared war on Germany in 1914 and easily conquered both the German Pacific islands north of the equator and German properties in Kiaochow and elsewhere in the Shantung Peninsula.[3]

Determined to consolidate her position, Japan confronted Chinese President Yuan Shih-k'ai in January, 1915, with the notorious Twenty-one Demands. Group 1 required China to consent to whatever disposition Japan might make of the former German leasehold at the end of the war and to grant additional railway and commercial privileges in Shantung; group 2 strengthened Japan's special position in Manchuria and Inner Mongolia; group 3 demanded exclusive mining and industrial privileges in the Yangtse Valley; group 4 required a Chinese promise not to cede or lease coastal areas to any foreign power; group 5 requested general Japanese supervision over Chinese political and social institutions. Although Japan tried to keep her demands secret, China allowed the news to leak out and sought British and American help in resisting Japanese pressure. The American Minister to China, Paul Reinsch, strongly sympathized with Yuan Shih-k'ai and gave him unofficial advice on how to deal with the situation. Secretary of State Bryan was more cautious. He strongly condemned the group 5 demands, which would have transformed China into a Japanese protectorate, but on the Shantung, Manchuria, and Mongolia issues he conceded that "territorial contiguity creates special relations between Japan and these districts." In a subsequent

[3] See chap. 28.

note Bryan took a somewhat stronger stand, laying down a principle later developed into Stimson's famous nonrecognition doctrine.[4] On May 11, 1915, he warned that the United States [5]

> cannot recognize any agreement or undertaking which has been entered into or which may be entered into between the Governments of Japan and China, impairing the treaty rights of the United States and its citizens in China, the political or territorial integrity of the Republic of China, or the international policy relative to China commonly known as the Open Door policy.

Although Great Britain also opposed the more drastic aspects of the Twenty-one Demands, China was obliged to deal with the crisis as best she could. To bluntly say no would have been suicidal, so Yuan resorted to quibbling and delay. In the end, Japan agreed to postpone the most controversial group 5 demands for future discussion and eased up on some of the others. Even so, however, the treaties signed by China and Japan in May, 1915, were loaded with substantial benefits to Japan both in Shantung and elsewhere.

Japanese diplomacy was now directed to getting the other great powers to assent to her recent gains. This she was able to do in secret treaties with England, France, and Russia, but the United States created difficulties. Japan's best opportunity to win over the Wilson administration came after the American declaration of war against Germany. Visiting Washington as the head of the Japanese war mission, Viscount Kikujiro Ishii arranged with the American Secretary of State the Lansing-Ishii agreement of November 2, 1917. This carefully worded document recognized that "territorial propinquity creates special relations between countries," and that Japan had "special interests in China, particularly in the part to which her possessions are contiguous." On the other hand, the two governments solemnly disclaimed any purpose "to infringe in any way the independence or territorial integrity of China," and they declared that "they always adhere to the principle of the so-called 'open-door' or equal opportunity for commerce and industry in China." Did the Lansing-Ishii agreement give American consent to Japan's domination of Shantung and Manchuria, or did it bind Japan to respect Chinese sovereignty and the Open Door? Each side hoped for the best, but each side proceeded much as though the document had never been signed. Japan tightened her tentacles on helpless China, and the United States girded itself for Wilson's brave but futile effort to reopen the Shantung question at the Paris Peace Conference.

[4] See chap. 30.
[5] *Papers Relating to the Foreign Relations of the United States, 1915* (Washington: Government Printing Office, 1924), p. 146.

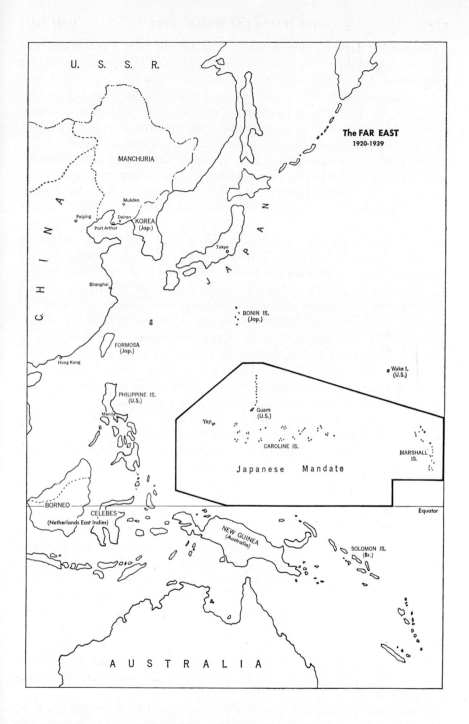

The FAR EAST
1920-1939

U. S. S. R.

MANCHURIA

CHINA

Mukden
Peiping
Dairen
Port Arthur
KOREA (Jap.)

JAPAN

Tokyo

Shanghai

BONIN IS. (Jap.)

FORMOSA (Jap.)

Hong Kong

Wake I. (U.S.)

PHILIPPINE IS. (U.S.)

Manila

Yap

Guam (U.S.)

CAROLINE IS.

MARSHALL IS.

Japanese Mandate

BORNEO
CELEBES
(Netherlands East Indies)

Equator

NEW GUINEA (Australia)

SOLOMON IS. (Br.)

AUSTRALIA

To combat Japanese imperialism under World War I conditions was difficult, yet Wilson did what he could. He even swallowed his earlier distrust of dollar diplomacy to ask American bankers to join a new consortium so that China would not be dependent solely upon Japan for loans. At the Paris Peace Conference and afterwards Wilson protested against the allocation of a Japanese mandate over the tiny island of Yap, of great importance as a base for trans-Pacific cable lines.

The United States also looked with grave suspicion upon Japanese activities in Siberia. Following the Bolshevik Revolution and the Soviet government's separate peace treaty with Germany, Allied armies had entered Russian territory at various points, ostensibly to prevent military supplies from falling into German hands. In the case of Siberia, there was the additional argument that 50,000 Czech prisoners of war might be evacuated through Vladivostok to strengthen the Allied armies on the western front. Rather than let Japan intervene in Siberia alone, Wilson arranged for an American force to go in too. Small British and French detachments also landed in Siberia, where they cooperated with the Japanese in helping the anti-Communist regime of Admiral Kolchak. Although Wilson extended some financial assistance to Kolchak, he ordered American General William S. Graves to avoid active participation in the Russian civil war. After the Kolchak regime collapsed in January, 1920, the United States withdrew its troops from Siberia, hoping that Japan would do the same. But Japan stayed on for two years more, thereby intensifying American suspicion that Japan was trying to dominate not only China but eastern Siberia as well.

The United States disliked the Anglo-Japanese alliance because it encouraged Japan in her ambitious policies and hampered Anglo-American countermeasures to hold Japanese imperialism in check. There was the additional fear that, in case of war between Japan and the United States, Britain might go to Japan's assistance, even though both British and Japanese spokesmen tried to reassure the United States on this point.

Canada, which had troubles of her own with Japan over the immigration question, also disliked the Anglo-Japanese alliance. Indeed, at a British Commonwealth conference in June, 1921, the Canadian Prime Minister protested so strongly against renewal of the alliance that the British government was forced to consider how it might end the partnership without antagonizing Japan. This was the situation that had impelled Lord Curzon, the British Foreign Secretary, to sound out the American government on the possibility of a conference on the Far East just at the time Secretary Hughes was initiating his own movement for a disarmament conference.

Since tension in the Far East was closely related to the naval question, Hughes readily agreed to broaden his original proposal to include this subject. China was invited to participate, as were also Belgium, Portugal, and the Netherlands. Hughes kept a firm hand on the preliminary arrangements, bluntly rejecting a British suggestion that the Washington meeting be preceded by one in London, where the British dominions could be heard on the Far Eastern problem. Unhappy at the thought that the conference might pass judgment on her recent conduct, Japan tried to limit the agenda, but Hughes would make only minor concessions. After two weeks of delay, Japan finally accepted the conference invitation.

The Washington Conference

The Conference on Limitation of Armament finally opened at Washington on November 12, 1921. The American delegation, carefully chosen to avoid such criticism as had been made of Wilson's peace commission, consisted of Secretary Hughes, Elihu Root, Senator Lodge, and Democratic Senator Oscar Underwood. Among the leaders representing other nations were Arthur Balfour of Great Britain, Baron Kato of Japan, Premier Aristide Briand of France, and Carlo Schanzer of Italy.

After a welcoming address by President Harding, Secretary Hughes was elected permanent chairman. When the dignified American rose to make his acceptance speech, the other delegates expected no more than the usual platitudes. Hughes, however, had decided that his best chance of achieving solid results lay in making a bold proposal at the very start of the conference. Spending a minimum of time on pleasantries, he plunged speedily into serious matters. "We can no longer content ourselves," he said, "with investigations, with statistics, with reports, with the circumlocution of inquiry.... Power and responsibility are here and the world awaits a practical program which shall at once be put into execution." This program, Hughes argued, should be based upon four principles: (1) that all capital shipbuilding programs, either actual or projected, should be abandoned; (2) that certain older ships should also be scrapped; (3) that naval ratios for the future should be based upon existing naval strength; and (4) that smaller naval vessels should be curtailed proportionately with capital ships. As evidence of good faith, the United States would sacrifice 15 battleships then under construction and 15 older ones, if Great Britain and Japan would scrap 19 and 17 respectively. "Thus, under this plan," Hughes summed up, "there would be immediately destroyed, of the navies of the three Powers, 66 capital fighting ships, built and building, with a total tonnage of 1,878,043." This reduction should be followed by a ten-year holiday on new construction.

As Hughes named the mighty ships that would be scrapped under his plan, admirals in the audience listened with amazement. This whiskered American, according to one English commentator, was sinking with a single speech more British battleships than "all the admirals of the world had destroyed in a cycle of centuries." Despite the dismay of professional sea dogs, Hughes's speech was received with fervent applause by its conference audience and was acclaimed by most of the world's newspapers.

Impressed by this global reaction, Balfour and Kato speedily accepted the Hughes plan in principle, although they reserved the right to object to specific points. In the Japanese case this haggling over details reached serious proportions. Kato asserted that the existing ratio among the United States, Great Britain, and Japan was not actually 5:5:3, as Hughes had assumed, but 10:10:7. When Hughes refused to budge on this point, Kato offered to accept the 5:5:3 ratio if the United States and Britain would agree not to increase their fortifications in the Pacific. A solution along this line was eventually worked out, but another Japanese objection caused more trouble. One of the ships proposed for scrapping was the *Mutsu*, a recently completed battleship for which Japanese school children had contributed their pennies and in which the entire nation took great pride. Since Japan refused to sacrifice the *Mutsu*, Britain and the United States insisted on keeping certain ships of their own to maintain the agreed ratio.

Annoyed because Britain, the United States, and Japan had proceeded this far before bringing France and Italy into the discussions, the French delegates would not submit tamely to the 1.75 ratio that Hughes suggested for them. Indeed, the American assumption that the French and Italian navies should be of equal size wounded French national pride so deeply that Franco-American relations felt the chill for years. In the end, the French accepted the designated ratio for battleships and aircraft carriers, but not for submarines. This refusal doomed Hughes's hope for a treaty that would extend to all types of naval craft.

By the Five-Power Naval Treaty, signed February 6, 1922, the signatories promised to limit their battleships and aircraft carriers to a ratio of approximately 5:5:3:1.75:1.75.[6] Except for a few specified exceptions they were to build no new battleships or aircraft carriers for ten years, and then only to replace twenty-year-old vessels. No battleships were to be constructed over 35,000 tons; no aircraft carriers of over 27,000 tons; no other ships of over 10,000 tons. The United States, the British Empire,

---

[6] The actual tonnages specified in the treaty were:

	Capital Ships	Aircraft Carriers
United States	525,000	135,000
British Empire	525,000	135,000
Japan	315,000	81,000
France	175,000	60,000
Italy	175,000	60,000

and Japan further agreed to maintain the *status quo* on Pacific fortifications with certain exceptions.[7] The treaty was to run until December 31, 1936.

Meantime, Balfour was looking for a way to end the Anglo-Japanese alliance without injuring Japanese pride. He suggested, with ready Japanese approval, that the alliance be broadened to include the United States. To this, Hughes had two objections: no such treaty could get past the Senate; and a tripartite partnership might be dominated by Britain and Japan. Hughes suggested, therefore, that France be brought in as a fourth member and that the obligations be watered down to a mere promise to respect each other's possessions and to confer in case of controversy. The Four-Power Treaty, signed December 13, 1921, accordingly bound the parties "to respect their rights in relation to their insular possessions and insular dominions in the region of the Pacific Ocean." In case of any controversy among the signatories over these rights, they were to meet in a conference "to which the whole subject will be referred for consideration and adjustment." Should their rights be threatened by some nonsignatory nation, the four powers should "communicate with one another fully and frankly in order to arrive at an understanding as to the most efficient measures to be taken. . . ." What did these words mean? American isolationists charged that they constituted a sinister alliance, but this was absurd. Much more accurate was the explanation that the Four-Power Treaty "had substituted a four-power agreement to talk for a two-power agreement to fight." Whether talk would suffice to keep peace remained to be seen.

Still a third major treaty emerged from the Washington Conference. Four principles suggested by Balfour as a basis for international policy toward China provided the core of what became the Nine-Power Treaty, signed February 6, 1922. This agreement, in the drafting of which Elihu Root played a key part, committed the signatories, among other things, (1) to respect the sovereignty, independence, and territorial integrity of China; (2) to provide the fullest opportunity for China to develop for herself an effective, stable government; (3) to maintain the Open Door, that is, equal opportunity for commerce and industry for all nations throughout China; and (4) to refrain from taking advantage of conditions in China to seek special rights or privileges.[8]

The American delegation was delighted with this agreement giving

---

[7] The ban on new fortifications did not apply to American islands off the West Coast, the Panama Canal Zone, and Alaska, nor to Hawaii. It did apply to the Philippines, Guam, and the Aleutians. Japan excluded her home islands; the British Empire excluded islands adjacent to Canada, Australia, and New Zealand.

[8] Nations signing the Nine-power Treaty were the United States, the British Empire, Japan, France, Italy, China, Belgium, Portugal, and the Netherlands.

international support to principles which John Hay and his successors had been preaching for more than twenty years, but which had never been formally accepted by the other powers. The moral victory was indeed great, yet the pledge to respect Chinese rights was based merely on self-restraint. No commitment was made to go to China's aid were these rights threatened. As in the Four-Power Treaty, the only promise was to confer in case of emergency—not to act, but to talk.

The Japanese delegates accepted the Nine-Power Treaty, but they did not always agree with the other delegates about how these principles applied to specific Far Eastern situations. The Shantung issue, so recently in controversy at the Paris Peace Conference, required particularly delicate negotiations between the Japanese and the Chinese. In the end, Japan agree to evacuate her troops from the province and return political control to the Chinese, retaining only certain economic concessions. This was a substantial victory for China, although not the complete Japanese withdrawal the Chinese had been demanding. In Manchuria, the Japanese insisted on retaining all the special interests they had accumulated since 1905. Raising the issue of Siberia, Hughes drew from the Japanese a pledge to respect Russian territorial integrity and to withdraw their troops in the near future.[9]

Shortly after the Washington Conference, Hughes rounded out his achievements by signing a treaty (February 11, 1922) under which Japan promised to grant American citizens cable, radio, and residential rights equal to those enjoyed by her own subjects on Yap, in return for American consent to Japan's mandate over the Pacific islands north of the equator.[10]

World public opinion, except for a few dissenting voices, acclaimed the Washington Conference as a great victory for the cause of peace. The *New York Herald* considered it "much the greatest" conference of all time, while the *Baltimore Sun* praised a "stupendous success—the results epochal." Senators Borah and Johnson, along with other incorrigible isolationists, tried to defeat the Four-Power Treaty, but, after the adoption of a reservation underlining what was obvious anyway—that the agreement involved "no commitment to armed force, no alliance, no obligation to join in any defense"—the treaty was approved by a vote of 67 to 27. The other treaties were virtually unopposed, the vote on the Naval Limitation Treaty being 74 to 1.

Despite this overwhelming approval, a few shrewd observers registered dissenting opinions. Unimpressed by Japanese concessions, Elmer Davis,

[9] Japan evacuated Siberia in October, 1922, but did not withdraw from northern Sakhalin until 1925.
[10] As another late dividend from the conference, the controversial Lansing-Ishii agreement was abrogated by mutual consent in December, 1922.

of the *New York Times*, pointed out that Japan had really retained "her strategic supremacy, military and political, on the continent of Asia." In fact, thought Davis, "Japan wins most; she wins Eastern Asia, to do with according to her pleasure. And on the wisdom and good sense of future Japanese policy on the continent of Asia must depend the ultimate estimate of the result of the Washington Conference." American naval experts could see that the 5:5:3 ratio did not actually hamper Japan. Because of the long distances involved, Japan's smaller navy controlled the western Pacific. Moreover, by banning new naval fortifications, the treaty ruled out the development of strong naval bases in Guam and the Philippines that might have equalized the American position.

Many years later, when the United States had to fight its way grimly across the western Pacific during World War II, these criticisms of the Washington Conference appeared particularly pertinent. Students began to describe the conference as a diplomatic defeat for the United States rather than a victory. Such criticisms, however, are not entirely fair, since they ignore the actual situation that Secretary Hughes faced in 1921. Well before the conference began, Congress had started to gamble on a policy of economy, denying to both Wilson and Harding the naval appropriations necessary to give the United States naval supremacy or to fortify the Pacific possessions. The alternatives that Hughes faced were not preponderant sea power versus disarmament, but rather unilateral American limitation versus limitation by international agreement. Given the situation as it actually existed, Hughes's diplomatic achievement still remains impressive.

Japanese Exclusion

Regardless of whether Japan or the United States had profited most, the Washington Conference had greatly aided Japanese-American friendship. Baron Shidehara, first as Japanese Ambassador to the United States and then as Foreign Minister, followed a policy of cooperation and tried to resist the growth of aggressive militarism. The friendship policy was strengthened by generous American aid in 1923, when Tokyo suffered a major earthquake.

These more cordial relations received a rude blow in 1924, when Congress totally excluded Oriental immigration. By so doing, the legislators trampled underfoot the Gentleman's Agreement under which Japan herself had barred the migration of Japanese laborers since 1907.[11]

Although Japan had carried out her agreement in good faith and Japanese immigration had been drastically curbed, certain loopholes in the plan had developed. Since nonlaborers and relatives of Japanese already in

[11] See chap. 23.

the United States were not covered, a substantial influx of Japanese women was possible—greatly to the alarm of California exclusionists, because the entrance of females provided the American Japanese with wives and led to the growth of Japanese families. Particularly resented was the arrival of wives whom the Japanese laborers had selected by photograph and married by proxy. In 1920 the Japanese government agreed to deny passports to these "picture brides," but this concession did not quiet the growing American demand for drastic restriction.

Just as the earlier exclusion movement had led to the San Francisco school controversy, so the new agitation resulted in discriminatory legislation against the Japanese residents of the West Coast. Despite a hurried trip to California in 1913, Secretary Bryan was unable to dissuade the state legislature from prohibiting aliens ineligible for citizenship from owning land and limiting alien land leases to three-year terms. By a referendum in 1920, the California voters prohibited Japanese leasing completely. The American Ambassador in Tokyo warned in 1921 of the "deep feeling of resentment" created by the California action. Japanese sensitivity was further wounded by Supreme Court decisions of 1922 and 1923, ruling that Japanese were ineligible for naturalization and upholding the constitutionality of both California and Washington bans on alien landholding.

Reading the warning signs, the State Department sought to reach a new understanding with Japan to tighten the old Gentleman's Agreement, but this proved impossible in the face of a rising demand for action, led by the American Legion and the American Federation of Labor, that would exclude the Japanese as drastically as the Chinese had been barred by earlier legislation.[12]

The demand for Japanese exclusion became part of a larger movement for curtailment of all immigration. Prejudice against the "new immigration"—that from southern and eastern Europe—led to increasingly severe restrictions, first in the literacy test imposed in 1917, then in the emergency acts of 1921 and 1922. This antiforeign drive reached its peak in the Johnson Bill of 1924, which proposed to restrict all non-Western Hemisphere immigration to 2 per cent of the foreign-born of any particular nationality, according to the census of 1890. Additionally, the measure would exclude aliens ineligible for citizenship, that is, Japanese, Chinese, and all other Orientals. Dismayed at this threat to his friendship policy, Secretary Hughes tried to get the exclusion provision stricken from the bill. If a quota for Japan were assigned on the same basis as for any other country, he argued, not more than 250 Japanese could enter in any year and these few would be nonlaborers, since the Gentleman's Agreement would continue in effect.

[12] See chap. 18.

In order to get a Japanese interpretation of the Gentleman's Agreement into congressional hands, Hughes invited Ambassador Masanao Hanihara to prepare a memorandum on the matter. Hanihara's resulting note was for the most part discreet and conciliatory, but it contained one unfortunate phrase, in which the Ambassador alluded to "the grave consequences" that exclusion would bring upon "the otherwise happy and mutually advantageous relations between our two countries." Senator Lodge and other nationalists denounced these words as a "veiled threat" to the United States. By a vote of 76 to 2 the Senate crushed an administration amendment to cut out the exclusion provision. The Johnson Bill as a whole then passed both houses by large majorities and was reluctantly signed by President Coolidge, who approved the general quota plan but regretted the unnecessary affront to Japan.

This American repudiation of the Gentleman's Agreement and the lumping together of Japanese, Chinese, and Koreans as undesirables provoked angry Japanese demonstrations. Crowds picketed the American Embassy in Tokyo and threatened American lives and property. "No nation retaining the least trace of its self-respect," said the newspaper *Jiji,* "could tolerate the discrimination aimed at by the Johnson bill."

In a letter to a friend, Secretary Hughes wrote: "It is a sorry business and I am greatly depressed. It has undone the work of the Washington Conference and implanted the seeds of an antagonism which are sure to bear fruit in the future.... The question is not one of war but of the substitution of antagonism for cooperation in the Far East, with all that that involves. Our friends in the Senate have in a few minutes spoiled the work of years and done a lasting injury to our common country." [13]

The World Court

Although reconciled to the impossibility of bringing the United States into the League of Nations, Hughes strongly hoped for American participation in the Permanent Court of International Justice, founded in 1920. Popularly known as the World Court, this tribunal was largely American in inspiration.

An earlier chapter [14] related the efforts of the American delegation at the Second Hague Conference of 1907 to achieve Secretary of State Elihu Root's goal of a permanent international court. The conference drafted a promising plan, but could not agree upon how the judges should be elected. In 1920, the League of Nations Council invited a committee of distinguished jurists to formulate a new project. Upon President Wilson's suggestion, Root was appointed to this group. Root soon convinced the

[13] Pusey, *Charles Evans Hughes,* vol. II, p. 516.
[14] See chap. 26.

others to use the draft plan of 1907 as the basis of the Court Statute. The method of electing judges, which had seemed so difficult, was easily resolved by making it a joint responsibility of the Council and the Assembly of the League of Nations, thus protecting the interests of both large and small states.

With a few modifications the jurists' plan was accepted by the League in December, 1920. Although the League was to elect the fifteen judges and pay the expenses, the World Court was to be open to non-League members on a basis of equality with members. The Court's jurisdiction was restricted to cases voluntarily referred to it, except where countries might agree to compulsory jurisdiction. The League elected John Bassett Moore, eminent American authority on international law, as one of the first judges.[15]

Although Harding was somewhat reluctant to take even this cautious step into unfamiliar waters, Hughes strongly urged American membership in the Court. "I am profoundly convinced," he wrote the President, "that this Government, under appropriate conditions, should become a party to the convention establishing the Court and should contribute its fair share of the expense of maintenance." He spelled out four appropriate reservations: (1) acceptance of the Court Statute should not involve the country in any legal relation to the League; (2) the United States should participate on a basis of equality when the League Council and Assembly elected judges; (3) the United States should pay its fair share of Court expenses, as determined by Congress; and (4) the Court Statute should not be amended without American consent.

Thus prodded, Harding submitted the World Court protocol to the Senate in February, 1923. In a brief but earnest plea for approval, he appealed to that body to make "effective all the fine things which have been said by us in favor of such an agency of advanced civilization." But no speedy action upon such a project was to be expected from a Senate Foreign Relations Committee still under the chairmanship of Henry Cabot Lodge. Investigation and delay prevented a vote in this congressional session. On August 2, 1923, Harding died, but Calvin Coolidge, his successor, renewed the World Court recommendation in his first message to Congress the following December.

Many of the tactics employed against the Treaty of Versailles were repeated in the fight over the World Court. While Coolidge and Hughes clung to a mild reservationist position, such opponents as Borah and Johnson again took an irreconcilable role, denouncing the Court as a mere tool of the League of Nations. Lodge characteristically professed to favor a court, but not this one; he called for a new Hague Conference to

[15] Later American judges on the World Court included Charles Evans Hughes, Frank B. Kellogg, and Manley O. Hudson.

draw up a different plan. In November, 1924, the great obstructionist died, but prospects for the World Court were by no means improved, since the new chairman of the Foreign Relations Committee was the isolationist Borah.

On March 3, 1925, the House of Representatives, by a vote of 302 to 28, expressed its "cordial approval" of the Court and its "earnest desire" that the United States adhere to the protocol. But this resolution failed to move the laggard Senate committee into action. Not until January 27, 1926, did the Senate finally get an opportunity to vote on the measure. Approval was given by a vote of 76 to 17, but adherence was made conditional upon written acceptance by the other countries of five reservations —the original four proposed by Hughes, plus a drastic fifth, which denied to the Court the right "to entertain any request for an advisory opinion touching any dispute or question in which the United States has or claims an interest," unless the United States gave its consent.[16]

Confronted by the American reservations, the League Council asked the United States to discuss the matter at a special conference of World Court members, but Secretary of State Frank B. Kellogg, who had succeeded Hughes in March, 1925, declined the invitation. The American reservations, Kellogg asserted, were "plain and unequivocal and, according to their terms, they must be accepted by the exchange of notes between the United States and each one of the forty-eight states signatory to the Statute of the Permanent Court before the United States can become a party and sign the Protocol." Despite this uncompromising stand, reflecting Kellogg's nervous fear of Senate criticism, the World Court members met in conference at Geneva in September, 1926. They decided to accept, with minor changes, the first four American reservations, but considered the fifth condition, demanding for the United States a veto over requests for advisory opinions, to be a more serious matter. Even on this point, however, the conference was conciliatory, offering to give to any American objection "the same force and effect as attaches to a vote ... by a Member of the League of Nations either in the Assembly or in the Council."

Elihu Root once remarked that President Coolidge "did not have an international hair on his head." Although this was probably an exaggeration, Coolidge and Kellogg made no response to the Geneva proposal and were content to allow the World Court issue to gather dust until Root visited Geneva in 1929 to serve on a new advisory committee on World Court matters. Now eighty-four years of age, the veteran American diplomat made a final effort to achieve American membership in the Court by working out a plan under which the League would inform the

[16] President Coolidge had suggested a more moderate reservation on the advisory opinion issue.

United States of any requests for advisory opinions. If the United States claimed an interest, there should be no reference to the World Court until the American government had had an opportunity to negotiate with the League, and an American objection should have the same weight as a vote by a League member. And, finally, if on this issue or any other the United States were dissatisfied with the World Court, she would retain the right to withdraw.

Once again hopes were kindled as the World Court members on one side and Herbert Hoover, now President, on the other, accepted the Root formula. But the Senate isolationists remained as suspicious as ever. Hoover, bedeviled with other problems, did not push the matter, nor did Franklin Roosevelt during his first two years in the White House. Not until 1935 did the Senate finally vote again on American membership in the Court, safeguarded with all the earlier reservations and with the Root formula. Supported by the popular New Deal President and by many influential sectors of public opinion, the project now seemed sure to win, but shrill cries of alarm from the Hearst press and from the influential radio priest, Father Charles Coughlin, brought so many last-minute telegrams into Washington that the more timid senators were afraid to vote for the Court. Although 52 favored American membership and only 36 opposed it, the vote fell 7 short of the necessary two-thirds.

Nothing better illustrates American irresponsibility in international affairs during these years than this melancholy story. American in origin, the World Court idea had had the support of every President from William McKinley to Franklin Roosevelt. Since no case involving the United States could have been referred to the Court without American consent, and since the members of the Court were willing to concede almost everything the United States demanded in the matter of advisory opinions, the nation would certainly have retained all its cherished sovereignty. Yet a determined minority, hating anything remotely connected with the League of Nations, succeeded in postponing action on the Court proposal for many years, then in loading American adherence with such conditions that difficulties arose with other nations, and finally, when these obstacles were removed, in defeating the project just the same.

The Pact of Paris

Divided though they were over United States membership in the League of Nations or the World Court, almost all Americans professed to hate war and love peace. Plans that seemed to contribute to peace and yet did not involve the nation in international organizations usually attracted overwhelming support. Such had been the response to the Washington Conference treaties; such was the reception of the movement to outlaw war that culminated in the Pact of Paris of 1928.

The phrase "outlawry of war" had been coined by Salmon O. Levinson, a wealthy Chicago corporation lawyer who had organized the American Committee for the Outlawry of War in 1921. Convinced that permanent peace would never be achieved until war had been declared illegal, Levinson's plan called for three steps: (1) an international treaty under which each nation would declare war to be an international crime and promise to punish its own warmongers, (2) codification of international law, and (3) a world court independent of the League of Nations. Levinson had made many influential converts, including the philosopher John Dewey; the editor of the *Christian Century*, Dr. Charles Clayton Morrison; and the famous reformer-lecturer Colonel Raymond Robbins. After some initial hesitation, Senator Borah also adopted Levinson's plan, which he incorporated in a resolution introduced into the Senate in 1923 and reintroduced in subsequent sessions.

Meanwhile, another branch of the American peace movement had been advocating the "renunciation of war as an instrument of national policy." Between this idea and the "outlawry of war" there was little difference visible to the naked eye, yet there was a wide divergence of viewpoint among the groups backing the two slogans. Whereas the Levinson plan appealed particularly to anti-League Americans, the renunciation of war drew its support from pro-Leaguers like Columbia President Nicholas Murray Butler and Professor James T. Shotwell, both powerful in the heavily endowed Carnegie Endowment for International Peace. Impressed by European efforts to supplement the League Covenant with new agreements condemning aggression, Butler and Shotwell hoped to bring the United States into closer cooperation with these projects.

In 1926 Butler had an opportunity to discuss his ideas with Aristide Briand, the French Foreign Minister. In a similar conversation the next year Shotwell made a specific suggestion: Why should not Briand demonstrate his love of peace by proposing a Franco-American treaty renouncing war? Briand not only agreed to do so, but allowed the American professor to draft a message to the American people. Dated April 6, 1927, the tenth anniversary of America's entry into World War I, Briand's appeal stressed the traditional friendship between the two nations and their mutual love of peace. "If there were any need between these two great democracies to testify more convincingly in favor of peace and to present to the peoples a more solemn example," Briand wrote, "France would be ready publicly to subscribe, with the United States, to any mutual engagement tending, as between those two countries to 'outlaw war,' to use an American expression."

Why had Briand adopted Shotwell's suggestion? The latter insisted that the French statesman had no other motive than a sincere desire for peace; but other scholars have doubted this, pointing out several other possible considerations. For one thing, Franco-American relations had been poor since the Washington Conference. Dissatisfied with her treatment as a second-class naval power, France had refused to attend a second conference at Geneva in 1927.[17] Because of this and because of France's insistence upon retaining a strong army, Americans had sharply condemned French militarism; the French, on the other hand, complained of American failure to understand France's need to protect herself against a possible German war of revenge. France and the United States had also been bickering over the war debt problem. By a friendly gesture, Briand probably hoped to smooth over these points of friction and restore the comradely relations of World War I days. France, moreover, was at just this time trying to increase her security through a network of alliances with such countries as Belgium, Poland, Czechoslovakia, Rumania, and Yugoslavia. Even though a Franco-American alliance was impossible, might not a treaty renouncing war between the two countries have the effect of a "negative alliance," assuring that the United States would at least remain neutral in any future conflict involving France?

The original Briand message, buried on the inside pages of American newspapers, attracted remarkably little attention. But on April 25, 1927, almost three weeks later, the *New York Times* published a letter from President Butler, which praised the French suggestion and asked the pointed question: "M. Briand, speaking the voice and expressing the soul of France, has called out to us across the ocean. What answer is he to hear?" The Butler letter had the effect of a bugle call in stirring peace zealots to fervent activity.

The first reaction of President Coolidge and Secretary of State Kellogg to this public clamor was one of annoyance. They thought Briand should have addressed his suggestion to them instead of to the American people, and they resented the amateur diplomacy of Butler and Shotwell. But the administration was soon forced out of its negative attitude as the campaign for an antiwar treaty mounted both in America and in Europe, where the tireless Levinson happened to be touring at this time. By an even more fortuitous circumstance, Charles A. Lindbergh landed at Le Bourget airfield on May 21, 1927, after the first nonstop flight from New York to Paris. The ecstatic welcome showered upon "Lucky Lindy" seemed to demonstrate the reality of Franco-American friendship and created a favorable climate for Briand's next move. In June the French Foreign Minister communicated to the American government his draft for a "Pact of Perpetual Friendship."

[17] See chap. 30.

Having received an official proposal, Coolidge and Kellogg could no longer ignore the outlawry issue, but they could and did stall for time. The State Department was convinced that the United States should not enter into any treaty with France seeming to establish a special tie between the two countries. Yet the public demand for an antiwar treaty was too strong to permit an abrupt rejection of the idea. On December 28, 1927, after six months of delay, Secretary Kellogg finally sent his reply. It had occurred to him, he wrote, that the two governments, instead of contenting themselves with a bilateral declaration, "might make a more signal contribution to world peace by joining in an effort to obtain the adherence of all the principal powers of the world to a declaration renouncing war as an instrument of national policy." He invited the French government to cooperate with the American in sponsoring such a multilateral treaty.

Who deserves the credit for finding this happy avenue of escape? Senator Borah was sure he had originated the idea of substituting the multilateral for the bilateral treaty; Secretary Kellogg was equally convinced the inspiration had been his own; certain subordinate State Department officials also claimed the glory. Perhaps they were all correct. Given the problem, the solution was sufficiently obvious so that it probably occurred to a number of people at about the same time.

The American note resulted in a remarkable reversal of roles. Hitherto the ardent suitor wooing the coy Kellogg, Briand suddenly became the reluctant maiden himself, while the American statesman impatiently pressed for action. Kellogg now aspired to go down in history as the diplomat who had led the way to the international outlawry of war. But for Briand there were serious difficulties. Relying upon the League of Nations and her various alliances for security against possible German aggression, France felt it impossible to renounce war unconditionally, nor did she want her allies to do so. Briand spun out the negotiations so long that Germany, Britain, and Japan had all indicated acceptance of the Kellogg project before France finally did so.

Actually all the replies were hedged with interpretations. Germany reserved the right of self-defense; Great Britain retained its freedom of action in "certain regions of the world" where she had special interests; France made it clear she would still abide by the League Covenant and the Locarno Treaty.[18] And Secretary Kellogg himself interpreted the proposed treaty as reserving the right of self-defense. "Every nation," he explained in a note of April 23, 1928, "is free at all times and regardless of treaty provisions to defend its territory from attack or invasion and it

[18] By the Locarno Treaty of 1925, Germany, France, and Belgium agreed to respect their common borders. In case of violation, Great Britain and Italy were obligated to assist the victim of aggression.

alone is competent to decide whether circumstances require recourse to war in self-defense." Since belligerent nations almost invariably claim to be acting in self-defense, it is obvious that the proposed treaty was never quite what it seemed to eager peace lovers.

Nevertheless, hopes ran high on August 27, 1928, when Kellogg, Briand, and the representatives of thirteen other nations gathered in Paris for the formal signing of the Kellogg-Briand Pact, otherwise known as the Pact of Paris. Of impressive simplicity, the treaty condemned "recourse to war for the solution of international controversies" and renounced it "as an instrument of national policy." The signatories agreed that the settlement of all disputes which might arise among them should "never be sought except by pacific means." The treaty was to remain open "for adherence by all the other Powers of the world"—an invitation promptly accepted by the Soviet Union, somewhat to the embarrassment of the United States, which had not yet recognized the Communist regime. Eventually more than sixty nations adhered to the pact.

With Senator Borah leading the fight for approval, the Pact of Paris entered the senatorial lions' den with much better prospects for coming out alive than had the Treaty of Versailles or the World Court Protocol. A nationalist faction did attempt to attach reservations, but Borah headed this off by issuing a Foreign Relations Committee report interpreting the treaty as preserving the right of self-defense and not obligating the United States to 'take any action to punish violators. Although some senators belittled the pact as worthless, practically none of them wished to go on record as opposing a project with such impressive popular support. On January 15, 1929, the upper house gave its consent by a vote of 85 to 1.[19]

Although the Pact of Paris was obviously powerless to prevent either small conflicts like the Italo-Ethiopian War or major ones like World War II, it was not without importance in international affairs during the 1930s and 1940s. It provided grounds for American protests against acts of aggression and served as a basis for the trial and execution of Nazi and Japanese war criminals.

Secretary Kellogg rounded out his peace efforts with a series of arbitration treaties to take the place of those originally negotiated by Elihu Root twenty years before. Although supposedly broader in coverage, the new treaties still required the consent of the Senate to each particular case. Kellogg also made Bryan-type conciliation treaties with many additional countries.

By the end of the Coolidge administration, the range and limitations of the Republican peace program had become clear. The United States had taken a leading part in the renunciation of war and in the limitation

[19] The sole negative vote was cast by the anti-British Senator John J. Blaine of Wisconsin.

of naval armaments by international agreement, but it had given no support to organizations like the League of Nations or the World Court, which were endeavoring to establish effective machinery for the maintenance of world order.

Development of the Foreign Service

During the 1920s Congress recognized the need to carry still further the professionalization of the diplomatic service begun under Roosevelt and Root. Secretary Bryan's tenderness to "deserving Democrats" had demonstrated that the system still left much to the patronage seekers, while the business of the State Department had been heavily increased by World War I and its aftermath. In 1919 Congress had authorized the appointment of an under secretary to serve as the Secretary's principal lieutenant.

The Rogers Act of 1924 attempted a final rooting out of the spoils system. The old distinction between the consular and diplomatic services was now wiped out with the establishment of a single Foreign Service with all permanent officials below the rank of minister designated as Foreign Service officers. These were divided into nine classes with salaries ranging from $3,000 in class 9 to $9,000 in class 1. Although the pay was certainly not munificent—even by the standards of the day—the way was now open for public-spirited young men to choose a career in the Foreign Service. Appointments and promotions were to be based solely on merit as determined by a Foreign Service Personnel Board. When the board was accused of favoritism in some of its policies, the situation was rectified by the Moses-Linthicum Act of 1931.

Although ambassadors and ministers were still presidential appointees, the Rogers Act provided that the Secretary of State might recommend for promotion to the grade of minister Foreign Service officers who had shown special capacity. From this time on, many of the minor legations were headed by career men, but the major posts continued to go to politicians and wealthy contributors to campaign funds.

30

SHIFTS OF POLICY

During the late 1920s and early 1930s American foreign policy underwent significant revision in all three major areas of the world. In Latin America the United States was still playing the role of policeman after World War I, but this cost so much in ill will that the State Department gradually shifted toward nonintervention and friendly collaboration—pointing the way to the later "Good Neighbor" policy. In Europe the new emphasis was toward closer relations with England and more concern for the shaky European economy. The London Naval Conference of 1930 patched up a senseless quarrel that had developed during the Coolidge administration, and Hoover's moratorium of 1931 repaired some of the damage caused by earlier American action on the war debts and tariff questions. In Asia better relations with Japan nurtured by Hughes at the Washington Conference broke down under the impact of two new forces: aggressive Chinese nationalism and intensified Japanese imperialism. The Stimson Doctrine, formulated to deal with Japanese aggression in Manchuria, provided a precedent for American policy makers confronted with many similar problems both before and after World War II.

Hoover and Stimson

Although the changed direction of American policy, at least toward Latin America, had begun well before 1929, the newer trends became particularly obvious during the Hoover administration. In part, this was a result of the Great Depression; in part, it reflected the personal influence of President Hoover and his Secretary of State, Henry L. Stimson.

Unlike the inept and poorly prepared Harding and the cautious and provincial Coolidge, Herbert Hoover was a man widely experienced in world affairs. First as mining engineer and promoter in remote parts of the globe, then as administrator of Belgian and Russian relief during and after World War I, and finally as wartime Food Administrator and peace-time Secretary of Commerce, Hoover had gained expert knowledge, particularly in the field of international trade and finance. Except for Article 10, he had been a strong supporter of the League of Nations, and years later he resented the "misrepresentation and demagoguery" by which Senate opponents had brought about its defeat. Yet, if Hoover was no isolationist, there were marked limitations to his internationalism. There were many things about Europe he did not like. He had been horrified by the human and material losses of World War I and repelled by devious European diplomacy seen at close hand during the Paris Peace Conference. He disapproved of European "doctrines of paternalism and state socialism." Defining his own attitude, he later wrote: [1]

> But Europe was infested with age-old hates and fears, with their offspring of military alliances, and increasing armament. Its rival imperialisms continued as smoldering fires which were the principal source of dangerous wars. Power politics was both the consequence and the cause. I had no desire to see the United States involved. . . .

Hoover is perhaps best understood as a war-hating Quaker and a waste-hating businessman. Thus he pinned great hopes on disarmament and the renunciation of war—earlier Republican achievements he hoped to implement as widely as possible. Similarly, he favored the World Court, arbitration and conciliation treaties, and full cooperation with the League of Nations "in its non-force activities." Convinced that the Depression was largely European in origin, he hoped to lead the world to safety through international economic cooperation. When the question arose of how the United States would deal with aggression, however, Hoover instinctively drew back from any commitment requiring the use of force.

Stimson, by training a lawyer and by temperament a soldier, was a man of quite different background and inclinations. The two great influences on Stimson's life were Elihu Root, in whose office Stimson began his legal career, and Theodore Roosevelt, who appointed him a Federal district attorney in 1906. He made them his heroes throughout a distinguished career that included service as Secretary of War under Taft, artillery colonel during World War I, special trouble shooter for Coolidge in Nicaragua, and Governor General of the Philippines. Nor was his service as Secretary of State the end, for in 1940 another Roosevelt summoned him to be Secretary of War during one of the most critical periods of American history. When he finally handed in his resignation to President Truman on his seventy-eighth birthday in September, 1945, he had the unusual distinction of holding Federal commissions under four Republican and three Democratic Presidents.

[1] Reprinted by permission of the publisher from *The Memoirs of Herbert Hoover* (Copyright 1951–1954 by The Macmillan Company, New York), vol. II, p. 331.

From Root and the first Roosevelt, Stimson inherited viewpoints quite unlike those of the Quaker Hoover. He had no great faith in disarmament and believed the ability to exert force was what counted most in world affairs.

> Temperamentally Stimson and Hoover were wholly different. One was by nature and training an advocate and a fighter; the other was an organizer and planner. Mr. Hoover liked to calculate his moves as he would the building of a bridge, while Stimson preferred to choose his main objective and then charge ahead without worrying, confident that aggressive executive leadership would win followers.[2]

During the first two years of the administration, Hoover and Stimson were in substantial agreement; it was only during the last two years that they found themselves differing on many issues: war debts, the Far East, disarmament, and "foreign entanglements." Yet Stimson loyally did his best to support the positions that Hoover took.

Mexican Oil

When General Alvaro Obregón became President of Mexico in 1920, the United States withheld recognition to see how the regime would deal with old and new American claims for losses. The State Department was particularly disturbed by reports that Obregón might enforce those articles in the Mexican constitution of 1917 that annulled land grants made to foreigners under Díaz and vested in the Mexican nation subsoil rights to oil and other minerals. As a condition for recognition, Secretary Hughes wanted a treaty guaranteeing that Mexico would not confiscate American-owned properties, but Obregón would have risked overthrow had he signed such an unpopular agreement.

Conveniently, the Mexican Supreme Court pointed a way out. In a series of decisions beginning in 1921 it interpreted the law as protecting the property of oil companies that had begun drilling or performed some other "positive act" before the constitution of 1917 had been adopted. Afraid that some later court might reverse this ruling, Hughes withheld recognition, still trying to get a treaty. Finally the two governments reached a compromise in the Bucareli Agreement of 1923,[3] under which Obregón promised to respect the property rights of Americans acquired before 1917 and confirmed by positive acts.

---

[2] Reprinted by permission of the publisher from Henry L. Stimson and McGeorge Bundy, *On Active Service in Peace and War* (Copyright 1948 by Harper & Brothers, New York), p. 196.

[3] The Bucareli Agreement also set up certain mixed claims commissions, but these had only a very limited success. American claims against Mexico were finally settled by direct diplomacy in 1934.

Although the Bucareli pact was only an executive agreement, Hughes accepted it as the best solution possible under the circumstances and recognized Obregón. Indeed, a few months later the United States saved Obregón from probable overthrow by providing him with arms to use against his domestic enemies.

When Obregón was assassinated in 1924, Plutarco Calles was elected to the presidency. Although belonging to the same faction as his predecessor, Calles refused to follow the spirit of the Bucareli Agreement. Despite American protests, the Mexican Congress enacted a new petroleum code in 1925, under which Mexican ownership of subsoil resources was re-affirmed. Foreign companies could obtain permission to operate oil wells only by putting themselves under Mexican law and renouncing the protection of their home governments; even then they would be granted rights for only fifty years, not in perpetuity as under the earlier agreement.

The American Ambassador to Mexico, James R. Sheffield, strongly sympathized with the American oil companies and besieged Washington with warnings and advice. Secretary Kellogg at first firmly backed Sheffield. In June, 1925, he declared the United States would continue to support the Calles regime

> ... only so long as it protects American lives and American rights. ...
> The Government of Mexico is now on trial before the world. We have
> the greatest interest in the stability, prosperity, and independence of
> Mexico. We have been patient and realize, of course, that it takes
> time to bring about a stable Government, but we cannot countenance
> violation of her obligations and failure to protect American citizens.

Throughout 1926 the United States and Mexico continued an acrimonious controversy over the petroleum code and other issues. Although some smaller American oil companies submitted to Mexican regulation, the larger ones resisted in hopes of active intervention. Certain other groups also called for stern action against Calles. Many American Catholics were upset by Mexican anticlericalism, reflected in the nationalization of church properties and the secularization of education. The Hearst press clamored for intervention with an ardor probably not unrelated to William Randolph Hearst's extensive Mexican holdings.

Most dangerous of all was the fact that Mexico and the United States were backing opposite sides in Nicaragua. Kellogg, highly suspicious and excitable by nature, regarded Mexican shipments of arms to the Nicaraguan rebels as evidence of a sinister Bolshevik plot to gain control of the whole region. Calles, on his side, was convinced Kellogg and Sheffield were trying to provoke an incident to serve as an excuse for intervention.

Yet for all this anti-Mexican clamor, the nation as a whole had no stomach for upholding American property rights by force. Dollar diplomacy, in its cruder forms, was now highly unpopular, as was demonstrated by a Senate resolution, unanimously passed in January, 1927, which called for arbitration of outstanding Mexican-American controversies. For their part, Coolidge and Kellogg, now realizing that the aggressive Sheffield was not the man for the delicate Mexican post, replaced him in September, 1927, with Dwight Morrow, Coolidge's Amherst classmate.

Since Morrow was a partner in the Wall Street banking firm of J. P. Morgan, newspapers at first regarded the appointment with suspicion. "After Morrow come the Marines," they predicted. Happily, however, they were completely mistaken. The new Ambassador went to Mexico City determined to follow Coolidge's only instruction: "Keep us out of war with Mexico." Without a trace of the condescension Americans often showed in dealing with Latin Americans, Morrow took every occasion to demonstrate his sympathetic interest in Mexican culture and development. His mission was marked by a dramatic improvement in Mexican-American relations, culminating in the good-will trip of Charles A. Lindbergh, Morrow's future son-in-law, then at the height of his fame.

In the new atmosphere, the oil controversy was speedily adjusted. The Mexican Supreme Court ruled unconstitutional the fifty-year limitation on oil rights, and the Mexican Congress, at Calles's request, amended the petroleum code of 1925 to bring it into harmony with the Bucareli Agreement. As we shall see, the settlement of these years was not permanent, but the United States had at least demonstrated a desire to put its relations with Mexico on a more satisfactory basis. By refraining from moral preachments and threats of intervention, the nation laid the basis for genuine friendship. These better relations were easier to maintain when Mexican politics became stabilized under the strong leadership of Calles and his successors.

Marines in Nicaragua

Coolidge's troubles with Mexico were minor compared to the hornets' nest stirred up in Nicaragua. Since 1912 a small detachment of American marines had been stationed in Managua, the Nicaraguan capital, as a warning to discontented Liberals not to rebel against the Conservative clique dominating the government. In 1925, however, the American force was withdrawn in the expectation that the recent election of a coalition ticket consisting of a Conservative president and a Liberal vice president would inaugurate an era of good feelings.

Within a few months, however, this truce was broken when General Emiliano Chamorro, a Conservative, compelled the President to resign and obtained his own election to the post. As the signer of the Bryan-Chamorro Treaty and an old friend of the State Department, the general hoped for speedy recognition, but Secretary Kellogg refused to overlook the unconstitutional way in which he had come to power.

In May, 1926, the Liberals began a civil war on behalf of their leader, Vice President Juan Sacasa, who had fled the country at the time of Chamorro's coup. From the Liberal point of view, the resignation of the constitutionally elected President had made Sacasa the rightful chief executive. In an effort to halt hostilities, Coolidge sent a cruiser to the scene and attempted to mediate between the parties. At American insistence Chamorro stepped aside, but Adolfo Díaz, who succeeded him, was no more acceptable to the Liberals. A member of the same Conservative clique as Chamorro, Díaz was well remembered as an earlier tool of dollar diplomacy. Nevertheless, the United States promptly recognized him in November, 1926, and American bankers quickly arranged a loan for him.

Insisting that Díaz was a usurper, Sacasa organized in December, 1926, the "Constitutionalist government," which Mexico recognized and allowed to buy arms. President Coolidge denounced Mexican interference and defended his own support of Díaz. Some 5,000 marines were landed in the country, and the Díaz army was supplied with arms and munitions. The American force tried to avoid hostilities, but the so-called neutral zones it established seriously hampered the Liberals, commanded by General José Moncada.

In April, 1927, Coolidge sent Henry L. Stimson to Nicaragua on a fact-finding mission. Not confining himself to observation, Stimson proceeded in true Rough Rider fashion to impose a settlement on the contestants. Díaz was to continue in office until the next regularly scheduled election in 1928, when a new president was to be elected under United States supervision. In the meantime, both sides were ordered to turn over their weapons to the United States marines; those who refused would be forcibly disarmed.

On May 15, 1927, the exultant Colonel Stimson wired Washington: "The civil war in Nicaragua is now definitely ended." Unhappily this was not so, for Augusto Sandino, one of Moncada's officers, continued guerrilla warfare against Díaz. In 1928, the marines policed an election in which General Moncada was rewarded for good behavior by winning the presidency, but Sandino, denounced as a "bandit," continued to harass the regime until he was killed in 1934. Well before that time, however, the country had been largely pacified, first by the marines, and later by a new American-trained constabulary. The strife of these years cost the lives of over 100 American marines and some 4,000 Nicaraguans.

Although Stimson defended American intervention as necessary to prevent anarchy in the vicinity of the Panama Canal, the use of marines was strongly condemned both in Latin America and in the United States. Even Stimson himself finally became eager to have the marines withdrawn—a step in which President Hoover, who strongly disliked the idea of intervention, heartily concurred. A new outburst of Sandino activity in 1931, which resulted in losses of American lives and property, gave Secretary Stimson an opportunity to show his change of tactics. Instead of taking strong action, he advised the threatened Americans either to move to the coast where the Navy could protect them, or to go home, because they "must not expect American forces to be sent inland to their aid." For the United States to undertake general protection of American citizens throughout the country "would lead to difficulties and commitments which this government does not propose to undertake." Also in line with this new policy, the withdrawal of marines began in 1931 and was completed early in 1933 after the Americans had patrolled one final Nicaraguan election.

Western Hemisphere Friendship

The storm clouds hovering over American relations with Mexico and Nicaragua were in contradiction to the more favorable weather elsewhere in the Hemisphere. There Republican secretaries of state found a promising field for advancing their favorite peace formulas: conciliation, arbitration, and renunciation of war.

Secretary Hughes, with the assistance of Latin-American expert Sumner Welles, made a first move by sponsoring a conference in Washington of the Central American countries in 1923. The resulting treaties covered some of the same ground as had the similar conference of 1907: a new arbitration tribunal was established; promises not to meddle in each other's domestic politics and not to recognize illegal seizures of power were exchanged. The treaties also provided for limitation of armaments and reduction of trade barriers.

This demonstration of regional cooperation served in some respects as a model for the general Pan-American conferences at Santiago, Chile, in 1923 and at Havana in 1928. The first of these produced the Gondra Convention, a multilateral conciliation treaty patterned on the Bryan cooling-off pacts. The Havana Conference branded aggression as an international crime and codified various categories of international law. At Washington the next year a special Conference on Conciliation and Arbitration strengthened the Gondra Convention and drafted a new general arbitration treaty, which condemned war as an instrument of national policy in harmony with the Pact of Paris and provided obligatory arbitration for several kinds of dispute.

Although the United States was eager to show its peaceful intentions by ratifying such treaties, it was not yet willing to renounce completely its policeman's role. Aware that Latin-American resentment might disrupt the 1928 Pan-American Conference, President Coolidge went to Havana to make a friendly speech. The main burden of defending American policy, however, fell upon the broad shoulders of former Secretary Hughes, the chief United States delegate. A proposed resolution stating that "no State has the right to intervene in the internal affairs of another" provoked excited debate, in which Latin-American delegates bitterly denounced recent American actions in Nicaragua. By a remarkable feat of oratory Hughes won the respectful attention of a hostile audience. Although he denied that the United States wanted to dominate any American republic, he asked: "What are we to do when government breaks down and American citizens are in danger of their lives? Are we to stand by and see them butchered in the jungle because a government in circumstances which it cannot control and for which it may not be responsible can no longer afford reasonable protection?" He refused to admit that action taken under such circumstances was intervention; "I would call it," he said, "interposition of a temporary character." [4]

Whether called intervention or interposition, however, the use of American troops in Caribbean countries was encountering increasing opposition both outside and inside the United States. Although a showdown on the issue had been avoided at Havana, it was clear that the attempt to condemn intervention would be repeated at future Pan-American conferences.

Actually, the United States was moving away from the Roosevelt Corollary throughout the 1920s. In 1921, the Senate finally ratified a treaty negotiated two years earlier under which the United States paid Colombia 25 million dollars to soothe the wounds left by Roosevelt's Panama intervention of 1903. Secretary Hughes was particularly eager to restore self-government to the Dominican Republic, which had been under American military rule since 1916. After careful preparation, American forces were successfully withdrawn in 1924. When reports of Cuban corruption and unrest raised the possibility that the United States might again be compelled to take action under the Platt Amendment, Hughes helped the Cubans make the necessary reforms without military intervention.

While still Secretary of Commerce, Hoover had developed "an increasing dissatisfaction" with American policy. "I was convinced," he later wrote, "that unless we displayed an entirely different attitude we should never dispel the suspicions and fears of the 'Colossus of the North' nor win the respect of those nations." [5] Specifically, he believed the Roosevelt Corollary and dollar diplomacy played into the hands of German, Italian,

---

[4] Reprinted by permission of the publisher from Merlo J. Pusey, *Charles Evans Hughes* (Copyright 1951 by The Macmillan Company, New York), vol. II, p. 560.
[5] *Memoirs of Herbert Hoover*, vol. II, p. 210.

and British trade interests seeking to stir up antagonism between the United States and Latin America.

To dramatize his desire for better relations, Hoover asked President Coolidge for the use of a battleship to make a postelection good-will tour of Latin America in 1928. Coolidge suggested that the President-elect take a cruiser—"it would not cost so much"—but finally approved the request, battleship and all. Visiting ten countries, Hoover laid a basis for the friendly cooperation later known as the Good Neighbor policy and even anticipated the phrase in some of his speeches. "We have a desire to maintain not only the cordial relations of governments with each other," he declared, "but the relations of *good neighbors*." As one of the happiest results of his trip, Hoover was able to offer a compromise by which Peru and Chile settled the long-standing Tacna-Arica dispute.

In the early months of his Presidency, Hoover struck blows against both dollar diplomacy and the Roosevelt Corollary. "I can say at once," said the President in 1929, "that it ought not to be the policy of the United States to intervene *by force* to secure or maintain contracts between our citizens and foreign states or their citizens." In 1930, Hoover ordered the publication of the important Clark Memorandum. This document had been prepared two years earlier by Under Secretary of State J. Reuben Clark at the request of Secretary Kellogg, who wanted a careful study made of the Monroe Doctrine in the light of the newly signed Pact of Paris. Clark's most important conclusion—confirming a position earlier taken by Secretary Hughes—was that the Roosevelt Corollary was not "justified by the terms of the Monroe Doctrine, however much it may be justified by the application of the doctrine of self-preservation." The Monroe Doctrine "states a case of the United States *vs.* Europe, and not of the United States *vs.* Latin America." As for Latin America, "the Doctrine is now, and always has been, not an instrument of violence and oppression, but an unbought, freely bestowed, and wholly effective guaranty of their freedom, independence, and territorial integrity against the imperialistic designs of Europe."

The Clark Memorandum, it will be noted, did not rule out the possibility of occasional United States intervention in Latin America—indeed, it suggested that this might be justified by the right of self-preservation; but it did reject the idea that such an intervention represented an application of the Monroe Doctrine. By purging the doctrine of its big-stick connotations, the United States hoped to eradicate Latin-American hostility to its traditional policy, but this could not be done overnight. A judge of the Mexican Supreme Court declared: "For Mexico the Monroe Doctrine does not exist," and added that it was "an infantile theory, to cloak a tutelage on the part of the United States toward Latin America." And in 1932, the Argentine legislature, voting to rejoin the League of

Nations, asserted that the Monroe Doctrine was a "unilateral political declaration which in its time performed a notable service to the cause of American emancipation," but which did "not constitute a regional agreement."

Once again, however, the Hoover administration found its most effective arguments in deeds rather than words. With the marines being withdrawn from Nicaragua, there remained only the problem of Haiti to be solved. Already Hoover had laid the basis for a change there. In 1930, the Forbes Commission, sent to study the situation, had recommended giving increased responsibility to the Haitians and otherwise preparing for the end of the American occupation. Although snags developed in the negotiation of a new agreement, the problem was so nearly solved that the American intervention could be terminated a year after Hoover left the White House. As still another evidence that the United States was renouncing Wilson's attitude of moral superiority, the Hoover administration returned to a policy of recognizing *de facto* governments.

Anglo-American Rift

During the Coolidge administration the United States and Great Britain seemed to be drifting into a new naval race. The Washington Treaty, it will be remembered, halted the construction of battleships and aircraft carriers; cruisers and other craft were dealt with only to the extent of limiting their individual size and gun power. Eager to extend the Washington ratios to these other categories, Coolidge sent representatives to the Preparatory Commission sponsored by the League of Nations to pave the way for an eventual general disarmament conference. But the Preparatory Commission, which met intermittently from 1926 to 1930, proceeded with frustrating slowness. For one thing, it was attempting to deal not only with naval armaments, but with the much more complicated question of land armaments as well. For another, it was confronted with the problem of security: France was unwilling to disarm to the level imposed upon Germany in the Treaty of Versailles or to permit Germany to rearm unless the danger of future aggression could be removed.

Impatient with this procedure, Coolidge and Kellogg proposed a new five-power conference to deal directly with the naval problem. From the beginning, this project seemed ill-fated. First, France and Italy, unwilling to ignore the general security problem, refused to attend. Great Britain, the United States, and Japan did send representatives to Geneva in the summer of 1927, but the three-power conference was a miserable failure. When the United States proposed a simple extension of the 5:5:3 ratio to all categories, the British argued that mathematical parity with the American Navy would not be equivalent to strategic parity because of the far different defense requirements of the two countries. With relatively few outlying territories to protect, the United States could concentrate its strength in a limited number of heavy cruisers. On the other hand, England needed both heavy and light cruisers—the former for striking power, the latter to protect its vital trade routes and overseas territories. The Japanese watched this hopeless deadlock from the sidelines.

Who was to blame for this disappointing failure? Some criticized Coolidge and Kellogg for calling the conference without preliminary negotiations that might have uncovered points of difference and possible compromises. Others laid the responsibility on the conference personnel. No statesmen of the caliber of Hughes or Balfour attended; instead, the governments were represented almost exclusively by professional navy men, extremely tenacious of their positions and opposed to drastic cuts. And a third source of blame rested on American shipbuilding firms, which allegedly sabotaged the conference through their lobbying.

The most glaring fallacy disclosed by the Geneva fiasco was the failure of the British and American governments to think realistically about world politics. If the two countries were potential enemies, such hard bargaining made sense to prevent one nation from gaining an advantage over the other. If, on the other hand, the British Empire and the United States were much more likely to be fighting on the same side in any future war, each should have dealt sympathetically with the other's defense needs.

The failure of the Geneva Conference made necessary a reassessment of American naval requirements. Complacency and love of economy had combined to halt naval building almost completely. Between 1922 and 1930 the United States began construction of only 11 vessels in the unrestricted categories, while Great Britain was building 74, Japan 125, France 119, and Italy 82. In December, 1927, Coolidge asked congressional authorization for a five-year building program to include 26 heavy cruisers and some 26 ships in other categories. Criticism from peace organizations and a reduction in British building plans resulted in the abandonment of this ambitious program and the substitution of a bill for the construction of fifteen 10,000-ton cruisers and an aircraft carrier. This Fifteen Cruiser Bill, passed by the House in March, 1928, became the subject of bitter controversy between advocates of preparedness and the peace forces, led by Senator Borah.

In the summer and fall of 1928, Anglo-American friction on the naval question increased. An Anglo-French agreement on the position to be taken by those two countries in the Preparatory Commission annoyed the Americans because it called for limitation of heavy cruisers, but not of light ones. In an Armistice Day speech, Coolidge pointed out that when present legislation was carried out, Britain would have 68 cruisers to only 40 for the United States. "It is obvious," the President said, "that, eliminating all competition, world standards of defense require us to have more cruisers." This speech was widely criticized as provocative of trouble and singularly inappropriate for an Armistice Day occasion. The *New York Times* reported that it excited "wonder at home and doubts abroad. . . . If his aim was to make this country still more disliked and suspected in Europe, he was all too successful." The London *Daily Herald* warned: "Despite all reassuring phrases, all the elements of an Anglo-American conflict are present." And President Nicholas Murray Butler scolded the President sharply: "To insist on naval expansion now, with the ink on the Pact of Paris hardly dry would be worse than a travesty. It would be the most complete confession of national insincerity." Yet in the absence of treaty restrictions, America's growing disparity in the lighter warships was too obvious to be ignored. The Fifteen Cruiser Bill finally passed Congress and was signed by Coolidge on March 2, 1929—just two days before he left the White House.

London Naval Conference of 1930

In Hoover's inaugural address he expressed his hope that the Pact of Paris would "pave the way to greater limitation of armament, the offer of which we sincerely extend to the world." The next month Hugh Gibson, American representative at the Geneva Preparatory Commission, suggested a way out of the Anglo-American deadlock through agreement upon a "yardstick" by which the relative value of heavy and light cruisers might be measured.

The prospects for a fresh attack on the disarmament problem brightened in June, 1929, when Ramsay MacDonald became British Prime Minister in a new Labor government. Like Hoover, MacDonald hoped to use his tenure of power to make a major contribution to peace. As a Socialist, moreover, he wanted to reduce expenditures for armaments so that more money would be available for social services. Soon after he took office, he expressed a desire to go to Washington to discuss Anglo-American relations with Hoover.

The American government, although welcoming MacDonald's suggestion, decided the proposed visit would be more helpful if it came after preliminary discussions. Consequently, Charles G. Dawes, the American Ambassador, was directed to carry on negotiations directly with the Prime Minister. Despite good will on both sides, the problem was a difficult one. The preceding Conservative government had set the goal of 70 cruisers as necessary for British defense; MacDonald reduced this to 60, but even this was far from satisfactory to Hoover. Explaining the Prime Minister's predicament, Dawes cabled Washington: "To secure real cruiser reduction, MacDonald has to scrap existing cruisers while Hoover has only to scrap cruiser programs in part and then build some cruisers." [6] Under further American pressure MacDonald reduced the British minimum to 50 cruisers, 15 of these to be heavy ones with 8-inch guns and the rest lighter cruisers with 6-inch guns. He was willing for the United States to have 18 heavy cruisers and 20 lighter ones, but opposed the American demand for 21 of the 8-inch type.

Although the two governments did not completely agree, they narrowed the gap between them sufficiently to have the British government issue invitations for a new five-power naval conference. To improve its prospects, Prime Minister MacDonald made a highly successful visit to Washington early in October, 1929. The press made much of his eloquent speech to the Senate and of his trip to Hoover's camp on the Rapidan River, where the two statesmen sat on a log, discussing world affairs.

By preliminary agreement with the British, Hoover had avoided one pitfall that had beset Coolidge's Geneva Conference. By a sharp rebuke to the shipbuilding lobby he sought to forestall any sabotage from that quarter. And, finally, he sent to London a strong civilian commission, [7] not likely to be overawed by its own naval experts.

At the London Conference, which opened in January, 1930, the United States and Great Britain soon compromised their remaining differences once the Americans agreed to limit their most heavily armed cruisers —those with 8-inch guns—to 18, instead of holding out for 21, as demanded by some admirals. The Japanese required careful handling, for they were opposed to extending the Washington ratio to all categories of vessels. They agreed, however, to accept the 5:5:3 ratio for heavy cruisers, provided they were allowed a 10:10:7 ratio in light cruisers and destroyers and a 10:10:10 ratio in submarines. [8]

[6] Reprinted by permission of the Estate of Charles G. Dawes from Charles G. Dawes, *Journal as Ambassador to Great Britain* (New York: The Macmillan Company, 1939), p. 45.

[7] Secretary Stimson was chairman; there were three ambassadors: Dawes (Britain), Gibson (Belgium), and Morrow (Mexico); and two senators: David Reed, Republican of Pennsylvania, and Joseph T. Robinson, Democrat of Arkansas.

[8] The total tonnage allocations in the London Naval Treaty were:

Categories	United States	Great Britain	Japan
8-inch gun cruisers	180,000	146,800	108,400
6-inch gun cruisers	143,500	192,200	100,450
Total	323,500	339,000	208,850
Destroyers	150,000	150,000	105,500
Submarines	52,700	52,700	52,700

A slightly larger total cruiser tonnage was allocated to Great Britain because her cruiser fleet consisted primarily of smaller vessels, weaker in gun power than those of the United States and Japan.

As in earlier disarmament negotiations, it was the French who were most stubborn. Worried not only by the danger of German revival but by the growing strength of fascist Italy, they demanded either naval superiority over Italy or an adequate security treaty. Stimson knew that no American promise to aid France in case of attack could get past the Senate, but he urged an Anglo-French security treaty. When the rumbling of English opinion warned MacDonald that he too must be careful, Stimson tried to resolve the difficulty by telling the press that the United States would be happy to see French demands for security settled by the British and that a pact involving only consultative obligations might then be acceptable to the Americans.

Although an agreement to talk in case of trouble would have been a no greater commitment than the Four-Power Treaty of 1921, strong senatorial opposition to the suggestion developed at once. President Hoover himself did not favor such a pact; he believed that it would morally commit the United States to aid France were France to reduce her fleet. "Camouflaged obligations" were not part of his policy.

Since without some concession to her security France would not admit Italy to full naval parity with herself, and since Italy would not accept less, all hope for a general five-power treaty evaporated. France and Italy did sign parts of the London Naval Treaty that extended the holiday on new capital-ship construction to 1936, thus saving the expense of new construction authorized under the Washington Treaty. They also agreed to restrictions on the use of submarines in future wars. But in its more important clauses limiting cruisers, destroyers, and submarines, the London Treaty was only a three-power agreement. Moreover, since British naval requirements might be affected by the Franco-Italian naval race, the treaty included an "escalator clause," whereby a signatory feeling itself threatened by a nonsignatory's construction might build ships in excess of the London quotas. In such a case, the other signatories would also be free to build.

Hoover was well pleased with the final treaty, signed April 22, 1930. He commended it to the Senate as "an important step in disarmament and in world peace." Not least among its merits was the fact that it promised to save American taxpayers more than 500 million dollars over the next six years. The Senate gave enthusiastic approval by a vote of 58 to 9. Stimson was happy for quite different reasons. For the United States to insist upon a reduction of the British navy seemed to him "utter nonsense," but the American public demanded "parity," so this is what he gave them. Far more important, he believed, was the Conference's impact on world politics. Much of the Anglo-American irritation had been ended, thereby paving the way for closer cooperation between the two countries in all future problems.

A behind-the-scenes tussle between Hoover and Stimson over disarmament policy gained force during the next two years. Eager to champion the cause of drastic land disarmament, the President placed bold proposals before the World Disarmament Conference, which opened at Geneva in 1932. First, he called for the scrapping of all offensive weapons; when this proposal was tabled, he suggested cutting world arms by nearly one-third. Stimson opposed what he privately called these "Alice-in-Wonderland" propositions. To him armaments were less a cause than a result of international insecurity. Substantial disarmament, he thought, would be impossible until the major tensions of European politics were eased. In 1932, he raised again the idea of a consultative pact to be tied to the Pact of Paris, but Hoover was still opposed.

War Debts and Reparations

Poisoning the international atmosphere throughout the twenties was the ill will caused by American insistence on war debt payments and by Allied demands for German reparations. American refusal to admit that the two issues were related was merely evidence of national unwillingness to face unpleasant facts.

While World War I was in progress, the United States had loaned more than 7 billion dollars to seven other governments fighting Germany.[9] After the war she had supplied almost 3.3 billion dollars more for relief and reconstruction to these and other countries. In all, twenty foreign governments had borrowed some 10.3 billion dollars, on which they had promised to pay interest of 5 per cent. Most Americans believed the United States should hold its debtors to repayment in full, or at least with only minor concessions on interest rates. From the American point of view this was not unreasonable, because the United States had borrowed the money from its own citizens through Liberty Bonds bearing $4\frac{1}{4}$ per cent interest. Unlike the Allies, who had exacted territory and reparations from the defeated enemy, the United States asked nothing except to collect its just debts.

But the European debtors regarded the matter quite differently. They had borne the brunt of the war and suffered millions of casualties before the United States could put an army into the field. They therefore thought that American advances of money and supplies ought to be considered as contributions to the mutual effort. An orator in the French Chamber of Deputies put the matter eloquently: "While war still raged, statesmen in every country appealed to the common cause. Some gave their ships, some munitions, some the lives of their sons, some money, and today only those who gave money come saying to us: 'Give back what we loaned.'" As a further reason for cancellation or drastic reduc-

[9] See chap. 28.

tion, Europeans pointed out that most of the money had been spent in the United States, with consequent profit to American business. Quite apart from the moral issues, they claimed that scarcity of gold and the American tariff made it impossible for them to make substantial debt payments—and in this contention they had the support of most American economists.

Although Congress would not hear of cancellation, it did authorize the appointment of a World War Foreign Debt Commission in 1922, with power to adjust the interest rates and terms of payment. Thirteen debtor nations took advantage of this opportunity to negotiate settlements based upon supposed ability to pay. An English delegation headed by Chancellor of the Exchequer Stanley Baldwin paved the way in 1923, accepting a plan under which the interest rate was reduced to 3.3 per cent and payments were stretched over a period of sixty-two years. The French, who particularly resented American pressure, did not negotiate an agreement until 1925, and then did not ratify it until 1929.

The Americans were impressed by their own generosity in these settlements. By forgiving past interest and accepting lower rates than the original 5 per cent, they calculated they had canceled about half the debt. Individual debtors had been forgiven amounts ranging from 30 per cent for Great Britain to 80 per cent for Italy. Yet Europeans continued to complain of "Uncle Shylock," while Americans reciprocated with grumblings about the ingratitude of their wartime associates.

Meanwhile, the reparations problem had reached a crisis in 1923, when France, alleging Germany to be in default, moved her army into the industrial Ruhr Valley. In the resulting struggle, Germany stopped all reparations and undertook measures of passive resistance that crippled her industry and inflated her currency to astronomical levels. As a way out of this costly contest, the various powers accepted a suggestion originally made by Secretary Hughes for a committee of experts to rehabilitate the German economy and put reparations on a workable basis. With former American Budget Director Charles G. Dawes serving as chairman, the experts finally drafted a plan that was accepted by all parties concerned in August, 1924. This provided for evacuation of the Ruhr, resumption of German reparations payments, and an international bankers' loan to stabilize German currency.

In 1928, the reparations problem was reviewed by a second committee of experts, headed this time by Owen D. Young, an American industrialist. By the resulting Young Plan, German reparations payments were substantially reduced, and the Allies promised to terminate their occupation of the Rhineland and to release Germany from other controls in 1930. Moreover, the Allies agreed to pass on to Germany any concessions that they themselves might receive in their war debt obligations to the United

States. By this provision the still-denied relationship between reparations and war debts was made explicit.

From 1924 to 1930 a kind of international pumping system was at work. American bankers loaned money to German industry, thereby facilitating a remarkable revival of the German economy; Germany made her reparations payments punctually to the Allies; and they in turn met their war debts installments to the United States. As the money went round and round, everyone felt happy, and ugly recriminations between the various creditors and debtors died down. The danger in this situation was obvious. If American loans to Germany were halted or if the pumping system broke down at some other point, all these gains would be lost.

Adventures of the Dollar

During the post–Civil War decades, European investors had supplied much of the capital for American railroads and other kinds of development. In 1914, Europeans held about 6.75 billion dollars of American securities. During World War I, however, they had been compelled to liquidate so many of these holdings that their total American investment fell to about 2.2 billion dollars. During these same years American bankers loaned money to the Allied governments, and the total private American investment abroad climbed from 3.5 to 6.5 billion dollars.

During the decade 1919–1929, American dollars provided capital for economic development in many parts of the world. Bolivian tin, Cuban sugar, Central American bananas, Indonesian rubber, Latin-American and Iraqi oil all offered promising fields for investment. American manufacturers built branch factories in many different countries. Foreign governments like Holland, France, Belgium, Italy, and Japan offered bonds to American investors with a higher return than comparable domestic securities. By 1929, American investments abroad had climbed to a total of 15.4 billion dollars. European investments in the United States had meanwhile revived to 6.5 billion, but the net movement of capital was still outward.

American investment abroad was in many ways highly desirable, because the postwar world desperately needed capital funds, and only in the United States was the necessary surplus available. Yet the situation posed many problems for Republican statesmen. "It is not the policy of our Government," declared Secretary Hughes in 1923, "to make loans to other governments, and the needed capital if to be supplied at all, must be furnished by private organizations." Even so, however, the State Department insisted that American bankers clear with Washington before offering foreign securities for sale. This gave the Department financial leverage to support its policies. Without its recognition, no government could hope to borrow money in the United States—a weapon extremely useful in policing Latin America. Similarly, by its veto power over private bankers' loans, the State Department compelled reluctant France and Italy to make war debt agreements. Sometimes official policy took a positive form. When the Morgan firm showed some reluctance to subscribe heavily to the Dawes loan to Germany, Secretary Hughes urged it to do so. Such urging was not necessary thereafter, because Americans were soon making German securities a favorite investment. At the other extreme, the Soviet Union was punished for its refusal to recognize the debts of previous Russian regimes by a veto on all borrowing in the American market.

The new position of the United States as a creditor nation should have induced a revision of American trade policy. An excess of exports over imports had been healthy in those pre-1914 years when foreign exchange was needed to pay interest and dividends on foreign-held American securities. Now the position was reversed, and Europe needed dollars, both for war debt payments and for the interest due to private American investors. But instead of lowering trade barriers, Republican Congresses raised them in the Emergency Tariff of 1921, the Fordney-McCumber Act of 1922, and the Hawley-Smoot Act of 1930. The result was inevitable: foreign imports into the United States lagged, reaching only 4.4 billion dollars in 1929, while American exports, stimulated by new trade associations and the helpful services of Secretary Hoover's Commerce Department, rose to 5.2 billion dollars. Like so many pitfalls of the twenties, this unhealthy situation was concealed as long as American loans continued to flow overseas; but when dollars for foreign adventures disappeared after 1929, Europe's inability to pay its debts soon became obvious.

The Hoover Moratorium

As the European economy began to totter ominously during the Great Depression, one of the most obvious danger spots was Austria, whose post–World War I boundaries were too constricted for a healthy economic life. In 1931, her government sought to lessen its problems by entering a customs union with Germany, but France sternly opposed any such step as likely to lead to political union as well. The French brought financial pressure to bear by withdrawing their German and Austrian loans, and this in turn caused other foreign investors to demand payment on their short-term credits. The threatened failure of Credit Anstalt,

Austria's largest private bank, was a warning of more disasters to come unless strong measures were taken. German President Paul von Hindenburg described the situation in an appeal to President Hoover: [10]

> The economic crisis from which the whole world is suffering hits particularly hard the German nation which has been deprived of its reserves by the consequences of the war. As the developments of the last few days show, the whole world lacks confidence in the ability of the German economic system to work under the existing burdens. Large credits received by us from foreign countries have been withdrawn. Even in the course of the last few days the Reichs Bank has had to hand over to foreign countries one third of its reserves of gold and foreign currency. The inevitable consequence of these developments must be a further serious restriction of economic life and an increase in the numbers of unemployed who already amount to more than one third of the total number of industrial workers. . . .

More than most Americans, Hoover realized the catastrophe to be feared in a complete collapse of the German economy, in which so much American money had been invested. Even before Hindenburg's cry for help arrived, the President had been lining up congressional support for a bold proposal. On June 20, 1931, he issued a statement to the newspapers suggesting "the postponement during one year of all payments on inter-governmental debts, reparations and relief debts, both principal and interest." He urged such a moratorium both to promote foreign recovery and to save the American recovery, which he contended had already begun, from "retarding influences from abroad." The abnormal movement of European gold to the United States was lowering the credit stability of foreign countries. "These and other difficulties abroad diminish buying power for our exports and in a measure are the cause of our continued unemployment and continued lower prices to our farmers."

Hoover's proposal for this one-year postponement had a dramatic impact both in the United States and in Europe. Rising prices on the stock exchange and in the commodity markets testified to the belief that resolute Presidential leadership had conquered the crisis. "We cannot but wonder with the rest of the world," said the *New York Times*, "at the happy revulsion of feeling which everywhere followed." Prime Minister MacDonald praised Hoover's action as one "of great wisdom, courage and deep insight."

Only in France were there strong misgivings. Because congressmen in whom Hoover had confided had leaked information to the press, the President had felt it necessary to make his moratorium proposal public

[10] Reprinted by permission of the publisher from William S. Myers and Walter H. Newton, *The Hoover Administration: A Documented Narrative* (Copyright 1936 by Charles Scribner's Sons, New York), pp. 90–91.

without prior negotiation with the French government. This the French, extremely sensitive on the whole reparations question, regarded as a breach of courtesy. They retaliated by placing obstacles in Hoover's path. They would promise at first only to relieve Germany of the so-called conditional payments under the Young Plan; the unconditional ones would have to be made. Hoover tried to mollify the French with public statements, but at the same time warned that if France insisted on collecting partial reparations from Germany, the United States would expect war debt installments from her. On July 6, 1931, France gave way to this pressure and accepted the Hoover plan, but her delay had created a new financial crisis in Germany and undone much of the good resulting from the original Hoover gesture.

As long as private bankers throughout the world continued to withdraw their short-term credits, the German situation must inevitably grow worse. England and France suggested meeting the crisis with an Anglo-French-American governmental loan, but Hoover strongly opposed the idea. Instead, he persuaded the other powers at a London conference to accept the "standstill agreement" of July 23, 1931, under which each government undertook to obtain the cooperation of its own private banks in halting the withdrawal of short-term credits to Germany. In combination with the moratorium, this solved the immediate crisis, but nothing had yet been done to remove the roots of the trouble.

The War Debts Fiasco

In Hoover's original proposal he had stressed the moratorium's one-year character. As soon as recovery materialized, he obviously expected war debt installments to the United States to be resumed. Not only did he rule out any permanent cancellation, but he took this occasion to deny once more that war debts and reparations were connected. Reparations, he declared, were "wholly a European problem with which we have no relation."

Yet as the Depression deepened rather than lifted, it was obvious that further steps would be necessary. The only result of Premier Pierre Laval's meeting with Hoover in October, 1931, was a vague joint statement recognizing that prior to the end of the moratorium, "some agreement" regarding intergovernmental obligations might be necessary, "covering the period of business depression." Any inclination of Hoover to make major war debt concessions was held in check by Congress, which approved the moratorium in December, but only after adding a resolution opposing any reduction or cancellation of the debts.

In July, 1932, Germany's reparations obligations were virtually wiped out by an agreement with the Allies releasing her from more than 90 per cent of her payments. This Lausanne Agreement eliminated a cause of controversy that had been poisoning European relations ever since the war, but there was one hurdle that first had to be removed. By a "gentleman's agreement," Great Britain, France, Italy, and Belgium had promised each other not to ratify the Lausanne plan unless they could obtain comparable relief from their war debt payments to the United States. Even though this meant that the cost of canceling reparations and war debts would be borne largely by the American taxpayer, Secretary Stimson believed the United States ought to cooperate in a policy so hopeful for promoting peace and economic recovery. With this opinion, however, Hoover disagreed violently. "He told me," Stimson recorded in his diary, "that he entirely differed with me, in fundamentals, that we really had no common ground; that he thought that the debts to us could and should be paid; and that the European nations were all in an iniquitous combine against us." [11] The President regarded the Europeans' failure to support substantial disarmament as proof that they could pay the debts if they so wanted.

Quite apart from his own feelings about the war debts, Hoover had the domestic political situation to worry about. The presidential campaign of 1932 had already begun. The Democratic platform explicitly opposed cancellation, and politicians of both parties tried to avoid the unpopular issue. Senator Borah was one of the few bold enough to advocate forgiveness of the debts. Hoover's defeat in the election made action on the Lausanne Agreement all the more difficult. Hoover himself lacked the political prestige to gain congressional support for a policy of major concessions, and Franklin D. Roosevelt was reluctant to assume responsibility in the matter.

The outcome of the tangled situation was thoroughly unsatisfactory. In December, 1932, war debt installments again fell due. France and four other governments "deferred" payment; Great Britain and the remaining countries paid, but made clear their belief that speedy adjustments were necessary. The Roosevelt administration proved no more able than its predecessor to solve the problem. During 1933, France and an increasing number of other debtor countries made no payment at all; Britain and most of the others sent partial or "token" payments; Finland alone paid in full—thereby gaining abundant dividends in American good will. In 1934, Congress responded by passing the Johnson Debt Default Act, which prohibited the sale in the United States of the securities of any government in default or arrears on its war debts. But this attempt at coercion resulted only in halting all debt payments, token as well as full.

In 1932, Secretary Stimson had written in his diary: "The quicker we

[11] Stimson and Bundy, *On Active Service*, p. 213.

get these damn debts out of the way in some settlement, in which I hope we may be able to get some quid pro quo for our concessions, the better off we will be." [12] By 1934, the "damn debts" were out of the way, but not through any amicable settlement. Convinced that they could no longer afford to meet these troublesome installments—particularly since German reparations had ended—the European debtors simply stopped paying. America received no *quid pro quo*, even in gratitude, and American isolationists were bitter in their determination that the nation should never play the role of "Uncle Sap" again.

Rise of Chinese Nationalism

During the early twenties China was in political turmoil. No single government was able to rule the country. Local war lords controlled the provinces, with first one faction and then another dominating the old capital at Peking. The most dynamic local regime was that headed by the idealistic Sun Yat-sen at Canton. Under Sun's leadership the Kuomintang, or Chinese Nationalist party, developed a broad program for political and social reform. Unable to obtain the help that he needed elsewhere, Sun turned to the Soviet Union. Young Nationalist officers, among them Chiang Kai-shek, were sent to Moscow for military instruction, and Russian military and economic advisers served with the Kuomintang government. After Sun's death in 1925, Chiang became Nationalist leader and won a series of victories that gradually extended Kuomintang rule over most of China. In the process, however, there was a split between the left and right wings of the movement. Siding with the latter, Chiang expelled Russian advisers and harassed the radicals. Out of this situation developed the civil war between the Nationalists and the Communists, which continued to plague China for many years.

However divided in their domestic politics, the Chinese shared a growing impatience with foreign interference. Student-led strikes, boycotts, and demonstrations swept the country in protest against the unequal treaties. In the face of rising Chinese nationalism, the Coolidge administration had to choose between joint action with the Western powers to maintain the old system or an independent policy more sympathetic with Chinese aspirations. Secretary Kellogg inclined toward the latter course, but outrages against foreign lives and property when the Nationalist armies captured Nanking in March, 1927, put a severe strain on his friendly inclinations. American and British gunboats protected foreigners who had taken refuge in the Standard Oil compound, and the State Department joined with Britain, France, Italy, and Japan in a strong protest to the Kuomintang regime.

[12] *Ibid.*, p. 216.

When Chiang's reply proved unsatisfactory, the other powers wanted to use military force to back their demands, but the United States refused. Believing that the day of "gunboat diplomacy" had passed, Secretary Kellogg settled the Nanking dispute through peaceful negotiation. A few months later, in July, 1928, he signed a treaty with the Nationalist government, restoring tariff autonomy to China. Implicit in this action was recognition of the Kuomintang regime as the *de facto* government of the country. The other nations followed the American lead in conceding tariff autonomy and otherwise conciliating Chinese nationalism.

A variety of considerations underlay Kellogg's decision to offer American friendship to Chiang. One was the force of American public opinion, now highly critical of imperialism and sympathetic with the Chinese demand to be masters of their own house. Another was the military situation. In 1927 and 1928 Kuomintang armies, by their capture of both Nanking and Peking, showed themselves as clearly the strongest force in the country. To recognize Chiang was, therefore, to accept the facts of life. And, finally, the Kuomintang leader's purge of the Communists offered a convincing argument for helping him.

Having broken with Moscow, the Chinese Nationalists were eager to dislodge the Russians from the special rights they held in northern Manchuria. During the spring and summer of 1929, Chinese police raided Russian consulates, arrested alleged Russian spies, and seized control of the telephone and telegraph system of the Chinese Eastern Railroad, which had been placed under joint Chinese-Russian management in 1924. The Soviet government retaliated with an ultimatum demanding release of arrested Russian railroad employees and an immediate conference on the whole controversy. With both sides breaking off diplomatic relations and mobilizing troops, a Russo-Chinese war might easily have begun at any moment.

Secretary Stimson, eager to transform the Pact of Paris from a pious pronouncement to a positive force for peace, reminded both China and Russia of their obligation to settle their dispute peacefully. Although both replied with assurances that they had no warlike intentions, this apparent victory for American policy was soon negated by developments in Manchuria. Sino-Russian negotiations broke down, armed clashes along the border became frequent, and finally in November, 1929, a Soviet army invaded Manchuria and forced the local Chinese commander to sue for peace.

On December 2, 1929, Secretary Stimson made a final attempt to mobilize world public opinion upon this Far Eastern situation. In identic notes, Great Britain, France, Italy, and the United States reminded Russia and China once again of their Pact of Paris obligations and appealed to them to desist from the use of force. The outcome was thoroughly unsatisfactory. Soviet Foreign Commissar Maksim Litvinov accused Stimson of favoring the Chinese by intervening while Sino-Russian negotiations were in progress. The Paris treaty, he said, did not "give any single State or group of States the function of protector of this pact." Furthermore, he could not forbear "expressing amazement that the Government of the United States, which by its own will has no official relations with the Soviet, deems it possible to apply to it with advice and counsel." Not strong enough to resist further, China promised to respect Russian treaty rights.

The ineffectiveness of the Paris Pact in this test reflected not only its lack of teeth, but the unreality of its definitions. Both China and Russia claimed to be acting in self-defense: China was trying to reassert sovereignty over its own territory; Russia was insisting upon its treaty rights.

Japan Grabs Manchuria

The Sino-Russian showdown over Manchuria was only a prelude to the more serious struggle between China and Japan. Although in the past Manchuria had been dominated by its own war lords and was often little more than nominally part of China, the victorious Chinese Nationalists hoped for a different future, in which this sparsely settled region might serve the same purpose as had the Western frontier for land-hungry Americans. By migration and the construction of competing railroads, the Chinese planned to combat the special position Japan had enjoyed since the Russo-Japanese War. This Chinese ambition ran head-long into the Japanese determination not only to hold onto what they already had won in Manchuria, but to develop new economic opportunities for the benefit of their own overcrowded country. Japan's desire to strengthen her position on the continent of Asia was linked to her fear of growing Russian strength in neighboring Siberia.

Rising tension between Japan and China was evident in a succession of minor disputes and frustrating attempts at diplomacy. Then, on September 18, 1931, the Japanese army suddenly struck. Alleging that the Chinese had exploded a bomb on the line of the South Manchurian Railroad, Japanese troops moved out of the railroad zone, where they had a treaty right to be, and occupied the Manchurian city of Mukden. China immediately appealed both to the League of Nations and to the United States on the basis of the Paris Pact.

Although he sent anxious notes of inquiry to Japan, Stimson discouraged any precipitous action. He believed that the Japanese military had probably acted without orders from the civilian government and that the best chance for peace lay in relying upon the good intentions of

Baron Shidehara, the moderate Foreign Minister well known for his "friendship policy."

Confidence that the Mukden incident could be easily adjusted began to falter in October, when Japanese planes bombed the Manchurian city of Chinchow far from the railroad zone. It now appeared that Japanese nationalists were determined to dominate the whole province. Looking for some way to restrain this aggression, Stimson convinced Hoover that the United States should collaborate much more closely with the League of Nations than ever before. Prentiss Gilbert, American consul at Geneva, was directed to sit with the League Council while it considered the Manchurian problem. Thus encouraged to take a firm stand, the League reminded China and Japan of their obligations under the Paris Pact, while the United States took independent but parallel action. A League resolution demanding immediate withdrawal of Japanese troops was defeated by a Japanese veto, but one authorizing an international commission of inquiry was passed.

Meantime, Japanese forces continued in a systematic conquest of Manchuria. When Baron Shidehara tried to halt this advance, the moderate ministry to which he belonged was overthrown and the militarists gained complete control. With the capture of Chinchow on January 2, 1932, the Japanese completed their conquest of southern Manchuria.

The Stimson Nonrecognition Doctrine

On January 7, 1932, Secretary Stimson sent identic notes to China and Japan notifying them that the United States "can not admit the legality of any situation de facto nor does it intend to recognize any treaty or agreement . . . which may impair the treaty rights of the United States or its citizens in China . . . and that it does not intend to recognize any situation, treaty or agreement which may be brought about by means contrary . . . to the pact of Paris. . . ." Stimson had taken as his model Bryan's 1915 note relating to the Twenty-one Demands.[13] He invited other signatories of the Nine-Power Treaty of 1922 to send similar warnings. The reply from London was highly disappointing: Japan had promised to respect the Open Door in Manchuria, and the British were disposed to accept this pledge at face value. Actually the British were not as trusting as this seemed; fully aware of the strength of Japanese imperialism, they preferred to see it find an outlet in Manchuria rather than in Central China, where their own interests were concentrated, or in countries like Australia or India. As for the Japanese, they replied with what Stimson called "cool cheek," asserting their intention to defend the sanctity of treaties and thanking the United States for its eagerness to "support Japan's efforts."

[13] See chap. 29.

Although their military defense of Manchuria had been pathetically weak, the Chinese had injured the aggressor nation through an energetic boycott of Japanese trade. Japan undertook to punish the boycotters by occupying the great port of Shanghai. This operation, begun January 28, 1932, provoked unexpectedly stubborn Chinese resistance, which held up the invaders for more than a month. Ruthless Japanese bombing attacks and Chinese bravery gained for China much more sympathy than she had won during the Manchurian hostilities. English complacency was shaken because the new Japanese aggression was in a region where British stakes were high.

Stimson hoped to capitalize on these new factors to build a stronger front against Japanese aggression. Personally he would have welcomed the imposition of economic sanctions by the League of Nations and American cooperation in their enforcement. But Hoover strongly opposed any course that might involve the nation in war. The President did agree with his Secretary in sending naval vessels to Shanghai to protect American lives and property and in holding the fleet at Hawaii after the conclusion of its 1932 maneuvers. Stimson was eager to use poker tactics to make the Japanese think the United States might take stronger measures, but Hoover, according to Stimson, had no heart for "even the fairest kind of bluff."

Groping about for some new weapon, the Secretary turned again to England with a proposal for a joint reassertion of the principles of the Nine-Power Treaty. But five trans-Atlantic telephone calls were ineffective in convincing Sir John Simon, the British Foreign Secretary, that he should accept such a program. Stimson then put his position on record, not in a new note to Japan that would have had little impact unless supported by other nations, but in an open letter to Senator Borah, chairman of the Foreign Relations Committee. This letter, dated February 23, 1932, reviewed John Hay's China policy, the Nine-Power Treaty, and the Pact of Paris. "We see no reason," Stimson wrote, "for abandoning the enlightened principles which are embodied in these treaties. We believe that this situation would have been avoided had these covenants been faithfully observed...." Calling attention to the nonrecognition principle of his January 7 note, he appealed to other nations to support him: [14]

If a similar decision should be reached and a similar position taken by the other governments of the world, a caveat will be placed upon such action which, we believe, will effectively bar the legality hereafter of any title or right sought to be obtained by pressure or treaty violation, and which, as has been shown by history in the past, will eventually lead to the restoration to China of rights and titles of which she may be deprived.

[14] Stimson and Bundy, *On Active Service*, p. 254.

The Secretary's biographer calls the Borah letter "in many ways the most significant paper Stimson ever wrote." It was intended for "at least five unnamed addressees." It was designed "to encourage China, enlighten the American public, exhort the League, stir up the British, and warn Japan." Stimson hoped to obtain a unanimous condemnation of Japan as a necessary first step toward sanctions. Although not a member of the League, the United States could—so Stimson argued—cooperate with League sanctions as a corollary to the Pact of Paris. But Hoover feared the implications of such a policy and was unwilling to go beyond moral pressure. In this caution the President had ample company among European statesmen. No economic or military measures against Japan were forthcoming, but at least Stimson had the satisfaction of seeing his nonrecognition doctrine widely accepted.

Japan withdrew from Shanghai at the end of May, 1932, partly because of world-wide condemnation of her occupation. But in Manchuria she persisted doggedly with her policy. A faction of pro-Japanese Man-churians were encouraged to declare the "independence" of the new state of Manchukuo under the rule of Henry Pu-yi, one-time Emperor of China. With this puppet regime Japan made treaties confirming all the privileges hitherto sought from the Chinese.

Meanwhile, the League wheels were slowly turning. The Lytton Commission,[15] sent to inquire into the situation, made an exhaustive report in October, 1932. Although it found some basis for Japanese grievances against China, it concluded that the Manchurian independence movement was a thoroughly synthetic Japanese product. It recommended a moderate program based upon Manchurian autonomy under Chinese sovereignty with recognition of Japan's special interests. After Japan rejected a settle-ment along these lines, the League Assembly finally voted on February 24, 1933, a strong resolution of censure against Japan and recommended that member states not recognize Manchukuo as either a *de facto* or a *de jure* government. The United States gave "general endorsement" to the Assembly resolution the following day. Japan took its final step of defiance by withdrawing from League membership.

The Manchurian affair gave grim warning of the new age of violence now beginning in world affairs. First Japan, then Germany and Italy, and finally Russia were to demonstrate their rejection of the *status quo* and their determination to extend their boundaries and influence. Against this rising flood of aggression, neither the Wilsonian League of Nations nor the Republican peace treaties offered any effective barrier.

[15] So-named for Lord Lytton, its chairman. The American expert, General Frank McCoy, served as a member.

31

GOOD NEIGHBORS—AND BAD

The first inauguration of President Franklin D. Roosevelt on March 4, 1933, took place amidst troublesome times at home and abroad. The domestic picture was anything but bright, for the Depression had not been conquered, and indeed most of the nation's banks had closed their doors. Millions of persons were unemployed, and business activity was at a low ebb. The international scene was similarly dark. Trade was falling off rapidly, and the more it declined, the more difficult it became for debtor nations to meet their obligations. Diplomatically there were thunderclouds gathering over both Europe and Asia. Germany, recently come under the control of Adolf Hitler, was chafing under the ignominy of the Treaty of Versailles, while Italy, dominated by Benito Mussolini, was looking forward to the restoration of an empire. Japan, having just thrown down the gauntlet before the League of Nations and the United States, was giving evidence of further aggression.

The American people, fearful lest these events portend another world conflagration, reverted to isolationism. War must be averted at all costs. This might be done by insulating both the country and the Western Hemisphere against the kinds of involvement believed responsible for bringing the United States into World War I.

Although the new President did profess belief in international cooperation and tried to ease world tensions, he generally went along with the isolationism of both Congress and the American people. Not until late 1937, when the New Deal had a firm foundation at home, did he assume the leadership among the peace-loving nations in attempting to thwart the aggressions of Germany and Japan.

Platform and Inaugural Promises

Despite the tense world situation, the Democratic platform of 1932 devoted most of its attention to domestic issues. Relegated to a secondary position were the planks dealing with international affairs: advocacy of "an international monetary conference called on the invitation of our government to consider the rehabilitation of silver and other questions"; the consummation of "reciprocal tariff agreements with other nations, and an international economic conference designed to restore international trade and facilitate exchange"; the formulation of "a firm foreign policy" that would promote "peace with all the world," arbitration of all disputes, "no interference in the internal affairs of other nations," "the sanctity of treaties" (especially the Paris Pact), and reduction of armaments by international agreement. There were, however, two planks tending toward isolationism: the desire to promote "the spirit of the Monroe Doctrine" and determined opposition to cancellation of the World War I debts owed the United States.

In the ensuing election in November, 1932, the voters cast their ballots overwhelmingly in favor of Franklin Roosevelt and his New Deal for the forgotten man. International issues played an insignificant role in the outcome. And Roosevelt's first inaugural address on March 4, 1933, was devoted almost entirely to glowing promises of a better United States. Indeed, he said that his major task was to establish "a sound national economy. I favor as a practical policy the putting of first things first." Yet the new President did announce his foreign policy formula:

> In the field of world policy I would dedicate this nation to the policy of the good neighbor—the neighbor who resolutely respects himself and, because he does so, respects the rights of others—the neighbor who respects his obligations and respects the sanctity of his agreements in and with the world of neighbors.

The London Economic Conference

Despite the emphasis on domestic recovery, an international problem of major importance immediately faced the Roosevelt administration—the world economic crisis. Trade among nations had fallen off more than 60 per cent in the preceding three years. One important cause was the economic nationalism expressed in the form of high tariff walls modeled after the Hawley-Smoot Tariff. As trade declined, debtor countries found it increasingly difficult to obtain the amounts necessary to take care of their World War I financial obligations. Inflationary experiments with national currencies likewise contributed to the economic upheaval because of the resulting difficulties in international exchange.

The stage had already been set to deal with these and other interrelated matters when the Lausanne Conference,[1] as one of its last actions, suggested that the League of Nations call a conference of nations—

[1] See chap. 30.

including the nonmember United States—to discuss means of improving the depressing situation. President Hoover immediately went on record as favoring American participation, as did also the Democratic platform of 1932. In August, an organizing committee and a preparatory committee of experts were set up, with the United States being represented on each, to draw up the agenda. It was during the course of these preliminary discussions that the United States insisted that the war debts question, the closely associated reparations problem, and the matter of tariff rates be excluded from the issues to be taken up. Although the representatives of other countries realized that the banned issues were closely tied up with the international economic crisis, they grudgingly accepted these prohibitions because American cooperation was essential to any satisfactory outcome.

Following Roosevelt's inauguration in March, 1933, every effort was made to ensure success for the forthcoming conference. In late April and early May the new President held a series of informal meetings with Prime Minister Ramsay MacDonald, Premier Édouard Herriot of France, Finance Minister Guido Jung of Italy, Doctor Hjalmar Schacht of Germany, and representatives of seven other countries to effect cooperative plans. Also on May 16, Roosevelt, in an appeal to the nations of the world, called for support of the meeting which "must establish order in place of the present chaos by a stabilization of currencies, by freeing the flow of world trade, and by international action to raise price levels." He believed that such "wise and considered international action" could well "supplement individual domestic programs for economic recovery." The heads of fifty-four other countries pledged their "best joint efforts" to make the conference a success.

The World Monetary and Economic Conference opened with high hopes at London on June 12, 1933.[2] Unfortunately, the welcoming address of Prime Minister MacDonald contained a tactless reference to war debts, which, he said, "must be dealt with before every obstacle to general recovery has been removed, and it must be taken up without delay by the nations concerned." The spokesmen of several other European countries voiced similar views. When the contents of these speeches were transmitted across the Atlantic, there was immediate criticism. Senator Hiram Johnson was particularly annoyed, accusing the British "not only of bad manners, but poor sportsmanship."

Despite this inauspicious start, the delegates began wrestling with the problem of currency stabilization, regarded as the *sine qua non* for the

---

[2] The American delegation, headed by Secretary of State Cordell Hull, included Senators James Couzens of Michigan and Key Pittman of Nevada and Representatives S. D. McReynolds of Tennessee, James Cox of Ohio, and Ralph Morrison of Texas.

revival of international trade. As long as there was no fixed relative value among the American dollar, the British pound, and the French franc, for example, trade among those countries was certain to be handicapped. The gold countries—France, Italy, Belgium, Switzerland, and the Netherlands—wanted currency to be stabilized on a gold base. To them this was the only sound way to restore world prices; currency depreciation would provide only "artificial" and temporary alleviation. They fully expected support from the United States; had not Roosevelt recently announced that he and Italian Finance Minister Jung "are in agreement that a fixed measure of exchange values must be reestablished in the world and we believe that this measure must be gold"? Although currently off the gold standard, Britain was divided on what course to follow. Many of her leading businessmen favored the return to gold as the best means of effecting prompt stabilization; others feared that such a policy would damage the British export position. The British delegation realized, however, that they must follow the course of the United States.

Therefore the British and Americans joined forces to draw up a preliminary plan to present to the rest of the conferees. Under this draft the pound and the dollar were to be stabilized at their current levels, and then it was expected that the gold countries would fall in line.

But the formal presentation of the Anglo-American solution necessarily had to await President Roosevelt's approval—and that approval never came. Suspension of the gold standard in March had been followed by a rise in the domestic price level, which the administration wanted to see continued. Roosevelt decided that a premature stabilization might jeopardize domestic recovery, and he charged the gold bloc with selfishness in attempting to force their wishes upon the majority. He also accused them of trying to sabotage the whole purpose of the conference by saying in effect that if the United States did not go along with a gold currency base, they would take no immediate action on the other agenda items.

The ultimate "bombshell," as Roosevelt subsequently called it, was his telegram to the American delegation on July 3:

> I would regard it as a catastrophe amounting to a world tragedy if the great Conference of Nations, called to bring about a more real and permanent financial stability and a greater prosperity to the masses of all Nations, should, in advance of any serious effort to consider these broader problems, allow itself to be diverted by the proposal of a purely artificial and temporary experiment effecting the monetary exchange of a few Nations only.

And with this message, to all intents and purposes the London Economic Conference came to an end. The general feeling was that without currency stabilization the other causes contributing to the world's economic ills could not be adequately considered. The blame for the failure of the conference was laid at the door of the United States, with the result that Roosevelt's profession about being a good neighbor in a world of neighbors was looked upon with skepticism. The spirit of the early New Deal was obviously one of economic nationalism.

The Johnson Debt Default Act

The troublesome matter of war debts had arisen again when the London Economic Conference was only three days old. Since there was no opportunity of discussing them at the meeting because of the United States prohibition, France and the other countries which had defaulted six months before again failed to meet their installments, Britain and most of the others continued to make token payments, while Finland was the only debtor to pay her obligation in full. Of the 143.6 million dollars due on June 15, 1933, only 11.3 million was paid. Although President Roosevelt refused to declare the token payers in default, he stated that any reconsideration of the debt problem was a congressional matter.

Congress, however, refused to heed the pleas of the European debtors for a lowering of their financial obligations. In line with majority American opinion, the legislators scoffed at European warnings that continued payment would ruin their economies. Congressmen pointed out that those nations could always find money for armaments, so why should it be so difficult to meet their semiannual installments? Another factor in the adamant position of Congress was its primary interest in the domestic economy. Failure to receive money from across the Atlantic might seriously weaken the efforts of the New Deal to promote national recovery.

It was in this spirit that Congress passed a measure indicative of growing isolationism—the Johnson Debt Default Act of April 13, 1934. This law prohibited loans to any country in arrears or in default of its World War I obligations and banned any future sales of its securities in the American market.

Instead of forcing the debtors to meet their installments, the Johnson Act caused even the token payers to default when the next payments became due on June 15, 1934. To the European nations, this act was another indication of United States failure to cooperate in alleviating the world economic situation, for it not only precluded the possibility of loans to those countries in dire straits, but also denied them any opportunity to negotiate a reduction of their debts. It had the more serious fault of discouraging Britain and France from taking a firm stand against

Hitler and Mussolini, since the door had been kicked shut to possible financial support from the United States.

The World Court Rejected

Another example of the isolationist trend was the senatorial action in reply to President Roosevelt's message of January 16, 1935:

> I hope that at an early date the Senate will advise and consent to the adherence of the United States [to the World Court].
>
> I urge that the Senate's consent be given in such form as not to defeat or to delay the objective of adherence.
>
> The sovereignty of the United States will be in no way diminished or jeopardized by such action. At this period in international relationships, when every act is of moment to the future of world peace, the United States has an opportunity once more to throw its weight into the scale in favor of peace.

The Senate had already opened debate on the issue two days before. The advocates of adherence were highly optimistic because of the initial public support and also because a newspaper poll of the Senate had indicated that two-thirds of the members apparently would vote in favor. But the optimists failed to take into consideration the strength of such isolationist senators as Huey Long, Borah, and Johnson, or of the influence of Father Charles Coughlin and the Hearst press. Father Coughlin appealed to his radio audience and the Hearst newspapers to their readers to send telegraph messages of protest to the upper house, and at least 200,000 did so.

Thus when the measure was brought to a vote on January 29, a sufficient number of senators had been so swayed by the avalanche of messages that United States adherence to the World Court was defeated.[3] Immediately Hiram Johnson happily announced that the upper house had "averted a serious danger to our beloved republic."

Failure of Arms Limitation

On the other hand, the United States had reason to find fault with European lack of cooperation. The Geneva Conference for the Reduction and Limitation of Armaments, which had temporarily disbanded in July, 1932, reconvened in February, 1933, to consider a series of proposals drawn up in the interim. During the first weeks of the new session, however, the deadlock continued. Prime Minister MacDonald sought to break it with a formula which allocated conscription quotas to each European country, including Germany. There was to be a ceiling placed

---

[3] The vote was 52 in favor, 36 against—7 less than the essential two-thirds.

on heavy ordnance and military planes. Finally, to safeguard France, much concerned about German rearmament, the signatories of the Paris Pact should promise to see that the foregoing terms were thoroughly adhered to. In general, the MacDonald proposals were well received except by Germany, which wanted to be allowed greater military strength—a demand that found no favor among the other delegations. Thereupon she announced her determination to rebuild her armed forces under any circumstances.

At this juncture, when again the meeting appeared to have reached an impasse, President Roosevelt tried to save the conference, first by conferring with representatives of several European powers and then by an open appeal to the heads of fifty-four nations. Although the replies to this were on the whole favorable, no specific action was taken on the Roosevelt suggestions. In an attempt to meet French demands for security, Norman H. Davis, recently named chairman of the United States delegation, promised that his country would not only consult with other nations in case of a threat to peace, but would refrain from taking any action tending to defeat sanctions imposed upon an aggressor state. This guarded language seemed to imply that the United States might cooperate with the League by cutting off trade with an aggressor, but the Senate Foreign Relations Committee weakened the President's offer by laying down the principle that any American embargo must be imposed against all belligerents alike. With Franco-German differences unsolved, the conference adjourned in June, 1933.

The ensuing summer did not clear the air; in fact when the conferees resumed their sessions in mid-October, the German delegates were conspicuously absent. Hitler felt that nothing could be solved by further discussion.[4] Not only did Germany withdraw from the conference, but she submitted the necessary notice for retirement from the League of Nations.

To all intents, the Geneva Conference had come to an end as far as its original objectives were concerned, even though there were sporadic sessions into early 1934. In the United States, already committed to isolationism, the failure to agree on arms limitation was further proof of Europe's incorrigible militarism.

The End of Naval Limitation

Scarcely had the Geneva Conference concluded its abortive sessions than preliminary meetings of American, Japanese, and British delegates opened in London in June, 1934, to discuss what should be taken up

[4] The United States, through Secretary Hull, had already announced that it would not be a party "to a plan for others to proceed to rearm."

at the Naval Conference scheduled for the following year. While both the British and Americans were in agreement that the existing ratios should be continued, they differed in other respects. The British wished to increase the number of cruisers, but desired a reduction in the size of capital ships and either elimination of submarines or a decrease in their number and size. The American delegates, on the other hand, favored an over-all 20 per cent reduction in the size of the respective navies. More serious was the Japanese demand for full equality with Britain and the United States. Now committed to an aggressive policy in the Far East, the Japanese would no longer tolerate the old 5:5:3 ratio. The Americans were adamant, however, in their position that the existing ratios be maintained, and the British, though at first showing signs of support for the Japanese stand, finally stood firm also. Therefore, on December 29, 1934, Japan gave the necessary two years' notice of her withdrawal from the Washington Naval Treaty of 1922 and the London agreements of 1930.

Thus when the second London Naval Conference opened a year later, the chances of success were dim. The American delegation still adhered to the existing ratios, while the Japanese continued to demand equality. When the Americans pointed out that the granting of Japanese wishes would be tantamount to recognition of the validity of Japan's recent aggression in Manchuria, the Japanese representatives angrily withdrew from the meeting. The four remaining delegations did draw up a treaty on March 25, 1936, which continued existing parities and provided for a few modest qualitative reductions. Since there were numerous "escape" clauses and Japan was no longer a party, the London Naval Treaty of 1936 was relatively worthless. Yet hoping that it was better than no agreement at all, the Senate unanimously ratified it on May 18. To increase the American Navy to safe strength, large appropriations were now made.

The failure of both arms reduction and naval limitation caused the isolationists to speed up legislation aimed at insulating the nation from the increasing world unrest.

Recognition of the Soviet Union

Diplomatic relations with Russia were still unrepaired when Franklin Roosevelt entered the White House, but the trend that had begun in the late 1920s toward American recognition of the Soviet government was gathering headway. The Russians were also showing a greater desire for international cooperation by 1933, possibly as a result of the growing strength of neighboring Germany. They had recently mended their political fences by drawing up a number of nonaggression treaties with nearby countries and trying to improve relations with England.

The first step taken by the United States to end the breach came on May 16, 1933, when President Roosevelt sent an appeal to the heads of fifty-four nations, including Russia, to cooperate in disarmament and in the ending of international economic chaos. The second step occurred at the London Economic Conference, where Maksim Litvinov, representing the Soviet Union, established a friendly accord with the American delegates. The third move came when the Reconstruction Finance Corporation approved a 4-million-dollar loan to assist American exporters in financing Russian purchases of American cotton. This action by a United States agency was not the same as official diplomatic recognition, but it was indicative of a changing administration position.

A culmination of these steps was the letter President Roosevelt sent to President Mikhail Kalinin on October 10, 1933:

> Since the beginning of my Administration, I have contemplated the desirability of an effort to end the present abnormal relations between the hundred and twenty-five million people of the United States and the hundred and sixty million people of Russia.
>
> ... The difficulties that have created this anomalous situation are serious but not, in my opinion, insoluble; and difficulties between two great Nations can be removed only by frank, friendly conversations. If you are of similar mind, I should be glad to receive any representative you may designate to explore with me personally all questions outstanding between our countries.

Kalinin's reply of a week later accepted Roosevelt's offer, and Litvinov, now the Commissar of Foreign Affairs, was named to conduct the negotiations.

After a week of conversations among Roosevelt, Hull, and Litvinov, a series of agreements was reached: the Soviet Union promised "to respect scrupulously the indisputable right of the United States to order its own life within its own jurisdiction in its own way and to refrain from interfering in any manner in the internal affairs of the United States"; it would check all organizations that were directing propaganda aimed at "bringing about by force a change in the political or social order" of the United States; American citizens resident in Russia were to be allowed the same "free exercise of liberty and conscience and religious worship" that they enjoyed at home; and they were also to be allowed the same civil rights as the citizens of the most favored nation. Finally, Roosevelt and Litvinov agreed that the debt issue should be treated at a later date, when they believed "a speedy and satisfactory solution" could be effected.

With these and lesser matters satisfactorily ironed out, President Roosevelt announced on November 16, 1933, that "the Government of the United States has decided to establish normal diplomatic relations with the Government of the Union of Soviet Socialist Republics and to exchange ambassadors." It was anticipated that restoration of diplomatic relations would lead to increased American exports to Russia, which in turn would help the United States emerge from the depression. Also behind this recognition must have been Roosevelt's wish to have a friendly Russia offset the mounting strength and aggressiveness of both Germany and Japan.

The Export-Import Bank

Immediately there were predictions that Russia would soon be purchasing at least 500 million dollars' worth of American goods, and some optimistic souls envisioned as much as a billion dollars in exports to the Soviet Union. In an attempt to speed up such anticipated buying, the first Export-Import Bank was established by the United States on February 2, 1934.[5] This institution was authorized to extend short-term credit in order to facilitate agricultural exports, long-term credit to help exporters of industrial commodities, and loans to American exporters doing business with foreign nations which did not provide their own citizens with sufficient credit exchange to meet their dollar obligations. As far as Russia was concerned, such credit and loans were dependent upon the successful settlement of the debt question.

But the expected trade boom did not materialize. The Russians not only refused to recognize the validity of the World War I obligations, but pushed embarrassing counterclaims arising out of American intervention in Russia from 1918 to 1920. The Soviet government, moreover, did not live up to its promise to curb Communist propaganda in the United States. Hopes for larger trade were given their ultimate chill by the passage of the Johnson Debt Default Act.

The Reciprocal Trade Program

In line with the Democratic platform, as well as in the belief that greater trade might improve conditions at home and abroad, President Roosevelt asked Congress on March 2, 1934, for authority "to enter into executive commercial agreements with foreign Nations." In the face of considerable opposition from those who believed that high tariffs were necessary to protect local interests or who felt that legislative powers were uncon-

[5] The second Export-Import Bank, set up a month later, was aimed at helping Cuba, and subsequently the rest of Latin America, recover economically.

stitutionally being granted to the President, the so-called Hull Trade Agreement Act was placed on the statute books on June 12.

Under this measure, Roosevelt was given authority to raise or lower the Hawley-Smoot Tariff rates up to 50 per cent in order to facilitate the negotiation of reciprocal trade agreements with other countries. Any nation discriminating against American exports was to be denied any concessions from the 1930 rates. Once an agreement was reached, the President was empowered to put it into effect by proclamation without the necessity of obtaining congressional approval.

The task of making these agreements was placed in the hands of Secretary Hull, who had been an advocate of reciprocity since 1916. He had a threefold objective: to obtain special concessions from the other party for American surplus goods; to lower the Hawley-Smoot rates on commodities needed in the United States; and to prevent undue competition with American manufactures and agricultural commodities. By such means it was hoped that both signatories would be benefited economically.

During the three-year life of the original Trade Agreement Act, Hull negotiated sixteen treaties, mainly with hemisphere countries.[6] Since the lower tariff rates were granted not only to the signatory country but to all other countries as well under the "most favored nation" principle, the effect of these treaties was to reduce the whole tariff structure. As soon as an agreement was signed, trade between the United States and the other country began to mount rapidly, sometimes as much as 40 per cent. Encouraged by this commercial improvement, Congress in 1937 extended the life of the act for another three years. Secretary Hull was thus able to broaden the scope of the trade agreements to include Great Britain and the majority of the other hemisphere republics.

The Good Neighbor

The unsettled situation in other parts of the world, especially the growth of totalitarian regimes in Europe, awakened the Roosevelt administration to the need of broadening the scope of the efforts of Coolidge and Hoover in promoting friendlier relations with the other hemisphere republics. Only through greater accord and unity might the menace of fascism and Nazism be kept from crossing the Atlantic.

Therefore, when President Roosevelt was called upon to address the governing board of the Pan American Union on April 12, 1933, he devoted a large portion of his speech to his definition of contemporary Pan-Americanism. Cogent parts of his talk were:

[6] The first agreement was with Cuba on August 24, 1934. The countries outside the hemisphere were Belgium, Finland, France, the Netherlands, Sweden, and Switzerland.

> The essential qualities of a true Pan Americanism must be the same
> as those which constitute a good neighbor. . . . Friendship among Nations
> . . . calls for constructive efforts to muster the forces of humanity in
> order that an atmosphere of close understanding and cooperation may
> be cultivated. It involves mutual obligations and responsibilities. . . . In
> this spirit the people of every Republic on our continent are coming
> to a deep understanding of the fact that the Monroe Doctrine . . . was
> and is directed at the maintenance of independence by the peoples of
> the continent. . . .

In order to ensure good neighborliness throughout the hemisphere, he
stressed the importance of having every country "abolish all unnecessary
and artificial barriers and restrictions which now hamper the healthy flow
of trade between the peoples of the American Republics."

The Roosevelt administration was not content to promote the Good
Neighbor policy by simply facilitating hemisphere commerce. It was soon
to show that the United States was desirous of and willing to cooperate
with the countries south of the Rio Grande in numerous other respects. In
promoting the hemisphere solidarity that the Good Neighbor implied,
Secretary of State Hull and Sumner Welles, his assistant, played prominent roles. Welles, through his keen knowledge of hemisphere problems,
proposed the means of achieving better relations, while Hull, through
his ability to engage in "shirt-sleeve" diplomacy, was able to persuade
the Latin Americans to accept the Good Neighbor policy.

It was at the seventh Pan-American Conference at Montevideo, Uruguay, held in December, 1933, that the United States first showed that this
policy was more than a pious wish. Perhaps the greatest achievement of
the session was the unanimous approval of the decision that "no State has
a right to intervene in the internal or external affairs of another." United
States support of this article was indicative of a shift of policy since 1928,
when the United States delegation to the Havana Conference had successfully opposed ratification of a similar proposal. And to supplement
this agreement, the delegates also provided for the establishment of a
series of commissions to investigate and possibly settle disagreements between hemisphere nations. In addition, Hull persuaded the other delegates
to use their utmost efforts to have their governments ratify the Paris Pact.
To show that these actions were not mere words, the conferees prevailed
upon Paraguay and Bolivia to cease temporarily their conflict over the
Gran Chaco.[7] It was also at this meeting that Hull set the stage for im-

[7] Friction had begun between the two countries in 1927 and had grown increasingly
worse until open war broke out in 1932. The Gran Chaco was practically a waste-
land, but a combination of nationalism and a belief that oil was there in abundance
led to this bloody conflict in which some 100,000 men were killed. A truce in 1935
was brought about through the good services of the United States, the ABC powers,
Peru, and Uruguay, but not until July, 1938, was the final peace treaty signed.

proved hemisphere commercial relations by obtaining promises of support for future reciprocal trade treaties. Finally, the delegates found time to consider means of improving cultural ties among the republics. As a result of this Montevideo meeting, President Roosevelt could say on December 28, 1933: "A better state of feeling among the neighbor Nations of North and Central and South America exists today than at any time within the memory of this generation," and for this feeling "much of the credit belongs to the Secretary of State of the United States, Cordell Hull."

The End of Intervention

Even before the conferees at Montevideo had agreed that no state had the right to intervene in the affairs of another, the United States had started to put the theory into practice. On August 7, 1933, President Roosevelt arranged an executive agreement with Stenio Vincent, President of Haiti, under which the Hoover plan would be speeded up and the last of the American marines would be withdrawn by October 1, 1934, when Haitian control of its national guard would be complete. So well did the agreement work that the withdrawal was accomplished a month and a half ahead of schedule.

The conclusion of American fiscal control was more difficult to arrange. The first step, that of naming a Haitian to collaborate with the American customs collector after January 1, 1934, did not wholly satisfy President Vincent and his people. After an exchange of visits in the spring and summer of 1934, however, the two executives worked out an arrangement whereby the Haitian government would buy from the National City Bank of New York its control of the National Bank of Haiti. This transfer was completed by the middle of 1935, and Haiti was thereby freed of dollar diplomacy.

The United States had previously acted to ensure financial stability for the island republic by concluding a reciprocal trade treaty with her. As a result, Haiti could dispose of her major export items—rum, fruit, and cocoa—in the American market at rates much lower than those of the Hawley-Smoot Tariff. Moreover, the Haitian market for American machinery and automotive equipment was opened with a similar lowering of the insular tariff wall.

Cuba presented a more complicated problem. During the late 1920s her economy had been hard hit, with sugar prices constantly falling. Accentuating this depression was the Hawley-Smoot Tariff, which levied high duties in the normal American market. In turn, hard times brought discontent with the dictatorial President, Gerardo Machado. Although he was able to suppress one revolt, he continued to sit on an uneasy throne. In June, 1933, President Roosevelt sent Sumner Welles to the island to try to mediate the political differences, but Machado refused to accept the American's solution—that of taking a leave of absence. Subsequently, the discontented Cubans called a general strike, and the army followed with a revolt that threw Machado out of office on August 12. His successor, Carlos Mendieta, suffered the same fate on September 5, leaving practical control in the hands of Fulgencio Batista and the army.

During several more months of disorder, the United States sent naval vessels to Cuban waters to protect American lives and property, but made no attempt to intervene by force. The Roosevelt administration also called upon the major countries of Latin America to work for Cuban peace. In the end, Mendieta once more became President in January, 1934, with the backing of both the army and the conservative factions.

In these troublesome times Cubans from all ranks charged that an underlying cause for the chaos was the Platt Amendment. Consequently, Welles and Mendieta drew up a treaty on May 29, under which both the Platt Amendment and the companion treaty of 1903 were abrogated by mutual consent. The upper houses of both countries promptly ratified the agreement, and President Roosevelt optimistically remarked: "By the consummation of this treaty this Government will make it clear that it not only opposes the policy of armed intervention but that it renounces those rights of intervention and interference in Cuba which have been bestowed upon it by treaty."

As in the case of Haiti, the United States came to the rescue of Cuban economy with a reciprocal trade treaty and, what was more important, through establishing a second Export-Import Bank on March 12, 1934, that provided credit for promoting trade not only with Cuba but with other countries as well.

The protectorate over Panama likewise came to an end in a series of steps beginning in October, 1933, when a conference between American and Panamanian officials resulted in a declaration that Panama would henceforth enjoy the commercial rights of a sovereign state in the Canal Zone. Further negotiations led to a treaty of March 2, 1936, under which the United States relinquished certain rights granted it in the Hay-Bunau-Varilla Treaty of 1903, especially those of intervention to protect the canal and of obtaining more land near the terminals under eminent domain. The United States also agreed that henceforth it would pay its annual rental in Panamanian currency at the preinflation rate. In turn, Panama promised to cooperate in defense of the canal. Concern over the tenseness of the world situation led American naval and military leaders to oppose the treaty vigorously, but the Senate finally ratified it in slightly amended form on July 25, 1939. Thereafter Panama, like Cuba, assumed full sovereignty.

Hemisphere solidarity was further extended by promoting closer relations between Canada and the United States, while American good neigh-borliness was extended across the Pacific in March, 1934, when Congress passed the Tydings-McDuffie Act. This measure corrected the weaknesses of the legislation of the Hoover administration as far as the Philippines were concerned and provided for a probationary period leading to ulti-mate Philippine independence.

The Buenos Aires Conference

Following the truce between Bolivia and Paraguay in the Gran Chaco War, President Roosevelt became convinced "that the moment has now arrived when the American Republics . . . should seize the altogether favorable opportunity to consider their joint responsibility . . . in guarding against the repetition" of such a disaster. Any accord among these re-publics, he believed, would also "advance the course of world peace" because it would implement "the efforts of the League of Nations and of all other existing or future peace agencies in seeking to prevent war."

Worried about the world situation, the other republics quickly ac-cepted Roosevelt's proposal for a hemisphere meeting. The general belief was that only through cooperation could the Americas be insulated against threats from abroad. The resulting Inter-American Conference for the Maintenance of Peace convened at Buenos Aires on December 1, 1936.

President Roosevelt was so anxious to have the meeting succeed that he made the long trip to the Argentine capital to deliver the opening address. He impressed the delegates with the fact that the objective was not "to form alliances, to divide the spoils of war, to partition countries, to deal with human beings as though they were pawns in the game of chance," but "to assure the continuance of the blessings of peace." Then he con-tinued:

> In the determination to live at peace among ourselves we in the Americas make it at the same time clear that we stand shoulder to shoulder in our final determination that others who, driven by war madness or land hunger, might seek to commit acts of aggression against us will find a Hemisphere wholly prepared to consult together for our mutual safety and our mutual good. . . . Each one of us has learned the glories of independence. Let each one of us learn the glories of interdependence.

The mutual fears of aggression from abroad, the general wish for peace, and the decline of suspicion toward the United States combined to make the Buenos Aires Conference a success. Eleven treaties and sixty-two reso-lutions were approved during the course of the cordial three-week session. One important convention reaffirmed existing treaties, especially those providing for settlement of differences by peaceful means; were war to break out between two hemisphere nations, the others would remain neutral. A second agreement declared that the republics would confer on the best means of safeguarding the hemisphere were its peace threatened by an internal or external war. And a third major action was to reaffirm the Montevideo declaration that "no State has the right to intervene in the internal or external affairs of another." The conferees also approved a number of significant resolutions aimed at improving economic and cultural ties.

By ratifying these agreements, particularly the one pledging hemisphere consultation to maintain peace, the United States showed a definite shift of policy. No longer was the Monroe Doctrine to be enforced by the United States alone; it had become a policy to be upheld by multilateral action.

Mexican Oil Again

The accord attained at Buenos Aires was soon threatened by a revival of the Mexican oil issue. In 1936, President Lazaro Cardenas inaugurated a Six-Year Plan of socioeconomic reforms. As part of this program, he ordered in March, 1938, the nationalization of the properties of American, British, and Dutch oil companies, valued by their owners at nearly half a billion dollars. Naturally those concerns appealed to their respective governments to intervene. On March 30, Secretary Hull, while admitting that the Mexican government had, under eminent domain, the right to expropriate, insisted that the American companies be given adequate compensation. When Mexico showed no sign of complying, the United States threatened Mexican economic stability by stopping purchases of Mexican silver at a price higher than the world market. On the other hand, despite the continued demands of the oil interests, Roosevelt avoided any direct intervention.

The combination of the silver action and Mexico's fear of more drastic steps caused her to agree in 1939 to the establishment of a joint commission of experts to fix a fair compensation for the oil companies. It was not until April, 1942, however, that a settlement was reached under which the Mexican government paid approximately 24 million dollars, in addition to the 9.6 million that it had already promised to two smaller concerns. On its part, the United States resumed the purchase of Mexican silver at an above-world-market price, cooperated in stabilizing the peso, and extended credit through the Export-Import Bank for Mexican highway construction. Mexico at the same time promised to settle American land claims to the extent of 40 million dollars.

Both governments were pleased with this solution of a long-standing controversy. By agreeing to accept the findings of the commission of experts, Mexico showed a financial stability that had been lacking in the past. The United States, despite the demands of powerful oil interests to force Mexico to pay huge sums, consistently followed the nonintervention resolutions of both Montevideo and Buenos Aires.

What Causes War?

But closer relations with Latin America were not paralleled with more intimate contacts with Europe. On the contrary, isolationism was running high during these years. No one incident but a number of interrelated factors brought on this trend. One was the appearance of a number of revisionist books that attempted to prove that World War I had been brought on by the selfish policy of virtually every European participant, and not by Germany alone. Moreover, the general feeling in the United States was that that titanic struggle had been fought in vain; certainly it had not made the world safe for democracy. The failure of the combatants to cooperate, as recently as the Geneva Conference, showed that they had not profited from World War I. Instead, political, military, and economic unrest in several parts of the world threatened to bring on another widespread conflagration.

More immediately, Americans were troubled by books and articles charging profit-hungry munitions makers with the responsibility of fomenting wars. Perhaps the article which made the greatest impact upon the American mind was "Arms and the Men," in the magazine *Fortune* for March, 1934.

So great was the furor raised by these accounts of profiteering that the Senate appointed a Munitions Investigating Committee in April, 1934, to study all "agencies in the United States engaged in the manufacture, sale, distribution, import or export of arms, munitions, or other implements of war." Furthermore, this committee was to determine whether existing legislation and treaties were sufficient to control the arms traffic and consider whether a government monopoly of the munitions industry should be established.

Under the chairmanship of Gerald Nye, an isolationist Senator from North Dakota, this committee held open hearings that lasted until 1936, when the final report was written. Based more on the biased views of the committee than on evidence revealed during the hearings, this report stated that the Departments of War and the Navy had done much to encourage sales of implements of war by American private companies to other governments; that such private firms had exerted considerable pressure on both the United States and foreign governments to go to war; that they also had attempted to fix prices for their military products; and that as a result they had made huge profits. In spite of the committee's efforts to do so, however, no concrete evidence was unearthed to prove that the lobbying and other forms of pressure by the munitions industry had in any way caused any country to go to war.

Yet much of the American public followed the hearings with avid interest and ultimately accepted the final report. Many came to believe that American participation in World War I had been a mistake and that everything possible should be done to avoid repeating that error. The stage was thereby set for subsequent congressional legislation aimed to prevent a recurrence of the incidents of 1914 to 1917 that had helped to drag the United States into a futile conflict.

Neutrality by Legislation

Much more in line with the isolationist trend than the Johnson Debt Default Act and the rejection of the World Court was a series of neutrality laws. Adding impetus to the first of these measures was the conduct of Benito Mussolini, who began rattling his saber as early as September, 1934, as the prelude to the reestablishment of the grandeur that was Rome. His objective was Ethiopia, then ruled by Haile Selassie, the Lion of Judah and the King of Kings. Although this monarch had done much to improve his impoverished nation, it was still weak militarily, having no modern equipment and being divided by feudal war lords. Mussolini, by conquering Ethiopia, would not only be able to unite his neighboring provinces of Eritrea and Somaliland, but wipe out the stain of Aduwa, where the Ethiopians had defeated an Italian army in 1896. In addition, Il Duce would be performing, so he said, a great service for Western civilization by bringing the blessings of liberty and civilization to a backward and barbarous nation alleged to be engaged in the slave trade. Moreover, the conquest would help relieve the depression in Italy, as well as provide an outlet for a rapidly increasing Italian population. Mussolini expected no trouble from his neighbors, for France was friendly and Germany was engaged in conscripting her army.

The first indication of trouble between Italy and Ethiopia reached the United States when Breckenridge Long, the Ambassador to Rome, reported to the State Department in September, 1934, that Italy was building up her war machine. In December, a border incident at Walwal between Ethiopian and Italian native troops served to make the situation more tense. Several months later Ambassador Long followed up his initial warning with accounts of round-the-clock activities in Italian war plants and of troop movements across the Mediterranean. During the spring and summer of 1935 disquieting news continued to arrive in Washington about the possibility of war.

The State Department did its best to prevent the anticipated struggle. Early in July Secretary Hull expressed to both the Ethiopians and the Italians his hope for peace, and in conversations with the British and French diplomatic representatives at Washington, stressed the need of upholding the Paris Pact. President Roosevelt added his voice to the cause of peace by declaring on August 1 that he hoped the League Council might settle the dispute.

Congress, more pessimistic about the fruits of conciliation and influenced by the early hearings of the Nye committee, showed its concern by resuming discussion of an embargo on arms.[8] If munitions makers had really been responsible for America's entrance into World War I, a ban on exports of arms would prevent future entanglements. The threat of such a prohibition might also deter other nations from resorting to war. After considerable debate and amendment, the so-called Neutrality Act of 1935 was passed on August 31. Under this measure, when the President proclaimed that a state of war existed between two or more foreign countries, an embargo on arms, munitions, and implements of war would immediately become effective. Moreover, American citizens would travel on belligerent-owned ships at their own risk.

In signing the Neutrality Act the President stated that "the purpose is wholly excellent" and that it would "to a considerable degree serve" to avoid war. He warned, however, that the embargo provision, which was to terminate in six months, needed "further and more complete consideration" because

> it is a fact that no Congress and no Executive can foresee all possible future situations. History is filled with unforeseeable situations that call for some flexibility of action. It is conceivable that situations may arise in which the wholly inflexible provisions...might have exactly the opposite effect from that which was intended. In other words, the inflexible provisions might drag us into war instead of keeping us out.

This measure had other weaknesses as well. From the isolationist point of view it would have been better to make the embargo mandatory upon the outbreak of any war instead of leaving it to the discretion of the President. Moreover, there should have been an adequate definition of implements of war included in the law instead of leaving the enumeration to the

[8] Just before leaving office, President Hoover, backed by Secretary Stimson, had proposed an arms embargo, which did not get beyond the discussion stage in Congress. Then in April, 1933, Secretary Hull had made a similar though much broader suggestion. To him a ban on exportation of arms could be effectively used by any President "to the sole end of maintaining the peace of the world and prudent regard for our national policies and national interests." The Senate Foreign Relations Committee amended the Hull plan in a way so unsatisfactory to the administration that it failed to become law.

President. From the internationalist point of view, the act's most serious fault was its inflexibility, leaving the President no discretion in distinguishing between an aggressor and his victim.

Neither the efforts of Secretary Hull, nor the threat of an embargo, nor the attempted conciliation by a divided and moribund League of Nations could stem Italy's imperialistic desires. On October 2, 1935, the invasion of Ethiopia began.

Within seventy-two hours President Roosevelt proclaimed the fact, thereby putting the Neutrality Act into effect. In addition to the embargo on implements of war and the warning to Americans that they would travel at their own risk, he announced that American citizens doing business with either belligerent likewise did so at their own risk. And with this proclamation the Wilsonian conception of neutral rights died.

The operation of the act brought some unexpected results. The failure to include on the embargo list indirect implements of war enabled American exporters, interested only in profit, to sell to Italy (Ethiopia had no money) materials such as copper, oil, and scrap iron, which were not proscribed but which could be quickly converted into war goods. The exports to Italy increased from a monthly average of $24,000 in 1934 to about $585,000 in November, 1935. President Roosevelt tried to dissuade these profiteers on October 30 with an appeal "to a comparatively small number of American citizens" who were tending to prolong the war to stop such trade. He warned that "the American Government is keeping informed as to all shipments consigned for export to both belligerents." American policy gave little encouragement to England and France to support effective League of Nations sanctions against Italy. If the League tried to stop oil shipments to the aggressor state, there was no provision in the American law to permit American cooperation. And if oil sanctions led to war, England and France could not hope to obtain either loans or arms in the United States.

Anticipating the legal termination of the embargo at the end of February, 1936, Congress began in January to debate the Pittman-McReynolds Bill, which would have extended the life of the embargo, as well as forbidden loans to belligerents and authorized the President to limit the exportation of nonprohibited war materials to "normal quantities." Neither Roosevelt nor Hull liked certain features of the bill, so used their influence to have it defeated. Instead, on February 29 the provisions of the original act were extended until May 1, 1937, plus a ban against loans and credit to the nations at war.

Meantime, the Italian armies were pushing steadily into the heart of Ethiopia in the face of a heroic but ever-weakening resistance. The capital, Addis Ababa, fell on May 5, and to all intents the conquest of Ethiopia was complete. Therefore, on June 20 President Roosevelt announced the termination of his neutrality proclamation. He believed that the embargo provisions had been effective, for although there were numerous attempts to violate them, "the combined efforts of the Departments of State, Treasury and Justice prevented the success of any attempt so far as any knowledge has come to the attention of the authorities."

The Spanish Civil War

Scarcely was this threat to world peace concluded than another menace appeared. In July, 1936, reactionary army officers, hating the liberal tendencies of the Spanish Republic, began a rebellion. This struggle between the Loyalists, as the government forces came to be known, and the rebels, under the leadership of General Francisco Franco, soon took on ideological and international aspects. From the beginning Franco received substantial aid from Nazi Germany and fascist Italy, and eventually the Loyalists received similar—though smaller—help from Communist Russia.

Public opinion in the United States was divided. About two-thirds of the people did not care what happened in Spain as long as their country was not involved in war. Slightly more than one-fifth, however, developed strong sympathies for the Loyalist cause. This element, hating fascism, organized committees to raise funds, collect clothing, and gather medical supplies for the Spanish government forces. Doctors, nurses, and thousands of military volunteers crossed the Atlantic to offer their services. On the other hand, about one-tenth of the American people, including many Catholic clergy and laity who feared the spread of communism, threw their support to the Franco side. Both groups of partisans were highly vocal in their advice on American foreign policy.

The broadening of the Spanish struggle and the vehement American partisanship worried the Roosevelt administration because the conflict was still theoretically a civil war not covered by the Neutrality Act. The only step that could be taken was a hands-off statement in early August, 1936:

> In conformity with its well-established policy of non-interference with the internal affairs of another country either in time of peace or in the event of civil strife, this Government will, of course, scrupulously refrain from any interference whatsoever in the unfortunate Spanish situation.

But while the government might maintain this policy, the exporters of implements of war saw in the Spanish conflict an opportunity for profit. At first most of them heeded the administration's admonitions against dealing in arms, but in December, 1936, some sought government export licenses to sell certain military equipment to the Loyalists.

These requests, plus continued agitation by American partisans, finally alarmed the isolationists in Congress. As a result, on January 8, 1937, President Roosevelt signed a measure—passed by Congress with only one dissenting vote—that extended the embargo provisions to both factions in the Spanish Civil War. Although the administration tried to justify its position by saying this action prevented the United States from giving aid to either contestant, actually it hurt the Loyalists. It cut them off from a potential source of supplies at a time when the Franco rebels were receiving an ever-increasing flow of war materials from Germany and Italy. Moreover, weak or not, the Loyalist government was the officially recognized one in Spain. Under international precedent, a legal government had always been entitled to import arms to cope with an internal uprising. Thus, as in the case of the Italo-Ethiopian War, the American desire for peace and neutrality superseded long-established diplomatic principles.

The Neutrality Act of 1937

As the time approached for the provisions of the existing neutrality measures to expire, the Spanish Civil War was still raging, and hostilities were threatening in other parts of Europe and in the Far East. Under the circumstances, Congress, still dominated by the isolationists, began debate on a new neutrality bill that would correct the deficiencies of the expiring laws, that would be more realistic and flexible, and that would be permanent in nature. To find the means of attaining such objectives was no easy matter, and it took long hours of discussion and compromise before agreement was finally reached on May 1, 1937.

This Neutrality Act of 1937 contained most of the mandatory features included in previous legislation: the arms embargo would become effective when the President proclaimed that a state of war, international or civil, existed; no loans could be made to belligerents; and no American vessels could carry war goods to belligerents. Now Americans were forbidden to travel on belligerent-owned ships, instead of being permitted to do so at their own risk. A ban was also placed on the arming of American merchant or passenger vessels. The most unusual feature of this act resulted from a compromise between those who believed that the sale of such items as copper, oil, and scrap iron, which could easily be converted into war goods, would help American economic recovery, and congressmen who were of the opinion that the embargo should include such materials. The result was the "cash-and-carry" clause, under which the President, at his discretion, could specify certain commodities, not direct implements of war, that might be exported only on condition that the belligerent paid cash and carried away the purchases in its own vessels.[9] Finally, the provisions of the act were not to be extended to Latin America.

While it is true that the Neutrality Act of 1937 sought to prevent practices held responsible for bringing the United States into World War I, it still contained some of the loopholes of earlier legislation. Some of its provisions tended to favor wealthy belligerents that had large merchant marines. Others helped to encourage Germany to embark on a broader policy of aggression because she was assured that her enemies would be unable to obtain direct implements of war from the United States. The act, like its predecessors, failed to make any distinction between the attacker and the attacked.

The Ludlow Amendment

Another example of the isolationist trend was the proposal by Representative Louis Ludlow of Indiana to amend the Constitution. Starting in 1934, he had regularly introduced a resolution that:

> Except in the event of an invasion of the United States or its Territorial possessions and attack upon its citizens residing therein, the authority of Congress to declare war shall not become effective until confirmed by a majority of all votes cast therein in a Nation-wide referendum. . . .

In each instance the proposed amendment had been killed in the House Judiciary Committee. Therefore in February, 1937, Ludlow started a petition to have it brought directly before the House, and by December, 1937, the requisite number of signatures had been obtained.

Speaker of the House William Bankhead, worried about possible passage of the resolution, sought the position of both President Roosevelt and Secretary Hull on the issue. On January 6, 1938, the President replied that he considered "that the proposed amendment would be impracticable in its application and incompatible with our representative form of government." Furthermore, it "would cripple any President in his conduct of our foreign relations, and it would encourage other nations to believe that they could violate American rights with impunity." And Hull was just as vehement in his opposition, saying that "from the standpoint of promoting peace and keeping this country out of war, I am unable to see either the wisdom or practicability of this proposal." Armed with these opinions, Bankhead was able to persuade the House on January 10, 1938, to turn down the amendment by a vote of 209 to 188.

A similar proposal was introduced into the upper house in February,

[9] Senator Borah, highly critical of this provision, undoubtedly voiced the opinion of many when he said of it: "We seek to avoid all risks, all dangers, but we make certain to get all the profits."

1939, by a group of Middle Western senators headed by La Follette. When both Hull and Secretary of War Harry Woodring voiced their vigorous opposition, the upper house rejected the La Follette amendment in July, 1939.

Renewed Japanese Aggression

Meantime, renewed Japanese aggression gave reason to question the whole policy of isolation. The trend toward such aggression had been apparent for several years, despite the fact that 1934 opened auspiciously for the cause of peace. On February 21, Koki Hirota, the Japanese Minister of Foreign Affairs, sent a message to Secretary Hull that "the two countries have always maintained a relationship of friendliness and cordiality . . . and that they are strengthening their relation of interdependence year after year." Under such circumstances Hirota did not doubt "that all issues pending between the two nations will be settled in a satisfactory manner." The Foreign Minister then went on to write:

> I can state with all emphasis at my command that the Japanese nation makes it its basic principle to collaborate in peace and harmony with all nations and has no intention whatever to provoke and make trouble with any power.

These conciliatory words of Hirota, however, were soon belied by the actual deeds of his country. Already Japan had announced her intention of withdrawing from the League of Nations after flouting both the League and the Pact of Paris, and she was soon to retire from the Naval Limitation Treaties. Moreover, in April, 1934—within two months after Hirota's message of friendship—Eiji Amau, Chief of the Bureau of Information and Intelligence of the Japanese Foreign Office, issued a statement regarded as a semiofficial pronouncement of his country's policy in the Far East:

> We oppose . . . any attempt on the part of China to avail herself of the influence of any other country in order to resist Japan: We also oppose any action taken by China, calculated to play one power against another. . . . Japan therefore must object to such undertakings [joint operations by foreign powers] as a matter of principle. . . .
>
> However, supplying China with war planes, building aerodromes in China and detailing military instructors or contracting a loan to provide funds for political uses would obviously tend to alienate friendly relations between Japan and China and other countries and to disturb peace and order in East Asia. Japan will oppose such projects.

In this so-called Amau Statement, Japan insisted that she was merely reiterating a long-standing policy because of the interference of Western nations in affairs of the Far East.

Despite Hirota's assertion that Amau had made this announcement without Foreign Office approval and that Japan had no intention of breaking the Nine-Power Treaty, the statement was one of the first pronouncements of what came to be known as Japan's New Order or the Greater East Asia Coprosperity Sphere. Under it, Japan would be to the Far East what the United States was to the Western Hemisphere under the Monroe Doctrine.

Secretary Hull's reply was that the relations of the United States with China, as well as with all countries, were governed "by the generally accepted principles of international law and the provisions of treaties to which the United States is a party." Under the circumstances, the United States would not countenance any interference with China such as the Amau Statement implied. Hirota continued to try to impress upon the Roosevelt administration that his government was interested in peace and had no desire to abrogate its treaty commitments, but Japan began to spend increasing amounts for her army and navy. Moreover, in 1935, her aggression was openly demonstrated by an "autonomy movement" in North China, which actually extended Japanese control over that area. American protests failed to stem the advance of the New Order.

Therefore the United States tried to obtain the support of other Western nations to check Japanese expansion, only to discover by the end of 1936 that even joint or parallel remonstrances were unavailing. For on November 25, Japan found a friend in Germany; the two countries signed the Anti-Comintern Pact, which was the beginning of the Axis partnership. Theoretically this was aimed at preventing the spread of communism; actually it meant a collaboration in aggression.

With Japan pressing her way southward into central China in 1937, open hostilities with the Chinese were inevitable. The incident that touched off the spark took place shortly before midnight on July 7, 1937, at the Marco Polo Bridge, some 10 miles west of Peiping, where shots were exchanged between Japanese troops and Chinese guards. It furnished the signal for Japan to start an all-out—though undeclared—war against China.

Trying to Aid the Victim

In an effort to stop this strife, the United States offered its good services, the League of Nations castigated Japan for defying the Nine-Power Treaty and the Paris Pact, the United States gave its unqualified backing to the League action, and both the League and the United States condemned the indiscriminate Japanese bombings of Chinese cities. None of these actions succeeded in swerving Japan from her objectives.

Despite the broadening of the Sino-Japanese struggle, President Roosevelt refused to invoke the provisions of the recently passed Neutrality

Act. His excuse was the absence of any formal declaration of war by either party; actually his position was based on his desire to help the underdog China. The President did proclaim, however, on September 14, 1937, that government-owned vessels could not carry implements of war to either belligerent and that privately owned ships would do so at their own risk.

Isolation Challenged

This refusal of President Roosevelt to invoke the Neutrality Act marked the beginning of a shift in administration policy. Until this time, the President, although criticizing some aspects of the neutrality legislation, had gone along with Congress and majority American opinion in support of isolationism.[10] By the fall of 1937, however, the major objectives of the New Deal had been enacted into law and the Supreme Court battle was over. Moreover, the international picture had grown steadily darker. Unless someone were found to lead the world forces of peace and order, the whole globe might be engulfed in the maelstrom presently localized in the Far East and parts of Europe. As President of the United States, Roosevelt was the logical leader.

The next action indicative of the President's shift came in a Chicago speech on October 5, 1937, when he announced that the progressive worsening of the world political situation was becoming a matter of "grave concern and anxiety to all the peoples and nations who wish to live in peace and amity with their neighbors." Without mentioning any by name, Roosevelt pointed out that some countries had completely disregarded the Paris Pact to bring about a "reign of terror and international lawlessness" that was spreading like an epidemic. This was his solution:

> When an epidemic of physical disease starts to spread, the community approves and joins in a quarantine of the patients in order to protect the health of the community against the spread of the disease.

Therefore he called upon the peace-loving states of the world to band together so that "nations that may be tempted to violate their agreements and the rights of others will desist from such a cause." The United States

[10] Critics of Roosevelt insist that he was really the leader of the isolationists. These critics assert that he had sufficient political strength to prevent or seriously weaken the isolationist trend had he so desired. To prove their position, they point out that Roosevelt, except for his stand on the World Court and reciprocal trade, advocated nothing between 1933 and 1936 to promote internationalism, preferring to sacrifice improved relations with Europe and Asia on the altar of domestic recovery. Supporters of the President counter these charges by declaring that he was an internationalist at heart, but accepted isolationism against his better judgment. Probably there is an element of truth in both positions.

would lead the way because "America hates war. America hopes for peace. Therefore, America actively engages in the search for peace." The quarantine speech met such a cool public response that Roosevelt realized he must go slow in his new policy of opposing aggression.

The "Panay" Incident

American hatred of war was subjected to a severe test when, on December 12, 1937, the United States gunboat *Panay* and three steamers owned by the Standard Oil Company were successively attacked by Japanese fighter and bombing planes in the Yangtze River nearly 30 miles above Nanking. The *Panay* and two of the merchantmen were sunk, with the loss of three lives and the wounding of seventy-four. To make the incident worse, all the vessels prominently displayed American flags; they were there, so the State Department insisted, "by uncontested and incontestable rights" on "legitimate and appropriate business."

The State Department, through Ambassador Grew, submitted a prompt note of protest on December 14, which demanded

> a formally recorded expression of regret, an undertaking to make complete and comprehensive indemnifications; and an assurance that definite and specific steps have been taken which will ensure that hereafter American nationals, interests and property in China will not be subjected to attack by Japanese armed forces or unlawful interference by any Japanese authorities or forces whatsoever.

Even before this note was delivered to Hirota, the Japanese realized that they had gone too far. On the same day the Foreign Minister, although insisting that the ships were mistaken for Chinese vessels, regretted "most profoundly" the casualties and damage and presented sincere apologies. He also promised that his government would pay an indemnity,[11] that strict orders had been given to prevent a recurrence of such incidents, and that the guilty would be punished.

The prompt Japanese apology prevented any possible American demand for forceful retaliation from mounting. To the isolationists, the war in the Far East was too remote to warrant a change of policy. Despite continued Japanese attacks on American property and bombings of defenseless cities in 1938, the United States confined its opposition to mere notes of protest.

Germany Returns to Power

Probably the reason for the failure of Americans to express more concern about events in the Far East was the greater worry about the grow-

[11] This was done on Apr. 22, 1938, when $2,214,007.36 was paid by Japan.

ing threat from Germany. Thanks in part to economic chaos and the wish to eradicate the ignominious stain of the Treaty of Versailles, the National Socialists or Nazis gained increasing strength in Germany as the 1930s opened, and by January, 1933, they practically dominated the country under their Fuehrer, Adolf Hitler. Space prevents more than an outline of Hitler's efforts to make Germany the dominant power in Europe. In October, 1933, Germany announced her withdrawal from the League of Nations. In 1935 she repudiated the restrictions imposed on her in the Treaty of Versailles and defied the Geneva arms limitation efforts by announcing a return to conscription. Then in 1936 the Rhineland was remilitarized, this time in open defiance of both the Versailles and Locarno treaties. In the same year Hitler paraded his anti-Communist professions in giving military assistance to Franco in the Spanish Civil War and in concluding the Anti-Comintern Pact, aimed at the Soviet Union, with Japan. The year 1937 witnessed a closer accord with Italy through the formation of the Rome-Berlin spoke of the Axis. Thus Hitler, supreme at home through purging his rivals, and with diplomatic fences mended elsewhere, was ready to fulfill the destiny of the Third Reich as originally outlined in *Mein Kampf*.

President Roosevelt indicated his grave concern about this state of affairs in a speech to Congress at the end of January, 1938. Although he insisted that the United States would continue to press for international cooperation in limiting armaments and in quarantining aggressors, it must in the meantime be ready to defend itself. Consequently he sought larger appropriations for the Army and Navy. The rising German menace did more than anything else to persuade an initially recalcitrant Congress to approve the President's request.

Neither American rearmament plans nor quarantine talks were sufficient to halt Hitler. After undermining Austria with fifth-column agents, the Nazis overran that neighbor in March, 1938, despite a three-year-old nonaggression treaty. With Roosevelt's full endorsement, Secretary Hull denounced this action and reiterated the need for a stronger United States. This strength would not be used to police the world alone, but, with the cooperation of other peace-loving states, it could attempt to deter aggressor countries from destroying "the fundamental principles of justice and morality and peace among nations." On the other hand, continued isolation and military weakness "would lay our country open to unpredictable hazards." Hull further believed that "we may seek to withdraw from participation in world affairs, but we cannot withdraw from the world itself. Isolation is not a means to security; it is a fruitful source of insecurity."

Appeasement at Munich

The German conquest of Austria left Czechoslovakia virtually surrounded by the Nazis, who now insisted that the Sudetenland, with its
majority of German-speaking people, must be turned over to the Reich.
Since Czechoslovakia had defensive alliances with both France and Russia,
the danger of war was obviously great. In any such conflict Britain too
was sure to be involved because of commitments to France.

Britain's Conservative government, headed by Prime Minister Neville
Chamberlain, was very reluctant to fight. For one thing, it realized the
weakness of British and French military preparations and feared the bombardment of London and Paris. For another, it hoped that through appeasement Germany could be wooed into better conduct, once the in-
justices of the Treaty of Versailles had been corrected. Flying twice to
Germany to confer with Hitler, Chamberlain first tried to persuade Hitler
to accept a proposal for a Czech grant of autonomy to the Sudetenland.
When the Fuehrer refused to accept anything less than annexation, Chamberlain, together with Premier Édouard Daladier of France, brought pressure to bear on Czechoslovakia to submit to the German demands. Just
when this step of appeasement appeared to be settled, complications developed over the method of transfer. Britain and France seemed ready to
fight rather than accept further humiliation, and the threat of general war
once more hung heavy over Europe.

Alarmed by this prospect, President Roosevelt personally appealed to
Hitler, Chamberlain, Daladier, and President Eduard Beneš of Czechoslovakia to try to compose their differences by peaceful means. To fail
to do so would mean the shattering of the economic and social structure
of every nation involved, as well as the destruction of "the lives of millions
of women and children." When Hitler insisted that Germany must be
allowed a free hand, Roosevelt called upon Mussolini to use his influence
to prevent the threatened hostilities. Dreading war for reasons of his own,
Mussolini did remonstrate at Berlin. As a result, a last-minute conference
of the heads of the governments of Germany, Italy, France, and Britain
was arranged at Munich on September 30. Here it was agreed that the
Sudetenland be promptly turned over to Germany in exchange for Hitler's
promise that this would end his territorial demands.

This Four-Power Accord did prevent war for the time being, but did
not bring the "peace for our time" that Chamberlain predicted. True, the
appeasement of Germany gave Britain and France a respite to prepare for
the conflict to come, but the rape of the Sudetenland caused the smaller
countries of Europe to regard those two democracies as betrayers who
could not be counted upon to support them in their struggle against Nazi

tyranny. Moreover, Russia definitely resented being excluded from this pact involving the future of Europe. The two totalitarian nations, Germany and Italy, saw in the Munich settlement a vacillating weakness of the Western democracies and were thereby encouraged to continue their aggression. Across the Atlantic, the United States shared in the responsibility for the dismemberment of Czechoslovakia; by placing peace above all else, it was apparently countenancing what Hitler had done.

The Lima Conference

Despite its acquiescence in appeasement, the United States realized that the threat of war had not been dispelled. Consequently it gladly participated in the Pan-American Conference at Lima, Peru, in November, 1938. There the delegates unanimously endorsed the Declaration of American Principles and the Declaration of Lima. The former reaffirmed the principles agreed to at both Montevideo and Buenos Aires; the latter not only upheld "continental solidarity" and the ideals "upon which the said solidarity is based," but promised that "in case the peace, security or territorial integrity of any American Republic" were threatened by external aggression, the foreign ministers of the several American states would meet to decide what cooperative steps must be taken to stem such a challenge to the hemisphere.

Thus the year 1938 closed with tensions still great in both Europe and Asia. The Roosevelt administration had awakened to the fact that neither isolation and the accompanying neutrality laws nor the efforts to quarantine aggressor nations had prevented totalitarian expansion. Obviously something more than burying the nation's head in the sand and resorting to moral speeches was needed to check the trend of events. It was not until war actually broke out in 1939, however, that Congress and the American people became wholly aware of the menace to the democratic way of life that the Axis partners posed, and two years more were needed before the realization came that force must be met with force.

32

BETWEEN PEACE AND WAR

During the first two years of World War II the American people were buffeted by two strongly felt but conflicting emotions. Detesting Hitler and his allies, they fervently hoped to thwart somehow the Axis bid for world supremacy. On the other hand, most Americans abhorred the thought of sending American boys to fight again on foreign battlefields. The strongly anti-Axis bias of majority opinion supported President Roosevelt in actions farther and farther divergent from true neutrality, yet antiwar sentiment insisted that these actions stop short of full hostilities. The policy emerging from these divergent forces—sometimes called nonbelligerency—resulted in the United States aiding nations defending themselves against Axis aggression with an increasing flow of war materials and with "neutrality patrols" and embargoes administered so as to hamper the totalitarian enemy. In the end, of course, the nation became involved in direct hostilities, but under circumstances that killed—for the time being at least—the isolationist opposition.

The Totalitarian Threat

Many Americans who had shared Neville Chamberlain's faith in the Munich settlement suffered a painful disillusionment just six months later when Nazi troops marched into Prague in March, 1939, and seized all of Czechoslovakia. Not only was this a flagrant violation of the Munich Agreement, but it destroyed the optimistic assumption that Hitler's ambition was limited to bringing all Germans together under one government. The Fuehrer then proceeded from his Czech coup to a successful demand upon Lithuania for the city of Memel and a brusque notification to Poland to give up Danzig. The Poles were determined to fight rather than submit, and their resolution was bolstered by a fateful pledge from Prime Minister Chamberlain on March 31, 1939: If Polish independence were threatened,

"His Majesty's Government would feel bound at once to lend the Polish Government all support in their power."

During the next few weeks the British further emphasized their shift from appeasement by feverish efforts to establish a "peace front" against new Nazi aggression. France, already allied with Poland, was a willing partner. After Italy seized Albania in April, Britain and France gave new pledges of assistance to Rumania and Greece. Since the Axis threat was directed against Central Europe and the Balkans, no really effective peace front could be built without Soviet Russia, but mutual suspicions made this difficult to achieve. Consequently, the course of events clearly threatened war: Germany would almost certainly press its demands against Poland; Poland would certainly resist; and England and France would assist her as best they could.

All of this posed momentous problems for the United States. Roosevelt and Hull demonstrated American opposition to aggression in public statements, by refusing to recognize the legality of the German and Italian seizures, and by administering the tariff laws in a way to hamper Nazi trade. These were mere popgun shots, however, and both men knew it. What else could they do to warn the dictators?

For one thing, the President personally appealed to Hitler and Mussolini on April 14, 1939, to promise not to attack some thirty-one countries of Europe and the Middle East. If the two dictators would give nonaggression pledges for a minimum of ten years, the United States would gladly participate in disarmament and trade discussions to improve world relations. The President concluded his appeal by saying:

> Heads of great governments in this hour are literally responsible for the fate of humanity in the coming years. They cannot fail to hear the prayers of their peoples to be protected from the foreseeable chaos of war. History will hold them accountable for the lives and the happiness of all—even unto the least.

Hitler reacted to the President's proposal with contempt. At the conclusion of a bellicose speech renouncing earlier German treaties with England and Poland, he boasted that none of the states mentioned by Roosevelt had felt any need for such nonaggression pledges, but they could have them if they addressed their requests to the German government. In an obvious bid to the American isolationists, Hitler added an assurance that he had no designs against the American continent.

Well aware that words were futile, Roosevelt and Hull could think of only one step that might actually have some weight as a deterrent to aggression. If the Neutrality Act were amended so that belligerent nations could buy arms in the United States, this would encourage England and France and serve as a warning to Germany and Italy. A public opinion poll in April, 1939, indicated that some 66 per cent of those interviewed favored the idea, but congressional isolationists were strong enough to postpone the issue. When the President argued against this delay in a conference with upper house leaders in July, Senator Borah waved aside Secretary Hull's warning of coming war with the blunt comment that he had better sources of information than the State Department and that these had assured him there would be no war.

Although congressional opposition tied the administration's hands in dealing with the European situation, Roosevelt had more support for a warning to Japan. Continued Japanese hostilities against China had been accompanied by frequent acts of violence against British, French, and American nationals in the Japanese-occupied zones. Even the isolationists, therefore, approved when, on July 26, 1939, the President gave Japan the required six-months' notice for terminating the Japanese-American commercial treaty of 1911. This would permit the government to impose embargoes against Japanese purchases—a serious matter since Japan was obtaining about half of its war materials in the United States.

World War II Begins

On August 23, 1939, the democratic world was stunned by the news of the signing of a Russo-German nonaggression pact, whose sinister significance was obvious. The British peace-front attempt had failed, and a German attack upon Poland was imminent. Indeed, by a secret protocol Stalin had granted Hitler a free hand in western Poland in return for a Soviet sphere of influence in eastern Poland and the Baltic states. Once again President Roosevelt sent a round of appeals to the heads of state of Germany, Poland, and Italy. These had no influence on the crisis, which reached its inevitable climax with the Nazi invasion of Poland on September 1, followed by British and French declarations of war on Germany two days later.

On September 3 Roosevelt discussed the situation in an informal radio talk. The nation, he said, would remain neutral, "but I cannot ask that every American remain neutral in thought as well. Even a neutral has a right to take account of facts. Even a neutral cannot be asked to close his mind or his conscience." Although these words reflected strong sympathy with England, France, and Poland, he promised that "as long as it remains within my power to prevent, there will be no blackout of peace in the United States." The President followed up his speech with a formal proclamation of neutrality, the imposition of the arms embargo required by the Neutrality Act, and the announcement of a state of limited national emergency.

Confronted by war in Europe, the United States participated eagerly in a conference of American foreign ministers at Panama. With impressive unanimity the conferees agreed upon cooperative measures to maintain their neutrality and meet anticipated economic problems. Their most unusual measure was the Declaration of Panama, establishing a 300-mile neutrality zone around the whole hemisphere with the exception of Canada. "As a measure of continental self-protection," the American republics asserted the right to have their adjacent waters "free from the commission of any hostile act by any non-American belligerent nation, whether such hostile act be attempted or made from land, sea, or air." Although many American experts in international law defended this as a legitimate extension of neutral rights, none of the belligerents consented to such a radical departure from the traditional 3-mile limit of national sovereignty. The Panama conference also authorized each country to police the waters off its own coast, but the United States Navy assumed the largest role in the neutrality patrol. In December, 1939, three British cruisers fought the *Graf Spee* off Uruguay and forced it to take shelter in Montevideo, where the Nazis scuttled it. This and other incidents demonstrated that the zone could not be fully enforced, yet American naval patrols did keep watch on belligerent ship movements in the western Atlantic—a watch that particularly handicapped German submarines.

During the early months of the conflict there was a series of incidents reminiscent of World War I. Twenty-eight American lives were lost the first week of the war when the British liner *Athenia* was torpedoed by a German submarine. Somewhat later the American freighter *City of Flint* was captured by the Germans, taken into Russian Murmansk, and then into a Norwegian port, where it was finally turned back to its American crew—an episode that strained American relations with both Germany and Russia. Meanwhile, the United States was having the usual disputes with Great Britain over British blockade measures and the censoring of American mail. Bickering over neutral rights, however, lacked the sharpness of World War I days—largely because it was overshadowed by more momentous developments.

Repeal of the Arms Embargo

With the outbreak of actual war Roosevelt renewed his effort to end the arms embargo. Summoning Congress in special session on September 21, 1939, he delivered a message criticizing the embargo as a reversal of traditional American foreign policy. He asked not only to have the law amended to permit belligerents to buy whatever they wished on a cash-and-carry basis, but to prohibit American merchant vessels from entering war zones.

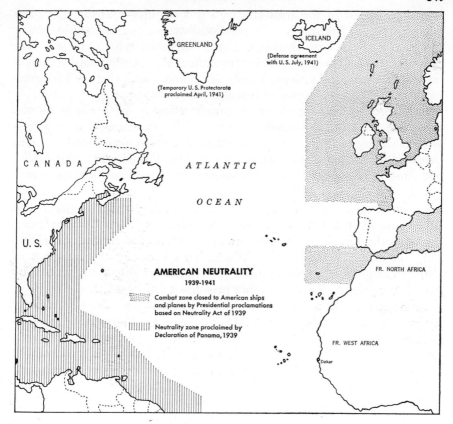

GREENLAND

ICELAND

(Defense agreement
with U. S. July, 1941)

(Temporary U. S. Protectorate
proclaimed April, 1941)

CANADA

ATLANTIC

OCEAN

U. S.

AMERICAN NEUTRALITY
1939-1941

Combat zone closed to American ships
and planes by Presidential proclamations
based on Neutrality Act of 1939

Neutrality zone proclaimed by
Declaration of Panama, 1939

FR. NORTH AFRICA

FR. WEST AFRICA

Dakar

To those who say that this program would involve a step toward war on our part, I reply that it offers far greater safeguards than we now possess or have ever possessed to protect American lives and property from danger. It is a positive program for giving safety. This means less likelihood of incidents and controversies which tend to draw us into conflict, as they unhappily did in the last World War. There lies the road to peace!

Although Roosevelt was probably sincere in arguing that the cash-and-carry principle would help keep the nation out of war, he purposely avoided spelling out his major hope—that repeal of the arms embargo would benefit England and France. In the prolonged congressional debate, there was a similar avoidance of this central issue. Both sides professed to abhor war, but they differed sharply on whether cash-and-carry would help keep the United States at peace or would involve it in the conflict.

Although the congressional debate was dreary and repetitious, the fight over repeal of the arms embargo was significant as the first great trial of strength between the internationalists and the isolationists under the impact of the new situation. The isolationists, who were still very powerful, ranging in respectability from the rabble-rousing Father Coughlin to the aviator-hero Colonel Lindbergh, bombarded Congress with resolutions and telegrams opposing repeal of the embargo.

But the crisis brought about an equally effective propaganda for the other side. Refusing to pussyfoot, Colonel Stimson warned that if Britain and France lost the war, the United States would be confronted by serious danger. "In the interests of our own safety we should repeal this foolish and dangerous embargo." Another prominent Republican, Colonel Frank Knox, strongly supported the cash-and-carry proposal through the columns of his *Chicago Daily News*. A particularly effective campaign was carried on by the newly organized Nonpartisan Committee for Peace Through the Revision of the Neutrality Law, headed by the liberal Republican editor, William Allen White. To counteract the influence of Father Coughlin, the Nonpartisan Committee arranged broadcasts by Monsignor John A. Ryan and other prominent Catholics.

In the end, the critics of the arms embargo won an impressive victory by passing the Neutrality Act of 1939, signed by the President on November 4.[1] This prohibited American ships from carrying either passengers or cargoes to any belligerent nation and required all exports to warring countries to change ownership before leaving American ports. American passengers were prohibited from traveling on the ships of a country at war, and the sale of such a nation's securities within the United States was banned—provisions continued from the earlier law. And finally, the President was authorized to proclaim war zones into which American ships might not go.

Although the new law benefited England and France by permitting them to buy American arms, it was obviously far less advantageous to them than the American neutrality policy of World War I days, which allowed American ships to deliver the goods and placed no bars in the way of buying on credit and borrowing money.

The Phony War

After Germany overran hapless Poland in a lightning campaign, the European war bogged down to boring inactivity through the winter of 1939–1940. Actually this was the deadly calm before the storm, as Hitler's mighty spring drives were to prove. Yet while it lasted, the

[1] The vote was 243 to 172 in the House, and 55 to 24 in the Senate. Most of the Republicans voted against repeal.

"phony war" or "sitzkrieg" fostered complacency not only in America, but even in France and England.

Roosevelt's diplomacy during these months was aimed at isolating Germany from her actual and potential allies. When the Japanese-American commercial treaty terminated in January, 1940, the administration resisted demands for a tight embargo because such a drastic step might drive Japan into full alliance with Germany and an attack upon British and French Far Eastern possessions. Instead, Roosevelt followed the much milder policy of putting Japanese-American trade on a day-to-day basis, somewhat extending the moral embargo list, and loaning money to China. He dealt even more gently with Mussolini, playing upon the latter's dislike for the Hitler-Stalin pact. In this effort to keep Italy neutral, Roosevelt found a useful ally in Pope Pius XII, to whom he sent his personal representative, Myron C. Taylor, an Episcopal businessman.

The most delicate problem was Soviet Russia. Never popular with most Americans, Stalin had antagonized opinion still further by his deal with Hitler, his occupation of eastern Poland and the Baltic states, and, most of all, his attack upon Finland. Although the administration showed disapproval of Soviet policy by public statements, by allowing Finland to buy American planes, and by a moral embargo against Russia on certain war materials, Roosevelt and Hull still played a cautious game, avoiding any drastic step that might push Stalin into full alliance with Hitler.

In February and March, 1940, Undersecretary of State Sumner Welles sounded out the governments at Rome, Berlin, Paris, and London on the possibilities of a negotiated peace. But this mission—so reminiscent of Colonel House's ventures during World War I—had no success. Hitler wanted peace on his own terms, which Britain and France could not honorably accept. Mussolini, foreseeing future dangers, was eager to have the war end, but believed that German demands would have to be met.

The End of Complacency

All through the early months of the war Americans dangerously underestimated German strength and exaggerated that of England and France. In September, 1939, a public opinion poll revealed that 82 per cent expected the Allies to win. British sea power and France's Maginot Line were believed to be too strong for the Nazis to overcome, especially after American war production was made available through cash and carry.

Disillusionment came in the spring. On April 9, 1940, the Germans suddenly struck against Norway and Denmark. Only the former attempted to resist, but her opposition was easily overcome with the help of traitors within the country, led by the pro-Nazi Major Vidkun Quisling. The Norwegian campaign was full of sobering instruction for Americans. Scrupulous neutrality had given no assurance against Nazi attack, and the failure of the British and French expeditionary force exposed both the fumbling leadership of the Chamberlain government and the weakness of sea power when confronted with overwhelming enemy superiority in the air.

On May 10, before these lessons could be well digested, the Nazis opened lightning attacks on three other neutrals—Holland, Belgium, and Luxembourg. British and French troops immediately moved into Belgium to help meet this assault, but during the next six weeks they suffered a series of disastrous defeats.

The day after the Nazi attack on the Lowlands, Winston Churchill succeeded Chamberlain as Prime Minister of England. Mobilizing every resource to deal with the crisis, Churchill frankly warned President Roosevelt on May 15 that if America hesitated too long, it might have "a completely subjugated Nazified Europe established with astonishing swiftness." Consequently, he asked the President to "proclaim non-belligerency, which would mean that you would help us with everything short of actually engaging armed forces." Britain's immediate needs were forty or fifty destroyers, several hundred planes, and a variety of other supplies. Roosevelt replied that he could not go too far without consulting Congress, but he would give what aid he could.

Despite the earlier strength of American isolationism, the administration was now able to move rather quickly away from neutrality and toward the kind of nonbelligerency that Churchill had described. The President's hands were freed for stronger measures by an impressive reversal of American public opinion. Complacency had given way to pessimism and alarm: a *Fortune* poll in May revealed that only 30 per cent now believed that the Allies would win the war; moreover, some 63 per cent believed that a victorious Hitler would attempt to seize territory in the Western Hemisphere. On May 17 William Allen White asked a number of prominent citizens to join a committee to agitate for maximum aid to the Allies. His argument was: [2]

> It would be folly to hold this nation chained to a neutrality policy determined in the light of last year's facts. The new situation requires a new attitude. From this day on America must spend every ounce of energy to keep the war away from the Western Hemisphere by preparing to defend herself and by aiding with our supplies and wealth the nations now fighting to stem the tide of aggression.

[2] Reprinted by permission of the author from Walter Johnson, *The Battle against Isolation* (Copyright 1944 by University of Chicago Press, Chicago), p. 70.

The resulting Committee to Defend America by Aiding the Allies soon lined up an impressive list of sponsors and established branches in all sections of the country. On June 10 newspapers in many cities carried a full-page advertisement headed STOP HITLER NOW!—an impassioned warning by playwright Robert Sherwood.

Actually, the United States could do very little to halt the immediate rush of events. Belgium surrendered on May 28; the left flank of the Allied army trapped at Dunkirk made an almost miraculous evacuation by sea, but left behind most of its equipment. On June 5 the Germans launched a new offensive against France itself; five days later Italy joined the attack. On June 22 the French had to accept Hitler's armistice terms at Compiègne in the very railroad car in which the Germans had submitted to Foch in 1918.

During these weeks Roosevelt directed Chief of Staff General George C. Marshall to locate any American arms and equipment that might be spared for the Allies. Packed away in warehouses, some 500,000 rifles, 80,000 machine guns, and a variety of field guns, bombs, and ammunition of World War I days were discovered. By the transparent fiction of selling them to a private firm, which then transferred them to Britain and France, Roosevelt started more than 600 freight cars of material rolling toward the New Jersey docks during the first week of June. Some 200 overage planes were also made available. "All this reads easily now," Winston Churchill later wrote, "but at that time it was a supreme act of faith and leadership for the United States to deprive themselves of this very considerable mass of arms for the sake of a country which many deemed already beaten." [3]

On June 11 Roosevelt made an eloquent appeal for his new policy in a speech at Charlottesville, Virginia. Referring bitterly to Mussolini's "stab in the back" of France, the President branded as a delusion the idea that the United States could exist as "a lone island in a world dominated by the philosophy of force." He called for the pursuit of two simultaneous courses: "We will extend to the opponents of force the material resources of this nation and, at the same time, we will harness and speed up the use of those resources in order that we ourselves in America may have equipment and training equal to the task of any emergency and every defense."

Roosevelt made a bid for bipartisan support for his own policies by appointing two prominent Republicans, Henry Stimson and Frank Knox, to the posts of Secretary of War and Secretary of the Navy respectively. Republican regulars denounced this as a political move on the eve of the presidential campaign, but less partisan observers applauded the strength-

[3] Reprinted by permission of the publisher from Winston Churchill, *Their Finest Hour* (Copyright 1949 by Houghton Mifflin Company, Boston), p. 143.

ening of the Cabinet by the addition of two outspoken advocates of aid to the Allies.

Another important response to the European crisis was the welding of stronger ties with both Latin America and Canada. A foreign ministers' conference took a further step toward making the Monroe Doctrine multilateral by drafting the Act of Havana of July 30, 1940, which asserted the right of the American nations to prevent the European aggressors from taking over the Western Hemisphere possessions of their victims. The act also stipulated that the American republics might establish provisional administrations over these colonies.[4] On August 18, the United States and Canada establish a joint defense board.

Destroyers for Bases

For a full year after the fall of France, Great Britain defended herself against the Nazi onslaught without the help of major allies. English cities were subjected to terrible nightly air attacks, and the threat of actual conquest hung over the island. Although the brilliant defense of the Royal Air Force prevented a Nazi invasion, the Germans' old World War I weapon, the submarine, threatened to do mortal injury. Now able to use the ports of western France, Nazi raiders became an ever more serious menace to British ships bringing essential supplies to the homeland.

Since Churchill had first asked for destroyers in May, the Roosevelt administration had pondered the problem of what might be done. Besides the inhibitions of traditional neutrality, there were specific American statutes prohibiting the transfer of military equipment unless it could be certified that this was not needed for national defense. The President at first believed that his hands were completely tied, but a group of private citizens that met regularly at the Century Club in New York City suggested a way to loosen the knots. If the United States could not legally give destroyers to Britain, could it not exchange them for something of greater value to American defense? And what would more obviously contribute to American defense than bases in the British Western Hemisphere possessions? Indeed, the isolationists themselves had been clamoring for American seizure of such bases as compensation for the defaulted war debts.

Although Roosevelt eagerly accepted this idea, he thought new legislation might be necessary. Through William Allen White, he tried

---

[4] Eventually the United States, Venezuela, and Brazil assumed the trusteeship of Surinam (Dutch Guiana), and the United States that of Greenland, a Danish possession. Vichy France was allowed to administer the French colonies, but the latter were kept under close observation to prevent collaboration with the Germans.

to enlist the help of Wendell Willkie, the Republican presidential candidate, in lining up the support of Republican congressmen. But Willkie, though personally favoring the deal, could not make the active alliance Roosevelt needed. To submit the issue to Congress—particularly in an election year—seemed certain to invite acrimonious debate and possible defeat. Once again the Century Club group came up with an attractive alternative. Four prominent lawyers argued in a letter to the *New York Times* that, under a proper interpretation of existing law, the President might make the destroyer deal on his own authority. Attorney General Robert H. Jackson prepared a formal opinion along these lines, and Admiral Harold Stark, Chief of Naval Operations, certified that the national defense would be strengthened, not weakened, by the exchange of overage destroyers for bases—which was obviously true.

Indeed, the desired bases were so much more valuable than fifty reconditioned World War I destroyers that Churchill would have preferred to separate the transactions, making a gift of the bases and receiving a free loan of the destroyers. This method, however, would not provide the legal device Roosevelt needed. Therefore, Secretary Hull and British Ambassador Lord Lothian on September 2, 1940, reached the final agreement: in exchange for fifty overage destroyers, the United States received the right to lease naval and air bases in the Bahamas, Jamaica, St. Lucia, Trinidad, Antigua, and British Guiana. The British granted similar rights in Newfoundland and Bermuda as gifts, "generously given and gladly received."

The President's bold assumption of authority encountered less criticism than he expected. While Willkie condemned the bypassing of Congress as "the most arbitrary and dictatorial action ever taken by any President in the history of the United States," he had to admit the advantages of the deal itself. Even the method did not shock William Allen White: "When you're negotiating a horse trade, you can't take all the neighbors into confidence."

The destroyers-for-bases deal was obviously a wide departure from traditional neutrality. According to Churchill, it was "a decidedly un-neutral act," which, "according to all the standards of history," would have justified a German declaration of war. This in fact was one of the deed's merits from the standpoint of the Prime Minister, who made no secret of his wish to see the United States directly involved in hostilities. For this very reason Hitler and Mussolini fumed, but took no drastic action. They did, however, seek to threaten America by joining with Japan in a Tripartite Pact on September 27, 1940, stipulating that in case one of them were attacked by a power not then involved in the European or Asian wars, the others would render full assistance.

Time Out for Politics

The policy of nonbelligerency was based on the premise that the defeat of Britain and China would place the Western Hemisphere in mortal danger in a world dominated by Germany, Italy, and Japan, with Soviet Russia as an uncertain factor. For its own defense, therefore, the United States had given up the pretense of impartial neutrality and undertaken to aid its friends and hamper its potential enemies. By preventing or at least delaying Axis victory, it hoped to gain time to build up its own defenses. Shocked by the fall of France, Congress had made huge appropriations for a two-ocean Navy and weapons for the Army. In September, 1940, it passed the first peacetime conscription act.

Although isolationism had been weakened by the events of the spring and summer, it revived strongly during the fall. The America First Committee, originally organized by a group of Yale law students, became a national movement, headed by General Robert E. Wood, a Sears Roebuck executive. America First grew rapidly and was soon carrying on an effective counterpropaganda against the Committee to Defend America by Aiding the Allies. Colonel Lindbergh was the most popular speaker at its rallies, but Senators Wheeler and Nye, General Hugh Johnson of NRA fame, and the well-known author Kathleen Norris were also active. Although America First was clean of foreign influence at the national level, local chapters were often heavily infiltrated with pro-Nazis and American fascists, some of them subsidized with German funds.

Against the background of this heated debate over foreign policy, the presidential campaign of 1940 was staged. The interventionists and isolationists both tried to influence the party platforms. The results were typical compromises: the Republican platform favored aid "not in violation of international law," but firmly opposed "involving this nation in foreign war"; the Democratic platform was stronger in its pledge of aid, but promised: "We will not participate in foreign wars, and we will not send our Army, naval or air forces to fight in foreign lands outside of the Americas, except in case of attack."

Roosevelt, running for an unprecedented third term, was of course defending the policies he had already developed. Willkie, the Republican candidate, really had little quarrel with these. A former Democrat, Willkie had been a fervent supporter of the League of Nations during the twenties, and in the present crisis was no less eager to aid the Allies than was Roosevelt. In his early speeches he criticized the President for "inflammatory statements," for secretiveness and lack of candor, and for bungling the defense effort, but reserved his major denunciations for the domestic New Deal.

During the closing weeks of the campaign, however, Willkie became much more emphatic in portraying himself as a man of peace who would save the country from Roosevelt's dangerous manipulations. "If you elect me President," he promised, "I will never send an American boy to fight in any European war." He ridiculed Roosevelt's similar pledges: "If his promise to keep our boys out of foreign wars is no better than his promise to balance the budget they're already almost on the transports." In another speech he predicted that the nation would be at war by April, 1941, if Roosevelt were reelected.

Democratic party workers, fearful of the effectiveness of Willkie's antiwar appeal, beseeched the President to reassure the nation. This Roosevelt did with increasing oversimplification as the campaign reached its climax. At first he was content merely to repeat the Democratic platform pledge to keep the country out of war, "except in case of attack." But at Boston on October 30 he dropped the qualifying phrase: "I have said this before, but I shall say it again and again and again: Your boys are not going to be sent into any foreign wars. . . . The purpose of our defense is defense."

Even more than the Democratic "He Kept Us Out of War" slogan of 1916, Roosevelt's Boston pledge was destined to embarrass the administration as it dealt with the difficult problems of the postelection months.

Arsenal of Democracy

As the smoke of the election battle lifted, the victorious Roosevelt turned again to serious national problems. For one thing, the tempo of war production was unsatisfactory. Administrative confusion at Washington, a "business as usual" attitude among industrialists, and a reluctance of labor unions to sacrifice their recent gains combined to restrict the level of output below the need of either national defense or aid to Britain. For another thing, embattled England was still in serious trouble. As Churchill described the situation to Roosevelt on December 8, 1940, the danger of British destruction through a swift, overwhelming blow had greatly receded, but in its place there was a menace "less sudden, less spectacular, but equally deadly," that of "the steady and increasing diminution of sea tonnage." To meet this threat, the Prime Minister suggested two alternatives. First, the United States might reassert its right to freedom of the seas by carrying goods to England in its own merchant ships, convoyed by the American Navy. If this could not be done, Churchill requested the transfer of more American destroyers and cargo ships, as well as an opportunity to place greatly expanded orders for planes and other military equipment. But these larger war orders raised the problem of finance. "The moment approaches when we shall no longer be able to pay cash for shipping and other supplies." Churchill did not suggest how the needed dollars might be supplied, but stressed the shortsightedness of limiting American aid to such commodities "as could be immediately paid for."

Even before the Prime Minister's appeal arrived, the administration had been studying these problems. Secretary Stimson and a few other officials urged repeal of the Neutrality Act of 1939 and the convoying of American merchant vessels to English ports, but the President doubted the feasibility or wisdom of this course, and neither Congress nor the general public was ready for such measures. Moreover, precipitate action might plunge the country into hostilities for which it was still unprepared. Attention therefore focused on two immediate and closely related objectives: the acceleration of war production and aid for the British in their dollar problem. The expansion of British war orders would encourage American munition factories to build new plants and to increase their total output—all to the benefit of American defense. Existing law, however, prohibited the delivery to the British of more than they could pay for in cash. Most of their American assets had already been liquidated; those remaining were not sufficient to cover orders already placed.

Pondering this problem on a vacation cruise in the Caribbean, the President hit upon an idea that he revealed in a Washington press conference on December 17, 1940. What he wanted to do was to "get rid of the silly, foolish old dollar sign." He explained what he meant in a way that caught the popular imagination:

> Suppose my neighbor's home catches fire, and I have a length of garden hose.... Now what do I do? I don't say to him... "Neighbor, my garden hose cost me $15; you have to pay me $15 for it." What is the transaction that goes on? I don't want $15—I want my garden hose back after the fire is over.

When Congress returned in January, said the President, he would ask for authority to loan American arms to Britain, these to be returned or replaced at the conclusion of the war.

Parallel with this move, Roosevelt tried to administer adrenalin to the lagging production effort. On December 29, 1940, he put his case to the public in one of his effective radio talks. He argued that an Axis victory would imperil the Western Hemisphere, whose vast resources constituted "the most tempting loot in all the round world." America's ability to keep out of war greatly depended on the outcome of Britain's fight. What the latter was asking was not for American troops, but for the implements of war.

> We must be the great arsenal of democracy. For us this is an emergency as serious as war itself. We must apply ourselves to our task with the same resolution, the same sense of urgency, the same spirit of patriotism and sacrifice as we would show were we at war.

Lend Lease

On January 6, 1941, Roosevelt presented his new aid plan to Congress. America could not tell nations defending themselves against Axis attack to surrender merely because they had exhausted their ready cash. Instead, they should be supplied with all that the nation could spare from its own defenses, postponing a decision on the form of repayment until after the war. The President concluded on a note of idealism, looking forward to "a world founded upon four essential human freedoms"—freedom of speech and expression, freedom of religion, freedom from want, and freedom from fear.

A few days later, a bill "to Promote the Defense of the United States" and felicitously numbered H.R. 1776 was introduced. This would grant the President broad powers to sell, lease, or lend defense articles to the government of any country whose defense the President deemed vital to the defense of the United States. The new proposal provoked a bitter exchange between Senator Wheeler, a leading isolationist, and President Roosevelt. Wheeler denounced "the New Deal's triple A foreign policy," which would "plow under every fourth American boy." Roosevelt retorted that this was "the rottenest thing that has been said in public life in my generation."

Characterizing the bill as a "blank check" that would enable the President to plunge the country into war, Father Coughlin, Colonel Lindbergh, and General Wood urged their followers to telegraph their congressmen to oppose the measure. Active in mobilizing public opinion on the other side were the Committee to Defend America by Aiding the Allies and such individual leaders as former New York Governor Alfred E. Smith and Wendell Willkie.

For two months this important debate continued both in Congress and in the country at large. In the end, lend-lease was enacted into law on March 11, 1941, with impressive majorities. In the Senate the final vote was 60 to 31; in the House, 317 to 71.

Among the advantages of lend-lease was that it prevented competition between American and British purchasing. Under the new arrangement, the United States placed all the orders and decided whether the finished equipment would best serve American defense by being sent to American friends abroad or kept at home. Britain and Greece—under Italian attack since October, 1940—were immediately declared eligible for lend-lease assistance; China was added to the list in May; later the Latin-American republics, Turkey, and the Soviet Union all benefited.

The Global Chessboard

Although Roosevelt still insisted that the United States would not fight unless attacked, the possibility of war grew steadily greater. Confronted by this situation, American military and naval officers began an informal exchange of information with their British counterparts in August, 1940. These staff conversations assumed a formal character in January, 1941, when the Anglo-American strategists started secretly planning "the best methods by which the armed forces of the United States and the British Commonwealth . . . could defeat Germany and the Powers allied with her, should the United States be compelled to resort to war." Long before Pearl Harbor the Americans and the British had prepared their general strategy, based on first defeating Germany while postponing a showdown with Japan.

For the time being, however, the United States was concentrating its effort on the diplomatic front, where Axis aggression threatened at many different points. Thwarted in their attempt to batter Britain into quick surrender, the Germans had turned to other strategems. A key objective was to cut British Empire lines of communication by gaining control of the Mediterranean. This involved gaining active collaboration with Spain for an assault upon Gibraltar and with Vichy France for bases and assistance in French North Africa, as well as Mussolini's breaking out of Libya, overrunning Egypt, and seizing the Suez Canal. As a further blow against the British Empire, the Fuehrer urged Japan to capture the great fortress of Singapore and cut the supply lines between Australia and England.

As the hard-pressed British made their countermoves, the United States found itself confronted with a series of difficult decisions. To prevent a joint German-Spanish attack on Gibraltar, Britain tried to capitalize on Spain's serious shortages of food and fuel by relaxing her blockade to allow supplies to trickle in and urging the United States to send aid. This the Americans did, but only to a very limited degree, because public opinion was still strongly anti-Franco and the State Department was reluctant to give substantial help to a notoriously pro-Axis and anti-democratic regime.

Whereas British policy toward Spain tended more to appeasement than the Americans liked, the situation was reversed in the case of Vichy France. Regarding Marshal Pétain's government as hopelessly infiltrated with pro-Nazi elements, Churchill dealt with it brusquely. Roosevelt and Hull, however, played a different game. By appointing as Ambassador to Vichy a professional Army or Navy man, they hoped to gain the ear of the aged Marshal and encourage him to resist collaboration with Germany. This delicate mission was entrusted to Admiral William D. Leahy, a former Chief of Naval Operations. Even more significant was the sending of the experienced diplomat, Robert D. Murphy, to North Africa to confer with the French military governnor, General Maxime Weygand. By agreeing to supply the North African colonies with desperately needed fuel and supplies, the United States gained the right to maintain control officers at strategic points, thus counteracting the influence of Nazi agents.

Held up by the vacillations of Franco and Pétain, Hitler shifted his main attention to the eastern Mediterranean, where Mussolini's invasion of Egypt had miscarried. Although penetrating some 60 miles in September, 1940, the Italians were driven back deep into Libya the following December, thereby providing Britain with her first real success of the war. Hitler thought it essential to avenge this reverse, not only to restore Axis reputation for invincibility, but to gain control of the Mediterranean and to prevent Greece from becoming the base for future

British operations. In preparation for new campaigns, German divisions were transferred to Libya and German diplomatic pressure bore down upon Yugoslavia, Bulgaria, and Turkey to permit Nazi troop movements across their territories to attack the defiant Greeks.

Once again the United States used its limited economic and diplomatic weapons to counter the German moves. American lend-lease materials made their way into Egypt over the long Red Sea route, while Colonel William A. Donovan, the President's personal representative, visited the Balkan capitals early in 1941, trying to encourage resistance to the Nazis. But neither America's moral support nor Britain's attempts to help with planes and troops could save Yugoslavia or Greece when the German thunderbolt finally struck in April, 1941, giving Hitler complete control of the Balkans. To make matters worse, British aid to Greece so weakened their position in Libya that the Germans and Italians launched an offensive into western Egypt. By May, 1941, the whole Middle East seemed likely to fall under Axis domination through a pincers movement from the Balkans and from Egypt.

Just when the situation seemed blackest, however, the British gained a breathing spell through Hitler's greatest mistake of the war. Instead of pushing his advantage in the Middle East, the Fuehrer turned against the Soviet Union, launching a vast offensive on June 22, 1941. Fatally miscalculating Russian military strength, he expected to defeat the new enemy within two months, after which he would be in a stronger position to force Britain to surrender. Although British and American military experts also anticipated a speedy German victory over Russia, every week of Soviet resistance was so valuable that Churchill and Roosevelt decided at once to offer aid to Stalin. The strongly anti-Communist Prime Minister explained his position thus: "I have only one purpose, the destruction of Hitler, and my life is much simplified thereby. If Hitler invaded Hell, I would make at least a favorable reference to the Devil in the House of Commons." Actual American aid to Russia was at first small, but, as the Soviets proved their ability to make an effective defense, more substantial shipments were sent. Not until November, 1941, however, was Russia made eligible to receive lend-lease supplies.

In still another quarter of the globe the British Empire was in grave danger during the winter of 1940–1941. The Japanese took advantage of the fall of France to occupy northern Indochina and to force the British into temporarily closing the Burma Road into China as an act of appeasement. This move into Southeastern Asia had a dual purpose: to open up the southern flank of China, thus helping to compel Chiang Kai-shek to surrender, and to provide a base for future campaigns against British Malaya, Singapore, and the Netherlands East Indies. Not only would such a Japanese operation create new troubles for the

British, but it might well involve the United States in a Pacific war, which would serve Nazi purposes by diverting American military supplies from England.

Since the British alone could not ward off the Japanese threat, Churchill urged Roosevelt to take some drastic action, such as sending an American fleet to Singapore. The President, however, continued to follow a cautious policy lest the United States become involved in a war for which it was unprepared. By the end of 1940 this policy had evolved as one of denying recognition to Japan's so-called New Order and of giving limited aid to China, yet of avoiding the kind of provocation that might result in drastic Japanese retaliation. Through the device of licensing strategic exports, Roosevelt gradually tightened the economic noose, cutting off aviation gasoline and high-grade scrap iron in July, 1940, and all other grades of scrap iron the following October. Nevertheless, he prudently refrained from a total embargo on the oil exports vital to the Japanese war machine; to do so might precipitate Japanese seizure of the oil-rich Netherlands Indies.

On the Japanese side, there was a division of counsels. Foreign Minister Yosuke Matsuoka and many of the army chiefs were strongly pro-Axis, eager to link Japan more closely with Germany and seize this opportunity to grab control of the rich resources of Southeastern Asia and the Indies. More conservative Japanese leaders, particularly businessmen, were alarmed by these rash proposals and advocated cutting loose from the Axis and bettering relations with America. The Premier, Prince Konoye, was in a middle position, sometimes siding with Matsuoka and sometimes with his critics. This gave Japanese policy a fluctuating character, with defiant public statements and intrigue in Southeastern Asia alternating with such mollifying gestures as the naming of the pro-American Admiral Kichisaburo Nomura as Ambassador to Washington early in 1941.

In the spring of 1941, Matsuoka paid important visits to Berlin and Moscow. In Germany he was not in a position to promise what Hitler wanted—an immediate attack upon Singapore—but he found the Russian leaders eager to make a mutually advantageous deal. On April 13 a Soviet-Japanese Neutrality Pact was signed, in effect assuring Japan against Russian attack in case of war with Britain or the United States, and assuring Russia against Japanese attack in case of war with Germany.

Stretching the Hemisphere

Despite his anxiety over the rest of the globe, Roosevelt told Churchill "that the outcome of this struggle is going to be decided in the Atlantic." By the spring of 1941 a grim situation had developed. Since the start of the war, the British had lost more than 900 merchant vessels, and the sinkings were now more frequent than ever because German submarines hunted in "wolf packs" instead of singly. On March 26 the Nazis announced a new operational zone extending as far west as Greenland; a week later they made good their threat by sinking 10 out of a 22-ship British convoy in those waters.

Of what use was lend-lease and the American "arsenal of democracy" if most of the exported arms were destined for the bottom of the sea? How could the United States assure delivery of the goods? The most obvious answer was to repeal the Neutrality Act of 1939 and permit American cargo ships to enter the war zones under protection of the American Navy. Even though such steps would probably lead to war, many of Roosevelt's advisers, and Wendell Willkie as well, urged him to go the whole way.

The interventionists, however, were strongly opposed. Senator Tobey of New Hampshire introduced a congressional resolution to prohibit convoying by the American Navy, and the America First Committee condemned any further step toward war. Although certainly not an isolationist, Secretary Hull was essentially a cautious man who advised against the more drastic plans of his colleagues. Under pressure from all these different sources, the President proceeded one step at a time, determined, on the one hand, to continue his policy of aiding the Allies, but, on the other, to keep the country out of a shooting war as long as possible.

The administration took the first of a new series of anti-Axis measures on March 30, 1941, when sixty-five Axis and Axis-controlled merchant ships lying in American ports were taken into protective custody, ostensibly to stop acts of sabotage that might menace navigation. Congress subsequently authorized turning over these seized ships to the American merchant marine. In April, ten Coast Guard cutters were transferred to the British for convoying duty, and the war zones were redefined to permit American merchant ships to enter the Red Sea. In June, the United States froze all German and Italian assets in the country and also ordered all German and Italian consuls to leave—measures intended to cripple Axis propaganda activities.

Yet such steps as these did nothing to meet the real crisis. To combat the submarines Roosevelt found a convenient weapon in the Declaration of Panama and the Act of Havana, under which belligerent acts were forbidden in a wide and vaguely defined neutrality zone and control over Western Hemisphere colonies likely to fall under Axis rule was established. Although no one knew just where the hemisphere ended, it was logical to include Greenland; under this premise an April agreement with the Danish Minister at Washington granted the United States a temporary protectorate over that strategic island.

The building of air and naval bases in Greenland permitted the American neutrality patrol to be extended much farther east. Even more important were the new orders given to the patrolling naval vessels on April 21 to trail Axis vessels and broadcast their positions at four-hour intervals. Although these were not the shoot-on-sight orders that the interventionists would have preferred, they did greatly help British convoys to evade lurking submarines and the British navy to locate and destroy them. To make the American patrol more effective, Roosevelt transferred about one-quarter of the Pacific fleet to the Atlantic. This reflected a major strategic decision: if the United States became involved in a two-ocean war, the defeat of Hitler was to be given priority and the war against Japan was to be at first a holding operation.

May, 1941, was a critical month. British defeats in the Middle East had been so serious that no one could predict where the next Nazi blow would fall. If Spain and Portugal were occupied, the Germans might then seize the Azores and the Canaries, strategically located along the South Atlantic route. Or the North Atlantic might be threatened by a move against Iceland. Churchill appealed to Roosevelt for the "one decisive counterweight" that might be effective—a United States declaration of war. Roosevelt was by no means ready for this, but he did try to galvanize the American people into a greater effort. In a radio talk on May 27 he warned that Nazi occupation of any of the Atlantic islands would jeopardize both North and South America. Explaining the importance of cutting down British cargo losses, he frankly stated that American patrols were "helping now to insure delivery of the needed supplies to Britain." Finally, he proclaimed the existence of an unlimited national emergency.

The next extension of American defense outposts was to Iceland in July. Britain and Canada had maintained troops there since May, 1940, with Icelandic consent, but now the pressure for reinforcements on other fronts made the British eager for American support. On July 1 the United States and Iceland signed an agreement providing for an American defense garrison, and a week later some 4,000 marines landed on the island. To protect the supply line to the new outpost, the President ordered the Navy to escort American and Icelandic ships and to destroy any hostile forces threatening them. German records captured at the end of the war show that Hitler fumed at these successive extensions of the defense zone, but ruled against any drastic retaliation until Russia could be beaten into submission.

The Atlantic Conference

Ever since becoming Prime Minister during the dark spring of 1940, Churchill had been exchanging personal letters with Roosevelt, yet the

two men had never met, except on one unimportant occasion during
World War I. In the summer of 1941 the President suggested that they
get together to discuss the world situation. The Prime Minister readily
agreed, and the result was a rendezvous at sea off the coast of Newfoundland. From August 9 to 12, 1941, earnest conversations were in
progress not only between Roosevelt and Churchill, but among high
diplomatic and military officers from both nations.[5]

Although the meeting was more important for its establishment of
face-to-face relations between the participants than for firm decisions,
the two leaders did agree on ways to speed up lend-lease deliveries and
on countermeasures to be taken in the Azores should Hitler occupy
Portugal. They also agreed that measures should be taken to increase
aid to Russia. Roosevelt rejected as unduly provocative Churchill's
proposal for a joint British–American–Netherland East Indies warning
against further Japanese aggression, but he did promise to warn Japan
personally.

Remembering how Wilson was embarrassed by the secret treaties of
World War I, Roosevelt sought assurances that Britain had not been
making similar deals in the present situation. Out of these discussions came
the two leaders' decision to publish to the world a statement of their
ideals. Eventually known as the "Atlantic Charter," this declaration of
August 14, 1941, set forth "certain common principles in the national
policies of their respective countries on which they base their hopes for
a better future for the world." Eight points followed, including a pledge
to "seek no aggrandizement, territorial or other"; agreement to make no
territorial changes that did not accord with the wishes of the peoples
concerned; respect for "the right of all peoples to choose the form of
government under which they will live"; equal access by all states to
necessary trade and raw materials; economic collaboration among all
nations to secure economic advancement and social security; a peace
that would afford safety to all nations and assurance "that all men in all
lands may live out their lives in freedom from fear and want"; and freedom of the seas. The eighth point read:

> ...they believe that all of the nations of the world, for realistic as
> well as spiritual reasons, must come to the abandonment of the use
> of force. Since no future peace can be maintained if land, sea, or air
> armaments continue to be employed by nations which threaten, or may
> threaten, aggression outside of their frontiers, they believe, pending
> the establishment of a wider and permanent system of general security,
> that the disarmament of such nations is essential. They will likewise

[5] On the American side the most important participants were Presidential adviser
Harry Hopkins, Under Secretary of State Sumner Welles, and General George C.
Marshall.

aid and encourage all other practicable measures which will lighten for peace-loving peoples the crushing burden of armaments.

Although somewhat reminiscent of Wilson's Fourteen Points, the Atlantic Charter differed from that famous document in several particulars. It represented not one individual's peace objectives, but a carefully phrased reconciliation of two points of view. The pledge of equality of trade, for example, compromised Hull's well-known preference for lowering all tariff barriers with Churchill's need to protect imperial preference so far as it already existed within the British Commonwealth. Unlike the Fourteen Points, the Atlantic Charter was limited to general principles and avoided the pitfalls involved in applying these to specific situations. When compared with Wilson's fourteenth point looking toward a league of nations, the eighth point of the new charter appears to have been purposely vague. Still disillusioned by the League, Roosevelt believed that the statement should place its emphasis on the immediate postwar objective of disarming the Axis, leaving for the future the establishment of some "wider and permanent system of general security." Although the Atlantic Charter was never embodied in a formal executive agreement and was, in reality, no more than a joint press release, it offered hope to a world still overshadowed by totalitarian aggression.

The Shooting War

By the fall of 1941, Congress had appropriated 13 billion dollars for lend-lease, and British transportation of the goods had been given vital help by the extension of the American neutrality patrol. Yet realistic observers knew that still stronger measures would be necessary if the Axis were to be finally defeated. In a memorandum to the President on September 25, 1941, the Army and Navy heads put the matter bluntly: [6]

> It is the opinion of the Joint Board that Germany and her European satellites cannot be defeated by the European powers now fighting against her. Therefore, if our European enemies are to be defeated, it will be necessary for the United States to enter the war, and to employ a part of its armed forces offensively in the Eastern Atlantic and in Europe or Africa.

Roosevelt, however, still shrank from the decisive plunge. In part, this probably reflected his reluctance to commit American troops to overseas combat, particularly after his campaign pledges of the preceding year. Still more must he have been influenced by evidence that majority

[6] Reprinted by permission of the publisher from William L. Langer and S. Everett Gleason, *The Undeclared War, 1940–1941* (Copyright 1953 by Harper & Brothers, New York), p. 739.

opinion—some 75 to 80 per cent, according to the public opinion polls —was opposed to direct participation in the war. As recently as August, 1941, isolationist strength had been impressively demonstrated by strong congressional opposition to extending the term of service for conscripted men; in the House the extension bill had passed by only one vote.

Consequently, the President edged along, leaving to Hitler the choice of countermeasures that might precipitate all-out war. Under the circumstances, sporadic incidents were inevitable. As early as April, the United States destroyer *Niblack*, reconnoitering off Iceland, had dropped depth bombs against a lurking German submarine, and in May the *Robin Moor*, an American freighter bound for Cape Town, had been sunk by a German submarine 700 miles off the coast of Brazil, leaving the crew and passengers to make a precarious escape by lifeboat.

Much more serious were the repercussions of an incident of September 4. The *Greer*, an American destroyer en route to Iceland, cooperated with a British patrol plane in locating and trailing a German submarine, periodically broadcasting its position. After several hours of this, the German vessel retaliated by firing first one, and later another torpedo, while the *Greer* fought back by dropping depth bombs. Reporting the affair in a radio talk on September 11, Roosevelt charged that the submarine had "fired first" with deliberate design to sink the destroyer. This he characterized as "piracy, legally and morally," part of a Nazi design to gain control of the oceans and dominate the Western Hemisphere. "In the waters which we deem necessary for our defense," the President warned, "American naval vessels and American planes will no longer wait until Axis submarines lurking under water, or Axis raiders on the surface of the sea, strike their deadly blow—first." Moreover, American patrolling vessels and planes were to protect "all merchant ships—not only American ships but ships of any flag—engaged in commerce in our defensive waters."

By seizing upon the *Greer* episode, the President was recruiting popular support for a policy decided upon, at least in part, at the Atlantic Conference. As early as August 26, the Navy had been ordered to escort all friendly shipping as far as Iceland. The shoot-on-sight orders inevitably increased the likelihood of German-American clashes, and new episodes soon occurred. On October 17, the United States destroyer *Kearny* was torpedoed when it went to the assistance of a westbound convoy under attack by a pack of German submarines 400 miles south of Iceland. Although suffering many casualties, the *Kearny* hobbled back to port. Not so fortunate was the destroyer *Reuben James*, sunk on October 31 with the loss of over 100 lives.

These Nazi attacks had a strong impact on Congress, which was then debating the President's request for drastic amendment of the Neutrality

Act of 1939 to permit American merchant ships to be armed and enter the war zones. If the American interest lay in delivering arms to the countries fighting the Axis, logic seemed to demand that American ships be permitted to carry the goods to their destination. Such was the case argued by Roosevelt in a message to Congress on October 9, but his proposal encountered bitter opposition. The isolationists, naturally alarmed at the whole course of recent events, put up a strong fight. Although Republicans like Wendell Willkie and Senators Bridges, Austin, and Gurney were ready to go even farther than the President, the Republican rank and file and many individual Democrats voted against any change. In the end, the *Kearny* and *Reuben James* episodes swung a majority to the President's side, but the final vote was close: 50 to 37 in the Senate, and 212 to 194 in the House.

The Neutrality Act amendments, passed on November 17, marked the final abandonment of the effort to keep the nation out of war by prohibiting American ships from carrying arms to belligerent ports. Even before this, German submarines had sunk eleven American merchant vessels and one destroyer and damaged many others. Now with armed merchant ships venturing into still more dangerous waters, an increasing number of attacks was to be expected. Since the Navy was under orders to shoot the German raiders on sight, a full-scale naval war was obviously in the making.

Threat to Southeast Asia

Throughout 1941 the Roosevelt administration faced the possibility that its aid-to-Britain policy might involve it in war not only with Germany, but with Japan as well because of the Tripartite Pact. In such an event, it had been decided that operations against Germany would be given priority and that hostilities against Japan would at first be merely defensive. For this reason, and also because the nation was still inadequately prepared for war, Roosevelt continued to follow a cautious policy. He gave an occasional jerk on the economic noose around the Japanese neck, but he refrained from any lethal tightening that might drive Japan to desperation. Explaining his position to Secretary Ickes, who wanted to impose a total oil embargo, the President wrote on July 1, 1941: "... it is terribly important for the control of the Atlantic for us to help keep peace in the Pacific. I simply have not got enough Navy to go round—and every little episode in the Pacific means fewer ships in the Atlantic."

Well aware that the Japanese government was divided between the pro-Nazi group headed by Foreign Minister Matsuoka and the more moderate elements represented by Prime Minister Konoye, Roosevelt and Hull continued to hope that the latter would gain control of the situation. Early in 1941 Bishop James E. Walsh and Father James M. Drought, Catholic missionary leaders, began to transmit confidential messages between the two governments, and Japanese businessmen served in a similar way. Meanwhile, the arrival of Admiral Nomura as the new Japanese Ambassador to Washington had brought on the scene a well-intentioned although somewhat inept diplomat. Hull and Nomura canvassed the whole field of Japanese-American relations during the spring of 1941, but failed to make significant progress. One reason for this was the sinister influence of Matsuoka, working to sabotage the negotiations whenever they seemed to take a more hopeful turn. But even without Matsuoka the two governments were so far apart in their objectives as to make compromise difficult or impossible. The Americans wanted a radical reversal of Japanese foreign policy, including a break with the Axis, withdrawal of Japanese troops from foreign soil, pledges against new aggression, and a commitment to the principles of territorial integrity and the Open Door in trade. This was going too far even for the Japanese moderates, who might have been willing to swear off further aggression and gradually withdraw their armies, but who expected in turn American acceptance of their "New Order" in Asia— particularly their paramount influence in China.

Although the Japanese were at first annoyed when Germany attacked Russia without consulting them, they speedily accepted the new situation as an opportunity to be turned to their own profit. Matsuoka, eagerly egged on by the Nazis, wanted Japan to invade Russian Siberia, but most of the other Japanese officials considered this too risky—at least until the Russian bear had been sufficiently mauled by the Germans. Instead, the Japanese leaders decided to strike south toward the oil-rich Netherlands Indies. This was a goal not to be won by a single blow, but by successive moves: first, the Japanese must build up their forces in southern Indochina and perhaps Siam; second, they must paralyze British power by campaigns against Malaya and Singapore; third, they must protect their flank against possible American attack, either by conquest of the Philippines or by diplomacy; only then could they swoop down on the main prize, the Netherlands Indies themselves.

Fear that the Japanese might embark on some such program of conquest had long been a nightmare to the Roosevelt administration. Economically, this would be disastrous, since Japan would gain control not only of precious petroleum, but of most of the world's supply of rubber, tin, and quinine. Strategically, it would paralyze the whole British position in the Far East and jeopardize the empire sea lanes. This explains the dismay with which Washington received the news in mid-July that Japan had forced Vichy France to turn over air and naval bases in southern Indochina. The Japanese explained that their action was purely defensive: to protect their position in the northern part of the country and prevent the strengthening of the Burma supply route into China. But Roosevelt and his advisers were not convinced: they regarded the Japanese build-up in southern Indochina as preparatory to campaigns against Malaya and Singapore. How right they were is evident from the secret word sent from Tokyo to Berlin. "The realization of this plan," explained Matsuoka, "is the first step for our push to the south."

Believing that only a drastic countermove could halt the Japanese, Roosevelt ordered the freezing of all Japanese funds and assets in the United States on July 26, 1941. Similar steps were taken by Great Britain, the British Commonwealth countries, and the Netherlands Indies. This latest move gave the President the means to enforce a total embargo, cutting off at last the oil supplies the Japanese war machine so desperately needed. Japanese-American relations now passed into a new and critical stage. The United States would agree to restore friendly trade relations only if Japan reversed her foreign policy; if Japan refused to retreat, then she could obtain the supplies she needed only by conquering them in Southeast Asia—and this probably meant war with America.

Diplomacy's Last Stand

In view of the conflicting aims of American and Japanese policies, an eventual clash was probable, yet on both sides there was still a desire to postpone the evil day as long as possible. At the Atlantic Conference, Roosevelt rejected British proposals that would have forced an early showdown in favor of temporizing tactics that would give the Armed Forces more time to prepare. After his return to Washington the President carried out a promise to Churchill by warning Ambassador Nomura that if Japan took any further aggressive steps, the United States would be compelled to take defensive countermeasures. But he tempered this with an offer to resume diplomatic talks if Japan would agree to suspend its expansionist policy.

On his side, Nomura began to press for a face-to-face meeting between President Roosevelt and Prime Minister Konoye somewhere in the Pacific. The Japanese moderates, having strengthened their position by forcing the pro-Nazi Matsuoka out of the Foreign Office, pinned their hopes on this proposal. At first prospects for the meeting seemed good. Ambassador Grew strongly urged it, and the President was much attracted to an idea so congenial to his flair for personal diplomacy. But in the end Roosevelt and Konoye never met. A cautious man by nature, Secretary Hull advised his impulsive chief not to go hurrying off to meet the Japanese Prime Minister before the ground had been prepared by agreement on matters of principle. The State Department's suspicion of Japanese intentions was deepened by information now being steadily supplied through the interception of secret diplomatic messages between the Japanese Foreign Office and its diplomatic representatives in various countries. American cryptographers had cracked the Japanese diplomatic code some months earlier and were now providing their superiors with disturbing reports.

On the Japanese side, Prince Konoye was apparently sincere in his desire for peace, but his freedom of action was narrowly circumscribed by the aggressive nationalists. An imperial conference in September set Japanese terms so high that American acceptance was extremely unlikely. In return for Japanese pledges not to use Indochina for attacking any other country and to withdraw after peace was established, the United States and Britain were to halt all aid to Chiang Kai-shek and help Japan gain needed supplies both from their own territories and from the Netherlands Indies. This demand that America actively support Japan's New Order was in fundamental conflict with the four principles repeatedly enunciated by Secretary Hull: the territorial integrity and sovereignty of all nations; noninterference in the internal affairs of other countries; the maintenance of equality, including that of commercial opportunity; nondisturbance of the *status quo* in the Pacific, except by peaceful means— principles that Konoye professed to accept but found troublesome to apply to the specific situation.

The chances for peaceful settlement, already dim, were further reduced in mid-October when the Konoye cabinet fell and the aggressive General Hideki Tojo became Prime Minister. The Roosevelt administration anxiously studied the new situation, wondering whether the Japanese militarists would strike out against Siberia in the north or against the Burma Road, Siam, or Malaya in the south.

In Tokyo there was still some sentiment against a final rupture with America. On November 5, an imperial conference charted the future in fateful outline. Japan was to present successively two final plans for American consideration: Plan A, for a general settlement of outstanding Japanese-American difficulties; Plan B, for a more limited temporary arrangement. If neither were accepted, negotiations were to be broken off and war commenced. How little the Japanese navy expected an agreement is revealed by the orders sent out the same day: "War with Netherlands, America, England inevitable; general operational preparations to be completed by early December."

To assist Ambassador Nomura in the final showdown, the Japanese government sent over a special envoy, Saburo Kurusu. This was largely window dressing—to impress public opinion with Japan's desire for peace on the eve of almost certain war. Even before Kurusu's arrival, preliminary discussion between Hull and Nomura had demonstrated that Japan and the United States were too far apart in their ideas on the future of China to make agreement on Japanese Plan A possible;[7] but Plan B, presented by Nomura and Kurusu on November 20, seemed to offer more possibilities. This proposed a modus vivendi, or stop-gap agreement, under which (1) Japan and the United States would promise not to make any new armed advance in Southeast Asia or the Southern Pacific area; (2) the Japanese would withdraw their troops from French Indochina after the establishment of peace; (3) Japan and the United States would cooperate in obtaining needed goods from the Netherlands Indies; (4) Japan and the United States would restore commercial relations to those prevailing before the freeze order, and the United States would supply Japan with a required quantity of oil; and (5) the United States would promise "to refrain from such measures and actions as will be prejudicial to the endeavors for the restoration of general peace between Japan and China."

Although Roosevelt and Hull objected strongly to points 4 and 5, which would have required the United States to desert Nationalist China while helping Japan to obtain oil and needed raw materials, they did explore the possibilities of a three-month modus vivendi on other terms. Such an idea, however, was strongly opposed by the Chinese and British, who feared any act of appeasement. Convinced by intercepted messages that the Japanese were even now preparing some new aggression, Hull abandoned the whole attempt to negotiate a temporary agreement. Instead, on November 26 he handed Nomura and Kurusu a stiff ten-point note, proposing among other things Japanese withdrawal from Indochina and China and a pledge not to support any rival Chinese government. In the obvious belief that war was imminent, Hull chose high moral grounds for his last stand. On November 27 the Navy warned its commanders: "Negotiations with Japan looking toward stabilization of conditions in the Pacific have ceased and aggressive move by Japan is expected within the next few days."

Where would the blow fall? Probably against Siam or Malaya, the experts believed, after studying reports of Japanese convoys sailing along the South China coast. There might be danger of an assault upon the Philippines, but this was not thought likely because an attack upon American soil would solidify American opinion behind the President,

[7] The principal features in Plan A were: (1) Japan to agree to the principle of nondiscrimination in trade in the entire Pacific area, including China, provided the same principle were applied to the rest of the world; (2) Japan to give a limited definition to its obligations under the Tripartite Pact; and (3) Japan to evacuate troops from most of China but to retain garrisons in North China and on the island of Hainan for an indefinite period.

while an attack on British or Siamese territory would pose a far more difficult problem. Indeed this question of what the President should do in case of an attack on Siam or Malaya preoccupied Washington attention for ten days. Roosevelt and his advisers were convinced that the United States should fight if Japan invaded this vital zone, yet they realized the difficulty of overcoming isolationist opposition in Congress to such a course. After many anguished conferences, a plan of procedure was finally approved. First, the President was to dramatize the situation in a direct appeal for peace to the Japanese Emperor; second, the President was to send a solemn message to Congress explaining why Japanese aggression in Southeast Asia threatened American security. Even yet Roosevelt had not finally decided on war; the appeal to Hirohito and the message to Congress were aimed at putting Japan clearly in the wrong and at laying the basis for possible American counteraction rather than announcing what that action would be.

In the end, events followed a Japanese rather than an American timetable. On November 25 the Japanese fleet had begun moving toward Hawaii, and on December 1 the Japanese Privy Council had made the final decision for war. Needing time to poise its thunderbolt, the home government ordered Nomura and Kurusu to string out the negotiations in Washington. On December 6, American officials learned that Japanese convoys were entering the Gulf of Siam, and Roosevelt hurried off his appeal to Emperor Hirohito, reviewing the long record of Japanese-American friendship and stressing the fear that the Japanese were planning to attack the Philippines, the Indies, Malaya, or Siam. "None of the peoples of whom I have spoken above can sit indefinitely or permanently on a keg of dynamite." The President asked the Emperor to remove this threat of aggression by withdrawing his forces from Indochina, assuring him that if he did so no other power would invade that area.

At 7:50 A.M. the next morning, the Sunday quiet of the Pearl Harbor naval base in Hawaii was shattered by Japanese carrier-based planes swooping down on their unwary prey. In Washington this was 1:20 P.M., and first reports of this attack were still coming in an hour later, when Secretary Hull kept a previously arranged appointment with Nomura and Kurusu to receive the Japanese reply to his note of November 26. Glancing through a long accusation that the United States and Great Britain were conspiring "to obstruct Japan's effort toward the establishment of peace through the creation of a New Order in East Asia," Hull angrily denounced it as crowded with "infamous falsehoods and distortions" on a scale "so huge that I never imagined any Government on this planet was capable of uttering them." Awed by this manifestation of Tennessee wrath, the Japanese envoys left without a word.

From the military point of view Japan had won a brilliant victory, paralyzing the Pacific fleet for months to come and easing the way for a rapid conquest of Southeast Asia and the western Pacific. In the realm of political warfare, however, she had been guilty of a tremendous blunder. The division of American opinion into interventionist and isolationist camps, which had so long limited the administration's freedom of action, was now swept away. When Roosevelt appeared before Congress on December 8 to ask for a declaration that "the unprovoked and dastardly attack by Japan" had initiated a state of war between the United States and the Japanese Empire, he received almost unanimous support. The Senate passed the war declaration by a vote of 82 to 0; the House by 388 to 1.

On December 11, Germany and Italy declared war on the United States, and that same day the President referred this new situation to Congress: "The long known and the long expected has thus taken place. The forces endeavoring to enslave the entire world now are moving toward this hemisphere." Congress thereupon adopted war resolutions against Germany and Italy without a dissenting vote.

The Problem of Responsibilities

Because Pearl Harbor solved so many problems for Roosevelt, the embittered isolationists eagerly accepted the thesis that the President had deliberately courted this attack. They seized particularly upon a puzzling passage in Secretary Stimson's diary, describing a White House meeting of top advisers on November 25, 1941, at which the President [8]

> brought up the event that we were likely to be attacked perhaps (as soon as) next Monday, for the Japanese are notorious for making an attack without warning, and the question was what we should do. The question was how we should maneuver them into the position of firing the first shot without allowing too much danger to ourselves. It was a difficult proposition.

On their face, these words seem almost to clinch the isolationist charge. Indeed, the explanation offered by the most careful student of Stimson's career that what the Secretary really had in mind was how to make the Japanese *seem* to fire the first shot may appear far-fetched.[9] Yet reflection on the actual situation gives strength to this interpretation. The blow that Roosevelt and his advisers expected was not a blow against American territory, but against Southeast Asia. This they regarded as very danger-

[8] Reprinted by permission of the publisher from Charles A. Beard, *President Roosevelt and the Coming of the War* (Copyright 1948 by Yale University Press, New Haven, Conn.), pp. 517–518.

[9] See Richard N. Current, "How Stimson Meant to 'Maneuver' the Japanese," *Mississippi Valley Historical Review*, vol. XL, June, 1953, pp. 67–74.

ous to American interests, since it would cut off the United States and its friends from the sources of vital raw materials, while opening up these same areas to the Axis. The real problem was how to alert the American people to their stake in the expected crisis and convince them that a Japanese move against Siam or Malaya in reality was a "first shot" against their security.

The Japanese assault upon Pearl Harbor was a genuine surprise, even though in earlier months Ambassador Grew and others had warned against such a possibility. In the critical early days of December all attention was focused on the Japanese forces moving toward the Gulf of Siam. The tragic failure of the Washington authorities to take with sufficient seriousness the possibility of a sudden blow against the American outposts resulted, not from sinister plotting, but from confusion and blundering.

In retrospect, Roosevelt's foreign policy from 1939 to 1941 was relatively simple. He was determined to prevent an Axis victory. At first he hoped to achieve this goal without involving the country in all-out war, but as the difficulty of bringing about the downfall of the Axis became more obvious, he was willing to take increasingly drastic action against Germany, no matter how serious the consequences. The Japanese problem was always secondary in the President's thinking. So long as he could, he delayed the showdown in the Pacific. The Japanese move into southern Indochina and the American freeze order brought Japanese-American relations to the danger point, but Roosevelt still played for time. Mistakes he may well have made. A meeting with Prince Konoye in September, 1941, might have strengthened the hands of the Japanese moderates, although this is doubtful in view of the strength of the more ardent expansionists. Still later, Roosevelt and Hull may have erred in giving up the effort to negotiate a modus vivendi and sending instead the drastic ten-point note of November 26. It is doubtful, however, whether the United States could have afforded to pay what it would have cost to divert Japan from the fatal course on which she embarked on December 7. To have reversed American foreign policy and helped Japan reduce China to the status of satellite state would have sacrificed principles upheld by Republican and Democratic secretaries of state since the days of John Hay.

In the end, the issue was clear: the Americans had either to acquiesce in German and Japanese domination of most of the world or to fight. They chose to fight.

33

THE GREAT COALITION

In December, 1941, the Axis aggressors dominated most of Europe, were strongly entrenched in northern Africa, and threatened to overrun all of eastern and southern Asia. China, weak and isolated from her friends, was in desperate trouble; Britain's resources were perilously low after two costly years of war; Russia had been cruelly hurt by six months of savage Nazi onslaught; and the United States, poorly prepared for so herculean a contest, had suffered the first of a serious of humiliating disasters. Four years later the picture had dramatically changed. Shattered and broken, the German, Italian, and Japanese empires lay completely at the mercy of their conquerors.

This great victory had been made possible by the combined resources of the United Nations, the countries that had pledged themselves to fight to the finish against Axis domination. Inevitably the Big Three—Great Britain, the Soviet Union, and the United States—had carried the major load. Born out of desperate necessity, this great coalition, despite frequent tensions and misunderstandings, held together until the enemy was defeated.

Conception of the United Nations

On December 22, 1941, after ten rough days at sea, Prime Minister Churchill arrived in Washington to confer with President Roosevelt about the new situation resulting from Pearl Harbor. This so-called "Arcadia Conference" reached important conclusions on the establishment of Combined Chiefs of Staff, the organization of a unified command in the Southwest Pacific, the fixing of war production goals, and other pressing matters of military coordination.

On New Year's Day, 1942, Roosevelt, Churchill, Russian Ambassador Maksim Litvinov, and Chinese Foreign Minister T. V. Soong gathered in the White House to sign a "Declaration by the United Nations." Secretary Hull was largely responsible for the text of the document, having worked out the details in discussions with other diplomats, but the name was a happy inspiration of Roosevelt himself. The day before the signing he had been pushed in his wheelchair into Churchill's bedroom and had made his suggestion just as his distinguished guest emerged from his morning bath. Churchill had agreed that "United Nations" stirred the imagination in a way that the pallid phrase "Associated Powers" of World War I days could not.

The declaration committed its signatories to the principles of the Atlantic Charter,[1] as well as to the defense of "life, liberty, independence, and religious freedom" and the preservation of "human rights and justice" against "savage and brutal forces seeking to subjugate the world." The signatory nations also pledged themselves to employ their full resources against the Axis enemies, to cooperate with each other, and not to make a separate armistice or peace. Provision was made for other countries to join, and the remaining twenty-two nations then at war with the Axis did so within the next few days.[2]

The American purpose in drafting the declaration was twofold. In its pledge to make war and peace together, the document served a purpose similar to a conventional treaty of alliance, and by committing its signatories to the Atlantic Charter it bound them to common peace aims— something Wilson had not achieved until just before the armistice, when the situation was already clouded by the secret treaties.

But general resolutions against sin are notoriously hard to enforce, and even while the United Nations Declaration was being drafted, British Foreign Secretary Anthony Eden discovered that Stalin's interpretation of no territorial aggrandizement was likely to be dangerously different from Churchill's and Roosevelt's. As one part of a formal treaty of alliance between Russia and Britain, Stalin wanted British consent to Soviet absorption of the Baltic states (Estonia, Latvia, and Lithuania), a rectification of the Finnish frontier, and annexation of eastern Poland. All these areas had been under Russian rule prior to 1918, but had been lost during post–World War I troubles. Under cover of the Hitler-Stalin pact of 1939 the Soviet Union had recovered these territories, only to lose them again after the Nazi invasion. From the Russian point of view, this was not territorial aggrandizement but the righting of an old wrong. To the

---

[1] See chap. 32.

[2] The twenty-six original United Nations were United States, United Kingdom, Soviet Union, China, Australia, Belgium, Canada, Costa Rica, Cuba, Czechoslovakia, Dominican Republic, El Salvador, Greece, Guatemala, Haiti, Honduras, India, Luxembourg, Netherlands, New Zealand, Nicaragua, Norway, Panama, Poland, South Africa, and Yugoslavia.

British and Americans, however, any such deal would negate the Atlantic Charter. In the end the Anglo-Russian alliance treaty omitted all reference to Soviet boundaries, thereby leaving the problem unsettled—a portent of future controversies.

The Second Front: Where and When?

Throughout most of 1942 the Red armies were under constant pressure from the Nazis, now deep in Russian territory. Only the most stubborn defense prevented the Germans from seizing Moscow, Stalingrad, and the oil-rich Caucasus. To help Stalin in this critical situation, Churchill and Roosevelt did whatever they could, but this was often less than the Russians were asking.

Anglo-American convoys loaded with desperately needed planes, tanks, and trucks crept along the northern route to Murmansk. So fierce were the Nazi submarine and plane attacks from Norwegian bases, however, that sometimes only one-half or one-third of the cargoes reached their destination. Often the convoys had to be suspended when the long Arctic days or other circumstances made the enterprise too hazardous. Delays and shortcomings in the scheduled deliveries led to recriminations. The situation was materially brightened in the fall of 1942, when American railroad experts improved the southern route from the head of the Persian Gulf across Iran.

In his hour of need Stalin asked repeatedly for a second front in Western Europe. If an Anglo-American force invaded France or Belgium, the Germans would be compelled to withdraw divisions from the eastern front to meet this threat, thus assuring the success of the Russian defense. Roosevelt and Churchill replied that they would establish a second front as soon as possible, but they could not promise when this would be.

Behind the scenes British and American strategists were already debating this very issue. Never forgetting the humiliation of Dunkirk, the British were determined not to attempt an invasion of the Continent until the Germans were sufficiently weakened on other fronts. At the Arcadia Conference Churchill proposed as the first great Anglo-American venture landings in French North Africa in order to destroy the German and Italian position in neighboring Libya. Although Roosevelt initially favored this idea, he was soon won over to a different strategic plan by his Chief of Staff, General George C. Marshall, who argued that instead of diverting men and equipment to diversionary forays, the United States should concentrate on a rapid increase of forces in the British Isles in preparation for a blow at the heart of the enemy position. The invasion of the Continent should take place not later than the spring of 1943, and perhaps much earlier if the Russian situation became too desperate.

In April, 1942, the British tentatively and reluctantly consented to the Marshall strategy. Such was the situation a month later when Vyacheslav Molotov, Soviet Commissar of Foreign Affairs, visited London and Washington. Without actually promising a second front in 1942, Roosevelt at least predicted one. Churchill was more cautious, emphasizing the difficulties of such a cross-Channel operation, yet not ruling one out before the year was over.

But the early invasion of Europe appeared to be still less feasible by July. The demands of other fronts—against the Japanese in the Pacific and against the Nazis and Italians in Libya—had delayed the build-up of forces in England. Churchill continued to urge the North African alternative, and in July he won over Roosevelt to this plan because it seemed to offer the only opportunity of opening some kind of front against the Germans in 1942.

It was Churchill's delicate mission to go to Moscow in August to inform Stalin of the change in plans. Although deeply disappointed, Stalin had to acquiesce in the decision.

The Two Frances

The decision to land British and American forces in French North Africa reflected a deep concern with the French political situation. At the time of France's defeat in June, 1940, French leaders had been sharply divided. Premier Reynaud and others wished to transfer the government to North Africa and move the navy to colonial bases where it could continue to fight in alliance with the British. But Marshal Pétain, a hero of World War I, and General Weygand insisted that it would be best for the government to remain in France and seek an armistice. In the resulting crisis Reynaud resigned, Pétain became Premier, and a Franco-German armistice was speedily signed, aided by certain Nazi concessions: about two-fifths of France was left unoccupied, and the French government remained in control of the French colonies and the navy.

After the armistice Marshal Pétain moved his seat of government to Vichy, a famous resort town in the unoccupied zone. Convinced that France's defeat had resulted from decadent democracy, Pétain liquidated the Third Republic and established an authoritarian regime. Although millions of Frenchmen placed a somewhat pathetic trust in this feeble old man to carry the nation through one of the most discouraging periods of its history, actual power soon fell largely into younger and more unscrupulous hands. Pierre Laval, the dominant figure most of the time, was an out-and-out collaborationist, convinced that France should win Nazi good will by effective help. Although the wavering Pétain toyed with collaboration at times, he was too much a nationalist to allow Laval a free hand. Instead, he resorted to evasions and delay, never giving the full collaboration Hitler wanted, yet yielding to specific German demands whenever the pressure became great. During a period of several months when Laval was dropped from the government, Admiral Jean François Darlan exercised power. Darlan was an anti-British opportunist, at first hardly less eager than Laval himself to collaborate with the Germans, but shrewd enough to change sides when the tide of battle subsequently moved in the other direction. After April, 1942, Laval and Darlan were both key figures: Laval, as Vice Premier, dominated domestic and foreign affairs; Darlan, as Pétain's Commander in Chief, controlled the armed forces.

Frenchmen wishing to continue to resist Hitler found a leader in General Charles de Gaulle, who had escaped to England at the time of the French defeat. Supplied with money and arms by the British, this group, first called the Free French and later the Fighting French, gradually gained strength. Some of the colonies, particularly in Equatorial Africa and the Pacific, threw off the rule of Vichy and supported de Gaulle.

Although in America liberal public opinion was strongly anti–Vichy and pro–de Gaulle, the State Department maintained diplomatic relations with Pétain and dealt with de Gaulle only at arm's length. Why did Hull and Roosevelt persist in so unpopular a policy?

At first the American leaders were motivated primarily by a concern lest the Germans gain control of the French fleet, a disaster that might seriously imperil the Western Hemisphere, particularly if the Nazis also seized Dakar in French West Africa, only 1,700 miles from the bulge of Brazil. By maintaining diplomatic relations with Vichy, Roosevelt and Hull hoped to encourage Pétain to resist Laval's intrigues. What the Americans wanted most, however, was French military resistance in case the Germans violated the armistice by attempting to seize either the fleet at Toulon or the French colonies in Africa. The Murphy-Weygand agreement, discussed in the preceding chapter, allowed a trickle of American supplies to flow into French North Africa under the supervision of American control officers. The intelligence reports submitted both by these men and by the Vichy Embassy provided a plausible argument for continuing relations with Pétain, even after he disappointed his American friends by so often giving in to Nazi demands.

The State Department's coolness to de Gaulle was a natural corollary of its Vichy policy. Pétain, hating his Free French rival, resented any recognition of de Gaulle's authority. Quite apart from this, however, Roosevelt and Hull were reluctant to give de Gaulle substantial support. Doubting that he had a large following within France itself, they resented his stubborn claim to speak for all Frenchmen.

Secretary Hull's dislike for de Gaulle was intensified in December,

1941, when the latter ordered a Fighting French naval force to seize St. Pierre, a tiny French island in the Gulf of St. Lawrence, important for its wireless station. The State Department condemned this highhanded act as a violation of the neutrality zone and an embarrassment to the United States, which had recognized the authority of Admiral Georges Robert, Vichy Governor of Martinique, over all French possessions in the Western Hemisphere. Although the strong de Gaulle sentiment in America deterred Hull from trying to restore St. Pierre to Vichy control, he never forgave the French general for his action.

Victory in North Africa

After Roosevelt finally consented to Churchill's plan for landings in French North Africa, United States intelligence agents redoubled their efforts to build up a pro-American clique among French officers so that they would not resist the invasion, but would cooperate in an offensive against the Germans and Italians in Libya. To achieve this goal, Roosevelt insisted on two conditions: so far as possible, the landings must be made to appear primarily an American operation, and de Gaulle's Fighting French must have no part in them.

What the American plan most needed was the cooperation of a high-ranking French officer, whose orders would be respected by the French local commanders at the invasion points. De Gaulle would not be the right man because of his unpopularity among the North African officer corps, which had sworn loyalty to Pétain. General Weygand, who had been dismissed from his North African post at German insistence, was unwilling to act behind Pétain's back. The only other possibility was General Henri Giraud, a French national hero who enjoyed the unusual distinction of having escaped from German prisons in both world wars. Friendly relations with Giraud were established, but he was not informed of the British and American plans until the last minute. Indeed, on November 7, 1942, the day before the invasion, General Eisenhower spent hours resisting Giraud's demand to be placed in supreme command of the incipient operation. The French general did not finally consent to cooperate until he was recognized as commander of all French forces in the region and governor of the French North African provinces.

The Anglo-American landings on November 8 were made in the vicinity of three ports: Algiers and Oran on the Mediterranean coast and Casablanca on the Atlantic. At each point the French put up initial resistance, especially in Morocco. To Eisenhower's disappointment, Giraud's cease-fire order was not recognized, but fate gave the American another chessman to play in this important game. A surprise prisoner taken at Algiers was none other than Admiral Darlan.[3] After extended negotiations with American Consul General Robert Murphy, General Mark Clark, and General Giraud, Darlan on November 10 ordered all French military and naval personnel to end their resistance. Darlan and Giraud also reached a compromise under which the admiral became political chief of North Africa and the general gained command of all French troops. When Pétain learned of these actions, he played a double game by publicly repudiating Darlan and ordering continued resistance, but secretly approving Darlan's steps. The Germans, incensed by these developments, occupied the rest of France and sent troops into Tunisia before the Anglo-American troops could invade that strategic colony.

Nevertheless, the Darlan deal brought substantial dividends. The British and Americans were able to establish themselves firmly in Algeria and Morocco with only a minimum of fighting. Morever, French West Africa voluntarily accepted Darlan's authority, thereby ending American apprehensions over Dakar. General Eisenhower, in his report to Washington, defended these steps as "the only possible workable arrangement" that would "secure advantages and avoid disadvantages." President Roosevelt upheld what had been done as "a temporary expedient, justified solely by the stress of battle."

However defensible from the military standpoint, American collaboration with so notorious a Vichyite as Darlan inevitably brought condemnation on the heads of all concerned. A spokesman for the Fighting French announced: "We and we alone have the right to speak for France and we know that France wants to have nothing more to do with the traitors of Bordeaux and Vichy, who sold their country once and are now trying to sell it again to the highest bidder." American liberals bewailed the continued slights to de Gaulle and the "shameless dickering" with French Quislings.

On December 24, 1942, a French assassin with royalist sympathies shot down Darlan at his office door in Algiers. The admiral's death opened the way for the less objectionable Giraud to become high commissioner and commander in chief in French North Africa.

The Casablanca Conference

On January 14, 1943, President Roosevelt arrived secretly at Casablanca, Morocco, to confer with Churchill and high-ranking British and

---

[3] Some commentators believe that Darlan's presence at this moment was too fortuitous to have been mere coincidence. Apparently the Americans did not invite or want him on the scene, but he may have heard rumors of the coming invasion and hastened to Algiers.

American officers on plans for the next blow to be struck after the conquest of Tunisia. General Marshall urged concentration on a cross-Channel invasion, while Churchill argued for a blow against Sicily and Italy, the "underbelly of the Axis." The conferees decided upon a Sicilian campaign because it offered the best employment for the large forces already in North Africa and would open the Mediterranean, thereby releasing naval strength for other fronts. American disappointment at further delay in crossing the Channel was assuaged by the establishment of a London headquarters to perfect plans for invading Europe—in 1943 were Germany to weaken suddenly, but more probably in 1944. The Americans were also pleased by the decision to speed up operations against Japan.

The Casablanca Conference is particularly remembered as the occasion upon which Roosevelt, with Churchill's somewhat startled concurrence, announced a policy of "unconditional surrender." In a press conference on January 24, 1943, the President asserted:

> The elimination of German, Japanese, and Italian war power means the unconditional surrender by Germany, Italy, and Japan. That means a reasonable assurance of future world peace. It does not mean the destruction of the population of Germany, Italy, or Japan, but it does mean the destruction of the philosophies in those countries which are based on conquest and the subjugation of other people.

Although Roosevelt confided to friends that he had spoken on impulse, basing his phrase on General Grant's famous Civil War precedent, it was only the occasion of his announcement that caused surprise. Actually the State Department had been advocating such a policy for some time, and Roosevelt and Churchill had also previously discussed the matter.

The "unconditional surrender" policy was intended to reassure liberal opinion that the recent Darlan deal would not provide a model for future bargains with the Nazis and Fascists. It reflected also a widespread conviction that the 1918 armistice had been a mistake because it had permitted the growth of the dangerous myth that the German army had not been defeated, but had been betrayed by a socialist "stab in the back." In retrospect, many critics have branded the "unconditional surrender" statement a mistake in that it stiffened Axis resistance and resulted in so thorough a destruction of German national power that Central Europe fell easily to communism. Yet the alternative policy of leaving the way open for a negotiated peace might have been even more dangerous, since it would have antagonized Stalin and encouraged the Germans to play Russia against the West to see which would offer the better terms.

Roosevelt and Churchill also attempted to clarify their policy toward France. Invited to come to Casablanca, General de Gaulle at first refused and only put in a sulky appearance after Churchill threatened to transfer British support to some other leader. Although de Gaulle and Giraud were induced to shake hands for the photographers, they reached no real agreement. After the Casablanca meeting each went his separate way, Giraud continuing to rule North Africa, while de Gaulle built up impressive support in other parts of the French empire and in the occupied homeland. On June 3, 1943, the two rivals agreed at Algiers to be co-presidents of a French Committee of National Liberation. While still cool to de Gaulle, Roosevelt joined Churchill in recognizing the authority of the new committee. As time passed, Giraud's political weakness became more and more evident, and in November he resigned his co-presidency, although continuing as commander in chief.

Focus on Italy

The Casablanca decision to attack Sicily still left the problem of whether this island was to be a terminal objective or a jumping-off place for an assault upon the Italian mainland. In May, 1943, Churchill argued for a push into Italy, and perhaps into the Balkans as well, both at the "Trident" Conference in Washington and at a subsequent meeting at Algiers attended by Generals Marshall and Eisenhower. The leaders finally decided that, if the Sicilian campaign were not too difficult, Eisenhower should continue on into southern Italy. Conceding somewhat to British opinion in this matter, the American planners took comfort in decisions to pursue a more aggressive strategy in the Pacific and to prepare for a cross-Channel invasion about May 1, 1944.

Churchill's desire for an Italian campaign was based quite as much on political as on military considerations. He believed that a sharp blow would topple Mussolini's house of cards and that any subsequent Italian government might surrender or even change sides and fight against Germany. These hoped-for gains were in part realized. The Anglo-American invasion of Sicily on July 10, 1943, was followed on July 25 by an Italian coup in which King Victor Emmanuel III and certain monarchist leaders collaborated in the dismissal and arrest of Mussolini and substituted a government headed by Marshal Pietro Badoglio. Although Badoglio announced that Italy would continue to fight, he immediately began secret negotiations with the British and Americans. On September 3, 1943, Eisenhower and the Italian representatives agreed on armistice terms— not made public until five days later—under which Italy pledged to cease all hostile acts against the United Nations, to deny cooperation to the Germans, and to transfer her navy and air force to United Nations control.

It had been hoped that a carefully timed announcement of the armistice would enable the Allies to gain control of Italy with a minimum of opposition. A small British landing had been made on the toe of Italy on September 3; the major Anglo-American assault on Salerno was scheduled for September 9; and American parachutists dropped on the airfields of Rome were to seize the capital and protect the King and Badoglio when they announced the surrender. Some key parts of this strategy miscarried, when the Nazis, suspicious of Badoglio, anticipated the news and made their countermoves with great swiftness. German capture of the Rome airfields forced a cancellation of the American paratroop move, while German reinforcements were rushed to southern Italy to contest every foot of the Anglo-American advance. Therefore it was not until June, 1944, that the United Nations fought their way as far north as Rome. In military terms, the Italian campaign proved unusually costly, demonstrating that General Marshall had had good reason to doubt its wisdom.

Nevertheless, the Italian armistice did bring substantial advantages. The Italian fleet was able to surrender to the United Nations. Victor Emmanuel and Badoglio fled from Rome and established a government behind the Allied lines at Brindisi. On October 13, the American, British, and Russian governments accepted Italy as a cobelligerent in the war against Germany. Meantime, however, Mussolini had been rescued by the Germans and installed as the head of a rival pro-German regime.

The recognition of Badoglio raised issues almost as controversial as those involved in the Darlan deal because both the King and the marshal had long collaborated with the Fascists. Sensitive to liberal criticism, Roosevelt carefully emphasized that these arrangements were only temporary and that the Italian people would ultimately be free to choose their own form of government. On the other hand, the more conservative Churchill wanted to preserve the monarchy as a bulwark against disorder and communism.

The Line to Moscow

Despite occasional disagreements, British and American cooperation became steadily more cordial. In August, 1943, the tireless Churchill again crossed the Atlantic to confer with Roosevelt at Quebec, where plans for the invasion of northern France were made more specific and Pacific war strategy discussed. The Prime Minister continued these talks at Washington during the stirring days when the Italian armistice and the invasion were making headlines.

Delighted with these comradely relations with Churchill, Roosevelt longed to develop a similar accord with Stalin. The British and American leaders had both urged their Russian counterpart to join them at Casablanca, but he had refused to make the trip on the excuse that he must remain close to the Russian military fronts. During the spring and summer of 1943 Roosevelt renewed his proposals either for a meeting directly with Stalin or for a Big Three conference to include Churchill. Stalin continued to postpone such a meeting on the ground that the war situation was much too critical.

During these months Russian relations with the Western allies were far from good. Still under fierce attack from the Germans, the Russians were impatient with the continued delay in opening a major second front. Suspension of the northern convoys during the summer of 1943 created disappointment, while Stalin did not conceal his suspicion that the British and Americans were dealing with French North Africa and Italy in a way to serve their own interests without consulting him.

During that same summer, however, there were signs that these frigid relations were beginning to soften. The Russians agreed to a Big Three conference of foreign ministers, which would prepare the way for an early meeting of Churchill, Roosevelt, and Stalin themselves. Contributing to a relaxation of tensions was the encouraging war news from all battle fronts. The Anglo-American invasion of Italy was tying up German forces in the West, while the Russians were opening a massive counter-offensive in the East.

The Moscow Conference of Foreign Ministers (October, 1943) proved unexpectedly harmonious. Secretary Hull and British Foreign Secretary Eden found Foreign Commissar Molotov in a relaxed and hospitable mood, which paved the way for speedy acceptance of certain declarations, largely American in origin. Despite British and Soviet objections that China was not really a great power, Hull obtained for Chiang Kai-shek's government the right to be associated in a Four-Power Declaration on General Security, pledging the signatories to act together in all matters relating to the surrender and disarmament of the Axis and to continue their united action in the postwar period. The four powers recognized "the necessity of establishing at the earliest practicable date a general international organization, based on the principle of the sovereign equality of all peace-loving states, and open to membership by all such states, large and small, for the maintenance of international peace and security." The signatories further promised that after the war they would "not employ their military forces within the territories of other states," except for peaceful purposes and after joint consultation.

In separate declarations to which China was not a party, the Big Three foreign ministers agreed that the Italian government should be made more democratic, that Austria be assured a free and independent future, and that Nazi war criminals be tried and punished after hostilities ceased. Just as the meeting was breaking up, Hull and Eden were delighted to receive an unsolicited promise from the Russians to join the war against Japan as soon as Hitler was defeated.

Secretary Hull returned to Washington, confident that Wilson's noble dream of a stable world order would at last be achieved. Reporting to Congress on the Moscow Conference, he declared: "As the provisions of the Four-Nation Declaration are carried into effect, there will no longer be need for spheres of influence, for alliances, for balance of power, or any other of the special arrangements through which, in the unhappy past, the nations strove to safeguard their security or to promote their interests." Congress was in an equally optimistic mood. Just before the Moscow Conference the House had passed the Fulbright resolution favoring the creation of "appropriate machinery with power adequate to establish a just and lasting peace"; before Hull reached home the Senate approved the Connally resolution recommending that the United States join in "the establishment and maintenance of international authority with power to prevent aggression and to preserve the peace of the world."

Cairo and Teheran

Even in the afterglow of the Moscow Conference Roosevelt did not find it easy to make final arrangements for a face-to-face meeting with Stalin. Still pleading the need to stay close to the war front, the Russian dictator would promise to go no farther than neighboring Iran. The President at first objected to the distance from Washington, but at length agreed to a meeting at Teheran.

On the way Roosevelt stopped off at Cairo, Egypt, where he conferred with Churchill and Chiang Kai-shek. Fearing that the Chinese had become discouraged because of the small amount of aid that Britain and the United States had been able to fly over the mountain "hump" between India and China, the President wanted to plan military campaigns that would reopen the Burma route. Although the Cairo discussions had only small success in dealing with this problem, Chinese morale was improved by a declaration in which the three nations promised to fight until Japan surrendered unconditionally. The enemy was to be stripped of all its conquests since the Sino-Japanese War of 1895; China was to regain Manchuria, Formosa, and the Pescadores; and Korea was to be free and independent.

At Teheran, Roosevelt, Churchill, and Stalin spent four days in lively and generally amicable discussion of war plans and postwar objectives. As in their earlier meetings, Roosevelt and Churchill differed somewhat on the degree of priority to be given to the cross-Channel invasion. Determined to adhere to the May 1 target date, Roosevelt was suspicious of any plans for further Mediterranean operations. Churchill, on the other hand, was intrigued by the possibilities for limited operations in the Adriatic or in the Aegean Sea, provided Turkey could be induced to enter the war. These, he argued, might be done without sacrificing forces needed for the trans-Channel invasion. Even if D day in France had to be delayed for a few months, he believed that Balkan operations might be worthwhile, since they would tie up German divisions that might otherwise be transferred to the Russian front or to France. Stalin did not particularly object to Churchill's fertile projects, but emphasized the supreme importance of fixing the date for the cross-Channel invasion so that the Russians could time their own spring offensive accordingly. He also supported the idea of a simultaneous attack upon southern France. In the end, Roosevelt and Stalin obtained Churchill's consent to fixing the month of May for both the trans-Channel and the southern France invasions, while Churchill gained approval for more support to the Tito partisans in Yugoslavia and for trying to persuade Turkey to enter the war.

Discussion at Teheran focused more on winning the war than planning for peace, but the Big Three did compare notes on such issues as the future of Germany and Poland, Russia's needs for warm-water ports, and the type of world organization most likely to succeed. Although it was obvious that Russia wanted to extend its frontiers in certain strategic areas and would insist on friendly neighbors, Roosevelt and Churchill heard nothing to cause them serious alarm.

The Problems of Success

After Teheran the United Nations entered upon a period of victorious campaigns. In the Pacific the United States Navy was now superior to the enemy fleet, and the marines were capturing one island group after another, thereby penetrating deeper into Japanese defenses so that the Japanese home islands might be brought under direct air attack. In October, 1944, General MacArthur began the reconquest of the Philippines. In the West, the Italian campaign continued to be difficult, yet the Anglo-American armies entered Rome on June 4, 1944, and then pushed on into the northern part of the country. On June 6, English and American forces successfully landed in Normandy; on August 15, a smaller invasion of southern France was opened; ten days later Paris was liberated; and by November the Germans had been hurled back into Holland and the Rhineland. On the Russian front—the most savagely contested of all—the Germans also suffered a series of disasters. In July, 1944, Soviet armies drove into Poland and soon thereafter entered Rumania and Bulgaria.

The British and Americans continued to have minor disagreements on strategy. Unenthusiastic toward the invasion of southern France, Churchill would have preferred operations in the northern Balkans, in which Anglo-American forces would cooperate with Yugoslav partisans in a drive toward Austria and Hungary. But this proposal was balked in part by American suspicion of all projects that might divert strength from the French front and in part by the stubbornness of German resistance in the Po Valley. Another point of friction developed between General Eisenhower, the Supreme Allied Commander, and British General Bernard Montgomery over how the United Nations strength should be deployed for the invasion of Germany. Montgomery wanted to concentrate overwhelming power in his own command so that he could break through German defenses along the North Sea and make a dash for Berlin; Eisenhower favored a more cautious strategy that would halt along the Rhine and then develop simultaneous crossings at points both north and south. Some postwar critics have regretted that British wishes were overruled on these two issues. If the British and Americans had opened a Balkan front or concentrated on beating the Russians into Berlin, so the argument runs, the Soviets would not have been in a position to dominate Central and Southeastern Europe during the postwar period. American planning is criticized as shortsighted because it was based solely on immediate military considerations without adequate provision for the future balance of power. Yet the Americans had good reasons for the positions they took: Churchill was often too optimistic in his strategic inspirations and his projects had a way of consuming many more troops and materials than originally planned; Montgomery's projected dash for Berlin, moreover, would have been risky, exposing a long Allied flank to German counterattack.

Despite these disagreements, general Anglo-American cooperation remained cordial, and Eisenhower was outstandingly successful in maintaining harmonious relations between the British and American officers. With the Russians there was no such close collaboration. British and American officials who attempted to build up liaison were frequently exasperated by Russian secretiveness and suspicion. Nevertheless, there were no major breaks among the wartime allies, since each fully realized its dependence on the others. At critical moments the Soviet armies timed their offensives to relieve pressure on the western front, and Russian air bases were opened to permit American shuttle bombing of all parts of Germany.

Whenever the Anglo-American armies or the Russians entered a new country, inevitable problems arose. The Moscow Conference of Foreign Ministers of 1943 had based its declarations on the premise that the Big Three powers would follow a joint policy. For this purpose a European Advisory Commission was established, and control councils were subsequently set up for each occupied country. Yet from the beginning it was obvious that possession would be nine points of the law: Great Britain and the United States dictated policy for Italy with only a minimum of consultation with the Soviet, while the latter was even more insistent upon a free hand in dealing with Finland, Rumania, and Bulgaria, all of whom sued for peace during the fall of 1944.

From the American point of view, the Italian political situation developed hopefully. After the liberation of Rome, Victor Emmanuel retired from active rule, turning his powers over to Crown Prince Humbert in a futile effort to save the crown. Marshal Badoglio also resigned, and Ivanoe Bonomi became Premier of an all-party government, to which the British and Americans turned over an increasing degree of responsibility.

Right up to D day Roosevelt and Hull continued to be cool to de Gaulle and insisted that the future government of France be decided by its liberated peoples. De Gaulle was not informed of Anglo-American plans until the eve of the invasion, when he was flown from Algiers to London. Despite wounded pride over this treatment, the general consented to broadcast an appeal to the French underground to help the invasion forces in every possible way. During the subsequent battle for France, two facts became evident: thousands of Frenchmen were ready to join in the battle for national liberation, and General de Gaulle was regarded as a hero by Frenchmen of every party and class. Impressed by this evidence, Roosevelt and Churchill made belated amends for earlier slights. Gaullist armies were given the honor of leading the triumphal entry into Paris; and the French Committee of National Liberation was recognized as the *de facto* government. De Gaulle promptly took advantage of the new turn of events to demand that France play an equal role with the Big Three in future dealings with Germany.

For nations like Czechoslovakia and Poland more likely to be liberated from Nazi rule by the Russians than by the Anglo-Americans, it became important to try to achieve an understanding with the Soviet government. In December, 1943, President Eduard Beneš of the Czech government-in-exile signed a mutual aid treaty with Stalin, which he hoped would assure full postwar independence for his country, and then advised Prime Minister Stanislaw Mikolajczyk of the Polish government-in-exile in London to follow a similar course. But Poland's problems were much more difficult. Soviet annexation of eastern Poland during the days of the Hitler-Stalin pact had naturally embittered Russo-Polish relations. To make matters worse, when the London Poles publicly charged the Soviets with massacring some 10,000 Polish military prisoners, Stalin had broken off diplomatic relations with the government-in-exile and supported a rival group, partly Communist in membership.

Since Great Britain had gone to war in 1939 to help Poland against Hitler, Churchill was particularly anxious that a strong independent Poland emerge from the war. Yet as a practical politician, he knew that the Soviet Union would never permit the restoration of an openly anti-

Russian government on its western border. Moreover, he deplored the London Poles' insistence on regaining all their eastern territory. In the interests of reconciliation, the Prime Minister believed that the Poles should give up territory to Russia in the East and accept compensation at Germany's expense in the West. After some discussion with Stalin at Teheran, Churchill had tried unsuccessfully to persuade Mikolajczyk to accept such a solution. Roosevelt was reluctant to become involved in the explosive Polish situation, but when Mikolajczyk visited him in June, 1944, the President advised the Polish leader to settle his difficulties directly with Stalin. Mikolajczyk made a trip to Moscow for this purpose in August, but he considered the Russian price too high to be honorably accepted.

The already bad relations between Stalin and the London Poles became even worse as a result of the tragic Warsaw uprising in August, 1944, which was finally crushed by the Nazis after the death of thousands of Polish patriots. The London Poles bitterly accused the Russians of making only a belated effort to help the rebels; the Soviet government retorted that the uprising had been recklessly ordered by the London Poles without consulting with Moscow. As the Soviet armies advanced across Poland, Stalin recognized as the provisional government a committee with headquarters at Lublin, but the London Poles regarded this to be no more than a Soviet puppet.

The need to plan future campaigns, particularly against Japan, as well as to agree on postwar policy, impelled Roosevelt to seek another Big Three conference. Once again it proved difficult to obtain Stalin's acceptance: during the summer of 1944 he excused himself on the ground that he was needed to direct operations on the eastern front; in the fall a siege of illness made him unwilling to travel outside Russia. Meanwhile, Roosevelt and Churchill reconciled many of their own views at the second Quebec Conference in September, 1944. The next month Churchill visited Stalin in Moscow with reassuring results. When the British leader suggested a division of Balkan responsibilities with Russia assuming most of the burden in Rumania and Bulgaria and the British and Americans in Greece, Stalin readily fell in with this suggestion for temporary spheres of influence. The two men further agreed that decisions affecting Hungary and Yugoslavia would be equally shared. Although the American government did not associate itself with this bargain, Ambassador Averell Harriman participated in subsequent discussions concerning Far Eastern strategy. Stalin promised to enter the war against Japan three months after the final defeat of Germany—the length of time needed to shift men and supplies to Siberian bases. A Soviet offensive would then be launched against the Japanese in Manchuria, as the American chiefs of staff had requested.

Yalta

Soon after winning election for a fourth presidential term, Roosevelt left for another meeting with Stalin and Churchill, this time at Yalta, a Black Sea resort in the Russian Crimea. Also present at this most important of World War II conferences were Harry Hopkins, the President's most trusted adviser; Edward R. Stettinius, Jr., the Secretary of State recently appointed to succeed the ailing Cordell Hull; and a numerous company of military and diplomatic advisers. Agreement was readily achieved on issues of grand strategy: the Russians and the Anglo-Americans each promised to keep unrelenting pressure on the Germans in order to prevent any shifting of German divisions from one front to the other; the Russians renewed their promise to attack the Japanese in Manchuria two or three months after the surrender of Germany.

The most fateful issue discussed at Yalta was what the Soviet Union might rightfully claim as her reward for entering the war against Japan. Earlier discussions had indicated that the price would be substantial, but Roosevelt was reconciled to the necessity of meeting Stalin's terms. Underestimating the degree to which Japan had already been weakened by blockade and air attack and not counting upon the yet untested atomic bomb, the chiefs of staff had warned the President that the defeat of Japan might require as much as eighteen months of further fighting, as well as a costly invasion of the home islands. Roosevelt consequently accepted Soviet demands in the hope of shortening the war and saving American lives. As finally signed, the Big Three agreement provided that the Soviet Union was to get the Kurile Islands and the southern half of Sakhalin; she was to have the right to lease Port Arthur as a naval base, while Dairen was to be internationalized in a manner to safeguard "the preeminent interests of the Soviet Union"; the principal Manchurian railroads were to be operated by a joint Soviet-Chinese company; and finally the *status quo* in Outer Mongolia was to be preserved—in other words, this region was to continue as a Communist puppet state. In so far as these decisions affected China, it was recognized that they would require the concurrence of Chiang Kai-shek, which Roosevelt promised to try to get. Regardless of China's reaction, the Big Three "agreed that these claims of the Soviet Union shall be unquestionably fulfilled after Japan has been defeated."

This particular Yalta agreement was kept rigorously secret—primarily in the interests of military security. When finally published a year later, the deal was sharply criticized by many Americans not only as a betrayal of China, but as a threat to the Far Eastern balance of power. Yet criticism of Roosevelt's diplomacy must be tempered both by a recognition of the military situation and by a realization that he hoped the agreement would work out to China's benefit. The document itself recognized China's "full sovereignty" over Manchuria and pledged the Soviet Union to make a treaty of friendship and alliance with "the National Government of China." For the most part, Russia was demanding no more than had been hers before the Russo-Japanese War. To Roosevelt, this seemed a not unreasonable price for Chiang to pay for the expulsion of the Japanese and the restoration of Chinese territories lost since 1895. With these questions settled, the President hoped that the Chinese Nationalists and the Communists would patch up their long-time quarrel and work together to restore their sadly devastated country.

On many aspects of the German question the Big Three found themselves in easy agreement. With only minor Russian opposition it was decided that France should share in the occupation and control of the defeated enemy. Each of the four powers was to have its own occupation zone, but they were to coordinate their policies through a central control commission with headquarters in Berlin. The Big Three agreed to disarm all German forces, to eliminate or control all industry that might be used for military production, to punish war criminals, and to end all Nazi influence. "It is not our purpose to destroy the people of Germany," the Big Three announced, "but only when Nazism and militarism have been extirpated will there be hope for a decent life for Germans and a place for them in the comity of nations."

None of the Big Three was in a mood to advocate leniency. Indeed, less than six months earlier at their Quebec meeting Roosevelt and Churchill had accepted much of the so-called Morgenthau Plan,[4] a drastic program for dismembering Germany, dismantling its industry, and reducing the country to dependence upon agriculture. Hull and Stimson had never liked the Morgenthau Plan and had warned the President of the unwisdom of such Draconian measures; Churchill had been skeptical from the beginning, and Roosevelt became so. By the time of the Yalta Conference, the Morgenthau Plan was nearly dead, but Churchill and Roosevelt had not clarified any alternative program. The Yalta Agreement kept alive the possibility of dismembering the defeated enemy in the interests of future peace, but postponed the issue for subsequent consideration.

The question of reparations proved a thorny one. Stalin grimly notified his guests that Germany should pay 20 billion dollars, with Russia getting half this sum; to avoid the difficulties of transferring so much money, he proposed that reparations be made in foreign assets, industrial equipment, and labor, thus serving the dual purpose of indemnifying the victors and destroying the enemy's war potential. Fearful of impoverishing and em-

[4] Proposed by Secretary of the Treasury Henry Morgenthau, but drafted mostly by a subordinate Treasury Department official, Harry Dexter White, later accused of Communist affiliations.

bittering the Germans, Churchill argued for moderation. Roosevelt undertook to mediate between the two. In the end, the three accepted the general principle of reparations in kind and labor, but assigned the working
out of details to an Allied reparations commission to sit at Moscow. The
Russians and Americans agreed that the Soviet plan for a 20-billion-dollar
total should serve as a basis for discussion; the British recorded their belief
that no figure should be mentioned until the Moscow commission made its
study.

The Polish question came again under debate. Churchill's hope to merge
the London and Lublin groups proved impossible to achieve. The most
that Stalin would concede was that the Russian-sponsored provisional government be "reorganized on a broader democratic basis with the inclusion
of democratic leaders from Poland itself and from Poles abroad." The resulting "Polish Provisional Government of National Unity" was to be
"pledged to the holding of free and unfettered elections as soon as possible on the basis of universal suffrage and secret ballot." Roosevelt urged
Stalin to relax his boundary demands to allow the Poles to retain the region
around Lvov, but the Russian leader insisted on the so-called Curzon line.[5]
On the other hand, Stalin wanted to compensate Poland at Germany's
expense more generously than either Churchill or Roosevelt considered
wise. To put the Poles' western boundary at the Western Neisse River, as
Russia proposed, would dispossess millions of Germans and provide a
cause for future wars. The Big Three finally agreed that the eastern
boundary should follow the Curzon line, but that the western boundary
be left for the peace conference to determine.

The pledge of free elections made for Poland was extended to all the
other countries being delivered from Nazi occupation. In the Declaration
on Liberated Europe the Big Three promised to "jointly assist the people
in any European liberated state or former Axis satellite state" to establish
peace, to provide emergency relief, "to form interim governmental authorities broadly representative of all democratic elements in the population and pledged to the earliest possible establishment through free elections of governments responsive to the will of the people," and "to facilitate where necessary the holding of such elections." Hopeful for the future of true democracy though these words were, the Yalta agreements
failed to establish any effective machinery for setting up such provisional
governments and policing early elections. Responsibility fell to the nation
in actual occupation of each particular country, and the battle lines of
1945 were bringing most of Central and Southeastern Europe within the
Soviet orbit.

[5] Lord Curzon was British Foreign Secretary in 1920, when the British government
had defined the eastern limits of the territory to which it believed Poland had a good
right on historic and ethnic grounds.

The Big Three found themselves in substantial agreement on procedure for establishing a new international organization. Much of the preliminary work had already been done at the Dumbarton Oaks Conference of September, 1944. Two issues unsettled at this lower level were compromised at Yalta: Stalin agreed to a somewhat narrower definition of the right of the big powers to veto Security Council proceedings, and Roosevelt and Churchill promised to support Stalin in his contention that the Soviet Union be entitled to three votes in the Assembly. In a confidential letter to the other two, Roosevelt warned that he might have to ask for additional votes for the United States in consequence. With these matters settled, the Big Three jointly announced their intention to bring about "the earliest possible establishment . . . of a general international organization to maintain peace and security." The charter of the new world order was to be written at a United Nations conference to open on April 25, 1945, at San Francisco.

Although Yalta decisions regarding the Far East and such other sensitive issues as the dismemberment of Germany were kept secret, the other accords for occupying and controlling Germany, for the summoning of a UN conference, and for democratic elections in Poland and other liberated countries were made public on February 11, 1945. In every country the response was enthusiastic. A war-weary world found hope in the belief that Russia, Great Britain, and the United States would work together both to gain final victory and to ensure future peace.

In subsequent months, when the secret bargains were revealed and when Russia used the postwar situation to achieve Communist domination over neighboring countries, the word Yalta changed from a symbol of hope to one of cynical betrayal. Republican critics were quick to blame most of the world's postwar troubles on Roosevelt's surrender to Stalin's demands. The more exaggerated charges against the President may be readily dismissed. Although it is true that his once rugged health was failing, there is no evidence that senility or illness affected his decisions. Even more fantastic is the idea that American interests were betrayed by Communists or fellow travelers in the American delegation.[6] Some of the Yalta agreements were of dubious wisdom on their face; others sounded reasonable in theory but worked out badly in practice. The mistakes were caused by a variety of factors: conservative military estimates that prompted the paying of too high a price for Soviet participation in the Pacific war; an unwise faith in high-sounding phrases that gave Eastern Europe too little protection for self-determination; hatred of the Nazis that motivated an unduly harsh statement of intentions toward Germany.

[6] It is true that Alger Hiss, State Department official later convicted of perjury in denying his Communist affiliations, was at Yalta, but he was not in a position to influence major decisions.

Yet with all their shortcomings, the Yalta agreements might have assured postwar peace if they had been carried out in the spirit in which Roosevelt and Churchill intended them. Most of the subsequent troubles arose out of violations and distortions of the Big Three accords. The pieces of paper signed at Yalta were not so much at fault as conflicting ambitions and the brute facts of postwar military power.

Gathering Storm Clouds

The Big Three had scarcely returned home after their cordial leave-taking at Yalta before new evidence of mistrust appeared. Roosevelt and Churchill had expected prompt action to broaden the base of the Polish government, but Stalin circumvented this by various devices. Within a month Churchill was complaining to Roosevelt of "a great failure and an utter breakdown of what was settled at Yalta." Equally disturbing was Russian policy in Rumania, where a pro-Soviet government was imposed upon the unwilling king in violation of the Yalta agreements. On the other hand, Stalin's suspicion of his allies was revealed in accusations that the British and Americans were going behind his back in carrying on secret negotiations for a German surrender on the Italian front. Remonstrating against such charges, Roosevelt warned Stalin: "It would be one of the greatest tragedies of history if at the very moment of the victory now within our grasp, such distrust, such lack of faith, should prejudice the entire undertaking after the colossal losses of life, material, and treasure involved."

On April 12, 1945, Roosevelt commented in a letter to Churchill:

I would minimize the general Soviet problem as much as possible because these problems, in one form or another, seem to arise every day, and most of them straighten out....

We must be firm, however, and our course thus far is correct.

These were the President's final reflections on the world situation, for that very day he was stricken with the cerebral hemorrhage that killed him.

Roosevelt's death brought to the presidency Harry S. Truman, whose nomination for Vice President in 1944 had resulted from a complex political situation. After a routine career in Kansas City politics, Truman had earned modest distinction as Senator from Missouri. In this position he had gained a knowledge of domestic problems, but he had had no opportunity to study the momentous issues of foreign policy now confronting the nation. During his initial weeks in the White House, Truman clung closely to the line of policy that he believed Roosevelt would have followed. The San Francisco United Nations Conference convened on schedule (April 25, 1945), and on July 17 Truman took his place at the conference in Potsdam in the Berlin suburbs, where the Big Three continued the planning for the postwar world begun at Teheran and Yalta. The new President leaned heavily on the advisers who had been closest to Roosevelt: he turned to General Marshall and Admiral William Leahy on military and naval matters; he even called upon the ailing Harry Hopkins to make an urgent trip to Moscow late in May to discuss directly with Stalin certain critical issues.

Truman did, however, feel the need to make a change in the State Department. Stettinius was a little-known former businessman, whose appointment to succeed Hull had really symbolized Roosevelt's intention to act as his own Secretary of State. Feeling the need of a stronger man in such a critical post, Truman appointed James F. Byrnes to the post on July 3. Byrnes, a former Senator from South Carolina and Supreme Court Justice, had held important responsibilities in the war administration and had been initiated into the mysteries of high-level diplomacy by accompanying Roosevelt to Yalta.

Meanwhile, the United Nations had crashed through to complete victory in Europe. The Anglo-American crossing of the Rhine was achieved with unexpected ease in March, and during April the invading armies overran the heart of the enemy country. Since the Nazis were resisting more strongly in the east than in the west, Churchill urged that the Anglo-Americans drive as deeply as possible into Germany in order to give leverage to the Western nations in settling outstanding issues with Stalin. But neither Truman nor Eisenhower, to whom the President allowed great discretion, wanted to jeopardize the lives of American soldiers by advancing farther east than necessary on military grounds. The Western armies were therefore ordered to halt at the Elbe River, where they presently made an amicable juncture with the Russians.

As a last desperate gamble, the Nazi chiefs who took over after Hitler's suicide on May 1, attempted to surrender to the British and Americans on terms that would have permitted them to continue the war against the Russians. But this effort to split the wartime coalition failed, and on May 7, in a little schoolhouse at Reims, France, German Chief of Staff Gustav Jodl accepted the unconditional surrender terms handed him by General Walter Bedell Smith, Eisenhower's Chief of Staff. At Berlin on the following day military representatives of Russia joined with those of the Western powers in accepting a formal German surrender to become effective at 12:01 A.M. (European time) on May 9, 1945.

Still holding together despite ominous cracks, the great coalition now concentrated its fire upon Japan, the last surviving Axis partner. On August 8—three months to the day after the Berlin surrender—the Soviet Union declared war on Japan and invaded Manchuria and Korea in accordance with its pledges. Two days earlier a single bomb dropped from an American plane had destroyed the Japanese industrial city of Hiroshima, thereby initiating the awesome age of nuclear weapons. Nagasaki was similarly pulverized on August 9. Stunned by these blows and already weakened by blockade and air bombardment, the Japanese government announced on August 10 its willingness to surrender, provided Emperor Hirohito were allowed to keep his throne.

The Allies replied that they would respect the Emperor's position only until they had completed an occupation of the country and supervised the carrying out of unconditional surrender. Then the Japanese people would decide their future form of government in a free election. On August 14, the Japanese government accepted these terms, and five days later a preliminary surrender document was signed at Manila. By a final act of impressive pageantry, General MacArthur accepted the formal Japanese surrender on September 2, 1945, aboard the American battleship *Missouri* in Tokyo Bay. World War II had thus culminated in complete victory for the United Nations and for the anti-Axis partnership of Great Britain, the Soviet Union, and the United States.

PART FIVE

Diplomacy of the Atomic Age

Awed by the terrible weapon placed in their hands by modern science, American statesmen in 1946 offered to surrender control of atomic energy to an international agency with adequate powers to save mankind from destruction and assure that this new source of energy should be used only for human welfare. Unfortunately, Stalin's suspicion of his recent allies was too great to permit the achievement of this goal.

For four years the United States enjoyed a power unique in its history. So long as it was the only nation possessing atomic bombs, it could destroy the cities of any enemy so completely as to force almost certain surrender. As Americans came to realize the danger of Communist expansion and initiated a policy of containment, they did so with confidence that in a final showdown their nation had sufficient power to achieve its goals. Yet even while the American monopoly lasted, responsible statesmen shrank from any rash employment of atomic bombs. Many American citizens felt a sense of guilt over the fate of Hiroshima and Nagasaki; they would countenance the further use of the new weapons only as a last resort. Outside the United States, the feeling was even stronger that the bomb imperiled the welfare of all mankind. Quite apart from humanitarian considerations, European shuddered in the knowledge that even without atomic weapons the Soviet Union had terrible potentialities for retaliation. With their huge armies well equipped with planes and tanks, the Russians could speedily overrun all Western Europe even while their own cities were being destroyed.

In August, 1949, the Soviets themselves tested an atomic bomb—long before complaisant American opinion had expected such a development. Trying desperately to keep ahead, the United States concentrated on producing the so-called hydrogen bomb, a weapon that would surpass the atomic bomb as decisively as that weapon had surpassed conventional explosives. In November, 1952, the Americans exploded an early version of the new weapon, and in March, 1954, they tested a fully developed H bomb of awe-inspiring strength, equivalent in explosive power to ten times all the Allied bombs dropped on Hitler's Germany. But Russian science was obviously cutting down the American lead, for the Soviets had tested their own first H bomb in August, 1953.

By this time it was clear that nuclear warfare would be a two-way street. If American bombers could destroy Moscow and Leningrad, Russian planes could almost as surely annihilate New York and Chicago. Indeed, the American public found it difficult to comprehend the full seriousness of the threat. A 10-megaton H bomb—by no means the largest possible one—would have an explosive force of 10 million tons of TNT or 500 times that of the atomic bomb that had destroyed Hiroshima. If such a bomb fell on New York City at the corner of 42d Street and Fifth Avenue, it would totally wipe out not only all Manhattan below 96th Street, but much of Queens and Jersey City as well, causing at least 3 million deaths. Beyond this would be another ring of heavy mortality extending over upper Manhattan and the other boroughs, where almost a million more deaths might be expected. Scarcely less terrifying would be the radioactive fall-out coming down in a deadly rain over an area as large as the state of New Jersey.

Since the most likely route for Soviet heavy bombers would be across Arctic wastes from northeastern Siberia or from the Kola Peninsula in the Northwest, the United States built a string of radar stations known as the Distant Early Warning (DEW) Line stretching across the Arctic Circle from Alaska through Canada to Baffin Bay. Below this was another detection system known as the Mid-Canada Line. Near the United States–Canada border was the first interception line, where enemy bombers would be opposed by intercepting American jet fighter planes. Below this were many guided missile bases capable of throwing up lethal anti-aircraft fire to protect vital American targets. Formidable though these defenses were, American strategists admitted that they could not count on destroying 100 per cent of any attacking force. Even though only a few enemy planes got through, it would not be possible to save American cities from heavy punishment.

The nation's best deterrent against attack was its Strategic Air Command (SAC), which maintained a string of bases extending around the globe from Okinawa and the Philippines through Saudi Arabia, Morocco, Spain, Great Britain, Iceland, and the United States itself. With crews and planes kept in readiness around the clock, long-distance bombers could start winging toward Moscow and other Russian targets within a matter of minutes after the order was given in Washington.

Regardless of whether the Soviet Union did or did not have more and better bombers than the United States—a matter of dispute—the United States had certain advantages so long as planes were necessary to deliver nuclear weapons. Whereas Russian attacks on the United States could be launched from only a relatively few points, American bombers could approach Soviet targets from many different directions, thereby multiplying Russian detection problems. Moreover, long-range American bombers could be refueled over friendly territory, but Soviet ones would face a major handicap in having to refuel over hostile soil.

But the strategic situation became much less favorable after October, 1957, when the Russians launched their first sputnik or earth satellite. Although the United States subsequently launched satellites of its own, the Soviet Union appeared to be substantially ahead in its development of rocketry. This and other evidence gave clear warning to the West that the Russians were rapidly improving ballistic missiles to the point where the deterrent power of the Strategic Air Command might be seriously challenged. Intercontinental ballistic missiles would travel through space so high and fast that detection and interception would be almost impossible.

However much Americans sighed for the good old days when the two oceans provided barriers behind which the nation could enjoy isolation, a return to such a policy was now out of the question. Conditions had changed so much since 1941 that even the precedents of World Wars I and II could not be followed. In those conflicts the United States had been able to remain neutral for two or three years while other nations stood the heat of battle. But this was not a possibility in dealing with the Soviet Union. So formidable was Communist power that no other country dared oppose it without assurance that instant American support would be available. The nation so long suspicious of entangling alliances now found itself entering mutual security treaties pledging it to help defend countries in every part of the globe—even including such recent enemies as Japan, Italy, and West Germany.

Beginning with the outbreak of the Korean conflict in 1950, foreign affairs dominated American politics to a degree almost unparalleled in American history. Although Republicans and Democrats really agreed on the fundamentals of policy and differed only on matters of detail, each party accused the other of criminal shortsightedness in foreign affairs. The Republicans charged that the Truman administration had permitted the Communists to take over China and involved the nation in futile and unnecessary war in Korea; the Democrats claimed credit for having stemmed the tide of communism through the Marshall Plan and NATO and accused their Republican successors of losing the strategic advantage that had thus been gained. Bewildered by these conflicting assertions, the American voters paradoxically elected Democratic congresses on most occasions, but twice gave thumping majorities to the Republican presidential candidate. In a time of anxiety they demonstrated an impressive trust in the sincerity and basic common sense of the World War II hero, General Eisenhower.

34

FROM ONE WORLD TO TWO

In 1943 Wendell Willkie had coined a phrase that conveyed much of the war-born idealism of the American people. In his book, *One World*, he told of a trip around the globe during which he had been impressed with the longing for peace and freedom shared by people everywhere, by Russians and Chinese as well as by Englishmen and Americans. To win the peace, said Willkie, three things were necessary: immediate planning, the extension of political and economic freedom to all countries, and an active and constructive role for the United States in championing freedom and keeping world peace. In harmony with this spirit the United States turned away from its old isolationism and became the most active sponsor of the new United Nations organization.

Unhappily the "one-world" ideal proved a mirage, drawing weary travelers on but melting into the desert whenever it seemed about to be reached. In actuality, there was not one world but two. There was the Communist world, where individual freedom was subordinated to the party's conception of the collective will, and the non-Communist world, where men sought to preserve the tradition of individual liberty. Within a few years these two worlds became engaged in a vast struggle for power and influence, popularly known as the "cold war."

No previous question in mankind's long history had been more vital than the one emerging after World War II. Could the Communist and non-Communist worlds coexist in an uneasy balance, or would they stumble into a gigantic collision in which both might be destroyed?

Birth of the United Nations Charter

American participation in World War II had resulted in a striking reversal in public attitudes toward international affairs. Isolationism of the type that had prevented American membership both in Woodrow Wilson's League of Nations and in Elihu Root's World Court appeared to be nearly dead after Pearl Harbor. Even so, Roosevelt moved warily, often seeming to lag behind Wendell Willkie and other crusaders for the "one-world" ideal. He took one cautious step toward closer economic co-operation by sponsoring a forty-four-nation Conference on Food and Agriculture at Hot Springs, Virginia, in May, 1943, and another by en-couraging the organization of a United Nations Relief and Rehabilitation Administration (UNRRA) the next November.

More ambitious planning was invited by the Fulbright and Connally resolutions, passed by the House and Senate respectively during the fall of 1943. At the international level, the idea of a postwar peace organiza-tion was accepted by the Big Four foreign ministers at Moscow and by the chiefs of state at Teheran and Yalta.

Throughout 1944 Secretary Hull and his State Department subordinates gave close study to the problem. As early as February, President Roosevelt approved a draft charter. Warned by Wilson's unhappy experience of the need to keep the project clear of politics, Hull sought the advice of respected elder statesmen like the Republican Charles Evans Hughes and the Democrat John W. Davis. He also invited key members of the Senate Foreign Relations Committee to study the American draft and make sug-gestions for its improvement. Meantime, Hull was negotiating with Britain and the Soviet Union. This preliminary work culminated in the Dumbarton Oaks Conference (August–October, 1944), held on a private estate in Washington, D.C. Out of these informal meetings of British, American, Russian, and Chinese diplomats there emerged a set of pro-posals complete in many respects, although postponing for later decision certain troublesome problems such as eligibility for membership, the extent of the veto, and the system of colonial trusteeships. The Big Three at Yalta settled some of these and planned the San Francisco Conference, at which representatives from all the United Nations would have their say.

So far as the United States was concerned, the San Francisco Conference could not have met in a more sympathetic atmosphere. Roosevelt's recent death had sobered the nation, and Republicans and Democrats had de-clared a temporary recess on politics to support the new President. Both parties were ready to welcome the proposed international organization with a minimum of fault finding. Before his death Roosevelt had made his own contribution to bipartisanship by appointing an outstanding Amer-ican delegation. Secretary Stettinius was named chairman, with former Secretary Hull as "senior delegate and senior adviser." [1] Congress was given full recognition with the appointment of two Democrats, Senator

[1] Illness prevented Hull from going to San Francisco, but he did telephone advice from his hospital bed.

Tom Connally and Representative Sol Bloom, and two Republicans, Senator Arthur Vandenberg and Representative Charles Eaton. To complete the delegation, Roosevelt had named Dean Virginia Gildersleeve of Barnard College and Commander Harold Stassen, former Republican Governor of Minnesota.

The forty-eight nations represented at the San Francisco Conference included all those who had declared war on the Axis. After the conference opened, White Russia and the Ukraine were admitted to separate representation at the insistence of Foreign Commissar Molotov, who called upon the United States to honor Roosevelt's Yalta promise.[2] On the other hand, the Russian request for a seat for Poland was denied on the grounds that the government reorganization promised at Yalta had not been carried out. Admitted to the conference after sharp controversy was Argentina, whose cause was championed by the other Latin-American republics despite her record of collaboration with the Axis throughout most of the war.

The initial disagreement over membership was followed by disputes on many other issues, with the Soviet representatives sometimes arguing against their big-power associates, the small powers disagreeing with the larger ones, and the American states with the European ones. Even the Russians, however, hesitated to press their contentions to the point of deadlocking the deliberations, and in the end the necessary words were found to bridge the fissures among the parties. On June 25, 1945, the Conference gave the final document its unanimous approval, while the delegates and the entire audience rose and cheered. Hopes for a brave new world were still bright.

The UN Charter

Although many Americans had embraced internationalism so warmly that they were clamoring for world federation, responsible statesmen were convinced that the United States was not ready to sacrifice its sovereignty. Their ambition was to build upon the experience provided by the old League of Nations and World Court, hoping that wholehearted American participation would make the new organization more successful than the old ones. While the framers hoped to make the UN Charter a stronger and clearer document than the Covenant of the League had been, they counted less on mechanical improvements than upon the complete support of the great powers.

The UN was to have as its most important organs a General Assembly and a Security Council. In the General Assembly each member nation

[2] Roosevelt had reserved a right for the United States to ask for two additional UN seats, but the American government decided not to do so.

was to have one vote; in the Security Council the five great powers—the United States, the Soviet Union, Great Britain, France, and China—were to have permanent seats, and there were to be six nonpermanent positions held by nations elected by a two-thirds vote of the General Assembly. The functions of the two bodies were more sharply defined than in the old League of Nations. The General Assembly, meeting in regular annual sessions and in special sessions when necessary, was primarily an international forum with broad powers to discuss international problems. The Security Council, on the other hand, was entrusted with "primary responsibility for the maintenance of international peace and security." Its members were to keep representatives near UN headquarters so that the Security Council could be immediately convened to deal with any emergency. To deal with acts of aggression or threats to the peace, it had broad powers including the breaking off of diplomatic relations and the use of air, land, and sea forces to be placed at its disposal by the member states.

Although impressive authority had been vested in the Security Council, the use of this power was carefully shackled by the so-called veto. No important action could be taken without seven affirmative votes, including those of all five permanent members. All those who had participated in the early planning for the UN had recognized that some kind of veto would be necessary: the United States Senate would, it was believed, reject out of hand any international document under which American troops might become involved in checking aggression without American consent; and Britain and Russia were equally insistent that great-power unanimity must be required for any UN attempt at coercion. When some of the smaller nations objected to the veto at the San Francisco Conference, they were bluntly told that without it there would be no UN organization at all.

Despite agreement that the veto was necessary, the Russians tried to carry the principle much farther than their allies thought desirable. At the Yalta Conference Roosevelt had argued that whenever the Security Council was trying to bring about a voluntary settlement, the parties to the dispute ought to abstain from voting; Stalin had at first opposed this idea, but had eventually conceded to the American position. At San Francisco, however, the Russians raised a new issue that threatened to break up the conference. How should the Security Council vote when the question was whether or not to discuss a particular issue? If this were to be considered as a mere matter of procedure, it might be decided by a majority of seven votes; if—as the Russians insisted—it were to be considered as a substantive matter, all the permanent members would have to concur. This Russian claim of a right to veto agenda items would severely constrict the principle of freedom of discussion, to which the Americans were strongly attached. The deadlock was broken in Moscow, where

Harry Hopkins was conferring on other critical Russian-American disagreements. Stalin waived the issue as of little importance and accepted the American interpretation of the Yalta formula. On the whole, therefore, the United States was successful in having the veto provisions written about as it had wanted; if the veto worked out badly in practice, it was because of the breakdown of the great-power community of interest upon which the whole UN plan depended.

Besides the General Assembly and the Security Council, the UN Charter provided for a Secretariat to be headed by a Secretary General as chief administrative officer of the entire organization, for a Trusteeship Council to supervise trust territories being administered by various UN members, for an Economic and Social Council to foster international cooperation in the nonpolitical sphere, and finally for a new International Court of Justice, almost identical with the old World Court.

Launching the One-world Ship

The UN Charter was to come into effect as soon as the Big Five powers and half of the other original signatories had ratified it. In the United States this was achieved with surprising ease. After only a week's debate the Senate approved the Charter on July 28, 1945, by a vote of 89 to 2. The "bitter-enders" of other days had now been reduced to the Republicans Langer of North Dakota, Shipstead of Minnesota, and Johnson of California—the last of these too ill to vote. Other ratifications were registered promptly, and on October 24 Secretary Byrnes formally proclaimed the United Nations Charter to be "now part of the law of nations."

The new organization began its actual functioning in London in January, 1946, moving after a few months to temporary quarters in the New York City suburbs. In harmony with the generous spirit of these days, John D. Rockefeller, Jr., offered to provide a site for permanent headquarters overlooking the East River in midtown Manhattan, and a beautiful group of buildings in modern architecture was completed in 1952. This bit of international territory in the heart of America's largest city proved a mecca for sightseers and helped to sustain a fairly warm American support for world cooperation.

Such Americans as had naïvely hoped that all world frictions would miraculously disappear once the UN were in operation were soon disillusioned. The true situation was dramatized during the new organization's first weeks of history. When Iran protested to the Security Council over continued occupation of her territory by Russian troops, the Soviet Union objected to discussion of the issue. Consistently with its stand at Yalta and San Francisco, the United States upheld the principle of freedom of discussion; the Soviet delegate thereupon walked out of the Council to show his disapproval. This particular issue was settled by direct negotiations between the Soviet Union and Iran, yet the portent was serious: the Russians intended to keep a free hand in dealing with their neighbors and would not meekly submit to UN supervision of their conduct.

Other evidence that the Soviet Union intended to play a lone hand soon accumulated. The UN Charter had specified that the member nations should make available to the Security Council certain armed forces, thus providing an international police force that might be employed to maintain peace. But the special agreements necessary to bring this into effect were never negotiated—largely because of Russian obstructionism. The Soviet Union failed to join the UN Educational, Scientific, and Cultural Organization (UNESCO) and certain of the economic agencies. Instead of reserving its Security Council veto for only the most serious issues— as the UN framers had intended—the Soviet Union employed it freely. Before the end of 1950 the Russians had used the veto on some fifty occasions and had also resorted to numerous boycotts of Council sessions. From the non-Communist point of view, the Soviet Union was sabotaging the UN to carry out a policy of dangerous aggression; in their own eyes, the Russians were protecting the minority interests of the Communist states against intrigues to use the UN machinery in the interests of hostile capitalism.

Inevitably this unhappy state of affairs led to a considerable degree of American disillusionment. Some nationalists wanted the United States to withdraw from all such international ties; others cried for expulsion of Russia from the UN, or if this were impossible for abandoning the UN and organizing anew without Russia. Yet more thoughtful students of the world situation realized that this would settle nothing. East-West frictions would only be intensified with a rising danger of annihilating war. So long as the United States and the Soviet Union both remained within the UN, its machinery was available for instant use whenever the two could find some basis for agreement. Moreover, the UN's failure to achieve great-power harmony was balanced by a substantial list of achievements not only in the nonpolitical field but in easing the birth pangs of such new states as Israel and Indonesia.

The Potsdam Agreements

The San Francisco Conference had by no means served the purpose of a peace conference. To fix the fate of the defeated enemies, direct negotiations among the victors would be necessary. As a first step, the Big Three heads of state with their advisers assembled at Potsdam in the suburbs of conquered Berlin in July, 1945. Faces around the conference table had strikingly changed since the Yalta meeting only five months before. Representing the United States were President Truman and his new Secretary of State, James F. Byrnes; representing Britain were Prime Minister Clement Attlee and Foreign Minister Ernest Bevin, key men in the new Labor government brought to power by a recent election.[3] Only the tough Russian team of Stalin and Molotov was the same.

Byrnes was convinced that the problems of 1945 were too complex to be settled in one great peace conference like the Paris meeting of 1919. He proposed as an alternative that the Big Five foreign ministers prepare draft peace treaties for each of the defeated powers and that these should then be submitted to a full UN conference for discussion, just as the UN Charter had been. Since the problems involved in the case of Italy and the Nazi satellite states promised to be less troublesome than that of Germany, Byrnes suggested that the foreign ministers take them up first. To this plan of action the Russians and British gave ready consent, insisting only that Chinese and French participation in the Council of Foreign Ministers should be limited to the treaties that particularly concerned them.

On issues involving the military occupation of Germany there was easy agreement along lines already well charted in earlier conferences. Although the Soviet Union, Great Britain, France, and the United States were each to have their separate zones, there was to be "uniformity of treatment of the German population throughout Germany." The guiding principles were to be complete disarmament and demilitarization and elimination or control of all German industry that could be used for military production, destruction of the Nazi party and all Nazi influence, and eventual reconstruction of German political life on a democratic basis. To implement these principles, there was to be a prompt trial of Nazi war criminals and a thoroughgoing reform of the German educational and judicial systems. Local self-government and free political parties were to be promptly restored; for the time being there was to be no central government, but "certain essential central German administrative departments" would be established to deal with economic matters under the direction of the Allied Control Council.

The Polish ghost that had haunted earlier Big Three meetings reappeared at Potsdam. In a bid for Polish friendship, the Soviets had turned over to Poland for administration all German territory east of the Western Neisse River—the very region Churchill and Roosevelt had been unwilling to transfer. Although the Russians defended their action as a temporary arrangement, leaving open the question of final borders, the step had grave implications. Once the Poles had occupied the disputed zone and

[3] Churchill and Eden, still in office until July 26, opened the conference, but they brought along Attlee and Bevin to take over in case the elections went against the Conservatives.

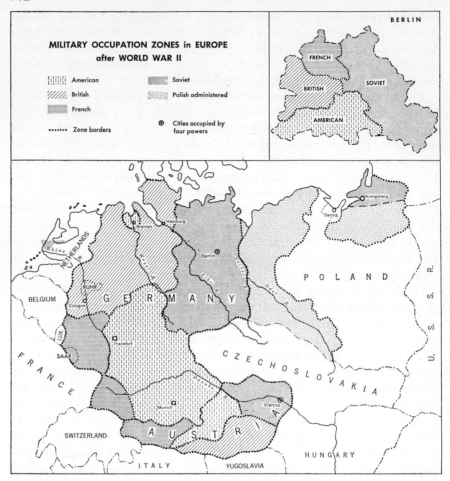

MILITARY OCCUPATION ZONES in EUROPE
after WORLD WAR II

||||||| American   Soviet
/////// British   Polish administered
French

.... Zone borders   ◉ Cities occupied by
                            four powers

its German population had fled to the west, it would be difficult to return any substantial part to Germany. Since the area included one-quarter of the agricultural lands of the defeated enemy as well as important industrial and mineral resources in Silesia, the economic consequences were likely to be serious. Unhappy though they were with this *fait accompli*, Truman and Attlee could do nothing about it, and the Big Three merely reaffirmed that "the final delimitation of the western frontier of Poland should await the peace settlement." [4] Also reaffirmed was the promise of free Polish elections with full freedom of the press in reporting them.[5]

[4] By a separate agreement the Big Three accepted the principle that the Königsberg area of East Prussia should be transferred to the Soviet Union.

[5] As a result of Harry Hopkins's mission to Moscow in May, Stalin had agreed that Mikolajczyk should join the Warsaw regime; and the United States had thereafter recognized the provisional government and supported Poland's admission to the UN.

Truman and Byrnes put up their sharpest fight on the reparations issue. Since the Yalta Conference the Reparations Commission had held long wrangling sessions at Moscow without agreement. Remembering the situation in the 1920s when annual German reparations payments had been made possible only through American loans, Byrnes opposed any collection of reparations out of current output until Germany exported enough goods to pay for essential imports like food and raw materials. On the other hand, indiscriminate Russian looting of German factories without systematic accounting had complicated the Yalta plan of collecting reparations by confiscating German machinery and equipment. Moreover, since the larger part of German industry was located in the western occupation zones, there was a problem of how much of this surplus Russia was entitled to. In the end, the Potsdam Agreement provided that the Soviet Union was to meet its reparations claims in part by removals from its own occupation zone and from appropriate German external assets; out of these seizures it was to settle Polish reparations claims as well. Similarly, the reparations claims of the United States, Great Britain, and other countries were to be met by removals from the western occupation zones and from external assets. In addition, the Soviet Union was to receive 25 per cent of the surplus equipment of the western zones— 15 per cent in exchange for food, fuel, and raw material from its own zone and 10 per cent outright.

Punishing the War Criminals

In at least one matter the Potsdam agreements were faithfully carried out. In November, 1945, at Nuremberg—scene of many Nazi spectacles in other days—an international tribunal composed of Russian, British, French, and American jurists convened for the trial of twenty-two alleged war criminals. The defendants included the famous Air Marshal Hermann Goering and other high military and civilian leaders charged with violations of the rules of war and crimes against humanity. Particularly controversial was the charge that they had broken international law by plotting aggressive war in violation of the Kellogg-Briand Pact. All but three of the defendants were found guilty; eleven were sentenced to death by hanging and the other eight were given prison terms.[6]

Critics of this procedure deplored the killing of enemy prisoners as an act of vengeance unworthy of the twentieth century. They could see no due process of law in proceedings where the victors served both as accusors and judges. This view was warmly combatted by Supreme Court Justice Robert H. Jackson, who was the chief United States prosecutor.

[6] Goering escaped by a last-minute suicide. Hitler, Goebbels, and Himmler had killed themselves during the last days of the war.

He and others defended the executions as just retribution for well-authenticated crimes and as a deterrent to future aggression.

The Nuremberg drama was followed by numerous other trials in the separate occupation zones. The American courts alone found over 1,500 Germans guilty of war crimes and imposed more than 400 death penalties. There were also a number of trials in conquered Japan, with such prominent leaders as former Premier Tojo and certain generals being sent to the gallows.

Progress in Peacemaking

In accordance with the Potsdam Agreement, a Big Four Council of Foreign Ministers convened at London in September, 1945, to begin the preparation of draft treaties for Italy, Bulgaria, Rumania, Hungary, and Finland. It soon became obvious that this would be no easy assignment. Molotov demanded Yugoslav annexation of Trieste, large reparations from Italy, and a Soviet trusteeship over some of the Italian colonies. Byrnes and Bevin pressed for policies that would broaden the governments of Bulgaria and Rumania and provide for some kind of international control over the Danube River. A deadlock on these and other issues broke up the London meeting, but the foreign ministers met again in Moscow in December, 1945, and in Paris in April and June of the next year.

Although these stubborn bargaining sessions had not settled all outstanding difficulties, Byrnes finally gained the approval of the other foreign ministers for submitting the draft treaties to a peace conference in which all twenty-one nations that had fought against the Nazis and their European allies would be represented. Meeting at Paris from July to October, 1946, the conference gave a hearing not only to the smaller powers on the victorious side but to the defeated states as well. The peace conference made some ninety recommendations, which the Big Four foreign ministers reviewed at a New York meeting in November. With Molotov in a somewhat more cooperative mood, over seventy of these recommendations were incorporated in the final treaties signed at Paris on February 10, 1947.

The most important of these treaties, that with Italy, provided for slight boundary rectifications in favor of France, the cession of the Dodecanese Islands to Greece, and of most of Venezia Giulia and certain Adriatic islands to Yugoslavia. Trieste was made a free city under the supervision of the UN Security Council.[7] The troublesome problem of the Italian colonies was postponed by placing them under temporary British trusteeship except for Ethiopia, which regained its independence.[8]

[7] In 1954 Italy and Yugoslavia agreed to partition the Free Territory of Trieste.

[8] Libya became independent in 1952; Eritrea was meanwhile federated with Ethiopia; and Somalia was placed under Italian trusteeship with a promise of early independence.

Italy's armed forces were reduced to 300,000 men, and she was required to pay 360 million dollars in reparations—100 million dollars of this to Russia.

The treaties with the other former Nazi satellites—Bulgaria, Rumania, Hungary, and Finland—required arms limitations and reparations, as well as some transfers of territory. British and American insistence resulted in the incorporation of clauses pledging the free navigation of the Danube and nondiscrimination in trade despite Soviet charges that the West was trying to perpetuate capitalist "enslavement" of the Balkan peoples.

The fifteen months or more of haggling required to negotiate the satellite treaties provided a disillusioning education in the difficulties of doing business with the Soviet Union. Frustrating though the experience was, there seemed to be a few modest compensations. For one thing, reasonably satisfactory treaties had finally been achieved. For another, Secretary Byrnes had been able to conduct negotiations on a bipartisan basis and to avoid trouble with the Senate by taking Senators Connally and Vandenberg, ranking Democratic and Republican members of the Foreign Relations Committee, along with him. The Byrnes-Connally-Vandenberg diplomatic team did not, however, escape all criticism. During the Paris peace conference Secretary of Commerce Henry Wallace made a speech sharply criticizing American policy as too harsh toward the Soviet Union. Byrnes threatened to resign, and President Truman somewhat belatedly exerted his authority to support his Secretary of State. Forced out of the Cabinet, Wallace became the principal critic of the tougher American policy. The former Vice President and Secretary of Commerce believed that patience and conciliation could still restore the Big Three cooperation of World War II days.

Deadlock on Austria and Germany

The peacemaking machinery that had ground out the satellite treaties so slowly broke down completely in dealing with the Austrian and German problems. Tiny Austria hardly seemed important enough for serious dissension, and indeed in 1945 she seemed to be advancing speedily toward full independence, treated more as a liberated than as an enemy country. But after Austrian elections in November, 1945, resulted in victories for the Socialist and Catholic parties, with the Communists receiving only 5 per cent of the vote, the Soviet position hardened. By demanding that Nazi assets be seized as reparations, the Soviets threatened to gain control of key Austrian industries. A draft treaty complete in most of its terms was approved in 1949, but the Russians still refused to complete the task, thereby necessitating a continuance of the four-power occupation. Not until 1955—ten years after V-E Day—was the Austrian peace treaty finally completed.

More important than any other European problem was the future of Germany. Even truncated by losses of territory in the East, a reunited Germany would contain some 67 million people with tremendous industrial resources. At Yalta and Potsdam the Big Three had agreed that Germany's military potential must be curbed before it would be safe to restore her sovereignty. Aware that the Soviet Union and France had particular reason to fear what might happen once the crippled giant regained his strength, Secretary Byrnes suggested a four-power treaty under which the victors would cooperate to keep Germany demilitarized for twenty-five years or more and would take common action against any new German aggression. Senators Connally and Vandenberg supported this radical departure from the old isolationism, but Stalin and Molotov rejected the idea—probably reluctant to having the United States involved in European affairs on a long-range basis.

The British and Americans stressed the Potsdam pledge to set up as quickly as possible central German administrative departments to deal with economic matters. They regarded this both as a desirable first step toward establishing a government with which a peace treaty could be signed and as a way of restoring Germany to a self-sufficient economic life. The inability of the western occupation zones to feed themselves was costing British taxpayers about 400 million dollars a year and American taxpayers about 200 million. But France and the Soviet Union, each for its own reasons, blocked reunification. De Gaulle, who had not been invited to Potsdam in 1945, felt no obligation to support the Big Three agreements. He demanded French annexation of the coal-rich Saar Basin, French administration of the strategic Rhineland, and international control over the heavy industry of the Ruhr. The United States supported the French Saar claim, but opposed French demands in the Ruhr and the Rhineland. Even more divisive was the Soviet position. Dissatisfied with the Potsdam settlement, the Russians had revived their demand for 10 billion dollars in reparations, to be taken largely out of current German production. They also had their eye on the Ruhr industries, proposing that these be placed under four-power control. The British and Americans resisted these Russian demands. They wanted German exports used to pay for necessary imports rather than as tribute to the Russians. Moreover, they suspected that both the reparations and the Ruhr demands were part of a scheme to paralyze German economic life and promote the interests of the Communist party.

During its several meetings in 1945 and 1946 the Council of Foreign Ministers was unable to make any progress toward a German peace treaty. The situation came to a showdown at Moscow in March, 1947. By this time Byrnes had retired and General George C. Marshall was the American Secretary of State. The Americans sought three immediate goals: the establishment of central German administrations to coordinate the four occupation zones, approval of a four-power pact to prevent German rearmament, and an Austrian treaty. To all these American proposals the Russians interposed objections and pushed for a program of their own. Instead of the federalized Germany favored by the Americans, Molotov now argued for a highly centralized German government. Marshall suspected that the real Soviet objective was to transform Germany into a Russian economic satellite by insisting on heavy reparations payments out of current production. Then by centralizing authority in Berlin, the Russians hoped to set up a situation favorable to a seizure of power by the German Communists. After seven weeks of deadlock, the Moscow Conference broke up without making any progress at all toward a German peace treaty. This failure combined with developments elsewhere to bring about a notable stiffening of American policy toward the Soviet Union in 1947.

The Hard Facts of Postwar Life

Underlying the important decisions of 1947 was a belated facing up to the harsh realities of the international situation. During 1945 and 1946 most Americans had been in a mood of penitence for their old isolationist sins. The United States had been wrong in its refusal to join the old League of Nations; it therefore sought atonement by wholehearted support of the new United Nations. It had been wrong in denying recognition and friendship to the Soviet Union; it now sought amends by offering to continue the wartime collaboration. By carrying out these good resolutions, Americans hoped to achieve a free and peaceful world. Not for many months did they come to the painful realization that they might have to make further sacrifices if the values of Western civilization were to be preserved.

The persistence of American illusions is better understood if certain facts are kept in mind. For one thing, millions of servicemen were eager to return to civilian life as soon as the enemy countries surrendered—a desire shared by their parents, wives, and sweethearts. Demobilization was so rapid that the nation's military power was reduced to a dangerously low level by the end of 1946. Even so, congressional hostility to peacetime conscription resulted in a suspension of the draft from March, 1947, to June, 1948. Under these pressures American occupation forces in the defeated countries were reduced to minimum strength, and American diplomats sought to negotiate the peace treaties that would make complete evacuation possible. But the weaker the American military position became, the more unyielding were the Russians. They appeared to hope that the United States would give up in disgust, bring its armed forces back to the Western Hemisphere, and wash its hands of the rest of the world. Such a reversion to isolationism would leave a clear field for Communist expansion.

The American reluctance to maintain a large postwar military establishment was paralleled by a yearning to reduce government expenditures and taxes. In August, 1945, President Truman had somewhat abruptly terminated American shipments under the lend-lease program. Since it was obvious that the war-devastated countries would need substantial help, American assistance was continued through other channels. The United States made large contributions to the United Nations Relief and Rehabilitation Administration (UNRRA), until this too was terminated in March, 1947. Two other international agencies, the International Monetary Fund and the International Bank for Reconstruction and Development (popularly known as the World Bank),[9] received strong American support, but these were administered on conservative business principles, as was the American Export-Import Bank. In addition, the United States had made substantial postwar loans to Great Britain, France, and Italy. Despite this generous record, the swelling demand for retrenchment and tax reduction, dramatized by Republican victory in the congressional elections of 1946, threatened to cut off American aid just when it was needed most.

Still a third factor inhibiting the United States from shouldering its full responsibility was a dislike for imperialism. Although it accepted a UN trusteeship over the Pacific islands that had been Japanese mandates before the war,[10] it had no desire to take over the white man's burden from Britain's sagging shoulders. On the contrary, by carrying out the prewar pledge of independence to the Philippines, it hoped to encourage the other colonial powers to make similar concessions. It was consistent with this anti-imperialist mood for many Americans to look with grave concern upon any action that tended toward United States interference in the affairs of smaller nations.

While America hesitated, evidence piled up that the postwar distribution of power was dangerously out of balance. United Nations victory over the old Axis had been shattering, and for the immediate future Germany, Japan, and Italy were helpless. But two of the victors were largely exhausted also. Although France had risen miraculously from the ashes of defeat, she faced paralyzing problems of reconstruction at home and a rising spirit of revolt throughout her colonial empire. British prospects

[9] The Monetary Fund and the World Bank had been established as a result of the Bretton Woods (New Hampshire) Conference of 1944.

[10] These included the Marshalls, Marianas, and Carolines. The Security Council entrusted their administration to the United States in 1947 as "strategic areas," which meant that they might be used as military bases.

were only slightly less grim. Attlee's Labor government was attempting a peaceful social revolution at home at the same time that it had to grapple with serious shortages of food and goods, disorganized world markets, and chaos in the money exchanges. If the British had less colonial trouble than the French, it was only because they had read the signs of the times and peacefully withdrawn their rule over India, Pakistan, Burma, Ceylon, and other outposts. As these new countries, along with formerly Dutch Indonesia, struggled with the problems of independence, another factor of uncertainty was added to the postwar situation.

The Soviet Union had its own problems of reconstruction, but these did not prevent it from taking advantage of the weakness of its neighbors. Communist control over the satellite states was usually achieved by stages. In Poland, for example, the Yalta agreement for a broadly based provisional government and free elections served only as window dressing for a process by which a coalition regime maintained itself in power by terrorizing all opposition parties and making a farce of the long-promised election finally held in January, 1947. The next stage was to squeeze out the non-Communist cabinet members and to transform the country into a full-fledged Communist state meekly subservient to Moscow. With variations this pattern of events was followed in Bulgaria, Rumania, Hungary, Czechoslovakia, Yugoslavia, Albania, and East Germany.

Although no longer in office, Winston Churchill still spoke with a prophetic voice. In a speech at Fulton, Missouri, in March, 1946, he declared: "From Stettin in the Baltic to Trieste in the Adriatic an iron curtain has descended across the continent." Condemning "the police governments" of Eastern Europe, he urged a firmer policy of resistance to be based on close Anglo-American cooperation.

Within the State Department George F. Kennan, a former counselor of the Moscow Embassy and in 1947 head of the Policy Planning Committee, exerted a strong intellectual influence. In a widely read article, whose authorship was at first a secret,[11] Kennan analyzed the peculiar nature of Soviet foreign policy with its assumptions of the innate antagonism between capitalism and communism, the necessity for constant opposition to capitalist intrigue, and the treatment of agreements as merely tactical devices to be sabotaged or renounced after they had served their immediate purposes. To appeal to the Soviets on moral grounds was futile because Communists and non-Communists did not share the same ideals. On the other hand, the Soviet leaders were more realistic than Napoleon and Hitler had been; believing time to be on their side, they were "more sensitive to contrary force, more ready to yield on individual sectors of the diplomatic front when that force is felt to be too strong. . . ." There-

---

[11] See "X," "The Sources of Soviet Conduct," *Foreign Affairs*, vol. XXV, July, 1947, pp. 566–582.

fore, Kennan argued "that the main element of any United States policy toward the Soviet Union must be that of long-term, patient but firm and vigilant containment of Russian expansive tendencies." Such "containment" must "confront the Russians with unalterable counter-force at every point where they show signs of encroaching upon the interests of a peaceful and stable world."

The Truman Doctrine

The region where President Truman first attempted a policy of containment was in the Near and Middle East. In this part of the world Russian foreign policy had shown continuity from the days of Peter the Great to Stalin, relentlessly pushing toward the Persian Gulf and the Mediterranean Sea with control of Constantinople and the Straits as a particularly cherished goal. In 1946 the Soviets tested the reflexes of the West first in Iran, then in Turkey. Failing to cow the Iranian government into subservience, the Russians postponed a showdown by withdrawing their occupation forces and trying to substitute Russo-Turkish control of the Straits for the international regime provided in the Montreux Convention of 1936. Under the new arrangement the Russians would gain the right to maintain air and naval bases in the Straits. Well aware of the danger of allowing the Russian camel to get his nose into the tent, the Turks refused. Once again the Russians did not insist, but the episode demonstrated the danger of the Turkish situation. If this sturdy little state were to continue to maintain its independence, it needed both the diplomatic support of the West and help in modernizing its armed forces.

In early 1947 the greatest danger was that by seizing power in Greece, the Communists might turn the Turkish flank and bring the whole region under Soviet domination. Greece's postwar history had diverged from that of the other Balkan states because of Churchill's resolute policy in 1944. Ordering British troops into Athens at the moment of Nazi withdrawal, Churchill throttled the attempt of the Communist-affiliated faction to gain control. A right-wing provisional government was established, and conservative victory in the election of 1946 was followed by the restoration of King George.

Yet Greece's position was full of perils. The country, poor under the best of conditions, was now so poverty-stricken as to be not far from famine. The corrupt and inefficient government had to maintain an expensive military establishment to deal with Communist-led guerrillas. Supplied with arms and recruits from Yugoslavia, Albania, and Bulgaria, the Communist rebels threatened to gain control over Macedonia and Thrace if not over all Greece. Only British troops and money were holding up the Greek government. But Britain herself was in serious difficulties.

In February, 1947, Foreign Minister Bevin warned Washington that his government could no longer aid either Greece or Turkey. If these two dikes against the Communist flood were to be strengthened, the United States would have to take the initiative.

Whatever Truman's shortcomings may have been, he was not lacking in courage and decisiveness. On March 12, 1947, he appeared before a joint session of Congress to depict in somber terms the crisis confronting Greece and Turkey. Contrasting the way of life represented by majority rule and free institutions with that based upon the domination of a minority through terror and oppression, the President declared:

> I believe that it must be the policy of the United States to support free peoples who are resisting attempted subjugation by armed minorities or by outside pressures.
> I believe that we must assist free peoples to work out their destiny in their own way.
> I believe that our help should be primarily through economic and financial aid, which is essential to economic stability and orderly political processes.

Specifically Truman asked Congress to appropriate 400 million dollars for aid to Greece and Turkey and to authorize the appointment of American missions to assist those countries in reorganizing their affairs.

To some critics the Truman Doctrine seemed only intervention with a sugar coating. Others complained that the United States was assuming a responsibility that more properly belonged to the United Nations. But majority opinion strongly upheld the President. Despite its Republican majority, Congress gave the President what he asked with only the mild proviso that American aid should be halted if the UN undertook an adequate aid program of its own. The Truman policy proved effective both in strengthening Greek and Turkish defenses and in ameliorating economic conditions. Tito's break with Stalin in 1948 was followed by a closing of the Yugoslav border to Communist raids on Greece. In 1949 the Greek civil war came to a close with the anti-Communist government still firmly in the saddle.

The Marshall Plan

Not in Greece alone was there danger that poverty and despair would play into Soviet hands by strengthening native Communist movements. In both France and Italy there were militant Communist parties, able to poll about one-third of the vote in elections. Since 1945 Communists had been included in Italian cabinet posts; in 1947 they achieved this goal in France. To alarmed observers, these two key Western nations seemed to be sliding down the slippery descent already traversed by countries like Poland and Hungary. Economic conditions during the winter of 1946–1947 intensified the discontent upon which communism fed. The most severe weather in modern European history destroyed the grain crop, and the farmers hoarded much of what had been earlier harvested. The hungry workers of the cities resorted to protest strikes, and industrial production, already seriously lagging, was still further reduced.

In England the Communists were much weaker, but the consequences of economic misfortune threatened to be equally serious. To import necessary food and raw materials from the United States, Britain had need of every dollar that she could get, yet she found it extraordinarily difficult to raise her exports to the necessary level. Her industrial production expanded only slowly because of shortages of manpower and outmoded equipment. To an already bad condition the paralyzing blizzards of January and February, 1947, were disastrous blows, threatening to bring the whole economic structure down in collapse. Lack of coal caused a shortage of electricity, which in turn closed half the factories of the country.

Europe's desperate needs obviously provided a powerful case for more rather than less American aid. Yet the piecemeal measures of the past had had disappointing results. They had alleviated suffering, but they had not restored the emaciated patient to sound economic health. American public opinion, somewhat critical of the negative anticommunism of the Truman Doctrine, called for a more constructive approach. Good evidence that the administration was pondering the problem was given in May, 1947, when Undersecretary of State Dean Acheson, speaking at Cleveland, Mississippi, called attention to the great gap between America's 16-million-dollar annual exports and its 8-million-dollar imports. Acheson appealed for more liberal tariff policies and for further financial aid to be concentrated "where it would be most effective in building world political and economic stability."

Visiting Harvard University on June 5, 1947, to receive an honorary degree, Secretary Marshall delivered a highly important address. After describing Europe's economic plight, he said:

> It is logical that the United States should do whatever it is able to do to assist in the return of normal economic health in the world, without which there can be no political stability and no assured peace. Our policy is directed not against any country or doctrine but against hunger, poverty, desperation, and chaos. Its purpose should be the revival of a working economy in the world so as to permit the emergence of political and social conditions in which free institutions can exist.

Marshall went on to explain the need for the European nations to take the initiative in drawing up "a program designed to place Europe on its feet economically." The role of the United States "should consist of friendly aid in the drafting of a European program and of later support of such a program so far as it may be practical for us to do so. The program should be a joint one, agreed to by a number, if not all, European nations."

Grasping at once the tremendous possibilities of Marshall's suggestion, the British and French governments took steps to meet the challenge. The American invitation had not excluded the Soviet Union; on the contrary, there had been some faint hope that by drawing the Communist countries into a plan for European recovery, the growing schism between East and West could be healed. But Stalin, after momentary hesitation, made the fateful decision not to cooperate. Communist propaganda denounced the plan as a form of capitalist imperialism, and none of the satellite states participated in the Paris conference of July, 1947, at which European planning was initiated. In the report eventually submitted to Secretary Marshall, the sixteen cooperating nations outlined production goals and measures for increasing trade and stabilizing their finances. To support this program, substantial American aid would be necessary.

Although Senator Taft and some of the other Republican leaders opposed what was bitterly called "Operation Rat Hole," the Marshall Plan had the support of Senator Vandenberg and other international-minded Republicans. The issue was, nevertheless, in doubt until a particularly brutal Communist coup in Czecholsovakia underlined the gravity of the European situation. On April 3, 1948, the President signed a Foreign Assistance Act appropriating 5.3 billion dollars for the first year of a four-year program. To head the new Economic Cooperation Administration, Truman appointed a liberal Republican businessman, Paul G. Hoffman.

Over the next four years the European Recovery Program (ERP) resulted in grants totaling about 12.3 billion dollars. This was spent largely for American goods to rehabilitate the European economy—grain, fertilizer, cotton and other raw materials, petroleum, coal, and machinery. The principal beneficiaries were the United Kingdom, France, West Germany, and Italy, but fourteen other countries also shared to some degree.[12] This aid combined with other factors to bring about an impressive economic recovery. By 1948 the ERP countries had restored their industrial production to pre–World War II levels; by 1951 they were producing at a level 40 per cent above 1938. In agriculture the results were less satisfactory, but by 1951 production was 10 per cent above the 1938 level. This did not mean that Europe was free of economic troubles: trade be-

[12] The others were the Netherlands, Austria, Greece, Belgium, Luxembourg, Denmark, Norway, Turkey, Ireland, Sweden, Portugal, Trieste, Iceland, and Yugoslavia.

tween the United States and Europe was still badly out of balance, and the European countries had made less progress than hoped for in eliminating tariff barriers and other obstacles to trade among themselves. Nevertheless, ERP had achieved a degree of success highly gratifying to General Marshall and its other sponsors.

Politically the Marshall Plan had even more striking results. The bleak despair of 1947 gave way to optimism. Elections in Italy, France, and West Germany indicated that for the time being at least, the Communist flood had reached its crest and was beginning to recede.

The Revival of Germany

Between 1945 and 1948 American policy toward Germany underwent striking change. At Potsdam the Big Three had readily agreed that German industry should be drastically curtailed, both to prevent German rearmament and to provide reparations. In 1946 the four occupying powers had agreed to a "level of industry" only about 55 per cent of that of 1938, with especially severe restrictions on steel production. Such a program might have been feasible if the German economy had been free to adjust itself on a nationwide basis, but it was totally unrealistic under the conditions brought about by four separate occupation zones. With the German economic machine compelled to operate on four cylinders instead of eight, British and American taxpayers had to pay heavy occupation costs. Even such neighbors as the Dutch, the Belgians, and the French, who had no reason to love the Germans, found themselves injured by the severe restrictions that had been placed on German industry. The goals of the Marshall Plan obviously demanded a substantial increase in German production.

Since it continued to be impossible to obtain four-power agreement on German policy, the Western nations began to take matters increasingly into their own hands. At the end of 1946 the British and Americans merged their occupation zones for administrative and economic purposes into the so-called "Bizonia." They halted most of the dismantling of factories and permitted a substantial rise in the level of industry. At first the French preferred to follow an independent course, but in 1948 they participated along with the Benelux countries (Belgium, the Netherlands, and Luxembourg) in a London conference at which important decisions for the creation of a new West German State were worked out. An International Authority was to allocate the production of the strategic Ruhr industries so that this could be used for the general benefit of Europe. To help stabilize German economic life, the Western powers agreed to issue new Deutsche marks in the place of the almost worthless currency then flooding the country.

Objecting bitterly to the whole tendency of Western policy, the Russians demonstrated their displeasure first by placing annoying restrictions upon British, American, and French land and water transport into Berlin and eventually by halting all such traffic through the hundred-mile Soviet corridor. By this Berlin blockade the Russians obviously hoped to make it impossible for the Western powers to keep garrisons within their three alloted sectors. To force their rivals out of the historic capital would be a great psychological victory and would end the embarrassing contrast between living conditions in West and East Berlin.

The Soviet policy boomeranged. By pressing every possible plane into service, the British and American air forces were able to keep their sectors of Berlin supplied with adequate food and fuel even during the winter months. By this heroic air lift the Western nations gave a dramatic demonstration of firmness that deeply impressed the Germans. Throughout western Germany a strong anti-Communist reaction set in. Tacitly recognizing the failure of their policy, the Russians ended the blockade on May 12, 1949. The Western powers made a concession of their own in consenting to a new four-power conference on the whole German problem, but no progress toward the much-needed German peace treaty was achieved.

Under encouragement from the Western powers German representatives from the British, American, and French occupation zones met at Bonn on the Rhine from September 1, 1948, to May, 1949, to draft a constitution for a Federal Republic of Germany. The relations between the new German government and its sponsors were defined in an Occupation Statute, dated April 8, 1949, which provided for continued occupation of the three western zones but substituted a civilian Allied High Commission for the earlier military government.

Although provision had been made in the Federal Republic constitution for the admission of the German states under Soviet occupation, the Russians would not permit any such unification. Instead, they sponsored a rival regime, the German Democratic Republic, with its capital at Berlin. The East German State, firmly in the Communist grip, had only half the population of its western rival and was much poorer in coal and industry, but it included some of the best German agricultural lands.

The West German State rapidly achieved political stability and economic vitality. In Konrad Adenauer, who became Chancellor after his Christian Democratic party and its middle-of-the-road allies won the first elections in 1949, the new state found an able leader, conservative in social philosophy but strongly committed to the democratic values of the West. Meanwhile, the German economy, freed more and more from Allied control and stimulated by the successful currency reform of 1948, was restored to flourishing condition. In May, 1952, West Germany signed a

"Peace Contract," which served as a provisional peace treaty with the Western powers.

The North Atlantic Alliance

In 1947 Western Europe's poverty and despair had threatened to deliver whole countries to communism without a struggle. The Marshall Plan and the restoration of the German economy had done much to reduce this danger, but the realities of Russian military power still remained. It was obvious that if the Soviet armed forces should start rolling, there would be little to stop them short of the Atlantic Coast. Warned by the mistakes of the 1930s, when nothing adequate had been done to build a collective defense system, the British had been taking cautious steps. In March, 1947, Britain and France had allied themselves through the Treaty of Dunkirk. A year later these two broadened their project to include the Benelux countries in the Brussels Pact.

But the crucial question was: What would the United States do? To enter into peacetime alliances was a sharp break with the whole tradition of American foreign policy, yet no combination to hold Communist aggression in check could have any chance of success without American participation. Well aware of the necessity of preparing Congress for new measures, President Truman enlisted the support of Senator Vandenberg, who in June, 1948, put through with only four dissenting votes a Senate resolution advising the President to develop collective defense arrangements within the UN Charter and to associate the United States with them.

Although the presidential campaign of 1948 and other distractions delayed the project for a few months, a collective defense treaty became an early order of business in Truman's second term, with Dean Acheson, the new Secretary of State, playing a major role. On April 4, 1949, the representatives of twelve nations [13] met at Washington to sign the North Atlantic Treaty. Announcing their purpose "to promote stability and well-being in the North Atlantic area," the signatories agreed:

> that an armed attack against one or more of them in Europe or North America shall be considered an attack against them all; and consequently they agree that, if such an armed attack occurs, each of them, in exercise of the right of individual or collective self-defense recognized by Article 51 of the Charter of the United Nations, will assist the Party or Parties so attacked by taking forthwith ... such action as it deems necessary, including the use of armed force, to restore and maintain the security of the North Atlantic area. ...

[13] The original NATO countries were United States, Canada, United Kingdom, France, Belgium, the Netherlands, Luxembourg, Norway, Denmark, Iceland, Italy, and Portugal. Greece and Turkey were admitted in 1951 and West Germany in 1955.

The Senate approved this historic commitment by a vote of 82 to 13.

Important though the treaty was, it would offer only a paper barrier against aggression unless implemented with a resolute strengthening of Western defenses. Although the new allies were ready to make heavy sacrifices to build up their armed forces, their financial and industrial position was still too weak to support effective measures without new forms of American aid. In September, 1949, Congress appropriated 1.3 billion dollars for a Mutual Defense Assistance program, under which military equipment and other necessities were to be supplied both to the North Atlantic Treaty Organization (NATO) allies and to other countries threatened with Communist attack. American military aid grants now became a continuing budget item, soon overshadowing economic aid intended for purely peaceful purposes.

When the North Atlantic Council, composed of the foreign ministers of the NATO powers, found it difficult to bring defense plans into firm coordination, it decided to establish an integrated military force "adequate for the defense of the freedom of Europe." General Eisenhower was appointed to the post of NATO Supreme Commander in December, 1950. The creation of a NATO army committed the United States to maintain substantial forces in Europe for the indefinite future. Although NATO helped to restore the European balance of power, the eagerly heralded NATO army continued to be little more than a skeleton force. The Korean conflict, the tying down of British and French troops in distant trouble spots like Indochina, Algeria, and Cyprus, and continuing budget problems all hampered the development of an adequate Western defense system. From the beginning the United States hoped to make West Germany a key link in the new chain, but French opposition to German rearmament postponed this until 1955.

Although Communist Yugoslavia and totalitarian Spain were not considered respectable enough to be invited into NATO, they both eventually received American aid. After Stalin denounced Tito in 1948 and branded the Yugoslav party as unorthodox, the United States undertook to encourage Tito in his independent course by trade deals and grants for relief. Similarly, American disapproval for Franco's collaboration with the Axis did not prevent the making of an agreement in 1953, whereby Spain was granted badly needed economic aid in return for American air and naval bases in her strategically located territory.

The Organization of American States

Even before the birth of NATO the United States had entered into a mutual defense agreement with other Western Hemisphere countries. Except for Argentina, which maintained a pro-Axis neutrality until early

1945, the Latin-American countries had shown strong sympathy and support for the UN cause during World War II. They broke off diplomatic relations with the Axis and sooner or later declared war.

In February, 1945, an Inter-American Conference on Problems of War and Peace was held at Mexico City, with all the American republics except Argentina in attendance. The resulting Act of Chapultepec declared that an attack against any one American state should be considered an act of aggression against them all and should result in mutual consultation for defense. To escape her threatened isolation, Argentina declared war on Germany and Japan and adhered to the Act of Chapultepec just in time to appear with freshly washed face on the doorstep of the UN Conference at San Francisco. At the insistence of the United States and over Soviet objections she was admitted as a charter member of the new world organization.

Even after these events the condition of affairs in Argentina was highly unsatisfactory to the American State Department. That important South American country had fallen under the domination of Colonel Juan Perón, who proceeded to establish a corrupt and tyrannical dictatorship. In 1946 the State Department published a "Blue Book," detailing Perón's unsavory pro-Nazi record in the hope that the Argentine voters would turn against him at the polls. But the effort miscarried, and the elections strengthened Perón's hold on the country. In June, 1947, the United States confessed the failure of its anti-Perón policy and indicated a willingness to have Argentina included in plans for a stronger Western Hemisphere defense pact.

The Treaty of Rio de Janeiro, signed by nineteen American states on September 2, 1947, went beyond the Act of Chapultepec by not only declaring that an attack against one American state was to be considered an attack against them all, but pledging each of the signatories "to assist in meeting the attack in the exercise of the inherent right of individual or collective self-defense recognized by Article 51 of the Charter of the United Nations."

During the spring of 1948 an Inter-American Conference at Bogotá, Colombia, provided for closer collaboration through the establishment of an Organization of American States (OAS), as one of the regional associations permitted under the UN Charter.

By 1949 the policy of containment seemed to have gained impressive strength throughout Western Europe and the two Americas. In Asia, however, it still remained uncertain just where the line between the Communist and non-Communist worlds would be drawn.

35

THE STRUGGLE FOR ASIA

In Asia the old distribution of power was completely shattered by World War II. Japanese rule over Formosa, Korea, and the occupied districts of China was ended, and Japan herself lay prostrate in defeat with her future destiny dependent upon the will of the United States. Liberation brought bitter fruit both to the Chinese and the Koreans, as Communists and anti-Communists became locked in savage warfare. The Asiatic situation was further confused by the upsurge of nationalism that loosened the British, Dutch, French, and American empires, bringing to birth such new nations as India, Pakistan, Burma, Indonesia, Vietnam, and the Philippines. As the world-wide struggle between Communism and anti-Communism deepened, some of these countries chose sides, but others, fearful of leaping from the old colonialism into a new, maintained a precarious neutrality. To formulate a wise foreign policy in so explosive a situation taxed the skill of presidents and secretaries of state, whether Democrats or Republicans.

Remodeling Japan

On July 26, 1945, Truman, Attlee, Stalin, and Chiang Kai-shek issued the Potsdam Declaration, calling upon Japan to surrender unconditionally but at the same time defining Allied intentions toward the vanquished enemy. Japan's militarist leaders were to be eliminated from all authority and influence; Japan's sovereignty was to be limited to her four home islands and minor neighboring ones; Japanese military forces were to be completely disarmed; all obstacles to democracy were to be removed; Japanese war industries were to be banned, but those necessary to sustain her economy would be permitted. The occupying forces would be withdrawn as soon as these objectives were achieved and "there has been established in accordance with the freely expressed will of the Japanese people a peacefully inclined and responsible government."

As events worked out, the implementation of this policy fell largely into the masterful hands of General Douglas MacArthur. Under the terms of surrender, the Emperor was allowed to retain his throne on condition that he carry out the orders of the Allied commander. Wisely concluding that full cooperation would shorten the occupation, Japanese officials made no attempt to obstruct American policy. After the British and Russians showed some unhappiness with MacArthur's almost dictatorial powers, the London Foreign Ministers' Conference of December, 1945, provided for an eleven-nation Far Eastern Commission to sit at Washington and a four-power Allied Council at Tokyo. Yet neither body exercised any effective power, so that for all practical purposes American policy controlled the occupation.

The Potsdam program was rapidly carried out. The Japanese army was disarmed, repatriated, and demobilized, while the air force and navy were destroyed. Private organizations that might cloak secret military activities were closely controlled. By the trial and punishment of alleged war criminals the occupation authorities weakened the dominance once held by professional militarists, and this reform was carried still further by purging old-line militarists and nationalists from government posts.

The growth of democratic institutions was fostered by insisting upon the classic civil liberties: free speech, freedom of the press, and freedom of association. Political prisoners were released, the secret police was abolished, and political parties, including the Communist, were allowed to function. To crown this process of democratization, the Japanese adopted a new constitution, largely drafted in MacArthur's headquarters. The Emperor was confirmed as head of the state, but his authority was defined as deriving "from the will of the people with whom resides sovereign power"—thus renouncing the classic dogma that the Emperor was of divine origin. The Emperor was to govern only through his constitutionally appointed officials, who in turn were responsible to the Diet, "the sole law-making organ of the state." Elections were to be by universal suffrage, including for the first time Japanese women. The most extraordinary provision of the MacArthur constitution read thus:

> Aspiring sincerely to an international peace based upon justice and order, the Japanese people forever renounce war as a sovereign right of the nation, and the threat or use of force as means of settling international disputes.
> In order to accomplish the aim of the preceding paragraph, land, sea, and air forces, as well as other war potential, will never be maintained. The right of belligerency of the state will not be recognized.

Ironically, within a few years the United States was encouraging Japan to circumvent the very prohibition upon which it had insisted.

The occupation authorities also attempted an ambitious program of economic reform, both to shackle Japan's war potential and to weaken the older privileged classes. Japanese workers were permitted to organize in labor unions and to strike. A land reform program providing for the redistribution of almost 5 million acres eased the lot of Japanese peasants. Certain factories were seized for reparations to China and the Philippines.

As time went on, however, the occupation authorities gave up their insistence on drastic economic reform. As in Germany, the United States faced the problem of high occupation costs because Japan could not produce and export enough to pay for imported food and raw material. In 1949 the United States halted the dismantling of Japanese plants, much to the discontent of the Asiatic nations still hopeful of receiving reparations. Also largely abandoned was the vigorous antitrust policy by which the occupation authorities had begun to break up the "zaibatsu," or family combines in control of Japanese industry.

As early as 1947 it was obvious that American policy toward Japan was turning toward new objectives. The desire to punish and cripple the defeated enemy was giving way to realization that worsening relations between the Communist and non-Communist worlds made it imperative to encourage Japanese recovery. On March 19, 1947, General MacArthur announced that "the time is now approaching when we must talk peace with Japan"; he wanted a peace treaty "as soon as possible." For the next three years, however, the United States was frustrated by disagreements with the Soviet Union over the proper peacemaking procedure. The situation was vastly complicated, moreover, by developments in China and Korea.

The China Puzzle

In the face of British and Russian skepticism, Roosevelt and Truman insisted on treating China as one of the major UN powers. Her weakness after years of struggle against the Japanese was admitted, but with American help it was hoped that a strong, united, and democratic nation could emerge from the war. Yet the situation in the spring of 1945 scarcely justified this optimism. There were in China two rival cores of power. The Kuomintang focal center was at Chungking, far up the Yangtse River in southern China, where Chiang Kai-shek had moved his capital to avoid capture by the Japanese. American military and diplomatic observers found many things to criticize in Chiang's government. Even if it were admitted that existing conditions made Western-type democracy impossible, the Nationalist regime seemed unnecessarily harsh and repressive. Although Chiang and some of his associates were honest men, many other officials were inefficient, corrupt, and cynical. The government was accused of being too subservient to the merchants and the landlords and doing too little to improve the lot of the Chinese peasantry. Nationalist generals were charged with hoarding troops and avoiding decisive measures against the Japanese.

At Yenan in northwestern China, a rival focus of power existed in the headquarters of the Chinese Communist party with Mao Tse-tung as its leader. Since 1937 the Kuomintang and the Communists had maintained an uneasy truce. In theory the Communists had recognized the authority of Chiang's government and incorporated their armies within the national forces; in actuality, they enjoyed complete autonomy over their own districts and followed their own strategy in fighting the Japanese. Although they were Marxist in philosophy, they had temporarily renounced extreme measures in favor of moderate land reform and cooperation with non-Communist liberals. This allowed some American observers to come to the comfortable but dangerous conclusion that the Chinese Communists were not really Communists at all, but merely agrarian reformers. Concealing its ultimate objectives, Mao's party was obviously growing in power. More honest and efficient than their Kuomintang rivals, the Communists had won the support of many peasants, while their guerrilla tactics were a constant harassment to the Japanese.

The United States became involved in Chinese politics, first, because it desired to increase Chinese military efficiency against Japan, and second, because it had based its postwar policy on a strong, friendly China. Disgusted with the poor training and morale of the Chinese troops, General Joseph Stilwell, UN commander of the China-Burma-India theater, made brusque demands for authority to reorganize the entire Chinese army, making greater use of the Communist forces. Fearful of measures that might strengthen his rivals, Chiang insisted that Stilwell be recalled. In October, 1944, General Albert C. Wedemeyer became commanding general of United States forces in the China theater. More tactful than Stilwell, Wedemeyer had some success in helping to improve the Chinese army, but much more thoroughgoing reform was necessary if China were to be genuinely unified. The Chinese Nationalists, the Communists, and the liberals who belonged to neither extreme must be brought together in a common effort to save the country. United States Ambassador Patrick J. Hurley, a former Republican Cabinet officer whom Roosevelt sent to China in the fall of 1944, tried hard to mediate among China's suspicious factions, but his efforts were frustrated. Even within the American Embassy there were divisions of counsel, with Hurley much more sympathetic to Chiang Kai-shek than were most professional Foreign Service men.

In June, 1945, President Truman informed Chiang of the Yalta arrangements and asked Chinese adherence to them. This resulted in negotiations between China and the Soviet Union in which Chiang tried to define Russian compensation in Manchuria as narrowly as possible, while Stalin made additional demands. China and Russia finally compromised their differences in a treaty of August 14, 1945. Although Chiang had to make unwelcome concessions in respect to Port Arthur, Dairen, the Manchurian railroads, and Outer Mongolia, he gained valuable advantages in recognition of Chinese sovereignty over the territories liberated from the enemy and in a pledge that Soviet support and aid would be "entirely given to the National Government as the central government of China." Stalin's promise not to help the Chinese Communists seemed of great importance because Russia had entered the war against Japan five days before and already her armies were deep within Manchuria. On the very day that the Sino-Russian treaty was signed, Japan surrendered.

Japan's final collapse, hastened by the atomic bomb, had occurred much earlier than expected. With their reform program still in the discussion stage and their armies still ragged and badly equipped, the Nationalists were ill-prepared to take the vigorous measures necessary to profit from the recent Soviet agreement. Although the Japanese in Manchuria were ordered to surrender only to Soviet commanders and elsewhere in China only to the Chinese Nationalists, the enemy troops were largely concentrated in districts far from Chiang's base of power and near to that of the Communists. General Wedemeyer was able to provide enough planes and ships to permit Chiang's forces to occupy key points in North China and Manchuria, but even so the Communists managed to strengthen their position. Stalin held to the letter of his bargain by avoiding direct intervention, yet he violated its spirit by policies that hampered the Nationalists. Soviet troops carried away as "war booty" Japanese-owned industrial machinery much needed for China's economic reconstruction. The Nationalists' occupation of Manchuria was delayed by Soviet red tape, while Chinese Communists were allowed to infiltrate the province and get possession of Japanese arms that had been surrendered to the Russians.

By early 1946, when the Soviet troops ended their occupation, Chinese Communist armies were dominating most of the rural districts of North China and Manchuria, even though the cities were under Nationalist control. Numerous local clashes threatened to widen into a resumption of the old civil war.

The Marshall Mission

Ambassador Hurley, in poor health and discouraged by the situation, resigned in November, 1945, thus opening the way for Truman to send General George C. Marshall to China as a special Presidential representative. Marshall was instructed "to bring to bear in an appropriate and practicable manner the influence of the United States" so that "the unification of China by peaceful, democratic methods" might be achieved.

For some weeks after Marshall arrived in December, 1945, prospects for his success appeared promising. In January the Nationalists and Communists agreed to a cease-fire while political talks were in progress. A Political Consultative Conference was set up, in which Kuomintang, Communist, and nonparty groups were all represented. This in turn passed resolutions calling for a coalition government and a national assembly to draft a constitution.

Paper agreements, however, were worthless without good faith in carrying them out. The Communists accused Chiang of trying to engineer the situation to break their movement; the Kuomintang, on the other hand, were convinced that the Communists were scheming to obtain complete power for themselves. Under these circumstances the promised coalition government was never established and, when the National Assembly finally met in November, 1946, the Communists refused to participate.

Although General Marshall worked hard at the thankless task of mediation, the tide of events soon turned against him. The truce broke down, and serious fighting began in the summer of 1946. Kuomintang leaders, convinced that they could defeat the Communists despite warnings to the contrary by Wedemeyer and Marshall, closed the door to further concessions. After almost thirteen months of striving for peace, Marshall acknowledged defeat in January, 1947, and came home to take on new responsibilities as Secretary of State. Reporting to the nation on his mission, Marshall blamed the extremists in both camps—the dominant group of Kuomintang reactionaries and the military elements within the ranks of communism. "The salvation of the situation," as Marshall saw it, "would be the assumption of leadership by liberals in the Government and in the minority parties, a splendid group of men, but who as yet lack the political power to exercise a controlling influence. Successful action on their part under the leadership of Generalissimo Chiang Kai-shek would, I believe, lead to unity through good government."

Communist Victory

Having rejected American advice, the Chinese rivals settled down to the grim business of trying to destroy each other. At first the Nationalists had some success, even capturing Yenan, but in 1948 the tide of battle turned strongly in the other direction. The Communists were in complete control of Manchuria by the fall of that year; and in 1949 they won victory after victory, taking Peiping in January, Nanking in April, and

Chungking in November. By January, 1950, the Nationalists had been forced to abandon the entire mainland and seek sanctuary on Formosa and other islands off the China coast. On October 1, 1949, a People's Republic of China, with Mao Tse-tung as President, was proclaimed at Peiping; and in February, 1950, this new government signed a thirty-year pact of friendship and mutual assistance with the Soviet Union.

What should the United States do about this situation? Two sharply conflicting schools of opinion had developed during the period of Nationalist defeats. Through his influential magazines *Time* and *Life*, Henry Luce argued for bold American aid to Chiang to stem the Communist flood. Also active in the so-called China Lobby were Congressman Walter Judd of Minnesota, a former missionary, and General Claire Chennault, whose "Flying Tigers" had fought for China during World War II. But many others believed that American aid to Chiang Kai-shek had proved futile. Much of it was diverted to the personal enrichment of corrupt officials; much was wasted through inefficiency; still more actually ended in Communist hands through easy capture of equipment and supplies. Only large-scale use of American troops would be effective, and this the American public would not tolerate.

Between 1945 and mid-1949 the United States granted some 3 billion dollars in aid to Nationalist China, equipping thirty-nine divisions or some 50 per cent of the national forces. In addition, American officers gave technical assistance in the training and reorganization of the Chinese units. The aid program had thoroughly unhappy results. Its open and large-scale character, in contrast to the less direct help given the Communists by the Soviet Union, led to charges of imperialist intervention. Not only did the Chinese Communists become implacably anti-American, but many non-Communists condemned American meddling. On the other hand, the American aid was not sufficient to avert debacle for the rot-permeated Nationalist forces. In August, 1949, the Truman administration attempted to wash its hands of the whole mess by issuing a thousand-page white paper, replete with documents showing the extent of American efforts and their frustration through the intransigence of the two sides and the failure of Chiang Kai-shek to make timely reforms. The *New York Times* characterized the white paper as "a sorry record of well-meaning mistakes." In January, 1950, President Truman announced that the United States would give no further military aid to Chiang, nor would it defend Formosa in case of attack.

Some Americans thought that a logical corollary to this reversal of policy would be to grant diplomatic recognition to the Communist government now in *de facto* control of the mainland. Indeed, Great Britain and a number of other European and Asiatic states did recognize Mao's regime early in 1950. But President Truman and Secretary of State Dean

Acheson decided against this course of action. Their reasons were varied. For one thing, Nationalist resistance to the Communist government was still continuing; for another, Communist hostility to the United States was obvious, not only in continuous anti-American propaganda, but in many arbitrary actions against American officials and civilians. And finally Truman and Acheson, already under bitter Republican attack for their China policy, could not afford to provoke a new storm by recognizing the Communist regime. Instead, the administration continued to treat Chiang's Formosa government as the legal one of China and stubbornly opposed all efforts to admit Communist China to the United Nations.

The Two Koreas

Although the postwar status of Korea had been briefly discussed at the Cairo, Yalta, and Potsdam Conferences, little had been decided other than that the country should ultimately be free and independent, but that some form of joint trusteeship might be necessary for an interim period. In August, 1945, when Japanese resistance suddenly collapsed, the United States proposed that Japanese forces in Korea north of the 38th parallel should be ordered to surrender to Soviet commanders and south of that parallel to American. Stalin assented, and in this casual arrangement a fateful division of Korea began.

Within the Soviet zone of occupation a façade of self-government was speedily erected at the local level. Like the Chinese Communists, their Korean brothers made a bid for mass support by using these local governing committees to institute a plausible program of land reform, labor legislation, and general enfranchisement. The Soviet occupation forces were thus able to develop North Korea as a complaisant puppet state while keeping their hand fairly well concealed.

In South Korea the American policy was more cautious. On the one hand, the occupation authorities wanted to encourage genuine democracy and a free political life; on the other, they feared the spread of communism. As a result, the Americans at first kept the reins of government quite firmly in their own hands; then they showed a preference for turning over responsibility to Korean conservatives.

As in Germany, the division of Korea into two occupation zones was unfortunate in its economic consequences. The country's heavy industry and hydroelectric power plants were largely in the north; the best agricultural land was in the south. The situation was complicated by the migration of thousands of Koreans from the northern to the southern zone. To restore the economy to health and pave the way for Korean independence, the United States pressed for unification of the country. When direct negotiations with the Soviet Union failed to bring an agreement, the Americans took the question to the United Nations in 1947.

Over the objections of its Communist members the UN Assembly resolved that Korea's future institutions should be decided by a Korean congress, freely elected under the observation of a UN Temporary Commission. When the Soviet commanders tried to block this program by refusing to admit the Temporary Commission to their zone, the UN Assembly directed the Commission to proceed with the elections in the other districts. In May, 1948, residents in the American occupation zone elected 200 representatives to the new Korean congress; 100 seats were reserved for the North Koreans in case the Soviets should change their policy.

The Korean congress adopted a constitution hopefully designed for the whole country and elected as first President Dr. Syngman Rhee, a tough Korean nationalist who had kept alive the independence movement over many years. American military government was terminated in August, 1948, and responsibility was turned over to the Rhee regime. The following December the UN General Assembly placed its stamp of approval on these proceedings. "This government," it asserted, "is based on elections which were a valid expression of the free will of the electorate ... and were observed by the Temporary Mixed Commission." It was, moreover, "the only such Government in Korea." The United States, Great Britain, Nationalist China, the Philippines, and some twenty-six other nations promptly recognized this new "Republic of Korea" with its capital at Seoul.

But Rhee's authority was vigorously disputed by a rival regime at Pyongyang in North Korea. In August, 1948, elections were held in the Soviet zone for a Supreme People's Assembly, which met and proclaimed a constitution the following month. Thus was born the "Democratic People's Republic of Korea," also claiming to be the rightful government of the whole country.

Confident that the North Korean government could maintain itself with its own army well equipped with Russian weapons, the Soviet Union completed the withdrawal of its occupation forces by January 1, 1949. The United States followed suit six months later, leaving behind only a few air force personnel and a military advisory group assigned to help organize a South Korean defense force. The American government made no promise to defend its protégé in case of attack; indeed, in a speech of January, 1950, Secretary Acheson defined the American "defensive perimeter" as running along the Aleutians to Japan, thence through the Ryukyus to the Philippines—thus omitting both Formosa and South Korea. As for other areas in the Pacific, said Acheson, their initial reliance must be upon their own resistance and then upon "the commitments of the entire civilized world under the Charter of the United Nations." In limiting the American obligation to defend South Korea to its duties under the UN, Acheson was probably trying to exert a sobering influence on Rhee, who showed some of the same authoritarian tendencies as Chiang Kai-shek.

The Korean Conflict

Early on the morning of June 25, 1950 (June 24 in Washington), North Korean forces began an invasion of South Korean territory, easily over-running the border outposts. Hurrying back to the capital from Inde-pendence, Missouri, President Truman had to face unpleasant alternatives. For the United States to rush to South Korea's defense would involve the nation in an unwanted war of unpredictable proportions; yet to stand aside and leave South Korea to resist alone might be fatal to the whole policy of containment. If Rhee's government established under UN super-vision and with American help were to be overwhelmed by sudden Com-munist onslaught, the prestige of the United States would drop to zero and small nations around the world would draw the lesson that resistance to communism was futile. Believing that World War II had been made inevitable by the weakness of the democratic nations in dealing with similar situations during the 1930s, Truman quickly decided on a policy of firmness.

American action proceeded simultaneously on two fronts, the diplo-matic and the military. At the request of the United States, the UN Se-curity Council met to consider the Korean situation only thirteen hours after news of the attack reached Washington. Fortunately for the anti-Communist cause, the Russians had for six months been boycotting the Council in protest against its failure to seat Communist China. With the threat of veto thus absent, the Council voted 9 to 0 (Yugoslavia abstain-ing) that the North Korean attack constituted a breach of the peace; it called upon the North Korean armies to withdraw to the 38th parallel and upon all UN members "to render every assistance to the United Na-tions in the execution of this resolution and to refrain from giving as-sistance to the North Korean authorities." On that same June 25 a con-ference between President Truman and his principal diplomatic and military advisers resulted in three preliminary decisions: American naval and air forces should be used to protect the evacuation of American civilians from South Korea; American arms and supplies should be rushed to the South Korean defenders; and the American Seventh Fleet should be moved from the Philippines to the Formosa Strait with orders not only to prevent any Communist attack on Formosa, but also to bar any Nationalist attack upon the mainland that might provoke a broadening of the conflict. The next day there were equally important decisions: to use the United States Navy and Air Force to assist the South Koreans and to give increased military aid to the Philippines and to French Indochina, important anti-Communist outposts.

These American decisions, announced on June 27, were given substantial UN support that same day. The Security Council by a vote of 7 to 1 [1] recommended "that the Members of the United Nations furnish such assistance to the Republic of Korea as may be necessary to repel the armed attack and to restore international peace and security in the area."

Truman had at first hoped that the South Korean army would be strong enough to repel the invasion with only naval and air assistance, but General MacArthur's inspection of the situation soon provided a more realistic picture. Not only was the South Korean army hopelessly inferior in manpower to the attacking forces, but it lacked planes and tanks. Unless the United States immediately sent in ground troops, the situation was hopeless. On June 29 the President therefore gave orders to move two American divisions from Japan to the Korean front. Within the next two weeks units from the United Kingdom, Australia, and New Zealand also responded to the emergency call. On July 7 the Security Council authorized these national units to use the United Nations flag as well as their own and requested the United States to designate a commander for these UN forces. Truman promptly named General MacArthur for this new responsibility.

Even these steps did not immediately save South Korea. The American troops sent from Japan were soft from occupation duty and far from ready for combat. To move reinforcements quickly from the West Coast involved serious problems of transportation. For several weeks the UN forces could fight only a costly delaying action. A sudden turn for the better came on September 15, when MacArthur made a surprise amphibious attack at Inchon behind the enemy lines. This bold move demoralized the North Koreans, and the UN forces speedily overcame most resistance below the 38th parallel.

The Chinese Thunderbolt

Although it might have been prudent to halt the UN offensive as soon as the invaders were driven out of South Korea, the Truman administration never seriously considered such a course. Accepting MacArthur's judgment that direct intervention by either the Soviet Union or Communist China was unlikely, the President authorized the general to extend his campaign north of the 38th parallel. Both military and political

[1] Yugoslavia voted no; India and Egypt abstained.

considerations seemed to dictate this policy. From the military point of view, South Korea would face the danger of new Communist attack if the North Korean army were not finally destroyed; from the political point of view, the opportunity to unify the country seemed too good to miss.

Even though MacArthur had been given a green light as early as September 27 and South Korean troops had actually crossed the 38th parallel on October 1, the movement of other troops was delayed while UN support was being sought. New strategy on the diplomatic front was now necessary, because on August 1 the Soviet Union had ended its boycott of the Security Council and had since made full use of its powers to delay and veto action. In the General Assembly, which convened September 19, the Korean problem was given extensive debate. The Indian representatives warned against the danger of extending the conflict north of the 38th parallel—a policy that would probably bring the Chinese Communists into the war, but the United States minimized this as a Peiping bluff. By a vote of 47 to 5, with 7 nations abstaining,[2] the General Assembly recommended on October 7 "all appropriate steps ... to ensure conditions of stability throughout Korea," to be followed by UN-sponsored elections for the establishment of "a unified, independent and democratic government."

At first General MacArthur's invasion of North Korea went very well, leading to hopes that the American troops would be home for Christmas. But as the UN spearheads approached the Manchurian borders, it became increasingly clear that the Chinese Communists had not been bluffing. Although small Chinese units were encountered late in October, the full danger of the new situation was not revealed until a month later when masses of well-equipped Chinese troops threw back the smaller UN forces with sickening losses. The new Communist offensive drove rapidly down the peninsula, and by the end of the year the UN forces had been compelled to withdraw far below the 38th parallel.

Pandora's Box

During the first few months of the Korean conflict President Truman received almost unanimous support. Republicans vied with Democrats in voicing approval of his decisive action. Many of the crucial Security Council sessions were televised, and American interest in the UN reached a higher level than ever before. Viewers were particularly impressed to see so many foreign diplomats loyally supporting the American position.

This honeymoon came to a depressing end, however, after Communist

[2] Voting no were three Soviet republics, Poland, and Czechoslovakia. Abstaining were Egypt, India, Lebanon, Saudi Arabia, Syria, Yemen, and Yugoslavia.

China entered the conflict. MacArthur's counteroffensive in March, 1951, drove the Communists back to the 38th parallel, but the conflict then bogged down, with neither side able to break the other's stubborn defense. As the casualty lists lengthened with each passing month, the conflict became increasingly unpopular. Truman and Acheson, acclaimed as heroes six months earlier, were now denounced as bunglers who had first permitted a Communist victory in China, then rashly defined the American defense perimeter in terms that excluded Korea and Formosa, and finally involved the nation in a conflict that they could neither win nor terminate. American public opinion also turned against the United Nations. Even though some forty-two countries had sent some kind of assistance to Korea, it remained true that 90 per cent of the UN forces were either American or South Korean. There were good reasons for this disparity: British and French troops, for example, were needed in Europe to preserve the Western balance of power against the Communist bloc. But this did not make the burden any more acceptable to the parents and wives of the American soldiers fighting on this distant front.

On the other hand, the anti-Communist nations that had accepted American leadership so readily early in the conflict were more hesitant after Communist China became involved. They feared some rash step that might widen this local conflict into World War III. When the United States urged the UN to brand Communist China as an aggressor and to employ sanctions against her, most of the other UN members wanted first to attempt conciliation. Although Communist China rejected a Security Council invitation to answer the American accusations, she did send a delegation to UN headquarters to present her own countercharge that the United States had been guilty of aggression both in Korea and Formosa. The Soviet Union championed the Chinese Communist cause, and the Security Council was thereby deadlocked.

Through the initiative of Secretary Acheson, the General Assembly had assumed more power in November, 1950. The so-called "Uniting for Peace" resolution provided that

if the Security Council, because of lack of unanimity of the permanent members, fails to exercise its primary responsibility for the maintenance of international peace and security in any case where there appears to be a threat to the peace, breach of the peace, or act of aggression, the General Assembly shall consider the matter immediately with a view to making appropriate recommendations to Members for collective measures, including ... the use of armed force when necessary, to maintain or restore international peace and security.

It was to the Assembly, accordingly, that the United States now turned for support, but instead of immediately condemning Chinese aggression, this body on December 14, 1950, authorized a commission to seek an armistice. Only when these negotiations failed did the Assembly on February 1, 1951, find Communist China guilty of aggression and call upon her to withdraw her forces. Still another three months elapsed before the Assembly recommended additional measures against North Korea and Communist China in the form of an embargo upon arms, petroleum, and other strategic goods.

A feeling that the UN was dragging its feet on the Korean issue contributed to a resurgence of American nationalism, greatly encouraged also by a public controversy between President Truman and General MacArthur. Viewing the situation purely as a military problem, MacArthur believed that he should not be required to confine hostilities to Korean territory. Since Chinese Communist planes were attacking the UN forces from bases across the Yalu River in Manchuria, he should have permission to bomb these bases. In a similar way he favored imposing a naval blockade of the China coast and helping Chiang Kai-shek reopen a front on the Chinese mainland. Truman and Acheson felt it necessary to keep a tight rein on the general. The MacArthur strategy, they were convinced, involved an almost certain broadening of the conflict. An all-out war against China would tie up more and more American forces in Asia, thus weakening the NATO front in Europe and opening the door to an extension of Russian influence. If the Soviet Union decided to come to China's aid, the United States would find itself involved in World War III on a front far distant from its allies. An Asia-first policy, in the view of the American joint chiefs of staff, would involve the nation "in the wrong war, at the wrong place, at the wrong time and with the wrong enemy." Opposition to MacArthur's proposals was particularly strong in Britain and France.

Disturbed by early signs of misunderstanding, President Truman flew halfway around the globe in October, 1950, to confer with MacArthur on Wake Island in the Pacific. For a time this conference appeared to clear the air, but after MacArthur's November setback relations between the general and the President became increasingly strained. Despite orders not to make policy statements unless they had been cleared with Washington, MacArthur wrote a letter to Republican House Leader Joseph W. Martin, strongly criticizing the Truman-Acheson policy, particularly on the point of not using Chinese Nationalist forces. The general also dealt severely with his European critics:

> It seems strangely difficult for some to realize that here in Asia is where the Communist conspirators have elected to make their play for global conquest, and that we have joined the issue thus raised on the battlefield; that here we fight Europe's war with arms while the diplomats there still fight it with words; that if we lose this war to Communism in Asia the fall of Europe is inevitable, win it and Europe most

probably would avoid war and yet preserve freedom. As you point out, we must win. There is no substitute for victory.

When MacArthur's letter to Martin found its way into the newspapers, the President reacted promptly, removing the general from his Far Eastern commands on April 11, 1951, to the great relief of most Europeans but much to the indignation of MacArthur's many American admirers. When MacArthur arrived back in the United States he was given a hero's welcome in numerous cities and was invited to address a joint session of Congress, where he made a highly emotional defense of his position. Subsequent congressional hearings kept the controversy alive for months. As in most such disputes, neither side convinced the other. Many Americans, particularly Republicans, strongly condemned Truman both for harsh treatment of a great American patriot and for his whole Korean policy. On the other hand, the President's courage in disciplining MacArthur was commended by many other citizens who believed that a major constitutional issue involving the subordination of the military to the civilian commander in chief was at stake and who also honored Truman for his determination to keep the Korean conflict localized.

The Korean Armistice

The Korean conflict continued to embitter American politics throughout the remainder of Truman's second term. In July, 1951, the opening of negotiations between military truce teams representing the two sides raised the hope of speedy peace, but bargaining with the the Communists proved to be a frustratingly slow process, interrupted by periodic suspensions. The Communists demanded that the truce line be established at the 38th parallel, but the UN commanders argued for a line that would follow the actual battle front, lying for the most part somewhat north of the parallel. The Communists eventually conceded this, but displayed new stubbornness on issues involving the exchange of prisoners and the policing of the armistice. In October, 1952, truce negotiations broke down completely. Meanwhile, fighting continued in Korea, often flaring up into savage battles, without clear advantage on either side.

Inevitably the Korean stalemate became an issue in the 1952 presidential campaign. The Republican platform was critical of Truman's whole Asia policy, and Republican campaign orators made Secretary of State Acheson a favorite whipping boy. Particularly effective was candidate Dwight D. Eisenhower's pledge to go to Korea to seek a solution on the spot, a pledge that he carried out by making a Far Eastern trip soon after his election.

The Republicans came to power in 1953 with a strong popular mandate to break the Korean stalemate, but just how was a difficult question. Should an attempt be made to win a clear-cut victory through intensified

The STRUGGLE for EASTERN ASIA

Communist countries
Anti-communist countries
Neutral countries

MONGOLIAN PEOPLE'S REPUBLIC

MANCHURIA

Sakhalin I.

KURILE ISLANDS

Dairen
Port Arthur
N. KOREA
Seoul
S. KOREA
Tokyo

PEOPLE'S REPUBLIC of CHINA

J A P A N

Quemoy
Formosa Strait
FORMOSA (Nationalist China)

BURMA
Hong Kong

THAILAND

PHILIPPINE REPUBLIC

INDONESIA

The KOREAN CONFLICT

MANCHURIA

N. KOREA
Pyongyang
SEA
1953 Truce Line
38th Parallel

YELLOW SEA

Seoul
S. KOREA

of

JAPAN

attack in full alliance with Nationalist China in the MacArthur spirit? Or should the emphasis be on trying to get a cease-fire on the best possible terms? President Eisenhower and his Secretary of State, John Foster Dulles, threatened the first alternative, but actually sought the second. To impress the Communists with the new firmness of American policy, Eisenhower announced that Truman's "shielding" of Communist China had been abandoned and Chiang Kai-shek was now free to carry on operations against the mainland—a permission that was in fact meaningless because the Nationalists were too weak to make more than the hit-and-run raids that had been tolerated under the Truman policy. Besides "unleashing Chiang," the Eisenhower administration made a show of toughness by sending more planes and atomic missiles to the Far East and warning Communist China through indirect channels that these might be used against the Manchurian air bases.

Either because they were impressed by these American measures or because Stalin's death on March 5, 1953, had changed the situation, the Communists modified their Korean policy during the spring months. They first permitted an exchange of sick and wounded prisoners, then proposed a resumption of cease-fire talks. After three months of hard bargaining the negotiators at Panmunjom finally agreed to an armistice on July 27, 1953. The agreement specified a truce line running somewhat north of the 38th parallel for most of its distance, but dropping south of it at its western end. A demilitarized zone 2½ miles wide was defined, and each side promised not to strengthen its armed forces within Korea. A Neutral Nations Supervisory Commission, with Swedish, Swiss, Polish, and Czech representatives, was to see that these pledges were kept. On the issue that had proved most troublesome—compulsory versus voluntary repatriation of war prisoners—a compromise favorable to the UN position had finally been worked out. Prisoners not wanting to go home were to be turned over to a Neutral Nations Repatriation Commission with members from India, Sweden, Switzerland, Czechoslovakia, and Poland. For ninety days Communist and UN representatives were to have an opportunity to "explain" to these men why they should be repatriated, but if they persisted in their position they were ultimately to be released and helped to find sanctuary. In the end, the prisoner exchange provided the UN with a substantial propaganda victory, since less than 3 per cent of the prisoners held by the Communists refused to return to non-Communist soil, while about 22 per cent of all prisoners in UN hands declined to go back to an uncertain fate in North Korea or Communist China.

Not everyone applauded the Korean armistice. President Rhee was bitterly disappointed to see the conflict come to an end on terms that left his country still divided and still in danger of attack. Indeed, he attempted to sabotage the negotiations by allowing some 27,000 North Korean prisoners of war to go free without regard to the armistice conditions. A hurried trip to Seoul by Assistant Secretary of State Walter F. Robertson and a pledge of American support in case of renewed Communist attack were necessary to wring from the South Korean government a reluctant promise to abide by the cease-fire and not to try to carry on the war alone.

In the United States the Korean armistice also encountered some criticism. Republican Senator William Knowland of California expressed the feelings of many strong nationalists in denying that this was an honorable settlement, while Democrats contended that Eisenhower had retreated from earlier positions taken by Truman. The general public, however, was too happy to have the Korean bloodshed stopped to give much weight to these lamentations. Although the Communists still controlled North Korea, their attempt to extend their rule over the whole country had been blocked. Casualties had been shockingly heavy, but they had not been in vain if the limited conflict in Korea helped to prevent a larger conflict elsewhere.

The armistice provided no solution to the fundamental Korean problem.

Not only was the country still divided, but foreign troops remained on both sides of the truce line. The armistice had recommended that a high-level political conference be convened within three months to seek a settlement, but this was delayed because of disagreements over whom to invite. Representatives of the United States, Britain, France, the Soviet Union, Communist China, North Korea, and South Korea did confer at Geneva in April, 1954, but promptly deadlocked over rival plans for Korean unification.

Japanese Peace Treaty

Events in China and Korea demonstrated the desirability of transforming Japan, if possible, from the status of defeated enemy to that of friendly ally. In 1950 the American State Department initiated a peace-making procedure that would avoid the frustrations of further Big Four conferences. The Department prepared a draft treaty and then delegated John Foster Dulles, Republican foreign policy expert, to carry on an intricate series of negotiations with each of the nations involved in the Pacific area. To provide reassurance against a revival of Japanese aggression, the United States entered upon mutual security agreements with Australia, New Zealand, and the Philippines.

Having obtained the assent of most of the interested countries to the American draft with certain modifications, the United States invited the fifty-four states which had been at war with Japan to send representatives to a peace conference at San Francisco in September, 1951. To avoid the difficult problem of deciding which government should represent China, neither party was invited and the negotiation of a Sino-Japanese peace treaty was postponed for later action by the two countries. Dissatisfied with this procedure and disapproving the draft treaty on other grounds, India and Burma refused to attend the San Francisco Conference, as did also Yugoslavia for its own reasons. On the other hand, the Soviet Union was represented—to the surprise of many observers. The Russians probably hoped to upset American plans, but Secretary Acheson so skillfully steered the proceedings that the treaty was rushed through for signature after only four days of speechmaking. The Soviet Union, Czechoslovakia, and Poland refused to sign, but forty-nine other nations, including Japan, did.[3]

The peace treaty required Japan to renounce all its modern empire and to restrict its rule to the four home islands and small adjoining ones. She had to concur in the establishment of a United States trusteeship under

[3] The Philippines signed, but put on record their dissatisfaction with the inadequacy of Japanese reparations. The reparations issue was also a source of bitterness with Burma, which did not sign.

UN auspices over the Ryukyus, the Bonins, and other Pacific islands. Although the treaty recognized that Japan ought to pay large reparations, it was conceded that this was economically impossible, and Japan's obligation was therefore limited to the surrender of certain foreign assets and the manufacture of goods out of raw materials supplied by claimant states. Japan agreed to abide by the UN peace-enforcement machinery; in return, she was granted the right of a sovereign power to "individual or collective self-defense," a stipulation that would permit her to rearm and to seek allies. Truman and Dulles characterized the treaty as one not "drawn in a spirit of revenge"; it was, so they hoped, a "treaty of reconciliation."

Within a few hours after the signing of the peace treaty, Japan and the United States signed a highly significant mutual security treaty. This stipulated that American military forces and installations were to continue in Japan until the two nations agreed that UN or other security arrangements made the American forces no longer necessary to the safety of Japan and the Far East. If requested by the Japanese government, the United States would assist "to put down large-scale internal riots and disturbances in Japan, caused through instigation or intervention by an outside power or powers"—an unmistakable warning to Communist troublemakers.

Two years later the effort to build a Far Eastern belt of containment took a further step in the signing of a Korean-American mutual security treaty on October 1, 1953. Although this obligated each to assist the other in case of armed attack, it also committed each to refrain from the threat or use of force in any way inconsistent with UN obligations. This was intended to reassure Rhee against renewed Communist aggression, but at the same time to restrain him from any rash act of his own.

The Problem of Indochina

There were many dangerously soft spots in the dike that American diplomacy was trying to erect around the Communist flood. One of these was in Southeast Asia, where French control over Indochina had been mortally weakened by the events of World War II. Following the Japanese withdrawal, an independent Republic of Vietnam was proclaimed in the three eastern states of the five that had constituted prewar French Indochina.[4] Although France recognized in principle the rights of the Vietnamese to self-rule, she insisted that the state remain under French tutelage as a part of the French Union. Consequent recriminations led to an outbreak of war between French troops and Vietnamese

[4] The states affected were Annam, Tongking, and Cochin China. The two western states, Laos and Cambodia, were evolving toward local constitutional monarchies.

nationalists. The anticolonial elements were of many different political colorations, but the most formidable faction was the Vietminh led by Ho-Chi-Minh, a Communist.

Unwilling to recognize Ho-Chi-Minh's government, the French tried to conciliate Vietnamese nationalism by sponsoring a rival regime headed by Emperor Bao Dai, but most native nationalists regarded Bao Dai as little more than a French puppet dependent on French military support. The Vietminh continued to fight a bold guerrilla-type war against the French. Disliking colonialism, the United States had at first given the French campaign in Indochina no encouragement, but events in 1949 and 1950—the Communist victory in China and the Korean conflict— brought a drastic change in American policy. Ho-Chi-Minh seemed no longer a potential George Washington, but rather a sinister pawn in the Communist game. Increasing American military and economic support was given to the French and to Bao Dai. In 1954 the United States was paying three-fourths of the French war costs.

Even with American support the French found it impossible to crush the Vietminh. In 1954 the anti-Communist cause suffered two major defeats, one on the military front, the other on the diplomatic. In May, the French garrison at Dienbienphu surrendered after fifty-five days of siege, thereby giving up control of most of northern Vietnam. Admiral Arthur Radford, chairman of the Joint Chiefs of Staff, had urged use of the American Air Force in an attempt to save Dienbienphu, but President Eisenhower had decided against this. As an alternative, Secretary Dulles had proposed joint military action by the United States and other nations. But the thought of turning Indochina into another Korea was abhorrent both to American public opinion and to America's allies. The French themselves were sick of the cost in lives and money. Consequently, a new government, headed by Premier Pierre Mendès-France, had come into office, pledged to seek an armistice.

Over American objections, therefore, the Indochina question was put on the agenda of the Geneva Conference, already scheduled for discussion of the Korean question. The negotiations at Geneva resulted in an armistice, dated July 21, 1954, under which Cambodia and Laos were recognized as independent, and Vietnam was divided at the 17th parallel, with the Communists in control of the north and the anti-Communists of the south. There was also a provision for elections under international supervision to choose a government for the entire country, but these were never held, largely because of fear that the Communists would win them.

Eisenhower and Dulles took a gloomy view of the Geneva armistice, which the United States promised to respect even though it was not a party. Not only did the agreement recognize Communist rule over strategic territory contiguous to Red China, but it placed the Communists in a favorable position to infiltrate the whole region of Southeast Asia—first in the weak and inexperienced states of South Vietnam, Laos, and Cambodia, then in neighboring Burma, Thailand, Malaya, and Indonesia, an area of great resources in rubber, tin, and petroleum. South Vietnam, expected by many observers to fall speedily to the Communists, managed to preserve its independence, thanks largely to the emergence of a local strong man, Ngo Dinh Diem. In 1955 Diem ousted the unpopular Emperor Bao Dai and assumed the presidency of a newly proclaimed republic, to which the United States made very substantial grants.

Allies and Neutrals

Worried by the Communist threat in Southeast Asia, Secretary Dulles invited interested nations to a conference at Manila in September, 1954. Eight countries—the United States, Australia, New Zealand, Britain, France, Thailand, Pakistan, and the Philippines—signed an agreement there creating the Southeast Asia Treaty Organization (SEATO), whose purposes were to strengthen defenses against external aggression, to counter subversion from within, and to develop economic measures for social well-being. Although Cambodia, Laos, and South Vietnam were barred by the Geneva armistice from entering any such alliance, the SEATO powers included these countries within the area to be protected against armed attack.

Although SEATO was obviously intended as the Asiatic counterpart to NATO, it was a much weaker combination. For one thing, only three truly Asiatic nations joined. Japan did not wish to commit herself to possible overseas operations; South Korea and Nationalist China were problem states not acceptable as allies by some of the SEATO members. The prestige of the alliance suffered particularly from the unwillingness of India, Burma, Ceylon, and Indonesia to participate. These nations that had recently won their independence from Britain and the Netherlands looked with suspicion on SEATO as a cover for the perpetuation of colonialism.

American relations with India were clouded by mutual suspicions and misunderstandings. Prime Minister Jawaharlal Nehru was determined that India should play a fully independent role in world affairs and refused to commit his country to either the Communist or anti-Communist blocs. From Nehru's point of view, the American China policy was all wrong: the results of the civil war showed that the Chinese people supported Mao Tse-tung rather than Chiang Kai-shek; United States persistence in supporting the Nationalists and refusing to recognize Communist China was, therefore, evidence of continued Western imperialism. Nehru similarly criticized American policy in Korea and Indochina as unduly aggressive.

From the American point of view, the Indian Prime Minister appeared to be unjustly suspicious of the United States, while failing to take seriously enough the imperialism of Communist China and the Soviet Union. Indian representatives in the UN were accused of playing the role of Communist stooges. Unable to anchor its Asiatic defense lines on India, the American State Department tied itself by alliance and military aid programs to India's rival, Pakistan—thereby still further embittering Indian-American relations.

Despite these recriminations, neither India nor the United States could afford a serious rupture, since each needed the other. Attempting an ambitious program of economic development to combat the nation's desperate poverty, India wanted American economic aid and technical assistance. And the American government, in turn, realized that to cut off aid to India would be to abandon a crucial front to the Soviet Union, already showing an eagerness to send equipment and technicians into underdeveloped countries as a means of enlarging its political influence. India was, after all, attempting to solve her problems through democratic methods; if she succeeded, her example might be of critical importance to other new nations otherwise tempted to follow the totalitarian methods of Communist China. Even so, the United States dealt much more generously with nations committed to the anti-Communist front than it did with the neutralist countries. In the year ending June 30, 1958, for example, India received only 45 million dollars in American grants and credits as compared with Pakistan's 98 million, while Indonesia received only 19 million dollars as contrasted with South Vietnam's 233 million.

The Formosa Question

When President Eisenhower issued orders for the Seventh Fleet to cease shielding Communist China from Nationalist attack, this "unleashing" of Chiang Kai-shek offered to "Asia First" partisans the hope that the Chinese Nationalists would soon invade the mainland. But it became obvious that Chiang's forces would never carry the war to the enemy except with large-scale American support—a support that Eisenhower had no more intention of giving than had Truman. The real question was not whether the Nationalists could reconquer the mainland, but whether they could keep Formosa and their other island possessions.

There was no question that the United States intended to defend Formosa itself and also the nearby Pescadores Islands. But the case of the so-called offshore islands—the Tachens, Quemoy, and Matsu—was fundamentally different in that they were close to the mainland and had remained under Chinese control even when Formosa had been under Japanese rule. These islands were valuable to the Nationalists because they served as ideal bases for hit-and-run raids upon the mainland and because they could be used to harass the trade of such Communist ports as Amoy. Possession of the offshore islands would also provide the Nationalists with invaluable stepping stones if they ever became strong enough to launch an invasion of the homeland.

The Communists were naturally as eager to capture the offshore islands as the Nationalists were to keep them. In September, 1954, the Reds began a heavy bombardment of Quemoy, only 5 miles from the mainland. Fearing an invasion attempt, Admiral Radford and certain other military men urged that American and Chinese Nationalist planes be used to bomb Communist bases, but General Matthew Ridgway, the Army Chief of Staff, opposed any such action as likely to involve the nation in full-scale war. President Eisenhower sided with Ridgway.

So far as Formosa itself was concerned, the United States made a definite commitment in a mutual defense treaty signed with Nationalist China on December 1, 1954. In case of an attack upon Formosa or the Pescadores, the United States promised to go to Chiang's assistance. Although no such open-and-shut commitment was made on the offshore islands, the treaty did leave room for including them by a stipulation that additional territories might be brought under the guarantee by mutual agreement. In an accompanying exchange of notes, Chiang promised not to attack the mainland without prior consultation with the American government. He was, in effect, "released."

The Communists avoided a showdown at Quemoy, but did test the American intentions by invading the Tachens, the northernmost of the Nationalist-held islands. Since these had only minor strategic value, Eisenhower decided against any attempt to oppose the Communist move. Instead, American naval units were ordered to assist the Nationalists in making a peaceful evacuation.

Lest American efforts to avoid trouble be misinterpreted, Congress passed on January 28, 1955, a resolution authorizing the President to use the Armed Forces of the United States "as he deems necessary for the specific purpose of securing and protecting Formosa and the Pescadores against armed attack, this authority to include the securing and protection of such related positions . . . as he judges to be required or appropriate in assuring the defense of Formosa and the Pescadores." Purposely vague, this wording left it in Eisenhower's discretion to help the Nationalists defend the remaining offshore islands if he thought it necessary.

For almost four years the Communists made no further move of consequence, but on August 23, 1958, they began shelling Quemoy on an unprecedentedly heavy scale, with the apparent intention of making the island untenable to the Nationalist garrison. At once the question left unanswered in 1954 again became urgent: What would the United States do if the Communists attempted to invade this tiny Pacific outpost? Chiang Kai-shek had bet on American support to the extent of committing about one-third of his best troops to the island. Were the United States to let him down, the blow to his prestige might topple the Nationalist regime even on Formosa itself. Yet to many Americans and to most Englishmen and Frenchmen, the idea that Quemoy was worth risking a major war seemed absurd. Only 5 miles from the Chinese Communist coast but 95 miles from Formosa, the island did not really seem part of Formosa's defenses.

Eisenhower and Dulles adopted a strategy that combined firmness and caution in almost equal ingredients. They warned Communist China not to attempt to invade the islands by publicly stating that "the security and protecting of Quemoy and Matsu have increasingly become related to the defense of Taiwan [Formosa]." Dwelling on this point in a radio talk to the nation, the President stressed the fact that the Communists were boasting that their ultimate objective was Formosa itself:

> Let us suppose that the Chinese Communists conquer Quemoy. Would that be the end of the story? ... They frankly say that their present military effort is part of a program to conquer Formosa.... This plan would liquidate all of the free world positions in the Western Pacific area.

By way of practical assistance, American naval vessels began convoying Nationalist supply boats across the Formosa Strait, but they avoided provocation by terminating their escort 3 miles off the Quemoy beaches, leaving the Nationalist boats to brave the storm of Communist bombardment as best they could. With similar prudence American officers vetoed Nationalist plans to make air attacks against the Communist mainland bases.

The Quemoy crisis continued to provoke tough talk from both sides, but each sought to avoid the outbreak of any full-scale war. Without departing from its nonrecognition policy, the United States did authorize a diplomatic representative in Warsaw to enter upon talks with an envoy from Communist China.[5] Since the American position was that the Communists should renounce the use of force in the Formosa Straits and the Communist was that American forces should completely withdraw from Formosa, the Warsaw talks inevitably failed. More important than this diplomatic fencing was Secretary Dulles's admission that the United States considered Chiang's heavy concentration of forces on Quemoy rather "foolish," a clear hint to Peiping that if the Communist bombardment of

[5] These talks were a continuation of an earlier series initiated at Geneva in 1955 that had dealt with the release of certain American prisoners held in China and other matters.

Quemoy were halted, the United States might insist on at least partial Nationalist evacuation. Also important was a statement from Chiang Kai-shek, obviously made under American pressure, renouncing the use of force to regain the mainland. American diplomacy was apparently orienting itself around a "two Chinas" policy, under which each side would give up its effort to conquer the other.

Communist reaction to these American overtures was bewildering. First, the bombardment of Quemoy was halted in a voluntary cease-fire of several days duration; then the shelling was resumed, but on an announced schedule of alternate days. In the end, the crisis petered out without any formal agreement. One explanation was that the Communists were as unhappy with the "two Chinas" policy as was Chiang Kai-shek and that they avoided pushing the Quemoy question to a final showdown in order to keep the issue alive for future use. Another explanation was that the Communists' principal objective in the whole affair had not been Quemoy itself, but rather to create divisions in the Western alliance and to gain support for Red China's admission to the UN.

Although the United States had shown some flexibility on the offshore islands, it had left no doubt of its determination not to allow a Communist capture of Formosa. American firmness on this issue reflected not so much love for Chiang Kai-shek as increasing reliance on Formosa as a key link in the American defense perimeter, now running from South Korea and Japan through Okinawa and the Ryukyus to Formosa, and then on to the Philippines. Formosa, in the eyes of American military planners, was an unsinkable aircraft carrier of tremendous importance in case of some future nuclear war.

The easing of the Quemoy crisis left American relations with Communist China still on a very unfriendly basis. Secretary Dulles continued to oppose diplomatic recognition of the regime on the ground that this would be "a well-nigh mortal blow to the survival of the non-Communist governments in the Far East. Such recognition and the seating of the Chinese Communists in the United Nations would so increase their prestige and influence in the Far East and so dishearten the free nations, that the Communist subversive efforts would almost surely succeed." Yet nonrecognition carried heavy risks of its own. Not only were the Communists in actual control of the country, but their ruthless efforts to industrialize and modernize the nation seemed likely to make China one of the world's most formidable powers in the not distant future.

Even in 1959, when India felt herself threatened by Communist China's moves into Tibet and other border territories, the Indian delegation continued to argue for the admission of China to the UN. Such a step, it was asserted, would not of itself curb Chinese aggressiveness, but it would at least bring her representatives into the forum of the nations, where the force of world opinion might have more influence upon her. Many American critics also believed that the quarantine of Red China was a self-defeating treatment, merely aggravating Chinese Communist hatred of the West. Yet general American opinion was so strongly opposed to recognition of the regime that few American politicians dared argue for a change of policy.

36

NUCLEAR STALEMATE

In January, 1954, Secretary of State John Foster Dulles warned potential aggressors that they could not count on prescribing battle conditions to suit themselves. To deter troublemakers, the United States would "depend primarily upon a great capacity to retaliate instantly, by means and at places of our choosing." In pronouncing this policy of "massive retaliation," Dulles was serving notice to the Communist world that the Eisenhower administration did not intend to dissipate national energies in a series of Korea-type conflicts. Repudiating the Truman-Acheson policies as unduly timid and negative, he threatened destructive punishment to any transgressor.

Yet the effort to give American foreign policy a new and more menacing look involved many difficulties. For one thing, Dulles's lightning often seemed to scare America's allies more than her enemies. For another, Russia's unexpectedly rapid scientific progress destroyed the margin of superiority needed to make massive retaliation an effective deterrent. And finally, serious though the growth of cancerous tissue in world affairs had become, nuclear warfare offered a surgery far too dangerous to employ.

New Policy Makers

The election of 1952 transferred power from the Democrats, who had been dominant for twenty years, and placed it in the hands of the Republicans; but just what this implied for American foreign policy was not at first clear. Although the new President, Dwight D. Eisenhower, enjoyed tremendous popularity as a military hero, the voters had little knowledge of how he stood on key issues. Yet one thing was certain: he had little sympathy with the ultranationalist wing of his party as represented by such Senators as Robert Taft and John Bricker of Ohio or William Knowland of California. Whereas these men regarded America's European allies with suspicion and favored strong independent action, Eisenhower came to the White House fresh from service as NATO's first Supreme Commander. Through this experience and his prior conditioning during World War II, the new President was firmly opposed to any "Fortress America" theory of foreign policy that would reduce American commitments abroad while concentrating on defense of the Western Hemisphere and giving Asia priority over Europe.

Despite his professional military background, Eisenhower was no sword rattler. On the contrary, firsthand knowledge of war's devastation gave a ring of sincerity to his frequent professions of devotion to peace. On several occasions the President overruled advisers who wanted to employ force to deal with some distant situation like Indochina or Quemoy.

Although Eisenhower faced his responsibilities manfully when hard decisions had to be made, he took only a minor role in day-to-day diplomacy. Accustomed as a general to delegate large responsibility to his staff officers, he carried the same practice into the White House. This placed extraordinary power in the willing hands of John Foster Dulles. Throughout a long career as a New York corporation lawyer, Dulles had dreamed of some day playing a key role in the formulation of American foreign policy. This ambition had its roots in family tradition: he had been named for his Republican grandfather, John Foster, Secretary of State under Benjamin Harrison, and had observed the career of his Democratic uncle, Robert Lansing, Secretary of State under Wilson.

Some confidants believed that Dulles was even more intrigued by the examples of Colonel House and Harry Hopkins than by the careers of his own relatives. What Dulles really wanted, in this view, was to be free of the formal burdens of the secretaryship so that he could travel from one world capital to another as some President's personal representative. As things worked out, Dulles played both these roles. He became Secretary of State, but he also served as roving diplomat, often stopping off at Washington only between hops from one continent to another. This did not mean, however, that Dulles relied extensively on his subordinates to run the shop while he ranged the globe. On the contrary, the Secretary of State kept direction firmly in his own hands. All in all, it was a performance of astonishing virtuosity, demonstrating that Dulles was a man of tireless energy and great intellectual powers. He had other obvious virtues as well: moral purposefulness, courage, personal charm, and technical competence in involved negotiations.

Despite his great abilities, Dulles was the target of much criticism. In many quarters his policy was regarded as dangerously negative, often seeming to involve an automatic "no" to every Soviet proposal. Critics complained that there appeared to be a dearth of fresh and challenging ideas. If this were so, perhaps it was the penalty of the Secretary's way of doing business. Always on the rush in dealing with the latest crisis, he seemed to lack the time for long-range planning. But Eisenhower regarded all such criticisms with impatience. Regarding Dulles as indispensable, he refused to replace him until it finally became necessary because of the Secretary's fatal illness.

Although not directly involved in foreign policy, Secretary of the Treasury George Humphrey and Secretary of Defense Charles E. Wilson were powerful figures in the first Eisenhower Cabinet. Deeply concerned with the unbalanced Federal budget, these two recruits from big business devoted their energies to getting "a bigger bang for a buck." This involved concentrating more heavily on nuclear weapons while saving money on conventional arms. The national defense came to rely increasingly on air power, particularly upon the striking force of the Strategic Air Command. This "new look" in American defense was obviously closely related to Dulles's massive retaliation policy.

Increasing reliance upon the deterrent power of nuclear weapons caused grave concern to many thoughtful critics, both European and American. Not only did it threaten to enlarge any small conflict into a major campaign of destruction, but it left the American Armed Forces with inadequate conventional weapons to deal with local situations. Lacking proper means to fight limited engagements, the West seemed vulnerable to a series of Communist provocations, each too serious to be ignored but not serious enough to run the risks of nuclear war.

Congress Challenges the Executive

During Eisenhower's first months in the White House there was some question whether the President or Congress would control foreign policy. Such conflicts inevitably arise from time to time under the American system of government, and one was to be expected when the Republicans returned to power. While in opposition, the congressional Republicans had accumulated a long list of grievances against the executive. Roosevelt and Truman, according to these critics, had acted in a highhanded fashion, involving the nation in unwise commitments through secret dealings with other governments. To many American ears, Yalta, Potsdam, and Korea were all evil words.

The Republican platform of 1952 had pledged that the government "under Republican leadership, will repudiate all commitments contained in secret understandings such as those of Yalta, which aid Communist enslavements." The nationalist wing of the party urged prompt congressional action to carry this out, but Eisenhower and Dulles counseled caution. To repudiate the war and postwar agreements would release the

Soviet Union from important promises; consequently the administration preferred a resolution rejecting "any interpretation or applications" of secret agreements "which have been perverted to bring about the subjugation of free peoples." But this tepid language did not satisfy the more partisan Republicans who tried to include a reference to the possible "invalidity" of the agreements. The Democrats would not support the intended rebuke to Roosevelt, and the whole project was eventually shelved without action.

A more serious challenge to the executive was contained in a constitutional amendment sponsored by Senator John W. Bricker of Ohio. This would have given Congress power to regulate all executive agreements and would also have stipulated that a treaty could become "effective as internal law in the United States only through legislation which would be valid in the absence of a treaty." [1] Many congressional nationalists of both parties supported the Bricker amendment not only because it would curb the President's power to make agreements like the Yalta one, but because it would prevent an alleged danger of UN-sponsored treaties that might invade national sovereignty or states' rights. Numerous patriotic societies and certain professional groups gave the proposal vociferous support.

Although President Eisenhower at first expressed some sympathy for the Bricker amendment, the State Department soon convinced him that the proposal was unwise. In January, 1954, he warned that the amendment would "so restrict the conduct of foreign affairs that our country could not negotiate the argeements necessary for the handling of our business with the rest of the world."

With administration influence thrown against it, the Bricker amendment had no chance of passage in its original form, but there was still danger that some scarcely less objectionable proposal might be substituted. In February, 1954, a formula proposed by Senator Walter George of Georgia failed by only one vote to obtain the necessary two-thirds approval in the upper house. The issue cut across party lines, with 32 Republicans and 28 Democrats voting for the George amendment, while 14 Republicans and 17 Democrats supported the President in opposing it.

The Quest for Disarmament

Ironically, throughout the years in which the United States and the Soviet Union were competing in the development of nuclear weapons, each was professing to believe that all such devices should be banned by

[1] In the case of *Missouri v. Holland* (1920), the Supreme Court upheld the validity of a Federal migratory bird law passed in conformity with an Anglo-American treaty, despite the fact that such legislation would under other circumstances have been invalid.

international treaty. For a few hopeful months after Hiroshima it had seemed that this might actually be accomplished. In November, 1945, President Truman, Prime Minister Attlee of Great Britain, and Prime Minister Mackenzie King of Canada had issued a joint declaration proposing that the UN establish a commission to plan for reserving atomic energy for peaceful purposes, for eliminating atomic weapons from national armaments, and for establishing effective international inspection. Stalin accepted this idea at the Moscow Foreign Ministers' Conference a month later, and in January, 1946, the UN Assembly authorized an Atomic Energy Commission.

Meanwhile, the American government had been carefully preparing a plan for dealing with the problem. An able team of consultants headed by David Lilienthal, chairman of the Tennessee Valley Authority, and J. Robert Oppenheimer, one of the key scientists in the development of the atomic bomb, prepared a report of striking boldness. Recognizing the difficulty of devising a feasible system of inspection, they advocated the establishment of an International Atomic Development Authority with sole power to mine uranium and refine critical metals, to construct and operate atomic reactors, and to conduct research on power development, nuclear explosives, and the like. Although national atomic energy authorities might carry on peaceful activities, no government would be permitted to make atomic weapons. Violations must be made punishable without Security Council veto.

On June 14, 1946, Bernard Baruch, representing the United States on the UN Atomic Energy Commission, officially presented an American proposal based squarely on the Lilienthal Report. The plan was breathtaking in scope: the United States was offering to hand over to an international authority the most valuable industrial secret ever known and capital assets worth at least 4 billion dollars, in addition to surrendering her monopoly of atomic weapons. Disbelieving such generosity, the Soviet leaders alleged that this was a sinister plot for "a sort of international trust . . . in which American financial and industrial monopolies would exercise command as they think fit." They were particularly hostile to the American insistence upon airtight control. "There must be no veto," Baruch had declared, "to protect those who violate their solemn agreements not to develop atomic energy for destructive purposes." This the Russians darkly regarded as an underhanded attempt to amend the UN Charter to put the Soviet Union at the mercy of American-controlled majorities.

Andrei Gromyko, the Soviet representative on the UN Atomic Energy Commission, countered the Baruch plan with one of his own, providing for an immediate prohibition on the making or use of the bomb and the destruction of all existing nuclear weapons within three months. Only after this was done would the Soviet Union cooperate in the establishment of international committees to encourage the peaceful use of atomic energy. Although this "ban the bomb" approach had propaganda appeal for unthinking pacifists, American leaders believed it would be the height of naïveté for the United States to give up atomic weapons without adequate assurance that no other nation would make them.

For three years the UN Commission struggled with the problem. Each side gave a little: the West conceded that with proper inspection more national atomic energy activity might be permitted; the Soviet Union admitted the need for some kind of inspection. But the Russians continued to insist on destruction of all existing bombs before they would enter any international agreement, and they still refused to accept the degree of control the West thought essential. On November 4, 1948, the UN Assembly passed a resolution approving the establishment of an International Atomic Development Authority along lines not greatly different from the original American proposal. With the Communist states still opposed, however, it was impossible to implement this action.

The issue of the atomic bomb was of course only one aspect of a much broader problem. A UN Commission on Conventional Armaments had also been established in 1946, but it could make no progress until the deadlock in the Atomic Energy Commission was broken. A fresh start was attempted in 1952, when both problems were assigned to a new UN Disarmament Commission. To this body the United States, Britain, and France proposed a program for establishing manpower ceilings for the armed forces of the principal powers. The United States, the Soviet Union, and China would be permitted quotas between 1 and 1.5 million men, while Britain and France would be limited to quotas between 700,000 and 800,000. In subsequent negotiations in a Disarmament Subcommittee, the Western delegates advocated a linking of the various aspects of the disarmament program: when 50 per cent of the agreed reduction of conventional armaments had been made, all new production of nuclear weapons should halt; when 75 per cent had been made, the use of nuclear weapons should be totally prohibited.

On May 10, 1955, the Soviet Union surprised the West by accepting the substance of these latest disarmament proposals. Although the Russian plan was vague on some important details of control, the two sides appeared to be closer to agreement than at any time since 1946. Such was the hopeful situation when the Big Four heads of state met in a summit conference at Geneva in July, 1955.

False Dawn at Geneva

The death of Stalin on March 5, 1953, had been followed by a period of some uncertainty over who would rule the Soviet Union and just what changes of policy this might involve. Stalin's nominal successor was

Georgi Malenkov, but the real power was in a collective leadership of Communist party bosses. From 1956 to 1958 Nikolai Bulganin served as Premier. Whoever occupied the front office, however, it soon became clear that Stalin's true heir was Nikita Khrushchev, who became Secretary General of the Russian Communist party in 1953 and steadily increased his power until he took over the premiership himself in 1958. Tough and shrewd, Khrushchev felt no compunction in reversing those Stalinist policies that he thought injurious to the Soviets' best interests. Within Russia there was some relaxation of the harshest features of Communist policy and an encouragement of more travel and cultural interchange between East and West. The quarrel with Tito's Yugoslavia was patched up, and the satellites were allowed somewhat more independence. Perceiving that Stalin's open hostility to the West had provoked countermeasures like the Marshall Plan and NATO, Khrushchev adopted more subtle tactics, alternating threats and blandishments in an effort to weaken the anti-Communist front.

Hopeful that this changed situation at Moscow might offer opportunities for bold diplomacy, Prime Minister Winston Churchill urged a "summit" conference in which a new Big Four would discuss world problems just as he, Roosevelt, and Stalin had done during World War II days. For months Eisenhower and Dulles resisted these suggestions. For one thing, they must have remembered the unhappy aftermath of Yalta; for another, they suspected the Russians of turning all such high-level meetings into propaganda circuses instead of honest and sincere bargaining sessions.

Yet in 1955 Eisenhower had to accept the summit conference idea. Senator Walter George, Democratic chairman of the Foreign Relations Committee, was urging such a meeting, as were also many other prominent American leaders. Even more insistent was the pressure from England. In April, 1955, Churchill resigned, turning over the prime ministership to Anthony Eden. Facing an immediate general election, Eden desperately needed some convincing evidence of peaceful intention to refute Labor charges that the Tories were perpetuating the cold war. And finally, a factor weakening American opposition was the currently more conciliatory aspect of Russian diplomacy. One evidence was Soviet concession on the disarmament issue; even more impressive was Russian acceptance of an Austrian peace treaty. Signed May 15, 1955, this restored Austria's pre-1938 boundaries and provided for the evacuation of foreign troops and the neutralization of the country. On May 10, 1955, Britain, France, and the United States jointly invited the Soviet Union to a meeting of heads of state, and the Russians promptly accepted.

Meeting from July 18 to 23, 1955, at Geneva, the Big Four [2] appeared to

[2] These included Eisenhower, Eden, Bulganin, and Premier Edgar Faure of France.

get along well. Eisenhower renewed his friendship with Marshal Georgi Zhukov, a comrade in arms of World War II days, and seemingly impressed the Russians with the sincerity of his pledge that the United States would never be a party to aggressive war. But when the conferees turned from generalities to specific issues, the old differences were at once apparent. The Western leaders urged a reunification of Germany based upon free elections; the Russians demanded as a prior condition the dissolution of NATO in favor of a collective security pact to which both the Communist and non-Communist states would be parties. On disarmament the Russians stood on their recent proposals, while the Americans insisted on more adequate inspection controls. As a challenging new idea, President Eisenhower presented an "open-skies plan." Each side should provide the other with complete information about all their military establishments and permit aerial reconnaissance to assure that no surprise attack was in preparation.

The summit conference resulted in no explicit commitments. Indeed, it had been agreed that its purpose should be merely that of exploration, with the detailed negotiations left to a later conference of foreign ministers. Nevertheless, the genial spirit of the meeting offered hope that a corner had been passed and that cold war tensions would now be permanently relaxed. Unfortunately this hope proved delusive. Not only did the foreign ministers, meeting during the following autumn, fail to agree, but within a few months a series of new episodes demonstrated that the two sides were still struggling for supremacy.

The Disarmament Labyrinth

The difficulty of translating the generally optimistic Geneva spirit into tangible results was demonstrated in the UN Disarmament Subcommittee in September, 1955. Instead of proceeding from the point of progress seemingly achieved by the Soviet's conciliatory proposal of the previous May, Harold Stassen, the American representative, announced that the United States was placing "a reservation upon all its pre-Geneva substantive positions." In effect, it was withdrawing all the proposals it had previously made.

Why had there been this apparent reversal of roles, with the Soviet Union now apparently eager to rush into some kind of disarmament treaty and the United States holding back? Stassen placed principal emphasis on the growing American realization that any system of international inspection and control would be only partially effective: with more and more countries using fissionable materials for peaceful purposes, it would become increasingly difficult to prevent some diversion of these materials to secret manufacture of weapons. As Stassen explained on a later occasion:

> On the basis of present scientific knowledge ... the United States has reluctantly concluded that it would not be sound, that it would not be consistent with the security of the United States or of other nations, to agree to the complete elimination of all nuclear weapons, and that such an agreement would be a bad agreement—a tragic mistake.

On other grounds as well, the Western powers now drew back from proposals to ban all nuclear weapons. Even if the control problem could be satisfactorily solved, there was serious danger that this type of disarmament would play into the hands of the Communists, with their great superiority in manpower and conventional weapons. Referring to the West's "atomic shield against aggression," Stassen said: "We wish to be very certain of the true worth of any arrangement which we put in its place before we agree to weaken this shield." Obviously the "new look" in American defense policy made Dulles more hesitant to rush into nuclear disarmament plans. Nor did the European allies put pressure on the United States to do so. Britain, struggling to pare its defense budget, was placing her bets even more strongly on nuclear weapons than the United States, while countries like France or West Germany without nuclear weapons of their own counted upon American strength in this field for their security against Communist aggression.

The West looked with equal suspicion upon the Soviet Union's professed willingness to accept earlier Western proposals for limiting Russian, Chinese, and American armed forces to the neighborhood of 1 to 1.5 million men, with proportionate cuts for the other nations. Sober second thought had made this kind of limitation seem less attractive to the West. Drastic cuts might destroy NATO as an effective agency and leave Western Europe at the mercy of Russia and her satellites.

As the difficulties in achieving any major disarmament agreement became more obvious, the two sides explored the possibility of more modest steps that might at least ease immediate tensions. Eisenhower's open-skies plan to reduce the danger of surprise attacks opened up one possibility after the Russians offered to accept it for limited zones. Another possibility seemed to be banning nuclear tests. Although scientists could not agree upon the extent to which such testing was endangering world health, there were growing protests, particularly from countries like Japan exposed to substantial fall-out from both the American and the Soviet blasts. Here again the Western leaders felt it necessary to be cautious. France and other nations objected to any test ban that would leave a monopoly of nuclear weapons in Russian, British, and American hands.

American authorities warned that a premature halt on testing would prevent the United States from producing a "cleaner" H bomb—that is, one with less fall-out, and also from perfecting the smaller atomic warheads necessary to equip ground forces with weapons for waging limited nuclear warfare.

For several months during 1957 the UN Disarmament Subcommittee meeting at London debated proposals for partial disarmament. Among other things the Russians urged an immediate two-year ban on nuclear testing and an open-skies inspection plan to apply to a limited zone on both sides of the Iron Curtain, but excluding most of industrial Russia and Eastern United States. The Western powers countered with a "package deal" that would link the two-year test ban with the establishment of an international control organization, effective inspection measures, safeguards against surprise attacks, and a cutoff of manufacture of new nuclear weapons. Once again the result was deadlock, with neither side willing to accept the other's program.

Although disarmament negotiations seemed invariably to lead into dead ends, neither side wanted to take the responsibility of refusing to talk. For one thing, the issues involved the lives and safety of millions of people. For another, they were closely intertwined with the global battle of propaganda, particularly in influencing the uncommitted nations of Asia and Africa. In March, 1958, the Soviet Union announced that it was suspending nuclear tests and invited the West to follow suit. Western statesmen retorted that this was no more than a propaganda maneuver since Russia had just completed an important series of tests, while the United States was about to begin one. Reversing roles in the fall, the United States and Britain offered to suspend tests for one year if the Soviet Union did not resume them, while Russia claimed a right to make as many new tests as the West had during its latest round.

A Geneva conference of scientists having reported in August, 1958, that it was technically possible to devise a foolproof system to detect nuclear explosions, a political conference on the subject was convened at Geneva the following October. Over the next several months the test-ban talks ran into familiar difficulties. The United States and Britain argued that it would be necessary to maintain teams of foreign observers on the soil of each nuclear nation with adequate powers to make on-the-spot investigations of suspected violations of any test ban. The Soviet Union opposed any such rigid system without some kind of veto. To sidestep this obstacle, Eisenhower suggested an immediate ban on lower atmosphere and underwater tests. These were the explosions carrying the greatest fall-out danger, but they were also the most easily detected without elaborate international policing. The Russian reply was discouraging. Claiming to want all tests stopped, they disdained the piecemeal approach—further proof in Western eyes that the Soviets were more interested in propaganda than in practical compromise.

Similar frustration was encountered in a separate series of Geneva talks in which Eisenhower's open-skies plan was further explored. Both sides professed to desire assurance against surprise attack, but each side had its own idea of which regions should be open to aerial inspection. Largely concerned with the possibility of Soviet attack from the direction of the Arctic, the Americans wanted inspection of the polar regions, but the Russians objected that this would open up more of their territory than that of the United States. On the other hand, the West objected to Soviet proposals for an inspection zone in Central Europe on the grounds that this would have the effect of perpetuating the existing political division.

Atoms for Peace

Fortunately, international cooperation for developing beneficial uses of the atom did not have to wait for the control of nuclear weapons. In December, 1953, President Eisenhower appeared in person before the UN Assembly to propose that the governments possessing atomic industries should make joint contributions from their stockpiles of uranium and other fissionable materials to an International Atomic Energy Agency. This body would devise methods whereby these precious supplies would be allocated "to serve the peaceful pursuits of mankind" in such fields as agriculture, medicine, and the production of electric power.

The President's initiative in this field led to modest but hopeful progress. In 1955 an International Conference on the Peaceful Uses of the Atom was held at Geneva, with sixty nations, both Communist and non-Communist, represented. Two years later a second such conference resulted in the freest exchange of nuclear data yet achieved between East and West.

Meanwhile the United States was loaning fissionable materials to friendly nations. Under a series of bilateral agreements it supplied over 7 tons of U235 to Italy and smaller quantities to France, West Germany, the Netherlands, and some twenty other countries. In 1957, six West European nations organized the European Community of Atomic Energy (Euratom) for the purpose of pooling resources for atomic power development.

In October, 1957, East and West both participated in the establishment of an International Atomic Energy Agency (IAEA), whose objective was "to accelerate and enlarge the contribution of atomic energy to peace, health, and prosperity throughout the world." To enable the agency to commence its work, the United States contributed a research reactor and other equipment, a complete library on the peaceful uses of atomic energy, and generous quantities of U235 and natural uranium. Some observers hoped that the development of inspection techniques by the IAEA might help solve the problems standing in the way of nuclear disarmament.

Danger Signals in the Middle East

After World War II the United States found itself increasingly involved in the turbulent politics of the Middle East. Even as a geographical term, this region was vaguely defined. Sometimes the phrase included all of North Africa and Southwest Asia from Morocco to Pakistan—a region inhabited by many different nationalities but mostly Moslem in religion. More accurately, the Middle East included Egypt and other Arab countries near the eastern Mediterranean, plus Israel, Turkey, and Iran.

Whichever the definition, this territory was of vast strategic and economic importance. So long as it remained under Western influence, it provided air and missile bases from which the Soviet Union might be brought under attack from many different directions. Should the Communists gain control of all or part of this region, the NATO countries in Europe would be outflanked and placed in grave danger. Soviet bases on the southern or eastern shores of the Mediterranean would also jeopardize communication lines between Europe and Asia. Particularly important prizes would be the Suez Canal and Arab air fields.

Still more vital were the oil fields of Saudi Arabia, Iraq, Kuwait, and Iran. Western Europe was almost wholly dependent on these sources, and the United States itself was counting increasingly on them for the future. The West viewed with unconcealed alarm any threat that the wells or the pipe lines to the Mediterranean might fall under hostile control.

Between World Wars I and II, Britain and France had held dominant influence throughout the whole region from Morocco to India, challenged only by the Italian possession of Libya; World War II and its aftermath, however, revolutionized this situation. Defeated Italy had to recognize the independence of its North African colony; France gave up its special position in Syria, Lebanon, Morocco, and Tunisia; Britain ended its mandates over Jordan and Israel and withdrew its troops from the Suez Canal Zone. As Western colonialism grew weaker, the flames of nationalism burned higher and higher. On the island of Cyprus the British struggled with an increasingly difficult situation until an independence plan recognizing rival Greek and Turkish interests was finally worked out in 1959. In Algeria, the French fought Moslem rebels in campaigns that drained the resources of the mother country.

Although American missionaries and oilmen had been active in the Middle East long before World War II, most Americans had their interest first aroused by the new state of Israel. American Jews, inspired by

Zionism and shocked by Nazi atrocities, contributed money, arms, and advisers to the Palestine colonists. Not unmindful of the Jewish vote, the Truman administration did what it could to aid the cause. During the 1948 campaign Truman said:

> ... it is my desire to help build in Palestine a strong, prosperous, free, and independent state. It must be large enough, free enough, and strong enough to make its people self-supporting and secure. As President of the United States, back in 1945 I was the first to call for the immediate opening of Palestine to immigration to the extent of at least 100,000 persons. The United States, under my administration, led the way in November 1947 and was responsible for the resolution of the United Nations setting up Israel, not only as a homeland but as a free and independent political state. The United States was the first to give full and complete recognition to the new state of Israel in April 1948....

Unfortunately, the birth of Israel, accompanied as it was by bitter warfare between the Israelis and their Arab neighbors, left ugly scars. Arab nationalists vowed that they would never recognize the new state, and even after the UN-sponsored truce of 1949 a succession of border incidents threatened to renew war at any time. The Arab-Israeli tension was intensified by Egyptian refusal to allow Israeli ships to use the Suez Canal and by the pathetic plight of almost a million Palestinian Arabs who had fled from Israel. Fearful that a spark might ignite a dangerous explosion, Britain, France, and the United States in 1950 joined in warning both Arabs and Israelis against resorting to force.

Believing that Truman's pro-Israel and pro-India policies had unduly antagonized the Moslem world, the Eisenhower administration sought to remedy this by gestures of friendship to the Arabs and by drawing Pakistan into the Southeast Asia Treaty Organization. Dulles hoped to complete the containment of the Communist world with an all-inclusive Middle East alliance, but rival ambitions within the region made this impossible. Instead, with American blessing, the "northern tier" states— Turkey, Iraq, Iran, and Pakistan—joined with Britain in the Baghdad Pact (1955), establishing a Middle East Treaty Organization (METO). The United States avoided an outright commitment, but gave the new alliance both moral support and military aid.

Since it aggravated Arab suspicion of the West, the Baghdad Pact was of dubious wisdom. Most Arabs resented British participation as a revival of colonialism and also deplored the strengthening of their traditional enemies, the Turks. Complicating an already complicated situation, Iraq's membership in METO alarmed Egypt, since these two nations were jealous rivals for dominant influence over the region. Even as a deterrent to the Soviet Union, the northern tier alliance was of little use. Except for Britain and Turkey—already committed to Western defense through NATO—the member nations possessed very little military power. Moreover, the Baghdad Pact provoked Russia into playing a much more active role than hitherto in the Middle East.

Western diplomacy found its most difficult problem in dealing with Colonel Abdul Gamel Nasser, who became a steadily more powerful figure in Egypt after the overthrow of the monarchy in 1952. Hoping to win Nasser's friendship, Secretary Dulles urged the British to pull their troops out of the Suez Canal Zone in 1954. Britain and the United States also promised to advance funds for the building of a high dam and hydroelectric plant at Aswan on the Nile.

In September, 1955, Nasser bitterly disappointed his would-be friends by announcing a deal under which Egypt would receive munitions from Communist Czechoslovakia in exchange for cotton, thereby circumventing the Middle East arms embargo by which the Western powers had been trying to prevent a renewal of war between Israel and her Arab neighbors. On the Communists' part, the British and Americans believed the arms deal to be a cynical betrayal of the peaceful professions of the Geneva summit conference only two months before. On Nasser's part, they regarded it as a piece of double-dealing to be sternly punished, particularly in view of Egypt's continued flirtation with the Communist world over the next few months. Consequently, in July, 1956, the United States and Britain publicly withdrew their support for the Aswan dam project.

The Suez Crisis

On July 26, 1956, just one week after Dulles struck his blow at the Aswan plan, President Nasser proclaimed the nationalization of the Suez Canal, whose profits would now be used for the dam. This in turn struck a blow at the Suez Canal Company, whose shares were owned by the British government and private French investors. Although Nasser promised compensation and open transit through the waterway, Britain and France protested against Egypt's sole control of an artery so vital to their own economic survival. Trying to avert serious trouble, Dulles sought some form of international control. Early in October the UN Security Council took up the issue and succeeded in persuading both sides to assent to six principles that included open transit of the canal, Egyptian sovereignty, and fair tolls. Russia and Yugoslavia combined to veto a resolution that would have added the principle of international control.

Meanwhile, Israel, alarmed by Communist arms shipments to her hostile neighbors, decided to gamble on preventive war. On October 29, Israeli forces launched a surprise attack against Egyptian bases in the Sinai Peninsula, capturing thousands of prisoners and large quantities of equipment. As the invaders pierced through surprisingly ineffective defenses to within 25 miles of the Suez Canal, Britain and France seized the opportunity to intervene. In an ultimatum of October 30, the two powers demanded that Israel and Egypt withdraw their forces from the vicinity of the canal and allow British and French troops to occupy key points. Israel accepted these terms, but Egypt rejected them angrily. The next day British and French planes began bombing Egyptian targets, and on November 5, Allied troops landed at Port Said, the northern terminal of the canal.

To Eisenhower and Dulles, the Franco-British action came as a most unpleasant surprise. During the preceding three months the Secretary of State had shown sympathy with British and French concern over the Suez situation, but he had insisted that there must be no resort to force in violation of UN obligations. Not only had America's European allies plunged into a dangerous adventure without informing Washington of their intention, but there was strong suspicion of Franco-British complicity in the Israeli attack.

The United Nations now became the scene of a strange drama, in which the United States and the Soviet Union found themselves on the same side in opposition to Britain, France, and Israel. Franco-British vetoes defeated two cease-fire resolutions in the Security Council, one sponsored by the United States, the other by Russia. But on November 2, the General Assembly, called into emergency session, passed an American-sponsored cease-fire resolution by a vote of 64 to 5, with Britain, France, and Israel finding their only support from Australia and New Zealand.

At first Britain and France stood firm, refusing to halt their invasion unless the UN would itself assume responsibility for policing the canal zone. Over the next few days, however, the dangers of defiance became all too obvious. The Arabs, who seldom cooperated on any issue, were now united in fierce resentment against what they regarded as a revival of imperialism. The Egyptians scuttled ships to block the Suez Canal, and their fellow Arabs cut vital pipe lines and threatened to sabotage or seize the oil fields. India and other neutralist countries condemned Britain and France strongly, and even Commonwealth countries like Canada were shocked. American bitterness found expression not only in public condemnation but in private warnings and financial pressure. To cap this mountain of woes, Prime Minister Eden found himself under bitter attack from the whole Labor party and a faction of his own Conservative party as well.

With the Western camp thus in angry confusion, the Soviet Union pressed its advantage ruthlessly, eager to divert world attention from

Hungary, where Russian tanks were crushing a serious anti-Communist uprising. On November 5, Premier Bulganin sent grim warnings to Britain, France, and Israel, stressing the "modern and terrible weapons" possessed by the Russians. This appeared to be a threat to destroy such cities as London, Paris, and Tel Aviv by nuclear attack unless the Suez campaign were halted. Bulganin even invited Eisenhower to join him in coercive measures, a proposal that the President rejected as "unthinkable," particularly at a moment when the Russian army was "brutally repressing the human rights of the Hungarian people." The United States, Eisenhower warned, would oppose "the introduction of new forces" into the Middle East—a position restated a few days later when Soviet spokesmen began to hint at a possible sending of "volunteers" to help Nasser.

Desperate to salvage something from the wreckage, Britain and France grasped at the opportunity provided by a Canadian-sponsored UN resolution for the establishment of a UN emergency force to police the Israeli-Egyptian boundary. This resolution was passed on November 5; and the next day Britain and France announced their willingness to accept a cease-fire, a decision already accepted by Egypt and Israel. Hostilities actually ended on November 7, but many weeks of negotiations were required to bring about the complete withdrawal of British, French, and Israeli troops.

In the end, Egypt and the Soviet Union gained decisively from the Suez affair and Israel came out not too badly, but everyone else was injured. Already badly defeated by Israel, Nasser would have lost not only the canal but his office as well if the Franco-British invasion had been allowed to run its course; instead, the Egyptian President emerged with the canal firmly in his grip and with his personal prestige greatly strengthened in the eyes of Arab nationalists. Khrushchev's gains were equally clear; in Arab eyes and in those of many other Africans and Asiatics he had appeared as the champion of small nations against the old imperialism. Although Israel suffered somewhat in world opinion by her act of aggression and was not permitted to keep any of her conquests, she could balance these losses with a few items on the profit side. Her impressive military victory over Egypt had ended for the time being the threat to her southern borders; she had even won tacit acquiescence in the right of her ships to use the Gulf of Aqaba.

For Britain and France the Suez adventure was a complete disaster. Not only had they failed to establish international control over the canal and to overthrow Nasser, but they had demonstrated to the whole world that they were only second-rate powers, helpless to persist in a policy opposed by the Soviet Union unless strongly backed by the United States. Eden's resignation from the prime ministership in January, 1957, was attributed to illness, but was probably hastened by the failure of his Suez policy.

The Suez crisis occurred just a week before the 1956 election. Politically the President did not suffer. Adlai Stevenson, the Democratic candidate, failed to convince the voters that the Franco-British attack proved the failure of Dulles's whole Middle Eastern policy; instead, the crisis probably increased the Eisenhower vote as frightened citizens clung to the popular hero. In sober review of the whole episode, however, many Americans believed that Dulles had handled matters badly. By first helping Nasser and then humiliating him, the Secretary had been largely responsible for the Egyptian President's angry seizure of the canal. Then when Britain and France took steps to protect what they believed were their vital interests, Dulles assumed a highly moralistic attitude. Probably this was necessary to prove to doubting neutrals that the United States was consistent in its opposition to all aggression, yet it was at the same time a damaging blow to the whole Western alliance for the United States to deal so harshly with its two oldest friends in world affairs.

Moves and Countermoves

The Suez affair destroyed most of what was left of British and French influence in the Middle East. Unless the United States assumed much more responsibility in the region, the Soviet Union was likely to win easy control of all the economic and strategic prizes of the eastern Mediterranean. Such at least was the premise on which was based the so-called Eisenhower Doctrine. On January 5, 1957, the President asked Congress for authority to extend economic and military aid to any Middle Eastern country that desired it and to employ American armed forces "to secure and protect the territorial independence of such nations ... against overt armed aggression from any nation controlled by international communism." Although some congressmen grumbled that Eisenhower was trying to shift to congressional shoulders a responsibility that was primarily his own, most of what he requested was granted in a resolution of March 9, 1957, together with an appropriation of 200 million dollars for economic and military aid to Middle Eastern countries.

At first the Eisenhower Doctrine seemed to have a measure of success. King Saud of Saudi Arabia and other Arab dignitaries made good-will trips to the United States, while former Congressman James P. Richards, acting as the President's special ambassador, visited fifteen Middle Eastern nations in an effort to line up a solid anti-Communist front. Most of these countries were glad of the opportunity to receive American military and economic aid.

Yet the Eisenhower Doctrine provided no magic key to all the intricate problems of the Middle East. For one thing, it was aimed only at "overt armed aggression" from Communist countries, and thus gave no security against breaches of the peace that might arise out of Israeli-Arab tensions or out of rivalries among the Arab states themselves. Moreover, it failed to recognize the increasingly obvious fact that threats to particular Middle Eastern governments were more likely to be internal than external. Most countries in the region contained explosive domestic situations likely at any moment to blow up into political assassinations, palace revolutions, or civil war. Since American aid had perforce to be granted to the dominant kings and sheiks, this created a dangerous situation in which discontented army officers and others agitating for change were almost invariably anti-American. Needless to say, these troubled waters were ideal fishing grounds for both Khrushchev and Nasser.

The dangers of internal subversion were first demonstrated in Jordan. Artificially created through the ramifications of the Palestine question, Jordan was dangerously divided between pro-Western and anti-Western factions. King Hussein inclined to the Western side, but he was under constant pressure from rabid Arab nationalists who hated Israel and admired Nasser. Yielding to these demands in 1956, the King had dismissed General John B. Glubb, the British officer long in command of the Arab Legion. A year later Britain's virtual protectorate over Jordan was ended with the announcement that British troops were being withdrawn and the British subsidy ended. Jordan seemed to be moving inexorably into the anti-Western camp until the King reversed gears in April, 1957. Dismissing his pro-Soviet premier and crushing a pro-Nasser army revolt, Hussein reasserted his personal authority. The United States moved its Sixth Fleet to the eastern Mediterranean as a warning against outside intervention and granted 10 million dollars in special aid to Hussein's new pro-Western government.

In Syria, on the other hand, events took a quite different turn. Spurning the Eisenhower Doctrine, the Syrian government accepted arms and economic aid from the Soviet Union, while looking to Nasser's Egypt for leadership in political affairs. These anti-Western tendencies were consolidated in August, 1957, when a leftist clique seized control of the Syrian army. In February, 1958, Syria joined Egypt in establishing the United Arab Republic. Strategic Yemen near the mouth of the Red Sea linked itself with the new republic the next month.

Syria's move into Nasser's camp was by no means unexpected, but the West received one of its worst surprises on July 14, 1958, when pro-Nasser and pro-Soviet elements rose in successful revolution in Iraq. Killing the King, the Crown Prince, and the strongly pro-Western Prime Minister, Nuri as-Said, the rebels proclaimed a republic and established a provisional government headed by General Abdul Karim el-Kassim.

Eisenhower and Dulles feared that the coup in Iraq might be only the first move in a campaign to overthrow all the pro-Western governments of the region. Lebanon and Jordan were believed to be in immediate peril.

On July 15, 1958, the President ordered United States marines into Lebanon at the request of President Camille Chamoun, who warned that Lebanese independence was threatened by Moslem rebels and reinforcements from Syria. Two days later British Prime Minister Harold Macmillan announced that British troops were being flown into Jordan at the request of King Hussein.

Not since the Suez affair had the threat of war hung so heavily over the Middle East. It seemed likely that the British and American troop landings would precipitate a parallel movement of Soviet forces into Iraq and elsewhere. The Russians demonstrated their displeasure in a note to Washington denouncing United States "aggression" and concluding that the Soviet government could not remain "indifferent to events creating a grave menace in an area adjacent to its frontiers." Moscow mobs, obviously acting on Communist orders, stoned the American Embassy.

Yet it was obvious that neither side wanted serious trouble. The United States and Britain made no attempt to intervene in Iraq; instead, they accepted at face value Kassim's promise to respect his international obligations and recognized his government early in August. Similarly, neither the Soviet Union nor Egypt attempted to contest the Anglo-American policy in Lebanon and Jordan. Indeed it was highly useful to Soviet propaganda for Russia to assume a posture of nonintervention that could be contrasted with the "aggressive" moves of the United States and Britain. Not only neutralist states like India, but such friends of the West as Sweden and Japan expressed alarm at Anglo-American policy.

The contest to influence world opinion found its natural forum in the United Nations. The United States tried to demonstrate that its intervention into Lebanon was necessary to prevent the overthrow of the legal government through infiltration of men and arms from hostile Syria; the Soviet Union denounced American policy as imperialist interference in a small country's internal affairs. In the Security Council the Soviet Union vetoed an American resolution that would have created a UN emergency force to replace American troops in Lebanon, but could muster no other vote than its own for a substitute proposal calling for the immediate withdrawal of the American forces. With the Security Council thus deadlocked, the issue went before an emergency session of the General Assembly. Here, after further acrimony, a way to save the faces of all concerned was provided from an unexpected quarter—the Arab nations themselves. Temporarily burying their rivalries, nine of these, including the United Arab Republic and Iraq on one side and Lebanon and Jordan on the other,[3] offered a resolution calling on members of the Arab League

[3] The other cooperating states were Libya, Sudan, Yemen, Tunisia, and Morocco. All but the last two were members of the Arab League, a loose grouping formed in 1945.

to observe their pledge of noninterference in one another's internal affairs and requesting the UN Secretary General to uphold the purposes of the UN Charter in relation to Lebanon and Jordan, thereby facilitating the withdrawal of foreign troops. Although vague in its phrasing, the Arab resolution appeared to mean that Nasser had promised to be good and the British and Americans had promised to withdraw their forces, leaving only token UN observation teams in their place.

American withdrawal was facilitated by the ending of the Lebanese civil war. American mediation between the pro-Western and the pro-Nasser parties facilitated a deal whereby a middle-of-the-road candidate, General Fuad Chehab, was elected President on July 31, 1958. Chehab was installed in his new post the following September, and American forces completed their withdrawal on October 25, followed soon after by British evacuation of Jordan.

It was characteristic of the Middle Eastern situation that no sooner was one fire extinguished than another broke out somewhere else. Early in 1959 it was the situation in Iraq that caused most concern. Although it was obvious from the start that the Iraqi revolution had deprived the Baghdad Pact of an important member,[4] Kassim at first followed a policy directed more toward keeping Iraq neutral than toward alliance with either the United Arab Republic or the Soviet Union. But the internal situation in Iraq was loaded with dynamite: many army officers were strongly pro-Nasser and many other groups of peasants, workers, teachers, and students were ardently Communist. In March, 1959, Kassim crushed a Nasserite revolt in the important Mosul oil district, but this victory appeared likely to increase Communist influence in the Iraqi government.

The contest for power between Khrushchev and Nasser in Iraq emphasized the fact that the earlier alliance between the two had been a largely unnatural one. Nasser had seen no inconsistency in receiving arms and loans from the Soviet Union, while suppressing Egyptian Communists; and Khrushchev, eager to fan Arab resentment against the West, had tolerated this. In the long run, however, rival ambitions to dominate the Middle East seemed likely to bring the two men into conflict. For the West, the problem became whether to return to a policy of aiding Nasser.

Dollars versus Rubles

Despite nerve-wracking ventures in "brinkmanship"[5] by both the Soviet Union and the United States, there was some basis for cautious

---

[4] To prevent the alliance's complete collapse, Secretary Dulles committed the United States to its full support in July, 1958. The name of the group was changed in October, 1959, to the Central Treaty Organization (CENTO).

[5] The term "brinkmanship" derived from a magazine article supposedly based on interviews with Dulles, in which the Secretary of State claimed that he had been

optimism that the two countries would never actually resort to reciprocal nuclear destruction. Unless some terrible human blunder occurred, it seemed possible that the grim struggle for power might continue to be fought with the weapons of diplomatic maneuver, propaganda, and economic aid.

When the Republicans first came to office, they talked rather irresponsibly about "liberating" the Soviet satellites, but events proved that this could not be done without precipitating a major war. Western hopes were unduly raised by anti-Communist riots in East Germany in 1953 and in Poland and Hungary in 1956. In dealing with these satellites Khrushchev demonstrated both the velvet glove and the iron fist. He held out the hope of more liberal policies by denouncing the dead Stalin. He renewed friendly relations with Tito of Yugoslavia and appeased Poland by tolerating the government of Wladyslaw Gomulka, a Communist with nationalist tendencies. Yet when a popular uprising in Hungary threatened to eradicate communism root and branch, Soviet tanks and troops crushed the movement ruthlessly. The UN General Assembly condemned the Russian action but was helpless to prevent it. Thousands of Hungarian refugees escaped into Austria, from which many of them eventually found asylum in America.

The Hungarian tragedy injured the reputation of both the Soviet Union and the United States. Neutral opinion was shocked by Soviet brutality, even though its impact was somewhat dulled by the coincidence of the Anglo-French invasion of Suez. Many observers felt, however, that the United States had some responsibility for the disaster. Through its propaganda the government appeared to have encouraged rebellion and then left the rebels to their fate with only the comfort of moral platitudes. After this little was heard of liberation as an object of American foreign policy.

Both sides in the cold war sought to gain predominant influence over the new nations of Asia and Africa. All these countries were desperately poor and eager to achieve a higher standard of living. To them the question seemed to be: Which was the more promising, communist totalitarianism or capitalist democracy? The former held great fascination. Russian material achievements since 1917 and Chinese since 1949 were likely to be more impressive to poor Asiatics than the slower if healthier growth of the Western democracies. Nor did the loss of liberties under a communist system necessarily scare peasants more concerned with empty stomachs than with free elections.

In his inaugural address of January 20, 1949, President Truman had called for "a bold new program for making the benefits of our scientific

---

successful in dealing with such problems as Korea, Indochina, and Formosa because of his willingness to go to the "brink" of war to call the Communist bluffs. See James Shepley, "How Dulles Averted War," *Life*, Jan. 16, 1956, pp. 78ff.

advances and industrial progress available for the improvement and growth of underdeveloped areas." Because of its position within a list of other foreign policy pronouncements, Truman's proposal became known as his "Point Four" program. The President hoped to help the underdeveloped countries by supplying them with American technical experts to train the native population in improved methods of agriculture and industry.

Many months were required to make Point Four a reality, with Congress providing the first modest appropriations in June, 1950. By 1953, when Truman left office, almost 2,500 American experts were at work in thirty-five different countries. Projects were in operation for improving food production and sanitation in India, controlling malaria and infantile diseases in Burma, improving rubber production in Brazil, and providing irrigation for Haiti. Besides its own technical assistance activities, the United States contributed to a similar program sponsored by the United Nations and to certain regional projects like the Colombo Plan for southern Asia and the economic program of the Organization of American States.

Eisenhower, like Truman, sought to put American dollars to work in eradicating the poverty upon which international communism fed. Since capital was often the vital need of the underdeveloped countries, Congress authorized in 1957 the establishment of a Development Loan Fund, which would be less rigid in its policies than the existing Export-Import Bank and the International Bank for Reconstruction and Development. The allocation of funds to the various foreign aid programs is shown in the following table:

THE MUTUAL ASSISTANCE PROGRAM *
(FISCAL YEARS—IN MILLIONS)

| | Budget Expenditures | |
Function and Program	1958 (actual)	1959 (estimate)
1. Military assistance	$2,187	$2,312
2. Defense support	874	815
3. Contingencies—other assistance	408	470
4. Technical cooperation	140	159
5. Development loan fund	2	125
Total	$3,611	$3,881

* See Gerard J. Mangone, *A Guide to United States Foreign Policy* (Syracuse: Syracuse University Press, 1959), p. 11.

Economic aid was beset by many perils. Whenever the budget-balancing mood was strong, either within the executive branch or within Congress, there was likely to be a demand for reducing foreign "giveaways." Often it was easier to obtain appropriations for military aid than for loans and grants for peaceful development. This raised the danger that poor countries would be encouraged to maintain armed forces beyond their means, thus jeopardizing sound economic growth.

Khrushchev was by no means inclined to sit back and allow the underdeveloped countries to look to America for all their technical assistance and loans. Between 1955 and 1958 the Soviet Union undertook economic aid programs of its own, totaling over 1.5 billion dollars and involving eighteen different countries. Although this was less than half the sum committed to similar purposes by the United States, the Russian program was shrewdly administered to obtain maximum political advantages.

The Machinery of Global Policy

In a feverish effort to keep abreast of its mounting responsibilities, the State Department expanded its personnel and tinkered with its organizational chart. By 1959 the Department was employing some 5,500 persons in Washington and another 16,000 overseas. To command this burgeoning force, Congress provided for not only a secretary of state and an undersecretary of state, but for an undersecretary of state for economic affairs, two deputy undersecretaries of state, and eleven assistant secretaries of state. In addition to the older regional divisions, the changing situation was reflected by the organization of new offices for dealing with the Near East and South Asia, with Africa, and with international organizations, as well as with other problems.

Large and powerful though the State Department had become, it shared responsibility for the implementation of American foreign policy with other branches of the government. The Department of Defense was obviously deeply involved, not only through the maintenance of its many overseas bases, but in administering programs for military assistance to some forty-seven different countries. Since all the new policies involved large expenditures of money, the Treasury Department also played a vital part. Indeed, the ramifications of foreign policy reached almost every Washington operation. American trade policies and foreign investments, the disposition of agricultural surpluses, and immigration policy all had important impact on United States relations with the rest of the world.

After the passage of the National Security Act of 1947 the nerve center of power became the National Security Council, composed of the President as chairman; the Vice President; the Secretaries of Defense, Treasury, and State; the chairman of the Joint Chiefs of Staff; and the directors of the Office of Defense Mobilization and the Central Intelligence Agency. The National Security Council was entrusted with responsibility for integrating the domestic, foreign, and military policies relating to national security. Since American diplomatic history had been replete with lighthearted assumptions of overseas obligations without thought of how these policies might be backed up in case of a showdown, the establishment of such an agency was evidence of growing maturity.

The National Security Council and other policy-making agencies could operate wisely only if they knew the hard facts of international life. In no branch of its operations had the United States been more negligent than in this. During World War II when President Roosevelt asked Colonel William J. Donovan to organize the Office of Strategic Services (OSS), he told him: "You will have to begin with nothing. We have no intelligence system." After the war, the OSS was disbanded and the old situation seemed likely to return until the National Security Act of 1947 established the Central Intelligence Agency (CIA). Since secrecy was essential to CIA efficiency, little was made public concerning the organization's size or activities, but several thousand persons were believed to be employed during the 1950s in domestic and overseas operations under the direction of Allen Dulles, brother of the Secretary of State.

If the government sought to gain its information about other nations as quietly as possible, its interest was quite the opposite when it came to explaining its own policies to the rest of the world. The United States Information Agency (USIA) broadcast in some thirty-seven different languages from radio transmitters both at home and overseas. It also issued news releases to newspapers and magazines, supplied motion picture and television programs, and maintained a world-wide network of libraries.

Warnings from the South

The East-West struggle for influence extended into Latin America. In 1954 President Jacobo Arbenz Guzmán of Guatemala was accused of dangerous complicity with the Communists, and the American State Department gave its blessing to an anti-Arbenz revolt, hatched by Guatemalan exiles on the soil of neighboring Honduras. Arbenz was forced into exile, some 2,000 Guatemalan Communists were imprisoned, and the strongely anti-Communist Colonel Carlos Castillo Armas became President.

In 1958, when Vice President Richard Nixon visited eight Latin-American countries upon what was supposed to be a "good-will" tour, he encountered anti-American demonstrations of shocking violence. He was heckled in Argentina and Paraguay, spat upon in Peru, and almost hit with flying rocks in Venezuela. So serious did the disorders become that President Eisenhower rushed paratroopers and marines into nearby Puerto Rico and Cuba as "a precautionary measure." Although the anti-Nixon demonstrations probably had their immediate provocation in Communist student circles, they gave alarming evidence of growing hostility to the United States among many other Latin-American groups.

Why had the Good Neighbor spirit now turned sour? For one thing, there was widespread poverty among the peasants and workers. The United States was accused of having taken its Latin-American neighbors for granted, while opening its purse strings to the rest of the world. Closely related to this was the charge that the American State Department was manipulating such economic and military aid as it did give to strengthen the position of certain Latin-American dictators. Beginning with the overthrow of Argentina's Perón in 1955, the Latin-American strong men began to go down like tenpins: Rojas of Colombia fell in 1957, Jiménez of Venezuela in 1958, and Batista of Cuba in 1959. The Cuban revolution, bringing Fidel Castro to power, was particularly explosive in its repercussions, threatening to spark similar outbreaks throughout the Caribbean region. In April, 1959, the Organization of American States nipped in the bud an attempt of Cuban adventurers to seize control of Panama.

The political ferment in Latin America had serious implications for the cold war. With or without reason the forces of change were deeply infected with hatred of the United States, thus playing into the hands of native Communists. Belatedly warned by the anti-Nixon demonstrations, Washington officials began to reorient their policies to refute the charge of hostility toward popular movements. As a first step, the State Department undertook a review of its trade and aid policies to see what more could be done to alleviate Latin America's serious economic problems.

But Washington's determination to be patient with Cuba was severely tried by the provocative behavior of Premier Fidel Castro. The new government alienated many Americans by the wholesale executions that followed its victory; this violence was followed by extensive seizures of American property as part of a radical program of agrarian reform. Castro and his colleagues carried on a violent propaganda campaign against the United States, accusing it of harboring Castro's enemies and permitting hostile flights against Cuban territory.

American distress at these developments was heightened by uncertainty over the underlying motives. Was Castro simply in the grip of an unusually virulent case of nationalism, or was he under the influence of Communist advisers, seeking to make Cuba a beachhead for Soviet intrigue in the Caribbean? There was a growing demand for American retaliation through withdrawal of the special privileges that Cuban sugar enjoyed in the United States market, but Eisenhower shrank from resorting to measures that might revive the old Latin-American charges of Yankee imperialism.

The Defense of Europe

As the struggle between the Communist and the anti-Communist nations expanded to global proportions, the maintenance of a balance of power in Europe became all the more important. The creation of NATO in 1949 had provided a hopeful beginning, but it proved difficult to build up NATO forces to a level likely to provide any real obstacle to Soviet armed might in case of war. France's contribution was severely limited both by continuing hostilities in Algeria and by internal political dissension that was not resolved until General de Gaulle was given extraordinary powers in May, 1958. Although by comparison Britain and Italy enjoyed relative stability, neither could afford to spend unlimited amounts on defense. This situation required the United States to keep substantial forces of its own in Europe and to seek new members for NATO.

West Germany, enjoying a rapid economic recovery, was the most obvious candidate, yet France was understandably reluctant to consent to the rearmament of the nation that had three times since 1870 invaded her soil. In 1952 it appeared that a way to include West Germany in a European Defense Community (EDC) under adequate safeguards had been discovered, but bitter opposition developed among French partisans of both the Communist left and the ultranationalist right. Annoyed by French procrastination in ratifying the EDC treaty, Secretary Dulles warned that the United States might be forced to "an agonizing reappraisal" of its policies. This thinly veiled threat to cut off American military aid only antagonized the French still further. In August, 1954, the French National Assembly finally rejected the EDC treaty.

Although this action at first seemed to torpedo the whole Western defense structure, a solution to the problem was eventually found, thanks largely to British Foreign Secretary Eden. To reduce French fear of a rearmed Germany, Britain promised to keep four divisions and a tactical air force in Europe as long as her Continental allies wanted them. The United States helped by asserting its intention of retaining its forces in Europe for the immediate future. With these reassurances Britain induced France to go along in a plan for enlarging the Western European Union (WEU) [6] to include West Germany and Italy. By the Paris Pact of October 23, 1954, it was agreed to invite West Germany to join NATO and provide twelve divisions (500,000 men) to the NATO army. The Western European Union was given substantial powers to assure that German rearmament was not carried farther than the permitted level.

In order to forestall remilitarization of West Germany, the Soviet

[6] The Western European Union, including Britain, France, and the Benelux countries, had originated in the Brussels Treaty of 1948.

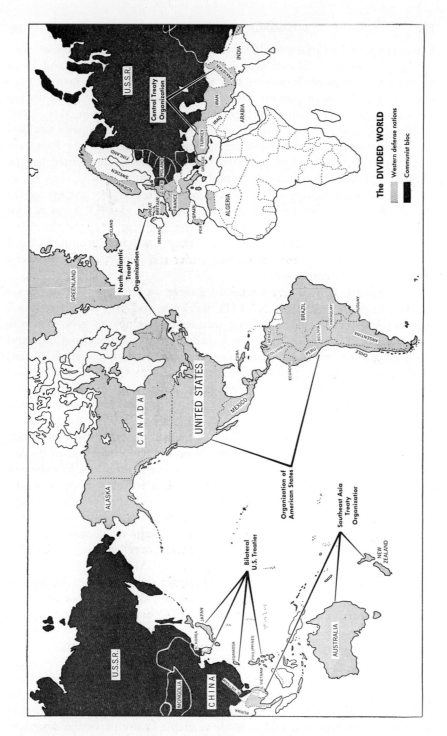

The DIVIDED WORLD

Western defense nations
Communist bloc

North Atlantic Treaty Organization

Central Treaty Organization

Organization of American States

Southeast Asia Treaty Organization

Bilateral U.S. Treaties

U.S.S.R.

GREENLAND

CANADA

UNITED STATES

ALASKA

MEXICO

CUBA

VENEZ.

COLOMBIA

ECUADOR

PERU

BRAZIL

BOLIVIA

PARAGUAY

CHILE

ARGENTINA

URUGUAY

U.S.S.R.

FINLAND

SWEDEN

NORWAY

GREAT BRITAIN

IRELAND

ICELAND

FRANCE

GER.

POLAND

GREECE

TURKEY

IRAQ

IRAN

ARABIA

SPAIN

PORT.

ALGERIA

PAKISTAN

INDIA

MONGOLIA

CHINA

BURMA

THAILAND

VIETNAM

JAPAN

N. KOREA

FORMOSA

PHILIPPINES

AUSTRALIA

NEW ZEALAND

Union suggested a variety of alternatives: a general collective security pact for Europe, general disarmament, or the reunification of East and West Germany. Convinced, however, that the Russians intended no real concessions, the Western powers ratified the Paris Pact, thereby restoring almost complete German sovereignty. As a countermove in May, 1955, the Soviet Union included East Germany and six other European satellites in a twenty-year mutual defense treaty known as the Warsaw Pact.

Although NATO's paper potential was enormously augmented by the admission of West Germany, its actual strength grew slowly, if at all. In 1959 the German contingent in NATO amounted to only 130,000 men—slightly more than one-quarter of the quota fixed in 1954. France continued to commit most of its strength to the Algerian war, and the other countries also contributed far less than they once had promised. Even the American forces tended to shrink under the impact of Eisenhower's "new look" in defense policy.

So long as the United States retained a clear superiority over the Soviet Union in nuclear weapons, NATO's weakness did not cause too much concern. Western Europe's defense seemed to rest not on ground forces with tactical air support, but on the United States Strategic Air Command ready on an instant's notice to employ massive retaliation against Russian cities. The launching of the first Soviet sputnik in October, 1957, however, gave notice that complacency was no longer possible. Many authorities warned of a growing "missiles gap"—a dangerous superiority that the Soviet Union appeared to be achieving both in IRBM's (intermediate range ballistic missiles) and in ICBM's (intercontinental ballistic missiles).

In December, 1957, the NATO heads of state met at Paris to discuss the changing situation. To emphasize his concern, President Eisenhower attended in person despite the fact that he had suffered a slight stroke only three weeks earlier. The Paris meeting resulted in a decision to establish a NATO nuclear missiles force with IRBM sites throughout Western Europe. By the use of short-range nuclear weapons it was hoped to strengthen the capabilities of NATO ground forces, while the IRBM's would add an additional strategic deterrent.

The new policy brought to the fore certain delicate issues arising out of the fact that the United States and Britain had the know-how to manufacture nuclear weapons, but the other NATO countries did not. American law, moreover, forbade the sharing of this knowledge. To meet this problem, the various national contingents were supplied with weapons capable of firing nuclear warheads, but the warheads themselves were stockpiled under the control of the NATO Supreme Commander, an American, without whose consent they could not be used. In effect, this gave to the United States the awesome responsibility of deciding whether or not nuclear weapons would be made available in any particular situation.

This dependence upon America was particularly galling to proud nations like France, and they therefore redoubled their efforts to develop nuclear weapons of their own—efforts that culminated in February, 1960, with the explosion of the first French atomic bomb in the Sahara Desert.

Although IRBM bases in Western Europe might temporarily restore the balance of deterrent power between East and West, the uneasy conviction grew that ICBM's would govern the future. If any American attempt to defend Western Europe might bring the threat of quick destruction to New York and Washington, could the United States be depended upon to oppose Soviet grabs for local objectives? Uncertainty on this point hung like a cloud over Paris, Bonn, and other NATO capitals.

The Continuing German Problem

From the point of view of the Communist nations, the admission of West Germany to NATO, the reemergence of a German army, and the prospect of nuclear missile bases close to the Iron Curtain were unwelcome developments, to be met with a combination of grim threats and offers to negotiate.

From time to time suggestions for "disengagement" were heard from both Eastern and Western sources. It was argued that world tensions would be materially lessened if rival forces in Central Europe could be somehow reduced and separated. Polish Foreign Minister Adam Rapacki made one such proposal in a speech to the UN in October, 1957. The Rapacki plan would have banned the production or stockpiling of nuclear weapons in East and West Germany, Poland, and Czechoslavakia. Attacking the problem from a different angle, George Kennan, a former high official of the American State Department, argued that the German question could best be settled by a pullback of Western and Soviet troops and the establishment of a unified, neutral Germany without modern military forces.

Although disengagement appealed to various sectors of Western opinion, the idea was vigorously opposed by both Secretary Dulles and former Secretary Acheson, his Democratic predecessor. They argued that any reduction of forces in Germany would dangerously weaken Western defenses and imperil the whole NATO alliance. Leaders like Adenauer of Germany and de Gaulle of France denounced the idea for the additional reason that they feared disengagement might hasten the dreaded day when American and British troops withdrew from Europe completely.

Both Eastern and Western leaders professed to sympathize with the Germans' desire to reunite their country. Yet neither side could afford to allow unification to take place on terms that would place all that nation's vast human and industrial resources under the control of its rivals. Adenauer's policy, encouraged by his NATO colleagues, was to insist upon nonrecognition of East Germany and unification only on the basis of a freely elected government for the whole country. This Khrushchev could not permit, so he urged an alternative program for reunion based upon confederation between East and West Germany and German withdrawal from both NATO and the Warsaw Pact—a program that would weaken the whole Western defense system.

Particularly galling to the Communists was the continued presence of British, French, and American troops in West Berlin. Not only did this detract from the prestige of the East German government, but it provided a Western showcase unsettling in its influence on all the Soviet satellites. On November 27, 1958, Khrushchev sent a brusque note to the three Western powers, complaining that they were "ruling the roost in West Berlin, making it a sort of state within a state, and using it as a center from which to pursue subversive activity." Consequently, the Soviet Union had resolved "to abolish the occupation regime in Berlin." As an alternative, Khrushchev proposed making West Berlin "a demilitarized free city." He allowed six months for East-West negotiations; if at the end of this period no agreement had been reached, the Soviet Union would put its plan into effect by a separate peace treaty with East Germany. The alternatives were unpleasant: if the West withdrew its occupation forces, West Berlin's status as a non-Communist enclave deep within Communist East Germany would be highly precarious; on the other hand, if the Western occupation troops remained and the Soviets turned over to the East Germans control of the communication routes between West Berlin and West Germany, a blockade of the city more serious than that of 1948 might be the result.

Khrushchev's ultimatum forced the Western powers to plan their countermoves with care. All were agreed that it would be a fatal mistake to withdraw from West Berlin, leaving the population dependent on the slender safeguards of free-city status. All also recognized the necessity of offering to discuss with the Russians not only the Berlin problem but the whole German situation. Yet there were significant differences of opinion on what form the East-West negotiations should take and what concessions, if any, should be offered. Disillusioned by the Geneva experience, Eisenhower and Dulles were reluctant to agree to another summit conference, but British Prime Minister Macmillan became convinced after a trip to Moscow that this was the most hopeful way out of the crisis. Arguing his case directly with the President, Macmillan gained his point, subject only to the qualification that the way should first be prepared by a four-power foreign ministers' conference. "As soon as developments in the foreign ministers' meeting justify holding a summit conference," read the American note to Moscow, "the United States would be ready to participate. . . ."

Macmillan, facing a general election, advocated a flexible Western position on such points as redefining the status of Berlin, granting *de facto* recognition to East Germany, and limiting armaments in Central Europe. Adenauer, believing that the security of West Germany was at stake, was much opposed to the British program. Adenauer found his strongest supporter in de Gaulle—impressive evidence of the remarkable improvement in Franco-German relations. To bridge these divergent viewpoints and build a solid Western front for the forthcoming East-West negotiations was the enormous task undertaken by Christian Herter, former governor of Massachusetts and Undersecretary of State, when he took over the office of Secretary of State from the desperately ill Dulles on April 22, 1959.

Eisenhower Steps Forward

Dulles's retirement, followed by his death on May 24, 1959, seemed to close a chapter in American diplomatic history. Although no less opposed to communism than his predecessor, Herter was more flexible in his methods and did not dominate the scene as Dulles had done. Essentially a self-effacing man, he became Eisenhower's faithful lieutenant, while the President assumed a much more active leadership than during the first six years of his term.

The Geneva Foreign Ministers' Conference, at which the American, French, and British representatives faced their Russian counterpart during the spring and summer of 1959, failed to bring any solution to either the German question or the disarmament problem. Yet even before its final adjournment events had been transpiring elsewhere that introduced a new type of personal diplomacy into the situation.

Khrushchev had all along been following a strange policy of alternating grim threats to the Americans with invitations to them to widen their social and cultural contacts with his country. American symphony orchestras met an enthusiastic reception in Russia, while Soviet ballet companies were delighting American audiences. A Soviet Exhibition in New York City was matched by an American Exhibition in Moscow. To open the latter, Vice President Nixon made a trip to the Russian capital in July, 1959. As a good-will gesture, the visit got off to a doubtful start when Khrushchev and Nixon became involved in a sharp public debate on the relative merits of capitalism and communism, but the Vice President's subsequent treatment was sufficiently friendly to pave the way for further and more significant steps. Early in August it was announced that Eisenhower had invited Khrushchev to pay an official visit to the

United States, and that the latter had reciprocated with an invitation to the President to go to the Soviet Union.

No sooner had these plans been announced than Eisenhower began a round of presidential globe-trotting unparalleled since Roosevelt's trips of World War II days. Visiting Adenauer in Bonn, Macmillan in London, and de Gaulle in Paris, the President exchanged views with the American allies and reassured them that he intended to make no Munich-like appeasement of the Russians.

Khrushchev's American visit in September, 1959, was a feverish affair in which the energetic Premier put in public appearances in American cities from New York to San Francisco and took quick looks at American supermarkets, cornfields, and steel mills. There were moments of serious tension when Khrushchev's local hosts needled him with unfriendly questions and speeches, to which he responded with sharp displays of temper. But in most places the Premier's reception was polite and his own mood genial. Eisenhower and Khrushchev treated each other with respect, and their face-to-face exchange of views at the President's Maryland retreat, Camp David, resulted in some clearing of the diplomatic air. By asserting that he had not intended to set a time limit on the Berlin negotiations, Khrushchev dissolved the ultimatum that the West had found so objectionable; President Eisenhower for his part conceded that the negotiations must not be prolonged indefinitely. This appeared to open the way for a summit conference on the issue. Speaking to the UN Assembly, Khrushchev made a typical propaganda bid by proposing total disarmament without spelling out the details of inspection and control that would make such a program practical. But the Premier's friendlier mood left hope that he might be prepared to make some concessions on the much more feasible matters of test bans and limited disarmament.

Eisenhower's new personal diplomacy soon took him on still more extensive trips. In December, 1959, he made a good-will tour to eleven countries of Europe, Asia, and the Middle East, and in February, 1960, he visited four South American nations. Everywhere he was greeted by huge and enthusiastic crowds. The President's friendliness and sincerity helped to convince many foreign doubters that he was a man of peace. This was of particular value to the United States in the neutralist countries. Khrushchev countered by making visits of his own to various countries in Asia and Europe, but his success seemed to be less than Eisenhower's —especially in nations like India, where the Soviet leader's fair words seemed to be contradicted by Communist China's unfriendly actions.

Meeting at Paris in December, 1959, the Western Big Four—Eisenhower, Macmillan, de Gaulle, and Adenauer—issued an invitation to Khrushchev to meet with them in the spring. Continued bickering over such issues as

Berlin, disarmament, and nuclear test bans gave little reason to believe that the projected Summit Conference could have any great success; yet optimists continued to hope for the best. All the more shocking, therefore, was the actual course of events in May when the long-awaited meeting at Paris broke up in failure before it ever really began.

On May 1, 1960, the Russians shot down a mysterious American plane over Sverdlovsk in the Urals, some 1,300 miles from the Soviet border. The Eisenhower administration at first made the mistake of denying the truth of Khrushchev's indignant announcement of the incident, but soon had to admit the essential truth of the Russian charge. An American U-2 plane, specially designed for high-flying espionage, had indeed been lost on a secret mission over Soviet territory. Sophisticated foreigners were not much shocked that the United States had been engaged in spying in view of Russia's reputation for maintaining a world-wide network of secret agents, but America's friends did regret that such secret activities had not been curbed on the eve of so important a diplomatic meeting. Even so the world was scarcely prepared for Khrushchev's violent re-action. Confronting President Eisenhower at the first meeting of the heads of state at Paris on May 16, the Russian Premier laid down an insulting ultimatum: either the President apologize for the incident and promise to punish those responsible or Khrushchev would go home. Eisenhower did announce that no more flights against Soviet territory would be made, but he refused to go farther in meeting the Russian demands. Khrushchev made good his threat of walking out on the conference.

Why had the Russian leader followed so drastic a course? Few believed that the plane incident had been more than an excuse. Perhaps the Russian leader was under pressure from other Communist leaders in Russia and China to halt his conciliatory policy; perhaps he himself had decided to wreck the conference rather than admit failure to move the Western leaders from their announced decision to stand firm on the Berlin question. At all events, the collapse of the long-anticipated Summit Conference removed any lingering hope that the Communist and non-Communist leaders could find some easy solution for the world's troubles.

The Road Ahead

In 1776, thirteen united colonies scattered along the Atlantic Coast from New Hampshire to Georgia had bravely asserted their claim to independent nationhood. Now, 183 years later, the United States had enlarged its roster of states to include the Pacific outposts of Alaska and Hawaii. American Armed Forces were stationed in bases around the world; the nation stood committed to defend more than forty different countries.

Atomic-powered submarines, projects for exploring outer space, and ever more ingenious weapons testified to the impressive might of the United States as a superpower.

In this new situation some Americans displayed a cockiness that was far from endearing them to other people. Yet these were the unthinking ones. For responsible citizens, America's place in the sun was one of sobering responsibilities. In the Soviet Union and Communist China the United States had two rivals already terrifyingly strong and getting more so all the time. Could the Communist and the non-Communist worlds continue to coexist, or would they blunder into some terrible nuclear holocaust?

If the rivalry between East and West were to continue, which side was likely to prevail? In part, the answer lay in the realm of material progress, in the ability to develop superior weapons and to excel in scientific research, technology, and industrial capacity. But in the long run, moral resources were likely to be still more important. America's most potent hidden weapon was her way of life based on constitutional government, individual liberty, and freedom from fear and want. If these values could be cherished at home and fostered abroad, American foreign policy might yet achieve its simplest but most difficult goal—a world order based on peace and justice.

SUGGESTIONS FOR FURTHER READING

The publisher's name, place, and date of publication are given only in the first citation of each work.

Bibliographical Guides. Indispensable tools for the serious student are SAMUEL FLAGG BEMIS AND GRACE G. GRIFFIN, *Guide to the Diplomatic History of the United States, 1775–1921* (Washington: U.S. Government Printing Office, 1935), and OSCAR HANDLIN AND OTHERS, EDS., *Harvard Guide to American History* (Cambridge: Belknap Press, Harvard University Press, 1955).

Important Source Collections. Many of the basic documents are to be found in HUNTER MILLER, ED., *Treaties and Other International Acts of the United States of America, 1776–1863* (Washington: U.S. Government Printing Office, 1931–48, 8 vols.), and WILLIAM M. MALLOY AND OTHERS, EDS., *Treaties, Conventions, International Acts, Protocols, and Agreements between the United States and Other Powers, 1776–1937* (Washington: U.S. Government Printing Office, 1910–38, 4 vols.). A convenient selection of materials is in RUHL J. BARTLETT, ED., *The Record of American Diplomacy* (New York: Alfred A. Knopf, Inc., 1947).

General Works. The most extensive account is SAMUEL FLAGG BEMIS, ED., *The American Secretaries of State and Their Diplomacy* (New York: Alfred A. Knopf, Inc., 1927–29, 10 vols.); particularly useful articles will be cited for the appropriate chapter of the text. For the organization of the State Department, see GAILLARD HUNT, *The Department of State of the United States: Its History and Functions* (New Haven, Conn.: Yale University Press, 1914), and GRAHAM H. STUART, *American Diplomatic and Consular Practice* (New York: Appleton-Century-Crofts, Inc., 1936). A provocative interpretation is CHARLES A. BEARD, *The Idea of National Interests: An Analytical Study in American Foreign Policy* (New York: The Macmillan Company, 1934). WILLIAM A. WILLIAMS, ED., *The Shaping of American Diplomacy* (Chicago: Rand McNally & Company, 1956), is a useful collection of readings and documents.

PART ONE. THE DIPLOMACY OF NASCENT NATIONALISM (1776–1815)

Chapter 1. The Struggle for Independence

General. The best account is SAMUEL FLAGG BEMIS, *The Diplomacy of the American Revolution* (New York: Appleton-Century-Crofts, Inc., 1935). See also CLAUDE H. VAN TYNE, *The War of Independence* (Boston: Houghton Mifflin Company, 1929), and JOHN R. ALDEN, *The American Revolution, 1775–1783* (New York: Harper & Brothers, 1954).

Special Phases. On relations with France, see EDWIN S. CORWIN, *French Policy and the American Alliance of 1778* (Princeton, N.J.: Princeton University Press, 1916), and ARTHUR B. DARLING, *Our Rising Empire, 1763–1803* (New Haven, Conn.: Yale University Press, 1940). On Franklin's diplomatic activities, see CARL VAN DOREN, *Benjamin Franklin* (New York: The Viking Press, Inc., 1938), and GERARD STOURZH, *Benjamin Franklin and American Foreign Policy* (Chicago: University of Chicago Press, 1954).

Sources. The standard collection is FRANCIS WHARTON, ED., *Revolutionary Diplomatic Correspondence* (Washington: U.S. Government Printing Office, 1889, 6 vols.). See also JOHN J. MENG, ED., *Despatches and Instructions of Conrad Alexandre Gérard, 1778–1780* (Baltimore: Johns Hopkins Press, 1939).

Chapter 2. Peace and Its Problems

Peace Negotiations. Useful accounts are BEMIS, *Diplomacy of the American Revolution,* CORWIN, *French Policy and the American Alliance of 1778,* and DARLING, *Our Rising Empire, 1763–1803.* On the American commissioners, see VAN DOREN, *Benjamin Franklin,* FRANK MONAGHAN, *John Jay* (Indianapolis: The Bobbs-Merrill Company, Inc., 1935), and GILBERT CHINARD, *Honest John Adams* (Boston: Little, Brown & Company, 1933).

Postwar Problems. Continuing difficulties with England are well described in SAMUEL FLAGG BEMIS, *Jay's Treaty* (New York: The Macmillan Company, 1924), and ALFRED L. BURT, *The United States, Great Britain, and British North America* (New Haven, Conn.: Yale University Press, 1940). For relations with Spain, see ARTHUR P. WHITAKER, *The Spanish-American Frontier, 1783–1795* (Boston: Houghton Mifflin Company, 1927), and SAMUEL FLAGG BEMIS, *Pinckney's Treaty* (Baltimore: Johns Hopkins Press, 1941).

Chapter 3. Politics and Diplomacy of the New Federal Union

Constitutional Development. For the framing of the Constitution, CHARLES WARREN, *The Making of the Constitution* (Boston: Little, Brown & Company, 1937), and MAX FERRAND, *The Framing of the Constitution* (New Haven, Conn.: Yale University Press, 1913), are excellent. On the treaty-making power, see DENNA F. FLEMING, *The Treaty Veto of the American Senate* (New York: G. P. Putnam's Sons, 1930), and R. EARL McLENDON, "The Origin of the Two-thirds Rule in Senate Action upon Treaties," *Amer. Hist.*

Rev., XXXVI (July, 1931), 768–772. For the organization of the State Department, consult HUNT, *Department of State*, and STUART, *American Diplomatic and Consular Practice*.

Diplomacy under Washington. Excellent biographies of key personalities are DOUGLAS S. FREEMAN, *George Washington* (New York: Charles Scribner's Sons, 1948–57, 7 vols.); NATHAN SCHACHNER, *Thomas Jefferson: A Biography* (New York: Appleton-Century-Crofts, Inc., 1951, 2 vols.); and NATHAN SCHACHNER, *Alexander Hamilton* (New York: Appleton-Century-Crofts, Inc., 1946). The controversy over foreign policy is well described in ALEXANDER DE CONDE, *Entangling Alliance: Politics and Diplomacy under George Washington* (Durham, N.C., Duke University Press, 1958). A standard study is CHARLES D. HAZEN, *Contemporary Opinion on the French Revolution* (Baltimore: Johns Hopkins Press, 1897). Genêt's intrigues are discussed in FREDERICK J. TURNER, *The Significance of Sections in American History* (New York: Henry Holt and Company, Inc., 1932). On relations with England, see BEMIS, *Jay's Treaty*, and MONAGHAN, *John Jay*.

Chapter 4. Wrestling with France and Spain

Relations with Spain. The best accounts are WHITAKER, *The Spanish-American Frontier, 1783–1795*, and BEMIS, *Pinckney's Treaty*. See also two articles by ARTHUR P. WHITAKER: "New Light on the Treaty of San Lorenzo," *Mississippi Valley Hist. Rev.*, XV (March, 1929), 435–454, and "Godoy's Knowledge of the Terms of Jay's Treaty," *Amer. Hist. Rev.*, XXXV (July, 1930), 804–810.

Relations with France. Adams's policy is sympathetically treated in CHINARD, *Honest John Adams*, and STEPHEN G. KURTZ, *The Presidency of John Adams* (Philadelphia: University of Pennsylvania Press, 1957). Volume 2 of ALBERT J. BEVERIDGE, *The Life of John Marshall* (Boston: Houghton Mifflin Company, 1916–19, 4 vols.), discusses the XYZ Affair. See also GARDNER W. ALLEN, *Our Naval War with France* (Boston: Houghton Mifflin Company, 1909). Scholarly studies of particular episodes are: SAMUEL FLAGG BEMIS, "Washington's Farewell Address: A Foreign Policy of Independence," *Amer. Hist. Rev.*, XXXIX (January, 1934), 250–268, and E. WILSON LYON, "The Franco-American Convention of 1800," *J. Modern Hist.*, XII (September, 1940), 305–333.

Chapter 5. Jefferson Flies the Flag

General. The best account is now IRVING BRANT, *James Madison, Secretary of State, 1800–1809* (Indianapolis: The Bobbs-Merrill Company, Inc., 1953). This modifies many of the judgments in the older but still highly useful HENRY ADAMS, *History of the United States during the Administrations of Jefferson and Madison* (New York: Charles Scribner's Sons, 1889–91, 9 vols.).

Relations with Barbary States. Useful studies are RAY W. IRWIN, *The Diplomatic Relations of the United States with the Barbary Powers, 1776–1816* (Chapel Hill, N.C.: University of North Carolina Press, 1931), and LOUIS B. WRIGHT AND JULIA H. McLEOD, *The First Americans in North Africa: William Eaton's Struggle for a Vigorous Policy against the Barbary Pirates, 1799–1805*

(Princeton, N.J.: Princeton University Press, 1945). See also CHARLES O. PAULLIN, *Diplomatic Negotiations of American Naval Officers, 1778–1883* (Baltimore: Johns Hopkins Press, 1912).

Louisiana. The best account is ARTHUR P. WHITAKER, *The Mississippi Question, 1795–1803* (New York: Appleton-Century-Crofts, Inc., 1934). For inter-relations with European diplomacy, see E. WILSON LYON, *Louisiana in French Diplomacy, 1759–1804* (Norman, Okla.: University of Oklahoma Press, 1934), and DARLING, *Our Rising Empire.* A basic source is the MARQUIS DE BARBÉ-MARBOIS, *The History of Louisiana* (Philadelphia: Carey & Lea, 1830). On the impact of events in Santo Domingo, see CHARLES C. TANSILL, *The United States and Santo Domingo, 1798–1873* (Baltimore: Johns Hopkins Press, 1938), and RAYFORD W. LOGAN, *The Diplomatic Relations of the United States with Haiti, 1776–1891* (Chapel Hill, N.C.: University of North Carolina Press, 1941).

Chapter 6. Dilemma of a Neutral

General. ADAMS, *History of the United States,* and BRANT, *James Madison, Secretary of State,* should be supplemented with IRVING BRANT, *James Madison: The President, 1809–1812* (Indianapolis: The Bobbs-Merrill Company, Inc., 1956); ALFRED T. MAHAN, *Sea Power in Its Relations to the War of 1812* (Boston: Little, Brown & Company, 1905, 2 vols.); and BURT, *The United States, Great Britain and British North America.*

Special Issues. On neutral trade, see CARLTON SAVAGE, *Policy of the United States toward Maritime Commerce in War* (Washington: U.S. Government Printing Office, 1934–36, 2 vols.). Important studies are JAMES F. ZIMMERMAN, *Impressment of American Seamen* (New York: Columbia University Press, 1925), and LOUIS M. SEARS, *Jefferson and the Embargo* (Durham, N.C.: Duke University Press, 1927). The influence of the war hawks is analyzed in JULIUS W. PRATT, *Expansionists of 1812* (New York: The Macmillan Company, 1925), which may be supplemented by BERNARD MAYO, *Henry Clay: Spokesman of the New West* (Boston: Houghton Mifflin Company, 1937), and CHARLES M. WILTSIE, *John C. Calhoun: Nationalist, 1782–1828* (Indianapolis: The Bobbs-Merrill Company, Inc., 1944). For other aspects, see LOUIS M. HACKER, "Western Land Hunger and the War of 1812: A Conjecture," *Mississippi Valley Hist. Rev.,* X (March, 1924), 365–395; GEORGE R. TAYLOR, "Agrarian Discontent in the Mississippi Valley Preceding the War of 1812," *J. of Political Economy,* XXXIX (August, 1931), 471–505; and WARREN H. GOODMAN, "The Origins of the War of 1812: A Survey of Changing Interpretations," *Mississippi Valley Hist. Rev.,* XXVIII (September, 1941), 171–186.

Chapter 7. Peace Again

Negotiations at Ghent. Highly useful are ADAMS, *History of the United States;* BURT, *The United States, Great Britain and British North America;* and MAHAN, *Sea Power in Its Relation to the War of 1812.* SAMUEL FLAGG BEMIS, *John Quincy Adams and the Foundations of American Foreign Policy* (New York: Alfred A. Knopf, Inc., 1949), is an outstanding study. For the other

American commissioners, see RAYMOND WALTER, *Albert Gallatin: Jeffersonian Financier and Diplomat* (New York: The Macmillan Company, 1957), and GLYNDON G. VAN DEUSEN, *The Life of Henry Clay* (Boston: Little, Brown & Company, 1937).

Convention of 1818. The older JAMES M. CALLAHAN, *The Neutrality of the American Lakes and Anglo-American Relations* (Baltimore: Johns Hopkins Press, 1898), should be supplemented with J. H. POWELL, *Richard Rush: Republican Diplomat, 1780–1859* (Philadelphia: University of Pennsylvania Press, 1942), and C. P. STACEY, "The Myth of the Unguarded Frontier, 1815–1871," *Amer. Hist. Rev.*, LVI (October, 1950), 1–18.

PART TWO. CONTINENTAL EXPANSION (1815–1890)

Chapter 8. The Florida Question

Earlier Phases. The most detailed account is ISAAC J. COX, *The West Florida Controversy, 1798–1813* (Baltimore: Johns Hopkins Press, 1918). See also ADAMS, *History of the United States;* BRANT, *James Madison: Secretary of State;* and BRANT, *James Madison: President.* CHARLES C. GRIFFIN, *The United States and the Disruption of the Spanish Empire* (New York: Columbia University Press, 1937), throws light on certain aspects.

Adams-Onís Treaty. The best account is PHILIP C. BROOKS, *Diplomacy and the Borderlands: The Adams-Onís Treaty of 1819* (Berkeley, Calif.: University of California Press, 1939). See also SAMUEL FLAGG BEMIS, *The Latin American Policy of the United States: An Historical Interpretation* (New York: Harcourt, Brace and Company, Inc., 1943); BEMIS, *John Quincy Adams and the Foundations of American Foreign Policy;* and DEXTER PERKINS, "John Quincy Adams," in BEMIS, ED., *American Secretaries of State,* vol. IV, pp. 3–111.

Chapter 9. The Monroe Doctrine

General. DEXTER PERKINS, *Hands Off: A History of the Monroe Doctrine* (Boston: Little, Brown & Company, 1941), is highly readable. Much more detailed for this period is the same author's *The Monroe Doctrine, 1823–1826* (Cambridge, Mass.: Harvard University Press, 1927). BEMIS, *John Quincy Adams and the Foundations of American Foreign Policy,* is excellent. For the general setting, see GEORGE DANGERFIELD, *The Era of Good Feelings* (New York: Harcourt, Brace and Company, Inc., 1952).

Special Phases. An authoritative study is ARTHUR P. WHITAKER, *The United States and the Independence of Latin America, 1800–1830* (Baltimore: Johns Hopkins Press, 1941). On the European situation, see EDWARD H. TATUM, *The United States and Europe, 1815–1830* (Berkeley, Calif.: University of California Press, 1936); HAROLD W. V. TEMPERLEY, *The Foreign Policy of Canning, 1822–1827* (London: G. Bell & Sons, Ltd., 1925); and J. FRED RIPPY, *Rivalry of the United States and Great Britain over Latin America, 1808–1830* (Baltimore: Johns Hopkins Press, 1929). On the Russian aspect, consult BENJAMIN P. THOMAS, *Russo-American Relations, 1815–1867* (Baltimore: Johns Hopkins

Press, 1930). GALE W. McGEE, "The Monroe Doctrine: A Stopgap Measure," *Mississippi Valley Hist. Rev.*, XXXVIII (1951), 233–250, provides a fresh point of view.

Chapter 10. Repairing Relations with France and England

Jacksonian Diplomacy. The most scholarly biography of Jackson is JOHN S. BASSETT, *The Life of Andrew Jackson* (New York: The Macmillan Company, 1916, 2 vols.). More lively is MARQUIS JAMES, *Andrew Jackson: Portrait of a President* (Indianapolis: The Bobbs-Merrill Company, Inc., 1937). F. LEE BENNS, *The American Struggle for the British West India Carrying-Trade, 1815–1830* (Bloomington, Ind.: Indiana University Press, 1923), and VERNON G. SETSER, *The Commercial Reciprocity Policy of the United States* (Philadelphia: University of Pennsylvania Press, 1937), are good special studies. For the spoliation claims, see RICHARD A. McELMORE, *Franco-American Diplomatic Relations, 1816–1836* (Baton Rouge, La.: Louisiana State University Press, 1941).

Troubles with Canada. The best account is ALBERT B. COREY, *The Crisis of 1830–1842 in Canadian-American Relations* (New Haven, Conn.: Yale University Press, 1941). See also JAMES M. CALLAHAN, *American Foreign Policy in Canadian Relations* (New York: The Macmillan Company, 1929), and JOHN B. BREBNER, *North Atlantic Triangle* (New Haven, Conn.: Yale University Press, 1945). Important special studies are ORRIN E. TIFFANY, "The Relations of the United States to the Canadian Rebellion of 1837–1838," *Buffalo Hist. Soc. Pubs.*, VIII (1905), 1–147, and ALASTAIR WATT, "The Case of Alexander McLeod," *Canadian Hist. Rev.*, XII (June, 1931), 145–167. On the Webster-Ashburton Treaty, see CLAUDE M. FUESS, *Daniel Webster* (Boston: Little, Brown & Company, 1930, 2 vols.), THOMAS LE DUC, "The Maine Frontier and the Northeastern Boundary Controversy," *Amer. Hist. Rev.*, LIII (October, 1947), 30–46, and RICHARD N. CURRENT, "Webster's Propaganda and the Ashburton Treaty," *Mississippi Valley Hist. Rev.*, XXXIV (1947), 187–200.

Chapter 11. Frontier Pressure

Texas. The most useful account is JUSTIN H. SMITH, *The Annexation of Texas* (New York: Barnes & Noble, Inc., 1941), but see also GEORGE L. RIVES, *The United States and Mexico, 1821–1848* (New York: Charles Scribner's Sons, 1913, 2 vols.); JAMES M. CALLAHAN, *American Foreign Policy in Mexican Relations* (New York: The Macmillan Company, 1932); JESSE S. REEVES, *American Diplomacy under Tyler and Polk* (Baltimore: Johns Hopkins Press, 1907); and THOMAS M. MARSHALL, *A History of the Western Boundary of the Louisiana Purchase, 1819–1841* (Berkeley, Calif.: University of California Press, 1914). Relations between the Texans and Mexico are discussed in EUGENE C. BARKER, *Mexico and Texas, 1821–1835* (Dallas: P. L. Turner Co., 1928); WILLIAM C. BINKLEY, *The Texas Revolution* (Baton Rouge, La.: Louisiana State University Press, 1952); and JOSEPH M. SCHMITZ, *Texan Statecraft, 1836–1845* (San Antonio: Naylor Co., 1941). For Tyler's policy, see OLIVER P. CHITWOOD, *John Tyler: Champion of the Old South* (New York: Appleton-Century-Crofts, Inc., 1939), and CHARLES M. WILTSIE, *John C. Calhoun: Sectionalist, 1840–1850* (Indianap-

olis: The Bobbs-Merrill Company, Inc., 1951). English policy is analyzed in
Ephraim D. Adams, *British Interests and Activities in Texas, 1838–1846* (Baltimore: Johns Hopkins Press, 1910).

Oregon. A good general account is Melvin C. Jacobs, *Winning Oregon: A
Study of an Expansionist Movement* (Caldwell, Idaho: Caxton Printers, Ltd.,
1938). For special phases, see Frederick Merk, *Albert Gallatin and the Oregon
Problem* (Cambridge, Mass.: Harvard University Press, 1950), and Joseph
Schafer, "The British Attitude toward the Oregon Question, 1815–1846,"
Amer. Hist. Rev., XVI (January, 1911), 273–299.

Chapter 12. Manifest Destiny

General. On the rise of expansionism, consult Albert K. Weinberg, *Manifest
Destiny: A Study of National Expansionism in American History* (Baltimore:
Johns Hopkins Press, 1935), and Julius W. Pratt, "The Origin of 'Manifest
Destiny,'" *Amer. Hist. Rev.*, XXXII (July, 1927), 795–798. On Polk's diplom-
acy, see Eugene I. McCormac, *James K. Polk: A Political Biography* (Berkeley,
Calif.: University of California Press, 1922), and St. George L. Sioussat,
"James Buchanan," in Bemis, ed., *American Secretaries of State*, vol. V, pp.
265–280. For the influence of Eastern merchants, an excellent study is Norman
A. Graebner, *Empire on the Pacific: A Study in American Continental Expan-
sion* (New York: The Ronald Press Company, 1955).

Oregon. Besides the works recommended for chap. 11, see the important articles by Frederick Merk: "The Oregon Pioneers and the Boundary," *Amer.
Hist. Rev.*, XXIX (July, 1924), 681–699; "British Party Politics and the Oregon
Treaty," *Amer. Hist. Rev.*, XXXVII (July, 1932), 653–677; "British Government Propaganda and the Oregon Treaty," *Amer. Hist. Rev.*, XL (October,
1934), 38–62; and "The British Corn Crisis of 1845–46 and the Oregon Treaty,"
Agricultural Hist., VIII (July, 1934), 95–123.

Mexican War. The outstanding study is Justin H. Smith, *The War with
Mexico* (New York: The Macmillan Company, 1919, 2 vols.). For the Treaty
of Guadalupe-Hidalgo, see Miller, ed., *Treaties and Other International Acts
of the United States*, vol. V, pp. 236–428; John D. P. Fuller, *The Movement
for the Annexation of All Mexico, 1846–1848* (Baltimore: Johns Hopkins Press,
1936); and Louis M. Sears, "Nicholas P. Trist: A Diplomat with Ideals," *Mississippi Valley Hist. Rev.*, XI (June, 1924), 85–98.

Chapter 13. Looking for New Worlds to Conquer

General. On Whig diplomacy, see Fuess, *Daniel Webster*, and Robert J.
Rayback, *Millard Fillmore: Biography of a President* (Buffalo: Henry Stewart,
1959). Merle E. Curti, "Young America," *Amer. Hist. Rev.*, XXXII (October,
1926), 34–55, throws light on the jingoism of the period.

Far East. An excellent study is Tyler Dennett, *Americans in Eastern Asia:
A Critical Study of the Policy of the United States with Reference to China,
Japan and Korea in the Nineteenth Century* (New York: The Macmillan Com-
pany, 1922). On China, see Kenneth S. Latourette, *The History of the Early
Relations between the United States and China, 1784–1844* (New Haven, Conn.:

Yale University Press, 1917); Foster Rhea Dulles, *China and America: The Story of Their Relations since 1784* (Princeton, N.J.: Princeton University Press, 1946); and Earl Swisher, *China's Management of the American Barbarians: A Study of Sino-American Relations, 1841–1861* (New Haven, Conn.: Yale University Press, 1953). On Japan, the standard authority is Payson J. Treat, *Diplomatic Relations between the United States and Japan, 1853–1905* (Stanford, Calif.: Stanford University Press, 1932–38, 3 vols.). See also Arthur Walworth, *Black Ships off Japan: The Story of Commodore Perry's Expedition* (New York: Alfred A. Knopf, Inc., 1947); Carl Crow, *He Opened the Door of Japan: Townshend Harris and the Story of His Amazing Adventures in Establishing American Relations with the Far East* (New York: Harper & Brothers, 1939); and Chitoshi Yanaga, *Japan since Perry* (New York: McGraw-Hill Book Company, Inc., 1949).

Central America. Outstanding studies are Dexter Perkins, *The Monroe Doctrine, 1826–1867* (Baltimore: Johns Hopkins Press, 1933), and Mary W. Williams, *Anglo-American Isthmian Diplomacy, 1815–1915* (Washington: American Historical Association, 1916). On William Walker, see William O. Scroggs, *Filibusters and Financiers: The Story of Walker and His Associates* (New York: The Macmillan Company, 1916).

Chapter 14. Diplomacy and the Slavery Issue

General. On Democratic expansionist policies during the 1850s, consult Roy F. Nichols, *Franklin Pierce: Young Hickory of the Granite Hills* (Philadelphia: University of Pennsylvania Press, 1931), and H. B. Learned, "William L. Marcy," in Bemis, ed., *American Secretaries of State*, vol. VI pp. 145–294.

Cuba. A good coverage is provided by Basil Rauch, *American Interest in Cuba, 1848–1855* (New York: Columbia University Press, 1948). On special phases, see Robert G. Caldwell, *The Lopez Expeditions to Cuba, 1848–1851* (Princeton, N.J.: Princeton University Press, 1915), and Amos A. Ettinger, *The Mission to Spain of Pierre Soulé, 1853–1855* (New Haven, Conn.: Yale University Press, 1932).

Other Issues. Relations with Mexico are discussed in Paul N. Garber, *The Gadsden Treaty* (Philadelphia: University of Pennsylvania Press, 1923). On reciprocity with Canada, see Lester B. Shippee, *Canadian-American Relations, 1849–1874* (New Haven, Conn.: Yale University Press, 1939), and Charles C. Tansill, *The Canadian Reciprocity Treaty of 1854* (Baltimore: Johns Hopkins Press, 1922). Maritime difficulties with England are discussed in Hugh G. Soulsby, *The Right of Search and the Slave Trade in Anglo-American Relations, 1814–1862* (Baltimore: Johns Hopkins Press, 1933).

Chapter 15. Civil War Diplomacy

General. Among many biographies of Lincoln, the most scholarly is James G. Randall, *Lincoln the President* (New York: Dodd, Mead & Company, Inc., 1945–55, 4 vols.), but see also Jay Monaghan, *Diplomat in Carpet Slippers: Abraham Lincoln Deals with Foreign Affairs* (Indianapolis: The Bobbs-Merrill Company, Inc., 1945). Frederick Bancroft, *The Life of William Seward* (New

York: Harper & Brothers, 1900, 2 vols.), should be supplemented with HENRY W. TEMPLE, "William H. Seward," in BEMIS, ED., *American Secretaries of State*, vol. VII, pp. 3–115.

Special Studies. FRANK L. OWSLEY, *King Cotton Diplomacy: Foreign Relations of the Confederate States* (Chicago: University of Chicago Press, 1931), is excellent. Equally outstanding is EPHRAIM D. ADAMS, *Great Britain and the American Civil War* (New York: Longmans, Green & Co., Inc., 1925, 2 vols.). For European public opinion, the best authorities are DONALDSON JORDAN AND EDWIN J. PRATT, *Europe and the American Civil War* (Boston: Houghton Mifflin Company, 1931), and LYNN M. CASE, ED., *French Opinion on the United States and Mexico, 1860–1867* (New York: Appleton-Century-Crofts, Inc., 1936). Useful articles are JAMES P. BAXTER III, "The British Government and Neutral Rights, 1861–1865," *Amer. Hist. Rev.*, XXXIV (October, 1928), 9–29; FRANK A. GOLDER, "The Russian Fleet and the American Civil War," *Amer. Hist. Rev.*, XX (July, 1915), 801–812; and THOMAS A. BAILEY, "The Russian Fleet Myth Reexamined," *Mississippi Valley Hist. Rev.*, XXXVIII (June, 1951), 81–90.

Chapter 16. Post–Civil War Expansionists

General. Among earlier works cited, the following are useful: WEINBERG, *Manifest Destiny;* BANCROFT, *Seward;* and TEMPLE, "William H. Seward," in BEMIS, ED., *American Secretaries of State*, vol. VII. An outstanding work of scholarship is ALLAN NEVINS, *Hamilton Fish: The Inner History of the Grant Administration* (New York: Dodd, Mead & Company, Inc., 1936). See also JOSEPH V. FULLER, "Hamilton Fish," in BEMIS, ED., *American Secretaries of State*, vol. VII, pp. 125–214.

Alaska. The most comprehensive study is VICTOR J. FARRAR, *The Annexation of Russian America to the United States* (Washington: W. F. Roberts Co., 1937), but also see FRANK A. GOLDER, "The Purchase of Alaska," *Amer. Hist. Rev.*, XXV (April, 1920), and THOMAS A. BAILEY, *America Faces Russia: Russian-American Relations from Early Times to Our Day* (Ithaca, N.Y.: Cornell University Press, 1950).

Other Regions. On Caribbean diplomacy, see CHARLES C. TANSILL, *The Purchase of the Danish West Indies* (Baltimore: Johns Hopkins Press, 1932), and CHARLES C. TANSILL, *The United States and Santo Domingo, 1798–1873* (Baltimore: Johns Hopkins Press, 1938). On the Pacific, see SYLVIA MASTERMAN, *The Origins of International Rivalry in Samoa, 1845–1884* (Stanford, Calif.: Stanford University Press, 1934), and GEORGE H. RYDEN, *The Foreign Policy of the United States in Relation to Samoa* (New Haven, Conn.: Yale University Press, 1933).

Chapter 17. War Scares and Peaceful Settlements

Maximilian Affair. The best discussion is PERKINS, *The Monroe Doctrine, 1826–1867.* See also J. FRED RIPPY, *The United States and Mexico* (New York: Alfred A. Knopf, Inc., 1931); EGON C. CORTI, *Maximilian and Charlotte of Mexico* (New York: Alfred A. Knopf, Inc., 1928, 2 vols.); and BANCROFT, *Seward.*

Relations with Great Britain. SHIPPEE, *Canadian-American Relations, 1849–1874*, is excellent. On the *Alabama* claims, see J. C. BANCROFT, *Mr. Fish and the Alabama Claims* (Boston: Houghton Mifflin Company, 1893), and NEVINS, *Hamilton Fish.* For the settlement, consult GOLDWIN SMITH, *The Treaty of Washington, 1871: A Study in Imperial History* (Ithaca, N.Y.: Cornell University Press, 1941), and FRANK W. HACKETT, *Reminiscences of the Geneva Tribunal of Arbitration* (Boston: Houghton Mifflin Company, 1911).

Cuba. Useful material is in FRANK E. CHADWICK, *The Relations of the United States and Spain: Diplomacy* (New York: Charles Scribner's Sons, 1909), and LELAND H. JENKS, *Our Cuban Colony: A Study in Sugar* (New York: Vanguard Press, Inc., 1928).

Chapter 18. Diplomacy in Low Gear

General. Diplomacy during the Hayes administration is discussed in CHESTER L. BARROWS, *William M. Evarts: Lawyer, Diplomat, Statesman* (Chapel Hill, N.C.: University of North Carolina Press, 1941). For Blaine's influence, consult ALICE F. TYLER, *The Foreign Policy of James G. Blaine* (Minneapolis: University of Minnesota Press, 1927); JOSEPH B. LOCKEY, "James Gillespie Blaine," in BEMIS, ED., *American Secretaries of State*, vol. VII, pp. 263–297, and vol. VIII, pp. 109–184; A. T. VOLWILER, "Harrison, Blaine, and American Foreign Policy, 1889–1893," *Proc. Am. Phil. Soc.*, LXXXIX (1938), 637–648. On Cleveland's policies, see CHARLES C. TANSILL, *The Foreign Policy of Thomas F. Bayard, 1885–1897* (New York: Fordham University Press, 1940), and GEORGE R. DULEBOHN, *Principles of Foreign Policy under the Cleveland Administration* (Philadelphia: [n.p.], 1941).

Latin America. The best general discussion is BEMIS, *Latin American Policy of the United States.* Outstanding for this period is A. CURTIS WILGUS, "James G. Blaine and the Pan-American Movement," *Hispanic Amer. Hist. Rev.*, V (November, 1922), 622–708. On the controversies with Chile, see HENRY C. EVANS, *Chile and Its Relations with the United States* (Durham, N.C.: Duke University Press, 1927); HERBERT MILLINGTON, *American Diplomacy and the War of the Pacific* (New York: Columbia University Press, 1948); and OSGOOD HARDY, "The *Itata* Incident," *Hispanic Amer. Hist. Rev.*, V (1922), 195–226.

Other Issues. On relations with Great Britain, see CHARLES C. TANSILL, *Canadian-American Relations, 1875–1911* (New Haven, Conn.: Yale University Press, 1943), and CHARLES S. CAMPBELL, JR., "The Dismissal of Lord Sackville," *Mississippi Valley Hist. Rev.*, XLIV (March, 1958), 635–648. On relations with Italy, consult J. A. KARLIN, "The Italo-American Incident of 1891 and the Road to Reunion," *J. Southern Hist.*, VIII (1942), 242–246. On relations with China, see MARY R. COOLIDGE, *Chinese Immigration* (New York: Henry Holt and Company, Inc., 1909).

PART THREE. THE AGE OF IMPERIALISM (1890–1917)

Chapter 19. The New Imperialism

General. FOSTER RHEA DULLES, *The Imperial Years* (New York: Thomas Y. Crowell Company, 1956), is a good summary. On the intellectual background, consult JULIUS W. PRATT, *Expansionists of 1898* (Baltimore: John Hopkins Press, 1936), and WILLIAM D. PULESTON, *Mahan* (New Haven, Conn.: Yale University Press, 1939). On the new Navy, see HAROLD AND MARGARET SPROUT, *The Rise of American Naval Power, 1776–1918* (Princeton, N.J.: Princeton University Press, 1939), and GEORGE T. DAVIS, *A Navy Second to None* (New York: Harcourt, Brace and Company, Inc., 1940). For Cleveland's relation to imperialism, see ALLAN NEVINS, *Grover Cleveland, A Study in Courage* (New York: Dodd, Mead & Company, Inc., 1933); MATHILDA GRESHAM, *Life of Walter Quintin Gresham, 1832–1895* (Chicago: Rand McNally & Company, 1919, 2 vols.); and HENRY JAMES, *Richard Olney and His Public Service* (Boston: Houghton Mifflin Company, 1923).

Samoa and Hawaii. A good general account is FOSTER RHEA DULLES, *America in the Pacific* (Boston: Houghton Mifflin Company, 1932). On Samoa, see RYDEN, *Foreign Policy of the United States in Relation to Samoa*, and TANSILL, *Foreign Policy of Thomas F. Bayard.* On Hawaii, consult SYLVESTER K. STEVENS, *American Expansion in Hawaii, 1842–1898* (Harrisburg, Pa.: Archives Publishing Co., 1945); PRATT, *Expansionists of 1898;* and RICHARD D. WEIGLE, "Sugar and the Hawaiian Revolution," *Pacific Hist. Rev.*, XIV (February, 1947), 41–58.

Venezuela. DEXTER PERKINS, *The Monroe Doctrine, 1867–1907* (Baltimore: Johns Hopkins Press, 1937), has a good discussion. For special phases, see NELSON M. BLAKE, "Background of Cleveland's Venezuelan Policy," *Amer. Hist. Rev.*, XLVII (January, 1942), 259–277; and GEORGE B. YOUNG, "Intervention under the Monroe Doctrine: The Olney Corollary," *Pol. Sci. Quart.*, LVII (June, 1942), 247–280.

Chapter 20. The United States Emerges as a World Power

General. FOSTER RHEA DULLES, *America's Rise to World Power, 1898–1954* (New York: Harper & Brothers, 1955), is a readable survey. JULIUS W. PRATT, *America's Colonial Experiment* (Englewood Cliffs, N.J.: Prentice-Hall, Inc., 1950), is excellent. CHARLES S. OLCOTT, *The Life of William McKinley* (Boston: Houghton Mifflin Company, 1916, 2 vols.), is very sympathetic to its subject.

Spanish-American War. CHADWICK, *Relations of the United States and Spain*, is very detailed. A brief account is in WILFRID CALCOTT, *The Caribbean Policy of the United States, 1890–1920* (Baltimore: Johns Hopkins Press, 1942). The Spanish side is well told in ORESTES FERRARA, *The Last Spanish War* (New York: Paisley Press, 1937). For Cuban propaganda activities, see GEORGE W. AUXIER, "The Propaganda Activities of the Cuban *Junta* in Precipitating the Spanish-American War, 1895–1898," *Hispanic Amer. Hist. Rev.*, XIX (August, 1939), 286–305. On the jingo press, consult JOSEPH E. WISAN, *The Cuban Crisis as Reflected in the New York Press, 1895–1898* (New York: Columbia University Press, 1934), and WALTER MILLIS, *The Martial Spirit: A Study of Our War with Spain* (Boston: Houghton Mifflin Company, 1931). Important special studies are FRED H. HARRINGTON, "The Anti-Imperialist Movement in the United States, 1898–1900," *Mississippi Valley Hist. Rev.*, XXII (September, 1935), 211–230; THOMAS A. BAILEY, "Was the Presidential Election of 1900 a Mandate on Imperialism," *Mississippi Valley Hist. Rev.*, XXIV (June, 1937), 43–52; THOMAS A. BAILEY, "Dewey and the Germans at Manila Bay," *Amer.*

Hist. Rev., XLV (October, 1939), 59–81; and Lester B. Shippee, "Germany and the Spanish-American War," *Amer. Hist. Rev.*, XXX (July, 1925), 754–777.

Chapter 21. John Hay and the Open Door

General. Robert E. Osgood, *Ideals and Self-Interest in America's Foreign Relations* (Chicago: University of Chicago Press, 1953), and George F. Kennan, *American Diplomacy, 1900–1950* (Chicago: University of Chicago Press, 1951), provide challenging interpretations of twentieth-century American foreign relations. Tyler Dennett, *John Hay: From Poetry to Politics* (New York: Dodd, Mead & Company, Inc., 1933), is an excellent biography. See also Alfred L. P. Dennis, "John Hay," in Bemis, ed., *American Secretaries of State*, vol. IX, pp. 115–189. Alfred L. P. Dennis, *Adventures in American Diplomacy, 1896–1906* (New York: E. P. Dutton & Co., Inc., 1928), contains useful material.

Relations with England. Lionel M. Gelber, *The Rise of Anglo-American Friendship* (New York: Oxford University Press, 1938); Charles S. Campbell, Jr., *Anglo-American Understanding, 1898–1903* (Baltimore: Johns Hopkins Press, 1957); and Nelson M. Blake, "England and the United States, 1897–1898," in D. E. Lee and G. E. McReynolds, eds., *Essays in History and International Relations in Honor of George Hubbard Blakeslee* (Worcester, Mass.: Clark University Press, 1949), pp. 257–283, all deal with the growing friendship between England and the United States. See also Robert B. Mowat, *The Life of Lord Pauncefote: First Ambassador to the United States* (Boston: Houghton Mifflin Company, 1929).

The Open Door Policy. The best study is A. Whitney Griswold, *The Far Eastern Policy of the United States* (New York: Harcourt, Brace and Company, Inc., 1938). See also Westel W. Willoughby, *Foreign Rights and Interests in China* (Baltimore: Johns Hopkins Press, 1927, 2 vols.); Charles S. Campbell, Jr., *Special Business Interests and the Open Door Policy* (New Haven, Conn.: Yale University Press, 1951); and Edward H. Zabriskie, *American-Russian Rivalry in the Far East* (Philadelphia: University of Pennsylvania Press, 1946).

Chapter 22. Roosevelt Gets His Canal

General. The best study of American diplomacy for these years is Howard K. Beale, *Theodore Roosevelt and the Rise of America to World Power* (Baltimore: Johns Hopkins Press, 1956). See also *Theodore Roosevelt: An Autobiography* (New York: Charles Scribner's Sons, 1916); Henry F. Pringle, *Theodore Roosevelt: A Biography* (New York: Harcourt, Brace and Company, Inc., 1931); Dennett, *John Hay;* and Philip C. Jessup, *Elihu Root* (New York: Dodd, Mead & Company, Inc., 1938).

Canal Diplomacy. The best accounts are Dwight C. Miner, *The Fight for the Panama Route* (New York: Columbia University Press, 1940), and Gerstle Mack, *The Land Divided* (New York: Alfred A. Knopf, Inc., 1944). For an important personal narrative, see Philippe Bunau-Varilla, *Panama: The Creation, Destruction, and Resurrection* (New York: McBride, Nast & Co., 1914). John Patterson, "Latin-American Reactions to the Panama Revolution of 1903,"

Hispanic Amer. Hist. Rev., XXIV (May, 1944), throws new light on the subject.

Caribbean Policy. Excellent for this period is HOWARD C. HILL, *Roosevelt and the Caribbean* (Chicago: University of Chicago Press, 1927). See also DEXTER PERKINS, *The United States and the Caribbean* (Cambridge, Mass.: Harvard University Press, 1947); J. FRED RIPPY, *The Caribbean Danger Zone* (New York: G. P. Putnam's Sons, 1940); and CALCOTT, *The Caribbean Policy of the United States.* On the Venezuelan debt controversy, see PERKINS, *The Monroe Doctrine, 1867–1907*, and SEWARD W. LIVERMORE, "Theodore Roosevelt, the American Navy, and the Venezuelan Crisis of 1902–1903," *Amer. Hist. Rev.*, LI (April, 1946), 452–471.

Chapter 23. Roosevelt and World Politics

General. The best account is BEALE, *Theodore Roosevelt and the Rise of America to World Power*, but see also DENNETT, *John Hay;* JESSUP, *Elihu Root;* and DENNIS, *Adventures in American Diplomacy.* NELSON M. BLAKE, "Ambassadors at the Court of Theodore Roosevelt," *Mississippi Valley Hist. Rev.*, XLII (September, 1955), 179–206, discusses personal factors in the diplomacy of the period.

Far East. GRISWOLD, *Far Eastern Policy of the United States*, is excellent. See also TYLER DENNETT, *Roosevelt and the Russo-Japanese War* (New York: Doubleday & Company, Inc., 1925); TREAT, *Diplomatic Relations between the United States and Japan, 1853–1905*, vol. III; THOMAS A. BAILEY, *Theodore Roosevelt and the Japanese-American Crisis* (Stanford, Calif.: Stanford University Press, 1934); and THOMAS A. BAILEY, "The Root-Takahira Agreement of 1908," *Pacific Hist. Rev.*, IX (March, 1940), 19–35. On Roosevelt's China policy, see JESSIE A. MILLER, "The United States and Chinese Territorial Integrity, 1908," in LEE AND McREYNOLDS, EDS., *Essays in History and International Relations in Honor of George Hubbard Blakeslee.* On Korea, consult FRED H. HARRINGTON, *God, Mammon, and the Japanese: Dr. Horace N. Allen and Korean-American Relations, 1884–1905* (Madison, Wis.: University of Wisconsin Press, 1944).

Moroccan Crisis. EUGENE N. ANDERSON, *The First Moroccan Crisis, 1904–1905* (Chicago: University of Chicago Press, 1930), is good on European aspects. For Roosevelt's part, see BEALE, *Theodore Roosevelt and the Rise of America to World Power*, and ALLAN NEVINS, *Henry White: Thirty Years of American Diplomacy* (New York: Harper & Brothers, 1930).

Chapter 24. Dollar Diplomacy

General. A good account of the Taft-Knox policies is in HENRY F. PRINGLE, *The Life and Times of William Howard Taft* (New York: Rinehart & Company, Inc., 1939, 2 vols.), and HERBERT F. WRIGHT, "Philander Chase Knox," in BEMIS, ED., *American Secretaries of State*, vol. IX, pp. 303–357. SCOTT NEARING AND JOSEPH FREEMAN, *Dollar Diplomacy* (New York: The Viking Press, Inc., 1925), gives a Marxist interpretation, which may be compared with BENJAMIN H. WILLIAMS, *Economic Foreign Policy of the United States* (New York: McGraw-Hill Book Company, Inc., 1929).

802 SUGGESTIONS FOR FURTHER READING

Latin America. BEMIS, *Latin American Policy of the United States;* PERKINS, *Hands Off;* and RIPPY, *The Caribbean Danger Zone,* all contain relevant material. ISAAC J. Cox, *Nicaragua and the United States, 1909–1927* (Boston: World Peace Foundation, 1927), contains both a scholarly narrative and important documents. THOMAS A. BAILEY, "The Lodge Corollary to the Monroe Doctrine," *Pol. Sci. Quart.,* XLVIII (1933), 220–229, is good.

Reciprocity with Canada. The best study is L. ETHAN ELLIS, *Reciprocity 1911: A Study in Canadian-American Relations* (New Haven, Conn.: Yale University Press, 1939). See also TANSILL, *Canadian-American Relations, 1875–1911.*

Far East. GRISWOLD, *Far Eastern Policy of the United States,* may be supplemented with CHARLES VEVIER, *The United States and China, 1906–1911* (New Brunswick, N.J.: Rutgers University Press, 1955); HERBERT CROLY, *Willard Straight* (New York: The Macmillan Company, 1924); and ZABRISKIE, *American-Russian Rivalry in the Far East, 1895–1914.*

Chapter 25. The Diplomacy of Morality

General. Wilsonian diplomacy is discussed in detail in RAY STANNARD BAKER, *Woodrow Wilson: Life and Letters* (New York: Doubleday & Company, Inc., 1927–1939, 8 vols.), especially vols. 4–6. For a more critical account, see the books of ARTHUR S. LINK: *Woodrow Wilson and the Progressive Era, 1910–1917* (New York: Harper & Brothers, 1954); *Wilson: The New Freedom* (Princeton, N.J.: Princeton University Press, 1956); and *Wilson the Diplomatist: A Look at His Major Foreign Policies* (Baltimore: Johns Hopkins Press, 1957). See also HARLEY NOTTER, *The Origins of the Foreign Policy of Woodrow Wilson* (Baltimore: Johns Hopkins Press, 1937), and EDWARD H. BUEHRIG, ED., *Wilson's Foreign Policy in Perspective* (Bloomington, Ind.: Indiana University Press, 1957).

Mexico. HOWARD F. CLINE, *The United States and Mexico* (Cambridge, Mass.: Harvard University Press, 1953), is excellent. See also RIPPY, *The United States and Mexico;* GEORGE M. STEPHENSON, *John Lind of Minnesota* (Minneapolis: University of Minnesota Press, 1935); and JULIUS GOEBEL, JR., *The Recognition Policy of the United States* (New York: Columbia University Press, 1915).

Caribbean Region. Wilson's policies are discussed in BEMIS, *Latin American Policy of the United States;* PERKINS, *Hands Off;* CALCOTT, *Caribbean Policy of the United States;* and DANA G. MUNRO, *The United States and the Caribbean Area* (Boston: World Peace Foundation, 1934). For Bryan's part, consult SELIG ADLER, "Bryan and Wilsonian Caribbean Penetration," *Hispanic Amer. Hist. Rev.,* XX (May, 1940), 198–226. On Haiti, see LUDWELL L. MONTAGUE, *Haiti and the United States, 1714–1938* (Durham, N.C.: Duke University Press, 1940); ARTHUR C. MILLSPAUGH, *Haiti under American Control* (Boston: World Peace Foundation, 1931); and CARL KELSY, "The American Intervention in Haiti and the Dominican Republic," *Annals Amer. Acad. Pol. and Social Science,* C (March, 1922), 109–122. On other countries, see WELLES, *Naboth's Vineyard: The Dominican Republic, 1844–1924;* Cox, *Nicaragua and the United States;* and TANSILL, *Purchase of the Danish West Indies.*

PART FOUR. THE SEARCH FOR WORLD ORDER (1917–1945)

Chapter 26. The Ideal of Peace

General. The most complete study is MERLE CURTI, *Peace or War: The American Struggle, 1636–1936* (New York: W. W. Norton & Company, Inc., 1936). Twentieth-century isolationism is analyzed in SELIG ADLER, *The Isolationist Impulse: Its Twentieth-Century Reaction* (New York: Abelard-Schuman, Inc., Publishers, 1957), and ALEXANDER DE CONDE, ED., *Isolation and Security* (Durham, N.C.: Duke University Press, 1957).

Hague Conferences. Useful accounts are JOSEPH H. CHOATE, *The Two Hague Conferences* (Princeton, N.J.: Princeton University Press, 1913); MARGARET ROBINSON, *Arbitration and the Hague Peace Conferences, 1899 and 1907* (Philadelphia: University of Pennsylvania Press, 1936); ERNEST LINDSEY, *The International Court* (New York: Thomas Y. Crowell Company, 1931); and MERZE TATE, *The United States and Armaments* (Cambridge, Mass.: Harvard University Press, 1948).

Arbitration. A mine of information is JOHN BASSETT MOORE, *History and Digest of the International Arbitrations to Which the United States Has Been a Party* (Washington: U.S. Government Printing Office, 1898, 6 vols.). The attempt to make a general arbitration treaty with England is described in NELSON M. BLAKE, "The Olney-Pauncefote Treaty of 1897," *Amer. Hist. Rev.*, L (January, 1945), 228–243. For similar efforts under Roosevelt and Taft, see DENNETT, *John Hay;* JESSUP, *Elihu Root;* and PRINGLE, *William Howard Taft.* Good articles on particular arbitrations are THOMAS A. BAILEY, "Theodore Roosevelt and the Alaska Boundary Settlement," *Canadian Hist. Rev.*, XVIII (June, 1937), 123–130; and ROBERT LANSING, "The North Atlantic Coast Fisheries Arbitration," *Amer. J. International Law*, V (January, 1911), 1–31. For the Wilson period, see MERLE E. CURTI, *Bryan and World Peace* (Northampton, Mass.: History Dept., Smith College, 1931).

Chapter 27. World War I: The Trials of a Neutral

General. Wilsonian diplomacy is defended in CHARLES SEYMOUR, *American Diplomacy during the World War* (Baltimore: Johns Hopkins Press, 1940), and the same author's *American Neutrality, 1914–1917* (New Haven, Conn.: Yale University Press, 1935). CHARLES C. TANSILL, *America Goes to War* (Boston: Little, Brown & Company, 1938), is critical. The influence of propaganda is emphasized in the highly readable WALTER MILLIS, *Road to War: America, 1914–1917* (Boston: Houghton Mifflin Company, 1935). Lively interpretation is provided by DEXTER PERKINS, *America and Two Wars* (Boston: Little, Brown & Company, 1944).

Memoirs and Biographies. On Wilson, consult the books by BAKER, LINK, NOTTER, and BUEHRIG, cited for chap. 25. For Wilson's most influential adviser, see CHARLES SEYMOUR, ED., *The Intimate Papers of Colonel House* (Boston: Houghton Mifflin Company, 1926–1928, 4 vols.). Other important men are covered in ROBERT LANSING, *War Memoirs* (New York: The Bobbs-Merrill

Company, Inc., 1935); DANIEL M. SMITH, "Robert Lansing and the Formulation of American Neutrality Policies, 1914–1915," *Mississippi Valley Hist. Rev.*, XLIII (June, 1956), 59–81; BURTON J. HENDRICK, *The Life and Letters of Walter Hines Page* (New York: Doubleday & Company, Inc., 1924–1925, 3 vols.); and JAMES W. GERARD, *My Four Years in Germany* (New York: Doubleday & Company, Inc., 1920).

Relations with Allies. The European background is emphasized in ERNEST R. MAY, *The World War and American Isolation, 1914–1917* (Cambridge, Mass.: Harvard University Press, 1958). On propaganda and related matters, see HORACE C. PETERSON, *Propaganda for War: The Campaign against American Neutrality, 1914–1917* (Norman, Okla.: University of Oklahoma Press, 1939); ARTHUR WILLERT, *The Road to Safety: A Study in Anglo-American Relations* (New York: British Book Centre, 1953); and ARMIN RAPPAPORT, *The British Press and Wilsonian Neutrality* (Stanford, Calif.: Stanford University Press, 1950). A recent study is MARION C. SINEY, *The Allied Blockade of Germany, 1914–1916* (Ann Arbor, Mich.: University of Michigan Press, 1957).

Relations with Germany. THOMAS A. BAILEY, "The Sinking of the *Lusitania*," *Amer. Hist. Rev.*, XLI (October, 1935), is good. For later developments, see KARL E. BIRNBAUM, *Peace Moves and U-Boat Warfare: A Study of Imperial Germany's Policy towards the United States, April 18, 1916–January 9, 1917* (Stockholm: Almquist & Wiksell, 1958), and BARBARA W. TUCHMAN, *The Zimmermann Telegram* (New York: The Viking Press, Inc., 1958). On antiwar sentiment, see HORACE C. PETERSON AND GILBERT C. FITE, *Opponents of War, 1917–1918* (Madison, Wis.: University of Wisconsin Press, 1957).

Chapter 28. The Light That Failed

General. Wilson's ideas are explained in BAKER, *Woodrow Wilson: Life and Letters*, and LINK, *Wilson the Diplomatist.* For the most important citizen group, consult RUHL J. BARTLETT, *The League to Enforce Peace* (Chapel Hill, N.C.: University of North Carolina Press, 1944), which should be supplemented with PRINGLE, *William Howard Taft.* On the armistice, see HARRY R. RUDIN, *Armistice 1918* (New Haven, Conn.: Yale University Press, 1944).

Paris Peace Conference. The most detailed treatments are HAROLD W. V. TEMPERLEY, *A History of the Peace Conference of Paris* (London: Hodder & Stoughton, Ltd., 1920–1924, 6 vols.), and RAY STANNARD BAKER, *Woodrow Wilson and the World Settlement* (New York: Doubleday & Company, Inc., 1922, 3 vols.). Excellent one-volume studies are PAUL BIRDSALL, *Versailles Twenty Years After* (New York: Reynal & Hitchcock, Inc., 1941), and THOMAS A. BAILEY, *Woodrow Wilson and the Lost Peace* (New York: The Macmillan Company, 1944). The role of the various American peace commissioners is discussed in SEYMOUR, ED., *Intimate Papers of Colonel House;* ROBERT LANSING, *The Peace Negotiations: A Personal Narrative* (Boston: Houghton Mifflin Company, 1921); NEVINS, *Henry White;* and FREDERICK PALMER, *Bliss: Peacemaker* (New York: Dodd, Mead & Company, Inc., 1934). For unusual points of view, consult HAROLD NICOLSON, *Peacemaking, 1919* (New York: Harcourt, Brace and Company, Inc., 1939); STEPHEN BONSAL, *Unfinished Business* (New

York: Doubleday & Company, Inc., 1944); STEPHEN BONSAL, *Suitors and Supplicants* (Englewood Cliffs, N.J.: Prentice-Hall, Inc., 1946); and HERBERT HOOVER, *Ordeal of Woodrow Wilson* (New York: McGraw-Hill Book Company, Inc., 1958).

The Far East. For the China problem, see RUSSELL H. FIFIELD, *Woodrow Wilson and the Far East: The Diplomacy of the Shantung Question* (New York: Thomas Y. Crowell Company, 1952). On complications with Russia, consult GEORGE F. KENNAN, *Soviet-American Relations, 1917–1920* (Princeton, N.J.: Princeton University Press, 1956–1958, 2 vols.); ROBERT P. BROWDER, *The Origins of Soviet-American Diplomacy* (Princeton, N.J.: Princeton University Press, 1953); WILLIAM S. GRAVES, *America's Siberian Adventure, 1918–1920* (New York: J. Cape & H. Smith, 1931); and BETTY M. UNTERBERGER, *America's Siberian Expedition, 1918–1920* (Durham, N.C.: Duke University Press, 1956).

The Treaty Fight. The most important studies are DENNA F. FLEMING, *The United States and the League of Nations, 1918–1920* (New York: G. P. Putnam's Sons, 1932), and THOMAS A. BAILEY, *Woodrow Wilson and the Great Betrayal* (New York: The Macmillan Company, 1945). More popular in its appeal is ALAN CRANSTON, *The Killing of the Peace* (New York: The Viking Press, Inc., 1945). For the opposition case, see HENRY CABOT LODGE, *The Senate and the League of Nations* (New York: Charles Scribner's Sons, 1925), and JOHN A. GARRATY, *Henry Cabot Lodge: A Biography* (New York: Alfred A. Knopf, Inc., 1953). Irish opposition to the treay is explained in CHARLES C. TANSILL, *America and the Fight for Irish Freedom* (New York: The Devin-Adair Company, 1957).

Chapter 29. Republican Peace Efforts

General. Diplomacy under Harding and Coolidge is intelligently discussed in MERLO J. PUSEY, *Charles Evans Hughes* (New York: The Macmillan Company, 1951, 2 vols.); DEXTER PERKINS, *Charles Evans Hughes and American Democratic Statesmanship* (Boston: Little, Brown & Company, 1956); and DAVID BRYN-JONES, *Frank B. Kellogg: A Biography* (New York: G. P. Putnam's Sons, 1937).

Disarmament. General accounts are in BENJAMIN H. WILLIAMS, *The United States and Disarmament* (New York: McGraw-Hill Book Company, Inc., 1931), and TATE, *The United States and Armaments*. For the Washington Conference, see HAROLD AND MARGARET SPROUT, *Toward a New Order of Sea Power: American Naval Policy and the World Scene, 1918–1922* (Princeton, N.J.: Princeton University Press, 1943); YAMOTO ICHIHASHI, *The Washington Conference and After* (Stanford, Calif.: Stanford University Press, 1928); RAYMOND L. BUELL, *The Washington Conference* (New York: Appleton-Century-Crofts, Inc., 1922); and C. LEONARD HOAG, *Preface to Preparedness: The Washington Disarmament Conference and Public Opinion* (Washington: American Council on Public Affairs, 1941). On the Four-Power Pact, see J. CARL VINSON, "The Parchment Peace," *Mississippi Valley Hist. Rev.*, XXXIX (September, 1952), 303–314.

The Far East. GRISWOLD, *Far Eastern Policy of the United States*, is excellent for this period. See also Rodman W. Paul, *The Abrogation of the Gentlemen's Agreement* (Cambridge, Mass.: Harvard University Press, 1936).

International Cooperation. Authoritative studies are Denna F. Fleming, *The United States and World Organization, 1920–1933* (New York: Columbia University Press, 1938), and the same author's *The United States and the World Court* (New York: Doubleday & Company, Inc., 1945). On the Pact of Paris, the best study is Robert H. Ferrell, *Peace in Their Time: The Origins of the Kellogg-Briand Pact* (New Haven, Conn.: Yale University Press, 1952), but see also James T. Shotwell, *War as an Instrument of National Policy: Its Renunciation in the Pact of Paris* (New York: Harcourt, Brace and Company, Inc., 1929); John E. Stoner, *S. O. Levinson and the Pact of Paris* (Chicago: University of Chicago Press, 1943); and John C. Vinson, *William E. Borah and the Outlawry of War* (Athens: University of Georgia Press, 1957).

Chapter 30. Shifts of Policy

General. The Hoover policies are ably defended in *The Memoirs of Herbert Hoover* (New York: The Macmillan Company, 1951–1952, 3 vols.), and also in William S. Meyers and Walter H. Newton, *The Hoover Administration: A Documented Narrative* (New York: Charles Scribner's Sons, 1936), and William S. Meyers, *The Foreign Policies of Herbert Hoover* (New York: Charles Scribner's Sons, 1940). For better balance, see Robert H. Ferrell, *American Diplomacy in the Great Depression: Hoover-Stimson Foreign Policy, 1929–1933* (New Haven, Conn.: Yale University Press, 1957). Henry L. Stimson and McGeorge Bundy, *On Active Service in Peace and War* (New York: Harper & Brothers, 1948), is a vigorous memoir. For a somewhat critical view, see Richard N. Current, *Secretary Stimson: A Study in Statecraft* (New Brunswick, N.J.: Rutgers University Press, 1954).

Latin America. An important study is Alexander de Conde, *Herbert Hoover's Latin-American Policy* (Stanford, Calif.: Stanford University Press, 1951). See also Bemis, *Latin American Policy of the United States;* Munro, *The United States and the Caribbean;* and Cline, *The United States and Mexico.*

Disarmament. An important firsthand account is Charles G. Dawes, *Journal as Ambassador to Great Britain* (New York: The Macmillan Company, 1939). See also Tate, *The United States and Armaments,* and Raymond G. O'Connor, "The 'Yardstick' and Naval Disarmament in the 1920's," *Mississippi Valley Hist. Rev.,* XLV (December, 1958), 441–463.

Economic Policy. Brief but suggestive is Herbert Feis, *The Diplomacy of the Dollar: First Era, 1919–1932* (Baltimore: Johns Hopkins Press, 1950). On other phases, see Joseph M. Jones, Jr., *Tariff Retaliation: Repercussions of the Hawley-Smoot Bill* (Philadelphia: University of Pennsylvania Press, 1934), and Harold G. Moulton and Leo Pasvolsky, *War Debts and World Prosperity* (New York: Appleton-Century-Crofts, Inc., 1932).

The Far East. Henry L. Stimson, *The Far Eastern Crisis: Recollections and Observations* (New York: Council on Foreign Relations, 1936), is the Secretary's own defense of his policy. For more detached views, see Griswold, *Far Eastern Policy of the United States;* Thomas A. Bisson, *America's Far Eastern*

Policy (New York: Institute of Pacific Relations, 1945); SARA R. SMITH, *The Manchurian Crisis, 1931–1932: A Tragedy in International Relations* (New York: Columbia University Press, 1948); REGINALD BASSETT, *Democracy and Foreign Policy: The Sino-Japanese Dispute, 1931–1933* (New York: Longmans, Green & Co., Inc., 1952); ROBERT LANGER, *Seizure of Territory: The Stimson Doctrine and Related Principles in Legal Theory and Diplomatic Practice* (Princeton, N.J.: Princeton University Press, 1947); and PAUL H. CLYDE, "The Diplomacy of 'Playing No Favorites': Secretary Stimson and Manchuria, 1931," *Mississippi Valley Hist. Rev.*, XXXV (September, 1948), 187–202.

Chapter 31. Good Neighbors—and Bad

General. A well-balanced account is ALLAN NEVINS, *The New Deal and World Affairs* (New Haven, Conn.: Yale University Press, 1950). Highly critical is CHARLES A. BEARD, *American Foreign Policy in the Making, 1932–1940* (New Haven, Conn.: Yale University Press, 1946). WILLIAM O. SCROGGS AND OTHERS, EDS., *The United States in World Affairs, 1933, 1934–35, 1936, 1937, 1938* (New York: Harper & Brothers, 1934–1939), provides a contemporary record of great value. For key Rooseveltian pronouncements, see WILFRED FUNK, ED., *Roosevelt's Foreign Policy, 1933–1941* (New York: Wilfred Funk, Inc., 1942). The *Memoirs of Cordell Hull* (New York: The Macmillan Company, 1948, 2 vols.) are highly detailed.

Good Neighbor Policy. EDWARD C. GUERRANT, *Roosevelt's Good Neighbor Policy* (Albuquerque, N.M.: The University of New Mexico Press, 1950), gives a brief analysis. Firsthand accounts are in SUMNER WELLES, *The Time for Decision* (New York: Harper & Brothers, 1944), and JOSEPHUS DANIELS, *Shirt-Sleeve Diplomat* (Chapel Hill, N.C.: University of North Carolina Press, 1947). See also BEMIS, *Latin American Policy of the United States;* PERKINS, *Hands Off;* and RIPPY, *The Caribbean Danger Zone.*

Economic Policy. Important studies are RAYMOND L. BUELL, *The Hull Trade Program* (New York: Foreign Policy Association, 1938); HERBERT FEIS, *The Changing Pattern of International Economic Affairs* (New York: Harper & Brothers, 1940); and SUMNER WELLES AND ALEXANDER STEVENSON, "Reciprocal Trade Agreements," in *International Conciliation*, no. 390 (May, 1943).

The Soviet Union. A good general account is WILLIAM A. WILLIAMS, *American-Russian Relations, 1781–1947* (New York: Rinehart & Company, Inc., 1952). See also MENO LOVENSTEIN, *American Opinion of Soviet Russia* (Washington: American Council on Public Affairs, 1941).

Neutrality. EDWIN M. BORCHARD AND WILLIAM P. LAGE, *Neutrality for the United States* (New Haven, Conn.: Yale University Press, 1937), reflects the trends of the day, as does also H. C. ENGELBRECHT AND F. C. HANIGHEN, *Merchants of Death: A Study of the International Armament Industry* (New York: Dodd, Mead & Company, Inc., 1934). Interesting special studies are JOHN NORMAN, "Influence of Pro-Fascist Propaganda on American Neutrality, 1935–1936," in LEE AND MCREYNOLDS, *Essays in History and International Relations in Honor of George Hubbard Blakeslee*, pp. 193–214; and F. JAY TAYLOR, *The United States and the Spanish Civil War, 1936–1939* (New York: Bookman

Associates, 1956). On Japan, see JOSEPH C. GREW, *Ten Years in Japan* (New York: Simon and Schuster, Inc., 1944); WILLIAM C. JOHNSTONE, *The United States and Japan's New Order* (New York: Oxford University Press, 1941); and FRANCIS C. JONES, *Japan's New Order in East Asia: Its Rise and Fall, 1937–45* (New York: Oxford University Press, 1954). On Roosevelt's shift of policy, see WILLIAM L. LANGER AND S. EVERETT GLEASON, *The Challenge to Isolation, 1937–1940* (New York: Harper & Brothers, 1952), and DOROTHY BERG, "Notes on Roosevelt's Quarantine Speech," *Pol. Sci. Quart.*, LXII (1957), 405–433.

Chapter 32. Between War and Peace

General. Roosevelt's policy has provided material for vigorous controversy. Generally favorable treatments are in the books of WILLIAM L. LANGER AND S. EVERETT GLEASON, *The Challenge of Isolation, 1937–1940*, and *The Undeclared War, 1940–1941* (New York: Harper & Brothers, 1953); and also in DONALD F. DRUMMOND, *The Passing of American Neutrality, 1937–1941* (Ann Arbor, Mich.: University of Michigan Press, 1955); BASIL RAUCH, *Roosevelt: From Munich to Pearl Harbor* (New York: Creative Age Press, Inc., 1950); and HERBERT FEIS, *The Road to Pearl Harbor* (Princeton, N.J.: Princeton University Press, 1950). Among the important "revisionist" or anti-Roosevelt works are the books of CHARLES A. BEARD, *American Foreign Policy in the Making, 1932–1940*, and *President Roosevelt and the Coming of the War, 1941* (New Haven, Conn.: Yale University Press, 1948); and also CHARLES C. TANSILL, *Back Door to War: The Roosevelt Foreign Policy, 1933–1941* (Chicago: Henry Regnery Company, 1952); HARRY E. BARNES, ED., *Perpetual War for Perpetual Peace: A Critical Examination of the Foreign Policy of Franklin Delano Roosevelt and Its Aftermath* (Caldwell, Idaho: Caxton Printers, Ltd., 1953); and WILLIAM H. CHAMBERLIN, *America's Second Crusade* (Chicago: Henry Regnery Company, 1950). For personal factors, see *Memoirs of Cordell Hull* and ROBERT E. SHERWOOD, *Roosevelt and Hopkins: An Intimate History* (New York: Harper & Brothers, 1948). Useful material is in *The United States in World Affairs, 1939, 1940, 1941.*

Public Opinion. HADLEY CANTRIL, ED., *Public Opinion, 1935–1946* (Princeton, N.J.: Princeton University Press, 1951), reports the results of public opinion polls. WALTER JOHNSON, *The Battle Against Isolation* (Chicago: University of Chicago Press, 1944), and WAYNE S. COLE, *America First: The Battle against Intervention, 1940–1941* (Madison, Wis.: University of Wisconsin Press, 1953), relate the efforts of rival pressure groups.

Relations with Belligerents. For Germany, see HANS L. TREFOUSSE, *Germany and American Neutrality, 1939–1941* (New York: Bookman Associates, 1951). For Japan, see JOSEPH C. GREW, *Ten Years in Japan*, and the same author's *Turbulent Era: A Diplomatic Record of Forty Years, 1904–1945*, ed. by Walter Johnson (Boston: Houghton Mifflin Company, 1952, 2 vols.); also PAUL W. SCHROEDER, *The Axis Alliance and Japanese-American Relations, 1941* (Ithaca, N.Y.: Cornell University Press, 1958).

Pearl Harbor. Graphic narratives are provided by WALTER MILLIS, *This Is Pearl! The United States and Japan* (New York: William Morrow & Company,

Inc., 1947), and WALTER LORD, *Day of Infamy* (New York: Henry Holt and Company, Inc., 1957). Roosevelt is blamed for the disaster in GEORGE E. MORGENSTERN, *Pearl Harbor: The Story of the Secret War* (New York: The Devin-Adair Company, 1947), and ROBERT A. THEOBOLD, *Final Secret of Pearl Harbor: The Washington Contribution to the Japanese Attack* (New York: The Devin-Adair Company, 1954).

Chapter 33. The Great Coalition

General. The indispensable work is WINSTON S. CHURCHILL, *The Second World War* (Boston: Houghton Mifflin Company, 1948–1953, 6 vols.). HERBERT FEIS, *Churchill, Roosevelt, Stalin: The War They Waged and the Peace They Sought* (Princeton, N.J.: Princeton University Press, 1957), is an outstanding work of scholarship. Also useful are *Memoirs of Cordell Hull;* STIMSON AND BUNDY, *On Active Service;* and SHERWOOD, *Roosevelt and Hopkins.*

Special Phases. For relations with France, see WILLIAM L. LANGER, *Our Vichy Gamble* (New York: Alfred A. Knopf, Inc., 1947), and WILLIAM D. LEAHY, *I Was There: The Personal Story of the Chief of Staff to Presidents Roosevelt and Truman* (New York: McGraw-Hill Book Company, Inc., 1950). For Russia, see JOHN R. DEANE, *The Strange Alliance: The Story of Our Efforts at Wartime Co-Operation with Russia* (New York: The Viking Press, Inc., 1947); FOSTER RHEA DULLES, *The Road to Teheran: The Story of Russia and America, 1781–1943* (Princeton, N.J.: Princeton University Press, 1944); and WILLIAMS, *American-Russian Relations, 1781–1947.* For Spain, consult CARLTON J. H. HAYES, *Wartime Mission in Spain, 1942–1945* (New York: The Macmillan Company, 1945). On military collaboration, see FORREST C. POGUE, *The Supreme Command* (Washington: Department of the Army, 1954). For a critical view, see CHESTER WILMOT, *The Struggle for Europe* (New York: Harper & Brothers, 1952), and HANSON W. BALDWIN, *Great Mistakes of the War* (New York: Harper & Brothers, 1950). On the Yalta Conference, consult EDWARD R. STETTINIUS, *Roosevelt and the Russians: The Yalta Conference* (New York: Doubleday & Company, Inc., 1949); JAMES F. BYRNES, *Speaking Frankly* (New York: Harper & Brothers, 1947); and JOHN L. SNELL, ED., *The Meaning of Yalta: Big Three Diplomacy and the Balance of Power* (Baton Rouge, La.: Louisiana State University Press, 1956).

PART FIVE. DIPLOMACY OF THE ATOMIC AGE (SINCE 1945)

Chapter 34. From One World to Two

General. Particularly useful are the publications of the Council on Foreign Relations: *The United States in World Affairs, 1945–47, 1947–48, 1948–49, 1949, 1950, 1951, 1952;* and *Documents on American Foreign Relations* for these years. HARRY S. TRUMAN, *Memoirs* (New York: Doubleday & Company, Inc., 1956, 2 vols.), defends the author's policies with characteristic vigor. See also LOUIS W. KOENIG, ED., *The Truman Administration: Its Principles and Practice* (New York: New York University Press, 1956). WALTER MILLIS, ED., *The Forrestal*

Diaries (New York: The Viking Press, Inc., 1951), gives the firsthand observations of a prominent Cabinet member. ARTHUR H. VANDENBERG, JR., *The Private Papers of Senator Vandenberg* (Boston: Houghton Mifflin Company, 1952), gives evidence of bipartisanship. See also H. BRADFORD WESTERFIELD, *Foreign Policy and Party Politics* (New Haven, Conn.: Yale University Press, 1955).

United Nations. RUTH B. RUSSELL AND JEANNE E. MUTHER, *A History of the United Nations Charter: The Role of the United States, 1940–1945* (Washington: Brookings Institution, 1958), carries the story through the San Francisco Conference in great detail. More concise is VERA M. DEAN, *The Four Cornerstones of Peace* (New York: McGraw-Hill Book Company, Inc., 1946). For subsequent developments, see CLARK M. EICHELBERGER, *UN: The First Ten Years* (New York: Harper & Brothers, 1955).

Origins of the Cold War. WALTER LIPPMANN, *The Cold War* (New York: Harper & Brothers, 1947), and ELLIS M. ZACHARIAS, *Behind Closed Doors* (New York: G. P. Putnam's Sons, 1950), reflect the growing tension. On the frustrations of postwar attempts at peacemaking, see BYRNES, *Speaking Frankly*, and REDVERS OPIE AND OTHERS, *The Search for Peace Settlements* (Washington: Brookings Institution, 1951). ARTHUR BLISS LANE, *I Saw Poland Betrayed* (Indianapolis: The Bobbs-Merrill Company, Inc., 1948), is the report of the American Ambassador of these years. Another Ambassador records his experiences in WALTER BEDELL SMITH, *My Three Years in Moscow* (Philadelphia: J. B. Lippincott Company, 1950). On Germany, see PHILIP E. MOSELY, "The Occupation of Germany: New Light on How the Zones Were Drawn," *Foreign Affairs*, XXVIII (July, 1950), 580–604; LUCIUS D. CLAY, *Decision in Germany* (New York: Doubleday & Company, Inc., 1950); and DREW MIDDLETON, *The Struggle for Germany* (Indianapolis: The Bobbs-Merrill Company, Inc., 1949).

Containment Policy. KENNAN, *American Diplomacy, 1900–1950*, reprints the article which coined the phrase. JOSEPH M. JONES, *The Fifteen Weeks (February 21–June 5, 1947)* (New York: The Viking Press, Inc., 1955), is excellent on the origins of the Truman Doctrine and the Marshall Plan. On subsequent developments, see A. C. TURNER, *Bulwark of the West: Implications and Problems of NATO* (Toronto: Ryerson Press, 1953), and THEODORE H. WHITE, *Fire in the Ashes: Europe in Mid-Century* (New York: William Sloane Associates, 1953).

Latin America. Useful studies are ARTHUR P. WHITAKER, *The United States and South America: The Northern Republics* (Cambridge, Mass.: Harvard University Press, 1948), and the same author's *The United States and Argentina* (Cambridge, Mass.: Harvard University Press, 1954). See also O. EDMUND SMITH, JR., *Yankee Diplomacy: U.S. Intervention in Argentina* (Dallas, Tex.: Southern Methodist University Press, 1953), and C. G. FENWICK, *The Inter-American Regional System* (New York: Declan X. McMullen Co., 1949).

Chapter 35. The Struggle for Asia

General. HAROLD M. VINACKE, *Far Eastern Politics in the Postwar Period* (New York: Appleton-Century-Crofts, Inc., 1956), is excellent. On evolving policy, see TRUMAN, *Memoirs;* ROBERT J. DONOVAN, *Eisenhower: The Inside*

Story (New York: Harper & Brothers, 1956); and MERLO J. PUSEY, *Eisenhower the President* (New York: The Macmillan Company, 1956).

Japan. Useful studies are BARON E. J. LEWE VAN ADUARD, *Japan from Surrender to Peace* (New York: Frederick A. Praeger, 1954); RUSSELL BRINES, *MacArthur's Japan* (Philadelphia: J. B. Lippincott Company, 1948); EDWIN M. MARTIN, *The Allied Occupation of Japan* (Stanford, Calif.: Stanford University Press, 1948); and EDWIN O. REISCHAUER, *The United States and Japan* (Cambridge, Mass.: Harvard University Press, 1950).

China. For the earlier phases, see HERBERT FEIS, *The China Tangle: The American Effort in China from Pearl Harbor to the Marshall Mission* (Princeton, N.J.: Princeton University Press, 1953). For the later situation, consult JOHN K. FAIRBANK, *The United States and China* (Cambridge, Mass.: Harvard University Press, 1958).

Korea. ROBERT T. OLIVER, *Why War Came to Korea* (New York: Fordham University Press, 1950), is the work of a warm admirer of President Rhee. More objective is LELAND M. GOODRICH, *Korea: A Study of U.S. Policy in the United Nations* (New York: Council on Foreign Relations, 1956). Two points of view on the MacArthur controversy are represented by COURTNEY WHITNEY, *MacArthur: His Rendezvous with History* (New York: Alfred A. Knopf, Inc., 1956), and RICHARD H. ROVERE AND ARTHUR M. SCHLESINGER, JR., *The General and the President, and the Future of American Foreign Policy* (New York: Farrar, Straus, & Young, Inc., 1951). On the armistice, see CHARLES T. JOY, *How Communists Negotiate* (New York: The Macmillan Company, 1955).

Other Regions. Useful studies are AMRY VANDENBOSCH AND RICHARD A. BUTWELL, *Southeast Asia among the World Powers* (Lexington: University of Kentucky Press, 1957); RUSSELL H. FIFIELD, *The Diplomacy of Southeast Asia, 1945–1958* (New York: Harper & Brothers, 1958); and PHILLIPS TALBOT AND S. I. POLAI, *India and America* (New York: Harper & Brothers, 1958).

Chapter 36. Nuclear Stalemate

General. Of continuing usefulness are *The United States in World Affairs* and *Documents on American Foreign Relations* for the relevant years. Eisenhower's policies are warmly defended in DONOVAN, *Eisenhower: The Inside Story*, and PUSEY, *Eisenhower the President*. For a more critical view, see MARQUIS CHILDS, *Eisenhower: Captive Hero* (New York: Harcourt, Brace and Company, Inc., 1958). JOHN FOSTER DULLES, *War or Peace* (New York: The Macmillan Company, 1957), is a new edition of an important statement of principles first laid down in 1950.

Armament and Disarmament. A good review of the problem is PHILIP NOEL-BAKER, *The Arms Race: A Programme for World Disarmament* (New York: Oceana Publications, 1958). For well-informed judgments, see HANSON W. BALDWIN, *The Great Arms Race: A Comparison of U.S. and Soviet Power Today* (New York: Frederick A. Praeger, Inc., 1958). Implications for foreign policy are thoughtfully drawn in HENRY A. KISSINGER, *Nuclear Weapons and Foreign Policy* (New York: Harper & Brothers, 1957), and LOUIS J. HALLE, *Choice for Survival* (New York: Harper & Brothers, 1958).

The Middle East. Good background material is provided by HALFORD L. HOSKINS, *The Middle East* (New York: The Macmillan Company, 1954), and JACOB C. HUREWITZ, *Middle East Dilemmas: The Background of United States Policy* (New York: Harper & Brothers, 1953). A. G. MEZERIK, *Suez Canal: Nationalization, Invasion, International Action* (New York: International Review Service, 1956), is a good summary. For subsequent problems, see JOHN C. CAMPBELL, *Defense of the Middle East* (New York: Harper & Brothers, 1958). CAROL A. FISHER AND FRED KRINSKY, *Middle East in Crisis: Historical and Documentary Review* (Syracuse: Syracuse University Press, 1959), contains useful material.

Underdeveloped Areas. Good studies are WILLIAM A. BROWN, JR., AND REDVERS OPIE, *American Foreign Assistance* (Washington: Brookings Institution, 1953); JONATHAN B. BINGHAM, *Shirt-Sleeve Diplomacy: Point 4 in Action* (New York: The John Day Company, Inc., 1954); and EUGENE STALEY, *The Future of Underdeveloped Countries: Political Implications of Economic Development* (New York: Harper & Brothers, 1954).

Debate over Methods and Objectives. Among many recent books on American foreign policy, the following are representative: DEAN ACHESON, *Power and Diplomacy* (Cambridge, Mass.: Harvard University Press, 1958); ADOLPHE A. BERLE, JR., *Tides of Crisis: A Primer of Foreign Relations* (New York: Reynal & Co., 1957); GEORGE F. KENNAN, *Realities of American Foreign Policy* (Princeton, N.J.: Princeton University Press, 1954); GEORGE F. KENNAN, *Russia, the Atom and the West* (New York: Harper & Brothers, 1958); and C. L. SULZBERGER, *What's Wrong with U.S. Foreign Policy* (New York: Harcourt, Brace and Company, Inc., 1959).

INDEX

ABC powers, 478, 479

Aberdeen, Lord, 169, 176, 179, 182, 201, 203, 207

Accessory Transit Company, 238–239

Acheson, Dean, 722, 737, 742; and China, 735–736; and Japan, 746–747

Adams, Charles Francis: minister to England, 267–268; favors neutrality, 269; opposes Confederate cruisers, 277–278; and recognition, 282; and Mexico, 310; supports *Alabama* claims, 317; at Geneva Tribunal, 326; as mugwump, 396

Adams, John: as diplomat, 4; in Holland, 20–21, 33; peace commissioner, 23–25, 27, 32; in England, 34, 39; as Vice President, 46; conflict with France, 70–76; in impressment issue, 97; opposes disloyalty, 105; enlarges navy, 356

Adams, John Quincy: opposes disloyalty, 105; and Treaty of Ghent, 118–119, 124, 126, 127; Secretary of State, 142; Florida issue, 144–146; and Monroe Doctrine, 149–151, 154–156, 158; on Panama Congress, 162–163; troubles with England, 167–168; and Texas, 189; on Oregon problem, 203; and Mexico, 211; on Cuban issue, 241

Adams, Samuel, 32

Adams, William, 119, 126

Adams-Onís Treaty, 1819, 144–146, 154, 193

Adamson Act, 1916, 531–532

Adenauer, Konrad, 725, 783, 786

Adet, Pierre, 67

Africa: Barbary pirates, 79–83; Boer War, 374; Morocco crisis, 445–447; Ethiopian War, 632–635; in World War II, 661–662, 679, 680, 682–685; and Suez crisis, 768–771

"Agreed memorandum," 1905, 443–445

Aguinaldo, Emilio, 395, 397

Aid, secret, from France, 12–14

Aix-la-Chapelle, Convention of, 1818, 153

Alabama in Civil War, 277, 332

Alabama claims, 316, 318–320, 324–327

"Alabama letters," 1844, 197

Alamo massacre, 1836, 187, 188

Alaska: purchase, 287–292, 303, 305, 342; boundary issue, 500–503

Albania, 646, 719, 720

Albert, Prince of England, 271

Albert, Heinrich, 518

Aleutian Islands, 290

Alexander I of Russia, 95, 102, 118, 130, 152, 154, 160

Alexander II of Russia, 283, 284, 289

Alexander VI, Pope, 7

Algeciras Conference, 1906, 445–447

Algiers: and pirates, 79–83; in World War II, 682, 685; revolt, 727, 766

Algiers Conference, 1943, 685

Alien and Sedition Acts, 1798, 74

Allen, Ethan, 38

Allen, William V., 404

Alliança incident, 1895, 379

Alliance: treaty of, with France, 1778, 16–17; suspended, 76

Allied Control Council, 711

Allied High Commission, 725

Almonte, Juan, 211

Altamonte, Juan, 312
Alverstone, Lord, 503
Amau Statement, 1934, 638, 639
Ambrister, Robert C., 143
America First Committee, 656, 664
American Asiatic Association, 1898, 408
American Revolution: independence, 4;
  diplomacy, 5–12; secret air, 12–14;
  French alliance, 14–17; relations with
  Spain, 17–19; and Holland, 19–20;
  Armed Neutrality, 21–22; peace nego-
  tiations, 23–32
American Russian Commercial Company,
  288, 290
American Society for the Judicial Settle-
  ment of International Disputes, 504
American West India Company, 295
Ames, Fisher, 61
Amiens, Peace of, 1802, 84
Ampudia, Pedro, 214
Anderson, Richard C., 163, 164
Andrews, Israel D., 257
Angell Commission, 1880, 334
Anglo-Japanese Alliance, 1902, 413, 439,
  443, 466, 572
Annexation Club, 1892, 362, 363
Annexation Manifesto, 1849, 256
Anti-Comintern Pact, 1936, 639, 642
Antietam, Battle of, 1862, 277
Apia, 304, 358–359
Appeasement, 1938, 643–644
Aqaba, Gulf of, 770
Arabic Pledge, 1915, 523
Arabs, post-World War II nationalism,
  767, 771–774
Aranda, Count of, 27, 33
Aranjuez, Convention of, 1779, 18, 22
Arbenz Guzmán, Jacobo, 778
Arbitration: definition, 493; Jay's Treaty,
  59–60; Treaty of Ghent, 125; Maine
  boundary, 177–178; Geneva Tribunal,
  326–327; Blaine's efforts, 337; Bering
  seals, 344–345; Venezuela boundary,
  374; Olney-Pauncefote Treaty, 494–
  495; Hague Conferences, 496–497, 499–
  500; Pious Fund, 497; Hay-Root treaties, 498; Alaska boundary, 502–503;
  Newfoundland fisheries, 504; Knox
  treaties, 504–505; Bryan treaties, 506–
  507; Kellogg treaties, 586
Arbuthnot, Alexander, 143

Arcadia Conference, 1941, 677, 679
Argentina: Drago Doctrine, 436; and
  Monroe Doctrine, 597; and UN, 707;
  under Perón, 728; anti-American feel-
  ing, 778–779
Arias, Desiderio, 485
Arman, M. L., 279, 280
Armed Neutrality, League of, 1780, 20–
  22, 24, 58, 119
Armed ships controversy: in World War
  I, 526–529, 537–538; in 1930s, 636; in
  World War II, 669
Armistice: 1918, 545–547; French, 1940,
  653; Italian, 1943, 685; Korean, 1953,
  743–746
"Arms and the Men," Fortune, 1934, 631
Arms embargo: and isolationism, 631–634,
  636; repealed, 648–650
Arms limitation, 620–621, 760, 762–763
Armstrong, John, 109, 136
Aroostook War, 1839, 178–179, 183
"Arsenal of democracy," 658–660, 664
Arthur, Chester A., 335, 337, 338, 415
Article 10 of League of Nations, 551, 558–
  560, 562, 565
Articles of Confederation, 33–35, 38–43,
  65, 79
Ashburton, Lord: and Webster, 176, 190;
  treaty with United States, 179–182
Assembly of Notables, 1863, 312
Astor, John Jacob, 128
Aswan Dam controversy, 767–768
Atchison, David R., 196
Athenia sinking, 1939, 648
Atlantic Charter, 1941, 666–667, 671, 678,
  679
Atlee, Clement, 711–713, 719, 729, 759
Atom bomb issue, 699, 758–766
Austerlitz, Battle of, 1805, 95
Austin, Alfred, 389
Austin, Moses, 183, 184
Austin, Stephen, 184, 186
Austin, Warren, 669
Australia: and Samoa, 304, 359; in World
  War II, 661; in Korean conflict, 739;
  and SEATO, 749
Austria: and France, 10; and American
  Revolution, 21; and Napoleon, 50, 95;
  in Holy Alliance, 152, 153, 157; and
  Monroe Doctrine, 160; Kossuth inci-
  dent, 221–223; in World War I, 510;

treaty, 567; war debts, 605–606; in World War II, 642, 689; World War II treaty, 715

Axis, 637, 645, 667, 676

Babcock, Orville, 298
Badoglio, Pietro, 685–686, 691
Baéz, Buenaventura, 293, 294, 296–297, 300
Baghdad Pact, 1955, 767, 768
Bagot, Charles, 126–127
Baily's Islands, 232
Bainbridge, William, 81
Baldwin, Stanley, 603
Balfour, Arthur, 543, 573–575, 598
Balkans in World War II, 662, 685, 690, 692
Balmaceda, José, 346
Baltimore incident, 1891, 347, 357
Bankhead, William, 637
Banks, Nathaniel, 297, 339
Bao Dai, 748
Barbary pirates: problem of, 34–35, 93; war against, 79–83
Barlow, Joseph, 75, 115
Barras, Paul, 71
Barron, James, 103
Barron, Samuel, 82
Baruch, Bernard, 759
Bases, World War II, 655–656
Basseno, Duc de, 115
Bates, George H., 358
Batista, Fulgencio, 628, 779
Baton Rouge, 137–138
Bay Islands, 233, 236–239
Bayard, James A., 118, 120
Bayard, Thomas: Pan-Americanism, 338; fisheries controversy, 340; sealing issue, 342–343; and Samoa, 358–360
Bayard-Chamberlain Convention, 1889, 340
Bayonne Decree, 1808, 106
Bazaine, François, 315–316
Bear Flag Republic, 210
Beaumarchais, Caron de, 10–13
Beckwith, George, 48
Belgium: in World War I, 510, 513; economic conference, 618; in World War II, 652, 653, 679; after World War II, 726
Belize, 233, 234, 236, 237

Benelux countries, 724, 726, 780
Beneš, Eduard, 643, 691
Benjamin, Judah P., 285
Bennett, James Gordon, 250
Benton, Thomas H., 182, 193, 196, 200, 207, 255
Beresford, Lord Charles, 409
Bering, Vitus, 154
Bering Sea Convention, 1892, 345, 346
Bering Sea seal controversy, 342–346
Berlin: Treaty of, 1921, 567; fall, 1945, 698; blockade, 725; division, 716–717, 784
Berlin airlift, 1948–1949, 725
Berlin Conference, 1889, 360
Berlin Decree, 1807, 101, 110, 115
Bermuda, 16, 656
Bernstorff, Johann von, 514, 520, 523, 529, 534, 537
Bethmann-Hollweg, von, Chancellor, 523, 532
Beveridge, Albert, 352
Bevin, Ernest, 711, 714
Biddle, James, 227
Bidlack, Benjamin, 234, 424–425
Bidlack Treaty, 1846, 234, 424–425
"Big-stick" diplomacy, 433–436
Bigelow, John, 279, 315
Bismarck, Otto von, 316, 358–360
Black Warrior incident, 1854, 246–249, 251
Blacklist, World War I, 531
Blaine, James G.: and *Alabama* claims, 319; opposes immigration, 334; revives Pan-Americanism, 335, 337–339; and sealing controversy, 343–345; the Chilean imbroglio, 346, 348; against Mafia, 349; and Samoa, 360; favors Hawaiian annexation, 361–363
Blair, Montgomery, 277
Blanco, Ramón, 382–383
Bliss, Tasker H., 547
Blockade: British, 101; in Civil War, 264, 269, 272–275; in World War I, 517–518; in World War II, 648, 661; of Berlin, 725
Bloom, Sol, 707
Blount, James H., 366–367
"Blue Book," 1946, 728
Bluefields, 233
Boer War, 1899–1902, 374, 403, 417, 437

Bolívar, Simón, 162, 164

Bolivia, 337, 338, 626, 629

Bolshevik Revolution, 1917, 544, 555, 572

Bonaparte, Joseph, 112, 133, 136, 147

Bonin Islands, 232, 747

Bonn, 725, 783

Bonomi, Ivanoe, 691

Bonvouloir, Archard de, 11

Borah, William: and World War I, 530; and League, 551–552, 557, 558, 562; favors naval limitation, 568, 576, 598; opposes World Court, 580–581; supports outlawry of war, 583, 585–586; stand on war debts, 608; favors Stimson Doctrine, 613–614; supports neutrality laws, 636, 647

Bordas Valdés, José, 485

Borden, Sir Robert, 465

Bowdoin, James, 136

Boxer Rebellion, 1900, 412–414

Boy-Ed, Karl, 518

Brandegee, Frank, 551–552

Brazil, 7, 152, 162, 325, 668

Briand, Aristide, 573, 583–587

Bricker, John, 755, 758

Bricker Amendment, 1953–1954, 758

Bridges, Styles, 669

Bright, John, 265, 281

"Brinkmanship," 774

British East Indies, 59, 126, 288

British Guiana: boundary controversy, 368–375; air bases in, 656

British North American Act, 1867, 322

British West Indies: and America, 16, 35, 36, 57, 59; trade controversy, 166–170

Brown, John, 64

Brussels Pact, 1948, 726, 780

Bryan, William Jennings: anti-imperialist, 352, 396, 400, 402; and dollar diplomacy, 468–469; beliefs, 470–474; Mexican policy, 474–478; and Haiti, 481–482; and Dominican Republic, 485–486; peace efforts, 506–507; in World War I, 511–522; and China, 569; and immigration, 578

Bryan Arbitration Treaties, 1913–1914, 506–507

Bryan-Chamorro Treaty, 1914, 486, 593

Bryce, James, 438, 472

Bucareli Agreement, 1923, 590–592

Buchanan, James: and Webster-Ashburton Treaty, 182; attitude toward Texas, 193; view on Oregon, 203–204, 207; and Mexico, 218, 255; on isthmian canal, 237; on acquisition of Cuba, 242; and Ostend Manifesto, 249, 252; on slave trade, 261; and Dominican Republic, 294

Buenos Aires, 148, 150–152

Bulganin, Nikolai, 761, 770

Bulgaria: in World War II, 662, 689, 691, 692; after World War II, 715, 719

Bullitt, William C., 555

Bulloch, James D., 276, 279

Bulwer, Henry, 236–238

Bunau-Varilla, Philippe, 420, 425–426

Burgess, John W., 356

Burgoyne, John, 16

Burke, Edmund, 35

Burlingame, Anson, 331–334

Burma, 662, 671, 688, 746

Burma Road, 662, 672

Butler, Anthony, 185, 188

Butler, Benjamin, 322

Butler, Nicholas Murray, 417, 583, 584, 599

Byrnes, James F.: appointed Secretary of State, 698; and UN, 709; at Potsdam, 711–713; and peace treaties, 714–716

Cabral, José, 296, 297

Cadore letter, 1810, 109

Cairo Conference, 1943, 688

Calderón, Don Angel, 245

Calhoun, John C.: and Florida problem, 143; on Monroe Doctrine, 158; and Texas annexation, 192; on Oregon issue, 207; opposes Mexican War, 215

California: early United States interest in, 131, 158, 196, 202, 204, 208; Bear Flag Republic, 210; United States attempts to purchase, 212; in Mexican War, 214–216, 219; opposes Chinese immigration, 333–335; against Japanese, 448–451

Calles, Plutarco, 591

Cambodia, 748, 749

Cambon, Jules, 393

Cameron, Don, 381

Camp David meeting, 1959, 786

Campos, Martínez, 377

Canada: gained by England, 8; in American Revolution, 16, 24, 26; and Northwest posts, 36–38; and War of 1812,

110–112, 115, 117, 120, 121; boundary dispute, 126–127; rebellion in, 173–174; *Caroline* affair, 174–177; Aroostook War, 177–178; Maine boundary, 178–182; and Elgin-Marcy Treaty, 256–259; and Civil War, 317; Fenian raids, 320–322; fisheries controversy, 322–324; seals issue, 342–346; reciprocity attempts, 464–465; Alaska boundary, 500–503; opposes Anglo-Japanese alliance, 572; in World War II, 654, 665; and hemisphere defense, 702

Canal diplomacy: in mid-nineteenth century, 232–238; in 1880s, 336–337; T. Roosevelt and Panama, 415–436; and dollar diplomacy, 458–463

Canning, George: British Foreign Secretary, 103, 107; and Monroe Doctrine, 155–158, 160–161, 194

Canning, Stratford, 156

Caperton, William B., 482, 485

Cárdenas, Lázaro, 630

Caribbean diplomacy: early interest, 155; after Civil War, 293–302; Venezuelan boundary, 368–375; Cuba, and war with Spain, 376–397; and Panama Canal, 415–436; under Wilson, 474–488

Carleton, Guy, 26, 56

Carlisle Commission, 1778, 17

Carlota of Belgium, 312, 316

Carmichael, William, 65

Carnegie Endowment for International Peace, 583

Caroline affair, 1837, 174–175, 183

Caroline Islands, 400

Carranza, Venustiano, 477–481

Casa Yrujo, Marquis de, 88

Casablanca Conference, 1943, 683–685

"Cash-and-carry" clause, 1937, 636, 649

Cass, Lewis, 205, 237, 261, 294

Castillo Armas, Carlos, 778

Castlereagh, Lord, 114, 118, 119, 122–127, 144, 150

Castrillo, Salvador, 461

Castro, Cipriano, 429–432

Castro, Fidel, 779–780

Catherine the Great of Russia, 21, 24, 119

Cazneau, William, 294, 298

Central America: independence, 152; in mid-nineteenth century, 232–239; and early canal problems, 336–337; Hay's diplomacy, 416–421; T. Roosevelt's interest, 421–427; dollar diplomacy, 458–463

Central American Court of Justice, 1907, 460, 476, 486

Central Intelligence Agency (CIA), 778

Céspedes, Carlos Manuel de, 327

Cevallos, Pedro de, 135

Ceylon, 344

Chamberlain, Joseph: as expansionist, 353; and Boer War, 374; favors United States alliance, 392, 402–403; supports Open Door, 406–407

Chamberlain, Neville: Munich appeasement, 643–645; replaced by Churchill, 652

Chamorro, Emiliano, 487, 592–593

Chamoun, Camille, 773

Chandler, William E., 371

Chapultepec, Act of, 1945, 728

Charles III of Spain, 12, 18

Charles IV of Spain, 65

Charles X of France, 170

Chatfield, Frederick, 235

Checks and balances of Constitution, 45

Chehab, Fuad, 774

Chennault, Claire, 735

Chesapeake incident, 1807, 103–104, 111, 113, 136

Chiang Kai-shek: gains power, 609–611; in World War II, 662, 672, 687, 688, 693; struggle with Communist China, 729–736; and Formosa question, 750–754

Chichester, Edward, 395

Chile: independence, 148, 151; United States recognition, 152; in War of Pacific, 337–338; troubles with United States, 346–348; and Hoover, 596

China: early Western interest in, 194, 223; Opium War, 224–225; Cushing mission, 225–226; Burlingame mission, 331–335; Open Door, 405–414, 454–455; and Russo-Japanese War, 439–443; dollar diplomacy, 465–468; and World War I, 554–555; Twenty-one Demands on, 569–570; and Nine-Power Treaty, 575; rise of nationalism, 609–611; troubles with Japan, 611–614; in World War II, 660, 662, 663, 668, 670, 673, 676, 688; and Yalta, 693–694; and UN, 706–709; post-World War II strife, 731–736, 750–754

China Lobby, 735
Chinese Exclusion Act, 1882, 333–335, 448
Choate, Joseph H., 416, 418, 472, 499
Choiseul, Duc de, 9, 10
Churchill, Winston: and World War II, 652–654, 656, 658, 662–663; and Atlantic Charter, 666–667; and UN, 677; supports second front, 679–680; at Casablanca, 683–686; at Yalta, 693–697; and Iron Curtain, 719; resigns, 761
City of Flint incident, 1939, 648
Civil War, diplomacy of, 263–285
Claiborne, William, 93, 137
Clarendon, Lord, 260
Clark, Champ, 464
Clark, George Rogers, 53
Clark, J. Reuben, 596–597
Clark, Mark, 683
Clark Memorandum, 1928, 596–597
Clay, Henry: as war hawk, 111, 113; at Ghent, 117–126; opposes Jackson, 143; favors Latin America, 149–151; and Panama Congress, 162–164; and West Indian trade, 168–169; stand on Texas, 190, 193, 196, 197
Clayton, John M.: Secretary of State, 220, 221, 243; canal diplomacy, 236–238
Clemenceau, Georges, 549, 555
Cleveland, Grover: and Pan-Americanism, 337–338; Sackville-West incident, 340–342; sealing controversy, 342–346; and Samoa, 358–359; opposes Hawaiian annexation, 365–368; Venezuelan boundary dispute, 368–375; and Cuban revolt, 379–381, 396; improves diplomatic service, 456; supports arbitration, 494–496
Clinton, George, 55
Clinton, Henry, 26
Coaling stations, 294
Cobb, Frank, 546
Cobden, Richard, 265
Cochin China, 224
Cockburn, Alexander, 326
Cole, Cornelius, 290
Colfax, Schuyler, 321
Collier, Sir Robert, 277
Colombia: independence, 151, 152; at Panama Congress, 162–164; early canal interest, 336, 338, 416; loss of Panama, 420–427; and Wilson, 474; revolt in, 779

Colombo Plan, 1951, 776
Columbia River, 128, 194–196, 204, 207, 208
Columbus, New Mexico, 479
Commerce: in American Revolution, 14, 16, 20, 21; during Confederation period, 34–37, 39–42; in Washington administration, 55–62; Jefferson and neutral trade, 94–106; Madison and neutral trade, 106–115; West Indies trade reopened, 166–170; slave trade, 181, 261–262; with the Far East, 223–232, 331–332; Canadian reciprocity, 256–259, 322–323, 464–465; in Civil War, 272–276, 280–281; with Hawaii, 303, 361–362; in 1890s, 354–355; and Open Door, 406–414; in World War I, 513–523, 526–531, 534–539; in 1920s, 604–605; under F. D. Roosevelt, 616–620, 622–625; and neutrality legislation, 632–637, 646–650, 669; aid to Allies, 651–654, 658–660; restrictions on Axis, 664, 669–673; after World War II, 721–724, 774–777
Commercial treaties: Plan of 1776, 14; France, 1778, 16, 34, 76; Netherlands, 1782, 20; Sweden, 1783, 34; Prussia, 1785, 34; Jay-Gardoqui, 1786, 41; Jay's, 1794, 58–62; with England, 1815, 126; Cushing, 1844, 225–226; Perry, 1854, 228; Japanese, 1858, 229; Elgin-Marcy, 1854, 258–259, 322; Hawaiian reciprocity, 1875, 303; Burlingame, 1868, 331–332; reciprocal, 1934, 624–625
Commission of Inquiry, definition, 493
Committee to Defend American by Aiding the Allies, 653, 656, 660
Committee for Foreign Affairs, 1777, 32
Committee on Public Information, 1917, 545
Committee of Secret Correspondence, 1775, 5, 6, 11, 12, 14, 32
Common Sense, 1776, 9
Communism: recognition of Soviet government, 622–624; Anti-Comintern Pact, 639; in Greece, 720–721; in rest of Europe, 721–724; in China, 731–736; in Korea, 738–746; in Indochina, 747–749; and Formosa, 750–754; in Central Europe, 774–775; in Latin America, 778–779
Communist China: and Yalta agreement,

693–694; and Kuomintang, 731–736; and Korea, 739–746; and Formosa, 750–753; and Tibet, 753

Compagnie Universelle du Canal Interocéanique, 416

Compromise of 1850, 240

Confederate cruisers, 276–280, 306

Confederate States, 263–284

Congress, Continental, 4, 5, 20, 23, 26, 32

Congressionalistas, 346

Connally, Tom, 707, 715–716

Connally Resolution, 1943, 688, 706

Constitution ("Old Ironsides"), 116, 125

Constitution of United States, 43–46

Containment policy, 720

Continental solidarity, 644

Continental system, 95, 104, 110, 113

Continuous voyage: in Napoleonic Wars, 121; in Civil War, 275–276; in World War I, 517

Contraband issue in World War I, 518

Convention of 1800, 75–77

Convention of 1818, 127–130, 144, 155, 193, 323

Cook, James, 128

Coolidge, Calvin: and League, 565; and immigration, 579; and World Court, 580–581; and Paris Pact, 584–585; and Mexico, 592; and Nicaragua, 593; and Havana Conference, 595; and naval limitation, 597–598, 600

Corinto, 369

Corn Islands, 486

Corn laws, 207

Cornwallis, Lord, 26

Corwin, Thomas, 309

Costa Rica: independence, 233; and early canal diplomacy, 235–236; and Walker affair, 239; and local disputes, 338; dollar diplomacy, 458–459

Coughlin, Father Charles, 582, 620, 650, 660

Council of National Defense, 1916, 532

Council of Ten, 1919, 549

Cowley, Lord, 269

Cox, James M., 562

Crampton, John F., 258–260

Cremer, Randolph, 494

Creole affair, 1841, 181

Crimean War, 1854–1856, 259, 283, 288, 293

Crittenden, William L., 243, 245

Cromwell, William N., 420, 422, 423

Cuba: question of future, 131, 155, 163; Lopez incident, 240–244; United States tries to buy, 245–253; and Southern expansionists, 256, 280; Ten Years' War, 327–330; insurrection, 376–390; Spanish-American War, 390–398; Platt Amendment, 428–429; and Hughes, 595; and F. D. Roosevelt, 627–629; under Castro, 779

Cullom, Shelby, 368, 371, 379

Curzon, Lord, 572, 695

Curzon line, 695

Cushing, Caleb, 225, 227, 231

Cyprus, 727, 766

Czechoslovakia, 572; overrun by Germany, 643–645; postwar problems, 691, 719, 723, 746, 768

D day, 689

Dakar, 681, 683

Daladier, Edouard, 643

Dale, Richard, 81

Dallas, George, 269

Dana, Francis, 21, 33

Dana, Richard Henry, 209

Danish West Indies (Virgin Islands): and trade, 168, 276; post-Civil War efforts to purchase, 300–302; purchased, 487

Darlan, Jean, 680, 683, 684

Dartiguenave, Sudre, 481–482

Darwin, Charles, 355

Davie, William R., 75

Davis, Cushman K., 393, 396

Davis, Elmer, 577

Davis, Henry W., 313

Davis, J. C. Bancroft, 326

Davis, Jefferson: and Cuba, 242; supports Gadsden Purchase, 253; President of Confederacy, 263; in Civil War, 268–270, 273

Davis, John W., 706

Dawes, Charles G., 599, 603, 605

Dawes Plan, 1924, 603

Dawkins, Edward J., 165

Dawson, Thomas, 461

Day, William R., 382, 393

Dayton, William L., 267, 279, 280, 310, 312

Deane, Silas, 6, 7, 11, 12, 14, 16

Debts: Revolutionary, 29, 30, 39, 57, 60, 61; World War I, 541–542, 602–603, 607–609, 617

Decatur, Stephen, 82

Declaration of Independence, 4, 14

Declaration on Liberated Europe, 1945, 695

Decrès, Denis, 89–90

de Gaulle, Charles: heads Free French, 681–682; cooperation with UN, 684–685, 691; promotes French interests, 716; gains control of France, 780, 783; and European defense, 785, 786

de Grasse, Count, 20

De Lassus, Carlos, 137

Delcassé, Théophile, 445, 446

de Lesseps, Ferdinand, 415

De Lôme, Enrique Depuy, 380, 384–385

De Lôme letter, 1898, 384–385

Demarcation Line, 1493–1494, 7

Denmark: in Armed Neutrality, 21, 58; and Civil War, 271, 280; refuses to sell Danish West Indies, 300–302; does sell to United States, 487; and World War II, 651, 664

Derne, 82

Destroyer-base deal, 1940, 654–656

Development Loan Fund, 1957, 776

Dewey, George, 394–395, 430, 432

Dewey, John, 583

Díaz, Adolfo, 462, 486, 593

Díaz, Porfirio, 459, 474–475, 590

Dickinson, John, 4, 6

Diederich, Otto von, 395

Dienbienphu, 748

Diplomacy, machinery of, 46–47

Diplomatic Service, 32–34, 456–457, 587

Directory, French, 68, 70

Disarmament attempts: in 1930s, 602, 620–621; after World War II, 758–766

Disraeli, Benjamin, 260, 318, 353

Distant Early Warning (DEW) Line, 702

Dole, Sanford B., 364–367

Dollar diplomacy: in Latin America, 458–463; in Far East, 465–468; criticisms of, 468–469; and Wilson, 471; end of, 627–629

Dominican Republic: troubles with Spain, 266, 311; United States annexation efforts, 293–300, 339; T. Roosevelt and intervention, 433–435; and dollar diplomacy, 463; and Wilson, 485–486;

Hughes ends intervention, 595 (See also Santo Domingo)

Donelson, Andrew Jackson, 201, 202

Donovan, William A., 662, 778

Dorchester, Lord, 56

Douglas, Stephen A., 237, 244, 245

Drago Doctrine, 1902, 436, 500

Drought, James M., 670

Du Barry, Madame, 10

Dulles, Allen, 778

Dulles, John Foster: and Korea, 744; Japanese treaty, 747; and Indochina, 748–749; and SEATO, 749; and Formosa, 750–754; background, 756–757; and disarmament, 63; and summit, 761; and Suez crisis, 768, 771; and Iraq, 772–773; and European defense, 780; and Germany, 784

Dumas, Charles W. F., 6, 7

Dumba, Constantin, 518, 522

Dumbarton Oaks Conference, 1944, 696, 706

Dunkirk: evacuation, 1940, 653; Treaty of, 1947, 726

Du Pont de Nemours, Pierre, 86

Durand, Sir Mortimer, 444

Durfee, Amos, 174, 175

East Florida, 31, 39, 88; acquired, 138–146

East Germany, 719, 724–726, 775, 783–785

East Indies, 7, 59, 126, 223, 288

Easter Week Rebellion, 1916, in Ireland, 530

Eaton, Charles, 707

Eaton, William, 82–83

Eckhardt, von, Minister, 537–538

Economic Cooperation Administration (ECA), 723

Eden, Anthony, 678, 687, 688, 762, 769, 780

Edward VII of England, 439

Egan, Patrick, 346, 348

Egypt, 281, 359, 445; in World War II, 661–662; and Suez crisis, 768–771; and Arab problems, 771–794

Eisenhower, Dwight D., in Africa, 682–683; and Italy, 685–686; and victory, 690, 698; and NATO, 727; and Korea, 743, 745; and Indochina, 748–749; and Formosa, 750–754; his advisers, 755–757; troubles with Congress, 757–758; first summit, 760–762; open-skies plan,

760; atoms for peace, 765–766; and Suez crisis, 770–771; and Lebanon, 772–773; and foreign aid, 776; and Germany, 782; meeting with Khrushchev, 786; good-will trips, 786; and 1960 summit, 786–787

Eisenhower Doctrine, 1957, 771, 772

Elbe River, 101

Elgin, Lord, 256, 258, 322

Elliot, Charles, 201, 202

Elliot, Jonathan, 294

Ellsworth, Oliver, 75

Emancipation Proclamation, 1863, 282

Embargo Act, 1807, 104–106

Empress of China, 223

England (*see* Great Britain)

Entente Cordiale, 438, 445–449

Erskine, David, 107

Escalator clauses, 601, 622

Essex case, 1805, 99

Estonia, 678

Ethiopia, 632–635

Etruria, 84

European Advisory Commission, 1943, 690

European Community of Atomic Energy (Euratom), 765–766

European Defense Community, 1952, 780

European Recovery Program (ERP), 1948, 723–724

Evarts, William, 334, 336

Everett, Edward, 192, 227, 244

Exclusion: Chinese, 333–335; Japanese, 448–455, 577–579

Expatriation, 264

Export-Import Bank, 1934, 624, 630, 718, 776

Extraterritoriality, 229

Fabens, James, 295, 297, 298

Falaba sinking, 1915, 519–520

Fallen Timbers, Battle of, 1794, 61

Family Compact, 10, 47, 65

Far East: early nineteenth century interest, 223–231; after Civil War, 331–335; during Spanish-American War, 394–398; and Open Door, 405–414; Russo-Japanese conflict, 439–445; immigration problems, 448–455; danger in 1920s, 569–573, 609–614; in 1930s, 638–641; in World War II and Yalta, 693–694; postwar problems, 729–754

Far Eastern Commission (1945), 730

Farewell Address, 1796, 68–70, 78

Fauchet, Joseph, 55, 63, 68

Fava, Baron, 349

Federal Republic of Germany (*see* West Germany)

Fenians, 320–321, 326

Ferdinand VII of Spain, 133, 136, 137, 141, 142, 147, 148, 150, 152, 153

Fifteen Cruiser Bill, 1929, 598–599

"Fifty-four forty or fight," 1844, 197, 205

Fighting French, 681, 682

Filibustering, 238–239, 242–244

Fillmore, Millard, 222, 227, 244, 257

Finland: and World War I debts, 608, 619; in World War II, 678, 691; peace treaty, 715

Fish, Hamilton: and expansion, 287; and Dominican Republic, 298; extends Monroe Doctrine, 300; and Danish West Indies, 302–303; and *Alabama* claims, 318, 320; signs Treaty of Washington, 324, 327; and Cuban revolt, 327–329; supports canal, 337; improves State Department, 456

Fisheries, Newfoundland, 20, 127, 128, 169, 257, 322–326, 503–504

Fiske, John, 355

Fiume, 554

Five-Power Treaty, 1922, 574–575

Flag, use of, 517, 519

"Flag-protection doctrine," 98

Florida: acquired by Spain, 8, 18; boundary issue, 29, 31, 39, 66; and Louisiana Purchase, 85, 87, 88; United States acquisition, 131–146, 155

Floridablanca, Conde de, 18, 19

Floyd Bill, 1824, 194

Foch, Ferdinand, 542, 546

Folch, Vizente, 137–138

Fonseca, Gulf of, 486

Food and Agriculture Commission, 1943, 706

Forbes Commission, 1930, 597

Fordney-McCumber tariff, 1922, 605

Foreign Affairs: Committee of, 32; Department of, 1781, 34

Foreign Assistance Act, 1948, 723

Foreign Enlistment Act, 276

Foreign Service, development of, 587

Forey, Elie, 312

Formosa, 232, 688; problem of, 750–754

Forster, William, 265
Forsyth, John, 167, 175, 190, 255
"Fortress America," 756
Fortune magazine, 631, 652
Foster, Augustus J., 113
Foster, John W., 345, 363, 365
Four Freedoms, 659
Four Power Accord, 1938, 643–644
Four-Power Consortium, 1911, 467
Four-Power Treaty, 1921, 575
Fourteen Points, 1918, 544–546, 549, 556
Fox, Charles James, 26, 27, 31, 35, 36, 100
Fox's Blockade, 1806, 101
France: and American Revolution, 6, 8,
    9–17, 22–32; Revolution in, 49–50; Genêt
    affair, 51–58; XYZ and undeclared war,
    67–68, 70–77; and Louisiana, 84–93; Na-
    poleonic war problems, 101–110; and
    Latin-American independence, 152,
    156–157; spoliations claims, 170–172; and
    Civil War, 264–283; Maximilian affair,
    307–316; late nineteenth-century expan-
    sion, 353–354; and Open Door, 406–
    414; and Dominican Republic, 434;
    relations with T. Roosevelt, 437–441,
    445–447; and Haiti, 481; in World War
    I, 509–564; and naval limitation, 567–
    569, 573–576, 597–602; supports Paris
    Pact, 582–586; war debts problem, 603,
    605–608, 619; and economic conference,
    616–619; at Munich, 643–644; in World
    War II, 647; fall, 653–654; divided coun-
    try, 680–685; and German treaty, 716;
    faces communism, 723; and divided
    Germany, 724–726, 783–785; enters
    NATO, 726–727; loses Indochina, 747–
    749; and SEATO, 749; at first summit
    conference, 760–762; on disarmament,
    762–766; and Middle East, 766–774; on
    postwar defense, 780; at 1960 summit,
    786–787
Francis Ferdinand, Archduke, 510
Francis Joseph of Austria, 221, 312
Franco, Francisco, 635–636, 661
Franco-Prussian War, 1870–1871, 324, 331,
    353
Franklin, Benjamin: as diplomat, 4, 5, 9,
    34, 36; mission to France, 14–17; and
    peace treaty, 23–30, 32
Free French, 681
"Free ships, free goods," 14, 76
Frelinghuysen, Frederick, 336, 337, 338,
    340

Frelinghuysen-Zavala Convention, 1884,
    337, 415
Frémont, John C., 209, 210
French Committee on National Libera-
    tion, 685
French and Indian War, 1754–1763, 8
French Revolution, 1789, 49, 149
French West Indies: and American Revo-
    lution, 13, 16; under Rule of 1756, 56;
    and Louisiana Purchase, 88–89, 98, 168;
    in World War II, 682
Frye, William P., 393, 396
Fukien, 414
Fulbright resolution, 1943, 688, 706

Gadsden Purchase, 1853, 253–255
Gallatin, Albert, 79, 118–120, 126, 128,
    130, 163, 168, 170, 194
Gambier, Lord, 119
Gardoqui, Diego de, 41
Garfield, James, 335, 337, 338, 415
Garrison, William Lloyd, 193
Gautier, Manuel, 298
Genêt, Edmond, 51–55, 57, 65
Geneva Conference: 1927, 597–599; 1932,
    620–621; 1955, 760–762, 765; 1958, 764
Geneva Preparatory Commission, 1926,
    597, 599
Geneva Tribunal, 1871–1872, 324–327
Gentleman's agreement, 1907, 448, 451–
    452, 578
George III of England, 4, 18, 25, 31, 109,
    182
George, Walter, 758, 761
George Washington, 81
Gérard, Conrad-Alexandre, 17, 19, 23, 25
Gerard, James, 520
German-Americans, 403–404
German Democratic Republic (*see* East
    Germany)
Germany: early interest in Samoa, 304–
    305; division of Samoa, 358–361, 400;
    and Spanish-American War, 388, 392,
    397, 400; and Open Door, 406–414; and
    Monroe Doctrine, 427–428; Venezuelan
    debt issue, 429–432; relations with
    T. Roosevelt, 437–438, 440–442, 445–447,
    467; peace efforts, 496–500; in World
    War I, 509–564, 566; end of war, 566–
    567; reparations issue, 603–604, 607–608;
    at economic conference, 616–619; and
    Spanish Civil War, 635–636, 642; rise

under Hitler, 641–645; in World War II, 647–699; disarmament, 711; World War II reparations, 713; trial of war criminals, 713–714; division, 724–725; peace contract, 726; post-World War II problems, 783–786

Gerry, Elbridge, 71–73

Ghent, Treaty of, 1814, 117–125

Gibraltar, 18, 22, 24, 29, 31, 79, 661

Gibson, Hugh, 599

Giddings, Joshua, 214

Gila River, 253, 254

Gilbert, Prentiss, 612

Gildersleeve, Virginia, 707

Gilmer letter, 1843, 191

Giraud, Henri, 682, 683, 685

Gladstone, William, 260, 265, 282, 318, 324

Glubb, John B., 772

Godeffray & Son, 304

Godkin, Edwin L., 373

Godoy, Manuel de, 65, 66

Goering, Hermann, 713

Goliad, Massacre at, 1836, 187, 188

Gómez, Máximo, 327, 377

Gomulka, Wladyslaw, 775

Gondra Convention, 1923, 594

Good Neighbor policy: under Coolidge-Hoover, 595–597, 625; under F. D. Roosevelt, 625–631

Good offices, 494

Gore-McLemore resolutions, 1916, 527–529

Goulburn, William, 119, 126

Graf Spee incident, 1939, 648

Gran Chaco War, 1932–1938, 626, 629

Grant, Ulysses S.: efforts to acquire Dominican Republic, 297–300; fails to gain Danish West Indies, 302; interest in Samoa, 304; and Mexico, 315; problems with England, 318, 321, 324, 327; and Cuba, 327–330; and Monroe Doctrine, 300, 339–340; favors canal, 415

Granville, Lord, 324, 336

Graves, William S., 572

Gray, George, 393, 396

Gray, Robert, 128

Great Britain: pre-Revolutionary conflicts, 4–5, 7–8; and American Revolution, 15, 16, 18, 20, 23–32; post-Revolutionary dealings with United States, 35–39; Nootka Sound incident, 47–49; and Jay's Treaty, 58–62; impressment and trade problems, 95–110; War of 1812, 110–125; improved relations with United States, 125–127; and Florida dispute, 143–144; Canning and Monroe Doctrine, 152, 155–162; opens West Indian trade, 166–170; Canadian problems in 1830s, 173–179; Webster-Ashburton agreements, 179–182; Oregon settlement, 193–196, 205–208; early interest in China, 224–226; Central American issues, 232–233, 235–238; mid-nineteenth-century disputes with United States, 256–262; and Civil War, 264–283; interest in Samoa, 304–305; Mexican intervention, 307–311; post-Civil War controversies with United States, 316–327; Sackville-West incident, 340–342; sealing dispute, 342–346; expansion at end of nineteenth century, 353–354; division of Samoa, 358–361, 400; Venezuela boundary dispute, 368–375; and Spanish-American War, 388–393; and Philippines, 395; relations with John Hay, 402–405; Open Door policy, 405–414; and Panama Canal, 415–419; naval policy, 427–428; Venezuelan debts, 429–432; relations with T. Roosevelt, 437–439, 441, 445–447; and Far East, 466–467, 570; tolls issue, 472–474; and Mexico, 477; supports arbitration, 494–500; Alaska boundary, 500–503; in World War I, 509–564; naval limitation, 567–569, 573–576, 597–602, 621–622; supports Paris Pact, 586; rift with United States, 597–599; and war debts, 603, 607–608, 619; economic conference, 616–619; trade relations, 625; at Munich, 643–644; in World War II, 647–699; at UN conference, 706–709; at Potsdam, 710–713; post-World War II treaties, 714–717; opposes communism, 722–723; division of Germany, 724–726; and NATO, 726–727; in Korean conflict, 738–746; supports SEATO, 749; at first summit meeting, 760–762; and disarmament, 763–766; in Middle East, 766–774; recent German problems, 783–785; and 1960 summit, 786–787

Great Depression, 588, 607

Great Lakes, 25, 29, 37, 116, 120, 122, 126, 181, 258

Great War for the Empire, 1754–1763, 8

Greater East Asia Co-Prosperity Sphere (*see* New Order)

Greece: independence, 159; in World
    War II, 646, 660, 662; post-World War
    II problems, 714, 720–721
Greeley, Horace, 193, 251
Greenland, 664–665
Greenville, Treaty of, 1795, 61
Greer incident, 1941, 668
Grenville, Lord, 27, 100
Grenville, Thomas, 27
Gresham, Walter Q., 345, 366, 367, 369
Grew, Joseph C., 641, 671, 676
Grey, Sir Edward, 466, 517, 525–526
Greytown, 235
Grier, Robert G., 274
Grimaldi, Jeronimo, 12
Gromyko, Andrei, 759
Grotius, Hugo, 493
Grundy, Felix, 111
Guam, 393, 397, 577
Guatemala, 233, 235, 237, 338, 459, 779
Gulflight incident, 1915, 519
Gullón, Pió, 382, 384
Gwin, William, 254, 288

Hague Conference: 1899, 496–497; 1907,
    436, 460, 498–500
Hague Court: in Venezuelan debts, 432,
    433, 497; established, 496–497; in Pious
    Fund, 497; and Newfoundland fisheries,
    504; and Knox treaties, 505
Hailie Selassie, 632
Haiti: in American Revolution, 13; inde-
    pendence, 162–164; attacks Dominican
    Republic, 293, 295, 297; and Monroe
    Doctrine, 340; and Wilson, 481–485;
    and Hoover, 597; and F. D. Roosevelt,
    627
Haldimand, Frederick, 38
Hale, Eugene, 453
Hamet Karamanli, 82–83
Hamilton, Alexander: favors England, 47;
    on Nootka Sound incident, 48–49; and
    neutrality, 50–57; supports Jay's Treaty,
    58–61; and Farewell Address, 69; fac-
    tional disputes, 70–71; troubles with
    France, 74, 76, 83; on Louisiana Pur-
    chase, 87
Hammond, George, 48, 49, 53, 58
Hanihara, Masanao, 579
Hanna, Mark, 381, 420

Harding, Warren G.: and Versailles, 562;
    and League, 562–566; and naval limita-
    tion, 568, 673; and World Court, 580
Harriman, Averell, 692
Harriman, Edward H., 465–466
Harris, Townsend, 228
Harrison, Benjamin: and Bering seals is-
    sue, 343; Chilean complications, 347–
    348; favors imperialism, 353; on annexa-
    tion of Hawaii, 361, 365; and Philip-
    pines, 396
Harrison, William Henry: at Tippecanoe,
    111; and McLeod affair, 175–176; as
    President, 182, 190
Hartford Convention, 1814, 116
Hartley, David, 36
Hartmont and Company, 297
Havana: sinking at, 385–386; Act of, 1940,
    654, 664
Havana Conference, 1940, 654, 664
Hawaii: early interest in, 223, 231–232;
    during Grant administration, 303; re-
    volt in, 361–368; annexation, 398–400;
    in World War II, 674
Hay, John: Ambassador to London, 393;
    relations with England, 401–405; and
    Open Door, 405–414; canal diplomacy,
    416–427, 456; and arbitration, 497–498;
    and Alaska, 500–503
Hay Act, 1916, 531
Hay Arbitration Treaties, 1904, 497–498
Hay-Bunau-Varilla Treaty, 1903, 426
Hay-Herrán Treaty, 1903, 422
Hay-Pauncefote Treaty, first, 1900, 417–
    418; second, 1901, 418–419
Hayes, Rutherford B.: and Samoa, 305;
    on Chinese immigration, 334, 335; and
    canal, 336, 339, 415
Hearst, William Randolph, 378, 384, 479,
    495, 582, 620
Helms, C. J., 266
Hennessy, David, 348
Henry Papers, 114
Hepburn Bill, 1902, 420
Herbert, Sir Michael, 438, 501–502
Herrán, Tomás, 422–423
Herrera, José, 202, 212–213
Herriot, Édouard, 617
Herter, Christian, 785
Hertz, Henry, 260
Hindenburg, Paul von, 606
Hippisley, Alfred E., 409–411

Hirohito, Emperor, of Japan, 674, 699, 730–731
Hiroshima, 699, 701
Hirota, Koki, 638, 639, 641
Hise, Elijah, 235
Hitler, Adolf: control of Germany, 615, 620; aggression, 641–647; and World War II, 647, 651, 653, 656, 661, 662, 665, 687, 691; death, 698
Ho-Chi-Minh, 748
Hoar, George F., 396, 397, 495
Hoffman, Paul G., 723
Holland (see Netherlands)
Holliben, Theodor von, 404, 429, 432
Holmes, David, 137, 138
Holy Alliance, 152–154, 158, 160
Honduras, 233, 235; and dollar diplomacy, 459, 462
Hongkong, 224, 406
Hoover, Herbert: and Versailles, 562; and World Court, 582, 589; background, 588–589; and Nicaragua, 594; and Good Neighbor, 595–597; and Haiti, 597; and naval limitation, 599–602; and foreign trade, 605; and moratorium, 605–607; and war debts, 607–609; and Manchuria, 613–614; and London Economic Conference, 617
Hopkins, Harry, 693, 698, 709
Hopkinson, Joseph, 74
Hortalez, Roderigue, & Co., 12, 13
Hotze, Henry, 266
House, Edward M.: and Pan-American Pact, 507; and World War I, 524–526, 532; and peace, 546, 547, 549
House-Grey Memorandum, 1916, 525–526, 530
Houston, Sam, 187, 188, 191, 192, 201, 202
Howe, Joseph, 260
Howe, William, 15
Hudson's Bay Company, 59, 194, 195, 207, 208, 288
Huerta, Victoriano, 475–478
Hughes, Charles Evans: in 1916, 532; and League, 553, 562, 566–567; and naval limitation, 567–577; and Japanese immigration, 579; and World Court, 579–581; and Mexico, 590–591; and reparations, 603; and investments, 604–605; and UN, 706
Hukuang Railroad, 467
Hull, Cordell: and recognition of Russia,

623; and trade, 624–625, 627; and Good Neighbor, 625–631; and Italo-Ethiopian War, 633; and Ludlow Amendment, 637; and Japan, 638, 639; and Hitler, 642, 646; and World War II, 669, 671–676, 678; and France, 681, 687, 688; retires, 693, 698; and UN, 706
Hull, William, 38
Hull Trade Agreement Act, 1934, 624–625, 627
Hülsemann, J. C., 223
Humbert, Prince, of Italy, 691
Humphrey, George, 757
Hungary: in mid-1800s, 221–223, 243; World War I treaty, 567; in World War II, 689; treaty, 715; post-World War II, 719; revolt, 769–770, 775
Hunt, Memucan, 189–190
"Hunters' Lodges," 174
Hurley, Patrick, 732, 733
Hussein, King, of Jordan, 773
Hydrogen bomb, 702

Iceland, 665, 668
Immigration control: Chinese, 333–335; in Hawaii, 362, 398; Japanese, 448–452, 577–579
Imperialism, 351–400
Impressment issue, 60, 95–101, 103–105, 110, 126
Independence, United States, 3
India, 223, 281; post-World War II problems, 746, 749–750, 766; and Tibet, 753
Indians, 37, 38, 55, 56, 59, 61, 94, 110–112, 121, 139, 141
Indochina, and World War II, 670, 672, 674; post-World War II strife, 727, 747–749
Indonesia, 719, 749
Industrialism, 354–355
Ingraham, David, 223
Inness, Harry, 64
Inter-American Conference for the Maintenance of Peace, 1936, 629
Inter-American Conferences: Mexico City, 1945, 728; Bogotá, 1948, 728
Intercontinental ballistic missiles (ICBM), 703, 782
Intermediate range ballistic missiles (IRBM), 782

International Atomic Development Authority, 1948, 759–760
International Atomic Energy Agency (IAEA), 1957, 765
International Bank for Reconstruction and Development, 1944, 718, 776
International Bureau of American Republics, 1890, 339
International Central American Bureau, 1907, 460
International Conference on the Peaceful Uses of the Atom, 1955, 765
International Monetary Fund, 1944, 718
Investments, foreign, 604–605
Iran, 679, 709–710, 767
Iraq, 767, 772–774
Ireland: in World War I, 530; and Versailles, 558, 560
Irish-Americans, 403–404, 495, 530, 558
Iron Curtain, 719, 764
Irreconcilables, 557–564, 566, 576
Isabella of Spain, 246, 248
Ishii, Kikujiro, 570
Isolationism: as American policy, 2; in World War I, 512, 527–529, 536–538; in 1920s, 576, 580–582; in 1930s, 619–620, 631–637, 649–650, 656–657; in World War II, 660, 669; post-World War II, 709
Israel, 767; and Suez crises, 768–771
Italo-Ethiopian War, 1935–1936, 586
Italy: at Geneva Tribunal, 325; on Bering seals, 345; Mafia incident, 348–350; Venezuelan debt issue, 429–432; in Triple Alliance, 437; in World War I, 543, 544; and naval limitation, 569, 573, 597, 601; at economic conference, 616–619; Ethiopian War, 632–635; Spanish Civil War, 643–644; in World War II, 685–686, 689; World War II treaty, 714–715; post-World War II problems, 718, 724, 726
Itata incident, 1891, 346
Izzard, Ralph, 33

Jackson, Andrew: as war hawk, 111; Florida campaign, 141–144; and Pan-American Congress, 163; relations with England, 166–170; relations with France, 170–172; and Maine boundary, 178; and Texas, 188, 189, 191, 193, 200, 201; and Mexico, 211
Jackson, Francis James, 107, 108, 125
Jackson, Robert H., 655, 713
Jagou, Gottlieb von, 524
Jameson Raid, 1896, 374
Jamaica, 329; as base, 656
Japan: early interest in, 224, 226–227; Perry mission, 227–228; Harris mission, 229; war with China, 335; Bering sealing, 342, 346; and Hawaii, 365, 398; view on Spanish-American War, 395, 397; immigration issues, 362, 577–578; Open Door, 405–414; war with Russia, 439–445; relations with T. Roosevelt, 448–455; Lodge Corollary, 460–463; Far East problems, 465–468; in World War I, 554, 555, 569–572; naval limitation, 567–569, 573–576, 597–602, 621–622; establishes Manchukuo, 611–614; aggression in 1930s, 638–641; in World War II, 647–699; surrender of, 698–699; trial of war criminals, 714; post-World War II reorganization, 730–731, 733; peace treaty, 746–747
Japanese and Korean Exclusion League, 1905, 448
Jay, John: as Revolutionary diplomat, 6, 18, 25, 27, 29, 32; Secretary of Foreign Affairs, 33; attempted treaty with Spain, 41–42; Chief Justice, 57; treaty with England, 58–62, 97, 167
Jay-Gardoqui Treaty, 1786, 41–42
Jay's Treaty, 1794, 57–62, 68, 72, 101, 117
Jecker claims, 311
Jefferson, Thomas: as peace commissioner, 14, 25; mission to Europe, 34–35, 39; Secretary of State, 46–47; Nootka Sound incident, 47–49; and French Revolution, 49–51, 71; Genêt affair, 51–55; Tripolitan War, 78–83; Louisiana Purchase, 83–93; impressment and neutral trade, 94–106; desire for Florida, 134; and Latin America, 148; and Monroe Doctrine, 157–158, 240
Jena, Battle of, 1806, 95
Jímenez, Juan Y., 485
Jodl, Gustav, 698
Johnson, Andrew: as expansionist, 287, 290, 340; Alaskan purchase, 291–292; and Dominican Republic, 297; and

Mexico, 315; differences with England, 317–318, 320–321

Johnson, Hiram: and League, 557, 558, 562; and naval limitation, 576; and immigration, 578–579; and World Court, 580, 620; and war debts, 608, 618–620; and UN, 709

Johnson, Hugh, 657

Johnson, Sir John, 38

Johnson, Reverdy, 318–320

Johnson-Clarendon Convention, 1869, 318–319, 324

Johnson Debt Default Act, 1934, 608, 619–620, 632

Johnson Immigration Act, 1924, 578–579

"Johnston, Mary," 12

Jones, Anson, 201, 202

Jones, Thomas A. C., 209

Jordan, 772, 773, 774

Juan de Fuca Strait, 194, 195, 208

Juárez, Benito, 255, 307, 309, 314, 316

Judd, Walter, 735

Jung, Guido, 617

Jusserand, Jean Jules, 438, 446–447, 505

Kalakaua, 362

Kalinin, Mikhail, 623

Kansas-Nebraska Act, 1854, 240–248, 254, 258

Kassim, Abdul Karim el, 772, 774

Kato, Baron, 573, 574

Katsura, Taro, 444–445

Kearney, Denis, 333

Kearny, Lawrence, 231

Kearny, Stephen, 215

Kearny attacked, 1941, 668–669

Keith, Minor, 459

Kellogg, Frank B.: and World Court, 581; and outlawry of war, 584–586; and Mexico, 591–592; and Nicaragua, 593; and naval limitation, 598–599; and China, 609–610

Kellogg-Briand Pact (see Paris Pact)

Kennan, George F., 719–720, 783

Kentucky, 40, 42, 51, 63, 66

Khrushchev, Nikita, 761

Kiaochow, 569

King, William R., 236

King Cotton, 268, 280–281

Knowland, William, 745, 755

Knox, Frank, 650, 653

Knox, Henry, 53

Knox, Philander: as Secretary of State, 458–469; and peace, 505, 561

Knox Arbitration Treaties, 1911, 505

Knox Resolution, 1920–1921, 561, 566–567

Kolchak, Admiral, 572

Konoye, Prince, 663, 669, 671, 672

Korea: claimed by Japan, 405, 439; and Agreed Memorandum, 444–445, 455; in World War II, 688–689; division after World War II, 736–738; conflict, 738–746

Kossuth, Louis, 221–222, 245

Koszta, Martin, 222–223

Kowloon, 406, 411

Kruger telegram, 1896, 374

Kuomintang, 609–610, 732–736

Kurile Islands, 228, 290, 693

Kurusu, Saburo, 672–674, 676

Kuwait, 766

Kwangchow, 406

La Petite Democrate incident, 1793, 54

Labrador, 30, 127, 128

Ladrone Islands, 393

Lafayette, Marquis de, 15, 49, 171

La Follette, Robert, Sr., 538–540

La Follette, Robert, Jr., 637

Laird rams, 278–279

Lake of the Woods, 29, 60, 62, 125, 127, 129, 181

La Luzerne, Chevalier, 25, 33

Lansing, Robert: Secretary of State, 471; and Caribbean, 479, 485; World War I, 521–522, 526–527, 529, 536, 538; and peace, 547

Lansing-Ishii Agreement, 1917, 570

Laos, 748, 749

Larkin, Thomas O., 209–210

Latin America: question of recognition, 147–154; Monroe Doctrine, 157–162; and Panama Congress, 162–165; mid-nineteenth century issues, 232–239; and Pan-Americanism, 335–340; Chilean problems, 346–348; Venezuelan boundary, 368–375; canal diplomacy, 415–436; dollar diplomacy, 458–463; and Hague Conference, 499–500; in 1920s, 590–594; improved United States relations, 594–

597; and F. D. Roosevelt, 625–631; in World War II, 644, 648, 654; and UN, 727; forms OAS, 728; Communist threat, 778–779

Latvia, 678

Laurens, Henry, 20, 25, 27

Laurier, Sir Wilfrid, 465, 500

Lausanne Conference, 1932, 608, 616

Laval, Pierre, 607, 680, 681

League to Enforce Peace, 543–544, 560

League of Nations: established, 543–545, 547–564; and World Court, 581–582; and Far East, 611–614, 638; and Germany, 642

Leahey, William D., 661, 698

Lear, Tobias, 82–83

Lebanon, 772–774

Leclerc, Charles, 89

Lee, Lord, 568

Lee, Arthur, 6, 7, 9, 11, 12, 33

Lee, Fitzhugh, 383, 385

Lee, Richard Henry, 4, 32

Lee, Robert E., 242, 285

Lee, William, 33

Lend-Lease: 1941, 658–660, 662, 664; terminated, 718

Leo XIII, Pope, 389

Leopard incident, 1807, 103–104

Lerdo, Miguel, 307

Letters of a Farmer in Pennsylvania, 6

Letters of marque, 45, 264, 269, 274

Levinson, Salmon O., 583–584

Lewis and Clark Expedition, 1803–1806, 92, 128

Lhuys, Drouyn de, 279

Liaotung Peninsula, 406, 410, 442

Libya, 661, 662, 679, 680, 682

Lilienthal, David, 759

Liliuokalani, 362–368

Limestone Ridge, Battle of, 1866, 321

Lincoln, Abraham: and Civil War, 263–264, 267; on Trent affair, 271; announces blockade, 273; Emancipation Proclamation, 272; and Dominican Republic, 294; opposes Mexican intervention, 309–310, 313

Lind, John, 476

Lindbergh, Charles, 584, 592, 650, 656, 660

Linn, Lewis F., 195

Lithuania, 678

Little Belt incident, 1811, 113

"Little England," 353

Little Sarah incident, 1793, 54

Litvinov, Maksim, 611, 623, 677

Liverpool, Lord, 124

Livingston, Edward, 167, 171

Livingston, Leonidas, 371

Livingston, Robert R.: Secretary of Foreign Affairs, 33; and Louisiana Purchase, 85, 88, 90–92, 134

Lloyd George, David: World War I, 533; and peace, 544, 549, 554–555; and navy, 568

Loans: in Revolution, 12, 13, 20; in World War I, 514–515, 541–542; in World War II, 718

Locarno Treaty, 1925, 585, 642

Lodge, Henry Cabot: supports navy, 357; and Venezuelan boundary, 371–372; imperialist, 400; and England, 408, 443; on Canal, 418–419; and Latin America, 435; and World War I, 540; attitude toward League, 543–544, 547–549, 551–553, 557–564; on naval limitation, 573; and immigration, 579; and World Court, 580, 620

Lodge Corollary, 1912, 351, 463

Lodge reservations, 559–564

Logan, George, 75

London: Convention of, 1861, 310–312; Declaration of, 1909, 499–500, 516–517

London Economic Conference, 1933, 616–619

London Naval Conference: 1908–1909, 499–500; 1930, 599–602; 1935, 621–622

London Poles, 691–692, 695

Long, Breckenridge, 633

Loochoo Islands, 231

López, Narciso, 242–244

Louis XV of France, 10

Louis XVI of France, 6, 10, 11, 13, 17, 18, 31, 49, 51, 52

Louis XVIII of France, 72, 170–172

Louis Philippe of France, 201, 293

Louisiana, 8, 47, 51, 65, 76, 83–93, 184

Louisiana Purchase, 1803, 42, 83–93, 112, 121, 125, 127, 133, 135, 170, 286, 301

L'Ouverture, Toussaint, 88–89

Lovell, James, 32

Lowell, James Russell, 318

Lower California, 239, 252, 255

Loyalists of Revolution, 29, 30, 38–40, 173

Lublin Poles, 692, 695

Luce, Henry, 735

Ludlow Amendment, 1937, 637
Lusitania incident, 1915, 520–523
Luxembourg, 726
Lyons, Lord, 272, 274
Lytton Commission, 1932, 614

McAdoo, William G., 513
Macao, 224
MacArthur, Douglas: in World War II, 689, 699; and Japan, 729–731; and Korea, 738–743
McCumber, Porter, 559–560
MacDonald, Ramsay, 599, 601, 606, 617, 620
MacDougal, John, 313
McGillvray, Alexander, 40
Machado, Gerardo, 627–628
Mackenzie, William Lyon, 173, 256
Mackenzie King, W. L., 759
McKinley, William: and Spanish War, 376, 381–397; and Hawaii, 399–400; relations with England, 401–405; and Open Door, 405–414; and peace, 495–496
McKinley Tariff, 1890, 361, 377
McLane, Louis, 167, 169, 171, 207, 456
McLane, Robert, 309
McLeod, Alexander, 175–177, 350
McLoughlin, John, 194, 195
Macmillan, Harold, 773, 784, 786
Macon, Nathaniel, 108, 113
Macon's Bill No. 2, 1810, 108
Madero, Francisco, 475
Madison, James: and Nootka affair, 48; on neutrality, 50; XYZ affair, 71; and Louisiana, 85; on impressment, 97, 99; dealings with England and France, 104, 106–113; war with England, 113–125; acquires West Florida, 136–138; and Latin America, 149; on Monroe Doctrine, 158
Madriz, José, 461
Maffitt, J. N., 276
Mafia, 348
Magdalen Islands, 30, 128
Magdalena Bay, 463
Maginot Line, 651
Mahan, Alfred Thayer, 351, 356–358, 394, 403
Mail censoring: in World War I, 517; in World War II, 648

Maine sunk, 1898, 385–387
Maine boundary problem, 116, 122, 177–179, 200
Malaya, 670–674, 676
Malenkov, Georgi, 761
Malietoa, 358–359
Malta, 89
Manchukuo, 614
Manchuria, 406, 439–443, 455; and dollar diplomacy, 465–468; troubles in 1920s and 1930s, 569, 576, 610, 612–614; in World War II, 688, 693, 699; postwar, 733
Mandates, World War I, 550
Manifest destiny, 199–219, 286–306, 352, 394
Manila, Battle of, 1898, 394–395, 399
Mann, A. Dudley, 221, 268, 272
Mao Tse-tung, 732–736
Marbois, François de, 89–90
Marburg, Theodore, 504
Marco Polo Bridge incident, 1937, 639
Marcy, William L.: and Hawaii, 231; fails to gain Cuba, 246–252; Canadian treaty, 257–258, 322; disputes with England, 254–260; and Declaration of Paris, 273; desires Alaska, 288–289; and Hawaii, 303
Mare clausum, 342, 343
Marroquin, José, 421–424
Marshall, George C.: in World War II, 653, 679, 680, 685, 698, 717; and plan, 721–724; and China, 733–734
Marshall, John, 71–73
Marshall Plan, 1947, 721–724
Martí, José, 377
Martinique, 13, 682
Mason, James M., 270–272, 274, 281
Mason, John Y., 249
Massive retaliation, 755
Mataafa, 359
Mathews, George, 139, 140, 143
Matsu Island, 750–754
Matsuoka, Yosuke, 663, 669, 670
Matta letter, 1891, 347
Max of Baden, 545
Maximilian, 306, 311–316, 339
Mayo, Henry T., 477
Meade, R. W., 304, 305
Mediation, definition of, 494
"Meiji Restoration," 1867, 229
Mellon, Andrew W., 566

Mena, Luis, 462
Mendès-France, Pierre, 748
Mendieta, Carlos, 628
Mercantilism, 34
Mercier, Henri, 266, 275, 283
Merry, Anthony, 96, 98
Metcalf, Victor, 450, 451
Metternich, Prince, 160
Mexican War, 1846–1848, 210–219, 234, 259
Mexico: independence, 144, 148, 151–152; problem of Texas, 183–193, 201–203; problem of California, 208–210; war with United States, 210–219; and William Walker, 252; Gadsden Purchase, 253–255; Maximilian affair, 306–316; and Central America, 459–460; Magdalena Bay, 463; and Wilson, 474–481; Pious Fund, 497; oil issue, 1920s, 590–592; 1930s, 630–631; and Monroe Doctrine, 596
Middle East, 353, 720; recent problems, 766–774
Middle East Treaty Organization (METO), 1955, 767
Midway Islands, 293, 303, 305
Mikolajczuk, Stanislaw, 691
Milan Decree, 1807, 102, 110, 115
Militia diplomats, 33
Mills Bill, 1888, 361
Minorca, 31
Miquelon, 31
Miramar, Convention of, 1864, 314
Missionaries, 351–352, 395–397, 670, 766
Mississippi River, 3, 8, 19, 23, 24, 27, 29, 39, 40–42, 60, 64–66, 83–93, 124, 127, 131
Mitchell, D. B., 141
Mobile Act, 1804, 134
Mobile Doctrine, 1913, 471–478
Mole St. Nicholas, 481
Molotov, Vyacheslav, 680, 687, 707, 711, 714, 716
Mon, Alexander, 367
Moncada, José, 593
Monroe, James: mission to France, 67–68; Louisiana Purchase, 87–88, 90–92; on neutral trade, 99; War of 1812, 113, 117, 118, 121, 125; improved relations with England, 126–130; acquires East Florida, 138–146; and Latin America, 149, 151; announces his doctrine, 157–162; and West Indian trade, 167

Monroe Doctrine: background, 152–157; promulgated, 157–162; and Oregon, 194; Polk corollary, 204–205, 234, 252; Grant's version, 299–300; and French in Mexico, 306, 309, 312–314, 316; and Canada, 322; and Cuba, 330; post-Civil War broadening, 339–340; Pacific extension, 359; Venezuela boundary, 369–375; Venezuelan debts, 429–432; Roosevelt corollary, 433–436, 595–596; and League, 548, 553, 559; Clark Memorandum, 596–597; becomes mutilateral, 629–630
Monterey, 209, 210, 217
Montgomery, Bernard, 690
Montreux Convention, 1936, 720
Montt, Jorge, 348
Moore, John Bassett, 424, 580
Morales, Carlos, 434
Morales, Juan, 86
Moratorium, 1931, 605–607
Morgan, J. P., 466; and World War I, 514–515
Morgan, John T., 303, 379, 417
Morgenthau Plan, 1944, 694
Morocco: and pirates, 35, 79–83; and Algeciras Conference, 445–447; in World War II, 682–685; after World War II, 766
Morris, Gouverneur, 48, 67
Morris, Roger, 4
Morrison, Charles C., 583
Morrow, Dwight, 592
Moscow Conference: 1943, 687, 690, 706; 1947, 716–717
Moses-Linthicum Act, 1931, 587
Mosquito Coast, 233–239
Most favored nation clause, 228, 332, 410
Motley, John Lothrop, 319, 320
Moultrie, William, 53
Munich Agreement, 1938, 643–644
Munitions Investigating Committee, 1934, 631–633
Murchison letter, 1888, 341–342
Murmansk, 648, 679
Murphy, Robert, 661, 681, 683
Murray, William Vans, 75
Muscat, 223
Mussolini, Benito: domination of Italy, 615, 620; and Ethiopian War, 632–635; at Munich, 643–644; World War II, 653, 661, 685

Mutual Defense Assistance Program, 1949, 727, 776

Naboth's Vineyard, 299
Nagasaki, 226, 227, 699, 701
Napoleon Bonaparte: gains power, 71; and undeclared war, 75–77; sells Louisiana, 83–95, 133; troubles with United States, 101–110; and Florida issue, 135, 136; intervention in Spain, 147–148
Napoleon III of France: and Civil War, 265, 266, 269, 275, 279, 283; intervention in Mexico, 308–316
Nashville, 425–426
Nasser, Abdul Gamel: and Suez crisis, 768–771; and United Arab Republic, 772, 774
National City Bank, 466, 481, 627
National Security Council, 777–778
Nationalist China: and Kuomintang, 609–613; and Yalta, 693–694; struggle with Communists, 731–736; and Formosa, 750–754
Naturalization issue, 96–97
Naval Construction Act, 1916, 531, 567
Naval limitation: background, 567–573; Washington Conference, 573–577; Geneva, 597–598; London, 1930, 599–602; London, 1935, 621–622
Navigation Acts, English, 35, 105, 167, 168, 257
Navy: and Barbary pirates, 35, 79–82; undeclared war with France, 74; *Chesapeake* incident, 103–104, 113; in 1812, 116, 120–121; and Rush-Bagot, 125–127; and California, 209; in Mexican War, 215; Perry mission, 227–228; mid-nineteenth century in Pacific, 230–232; in Civil War, 270–276; and post-Civil War bases, 286–305; and sealing controversy, 342–346; *Baltimore*, 346–348; birth of modern navy, 356–358; and Samoa, 360–361; and Hawaii, 364, 366; and Spanish War, 385–387, 393–395; and Far East, 414; and Panama Canal, 415–428; and Venezuelan debts, 430–432; demonstration in 1907, 452–454; and Mexico, 477–478; Caribbean interventions, 481–488; in World War I, 541; limitations, 567–577, 597–602, 621–622; *Panay* incident, 641; neutrality patrol, 648, 663–665; destroyer deal, 654–656; shooting war, 1941, 667–669; Pearl Harbor attack, 674–676; World War II, 682–683, 689, 699; Korean conflict, 738–739; and Formosa, 750–753; and Middle East, 771–777
Navy Island, 173
Nehru, Jawaharlal, 749
Netherlands: and American Revolution, 19–20, 22, 24, 26; treaty with United States, 60; and early Japan, 226, 228, 229; on continuous voyage, 276; economic conference, 618; in World War II, 652, 662, 663, 670–672, 674; after World War II, 726, 765
Netherlands East Indies, 7, 223; and World War II, 662, 663, 666, 670–672, 674
Neutral Nations Supervisory Commission, 1953, 745
Neutral rights: in Plan of 1776, 14; and Armed Neutrality, 21; in commercial treaties, 34; and Napoleonic wars, 56–60, 67; under Jefferson and Madison, 94–110; in World War I, 515–539; in World War II, 634
Neutrality: in Napoleonic wars, 50–51, 53–54, 94–110; in Latin-American wars, 150; and Civil War, 268–270; in World War I, 511–534; pre-World War II, 633–640; in World War II, 648–650
Neutrality Acts: 1815, 185; 1818, 259–260, 317, 321; 1935, 633–635; January, 1937, 636; May, 1937, 636–637, 639–640; 1939, 648–650; amended, 669
Neutrality proclamations: 1793, 50–51, 53; 1861, 268–270; 1914, 511–512; 1939, 647
Neutrality zone, 1939, 648, 665
New Brunswick, 177–179, 257
New Granada, 233–234
New Mexico, 131, 201, 212, 215, 216, 286
New Order, 639, 663, 670, 674
New Orleans, 8, 40, 55, 64–67, 76, 83–93, 112, 125, 134, 141, 188, 242–244, 348, 349
New Panama Canal Company, 416, 420–425
New Zealand, 739, 749
Newfoundland: as base in World War II, 656; and Atlantic Charter, 666–667 (*See also* Fisheries)
Ngo Dinh Diem, 749
Niagara Falls, 478, 479
Niblack incident, 1941, **668**

Nicaragua: independence, 233; canal interest, 235, 236, 415, 420, 421, 424; and filibusters, 238, 239; rivalries, 337, 351, 369; and dollar diplomacy, 458–462; and Wilson, 486–487; internal strife, 1920s, 592–594; and Hoover, 597
Nicholas II of Russia, 441–442, 496–500
Nicholls, Edward, 141
Nicholls, F. T., 349
Nine-Power Treaty, 1922, 575–576, 612, 613, 639
Nixon, Richard, 778–779, 785
No-transfer doctrine, 240, 340
Nomura, Kichisaburo, 663, 670–674
Non-Importation Act, 1806, 100, 104, 107
Non-Intercourse Act, 1809, 107–109
Nootka Sound incident, 1789–1790, 47–49, 64, 128
Norris, George, 538, 540
Norris, Kathleen, 657
North, Lord, 16, 31, 36
North Africa campaigns in World War II, 661–662, 679, 680, 682–685
North Atlantic Treaty Organization (NATO) 1949, 726–727, 762, 763, 780–784
North West Company, 128, 194
Northeast boundary, 177, 181
Northwest posts, 38, 47, 48, 59, 61, 111
Northwest Territory, 28, 49, 55–56, 61–62, 110, 122, 127, 129
Norway, 226, 651–652, 679
Nova Scotia, 24, 30, 36, 108, 257, 260
Nuclear efforts, 782
Nueces River, 212, 214, 217
Nuremberg trials, 713–714
Nur as-Said, 772
Nye, Gerald, 631, 657
Nye Committee, 1934, 631–633

Obregón, Alvaro, 479–480, 590
Ochs, Adolph, 568
Office of Strategic Services (OSS), 778
Offshore islands, 750–754
Oil problem: in Mexico, 590–592, 630–631; in Middle East, 766
Olney, Richard: and Hawaii, 366; and Venezuela, 369–371, 374–375; against colonialism, 396; and Britain, 416; and arbitration, 494–496
Olney Doctrine, 1895, 369–372

O'Mahony, John, 321
One World, 1943, 705
Onís, Luis de, 141–146
Open Door policy: tradition, 2; foundations, 225; and other countries, 351, 389; and John Hay, 405–414; and T. Roosevelt, 440, 454–455; and William H. Taft, 465–468; and Nine-Power Treaty, 1922, 575; and Manchuria, 612; and World War II, 670
"Open-skies" plan, 1955, 762–765
Opium war, 1839–1842, 224–225
Oppenheimer, J. Robert, 759
Oran, 682
Orders in Council, English, 56, 102, 104
Oregon: rival claims to, 128–129, 144, 183; growing American interest in, 193–198, 201, 354; Polk's policy toward, 203–208, 213; results of annexation, 227, 264, 288; dispute over Puget Sound, 323–324, 326
Oregon, 415
Organization of American States (OAS), 1948, 728, 776
Orlando, Vittorio, 549, 554
Orth, Godlove, 297
Ostend Manifesto, 1854, 249–252
O'Sullivan, John L., 199, 245
Oswald, Richard, 26–27, 32
Outlawry of war, 582–587

Pacific Fur Trading Company, 128
Page, T. Jefferson, 280
Page, Walter Hines, 520
Pago Pago, 304–305, 360, 400
Paine, Thomas, 9
Pakenham, Richard, 192, 203–204, 207–208
Pakistan, 749–750
Palma, Tomas Estrada, 429
Palmerston, Lord: and Caroline affair, 175–176; and "red-line" map, 179, 182; and Central America, 236–237; and Crimean War, 260; and Civil War, 265, 275
Panama: Congress plan, 162; proposed canal through, 234, 236, 253; French canal project, 336; United States protectorate over, 351, 628; revolution in, 424–427; Declaration of, 1939, 648, 664
Panama Canal: proposed, 234, 236, 253; United States negotiations with Great Britain, 236–238, 415–419; route selected,

419–421; negotiations with Colombia, 421–425, 474; negotiations with Panama, 425–427; influence on United States foreign policy, 427–436, 459–463, 486–487; tolls issue, 472–474; and Good Neighbor policy, 628

Panama Conference, 1939, 648

Panama Congress, 1826, 162–165, 232

Panama Tolls Act, 1912, 472–474

Pan-American Conferences: Washington, 1889–1890, 338–339; Rio de Janeiro, 1906, 435–436; Santiago, 1923, 594; Havana, 1928, 594–595, 626; Montevideo, 1933, 626–627, 644; Buenos Aires, 1936, 629–630; Lima, 1938, 644; Panama, 1939, 648; Havana, 1940, 654; Mexico City, 1945, 728; Bogotá, 1948, 728

Pan-American Union, 339, 625

Pan-Americanism, 335–339, 348

Panay incident, 1937, 641

Panmunjom, 745

Panton, William, 40

Papen, Franz von, 518

Papineau, Louis, 173

Paraguay, 626, 629

Paredes, Mariano, 213

Paris, Declaration of, 1856, 269, 273, 516

Paris, Treaty of: 1763, 8, 10; 1783, 31–32, 37–39, 60–62; 1898, 393–398

Paris Pact: 1928, 582–587, 594; and Far East, 610–614, 638, 640; and Latin America, 626; and war criminals, 713

Paris Peace Conference, 1919, 547–556

Parker, Peter, 232

Pauncefote, Sir Julian: and American offer, 345; and Spanish-American War, 390–392; and China, 408; and canal treaties, 416–420; death, 1902, 438; and arbitration, 494–496

Payne-Aldrich tariff, 1909, 464

Peace movement, 492–508

"Peace without victory," 533, 543

Peaceable coercion, 104–110

Pearl Harbor, 414, 674–677

Peel, Sir Robert, 207

Peking, 226, 332, 412, 609–610

Peña y Peña, Manuel de la, 217

Peninsular War, 1808–1813, 147

People's Republic of China (*see* Communist China)

Perdido River, 134–135, 138, 141, 146

Permanent Court of International Justice (*see* World Court)

Perón, Juan, 728, 779

Perry, Matthew C., 227–228, 232, 257

Perry, Oliver H., 116, 121

Pershing, John J., 479–480, 542, 546

Persia sunk, 1915, 526

Peru, 151–152, 162, 280; and War of the Pacific, 337–338; and Hoover, 596

Pescadores Islands, 688, 750

Pétain, Marshal Henri, 661, 680–681

Peterhoff case, 1863, 276

Petrel case, 1861, 274

Phelps, Edward, 341, 343

Philadelphia, 82

Philippines: and Spain, 7, 352; United States annexation, 392–398; Japan and, 444–445, 577; in World War II, 673–674, 689; independence, 718; and SEATO, 749

"Phony war," 1939–1940, 650

Pichon, Louis, 85, 88

Pickering, Timothy, 63, 70, 105

Pierce, Franklin K.: expansionist policy, 220, 240; and Hawaii, 231; and Cuba, 244–252; and Mexico, 253–255; and Canada, 257–259

Pinckney, Charles Cotesworth, 68, 70–73, 135

Pinckney, Thomas, 48, 63, 141

Pinckney Treaty, 1795, 63, 65–67

Pinkney, William, 100, 107, 109

Pious Fund, 497

Piracy, 79–83, 344

Pitt, William, 35–36, 100

Pius XII, Pope, 651

Plan of 1776, 14, 21, 34

Platt Amendment, 1903, 428, 595, 628

Poinsett, Joel, 164, 185

Point Four Program, 1949, 775–776

Poland: attacked by Germany, 645–647; in World War II, 689, 691–692; and Yalta, 694–695; and UN, 707; after World War II, 711–712, 719, 775

Polignac, Count Jules de, 157

Polk, James K.: elected President, 196–199; Oregon policy, 203–208; reasserts Monroe Doctrine, 204–205; and Mexico, 211–219; and Central America, 234–235; and Cuba, 242, 246; and Canada, 257; and Alaska, 288

Polk Doctrine, 1845, 205

Polly case, 1802, 99
Pompadour, Madame de, 9–10
Port Arthur, 406, 442, 693
Portsmouth, Treaty of, 1905, 442–443
Portugal: and Demarcation Line, 7; and Revolutionary War, 14, 21; and Latin American independence, 152, 162; and Far East, 226; and World War II, 665–666
Potsdam Conference, 1945, 710–713
Pozzo di Borgo, Carlo, 153
Preble, Edward, 81
Preparedness; during World War I, 531–532; during World War II, 653–656, 658–660
President, diplomatic powers, 43–45
President incident, 1811, 113
Preston, William, 294–295
Pribilof Islands, 342, 346
Princeton, 192
Privateering: and French Revolution, 51, 53–54, 60, 67; and Napoleon, 115; and Declaration of Paris, 273
Privy Council, 36
Proctor, Redfield, 386–387
Propaganda, World War I, 512–513
Prophet, 111
Provision Order, 1793, 56
Prussia: relations with France and Austria, 10, 50; and Revolutionary War, 21; commercial treaty with, 34, 60; and Napoleon, 95; and arbitration, 211; and Civil War, 271, 280; expansion, 300, 316
Pu Yi, Henry, 614
Puerto Rico, 163–164, 393, 397
Pufendorf, Samuel, 493
Puget Sound, 195, 323
Pujol, Pablo, 295
Pulitzer, Joseph, 373, 378
Pyramid Harbor, 500–501

Quadruple Alliance, 1815, 152–153
Quarantine speech, 1937, 640–641
Quebec Conference: 1943, 686; 1944, 692, 694
Quemoy Island, 750–754
Quisling, Vidkun, 652

Raasloff, Waldemar, 300–302
Radford, Arthur, 748
"Raleigh Letter," 1844, 197

Rambouillet Decree, 1810, 109
Randolph, Edmund, 55, 63
Randolph, John, 105, 163
Rapacki, Adam, 783
Rawlins, John, 328
Rayvenal, Gérard, 27
Reciprocity: in West Indies, 169; with Canada, 256–259, 322–323, 465–466; with Hawaii, 303, 361; Hull program for, 624–625, 627
Recognition: Jefferson's policy, 52; of Latin American independence, 147–152; and Civil War, 281–283; and Mexico, 476–481; Stimson Doctrine on, 612–614; of Soviet Union, 622–624; and Communist China, 735–736, 753
Reconcentration in Cuba, 378, 382, 386–388
Red-line map, 179, 182
Reform, War of, 1858–1861, 307
Reid, Whitelaw, 358, 393, 396
Reinsch, Paul, 569
Reparations: World War I, 554, 603–604; World War II, 694–695, 713, 715, 731
Reparations Commission, World War I, 603
Reservations, Versailles Treaty, 557–564
Restoration, War of, 1863–1865, 295
Reuben James sinking, 1941, 668–669
Reynaud, Paul, 680
Reynolds, William, 293
Rhea, John, 137, 143
Rhee, Syngman, 737–745
Rhineland, 554, 642, 689, 716
Rhodes, Cecil, 374
Richards, James P., 771
Ridgway, Matthew, 751
Rio Grande, 135, 144, 187; Texas claims boundary at, 201, 208, 212–214
Rives, William, 170–171
Robbins, Raymond, 583
Robert, Georges, 682
Roberts, Edmund, 223–224, 227
Robertson, Walter F., 745
Robin Moor sinking, 1941, 668
Robinson, Sir Frederick, 126
Rockefeller, John D., Jr., 707
Rockhill, William W., 409–411
Rockingham, Lord, 26–27
Rocky Mountains, 8, 129, 203, 206
Rodgers, John, 82, 113
Rogers Act, 1924, 587
Rome, fall of, 1944, 689

Roosevelt, Franklin D.: and World Court, 582, 620; and war debts, 608; inaugural, 615–616; and London Economic Conference, 616–619; and disarmament, 620–622; and Soviet Union, 622–624; and trade, 624–625; and Latin America, 625–631, 644; and neutrality legislation, 632–636; and Japanese aggression, 638–641, 647; and German aggression, 639–640, 641–647; World War II neutrality policy, 647–650; destroyers-for-bases deal, 654–656; reelected, 1940, 656–657; Lend Lease, 658–660; Atlantic Charter, 666–667; shooting war, 667–669; and France, 680–683; at Casablanca, 683–685; at Cairo, 688; at Teheran, 688–689; at Yalta, 693–697; death, 698

Roosevelt, Theodore: as expansionist, 358, 372; and Spanish-American War, 394, 398; and John Hay, 401–402; and Boer War, 403; canal diplomacy, 417–427, 474; and Venezuelan debt controversy, 429–432; and Europe, 437–439; and Russo-Japanese War, 439–445; and Morocco, 445–447; and Japanese immigration, 448–452; naval demonstration by, 452–454; and China, 454–455; and diplomatic service, 457; and Central America, 479; and arbitration, 497–505; and World War I, 520, 523, 540; and League of Nations, 543, 548

Roosevelt Corollary, 1904–1905, 433–436, 595–596

Root, Elihu: and Roosevelt Corollary, 433–435; and Russo-Japanese War, 440; and San Francisco school law, 450; and Root-Takahira Agreement, 454–456; and State Department, 456; and Latin America, 459–460; and peace movement, 498–499; and Alaska, 502; and Newfoundland, 503–504; and League of Nations, 553, 562; and Naval limitation, 573, 575; and World Court, 579, 581–582

Root-Takahira Agreement, 1908, 454–455
Rose, George, 104–105
Rose, John, 324
Ross, James, 88
Rost, Pierre A., 268
Round Robin, 1919, 552
Rousseau, Jean Jacques, 15
Rousseau, Lovell, 292
Rouvier, Pierre Maurice, 446

Rowcroft, Charles, 260
Rudini, Marquis, 349
Ruhr, 603, 716, 724
Rule of 1756, 14, 56–57, 98–99
Rumania, 646, 689, 691–692, 697, 715
Rush, Richard, 126–128, 144, 149, 155–156, 161
Rush-Bagot Agreement, 1817, 126–127, 144, 155
Russell, Lord John: attitude toward Civil War, 265; recognizes Confederate belligerency, 268–269; and *Trent* affair, 271-272; and blockade, 275; and Confederate cruisers, 277–278, 317; and recognition question, 282; and Danish West Indies, 301; and Mexico, 308, 310
Russell, Jonathan, 117, 119, 120
Russia: and Revolutionary War, 21–24; and War of 1812, 118–119; and Monroe Doctrine, 150, 153–155, 158–160; and Oregon, 193; Asiatic expansion, 226, 228, 353; and Civil War, 271, 283–285; sells Alaska, 287–292; and sealing controversy, 342, 344, 346; and Open Door, 406–414, 455; Russo-Japanese War, 439–443; Taft's policy toward, 465–468; and Hague Conferences, 496–500; during World War I, 538, 542, 544–545, 570; Allied intervention, 555, 572, 576; and China, 609–611; United States recognition of Soviet government, 622–624; and Spanish Civil War, 635–636; in World War II, 647–699; and UN, 706–710; at Potsdam, 710–713; and post-World War II treaties, 714–717; and Germany, 724–726, 783–785; and China, 733; and Korea, 738–746; and Japanese peace treaty, 746–747; and disarmament, 759–760, 762–766; and Geneva Conference, 1955, 761–762; and Middle East, 766–774; and Hungary, 775; and summit conference, 1960, 786–787
Russian-American Company, 154, 288–290
Russian Revolution, 538, 544–545
Russo-Japanese War, 1904–1905, 413, 439–443
Ryan, John A., 650
Ryukyu Islands, 231, 747

Saar, 554
Sabine River, 146, 208
Sabotage: in World War I, 518; in World War II, 664

Sacasa, Juan, 593
Sackville-West, Lionel, 341–342, 404
Sagasta, Praxedes, 382, 387
St. Clair, Arthur, 55
St. Croix Island, 302
St. Croix River, 29, 60–61, 125
St. Eustatius, 19–20
St. John Island, 300–301
St. Lawrence River, 29–31, 180, 258, 326
St. Pierre, 31, 682
St. Thomas, 300–301
Sakhalin Island, 228, 442, 693
Salazar, José María, 162
Saligny, Count de, 202
Salisbury, Lord: and Murchison letter, 341; and sealing controversy, 344; and Samoa, 359; and Venezuela, 371–375; and Spanish-American War, 388–390; and isthmian canal, 418; and arbitration, 495
Salvador, 233
Sam, Vilbrun, 482
Samaná Bay, 294, 297–298, 300
Samsah Bay, 414
San Diego, 208, 217, 346
San Francisco: American interest in, 154, 209, 212, 217; trade, 279, 304; entertains Russian fleet, 284; anti-Chinese demonstrations, 333; Japanese school children, 448–451
San Francisco Conference, 1945, 697, 706–709
San Francisco school law, 1906, 448–451
San Ildefonso, Treaty of, 1800, 76, 84–86, 90, 93, 133–134
San Jacinto, 270
San Jacinto, battle of, 1836, 187–189
San Juan Island, 323, 326
San Lorenzo, Treaty of, 1795, 65–67, 84, 86
Sanders, George, 222
Sandino, Augusto, 593
Santa Anna, Antonio Lopez de, 186–187, 216, 253–255, 306
Santana, Pedro, 293–295
Santo Domingo, 88–89, 241, 311 (See also Dominican Republic)
Sarajevo, 510
Saud, King, 771
Saudi Arabia, 771
Savannah case, 1861, 273
Schacht, Hjalmar, 617

Schanzer, Carlo, 573
Schenck, Robert, 323
Schley, Winfield S., 347
Schofield, John M., 315
Schomburgk line, 368, 371, 375
Schurman, Jacob G., 410
Schurz, Carl, 295, 310, 396
Scott, Sir William, 98–99
Scott, Winfield, 173, 216–217
Scruggs, William L., 369
Sealing controversy, 342–346
Second front problem, 679–680, 684, 688–689
Secret treaties, World War I, 543–544, 554
Secretary of Foreign Affairs, 40–41
Senate, treaty-making power, 44
Serbia, 510
Sergeant, John, 163–164
Serrano, Francisco, 307
Seven Years' War, 1756–1763, 8
Sewall, Harold M., 359
Seward, William: and McLeod affair, 175; visit and search, 262; and Civil War, 266–268, 271–273, 279, 283; and territorial expansion, 286–287; purchase of Alaska, 290–292; and Dominican Republic, 294–297; and Danish West Indies, 300–303; and Maximilian affair, 309–311, 313, 315–316; and China, 331–332, 334; and canal, 336–337
Shanghai, 613
Shantung, 406, 554–555, 569–570, 576
Sheffield, Earl of, 35
Sheffield, James R., 592
Shelburne, Lord, 26–27, 31, 35
Sheridan, Philip, 315
Sherman, John, 372, 382, 407
Shidehara, Baron, 577
Shih-k'ai, Yuan, 569
Shimonoseki, 229
Shooting war, 1941, 664, 667, 669
Short, William, 65
Shotwell, James T., 583–584
Siam, 223, 670, 672–674, 676
Siberia: and Russian expansion, 228, 611; World War I expedition to, 555, 572, 576; in World War II, 670, 672
Sicily, invasion of, 685
Sickles, Daniel, 327, 329
Simon, Sir John, 613
Singapore, 661–662, 670–671

Sino-Japanese War, 1894–1895, 335, 405
Six-Power Consortium, 1912, 468, 471
Slave trade, 129, 181
Slavery issue, 191, 240–256, 261–262
Slidell, John, 212–214, 270–272, 279
Smith, Adam, 35
Smith, J. Somers, 296–297
Smith, Robert, 106–108
Social Darwinism, 355
Sonoma, 210
Soong, T. V., 677
Soulé, Pierre, 244–246, 249–252
South Manchurian Railroad, 611
Southeast Asia: in World War II, 662, 669–671, 674–675; in post-World War II, 747–749
Soviet Union (see Russia)
Spain: colonial empire, 7; and Revolutionary War, 10, 12–13, 17–19; and peace negotiations, 19, 23, 26–29, 31–32; early controversies with, 39–42; Nootka Sound incident, 47–49; Pinckney's Treaty with, 64–67; and Louisiana, 83–93; and Florida, 112, 133–146; and Latin America, 147–162; and Texas, 183–185; and Oregon, 193; and Central America, 232–233; and Cuba to 1860, 241–252; and Mexico, 255, 267, 306–307; and Dominican Republic, 266–267, 293–294; Ten Years' War in Cuba, 327–330; and Cuba during 1890s, 376–381; Spanish-American War, 381–398; Civil War, 1936–1939, 635–636; during World War II, 661, 665; American bases in, 702, 727
Spanish-American War, 1898: origins, 377–392; campaigns, 392; peacemaking after, 392–398; results, 398–405
Spanish Armada, 1588, 7
Spanish Civil War, 1936–1939, 635–636
Spanish Succession, War of, 1702–1713, 18
Sparks, Jared, 179
Spoliation claims, 170–172
Spoliations Commission, 1802. 61–62
Spooner Act, 1902, 421
Spring-Rice, Cecil, 444–445, 517
Springbok case, 1862, 276
Sputnik, 703, 782
Squier, Ephraim G., 235
Stab-in-the-back speech, 1940, 653
Stalin, Joseph: and World War II, 662, 678–680, 686, 691–692; at Yalta, 693–697;

and UN, 709; at Potsdam, 711; and peace treaties, 716, 723; and NATO, 727
Stamp Act, 1765, 10
Stanley, Lord, 317
Stassen, Harold, 707, 762–763
State Department, 5, 46; reorganizations, 456–457, 777
Steinberger, A. B., 304
Stephens, Alexander, 214
Stephens, James, 99
Sternberg, Speck von, 432, 438–440, 445–447
Stettinius, Edward R., Jr., 693, 698, 706
Steuben, Baron von, 15
Stevens, John L., 363–367
Stevenson, Adlai, 771
Stilwell, Joseph, 732
Stimson, Henry L.: early career, 588–590; and Nicaragua, 593; and naval limitation, 601–602; and reparations, 608–609; nonrecognition doctrine, 612–614; and World War II, 650, 653, 658, 675
Stimson Doctrine, 1932, 612–614
Stoeckl, Edouard de, 288–292
Stone, William, 528
Strachey, Henry, 29
Straight, Willard, 485
Strategic Air Command (SAC), 702, 757, 782
Strong, Josiah, 356
Submarine warfare: in World War I, 518–523, 527–530, 534–539; in World War II, 664, 667–669
Sudetenland, 643–644
Suez Canal, 416–417, 661
Suez crisis, 1956, 768–771
Sullivan, James M., 485
Summit Conference: 1955, 760–762; 1960, 786–787
Sumner, Charles: and Alaska, 291; and Dominican treaty, 298–299; and Alabama claims, 317–320, 326; and Cuba, 328
Sun Yat-sen, 609
Sussex pledge, 1916, 529–530, 534–536
Sweden: and Armed Neutrality, 21, 58; commercial treaty with, 34, 60; and arbitration, 345; and Lebanon crisis, 1958, 773
Switzerland, 89, 259, 325, 618
Syria, 766, 772–773

Tachen Islands, 750–754
Tacna-Arica problem, 596
Taft, Robert A., 723, 755
Taft, William Howard: Secretary of
War, 444; President, 457; and dollar
diplomacy, 458–463, 465–469; and Cana-
dian reciprocity, 464–465; and arbitra-
tion, 504–505; and World War I, 543;
and League of Nations, 543–544, 551–
553, 560
Taft-Katsura Memorandum, 1905, 443–
445
Taiwan (see Formosa)
Talleyrand, Charles Maurice de, 71–76,
89, 135
Tamasese, 358–359
Tampico incident, 1914, 477–478
Taney, Roger, 171
Tariffs: and Oregon question, 207; and
Civil War, 283; and Hawaii, 361; and
Cuba, 377; during 1920s, 605; during
1930s, 617, 624–625 (See also Reciproc-
ity)
Taylor, Admiral H. C., 433
Taylor, Myron C., 651
Taylor, Zachary, 214–216, 220–221, 257
Tecumseh, 111
Teheran Conference, 1943, 688, 706
Tehuantepec, 236, 253, 255
Teller Resolution, 1898, 391
Ten Years' War, 1868–1878, 319, 327–330,
376
Tennessee, 40, 42, 60
Texas: and Louisiana Purchase, 133, 135,
144–145; American settlement, 183–185,
354; wins independence, 186–188; pro-
posed annexation, 188–193; annexation
completed, 199–203; disputed boundary
with Mexico, 212–214, 217
Thailand, 749
Théodore, Davilmar, 482
Thornton, Ernest, 321
Thouvenel, Edouard: pro-Confederate
policies, 266, 269, 275, 283; and Trent
affair, 271; and Maximilian affair, 312
Thrasher, Leon, 519
Thurston, Lorrin A., 363
Tibet, 753
Tippecanoe, Battle of, 1811, 111
Tito, 727, 761, 775
Tobago, 31
Tojo, Hideki, 672, 714

Tordesillas, Treaty of, 1494, 7
Torres, Manuel, 152
Townshend Acts, 1767, 6, 10
Trafalgar, Battle of, 1805, 95
Treaty-making power, 44–46
Trent affair, 1861, 270–272
Trescot, William H., 337
Trident Conference, 1943, 685
Trieste, 714
Tripartite Pact, 1941, 669
Tripartite Treaty, 1889, 360–361
Triple Alliance, 438
Tripoli, 35, 79–83
Tripolitan War, 1801–1805, 98–100
Trist, Nicholas, 216–219
Troppau, Congress of, 1821, 153
Truman, Harry S.: becomes President,
697–698; and Potsdam Conference, 710–
713; and peace treaties, 715; and eco-
nomic aid, 723–724; and NATO, 726–
727; and Latin America, 727–728; China
policy, 731–734; and Korea, 736–744;
and atomic energy, 758–759; and Israel,
767; and Point Four program, 775–776
Truman Doctrine, 1947, 720–721
Trusteeships, 718
Tunis, 35, 79–83
Tunisia, 683
Turgot, Marquis de, 11
Turkey, 79, 81, 152; and Hungarian pa-
triots, 222–223; and Crimean War, 259;
and World War I, 510, 550; and World
War II, 660, 662; United States aid to,
720–721; and Middle East defense, 766–
768
Turner, George, 502
Tutuila, 304, 376, 400
Twenty-one Demands, 1915, 569–570, 612
Two Sicilies, Kingdom of, 21
Tyler, John: President, 166, 176; and
Webster-Ashburton Treaty, 180–182;
and Texas, 190–192, 200–203; and Mex-
ico, 210–211; and China, 225; and Ha-
waii, 231

U-2 incident, 1960, 787
Ukraine, 707
Unconditional surrender, 684, 688
Undeclared war with France, 1798–1800,
74–75, 172
Underwood, Oscar, 573

United Arab Republic, 772–774
United Fruit Company, 459
United Nations (military), 677–699
United Nations (political): and Yalta
  Conference, 695–696; background, 705–
  706; San Francisco Conference, 706–
  707; and Korea, 738–746; and atomic
  control, 758–760; and Suez crisis, 768–
  771; and Lebanon-Jordan incident, 773–
  774; and Hungary, 775
United Nations Charter, 1945, 707–710
United Nations Commission on Conven-
  tional Armaments, 1946, 760
United Nations Declaration, 1942, 677–
  678
United Nations Educational, Scientific,
  and Cultural Organization (UNESCO),
  1945, 710
United Nations Relief and Rehabilitation
  Administration (UNRRA), 1943, 706,
  718
United States Information Agency
  (USIA), 778
Uniting for Peace Resolution, 1950, 741
Upshur, Abel, 192
Uruguay, 648

Van Buren, Martin: Secretary of State,
  166–169; President, 171, 211; and Can-
  ada, 173–174, 178; and Texas, 189–190,
  193, 196–197; and Alaska, 288
Vancouver Island, 47, 195, 203, 208, 323
Vandenberg, Arthur, 707, 715–716
Vanderbilt, Cornelius, 238–239
Van Zandt, Isaac, 192
Vattel, Emeric de, 493
Venezia Giulia, 714
Venezuela, 148, 151; boundary dispute,
  368–375, 497; and debts, 429–433
Vera Cruz, 308, 311, 477–478
Vergennes, Count de: and secret-aid pol-
  icy, 6, 10–11, 13; and Franco-American
  alliance, 16–17; and Spain, 18–19; and
  peace negotiations, 24–25, 30–31
Verona, Congress of, 1822, 153
Vichy France, 661, 670, 680–683
Victor Emmanuel III, King of Italy, 685–
  686, 691
Victoria, Queen of England, 271, 391–392
Vienna, Congress of, 1815, 119, 124, 152
Vietminh, 748
Vietnam, war in, 747–749

Villa, Francisco, 478–480
Vincent, Stenio, 627
Virgin Islands purchased, 487 (See also
  Danish West Indies)
Virginius incident, 1873, 328–330
Visit and search, 261–262, 516
Voruz Company, 279

Wake Island, 400
Walker, Robert, 193, 218, 288
Walker, William, 238–239, 252
Walker Commission, 1899, 420
Wallace, Henry, 715
Walsh, James E., 670
War of 1812, 113–127
War of the Pacific, 1879–1884, 337
War criminals, trial of, 713–714
War hawks, 110–113
Warren, Sir John, 117
Warsaw Pact, 1955, 782, 784
Washington, George: in Revolutionary
  War, 5, 14, 26; becomes President, 43,
  46–48; and France, 50–55, 67–68; and
  Great Britain, 55–62, 97; and Spain,
  63–67; Farewell Address, 68–70, 163
Washington Conference: 1887, 359;
  1921–1922, 573–577, 638
"Watchful waiting," 1914, 475–478
Wayne, Anthony, 55–56, 61
Webb, William H., 304
Webster, Daniel; advocate of peaceful
  measures, 169, 207, 209, 220; and
  McLeod affair, 175–176; and Webster-
  Ashburton Treaty, 179–182; and Texas,
  191–192; and Hungary, 221–223; and
  Far East, 225, 227; and Cuba, 243; and
  Mexico, 253
Wedemeyer, Albert C., 732–733
Weihaiwei, 406
Welles, Gideon, 271
Welles, Sumner, 594; and Good Neigh-
  bor policy, 626, 628; and World War
  II, 651
Wellington, Duke of, 123
Wellington House, 512
West Florida: and Revolutionary War,
  18; and Treaty of Paris, 29, 31, 39; and
  Louisiana Purchase, 85, 88, 90; United
  States annexation, 136–138, 188
West Germany, 724–726, 765, 780, 783–
  785

West Indies (*see* British West Indies; Danish West Indies; French West Indies)

Western European Union (WEU), 780

Weygand, Maxime, 661, 680–682

Weyler, Don Valeriano, 377, 382

Wharton, William F., 189

Wheeler, Burton K., 657, 660

White, Andrew D., 496

White, Henry, 405, 408, 447; at Paris Peace Conference, 547–548

White, William Allen, 650, 654

"White man's burden," 353–354, 718

White Russia, 707

Whitthorne, Washington C., 356

Wilkes, Charles, 270–272, 304

Wilkinson, James, 42, 64, 93, 138

"Willful men," 1917, 538

William II, Emperor of Germany: Mahan's influence on, 357; and Kruger telegram, 374; and Spanish-American War, 388; and European rivalries, 427; and Venezuelan debt controversy, 431–432; and T. Roosevelt, 438–439, 441; and Morocco, 445–447; abdication, 546

Willis, Albert S., 367

Willkie, Wendell, 655, 657, 664, 669

Wilson, Charles E., 757

Wilson, Henry Lane, 475–476, 547–548

Wilson, Woodrow: and American influence, 352; and Far East, 468–469; diplomatic principles, 470–474; and Mexico, 474–481; Caribbean policy, 481–488; and peace movement, 506–508; and World War I neutrality, 509–539; and United States participation in World War I, 539–542; and Treaty of Versailles, 542–564

Witte, Serge, 442

Wood, Leonard, 428

Wood, Robert E., 656, 660

Woodford, Stewart L., 382, 387–388, 390

World Bank, 718, 776

World Court: establishment, 550; rejected, 579–582, 620; and UN, 709

World Disarmament Conference, 1932, 602

World Monetary and Economic Conference, 1933, 616–619

World War I: origins, 509–511; United States neutrality, 511–539; United States enters, 539–540; United States participation, 541–542; war aims, 542–545; armistice, 545–547; peace negotiations, 547–564

World War II: begins, 647–648; United States neutrality, 648–654; destroyers-for-bases deal, 654–656; Lend Lease, 658–660; campaigns, 1940–1941, 661–663; United States aid to Allies, 663–665; Atlantic Conference, 665–666; shooting war, 667–669; United States policy toward Japan, 669–674; Pearl Harbor, 675–676; UN cooperation, 676–698; UN victory, 698–699

World War Foreign Debt Commission, 1923, 603

Wyke, Charles, 308, 314

XYZ affair, 1797, 73–75

Yalta Conference, 1945, 693–697, 706

Yalu River, 742

Yancey, William L., 268, 272

Yap, 572, 576

Yazoo River, 29, 40, 64

Yedo, 226–228

Yemen, 772

Yorktown, Battle of, 1781, 20, 26

Young, Owen D., 603

Young Plan, 1929, 603–604, 607

Young America, 222, 245

Yucatan, 202, 242, 252

Yugoslavia: during World War II, 662, 692; Communist control, 719–720; Tito's policies, 727, 775; and Suez crisis, 768

Yusuf, Karamanli, 82–83

Zamor, Orestes, 482

Zavala, Joaquín, 337, 340

Zelaya, José, 459–461

Zhukov, Georgi, 762

Zimmermann telegram, 1917, 537–538